The Law in Context Series

Editors: William Twining (University College London)
Christopher McCrudden (Lincoln College, Oxford)
Bronwen Morgan (University of Bristol).

Since 1970 the Law in Context series has been in the forefront of the movement to broaden the study of law. It has been a vehicle for the publication of innovative scholarly books that treat law and legal phenomena critically in their social, political and economic contexts from a variety of perspectives. The series particularly aims to publish scholarly legal writing that brings fresh perspectives to bear on new and existing areas of law taught in universities. A contextual approach involves treating legal subjects broadly, using materials from other social sciences, and from any other discipline that helps to explain the operation in practice of the subject under discussion. It is hoped that this orientation is at once more stimulating and more realistic than the bare exposition of legal rules. The series includes original books that have a different emphasis from traditional legal textbooks, while maintaining the same high standards of scholarship. They are written primarily for undergraduate and graduate students of law and of other disciplines, but most also appeal to a wider readership. In the past, most books in the series have focused on English law, but recent publications include books on European law, globalisation, transnational legal processes, and comparative law.

Books in the Series

Anderson, Schum & Twining: *Analysis of Evidence*
Ashworth: *Sentencing and Criminal Justice*
Barton & Douglas: *Law and Parenthood*
Beecher-Monas: *Evaluating Scientific Evidence: An Interdisciplinary Framework for Intellectual Due Process*
Bell: *French Legal Cultures*
Bercusson: *European Labour Law*
Birkinshaw: *European Public Law*
Birkinshaw: *Freedom of Information: The Law, the Practice and the Ideal*
Cane: *Atiyah's Accidents, Compensation and the Law*
Clarke & Kohler: *Property Law: Commentary and Materials*
Collins: *The Law of Contract*
Cranston: *Legal Foundations of the Welfare State*
Davies: *Perspectives on Labour Law*
Dembour: *Who Believes in Human Rights?: The European Convention in Question*
de Sousa Santos: *Toward a New Legal Common Sense*
Diduck: *Law's Families*
Elworthy & Holder: *Environmental Protection: Text and Materials*
Fortin: *Children's Rights and the Developing Law*
Glover-*Thomas: Reconstructing Mental Health Law and Policy*

Children's Rights and the Developing Law

3rd Edition

JANE FORTIN

CAMBRIDGE
UNIVERSITY PRESS

CAMBRIDGE UNIVERSITY PRESS
Cambridge, New York, Melbourne, Madrid, Cape Town, Singapore, São Paulo, Delhi

Cambridge University Press
The Edinburgh Building, Cambridge CB2 8RU, UK

Published in the United States of America by Cambridge University Press, New York

www.cambridge.org
Information on this title: www.cambridge.org/9780521698016

First published 1998
Second edition 2003
Third edition 2009

Printed in the United Kingdom at the University Press, Cambridge

A catalogue record for this publication is available from the British Library

ISBN 978-0-521-69801-6 paperback

Contents

Preface

Many of those who work with legal principles affecting children are fully committed to the notion that children have rights. Nevertheless, they may be unclear how to promote such a notion in a way that enhances children's lives at a practical level, rather than allowing it to remain a theoretical ideal. The law does not stand still and the purpose of this book is to consider the extent to which the emerging legal principles can be harnessed to achieve such a goal.

Interest in the concept of children's rights has grown significantly since the first edition of this work was published in 1998. By the time the second edition was published in 2003, there was already an increasing appreciation, amongst lay people and lawyers, of the UK's obligations under the United Nations Convention on the Rights of the Child (CRC). But the delayed implementation of the Human Rights Act (HRA) 1998 meant that it was then still difficult to gauge the extent to which the principles of law governing children's lives would change under the impact of a rights-based approach. Since then we have seen the courts gradually accommodating the fact that the rights guaranteed by the European Convention on Human Rights and Fundamental Freedoms (ECHR) are also available to children. These two international conventions are undoubtedly having a dramatic impact on adults' perceptions of children's status. Meanwhile, during the last ten years, we have had a government in power with a real interest in children's lives, reflected by the huge body of child-related legislation it has introduced. Nevertheless, New Labour is not committed to the concept of children having rights, and its legislation reflects this. Indeed, at times the developing law and policy in England and Wales are simultaneously promoting and undermining the rights of children.

This work considers the developing law in England and Wales within a traditional range of legal topics, which reflect children's own activities and the principles used by lawyers to assist them. The first part considers the theoretical sources of ideas about children's rights and the extent to which international activity in the field of human rights can inform the domestic law. The next and largest part of the book contains chapters all broadly considering the extent to which the law acknowledges the growing maturity of adolescents and their capacity for independent thought and action. These chapters review the extent to which the law encourages adults to consult adolescents and older children over decisions regarding their future and the scope they are given to reach legally binding decisions of their own. The work's third part assesses the way in which the law balances the rights of younger children who are incapable of making decisions for themselves, against parents' powers and responsibilities regarding their upbringing. It considers how the law's support for parental autonomy, at times, hampers the legal fulfilment of children's own rights in various contexts. The fourth part of the work contains chapters considering the manner in which the state fulfils children's rights to protection against parental abuse and the extent to which children are protected from abuse whilst in state care. It also considers the rights of young offenders to be protected against a society which continues to maintain savagely punitive attitudes towards those who offend against its rules. The last chapter assesses the dilemmas that the law poses and the ways in which children's rights could be enforced more effectively and coherently.

Placing the legal principles affecting children in a rights-based framework can achieve little when they lack practical relevance. This lack of relevance often occurs quite simply because adult assumptions about children's interests are entirely unrealistic. To redress this weakness, readers of this work will find that there are numerous references to the steadily growing body of research on children's real needs. This is used throughout the work to test and inform the legal principles under discussion. It should also be noted that a work of this nature cannot cover all the topics at a sufficient depth to do justice to the wealth of research and academic comment underpinning them. It is hoped that the many footnoted references to much of this material will provide signposts for those tempted to delve more deeply into some of the subject areas. The work will have fulfilled its task if it provokes further thought and speculation over the way in which the law is developing and how it should develop to promote children's rights effectively.

Acknowledgements

As with the preceding editions, I am immensely grateful to numerous colleagues and practitioners who have assisted me when researching and writing this work. Amongst the countless busy people who responded to my queries with unfailing generosity, I would like to thank Janet Allbeson, Jenny Driscoll, Joan Hunt, Byron James, Heather Keating, Laurence Koffman, Daniel Monk, Camilla Parker, Lisa Payne, Euan Ross and James Ross. I owe a particular debt of gratitude to Tim Bateman, Julie Doughty, Neville Harris and Sarah McKimm who worked their way through whole drafts of chapters and gave me many very detailed comments. The mistakes that remain are mine alone. I am again endlessly indebted to my husband not only for reading and commenting on huge chunks of draft material, but also for keeping me and himself sane whilst this work was in preparation. Our daughters, Abigail, Elizabeth and Katharine have again patiently suffered my lack of attention during its production and as before, this book is dedicated to them.

Table of cases

Table of statutes

Table of statutory instruments

Table of international instruments

Part One

Theoretical perspectives and international sources

Chapter 1

Theoretical perspectives

(1) Introduction

Children's lives are underpinned by an incoherent hotchpotch of legal principles and government policies. A rights-based approach might address at least some of their weaker aspects very effectively if the government and judiciary were prepared to utilise it more wholeheartedly. In particular, such an approach can address the problem experienced by children, alongside other minority groups, of being the focus of various specialised branches of law and policy, all with their own distinctive character, with no coherence or similarity in objectives. By placing the differing aspects of childhood in a framework of rights, rather than, for example, in a medical or educational-based context, the boundaries between the various disciplines start becoming irrelevant, with a far more coherent outcome being possible.

The time is right for such a change in approach, given the greatly increased level of 'rights consciousness' in the country today. The UK's ratification, in 1991, of the United Nations Convention on the Rights of the Child (CRC) and the incorporation of the European Convention for the Protection of Human Rights and Fundamental Freedoms (1950) (ECHR) by the Human Rights Act (HRA) 1998, into domestic law, have undoubtedly played their part in achieving this. There appears now to be more sympathy with a desire to promote children's rights in more realistic and practical ways. Nevertheless, it would be foolish to ignore the real concerns that many retain over the wisdom of utilising the concept of rights to increase children's well-being.

Important though they are, the CRC and the HRA 1998 have had a relatively late impact on the development of thought on the concept of children's rights. The idea that children enjoy rights is not a new one – rather, it has been the topic of speculation and comment for over 30 years. Certain themes constantly recur. Indeed, although writers have often approached this field of thought from a variety of viewpoints, they have all identified common areas of concern, principally surrounding how to identify children's rights, how to balance one set of rights against another in the event of a conflict between them, and how to mediate between children's rights and those of adults. Practitioners are wrong to assume that such a voluminous body of theoretical inquiry should be confined to the realm of intellectual speculation. If made more accessible, it might usefully inform their own attempts to apply legal principles to individual children in a way which promotes those children's moral and legal rights more effectively. Better still, when it can be demonstrated that existing legal principles clearly reflect such theoretical ideals, the law gains a greater intellectual validity. This chapter sets out to identify these recurring themes and provide a brief summary of their treatment.

(2) Rights awareness and rights scepticism

(A) Children's liberation

The ideas of the American 'children's liberationists' generated a wealth of valuable debate about the extent to which society should encourage children to develop their powers of self-determination. The American civil rights movement had encouraged, in the 1960s and early 1970s, a far more sympathetic attitude to the treatment of all minority groups, including children. In the long run, however, the early American children's liberationists probably did the concept of children's rights a disservice, in so far as they conveyed the misleading impression that it is almost wholly concerned with giving children adult freedoms. It was Foster and Freed, writing in the 1970s, who claimed that adults exploited their power over children and that children's inferior status should be radically reassessed.[1] They gathered inspiration from a series of decisions reached by the United States Supreme Court.[2] Most notable of these was the landmark decision of *Re Gault* in which the court ruled that 'neither the Fourteenth Amendment nor the Bill of Rights is for adults alone'[3] and that as 'persons', children were entitled to claim the same procedural safeguards as those offered to adults by the United States Constitution.

Holt and Farson, the most well-known of the children's liberationists, adopting the view of Ariès[4] that childhood is a relatively recent Western social 'invention', argued that it was a form of oppressive and unwarranted discrimination to exclude children from the adult world. They maintained that since children's ability for self-determination was greatly underestimated, there was little reason to exclude them from the freedoms granted by the state to adults. Thus Holt argued that children of any age should have, amongst other things, the right to vote, to work for money, to own and sell property, to travel, to be paid a guaranteed minimum state income, to direct their own education, to use drugs and to control their own private sexual lives.[5] The fact that children might

---

[1] H. Foster and D. Freed (1972).

[2] E.g. *Tinker v. Des Moines Independent Community School District* 393 US 503 (1969) and *Goss v. Lopez* 419 US 565 (1975).

[3] 387 US 1 at 13 (1967).

[4] P. Ariès (1962). The strength of his view has been undermined by later historical research. See e.g. L. Pollock (1983).

[5] J. Holt (1974) p. 18. Farson's list of rights was very similar to that set out by Holt, R. Farson (1974). See also the list of rights proposed by H. Foster and D. Freed (1972) p. 347.

be too young to wish to exercise any of these rights was merely part of their freedom of choice; they could exercise them, when and if they chose, in precisely the same way as adults do. The publicity these radical views attracted led to the movement for children's rights becoming inextricably associated with giving adult rights to children[6] and being treated with considerable scepticism.[7]

To modern readers the claims of writers like Holt and Farson for children to enjoy adult freedoms might seem not only unrealistic but reckless. Indeed, the views of the child liberationists were, from the first, extremely controversial. Much of the criticism, both in the 1970s[8] and after,[9] has focused on a variety of relatively practical issues. Two main topics have been recurrent themes. The first is that there are obvious dangers in ignoring the slow rate of children's physical and mental development by giving them the same rights and responsibilities as fully mature adults. The second is the danger of interfering with the relationship between children and parents, including the potential damage to the family unit as a whole.

Many writers have voiced considerable concern over the liberationists' failure to accord sufficient attention to the physical and mental differences between childhood and adulthood. Indeed, this is the most obvious weakness of the liberationists' ideas. They appeared to ignore the evidence on developmental growth through childhood, which establishes clearly that children are different from adults in development, behaviour, knowledge, skills and in their dependence on adults, most often their parents. Research evidence now reinforces the view that the liberationists' ideas were based on an unrealistic perception of children's capacities.[10] It is obviously impossible to set a single age when all children can be deemed competent to reach any particular type of decision. It seems clear, however, that the relatively slow development of children's cognitive processes makes the *majority* of children unfit to take complete responsibility for their own lives by being granted adult freedoms before they reach mid-adolescence.[11] Moreover, as Fox Harding cogently points out, a failure to regulate childhood would lead to more exploitation of children, rather than less.[12]

The need to protect children from being forced into adulthood before they are sufficiently mature is also a common theme of those opposing calls for recognition of children's autonomy rights. Campbell points to the constant stress on children's adult-like competence to make rational decisions for themselves, which in his view is tantamount to claims to redraw the boundaries between childhood and adulthood. He urges that the current needs of the child *here and now*, should not be sacrificed to those of the future child. Children have a right to be children and not adults.[13] The frequency with which these arguments and

---

[6] The work of the children's liberationists is described by D. Archard (2004) Part II.
[7] Eg B Hafen (1976).   [8] Inter alia, M. Wald (1979) and B. Hafen (1976).
[9] Inter alia, L. Fox Harding (1997) ch. 5; see also D Archard (2004) chs. 5 and 6.
[10] Discussed in Chapter 3.   [11] L. Fox Harding (1997) pp. 128–37.
[12] Ibid. at p. 134.   [13] T. Campbell (1992) p. 20.

counter-arguments are raised reinforces the notion that the same child may need both care for one purpose and autonomy or self-determination for another.[14]

The more recent proponents of the children's liberation school, such as Franklin,[15] though less radical than the early writers, continue to promote their central premise – that even quite young children are capable of competent thought and of making informed choices, and some are far more competent to make decisions than many adults. Indeed, adults, like children, make mistakes; they too may be ignorant and lack education and experience. There is also the not unreasonable criticism that until quite young children are trusted with more decision-making, they are denied the opportunity of gaining experience in doing so and, more importantly, of developing any decision-making skills. It is certainly difficult to defend some of the more arbitrary and inconsistent age limits determining children's competence to take part in various activities.[16] Such arguments came to the fore once again in the debate over lowering the minimum age for voting. Those advocating reform criticised the laws prohibiting intelligent 17-year-olds from voting, whilst allowing incompetent adults to exercise such rights.[17]

The answer to the criticism of arbitrary age limits is, of course, that all lines are essentially arbitrary and that they must be drawn somewhere.[18] Nevertheless, at the very least, the views of the liberationists justified a more critical examination of the law's treatment of children. The majority of the House of Lords in *Gillick v. West Norfolk and Wisbech Area Health Authority*[19] obviously sympathised with the notion of adopting a more intelligent approach to assessing children's legal competence. Lord Scarman commented:

> If the law should impose on the process of 'growing up' fixed limits where nature knows only a continuous process, the price would be artificiality and a lack of realism in an area where the law must be sensitive to human development and social change.[20]

Freeman wisely suggests that whilst the special treatment of children can be justified on the basis of the child's incapacity or immaturity, at the same time they should be brought 'to a capacity where they are able to take full responsibility as free, rational agents for their own system of ends'.[21]

(B) Children's rights and the parental role

A constant theme of those questioning the notion of children being rights holders concerns their relationship with their parents. These doubts are often rooted in the assumption that the concept of children's rights revolves solely around children's autonomy, as strongly suggested by the children's liberationists. Such

---

[14] M. Minow (1986) p. 14.   [15] B. Franklin (2002) pp. 22–8.
[16] J. Claridge (2008).   [17] Discussed further in Chapter 4.   [18] D. Archard (2001) p. 47.
[19] [1986] AC 112.   [20] Ibid. at 186.   [21] M. Freeman (1983) p. 57.

an assumption is false; children have a whole range of rights and many, such as the right to care and protection, have little to do with making decisions. Acknowledging these may be much more important to young children than acknowledging any claimed right to autonomy. Nevertheless, children soon move out of dependence and into a developmental stage where their capacity for taking responsibility for their lives needs encouraging. Indeed, there is a growing view in wealthy nations that teenagers should be provided with far greater opportunities for developing their decision-making capacities and their sense of responsibility, not only for their own sake, but also for the sake of the communities in which they live. Industrialised societies expect children to emerge from minority immediately ready to take their place as newly minted citizens. In truth, childhood is short and it is unrealistic to argue that a child who is protected throughout from responsibility and from participation in important decisions regarding his or her upbringing will become a confident young person and responsible citizen.[22] A sympathy for these ideas underlies the establishment of the citizenship education programme in schools.[23]

Schools undoubtedly play an important part in producing confident young people, but most writers agree that the parent's role is infinitely more important. Whilst in Victorian times it might have suited society well to promote the idea that children should be seen and not heard and that parents could treat their children with some disdain, today such ideas have lost their appeal, quite simply because society needs more sophisticated children. 'Good' parents should help their children develop 'the ability to conceive, evaluate alternatives, and act on a life plan – to pursue, in other words, a self-given system of ends that has at least rough internal consistency'.[24] However mature, they will be unable to make a successful transition to adulthood unless they are given opportunities for practising their decision-making skills and are provided with 'a dry run' at adulthood.[25] Indeed, contemporary society may have contrived a situation whereby its children can only thrive if they are able to take on more responsibility for their own lives at an earlier age than before and in more complex situations. As Gardner has said:

> We have remade childhood experience in a way which requires an earlier engagement with adult concerns, and hence an earlier submission to ideals of adulthood such as autonomy.[26]

Is it reasonable to make such demands on parents? Requiring them to promote their children's capacity for autonomy may result in a diminution of their own confidence and ability to bring up their children according to their family beliefs and values. A recurring concern is that by promoting the rights of children, law and policy will undermine the status and authority of parents.

---

[22] M. de Winter (1997) p. 26.   [23] Discussed in Chapter 6.
[24] P. Brown (1982) pp. 210–12.   [25] I am grateful to John Gardner for his 'dry run' idea.
[26] J. Gardner (1996) unpublished communications with author.

Anxieties such as these drove Victoria Gillick and Sue Axon to seek legal confirmation of their right to bring their daughters up as they thought fit.[27] These concerns are well expressed by O'Brien Steinfels:

> There is a deep contradiction between the political theory underlying our law with its impulse to protect individuals by an appeal to rights, and the biological and psychological requirements for successfully rearing children to participate as adults in such a polity. In effect, one of the most perplexing questions raised by these changes is whether the efforts to extend rights of citizens to minors will not inhibit and undermine the kind of parental authority and family autonomy necessary to foster the qualities and virtues adult citizens must possess and be able to exercise in our society.[28]

Many of the children's liberationists were sceptical of parents' capacity to adopt a more liberal family regime. Indeed, Holt saw childhood as an oppressed state and parents as the chief oppressors. Rather than the family being a protective haven, it was the place where, at best, parents might exploit their children and treat them as a mixture of expensive nuisance, slave and 'Ideal Cute Child';[29] at worst, a place where parents could abuse their children in private. Holt undoubtedly had a distorted view of the parent-child relationship in the majority of modern homes. He failed to recognise that, although parents may once have treated their children like chattels, this is no longer the case. Furthermore, although a minority of parents abuse their children, most parents are, in reality, the adults who know and love their children best and are therefore rightly cast by the state in the caring role and in a position to exercise powers over their children.

Admittedly, the privacy of family life does allow a minority of parents to undermine their children's self-confidence and capacity for self-determination. Does it follow that the government should intervene to promote a 'better' relationship between all parents and children? The more radical children's liberationists certainly considered parents quite incapable of giving children greater freedom without being forced to do so. Nevertheless, the prospect of government interference with the parental role has traditionally provoked strong hostility. Fox Harding notes that nineteenth century laws restricting child labour and introducing compulsory education were opposed on grounds that they constituted an unacceptable interference with family responsibility and parental rights.[30] Today, anxieties about family privacy are often linked with the fear that if children's capacity for autonomy were promoted by the state, this would involve a much closer monitoring of the way parents bring up their children, with the consequent undermining of their authority. Goldstein,

---

[27] *Gillick v. West Norfolk and Wisbech Area Health Authority* [1986] AC 112 and *R (Axon) v. Secretary of State for Health and the Family Planning Association* [2006] EWHC 37 (Admin), [2006] 2 FLR 206; discussed further in Chapters 3 and 5.

[28] M. O'Brien Steinfels (1982) p. 232.   [29] J. Holt (1974) p. 126.

[30] L. Fox Harding (1997) p. 35.

Freud and Solnit, the most famous proponents of a 'laissez-faire approach', argued strongly that privacy is essential to family life and that state interference detracts from its value to its members.[31] Guggenheim adopts a not dissimilar approach, proposing a 'parental rights doctrine' which, he asserts:

> guarantees children at least that the important decisions in their lives will be made by those who are most likely to know them best and to care the most for them. There may be no assurances that, in any given case, parents will make the best choice for their children ... But the alternative of unleashing state oversight is also unable to promise any of these things.[32]

He continues:

> Children do not need rights within the family. What they need are rules that work. Keeping families free from state oversight will do more for children than encouraging litigation and judicial intervention.[33]

Such views are diametrically opposed to those of the children's liberationists, but as extreme. Although a degree of family privacy is obviously desirable, a hands-off presumption endangers the concept of children's rights by fostering the view that parental behaviour towards their children should largely be outside the scope of the law. The family may be likened to a state within a state; interference by the public state within family affairs is a grave matter, comparable to interference by one state with the internal affairs of another.[34] The consequence of such an approach is that children are doubly dependent. Not only are they themselves excluded from a rights-bearing status, but they are also within the sphere of the private family, with parents standing between them and the state.[35]

(C) The dangers of 'rights talk'

The view that rights claims can protect the minority of children who need protection against their parents seems irrefutable. Nevertheless, 'rights talk' has, on a more general basis, a variety of opponents. Wellman urges far greater restraint over employing the language of rights. As he points out, asserting the existence of unreal moral rights discredits the genuine ones and even produces public scepticism over the very existence of such a concept.[36] Similarly, Freeman has observed: 'Many references to children's rights turn out on inspection to be aspirations for the accomplishment of particular social or moral goals.'[37] As discussed below, this comment is particularly apposite to the development of international human rights law. A failure to distinguish

---

[31] J. Goldstein, A. Freud and A. Solnit (1973) and J. Goldstein, A. Freud and A. Solnit (1980). For a more detailed assessment of their views and those of their critics, see J. Fortin (2003) pp. 8–9.
[32] M. Guggenheim (2005) p. 46.   [33] Ibid. p. 249.
[34] J. Bigelow *et al.* (1988) p. 185.   [35] M. Minow (1986) p. 18.
[36] C. Wellman (1999) pp. 3 and 176–81.   [37] M. Freeman (1983) p. 37.

between real and illusory rights undoubtedly plays into the hands of the media, who are only too keen to lampoon the concept of children having rights. The cartoons depicting small children consulting their solicitors over trivial griev-ances provoke derision. Furthermore, the language of rights sometimes becomes a form of political correctness used to mask claims made by adults on behalf of children, which might not otherwise escape critical analysis. Thus practitioners from various disciplines tend to assert that children have rights to a range of services, without pausing to reflect on the theoretical strength of such claims.[38]

The language of rights should not be used loosely. But from a slightly differ-ent perspective, another group of commentators are united in their view that rights themselves are a destructive concept. They argue that a rights-based society is 'a cold, hollow one, drained of the sentiments of mutual care and love', where individuals assert their rights *against* each other.[39] Sir John Laws asserts the view that rights are not a moral but a legal construct,[40] and that whilst the language of rights is a necessary ingredient in any developed system of law,[41] interpersonal morality is not a function of law and not governed by a frame-work of moral rights, but of duties.[42] Indeed, when discussing the then impend-ing introduction of the HRA 1998, he pointed out the limitations of the concept of rights:

> the idea of a rights-based society represents an immature stage in the develop-ment of a free and just society … nothing is more important, if we are truly dedicated to freedom and justice, than to see the shortcomings of this fragile pedestal. A society whose values are defined by reference to individual rights is by that very fact already impoverished. Its culture says nothing about individual duty – nothing about virtue. We speak of respect for other people's rights. But, crudely at least, this comes more and more to mean only that we should accept that what someone wants to do, he should be allowed to do. Self-discipline, self-restraint, to say nothing of self-sacrifice, are at best regarded as optional extras and at worst (and the worst is too often the reality) as old-fashioned ideas worth nothing but a scoff and a gibe.[43]

Many authors consider that children's worlds are genuinely different from those of adults, due to their vulnerability and their dependence on their parents and other carers. As noted above, O'Brien Steinfels argues that loving family relationships can be damaged by assertions which not only promote individu-alism but also inhibit and undermine parental authority and family autonomy.[44] Some feminist theorists also argue that a rights approach focuses on the wrong things, downplaying the relationships which underlie the reality of daily life.[45] Their ideas on women's powerlessness throw light on the way

---

[38] E.g. a health practitioner's enthusiastic assertion to the author that 'babies have a *right* to be breast fed by their mothers'.
[39] D. Archard (2004) p. 119.   [40] J. Laws (1998) p. 255.   [41] J. Laws (2003) p. 273.
[42] Ibid. at pp. 265–8.   [43] J. Laws (1998) p. 255.   [44] M. O'Brien Steinfels (1982) p. 240.
[45] E. Kiss (1997) and V. Held (2006), ch. 1.

that rights theories relating to children are similarly influenced by children's dependence.[46]

Nevertheless, as Archard points out, such views would lead to the dubious proposition that even if children are to be deemed rights-holders, they should not be permitted to enforce them against their parents, because of their dependence and interdependence. Furthermore, this type of criticism implies that family relationships can *either* be based on mutual affection *or* the existence of rights and duties, but not both. Archard refutes this as being far from the truth. For a child to have rights against its parents is not evidence that parental love is not forthcoming. It is regrettable if that love has broken down and recourse to rights may be second best, but this is not a reason not to have rights.[47] The position is summed up well by Waldron:

> the structure of rights is not constitutive of social life, but is instead to be understood as a position of fallback and security in case other constitutive elements of a social relationship ever come apart.[48]

Articulating children's interests in terms of rights may indeed lead to the behaviour of their caretakers being submitted to far more intensive examination than before, however well-intentioned such behaviour is. This, in turn, may risk undermining the relationships through which their needs are usually met. Nevertheless, as Minow asserts, children would not be better off if schools and families were removed from the purview of public scrutiny permitted by rights claims. She suggests that if rights need asserting, conflict has occurred already, and the process of enforcing the right often gives it expression and provides a method of resolution.[49] The validity of Minow's approach is borne out by the case law, particularly that involving children who apply to court for legal authority to reside with an adult other than their parents.[50] It seems quite unrealistic to argue that without the prospect of court proceedings, the child and parents would become reconciled. Whilst mediation might avoid the polarising effect of litigation, the damage to the relationships between child and parents probably predates the litigation. In summary, many authors conclude that it is better to be a rights-holder than to 'depend on the kindness and favors of others'.[51]

(3) Do children have any rights and, if so, which ones?

Moral philosophers have devoted much theoretical thought to the nature of rights, and, in the context of children's rights, whether children can be rights-holders at all. Practitioners and policy-makers, assuming that children must be rights-holders, worry more about the rights children have or should have and

---

[46] H. Lim and J. Roche (2000) esp. at pp. 235–41.   [47] D. Archard (2004) pp. 120–1.
[48] J. Waldron (1993) p. 374.   [49] M. Minow (1987) pp. 1890–1.
[50] Under the Children Act (CA) 1989, s. 8; discussed in Chapters 4 and 7.
[51] B. Bandman (1973) p. 236.

the need to balance one right against another when attempting to enforce them. Practitioners' assumption that children are rights-holders is borne out by their knowledge that ever since the HRA 1998 was implemented in October 2000, we have all been living in a rights-based culture. Depending on their interpretation, children are as entitled to the rights listed by the ECHR as are adults. Naturally, the extent to which children will benefit from this development will ultimately depend on the courts' interpretation of these provisions. Furthermore, a conceptual analysis of moral rights provides no final answers on how the law should be interpreted. Nevertheless, a clearer understanding of rights theory will help practitioners and policy-makers to shape the law in a way that promotes children's interests.

(A) Children as rights-holders

An acceptance of the existence of the rights of the individual underlies most liberal political theories. Indeed, whilst there have been endless theoretical debates over the part to be played by the concept of rights in the social order and over how rights are to be defined, the premise central to rights theories is that moral rights do exist.[52] First though, no assessment of children's rights would be complete without a brief reference to the philosophical and jurisprudential controversies over whether children can justifiably be described as rights-holders at all.[53] The main doubt over this issue stems from disagreements over the nature of rights themselves – which in turn are linked with a related controversy over the relevance of choice. There is the view that a person cannot be described as a rights-holder unless he or she is able to exercise a choice over the exercise of that right. The 'choice' or 'will'[54] theory of rights invests the importance of choice with such significance that it alone is capable of grounding all rights. Since the existence of a right is therefore dependent on the right-holder's interest in choosing and since the majority of children lack the competence to make choices, proponents argue they cannot be described as having any rights. Thus Hart considers the term 'rights' inappropriate for application to babies, or indeed to animals.[55]

The assertion that children, who are too young and incompetent to claim rights, therefore have no rights, has an unattractive logic. It negates the intuitive view that children must have rights because it would be wrong to deny such a

[52] J. Waldron (1984) provides a usefully brief but seminal consideration of general rights theories.
[53] M. Freeman (1983) ch. 2 provides an exhaustive theoretical discussion of the concept of children's rights.
[54] Alternatively sometimes described as the 'power' or 'claim' theory of rights. For proponents see, inter alia, H.L.A. Hart (1984) and J. Feinberg (1980a).
[55] H.L.A. Hart (1984) p. 82. In Hart's view the fact that it is considered *wrong* to ill-treat babies or animals does not justify utilising the expression 'rights' when describing such situations (emphasis supplied).

proposition. Fortunately, theorists such as MacCormick,[56] Raz[57] and Campbell[58] provide a competing view that the concept of rights need not be confined only to those who can lay claim to or waive them. They present an interest theory of rights which posits that a person has a right where his *interests* are protected in certain ways 'by the imposition of (legal or moral) normative constraints on the acts and activities of other people with respect to the object of one's interests'.[59] Children, like adults, have interests which require protecting in such a way and the use of this model avoids denying them moral and legal rights until they have acquired the capacity to reach reasoned decisions. Such a rights model fully accommodates the view that children are no less precious because of their lack of adult capacities.[60] MacCormick forcefully sets out the value of applying such a model to children:

> To argue, on the other hand [when countering the choice or will theory of rights], that each and every child is a being whose needs and capacities command our respect, so that denial to any child of the wherewithal to meet his or her needs and to develop his or her capacities would be wrong in itself (at least in so far as it is physically possible to provide the wherewithal), and would be wrong regardless of the ulterior disadvantages or advantages to anyone else – so to argue, would be to put a case which is intelligible as a justification of the opinion that children have such rights.[61]

MacCormick proceeds to criticise the proponents of the choice theory of rights for putting the cart before the horse in their insistence on there being a means of remedying a child's right, through the enforcement of someone else's correlative duty, before they can accept the existence of the right itself.[62] He considers this to be an obsession with the existence of remedies, *ubi remedium ibi ius*, rather than with rights themselves. By contrast, he maintains that it is *because* children have the right, for example, to care and nurture, that the imposition of legal provisions requiring others to provide that care and nurture is justified. In other words, the existence of the right presupposes the remedy, *ubi ius, ibi remedium*.

Before gratefully accepting these assurances that children are respectable rights-holders, brief attention should be paid to the theoretical concerns revolving around the difficulties involved in enforcing children's rights, in the light of their innate powerlessness. In the first place, children are often dependent on those very adults who are acting in breach of their rights, most commonly their parents, and, secondly, they may be too young to take steps to enforce their rights. O'Neill, who considers that adopting a rights-based approach for

---

[56] N. MacCormick (1982) ch. 8. MacCormick (pp. 154–6) clearly sets out the basis for the two competing views on the importance of choice.

[57] J. Raz (1986) esp. at pp. 165–92.   [58] T. Campbell (1992) pp. 1–23.

[59] N. MacCormick (1982) p. 154. See also J. Raz (1984b) and J. Raz (1986) esp at pp. 165–92.

[60] T. Campbell (1992) p. 5.   [61] N. MacCormick (1982) p. 160.

[62] The choice model of rights is underpinned by Hohfeld's classification involving the existence of duties in others, correlative to the rights asserted. See W. Hohfeld (1919).

children suffers from many theoretical problems, including that of enforcement, would prefer to couch children's rights in terms of the obligations owed
to them by others. Although the 'rhetoric of rights' has relevance for oppressed
adults, she considers that an appeal to rights has little chance of empowering
children. If they are too young they will be unable to respond to such an appeal,
and if they are old enough to respond, they are well on their way to adulthood
and freedom from dependence. Indeed, as she points out, the fundamental
difference between children and groups of oppressed adults is that children
emerge from their powerless state. This leads her to conclude that the main
remedy for children's powerlessness 'is to grow up'.[63]

Fortunately, not everyone agrees with O'Neill's diagnosis or remedy,
which might, to children, appear to be a counsel of despair. According to
MacCormick, neither problem prevents rights vesting in children. Indeed, in
his view children may have moral rights *prior* to any correlative duties vesting
in anyone to fulfil them or indeed without it being clear who is obliged to fulfil
the right. He cites, by way of example, the child's right to be educated to the
limit of his or her abilities. Although such a right exists, it may be unclear whose
is the power to enforce it and whose the duty to provide it. He nevertheless
concedes the purely practical difficulty which attaches to the enforcement of
children's rights.[64]

Ultimately, agreement over a universally acceptable theory of rights for
dependent children may always prove elusive.[65] Some feminist theorists consider that the interest theory of rights disadvantages children, in so far as it
recognises their need for protection and care, as opposed to recognising their
competency and autonomy.[66] This surely misinterprets the interest theory of
rights which accommodates the view that children acquire freedom of action
like adults, as they become the best judge of what is for their own good.[67] In
other words, children have an interest *in* choice, as they develop an ability to
reach choices.[68] Such issues are discussed below. Meanwhile, MacCormick's
description of a moral right as 'a good of such importance that it would be
wrong to deny it to or withhold it from any member of C (a given class)'[69] has
an arresting simplicity that many non-theorists may find attractive. Without
underestimating the difficulties implicit in its generality, it provides a scheme of
thought which promotes a compelling and flexible assessment of the concept of
children's rights. Its drawback is that it provides little guidance over defining
what interests may become translated into moral rights.

---

[63] O. O'Neill (1992) pp. 38–9.   [64] N. MacCormick (1982) pp. 162–6.

[65] Some maintain that the theorists are striving to describe with the term 'rights' what are in truth
   totally different concepts. See J. Harris (1980) p. 86.

[66] K. Federle (1994) p. 353.   [67] N. MacCormick (1982) p. 165.

[68] Discussed below. S. Brennan (2002) pp. 63–4, considers that children progress from having
   their interests protected by rights to having their choices protected as they become better able to
   judge for themselves what is in their interests.

[69] N. MacCormick (1982) p. 160.

(B) What rights do children have?

There are two questions that follow on from the adoption of MacCormick's interest model of rights. What interests can be translated into moral rights and what moral rights might be translated into legal rights? The second question is slightly easier to answer than the first. Most commentators accept that moral rights are translated into legal rights[70] if there is some recognition of their importance by the rest of society and consequently the imposition of correlative legal duties on others regarding the fulfilment of those rights.[71] The law thereby makes it unlawful to withhold a particular moral right from any one of a class of individuals. Meanwhile, unhappily, there appear to be no clear answers to the first question. Indeed, proponents of the interest theory of rights often tend to refer to children's interests rather than their rights, because of their uncertainty over whether there is sufficient unanimity over the wrongness of denying any particular good for it to be translated into a moral right. Eekelaar's words reflect this dilemma:

> whether these interests can also be said to be 'rights' depends on the extent to which it is generally believed that children have them and that they should be protected by law. If such beliefs were part of 'official' ideology it might make sense to say that children had those rights. It is not claimed that such an ideology actually exists. But it could be put forward as a challenge. Should not our community behave towards its children as if they had rights? If so, are these not the rights which they should have?[72]

Perhaps inevitably, a common criticism of the interest theory is that it is far too broad; the interests relevant to the justification of rights are without clear demarcation.[73] Adoption of MacCormick's description of a moral right as 'a good of such importance that it would be wrong to deny it to or withhold it from any member of C (a given class)' inevitably leads to uncertainty over the 'wrongness' of denying the importance of many potential interests. MacCormick acknowledges this and merely responds, a little unhelpfully, that 'rights belong to the class of essentially contested concepts'.[74] Campbell, who uses a description

---

[70] D. Lyons (1984) pp. 113–17, discusses Bentham's rejection of the concept of moral rights being an essential ingredient of legal rights. The extent to which Bentham's arguments undermine the concept of natural law is considered at length by J. Finnis in his seminal work (1980).

[71] E.g. J. Raz (1984b) pp. 13–14, proposes that 'a law creates a right if it is based on and expresses the view that someone has an interest which is sufficient ground for holding another to be subject to a duty … His right is a legal right if it is recognized by law, that is if the law holds his interest to be sufficient ground to hold another to be subject to a duty'. But it does not follow that moral rights once asserted should always be followed by endorsement as legal rights. J. Eekelaar (2004) p. 187, suggests that such an assumption is a dangerous one.

[72] J. Eekelaar (1991) p. 103. He subsequently suggests that the concept of rights is bound up with promoting a person's well-being, as opposed to his interests. See J. Eekelaar (2004) pp. 182–4.

[73] E.g. O. O'Neill (1992) who criticises the whole concept of children having 'fundamental rights', considering that far more would be achieved by way of improving children's lives if a theoretical framework of obligations were adopted.

[74] N. MacCormick (1982) p. 160.

of moral rights not dissimilar to that adopted by MacCormick,[75] claims neither that all children's interests give rise to rights nor underestimates the difficulty of identifying and classifying the full range of the sometimes conflicting interests protected by rights. Indeed, he admits that it may be a weakness of the interest theory of rights that 'it leaves us with a very open ended basis for determining which interests are to serve as the ground of rights'.[76] Nevertheless, the extent of children's rights cannot be left in the realms of philosophical debate. An appreciation of this problem has led to various attempts to provide a more practical framework for children's rights, not by attempting to list them, but by classifying them into identifying groups.

In a seminal article, Eekelaar explores the type of children's interests that might deserve recognition and protection.[77] He reviews what benefits children 'might plausibly claim for themselves' and produces a threefold classification.[78] In doing so, he adopts a 'hypothetical retrospective judgement' approach: he makes an 'imaginative leap' to 'guess what a child might retrospectively have wanted once it reaches a position of maturity'.[79] Although Eekelaar subsequently reformulates this method of discerning what interests children might claim,[80] the classification he adopts remains of considerable value. In his view, children's interests fall into three groups: basic, developmental and autonomy interests.[81] Their 'basic' interests arise from children's claims regarding their immediate physical, emotional and intellectual care and well-being. Children's 'developmental' interests revolve round their claims on the wider community to maximise their potential. All children should have an equal opportunity to maximise the resources available to them during their childhood. A child's autonomy interests relate to 'the freedom to choose his own lifestyle and to enter social relations according to his own inclinations uncontrolled by the authority of the adult world, whether parents or institutions'.[82] In the event of a child's autonomy interest conflicting with his developmental or basic interest, Eekelaar suggests that the latter interests should prevail. As discussed below, this suggestion has obvious and far-reaching implications if applied to practical situations involving adolescents refusing to accept life-saving medical treatment.[83] He justifies this view by asserting that few adults would retrospectively approve of the exercise of their autonomy interest being allowed to prejudice their life-chances in adulthood.

[75] T. Campbell (1992) p. 9: 'Moral rights may be regarded as those interests which are thought to be of such significance to the life of the human individual that they ought to be given priority in the organization of societal existence wherever possible.'

[76] Ibid. at p. 16; see also pp. 6–7.

[77] J. Eekelaar (1986) p. 166ff. He adopts an interest theory of moral rights similar to that set out by J. Raz (1984b).

[78] J. Eekelaar (1986) p. 169.   [79] Ibid. at p. 170.   [80] Discussed below.

[81] J. Eekelaar (1986) pp. 170–1.   [82] Ibid. at p. 171.

[83] Discussed below and further in Chapter 5.

Many other classifications of children's rights have been formulated. Freeman proposes four categories: welfare rights, protective rights, those grounded in social justice and those based on children's claims to more freedom from control and more autonomy over their lives.[84] This is similar to another fourfold classification of rights proposed by Wald, described as: 'Rights Against the World', 'Protection from Inadequate Care', 'Rights to an Adult Legal Status' and 'Rights Versus Parents'.[85] Campbell suggests a fourfold classification according to the minor's status as person, child, juvenile and future adult.[86] Arguably, Bevan's scheme which simply divides children's rights into two broad categories: protective and self-assertive,[87] has a more pragmatic relevance. It reflects the fundamental conflict currently underlying the whole of child law as it is developing in practice – that is the conflict between the need to fulfil children's rights to protection and to promote their capacity for self-determination. Children's 'protective rights' arise from their innate dependence and vulnerability and an obvious need for nurture, love and care, both physical and psychological. These rights must include the right to protection from ill-treatment and the right to state intervention in order to achieve such protection. Bevan's term 'assertive rights' is usefully broad enough to include their claims to adult human rights, such as the right to bodily integrity and to freedom of expression and thought, conscience and religion and to certain 'decision-making rights'.

Whilst many theorists currently accept that children can be rights-holders, there remains no clear test providing guidance over what rights they have or should have. Eekelaar's threefold classification, basic, developmental and autonomy interests, is posed in terms of the '*interests*' children have, rather than the rights that they have. His uncertainty over whether they can be correctly described as rights is emphasised by his words quoted above. But, as these words suggest, perhaps strict theoretical justifications for the existence of moral rights do not matter so much as believing that children have rights. More pragmatically, as noted below when discussing the rights protected by international conventions, the language or 'rhetoric' of rights is a politically useful tool to ensure the achievement of certain goals for children.

(C) International human rights

When considering whether children have rights, many practitioners appear to draw more support from the widely held view that children are holders of 'human rights' than from the work of the moral philosophers referred to above. As discussed in more detail elsewhere in this work,[88] the term 'human rights' derives from the writings of the eighteenth century philosophers who were concerned with natural rights or the rights of man. Lists of these rights became the basis of the famous declarations of rights associated with the American and

---

[84] M. Freeman (1983) p. 40.   [85] M. Wald (1979) p. 260ff.   [86] T. Campbell (1992) p. 22.
[87] H. Bevan (1989) p. 11.   [88] See Chapter 2.

French revolutions. Many years later, the draftsmen of the CRC considered children to be entitled to a vast array of human rights.

Their inclusion in international instruments tends to give the rights defined therein credibility as respectable moral rights. Nevertheless, a variety of writers are sceptical about the 'rights talk' adopted in such documents. It is arguable that many of the economic, social and cultural rights included in international treaties are, in reality, social ideas rather than individual rights. Whilst some human needs are undoubtedly sufficiently fundamental to ground moral rights, some writers question the moral and legal reality of these social welfare rights.[89] In a similar vein, the fact that the CRC contains a long list of substantive rights does not necessarily legitimise the belief that children enjoy all the rights it contains. Indeed, one might argue that some of the economic, social and cultural rights contained in the CRC are not rights at all but merely claims based on ideals regarding children's needs in a perfect world. These provisions describe how children should be treated and what they should be granted, were governments to take their rights seriously.[90]

Feinberg suggests that many of the rights contained in international documents are no more than 'manifesto' rights.[91] But he, like O'Neill,[92] sympathises with the manifesto writers who describe claims based on need and aspirations alone, as if they were rights already, considering it a powerful way of expressing the conviction that they ought to be recognised by states here and now as potential rights. He considers such language to be 'a valid exercise of rhetorical licence'.[93] These views are borne out by the CRC's growing impact on the development of laws and policies throughout the world. Some writers, however, have less sympathy with such an approach. King, with some prescience, argued that by transforming ambitions regarding children's welfare and autonomy into treaty rights, international documents like the CRC let governments 'off the hook', by allowing them to couch their responses in formalistic terms, without achieving real progress towards promoting such rights.[94]

The fact that the CRC has not been made part of domestic law allows the UK government to avoid determining the precise scope of its more ambitiously worded articles. For example, despite its inclusion in a document which is binding on those countries which have ratified it, it is difficult to argue that Article 27 of the CRC can ever be legally enforced, due to its extreme vagueness.[95] By contrast, the HRA 1998 ensured that all the rights listed in the ECHR became part of domestic law. Like adults, children are entitled to claim the protection of all its articles. Consequently, society is confronted with a dilemma – are children guaranteed the protection of all the ECHR rights listed

---

[89] C. Wellman (1999) esp at pp. 20–9 and 155ff.   [90] O. O'Neill (1992) p. 37.

[91] J. Feinberg (1980a) p. 153.   [92] O. O'Neill (1992) pp. 37–40.

[93] J. Feinberg (1980a) p. 153.   [94] M. King (1994) p. 396.

[95] The 'right of every child to a standard of living adequate for the child's physical, mental, spiritual, moral and social development'. This phrasing partially reflects the wording of Art. 25 of the Universal Declaration of Human Rights of 1948.

in precisely the same manner as adults? As discussed below, this dilemma comes to the fore when considering the claims of older children who value personal freedom more than younger children and, furthermore, consider themselves the best judges of what is for their own good.

(D) Children's rights and the role of paternalism

(i) Children's 'autonomy' and the role of paternalism

Claims that children have a right to autonomy are derived from liberal political philosophies which emphasise the need to promote as fully as possible an individual's freedom to make rational autonomous decisions. It is argued that children, as human beings, should, like adults, also be free to lead their own lives according to their own conception of a good or worthwhile life, provided that this does not illegitimately restrict the liberty of others to do the same.[96] The early children's liberationists saw the child's right to autonomy as of overriding importance. Farson made his views on this clear:

> the issue of self-determination is at the heart of children's liberation. It is in fact, the only issue, a definition of the entire concept. The acceptance of the child's right to self-determination is fundamental to all the rights to which children are entitled.[97]

As these words suggest, the children's liberationists deplored any paternalistic restrictions on children's freedom. In their view it was a mistake to assume that children lacked the competence for it. These extreme views gathered little support. Few deny that mature children are often able to take on far more responsibility than many adults give them credit for. But many contemporary writers are now chary of claiming for children a moral right to autonomy identical to that claimed by adults. There are good theoretical grounds for their reluctance to do so; few philosophers today consider that children have the competence for complete autonomy and some see paternalism as having an important role to play in restricting their powers of self-determination.

John Stuart Mill gave a classic exposition of the concept of an adult's right to autonomy[98] and other philosophers have constantly reassessed it.[99] Despite the importance Mill attached to autonomy, he considered it self-evident that children are too immature to be autonomous. Since they lacked the capacity for autonomy, for them there was an obvious need for paternalism:

> It is, perhaps, hardly necessary to say that this doctrine is meant to apply only to human beings in the maturity of their faculties. We are not speaking of children, or of young persons below the age which the law may fix as that of manhood or

---

[96] R. Lindley (1989) p. 75.   [97] R. Farson (1974) p. 27.   [98] J.S. Mill (1859).
[99] E.g. J. Rawls (1971) pp. 90–5 and 130–6. See also J. Raz (1986) pp. 245–50.

womanhood. Those who are still in a state to require being taken care of by others, must be protected against their own actions as well as against external injury.[100]

Mill considered that adults should make choices on behalf of children, mainly because children are not capable of rational autonomy. They have not yet developed the cognitive capacity to make intelligent decisions in the light of relevant information and their judgment is prone to be wild and variable under the influence of 'emotional inconstancy'.[101]

A variety of writers have subsequently discussed the concept of paternalism, in the context of children's decision-making powers.[102] Many point to the danger of adopting a rights theory which accepts that children have a right to make choices, when, in fact, they may lack the ability to make good choices.[103] The varying theoretical models of rights appear to place a different weight on the importance of children's autonomy. Adoption of the choice or will theory of rights leads to particular emphasis being placed on a child's capacity for rational choice, an obvious prerequisite of autonomy.[104] As Brennan points out, whilst a child's capacity to plan and choose develops gradually, the choice theory seems to 'commit us to the view that, prior to this acquisition of choosing skills, children have no rights'.[105] But after that they apparently have complete autonomy, an equally problematic notion. Indeed, MacCormick attacks the choice theory of rights for presuming that children's rights carry the option of waiver or enforcement by the children themselves or on their behalf. He argues that whilst such a theory can be appropriate for adults, who may be the best judge of what is good for them, it is not appropriate for children, who are not.[106]

Brennan considers that neither the interest nor choice theory of rights adequately accommodates the problem of young children being poor choosers and prefers a 'gradualist account of children's rights', which, she argues, includes protections for both interests and choices.[107] Under such an account, as 'children acquire the ability to choose, their rights will change from protecting interests primarily to protecting primarily choices'.[108] But this surely overlooks the fact that the interest theory of rights itself accommodates such a proposition, since children may indeed gradually acquire rights to self-determination based on their interest *in* choice, without having a right to complete autonomy.[109] As Campbell points out, during the transitional period between childhood and 'full-blown adulthood', a child's capacity for different

---

[100] J.S. Mill (1859) p. 73.   [101] Archard discusses Mill's approach in D. Archard (2004) pp. 77–8.
[102] Freeman discusses the paternalistic ideas of Hobbes, Locke and Mill relating to the dependence of children, in M. Freeman (1983) pp. 52–4. See also D. Archard (2004) ch. 1 for a discussion of Locke's approach to childhood.
[103] E.g. L. Purdy (1992) opposes the concept of children having *equal* rights to those of adults, because of her view that children's choosing can go wrong; discussed by S. Brennan (2002) p. 60. See also H. Brighouse (2002) pp. 39–51, who argues that unlike adults, children lack the competence and rationality to exercise 'agency rights' involving the exercise of choice.
[104] T. Campbell (1992) p. 20.   [105] S. Brennan (2002) p. 62.   [106] N. MacCormick (1982) p 166.
[107] S. Brennan (2002) p. 62.   [108] Ibid. at p. 66.
[109] The author is grateful to J. Gardner for his lucid explanation of this point.

sorts of adult activity emerges at different points of his or her development: 'As a juvenile the child has considerable autonomy interests and many of the rights of the child may be seen as recognizing this fact.'[110]

Feinberg similarly distinguishes between a child's right to 'an open future' and an adult's right to get what he wants now. Whereas an adult's right to autonomy now takes precedence over his probable future good, respect for a child's future autonomy as an adult often means preventing his free choice now.[111] Many authors take as an example the child's right to education, a right unaffected by his or her choices. A young child may not wish to go to school and may adversely affect his or her own potential development by refusing to do so. MacCormick explains his position persuasively:

> Children are not always or even usually the best judges of what is good for them, so much so that even the rights that are most important to their long-term well-being, such as the right to discipline or to a safe environment, they regularly perceive as being the reverse of rights or advantages.[112]

But by utilising an interest model of rights he is:

> at once glad and regretful to discover that it is possible for me to acknowledge that my children have rights, without being thereby committed to the outrageous permissiveness to which my natural indolence inclines me.[113]

Raz also points out that independence is not all or nothing. In his view, various reasons may justify coercion: it may be necessary to protect someone else, or to protect the coerced person's own long-term autonomy, or some other interest. He suggests that paternalistic coercion may be justified by the trust reposed in the coercer by the coerced person.[114] This idea is presented in the context of paternalistic coercion by government against its adult citizens, but it may similarly be applied to situations involving children. An uncooperative child may sufficiently trust parents, doctors, or indeed representatives of the education authority, to justify their adopting a degree of coercive paternalism, with a view to achieving school attendance, or compliance with medical advice or some other course of action.

As this discussion demonstrates, when considering theoretical accounts of children's rights, many theorists see little need to accord children choice rights before they gain the capacity to reach wise choices. Such views provide a morally coherent justification for a paternalistic interpretation of children's rights,[115] but they fill some authors with dismay. As discussed more fully below, Eekelaar considers that it is quite wrong to assert that an individual's interests can be determined and asserted by someone else.[116] Furthermore, these explanations do not sufficiently clarify *when* interventions to restrict children's choices could be fully justified. This question assumes an obvious relevance when

---

[110] T. Campbell (1992) p. 19.   [111] J. Feinberg (1980b) pp. 126–7.
[112] N. MacCormick (1982) p. 166.   [113] Ibid.   [114] J. Raz (1996) p. 121.
[115] T. Campbell (1992) p. 15.   [116] J. Eekelaar (2004) p. 183.

attempts are made to incorporate theoretical analyses of children's rights into legal principles. At this point, the HRA 1998 also produces a number of dilemmas, the most important being whether children can claim Convention rights in precisely the same way as adults or whether such rights can be interpreted paternalistically. As discussed below, a growing emphasis on adults' right to autonomy under the ECHR are inevitably influencing ideas about adolescents' decision-making rights.

(ii) Welfare 'versus' rights – restraining paternalism?

As this discussion has demonstrated, many theorists see little need to rule out paternalistic interventions to restrict the actions of adults or children; indeed they consider them justified by reference to the rights of those constrained.[117] On this basis, it is right to restrain or require activity simply because this will better promote that which the individual is interested in. Whatever their age, child or adult, their interests are not always achieved by letting them follow their own views on how to contribute to their achievement.[118] MacCormick, in his words quoted above, seems to assume that his paternalism, as a parent, will be 'good' for his children. Certainly, parents are those most obviously fitted to exercise paternalism in relation to children. Society recognises this by imposing legal and moral duties on those who brought the children into the world, on the basis that they are the most likely to have their interests at heart.[119] Indeed, there is the view that paternalism, rather than being seen as 'an odious tyranny'[120] is essential to the relationship of parent and child and that an abandonment of parental authority would be 'an act of immorality, as well as a failure in nurturing'.[121]

One can certainly argue that '[G]oing to school is necessary for maturation into a rational autonomous individual. Present compulsion is a precondition for subsequent choice',[122] but it is far less clear how much should be denied to children and the precise ends to be served by such denial. Indeed, the prospect of unrestricted paternalism being applied to override children's choices leaves many writers with a sense of unease, particularly because powers of coercion are largely vested in parents and sometimes the judiciary. Whilst it may be possible to justify paternalistic coercion to ensure that children fulfil their potential for future choices, it should not unduly restrict their capacities for decision-making. Furthermore, the ability to exercise paternalism may be exploited by

---

[117]   Hart was well known for his view that society may prevent people doing themselves physical harm. See H.L.A. Hart (1963).

[118]   T. Campbell (1992) p. 15. Nevertheless, he concedes that there are risks involved in considering children's concerns from an adult-centred point of view.

[119]   G. Dworkin (1982) p. 204: these are the reasons for society selecting parents as proxies for their children when reaching decisions, for example, decisions on health care.

[120]   D. Archard (2004) p. 13.   [121]   W. Gaylin (1982) pp. 30–1.

[122]   D. Archard (2004) p. 81. This is presented as part of Archard's 'caretaker thesis', one of a number of approaches to children's rights.

those in a position of power over children. Some suggest that paternalism comes in all shapes and sizes, and what Olsen describes as 'bad faith' or negative paternalism may oppress children just as much as it does some groups of adults.[123] It was the abuse of parents' power over their children that in part influenced the children's liberationists to claim that the only remedy was to empower children against their parents.

Such concerns have a practical relevance for academics and practitioners anxious to ensure that the developing law adequately protects children's interests. As noted below, the courts in this country are under increasing pressure to give greater weight to the concept of children's rights, often with an enthusiasm for seeing children's rights solely in terms of their right to reach choices of their own. Indeed, the courts are directed by statute to have regard to 'the ascertainable wishes and feelings of the child concerned (considered in the light of his age and understanding)'.[124] Nevertheless, the overtly paternalistic welfare principle[125] obliges the judiciary to reach a decision which in their view most accords with the child's best interests, whether or not it accords with his or her views. When doing so, should they assimilate the ideas of the theorists regarding the weight to be placed on a child's gradual interest in choice – and if so, how?

In many of his papers, Eekelaar discusses his concern that when the courts reach decisions that are said to conform with the 'welfare' or 'best interests' principle, this formula is sufficiently indeterminate to take little account of the child's true views. Indeed, he fears that adults, and particularly the judiciary, subject children to 'coercive paternalism' and, in so doing, may ignore their interest in making choices in their lives.[126] Maintaining his concern to ensure that children's interest in choice should not be overlooked, he develops a sophisticated approach to promoting children's own views. He proposes a method of decision-making in the place of the best interests test, described as the concept of 'dynamic self-determism' which is intended 'to bring a child to the threshold of adulthood with the maximum opportunities to form and pursue life-goals which reflect as closely as possible an autonomous choice'.[127]

Eekelaar's concept of 'dynamic self-determism' is not unlike Feinberg's suggestion that children have a right to an 'open future', or Brennan's gradualist account of children's rights, discussed above. Nevertheless, Eekelaar goes further than this when considering ideas about children's welfare, in the context of children's rights. He rejects what he describes as the 'welfarist' stance that a child may be described as having a 'right' to have performed for him or her what someone else considers to be in accordance with that child's welfare.[128]

---

[123] F. Olsen (1992) pp. 206–7.   [124] CA 1989, s. 1(3)(a).

[125] Ibid., s 1(1): 'The child's welfare shall be the court's paramount consideration.' Note the terms 'paramountcy principle', 'welfare principle' and 'best interests test' are often used interchangeably.

[126] See particularly, J. Eekelaar (1986), (1992) and (1994b).   [127] J. Eekelaar (1994b) p. 53.

[128] J. Eekelaar (1994a) p. 301. See also J. Eekelaar (2004) p. 183.

Although it might logically be held that B has the right that A should promote B's welfare in accordance with A's conception of that welfare, such a right is really no right at all. A person who surrenders to another the power to determine where his own welfare lies has in a real sense abdicated his personal autonomy.[129]

He subsequently suggests that although 'it is not necessarily wrong to force an outcome on people which they do not want, it is wrong to do this under the guise of protecting their rights'.[130] Although he acknowledges that autonomy depends on the child's competence for self-determination,[131] such views might suggest to some that sympathy with the concept that children are rights-holders dictates an inability to override children's wishes, because doing so thereby undermines their rights. When applied in the context of judicial decision-making, it implies that the judiciary cannot respect children's rights and ignore their choices at one and the same time.

A practical example of the tensions involved in the two approaches is provided by *Re W (contact: joining child as party)*.[132] Dame Elizabeth Butler-Sloss P disapproved of the way in which the trial judge had accepted the independent social worker's view that the 7-year-old boy needed the finality of knowing that there would be no more litigation about contact with his father. She said:

> The child has a right to a relationship with his father even if he does not want it. The child's welfare demands that efforts should be made to make it possible that it can be.[133]

This assertion is in tune with the views of the theorists discussed above, that a child may well have a right to an outcome which keeps his options open, rather than complying with his own short-term wishes. Nevertheless, such an approach has attracted criticism.

> This particularly legal construction of the concept of the child's right has the effect of transforming the child's right into a responsibility or even duty to see his father, since such a conception of rights fails to endow the child with the equivalent right *not* to have such contact. It also clearly demonstrates not only the readiness of courts to set aside children's wishes and feelings but also the power of the language of welfare to deny children's agency.[134]

James *et al.* clearly consider that the court here adopted a particularly legal-istic and skewed version of what rights children really have. In their view, a correct interpretation of a child's true rights would take account of his or her own wishes. James *et al.* are not alone in their view that by acknowledging the concept of children's rights, the courts are committed to respecting their

---

[129] J. Eekelaar (1994a) p. 301.   [130] J. Eekelaar (2004) p. 183.
[131] J. Eekelaar (2006) p. 157. See also discussion below in the context of adolescents and paternalism.
[132] [2001] EWCA Civ 1830, [2003] 1 FLR 681.   [133] Ibid. at [16].
[134] A. James *et al.* (2004) p. 201.

choices rather than reaching a decision according with their welfare. Indeed, many academics, researchers and members of the judiciary increasingly refer to the 'welfare' and 'rights' perspectives. They commonly suggest that under a 'welfare' approach, the child's wishes can be overborne, whereas under a 'rights' approach they cannot. In other words, the two concepts are diametrically opposed.[135]

Such ideas have come more to the fore since 2000 when the HRA 1998 was implemented. The 1998 Act makes it plain that the domestic courts have little choice but to acknowledge, not only that children have rights of their own, but that they have access to the same list of rights as are available to adults. Furthermore, as commented elsewhere, many of the rights embodied in the ECHR reflect a belief in liberty and autonomy.[136] Their interpretation by the European Court of Human Rights reflects society's increasing commitment to the notion of adult autonomy,[137] with such ideas inevitably influencing domestic decision-making relating to adults[138] and to adolescents.[139] These developments may eventually force the judiciary here to reassess their paternalistic stance regarding children, particularly adolescents who refuse to accept life-saving medical treatment.[140] Nevertheless, as Sir John Laws comments, albeit in the context of constitutional issues:

> the Convention's Articles are expressed in very broad terms, quite unlike the usual formula of a British statute … So the argument is that the Convention text invites the judges to apply their subjective judgment to broad questions of policy[141]

The judiciary clearly have similar leeway when considering how to interpret children's rights under the broadly phrased articles of the Convention. Furthermore it is worth recalling Sir John's warning set out above about the impoverishing effect of rights-based arguments on society generally. The challenge for the courts is to find a balance between interpreting children's Convention rights too liberally, and withholding their availability in situations

---

[135] Inter alia, F. Kaganas and A. Diduck (2004) pp. 972 and 978; G. Douglas *et al.* (2006) pp. 23–4; J. Herring and R. Taylor (2006) pp. 529–34. See also Thorpe LJ in *Mabon v. Mabon* [2005] EWCA Civ 634, [2005] 2 FLR 1011 at [28]–[29] (discussed further in Chapter 7). Most authors use the term 'welfare' or 'welfarism' instead of 'paternalism' as a short-hand way of describing the courts overriding children's wishes. S. Parker (1992) p. 321, however, employs the term 'utility' as a means of describing a 'welfare' dominated approach to family law debates, which he argues is inconsistent with a 'rights based' or 'justice' model. But, as Raz explains (J. Raz (1984a) esp. at p. 128), it is logically perfectly possible to combine utilitarianism with a conception of prima facie rights, despite some people finding such a conclusion unacceptable.

[136] J. Fortin (2006) p. 317.   [137] E.g. *Pretty v. UK* [2002] 2 FLR 45 at [61].

[138] E.g. *Re B (adult: refusal of medical treatment)* [2002] EWHC 429 (Fam), [2002] 2 All ER 449; discussed in Chapter 5.

[139] E.g. *Re Roddy (a child)(identification: restriction on publication)* [2003] EWHC 2927 (Fam), [2004] 2 FLR 949; *R (Axon) v. Secretary of State for Health and the Family Planning Association* [2006] EWCA 37 (Admin), [2006] 2 FLR 206; *Mabon v. Mabon* [2005] EWCA Civ 634, [2005] 2 FLR 1011.

[140] Discussed further in Chapter 5 and J. Fortin (2006) p. 317.   [141] J. Laws (1998) p. 257.

where their long-term well-being is not being threatened. The ECHR does not accommodate children's needs particularly effectively, but arguably, it should not be interpreted ignoring the theoretical models of children's rights which take account of children's inability to reach wise choices.

More importantly, as noted by this author:

> The rights contained in the European Convention are formulations, albeit some-times in awkward phraseology, of aspects of the good life, not the bad and should be interpreted in a way that enhances a person's life. Admittedly, a person may suffer a deficit in well-being if his or her rights are displaced by those of another, but no concept of rights can prevent such an occurrence nor can the courts always balance the rights of one person against another in an ideal fashion. Developing this notion, and adopting an interest theory of rights as a basis for the proposition that children are rights holders, it follows that a child's welfare cannot be inconsistent with his rights.[142]

The assumption that rights and welfare are discrete matters and that appeals to children's rights may produce a potentially damaging outcome for the child produces deep confusion in the case law. Such an approach is not supported by the works of the theorists and, indeed, appears to be a contradiction in terms.[143]

(iii) Adolescents and paternalism

The ideas discussed above have a particular relevance to claims made on behalf of adolescents to greater freedom. As noted, theorists are able to justify pater-nalistic coercion to restrict children's liberty, whilst accepting the need to promote their capacities for decision-making and responsibility. Nevertheless, the need to find an acceptable balance between respecting children's choices and retaining the power to override decisions which may destroy their future lives is a theme constantly returned to by commentators on children's rights, particularly when adolescents are concerned.

The claims of the children's liberationists that children should be autonomous and free of paternalistic restraints become most cogent when applied to mature adolescents. Freeman points out that 'no one can seriously believe that there is a real distinction ... between someone of 18 years and a day and someone of 17 years and 364 days'.[144] Although the argument that childhood is a social con-struct[145] is difficult to justify in relation to young children, the suggestion that adolescence, as a new stage after infancy and before adulthood, artificially pro-longs the inferior status of childhood is rather more plausible. The increase in the compulsory school age to 18, together with legislation banning children from full-time employment until that age, artificially postpones the time when adoles-cents can start engaging in activities carrying fuller responsibility.[146]

---

[142] J. Fortin (2006) p. 311. I am grateful to my ex-colleague, Kenneth Campbell, for spending much time with me discussing this area of thought.
[143] J. Fortin (2006) pp. 310–11.   [144] M. Freeman (1992) p. 35.
[145] See P. Ariès (1962).   [146] Discussed further in Chapter 4.

As commented earlier, adoption of MacCormick's description of a moral right as 'a good of such importance that it would be wrong to deny it to or withhold it from any member of C (a given class)' inevitably leads to controversy over the 'wrongness' of denying the importance of certain interests to certain groups. It is unlikely that there could ever be agreement over the wrongness of denying complete autonomy to all mature adolescents. Nevertheless, many adults would approve of their having a degree of personal autonomy, by acknowledging their right to reach certain major decisions for themselves. Inevitably though, there would be disagreement over which decisions such adolescents should and should not have a right to determine. Gerald Dworkin considers that: 'Our self-esteem and sense of worth are bound up with the right to determine what shall be done to and with our bodies and minds.'[147] Whilst not underestimating the younger child's right to dignity and self-respect, these words are particularly apposite when applied to adolescents. As Archard comments:

> While it is easy to represent an infant as evidently not an adult, lacking all but the most basic, and unimportant, characteristics of the mature human being, it is correspondingly harder to do so for a late adolescent. What is true of the six-month-old baby by contrast with an adult is false of a sixteen-year-old adolescent. To the extent that this is true it is problematic to deny to the adolescent that standing which is denied to all children in virtue of their not being adults.[148]

In a landmark decision reached in the late 1980s, the House of Lords accepted that adolescents need formal acknowledgment of their right to reach decisions for themselves over a variety of matters, particularly regarding their own bodily integrity. The *Gillick* decision marked an acceptance that adolescents have the right to decide a variety of matters long before they reach legal maturity.[149] More recently, the courts have confirmed that the notions of autonomy developed by the House of Lords are reinforced by the values underlying many Convention rights. The HRA 1998 is clearly able to provide adolescents with extra protection against attempts to restrict their personal freedom.[150]

But what if adolescents foreclose on their future opportunities by reaching decisions which adults consider unwise or even dangerous? They may truant from school, take up smoking or drinking and, more dramatically, take risks with their health by refusing life-saving medical treatment. Though adolescents are individuals nearing adulthood and respect for their views is arguably more important to their own self-respect than it is to a toddler, many theorists are reluctant to allow them the freedom to make life-threatening mistakes. Many

---

[147] G. Dworkin (1982) p. 203.   [148] D. Archard (2001) p. 47.

[149] *Gillick v. West Norfolk and Wisbech Area Health Authority* [1986] AC 112. Discussed in more detail in Chapters 3 and 5.

[150] E.g. *Re Roddy (a child)(identification: restriction on publication)* [2003] EWHC 2927 (Fam), [2004] 2 FLR 949; *R (Axon) v. Secretary of State for Health and the Family Planning Association* [2006] EWCA 37 (Admin), [2006] 2 FLR 206; *Mabon v. Mabon* [2005] EWCA Civ 634, [2005] 2 FLR 1011.

theorists seem prepared to grant more autonomy generally to adolescents, whilst still supporting a paternalistic role for the state in protecting them against foolish, self-destructive choices. This is variously described as a form of 'justified paternalism',[151] or 'liberal paternalism'.[152] Freeman considers that protection against a teenager reaching decisions which threaten death or serious physical or mental harm to him or her can be justified and suggests the following formula:

> The question we should ask ourselves is: what sorts of action or conduct would we wish, as children, to be shielded against on the assumption that we would want to mature to a rationally autonomous adulthood and be capable of deciding on our own system of ends as free and rational beings?[153]

Similarly, Eekelaar's concept of 'dynamic self-determinism' also avoids the position whereby even 'competent'[154] adolescents are given complete powers of self-determination if their decisions are contrary to their self-interests, in terms of their physical and mental well-being.[155] More recently he acknowledged that there are major constraints on a child's competence[156] and that: 'Self determination under a mistake is a cruel illusion. This possibility permits certain restraints on children's freedom to be imposed in order to further the[ir] basic and developmental interests.'[157] Nevertheless, the balance is a sensitive one. Paternalistic restrictions should not deny adolescents all opportunity to take risks, for as Freeman states: 'We cannot treat persons as equals without also respecting their capacity to take risks and make mistakes.'[158] Moreover, a 'dry run' at adulthood loses all credibility if it contains no risks.

Such questions have a practical relevance, as was made clear in two cases decided by the Court of Appeal soon after the *Gillick*[159] decision. Though controversial, the outcome achieved by the judiciary in these and later decisions, which was to force the adolescents involved to undergo life-saving treatment, was fully consistent with the model of rights advocated above.[160] Today, however, such decision-making must fulfil the demands of the HRA 1998. Adolescents could now argue that they are entitled to precisely the same protection from the ECHR as any adult and that therefore the courts can no longer override their wishes by reference to their best interests.

---

[151] R. Macklin (1982) pp. 293–4.   [152] M. Freeman (1983) p. 57.   [153] Ibid. at p. 57.

[154] Eekelaar devotes some discussion to the significance of this term in J. Eekelaar (1994b) pp. 54–7. A child's legal competence to reach decisions is discussed in Chapter 3.

[155] J. Eekelaar (1994b) esp. at p. 57.

[156] J. Eekelaar (2006) p. 157: i.e. insufficient comprehension of the 'workings of the world', instability in the child's appreciation of his or her own medium term life-goals, and the presence of excessive or improper pressure.

[157] Ibid.   [158] M. Freeman (1992) p. 38. But now see M. Freeman (2005) pp. 212–13.

[159] *Gillick v. West Norfolk and Wisbech Area Health Authority* [1986] AC 112.

[160] This case law is discussed further in Chapter 3 and 5.

To date, no such challenge has been taken to the courts. But, as discussed above, there is a substantial body of theoretical opinion supporting the view that protecting the older child's long-term well-being against his short-term wishes is morally justifiable. The courts might draw confidence from the theorists' views and simply refuse all such challenges, arguing that the Convention rights are not available to any minor in the same way as they are to adults. Nevertheless, as discussed elsewhere, given the Strasbourg jurisprudence developing notions of adult autonomy and given the fact that teenagers are themselves fast approaching adulthood, the courts may come under pressure to review their position.[161] Any change would, however, undermine the protective status of minority. The ideal formula would authorise paternalistic interventions to protect adolescents from making life-threatening mistakes, but restrain autocratic and arbitrary adult restrictions on their potential for autonomy. Finding it may prove problematic.

(4) Conclusion

The considerable wealth of scholarship discussed above reflects a common assumption that children's rights are of immense importance but that attempts to satisfy them require considerable care. The concerns expressed by the theorists often resurface in the conflicts involving children that practitioners tussle with on a day-to-day basis. There is, though, an unfortunate disjunction between theory and practice. Practitioners and members of the judiciary who deal with the here and now may not see any relevance in theories which have been developed for hypothetical children as a class. They may perceive no clear and practical message which assists them when applying the law to individual children in situations involving considerable complexity. Even if sympathetic with the need to fulfil the individual child's rights, they may find it difficult to find a means of doing so. Furthermore, a child's rights may not only conflict with each other, but also with those of adults in his or her life, such as parents and other carers.

The ideas of the theorists can obviously be of more practical assistance if translated into a set of legal principles which provides clear guidance over the extent to which children's rights can be fulfilled. This sometimes occurs, but even when it does not, their theories should not be dismissed as having little practical impact. They may provide a sound intellectual basis for preferring one course of action to another. Despite the fact that this body of intellectual thought has not taken particular account of the needs of practitioners, it does provide a far better basis for translating the concept of children's rights into practice than mere intuition or prejudice. It has become of particular importance now that all those concerned with the principles of child law must come to terms with the fact that children are important rights-holders under the CRC

---

[161] Discussed further in Chapters 3 and 5 and in J. Fortin (2006) pp. 314–26.

and ECHR. Indeed, without a clearer understanding of rights theory, there is a risk that children's challenges will be dealt with on an ad hoc basis and in an increasingly confused and inconsistent manner.

BIBLIOGRAPHY

Archard, D. (2001) 'Philosophical Perspectives on Childhood' in Fionda, J. (ed.) *Legal Concepts of Childhood*, Hart Publishing.

(2004) *Children: Rights and Childhood*, Routledge.

Ariès, P. (1962) *Centuries of Childhood*, Jonathan Cape.

Bandman, B. (1973) 'Do Children Have Any Natural Rights? A Look at Rights and Claims in Legal, Moral and Educational Discourse'. Proceedings of the 29th Annual Meeting of the Philosophy of Education Society.

Bevan, H. (1989) *Child Law*, Butterworths.

Bigelow, J., Campbell, J., Dodds, S., Pargetter, R., Prior, E. and Young, R. (1988) 'Parental Autonomy' 5 *Journal of Applied Philosophy* 183.

Brennan, S. (2002) 'Children's Choices or Children's Interests: Which Do Their Rights Protect?' in Archard, D. and Macleod, M. *The Moral and Political Status of Children*, Oxford University Press.

Brighouse, H. (2002) 'What Rights (If Any) Do Children Have?' in Archard, D. and Macleod, M. *The Moral and Political Status of Children*, Oxford University Press.

Brown, P. (1982) 'Human Independence and Parental Proxy' in Gaylin, W. and Macklin, R. (eds.) *Who Speaks for the Child*, Plenum Press.

Campbell, T. (1992) 'The Rights of the Minor' in Alston, P., Parker, S. and Seymour, J. (eds.) *Children, Rights and the Law*, Clarendon Press.

Claridge, J. (updated by) (2008) *At What Age Can I? A Guide to Age-based Legislation*, The Children's Legal Centre.

Douglas, G., Murch, M., Miles, C. and Scanlan, L. (2006) *Research into the Operation of Rule 9.5 of the Family Proceedings Rules 1991, Final Report to the Department of Constitutional Affairs*, Department of Constitutional Affairs.

Dworkin, G. (1982) 'Consent, Representation and Proxy Consent' in Gaylin, W. and Macklin, R. (eds.) *Who Speaks for the Child*, Plenum Press.

Eekelaar, J. (1986) 'The Emergence of Children's Rights' 6 *Oxford Journal of Legal Studies* 161.

(1991) *Regulating Divorce*, Clarendon Press.

(1992) 'The Importance of Thinking that Children Have Rights' in Alston, P., Parker, S. and Seymour, J. (eds.) *Children, Rights and the Law*, Clarendon Press.

(1994a) 'Families and Children: From Welfarism to Rights' in McCrudden, C. and Chambers, G. *Individual Rights and Law in Britain*, Clarendon Press.

(1994b) 'The Interests of the Child and the Child's Wishes: The Role of Dynamic Self-Determinism' 8 *International Journal of Law and the Family* 42.

(2004) 'Personal Rights and Human Rights' in Lødrup, P. and Modvar, E. (eds.) *Family Life and Human Rights*, Gyldendal.

(2006) *Family Law and Personal Life*, Oxford University Press.

Farson, R. (1974) *Birthrights*, Collier Macmillan.

Federle, K. (1994) 'Rights Flow Downhill' 2 *International Journal of Children's Rights* 343.

Feinberg, J. (1980a) *Rights, Justice and the Bounds of Liberty*, Princeton University Press.

(1980b) 'The Child's Right to an Open Future' in Aiken, W. and LaFollette, H. (eds.) *Whose Child?*, Littlefield, Adams & Co.

Finnis, J. (1980) *Natural Law and Natural Rights*, Clarendon Press.

Fortin, J. (2006) 'Accommodating Children's Rights in a Post Human Rights Act Era' 69 *Modern Law Review* 299.

(2003) *Children's Rights and the Developing Law*, LexisNexis Butterworths.

Foster, H. and Freed, D. (1972) 'A Bill of Rights for Children' 6 *Family Law Quarterly* 343.

Fox Harding, L. (1997) *Perspectives in Child Care Policy*, Longman.

Franklin, B. (ed.) (2002) *The New Handbook of Children's Rights: Comparative Policy and Practice*, Routledge.

Freeman, M. (1983) *The Rights and Wrongs of Children*, Frances Pinter.

(1992) 'The Limits of Children's Rights' in Freeman, M. and Veerman, P. (eds.) *The Ideologies of Children's Rights*, Martinus Nijhoff Publishers.

(2005) 'Rethinking *Gillick*' 13 *International Journal of Children's Rights* 201.

Gaylin, W. (1982) 'Who Speaks for the Child?' in Gaylin, W. and Macklin, R. (eds.) *Who Speaks for the Child*, Plenum Press.

Goldstein, J., Freud, A. and Solnit, A. (1973) *Beyond the Best Interests of the Child*, New York Free Press.

(1980) *Before the Best Interests of the Child*, Burnett Books Ltd.

Guggenheim, M. (2005) *What's Wrong with Children's Rights?*, Harvard University Press.

Hafen, B. (1976) 'Children's Liberation and the New Egalitarianism: Some Reservations About Abandoning Youth to their "Rights"', *Brigham Young University Law Review* 605.

Harris, J. (1980) *Legal Philosophies*, Butterworths.

Hart, H. L. A. (1963) *Law, Liberty and Morality*, Oxford University Press.

(1984) 'Are There Any Natural Rights?' reproduced in Waldron, J. *Theories of Rights*, Oxford University Press.

Held, V. (2006) *The Ethics of Care*, Oxford University Press.

Herring, J. and Taylor, R. (2006) 18 *Child and Family Law Quarterly* 517.

Hohfeld, W. (1919) *Fundamental Legal Conceptions as Applied in Judicial reasoning*, Yale University Press.

Holt, J. (1974) *Escape from Childhood: The Needs and Rights of Childhood*, E P Dutton and Co Inc.

James, A., James, A. and McNamee, S. (2004) 'Turn down the volume? – not hearing children in family proceedings' 16 *Child and Family Law Quarterly* 189.

Kaganas, F. and Diduck, A. (2004) 'Incomplete Citizens: Changing Images of Post-Separation Children' 67 *Modern Law Review* 959.

King, M. (1994) 'Children's Rights as Communication: Reflections on Autopoietic Theory and the United Nations Convention' 57 *Modern Law Review* 385.

Kiss, E. (1997) 'Alchemy or Fool's Gold? Assessing Feminist Doubts About Rights' in Shanley, M. and Narayan, U. (eds.) *Reconstructing Political Theory*, Polity Press.

Laws, J. (1998) 'The Limitations of Human Rights' *Public Law* 254.

Laws, J. (2003) 'Beyond Rights' 23 *Oxford Journal of Legal Studies* 265.

Lim, H. and Roche, J. (2000) 'Feminism and Children's Rights' in Bridgeman, J. and Monk, D. (eds.) *Feminist Perspectives on Child Law*, Cavendish.

Lindley, R. (1989) 'Teenagers and Other Children' in Scarre, G. (ed.) *Children, Parents and Politics*, Cambridge University Press.

Lyons, D. (1984) 'Utility and Rights' in Waldron J. (ed.) *Theories of Rights*, Oxford University Press.

MacCormick, N. (1982) *Legal Right and Social Democracy: Essays in Legal and Political Philosophy*, Clarendon Press.

Macklin, R. (1982) 'Return to the Best Interests of the Child' in Gaylin, W. and Macklin, R. (eds) *Who Speaks for the Child*, Plenum Press.

Mill, J.S. (1859), On Liberty from Acton, H. (ed.) (1972) *Utilitarianism, Liberty, Representative Government*, Dent.

Minow, M. (1986) 'Rights For the Next Generation: A Feminist Approach to Children's Rights' 9 *Harvard Women's Law Journal* 1.

(1987) 'Interpreting Rights: An Essay for Robert Cover' 96 *Yale Law Journal* 1860.

O'Brien Steinfels, M. (1982) 'Children's Rights, Parental Rights, Family Privacy, and Family Autonomy' in Gaylin, W. and Macklin, R. (eds.) *Who Speaks for the Child*, Plenum Press.

O'Neill, O. (1992) 'Children's Rights and Children's Lives' in Alston, P., Parker, S. and Seymour, J. (eds.) *Children, Rights and the Law*, Clarendon Press.

Olsen, F. (1992) 'Children's Rights: Some Feminist Approaches to the United Nations Convention on the Rights of the Child' in Alston, P., Parker, S. and Seymour, J. (eds.) *Children, Rights and the Law*, Clarendon Press.

Parker, S. (1992) 'Rights and Utility in Anglo-Australian Family Law' 55 *Modern Law Review* 311.

Pollock, L. (1983) *Forgotten Children: Parent-Child Relations from 1500–1900*, Cambridge University Press.

Purdy, L. (1992) In *Their Best Interest? The Case Against Equal Rights for Children*, Cornell University Press.

Rawls, J. (1971) *A Theory of Justice*, Oxford University Press.

Raz, J. (1984a) 'Hart on Moral Rights and Legal Duties' 4 *Oxford Journal of Legal Studies* 123.

(1984b) 'Legal Rights' 4 *Oxford Journal of Legal Studies* 1.

(1986) *The Morality of Freedom*, Clarendon Press.

(1996) 'Liberty and Trust' in George, R. (ed.) *Natural Law, Liberalism and Morality*, Oxford University Press.

Wald, M. (1979) 'Children's Rights: A Framework for Analysis' 12 *University of California Davis Law Review* 255.

Waldron, J. (ed.) (1984) *Theories of Rights*, Oxford University Press.

(1993) *Liberal Rights: Collected Papers 1891–1991*, Cambridge University Press.

Wellman, C. *The Proliferation of Rights: Moral Progress or Empty Rhetoric?*, Westview Press.

de Winter, M. (1997) *Children as Fellow Citizens: Participation and Commitment*, Radcliffe Medical Press Ltd.

Chapter 2

International children's rights

(1) Introduction

A large body of international human rights law exists today which informs the way that domestic law promotes children's rights in the UK. The translation of ideas about children's rights into principles of English law was undoubtedly accelerated by the British government ratifying a series of international instruments prepared by the General Assembly of the United Nations and by the Council of Europe. An event of outstanding importance was the ratification by the UK of the United Nations Convention on the Rights of the Child (CRC) in 1991. This long and ambitious list of children's rights constitutes a painstaking attempt to define children's needs and aspirations and to commit ratifying states to their accomplishment. Although not part of English law as such, it currently exerts an increasingly powerful influence on the developing law and is often used as an international template against which to measure domestic standards.

Unlike the CRC, the European Convention on Human Rights and Fundamental Freedoms (ECHR) was not designed specifically to protect children as a group. But they, as human beings, are entitled to claim its protection and it has a direct influence on the way in which children's rights are protected in this country. Indeed, on 2 October 2000, the day on which the Human Rights Act (HRA) 1998 was implemented, the rights listed in the ECHR left the international domain and formed part of the slowly accumulating layers of domestic case law and legislation. Despite its status as part of the UK's domestic law, no chapter devoted to an assessment of children's rights from an international perspective would be complete without a discussion of the ECHR's singular significance, alongside the CRC.

The following chapter discusses the importance of these two international treaties and the manner in which they have been interpreted. It also considers briefly a variety of other international instruments produced by the United Nations and the Council of Europe which provide insight on international expectations regarding the treatment of children in various areas of activity. First, though, it devotes a short discussion to the links between theories about children's moral and legal rights and those underlying their international human rights.

(2) Rights theories and international human rights

The jurisprudential doubts underlying the existence and scope of children's rights[1] did not inhibit the efforts of those seeking to promote children's protection in an international context. Indeed, had it not been for the driving force of international human rights lawyers, ideas and theories about children's rights might have remained in the realms of intellectual speculation. At first sight, the academics and legal practitioners concerned with the field of international human rights appear to be interested in entirely different concepts from the pure rights theories which concern the moral philosophers and jurists. These differences, more apparent than real, are exacerbated by the different language they employ. Indeed, Eekelaar argues that '[H]uman rights have the same structure as all rights. My thesis is that the only difference lies in the nature of the social base through which the entitlement is claimed ... *the social base is the whole of humanity.*'[2]

It was not until the aftermath of the Second World War that the term 'human rights' crept into common parlance as a way of describing the moral rights considered fundamental to civilised existence.[3] The draftsmen of the post-War international treaties adopted the new term in preference to the well-known phrase 'rights of man' favoured by natural law theorists. Thus the United Nations in its founding charter of 1945 stated that one of its primary purposes was to promote and encourage 'respect for human rights and for fundamental freedoms for all without distinction as to race, sex, language, or religion'. Only three years later, in 1948, the Universal Declaration of Human Rights, adopted by the United Nations General Assembly, contained a general statement guaranteeing 'the inherent dignity and ... equal and inalienable rights of all members of the human family'.[4]

It was the civil and political rights selected for protection by the post-War treaties that were most clearly based on the ideas of the earlier natural law philosophers. They were derived from those inalienable rights of man that seventeenth-century theorists, like Hugo Grotius and John Locke, considered to be fundamental to human nature. Locke argued that, according to the laws of nature, each human being is entitled to the inalienable moral right to life, liberty and property.[5] These ideas had grounded the eighteenth-century bills of rights emanating from America and France – the American Declaration of Independence of 1776 and the French Declaration of the Rights of Man and of the Citizen of 1789. Although interest in natural rights theories waned during the nineteenth century, it revived in the 1940s in response to the manner in

---

[1] Discussed in Chapter 1.   [2] J. Eekelaar (2004) p. 188. See also J. Eekelaar (2006) p. 340.
[3] C. Wellman (1999) esp. at pp. 13–21: the historical development of the concept of natural rights and their later translation into 'human rights', as set out in a series of international treaties.
[4] K. Marshall and P. Parvis (2004) pp. 103–6 and pp. 129–31. See also pp. 114–16 for a useful analysis of the term 'inalienable,' as used in many human rights documents.
[5] C. Wellman (1999) esp. at pp. 13–21. See also K. Marshall and P. Parvis (2004) pp. 95–103.

which totalitarian regimes, such as that of Nazi Germany, had been able to commit atrocities on a horrifying scale. As Feldman observes:

> the idea at the root of human rights thinking is that there are certain rights which are so fundamental to society's well-being and to people's chance of leading a fulfilling life that governments are obligated to respect them, and the international order has to protect them.[6]

The ECHR 1950 and the International Covenant on Civil and Political Rights (ICCPR) 1966 were both primarily concerned with fundamental liberties. The 'first generation human rights' they listed sought to protect the individual from oppressive interference by a nation state. Their provisions typically guarantee freedom from torture, from conviction without a fair trial, of expression and the right to peaceful assembly. By contrast, documents such as the Universal Declaration of Human Rights 1948[7] and the International Covenant on Economic, Social and Cultural Rights (ICESCR) 1966, which contain a list of 'second generation rights', reflect a more developed theory of human rights.[8] These seek to ensure that the first generation of 'negative' liberties are complemented by requiring states to take positive action to promote the welfare of individual human beings. In an approach later echoed in the CRC, the ICESCR reflects the view that it is not enough for human rights documents to identify certain liberties essential to individual autonomy, such as freedom of speech and assembly.[9] These rights may be of no value to those too poor or ill to benefit from them, whose time is taken up surviving from day to day.[10] Consequently, the Covenant obliges states to take a more active role. They are required to make resources available for certain additional social welfare rights; for example by guaranteeing the right to an adequate standard of living[11] and to the highest attainable standard of physical and mental health,[12] thereby enabling people to take advantage of their innate freedoms. Some international lawyers refuse to acknowledge that these social welfare rights can have the force of international law, because there is no obvious means of enforcing them.[13] Nevertheless, their inclusion in a variety of international documents, including the CRC, constantly reminds states of their wider obligations regarding their citizens.

The notion that children are, as human beings, entitled to human rights, was gradually accepted in an international and domestic context. Indeed, during the second half of the twentieth century it became widely acknowledged that

---

[6] D. Feldman (2002) pp. 34–5.

[7] Esp. Arts. 22–9; cf. arts. 1–21 which embrace the traditional civil and political rights.

[8] C. Wellman (1999) pp. 29–30, discusses the emergence of a third generation of human rights – the 'solidarity rights' or the rights of normally vulnerable groups to protection, *as a group*, rather than as individuals. E.g., inter alia, the Convention on the Prevention of the Crime of Genocide 1948, which was motivated by the German attempts to destroy the Jewish race throughout Europe; the Convention on the Elimination of All Forms of Discrimination against Women 1979.

[9] This approach was also evident in arts 22–9 of the Universal Declaration of Human Rights.

[10] D. Feldman (2002) pp. 12–14.   [11] ICESCR, Art. 11.   [12] Ibid. Art. 12.

[13] Arguments summarised by C. Wellman (1999) pp. 20–9.

children's human rights were theoretically no different from those of adults – they too were entitled to certain fundamental moral rights carrying the force of international law. This perception underpins the CRC. That document not only contains the civil and political rights derived from the inalienable 'rights of man', but also the second generation social welfare rights guaranteed by documents like the ICESCR. The concept of children's rights thereby acquired an important international dimension which is difficult for government and public agencies to ignore.

(3) The United Nations and the aftermath of the Second World War

The atrocities perpetrated before and during the Second World War led to a firm resolve to strengthen international unity. Indeed, the main spur to identify the human rights important to mankind, to include them in international treaties and to persuade governments to recognise them on a worldwide basis has always been some serious disregard for humanitarian values.[14] A determination to prevent such appalling events occurring again was accompanied by the promulgation of a large number of human rights instruments setting out those rights deemed essential to civilised life. Attempts to strengthen international unity included establishing the United Nations, whose charter came into force in 1945.

This post-War activity was intended to strengthen human rights generally. Although children implicitly benefited from it, they received no special protection as a group. The charter of the United Nations simply seeks to promote and encourage the human rights and fundamental freedoms 'for all without distinction as to race, sex, language or religion'. Whilst it certainly does not exclude children from its ambit, it contains no specific reference to them.[15] Similarly, the Universal Declaration of Human Rights adopted in 1948 contains references to children[16] and guarantees the 'equal and inalienable rights of all members of the human family',[17] but makes no attempt to provide for a range of rights more suitable for children with needs of their own.

A wide variety of UN human rights instruments now exists which refer to children's rights in various different contexts,[18] but again their main emphasis is not on children specifically. Admittedly, some, like the twin covenants adopted by the General Assembly of the United Nations in 1966, the ICCPR and the ICESCR, do refer specifically to children's special needs.[19] The former

---

[14] D. Feldman (2002) p. 35. See also C. Wellman (1999) pp. 20–9.   [15] Art. 55(c).

[16] Art. 25(2) refers to motherhood and childhood both requiring special care and assistance; see also Art. 26, which concerns educational rights.

[17] Preamble.   [18] R. Hodgkin and P. Newell (2007) Appendix 4.

[19] E.g. Art. 10(3) of the ICESCR seeks to protect children from economic and social exploitation, particularly in the workplace, whilst Art. 13 enshrines the right of everyone to education. Similarly, Art. 10 of the ICCPR deals with the rights of juvenile offenders, whilst Art. 24 guarantees children's right to protection by his family, society and the state.

covenant provides particularly important safeguards for the religious rights of minority groups.[20] Nevertheless, these general human rights documents make no attempt to deal with the broad spectrum of children's needs or to make them their main focus of attention. By contrast, the CRC, adopted by the General Assembly over 20 years later in 1989, achieves both aims outstandingly well, with many of the provisions listed in these earlier documents reappearing in the new children's convention.

A second remarkable document is the Beijing Rules, whose official title is the United Nations Standard Minimum Rules for the Administration of Juvenile Justice. These were adopted by the General Assembly in 1985 and, like the CRC, relate only to children. They are, nevertheless, limited to a very narrow focus of their activities. They provide a complete and detailed framework for the operation of a national youth justice system. Their weakness is that they have no legal status, merely providing guidance on good practice. Despite this, the Beijing Rules provide a complete and realistic coverage of what an ideal youth justice system should aim to achieve at every stage of the process for dealing with children caught up in youth crime. As discussed later,[21] they display an impressively thorough understanding of the whole area of youth crime and of the need to avoid dealing with young offenders in an over-aggressive and inhumane way.[22]

(4) The United Nations and children's rights

Although the special vulnerability of children as a group had been recognised much earlier than the international human rights activity generated by the Second World War, little progress was made towards producing an instrument which had binding force, covering the full scope of their needs. The first important international document devoted entirely to protecting the rights of children was adopted by the Fifth Assembly of the League of Nations in 1924. This was the Declaration of the Rights of the Child, known as the Declaration of Geneva.[23] It contained only five basic principles, all of which were couched in forthright terms. Thus the first commenced with the words: 'The child must be given the means requisite for its normal development, both materially and spiritually.' The second went on to state that: 'The child that is hungry must be fed; the child that is sick must be nursed'. The third was even more to the point, stating merely that: 'The child must be the first to receive relief in times of distress.'

The Declaration of Geneva was brief and aspirational; it merely invited the member states to be 'guided by its principles in the work of child welfare'. Of far

---

[20] Art. 27; discussed further in Chapter 11.   [21] Chapter 18.

[22] See also the Riyadh Guidelines (the UN Guidelines for the Prevention of Juvenile Delinquency), adopted in 1990.

[23] D. Hodgson (1992) pp. 260–1. See also P. Alston and J. Tobin (2005) p. 4.

greater importance was the Declaration of the Rights of the Child adopted in 1959 by the General Assembly of the United Nations.[24] This longer document contained ten principles, but again, it had the limited status of a declaration. It did not attempt to claim that the 'rights' listed constituted legal obligations. Instead, states were merely required to take note of the principles contained therein, on the basis that they were universally accepted as being applicable to all children.

Some of the principles set out in the 1959 Declaration now appear idealistic, others simply vague and outdated. Nevertheless, as Alston and Tobin point out, the document is significant for the way it emphasises children's emotional well-being.[25] Principle 6 refers to a child's need for 'love and understanding', and to grow up in an atmosphere of 'affection and of moral and material security'. Other parts, however, reflect outmoded stereotyped ideas about the roles to be played by mothers and fathers in the lives of their children. Principle 6 also asserts that a 'child of tender years shall not, save in exceptional circumstances, be separated from his mother'. As Thorpe LJ emphasised, when trenchantly rejecting a mother's claim that Principle 6 strengthened her application for a residence order:

> The relevance and value of the UN 1959 Declaration is most doubtful. In terms of relevant social policy it could be said to be almost antiquated since it is now nearly 40 years old and in terms of social development and in terms of understanding of child development and welfare that is an exceedingly long time.[26]

The real importance of the 1959 Declaration lies in the fact that it embodies the first serious attempt to describe in a reasonably detailed manner what constitutes children's overriding claims and entitlements. Whilst not overlooking its weaknesses, some of the ideas it contains are surprisingly modern and reappear in an elaborated form in the CRC, introduced 30 years later in 1989. For example, the references to the child's right to name and nationality; to treatment without discrimination; to socioeconomic rights, such as housing, medical care and food; to rights to education and protection from exploitation, neglect and cruelty; all found their way into the 1989 Convention.

To a modern eye, the greatest weakness of the 1959 document was its failure to list any of the first generation human rights, the freedoms from state oppression. Indeed, barring the reference to name and nationality, there is no mention of children's civil and political rights.[27] The CRC was borne out of calls for a more systematic approach to protecting children's rights. By the 1970s, growing concern over the violations of children's rights throughout the world led finally to a move to establish an international document guaranteeing children's rights through the imposition of legal obligations.[28] In 1976, the

---

[24] P. Alston and J. Tobin (2005) pp. 5–6.   [25] Ibid. at p. 5.

[26] *Re A (children: 1959 UN Declaration)* [1998] 1 FLR 354 at 358. The father successfully appealed their 3½-year-old son being the subject of a residence order in the mother's favour.

[27] P. Alston and J. Tobin (2005) p. 5.   [28] Ibid. at pp. 6–7 and D. Hodgson (1992) pp. 275–6.

United Nations General Assembly, fulfilling a request from the executive board of UNICEF, declared 1979 the International Year of the Child and urged governments to commemorate the year by making special contributions to improving the well-being of children. As its contribution to the year, the Polish government, in 1978, submitted to the United Nations Commission on Human Rights a draft for a new CRC. It was virtually identical in format to the 1959 Declaration and it was hoped that it could be adopted by the United Nations the following year, as a legally binding international document. Such an optimistic timescale proved unrealistic. Although there was general agreement that a document of this nature should be created, it was considered that there was little point in repeating the mistakes of the 1959 Declaration. Governments would continue to ignore their obligations to children unless the provisions were sufficiently specific and realistic. Nearly ten years were to elapse before a final draft of the CRC was completed in 1988 and submitted to the Commission on Human Rights for approval in 1989. It was finally adopted by the General Assembly in November 1989, entering into force in 1990. It was ratified by the UK in 1991 and came into force in the UK in January 1992.

(5) The Convention on the Rights of the Child

(A) A broad spectrum of rights

The Preamble to the CRC makes plain the size of the task taken on by its draftsmen and the conflicting ideals that required accommodation within a document commanding international respect. Whilst recognising the importance of the family as 'the fundamental group of society' and the child's need to 'grow up in a family environment' with love and understanding, it also asserts that 'a child should be fully prepared to live an individual life in society, and brought up in the spirit of the ideals proclaimed in the Charter of the United Nations, and in particular in the spirit of peace, dignity, tolerance, freedom, equality and solidarity'.[29] Despite these conflicts, the decade of drafting produced a document which, if fully complied with, would indeed achieve many of these aims.

The rights listed cover the broad spectrum of children's needs and aspirations. Its fifty-four articles, some forty of which are concerned with substantive rights, cover civil, political, economic and social issues. Unlike most other international human rights treaties, notably the ICCPR and the ICESCR, the CRC contains both sets of rights in one single document. The Convention applies to 'every human being below the age of eighteen years'[30] and by including all the traditional civil and political rights, such as freedom of expression,[31] religion,[32] association and assembly,[33] it departs radically from

---

[29] Preamble to the CRC, para. 7.   [30] Unless the age of majority is attained earlier; see Art 1.
[31] Art. 13.   [32] Art. 14.   [33] Art. 15.

the earlier international documents which primarily aimed to address children's immaturity and need for care. By including children's social and economic rights, the Convention also emphasises that states must not only protect children and safeguard their fundamental freedoms, but also devote resources to ensuring that they realise their potential for maturing into a healthy and happy adulthood. Indeed, although the wording of Article 4 reflects 'a realistic acceptance that lack of resources – financial and other resources – can hamper the full implementation of economic, social and cultural rights in some States … States need to be able to demonstrate that they have implemented "to the maximum extent of their available resources"'.[34]

The CRC's provisions demonstrate a strange mixture of idealism and practical realism. Some, like Article 28 on education, descend into the detailed aspects of schooling, such as ensuring regular attendance and 'the reduction of drop-out rates'.[35] Others, like Article 12, assuring respect for the child's views, maintain a more philosophical approach to their capacity for autonomy. When interpreting some of the more opaque provisions, valuable assistance can be derived from the research which has analysed the 'Concluding Observations'[36] of the Committee on the Rights of the Child. This throws light on the Committee's view of the Convention's intentions.

Although the Committee has stressed that the articles of the Convention are interrelated and should be considered together, it has itself elevated Articles 2,[37] 3,[38] 6[39] and 12[40] to the status of general principles,[41] with a suggested greater priority being given to their implementation.[42] Theoretically, none of these four principles is more important than any other; nevertheless Article 3, requiring a commitment to the child's best interests, underpins all the other provisions. It should be noted, however, that unlike the Children Act (CA) 1989, section 1, which provides that the child's best interests are paramount,[43] Article 3(1) only provides that 'the best interests of the child shall be *a* primary consideration'. This rather grudging approach to a principle overriding an entirely child-centred document is attributable to the concerns of delegates that there might be other competing interests, for example, those of justice and society, at times making paramountcy inappropriate.[44] Despite the 'best interests' formula not adopting the paramountcy criterion, the Committee on the Rights of the Child is keen not to allow it to be downplayed.[45] It constantly emphasises that Article 3 must be used as 'a guiding principle' when interpreting all

---

[34] Committee on the Rights of the Child (2003) para. 7.   [35] Art. 28(1)(e).

[36] Discussed below.   [37] Freedom from discrimination.   [38] The child's best interests.

[39] The right to life.   [40] Respect for the child's views.

[41] Committee on the Rights of the Child (2003) para. 12.

[42] Committee on the Rights of the Child (1995) para. 27.

[43] See also Principle 2 of the 1959 Declaration of the Rights of the Child which made the child's interests paramount.

[44] R. Barsh (1989) pp. 143–4; D. McGoldrick (1991) pp. 135–7; U. Kilkelly and L. Lundy (2006) p. 337.

[45] R. Hodgkin and P. Newell (2007) pp. 39–48.

Convention provisions. Consequently it should be reflected in all 'legislative and policy matters affecting children',[46] including legislation on health, education and social security.[47] Furthermore, it should underwrite all obligations regarding the allocation of resources.[48] In other words, *all* children's rights must be interpreted in accordance with their best interests.[49]

(B) Classifying the Convention rights

Important though they are, the four general principles cannot stand alone. They are underpinned by a broad array of substantive rights, together comprising a bewildering hotchpotch of provisions, some overlapping considerably in their aims.[50] The contents of the Convention have been classified in a variety of ways, none of which avoids overlap.[51] Although not ideal, LeBlanc's classification,[52] by including 'membership rights', emphasises the way in which the Convention addresses children's need for community. According to his arrangement, the rights are classified into 'survival rights', 'membership rights', 'protection rights' and 'empowerment rights'.[53] The survival rights include not only the right to life itself, but also the right to all those rights which sustain life, such as the rights to an adequate standard of living and to health care. Membership rights include those which treat the child as a member of his or her community and family. Protection rights guard the child against abuses of power by individuals and the state. Finally, empowerment rights secure a respect for children as effective members of the communities in which they live, through protecting their freedom of thought and conscience and encouraging their capacity for self-determination.[54]

The empowerment rights listed by the Convention are the most remarkable given that many of the delegates involved in the drafting sessions were from Islamic countries whose conceptions of the role of children in families and the wider community were relatively narrow.[55] The Convention recognises that children are active and creative and may need encouragement to shape their own lives. As such they must be assisted to develop their independence and ability to take responsibility for their future. In particular, by extending the traditional civil and political rights to children, the Convention indicates that all

---

[46] Committee on the Rights of the Child (2008) para. 26.   [47] Ibid. (1995) para. 11.
[48] I.e. under Art. 4; ibid. (1995) para. 24.   [49] R. Hodgkin and P. Newell (2007) p. 39.
[50] K. Marshall and P. Parvis (2004) pp. 12–20.
[51] E.g. T. Hammarberg (1990) suggests a classification involving the four 'P's: the participation of children in decisions involving their own destiny; the protection of children against discrimination and all forms of neglect; the prevention of harm to children; and the provision of assistance for their basic needs.
[52] Adapted from that proposed by J. Donnelly and R. Howard (1988).
[53] L. LeBlanc (1995) Part Two.   [54] Ibid. at p. xviii.
[55] See J. Fortin (2003) pp. 38–40, for a more detailed analysis of the survival rights, the membership rights and protection rights.

children, irrespective of age, have the same dignity and worth as adults.[56] In particular, they require the liberties essential to notions of adult autonomy if they are to develop their own capacity for autonomy and play an active part in society.

Article 12 is often singled out as being one of the most important in the Convention.[57] It assures to children capable of forming their own views 'the right to express those views freely in all matters affecting (them), the views of the child being given due weight in accordance with the age and maturity of the child'.[58] Moreover, Article 12(2) provides children with the procedural right to be heard in any judicial or administrative proceedings affecting them – this latter provision being crucially important to children who are the subject of parental disputes.[59] When responding to each state's periodic reports on the progress made towards implementation, the Committee on the Rights of the Child often stresses that the principles set out in Article 12 should be given 'greater priority' and that this should be seen as a right and not merely a matter of discretion for individual governments. Involving and consulting children must also 'avoid being tokenistic'.[60] States are constantly urged to make further efforts to ensure children's active participation in the family, schools and other institutions.[61]

Closely linked with and complementing Article 12, is Article 13 securing the right to freedom of expression, including the right to seek, receive and impart information and ideas. As Newell and Hodgkin point out, this is the first of a series of articles contained in the Convention specifically confirming that children are, like 'everyone' else, entitled to the civil rights guaranteed by the more general human rights documents.[62] The Convention also recognises that in order to form and express their own views, children need access to information and material from a variety of sources.[63] Even more fundamental, they are entitled to respect and dignity, as they mature to adulthood. States must secure their rights to freedom of thought, conscience and religion,[64] to privacy[65] and a freedom to meet and mix with others and share views.[66] Crucially, children cannot develop their views and critical thought without a right to education. This too is fully recognised, with detailed provisions regarding the practical aspects of providing schooling,[67] and additionally setting out the more philosophical aims of education, including the need to promote a respect for the child's parents and his or her cultural identity.[68]

---

[56] The second paragraph of the Preamble to the Convention reminds states that the UN Charter reaffirmed faith in 'fundamental human rights and in the dignity and worth of the human person'.
[57] R. Hodgkin and P. Newell (2007) pp. 149–71.   [58] Art. 12(1).
[59] Discussed further in Chapter 7.   [60] Committee on the Rights of the Child (2003) para. 12.
[61] E.g. Committee on the Rights of the Child (1995) para. 27; ibid. (2002a) paras. 29 and 30; ibid. (2008), paras. 32–3. See also R. Hodgkin and P. Newell (2007) pp. 149–71.
[62] E.g. the Universal Declaration of Human Rights. R. Hodgkin and P. Newell (2007) p. 177.
[63] Art. 17.   [64] Art. 14(1).   [65] Art. 16.   [66] Art. 15.   [67] Art. 28(1)(a)–(e).   [68] Art. 29.

(C) Internal inconsistencies

The aims of the Convention, as set out in the Preamble, are ambitious. In particular, it emphasises the need to promote children's capacity for eventual autonomy, whilst simultaneously supporting the traditional role of the family in society and the authority of parents over their children. Some might argue that these aims are irreconcilable. Certainly the wording of the Preamble and some of the other articles containing internal inconsistencies reflect the many disagreements during the drafting sessions. Conflicting views were expressed by the delegates from the Islamic countries, who were deeply opposed to giving children freedom from parental direction and religious teaching and by those from countries like the US, who, influenced by their own constitutional history, strongly favoured the concept of children enjoying similar civil and political rights to adults.[69] Some delegates also feared that providing families with protection from state interference would provide parents with arbitrary control over their children, thereby inhibiting children from being able to develop their own views.

The compromises resulting from attempts to balance these differing approaches to the family are reflected in many of the articles. Thus whilst Article 3(2) requires states to ensure the child 'such protection and care as is necessary for his or her well-being', they must do so 'taking into account the rights and duties of his or her parents.' Similarly, Article 5, which respects the parents' right to direct and guide their children, conflicts with the position adopted by other provisions which promote a child's capacity for independence. As McGoldrick observes, the wording of Article 5 itself is fraught with difficulty, since those obliged to fulfil it are the very individuals who may have a personal interest in ensuring that children do not exercise their rights.[70] Significantly, neither Article 12, which requires states to ensure that children's opinions are sought, nor Article 13 regarding a child's right to freedom of expression, contains any qualifying phrase requiring states to take account of parental wishes. Indeed, Article 12(1) makes it clear that *every* child who is capable of forming his or her own views should have the right to express them freely over all matters affecting him or her.[71] The fact that Article 12(1) ends with the phrase 'the views of the child being given due weight *in accordance with the age and maturity of the child*'[72] might apparently offer scope for a paternalistic restriction of the underlying aims of the article. Nevertheless, the Committee on the Rights of the Child has criticised attempts to exploit this phrase in a way which dilutes children's participation rights.[73]

The inclusion of the traditional human right to freedom of religion provoked considerable disagreement amongst those attending the drafting sessions.

---

[69] L. LeBlanc (1995) ch. 1 and pp. 112–17.   [70] D. McGoldrick (1991) pp. 138–9.
[71] R. Hodgkin and P. Newell (2007) p. 153.   [72] Emphasis supplied.
[73] E.g. by Finland making the right to be heard dependent on a child attaining the age of 12. R. Hodgkin and P. Newell (2007) pp. 153–4.

Islamic states were strongly opposed to any suggestion that the child should have complete freedom of religious choice.[74] It is notable that Article 14 does not, unlike its counterpart in the ICCPR, specifically set out a correlative right to 'have or adopt a religion or belief of his choice'.[75] This could imply that the CRC merely gives children the right to *practise* their own religion, rather than the freedom to 'choose' it, thereby maintaining the parental right to impose a 'choice' of religion on their children. Belgium and The Netherlands made declarations indicating their intention to expand the meaning of Article 14 by interpreting it in accordance with the provisions of Article 18 of the ICCPR.[76] Reflecting the Islamic states' concerns, Article 14(2) stresses the parental right 'to provide direction to the child in the exercise of his or her right in a manner consistent with the evolving capacities of the child'. Nevertheless, as Hodgkin and Newell emphasise, the wording of Article 14(2) does not suggest that children should automatically adopt their parents' religion. Indeed, the right to freedom of religion is unambiguously that of the child, with parents only able to provide direction, and then direction which is consistent with the child's own developing competence, and with the child's own rights under Articles 12 and 13.[77] Perhaps predictably, there are more reservations made against Article 14 (1) than any other article.[78] Freedom of religion in schools is of particular importance to children of minority groups, but these children's interests may not be identical to those of their parents. Again, these tensions are not resolved by the Convention which expresses a need to allow children their own independence, whilst supporting their cultural heritage. This conflict comes out most clearly in the context of the child's right to education.[79] Although the child's need for a broad education is recognised by Article 29,[80] that provision also refers to the need for education to develop 'respect for the child's parents, his or her own cultural identity, language and values'.[81]

It would be foolish to deny the existence of compromises and internal inconsistencies within the Convention. Indeed, as in many domestic legal systems, including our own, it reflects an obvious ambivalence over the need to promote children's capacity for self-determination, whilst at the same time maintaining the traditional rights of parents to provide direction, support and discipline.[82] Inevitably, its drafting could, with hindsight, be improved upon, for example, to give greater attention to certain groups of children, such as the disabled.[83] Like many other international conventions, it contains little very

---

[74] L. LeBlanc (1995) pp. 168–75.   [75] ICCPR, Art. 18(1).

[76] R. Hodgkin and P. Newell (2007) p. 189 and K. Marshall and P. Parvis (2004) p. 23.

[77] Ibid. at p. 188.

[78] Ibid. and K. Marshall and P. Parvis (2004) p. 23: reservations placed against it by countries where Islam is the state religion commonly specify that children have no right to choose or change their religion.

[79] Art. 28(1).   [80] Art. 29(1)(a).

[81] Art. 29(1)(c); this conflict is discussed further in Chapter 12.   [82] J. Fortin (2002) p. 19.

[83] M. Freeman (2000) pp. 282–9; U. Kilkelly and L. Lundy (2006) p. 336.

practical or specific advice. Indeed, as King rightly says, it 'contains a wide range of rather vague political and economic rights and duties which require further precision and transformation at the national level if they are to become amenable to lawful/unlawful decisions'.[84] But for all its faults, the Convention remains a remarkable document, which provides a comprehensive set of standards against which ratifying states may measure the extent to which they fulfil children's rights.

(D) Success or failure?

The CRC had a startling success in so far as it was quickly ratified by every country in the world, bar the US and Somalia.[85] Despite this near universal acclaim, the Convention is not without its critics. The American refusal to ratify the Convention is based on a number of concerns,[86] the more vocal largely emanating from politically conservative Christian organisations.[87] Much of it is based on an incorrect interpretation of its provisions and of its underlying aims. Contrary to the beliefs of some American parents, the Convention provides a framework for implementation through government policies and programmes, not through interference with individual families. The provisions that produce greatest unease from a variety of quarters are those encouraging children to assert their independence. American critics suggest that the Convention will undermine parents' authority over their children through 'its sweeping and unprecedented creation of autonomy rights for children [which] may, in the long run, threaten children's well being'.[88] But Americans are not the only critics of the Convention. From a different perspective, others argue that by encouraging children's independence, the Convention is attempting to impose on non-industrialised countries the ideas and values of the richer Western states.[89] There are also those who consider that whilst the ruling elites in many non-Western countries enthusiastically endorse the Western human rights ideals implicit in the CRC, the local populations have very different cultural norms.[90] Large numbers of Islamic countries placed sweeping reservations against some of the articles (notably Article 14) indicating their intention to abide by the CRC, but only in so far as it is consistent with Islamic law; information which must reflect a relatively widespread concern about some of its aims.[91]

[84] M. King (1994) p. 395.
[85] P. Alston and J. Tobin (2005) p. x: 192 countries have ratified the CRC, a number unmatched by any other international convention.
[86] S. Kilbourne (1998) discusses the ways in which the American federal system undermines attempts to ratify the Convention.
[87] Ibid.; K. Marshall and P. Parvis (2004) pp. 52–63; P. Alston and J. Tobin (2005) p. 12.
[88] R. Wilkins (2004) p. 998.   [89] S. Timimi (2006) p. 38.   [90] S. Harris-Short (2003).
[91] K. Marshall and P. Parvis (2004) pp. 20–4.

From a more theoretical viewpoint, there are also the jurisprudential doubts about the true status of some of the 'rights' listed in the Convention.[92] It is argued that although acceptable as moral claims, many of the 'rights' listed by the Convention are far too vague to be translated into international or domestic law.[93] Indeed, by asserting so many 'legal rights' on behalf of children, the Convention certainly contributes to the process of rights 'devaluation' described by Wellman.[94] Such lack of clarity also undermines the CRC's usefulness as a practical monitoring tool.[95] Many of the rights listed are, in reality, no more than aspirations regarding what *should* happen if governments were to take children's needs seriously – an insistence on certain ideals or goals. Indeed, as noted above, Article 4 clearly acknowledges that the resource implications of such provisions may rule out their immediate or even long-term fulfilment. Its use of the future tense, when enlarging on states' obligations under these articles, emphasises this realism.[96] Nevertheless, many authors consider that the 'rhetoric of rights' is justified,[97] expressing the conviction that these aspirations ought to be recognised by states here and now as potential rights and that they provide guides to present policies.[98] Eekelaar is surely right to argue that the symbolism of the CRC is as important as its practical efficacy. In his view, 'to recognize people as having rights from the moment of their birth continuously into adulthood could turn out, politically, to be the most radical step of all'.[99]

A more practical, though fundamental, weakness is that the Convention has no direct method of formal enforcement, either available to the rights-holders themselves, or to the United Nations Commission. By contrast with the ECHR, there is no court which can assess claims that its terms have been infringed. Governments are merely directed to undertake 'all appropriate legislative, administrative and other measures' to implement the rights contained in the Convention.[100] The implementation mechanism is similar to that of other United Nations human rights treaties. Thus the only body with responsibility for 'examining the progress made by States Parties in achieving the realisation of the obligations' contained therein is the Committee on the Rights of the Child, established under the auspices of the General Assembly of the United Nations.[101] The Committee sits in Geneva and consists of 18 experts elected from within the ranks of states parties who have ratified the Convention. In the absence of any formal method for requiring governments to account for

---

[92] Discussed in Chapter 1.   [93] E.g. Arts. 23, 24 and 27.   [94] C. Wellman (1999) esp. at ch. 7.

[95] U. Kilkelly and L. Lundy (2006) pp. 335–8.

[96] See also Art. 24(4), which directs states, regarding children's health rights, to 'promote and encourage international co-operation *with a view to achieving progressively* the full realization of the right recognized in the present article' (emphasis supplied).

[97] Discussed in Chapter 1.   [98] J. Feinberg (1980) p. 153 and M. Minow (1987) p. 1887.

[99] J. Eekelaar (1992) p. 234.   [100] Art. 4.

[101] Art. 43 sets out the reporting mechanism and establishes the Committee on the Rights of the Child. See R. Hodgkin and P. Newell (2007) pp. 639–41.

infringements of the Convention, the reporting mechanism is extremely important.[102] Two years after ratification, each government is expected to send an initial report to the Committee on the Rights of the Child, detailing the progress it has made in fulfilling its obligations and any difficulties experienced in doing so. Thereafter, it is normally required to submit periodic reports at five-year intervals.[103] After receiving a report, the Committee will obtain additional information on the government's record on implementation from other UN organisations and domestic non-governmental organisations (NGOs) by inviting them to comment on the report itself.[104] In the Committee's final report, its 'Concluding Observations', the Committee may identify and criticise areas of non-compliance and make suggestions for remedy.

The CRC's nearly universal acceptance soon led to problems for the Committee on the Rights of the Child. Over 80 governments produced initial reports within a very short time of the Convention itself having come into force. The Committee then faced the overwhelming task of considering their reports and producing detailed concluding observations on each. This enormous workload led to the Committee adapting its procedures to tackle the increasingly long backlog of reports awaiting review.[105] The Committee wields considerable influence in its interpretation of the Convention. Its Concluding Observations, which have gradually become more detailed and complex, are read with considerable interest by human rights experts throughout the world. It also eventually followed the model of the Human Rights Committee responsible for monitoring the ICCPR, by producing a series of 'General Comments' explaining how the Committee interprets many of the articles of the Covenant.[106] Researchers have been able to gain, from this growing body of jurisprudence, some insight into the way in which the Committee interprets the Convention and the relative importance it places on states' obligations thereunder.[107] This guidance is available for use by governments to inform their policies regarding implementation.

(E) The reporting mechanism and the United Kingdom

Unlike many other countries,[108] although the UK has ratified the CRC, it has not incorporated it into domestic law. Consequently, in this country the

---

[102] Ibid. at pp. 645–52 and C. Price Cohen and S. Kilbourne (1998) pp. 640–42.

[103] Art. 44(1)(b). But due to the backlog of work, some countries have recently been requested to consolidate their next two periodical reports into one; see below.

[104] E.g. CRAE (2008) and UK Children's Commissioners (2008). See also R. Hodgkin and P. Newell (2007) p. 647.

[105] The Committee increased its membership from 12 to 18, enabling it (in 2005–06) to divide into two chambers to deal with the increasing backlog of unexamined periodical reports. The UK (along with some other states) was requested to consolidate its 3rd and 4th periodic reports, the combined report (HM Government (2007)) being submitted to the Committee in 2007.

[106] E.g. Committee on the Rights of the Child (2006).

[107] E.g. C. Price Cohen and S. Kilbourne (1998) and R. Hodgkin and P. Newell (2007).

[108] UNICEF (2006).

Convention is of persuasive influence only. It was hoped that the need to produce periodic reports and the knowledge that they would be subjected to detailed consideration by the Committee on the Rights of the Child, would encourage states who had not incorporated the CRC to implement its provisions effectively. Certainly the publication of the Committee's detailed observations on these reports produces media attention and a heightened public awareness of the principles contained in the Convention as well as the extent to which governments are implementing its obligations. Indeed, media fury at the Committee's criticisms of the UK's record of implementation following its initial report led to such headlines as 'How dare the UN lecture us'.[109]

The reporting mechanism relies on governments to subject their implementation programme to an objective and critical analysis before compiling their reports. Reports must indicate to the Committee 'factors and difficulties, if any, affecting the degree of fulfilment' of their obligations under the Convention.[110] Nevertheless, the absence of any supervision or coercion over this can lead to reports painting an over-optimistic and complacent picture of governmental achievements. This weakness in the reporting procedure has led to many countries providing reports indicating little or no difficulty with implementing some of their more onerous obligations.[111] The UK's own performance has been no exception. Its initial report in 1994[112] failed to identify any real difficulties over doing so, providing vague and superficial information about compliance with each right or groups of rights. Although its later reports have been far more detailed and specifically addressed some of the Committee's concerns, the government has been highly selective and unbalanced in its coverage of the Convention's requirements. Indeed, the Joint Committee on Human Rights (JCHR) caustically stated that it gave:

> the common reader little sense of how the information it provides relates to the principles of the Convention, or what the Government's strategic priorities for advancing children's rights are.[113]

In all its reports to date, the government has, time and again, fulfilled King's predictions and exploited the Convention's internal incoherence by choosing the policies which suit them and ignoring those that do not.[114] At times, it has even distorted the aims of current legislation to justify spurious claims of compliance with the Convention's provisions. For example, in its second report, the government made the astonishing claim that changes made to the law on youth offending, notably the abolition of the presumption of *doli incapax* for accused children between the ages of 10 and 14,[115] would promote children's rights, on the basis that it would:

---

[109] *Daily Mail*, 28 January 1995.   [110] Art. 44(2).

[111] L. Scherer and S. Hart (2001) pp 84–85: an analysis of the initial reports of 49 countries (regarding compliance with Articles 28 and 29) found that most failed to specify any difficulties relating to education.

[112] DH (1994).   [113] JCHR (2003) para. 10.   [114] M. King (1994) p. 397.

[115] Crime and Disorder Act 1998, s. 36.

ensure that, if a child has begun to offend, he or she is entitled to the earliest possible intervention to address that offending behaviour and eliminate its causes. The changes will also have the result of putting all juveniles on the same footing as far as courts are concerned, and will contribute to the *right* of children appearing there to develop responsibility for themselves.[116]

The Committee was plainly not deceived by such disingenuous claims and emphasised its 'serious concern' that the 'law has worsened since the consideration of the initial report' with the age of criminal responsibility being retained at 10 and the *doli incapax* presumption being abolished.[117]

As Kilkelly points out, a government's failure to participate in critical self-analysis undermines the value of the reporting mechanism.[118] It has only been due to the well co-ordinated response of NGOs to the UK's reports that the Committee on the Rights of the Child has received a clear picture of the weaknesses in the government's implementation programme.[119] In particular, the NGOs have drawn to the Committee's attention the UK's relatively low spending on basic services for children, such as health, education, housing and social security, judged against other European countries. This material enabled the Committee to produce relatively hard-hitting sets of concluding observations.[120] But when responding to its second and third reports, the Committee noted with commendable restraint its 'regret' that some of its recommendations had still not been fully implemented.[121]

The various ways in which the law in the UK still fails to comply with the aims of the Convention are discussed throughout this work, in the context of the developing principles of domestic law. In terms of overall progress towards implementation, the Committee on the Rights of the Child has made it reasonably plain that for a wealthy nation our record is relatively poor.[122] In particular, it has criticised the absence of any 'consistent budgetary analysis and child rights impact assessment' which hinders identification of how much expenditure is allocated to children.[123] As the Committee has pointed out, no state can tell whether it is fulfilling children's rights to the maximum extent of its available resources, as required by Article 4, unless it can identify the budgetary allocation to children, both directly and indirectly.[124] In general terms, the UK government shows little sign of taking seriously the advice to all states to 'see

---

[116] DH (1999) para. 10.30.1 (emphasis supplied); see also HM Government (2007) p. 160, para. 54.

[117] Committee on the Rights of the Child (2002a) para. 59. See also Committee on the Rights of the Child (2008) para. 78. The age of criminal responsibility is discussed in Chapter 18.

[118] U. Kilkelly (1996) pp. 119–20.

[119] Children's Rights Development Unit (1994), Children's Rights Alliance (2002), CRAE (2008). See also the UK Children's Commissioners (2008).

[120] Committee on the Rights of the Child (1995), (2002a) and (2008).

[121] Committee on the Rights of the Child (2002a) para. 4; ibid. (2008) para. 6.

[122] Committee on the Rights of the Child (1995) para. 9; ibid. (2002a) paras. 10–11; ibid. (2008), paras. 18–19.

[123] Committee on the Rights of the Child (2008) paras. 15 and 18–19; see also ibid. (2002a) para. 11.

[124] Committee on the Rights of the Child (2003) para. 51.

their role as fulfilling clear legal obligations to each and every child. Implementation of the human rights of children must not be seen as a charitable process, bestowing favours on children'.[125]

(F) More effective enforcement procedures

(i) Incorporation into domestic law?

The overall impression created by the UK's reports to the Committee on the Rights of the Child is that the government is relatively untroubled by fear of its criticism. This impression is reinforced by the government's failure to address the more obvious breaches in compliance noted by the Committee when responding to its earlier reports. When reviewing the UK's implementation record, the JCHR commented that progress towards fuller compliance with the Convention 'cannot be sustained if it is only measured once every five years or so. It requires more sustained attention'.[126]

An obvious way of ensuring greater compliance with its provisions would be to incorporate the Convention into domestic law, as has been done by many other ratifying countries and has been urged on the government here by the Committee on the Rights of the Child.[127] Criticising the government's current lack of enthusiasm for such a step,[128] the JCHR considered that at least some of the rights, principles and provisions of the Convention should be incorporated into UK law.[129] Although well-intentioned, such a recommendation would allow the government to incorporate only those parts of the Convention it can implement with little expenditure, leaving the more onerous obligations unincorporated. The answer must surely be to incorporate the Convention in its entirety or not at all.

The prospects for incorporation are now beginning to look far more realistic. When discussing the introduction of a Bill of Rights into this country, the government agreed that any such document could include specific provision for the rights of vulnerable groups such as children.[130] Notably, the JCHR considered there to be a 'strong case' for such a step.[131] It was impressed by the fact that the South African Bill of Rights makes specific provision for children's rights.[132] Obviously influential was Baroness Hale of Richmond's view that protection of children's rights within a new Bill of Rights would redress the fact that 'There is virtually nothing in the ECHR about children'.[133] It was also pointed out that unlike the ECHR, which only concentrates of civil and political rights, the CRC additionally protects all children's social and economic

---

[125] Ibid. at para. 11.   [126] JCHR (2003) para. 116.

[127] Committee on the Rights of the Child (2002a) paras. 8–9; ibid. (2008) para. 11.

[128] JCHR (2003) para. 21: when asked to comment on this proposition, the then Minister for Children and Young People rejected it because 'the very aspirational language' of the Convention was not easy to put into primary legislation.

[129] Ibid. at para. 22.   [130] JCHR (2008a) para. 139.   [131] Ibid. at para. 145.

[132] Ibid. at para. 138.   [133] Ibid. at para. 141.

rights.[134] Whether or not a Bill of Rights is introduced in the UK, there are now powerful arguments favouring incorporation of the CRC. It would give children 'entrenched, inalienable and enforceable rights, with the potential to effect real change for the better'.[135]

(ii) An effective Children's Commissioner?

Alston and Tobin note the strong and growing emphasis in the human rights domain for the establishment of national independent human rights institutions (NHRIs).[136] The provisions of the CRC require states to establish specialised institutional arrangements to promote and protect children's rights[137] and the Committee on the Rights of the Child regularly criticises those who fail to do so.[138] In 1981, Norway appointed the first Children's Ombudsman, Målfrid Flekkøy; other countries soon followed suit, establishing NHRIs with a variety of titles and functions.[139] Many have a great deal of power and influence and thereby achieve considerable improvements in the treatment of children in their respective countries.[140] The activities they fulfil vary throughout the world, but most have the powers and duties recommended by the Committee on the Rights of the Child. These are, inter alia, to undertake investigations into violations of children's rights, on complaint or on their own initiative; to prepare and publicise opinions and recommendations regarding children's rights; to review and report on the government's implementation and monitoring of such rights; to promote public understanding and awareness of children's rights.[141]

It was not until 2005[142] that English children finally acquired a children's commissioner, some time after their peers in Wales,[143] Northern Ireland[144] and Scotland.[145] But the terms of his office made it immediately clear that his position was weaker than any other ombudsman or children's commissioner in the UK and Europe. The absence of real independence from government deemed so essential to a post of this kind[146] fundamentally undermines his role.[147] The government was also reluctant for his role to be linked with the

---

[134] JCHR (2008b), Memorandum of Evidence from the Children's Rights Alliance for England, Ev. 112–13.

[135] Ibid. at Ev. 111.   [136] P. Alston and J. Tobin (2005) p. 40.   [137] Arts. 4 and 42.

[138] R. Hodgkin and P. Newell (2007) pp. 66–8.   [139] P. Alston and J. Tobin (2005) pp. 40–51.

[140] M Flekkøy (1991).

[141] Committee on the Rights of the Child (2002b) para. 19, lists 20 recommended activities.

[142] CA 2004, Part 1.

[143] Care Standards Act 2000, Part V and Children's Commissioner for Wales Act 2001.

[144] Commissioner for Children and Young People (Northern Ireland) Order 2003 (SI 2003/439 (NI11)).

[145] Commissioner for Children and Young People (Scotland) Act 2003.

[146] Committee on the Rights of the Child (2002b) para. 7.

[147] Inter alia: the Secretary of State can direct the Children's Commissioner for England to carry out an inquiry (CA 2004, s. 4(1)); the Commissioner must consult the Secretary of State before holding an independent inquiry (CA 2004, s. 3(3)); unlike his counterparts elsewhere, the Commissioner's annual reports do not go directly to Parliament but must be submitted to the Secretary of State who 'must as soon as possible' lay it before Parliament (CA 2004, s. 8(3)).

need to promote children's rights under the Convention. He must instead merely promote an '*awareness* of the views and interests of children in England'[148] and his functions are tied to promoting government policies, as specified in the 'Every Child Matters' policy programme,[149] rather than an independent rights agenda. Indeed, the legislative provisions setting out his powers and duties contain a single reference to the word 'rights' when requiring the Commissioner to 'have regard to the United Nations Convention on the Rights of the Child'.[150]

Fortunately, the roles of the children's commissioners in Wales, Northern Ireland and Scotland are not hampered by a similar antipathy to 'rights talk', with their official functions being clearly linked with promoting the aims of the CRC and children's rights generally.[151] Admittedly the present commissioner for England[152] has interpreted his terms of reference broadly in a way that allows him to use the CRC as 'the framework for many of the themes and activities' he undertakes and to formulate a long list of 'children's *rights* issues of concern' to work on.[153] Nevertheless, as Williams points out, the stark differences between his role and that of the three other commissioners are likely to prove problematic. Indeed, she suggests that these differences reflect 'a growing divergence between the UK Government and the devolved administrations as to the value of a rights based framework for child policy'.[154]

(iii) An individual right of petition?

A cynic might argue that a casual approach to the Convention will continue until there is a more obvious way of holding the government to account for its failures. The impact of the CRC would be significantly strengthened were enforcement procedures to be grafted on to it. The most effective would be the establishment of an international court to consider individual petitions, as was done for the ECHR. Such procedures were not considered to be appropriate at the Convention's drafting stage because it was feared that it would discourage some developing nations from ratifying it.[155] Those opposing an individual petitioning system being provided for all children argue that it would be appropriate only for children's civil and political rights, rather than the economic, social and cultural rights, which require the injection of financial resources. But such an argument seems to lack real credence, particularly when it is so difficult to distinguish logically between many of the rights.[156]

---

[148] CA 2004, s. 2(1), emphasis added.   [149] CA 2004, s. 2(3); discussed in Chapter 15.

[150] There were fruitless attempts to insert the word 'rights' into various parts of the CA 2004 when it was still in Bill form (see House of Commons Standing Committee B (parts 2 and 3), cols 9–16 (2004)). These were all opposed by Margaret Hodge, then the Minister for Children, Young People and Families; discussed further in Chapter 19.

[151] J. Williams (2005) pp. 40–8. She notes (at pp. 40–1) that the Welsh Children's Commissioner only subsequently, by regulations, became obliged to pay regard to the CRC.

[152] Sir Albert Aynsley-Green took up the position of Children's Commissioner for England in 2005.

[153] Emphasis supplied. Children's Commissioner for England (2006) p. 3.

[154] J. Williams (2005) p. 53.   [155] U. Kilkelly (1996) p. 117.   [156] G. Van Bueren (1995) p. 411.

As Van Bueren observes, the African Charter on the Rights and Welfare of the Child, which protects not only civil and political rights but also economic, social and cultural rights, incorporates the right of individual petition for all children.[157] Other doubts have been voiced regarding children's capacity to petition a court and the practicality of their doing so when their complaints may focus on their own parents' behaviour[158] – but these are not insurmountable. Experience shows that although most applications to the European Court of Human Rights (ECtHR) are made by parents on their children's behalf, someone other than the child's parents may sometimes be sufficiently motivated to do so instead.[159]

One way of compensating for the lack of a court is for the Children's Commissioner to have power to investigate children's individual complaints and petitions and ensure that they are remedied. Indeed the Committee on the Rights of the Child considers such a power to be essential for *all* NHRIs, alongside the ability to support children taking cases to court.[160] Målfrid Flekkøy's list of those functions considered to be fundamental to an ombudsman's work, places 'responding to complaints and/or violations' as a 'core function', enabling children 'to overcome a faceless, inhuman bureaucracy by having their grievances identified and pursued by a personal advocate'.[161] The children's commissioner in Wales and Northern Ireland[162] has the power to investigate individual complaints; not so their colleagues in Scotland and England. Predictably, the Committee on the Rights of the Child has noted with concern the limitations on the independence and powers of the UK children's commissioners.[163] It recommends that all four commissioners be mandated to receive and investigate complaints from or on behalf of children concerning violations of their rights and be given the resources necessary to carry out this role.[164]

(G) The practical influence of the CRC

The CRC has been enormously influential – indeed, to many it is regarded as the touchstone for children's rights throughout the world. It constitutes the most comprehensive list of human rights created for a specific group. International bodies refer to it with approval on the basis that it can be utilised to promote 'a change in the way children, as individuals with rights, are viewed

---

[157] Ibid. See also P. Alston and J. Tobin (2005) pp. 12–14 for an assessment of the African Charters.

[158] U. Kilkelly (1996) pp. 117–18.

[159] E.g. the Official Solicitor took a complaint to the European Commission and Court on Human Rights on behalf of the children involved in *X v. Bedfordshire County Council* [1995] 3 All ER 353; discussed in Chapter 16.

[160] Committee on the Rights of the Child (2002b) paras. 13–14.   [161] M. Flekkøy (2001) p. 159.

[162] But the Welsh Commissioner may only investigate individual cases if they have wider implications, whereas the Northern Irish Commissioner can investigate cases and take legal action on behalf of children; see J. Williams (2005).

[163] Committee on the Rights of the Child (2008) para. 17.   [164] Ibid. at para. 17.

and also to encourage their active and responsible participation within the family and society'.[165] The ECtHR increasingly refers to its provisions as being of persuasive authority when reaching their decisions.[166] Equally the English courts, when dealing with children's cases, are now quite commonly drawing attention to its provisions.[167] Indeed, having reviewed the extensive protection of children's rights provided by the CRC,[168] Silber J suggested that there had been a 'change in the landscape of family matters, in which the rights of children are becoming increasingly important'.[169]

But whilst many countries have been extremely active in fulfilling their duty under Article 42 to make its principles widely known to adults and children alike,[170] the Committee on the Rights of the Child has been unimpressed by the UK's record on this. It has indicated its concern at the absence of any systematic 'awareness raising of the Convention' and at the low level of knowledge about it amongst children, parents and professionals working with children.[171] Hopefully, the citizenship education programme[172] will gradually improve British school children's awareness of the UN Convention and thereby ensure that the UK better fulfils its obligations in this respect.[173] Similarly, those working with children in this country are increasingly aware of the Convention's existence and their obligations thereunder.[174] But as the JCHR made clear, the government's own overall record needs considerable attention:

> The Convention should function as the source of a set of child-centred considerations to be used as yardsticks by all departments of Government when evaluating legislation and in policy-making, whether in respect of the progressive realisation of economic, social and cultural rights or in relation to guarantees of civil and political rights. We recommend, particularly in relation to

---

[165] E.g. Council of Europe (1996) para. 4.

[166] E.g., inter alia, *Costello-Roberts v. United Kingdom* [1994] 1 FCR 65, at paras. 27 and 35; *A v. United Kingdom (human rights: punishment of child)* [1998] 2 FLR 959, at para. 22; *V v. United Kingdom* (1999) 30 EHRR 121, at paras. 73, 76, 97.

[167] E.g. *R (on the application of Williamson and others) v. Secretary of State for Education and Employment and others* [2005] UKHL 15, [2005], 2 All ER 1 at [81]–[83], per Baroness Hale of Richmond; *Mabon v. Mabon* [2005] EWCA Civ 634, [2005] 2 FLR 1011, per Thorpe LJ, at [26] and [28]; *R (on the application of R) v. Durham Constabulary and another* [2005] UKHL 21, 369, per Baroness Hale of Richmond, at [41]–[42].

[168] *R (Axon) v. Secretary of State for Health and the Family Planning Association* [2006] EWHC 37 (Admin), [2006] 2 FLR 206, at [76]–[80].

[169] Ibid. at [80].

[170] E.g. Spain, which, on implementing the Convention, launched a mass media campaign designed to ensure the aims of the Convention were widely known.

[171] Committee on the Rights of the Child (2008) para. 20. See also ibid. (2002a) para. 20.

[172] Discussed in Chapter 6.

[173] UK Children's Commissioners (2008) para. 14: according to survey findings, 44% children in Scotland in 2007, 13% of children in England in 2006 and 8% of children in Wales in 2007, had heard of the CRC.

[174] V. Combe (2002) provides examples of local good practice.

policy-making, that Government demonstrate more conspicuously a recognition of its obligation to implement the rights under the Convention.[175]

(6) The European Convention on Human Rights

(A) The post-War background

On 2 October 2000, the HRA 1998 incorporated the ECHR into the domestic law of the UK – a dramatic event indeed. The importance of this change can only be fully appreciated if it is placed within the Convention's own historical context. The ECHR was a product of the late 1940s, a period when there was considerable enthusiasm for the concept of a united Europe – an enthusiasm provoked by the destructive havoc wreaked on European countries by the Second World War. The Statute on the Council of Europe, signed in 1949, provided for a Committee of Ministers and a Parliamentary Assembly. The Council of Europe soon initiated and became involved in many cultural, economic and scientific activities and in 1961 adopted the European Social Charter with a view to protecting economic and social rights.[176] Possibly its greatest achievement in the human rights field, however, was to adopt the ECHR, signed in 1950.

The ECHR reflected a revived interest, in the late 1940s, in the natural rights theories of an earlier generation of political philosophers.[177] Strongly influenced by the Universal Declaration of Human Rights 1948,[178] the intention was to guarantee certain inalienable freedoms, namely those first generation civil and political rights considered essential to life in a civilised society. Consequently, the Convention's aims are relatively limited. Its main focus is to prevent governments from interfering with certain fundamental but negative liberties, rather than obliging them to promote, in positive ways, people's civil, economic, social, and cultural rights.[179] Overarching those listed is Article 14, which has no independent existence,[180] but which governs the interpretation of all the other rights, ensuring that they are all secured 'without discrimination on any ground such as sex, race, colour, language, religion, political or other

---

[175] JCHR (2003) para. 25.

[176] This has achieved important protection for children in the context of regulating their employment, further discussed in Chapter 4. In July 2006, the European Commission launched the European Strategy on the Rights of the Child whose aim is to ensure all EU policies respect children's rights in accordance with Community law and that they are fully compatible with the principles of the UNCRC. For more information about the role of the EU generally, see, inter alia: J. Wadham *et al.* (2003) ch. 7; D. Feldman (2002) pp. 117–21; and in relation to families and children see, inter alia: C. McGlynn (2000); C. McGlynn (2001); C. Henricson and A. Bainham (2005) pp. 24–31 and 97–8; P. Alston and J. Tobin (2005) pp. 20–1.

[177] Discussed above.   [178] Arts. 1–21.

[179] Art. 2 of the First Protocol is a notable exception, in so far as it protects a social welfare right, the right to education.

[180] An infringement of Art. 14 cannot be complained about discretely, it must instead be linked with one of the other articles.

opinion, national or social origin, association with a national minority, property, birth or other status'.

The ECHR quickly became immensely influential, largely because it was the first international instrument of its kind to provide a mechanism for its own interpretation and enforcement. The Commission and Court of Human Rights were established to receive and examine complaints about infringements of the Convention by state parties, thereby providing an authoritative interpretation of its terms.[181] This special feature undoubtedly enhanced the Convention's reputation for being one of the world's foremost human rights instruments. The original complicated procedure[182] was simplified in 1998,[183] with the part-time Commission and Court being replaced by a single full-time Court, which has thereafter decided both on the admissibility and merits of each case. In the event of the Court finding a violation of the Convention, it can order adequate reparation,[184] but in practice its most important function is often to bring it to the attention of the state in question, together with the need for a change in its domestic law.

(B) Incorporation of the European Convention on Human Rights into domestic law

Even before implementation of the HRA 1998, the list of rights embodied by the ECHR had already become a relatively familiar one to people living in the UK. The domestic courts were entitled to assume from the Convention's ratification that domestic legislation and case law should be interpreted, as far as possible, consistently with the UK's obligations under the Convention.[185] Furthermore, from the mid-1960s, having exhausted the remedies offered by the domestic courts, UK residents could petition the European Commission and Court in Strasbourg,[186] arguing that English law was violating the ECHR and should be amended. Consequently long before it had become part of English law in 2000, the Convention's contents had had considerable influence on the development of law here. English law was adjusted from time to time to take account of decisions of the Strasbourg institutions in cases where they concluded that the

---

[181] The ECtHR was established in 1959.

[182] Whereby the European Commission on Human Rights (EComHR) investigated and filtered out manifestly ill-founded applications before referring well-founded cases to the ECtHR for adjudication.

[183] The new system was implemented by the Eleventh Protocol of the ECHR, which came into force on 1 November 1998.

[184] Unless a friendly settlement is reached between the two parties.

[185] E.g. *Re KD (a minor) (ward: termination of access)* [1988] 1 All ER 577, in which the House of Lords took full account of the need for all domestic legislation and case law to comply with the Convention's terms. See, particularly, Lord Oliver's attempts (at 587–9) to reconcile English law with the terms of Art. 8.

[186] In 1966, the British government made a declaration, under Art. 25, recognising the jurisdiction of the European Commission to consider individual petitions.

human rights of those living in the UK had been infringed.[187] Nevertheless, procedurally such a system was so expensive and lengthy that only the most determined were prepared to utilise this remedy of last resort.[188]

The 2 October 2000 marked the point when anyone of any age, including children, could challenge the existing law in any domestic court anywhere in the UK, arguing that it ignored their rights under the ECHR. The HRA 1998 thereby produced a vastly improved system, both procedurally and substantively. But incorporation of the ECHR into domestic law also marked a radical change of approach towards protecting the fundamental rights of those who live in the UK. Before then, it had been considered that our innate freedoms were properly protected by a democratically elected Parliament and that they existed, unless and until they were expressly abrogated by common law or legislation. Many considered that to adopt a written constitution, as in France and the US, would endanger our underlying liberties, since only those listed would gain recognition.[189] By enacting the HRA 1998, the government signalled the view that it was not enough to assert the theoretical existence of fundamental liberties, everyone's constitutional rights should now also have formal guarantees and direct modes of protection.[190]

The ECHR guarantees the fundamental human rights of all people living within the boundaries of those states which ratified it, irrespective of age. From October 2000, all children living in the UK have been able to complain to the domestic courts that their rights are being infringed by any public authority,[191] such as a hospital trust, a local education authority, or a children's services authority. Similarly, they can complain if the state, through its laws, has failed to protect them adequately from the behaviour of some private individual – even a parent.[192] To assist them, children's lawyers must be familiar with the operation of the HRA 1998[193] and with the Strasbourg institutions' own interpretation of the ECHR itself.[194] But although this existing body of jurisprudence is extremely influential, the Convention is a 'living instrument' and its interpretation by the domestic courts must keep abreast with changes in society's needs.[195] In other words, the judiciary here are not obliged to follow the Strasbourg case law slavishly, if they can be persuaded that it is anachronistic.

---

[187] E.g. *W v. United Kingdom* (1987) 10 EHRR 29. This decision led to reform of the legislative methods whereby local authorities gained authority to care for children.

[188] HO (1997) para. 1.14: it took on average five years to get applications into the ECtHR and cost an average of £30,000.

[189] For a comprehensive discussion of the legal and political background to the campaign to incorporate the Convention see, inter alia: C. Gearty (1997) pp. 65–83; D. Feldman (2002) pp. 45–105; J. Wadham *et al.* (2003) ch. 2.

[190] HO (1997) esp. paras. 1.16–19.   [191] HRA 1998, s. 6.   [192] Discussed below.

[193] For a usefully concise summary of the operation of the HRA 1998, see J. Wadham *et al.* (2003) chs, 4–6. For an even briefer summary, see M.-B. Dembour (2006) ch. 2.

[194] HRA 1998, s. 2: the domestic courts, when considering any alleged infringement of Convention rights, must be guided by the way in which the Convention has been interpreted in the past by the European Commission and Court.

[195] *Cossey v. United Kingdom* [1991] 2 FLR 492 at 501.

If a child's legal adviser successfully persuades a domestic court that the infringement of the child's rights stems from the terms of old legislation, the court may itself be able to interpret that legislation afresh to ensure compatibility.[196] If that is impossible,[197] the court, providing it is sufficiently senior,[198] may promote the legislation's speedy amendment by making a declaration of incompatibility.[199] Theoretically, a child's rights will not be endangered by any legislation introduced after 2000, since it should have been drafted in Convention compatible terms.[200] But some children's Convention rights are infringed not by any legislative provision but by the existing principles of the common law itself. A court agreeing with such an argument must, as a 'public authority',[201] act compatibly with the Convention and adapt the principles of common law to secure their rights. In so doing, the court may feel obliged to override existing case law, irrespective of its age or the level of court from which it emanated. If all else fails, the ECtHR remains a court of last resort for children who, having exhausted their domestic remedies in this country, still feel aggrieved by an alleged infringement of their rights.[202]

(C) The role of the European Court of Human Rights and children's claims

When considering how to use the Strasbourg jurisprudence on behalf of children, it is important to bear in mind the principles underlying the interpretation of the Convention rights, together with the ECtHR's own role. Whilst some of the rights are absolute,[203] others are limited by specific exceptions,[204] whilst others again, notably Article 8, the article most relevant to family life, are qualified in such a way as to make it plain that the rights of the individual must be balanced against the needs of society as a whole.[205] Thus society can only infringe these qualified rights if the limitations fulfil three requirements: they are prescribed by law, they are intended to achieve a legitimate objective and are

---

[196] Under HRA 1998, s. 3(1), the courts must 'read' the terms of existing legislation deemed incompatible with Convention rights, 'so far as it is possible to do so' in accordance with the Convention's terms. See G. Phillipson (2003).

[197] There may be judicial disagreement over whether HRA 1998, s. 3 allows express statutory provisions to be given a strained or non-literal construction in order to comply with Convention demands. See, inter alia: *R v. A (No. 2)* [2001] UKHL 25, [2001] 3 All ER 1, per Lord Steyn, at [44]–[45]; cf. *R v. Lambert* [2001] UKHL 37, [2001] 3 All ER 577, per Lord Hope, at [80]–[81]; and *Re S (children: care plan); Re W (children: care plan)* [2002] UKHL 10, [2002] 2 All ER 192, per Lord Nicholls of Birkenhead at [37]–[39].

[198] HRA 1998, s. 4(2) and (5): only the House of Lords, Court of Appeal and High Court have jurisdiction to make a declaration of incompatibility.

[199] E.g. *R (on the application of Morris) v. Westminster City Council (No. 3)* [2005] EWCA Civ 1184, [2006] 1 WLR 505.

[200] HRA 1998, s. 19: any government minister introducing draft legislation in Parliament must annex to it a written statement confirming that it is compatible with the terms of the ECHR.

[201] HRA 1998, s. 6.

[202] J. Wadham *et al.* (2003) ch. 9, briefly describes how to take a case to Strasbourg.

[203] E.g. Art. 3, protection from torture.   [204] E.g. Art. 5, right to liberty.

[205] NB Arts. 9–11 are all similarly qualified.

'necessary' in a democratic society.[206] It is not intended here to discuss the detailed principles underlying these three requirements.[207] Suffice it to say that the first two requirements are normally unproblematic in children's cases since any intervention will normally have accorded with clear legal principles and its legitimate objective will have been to promote the child's interests. The last is more demanding, since the state can only justify an infringement of a Convention right if the interference is 'necessary', if it is both relevant and sufficient and the minimum needed to secure a pressing social need – in other words, it must comply with the doctrine of proportionality.[208] Thus the greater the interference, the less likely it is that a justification can be established, especially if there is some less restrictive alternative.[209] When deciding on proportionality and whether the infringement was 'necessary in a democratic society', the ECtHR has acknowledged that the state itself may be in a better position to judge what is necessary to meet the needs of its own people, than an international body such as itself.[210] In other words, states have a margin of appreciation – they are free to evaluate their own public policy decisions, though subject to review by the Strasbourg institutions.[211] Thus the ECtHR's task is not to substitute its decision-making for that of the domestic court, but to review the decision and how it was reached.

When dealing with an application arguing that the domestic court's decision unduly infringed the rights of one or more of the parties involved in a children's case, the ECtHR must consider whether the domestic court has balanced the parties' rights against each other appropriately and, in so doing, whether the measures taken were relevant and sufficient for the purposes of Article 8(2).[212] But the ECtHR is aware that such a decision will have been influenced largely by the domestic court's assessment of how to promote the child's best interests and that that decision will have been reached with the court having had the benefit of seeing the adults concerned.[213] The ECtHR has repeatedly stressed in children's cases that its task is not to substitute its decision-making for that of the domestic courts.[214] The ECtHR has also stressed that countries have a wide margin of appreciation when assessing the justification for the infringement.[215] In other words, it does not normally second guess the domestic court's decision over whether it was necessary to infringe an applicant's rights in the first place or the balance achieved by the domestic court between the parents' interests inter se and those of the child. Thus in public law cases, it only rarely criticises the reasons for a child being taken into state care; similarly in private law cases it

---

[206] See the wording of Art. 8(2).   [207] J. Wadham *et al.* (2003) ch. 2.
[208] Ibid. at pp. 35–9.   [209] J. Wadham *et al.* (2003) p. 36.
[210] *Handyside v. United Kingdom* (1979–80) 1 EHRR 737, para. 48.
[211] J. Wadham *et al.* (2003) p. 44.
[212] Inter alia: *Hokkanen v. Finland* (1995) 19 EHRR 139, para. 55; *Sahin v. Germany* [2003] 2 FLR 671, at para. 64.
[213] E.g. *Sahin v. Germany* [2003] 2 FLR 671, at para. 64.
[214] Ibid.   [215] Ibid. at para. 65.

only rarely criticises the reasons for making an order in favour of one parent, as opposed to the other. It may, however, scrutinise carefully *how* the decision was reached – whether the decision-making process, seen as a whole, provided the applicant with the requisite protection of his interests.[216] Thus, it may decide that the procedural aspects of the decision-making did not adequately and fairly involve the applicant, perhaps due to an insufficiency of expert evidence.[217] But as the Grand Chamber has made clear, even in the context of procedural matters, the ECtHR must resist the temptation not to exceed its power of review; it must allow the domestic courts a sufficient margin of appreciation and leave it to them to establish the evidence underlying the case.[218]

The ECtHR has traditionally allowed state authorities a narrower margin of appreciation when considering whether the state has made sufficient efforts to ensure the child is reintegrated into his or her family after being removed into care, or to avoid a non-resident parent remaining out of contact with his child. Thus the ECtHR has stressed that a child's removal into state care must be seen as a temporary measure only, expecting states to make real efforts to ensure the child's rapid integration into his family.[219] Similarly when considering a parental dispute, it will also scrutinise carefully any restrictions placed on a parent's right to have contact with his child, given that such limitations curtail the family relations between them.[220]

(D) The European Convention on Human Rights and its interpretation – strengths and weaknesses for children

(i) Offsetting the Convention's narrow focus

The list of rights set out in the ECHR looks relatively unprepossessing so far as children are concerned. Indeed, as Alston and Tobin observe, 'it contains not a single provision which is specifically addressed to children'.[221] A fundamental problem is that its very limited scope prevents its addressing the wide variety of children's needs. With the exception of Article 2 of the First Protocol (A2P1) of the ECHR, which protects the right to education, the Convention is principally concerned with civil and political rights – the basic freedoms deemed essential to individual autonomy and to privacy from state interference, such as freedom from torture and the right to a fair trial. Unlike the CRC, which guarantees both children's basic civil and political freedoms and their social, economic and

---

[216] Inter alia: *W v. United Kingdom* (1988) 10 EHRR 29, at para. 64; *Haase v. Germany* [2004] 2 FLR 39, at para. 97; *Elsholz v. Germany* [2000] 2 FLR 486, at para. 52.

[217] E.g. *Elsholz v. Germany* [2000] 2 FLR 486.

[218] *Sahin v. Germany* [2003] 2 FLR 671, at para. 73.

[219] Inter alia: *Johansen v. Norway* (1996) 23 EHRR 33, at para. 64; *K and T v. Finland* [2001] 2 FLR 707, at paras. 155 and 178; discussed further in Chapter 15.

[220] Inter alia: *Sahin v. Germany* [2003] 2 FLR 671, at para. 63; *Elsholz v. Germany* [2000] 2 FLR 486, para. 49; discussed further in Chapter 13.

[221] P. Alston and J. Tobin (2005) p. 16.

cultural rights, the ECHR primarily seeks to protect individuals from state interference with their lives. Civil and political rights of this kind are usually relatively unimportant to children brought up in the protected environment of their own homes. This probably explains why there have been relatively few applications taken to the ECtHR testing the scope of children's right to enjoy some of the more traditional political and civil rights.[222]

Some of the more obvious weaknesses of the Convention have, however, been addressed by the ECtHR interpreting its provisions in a surprisingly purposeful way. An imaginative interpretation of its awkwardly worded provisions has produced unexpectedly effective protection for children. Many parents might balk at the suggestion that using physical punishment could, in some circumstances, be described as a form of 'torture' or even as 'inhuman or degrading treatment'. Nevertheless, Article 3 has been pressed into service to protect children from severe forms of physical punishment.[223] Equally, it is unlikely that the draftsmen of the Convention ever considered the need to prevent parental child abuse. But through a combination of Articles 2, 3 and 8, the Convention now imposes an obligation on child welfare authorities to protect children from abusive treatment.[224]

An increasingly broad interpretation of the concept of respect for a person's private and family life, as protected by Article 8, has probably borne the most fruit, so far as children are concerned. The concept of family life itself has been interpreted flexibly, so that it protects the relationships between children and unmarried, as well as married parents,[225] and their relationships with other members of de facto family groupings.[226] The protection Article 8 offers family life is not only substantive but procedural as well. Thus any form of decision-making, judicial or administrative, which might infringe it is within its scope.[227] The right to respect for private life has also been widely interpreted. It has secured for children the right to obtain information about themselves held by any public agencies which enables them to know and understand their childhood and early development.[228] It also recognises their need to have uncertainty over their personal identity (arising from ignorance of their parents' identity) eliminated without unnecessary delay.[229] Its interpretation to include

---

[222] J. Fortin (2004) pp. 254–6.

[223] *A v. United Kingdom (human rights: punishment of child)* [1998] 2 FLR 959; discussed further in Chapter 9.

[224] *Z v. United Kingdom* [2001] 2 FLR 612, esp at paras 73–5. Whilst Art. 2 protects children from life-threatening abuse, Art. 3 protects them from abusive treatment amounting to inhuman or degrading treatment and Art. 8 protects them from infringements of their physical integrity.

[225] *Marckx v. Belgium* (1979) 2 EHRR 330.

[226] E.g., inter alia: *X, Y and Z v. United Kingdom* [1997] 2 FLR 892 (transsexual parent); *Marckx v. Belgium* (1979) 2 EHRR 330 (grandparent); *Boyle v. United Kingdom* (1994) 19 EHRR 179 (uncle); discussed further in Chapter 14.

[227] *McMichael v. United Kingdom* (1995) 20 EHRR 205; *W v. United Kingdom* (1987) 10 EHRR 29; *Venema v. The Netherlands* [2003] 1 FLR 552; *B v. United Kingdom* (1998) 10 EHRR 87.

[228] *Gaskin v. United Kingdom* (1989) 12 EHRR 36; J. Fortin (1999) pp. 362–3.

[229] *Mikulic v. Croatia* [2002] 1 FCR 720; discussed further in Chapter 13.

respect for private sexual life has ensured that homosexual adolescents have a sexual freedom equal to that enjoyed by their heterosexual and lesbian counterparts.[230]

Arguably, the full protection that Article 8 could offer children, through the concept of respect for their private life, has not yet been fully realised. The ECtHR's recent jurisprudence exploring this aspect of the article's protection has been in the context of adults' claims. But, as Munby J has pointed out, it also has considerable potential for protecting children in a variety of ways.[231] Since respect for a person's private life includes psychological integrity, its protection should enable children not only to live their own personal lives as they choose, but also to establish relationships with others. According to the case law, Article 8 protects their right to develop their own personalities free from interference,[232] and with their mental stability fully preserved.[233] Indeed, Munby J suggests 'that a child's Art 8 rights may be engaged if he is being brought up in surroundings that isolate him socially or confine or stultify him emotionally'.[234] The ECtHR's affirmation that the notion of personal autonomy is an important principle underlying the interpretation of Article 8[235] also has an obvious relevance for adolescents, particularly in the context of unwanted medical treatment.[236]

(ii) Positive obligations

As can be seen, the Strasbourg jurisprudence has forcefully extended the protection available to children. The Convention's ability to promote children's rights has also been greatly strengthened through the notion of positive obligations attaching to many of its provisions. Thus the view has been taken by the ECtHR that certain parts of the Convention impose more onerous duties on member states than others. In other words, these provisions not only compel states to abstain from interfering with the rights they protect, they require them to take active steps to secure these rights effectively.[237] Thus it is not enough for states to refrain from the intentional and unlawful killing of a child under Article 2, they must also take appropriate steps to safeguard his or her life.[238] Local authorities must therefore protect children effectively from abusive parental behaviour, in order to fulfil their positive obligations under Article 3 to protect children against inhuman or degrading treatment. They must not

---

[230] *Sutherland v. United Kingdom* (1997) 24 EHRR CD 22 led to the introduction of the Sexual Offences (Amendment) Act 2000 which lowered the age of consent to homosexual activity from 18 years to 16 years.

[231] Munby J (2004) pp. 341–2 and in *Re Roddy (a child)(identification: restriction on publication)* [2003] EWHC 2927 (Fam), [2004] 2 FLR 949, at [29]–[30].

[232] *Niemitz v. Germany* (1993) 16 EHRR 97, at para. 29; *Botta v. Italy* (1998) 26 EHRR 97, at para. 32.

[233] *Bensaid v. United Kingdom* (2001) 33 EHRR 1, at para. 47.

[234] Munby J (2004) p. 341.   [235] *Pretty v. United Kingdom* [2002] 2 FLR 45, at para. 61.

[236] Discussed further in Chapter 5.   [237] J. Wadham *et al.* (2003) pp. 25–9.

[238] *Osman v. United Kingdom* [1999] 1 FLR 193, at para. 115.

stand back and allow abuse that they are aware of to continue, they must intervene to prevent its continuation.[239] Similarly, rather than merely refraining from interfering with a child's private life under Article 8, a state must take appropriate steps to ensure that laws are in place to make such a right practical and effective,[240] including those safeguarding his or her right to physical integrity.[241] The positive obligations attaching to Article 8 are particularly relevant in cases involving parents who, having successfully obtained orders in the domestic courts aimed at reuniting them with their children, find it impossible to enforce such orders, due to the recalcitrance of the children's carers. In such cases, the ECtHR has repeatedly stressed that although not absolute,[242] the state has a positive obligation to take all necessary steps as can reasonably be demanded in the circumstances of the case to facilitate such a reunion, and as swiftly as possible.[243]

It was through employing the concept of positive obligations when interpreting the Convention, that the Strasbourg institutions achieved a truly dramatic extension of its jurisdiction. The Convention is not confined to a 'vertical' application, whereby individuals are only protected from public agencies. A 'horizontal approach'[244] to interpreting the Convention extends its jurisdiction sideways from the public domain into the realm of private relationships and disputes.[245] Consequently, states must prevent infringements occurring, irrespective of the circumstances and whether or not this involves interfering with private relationships between individuals. Such an approach has particularly far-ranging implications for children, since it requires states to establish laws ensuring that private individuals behave towards each other in a way which does not infringe their rights under the articles in question. For example, the ECtHR has ruled that Article 3 does not merely require public authorities like schools to refrain from punishing children in a way which infringes their right to freedom from inhuman or degrading treatment.[246] States must also ensure that children are protected from such behaviour in the privacy of their own homes, even when it is administered by their parents under the guise of physical punishment.[247] Similarly, whilst Article 8 clearly protects individuals against arbitrary interference by public authorities, states are also under a positive

---

[239] *Z v. United Kingdom* [2001] 2 FLR 612, at paras. 73–4; *Mayeka v. Belgium* [2006] 3 FCR 367, at para. 53.

[240] *Marckx v. Belgium* (1979) 2 EHRR 330, at para. 31; the Convention is intended to guarantee rights which are not merely 'theoretical and illusory' but 'practical and effective'.

[241] E.g. *X and Y v. Netherlands* (1985) 8 EHRR 235.

[242] E.g. if the child strongly opposes such a reunion, as in *Hokkanen v. Finland* (1995) 19 EHRR 139.

[243] E.g. *Ignaccolo-Zenide v. Romania* (2001) 31 EHRR 7, at paras. 94–6 and 102; discussed further in Chapters 8 and 13.

[244] M. Hunt (2001).   [245] See *Douglas v. Hello! Ltd* [2001] 2 All ER 289.

[246] Successful challenges taken to the ECtHR based on Art. 3 led to legislation abolishing the use of physical punishment in all schools; discussed further in Chapter 9.

[247] *A v. United Kingdom (human rights: punishment of child)* [1998] 2 FLR 959.

obligation to adopt measures to ensure that private individuals respect each others' private and family life.[248]

(iii) Articulating children's claims?
(a) Differing approaches

As discussed above, the ECtHR has played an important part in developing the protection available to children under the ECHR. Furthermore, it is increasingly willing to be guided by the principles set out by the CRC, with regular references to its provisions in its decisions.[249] The Court has, however, singularly failed to develop a robust body of jurisprudence analysing the rights that children themselves may enjoy under the Convention – it often fails to articulate children's claims at all. Applications to the ECtHR which might focus on children's rights will inevitably be brought on their behalf by adults, quite simply because children are too young to cope with the procedural complications of making claims themselves. The adults bringing such applications are usually parents and their claims largely centre on their own rights, rather than those of their children. Thus in public law cases, parents object to attempts to interfere with what they see as their right to bring up their children, free of state interference. In private law cases, they will often argue that their right to enjoy their children's company under Article 8 has been unnecessarily infringed through the domestic courts favouring the other parent.

A much smaller group of cases involves applications brought by adults on children's behalf, who are genuinely objecting to the way that the state has interfered with the children's own rights. There is a stark contrast in the manner the two types of challenges are dealt with. Indeed, it is arguable that the ECtHR often plays a poor part in championing children's rights, as opposed to those of their parents.

(b) State interference

In the context of child protection law, the focus will usually be on the parents' right to family life under Article 8, the wording of which appears to suggests that as long as families are protected from undue state interference, the regulation of family life can be safely left to its adult members.[250] But when considering a parent's claim that his rights under Article 8 have been infringed, the ECtHR makes little attempt to assess the evidence in terms of the child's own rights under the Convention. Instead, the early case law established a rigidly formal manner of processing such cases.[251] Evidence suggesting that the child might have suffered considerable harm at the hands of his or her parents is dealt with only within a discussion of whether the infringement of the parents' rights under Article 8(1) of

---

[248] *X and Y v. Netherlands* (1985) 8 EHRR 235.
[249] E.g. *Sahin v. Germany* [2003] 2 FLR 671, at paras. 39–41. See further U. Kilkelly (2001).
[250] J. Fortin (1999) p. 357.   [251] E.g. *Olsson v. Sweden (No. 2)* (1992) 17 EHRR 134.

the Convention can be justified under Article 8(2), as being a 'necessary' infringement, with the discussion being couched in terms of the child's best interests.[252] There is therefore no analysis of the infringement of the child's own rights, say under Articles 3 and 8. The consistent theme in these cases is that adults have rights, whilst children have interests, albeit 'best' interests.[253]

When reviewing the 'necessity' of the state's intervention (within the terms of Article 8(2)), and asserting the state's wide margin of appreciation when considering the need for state intervention, the ECtHR adopts a viewpoint which focuses on the rights of the adult applicants – the parents.[254] As Woolf points out, the child's best interests are sidelined, with the Court concentrating on whether the authorities have acted proportionately when interfering with the parents' right to family life.[255] This was certainly the view of Judge Bonello in *EP v. Italy*,[256] who passionately opposed the majority decision of the ECtHR concluding that the Italian authorities had failed to take necessary steps to reunite a mother and her 7-year-old daughter.[257] He pointed to the well-based concerns that the way the mother had constantly sought medical attention for her daughter was pathological and argued:

> The core question, in my view, should have been: did this unfortunate child have a right to a normal family and a happy home once her mother became unable to provide her with those basic minima? Saying, as the majority did, that the child's adoption was wrong is tantamount to saying that this particularly wretched child, did not, for reasons undisclosed, deserve a normal family life.[258]

Similarly, the Court's criticism of state authorities for using emergency powers over-precipitously to protect very young children, may to child care practitioners, appear to stem from an unduly adult-orientated position. Whilst it is understandable for the ECtHR to stress that removing very young babies from their mothers soon after birth can only be justified by extraordinarily compelling reasons,[259] the child welfare authorities are confronted by an obvious dilemma if they doubt a mother's ability to care for her baby.[260] Babies are particularly vulnerable to abuse.[261] Whilst the ECtHR criticises them for unacceptably intervening they would have been blamed by the public had they not intervened and the child had been harmed.[262] In none of this case

---

[252] E.g. *K and T v. Finland* [2001] 2 FLR 707, at paras. 154–5.   [253] Discussed further below.

[254] M. Woolf (2003) pp. 211–12.   [255] Ibid at p. 220.   [256] (2001) 31 EHRR 17.

[257] Judge Bonello's dissent, at paras. 4–6.   [258] Ibid. at para. 13.

[259] *K and T v. Finland* [2001] 2 FLR 707, at para. 168 and *Haase v. Germany* [2004] 2 FLR 39, at para. 102.

[260] E.g. in *K and T v. Finland* [2001] 2 FLR 707 the mother was a paranoid schizophrenic with a poor parenting record regarding her older child.

[261] Discussed in Chapter 15.

[262] *K and T v. Finland*, ibid., per dissenting judges, Judge Palm, joined by Judge Gaukur Jörundsson, (see esp. at 752) and Judge Bonello (see esp. at 755). The latter complained that those who had wanted to place the baby beyond reach of harm were now themselves 'branded violators of human rights' (at 756).

law is there any specific mention of the child's own Convention rights which might have counter-balanced those of the parent.

(c) Parental disputes

When it comes to dealing with disputes between private individuals over children, the ECtHR takes an equally formalistic and adult-centred approach. Whilst children are the focus of such complaints, these applications are brought by adults unhappy about the way that their right to enjoy their children's company under Article 8 has been infringed through the domestic courts favouring the other parent. Admittedly the ECtHR considers whether the disputed order can be justified under Article 8(2), by reference to protecting the 'rights and freedoms of others', including the rights of the children concerned. But again, it does so without articulating their specific Convention rights, merely assessing the evidence relating to their best interests. Such an approach may lead to a relatively superficial assessment of the child's own position in any given case. Thus in cases like *Hoffmann v. Austria*,[263] and *Yousef v. Netherlands*,[264] the complexities of the children's own position are hardly referred to. In the first there is no discussion of the children's own religious rights and in the second, no mention of the child's own right to retain a relationship with her father, or indeed, any discussion of her relationship with her maternal grandparents. In *Yousef*, the ECtHR gave the following guidance:

> The court reiterates that in judicial decisions where the rights under Art 8 of parents and those of a child are at stake, the child's rights must be the paramount consideration. If any balancing of interests is necessary, the interests of the child must prevail (see *Elsholz v Germany* [refs] and *TP and KM v United Kingdom* [refs].[265]

By using the word 'rights' in relation to the child, the Court appeared to acknowledge that the child did have rights of her own, but this concept was not developed. Indeed, the use of the word 'interests' was swiftly reverted to – the word employed throughout the remainder of the discussion devoted to the child's own position.

The ECtHR adopts a similarly myopic approach to children's own Convention rights when considering the claims of parents whom states fail to assist adequately with enforcing orders aimed at reuniting them with their children.[266] There is often the additional complication that time has elapsed, and the child him or herself, perhaps due to indoctrination by the residential

---

[263] (1993) 17 EHRR 293: per ECtHR (five votes to four), by denying the Jehovah's Witness mother custody on the grounds of her religion, the Austrian courts had violated her rights under Art. 8, in conjunction with Art. 14. See also *Palau-Martinez v. France* [2004] 2 FLR 810; cf. *Ismailova v. Russia* [2008] 1 FLR 533.

[264] [2003] 1 FLR 210: an unmarried father unsuccessfully challenged the Dutch courts' refusal to allow him to recognise or take over the care of his 5-year-old child who was being cared for by her maternal grandparents after her mother's death.

[265] Ibid. at para. 73.   [266] Discussed further in Chapter 13.

parent or carer, now refuses contact with the applicant parent.[267] In all these cases, the ECtHR constantly stresses that:

> Whilst national authorities must do their utmost to facilitate such co-operation [leading to reunion], any obligation to apply coercion in this area must be limited since the ... rights and freedoms of all concerned must be taken into account ... and more particularly the best interests of the child and his or her rights under Art 8 of the Convention.[268]

Nevertheless, this rather vague reference to the child's rights is normally followed by a discussion of the strength of evidence acceding to the child's wishes on the matter, all in the context of finding an outcome which safeguards the child's best interests.[269] Again there is no systematic analysis of what Convention rights a child might have in circumstance of this kind.

(d) Children's own applications

The ECtHR appears only to explore the full scope of children's own rights within the Convention's framework when the applications are brought on behalf of children themselves. Their rights are then specifically articulated. Thus the ECtHR has explored the scope of Article 3 when addressing the claims of children objecting to being physically punished in school,[270] or at home.[271] Furthermore, whilst, as noted above, there is a large body of Strasbourg jurisprudence considering parents' complaints over the way in which their children have been removed into state care, a tiny number of applications is also brought on behalf of abused children themselves. These have produced decisions exploring the scope of Articles 2, 3 and 8 of the Convention, all of which offer abused children important forms of protection.[272] Equally well known are the important principles that have emerged from applications brought by young people objecting to being restrained in secure units of various kinds[273] and by young offenders objecting to their methods of trial.[274]

In some cases, because parent and child are both actively involved in a family dispute, it appears almost coincidental who takes a case to Strasbourg. But an application may assume an entirely different set of perspectives when it is the child's application and not that of the parent. Thus in *Mikulic v. Croatia*,[275]

---

[267] E.g. *Hansen v. Turkey* [2004] 1 FLR 142.

[268] *Kosmopoulou v. Greece* [2004] 1 FLR 800, at para. 45.

[269] E.g. *Süss v. Germany* [2006] 1 FLR 522, at para. 90.

[270] E.g. *Tyrer v. United Kingdom* (1978) 2 EHRR 1 and *Campbell and Cosans v. United Kingdom* (1982) 4 EHRR 293. In the latter case, the parents, who claimed an infringement of the child's Art. 3 rights, fell back on a claim based on their own rights under A2P1 of the ECHR.

[271] *A v. United Kingdom* (1998) 27 EHRR 611.

[272] E.g. *Z v. United Kingdom* [2001] 2 FLR 612; *TP and KM v. United Kingdom* [2001] 2 FLR 549; *E v. United Kingdom* [2002] 3 FCR 700.

[273] E.g. *Bouamar v. Belgium* (1988) 11 EHRR 1 and *Koniarska v. United Kingdom* (App. No. 33670/96) (12 October 2000, unreported).

[274] *V and T v. United Kingdom* (1999) 30 EHRR 121; *SC v. United Kingdom* (2004) 40 EHRR 10.

[275] [2002] 1 FCR 720.

instead of focusing on the lack of effective procedures enabling an unmarried mother to establish the paternity of her child's father and obtain financial support for her child, the ECtHR explored her daughter's own right to respect for her private life within Article 8.[276] It concluded that states should have in place a procedure striking a fair balance between the need of a child to have eliminated without unnecessary delay any uncertainty over his or her personal identity (arising from ignorance of a parent's identity)[277] and those of the alleged father not to be forced into DNA testing.[278]

Unfortunately, even when dealing with individual child applicants, the ECtHR's record is not entirely consistent. Indeed, the Court is not always enthusiastic about the notion of children being rights-holders themselves, particularly in situations where the rights of parent and child are both at stake. Thus in *Valsamis v. Greece*,[279] the ECtHR saw no reason to subject a 12-year-old girl's claim to religious freedom under Article 9 to a separate examination, once it had considered and rejected her parents' claim that their own religious rights had been infringed. The ECtHR has also found it particularly difficult to grasp the nettle in cases where, as in *Nielsen v. Denmark*,[280] there is an apparent conflict between a child's rights and those of his or her parent. It was the ECtHR's obvious concern about the way in which a boy's rights under Article 5 might conflict with those of his mother, under Article 8, to reach decisions about his upbringing, that led it to reject the proposition that Article 5 was engaged in favour of the boy. The *Nielsen* decision reinforces the view that the Convention is ill-equipped to help courts find an appropriate balance between parents' powers and children's rights.[281] This view is also borne out by the EComHR's inconsistent approach to interpreting Article 8 in cases involving adolescents challenging their parents' rights to force them to live at home.[282] The Strasbourg institutions obviously find it difficult to acknowledge that an older child may have a right to family privacy alongside his or her parents' right to run their household as they please. This approach sits a little uncomfortably with its burgeoning emphasis on adult autonomy,[283] an emphasis which may lead into its adapting its views on adolescents' position within the family.[284]

It is perhaps the formalised procedure utilised by the ECtHR that has undermined its ability to explore children's own position in applications brought by adults but focusing on children. For example, its rejection of the parents' claim in *Kjeldsen, Busk Madsen and Pedersen v. Denmark*[285] implies that it was very

---

[276] Ibid. at paras. 53–5.   [277] Discussed further in Chapter 13.   [278] Ibid. and paras. 64–6.

[279] (1996) 24 EHRR 294; discussed further in Chapter 11.   [280] (1988) 11 EHRR 175.

[281] J. Fortin (2002) p. 22; see also Chapters 3, 5 and 10.

[282] *X v. Netherlands* (1974) Application No 6753/74 (1975–76) 1–3 DR 118; cf. *X v. Denmark* (1978) Application No 6854/74 (1977–78) 7–9 DR 81; discussed further in Chapter 4.

[283] E.g. inter alia: *YF v. Turkey* (2004) 39 EHRR 34, at para. 33; *Storck v. Germany* (2006) 43 EHRR 6, at paras. 150–2; *Pretty v. United Kingdom* [2002] 2 FLR 45, at para. 41.

[284] Discussed further in Chapter 3.   [285] (1976) EHRR 711.

aware of the children's own needs in such a scenario.[286] Nevertheless, the Court dealt with the parents' challenge that the Danish government had violated their rights under A2P1 of the ECHR by providing compulsory sex education in schools without any reference to the children's Convention rights. Admittedly, a response focusing on the terms of the parents' application was predictable but a more child-orientated court might have initiated an assessment of the children's own possible rights. For example, the ECtHR could have discussed the children's right, under Article 10, to receive informative sex education in school alongside their peers. Dembour criticises the ECtHR for failing to promote women's rights more effectively.[287] Arguably, the Court's record is even worse in its dealings with children.

(iv) No 'welfare or best interests' formula

One explanation for the ECtHR's failure to analyse challenges involving children, in terms of the children's own Convention rights, may be the fact that children are seldom separately represented in Strasbourg. Even in the rare event of this occurring, the Court often sees no reason to differentiate the parents' position from that of the child.[288] A far more fundamental reason, however, must be the way in which the ECtHR deals with the fact that the Convention contains no formula referring to the child's best interests. Unlike the paramountcy principle which governs decision making in our domestic courts,[289] none of the Convention's articles indicates that a child's position commands a paramount place. In children's cases which normally involve a conflict between the rights of several individuals, the ECtHR sees its job as to balance one set of rights against another, without any *initial* presumption favouring one over the other. Within these parameters, the Court goes as far as it can to give children's interests a special weighting. As Woolf points out, a consideration of the child's best interests by the ECtHR has concentrated on the Article 8 right to family life. Subject to its practice of allowing states a margin of appreciation when considering what outcome is in the child's best interests,[290] the Court has stressed time and again the importance of this factor. Thus, in the context of public law cases, it maintains that whilst a fair balance must be struck between the interests of the child and those of the parent,[291] 'crucial'[292] or 'particular'[293] importance is attached:

> to the best interests of the child, which, depending on their nature and seriousness, may override those of the parent. In particular ... the parent cannot be

---

[286] Discussed further in Chapter 6.   [287] M.-B. Dembour (2006) p. 219.

[288] E.g. *P, C and S v. United Kingdom* [2002] 2 FLR 631, where although the child was separately represented, the ECtHR failed to differentiate her position from that of her parents and refused her damages for breach of her Art. 8 rights, alongside those awarded to her parents. I gratefully acknowledge Professor Judith Masson's assistance on this point.

[289] CA 1989, s. 1(1); discussed further in Chapter 8.   [290] M. Woolf (2003) pp. 209–10.

[291] *Olsson v. Sweden (No. 2)* (1992) 17 EHRR 134, at para. 90.

[292] *Johansen v. Denmark* (1996) 23 EHRR 33, at para. 64.   [293] Ibid. at para. 78.

entitled under article 8 of the Convention to have such measures taken as would harm the child's health and development.[294]

Similarly, in private law disputes, the ECtHR advises domestic courts to consider 'the rights and freedoms of all concerned … and *more particularly* the best interests of the child and his or her rights under Article 8 of the Convention'.[295] In this way the ECtHR has skilfully compensated for the absence of any best interests formula within the Convention itself. Nevertheless the way it has done so involves all evidence regarding the child being treated by the ECtHR as 'best interests' material and used to counter-balance parents' claims regarding their own rights. Excepting those cases where applications are made on behalf of children themselves, such evidence is there-fore not examined to see whether it could support claims that the child has specific Convention rights. Woolf argues that by largely allowing states to decide for themselves, under the margin of appreciation, what outcome is in a child's best interests, limits its ability to scrutinise adequately decisions reached by the domestic courts.[296]

At this point it should be noted that to some, the ECtHR's decision in *Yousef v. Netherlands*,[297] now followed by more recent case law,[298] suggests that the child's best interests have become the *paramount* consideration in Strasbourg jurisprudence.[299] But as the quotation above makes clear, this is not what the Court said. Following its statement that the child's rights must be the para-mount consideration, it proceeds to emphasise that 'If any balancing of interests is necessary, the interests of the child must prevail'.[300] As these words make clear, if, when deciding whether it is *necessary* to infringe the rights of the adult applicant, the court finds that each of the scales containing evidence relating to child and adult is evenly weighted against the other, *then* the child's rights or interests must prevail. Indeed, the ECtHR commonly reverts to the standard and far more familiar formula:

> a fair balance must be struck between the interests of the child and those of the parent and that, in striking such a balance, particular importance must be attached to the best interests of the child which, depending on their nature and seriousness, may override those of the parent.[301]

---

[294] Ibid.

[295] *Hokkanen v. Finland* (1994) 19 EHRR 139, at para. 58: emphasis supplied. See also *Hoffmann v. Austria* (1993) 17 EHRR 293, per EComHR, at para. 91: 'the *predominant* consideration in this respect [for the domestic court] must be the best interest of the children, including the protection of their health and morals' (emphasis supplied).

[296] M. Woolf (2003) p. 220.   [297] [2003] 1 FLR 210.

[298] *Kearns v. France* [2008] 1 FLR 888, at para. 79.

[299] E.g. Dame Elizabeth Butler-Sloss P, in *Re S (contact: promoting relationship with absent parent)* [2004] EWCA Civ 18, [2004] 1 FLR 1279, at [15].

[300] [2003] 1 FLR 210, at para. 73. See also *Kearns v. France* [2008] 1 FLR 888, at para. 79: 'In striking a balance between these different interests, the child's best interests should be paramount.'

[301] Inter alia: *Hoppe v. Germany* [2003] 1 FLR 384, at para. 49; *Görgülü v. Germany* [2004] 1 FLR 894, at para. 43; *Süss v. Germany* [2006] 1 FLR 522, at para. 88.

As Choudhry points out, this more traditional formula avoids suggesting that the child's best interests are paramount.[302] Indeed, the ECtHR's position appears to be clear. It cannot give 'crucial' or 'particular' importance to the child's interests until it has completed the balancing act between the various interests. As argued by Herring, in the context of Article 8, there is a significant difference between *starting* from the premise that a parent's rights must not be infringed *unless* the court is satisfied that such an infringement can be justified under Article 8(2), with reference to the child's best interests, and determining the outcome of the dispute by reference to the child's best interests, and *then* taking account of the rights of the others involved.[303] Despite the domestic courts' confidence that the two approaches are identical,[304] the Convention dictates a process which signally fails to make the child's interests paramount.

Cases like *Elsholz v. Germany*[305] and *Görgülü v. Germany*[306] demonstrate only too clearly the difference between according a child's best interests a paramount status and acknowledging its 'crucial' or 'particular' significance when deciding whether it is 'necessary' to infringe an adult's Article 8 rights. In the former, the German courts, relying on the child's own strongly stated hostility towards his father (in oral hearings and two lengthy interviews), had considered that contact would be not be in his best interests. In *Görgülü v. Germany*, the German court considered that it would be against a 4-year-old boy's best interests for his father to take over his care, having been in foster care since birth. In each case, the ECtHR concluded that despite the German courts' findings that it would have harmed these children for the respective fathers to obtain the orders sought, it had not been *necessary* to infringe the fathers' rights in such a way. So it was not enough to show that such an order was against the child's best interests – the justification for infringing the fathers' rights required 'very strong evidence indeed'.[307] Eekelaar strongly urges that the ECtHR could avoid placing a child's interests 'too low' if it started considering the evidence in terms of his Convention rights, rather than in terms of his best interests.[308]

One wonders whether Eekelaar's suggested approach would have produced a different result in *Elsholz v. Germany*[309] or *Görgülü v. Germany*.[310] In both there was evidence explaining the ECtHR's view that the fathers' claims should be upheld. Nevertheless, had it been analysed and couched in terms of the child's own rights under Article 8(1), a more considered and child-centred approach might have emerged. Whilst both children certainly had a long-term right to know and enjoy the company of their fathers, both also had the right to the preservation of their mental stability, this being 'an indispensable precondition to effective enjoyment of the right to respect for private life'.[311] Damage to their mental stability with their present carers might well undermine their ability to

---

[302] S. Choudhry (2003) pp. 130–1.   [303] J. Herring (1999) p. 231.
[304] Further discussed in Chapter 8.   [305] [2000] 2 FLR 486.   [306] [2004] 1 FLR 894.
[307] J. Eekelaar (2002) p. 241, commenting on *Elsholz v. Germany*.   [308] Ibid.
[309] [2000] 2 FLR 486.   [310] [2004] 1 FLR 894.
[311] *Bensaid v. United Kingdom* (2001) 33 EHRR 1, at para. 47.

enjoy their longer term relationships with their respective fathers. Neither right was referred to or discussed.

(7) The Council of Europe and children's rights

As noted above, perhaps the greatest achievement of the Council of Europe was to adopt the ECHR. This had no specific remit to protect children's rights; had it been designed with this purpose in mind, it could have done so far more efficiently. Nevertheless, the Council of Europe has also played a direct part in encouraging important reforms in the area of family law, many of which have promoted children's rights.[312] This has been achieved through the work of the European Ministers of Justice, the Parliamentary Assembly, and the Committee of Experts on Family Law. Whilst the Resolutions and Recommendations of the Parliamentary Assembly[313] and of the Committee of Ministers[314] only have persuasive influence, many reflect a clear and refreshingly forthright approach to the concept of children's rights and to the part children could play in Europe were they given appropriate encouragement.[315] Some of these recommendations have achieved concrete results, in so far as they have led to the preparation of international instruments whose specific aim is to harmonise the laws of European member states in order to promote children's welfare more effectively.[316] Many, for example, the European Convention on the Legal Status of Children Born Out of Wedlock, achieved improvements in domestic law. It was

---

[312] Council of Europe (2002). The Council of Europe launched in April 2005, a three-year action programme 'Building a Europe for and with Children'.

[313] E.g., inter alia: Recommendation 1065 (1987) On the Traffic in Children and other Forms of Child Exploitation; Recommendation 1071 (1988) Providing Institutional Care for Infants and Children; Recommendation 1286 (1996) on a European Strategy for Children; Recommendation 1336 (1997) on Combating Child Labour Exploitation; Recommendation 1666 (2004) on a Europe-wide Ban on Corporal Punishment of Children; Resolution 1468 and Recommendation 1723 (2005) on Forced Marriage and Child Marriages.

[314] E.g., inter alia: Recommendation 16 (2001) on the Protection from Sexual Exploitation of Children and Young Adults; Recommendation 20 (2003) on New Ways of Dealing with Juvenile Justice and the Role of Juvenile Justice; Recommendation 5 (2005) on the Rights of Children Living in Residential Institutions; Recommendation 12 (2006) on Empowering Children in the New Information and Communications Environment.

[315] E.g. the Committee of Ministers has emphasised the importance of enabling children to influence the conditions of their own lives through full and effective participation in family and society: see Council of Europe, Committee of Ministers, Recommendation (No R (98) 8) on Children's Participation in Family and Social Life.

[316] Inter alia: the European Convention on the Legal Status of Children Born Out of Wedlock 1975; the European Convention on Recognition and Enforcement of Decisions Concerning Custody of Children and on Restoration of Custody of Children 1980; the European Convention on the Exercise of Children's Rights 1996; the European Convention for the Protection of Human Rights and Dignity of the Human Being with Regard to the Application of Biology and Medicine 1997; the European Convention on Contact Concerning Children 2003; the European Convention on the Protection of Children from Sexual Exploitation and Abuse 2007; the European Convention on the Adoption of Children (Revised) 2008.

the combination of the *Marckx* decision[317] and the UK's ratification of this Convention in 1981, which led the English Law Commission to recommend the widespread reform of the English law relating to children born out of wedlock.[318]

The Committee of Experts on Family Law were also responsible for a further initiative designed to promote children's rights in the context of family litigation. They prepared and introduced the European Convention on the Exercise of Children's Rights, opened for signature in 1996. The intention of this Convention was to supplement the CRC by assisting children to exercise their substantive rights set out in the Convention. It recognises that the most practical means for children to claim and enforce their rights is through legal proceedings. The European Convention on the Exercise of Children's Rights therefore confines itself to creating and strengthening procedural rights to be exercised by children when becoming involved in family proceedings.[319] Meanwhile, the Council of Europe continues to pay special attention to its law reform role. Through its Committee of Experts on Family Law, it identifies areas of law requiring reform and harmonisation with a view to improving the lives of children living in member states, both in their families and in their wider communities.

Though these developments have been of some significance, the Council of Europe has not initiated any reforms broad enough in scope to match the impact of the United Nation's CRC. Calls have been made from time to time for the Council to adopt a specialist treaty dealing with children's rights.[320] Its failure to do so may stem from the view that a European Charter on the Rights of the Child could do little more than reproduce a list similar to that provided by the CRC. Nevertheless, Alston and Tobin argue that the ECHR's weaknesses so far as children are concerned justify the Council pressing ahead with a specialist convention of its own. An alternative would be for it to adopt a protocol to the ECHR, ensuring the addition of various rights contained in the CRC which are not already adequately covered.[321]

(8) Conclusion

The contribution made by international human rights law to promoting the rights of children has been of inestimable importance. Ratification of the CRC by nearly all countries throughout the world means that it has become an international treaty of major significance. Its influence is undoubtedly growing in this country, despite the current government's apparent reluctance to give it greater standing. For children in this country, the work of the Council of

---

[317] *Marckx v. Belgium* (1979) 2 EHRR 330.
[318] Law Commission (1982) paras. 4.11–12, followed by the Family Law Reform Act 1987.
[319] Council of Europe (1997) p. 18; discussed further in Chapter 7.
[320] P. Alston and J. Tobin (2005) p. 17.   [321] Ibid.

Europe, both in establishing the ECHR and through its reforming initiatives, has also had considerable impact. Even before implementation of the HRA 1998, these developments had combined to produce a practical rights-oriented consciousness amongst those dealing with legal problems affecting children on a day-to-day basis. It was also becoming increasingly common for domestic courts to justify their decisions on matters affecting children by reference to children's rights and to draw on both these treaties to substantiate such an approach. Now that it has become part of domestic law, the ECHR has gained an even greater impact on the legal principles underpinning children's rights than the CRC, hampered as the latter treaty is by its weak enforcement mechanism. Be that as it may, practitioners and the judiciary are now not only far more open to arguments based on children's rights, but also more willing to consider international instruments as an important source of guidance over the standards to be reached by domestic law.

BIBLIOGRAPHY

NB Some of these publications can be obtained on the relevant organisation's website.

Alston, P. and Tobin, J. (2005) *Laying the Foundations for Children's Rights*, UNICEF.

Bainham, A. (2002) 'Can We Protect Children and Protect their Rights?' *Family Law* 279.

Barsh, R. (1989) 'The Convention on the Rights of the Child: a Re-assessment of the Final Text' 7 *New York Law School Journal of Human Rights* 142.

Children's Commissioner for England (2006) *Memorandum from the Office of the Children's Commissioner to the Joint Committee on Human Rights*, Office of the Children's Commissioner.

Children's Rights Alliance (2002) *Report to the Pre-Sessional Working Group of the Committee on the Rights of the Child, preparing for examination of the UK's second report under the CRC*, unpublished.

Children's Rights Alliance for England (CRAE) (2008) *UK Implementation of the Convention on the Rights of the Child: NGO alternative report to the Committee on the Rights of the Child – England*, unpublished.

Children's Rights Development Unit (1994) *UK Agenda for Children*, Children's Rights Development Unit.

Choudhry, S. (2003) 'The Adoption and Children Act 2002, the Welfare Principle and the Human Rights Act 1998 – a Missed Opportunity' 15 *Child and Family Law Quarterly* 119.

Combe, V. (2002) *Up for it: Getting Young People Involved in Local Government*, The National Youth Agency.

Committee on the Rights of the Child (1995) *Concluding Observations of the Committee on the Rights of the Child: United Kingdom of Great Britain and Northern Ireland*, CRC/C/15/Add 34 1995, Centre for Human Rights, Geneva.

Committee on the Rights of the Child (2002a) *Concluding Observations of the Committee on the Rights of the Child: United Kingdom of Great Britain and Northern Ireland*, CRC/C/15/Add 188 2002, Centre for Human Rights, Geneva.

Committee on the Rights of the Child (2002b) *The Role of Independent National Human Rights Institutions in the Promotion and Protection of the Rights of the Child*, General Comment No. 2, CRC/GC/2002/2, Centre for Human Rights, Geneva.

Committee on the Rights of the Child (2003) *General Measures of Implementation of the Convention on the Rights of the Child (arts 4, 42 and 44, para 6)*, General Comment No. 5, CRC/GC/2003/5, Centre for Human Rights, Geneva.

Committee on the Rights of the Child (2006) *The Rights of Children with Disabilities*, General Comment No. 9, CRC/C/GC 9, Centre for Human Rights, Geneva.

Committee on the Rights of the Child (2008) *Concluding Observations of the Committee on the Rights of the Child: United Kingdom of Great Britain and Northern Ireland* CRC/C/GBR/CO/4, Centre for Human Rights, Geneva.

Council of Europe (1996) *Report on a European Strategy for Children*, Parliamentary Assembly of the Council of Europe, Recommendation 1286.

Council of Europe (1997) *European Convention on the Exercise of Children's Rights and Explanatory Report*, Council of Europe Publishing.

Council of Europe (2002) *Council of Europe Achievements in the Field of Law: Family Law and the Protection of Children* DIR/JUR 9.

Dembour, M.-B. (2006) *Who Believes in Human Rights? Reflections on the European Convention*, Cambridge University Press.

Department of Health (DH) (1994) *The UN Convention on the Rights of the Child: The UK's First Report to the UN Committee on the Rights of the Child*, HMSO.

Department of Health (DH) (1999) *United Nations Convention on the Rights of the Child: Second Report to the UN Committee by the United Kingdom 1999*, The Stationery Office.

Detrick, S. (ed.) (1992) *The United Nations Convention on the Rights of the Child: A Guide to the 'Travaux Préparatoires'*, Martinus Nijhoff Publishers.

Donnelly, J. and Howard, R. (1988) 'Assessing National Human Rights Performance: A Theoretical Framework' 10 *Human Rights Quarterly* 214.

Eekelaar, J. (1992) 'The Importance of Thinking that Children Have Rights' in Alston, P., Parker, S. and Seymour, J. (eds.) *Children, Rights and the Law*, Clarendon Press.

(2002) 'Beyond the Welfare Principle' 14 *Child and Family Law Quarterly* 237.

(2004) 'Personal Rights and Human Rights' in Lødrup, P. and Modvar, E. (eds.) *Family Life and Human Rights*, Gyldendal.

(2006) 'Invoking Human Rights' in Endicott, T., Getzler, J. and Peel, E. (eds.) *Properties of Law: Essays in Honour of Jim Harris*, Oxford University Press.

Feinberg, J. (1980) *Rights, Justice and the Bounds of Liberty*, Princeton University Press.

Feldman, D. (2002) *Civil Liberties and Human Rights in England and Wales*, Oxford University Press.

Flekkøy, M. (1991) *A Voice for Children: Speaking Out as their Ombudsman*, Jessica Kingsley Publishers.

(2001) 'The Role of an Ombudsman for Children: Securing the Child's Right to Education' in Hart, S., Price Cohen, C., Farrell Erickson, M. and Flekkøy, M. *Children's Rights in Education*, Jessica Kingsley Publishers.

Fortin, J. (1999) 'Rights Brought Home for Children' 62 *Modern Law Review* 350.

(2002) 'Children's Rights and the Impact of Two International Conventions: The UNCRC and the ECHR' in The Rt Hon L J Thorpe and Cowton, C. (eds.) *Delight and Dole: The Children Act 10 years on*, Jordan Publishing Ltd.

(2003) *Children's Rights and the Developing Law*, LexisNexis Butterworths.

(2004) 'Children's Rights: Are the Courts Now Taking Them More Seriously?' 15 *King's College Law Journal* 253.

Freeman, M. (2000) 'The Future of Children's Rights' 14 *Children and Society* 277.

Gearty, C. (1997) 'The United Kingdom' in Gearty, C. (ed.) *European Civil Liberties and the European Convention on Human Rights: A Comparative Study*, The Hague.

HM Government (2007) *The Consolidated 3rd and 4th Periodic Report to UN Committee on the Rights of the Child*, DCSF.

Hammarberg, T. (1990) 'The UN Convention on the Rights of the Child – and How to Make it Work' 12 *Human Rights Quarterly* 97.

Harris-Short, S. (2003) 'International Human Rights Law: Imperialist, Inept and Ineffective? Cultural Relativism and the UN Convention on the Rights of the Child' 25 *Human Rights Quarterly* 130.

Henricson, C. and Bainham, A. (2005) *The Child and Family Policy Divide*, Joseph Rowntree Foundation.

Herring, J. (1999) 'The Human Rights Act and the Welfare Principle in Family Law – Conflicting or Complementary?' 11 *Child and Family Law Quarterly* 223.

Hodgkin, R. and Newell, P. (eds.) (2007) *Implementation Handbook for the Convention on the Rights of the Child*, UNICEF.

Hodgson, D. (1992) 'The Historical Development and "Internationalisation" of the Children's Rights Movement' 6 *Australian Journal of Family Law* 25.

Home Office (HO) (1997) *Rights Brought Home: The Human Rights Bill* Cm 3782, HMSO.

Hunt, M. (2001) 'The "Horizontal Effect" of the Human Rights Act: Moving Beyond the Public-Private Distinction' in Jowell, J. and Cooper, J. (eds.) *Understanding Human Rights Principles*, Hart Publishing.

Joint Committee on Human Rights (JCHR) (2003) House of Lords, House of Commons, Joint Committee on Human Rights, *The UN Convention on the Rights of the Child*, Tenth Report of Session 2002–03 HL Paper 117/HC 81.

Joint Committee on Human Rights (JCHR) (2008a), *A Bill of Rights for the UK? Twenty-ninth Report of Session 2007–08*, HL Paper 165-I, HC 150-I, The Stationery Office.

Joint Committee on Human Rights (JCHR) (2008b), *A Bill of Rights for the UK? Twenty-ninth Report of Session 2007–08*, *Volume II*, HL Paper 165-II, HC 150-II, The Stationery Office.

Kilbourne, S. (1998) 'The Wayward Americans – Why the USA has not Ratified the UN Convention on the Rights of the Child' 10 *Child and Family Law Quarterly* 243.

Kilkelly, U. (1996) 'The UN Committee on the Rights of the Child – an Evaluation in the Light of the Recent UK Experience' 8 *Child and Family Law Quarterly* 105.

(2001) 'The Best of Both Worlds for Children's Right? Interpreting the European Convention on Human Rights in the Light of the UN Convention on the Rights of the Child' 23 *Human Rights Quarterly* 308.

Kilkelly, U. and Lundy, L. (2006) 'Children's Rights in Action: Using the UN Convention on the Rights of the Child as an Auditing Tool' 18 *Child and Family Law Quarterly* 331.

King, M. (1994) 'Children's Rights as Communication: Reflections on Autopoietic Theory and the United Nations Convention' 57 *Modern Law Review* 385.

Law Commission (1982) *Family Law Report on Illegitimacy* Law Com No 118, HMSO.

LeBlanc, L. (1995) *The Convention on the Rights of the Child: United Nations Lawmaking on Human Rights*, University of Nebraska Press.

McGlynn, C. (2000) 'A Family Law for the EU?' in Shaw, J. (ed.) *Social Law and Policy in an Evolving EU*, Hart Publishing.

(2001) 'The Europeanisation of Family Law' 13 *Child and Family Law Quarterly* 35.

McGoldrick, D. (1991) 'The United Nations Convention on the Rights of the Child' 5 *International Journal of Law and the Family* 132.

Marshall, K. and Parvis, P. (2004) *Honouring Children*, Saint Andrew Press.

Minow, M. (1987) 'Interpreting Rights: An Essay for Robert Cover' 96 *Yale Law Journal* 1860.

Munby, J. (2004) 'Making Sure the Child is Heard' 34 *Family Law* 338.

Phillipson, G. (2003) '(Mis)-reading section 3 of the Human Rights Act' 199 *Law Quarterly Review* 183.

Price Cohen, C. and Kilbourne, S. (1998) 'Jurisprudence of the Committee on the Rights of the Child: A Guide for Research and Analysis' 19 *Michigan Journal of International Law* 633.

Scherer, L. and Hart, S. (2001) 'Reporting on the Status of Education to the Committee on the Rights of the Child' in Hart, S., Price Cohen, C., Farrell Erickson, M. and Flekkøy, M. *Children's Rights in Education*, Jessica Kingsley Publishers.

Timimi, S. (2006) 'Children's Mental Health: The Role of Culture, Markets and Prescribed Drugs' 13 *Public Policy Research* 35.

UK Children's Commissioners (2008) *UK Children's Commissioners' Report to the UN Committee on the Rights of the Child*, 11 million.

UNICEF Innocenti Research Centre (2006) *The General Measures of the Convention on the Rights of the Child: The Process in Europe and Central Asia*, UNICEF.

Van Bueren, G. (1995) *The International Law on the Rights of the Child*, Martinus Nijhoff Publishers.

Wadham, J., Mountfield, H. and Edmundson, A. (2003) *Blackstone's Guide to the Human Rights Act 1998*, Oxford University Press.

Wellman, C. (1999) *The Proliferation of Rights: Moral Progress or Empty Rhetoric?*, Westview Press.

Wilkins, R. (2004) 'International Law, Social Change and the Family' in Lødrup, P. and Modvar, E. (eds.) *Family Life and Human Rights*, Gyldendal.

Williams, J. (2005) 'Effective Government Structures for Children?: The UK's Four Children's Commissioners' 17 *Child and Family Law Quarterly* 37.

Woolf, M. (2003) 'Coming of Age? – The Principle of "The Best Interests of the Child"' *European Human Rights Law Review* 205.

Part Two

Promoting consultation and decision-making

Chapter 3

Adolescent autonomy and parents

(1) Introduction

Adolescents are fast approaching adulthood, but they cannot be expected to make the transition from childhood to an adult legal status successfully without assistance. They need to develop complex skills for independent life in our relatively wealthy and technologically sophisticated society. Although parents have an essential part to play in this process, the law should also assist by ensuring that an adolescent's decisions are, as far as possible, respected. The growing emphasis on adult autonomy encouraged by the implementation of the Human Rights Act (HRA) 1998 has produced a judicial willingness to accommodate such ideas when interpreting adolescents' interests. The words of Baroness Hale of Richmond exemplify such an approach:

> Important physical, cognitive and psychological developments take place during adolescence. Adolescence begins with the onset of puberty; from puberty to adulthood, the 'capacity to acquire and utilise knowledge reaches its peak efficiency'; and the capacity for formal operational thought is the forerunner to developing the capacity to make autonomous moral judgments. Obviously, these developments happen at different times and at different rates for different people. But it is not at all surprising to find adolescents making different moral judgments from those of their parents. It is part of growing up.[1]

It is, however, unrealistic to expect children of any age to make decisions for themselves before they are developmentally ready to do so. Those who argue over the extent to which children should be allowed greater legal responsibilities seldom refer to the extensive body of research on children's mental processes and cognitive powers. This chapter briefly summarises some of this material and explores how it might inform decision-making relating to children as they mature into adolescence.

The second part of the chapter considers, in general terms, the confused legal principles now governing the relationship between adolescents and their parents. In practice, parents play an enormously influential role in their children's lives.

---

[1] *R (on the application of Begum) v. Head Teacher and Governors of Denbigh High School* [2006] UKHL 15, [2007] AC 100 at [93].

Parents are the people who can most effectively encourage them to develop a capacity for independence. Parents are also excellently placed to undermine the self-confidence of their teenage offspring so effectively that they emerge into adulthood quite unable to fend happily for themselves. The law is ambivalent both over the extent to which parents should be encouraging their children to become independent and over the legal limits to their own authority.

(2) Child and adolescent developmental capacity for decision-making – the research evidence

Ideas about children's competence for various tasks are formed by practitioners and academics alike in a variety of different contexts, but often without any cross-referencing, or exploration of common themes. Thus those involved in the field of youth crime are well aware that they should have some understanding of children's ability to take responsibility for their wrongdoing.[2] Equally, no practitioner should consider calling a child as a witness in a criminal trial without a good understanding of children's mental processes and capacity to recall events.[3] Similarly, doctors treating children and adolescents require a reasonably accurate idea of their young patients' ability to comprehend and consent to treatment.[4] Legal practitioners may have to decide whether a young person has the legal capacity to instruct his or her own solicitor in litigation involving both parents.[5] There is a huge body of research literature on developmental psychology which provides information about children's decision-making processes. Nevertheless, its very complexity defies those wishing to find straightforward answers to specific questions about a particular child's competence in any given context. Indeed, different aspects of the research may be exploited for different purposes. Thus critics of the punitive aspects of the law on youth crime point to the developmental research indicating that adolescents' ability to take responsibility for their criminal acts may develop far later than their physical and intellectual ability suggests.[6] By contrast, those arguing that children and young people should be allowed to take earlier responsibility for a variety of activities, including voting and medical decision-making, emphasise the research indicating the development of cognitive and social skills in some children at relatively early ages.[7]

Generalisations are, of course, always misleading. Ideally, a child's capacity for decision-making should always be considered on an individual case-by-case basis, since it will hinge largely on the type of decision, its context and the child's own personal circumstances.[8] Nevertheless, research does provide information about the cognitive skills of the average child, depending on his or her developmental growth and it clearly challenges the arguments of those

---

[2] See Chapter 18.   [3] See Chapter 17.   [4] See Chapter 5.   [5] See Chapter 7.
[6] E.g. Royal College of Psychiatrists (2006).
[7] E.g. P. Alderson (1993) and L. Ferguson (2004).   [8] M. Rutter and M. Rutter (1993) p. 197.

advocating equal rights for children, irrespective of age. In the first place, there are important developmental differences between children and adults which cannot be ignored. Piaget's ideas relating to the existence of discrete and successive stages of developmental growth have been largely discredited.[9] Indeed, most agree that his abstract construction of cognitive competence is insufficient in itself. Nevertheless, Rutter and Rutter maintain that it is impossible to discount the concept of stages altogether: 'No amount of training will cause, say, a four-month-old to walk or talk, or a six-year-old to learn differential calculus.'[10] Cognitive performance is dependent on the emergence of specific metacognitive skills which are simply not available to young children.[11] Those who argue that it is wrong to exclude children from adult freedoms should study this evidence regarding children's decision-making abilities.

Research on the way in which children and young people think and reason can take matters further than merely distinguishing between the cognitive skills of children and adults. Researchers broadly agree that there are fundamental differences between childhood thought, preoccupied as it is with practical issues to do with the here and now, and adolescent thinking which is much more sophisticated. Adolescents are increasingly able to cope with abstractions and to distinguish between the real and concrete and the abstract or possible. They can test hypotheses and think and plan about the future. They become aware of their own thought processes and become self-reflective, even introspective.[12] Their thinking is multidimensional, with a greater use of relative, rather than absolute, concepts.[13] These findings correlate with research on the human brain which shows that the frontal lobes of the brain undergo more change in adolescence than in any other stage of life.[14]

> The frontal lobes are involved in an individual's ability to manage the large amount of information entering consciousness from many sources, in changing behaviour, in using acquired information, in planning actions and in controlling impulsivity. Generally the frontal lobes are felt to mature at approximately 14 years of age.[15]

Most therefore agree that the intellectual competence of young children aged up to about 11–12 is far less sophisticated than that of adolescents between the ages of 12 and 18.[16] Important changes occur even within the adolescent period. Thus the manner in which the older adolescent deals with moral dilemmas is

---

[9] Piaget's research and writings, which had considerable influence in the field of developmental psychology, spanned nearly 50 years from the early 1920s to the late 1970s. See, inter alia, J. Piaget (1924). J. Coleman and L. Hendry (1999) pp. 36–43, summarise the main criticisms of his work.

[10] M. Rutter and M. Rutter (1993) p. 195.   [11] Ibid. at p. 197.

[12] Much of this material is summarised by T. Gullotta et al. (2000) pp. 59–62 and by L. Ferguson (2004) pp. 42–55.

[13] M. Rutter and M. Rutter (1993) p. 253.

[14] E. Sowell et al. (1999) and J. Margo and A. Stevens (2008) p. 42.

[15] Royal College of Psychiatrists (2006) p. 38.   [16] M. Rutter and M. Rutter (1993) pp. 6 and 7.

significantly more sophisticated than that adopted by children between the ages of 8 and 12, which is, in turn, more sophisticated than that of children below the age of 8.[17] This material is reinforced by research on adolescents' ability to involve themselves in political thought and reasoning.[18] According to this research, there are important and subtle differences between the approach of a 12-year-old to political dilemmas, from that of the 14- or 15-year-old, and again from that of a 16-year-old. It shows that the typical adolescent of 12 or 13 years of age cannot appreciate that there may be more than one solution to a problem or that individual acts or political solutions are not necessarily absolutely right or wrong. Whereas the concept of moral relativism is not yet available for the 12-year-old, by the age of 14 or 15, the adolescent is able to think in a more critical and pragmatic way.[19] Indeed most researchers seem agreed that 'a considerable degree of intellectual maturation may have occurred by 14 years'.[20] Interestingly, the growth in competence which takes place at around the age of 15 corresponds with the belief of many adolescents themselves that the age of 15 is an appropriate age for gaining the right to make major personal decisions.[21]

It is also during later adolescence that young people start understanding themselves and becoming aware of their own personalities.[22] Although Erikson's theory[23] that adolescents have to pass through a series of identity 'crises' to achieve a coherent sense of identity or self-concept has been much criticised,[24] it is nevertheless generally accepted that it is during the teenage years that young people establish a clearer sense of personal identity.[25] Indeed, in summary, it is the older adolescents' ability to conceptualise, to think about the meaning of their experiences and to establish concepts about themselves as distinctive persons that marks out adolescence from the earlier years of life.[26] This research material suggests that the majority of older adolescents are equipped with developmental skills for relatively sophisticated decision-making.[27]

Researchers have not confined their attentions to the distinctions between the cognitive processes of children and adolescents.

> Improved cognitive or thinking capacities are only one aspect of the maturational and learning processes which need to occur to turn the naturally impulsive, self-centred, short-term thinking toddler into a reasonably self-controlled, reflective young adult, able to take a long-term view.[28]

[17] J. Coleman and L. Hendry (1999) pp. 43–8.
[18] Ibid. at pp. 194–6. See also J. Adelson and R. O'Neill (1966).
[19] J. Coleman and L. Hendry (1999) pp. 195–6.
[20] M. Rutter (2005) p. 33. See also L. Ferguson (2004) p. 43, who notes general agreement amongst researchers that minors become 'mature abstract cognitive thinkers' from age 14 onwards.
[21] L. Taylor et al. (1984) and L. Taylor et al. (1985).
[22] J. Coleman and L. Hendry (1999) ch. 4.   [23] E. Erikson (1968).
[24] J. Coleman and L. Hendry (1999) pp. 59–65 and J. Margo and M. Dixon et al. (2006) p. 103.
[25] M Rutter and M Rutter (1993) pp 253–254.   [26] Ibid. at p. 252.
[27] J. Coleman and L. Hendry (1999) pp. 195–6.   [28] Royal College of Psychiatrists (2006) p. 33.

As critics of the harsh juvenile justice system emphasise, cognitive capacity to reach decisions does not necessarily correlate with mature judgment. Most agree that 'mature' decision-making is greatly influenced by such matters as context and by an individual's emotional and social development.[29] Indeed, although an individual's intellectual development may have reached adult levels by the time he or she reaches the age of 17:

> the development of good judgement, emotional and social maturity usually takes much longer to achieve … although adolescents may have the intellectual equipment to attempt adult reasoning, they do not have the experience and range of information on which to base sensible judgements. In addition, adolescents, by dint of their immaturity, may be more susceptible to external social and environmental factors and this may mean that their intellectual capacity is not used to make good judgements, such as avoiding drugs or crime opportunities.[30]

The development of mature or good judgment is inevitably delayed by emotional and social instability – the adolescent years are characterised by change and transition. In addition to physical changes in the brain structure, adolescents often undergo dramatic hormonal and emotional changes.[31] They start questioning the belief-system with which they were brought up and discard their parents' values as they respond to influences outside the family. It is a time for experimenting with new ideas, clothes, sexual behaviour. They may engage in behaviour which endangers their health and well-being and that of society as a whole. Some indulge in alcohol abuse, drug abuse, unprotected sexual activity, dangerous driving and criminal activities.[32] Indeed, youthful recklessness, leading to self- and socially destructive behaviour is the topic of much speculation, both as to its causes and as to appropriate interventions.[33] Research suggests that those who become involved in such activities often do so because they feel obliged by peer pressure to gain esteem by joining the activities of others.[34] They also commonly believe that they are immune from their dangerous consequences; for example, that they will not become infected from sexually transmitted diseases as a result of unprotected sexual activity. They assume that they can control and prevent any damaging outcome.[35] Researchers also argue that risk-taking experimentation, particularly when it comes to taking health risks through alcohol and drug misuse, is an important educational element on the path to adulthood.[36]

---

[29] L. Ferguson (2004) pp. 43–50: research summary.
[30] Royal College of Psychiatrists (2006) p. 33. See also J. Margo and A. Stevens (2008) p. 39.
[31] Juvenile Justice Center (2004) p. 2.   [32] See Chapter 18.
[33] Inter alia: R. Muuss and H. Porton (1998) and L. Furby and R. Beyth-Marom (1992).
[34] Inter alia: D. Santor et al. (2000); K. Michael and H. Ben-Zur (2007); L. Coleman and S. Cater (2005) esp. ch. 3.
[35] A. Benthin et al. (1993) esp. p. 166. But see S. Millstein (1993) p. 55ff: there is little or no empirical evidence supporting the concept of 'adolescent invulnerability'.
[36] J. Coleman and L. Hendry (1999) p. 135.

Clearly the research on the thought processes of young children and adolescents cannot provide generalisations or 'rule of thumb' guidelines to assist with assessing an individual's capacity to reach decisions. Competence for decision-making will vary enormously, depending on a variety of factors, such as peer pressure and family environment. It not only depends on the maturity and social circumstances of the person reaching the decision but also on the content and context of the decision in question. Thus whilst a person of any age may need a variety of skills, and therefore a relatively sophisticated type of competence before being able, for example, to consent to surgery, they will require a much lower level of competence to activate a machine. Some of the relevant skills manifest earlier and there is a gradual increase in the ability, for example, to conceptualise, with decision-making depending on context and task. Nevertheless, whilst individual children will demonstrate different abilities, the average child will develop along similar lines to his or her contemporaries. Furthermore, it appears that before early adolescence, the *majority* of children do lack the cognitive abilities and judgmental skills to make major decisions that might seriously affect their lives. So although the significance given by society to chronological age is probably excessive, the relative youth of a child is very relevant to the reasonableness of the choices put to him or her.[37]

When considering the capacity of children and adolescents to reach decisions for themselves, writers, practitioners and the judiciary often use imprecise terms such as 'competence', 'maturity' and 'understanding'. It appears that these are essentially meaningless without much further refinement. As the body of psychological research on children's developmental processes discussed above makes clear, the assessment of competence will be influenced by a raft of overlapping considerations, including context and external factors.

(3) Child and adolescent capacity for decision-making – liberalising the law on minority status?

Children in this country remain minors until they reach the age of 18.[38] Even so, the research on child development discussed above substantially undermines the calls made by children's liberationists like Holt and Farson for virtually all important adult freedoms to be extended to any child wishing to exercise them.[39] Such views are not confined to the US. Harris similarly claims that children should acquire full political status with the right, inter alia, to vote, work, initiate and defend legal proceedings, own property, write wills and enter into contracts.[40] He asserts:

> Bold quick, ingenious, forward and capable young people are by no means a rarity, neither, unfortunately, are dull-witted incompetent adults. If freedom from control and full political status are things that we qualify for by the

[37] J. Hughes (1989) p. 38.   [38] Family Law Reform Act (FLRA) 1969, s. 1.
[39] J. Holt (1974) and R. Farson (1974); see Chapter 1.   [40] J. Harris (1982) p. 51.

acquisition of a range of capacities, then as soon as anyone possesses those capacities they qualify, and if they never acquire them they never qualify. So if it is supposed that it is the comprehensive possession by adults of capacities lacked equally comprehensively by children that sustains and justifies the political disabling of children and the rule of adults, the supposition is false.[41]

Harris later deftly dilutes his remarkably liberal approach by emphasising that it is only children who are capable of making 'maximally autonomous' decisions who can be in control of their own destinies.[42] His Draconian qualifying conditions which exclude children from the capacity to reach 'maximally autonomous' decisions, for example, if they lack the ability to control their desires or actions, or have defects in their reasoning, restrict the practical impact of his ideas. Other writers, although not making claims as apparently radical as Harris's, point out that Piaget's assumptions about the stages of children's cognitive ability can be refuted by the activities of children themselves and that the law should recognise and respect their decision-making abilities.[43] Like Harris, they criticise the traditional assumptions regarding adult and childhood intellectual and psychological capacities. They point to the many children under the age of 18 who care for ill or disabled parents with little or no help, the street children in the world's major cities who exhibit survival strategies equal to those of many adults, and the children who happily take on a responsible role in working parents' households, if properly involved in the division of labour.[44] Alderson's research with children in hospital led her to conclude that children develop the competence to make complex decisions about their medical treatment at far earlier ages than adults realise or accept. Indeed she argues that since many children exceed many adults in qualities such as intelligence, ability and prudence, differences between adults and children lie mainly in social beliefs about childhood, rather than in children's actual abilities.[45]

Despite claims of this kind, the research material discussed above shows that there are significant and subtle differences between the thought processes of young children and adolescents and between younger and older adolescents. As noted, younger children are far less able than adolescents to weigh up alternatives and cope rationally with major decisions. Although some children may, through experience, become competent to deal with the challenges that life throws up and able to make decisions in the face of pain, hardship and ill-health, this may be at considerable psychological cost. Maturity also depends on a number of other factors; for example, being good or even amazingly good at maths, does not indicate that a young child knows enough about the working of a democratic society to vote,[46] or assess the implications of surgery.[47] Indeed, it is surely appropriate to shield the average child from making significant choices

---

[41] Ibid. at p. 37.   [42] J. Harris (1985) p. 215.
[43] G. Lansdown (2005) pp. 24–31: research summary.   [44] Ibid.   [45] P. Alderson (1993) p. 190.
[46] Lowering the voting age is discussed in Chapter 4.   [47] J. Hughes (1989) p. 40.

before he or she acquires the cognitive tools to do so adequately. Such an approach readily accords with the interest theory of rights which presupposes that although children may have an interest in making choices, they do not necessarily have a moral right to do so. Under MacCormick's test, an interest in choice could only be deemed a moral right if it is so important to the child that it would be wrong in itself to deny or withhold it from him or her.[48]

The slow rate of children's developmental growth indicates that far from being wrong to deny the younger child a choice, it may be wrong to ask him or her to make a decision over a variety of matters, at least before reaching adolescence. In any event, children's interest in choice may be fulfilled by acknowledging their moral right to have their decision-making capacity *promoted*, rather than a right to have their choices respected. This would involve consulting them, rather than giving them complete responsibility for choice. Giving them the opportunity to participate in decisions over their future may be appropriate when they are capable of making a sensible contribution, but lack the maturity to reach a decision, given its context and seriousness. To argue otherwise is to overlook the fact that children have a variety of rights, all of which need fulfilling, in particular their right to protection. It is perfectly appropriate for society to protect children from being required to make significant choices if it considers that they may suffer unnecessarily from being involved in decision-making before they are sufficiently mature. Furthermore, if their decisions interfere with and restrict their ability for future choices, then they should be overborne.[49]

The research on the older adolescent's psychological development suggests that a different approach might be justified for those at the upper end of adolescence. It certainly supports those who argue that the current law is too restrictive in its approach to recognising the decision-making capacity of older children. Some writers, like Lindley, argue in favour of a more sophisticated approach to children's liberation. In his view there are good reasons for rejecting the claim that all children should have equal rights to self-determination because of the significant correlation between childhood and incompetence.[50] As he points out:

> it is clear that allowing five-year-olds to decide whether they will go to school and what they will learn would actually reduce their chances of *developing* autonomy. Furthermore, a lack of education is most likely to reduce a person's chances of the *exercise* of autonomy later.[51]

Although less obviously radical than Harris, he considers it difficult to justify paternalistic restrictions on all adolescents under the age of 18, simply by reason of their minor status. He suggests that by the time children are 13, they are sufficiently stable and have sufficient conceptual competence to be able

---

[48] N. MacCormick (1982) p. 160; see Chapter 1.   [49] See Chapter 1.
[50] R. Lindley (1989) p. 79.   [51] Ibid. at p. 85.

to have the objectives of a life plan. On that basis, he advocates that laws relating to the 13- to 16-year-old category should be liberalised. Citing the high rates of adolescent sexual activity below the age of 16, he criticises the laws which prevent girls under the age of 16 from consenting to sexual intercourse.[52] He also argues that the high levels of truancy in schools indicates that young people between the ages of 13 and 16 should not be forced to remain in full-time compulsory education, but should be allowed to take full-time employment instead. Furthermore, in his view, adolescents should be given political education in schools and allowed to vote.[53]

The developmental research discussed above suggests that Lindley's proposal is flawed. He does not take sufficient account of the fact that the development of maturity is a gradual process, and that adult maturity does not emerge suddenly on attaining adolescence, or indeed on a child's 13th birthday. The research showing important differences between the thinking of younger and older adolescents suggests that it would be ill-judged to assume that the young adolescent should be given the same degree of independence as the older category . Indeed, the rates of truancy indicate that there is a good number of adolescents within this age group who would not appreciate the educational advantages of remaining at school beyond that age.[54]

Although it is sensible for adolescents to be allowed greater responsibility for taking decisions for themselves, the liberationists are rash to advocate the age governing the attainment of adult status being lowered. By leaving it at the age of 18, the older adolescents still prone to youthful recklessness gain a few extra years of legal protection. These may ensure that they attain sufficient maturity to emerge into adulthood with a degree of confidence. But this cautious approach should not be taken as signalling complete approval of the existing law. There are clear arguments in favour of giving 16-year-olds voting rights.[55] Furthermore, as discussed below, there is a need for considerably greater clarity in the legal principles applying to adolescents and for the law to maintain a better balance between allowing young people as much freedom as they have the capacity for, whilst restraining them from making choices which restrict their own future development.

(4) Adolescents and parents – legal boundaries?

(A) Legislative persuasion

The law provides a series of mixed messages about the limits to parental authority once children reach adolescence.[56] No doubt this incoherence springs

---

[52] See also *R v. K* [2001] UKHL 41, [2001] 3 All ER 897, per Lord Millett, at [44]: the age of consent 'has long since ceased to reflect ordinary life, and in this respect Parliament has signally failed to discharge its responsibility for keeping the criminal law in touch with the needs of society'.
[53] R. Lindley (1989) pp. 88–92.   [54] See Chapter 6.
[55] See Chapter 4.   [56] J. Fortin (2001) pp. 247–50.

from the fact that society itself is uncertain about how parents should adapt to their children's growing maturity. Although children mature at different rates, the law withholds the right to full adult autonomy from all adolescents until they attain the age of 18.[57] But on attaining that age, adolescents are expected to make an immediate successful transition from the legal status of childhood to responsible citizenship.[58] Giving them a chance to develop the skills needed for adulthood is therefore essential. Whether they get it depends enormously on their parents' willingness to encourage in their children a capacity to take responsibility for their own future. But should the law make parents undertake this task? Research provides practical support for the views of the theorists who argue that parents have a duty to encourage children to develop decision-making capacities from as early an age as possible. It suggests not only that family environment and family dynamics are major factors in adolescent psychological development,[59] but that parents help shape adolescents' capacity for reaching decisions competently and influence the extent to which they participate in decision-making.

Most parents agree that they have an important part to play in helping their children gain emotional independence,[60] but this may not always be as easy as it sounds. Whilst many parents subscribe to the idea of the family becoming an increasingly democratic unit, they often find that life with teenagers 'presents fundamental contradictions between ideals and lived reality'.[61] The following words have a ring of truth for parents with teenage children:

> The teenage years herald a period of re-negotiation as budding adults take up the banner of freedom – freedom to make choices, such as what to wear, who to associate with or when to engage in sexual relations. On the other side, parents and carers wave the flag of responsibility, struggling to push recalcitrant adolescents towards maturity, sobriety, practical skills and 'appropriate' behaviour.[62]

Parents' proximity to their children may lead them to underestimate their children's maturity and abilities, particularly their ability to discuss sensibly decisions relating to their own future. They may effectively undermine their children's self-confidence and hamper their decision-making skills by involving them very little in family decisions.[63] In particular, many parents find it extremely difficult to allow even quite mature children to make up their own minds on major matters affecting their upbringing and future. Knowledgeable parents might argue that they are supported in such an approach by Article 5 of the United Nations Convention on the Rights of the Child (CRC). This requires governments to respect parents' rights and duties to provide 'appropriate

---

[57] FLRA 1969, s. 1.   [58] M. de Winter (1997) p. 26.
[59] See J. Coleman and L. Hendry (1999) ch. 5.
[60] W. Langford *et al.* (2001) p. 25.   [61] Ibid. at p. 47.
[62] Department of Health (1996) p. 18. See also W. Langford *et al.* (2001) ch. 4.
[63] E.g. many divorcing parents fail to consult even quite mature children over their proposed arrangements for their children's future upbringing; see discussion in Chapter 7.

direction and guidance in the exercise by the child of the rights recognised'. Nevertheless, parents should not overlook the article's qualifying phrase, which emphasises that parental direction and guidance should only be provided 'in a manner consistent with the evolving capacities of the child'. Furthermore, Articles 12, 13 and 14 of the Convention all emphasise the child's right to develop a capacity for independent thought and action. Whilst Article 12 guarantees the right of all children who are capable of forming their own views, the right to express those views over matters to do with their upbringing, Articles 13 and 14 secure their freedom of expression and their freedom of thought, conscience and religion.

Although domestic legislation could usefully encourage changes in parental attitudes, the Children Act (CA) 1989 and subsequent amending legislation signally failed to seize the opportunity to do so. Admittedly, the substitution of the new concept of 'parental responsibility' for the old 'parental rights and duties' 'reflect[s] the everyday reality of being a parent';[64] it also discourages the idea that children are under parents' absolute control. Nevertheless, the failure to impose a duty on parents to consult their children over important matters regarding their own future is disappointing. Indeed, given the Law Commission's view that requiring the courts to consider children's views[65] would reflect 'the increasing recognition given both in practice and in law to the child's status as a human being in his own right, rather than the object of the rights of others',[66] it is surprising that no one apparently thought of requiring parents to do the same. Equally surprising was the failure to remedy this gap in the law when the CA 1989 was amended by later legislation. Thus although the duty imposed on local authorities to consult children before reaching decisions relating to them[67] was extended by the CA 2004,[68] the legislative opportunity then to impose consultative duties on parents was missed.

This gap in the English legislation compares unfavourably with the Children (Scotland) Act 1995, section 6(1) which requires any parent, when reaching 'any major decision' involving his child's upbringing, to 'have regard so far as is practicable to the views (if he wishes to express them) of the child concerned'.[69] Many parents aspire to moving into a more democratic, negotiated and 'open'

---

[64] Law Commission (1988) para. 2.4.   [65] CA 1989, s. 1(3)(a).
[66] Law Commission (1988) para. 3.24.   [67] CA 1989, s. 22(4)(a) and (5)(a).
[68] CA 2004, ss. 53(1) and (3).
[69] Children (Scotland) Act 1995, s. 6(1) provides: 'A person shall, in reaching any major decision which involves –
   (a) his fulfilling a parental responsibility or the responsibility mentioned in section 5(1) of this Act; or
   (b) his exercising a parental right or giving consent by virtue of that section, have regard so far as practicable to the views (if he wishes to express them) of the child concerned, taking account of the child's age and maturity ... and without prejudice to the generality of this subsection a child twelve years of age or more shall be presumed to be of sufficient age and maturity to form a view.'

style of communication with their teenage children,[70] but find it difficult to put them into practice.[71] Unlike their English counterparts, Scottish parents are under a legislative duty to do so. Furthermore the legal presumption that a child of 12 years of age or more is 'of sufficient age and maturity to form a view' on such decisions, requires a Scottish parent to justify reaching a decision without consulting his child, if the latter has attained such an age.[72] Interestingly, the Scottish Law Commission considered that the age limit of 12 was in line with psychological evidence on children's intellectual development, but recommended that the word 'maturity' was used, rather than 'understanding', to ensure that it is not merely a child's cognitive development which is considered.[73] Although this recommendation was not supported by reference to any particularly weighty psychological research, such a view seems reasonably consistent with the research evidence discussed above. Although, at the age of 12, the average child is probably too young to reach important decisions for him or herself, since children of such an age lack the ability to weigh up alternatives and conceptualise or plan, they do have the intellectual capacity to be involved in the decision-making process.

The imposition of a duty on Scottish parents to consult their children was prompted by the Scottish Law Commission's view that such a provision would emphasise 'that the child is a person in his or her own right and that his or her views are entitled to respect and consideration'.[74] It also noted that legislation incorporating such a provision would be consistent with Article 12 of the CRC and that a number of other legal systems had already introduced a similar provision, including Germany, Sweden, Norway and Finland. The Scottish Law Commission openly acknowledged the difficulties involved in introducing such a 'vague and unenforceable' provision, in particular the fact that there is no obvious sanction. It also admitted that it would not always be easy to distinguish 'major' decisions from 'minor' ones. Nevertheless, it considered the benefits of introducing such a provision outweighed the difficulties, particularly because it could influence behaviour.

The failure of the English legislation to introduce a similar provision suggests to parents here that there is no need for them to consult their children, whatever their age and irrespective of the importance of the decision. This omission reflects the government's assumption in this context that parents will comply with their parental responsibilities, with no guidance on how to do so. One might excuse the English legislation by pointing out that, unlike the Children (Scotland) Act 1995, the CA 1989 was drafted before the publication of the CRC; consequently its draftsmen were not privy to the terms of Article 12, which was to become so influential throughout the world. But this excuse overlooks not only the wider implications of the decision in *Gillick v. West Norfolk and Wisbech Area Health Authority*,[75] decided well before the introduction of the CA 1989, but also the much later CA 2004, which, as noted

---

[70] W. Langford *et al.* (2001) p. 36.   [71] Ibid. at chs 7 and 8.
[72] Scottish Law Commission (1992) paras. 2.63–2.65.   [73] Ibid.
[74] Ibid. at para. 2.62.   [75] [1986] AC 112.

above, tacked onto the CA 1989 various duties on local authorities, but omitted any mention of parents.

(B) Lessons from *Gillick*

Although the legislation has made little real attempt to liberalise the parent-child relationship, well-informed parents could learn a great deal from the House of Lords' decision in *Gillick v. West Norfolk and Wisbech Area Health Authority*.[76] This showed that by the mid-1980s, a far more enlightened approach to the parental role was emerging, compared with that of earlier generations. Indeed, the *Gillick* decision established new legal boundaries for parents' relationships with their adolescent children. It reflected the view that the law should encourage parents to stand back and permit their adolescents to reach important decisions with as little interference as possible. Both Lord Fraser and Lord Scarman cited with approval Lord Denning's famous words in *Hewer v. Bryant*[77] in which he emphasised that:

> the legal right of a parent to the custody of a child ends at the 18th birthday: and even up till then, it is a dwindling right which the courts will hesitate to enforce against the wishes of the child, and the more so the older he is. It starts with a right of control and ends with little more than advice.[78]

Similarly, Lord Scarman was uncompromising regarding the position of parents. In his view:

> [the] parental right yields to the child's right to make his own decisions when he reaches a sufficient understanding and intelligence to be capable of making up his own mind on the matter requiring decision.[79]

These words indicate very plainly that he was concerned with the broad issue of potential conflicts between parent and child, in the light of adolescents' developing capacity for adult autonomy. There seemed little doubt in his mind that parents had no right to oppose their children once they had reached sufficient understanding and intelligence to make up their own minds on the matter in question. Lord Fraser's views were, in the main, restricted to the narrow confines of consenting to contraceptive treatment and advice. Nevertheless, he too made some general remarks about the need to encourage adolescents' capacity for independence:

> It is, in my view, contrary to the ordinary experience of mankind, at least in Western Europe in the present century, to say that a child or young person remains in fact under the complete control of his parents until he attains the definite age of majority ... In practice most wise parents relax their control gradually as the child develops and encourage him or her to become increasingly independent.[80]

---

[76] Ibid.   [77] [1970] 1 QB 357.   [78] Ibid. at 369.   [79] [1986] AC 112 at 186.   [80] Ibid. at 171.

Such an approach was remarkably enlightened, particularly bearing in mind that their Lordships were dealing with the legal capacity of adolescents under the age of 16 to reach decisions for themselves. Their finding that doctors could provide mature teenage girls with contraceptive treatment without requiring parental consent was timely.[81] But it went much further and translated into law what their Lordships clearly perceived to be the moral right of adolescents to take responsibility for *all* important decisions in their lives, when competent to do so. It also went considerably further than Article 12 of the CRC, which merely requires participation in decision-making, not that children's choices should be complied with. At the most, Article 12(1) requires a child's views to be given 'due weight', depending on his or her age and maturity.

The *Gillick* decision sent a strong message to parents that their own rights of decision-making are constrained and that they have a duty to allow their adolescents to make a gradual transition into adulthood. An interpretation of the law in these terms does not, however, provide clear guidance over the point at which adolescents reach a stage of maturity when they can reach decisions for themselves. Indeed, the weakness of the concept of *Gillick* competence is its uncertainty. By making an adolescent's legal capacity hinge on notions as debatable as understanding and maturity fundamentally hampers its effectiveness as a means of settling internal family conflicts. Parents struggling to impose restrictions on recalcitrant adolescents may find it impossible to retain their objectivity when deciding whether their offspring can comply with Lord Scarman's test of capacity. Many parents might assume that their offspring have no legal right to reach major decisions regarding their lives because they are not sufficiently mature to consent to take part in any one of a variety of dangerous activities. They might gain support for such a view from the research evidence discussed above, indicating that adolescents' ability to make wise decisions is fundamentally undermined by various factors, such as peer pressure. Indeed, the Scarman test contains no guidance over the extent to which an adjustment should be made for factors affecting the adolescent's understanding, such as peer pressure, drug and substance abuse, family stress, emotional disturbance, physical and mental illness. In practice, a definitive ruling on an adolescent's legal competence in various situations can only emerge through applying for the courts' assistance over the matter. There is the further complication that the HRA 1998 introduced a different and rights-based approach to family life.

(C) *Gillick* and the HRA 1998

Arguably the HRA 1998 strengthened parents' ability to control their teenage offspring by reference to their own rights under Article 8. But contrarily, teenagers might themselves claim Convention rights against their parents. How would Mrs Gillick have fared had she gone to court after the

---

[81] Discussed in Chapter 5.

implementation of the HRA 1998, instead of when she did, in the mid-1980s? Some of these issues were clarified when Ms Axon adopted a very similar position to that of Victoria Gillick in 2006. *R (Axon) v. Secretary of State for Health and the Family Planning Association*[82] provided Silber J with a good opportunity to show how the *Gillick* principles regarding the interrelationship between parents and adolescents can be aligned within the European Convention on Human Rights and Fundamental Freedoms (ECHR) framework of rights. Ms Axon had claimed that parents are legally responsible for all aspects of their children's welfare, including matters to do with their health and sexuality, and that if doctors keep consultations with children secret, this undermines parents' ability to advise and help them on sexual matters.[83] She also claimed that such rights and responsibilities are reinforced by Article 8 of the ECHR. Whilst the narrow medical focus of medical confidentiality, alongside the *Gillick* decision,[84] is discussed elsewhere in this text,[85] Silber J's treatment of the more general aspects of the parent-child relationship in the light of the HRA 1998 is instructive.

In Silber J's view, a close reading of the *Gillick* decision refuted all Ms Axon's claims; it remained good law and was unaffected by Ms Axon's right under Article 8 of the ECHR to have her family life respected by the state. That being so, he attempted valiantly to translate the scope of parents' rights, as delineated by *Gillick*, into Convention compatible terms. His conviction that any parental right or power under Article 8 is no wider than that delineated by the common law,[86] led to his translating their Lordships' idea that parental authority dwindles as the child develops decision-making skills into the confines of Article 8. Thus, in his view, a parent's right to exercise control over his child, including the right to be notified over medical consultations, dwindles and then comes to an end as her teenage offspring reaches an age when (in Lord Scarman's words) 'he reaches a sufficient understanding and intelligence to be capable of making up his own mind on the matter requiring decision'.[87] Ms Axon's parental rights under Article 8, to advise and guide her daughters had therefore terminated on their attaining *Gillick* competence. This idea of parents simply *losing* their right to respect for family life, as soon as their children gain sufficient understanding to reach decisions for themselves, is not supported by Strasbourg jurisprudence,[88] despite its representing the House of Lords' view in *Gillick* of the common law.[89] Furthermore, as Taylor cogently argues, the retention of a parent's right to enjoy family life under Article 8 does not necessarily carry a right to control his or her children throughout their lives. Family life exists between parents and children but may not require 'respect' or legal promotion once the child matures.[90]

---

[82] [2006] EWHC 37 (Admin), [2006] 2 FLR 206.   [83] Ibid. at [44]–[45].
[84] *Gillick v. West Norfolk and Wisbech Area Health Authority* [1986] AC 112.
[85] In Chapter 5.   [86] [2006] EWHC 37 (Admin), [2006] 2 FLR 206, at [132].
[87] Ibid. at [130].   [88] R. Taylor (2007) pp. 90–2.
[89] Ibid. at p. 90.   [90] Ibid. at p. 91.

It would surely have been more plausible for Silber J to approach a situation of this kind, where parent and child obviously have conflicting Convention rights, on the basis that an appropriate balance must be found between them.[91] The balance will tip in the child's favour as he or she grows in understanding and intelligence – at which point, the state can justify (under Article 8(2)) infringing the mother's rights under Article 8(1) by reference to the child's own rights under Article 8(1). But Silber J did not pursue such an approach when he dealt with the alternative argument – that (in the event of his being wrong in his view that Ms Axon's Article 8 rights had simply terminated) the state could justify infringing her rights by reference to Article 8(2). When considering this issue, he referred rather generally to a variety of reasons justifying the state infringing her right to family life. Admittedly he stated that young people have the same rights under Article 8(1) to medical confidentiality as adults,[92] but he made no real attempt to analyse all the specific Convention rights enjoyed by Ms Axon's daughters which might conflict with those of their mother.

Such an omission is odd given Silber J's careful assessment of the developing recognition of children's rights generally. Having reviewed the extensive protection of children's rights provided by the CRC,[93] he referred to the case law endorsing the view that:

> the right of young people to make decisions about their own lives by themselves at the expense of the views of their parents has now become an increasingly important and accepted feature of family life.[94]

He referred also to 'this change in the landscape of family matters, in which the rights of children are becoming increasingly important'.[95] Taylor argues that Silber J's decision is important for the way that it is part of a 'growing movement towards greater recognition and autonomy of children'.[96] Whilst undoubtedly true, his judgment is weakened by the absence of any detailed analysis of the Axon daughters' own position in the light of their mother's claim of a right to control their lives in important ways. Indeed, his reasoning is not dissimilar to that adopted in a host of family law cases involving a potential clash between the rights of parents and children. The judiciary not uncommonly analyse the rights that *adults* have, but fail to articulate those of the children.[97] In this instance, *Axon* was an important decision affecting the lives of teenage girls generally which failed to clarify exactly what Convention rights they have and how they might be balanced against those of their mother. What

---

[91] For a discussion of the 'ultimate balancing test' see J. Fortin (2006b) pp. 306–10.

[92] [2006] EWHC 37 (Admin) at [127].

[93] *R (Axon) v. Secretary of State for Health and the Family Planning Association* [2006] EWHC 37 (Admin), [2006] 2 FLR 206, at [76]–[79].

[94] Ibid. at [79]. The case law he referred to was *Mabon v. Mabon* [2005] EWCA Civ 634, [2005] 2 FLR 1011, per Thorpe LJ, at [26] and [28] and *R (on the application of Williamson and others) v. Secretary of State for Education and Employment and others* [2005] UKHL 15, [2005] 2 All ER 1, per Baroness Hale of Richmond, at [80].

[95] Ibid. at [80].   [96] R. Taylor (2007) p. 93.   [97] J. Fortin (2006b) pp. 302–3.

is interesting about the *Axon* case is that six years after the HRA 1998's implementation, Ms Axon and her legal advisers thought that she had a good chance of succeeding in her application.[98] This suggests a reluctance to engage with the notion that children have rights under the ECHR which may actually override those of their parents.

The absence of any specific discussion in *Axon* about the extent to which children can themselves claim rights under Article 8 when opposed by their parents avoided an assessment of how the concept of *Gillick* competence itself might translate into ideas about adolescents' own Article 8 rights. This issue is of obvious importance in situations where, as in *Axon* itself, there is a conflict between the parent's interests and those of their children. *Re Roddy*[99] did not involve the interplay between children's rights and parents' rights. Nevertheless, Munby J's judgment contains an instructive review of *Gillick* competence in Convention terms. Drawing attention to the Strasbourg case law developing the meaning of the right to respect for private life,[100] he emphasised that children are as much entitled to the Convention's protection as anyone else.[101] But he clearly considered that some aspects of these rights hinge on capacity to enjoy them. Having reviewed the House of Lords' *Gillick* competence test and its subsequent judicial treatment,[102] he emphasised the courts' duty not only to recognise, but to defend the *right* of the child who has sufficient understanding to make an informed decision, to make his or her own choices.[103] In so doing, he stressed, the courts recognise her dignity and integrity as a human being, as protected, in this case, by Articles 8 and 10.[104]

A competence qualification of this kind is consistent with the underlying properties of some Convention rights which might support the notion of children's autonomy. Certain aspects of the right to private life under Article 8, notably those encompassing an individual's right to socialise with other people, require a capacity for mature thought. Requiring compliance with the *Gillick* competence test before children can claim such Article 8 rights neatly translates the common law concept of children's legal competence into Convention terms. This approach accords with parents' own Article 8 right to

---

[98] J. Fortin (2006a) p. 764.

[99] *Re Roddy (a child)(identification: restriction on publication)* [2003] EWHC 2927 (Fam), [2004] 2 FLR 949: Munby J acceded to the request of Angela Roddy, a 17-year-old teenage mother, to lift a series of injunctions (designed to protect the identities of her, her baby and the child's father), thereby enabling her tell her story to the press.

[100] Inter alia: *Niemitz v. Germany* (1993) 16 EHRR 97, para. 29; *Botta v. Italy* (1998) 26 EHRR 97, para. 32; *Bensaid v. United Kingdom* (2001) 33 EHRR 1, para. 47; discussed in Chapter 2.

[101] *Re Roddy (a child)(identification: restriction on publication)* [2003] EWHC 2927 (Fam), [2004] 2 FLR 949, at [37].

[102] Inter alia: *In re W (a minor) (medical treatment: court's jurisdiction)* [1993] Fam 64; *Re W (wardship: discharge: publicity)* [1995] 2 FLR 466.

[103] *Re Roddy (a child)(identification: restriction on publication)* [2003] EWHC 2927 (Fam), [2004] 2 FLR 949, at [57].

[104] Ibid.

reach decisions on behalf of their *Gillick in*competent children.[105] Splicing the *Gillick* competence test onto Article 8 rights also suggests that *Gillick* competent adolescents may now have complete autonomy in all matters that they fully comprehend, whether or not their parents agree with their views. Such an approach does not necessarily involve accepting Silber J's proposition that parents' Article 8 rights and responsibilities simply disappear on an adolescent becoming *Gillick* competent. The common law principles, as set out by the House of Lords in *Gillick* itself, do not coincide, in this instance, with the Convention position. Instead, as discussed above, parents' rights of responsibility for their older children, as protected by Article 8, must be balanced against the Article 8 rights of the children themselves. Confronted by a *Gillick* competent adolescent, the court would be entirely justified in concluding that the parent's Article 8 rights can be infringed by reference to the adolescent's own Article 8 rights,[106] as long as the infringement is proportionate to the risk averted.[107] So the Convention position may in some cases approximate with that established by the common law, but this must be established on a case-by-case basis.

(5) Adolescents' right to refuse and parents' to agree

What is the legal position of the parents, who, having struggled to apply the *Gillick* test, decide as objectively as possible that although their adolescent son or daughter is *Gillick* competent, they require a measure of control over their activities?[108] Their Lordships' proposition in *Gillick*[109] that parents lose *all* rights to influence their son or daughter regarding any decisions reached within his or her competence was unlikely to be embraced with enthusiasm by parents, or indeed, by a conventional and paternalistic judiciary. Only a short time elapsed before the Court of Appeal, in *Re R (a minor) (wardship : consent to treatment)*[110] and *Re W (a minor) (medical treatment : court's jurisdiction)*,[111] comprehensively undermined their Lordships' attempt to ensure that parents respected their adolescents' capacity for autonomy. In each case, the subject of the application was resisting life-saving medical treatment and in each the Court of Appeal held that under its inherent jurisdiction, a court can override a young patient's wishes and authorise life-saving treatment.[112]

---

[105] As confirmed in *Nielsen v. Denmark* (1988) 11 EHRR 175 and *Glass v. UK* [2004] 1 FLR 1019, at para 70.

[106] I.e. under Art. 8(2).   [107] The doctrine of proportionality is discussed in Chapter 2.

[108] Discussed in more detail by J. Fortin (2001) pp. 247–50.   [109] [1986] AC 112.

[110] [1992] Fam 11: the Court of Appeal authorised the compulsory use of anti-psychotic drugs to treat a 15-year-old suffering from increasingly paranoid and disturbed behaviour.

[111] [1993] Fam 64: the Court of Appeal authorised the compulsory treatment of a 16-year-old in a dangerously anorexic state.

[112] *Re R (a minor) (wardship: consent to treatment)* [1992] Fam 11, per Lord Donaldson of Lymington MR, at 25.

Such a judicial response is not surprising, given that a court may find it impossible to conclude that it is in the child's best interests to be allowed to die.[113] Indeed, such an approach could be justified by reference to the rights of the children themselves – they have a right to be protected from the outcome of such choices. It is, though, imperative that if their wishes are to be overridden, appropriate methods should be adopted to constrain them. Those utilised by the Court of Appeal, however, were controversial. Rather than confining their reasoning to the courts' own powers to override the wishes of a teenage patient, the Court of Appeal established the principle that *anyone* with parental responsibility for a minor can provide legal authority to others to go ahead with a procedure concerning the adolescent, despite the latter's own clear opposition.[114] Accordingly, Lord Scarman's view in *Gillick* that 'the parental right *yields* to the child's right to make his own decisions when he reaches a sufficient understanding and intelligence to be capable of making up his own mind on the matter requiring decision',[115] apparently has no effect on parents' right to consent on the child's behalf. Since their right to consent survives the child's achieving *Gillick* competence,[116] that phrase merely means that parents cannot veto *affirmative* decisions reached by such a child. According to *Gillick*, whatever his or her age, parents cannot overrule an adolescent's consent to any procedure that he or she has the competence to comprehend fully. But, according to the Court of Appeal, those very same parents can themselves consent to any procedure on behalf of an adolescent of any age or competence, as long as they consider it to be in his or her best interests, and even if the adolescent objects violently. In this respect, the law not only created inordinate confusion, but retreated significantly from *Gillick*. Predictably, this case law attracted a storm of criticism.[117]

Both Lord Donaldson MR and Balcombe LJ seemed clearly aware of the implications of undermining *Gillick* in this way and were keen in *Re W* to stress that the wishes of a mature adolescent should always be given great weight. Lord Donaldson MR made this clear when he said:

> Adolescence is a period of progressive transition from childhood to adulthood and as experience of life is acquired and intelligence and understanding grow, so will the scope of the decision-making which should be left to the minor, for it is only by making decisions and experiencing the consequences that decision-making skills will be acquired ... 'good parenting involves giving minors as

---

[113] Discussed further in Chapter 5.

[114] This proposition was introduced in *Re R (a minor) (wardship: consent to treatment)* [1992] Fam 11 and fully developed in *Re W (a minor) (medical treatment: courts' jurisdiction)* [1993] Fam 64.

[115] [1986] AC 112 at 186 (emphasis supplied).

[116] *Re W (a minor) (medical treatment: courts' jurisdiction)* [1993] Fam 64, per Lord Donaldson MR at 78 and Balcombe LJ at 87.

[117] Inter alia: G. Douglas (1992); M. Freeman (2005); discussed in more detail in Chapter 5.

much rope as they can handle without an unacceptable risk that they will hang themselves'.[118]

He and his colleagues in the Court of Appeal suggested that the courts would be extremely slow to overrule the decisions of adolescents who had already attained the age of 16. But they appeared to overlook the fact that such moderation in the hands of the judiciary is of little relevance to an adolescent whose tyrannical and obsessive parents are endeavouring to force on him or her a wholly unwanted course of action. Lord Donaldson and Balcombe LJ acknowledged in *Re W* that parents might endeavour to force adolescents to undergo procedures against their will. But they only envisaged this happening in a medical context, more particularly in the context of a teenage girl being forced by her parents to have an abortion against her wishes. This overlooks the fact that the principle they established is not confined to medical matters and has a general application. More remarkably, the principle applies to all adolescents up to their 18th birthdays. The legal limitation on the parents' activities is that their choices for their child must be consistent with the child's best interests. But the best interests test is too subjective to deter bullying parents from seeing only their own point of view. Whilst their refusal to allow their daughter to leave school on her 16th birthday might be tenable, few would agree with their view that she would benefit from being sent back to their country of origin to be married against her will to a man she has never met.[119] Many adolescents are law abiding and will feel obliged to comply with their parents' wishes, if told that they are backed by the law.

Whilst it is arguable that the judiciary should be able to override those minors who refuse life-saving treatment, the Court of Appeal did not perceive the dangers of handing back to parents so much of the power removed from them by the House of Lords in *Gillick*. Only a radical reassessment of the law can address the complete lack of coherence between the *Gillick* principle and that contained in the later case law. The *Gillick* decision contained a powerful message to parents intent on maintaining a repressive and authoritarian family regime. They should heed the law which acknowledges adolescents' increasing ability to make important decisions for themselves. The later decisions appeared to be saying the opposite. The fact that a court is unlikely to uphold the repressive decisions of domineering parents is neither here nor there. Unlike the exercise of paternalism by the judiciary, which is at least open to public scrutiny, parental paternalism is restrained only by the indeterminacy of the best interests test and hidden from view by the curtain of family privacy.

As discussed in more detail in the context of medical decision-making,[120] there are good grounds for arguing that the principle established by the Court of Appeal in *Re R* and *Re W* should be reviewed judicially and that the HRA 1998 can assist this process.[121] In a more general context, it could be claimed that

---

[118] *Re W (a minor) (medical treatment: courts' jurisdiction)* [1993] Fam 64 at 81.
[119] Discussed in Chapter 4.   [120] Discussed in Chapter 5.   [121] R. Taylor (2007) pp. 94–7.

authoritarian parents are infringing their children's own rights under Articles 5 and 8 of the ECHR by forcing them to comply with parental demands against their will. As discussed above, there is a growing body of case law suggesting that the domestic judiciary are far more aware than before of the importance of respecting children's rights, as guaranteed by the CRC. Nevertheless, the European Court of Human Rights' (ECtHR) controversial decision in *Nielsen v. Denmark*[122] cannot be ignored when considering the boundaries between parents' rights and those of their uncooperative children. The ECtHR accepted that parents' rights cannot be unlimited and that children must be protected from abuse,[123] but the majority concluded that the mother's authorisation of the lengthy restrictions placed on her nervous (but not mentally ill) son of 12, was for 'a proper purpose'[124] and well within the normal exercise of parental authority.

The fact that the restrictions placed on the boy in *Nielsen* were at his mother's request had clearly presented the ECtHR with a problem. Its decision that the boy's Article 5 rights were not engaged avoided Article 5 conflicting with Article 8 and undermining the way the latter article protects family life and parental autonomy from undue state interference. In the Court's view, Article 8 protects parental decisions over how their children should spend their time, including where they should reside, whether they should go to an educational or recreational institution, or to hospital and whether they should receive medical treatment.[125] It is notable that the Strasbourg judiciary were far from united in their treatment of the boy's application.[126] Their conclusion that the mother's decision had been for a 'proper purpose' also reflected the view that parental decision-making has clear boundaries – albeit rather more widely drawn than the minority thought appropriate. Furthermore, the boy concerned was only 12 years old; the strong implication of the majority decision of the ECtHR being that had he been older, they would not have considered the mother's actions to be so reasonable.[127] Nevertheless, given that a 12-year-old is normally quite old enough to have strong views, the majority of the judges had a peculiarly authoritarian view of the parental role. The Court's decision represented a particularly cautious way of dealing with the interplay between the rights of parents and adolescents.[128]

Notably, Silber J rejected Ms Axon's argument that since, according to *Nielsen v. Denmark*,[129] her parental Article 8 rights (to respect for her family life) included a wide range of rights and responsibilities, these would be

---

[122] (1988) 11 EHRR 175: a 12-year-old boy was placed, at his mother's request, in the closed psychiatric ward of a state hospital for 5½ months. The majority of the European Court decided that his rights under Art. 5 had not been infringed; discussed in Chapter 2.

[123] Ibid. at para. 72.   [124] Ibid. at para. 69.   [125] Ibid. at para. 61.

[126] The European Commission of Human Rights had favoured the boy's claim, finding, 11 votes to 1, a violation of Art. 5(1) and 10 votes to 2, a violation of Art. 5(4). The ECtHR concluded by only 9 votes to 7 that Art. 5 was inapplicable.

[127] (1988) 11 EHRR 175 at para 72.   [128] J. Fortin (2004) p. 255.   [129] (1988) 11 EHRR 175.

undermined by depriving her of a chance to discuss such matters as contraceptive advice and treatment with her teenage children.[130] On this, he maintained that *Nielsen* was irrelevant for a number of rather implausible reasons, including the fact that it had involved an application under Article 5, rather than Article 8, and that it related to a parent's rights to exercise control over her own child and not to a parent's right to obtain information about her child from a third person, such as a doctor.[131] Whilst one can sympathise with Silber J's desire to limit *Nielsen*'s scope, it would have been more prudent simply to reject its now anachronistic interpretation of parental rights. Hopefully the ECtHR's greater emphasis on adult autonomy[132] may lead to its reassessing its own rather immoderate approach to adolescents' position in the family.

The decision in *Re K (a child)(secure accommodation order: right to liberty)*[133] provides further insight into this area of law, in so far as it explored the extent of a local authority's power to control a teenager who is the subject of a secure accommodation order. The Court of Appeal's views provided some useful, albeit obiter, ideas on the limits to parental powers of control. The Appellate judges seemed ambivalent about the ECtHR's assessment in *Nielsen* of parents' power to control their children's movements. They suggested that within normal parent-child relationships its authority is assured. But they sounded a note of warning. Thus according to Dame Elizabeth Butler-Sloss P:

> There is a point, however, at which one has to stand back and say – is this within ordinary acceptable parental restrictions upon the movements of a child or does it require justification?[134]

Judge LJ considered it an easy matter to distinguish normal from abnormal family life, the former involving parents:

> for example, putting young children into bed when they would rather be up, or 'grounding' teenagers when they would prefer to be partying with their friends, or sending children to boarding schools, entrusting the schools with authority to restrict their movements. All this reflects the normal working of family life, in which parents are responsible for bringing up, teaching, enlightening and disciplining their children as necessary and appropriate, and into which the law and local authorities should only intervene when the parents' behaviour can fairly be stigmatised as cruel or abusive.[135]

These comments lack clarity – what is an 'acceptable parental restriction' and what is the 'normal working of family life'? Nevertheless, they are not dissimilar to the concept of the 'parental zone of control' described in the Mental Health Code of Guidance discussed later in this work.[136] Doctors are advised not to act on a parent's authority unless they are sure that the parent's decision is within

---

[130] [2006] 2 FLR 206, at para. 124.   [131] Ibid at para. 126.

[132] E.g., inter alia: *YF v. Turkey* (2004) 39 EHRR 34, at para. 33; *Storck v. Germany* (2006) 43 EHRR 6, at paras. 150–2; *Pretty v. United Kingdom* [2002] 2 FLR 45, at para. 41.

[133] [2001] 1 FLR 526.   [134] Ibid. per Dame Elizabeth Butler-Sloss P, at para 28.

[135] Ibid. at para. 99.   [136] In Chapter 5.

the 'zone of parental control'. When deciding whether it is, they should ask first whether 'the decision is one that a parent would be expected to make, having regard both to what is considered to be normal practice in our society and to any relevant human rights decisions by the courts'.[137] But what is 'normal practice in our society'? Is this question any clearer than that asked by the Court of Appeal? Nevertheless, these views suggest that a domestic court might today reject parental restrictions considered to be outside 'normal' family life or societal views, thus infringing an adolescent's own Article 5 rights, combined with his or her own rights under Article 8 to respect for privacy and personal autonomy.

(6) Conclusion

The research evidence discussed at the beginning of this chapter suggests that children should not be expected to reach decisions for themselves before entering adolescence. By then, however, despite starting to develop the skills they need for independent life, they also need their parents' assistance to establish the confidence to exercise them. The *Gillick* decision acknowledged that adolescents' sense of responsibility and ability to take control of their own lives are qualities which should be respected. Most parents will happily, or grudgingly, comply with the law's expectations and provide adolescents with an increasing measure of independence. Nevertheless, for those adolescents caught up in family disputes and crises, the law does not provide an effective framework for dealing with their problems. The ad hoc decision-making of the Court of Appeal was intended to fill a gap left by the *Gillick* decision – how to ensure that medical care was provided for ill and incapacitated adolescents, even against their wishes. The pity is that, by going too far, it developed legal principles which are at odds with the ability of 'average' adolescents to judge for themselves what is in their own best interests. A growing realisation that children have rights to be respected may augur a new judicial approach to this sensitive balance between parents' rights and those of their maturing children.

BIBLIOGRAPHY

NB Some of these publications can be obtained on the relevant organisation's website.

Adelson, J. and O'Neill, R. (1966) 'The Development of Political Thought in Adolescence' 4 *Journal of Personality and Social Psychology* 295.

Alderson, P. (1993) *Children's Consent to Surgery*, Oxford University Press.

Alderson, P. and Montgomery, J. (1996) *Health Care Decisions: Making Decisions with Children*, IPPR.

Bainham, A. (1993) 'Reforming Scottish Children Law – Sense From North of the Border' 5 *Journal of Child Law* 3.

---

[137] Department of Health (2008) para. 36.10.

Bell, N. and Bell, R. (eds.) (1993) *Adolescent Risk Taking*, Sage Publications.

Benthin, A, Slovic, P. and Severson, H. (1993) 'A Psychometric Study of Adolescent Risk Perception' 16 *Journal of Adolescence* 153.

Coleman, J. and Hendry, L. (1999) *The Nature of Adolescence*, Routledge.

Coleman, L. and Cater, S. (2005) *Underage 'Risky' Drinking* Joseph Rowntree Foundation.

deWinter, M. (1997) *Children as Fellow Citizens: Participation and Commitment*, Radcliffe Medical Press Ltd.

Douglas, G. (1992) 'The Retreat from Gillick' 55 *Modern Law Review* 569.

Department of Health (DH) (1996) *Focus on Teenagers: Research into Practice*, HMSO.

Department of Health (DH) (2008) *Code of Practice: Mental Health Act 1983*, TSO.

Erikson, E. (1968) *Identity, Youth and Crisis*, Norton.

Farson, R. (1974) *Birthrights*, Collier Macmillan.

Ferguson, L. (2004) *The End of an Age: Beyond Age Restrictions for Minors' Medical Treatment Decisions*, Law Commission of Canada.

Fortin, J. (2001) 'Children's Rights and the Use of Physical Force' 13 *Child and Family Law Quarterly* 243.

(2004) 'Children's Rights: Are the Courts Now Taking Them More Seriously?' 15 *King's College Law Journal* 253.

(2006a) 'Children's Rights – Substance or Spin?' *Family Law* 759.

(2006b) 'Accommodating Children's Rights in a Post Human Rights Act Era' 69 *Modern Law Review* 299.

Freeman, M. (2005) 'Rethinking *Gillick*' 13 *International Journal of Children's Rights* 201.

Furby, L. and Beyth-Marom, R. (1992) 'Risk-taking in Adolescence: A Decision-making Perspective' 12 *Developmental Review* 1.

Gullotta, T., Adams, G. and Markstrom, C. (2000) *The Adolescent Experience*, Academic Press.

Hall, A. (2006) 'Children's Rights, Parents' Wishes and the State: the Medical Treatment of Children' *Family Law* 317.

Harris, J. (1982) 'The Political Status of Children' in Graham, K. (ed.) *Contemporary Political Philosophy*, Cambridge University Press.

(1985) *The Value of Life: An Introduction to Medical Ethics*, Routledge and Kegan Paul.

Holt, J. (1974) *Escape from Childhood: The Needs and Rights of Children*, E P Dutton and Co Ltd.

Hughes, J. (1989) 'Thinking about Children' in Scarre, G. (ed.) *Children, Parents and Politics*, Cambridge University Press.

Juvenile Justice Center (2004) *Adolescence, Brain Development and Legal Culpability*, American Bar Association.

Langford, W., Lewis, C., Soloman, Y. and Warin, J. (2001) *Family Understandings: Closeness, Authority and Independence in Families With Teenagers*, Joseph Rowntree Foundation.

Law Commission 594 (1988) *Family Law Review of Child Law, Guardianship and Custody* Law Com No 172 HC, HMSO.

Lansdown, G. (2005) *The Evolving Capacities of the Child*, Innocenti Insight, United Nations Children's Fund (Unicef).

Lindley, R. (1989) 'Teenagers and Other Children' in Scarre, G. (ed.) *Children, Parents and Politics*, Cambridge University Press.

MacCormick, N. (1982) *Legal Right and Social Democracy: Essays in Legal and Political Philosophy*, Clarendon Press.

Mann, L., Harmoni, R. and Power, C. (1989) 'Adolescent Decision-making: the Development of Competence' 12 *Journal of Adolescence* 265.

Margo, J. and Dixon, M, with Pearce, N. and Reed, H. (2006) *Freedom's Orphans*, IPPR.

Margo, J. and Stevens, A. (2008) *Make Me a Criminal: Preventing youth crime*, IPPR.

Michael, K. and Ben-Zur, H. (2007) 'Risk-taking Among Adolescents: Associations with Social and Affective Factors' 30 *Journal of Adolescence* 17.

Millstein, S. (1993) 'Perceptual, Attributional, and Affective Processes in Perceptions of Vulnerability Through the Life Span' in Bell, N. and Bell, R. (eds.) *Adolescent Risk Taking*, Sage Publications.

Muuss, R. and Porton, H. (1998) 'Increasing Risk Behaviour Among Adolescents' in Muuss, R. and Porton, H. (eds.) *Adolescent Behaviour and Society: A Book of Readings*, McGraw Hill.

Piaget, J. (1924) *The Language and Thought of the Child*, Routledge.

Royal College of Psychiatrists (2006) *Child Defendants* Occasional Paper OP 56, Royal College of Psychiatrists.

Rutter, M. (Chairman) (2005) *Commission on Families and the Wellbeing of Children, Families and the State: Two-way Support and Responsibilities*, The Policy Press.

Rutter, M. and Rutter, M. (1993) *Developing Minds: Challenge and Continuity across the Life Span*, Penguin.

Santor, D., Messervey, D. and Kusumakar, V. (2000) 'Measuring Peer Pressure, Popularity, and Conformity in Adolescent Boys and Girls: Predicting School Performance, Sexual Attitudes, and Substance Abuse' 29 *Journal of Youth and Adolescence* 163.

Scottish Law Commission (1992) *Report on Family Law* Scot Law Com No 135, HMSO.

Sowell, E. *et al.* (1999) 'In Vivo Evidence From Post-adolescent Brain Maturation in Frontal and Striatal Regions' 2 *Nature Neuroscience* 10.

Taylor, L, Linda, I., Adelman, H., Kayser-Boyd, N. (1984) 'Attitudes Toward Involving Minors in Decisions' 15 *Professional Psychology: Research and Practice* 436.

Taylor, L. *et al.* (1985) 'Minors' Attitudes and Competence Toward Participation in Psychoeducational Decisions' 16 *Professional Psychology: Research and Practice* 226.

Taylor, R. (2007) 'Reversing the Retreat from *Gillick*? *R (Axon) v Secretary of State for Health*' 18 *Child and Family Law Quarterly* 81

Chapter 4

Leaving home, rights to support and emancipation

(1) Introduction

One of the most emphatic ways in which children and young people can assert their right to take responsibility for their own lives is by simply walking out – leaving their home and parents behind them. This is a drastic step. Most children, particularly teenagers, sometimes find their parents' ideas outdated and their attempts to discipline them tedious. In turn, parents may be reluctant to allow their offspring greater independence before they consider them ready to cope with it. Nevertheless, in well-functioning families, negotiation and compromise will ensure that both 'sides' emerge relatively unscathed. Sadly, increasing numbers of children and young people find life at home so unbearable that they vote with their feet and leave. The law presents them with a contradictory set of principles. There is confusion over whether they have the right to leave home at all, at what age they may do so, what rights they have on leaving and what rights their parents have to force their return.

Although it is currently impossible to obtain accurate estimates of the number of children and young people running away from home,[1] it is clear that too many take this step.[2] Young people leave for a variety of reasons: to escape 'maltreatment';[3] arguments and family conflict;[4] general unhappiness at home;[5] problems

---

[1] Children Society (2007) pp. 9–10: exacerbated by the definitional confusion between 'running away' and 'missing'; as many as two-thirds of young 'runaways' are not reported to the police as 'missing persons'. DCSF (2008a) para. 48: an improved system of data collection is being introduced.

[2] G. Rees and J. Lee (2005) pp. 6–7: 11% teenagers under 16 (i.e. 1 in 9 of the youth population) run away for one night or more on more than one occasion; around 66,000 young people run away for the first time each year in England. Ibid. at p. 9: 30% of the first time runaways had first run away before the age of 13, with more than 1 in 10 having done so before the age of 11. See also Children's Society (2007) p. 10, summarising research statistics.

[3] G. Rees and J. Lee (2005) p. 16: approximately 12% of young people surveyed gave 'maltreatment' (physical abuse or violence, emotional abuse or neglect, domestic violence, sexual abuse, or feeling scared) as the reason for running away. See also N. Pleace et al. (2008) para. 12.52: 45% of statutorily homeless 16–17-year-olds reported violence. See also, ibid., Table 12.4.

[4] G. Rees and J. Lee (2005) p. 16.

[5] Family formation underlies variations in rates of running away. See inter alia: G. Rees and J. Lee (2005) p. 11: 18% of young people living in step families were likely to have run away, cf. 6.7% of those living with both birth parents, with even higher rates for those living with relatives etc.;

at school, including bullying and exclusions.[6] Surprisingly large numbers are quite simply told by their parents or step-parents to leave,[7] or they feel forced to go.[8] Housing authorities throughout the country are increasingly being asked to accommodate young people who have been asked to leave by their parents.[9] This problem may have been exacerbated by social landlords' greater powers to obtain orders excluding tenants from their homes because of their children's bad behaviour.[10] More parents may now feel obliged to eject their ill-disciplined teenage offspring in order to avoid homelessness themselves. 'Looked after children'[11] and young people cared for in children's homes or foster care also form a significant proportion of young runaways.[12] They often have slightly different reasons for leaving, including bullying by other residents, being separated from siblings and parents, and being frustrated by rules.[13] Many leave home with nowhere to go and some end up sleeping rough[14] in situations often involving risk. A significant number turn to theft, drugs[15] and/or prostitution to survive.[16]

Although, outwardly, those who leave home demonstrate their capacity for independence, the fact that they do so does not necessarily indicate that they are sufficiently mature to look after themselves. Indeed, they are often at their most vulnerable and need considerable support. Despite the apparent liberality of the House of Lords' decision in *Gillick v. West Norfolk and Wisbech Area Health Authority*,[17] the relevant legal principles and policies are quite inappropriate for

---

N. Pleace *et al.* (2008) para. 12.20: the parents of 67% of statutorily homeless 16–17-year-olds had separated or divorced and a step-parent had moved into the home of 51%.

[6] G. Randall and S. Brown (2001) pp. 15–16 and at p. 2: many homeless young people mention problems at school.

[7] N. Pleace *et al.* (2008) Table 12.2: 70% of statutorily homeless 16–17-year-olds reported relationship breakdown as the reason for their homelessness.

[8] G. Rees and J. Lee (2005) p. 18: 26% of overnight runaways had been forced to leave home on the most recent occasion that they were away.

[9] Office of the Deputy Prime Minister (2004a) para. 3.139.

[10] I.e. by obtaining anti-social behaviour injunctions (ASBIs) excluding the tenant from the premises under the Housing Act 1996, ss. 153A and 153D. E.g. *Moat Housing Group South Ltd v. Harris and anor* [2005] EWCA Civ 287, [2005] 4 All ER 1051. See also DCLG (2006c) p. 42: 62% of the families at risk of eviction had three or more children; p. 38: 37% of anti-social behaviour associated with these families was youth nuisance.

[11] Children Act (CA) 1989, s. 22(1) and (2): a 'looked after child' is either a child who is the subject of a care order or a child being provided with accommodation under s. 20 for a continuous period of more than 24 hours.

[12] Estimates vary over precise numbers of young people running away from residential and foster care. G. Rees *et al.* (2005) pp. 19–20: 17.3% of referrals to young runaways projects came from residential or foster care.

[13] R. Morgan (2006a) pp. 7–9.

[14] Inter alia: G. Rees and J. Lee (2005) pp. 18–19: 1 in 6 of their sample had slept rough whilst away, whilst the most common place for the remainder to stay was with friends or relatives; N. Pleace and S. Fitzpatrick (2004) p. 17: 11% of statutorily homeless 16–17-year-olds had experienced rough sleeping.

[15] But some young people's drug use may prompt their being told to leave. Inter alia: G. Rees and J. Lee (2005) p. 14; N. Pleace *et al.* (2008) para. 12.51. NB (N. Pleace *et al.*, ibid) parents' and step-parents' own drug or alcohol problems may prompt young people to leave home.

[16] G. Rees and J. Lee (2005) pp. 19–20.   [17] [1986] AC 112.

a group of young people who often feel obliged to leave home. Admittedly, the current government has recognised that tackling the problems of young people requires a new approach, particularly regarding those with multiple disadvantages – the groups of 'socially excluded' young people, who through a combination of poverty, family conflict, poor educational opportunities and poor services, 'find themselves apparently destined for a life of underachievement and social exclusion'.[18] Various groups of young people, including young runaways,[19] attracted the attention of the Social Exclusion Unit (SEU), whose reports produced a range of valuable recommendations and initiatives.[20] Nevertheless, as discussed below, many policies, including the whole emphasis of the benefits system and the governments' initiatives on youth unemployment[21] remain firmly focused on relieving the hardships of young people between the ages of 18 and 24, rather than on those under that age. By and large, law and policy reflect an official view that all young people under the age of 18 should be living at home and that, if they are not, they only have themselves to blame. Matters are, however, confused by the way that many legal principles distinguish between minors under the age of 16 and those aged between 16 and 18. But whilst this older group are, in many ways, treated like adults, in others, they are still treated like children. This confusion will be exacerbated once the government's plans to keep young people in education or training up to the age of 18 come to fruition; indeed the legislative changes will further extend childhood. The following chapter considers the inconsistencies in the law and the extent to which it could be improved.

(2) Legal age limits

The law reflects a sense of deep confusion regarding the point at which children should be allowed to take full responsibility for their activities. Section 1 of the Family Law Reform Act 1969 bars all those under the age of 18 from full legal 'emancipation'. A range of disqualifications makes all minors of any age broadly incapable of entering into a legally binding contract, hold a legal estate in land, make a will or vote. Nevertheless, as discussed below, a number of adult freedoms are available to 16 and 17-year-olds, leaving those under the age of 16 the subject of much wider restrictions.

(A) Under 16 – supplementing pocket money?

For those under 16, a series of legislative provisions have, over the years, thrown up a collection of bizarrely arbitrary age limits governing a range of activities,

---

[18] Paul Boateng, SEU (2000) Foreword, p. 1. See Chapter 19 for further discussion of 'social exclusion'.

[19] SEU (2002).

[20] E.g. the Children and Young People's Unit funded 27 short-term development projects to test the viability of a variety of ways of assisting young runaways. See G. Rees and J. Lee (2005).

[21] E.g. the 'New Deal for Young People' designed for those aged between 18 and 24.

such as buying a pet[22] and riding a horse without a safety helmet.[23] These are more a source of amusement than of any practical utility and certainly have little logical rationale. The simple explanation for this legislative hotchpotch is that the qualifying ages have been adopted on an ad hoc and piecemeal basis. Of more practical significance are the provisions of the criminal law making the age of 16 govern the point at which young people can agree to sexual inter-course[24] and of the child abduction legislation which makes it so difficult for those under 16 to gain assistance in leaving home.[25] The importance of these legal principles, however, pales into insignificance compared with the current legislation making full-time education compulsory for those under the age of 16. All young people under the age of 18 will eventually be obliged to remain in formal education or accredited training.[26] Meanwhile, those under 16 must remain in school on a full-time basis; and are thereby prevented from gaining financial independence through full-time employment.[27] Despite this, large numbers of children and young people under that age supplement their pocket money, or provide their own, by working in their spare time out of school, often for very low rates of pay.[28]

The rules presently governing the extent to which school children under the age of 16 can take part-time work are not only extremely confusing, but fail to protect them adequately. Article 32(1) of the United Nations Convention on the Rights of the Child (CRC) requires states to protect children against economic exploitation and work that is likely to harm their safety, health, development or jeopardise their education. Article 32(2) details the measures states should take to regulate ages and hours for admission to employment. Such duties would be fulfilled were employers in the UK to comply fully with the Council of Europe's requirements[29] protecting children from being employed for over-long hours and in unsuitable conditions.[30] Unfortunately the domestic regulations introduced to implement these measures simply ensure that even fewer prospective employers than before understand the complicated laws limiting the part-time work of children under the age

---

[22] Allowed at age 12. J. Claridge (2008).

[23] Allowed at age 14. A 16-year-old can, inter alia, buy lottery tickets and aerosol paint, sell scrap metal and join the army. Ibid.

[24] See *R v. K* [2001] UKHL 41, [2001] 3 All ER 897, per Lord Millett, at [44]: he clearly considers that the age of 16 is far too high.

[25] Discussed below.

[26] Education and Skills Act (ESA) 2008, s. 2; see also policy papers, DfES (2007a), DCSF (2007) and DCSF (2008b). DCSF (2007), para. 5.1: the participation age is to be raised in stages: from 2013, young people will participate until the end of the academic year in which they attain 17; until the age of 18 from 2015.

[27] Discussed in Chapter 6.   [28] N. Stack and J. McKechnie (2002) pp. 93–5.

[29] European Council Directive on the Protection of Young People at Work (94/33/EC).

[30] Children (Protection at Work) Regulations 1998 (SI 1998/276) and Children (Protection at Work) Regulations 2000 (SI 2000/1333) and the Children (Protection at Work) (No. 2) Regulations 2000 (SI 2000/2548).

of 16.[31] These now differ considerably, depending on a child's precise age and the type of work he or she is undertaking.[32] The confusing nature of the provisions restricting the hours and days of the week on which children below 16 may work[33] enables them to be widely flouted, not only by employers, but by local authorities (LAs) who are responsible for their enforcement.[34] This is regrettable, since they are intended to protect the younger child's ability to attend school and do their homework. The need to produce a more coherent and comprehensible body of law will become particularly urgent when the legislation requiring young people to participate in education or training until the age to 18 is fully implemented.

(B) Over 16 and under 18

This age group is treated in a strangely ambivalent way. They face a number of formal legal barriers which, inter alia, exclude them from voting, standing for Parliament, being a school governor, acquiring a legal estate in land or making a will. Furthermore, as discussed below, those contemplating leaving home will find that there are further severe legal restrictions on their financial independence. They can claim only very limited social security benefits, and, with the exception of contracts for the supply of 'necessaries' and beneficial contracts of service, they cannot enter into any legally binding contract.[35] Meanwhile, certain important freedoms become available to 16-year-olds. They may consent to surgical, medical or dental treatment,[36] marry with the consent of their

---

[31] Inter alia: Better Regulation Task Force (2004); C. Hamilton and B. Watt (2004); C. Hamilton (2005), ch. 14 and S. Hobbs *et al.* (2007).

[32] Children and Young Persons Act (CYPA) 1933, s. 18 (as amended) regulates children's part-time work, regarding the hours they can work and the type of work they can undertake, depending on whether they are aged 13, 14 or 15.

[33] CYPA 1933, ss. 18–21 (as amended by the Children (Protection at Work) Regulations 1998–2000), *broadly* prohibit employers from employing children under 14 at all (unless employed by a parent or guardian in specified light work). Those between 14 and 16 cannot be employed before 7 a.m. and after 7 p.m. on any day and on school days, they can only be employed for a maximum of two hours, only one of which can be before school, or a maximum of 12 hours in any school week. In the school holidays, a 14-year-old may not work for more than 25 hours in any week, or more than four hours in any day without a rest break of one hour. These provisions are all subject to the provisions of local byelaws, themselves amended to comply with EC Directive 94/33/EC. See DCSF (2008c) for a reasonably clear explanation of the existing law.

[34] C. Hamilton and B. Watt (2004) pp. 136–7: assess the evidence indicating many LAs' failure to comply with the EC regulations. See also Better Regulation Task Force (2004) and S. Hobbs *et al.* (2007).

[35] The anachronistic rules of contract (see A. Bainham (2005) pp. 673–9) ensuring that minors can only enter into binding contracts for the supply of 'necessaries' and beneficial contracts of service are widely misunderstood. E.g. *Proform Sports Management Ltd v. Proactive Sports Management Ltd and anor* [2006] EWHC 2812 (Ch), [2007] 1 All ER 542: since an agreement entered into by Wayne Rooney, a professional footballer, at the age of 15 was a voidable contract and not a contract for necessaries, it could be avoided.

[36] Family Law Reform Act 1969, s. 8(1), discussed in more detail in Chapter 5.

parents, join the army and consent to sexual intercourse.[37] Furthermore, under current law they are free to leave school and take full-time work.

No clear policy is discernable in the law presently governing those aged between 16 and 18 who seek employment. By and large, it treats them like adults, requiring them to pay national insurance contributions and taxes. But in practice, even at 16, they are far more vulnerable than adult employees. Until recently, the UK government's position on their employment was an uneasy one. It appeared to recognise the vulnerability of this group of young employees by implementing the Council of Europe's protective employment restrictions.[38] But it was not until 2004, following international criticism,[39] that the statutory minimum wage scheme was extended to 16–17-year-olds. The niggardly intro-ductory rate[40] was officially justified as striking a balance between stopping exploitation and avoiding young people being enticed out of much-needed education or training by better employment rates.[41] Despite continuing criticisms that the present arrangements are discriminatory and encourage the use of younger employees as a source of cheap labour,[42] there seems little official enthusiasm for bringing their statutory minimum wage into line with that for 18–21-year-olds.[43] Even at its present level,[44] at least some employers are either unaware of the minimum wage regulations or deliberately ignore them.[45] Indeed, the 16–17-year-old minimum wage is apparently seen merely as 'providing a wage floor to prevent exploitation'.[46] One wonders how effec-tively LAs will be able to enforce regulations prohibiting age-discriminatory provisions[47] once they take responsibility for monitoring the large numbers of 16–18-year-olds embarking on accredited training and apprenticeships under the new education legislation.

Entitlement to a minimum wage presupposes an ability to find work. For those over 16 who do so, the chances are that it will be far less well paid than

---

[37] Sexual Offences (Amendment) Act 2000 ensured that homosexual males finally acquired sexual parity with their heterosexual male and lesbian female counterparts.

[38] European Council Directive on the Protection of Young People at Work (94/33/EC) requires inter alia, strict regulation and protection of work done by 'adolescents' (those between minimum school leaving age and 18). Management of Health and Safety at Work Regulations 1999 (SI 1999/3242), require employers to make a risk assessment of certain types of employment for employees between the ages of 16 and 18. Explained by LAC 92/3 Rev and discussed by C. Hamilton and B. Watt (2004) pp. 147–8. Failure to comply with these regulations is common, e.g. in 2005, a verdict of unlawful killing was reached by a Newport inquest into the death of a 17-year-old employed by a roofing company, who within a week of starting his job fell through a skylight. He had received no prior safety training.

[39] Committee on Economic, Social and Cultural Rights (2002) paras. 15 and 33 and Committee on the Rights of the Child (2002) paras. 55 and 56.

[40] £3 per hour.   [41] Low Pay Commission (2006) para. 3.3.   [42] Ibid. at para. 3.46.

[43] As suggested by various trade unions and the Children's Rights Alliance for England. Ibid.

[44] Current (as from October 2008) minimum wage rates: £5.73 per hour for workers aged 22 and over; £4.77 per hour for 18–21-year-olds (development rate); £3.53 per hour for 16–17-year-olds.

[45] Low Pay Commission (2006) paras. 3.56–3.59.   [46] Ibid. at para. 3.52.

[47] The Employment Equality (Age) Regulations 2006 (SI 2006/1031).

adult work[48] and often with poor training prospects.[49] But not all find work; underlying the government's enthusiasm for forcing 16–18-year-olds to acquire greater skills is the research showing their particular vulnerability to unemployment.[50] The demand for young employees has fallen significantly since the 1970s; young male school leavers, finding fewer craft jobs, have moved into low-skilled occupations, and young women school leavers have moved from administrative and clerical jobs into sales and personal service occupations.[51] Indeed, research indicates the dire consequences, both to the individual and to society as a whole, of young people leaving school at 16 with few, if any, qualifications, only to swell the ranks of those not in education or training (NEETs).[52] This dismal picture is reinforced by indications that an unemployed status for this age group is not only likely to have long-term effects well into adulthood, but is also strongly associated with homelessness, crime, drug use and teenage pregnancy.[53] There is also the need for the UK to compete with other countries with more highly skilled work forces.[54] Workers' skills are important to the economy and the UK's relatively poor record[55] in persuading young people to stay on in school or training after that age is hampering its performance.[56] These are the concerns underpinning the introduction of a new legal duty to participate in education or training up to the age of 18.[57]

Measures have already been introduced designed to encourage more young people to acquire good skills, with waged apprentices now entitled to a minimum wage from training providers. Those on unwaged schemes are eligible for the education maintenance allowance (EMA).[58] The fact that entitlement to

---

[48] Low Pay Commission (2006) para. 3.36: in 2004 and 2005, approximately 60% of 16–17-year-olds earned less than the adult minimum wage and just under 30% earned less than the youth development rate (see above). See also R. MacDonald and J. Marsh (2005) pp. 114–15: their young research participants worked long unsupervised shifts for pay well below the minimum wage.

[49] J. Heyes (2004) pp. 16–18.

[50] Low Pay Commission (2006) paras. 3.16–3.42: despite fluctuations, the overall trend of unemployment amongst 16–17-year-olds not in full-time education has steadily been upwards since 1998. In 2004, approximately 9% of 16–17-year-olds were not in education, employment or training (NEETs) (a figure which has remained stable since 1997). Ibid. at para. 3.23: whilst economically active 16–17-year-olds only form about 2.6% of the whole economically active population, they also comprise over 10% of the unemployed population.

[51] J. Bynner et al. (2002) pp. 6–7 and ch. 2 for a detailed analysis of changing employment patterns.

[52] Inter alia: SEU (1999a); B. Coles et al. (2002); DfES (2005) paras. 9.3–9.4; DfES (2007a) paras. 2.2–2.7.

[53] DfES (2007a) para. 2.7.   [54] Ibid. at para. 2.6.

[55] UNICEF (2007) Fig. 3.3a: UK has one of the highest percentage of 15–19-year-olds not in education, training or employment amongst OECD countries.

[56] DfES (2007a) pp. 11–12.

[57] ESA 2008, s. 2; DCSF (2007) para. 5.1: the 'participation age' will be raised in stages; from 2013, until the end of the academic year young people turn 17; from 2015, until the age of 18.

[58] I.e. a weekly payment of up to £30 per week, depending on household income, intended to help pay for the day-to-day costs of staying on in education or training. SEU (2004) p. 50 and J. Bynner and M. Londra (2004) pp. 35–7: the EMA scheme has successfully encouraged a small but significant proportion of young people to remain in school.

EMA is not treated as income, and does not therefore affect their entitlement to other benefits, such as housing allowance and income support,[59] gives those living away from their families more financial stability, albeit within these educational confines. Nevertheless, it is difficult to understand the government's confidence that it can successfully fulfil its 'existing aspiration for 90% participation amongst 17 year olds by 2015'.[60] In particular it must address the problems currently dogging 'work based learning' – the relative scarcity of training schemes and apprenticeships for those under 18,[61] the poor quality of some schemes and the relatively low pay for trainees.[62] One wonders how employers can be persuaded to join others in 'playing their part'[63] in providing sufficient work-based training in areas of high deprivation and unemployment.

There is also considerable unease over the possible criminalisation of those 16–18-year-olds who refuse to 'engage voluntarily' in regular participation.[64] In many deprived areas, the majority of young people currently leave school at 16 and move into unemployment or jobs at the bottom end of the labour market.[65] They often consider any job, however menial and poorly paid, as preferable to remaining in youth training schemes or further education. Such an approach is influenced by their seeing friends emerging from two extra years of school or training, in courses which, in their view often lack rigour or intellectual challenge, without then achieving any obvious reward.[66] 'Serving in cake-shops or stacking supermarket shelves does not, in their view, require GCSEs'.[67] Worryingly for the government, ignorance of the allowances available does not underlie their plans to find work as soon as possible.[68] Nor should the homeless 16 and 17-year-olds be forgotten.[69] The fact that the disruption of homelessness[70] contributes greatly to their current very low participation in education, employment and training,[71] suggests that their housing problems need addressing long before their lack of formal skills. Admittedly, the government advocates overcoming 'significant barriers to young people's engagement', such as homelessness or drug or alcohol problems, before criminal sanctions are used.[72] Nevertheless, it is an unedifying prospect that LAs will be obliged to use such sanctions against vulnerable teenagers who fail to

---

[59] Discussed below.   [60] DCSF (2007) para. 4.11.   [61] DfES (2007a) para. 4.13.

[62] R. MacDonald and J. Marsh (2005) pp. 94–6.

[63] DfES (2007a) p. 44. See also DCSF (2008d) ch. 2. Entitlement to apprenticeships is placed on a statutory footing by the Apprenticeship, Skills, Children and Learning Bill 2009.

[64] DCSF (2007) paras. 4.29–4.31.

[65] R. MacDonald and J. Marsh (2005) ch. 6 and pp. 214–17.

[66] Ibid. at p. 96.   [67] Ibid. at p. 65.

[68] A Anderson *et al.* (2006), p 22: the young people in this research were aware of the financial incentives to stay in education and training eg the EMA and training allowances.

[69] Discussed below.   [70] N. Pleace *et al.* (2008) paras. 12.107–12.117.

[71] Ibid. at para. 12.110: 57% of statutorily homeless 16–18-year-olds were not in education, employment or training, cf. 11% of those with homes.

[72] DCSF (2007) para. 4.29.

participate in the education and training they consider to be entirely irrelevant to their present situation.[73]

(C) Liberalising the law for 16–18-year-olds?

Activities not specifically covered by legislation are governed by the House of Lords' decision in *Gillick*.[74] Their Lordships rejected the proposition that fixed age limits could ever be a satisfactory method of determining a child's legal competence. For otherwise, Lord Scarman declared, the price would be 'artificiality and a lack of realism'.[75] Providing every child with legal capacity to make his own decisions, 'when he reaches a sufficient understanding and intelligence to be capable of making up his own mind on the matter requiring decision',[76] is a refreshingly liberal approach. But it fails to prevent this body of law lapsing into incoherence. Indeed, it creates a layer of uncertainty superimposed on an ill-assorted list of inflexible age limits, below which there is no capacity and above which there is total freedom to perform the activity in question.

Greater clarity would undoubtedly be achieved by lowering the age of majority to 16 years. But despite the logical attraction of such a change, it would be at total odds with the new law requiring young people to stay in education or training until the age of 18. It would also jettison those important methods by which those over 16 can be protected from danger up to the age of 18. A care order, once made, will endure until a child attains that age[77] and the High Court's inherent jurisdiction is available for providing protection regarding any child below that age. Arguably then, the age of majority itself should remain at 18.

Meanwhile, liberalising the law by extending the right to vote to 16-year-olds would reflect their growing ability to play a part in the community.[78] Nevertheless, in 2004, the Electoral Commission, having consulted widely, rejected widespread calls for such a change.[79] Unimpressed by the arguments that 16-year-olds can join the armed forces, work full-time, apply for a passport without parental consent and are liable for taxation, it pointed out that very few young people of such an age are involved in such activities[80] and that other more important rights are withheld from them. The Commission seemed particularly influenced by those asserting that 16-year-olds have insufficient social responsibility and emotional maturity.[81] It also considered that the relatively new citizenship educational programme should become better established in schools before such a reform was introduced.[82] Furthermore, the low voting rates of 18–24-year-olds had led to the fear that lowering the voting age to 16 might lead to even lower voting turnouts than before.[83]

---

[73] Discussed in Chapter 6.   [74] [1986] AC 112.   [75] Ibid. at 186.   [76] Ibid.
[77] CA 1989, s. 91(12). See also s. 31(3): a care order can be made regarding a teenager up to the age of 17.
[78] Also discussed in Chapter 3.   [79] Electoral Commission (2004).
[80] Ibid. esp at para 3.6.   [81] Ibid. at paras. 3.16–3.28.   [82] Ibid. at ch. 4.   [83] Ibid. at ch. 6.

Given that a majority of the general public, together with many young people themselves, favoured retaining the present age limit, the Commission's conclusion was probably inevitable.[84] Nevertheless, the Commission emphasised that circumstances might change and recommended that this issue should be reviewed periodically.[85] Soon after this decision, the 2005 election produced an even lower turnout amongst the 18–24-year-olds than in 2001.[86] Nevertheless, many still argue that lowering the voting age might actually reverse a disengagement with politics,[87] by instilling in young people the habit of voting earlier.[88] It might also increase the likelihood of their taking an interest and part in political and democratic debate by demonstrating that political institutions are there to represent not only older people.[89] Such a change would also be in tune with the government's current concern to encourage young people into 'active citizenship' through, for example, volunteering in a range of operations and becoming more involved in local activities.[90]

(3) Legal rights to leave home

(A) Can parents stop young people leaving?

'When can I leave home?' Unfortunately, those working with young people can give them no simple answer. Of greater relevance are two further questions: do their parents have a legal right to stop them leaving in the first place and can their parents force them to return home if they do leave?[91] The answer is not always clear, due to the law's ambivalence over the limits to parental control. In relation to the first question, there has always existed a principle of common law that parents have a power to control the person and property of their children, as long as such a right is exercised in accordance with the welfare principle. As Lord Scarman pointed out in *Gillick*,[92] although the parental 'right or power' exists, it does so 'primarily to enable the parent to discharge his duty of maintenance, protection, and education until he reaches such an age as to be able to look after himself and make his own decisions'.[93] Implicit in his decision is the view that parents who consider that their offspring have reached 'a sufficient understanding and intelligence to be capable of making up his own mind on the matter requiring decision',[94] should not attempt to prevent them

---

[84] Ibid. at ch. 5.   [85] Ibid. at para 8.17.

[86] Using the 2005 turnout statistics, estimates indicated that only 37% (cf. 39% in the 2001 election) of young voters aged 18–24 had voted, cf. 61% of the 35–44 age group. Electoral Commission (2005) p. 25.

[87] Despite a modest improvement in the 2005 election, voting patterns show a consistent decrease in turnout since 1950. See Electoral Commission (2004), ch. 1.

[88] H. Kennedy (2006) pp. 200–1.   [89] Ibid. at p. 199.

[90] DfES (2005) esp ch. 4 and DfES (2006); discussed in Chapter 19.

[91] Discussed in more detail by J. Fortin (2001) pp. 247–50.

[92] *Gillick v. West Norfolk and Wisbech Area Health Authority* [1986] AC 112.

[93] Ibid. at 185.   [94] Ibid. at 186.

leaving home. Some parents might of course be reluctant to acknowledge that their offspring had reached such maturity.

The criminal law has, like the civil law, maintained a disapproving attitude towards parents who assume a right to control their children by force.[95] But there is no real clarity over the point at which parental behaviour changes from being a reasonable form of discipline to abusive behaviour amounting to false imprisonment.[96] Indeed, the law's failure to clarify when young people acquire the right to legal independence from their parents may have contributed to a climate in which some parents even feel entitled to force their daughters to marry against their will.[97] Such confusion undoubtedly hampers campaigners' efforts to stamp out forced marriage in this country, a practice also linked with violence and honour-related killings.[98] Fears of deterring victims from seeking help and driving the practice further underground prevented the introduction of legislation creating a specific criminal offence of forcing someone into wedlock.[99] Instead, legislation has provided civil remedies for those faced with forced marriage and for victims of forced marriage.[100] Hopefully, such marriages will become things of the past when parents adjust to the idea that their offspring have legal rights of their own which must be respected.

At first sight, one might have assumed that children faced by authoritarian parents seeking to prevent their leaving would gain assistance from the Human Rights Act (HRA) 1998, more particularly from Article 5 of the European Convention for the Protection of Human Rights and Fundamental Freedoms (1950) (ECHR).[101] It appears to provide children with protection against deprivation of liberty. Nevertheless, the European Court of Human Rights (ECtHR) in *Nielsen v. Denmark*[102] emphasised that that a parent's right to family life under Article 8 includes a broad range of parental rights and

---

[95] E.g. *R v. D* [1984] 2 All ER 449: the House of Lords confirmed that a parent could be charged with the common law offence of kidnapping if he 'stole and carried away' a child against that child's consent.

[96] E.g. in *R v. Rahman* (1985) 81 Cr App Rep 349, Lord Lane CJ disapproved of a father who had bundled his teenage daughter into a car against her will in order to return her to Bangladesh. Such behaviour could amount to false imprisonment if, as in this case, it was outside the realms of reasonable parental discipline. But such a qualification creates further uncertainty: what is 'reasonable parental discipline'?

[97] E.g. *NS v. M I* [2006] EWHC 1646 (Fam), [2007] 1 FLR 444. According to Forced Marriage Unit case statistics, West Yorkshire police recorded 211 forced marriage victims in 2005 (169 of Pakistani origin). Most victims are aged between 16 and 20, although some are much younger.

[98] Families sometimes resort to violence or kidnap to force reluctant girls into marriage. E.g. *NS v. MI* [2006] EWHC 1646 (Fam), [2007] 1 FLR 444.

[99] Announcement made by Home Office Minister, The Rt Hon Baroness Scotland, 7 June 2006.

[100] Under the Family Law Act 1996, s. 63A (as amended by the Forced Marriage (Civil Protection) Act 2007, s. 1) a forced marriage protection order can be made, on notice or ex parte, to stop anyone from forcing another person into marriage through mental or physical coercion, with (s. 63H) a power of arrest attached. The application can be brought by the victim or by a 'relevant third party' with court leave; ibid. at s. 63C(2).

[101] Art. 8 might also assist, protecting the child's private life and physical integrity.

[102] (1988) 11 EHRR 175. Discussed in more detail in Chapter 3.

responsibilities including the right to decide where the child must reside and to 'impose, or authorise others to impose, various restrictions on the child's liberty'.[103] Although the ECtHR acknowledged that a parent's rights 'cannot be completely unlimited and that it is incumbent on the State to provide safeguards against abuse',[104] it was satisfied that this 12-year-old child was still of an age when it was 'normal' for a decision to be made by a parent even against his wishes. Consequently the boy's challenge fell completely outside the ambit of Article 5 of the ECHR.[105] Crucially, the ECtHR failed to clarify the outer limits of parental behaviour or what might amount to an 'improper' purpose or 'bad faith', thereby excluding Article 8 protection.

Children arguing that their rights under Article 5 of the ECHR have been infringed by parents obstructing their efforts to leave home may find that the domestic court happily set aside *Nielsen v. Denmark*[106] as being anachronistic. As discussed earlier,[107] the Court of Appeal in *Re K (secure accommodation order: right to liberty)*[108] suggested that its authority was restricted to normal parent-child relationships. Although their approach needs clarification, Judge LJ and Dame Elizabeth Butler-Sloss P both suggested that the domestic courts might withdraw Article 8 protection from parents who behave in an outrageously over-authoritarian manner. Judge LJ thought he could easily distinguish between parents disciplining their children 'as necessary and appropriate' and parents behaving in a cruel or abusive way.[109] Similarly, Dame Elizabeth Butler-Sloss P considered that a court's response should depend on whether the parent's actions were 'within ordinary acceptable parental restrictions upon the movements of a child'.[110] But surprisingly, she also considered that 'It might be permissible' for a parent to detain a child 'for a few days'.[111] This is regrettable; surely 'ordinary acceptable parental restrictions' would exclude restricting the liberty of an older child for more than a few *hours*? Fortunately, unlike Thorpe LJ, neither she nor Judge LJ considered that a parent could restrict the liberty of a child for *more* than a few days.[112] If this majority, albeit obiter, view is adopted in subsequent cases, parents today would find it difficult to justify preventing, for more than a few days, a child from leaving home.

(B) Can parents force a child or young person to return home?

Once a child leaves the premises, the law remains confused over whether the parent can force him or her to return. The eighteenth and nineteenth-century

---

[103] Ibid. at para. 61.   [104] Ibid. at para. 72.   [105] Ibid.   [106] (1988) 11 EHRR 175.
[107] Discussed in Chapter 3.   [108] [2001] 1 FLR 526.   [109] [2001] 1 FLR 526 at para. 99.
[110] Ibid. at para. 28.   [111] Ibid. at para. 29.
[112] [2001] 1 FLR 526, per Butler-Sloss LJ, at para. 29 and per Judge LJ, at para. 101. By contrast, Thorpe LJ, at para. 61, considered that 'the deprivation of liberty was a necessary consequence of an exercise of parental responsibility for the protection and promotion of his welfare', and that therefore a LA (like a parent) has the authority to deprive a child of his or her liberty for longer than 72 hours, if necessary.

judiciary were unexpectedly liberal, refusing to issue writs of habeas corpus ordering children to return home against their will once they had attained the 'age of discretion' – 14 for boys and 16 for girls.[113] Today, this concept has disappeared but without replacement by a clear set of legal principles. Whilst it is arguable that a teenager could now claim the protection of the ECHR, there is little case law supporting such an approach. Indeed, the European Commission of Human Rights has responded inconsistently to runaway teenagers. It rejected the claim of a 14-year-old Dutch runaway that her rights under Article 8 had been infringed by the actions taken by the welfare authorities to return her home. Any infringement of her rights was justified by their need to protect her health and morals under Article 8(2).[114] But in a later decision, the European Commission rejected the parents' arguments that by refusing to force their 14-year-old daughter to return home against her will, the Danish welfare authorities had infringed the parents' own rights under Article 8.[115] Today, those advising a runaway would seek to convince a domestic court that he or she has a right to respect for his or her private life under Article 8, free from parental interference and to freedom from restraint under Article 5. But in the absence of any clearer guidance from Strasbourg, the domestic courts might instead turn to the common law principles, which though incoherent, broadly distinguish between those below and above the age of 16.

(i) Under 16s

Even very young children run away from home,[116] often for very good reasons. Indeed, as discussed above, due to family disruption and reconstitution, children are often told by their parents to leave or feel forced to do so. Nevertheless, the provisions of criminal law and those contained in the CA 1989 reflect a view of family life which is radically out of step with this reality experienced by so many. The law implicitly assumes that those assisting runaways under the age of 16 are breaking up happy family units – a situation which can be simply solved by the child's rapid return. Whilst returning such children to the source of their unhappiness solves nothing, the child care agencies know that parents are those with parental responsibility for their children. Indeed, the law strengthens the parental role by adding criminal sanctions. Thus until their children attain their 16th birthday, parents are subject to criminal sanctions if they neglect them,[117] or more specifically, fail to provide them with adequate food, clothing, medical aid or lodging.[118]

---

[113] Lord Scarman summarises this old case law in *Gillick v. West Norfolk and Wisbech Area Health Authority* [1986] AC 112 at 187–188. *Krishnan v. London Borough of Sutton* [1970] Ch 181 provides a contemporary example of the age of discretion cases. There the court refused to order the LA to require a girl of nearly 18 to return to her father against her will, since, in practical terms, such an order could not be enforced.

[114] *X v. Netherlands* (1974) 2 DR 118.   [115] *X v. Denmark* (1977–78) 7–9 DR 81.

[116] See fn. 2 above.   [117] CYPA 1933, s. 1(1).   [118] CYPA 1933, s. 1(2)(a).

Children's aid agencies advising runaways under the age of 16 are principally deterred from assisting them by the criminal law on 'harbouring'. The scope of section 2 of the Child Abduction Act 1984 is extremely wide.[119] Even providing a child under the age of 16 with advice or assistance over running away from home could theoretically amount to an offence. It is little used but case law bears out arguments suggesting its broad scope.[120] It is, however, unlikely that an offence could be proved against someone assisting a *Gillick* competent child, given the statutory defence of 'reasonable excuse'. Furthermore, a prosecution is unlikely to succeed if the adult has merely responded to a child's plea for support, rather than actively encouraging him or her to run away.[121] Whatever its real scope, the 1984 Act has produced a situation in which child runaways under the age of 16 come under considerable pressure from aid workers and the police to return home. It was hoped, following implementation of the CA 1989, that as a last resort, runaways under the age of 16 could avoid being returned home by seeking accommodation at a 'child refuge'. Exempted from the harbouring laws,[122] refuges are authorised to provide children with a place if it appears that they are at risk of harm if not taken in.[123] Although immensely valuable, these establishments have proved expensive and difficult to maintain;[124] there is a grave lack of emergency accommodation for young runaways.[125] Indeed, few LAs currently provide any specific services for runaways.[126]

---

[119] Child Abduction Act 1984, s. 2(1) provides that a person unconnected with the child (i.e. not a parent or guardian) commits an offence – 'if, without lawful authority or reasonable excuse, he takes or detains a child under the age of 16 – (a) so as to remove him from the lawful control of any person having lawful control of the child; or (b) so as to keep him out of the lawful control of any person entitled to lawful control of the child.'

   S. 2(3) provides a statutory defence in the event of the person charged showing that he believed the child to have attained the age of 16 or in the case of a non-marital child, that he reasonably believed himself to be the child's father.

   See also the CA 1989, s. 49 which creates an offence for any person knowingly and without lawful authority or reasonable excuse, to take away and keep children or induce or incite them to stay away from those responsible for their care under a care or emergency protection order, or police protection.

[120] E.g. *R v. Leather* [1993] 2 FLR 770: on separate occasions, the appellant persuaded small numbers of unsupervised children to leave activities authorised by their parents, to accompany him to places they had previously visited with their parents, but without parental consent. The appellant had not attempted to touch the children and they had felt free to leave him at any time. The Court of Appeal dismissed his appeal against conviction under the Child Abduction Act 1984, s. 2.

[121] C. Hamilton (2005) p. 43.   [122] CA 1989, s. 51.

[123] A child can only stay for a maximum of 14 days. See the Refuges (Children's Homes and Foster Placement) Regulations 1991 (SI 1991/1507).

[124] SEU (2002) paras. 5.30–5.35.

[125] Children's Society (2007) pp. 32–4 and 49; DCSF (2008a) para. 55: the government accepts the lack of suitable emergency accommodation and indicates its 'support for' the development of more local provision after consultation.

[126] Children's Society (2007) p. 30: just over 12% of LAs.

Given the high numbers of children running away from home and the reasons for this happening, it is regrettable that the harbouring laws constrain those providing them with assistance. Those who go missing from LA care should not be peremptorily returned, given the clear guidance given to children's services authorities over the steps to take when runaways are found. But whilst the reasons for the running away should be established before returning the child to an establishment he or she may find intolerable,[127] not all authorities provide such interviews, often expecting them to be carried out by the police, if at all.[128] Young runaways themselves endorse the importance of their being supported on return and being given an opportunity to talk confidentially about their problems.[129]

By contrast, in the absence of child protection concerns, LAs tend to place a relatively low priority on the child who runs away from his or her own family. So the child is, normally, simply returned home by the police.[130] Runaways often strongly resent this response, considering it quite inappropriate that they should be made to feel 'as though you've done something wrong – not to try to find out why you ran'.[131] It may, in any event, be ill-advised, given that the police often find it difficult to establish the true reasons for the child leaving.[132] It also ignores the official guidance[133] which points out that any children who run away are likely to be children in need[134] and therefore entitled to services provided by the LA, including advice, guidance and counselling.[135] It directs LAs, the police and other agencies to establish inter-agency protocols so that appropriate referrals are made to the LA.[136] The guidance states that all runaways should be offered access to an independent interview to identify the reasons for running away.[137]

It appears that this guidance is seldom followed unless a child's reluctance to return home (leading to repeat running away) triggers child protection

---

[127] DH (2002) pp. 16–17.   [128] Children's Society (2007) pp. 30–1.

[129] R. Morgan (2006a) pp. 16–17 and DH (2002) p. 17.

[130] SEU (2002) para. 5.54. Some are initially removed into police protection. Children cannot be held under these provisions for more than 72 hours, and the police must inform the LA and the child's parents of the steps taken. See CA 1989, s. 46 esp. s. 46(3)(a) and (4)(a). The police protection powers are often used to deal with runaways located 'out-of-hours', when the short-staffed children's social care Emergency Duty Teams are unable to help.

[131] R. Morgan (2006a) p. 18.

[132] Police forces conduct 'welfare interviews' to establish the reasons for the young person leaving. They are less useful if conducted by uniformed officers with young runaways who are often distrustful of the police, especially if conducted in the presence of the child's parents. SEU (2002) paras. 6.10–6.13. See also G. Newiss (1999) p. 21: 'welfare interviews' with missing persons being returned home 'may often amount to little more than a "word in the back of the car"'.

[133] DH (2002) pp. 24–5.

[134] Under the CA 1989, s. 17. Discussed in more detail in Chapter 16.   [135] DH (2002) p. 24.

[136] Children's Society (2007) p. 24: whilst most LAs and police forces operate inter-agency protocols for responding to children running away, at least half relate only to 'looked after' young people.

[137] DH (2002) p. 26.

concerns.[138] The LA will then investigate his or her home circumstances,[139] to establish any evidence of parental ill-treatment which might justify an application for a care order or emergency protection order,[140] or even for criminal proceedings to be instituted. But unless and until the LA acquires an order authorising them to care for the child, they are under no legal duty to accommodate him or her unless the child is orphaned, lost or abandoned, or his or her present carers are prevented from doing so themselves.[141] More to the point, they are powerless to do so against his or her parents' wishes.[142] Social workers know that parents are legally responsible for accommodating their children aged under 16 themselves and additionally, that there is a serious lack of emergency accommodation for this age group. In any event, LAs may be reluctant to accommodate young people in all but the most extreme circumstances. Researchers found that young runaways were being urged to return home by social workers, despite it being unsuitable for them to do so, in order to avoid activating LAs' leaving care obligations by the provision of accommodation. Indeed, the Children's Society reports 'many' LAs operating 'unwritten policies' to avoid accommodating 14 and 15-year-olds, and even 13-year-old runaways.[143] As discussed below, in their anxiety to avoid longer-term legal responsibilities, social workers are failing to provide vulnerable teenagers with appropriate support. Hopefully improvements in practice will be achieved by new guidance requiring 'a full needs assessment/welfare interview' for all those who runaway.[144]

(ii) Over 16s

Once over the age of 16, young people may gain the false impression that parental responsibility has terminated, that they are therefore legally 'emancipated' and can behave as adults. Nevertheless, it is quite incorrect to give them such advice – the law is clear that they do not attain full legal independence until their 18th birthday. Until then parents retain parental responsibility and the young person, as a legal minor, is subject to all the confusing legal incapacities affecting his or her ability to follow an independent existence.[145] Despite this, attaining the age of 16 does have considerable legal significance, so far as leaving home is concerned. The criminal provisions on 'harbouring' and the criminal sanctions available against neglectful parents drop away from children once they attain the age of 16. Indeed, it appears that for these reasons, some parents

---

[138] Only 4% of current Children and Young People's Plans, out of 75 LAs, make specific reference to runaway children. Written answer by the Parliamentary Under-Secretary, Department for Education and Skills, 8 February 2007. See also Children's Society (2007) p. 28.

[139] Under the CA 1989, s. 47(1). Discussed in more detail in Chapter 16.

[140] CA 1989, s. 31 or 44.   [141] CA 1989, s. 20(1).

[142] CA 1989, s. 20(7). See also s. 20(8): the child's parents may remove him or her from LA accommodation at any time.

[143] Children's Society (2007) pp. 34 and 52.

[144] DCSF (2008a) para. 58: to be introduced by Spring 2009.   [145] Discussed above.

regard 16 as the point at which they can reasonably 'kick out' their offspring if they are causing trouble in the home.[146] Strangely, the government does not appear to have considered changing the law by extending the scope of such criminal sanctions to the age of 18, thereby ensuring the law's consistency with plans to require young people to remain in education or training until they attain such an age.[147]

Parents who wish to persuade sons and daughters over the age of 16 to return home will have an uphill battle. The courts' power to make any section 8 orders normally ends on a child attaining such an age[148] – reflecting the realistic view that it is pointless for courts to make residence orders contrary to the wishes of those over 16. It is also unlikely that parents can force a 16-year-old to return home by involving the LA. If the LA considers him or her to be suffering significant harm, they can apply for a care order,[149] but it is unlikely they would contemplate seeking such an order against the wishes of an 'elderly' child, unless exceptional circumstances existed.[150] Admittedly, a young person over the age of 16 who is opposed to returning home, might avoid doing so by persuading the LA to provide him or her with accommodation, as the LA is entitled to do,[151] even against his or her parents' wishes. The parents would then have no right to remove him or her from such accommodation.[152] In practice, however, as noted below, children's services are unlikely to accede to such persuasion since the provision of accommodation might activate costly leaving care obligations towards such a child.

(4) Leaving home – state assistance with financial support

The list of rights contained in the CRC reflects the view that it is not enough to identify certain liberties essential to a child's capacity for eventual autonomy, such as freedom of speech. These are of no value to those too poor or ill to benefit from them, particularly if their time is taken up surviving from day to day. These rights must therefore be complemented by more positive action on the part of the state to enable children to enjoy fully their basic liberties.[153] Article 26 reserves the right of every child 'to benefit from social security, including social insurance' and Article 27(1) states that governments should 'recognise the right of every child to a standard of living adequate for the child's physical, mental, spiritual, moral and social development'. Unfortunately, the

---

[146] G. Randall and S. Brown (2001) p. 11.   [147] DfES (2007a) ch. 5.
[148] CA 1989, s. 9(6) and (7): unless the circumstances are exceptional.
[149] CA 1989, s. 31(3).
[150] E.g. *Re V (care or supervision order)* [1996] 1 FLR 776; discussed in Chapter 12.
[151] CA 1989, s. 20(3), discussed further below.
[152] CA 1989, s. 20(11). See also *Krishnan v. London Borough of Sutton* [1970] Ch 181.
[153] Discussed in Chapter 2.

principles of English law fail to match up to both these international obligations when dealing with children who leave home.

Children who leave their homes before attaining adulthood quickly discover that, although the law may recognise their rights to express their views and to reach certain decisions, such rights may be of little value to them. Freedom from the restrictions of family life is often a bleak experience for those who have no correlative rights to financial help or accommodation. Official policy continues to categorise minors very differently, according to their situations. They are dependent children if living at home and in full-time education, in which case their parents are still entitled to child benefit. They are young adults if on training programmes, with their own training allowance.[154] If unemployed and not in school, they are neither.[155] Homelessness and poverty combine to produce a host of practical difficulties, so that those without a home have no address and therefore no obvious credentials to offer prospective employers. Those who leave home hurriedly may have no formal identification documents with which to satisfy the demands of the benefits system. Those who are still under the age of 16 will find life particularly difficult with no legal means of support. They should be in full-time school and so are not entitled to take full-time employment. They have no right to welfare benefits and are not entitled to work-based training places. If they are determined to stay away from home and the LA fails to assist them, they will have no alternative but to find friends and relatives to care for them, or take to the streets.

Those over 16 who are not in training or employment may turn to the benefits system for financial assistance. The 16 and 17-year-olds who manage to obtain state support are the lucky few who find their way through a bizarrely complex system of interrelated benefits so confusing that most do not know what they are entitled to.[156] It continues to attract considerable criticism for its harsh discrimination against those under the age of 18. Successive governments have defended the controversial withdrawal of an automatic right to draw supplementary benefit (now income support) from those under 18.[157] They have maintained the view that this age group should either be capable of supporting themselves through work or youth training or should be supported by their parents whilst remaining in full-time education. Admittedly there are exceptions to the overall exclusion of this age group from entitlement to income support. Those 16–18-year-olds who cannot work, for example, because they are still in education, remain entitled to it, but only if they are able to satisfy the Department of Work and Pensions that they are estranged from their parents.[158] Furthermore, until recently, they were

---

[154] Discussed above.   [155] N. Harris (1992) p. 184.   [156] SEU (2000) para. 3.52.

[157] Change introduced by Social Security Act 1986 (implemented in 1988).

[158] Under the Income Support (General) Regulations 1987 (SI 1987/1967), reg. 42A and Sch. 1B (as amended), claimants are, in exceptional circumstances, eligible for income support on the basis that they do not have to be available for work. These include, inter alia, if the claimant is a single parent, or pregnant, or is in full-time education but living away from home because of being

paid a lower rate of benefit than adults over the age of 18, despite having precisely the same needs.[159]

Admittedly, the extension of the EMA to work-based trainees has significantly reduced the number of young people still dependent on benefits. The entitlement of those in education or unwaged training to EMA, without affecting the level of their income support or housing benefit, has undoubtedly done much to improve their general financial well-being.[160] Furthermore, care leavers eligible for 'leaving care' support[161] have all their financial assistance provided by their LAs,[162] and none at all from the benefits system. Whilst the leaving care legislation has considerably improved the outcomes for some care leavers,[163] there are enormous variations in support paid by LAs.[164] These should disappear once LAs lose their current freedom to determine the amount of financial support to be paid to those engaging in higher education or training.[165] Hopefully, the standardisation of support will provide care leavers with far greater financial security and clarity over their entitlement to financial assistance when in education, employment or training.[166] In particular, it should prevent LAs suddenly withdrawing financial help with tuition fees, as sometimes occurs at present.[167]

Meanwhile, although reduced in number, there remains a significant group of 16 and 17-year-olds outside the scope of the EMA system and the care system. Those who leave home suddenly will be often unable to take up any education, employment or training options, at least for the time being, thereby ruling out eligibility for EMA.[168] Indeed, many NEET 16–18-year-olds cite the disruption caused by homelessness as a barrier to their participation in education, employment and training.[169] This group remains dependent on a benefits system described by the government itself as involving 'myriad rules [which]

estranged from his or her parents, or being in physical or moral danger, or at serious risk to his or her physical or mental health. Alternatively, unemployed young people aged 16 or 17 may, in certain circumstances, be eligible for Jobseeker's Allowance on a temporary basis after leaving education if living away from home. See below.

[159] HM Treasury (2007) para. 5.37: rates of Jobseeker's Allowance (JSA) and Income Support (IS) raised (as from April 2008) to align with 18–24 rates.

[160] Discussed above.

[161] CA 1989, ss. 22–24 and Sch. 2, para. 19; discussed further in Chapter 16. NB a 16 or 17-year-old who is in LA care or who has left care since October 2001 can claim IS if a lone parent or sick or disabled.

[162] DH (2001) ch. 9 and The Children (Leaving Care)(England) Regulations 2001 (SI 2001/2874).

[163] J. Wade and J. Dixon (2006).

[164] DfES (2007b) para. 6.69: the most common weekly allowance paid to care leavers across 52 leaving care teams is £42.70 and the grant paid to young people on leaving care varies from £400 to £2,000.

[165] CA 1989, s. 23C (5A)–(5C): LAs must pay 'the relevant amount', as specified by regulations, to a former relevant child who pursues higher education or training.

[166] M. Allen (2003) p. 15.   [167] R. Morgan (2006b) p. 13.

[168] N. Pleace *et al.* (2008) para. 12.107: 33% of statutorily homeless 17-year-olds were in full-time education, cf. 66% of 17-year-olds nationally.

[169] Ibid. at para. 12.117: 37%.

make it incomprehensible to all but the most expert'.[170] To ensure that 'young people in genuine need and hardship are not left destitute',[171] there is a safety net of welfare arrangements (JSA, severe hardship (SH)), as long as they are available for work. But these discretionary payments are only paid over in exceptional circumstances involving severe hardship.[172] Claiming income support or JSA(SH) payments is often a harrowing experience for 16–17-year-olds. The government accepted that job centre interviews involving young people being forced to prove 'estrangement' or inability to return home could often create further distress for those already in desperate situations, particularly if they had been abused at home.[173] It might even result in 'their severing contact with the very agencies which can support them, potentially placing themselves at further risk'.[174] Jobcentre Plus staff are now required to accept the word of the young person on the justification for the estrangement and to accept corroboration (if considered necessary)[175] from third party professionals, such as Connexions staff or voluntary and community organisations, rather from the young person's parents or carer.

Most agree that the system of benefits governing those aged 16 and 17 is unsatisfactory, with the Committee on the Rights of the Child strongly criticising this field of law.[176] A series of official reports and papers have criticised its complexities and extreme anomalies.[177] Those assisting homeless young people find that some young claimants never complete the process of claiming benefits; those that do find that what they receive is very hard to live off,[178] with many suffering from financial difficulties.[179] The SEU had, in 1999, suggested, as a long-term objective, a complete overhaul of the wide range of benefits presently available, by introducing a single youth allowance, as in Australia.[180] Some years later, in 2004, after echoing the SEU's views, the government confirmed that it 'has a long-term vision of a single coherent system of financial support for 16–19 year olds'.[181] This 'long-term vision' of a UK youth allowance seems now to have faded away, probably because there are far fewer 16 and 17-year-olds still affected by the present chaotic benefits system. Presumably the government now considers such reforms to be unnecessary given that

---

[170] HM Treasury (2004) para. 3.1.   [171] Learning and Skills Council (2006).

[172] Under the Jobseekers Act 1995, s. 16(1). E.g. homelessness, inadequate accommodation, parents' inability to support, lack of income or vulnerability.

[173] HM Treasury (2004) paras. 3.11–3.16 and HM Treasury (2005) paras. 2.5–2.8.

[174] HM Treasury (2004) para. 2.5.

[175] Current DWP guidance, para. 7: only if 'we have valid evidence of doubt' will third party corroboration be required.

[176] Committee on the Rights of the Child (1995) para. 15 and (2002) para. 46(c).

[177] SEU (1999a) paras. 5.20–5.24: money being paid through at least eight different routes by eight different agencies on behalf of two government departments. See also HM Treasury (2004), HM Treasury (2005), Centre for Economic and Social Inclusion (2005).

[178] D. Quilgars et al. (2008) p. 53.   [179] N. Pleace et al. (2008) para. 12.127.

[180] SEU (1999a) para. 9.4, Action 9. Annex F describes the working of the Australian Youth Allowance. See also HM Treasury (2004) App. C.

[181] HM Treasury (2004) para. 4.1.

education or training will be eventually compulsory for all those under 18, with benefits linked to education.[182] But this overlooks the fact that young people who require state support at the age of 16 and 17 have left home and often have far more and complex personal problems than their peers nationally.[183] It is surely unrealistic to assume there will be no need for a safety net of benefits for young people like this who may be incapable of engaging in education or training in the short term.

(5) Leaving home – assistance with housing

There are no accurate national statistics measuring the extent of youth homelessness. The official statistics on the numbers of homeless young people relate only to those accepted by LAs as having a priority need for rehousing due to their age.[184] These figures do not, however, provide a true picture of the problem, since many young people do not approach the statutory agencies.[185] Some homeless young people find accommodation with friends and relatives, and others, perhaps inevitably, end up living rough on the streets.[186] Many children and young people who leave home are caught in a vicious spiral of no home, no address, no job prospects. The Committee on the Rights of the Child has twice urged the government to improve its efforts to deal with the phenomenon of youth homelessness.[187]

(A) Homelessness provision

As long as they are over the age of 16, young people who leave home today are better catered for by the law than those who did so a decade ago. For those under 16, even if the children's services authority are prepared to assist, parental objections may prevent such a move.[188] In relation to the older group, the picture is now very different, due to changes made in 2002 to the homelessness legislation. Now the categories of 'priority need' include homeless 16 and 17-year-olds and care leavers aged between 18 and 21,[189] thereby imposing a legal obligation on

[182] DfES (2007a) para. 5.28: 16 and 17-year-olds who are estranged from their parents should obtain extended support but probably conditional on their seeking education or training.

[183] N. Pleace *et al.* (2008) para. 12.116. See also p. 280: 52% of statutorily homeless 16–17-year-olds reported having had anxiety, depression or other mental health problems; 33% had current mental health problems – three times that of young people of the same age in the general population.

[184] D. Quilgars *et al.* (2008) ch. 2: analysis of scale and patterns of youth homelessness; see esp Table 4 which cites statistics showing 5,652 acceptances of applicants aged 16/17 for 2006–7 in England. But the true numbers of 16 and 17-year-olds accepted as being in priority need may be higher since some are accepted for reasons other than their age, e.g. having children of their own.

[185] Shelter (2005a) pp. 6–7.   [186] See fn. 14.

[187] Committee on the Rights of the Child (1995) para. 15 and (2002) para. 46(b).

[188] CA 1989, s. 20 (7) and (8); discussed above.

[189] Homelessness (Priority Need for Accommodation) (England) Order 2002 (SI 2002/2051).

housing authorities to provide them with accommodation.[190] This change ensures that housing authorities can no longer refuse to house these homeless young people on the assumption that the children's services authority will do so instead.

Many of this older group will have left home precipitately. Indeed, housing authorities are increasingly finding that a major cause of homelessness throughout the country is young people being asked to leave by their parents.[191] Official guidance states that since it is generally in the best interests of 16 and 17-year-olds to live at home, the possibility of a reconciliation should be explored through family mediation strategies, unless relations have broken down irretrievably or it would not be safe for the young person to return.[192] Research suggests that mediation is very commonly used as part of the homelessness assessment process for 16 and 17-year-olds,[193] and that it can be effective.[194] Whilst ostensibly sensible, there is a real danger that some young people feel pressurised into returning to an unsafe home as a short-term 'fix'.[195] The guidance warns of collusive arrangements being made between parents and young people, with the parents telling the young person to leave, knowing that all 16 and 17-year-olds have a priority need for accommodation. If this is found to be the case, the young person must be designated intentionally homeless with no legal entitlement to long-term accommodation.[196] But again there is the risk that poorly trained staff will make such assessments incorrectly.[197]

The accommodation needs of homeless 16 and 17-year-olds are now well recognised. If estranged from their families, they will be particularly vulnerable and may need a range of extra support.

> These young people's childhoods were very often marred by extremely difficult and fractured family relations – with family restructuring, violence, parents with mental health problems, and frequent moves commonly experienced – and many had also had a very disrupted education. Large proportions had experienced mental health and/or substance misuse problems[198]

Accommodation alone is seldom sufficient, since they will often lack skills at managing their affairs and will need the advice and support normally available to that age group from their own families. Nevertheless, a continuing problem has been ensuring that housing and children's services cooperate in providing these young people with an appropriate package of services. The housing guidance has constantly directed both services to establish joint protocols for liaising over this group of applicants,[199] to ensure that joint assessments of the

---

[190] I.e. under the Housing Act 1996, s. 193(2).   [191] ODPM (2004b) para. 3.139.

[192] DCLG (2006b) ch. 5. See also DCLG (2007) pp. 11–15.

[193] Shelter (2005b) ch. 3; D. Quilgars *et al.* (2008) pp. 65–8.

[194] DCLG (2006b) paras. 3.139–3.14 and G. Randall and S. Brown (2001) ch. 3.

[195] Inter alia: Shelter (2005b) pp. 9–10; SEU (2005) para. 5.34; D. Quilgars *et al.* (2008) pp. 66–8.

[196] Under the Housing Act 1996, s. 191(3).   [197] Shelter (2005b) p. 10.

[198] N. Pleace *et al.* (2008) para. 12.134.

[199] DCLG (2006a) paras. 5.16–5.17. See also DCLG (2007) pp. 15–16 and DCLG/DCSF (2008) chs. 2–3.

young person's needs are carried out,[200] with any non-housing support, such as care, health or other support being provided by children's services.[201] The need to cooperate has now been reinforced by new duties under the CA 2004.[202] A complicating feature of the relationship between the two agencies is that a 16 or 17-year-old may be both a child in need, requiring specialised support, which only children's services can provide after appropriate assessment, and homeless, with a need for specialist accommodation, which only housing can provide. This complexity also arises in relation to young people leaving care, for whose welfare children's services have a continuing responsibility, but whose housing needs may need fulfilling by the housing authority.[203]

The homelessness guidance emphasises that 16 and 17-year-olds are not in 'priority need' of housing if they are 'children in need'[204] and that in relation to the latter, children's services have a duty to accommodate them under section 20 of the CA 1989. It also directs that 'in cases of uncertainty as to whether a 16 or 17 year old applicant may be a relevant child[205] or a child in need, the housing authority should contact the relevant children's services authority, and *where necessary*, should provide interim accommodation under s188 [of the Housing Act 1996], *pending clarification*'.[206] So as Baroness Hale of Richmond observed in *R (M) v. Hammersmith and Fulham London Borough Council*,[207] the statutory guidance and Priority Need Order 'clearly contemplates that, if the criteria in section 20 of the 1989 Act are met, social services rather than housing should take the long term responsibility'.[208] Even so, section 20(3) of the CA 1989 imposes no *absolute* legal obligation on children's services to accommodate this group of older teenagers, unless they are care leavers. Since they are only obliged to provide accommodation for children in need over the age of 16 *if* their welfare is considered 'likely to be seriously prejudiced' without it, children's services may conclude that such 'serious prejudice' will be avoided by the housing authority's provision of accommodation, in the short and long term.

Underlying the reluctance of children's services authorities to accommodate children themselves is the leaving care legislation introduced in 2000. Whereas prior to that legislation, housing authorities would routinely refuse to assist children's services over accommodating young people,[209] now the boot is on

---

[200]   DCLG/DCSF (2008) para. 2.7: using the common assessment framework (CAF).
[201]   DCLG (2006a) paras. 12.12–12.15.   [202]   CA 2004, ss. 10–11.
[203]   DCLG (2006a) para. 5.17; LAs' duties to children leaving care are discussed below.
[204]   The term 'child in need' is defined by CA 1989, s. 17(1); discussed further in Chapter 15.
[205]   I.e. a care leaver, entitled to accommodation under the leaving care legislation.
[206]   DCLG (2006a) para. 12.6, emphasis added. See also Homelessness (Priority Need for Accommodation)(England) Order 2002 (SI 2002/2051), art. 3(2).
[207]   [2008] UKHL 14, [2008] 1 WLR 535.   [208]   Ibid. at [31].
[209]   CA 1989, s. 27 authorises children's services authorities to request the help of other authorities, e.g. the local housing authority, with the exercise of any of their functions. But the extent to which housing authorities could be persuaded to assist with housing for young people was substantially undermined by *R v. Northavon District Council, ex p Smith* [1994] 2 AC 402; discussed further in Chapter 15.

the other foot, so to speak. Children's services may refrain from accommodating a young person under CA 1989, section 20, to avoid triggering long term
and expensive leaving care liabilities to him or her.[210] Thus although housing
authorities may contact children's services, particularly if a homeless young
person has had some previous contact with them or if there are serious concerns
about the young person's welfare due to violence or abuse, it is now less likely
that children's services will take any responsibility for supporting homeless 16
and 17-year-olds.[211] Indeed, although as Baroness Hale of Richmond specifically stated 'It was not intended that social services should be able to avoid those
responsibilities by looking to the housing authority to accommodate the
child'[212] this is precisely what happens. Through being defined as in priority
need, some homeless teenagers are, as in the *Hammersmith and Fulham* case,[213]
provided with short-term accommodation without any involvement of children's services at all, and certainly without the statutory assessment that they are
entitled to.[214]

Baroness Hale of Richmond was in no doubt that the housing authority in
the *Hammersmith and Fulham* case should have referred that homeless 17-
year-old to the children's services authority and that they should have accepted
responsibility for her, given her deeply troubled background and her need for
far more than a roof over her head.[215] She also warned that it would be unlawful
for a LA to operate a deliberate policy of shifting their duty to provide
accommodation under the CA 1989 onto housing.[216] This warning was followed by fresh guidance stressing the need for housing and children's services
authorities to work together to eliminate the risks of homelessness amongst 16
and 17-year-olds.[217] It emphasises that 'systems should eliminate the risk of
young people being passed between Housing and Children's Services unnecessarily',[218] with each young person being provided with a 'personalised support
package' based on a full assessment of their needs.[219] Cynics might wonder why
a new volume of guidance should have any more effect than previous volumes

---

[210] A child becomes eligible for leaving care services if he or she is aged between 16 and 17 and has
been looked after (i.e. provided with accommodation under CA 1989, s. 20) for at least 13 weeks
since the attainment of 14.

[211] Inter alia: Shelter (2005b) p. 35; Children's Commissioner (2007) p. 9; Children's Society (2007)
pp. 34 and 52 (in relation to young runaways); Howard League (2006) pp. 14–15 (in relation to
youth offenders leaving custody).

[212] *R (M) v. Hammersmith and Fulham London Borough Council* [2008] UKHL 14, [2008] 1 WLR
535 at [31].

[213] A 17-year-old girl, on being refused accommodation by her terminally ill mother, had been
referred by social services to housing and accommodated by housing in bed and breakfast and
hostel accommodation, both before and after her stay in custody for robbery.

[214] E.g. *R(S) v. Sutton London Borough Council* [2007] EWHC 1196 (Admin), [2007] 2 FLR 849, per
Stanley Burnton J, at [50]–[59]: the LA should not have decided that it need not accommodate a
17-year-old under CA 1989, s. 20 on her release from custody without having carried out a
detailed assessment of her needs.

[215] [2008] UKHL 14, [2008] 1 WLR 535 at [33].   [216] Ibid.

[217] DCLG/DCSF (2008) ch. 3.   [218] Ibid. at para. 3.4.   [219] Ibid. at para. 3.3.

carrying precisely the same message. In such circumstances, it is crucial that 16 and 17-year-olds are placed by housing authorities in appropriate accommodation. As noted below, it is still somewhat of a lottery whether this occurs.

(B) Care leavers

During the late 1990s, increasing concern was voiced over the way that young people in care were discharged early by their LAs, often at the age of 16 – such treatment contrasting starkly with the way that other young people typically leave home at the age of 22.[220] Even if suitably accommodated, given their childhood histories, many of these care leavers were quite unable to cope with independent living and were greatly over-represented amongst those who ended up sleeping rough.[221]

Appropriate accommodation for care leavers is essential. Under the leaving care provisions introduced in 2000, eligible looked-after children leaving care[222] should obtain a package of care more akin to that received by young people growing up with their families,[223] with settled accommodation being a crucial element of their 'pathway plan'. The leaving care obligations obviously have considerable resource implications for LAs, given that care leavers' entitlement to financial support and accommodation continues for those in tertiary education, well beyond their 18th birthday. Case law has established that a LA cannot avoid its legal liabilities under the leaving care legislation by claiming to accommodate children under CA 1989, section 17, as opposed to section 20.[224] Since any child over 14 qualifies for leaving care assistance, once the 13 weeks of accommodation under section 20 have accumulated, some LAs avoid embarking upon providing any accommodation at all.[225] Instead, as discussed above, they simply rely on the housing authority to provide short-term accommodation. In future, instead of providing a young person with accommodation as such, LAs may exploit their new wider power to make cash payments to children in

---

[220] DH (1999) para. 2.1.   [221] Discussed above.   [222] See fn 210 above.

[223] Children (Leaving Care) Act 2000 and Children (Leaving Care)(England) Regulations 2001 (SI 2001/2874); discussed in more detail in Chapter 16.

[224] *H, Barhanu and B v. London Borough of Wandsworth and ors* [2007] EWHC 1082 (Admin), [2007] 2 FLR 822, per Holman J, esp. at [55]–[60]: the LA could not simply assert that they had accommodated two unaccompanied asylum seekers under CA 1989, s. 17, as opposed to s. 20, thereby avoiding their leaving care obligations. See also *R (W) v. North Lincolnshire Council* [2008] EWHC 2299 (Admin), [2008] 2 FLR 2150, per HHJ Mackie QC, at [39]–[41]: the LA had sought to fulfil a duty under s. 17 when one was owed under s. 20; the s. 17 route had been taken when on the facts the LA were obliged to follow s. 20. But see also *R (G) v. Southwark London Borough Council* [2008] EWCA Civ 877, [2008] 2 FLR 1762, per Longmore and Pill LJJ (Rix LJ strongly dissenting): a LA is entitled to conclude that some homeless young people do not require accommodation under s. 20, but can be 'helped with accommodation' under s. 17 if they are sufficiently capable and resourceful to find their own accommodation.

[225] Children's Commissioner (2007) p. 9: some LAs are reluctant to bring 14–18-year-olds into the care system at all, or they 'de-accommodate' them, in order to avoid assuming leaving care obligations.

need,[226] by paying the rent of a young person needing accommodation, thereby, once again, avoiding the letter of the law regarding the leaving care provisions.

(C) Specialised accommodation

'Housing emerged as the life area most closely associated with mental well-being, outstripping the contribution made by involvement in education and training.'[227] The need to develop more suitable supported accommodation for the 16–18 year age group has been recognised for many years. Indeed, housing authorities were in 2002 required to formulate an over-arching homelessness strategy within their areas, to prevent homelessness and to secure that appropriate accommodation is available.[228] The housing guidance also emphasises that most 16 and 17-year-olds are likely to benefit from a period of supported accommodation before moving into a tenancy of their own.

Most LAs do make use of a range of accommodation for 16 and 17-year-olds, including supported lodgings, trainer flats, hostels, and foyers.[229] But whilst significant improvements have taken place,[230] progress is geographically patchy,[231] with some areas still experiencing an inadequate supply of affordable, secure, social rented housing.[232] Young people are still being placed in very unsuitable accommodation in rough areas, in which they sometimes feel very unsafe,[233] and/or far from their support networks.[234] Despite official guidance stressing that bed and breakfast (B and B) accommodation is unsuitable and should not be used except as a last resort,[235] a surprisingly high number of 16–17-year-olds are still being placed in B and B 'hotels', albeit for relatively short periods.[236] Similarly, accommodation in large hostels continues, despite its often carrying the risk of violence, theft, bullying, and exposure to alcohol and drug misuse.[237] Some of this age group remain in 'temporary accommodation' for relatively long periods,[238] in some cases until they reach their 18th

---

[226] Children and Young Persons Act 2008, s. 24: amends CA 1989, s. 17(6) by removing 'in exceptional circumstances', thereby enabling cash payments to be made to children in need as a means of regular and continuing support.

[227] J. Wade and J. Dixon (2006) p. 203.   [228] Homelessness Act 2002, ss. 1–4

[229] J. Wade and J. Dixon (2006) p. 202.

[230] D. Quilgars et al. (2008) pp. 30–1: in some areas, the Supporting People programme (established in 2003) has helped provide housing related support services for vulnerable groups, such as young homeless people.

[231] J. Wade and J. Dixon (2006) p. 203 and B. Broad (2005) p 377–8.

[232] Shelter (2005b) p. 30.   [233] D. Quilgars et al. (2008) pp. 52–3.

[234] J. Wade and J. Dixon (2006) p. 204. See also R. Morgan (2006b) p. 12.

[235] DCLG (2006a) paras. 12.13–12.14. See also DCLG/DCSF (2008) p. 28.

[236] D. Quilgars et al. (2008) p. 22: 25% statutorily homeless 16 and 17-year-olds were placed in B and B during 2006–7, but only 9% for longer than 6 weeks. The government is committed to end B and B accommodation for 16–17-year-olds by 2010: 14 November 2006, speech by Ruth Kelly, Secretary of State for DCLG.

[237] Shelter (2005b) p. 30.

[238] N. Pleace et al. (2008) para. 12.58: 49% of statutorily homeless 16–17-year-olds had spent 7–12 months in temporary accommodation; only 3% for over a year.

birthday to simplify matters for the housing authority when it comes to their taking a longer-term tenancy.[239] Care leavers are particularly vulnerable. But they presently experience far too many moves,[240] even homelessness,[241] with long delays in obtaining promised accommodation, intervening periods in unsuitable B and B or hostel accommodation and promised funding not materialising.[242] Hopefully, the new legislative duty on LAs to secure a range of suitable accommodation sufficient to meet the differing needs of looked after children[243] will feed through into improving the accommodation available for care leavers.

The lack of appropriate accommodation for homeless young people is exacerbated by the scarcity of affordable accommodation in the rented sector. Many are chary of taking privately rented accommodation because of their concerns about insecurity of tenure and unscrupulous landlords.[244] In any event, the single room rent restrictions put a ceiling on the amount of housing benefit for which they are eligible.[245] Furthermore, the little understood principle of property law barring those under 18 from executing a legal lease on a flat greatly exacerbates the difficulties of homeless 16 and 17-year-olds seeking housing authority accommodation. A widespread misunderstanding of the law prevents this principle being avoided by relatively simple expedients.[246] For example, since a minor can hold an equitable tenancy in any property,[247] if a minor arranges to take a tenancy, it will operate as a contract for a lease,[248] binding on him or her, unless and until repudiated.[249] Nevertheless, housing authorities often refuse to offer tenancies to under 18-year-olds unless the children's services authority act as guarantor, which they may not wish to do.[250] Young people fending for themselves for the first time may, in any event, be far more appropriately accommodated in specialised hostels and foyers offering support, some of which also provide training schemes.

---

[239] Discussed below.
[240] J. Wade and J. Dixon (2006) p. 202: almost 1 in 5 more than four or more times.
[241] Ibid over one-third.   [242] R. Morgan (2006a) pp. 12–13.
[243] CA 1989, s. 22G (2) and (4), as inserted by CYPA 2008, s. 9.
[244] D. Quilgars et al. (2008) pp. 79–83.
[245] The amount of housing benefit for those under 25 (based on the assumption that people under 25 do not need one-bedroom single flats) is limited to the average rent for a room in a shared house.
[246] D. Cowan and N. Deardon (2002) pp. 173–82: a detailed exposition of the legal pitfalls and remedies regarding the grant of tenancies to under-age tenants.
[247] Taking effect under the Trusts of Land and Appointment of Trustees Act 1996, Sch. 2, para. 2. See D. Cowan and N. Deardon (2002) pp. 173–82 and J. Morgan (2000).
[248] Suitable accommodation for a minor will also inevitably be deemed 'a necessary'.
[249] See Hale J's explanation of a minor's position regarding leases of land in *Kingston upon Thames Borough Council v. Prince* [1999] 1 FLR 593.
[250] Shelter (2006) pp. 25–6.

(6) Children 'divorcing' their parents

(A) The child applicant

A child leaving home will often turn to friends or relations for accommodation and help. In such circumstances, obtaining a court order approving such an arrangement clarifies the carer's legal position. Indeed, obtaining a residence order under section 8 of the CA 1989 is a simpler way of obtaining a judicial stamp of approval for a child now living with someone outside his or her immediate family. Children may take the initiative and apply for such orders themselves.[251] A residence order confirming the new carer's parental responsibility for the child[252] not only avoids the risk of criminal charges under the Child Abduction Act 1984[253] and under the legislation designed to protect girls from sexual offences,[254] but also persuades schools and other agencies that the carer has authority to make decisions regarding the child.[255]

It is a remarkably liberal aspect of English law that the CA 1989, by permitting children to apply for section 8 orders, enables them to instruct their own solicitors and initiate proceedings, thereby forcing their parents into court to answer their claims. It in no way detracts from the liberality of these provisions that they do not guarantee that the outcome will necessarily be what these children want. The court may ultimately decide that an order complying with a child's own wishes would not be in his or her best interests. Despite this, embarking on litigation is, in itself, a dramatic way of taking independent action. The fact that a solicitor who considers a child competent to give instructions is able to respect that child's wishes on this and treat him or her as a client, indicates the extent to which English law currently acknowledges children's capacity for making important choices in their lives and taking the responsibility to pursue them.

It is unlikely that many solicitors would take instructions from a child very much below adolescence. Indeed, children face at least two procedural hurdles before the courts hear their applications for section 8 orders under the CA 1989. They must first convince their solicitors that they have sufficient understanding to instruct them without a guardian or next friend.[256] Next they must obtain leave from the court under section 10(8) to proceed with an application for a residence order. Leave can only be obtained if they convince the court that they have 'sufficient understanding' to apply for the section 8 order in question.

---

[251] Having first obtained leave to do so under CA 1989, s. 10(8). See discussion below and in Chapter 7, in the context of children instructing their own solicitors.

[252] CA 1989, s. 12(2).   [253] Discussed above.

[254] E.g. the various offences under Sexual Offences Act 1956.

[255] E.g. B v. B (a minor) (residence order) [1992] 2 FLR 327: the High Court agreed that although under the CA 1989, s. 3(5) the child's grandmother could, as her carer, take decisions necessary to safeguard her welfare, a residence order would provide her granddaughter's school with legal confirmation of her authority to do so.

[256] Both solicitor and court must be convinced on this score; discussed further in Chapter 7.

A solicitor considering that the child would pass this test may nevertheless suggest that the adult with whom the child intends to live makes the application instead, perhaps to avoid the child being closely involved in potentially unpleasant litigation. But there are tactical reasons why an application by the child might be preferable. In the first place, a mature child, with no income of his or her own, will probably obtain public funding for the litigation, whereas an adult in paid employment will not.[257] The Legal Services Commission will, however, normally scrutinise a child's application to ensure that it does not disguise an adult's attempt to obtain indirect public funding for his own cause. Secondly, the child might be more successful in obtaining leave to proceed because the qualifying formula applicable to a child under section 10(8) is less rigorous than the checklist of factors to be complied with by an adult in order to obtain leave under section 10(9).[258] The legal outcome will be no different, whether the child takes the initiative and obtains leave under section 10(8) to apply for a residence order, or the third-party residential carer does so under section 10 (9).[259] As noted below, in each case the residence order will be in the adult's 'favour', in so far as it vests parental responsibility in the person with whom the child now wishes to live.

(B) Applying for court leave

Children's applications for leave under CA 1989, section 10(8), to proceed with applications for section 8 orders have received a mixed judicial response.[260] Indeed, this method of resolving family disputes very obviously challenges well-established perceptions about the appropriate roles of parent and child. There is a variety of misgivings about children's ability to litigate in this fashion. It can be particularly damaging for a child to become drawn into what may essentially be a dispute between the child's own parents over the child's future care.[261] Furthermore, those with a specialised knowledge of child development often doubt their ability to maintain a sense of proportion if they get involved in their parents' disputes, and fear that they will thereby gain a false idea of their own

---

[257] E.g. *Re HG (specific issue order: sterilisation)* [1993] 1 FLR 587: parents applied on behalf of their learning disabled daughter for leave under CA 1989, s 10(8) to obtain a specific issue order authorising her sterilisation. The parents were unable to obtain legal aid to bring the application themselves.

[258] E.g. *Re SC (a minor) (leave to seek residence order)* [1994] 1 FLR 96: the foster carer with whom the child, S, wished to live had been considered and rejected by the LA as a prospective foster parent for S and so was unlikely to satisfy the test under s. 10(9) for obtaining leave to apply for a residence order.

[259] E.g. *Re O (minors) (leave to seek residence order)* [1994] 1 FLR 172: a distant cousin of two boys aged 13 and 10 was persuaded by them to go to the magistrates' court to seek a residence order authorising them to stay with him rather than returning to their mother and their alcoholic stepfather.

[260] NB all children's applications for leave to apply for a s. 8 order must be initiated in the High Court. See *Practice Direction* [1993] 1 All ER 820.

[261] R. Emery *et al.* (2005).

importance.[262] In the more typical running away scenario, where the child has fallen out with *both* parents,[263] the parents may argue that strangers to the family are unaware of the dangers of allowing a young person's wishes to cloud adult perceptions of their safety.[264] Hopefully these days, the family might gain support from Cafcass in the context of a family assistance order to help them overcome the corrosive effects of the litigation.[265] Otherwise, the child's relationship with his or her parents may become irrevocably damaged.[266]

There is also the view that articulating the interests of family members in terms of rights, merely polarises domestic disputes and undermines family relationships. Even so, Minow is surely correct to claim that if rights need asserting, serious conflict already exists. The process of enforcing the right gives it expression and provides a method of resolution which would not be arrived at otherwise.[267] Family disputes will not be resolved by simply closing off the child's route to judicial assistance. In any event, a procedural restriction in the form of refusing a child leave under section 10(8) probably comes far too late to protect him or her from involvement in damaging litigation. Attempting to protect the child at this stage is tantamount to shutting the stable door after the horse has bolted. Refusing them leave despite their having shown sufficient determination to commence proceedings against their parents, risks alienating them entirely. Indeed, adolescence is a volatile time and a young person may respond to a court's refusal of leave by simply leaving home and community behind him.

Case law has clarified the fact that the leave application under section 10(8) is not governed by the paramountcy criterion.[268] Thus it is the court hearing the substantive application for a residence order after leave has been granted which must determine whether a residence order would be in the child's best interests, not the court hearing the leave application itself. Nevertheless, concerns over the wisdom of allowing children's applications for section 8 orders continue to

---

[262] See the child psychiatrist's doubts about the boy, N's, ability to instruct his own solicitor in *Re N (contact: minor seeking leave to defend and removal of guardian)* [2003] 1 FLR 652 at 658.

[263] E.g. *Re CE (section 37 direction)* [1995] 1 FLR 26: CE, a girl of 14, ran away to live with her boyfriend and his parents, against the wishes of her own parents. Her parents applied for a residence order, to determine where she should live. Their application was countered by CE herself instructing a solicitor to do the same on her own behalf.

[264] Per W. Utting (1997) paras. 8.48–8.53: some parents criticise social workers for listening to their children's views of unhappy home situations (whilst ignoring their own) without apparently realising the dangers of exploitative adults weaning the children away from their parents.

[265] CA 1989, s. 16.

[266] E.g. *Re C (family assistance order)* [1996] 1 FLR 424: the LA had insufficient resources to service such a family assistance order thus dashing Johnson J's hopes of thereby restoring the boy's poor relationship with his mother. The boy's relationship with his mother had been soured by his successful application for a residence order approving of his living with his uncle and aunt.

[267] M. Minow (1987) p. 1890.

[268] *Re SC (a minor) (leave to seek residence order)* [1994] 1 FLR 96; *Re C (residence: child's application for leave)* [1995] 1 FLR 927; *Re H (residence order: child's application for leave)* [2000] 1 FLR 780.

colour the way leave applications are themselves dealt with.[269] For example, refusing to allow S, a highly intelligent 12-year-old boy, to proceed with his application for a section 8 order is open to criticism on a number of fronts.[270] Despite concluding that S had 'sufficient understanding' for the purposes of the CA 1989, section 10(8),[271] Johnson J did not consider that his evidence would add anything to the evidence provided by S's father in support of his own application for a residence order.[272] Admittedly, the court would inevitably hear the evidence supporting these parents' respective applications for residence orders, whether or not S provided his own interpretation of the situation. Nevertheless, the legislative formula contained in section 10(8) does not obviously allow the judiciary to refuse leave merely because the child intends to give similar evidence to his parent. More seriously, such an approach discounted the boy's own perspectives. Nor would such a refusal enhance his respect for the judicial process given the legislation apparently providing him with a procedural right to give his side of the picture, once he had established sufficient maturity to do so. This approach adds an extra obstacle in the way of children seeking leave under section 10(8).[273] Although it now seems unlikely that children need persuade the court that their applications are likely to succeed,[274] they must convince the court that their prospects of success are not so remote as to be unsustainable;[275] they must have sufficient understanding to apply; and their own case must be different from that of any other party in the dispute.

Not all section 10(8) applications brought by children are interpreted so restrictively. Stuart-White J approached a teenager's application for leave very differently in *Re C (residence: child's application for leave).*[276] There, despite her father's claims that C lacked objectivity and insight, the court accepted evidence indicating that she had the understanding needed by section 10(8). She was aged 14, articulate, with very decided views of her own, and she was not content with these being presented for her by the court welfare officer. Stuart-White J appreciated that if he now refused her leave she would be unable to explain what her real views were.

The dearth of case law testing out these provisions may suggest that they are little used. Perhaps there are very few children troubled enough or bold enough to seek judicial assistance over establishing where they should live. When they

---

[269] E.g. *Re C (a minor) (leave to seek section 8 orders)* [1994] 1 FLR 26: a 15-year-old was refused leave to apply for a specific issue order to gain judicial authority to go to Bulgaria for a 2-week holiday with another family against her parents' wishes. Per Johnson J, a disagreement over a holiday was not sufficiently important to justify litigation.

[270] *Re H (residence order: child's application for leave)* [2000] 1 FLR 780.

[271] Perhaps predictable, given that the boy had been placed by an educational psychologist in the 99th intelligence percentile.

[272] *Re H (residence order: child's application for leave)* [2000] 1 FLR 780 at 783.

[273] C. Sawyer (1995) p. 205.

[274] *Re J (leave to issue application for residence order)* [2003] 1 FLR 114, per Thorpe LJ, at para. 18.

[275] *Re W (care proceedings: leave to apply)* [2004] EWHC 3342 (Fam), [2005] 2 FLR 468, per Sumner J, at [28], in the context of a s. 10(9) application.

[276] [1995] 1 FLR 927.

do, their way should be cleared rather than obstructed. Dame Margaret Booth strongly opposed children still being required to seek permission to commence proceedings because of the difficulties and delays such a process produces. She also saw no need to keep such applications within the confines of the High Court.[277] Regrettably her views were not acted on.

(C) Effect of a residence order obtained on a child's application

Having granted a child leave to apply for a section 8 order, the court must decide the substantive application; at that stage it must arbitrate between a child totally opposed to returning home and parents strongly opposed to the child staying away. But despite the media's predilection for the term, if the child is successful, the result achieved does not involve that child 'divorcing' his or her parents.[278] As Freeman points out, unlike the situation on divorce, which enables the parties to remarry with the possibility of an entirely new legal relationship, the child-parent legal relationship persists.[279] Indeed, the law has contrived an incoherent situation regarding children who obtain residence orders. By making section 8 orders available to them, it acknowledges their growing capacity for autonomy. The procedure enables them to force essentially private family disputes into the public arena, and provides them with an opportunity to ensure that their own viewpoint is heard. Their ability to initiate an application for a section 8 order to resolve a situation which they find unbearable, may prevent them from simply disappearing from view, in company with the many other young people who inhabit the streets of large cities.

In the event of a residence order being granted, its subject is left in a kind of legal limbo. Whilst the order remains in being, responsibility for all major decisions remain within the purview of adults – the child's present carers, but shared with his or her natural parents. The child has no greater legal status than before and remains under his or her parents' tutelage, despite their having been rejected by the child and the court as suitable carers. This must appear incomprehensible to child applicants, since it is intrinsically unlikely that a court will willingly grant a residence order on their application, unless their home circumstances have deteriorated very seriously. Given its drastic effect, few would advocate allowing young people here to obtain declarations of emancipation from their parents, as in some states of the US.[280] Nevertheless, the law's failure

---

[277] Children Act Sub-Committee of the Advisory Board on Family Law (2002) para. 12.6.
[278] The effect of the CA 1989, ss. 2(6) and 12(2) is that the adult acquiring a residence order shares parental responsibility for the child with the child's parents.
[279] M. Freeman (1996) p. 159.
[280] J. Fortin (2003) pp. 115–16: discusses the American system of emancipation. Once child petitioners in the US obtain declarations of emancipation, their parents have no further obligation to provide moral or financial support for them of any kind at all. See also C. Sanger and E. Willemsen (1992) pp. 250–8: a detailed history of California's emancipation laws.

then to provide children here with any legal acknowledgment of their changed situation seems unreasonable. Indeed, as Harries points out, it is anomalous that a child has the means of persuading a court to terminate her unmarried father's parental responsibility[281] but none of ensuring that an abusive but married father's parental responsibility is similarly terminated.[282] The legal restrictions which continue to affect such children, despite their having successfully obtained residence orders authorising them to live apart from their parents, are particularly inappropriate in the context of their being unable to initiate proceedings against their parents for financial support.[283]

(7) Children's right to parental money

The young person who becomes estranged from his or her parents and leaves home under the age of 18 is in an anomalous position. Even those who, through a residence order, have gained judicial permission to live with someone other than their parents, have no means of gaining complete financial independence without considerable assistance from some well-meaning adult. As noted above, they have very limited entitlement to social security benefits and will therefore suffer severe poverty, unless they can obtain reasonably paid employment or financial support from their parents or other carers.

A young person wishing to extract financial support from a parent will find that the legal principles governing the child-parent relationship produce a bizarre situation, even in the event of that parent being exceptionally wealthy. These principles reflect the assumption that if money is to be extracted, it should be done by an adult and not by the child. If parents are separated, it is, of course, perfectly feasible for one parent to apply for child maintenance for their son or daughter, from the other parent, through CMEC.[284] But a parent cannot do so unless the child has remained at home in the parent's care. So those who refuse to live with either parent are in an anomalous position. One might assume that an older child could independently initiate maintenance proceedings against a parent, particularly if the parent is extremely wealthy and the teenager is living in impoverished circumstances. But unlike Scottish law, which allows any child having attained the age of 12 to initiate an application under the Child Support Act 1991,[285] children in England and Wales are not provided with any direct method of doing so. This gap in the English law seems odd, particularly given Baroness Hale of

---

[281] CA 1989, s. 4(3)(b): a child can apply for an order terminating the father's parental responsibility provided he or she first obtains leave of the court.

[282] N. Harries (2000) p. 848.   [283] Discussed below.

[284] The Child Maintenance and Enforcement Commission; further discussed in Chapter 9.

[285] CSA (CSA) 1991, s. 7(1) enables children habitually resident in Scotland, having attained the age of 12 years to apply for a maintenance assessment under the Act; discussed in Chapter 9.

Richmond's conviction that children themselves have a civil right to be maintained by their parents and that this survives the child support legislation.[286]

The child support legislation only allows maintenance proceedings to be taken by an adult who is providing the child with a home and day-to-day care.[287] If an adult with whom an older child has taken refuge is prepared to take such a step, the child maintenance will obviously provide the child with much needed financial assistance. Furthermore, an adult who has first obtained a residence order authorising him or her to provide the child with a home, can then apply to the courts for an additional order, forcing the parents to assist even more generously with the child's maintenance.[288] Such a carer could, for example, apply to the courts to obtain an order against a child's wealthy parents for additional periodical payments by way of 'topping up payments'[289] and school fees.[290] But adults with whom a runaway takes refuge may simply decide that they do not want the unpleasantness of initiating either set of proceedings against the parents – in which case the child has no means at all of taking the matter into his or her own hands.

Only elderly 'children' over the age of 18 seem to attract legislative attention[291] in so far as they can utilise the legislative methods available to separating parents[292] and divorcing parents[293] to force their parents to maintain them. But applicants must justify such claims by reference to their educational or other special needs,[294] and can only apply at all if their parents are already separated[295] or have instituted matrimonial proceedings against each other.[296] It seems unsupportable that despite children being able to 'divorce their parents', there is no obvious way for a child under the age of 18 to initiate maintenance proceedings against such parents, unless those parents divorce each other.[297]

---

[286] *R (Kehoe) v. Secretary of State for Work and Pensions* [2005] UKHL 48, [2006] 1 AC 42 at [71] and [73].

[287] CSA 1991, s. 3(3). The person with care does not need to be a parent of the child, as long as he usually provides day-to-day care for the child and the child has his home with that person.

[288] I.e. under CA 1989, Sch. 1, para. 1, for an order outside the jurisdiction of the Child Support Agency, as authorised by CSA 1991, s. 8.

[289] CSA 1991, s. 8(6). The courts might consider such an order appropriate against a wealthy parent, in cases where the maximum child maintenance assessment is already in force.

[290] CSA 1991, s 8(7).   [291] M. Letts (2001) pp. 840–3.

[292] CA 1989, Sch. 1, para. 2(1). But under para. 2(3) a child can only apply on attaining the age of 18 if a periodical payments order has not been in force with respect to him prior to his attaining the age of 16. The teenager who has been the subject of a periodical payments order prior to attaining 16, can himself apply for a variation of that order, on attaining that age. N. Lowe and G. Douglas (2007) pp. 966–76.

[293] Matrimonial Causes Act 1973, s. 23(1).   [294] CA 1989, Sch. 1, para. 2(1).

[295] CA 1989, Sch. 1, para. 2 (4).

[296] Family Proceedings Rules 1991 (SI 1991/1247), r. 2.54: a child (if under the age of 18, he or she would require the assistance of an adult, as next friend) may apply, after obtaining leave to intervene as party to the parents' divorce proceedings, for a maintenance order under the Matrimonial Causes Act 1973, s. 23. E.g. *Downing v. Downing (Downing intervening)* [1976] Fam 288.

[297] The *Downing* route does not appear to be confined to 'children' over the age of 18.

This gap in the law suggests that the legislation is not designed for teenagers trying to sort out financial disputes with their parents themselves.

The type of family conflict which results in parents refusing to support their offspring might continue beyond the grave. A wealthy parent may die leaving a will excluding his or her estranged son or daughter entirely. The terms of the will could, of course, be disputed by the disinherited child (assisted by an adult next friend) bringing an application for reasonable provision out of the parents' estate.[298] Although the success of such an application is by no means a foregone conclusion, since it will depend on the court's view of the merits of the child's case, it seems unlikely that the court would refuse such an application entirely.[299] The dearth of relevant case law suggests that these situations rarely occur. If the parent dies intestate, the principles of law governing the distribution of his or her estate ensure that there is often little or nothing left from the estate for any issue after the surviving widow or widower takes their share.[300] Well-established case law demonstrates the inequities that such rules can produce.[301]

(8) Conclusion

Children and young people living in well-functioning families are not particularly affected by the confused hotchpotch of legal principles governing their gradual attainment of legal autonomy. These principles, though bewildering, do not impinge greatly on their everyday life. In the event of family life going badly wrong, however, the law's apparent liberality, in terms of recognising legal competence to obtain a residence order, is not accompanied by its providing a financial safety net for those who feel obliged to leave home.

Young people are not always sufficiently realistic to know that the prospect of gaining freedom from their parents is, in practice, often accompanied by considerable financial and emotional hardship. The destitution and despair experienced by minors of all ages who run away from home shows the extent to

---

[298] A child of married or unmarried parents can claim, under the Inheritance (Provision for Family and Dependants) Act 1975, a share in a deceased parent's estate on the basis that the will did not make reasonable provision for him or her. See A. Bainham (2005) pp. 362–8.

[299] See Inheritance (Provision for Family and Dependants) Act 1975, s. 3, for the factors relevant to such an application, such as the financial resources and needs of the applicant. The child's potential need for education and training would be particularly relevant.

[300] Under the Administration of Estates Act 1925, the surviving spouse is treated generously – i.e. a statutory legacy of the first £125,000 of the estate, and a life interest in half the residue. Although legally, the remaining half of the residue is held on trust for the children, the surviving spouse's statutory legacy may entirely drain the estate. See N. Lowe and G. Douglas (2007) pp. 1096–100.

[301] E.g., inter alia: *Sivyer v. Sivyer* [1967] 1 WLR 1482 (the intestate's entire estate went to his widow, who had been his second wife, with nothing left for his 13-year-old daughter by a previous marriage); *Re Collins (decd)* [1990] Fam 56 (the deceased died having obtained a decree nisi (but not a decree absolute) of divorce against her husband. Her husband was duly entitled to the whole of her estate on her intestacy, with nothing left for their son and her illegitimate daughter).

which English law is failing to live up to its international obligations under the CRC. The law neither protects their wage-earning nor provides them with appropriate welfare benefits when out of work. Indeed, this group of children slip through the net at every turn and simply do not obtain the special protection and support that should attend the legal status of minority. Overall, it appears that the law is attempting to have its cake and eat it. On the one hand it withholds an adult legal status from all children under the age of 18, on the basis that they require special protection. But on the other hand, it also assumes that the source of this protection will be provided by parents and withholds it from those children who inconveniently refuse to fit into family life.

BIBLIOGRAPHY

NB many of these publications can be obtained on the relevant organisation's website.

Allen, M. (2003) *Into the Mainstream: Care Leavers Entering Work, Education and Training*, Joseph Rowntree Foundation.

Anderson, A., Brooke, B., Doyle, A., Finn, D. and Moley, S. (2006) Research Report RR 736, *Understanding Young People in Jobs without Training*, DfES.

Bainham, A. (2005) *Children: The Modern Law*, Family Law.

Better Regulation Task Force (2004) *The Regulation of Child Employment*, Cabinet Office.

Broad, B. (2005) 'Young People Leaving Care: Implementing the Children (Leaving Care) Act 2000?' 19 *Children and Society* 371.

Bynner, J., Elias, P., McKnight, A., Huiqi, P. and Gaëlle, P. (2002) *Young People's Changing Routes to Independence*, Joseph Rowntree Foundation.

Bynner, J. and Londra, M. (2004) *The Impact of Government Policy on Social Exclusion Among Young People: A Review of the Literature for the Social Exclusion Unit in the Breaking the Cycle Series*, Office of the Deputy Prime Minister (ODPM).

Centre for Economic and Social Inclusion (2005) *A UK Youth Allowance? Inclusion Policy Paper 4*, www.cesi.org.uk.

Children Act Sub-Committee of the Advisory Board on Family Law (2002) *Making Contact Work*, Lord Chancellor's Department.

Children's Commissioner (2007) *Care Matters: Transforming the Lives of Children and Young People in Care: A Response by the Children's Commissioner*, Office of the Children's Commissioner.

Children's Society (2007) *Stepping Up: The Future of Runaways Services*, Children's Society.

Claridge, J. (updated by) (2008) *At What Age Can I? A Guide to Age-based Legislation*, The Children's Legal Centre.

Coles, B., Hutton, S., Bradshaw, J., Craig, G., Godfrey, C. and Johnson, J. (2002) *Literature Review of the Costs of Being 'Not in Education, Employment or Training' at Age 16–18*, Social Policy Research Unit, DfES Research Report No 347, DfES.

Committee on Economic, Social and Cultural Rights (2002) *Concluding Observations of the Committee on Economic, Social and Cultural Rights: United Kingdom of Great Britain and Northern Ireland – Dependent Territories 2002* E/C12/1/Add 79, Centre for Human Rights, Geneva.

Committee on the Rights of the Child (1995) *Concluding Observations of the Committee on the Rights of the Child: United Kingdom of Great Britain and Northern Ireland* CRC/C/15/Add 34, Centre for Human Rights, Geneva.

Committee on the Rights of the Child (2002) *Concluding Observations of the Committee on the Rights of the Child: United Kingdom of Great Britain and Northern Ireland* CRC/C/15/Add 188, Centre for Human Rights, Geneva.

Cowan, D, and Deardon, N. (2002) 'The Minor as (a) Subject: The Case of Housing Law' in Fionda, J. (ed.) *Legal Concepts of Childhood*, Hart Publishing.

Department for Children, Schools and Families (DCSF) (2007) *Raising Expectations: Staying in Education and Training Post-16. From Policy to Legislation*, DCSF.

Department for Children, Schools and Families (DCSF) (2008a) *Young Runaways Action Plan*, DCSF.

Department for Children, Schools and Families (DCSF) (2008b) Cm 7348, *Raising Expectations: enabling the system to deliver*, TSO.

Department for Children, Schools and Families (DCSF) (2008c) *Guidance on the Employment of Children*, DCSF.

Department for Children, Schools and Families (DCSF) (2008d) *Delivering 14–19 Reform: Next Steps*, DCSF

Department for Communities and Local Government (DCLG)/Department for Education and Skills/Department of Health (2006a) *Homelessness Code of Guidance for Local Authorities*, DCLG Publications.

Department for Communities and Local Government (DCLG) (2006b) *Homelessness Prevention: a Guide to Good Practice*, HMSO.

Department for Communities and Local Government (DCLG) (2006c) *Anti-social Behaviour Intensive Family Support Projects: An evaluation of six pioneering projects*, DCLG.

Department for Communities and Local Government (DCLG) (2007) *Tackling Youth Homelessness: Policy Briefing 18*, DCLG.

Department for Communities and Local Government (DCLG) and Department for Children, Schools and Families (DCSF) (2008) *Joint working between Housing and Children's Services*, DCLG.

Department for Education and Skills (DfES) (2005) Cm 6476, *14–19 Education and Skills*, HMSO.

Department for Education and Skills (DfES) (2006) *Youth Matters – Next Steps*, DfES Publications.

Department for Education and Skills (DfES) (2007a) Cm 7065, *Raising Expectations: Staying in Education and Training Post-16*, TSO.

Department for Education and Skills (DfES) (2007b) Cm 7137, *Care Matters: Time for Change*, TSO.

Department for Work and Pensions, *Jobseekers' Allowance for 16–17-year-olds Guidance: Severe Hardship Direction*, www.dwp.gov.uk/advisers/.

Department of Health (DH) (1999) *Me Survive Out There?: New Arrangements for Young People Living in and Leaving Care Consultation Paper*, Department of Health.

Department of Health (DH) (2001) *Children (Leaving Care) Act 2000: Regulations and Guidance*, Department of Health.

Department of Health (DH) (2002) *Children Missing from Care and from Home: a Guide to Good Practice*, Department of Health.

Electoral Commission (2004) *Age of Electoral Majority: Report and Recommendations*, The Electoral Commission.

Electoral Commission (2005) *Election 2005: Turnout, How Many, Who and Why?*, The Electoral Commission.

Emery, R., Otto, R. and O'Donohue, W. (2005) 'A Critical Assessment of Child Custody Evaluations: Limited Science and a Flawed System' 6 *Psychological Science in the Public Interest* 1.

Fortin, J. (2001) 'Children's Rights and the Use of Physical Force' 13 *Child and Family Law Quarterly* 243.

    (2003) *Children's Rights and the Developing Law*, LexisNexis Butterworths.

Freeman, M. (1996) 'Can Children Divorce Their Parents?' in Freeman, M. (ed.) *Divorce – Where Next*, Dartmouth.

HM Treasury, Department for Work and Pensions and Department for Education and Skills (2004) *Supporting Young People to Achieve: Towards a New Deal for Skills*, HMSO.

HM Treasury, Department for Work and Pensions and Department for Education and Skills (2005) *Supporting Young People to Achieve: the Government's Response to the Consultation*, HMSO.

HM Treasury (2007) Cm 7227, *Meeting the Aspirations of the British people: 2007 Pre-Budget Report and Comprehensive Spending Review*, TSO.

Hamilton, C. (2005) *Working With Young People: Legal Responsibility and Liability*, The Children's Legal Centre.

Hamilton, C. and Watt, B. (2004) 'The Employment of Children' 16 *Child and Family Law Quarterly* 135.

Harries, N. (2000) 'Removal of Parental Responsibility: The Child's Perspective' 30 *Family Law* 848.

Harris, N. (1992) 'Youth, Citizenship and Welfare' *Journal of Social Welfare and Family Law* 175.

Heyes, J. (2004) *Firms' Attitudes to Employing 16 and 17 Year Olds*, Report Prepared for the Low Pay Commission.

Hobbs, S., Anderson, S. and McKechnie, J. (2007) 'Protection of Children at Work' 232 *Childright* 9.

Howard League for Penal Reform (2006) *Chaos, Neglect and Abuse: Looking After Children Leaving Custody. the Duties of Local Authorities to Provide Children With Suitable Accommodation and Support Services.*

Jones, G. (2002) *The Youth Divide: Diverging Paths to Adulthood*, Joseph Rowntree Foundation.

Kennedy, H. (chairman) (2006) *Power to the People: The Report of Power: An Independent Inquiry into Britain's Democracy*, York Publishing.

Learning and Skills Council (2006) *EMA Extension Update Benefits Special*, www.lsc.gov.uk.

Letts, M. (2001) 'Children – The Continuing Duty to Maintain' 31 *Family Law* 839.

Low Pay Commission (2006) Cm 6759, *National Minimum Wage: Low Pay Commission Report 2006*, TSO.

Lowe, N. and Douglas, G. (2007) *Bromley's Family Law*, Oxford University Press.

MacDonald, R. and Marsh, J. (2005) *Disconnected Youth? Growing up in Britain's Poor Neighbourhoods*, Palgrave Macmillan.

Minow, M. (1987) 'Interpreting Rights: An Essay for Robert Cover' 96 *Yale Law Journal* 1860.

Morgan, J. (2000) '*Kingston upon Thames Borough Council v Prince*: "Children are people too"' 12 *Child and Family Law Quarterly* 65.

Morgan, R., Children's Rights Director for England (2006a) *Running Away: A Children's Views Report*, Commission for Social Care Inspection.

(2006b) *Young People's Views on Leaving Care*, Commission for Social Care Inspection.

Newiss, G. (1999) *Missing Presumed ...? The Police Response to Missing Persons*, Police Research Series Paper 114, Home Office.

Office of the Deputy Prime Minister (2004a) *Homelessness Statistics September 2004 and Delivering on the Positive Outcomes*, Policy Briefing 10, Homelessness and Housing Support Directorate.

Office of the Deputy Prime Minister (2004b) *Local Authorities' Homelessness Strategies: Evaluation and Good Practice Guide*, Housing Quality Network Services, ODPM Publications.

Office of the Deputy Prime Minister (2006) *Statutory Homelessness: Supplementary Report 2004/5*, ODPM Publications.

Pleace, N. and Fitzpatrick, S. (2004) *Centrepoint Youth Homelessness index*, Centrepoint.

Pleace, N., Fitzpatrick, S., Johnsen, S., Quilgars, D. and Sanderson, D. (2008) *Statutory Homelessness in England: The Experience of Families and 16–17 Year Olds*, Department for Communities and Local Government.

Quilgars, D., Johnsen, S. and Pleace, N. (2008) *Youth Homelessness in the UK: A Decade of Progress?*, Joseph Rowntree Foundation.

Randall, G. and Brown, S. (2001) *Trouble at Home: Family Conflict, Young People and Homelessness*, Crisis.

Rees, G. and Lee, J. (2005) *Still Running II: Findings from the Second National Survey of Young Runaways*, The Children's Society.

Rees, G., Franks, M., Raws, P. and Medforth, R. (2005) *Responding to Young Runaways: An Evaluation of 19 Projects, 2003 to 2004*, DfES Research Report RR 634, Children's Society/University of York.

Sanger, C. and Willemsen, E. (1992) 'Minor Changes: Emancipating Children in Modern Times' 25 *University of Michigan Journal of Law Reform* 239.

Sawyer, C. (1995) 'The Competence of Children to Participate in Family Proceedings' 7 *Child and Family Law Quarterly* 180.

Shelter (2005a) *Young People and Homelessness*, Shelter.

(2005b) *More Priority Needed: The Impact of Legislative Change on Young Homeless People's Access to Housing and Support*, Shelter.

(2006) *How Registered Social Landlords Can Work With Young People: A Good Practice Guide*, Shelter.

Social Exclusion Unit (SEU) (1999a) Cm 4405, *Bridging the Gap: New Opportunities for 16–18 Year Olds Not in Education, Employment or Training*, Cabinet Office.

Social Exclusion Unit (SEU), (1999b) Cm 4342, *Teenage Pregnancy*, Cabinet Office.

Social Exclusion Unit (SEU) (2000) *Report of Policy Action Team 12; Young People*, Cabinet Office.

Social Exclusion Unit (SEU) (2002) *Young Runaways*, Cabinet Office.

Social Exclusion Unit (SEU) (2004) *Breaking the Cycle: Taking Stock of Progress and Priorities for the Future*, Office of the Deputy Prime Minister.

Social Exclusion Unit (SEU) (2005) *Transitions: Young Adults with Complex Needs*, Office of the Deputy Prime Minister.

Stack, N. and McKechnie, J. (2002) 'Working Children' in Goldson, B., Lavalette, M. and McKechnie, J. *Children, Welfare and the State*, Sage.

Stein, M. (2005), 'Young People Leaving Care: Poverty Across the Life Course' in Preston, G. (ed.) *At Greatest Risk: The Children Most Likely to be Poor*, Child Poverty Action Group.

UNICEF, Innocenti Research Centre (2007) *Child Poverty in Perspective: An Overview of Child Well-Being in Rich Countries*, Innocenti Report Card 7, UNICEF.

Unison (2005) *One Year on: 16 and 17 Year Olds and the Minimum Wage*, Submission to the Low Pay Commission, Unison.

Utting, W. (1997) *People Like Us: The Report of the Review of the Safeguards For Children Living Away From Home*, The Stationery Office.

Wade, J. and Dixon, J. (2006) 'Making a Home, Finding a Job: Investigating Early Housing and Employment Outcomes for Young People Leaving Care' 11 *Child and Family Social Work* 199.

Chapter 5

Adolescent decision-making and health care

Introduction

It is no accident that many of the boundaries to adolescent legal independence have been mapped out by the courts in the context of health care. Medical treatment often involves an invasion of bodily and personal privacy which would be intolerable if patients had no right to control its delivery. International human rights law recognises that an important aspect of an adult's right to self-determination includes the right to decide what should happen to his own body.[1] Long before the Human Rights Act (HRA) 1998 was implemented, the common law had emphasised that adult patients enjoy such a right.[2] Precisely the same reasoning can be applied to adolescents. Although young children, particularly if they are unwell, might not be equal to reaching decisions on their medical treatment,[3] adolescents are different. They are not only fast reaching maturity, but society has an interest in ensuring that they take responsibility for decision-making over important aspects of their lives. Furthermore, they are being taught to value their status as rights-holders and can justifiably argue that they, like adults, have the right to make choices over their medical treatment, if competent to do so.

This chapter is divided into two sections. It first assesses the extent to which the general principles of law recognise an adolescent's capacity to consent to and refuse medical treatment. It then goes on to consider the application of these general principles in the context of two specific areas of decision-making

---

[1] E.g. inter alia: *YF v. Turkey* (2004) 39 EHRR 34 at [33]: Art. 8 of the European Convention for the Protection of Human Rights and Fundamental Freedoms (1950) (ECHR) protects against compulsory medical intervention, even if that intervention is of minor importance. 'A person's body concerns the most intimate aspect of one's private life'; *Storck v. Germany* (2006) 43 EHRR 6: an adult's rights to liberty under Art. 5 ECHR had been infringed by her being detained in a psychiatric clinic against her will on her father's authorisation alone, without a court order.

[2] See inter alia: *Re F (mental patient: sterilisation)* [1990] 2 AC 1, per Lord Goff, at 72. There 'is the fundamental principle, long established, that every person's body is inviolate'. See also *Sidaway v. Board of Governors of the Bethlem Royal Hospital and the Maudsley Hospital* [1985] AC 871, per Lord Scarman, at 882 and *Re B (adult: refusal of medical treatment)* [2002] EWHC 429 (Fam), [2002] 2 All ER 449, per Dame Elizabeth Butler-Sloss P, at [94] and [100].

[3] See Chapter 10 for a discussion of the medical treatment of children too young to consent for themselves.

which cause particular difficulties: the control of fertility and the treatment of mentally disturbed young people.

Section A Adolescent decision-making – the general principles

(1) Adolescents' legal right to consent to medical treatment

(A) Legal competence to consent – adolescents under 16

Until the mid-1980s, the traditional legal approach was to assume that parents were the appropriate people to determine what happened to their children's bodies when receiving medical treatment. Consequently, parents were automatically treated by the medical profession as proxy consent-givers. This was convenient, in so far as doctors could avoid asking their young patients their own views on the matter. But latterly, the needs of society have changed and the law has adapted its approach to adolescents. It now acknowledges that, as a group, they are approaching mental and physical maturity. Thus the Family Law Reform Act (FLRA) 1969, section 8(1) established that on attaining the age of 16, adolescents could be assumed to have sufficient capacity to make choices over their own health care.[4] Nevertheless, to ignore the decision-making capacities of adolescents under the age of 16 might be counter-productive, given the increase in their sexual activity.[5] The decision of the House of Lords in *Gillick v. West Norfolk and Wisbech Area Health Authority*[6] signified a much more liberal approach to this younger age group. Although it specifically dealt with the issue of adolescent competence to consent to contraceptive advice and treatment, the principles it established have a general application to all forms of medical treatment and assistance. It introduced the idea that adolescents' rights over their own bodies grow with their competence to understand the implications of the procedure involved. As Feldman has pointed out, this approach is 'consistent with the theory that autonomy is the value at the root of the moral justification of freedom: the greater one's capacity to exercise a choice in an informed way, the stronger is one's claim to be free to exercise it'.[7]

English law, as delineated by *Gillick*, accepts that minors under the age of 16 have the right to consent on their own behalf to a variety of medical procedures, as long as they fully understand what is involved. The House of Lords emphatically rejected Mrs Gillick's claim that section 8(1)[8] of the FLRA 1969 implicitly precluded adolescents under the age of 16 from giving a valid consent to medical treatment. Indeed, they asserted that section 8(3) had left intact the

---

[4] FLRA 1969, s. 8(1): 'The consent of a minor who has attained the age of sixteen years to any surgical, medical or dental treatment which, in the absence of consent, would constitute a trespass to his person, shall be as effective as it would be if he were of full age; and where a minor has by virtue of this section given an effective consent to any treatment it shall not be necessary to obtain any consent for it from his parent or guardian.' Discussed further below.

[5] Discussed below.   [6] [1986] AC 112; also discussed in Chapter 3.

[7] D. Feldman (2002) p. 287.   [8] Fn 4 above.

existing principles of common law which allow adolescents under 16 to consent to whatever procedures they can adequately comprehend.[9]

According to Lord Fraser:

> It seems to me verging on the absurd to suggest that a girl or a boy aged 15 could not effectively consent, for example, to have a medical examination of some trivial injury to his body or even to have a broken arm set. Of course the consent of the parents should normally be asked, but they may not be immediately available. Provided the patient, whether a boy or a girl, is capable of understanding what is proposed, and of expressing his or her own wishes, I see no good reason for holding that he or she lacks the capacity to express them validly and effectively and to authorise the medical man to make the examination or give the treatment which he advises.[10]

Similarly, Lord Scarman considered that parents lost the right to consent to medical procedures on behalf of their children:

> [the] parental right yields to the child's right to make his own decisions when he reaches a sufficient understanding and intelligence to be capable of making up his own mind on the matter requiring decision.[11]

He stressed, however, that it would be 'a question of fact whether a child seeking advice has sufficient understanding of what is involved to give a consent valid in law'.[12]

Although there is an expanding body of case law establishing the level of competence required of an adolescent who wishes to reject much needed medical treatment,[13] the *Gillick* decision remains authoritative so far as consent to treatment is concerned. Lord Scarman's *Gillick* competence formula, to all intents and purposes, provides an excellent method whereby doctors can identify those teenage patients who are sufficiently mature to reach responsible decisions for themselves. It allows a doctor to adopt a far more intelligent approach to the concept of capacity than one merely relying on age or even on the research evidence on children's cognitive growth.[14] The test is a functional one – whether the minor has capacity to comprehend, and therefore consent to, the procedure depends on the gravity of what is proposed. Even so, the difficulty implicit in the test for assessing *Gillick* competence is its deceptive simplicity. Indeed, it was only in the context of the provision of contraceptive advice and treatment that such guidance was developed further.[15] In more general medical contexts, *Gillick* left doctors with no clear guidelines over the circumstances in which they can accept that an adolescent can consent to a particular procedure without involving his or her parents.[16]

Nevertheless, and despite variations in medical practice, *Gillick* appears to have influenced practice in so far as young patients are sometimes being given

---

[9] Lord Fraser [1986] AC 112 at 167 and Lord Scarman [1986] AC 112 at 182.
[10] [1986] AC 112 at 169.   [11] Ibid. at 186.   [12] Ibid. at 189.   [13] Discussed below.
[14] Discussed in Chapter 3.   [15] Discussed below.   [16] M. Brazier and C. Bridge (1996) pp. 91–2.

considerable responsibility for reaching medical decisions on their own behalf at relatively early ages.[17] But the uncertainty underlying the concept of *Gillick* competence undoubtedly weakens its practical usefulness. It places even the most mature adolescent entirely in the hands of the medical profession. The doctor holds considerable power over his young patients. It is he who occupies a gate-keeping position, so far as treatment is concerned. He must decide not only whether treatment is medically indicated, but also whether his patient is competent to consent to the procedure. The fact that such decisions must be taken on a case-by-case basis, according to the circumstances of each patient and each procedure, produces uncertainty for the adolescent patient. A teenage girl may, for example, be desperately anxious to undergo extensive plastic surgery. If satisfied that the procedure is in her best medical interests and that she can adequately understand all the issues involved, in terms of length of treatment, pain and suffering and the success rate, the decision in *Gillick* allows the doctor to proceed with treatment without involving her parents at all. They have no legal right of veto and she, like any adult patient capable of giving consent to treatment, is normally entitled to medical confidentiality, unless she agrees to disclosure.[18] Consequently, her parents might not discover the treatment until after it has occurred. But the *Gillick* test's lack of clarity implicitly encourages a doctor to refuse to go ahead with any treatment for an adolescent which is not trivial or life-saving, unless he can involve the parents. In this scenario, he knows that if they violently object to his having carried out the plastic surgery, they might challenge his assessment of their daughter's legal capacity to consent, by suing in tort. If the court finds her *Gillick* incompetent, he would be liable on an action in battery, although it is unlikely that the damages would be more than nominal. Such uncertainty may therefore reinforce an over-protective attitude towards adolescents, which might be appropriate if they are ill and incapable of comprehending the implications of the procedure under consideration, but quite inappropriate if they are perfectly capable of making up their own minds.

Specialised guidance produced for medical practitioners has sought to amplify the *Gillick* test by introducing more practical considerations.[19] Although mostly useful, at times it places an unrealistic emphasis on the ability of a child or young person to reach a decision over treatment 'free from undue external influences'.[20] Thus the British Medical Association (BMA) warns doctors that young people can be strongly influenced by their parents over treatment options, and suggests that although parents will often be asked for advice by a child patient, it is important that the ultimate decision is the 'person's own independent choice'.[21] This crucial issue was not touched on by their Lordships in their *Gillick* decision. Nevertheless, guidance of this kind

---

[17] K. Stalker *et al.* (2003).   [18] Discussed below.
[19] BMA (2001), esp. ch. 5; BMA (2004); GMC (2007), esp. paras. 20–2.
[20] BMA (2001) p. 93.   [21] Ibid. at p. 94.

withholds competence from any children brought up by strongly religious parents, such as Jehovah's Witnesses, since they will inevitably adopt their parents' faith. It would be virtually impossible for such a child, even when an adolescent, to adopt his or her 'own independent choice'.

Many of the limitations of the *Gillick* test of medical competence could be remedied by reference to the developing legal principles governing adult capacity to consent to medical procedures. Refinements were introduced first by case law[22] and later by legislation, in the context of adult *in*capacity. The test of incapacity set out by the Mental Capacity Act (MCA) 2005 might usefully be adopted to inform assessments of *Gillick* competence in a medical context.[23] Thus an adolescent's inability to understand the information relevant to the decision, to retain the information, to use or weigh that information as part of the decision-making process or to communicate that decision (by talking, signing or by other means) would connote an inability to consent to medical treatment;[24] similarly the reverse should follow regarding competence to consent. Equally helpful is the additional advice regarding assessments of incompetence. Thus the MCA 2005 stresses that a person should not be treated as incompetent in the absence of practicable help to assist him to reach a decision,[25] nor simply because he has reached an unwise decision,[26] nor because he can only retain information relevant to the decision for short periods only.[27] The value of these additional refinements is that they would make the *Gillick* competence formula more workable. With their assistance, doctors might be more ready to rely on their own assessments of adolescent competence without always feeling obliged to seek additional consent from parents.

(B) Legal competence to consent – adolescents over 16

The research evidence on developmental growth suggests that later adolescence brings a more developed ability to deal with major decisions over health care. By this time adolescents are more able to identify a range of risks and benefits,

[22] *Re C (refusal of treatment)* [1994] 1 FLR 31, per Thorpe J, at 33. The test (as later refined by Butler-Sloss LJ, in *Re MB (medical treatment)* [1997] 2 FLR 426 at 437) requires an ability to comprehend and retain treatment information relevant to the decision, especially as to the likely consequences of having or not having the treatment in question, to use it, and to weigh it in the balance when arriving at a decision. This test of capacity influenced the test of *in*capacity adopted by the Mental Capacity Act (MCA) 2005, s. 3(1).

[23] The MCA 2005 primarily governs adult decision-making (including medical decision making) but also governs decision-making on behalf of minors aged between 16 and 18 whose incapacity to reach decisions for themselves is attributable to an impairment of or a disturbance in the functioning of his or her mind or brain; discussed further below.

[24] MCA 2005, s. 3(1).

[25] MCA 2005, s. 1(3). See also s. 3(2) and (4) which stress that the person should be given an explanation of the information relevant to the decision in a way appropriate to his circumstances (e.g. using simple language or visual aids), including information about the reasonably foreseeable consequences of deciding one way or the other or of failing to decide.

[26] MCA 2005, s. 1(4).   [27] MCA 2005, s. 3(3).

foresee the consequences of alternatives and gauge the credibility of information provided by experts.[28] Section 8(1) of the FLRA 1969 recognises this by assuming that on attaining the age of 16, but before they attain 18 (the age of majority), young people have the capacity and therefore the legal right to consent on their own behalf to 'any surgical, medical or dental treatment'.[29] Thus whilst the decision in *Gillick*[30] indicated that the law should recognise the decision-making rights of adolescents below that age, but on a case-by-case basis, section 8 introduces the presumption that all adolescents over that age are competent to consent for themselves.

The consent rights of the adolescent over the age of 16 are nevertheless more limited than those of an adult patient simply because the scope of section 8 is relatively narrow. It only authorises adolescents over the age of 16 to consent to surgical, medical or dental treatment and diagnostic procedures. Blood and organ donations are therefore outside the scope of section 8. Nevertheless, in Lord Donaldson's view, the donation of blood would not present problems, since '"a *Gillick* competent" minor of any age would be able to give consent [to giving blood] under the common law'.[31] But he warned, organ donations are quite different. They are not only excluded from the scope of section 8 but, in his view, it would be 'highly improbable' that an adolescent under the age of 18 wishing to become an organ donor could be *Gillick* competent 'in the context of so serious a procedure which could not benefit the minor'.[32] That being the case, a doctor should not proceed with an organ transplant without securing the consent of a parent on the adolescent's behalf.[33]

There is, of course, nothing to prevent adolescents over the age of 16 consenting to any other procedure outside the section's scope, as long as they are *Gillick* competent. But in those circumstances, the adolescent's competence is not presumed and must be assessed, as for the under 16-year-old, on a case-by-case basis, depending on the seriousness of the procedure involved. If a 16-year-old is deemed to be *Gillick* incompetent, then treatment in his or her best interests can be authorised by anyone with parental responsibility over him or her, on the authority of *Gillick*[34] itself. It should be noted, however, that in many cases, adolescents over the age of 16 considered to be *Gillick* incompetent, will *also* be deemed to lack capacity by the MCA 2005. This will almost certainly be the case if the adolescent's lack of capacity is attributable to an impairment of or a disturbance in the functioning of his or her mind or brain.[35] Although in such circumstances, the medical team must still gain authority to treat such a patient from his or her parents,[36] they can only consent to the treatment if it is

---

[28] Discussed in Chapter 3.   [29] See fn 4 above.

[30] [1986] AC 112, per Lord Scarman, at 184.   [31] Ibid.   [32] Ibid.

[33] Ibid at 79. Medical practitioners in the UK do not in practice countenance organ donation by minors; discussed in Chapter 10.

[34] [1986] AC 112, per Lord Scarman, at 184.   [35] MCA 2005, s. 2(1) and DCA (2007) para. 12.13.

[36] Unless there is a disagreement over this, in which case a decision may be sought from the Court of Protection.

deemed to be in the patient's best interests, as determined by the MCA 2005[37] and its accompanying Code of Practice.[38] Consequently, the team should familiarise themselves with these provisions. But, as discussed below, there may be situations where a young patient is unable to make a decision for some other reason, for example, because they are overwhelmed by the implications of the decision.[39] Since the MCA 2005 does not then govern the situation, the parents (or those with parental responsibility for the child) must decide for themselves what is in their son or daughter's best interests, assisted by the medical team.[40]

(2) Adolescents' legal rights to refuse medical treatment

(A) Legal competence to refuse life-saving treatment

The decision in *Gillick* appeared to give young patients the right to martyr themselves by refusing life-saving medical treatment, providing they possessed sufficient maturity to be considered *Gillick* competent. The judiciary, however, found it impossible to stand aside and allow young patients to endanger their lives in such a way. Subsequent case law preserved society's right to override their more dangerous choices.[41] Despite this, the courts have explored what level of competence an adolescent *theoretically* requires in order to refuse treatment. A finding that a young patient has the legal capacity to refuse consent to the treatment under consideration results in the court giving an increased weight to his or her views, whilst recalling that they are not determinative.[42] But as Downie comments:

> the application of the principle in *Re W (a minor) (medical treatment)*[43] that the court can always override a refusal of consent even by a *Gillick* competent minor, means that the assessment of his competence is almost a pretence.[44]

Nevertheless, if, as argued below, Articles 3, 5 and 8 of the ECHR provide adolescents with protection from being forced to have medical treatment against their will, their competence to refuse consent becomes far more relevant than hitherto. A court might hesitate before asserting its own duty to preserve the life of a resisting patient if it considers that the patient is legally capable of making up his or her own mind over the matter. On this basis, the case law analysing an adolescent's competence to refuse treatment is of considerable current interest. This issue has arisen in the context of two kinds of cases; those

---

[37] MCA 2005, s. 4.   [38] DCA (2007), chs. 4 and 12. See esp. para. 12.16.   [39] Ibid. at para. 12.13.
[40] NB DH (2008) para. 36.9–36.15: parents' right to consent to medical treatment is restricted to decision-making within the 'zone of parental control'; discussed further below.
[41] See *Re R (a minor) (wardship: consent to treatment)* [1992] Fam 11 and *Re W (a minor) (medical treatment: court's jurisdiction)* [1993] Fam 64, discussed below. The concept of overriding the wishes of adolescents is discussed at a more theoretical level in Chapter 1, and more generally in Chapter 3, regarding adolescents and their legal relationship with their parents.
[42] Per Wall J in *Re C (detention: medical treatment)* [1997] 2 FLR 180 at 195.
[43] [1993] Fam 64.   [44] A. Downie (1999) p. 819.

involving mentally disturbed adolescents and those opposed to treatment on religious grounds.

On the face of it, there seems no logical reason why any adolescent patient should need a higher level of competence to refuse to undergo treatment than to consent to it. Although the courts may adopt similar criteria to those used when assessing an adult's competence,[45] in most cases they require much higher levels of competence from uncooperative adolescents – thereby ensuring that they receive the medical treatment deemed essential to safeguard their health. In other words, the courts simply adjust the level of competence required, in the light of the implications of the minor's decision. The more dangerous the outcome, the higher is the competence required. The outcome in *Re R (a minor) (wardship: medical treatment)*[46] was that, without treatment, R would again lapse into a dangerously psychotic state. Lord Donaldson MR did not consider her to be *Gillick* competent. To qualify he demanded:

> not merely an ability to understand the nature of the proposed treatment ... but a full understanding and appreciation of the consequences both of the treatment in terms of intended and possible side effects and, equally important, the anticipated consequences of a failure to treat.[47]

Such a test demands a higher threshold than the test of competence established by case law for mentally disordered adults.[48] It also remains more demanding than that required by the MCA 2005,[49] which stresses that an unwise decision does not connote incapacity.[50] Lord Donaldson's test of competence in *Re R* becomes even more onerous when combined with his other demand that *Gillick* competence must be a permanent aspect of an adolescent's development and not a form of competence which exists on some days and not on others. Since the adolescent in *Re R* was subject to 'fluctuating mental disability', being not only *Gillick* 'incompetent', but 'sectionable' on some days,[51] she could not satisfy the requirements of *Gillick* competence.[52] Given that the state of mind of many mentally disturbed adolescents fluctuates from day to day, this requirement is particularly demanding.

---

[45] E.g. Wall J in *Re C (detention: medical treatment)* [1997] 2 FLR 180 at 195, assessed the competence of C, a severely anorexic girl of 16, using the criteria established for adult patients by Thorpe J in *Re C (refusal of treatment)* [1994] 1 FLR 31 at 33. I.e. the patient should have an ability to comprehend and retain treatment information, believe it and weigh it in the balance to arrive at a decision. In his view, C lacked competence due to her inability to consider the long-term impact of refusing treatment for her anorexia.

[46] [1992] Fam 11.　　[47] Ibid. at 26.

[48] E.g. *Re JT (adult: refusal of medical treatment)* [1998] 1 FLR 48: the High Court refused to overrule a woman patient's refusal to undergo dialysis for renal failure, despite her learning difficulties and extremely severe behavioural disturbance, considering her capable of refusing agreement to treatment under the test in *Re C (refusal of medical treatment)* [1994] 1 FLR 31 (see fn 22 above).

[49] Discussed above.　　[50] MCA 2005, s. 1(4).

[51] I.e. liable to compulsory admission under the Mental Health Act (MHA) 1983, s. 2 or 3.

[52] Per Lord Donaldson MR [1992] Fam 11 at 26.

A similar approach was developed for young Jehovah's Witness patients, who, regardless of age, normally refuse treatment involving the use of blood products. In a series of cases, the courts found it impossible to stand aside and allow such patients to bring about their own deaths. So, instead, they simply decided that the adolescent involved had insufficient capacity to be *Gillick* competent, that therefore his or her refusal could be ignored and a decision substituted by the court, in the minor's best interests. A finding of *Gillick incompetence* became readily available, given the courts' insistence on the patient not only understanding his or her impending death but also possessing 'a greater understanding of the manner of the death and pain and the distress'.[53] *Re E (a minor) (wardship: medical treatment)*,[54] remains the most well known of these cases, possibly because of its tragic sequel.[55] Although he was of sufficient intelligence to be able to take decisions about his own well-being, the court overrode the refusal of a 16-year-old Jehovah's Witness to receive blood transfusion treatment for his leukaemia. Ward J did not deem him to be *Gillick* competent because there was a range of decisions facing him outside his full comprehension; furthermore he lacked a full understanding of the implications of refusing treatment and the manner of his own death. Subsequent courts confronted by young uncooperative Jehovah's Witness patients[56] were similarly reluctant to allow 'an infant to martyr himself'.[57] But as critics have pointed out, it seems particularly inappropriate to judge adolescent patients incapable of comprehending the detailed manner of their death, when information about this is deliberately withheld from them by their doctors because of its distressing nature.[58] Indeed, neither case law[59] nor legislation[60] allows medical teams to overrule adults' refusal to undergo treatment for similar reasons. The MCA 2005 makes it clear that a person's capacity for decision-making should only be determined once he has been given 'the information relevant to the decision'.[61]

---

[53] *Re E (a minor) (wardship: medical treatment)* [1993] 1 FLR 386, per Ward J, at 394.   [54] Ibid.

[55] Although the 16-year-old patient was forced to undergo treatment, tragically, when he reached the age of 18, he exercised his right as an adult to refuse treatment and died. This sequel to the decision was revealed in *Re S (a minor) (consent to medical treatment)* [1994] 2 FLR 1065.

[56] *Re S (a minor) (consent to medical treatment)* [1994] 2 FLR 1065: a 15½-year-old Jehovah's Witness patient suffering from thalassaemia virtually since birth, was kept alive by monthly blood transfusions and daily injections. The court authorised continued treatment despite her expressed wish to the contrary. See also *Re L (medical treatment: Gillick competency)* [1999] 2 FCR 524: a deeply religious 14-year-old Jehovah's Witness patient suffered life-threatening scalds sustained whilst bathing. The court authorised blood transfusion treatment alongside the required surgical intervention, despite her strong opposition.

[57] [1993] 1 FLR 386, per Ward J, at 394.

[58] As in *Re E (a minor) (wardship: medical treatment)* [1993] 1 FLR 386 and *Re L (Medical treatment: Gillick competency)* [1999] 2 FCR 524. See C. McCafferty (1999).

[59] E.g. *Re C (refusal of medical treatment)* [1994] 1 FLR 31: the court respected the right of a paranoid schizophrenic to refuse an amputation of his leg to cure potentially fatal gangrene. There was no indication that he fully realised the implications which lay before him as to the process of dying.

[60] MCA 2005.   [61] MCA 2005, s. 3(1)(a).

Despite objections to the *Gillick* competence test being adjusted in this way, jurisprudential theory allows us to argue that seriously ill adolescents have a right to greater protection than adult patients. This approach is in tune with an interest theory of rights which affirms the part to be played by paternalism to protect future choice.[62] Nevertheless, it remains questionable whether the levels of legal competence should be adjusted so blatantly. Where an adolescent refuses to undergo life-saving treatment and parental consent is not available, it may be more honest to accept that the patient is *Gillick* competent, and then to override his or her wishes.[63] This approach does not demean the minor by suggesting that his or her emotional maturity is fundamentally flawed. The court can legitimately argue that society has an interest in protecting under-age minors, irrespective of their legal competence until they attain their majority.

(B) Overriding an adolescent's refusal to be treated

Lord Scarman, in his following words, implied that *Gillick* competence carries the right both to refuse and consent to medical treatment:

> In the light of the foregoing I would hold that as a matter of law the parental right to determine *whether or not* their minor child below the age of 16 will have medical treatment terminates if and when the child achieves a sufficient understanding and intelligence to enable him or her to understand fully what is proposed.[64]

But, as the Court of Appeal in *Re R (a minor) (wardship: medical treatment)*[65] and *Re W (a minor) (medical treatment: court's jurisdiction)*[66] pointed out, such a statement was not made in the context of a desperately ill minor intent on rejecting essential medical treatment. Lord Donaldson MR argued that Lord Scarman had never intended to suggest that parents lost their right to consent to their child's treatment; but if Lord Scarman had so intended, he considered such a view to have been obiter.[67] According to the Court of Appeal in these later decisions, a medical team can obtain legal authority to treat a dissenting minor patient, whatever his or her age or legal competence, from anyone with parental responsibility (normally parents), or from the court itself.[68] The Court of Appeal emphasised that the courts would normally assume that it is in the best interests of a *Gillick* competent child to respect his wishes:

> and not lightly override its decision on such a personal matter as medical treatment, all the more so if that treatment is invasive.[69]

---

[62] Discussed in Chapter 1.

[63] E.g. *Re M (medical treatment: consent)* [1999] 2 FLR 1097 and *Re P (medical treatment: best interests)* [2003] EWHC 2327 (Fam), [2004] 2 FLR 1117.

[64] *Gillick v. West Norfolk and Wisbech Area Health Authority* [1986] AC 112 at 188–9, emphasis added.

[65] [1992] Fam 11.   [66] [1993] Fam 64.

[67] *Re R (a minor) (wardship: medical treatment)* [1992] Fam 11 at 23–24 and *Re W (a minor) (medical treatment: court's jurisdiction)* [1993] Fam 64 at 76.

[68] The High Court deals with such requests in the exercise of its inherent jurisdiction.

[69] *Re W (a minor) (medical treatment: court's jurisdiction)* [1993] Fam 64, per Balcombe LJ, at 88.

Despite these sentiments, the court felt obliged to override the strong objections of the seriously ill teenage patients in *Re R* and *Re W*, to ensure that they received the treatment they needed. In *Re R*, the court authorised compulsory treatment for R, a 15-year-old, in the form of anti-psychotic drugs for her increasingly paranoid and disturbed behaviour. In *Re W*, the patient was so dangerously ill with anorexia that the court considered it essential to override her refusal of treatment, despite her being over 16 and apparently being of sufficient understanding to make an informed decision.[70]

These two Court of Appeal decisions contrived a situation whereby legal authority for such treatment could readily be obtained from the courts[71] or from well-intentioned parents desperate to save the life of their son or daughter. They produced great confusion, in that the legal principles depend entirely on whether an adolescent refuses to undergo medical treatment, or consents, even when the proposed treatment is precisely the same.[72] According to *Gillick*, a minor patient of any age can consent to treatment, without parental involvement and however dangerous that treatment may be, as long as he or she passes the *Gillick* competence test. But according to the principles explored in *Re R* and more fully developed in *Re W*, a young patient's refusal to undergo treatment can be overridden, if legal authorisation can be secured from his or her parents or from the court. As Brazier and Bridge comment, according to this case law 'the right to be wrong applies only where minors say yes to treatment'.[73]

This exercise in paternalism on the part of the Court of Appeal was not surprising, given that a court may find it impossible to conclude that it is in the child's best interests to be allowed to die.[74] Balcombe LJ considered that a child's refusal should be overridden to avoid 'death or severe permanent injury'.[75] In such circumstances it is obviously extremely tempting for a court to authorise the treatment available. As Nolan LJ stated in *Re W (a minor) (medical treatment: courts' jurisdiction)*:

> In general terms, however, the present state of the law is that an individual who has reached the age of 18 is free to do with his life what he wishes, but it

---

[70] Ibid. at 80: Lord Donaldson MR doubted the correctness of Thorpe J's view (at first instance) that, despite her anorexic condition, W was sufficiently competent to reach an informed decision. But in any event, the courts' powers were sufficient to override her wishes, irrespective of her age (over 16) and her competence to refuse treatment. [1992] Fam 11 at 26.

[71] E.g. *Re C (detention: medical treatment)* [1997] 2 FLR 180: Wall J overrode the anorexic girl's refusal to accept treatment irrespective of her capacity to consent on her own behalf to medical treatment.

[72] NB the MCA 2005 has introduced further confusion. If a 16 and 17-year-old patient lacks capacity to consent, as determined by the MCA 2005, ss. 2–3, his parents can only override his refusal to undergo treatment if such treatment fulfils the requirements of the best interests test set out by s. 4 and DCA (2007) ch. 4. See also DCA (2007) para. 12.17: if the parents of such a patient are unavailable or refuse to consent, the medical team can still treat the young patient without incurring medical liability (s. 5), as long as the treatment is deemed to be in the patient's best interests (s. 4).

[73] M. Brazier and C. Bridge (1996) p. 88.   [74] B. Hale and J. Fortin (2008) p. 106.

[75] *Re W (a minor) (medical treatment: courts' jurisdiction)* [1993] Fam 64, per Balcombe LJ, at 88.

is the duty of the court to ensure so far as it can that children survive to attain that age.[76]

Furthermore, despite its outward appearance of illogicality, the distinction between consent to and refusal of treatment is sustainable, since doctors only recommend treatment which is necessary and in the patient's best interests. Lowe and Juss point out that it is reasonable to withhold an adolescent's right to veto treatment designed for his or her benefit, particularly if refusal would lead to death or permanent damage.[77] Refusal of medical treatment not only rejects the advice of qualified doctors who know more about treatment for disease than children, but closes down options, rather than opening them up, in such a way which may be regretted later.[78] In any event, an adolescent may welcome matters being taken out of his own hands.[79]

Although their underlying rationale is logically sustainable, the decisions in *Re R* and *Re W* provoked considerable criticism.[80] Whilst it may be morally justifiable to override the wishes of an adolescent to prevent his or her death or severe permanent injury, doing so where failure to treat will not produce such dire consequences is far less justifiable.[81] Indeed, the courts have sometimes found themselves on a slope too slippery to resist when appealed to by doctors keen to provide much needed treatment.[82] Furthermore, critics argue that it is an arbitrary and status-driven form of decision-making which allows the patient's legal competence to be treated as irrelevant, solely because he or she is under the age of 18.[83] They urge the courts to adopt a more critical approach to the assumption that minors, unlike adults, must always be forced to live. Thus as Lewis argues:

> It may be that in a small minority of cases, an adolescent will be able to make a competent, maximally autonomous choice to refuse life-saving treatment. Respecting such a choice will be difficult, but it is preferable to arbitrary discrimination on the basis of age alone.[84]

The courts might, for example, justifiably distinguish the case where doctors are seeking to force an adolescent to continue with years of regular invasive

---

[76] Ibid. at 94.   [77] N. Lowe and S. Juss (1993) pp. 871–2.

[78] J. Mason and G. Laurie (2006) p. 371–2.

[79] R. Lansdown (1998) p. 460: 'a very large fifteen-year-old' needle phobic patient, who having been counselled, but then held down to undergo a blood test, told his doctor: 'That's better. Next time I have to have a needle you hold me down, forget all that psychological rubbish.'

[80] Inter alia: G. Douglas (1992); J. Masson (1993); J. Eekelaar (1993); R. Huxtable (2000); M. Freeman (2005).

[81] E.g. *Re K, W and H (minors) (medical treatment)* [1993] 1 FLR 854: a psychiatric treatment unit obtained legal authority for the use of 'emergency medication' when treating three mentally disturbed teenagers; *South Glamorgan County Council v. W and B* [1993] 1 FLR 574: a local authority (LA) obtained judicial authority for the forcible removal of a disturbed 15-year-old from home and her transfer to a specialised psychiatric unit for assessment and treatment. See both cases discussed below.

[82] B. Hale and J. Fortin (2008) p. 107.

[83] R. Huxtable (2000) pp. 84–6; P. Lewis (2001) p. 159; L. Ferguson (2004), Part Five.

[84] P. Lewis (2001) p. 159.

treatment,[85] from that involving a one-off blood transfusion or even major surgery. As Bridge argues 'there must come a time when a mature adolescent, like an adult suffering from chronic disability, can say "enough is enough" and reject treatment'.[86]

Perhaps the most worrying aspect of this case law, however, relates not to the *courts'* ability to override the objections of seriously ill adolescents, but to parents' power, in consultation with the doctors, to do so, irrespective of their age (over or under 16) and competence. As a matter of good practice, medical teams now try to involve all children in medical decisions and do not generally feel it appropriate to force treatment on unwilling patients, however young.[87] Nevertheless, a doctor, considering it essential for a young patient to receive the treatment he recommends, can simply appeal to the parents for authority to go ahead, in circumstances far less serious than those described by the judiciary in *Re W*. In such circumstances, a court will not be involved and so cannot withhold authority for treatment on the basis that an adolescent's wishes should *only* be overridden to avoid death or severe permanent injury.

(C) Time for reassessment?

The legal principles underpinning *Re R* and *Re W* require urgent reassessment now that the HRA 1998 has heightened a general awareness of rights entitlement, both for adults and children. Without a changed approach, an increasingly stark divide will emerge between the legal principles governing the treatment of adolescent patients and those governing adult patients.[88] Perhaps the most cogent reason for reassessing these principles is that overcoming refusal inevitably involves interfering with a person's bodily and intellectual autonomy.[89] The use of physical force may be unavoidable in cases involving the treatment of an uncooperative but a fully grown adolescent.[90] As Gostin says:

> Nothing degrades a human being more than to have intrusive treatment thrust upon him despite his full understanding of its nature and purpose and his clear will to say "no".[91]

The courts have emphasised that the protection provided by the common law and by the ECHR[92] should be taken seriously by those responsible for treating adult patients.[93] In relation to the withdrawal of unwanted life-prolonging

---

[85] In *Re S (a minor) (consent to medical treatment)* [1994] 2 FLR 1065, the 15-year-old sufferer of thalassaemia was to be forced to undergo monthly blood transfusions for a further two and a half years until, at the age of 18, she could refuse treatment.
[86] C. Bridge (1999) p. 593.   [87] GMC (2007) paras. 27–30.
[88] J. Fortin (2006a) pp. 324–5.   [89] G. Douglas (1992) p. 576.
[90] In *Re S (a minor)(consent to medical treatment)* [1994] 2 FLR 1065 at 1074, Johnson J acknowledged that the possible use of force was 'extremely distasteful'.
[91] L. Gostin (1992) p. 76.   [92] E.g. *YF v. Turkey* (2004) 39 EHRR 34; see fn 1 above.
[93] E.g. *Re B (adult: refusal of medical treatment)* [2002] EWHC 429 (Fam), [2002] 2 All ER 449.

treatment from a tetraplegic adult patient, Dame Elizabeth Butler-Sloss P stated:

> Unless the gravity of the illness has affected the patient's capacity, a seriously disabled patient has the same rights as the fit person to respect for personal autonomy. There is a serious danger, exemplified in this case, of a benevolent paternalism which does not embrace recognition of the personal autonomy of the severely disabled patient ... If mental capacity is not in issue and the patient, having been given the relevant information and offered the available options, chooses to refuse the treatment, that decision has to be respected by the doctors. Considerations that the best interests of the patient would indicate that the decision should be to consent to treatment are irrelevant.[94]

In other contexts, current case law suggests an increasing judicial sympathy with the notion of adolescent autonomy.[95] A reassessment of the law would also placate those who so strongly condemned the way in which the Court of Appeal had undermined the House of Lords' attempt in *Gillick* to provide adolescents with a degree of legal autonomy.[96]

An adolescent now being forced to undergo life-saving treatment may find that Articles 3 and 5 of the ECHR, perhaps in conjunction with Article 14, offer the strongest vehicles for a successful challenge. At first sight, Article 8 might appear to be the best candidate for such a challenge, guaranteeing as it does, the right to a patient's 'physical and moral integrity'.[97] But a medical team might justify infringing a young patient's rights thereunder by arguing that enforced treatment was *necessary* to save his or her life and that such an intervention was therefore proportionate to the risks involved in their failing to treat.[98] Strasbourg jurisprudence developed in relation to adult patients indicates that an Article 3 challenge might be more fruitful. Forcing an adult patient to undergo medical treatment can involve 'inhuman or degrading treatment', even if he or she is mentally incompetent, unless the treatment is perfectly orthodox medically and is deemed essential by the medical experts consulted.[99] Arguably, the same principle should apply to minors. Similarly, Article 5, which

---

[94] Ibid. at [94] and [100].

[95] Inter alia: *Re Roddy (a child)(identification: restriction on publication)* [2003] EWHC 2927 (Fam), [2004] 2 FLR 949; *Mabon v. Mabon* [2005] EWCA Civ 634, [2005] 2 FLR 101; *R (Axon) v. Secretary of State for Health and the Family Planning Association* [2006] EWHC 37 (Admin), [2006] 2 FLR 206; discussed by R. Taylor (2007).

[96] See above.   [97] *YF v. Turkey* (2004) 39 EHRR 34, see fn 1 above.

[98] I.e. under Art. 8(2). But the treatment must have been proportionate both to the risks involved in the patient not receiving the treatment and to the infringement of the patient's autonomy.

[99] See *Herczegfalvy v. Austria* (1992) 15 EHRR 437: a dangerously aggressive mental patient had been confined to a security bed and suffered the forcible administration of food and drugs whilst handcuffed and strapped by his ankles. The European Court of Human Rights (ECtHR) held (at paras. 82–6) that forcible treatment may infringe a psychiatric patient's rights under Art. 3, unless it amounts to 'a measure which is a therapeutic necessity' according to the 'psychiatric principles generally accepted at the time'. In this case, however, despite the worrying two-week duration of the treatment, there was no infringement because these measures had fulfilled both conditions.

protects the right to liberty and security of a person, undermines the ability of the courts and doctors to force an adult patient to undergo treatment in any situation involving the need for restraint or detention.[100] Depending on their degree and intensity, even very short periods of restraint have been held to infringe its terms.[101] Consequently, it is arguable that Article 5 is available if a medical team, acting on the authority of the parents of an uncooperative adolescent, either forces his admission to a hospital ward for treatment (and then refuses to allow him to go home) or holds him down for only a few minutes in order to administer sedating medication, as a prelude to treatment – or the team does both.

The medical team might certainly have a defence to infringing the Article 5 rights of an unwilling minor if they can argue that such a patient is of 'unsound mind'.[102] But such an argument becomes implausible in the context of a *Gillick* competent adolescent who refuses to undergo life saving treatment. It is also unlikely that the domestic courts would today accept that a medical team could shelter behind the *Nielsen* decision which so blatantly undermined the usefulness of Article 5 in situations where a parent has Article 8 rights.[103] In any event, as discussed below, the ECtHR considered that a parent's rights under Article 8 of the ECHR were confined to authorising medical decisions for a 'proper purpose'.[104] In summary, the principle established in *Re R* and *Re W* is vulnerable to challenges based on Articles 3 and 5 and 8 of the ECHR, combined with Article 14. *Gillick* competent adolescents resisting treatment might argue that they are as intellectually mature as many adults and are therefore entitled to the same rights to freedom from forcible treatment as those available to adult patients. A denial of such rights would not only infringe their rights under these articles, but would unlawfully discriminate against them on the grounds of age alone, under Article 14.

The law relating to the treatment of mentally disturbed adolescents is discussed in more detail below. It is important to note at this point, however, that the government itself is obviously persuaded that the legal principles established by the Court of Appeal in *Re R* and *Re W* are no longer reliable, at least in relation to the admission to hospital for treatment of 16 and 17-year-olds for a mental disorder. Presumably prompted by the greater judicial willingness to respect teenage autonomy in other contexts,[105] new legislation ensures that doctors can

---

[100] *Storck v. Germany* (2006) 43 EHRR 6; see fn 1 above.

[101] E.g. *X v. Austria* (Application No. 8278/78) 18 DR 154 (1979) – detention in order to subject the detainee to a blood test, though short, could, in principle, amount to a breach of Art. 5. See also *Guzzardi v. Italy* (1981) 3 EHRR 333, at para. 92: whether there is an infringement depends on a range of criteria, including the type, duration, effects and manner of implementation.

[102] I.e. the Art. 5(1)(e) exception: 'the lawful detention of persons for the prevention of the spreading of infectious diseases, of persons of unsound mind, alcoholics or drug addicts or vagrants'. But the rigorous requirements of *Winterwerp v. Netherlands* (1979) 2 EHRR 387 dictate full compliance with the mental health legislation in order to fulfil the requirements of this exception; see treatment of mentally disturbed teenagers discussed below.

[103] *Nielsen v. Denmark* (1988) 11 EHRR 175; discussed below.

[104] Ibid. at para. 69.   [105] See fn 95 above.

only admit 16 and 17-year-olds for treatment as a 'voluntary' or 'informal' patients,[106] if they themselves consent to such admission, being deemed competent to do so by the MCA 2005.[107] If they oppose such a step, doctors can no longer obtain legal authority for admission from their parents.[108] The government had undoubtedly feared that admission on the authority of parental consent alone would be successfully challenged under the HRA 1998.[109] As explained below, the new law means that if doctors want to force admission on a 16 or 17-year-old against their wishes, they must use the mental health legislation, as in the case of adult patients. Notably, this legislation only prohibits admission; it does not prohibit doctors from relying on parental authority for unwanted treatment of a 16 or 17-year-old *Gillick* competent adolescent, once admitted onto a treatment unit. Nevertheless, the Mental Health Code warns doctors that, although in the past, the courts have found that parents can overrule such an adolescent's refusal of consent 'in non-emergency cases', doctors should not rely on this principle still applying and should consider instead, obtaining authority for treatment by using the mental health legislation or they should obtain court authorisation:[110]

> there is no post-Human Rights Act decision on this, and the trend in recent cases is to reflect greater autonomy for under 18s in law. In the Department of Health's view, it is not wise to rely on the consent of a person with parental responsibility to treat a young person who refuses in these circumstances.[111]

This very clear guidance is, however, significantly qualified by the confident assertion that in an emergency, 'the clinician could act without anyone's consent if the refusal would in all likelihood lead to their death or severe permanent injury', since the 16 or 17-year-old's refusal to undergo treatment 'could be overruled'.[112] This is mysterious; it perhaps reflects the fact that doctors have always had the right to treat a patient without consent in an emergency to save his or her life, under the doctrine of necessity.[113] But the scope of this doctrine is unclear and is normally reserved for the treatment of unconscious patients.[114] Alternatively, the Code's wording may reflect an expectation that the courts will review the principle in *Re R* and *Re W*, but not overrule it entirely. Instead, they are perhaps expected to restate the basic premise more firmly – that a *Gillick*

---

[106] I.e. as a patient who consents to treatment, thereby obviating the need to comply with the requirements of the mental health legislation when treating patients against their wishes.

[107] Mental Health Act (MHA) 1983, s. 131(2), as amended by MHA 2007, s. 43.

[108] MHA 1983, s. 131(4).   [109] I.e. under Art. 5 ECHR.   [110] DH (2008) para. 36.33.   [111] Ibid.

[112] Ibid. at para. 36.34. See also para. 36.44 for similar advice regarding *Gillick* competent under 16-year-olds.

[113] *Sidaway v. Board of Governors of the Bethlem Royal Hospital and the Maudsley Hospital* [1985] AC 871, per Lord Scarman, at 882: medical treatment of an adult without consent normally, unless life-saving treatment is required in an emergency when it can be carried out under the doctrine of necessity, amounts to a trespass to the person and to a criminal assault. See also *Gillick v. West Norfolk and Wisbech Area Health Authority* [1986] AC 112, per Lord Scarman, at 189: children can be treated without consent in emergencies.

[114] J. Mason and G. Laurie (2006) pp. 350–3.

competent patient's refusal of treatment can be overridden, but only to avoid death or severe permanent injury. More significantly, however, the guidance also seems to envisage the courts restricting the principle in *Re R* and *Re W* even further, with the power to authorise treatment against a *Gillick* competent patient's wishes being confined to the courts alone. In other words, parents' power to authorise treatment against the will of their *Gillick* competent sons and daughters is expected to disappear. Such a proposition would involve the courts retaining power to prevent adolescents from killing themselves but not parents.

The government obviously assumes that neither the judiciary nor society is ready to allow adolescents to martyr themselves.[115] It is difficult, however, to see how the courts could achieve such a result, bearing in mind their duty to promote a young patient's rights under the ECHR. They might turn to Article 2 for assistance. As the Strasbourg jurisprudence shows, certain situations produce a conflict of rights which, in the context of forcing medical treatment on uncooperative or incompetent adult patients, the ECtHR has been content to allow states to resolve themselves.[116] It is therefore arguable that whilst a minor patient is certainly entitled to the basic freedoms guaranteed by Articles 3, 5 and 8, these rights might be outweighed by his or her right to life itself. Given that Article 2 imposes a positive obligation on all public authorities, including the courts and other state agencies, to take appropriate steps to safeguard life,[117] a court might maintain that it cannot ignore its duty to save the life of a desperately ill adolescent, despite his or her own strong opposition to treatment. An adolescent would, however, undoubtedly find such an approach objectionable. It would involve the courts promoting the dubious proposition that by overriding an adolescent's autonomy rights, through enforced medical treatment involving bodily restraint, they are in fact safeguarding his or her rights to future health and self-fulfilment.[118] Only the courts can tell us whether

---

[115] J. Fortin (2006a) p. 325.

[116] E.g. *X v. Germany* (Application No. 10565/83) (1984) 7 EHRR 152, per the European Commission on Human Rights (EComHR): although force-feeding a prisoner might, in certain circumstances, amount to a breach of his rights under Art. 3, the state had a positive obligation under Art. 2 to preserve his life. The ECHR provides no guidance on how to resolve the conflict between the two obligations, and here, since the state had acted in the prisoner's best interests in taking action to save his life, rather than to respect his will not to accept nourishment, the complaint was ill-founded; *Keenan v. United Kingdom* (2001) 33 EHRR 28: a young prisoner's mother failed in her complaint that by not preventing her son from committing suicide, the prison authorities had infringed his right to life under Art. 2. Per ECtHR at [92], any measures taken to promote his rights under Art 2 were limited by the constraints imposed by his rights under Arts. 5 and 8.

[117] Inter alia: *LCB v. United Kingdom* (1999) 27 EHRR 212 at para 36; *Osman v. United Kingdom* [1999] 1 FLR 193 at paras 115–16); *Keenan v. United Kingdom* (2001) 33 EHRR 28 at para. 89; *R (on the application of Pretty) v. Director of Public Prosecutions* [2001] UKHL 61, [2002] 1 All ER 1, per Lord Hope, at [87]; *Savage v. South Essex Partnership NHS Foundation Trust* [2008] UKHL 74, [2009] All ER 1053, per Lord Rodger of Earlseferry, at [45].

[118] J. Fortin (2006a) pp. 323–5.

the Department of Health's confident advice is correct; hopefully a test case will soon provide a suitable vehicle for reviewing this area of law.

Section B Adolescent decision-making – the difficult cases

(1) The control of fertility

(A) Contraception

Adults may find it unpalatable to come to terms with adolescent sexual activity.[119] Teenagers in the UK reach physical, if not psychological, maturity extremely rapidly. This is clearly reflected in the high rate of teenage pregnancy in the UK,[120] noted with concern by the Committee on the Rights of the Child.[121] In a much researched area,[122] there seems to be general agreement that the outcomes for teenagers who complete their pregnancies and for their babies[123] are poorer than for older mothers, both in health and in socio-economic terms.[124] Research indicates that the adverse outcomes pass to the next generation who, in turn, are more likely to become teenage mothers themselves, more likely to experience poverty, poor housing and nutrition and to live in a single parent family.[125] The government's increased efforts[126] to drive down the rates of teenage pregnancy are slowly producing results,[127] as are attempts to provide teenage mothers with better services.[128] Researchers currently stress that the disadvantages connected with teenage pregnancy and parenthood are a function of the conditions in which these mothers grow up themselves and are not necessarily related to their age *per se*.[129] They also urge

---

[119] Inter alia: J Bradshaw *et al.* (2004) para. 5.4.3: numbers of teenagers under 16 who report having had sex has doubled in a generation; UNICEF (2007) Figure 5.2d: cf. other OECD nations, UK has the highest percentage of 15-year-olds who reported having had sex. See also Parliamentary Office of Science and Technology (2004) and Health Protection Agency (2006): diagnosis of sexually transmitted diseases in teenagers under the age of 19 has steadily increased since 1996.

[120] UNICEF (2007) Figure 5.2f: UK has the highest teenage pregnancy rate in Europe and third highest of all OECD countries.

[121] Committee on the Rights of the Child (2002) para. 43; ibid. (2008) para. 60.

[122] Much of the earlier research on teenage pregnancy is usefully summarised in Health Development Agency (2004).

[123] Healthcare Commission (2007) p. 65: infant mortality for babies with mothers under 20 is 60% higher than for babies of older mothers aged 20–39.

[124] Research summaries: J. Bynner and M. Londra (2004) para. 3.2.1; J. Bradshaw *et al.* (2004) para. 5.4; Health Development Agency (2004) p. 7; DCSF and DH (2008) Section 1.

[125] Inter alia: SEU (1999) paras. 3.9–3.10; UNICEF (2001) Figures 5 and 12; J. Hobcraft and K. Kiernan (2001); T. Moffitt *et al.* (2002). By the age of 33, teenage mothers have, inter alia, a higher likelihood of lacking any qualification, being on substantially lower income, and being more likely to be divorced or separated.

[126] Inter alia: DfES (2006a) and DfES (2006b).

[127] Despite the work of the Teenage Pregnancy Unit, established in 2000, statistics show only small reductions in some areas and significant rises in 'teenage pregnancy hotspots' (see annual statistics published by the Teenage Pregnancy Unit).

[128] DCSF and DH (2008).

[129] M. Wiggins *et al.* (2005) p. 9. See also S. Cater and L. Coleman (2006) ch. 4.

policy-makers to accept that some teenage mothers from disadvantaged and insecure backgrounds choose pregnancy as a means of providing themselves with a positive change in their lives.[130]

It seems unlikely that teenagers can be persuaded that complete abstinence from sexual activity is the best way of forcing down the rate of teenage pregnancies. Since the statistics suggest that adolescents in the UK are starting intercourse at increasingly early ages, official policy is to encourage an increased use of contraception and better sex education in schools.[131] The contraceptive pill continues to be a relatively safe and easy method for teenage girls to adopt; indeed, Lord Scarman noted that:

> women have obtained by the availability of the pill a choice of life-style with a degree of independence and of opportunity undreamed of until this genera-tion … The law ignores these developments at its peril.[132]

The decision in *Gillick v. West Norfolk and Wisbech Area Health Authority*[133] was a victory of realism over idealism; certainly it was an exercise in pragma-tism. The House of Lords accepted the common-sense advice from the Department of Health that increased pregnancy and sexually transmitted dis-eases would result from a law requiring adolescents under 16 to obtain parental permission before seeking contraceptive advice and treatment. The decision legally affirmed that adolescents are entitled to act responsibly by seeking support and help outside their families, even if doing so offends their parents' own convictions. Moreover, their Lordships held that a doctor does not incur criminal liability[134] by providing such help, if the prescription of contraceptive treatment is medically indicated. He has a defence if it involves the bona fide exercise of his clinical judgment in deciding what is best for his patient's health.[135]

Despite the *Gillick* decision being regarded as the high-water mark for recognising adolescent decision-making rights, within its own context its demands are relatively rigorous. A teenage girl cannot demand contraceptive services from her doctor, irrespective of her circumstances. Both Lord Scarman and Lord Fraser stressed the complexities she must comprehend before a doctor can judge her competent to receive contraceptive advice and treatment. Lord Scarman emphasised that it is not enough for her to simply understand the nature of the advice given, she must also have sufficient maturity to 'understand what is involved'. A doctor must be satisfied that she understands the long-term problems and risks associated with sexual intercourse, pregnancy and its termination.[136] Lord Fraser's judgment provided doctors with detailed practical

---

[130] S. Cater and L. Coleman (2006) chs. 5 and 6. See also M. Wiggins *et al.* (2005) pp. 62–4.
[131] Sex education in schools is discussed in Chapter 6.
[132] *Gillick v. West Norfolk and Wisbech Area Health Authority* [1986] AC 112 at 183.   [133] Ibid.
[134] I.e. aiding and abetting unlawful intercourse with a girl under 16 under the sexual offences legislation.
[135] *Gillick v. West Norfolk and Wisbech Area Health Authority* [1986] AC 112, per Lord Scarman, at 190–1 and Lord Fraser at 175.
[136] Ibid. at 189.

advice which became immediately influential (known as the 'Fraser guide-lines'). A doctor should only provide a girl with treatment or advice without involving her parents, if fully satisfied over five rigorous requirements:[137] (i) that the girl must understand his advice; (ii) she cannot be persuaded to inform her parents of the matter; (iii) she is likely to have sexual intercourse with or without contraceptive treatment; (iv) it is likely that her physical or mental health will suffer should she not receive the treatment; and (v) her best interests require her to receive the treatment without her parents' consent. All five requirements were adopted by the revised government guidance[138] and by the medical profession and are regarded as the rules governing those prescribing teenagers with contraceptive services.[139]

The decision in *Gillick* would never have reached the House of Lords had Mrs Gillick not been so determined to prevent her adolescent daughters obtaining contraceptive advice and treatment without her consent. Many years later, Ms Axon, a mother with similarly strong views, received similarly robust judicial treatment.[140] Silber J rejected her argument that a mother's own Article 8 rights are unjustifiably infringed by her daughter being allowed to gain contraceptive advice from a doctor without her prior knowledge.[141] His decision confirmed that the HRA 1998 had not affected the principles established by *Gillick* in this context. Adolescents remain entitled to seek contraceptive advice and treatment and to medical confidentiality,[142] provided they comply with the tests of legal competence established by Lord Scarman and Lord Fraser.

(B) Abortion

Despite the UK having the highest rate of teenage birth in Western Europe, the abortion rate amongst teenagers is comparatively low,[143] but with large regional variations.[144] It appears that young women from the most socially deprived areas are the most likely to become teenage mothers and the least likely to choose abortions. Indeed, it appears that many young people in more deprived areas disapprove strongly of abortion[145] and that whilst teenage pregnancy is often a common phenomenon in these areas,[146] abortion is not seen as a positive option, and is often not considered at all.[147] Indeed, disapproval of abortion expressed by their own close families, particularly by their own parents, and by the baby's father, persuades some teenagers to keep their

---

[137] Ibid. at 174.   [138] DH (1986) replaced by subsequent guidance.
[139] DH (2004a) and GMC (2007) paras. 70–2.
[140] *R (Axon) v. Secretary of State for Health and the Family Planning Association* [2006] EWHC 37 (Admin), [2006] 2 FLR 206.
[141] See also Chapter 3.   [142] Discussed below.
[143] ONS (2008) p. 26, Table 2.18 and Figure 2.19.   [144] E. Lee *et al.* (2004) p. 12, map 1.
[145] Inter alia: SEU (1999) para. 8.18; E. Lee *et al.* (2004) pp. 16–18; S. Cater and L. Coleman (2006) p. 20.
[146] E. Lee *et al.* (2004) pp. 45–6; S. Cater and L. Coleman (2006) pp. 26–7.
[147] S. Tabberer *et al.* (2000) pp. 19 and 44.

babies.[148] Research suggests that more open discussion about abortion might encourage young people, their parents and their communities to see it as a positive, rather than a negative choice.[149]

Sometimes a pregnant teenager, knowing her parents' views and the baby's father's opposition to the concept of abortion,[150] feels obliged to seek a termination secretly. Does she have the right to proceed with such a procedure without involving her parents? Silber J considers that *Gillick* competence for these purposes requires a higher threshold of capacity than that required for receiving contraceptive advice and treatment.[151] Unlike contraceptive treatment, abortion involves invasive and irreversible surgical procedure with potential risks and side effects.[152] Even so, according to Silber J, the guidance on legal competence provided by Lord Scarman and Lord Fraser in *Gillick*[153] can be used in the context of abortion, but with some adaptation, given that abortion raises more serious and complex issues.[154] Consequently, a doctor providing an adolescent under the age of 16 with abortion services must fulfil Lord Fraser's five guidelines, but also taking additional account of Lord Scarman's requirement that the young person 'understands properly "what is involved"',[155] a requirement which in itself involves a 'high threshold' of legal competence.[156] A doctor providing abortion services without complying with such guidance must expect to be professionally disciplined.[157] As discussed below, the decision in *Axon* also usefully confirmed the common assumption that if a doctor considers the girl to be sufficiently competent to consent to an abortion and that an abortion is medically advised, he need not insist on consulting her parents over the matter.[158]

English law remains confused over what happens if the girl's parents wish to take legal steps to oppose her arrangements for an abortion. As noted above, research suggests that some parents may exert considerable pressure on their daughters to keep their babies due to their own antipathy towards abortion. Legally, although her parents are not entitled to veto any medical procedure a *Gillick* competent girl has consented to, this does not prevent them seeking the assistance of the courts to stop her going ahead with an abortion against their wishes.[159] The case law relevant to this issue suggests that the courts are not

---

[148] Ibid. at ch. 5 and E. Lee *et al.* (2004) pp. 40–1 and 44.

[149] S. Tabberer *et al.* (2000) pp. 44–5 and E. Lee *et al.* (2004) ch. 4.

[150] NB the father of an unborn child has no legal right to prevent the mother undergoing an abortion, as long as she and her medical advisers comply with the procedures established by the Abortion Act 1967. See *Paton v. British Pregnancy Advisory Service Trustees* [1979] QB 276; *Kelly v. Kelly* [1997] 2 FLR 828; *Paton v. United Kingdom* (1980) 3 EHRR 408.

[151] *R (Axon) v. Secretary of State for Health and the Family Planning Association* [2006] EWHC 37 (Admin), [2006] 2 FLR 206 at [90].

[152] Ibid. at [83].   [153] [1986] AC 112.   [154] *R (Axon)*, ibid. at [90]–[91].

[155] *Gillick v. West Norfolk and Wisbech Area Health Authority* [1986] AC 112 at 189.

[156] *R (Axon)*, ibid. at [90].   [157] Ibid.   [158] Ibid. at [87] and [90].

[159] I.e. by seeking the court's assistance through its inherent jurisdiction, or by seeking a specific issue order or prohibited steps order under the Children Act (CA) 1989, s. 8.

particularly receptive to such parental applications.[160] Nevertheless, depending on her age and maturity, an open disagreement between an adolescent and her parents over whether her pregnancy should be terminated may make doctors reluctant to go ahead without obtaining prior court authorisation.

Has a *Gillick* competent pregnant girl the right to resist the wishes of her parents who want her to undergo an abortion? In *Re W (a minor) (medical treatment: court's jurisdiction)*,[161] both Lord Donaldson MR and Balcombe LJ admitted that, according to their interpretation of the law, a teenage girl could be forced to undergo an abortion against her wishes, merely on the consent of her parents. Nevertheless, Balcombe LJ thought it difficult to conceive of a court ordering an abortion against the wishes of a mentally competent 16-year-old.[162] Given the growing judicial sympathy for the notion of adolescent autonomy, a court today is unlikely to override a pregnant girl's wishes, unless her doctors advise that continuing with her pregnancy is likely to jeopardise her future survival. A challenge enlisting Articles 3,[163] 5 and 8 of the ECHR would almost certainly protect her from undergoing an abortion against her will. Few would quarrel with the proposition that an adolescent has a right to have her choices respected over whether she carries her baby to term or not and that this right should be translated into clear legal principles.

(C) Confidentiality

Adults are entitled to assume that their doctors will not divulge their medical secrets[164] – an entitlement which has been reinforced by Strasbourg jurisprudence and domestic case law maintaining that the right to respect for personal privacy[165] embraces the right to medical confidentiality.[166] Acceptance of the research evidence on adolescents' similar need for medical confidentiality[167]

---

[160] *Re P (a minor)* [1986] 1 FLR 272: the court authorised a 15-year-old girl in LA care to undergo an abortion despite her parents' opposition to this procedure.

[161] [1993] Fam 64.   [162] Ibid. at 90.

[163] It is unlikely that the doctors could argue that performing an enforced abortion is a therapeutic necessity and in accordance with accepted medical practice, as required by *Herczegfalvy v. Austria* (1992) 15 EHRR 437.

[164] But in rare circumstances, disclosure may be justified 'in the public interest' (*W v. Egdell* [1990] Ch 359), e.g. where failure to disclose appropriate information would expose a third party to risk of death or serious harm.

[165] I.e. under Art. 8 ECHR.

[166] See *Z v. Finland* (1997) 25 EHRR 371 at para. 95 and *Campbell v. MGN Ltd* [2004] UKHL 22, [2004] 2 AC 457, esp. Baroness Hale of Richmond, at [145]. J. Loughrey (2008) pp. 313–17, assesses the case law developing the right to medical confidentiality.

[167] Inter alia: SEU (1999) para. 7.7: young people had an overriding fear that their doctors would inform their parents of their medical consultations; BMRB International (2004) para. 2.9: 42% of young people aged between 13–21 considered 'confidentiality/privacy' to be the most important factor when seeking advice on sex and relationships (a similar finding was obtained in earlier 'waves' carried out by BMRB International); see also similar evidence summarised by Silber J in *R (Axon) v. Secretary of State for Health and the Family Planning Association* [2006] EWHC 37 (Admin), [2006] 2 FLR 206 at paras. 67–71.

undoubtedly underpinned the Department of Health's assertion that those under 16 were owed the same duty of confidentiality as that owed to any adult.[168] Fortunately Ms Axon failed in her bid to establish that this guidance was unlawful. Silber J acknowledged that their Lordships in *Gillick*[169] had not specifically stated that *Gillick* competent adolescents were entitled to absolute confidentiality when consulting a medical practitioner over contraception and other sexual matters. Nevertheless, he concluded that such an assumption was implicit in their decision.[170] Consequently, although a doctor should always encourage a *Gillick* competent patient to confide in her parents, if she refuses to do so, she has a right to absolute, not qualified medical confidentiality.[171] This duty of confidentiality applies whether it is advice or treatment that is sought and whether such advice or treatment involves contraception, sexually transmitted infection or abortion.[172] Despite its limitations,[173] Silber J's decision usefully confirmed that the Department of Health's guidance is unaffected by the implementation of the HRA 1998. Its importance lies in his confirmation that Ms Axon's rights under Article 8 could justifiably be infringed by reference to the need, under Article 8(2), to protect her daughters' right to medical confidentiality.[174] Indeed, Ms Axon, like Ms Gillick before her, achieved precisely what she wished to prevent – in this case that medical practitioners must respect the medical secrets of all *Gillick* competent adolescents.[175]

Since Ms Axon's daughters were assumed to be *Gillick* competent, the decision in *Axon* left untouched the official assumption that the *Gillick* incompetent adolescent is also entitled to medical confidentiality.[176] The law has been unclear over whether an adolescent not deemed sufficiently mature to understand the contraceptive advice or treatment is also entitled to medical confidentiality. Case law establishes that doctors should not disclose the medical details of very young children to anyone other than their own parents.[177] Recent case law shows that children may be protected against invasions of privacy by the press, reinforced by their right to privacy under Article 8 of the ECHR.[178] But can a doctor divulge details of a *Gillick* incompetent adolescent's medical consultation to her parents? Some have argued that a doctor does not

---

[168] DH (2004a) p. 2.   [169] [1986] AC 112.   [170] *R (Axon)*, ibid. at [55]–[65].

[171] Ibid. at [6]: Ms Axon unsuccessfully argued that doctors should not provide teenagers under the age of 16 with any advice and treatment on contraception, sexually transmitted infections or abortion without their parents' knowledge, *unless* passing on such information would prejudice their physical or mental health, thereby rendering it against their best interests so to do.

[172] Ibid. at [87].   [173] Discussed in Chapter 3.   [174] *R (Axon)*, ibid. at [136]–[150].

[175] See R. Taylor (2007) for a critique of the *Axon* decision.

[176] Successive health guidance documents have all suggested without qualification that doctors unable to persuade teenagers under 16 to involve their parents in any treatment decisions involving contraception, sexually transmitted infections or abortion, must always maintain strict medical confidentiality. E.g. DH (2004).

[177] *Re C (a minor) (wardship: medical treatment) (No. 2)* [1990] Fam 39.

[178] *Murray v. Express Newspapers Plc* [2008] EWCA Civ 446, [2008] HRLR 33, per Sir Arthur Clarke MR, at [16]. But the right to an expectation of privacy is not absolute, ibid. at [58]; discussed by J. Loughrey (2008) pp. 321–3.

owe a duty of confidentiality to a minor legally incapable of entering into a legal relationship with him.[179] This controversially means that a teenage girl will not know until the end of her consultation whether her doctor considers her to be *Gillick* competent and cannot be guaranteed secrecy at the outset. It also implicitly links competence for reaching decisions over treatment to competence for expecting medical confidentiality – whereas, as Loughrey points out, children who lack competence for medical decision-making may comprehend the concept of confidentiality.[180] Nevertheless, Ms Axon's claim that a parent's Article 8 rights are infringed by a doctor withholding information from her about her child's medical needs becomes more sustainable in the case of an adolescent deemed to be *Gillick in*competent. Loughrey points out that a doctor could certainly justify (under Article 8(2)) divulging the information to a parent who needs it in order to authorise the child's medical treatment.[181] In other circumstances, the child's own right to privacy might trump those of the parents.

Whatever the strict state of the law, the younger, more immature adolescent will be deterred from seeking contraceptive advice without guarantees of privacy. It is therefore undoubtedly sensible for the official guidance to encourage doctors to respect the confidentiality of all patients under the age of 16.[182] Nevertheless, issues of medical confidentiality can arise in other contexts. A doctor may fear, for example, that a young girl's pregnancy can only be explained by sexual abuse within her own family. In such cases, irrespective of the adolescent's competence, medical confidentiality cannot be absolute. Official guidance emphasises that medical practitioners must be prepared to pass on medical information, in the public interest, perhaps to assist a child protection investigation into alleged abusive practices. It stresses that a child or young person must always be encouraged to agree to such disclosure before it occurs.[183] Hopefully, aided by an appropriate explanation of such steps, most adolescents will understand why their confidences have to be broken in such a way.

(2) Treatment for mentally impaired adolescents

(A) The background

Adolescence is a time when young people commonly experience mood swings, ranging from intense exhilaration to extreme depression, explained in part by the fact that their brains are still undergoing profound physical changes, combined with hormonal development.[184] During this time the prevalence of

---

[179] I. Kennedy (1992) pp. 111–17; J. Mason and G. Laurie (2006) p. 273.
[180] J. Loughrey (2008) p. 317.   [181] Ibid. at pp. 322–3.   [182] DH (2004a).
[183] HM Government (2008) para. 3.38: e.g. evidence that the child is suffering or is at risk of suffering significant harm; or where there is reasonable cause to believe that a child may be suffering or at risk of significant harm (para. 3.42). See also GMC (2007) paras. 46–9.
[184] Discussed in Chapter 3.

many psycho-social disorders increases.[185] Indeed, there seems to be a consensus that the overall prevalence rate for child and adolescent mental health problems has been rising in nearly all developed countries.[186] Severe eating disorders, suicidal or self-mutilating behaviour,[187] aggression and violence often need urgent treatment and may even endanger others if left untreated. Furthermore, all those under 18 clearly have a right to the 'highest attainable standard of health'.[188] The government has certainly made considerable efforts to improve their health care generally[189] and to improve provision for their mental health care.[190] Meanwhile, not all young people are willing to admit that they require mental health treatment. If they resist treatment, medical teams must also take account of their young patients' other rights: their right to freedom from arbitrary deprivation of liberty[191] and to protection from all forms of physical violence.[192] Indeed, a report prepared for the Council of Europe maintained that protective measures for minors undergoing involuntary placement and treatment should be *more* stringent than for adult mental health patients.[193] Under domestic law in England and Wales, however, as the discussion below indicates, minors' liberty may, depending on their age, currently be restricted for indeterminate lengths of time, with no independent safeguards.

The case law also shows the courts, parents, treatment units and LAs using a bewildering variety of overlapping methods to authorise admission, detention and treatment against a young patient's will. Considerable confusion is created by the availability of various procedures whereby an adolescent may be admitted to a specialised treatment unit against his or her wishes. The distinction between legal authority for admission and that for treatment is an important one. In many cases the admission itself is unproblematic, but the patient objects to the form of treatment. Depending on his or her age, medical practitioners can very quickly and simply get round such objections by obtaining parental authority first for 'informal admission' and then for treatment. In complex cases, however, clinical teams may prefer to seek the High Court's assistance under its inherent jurisdiction to authorise compulsory admission and/or treatment. Alternatively, a LA may obtain a secure accommodation order (SAO) under the CA 1989, section 25(1) which authorises admission and

---

[185] Inter alia: S. Collishaw *et al.* (2004); H. Green *et al.* (2005); J. Cyranowski *et al.* (2000).

[186] S. Collishaw *et al.* (2004).

[187] SEU (2000) ch. 1: research summary – the rate of self-harm amongst young people has increased since the mid-1980s.

[188] United Nations Convention on the Rights of the Child (CRC), Art. 24(1).

[189] E.g. by the launch in 2004 of the Children's National Service Framework (DH (2004b)) setting out 11 standards for the improvement of health and other services over a 10-year period, standards 6–10, governing children's health care in various contexts.

[190] See DH (2004b) standard 9: all children and young people under 18 with mental health problems and disorders to 'have access to timely, integrated, high quality, multi-disciplinary mental health services'. See also DH (2006) esp. pp. 11 and 28: greater government investment in Child and Adolescent Mental Health Services (CAMHS).

[191] CRC, Art. 37(b); Art. 5 ECHR.   [192] CRC, esp. Arts. 19(1) and 37; Arts. 3 and 8 ECHR.

[193] Council of Europe (2000) para. 8.1.

detention. Such an order cannot, however, govern treatment; so authority for compulsory treatment must be obtained by some other means, either from the patient, the parent or from the court. Despite being available, many commentators suggest that none of these methods should be used in preference to the procedures available under the mental health legislation, which has the advantage of providing both for compulsory admission *and* treatment, albeit carefully regulated.

(B) The mental health legislation

A seriously ill adolescent confronting compulsory admission for treatment might quite reasonably conclude that there are considerable advantages to being admitted to hospital under the mental health legislation, rather than under the common law. This legislation, which has undergone radical reform,[194] applies to all patients requiring compulsory assessment and treatment for mental disorders, irrespective of their age. It recognises that removing an individual's liberty in order to treat them on a compulsory basis is a drastic step and it contains a set of strict legislative safeguards which apply to all mental health patients. Many of its provisions are specifically intended to protect all such patients from arbitrary restrictions on their liberty and unsupervised treatment regimes.[195] Admission is strictly regulated,[196] and there are clear procedures for gaining an independent review of the need for detention.[197] In broad terms, detention and compulsory treatment can only be authorised if it is necessary for the patient's health or safety, or for the protection of others,[198] whether or not the patient has the capacity to agree to or refuse treatment.[199] Many of the safeguards introduced by the MHA 1983 were designed to compensate for the fact that a patient's competence to consent to or refuse treatment does not prevent treatment taking place. Nevertheless, the use of compulsory powers to restrain and treat a mental health patient would, in normal circumstances, infringe his or her rights under Article 5 of the ECHR, unless it falls within the 'of unsound mind' exception,[200] and to do so, there are certain rigorous human rights criteria to be fulfilled.[201] The new mental health legislation was designed, through a range

---

[194] The MHA 2007 significantly amended the MHA 1983.

[195] P. Fennell (2007) pp. 28–33 and ch. 6.

[196] An application can be made for compulsory admission for assessment under s. 2, or for treatment under s. 3 of the MHA 1983.

[197] P. Fennell (2007) ch. 9.

[198] MHA 1983, s. 3. But (s. 3(2)(d)) appropriate medical treatment must be available for him.

[199] MHA 1983, s. 63.   [200] Art. 5(1)(e), see fn 102.

[201] Inter alia: *Winterwerp v. Netherlands* (1979) 2 EHRR 387 at para. 39: the medical disorder must exist, according to objective medical advice, must be sufficiently extreme to justify the detention and detention must last only as long as the disorder itself; *Ashingdane v. United Kingdom* (1985) 7 EHRR 528: detention must take place within a hospital, clinic or other appropriate institution; *HL v. United Kingdom* (2005) 40 EHRR 32: the informal admission of a 'compliant' patient into psychiatric care must comply with the requirements of Art. 5(1)(e); *Storck v. Germany* (2006) 43 EHRR 6: the domestic legislation and procedures governing

of new safeguards, to ensure that its provisions were fully compliant with these human rights requirements.

Those treating mentally ill minors were, in the past, often reluctant to use the mental health legislation for their treatment,[202] due to the perceived stigma attached to compulsory powers. It is arguably disadvantageous in later life for it to become known that an individual was formerly treated under the mental health legislation.[203] Furthermore, as explained above, a simpler route has long been available to any clinical team whereby they could obtain authority for treatment from the adolescent's parents under the legal principles established by the Court of Appeal in the early 1990s.[204] Nevertheless, attitudes to the use of the mental health legislation have been gradually changing. Particularly when treating eating disorders in older children, some practitioners seem more prepared to envisage its use.[205] Today they may be deterred by the law's extreme complexity, with legislative changes concerning children having been grafted on to the common law by the Mental Capacity Act (MCA) 2005 and the MHA 2007 with little concern for clarity or coherence.[206]

As discussed above, the new legislation and the official guidance accompanying it prevents doctors from informally admitting an unwilling *Gillick* competent adolescent aged between 16 and 18 to hospital for treatment on his or her parents' authority alone.[207] They should therefore only attempt compulsory admission by using the mental health legislation, as in the case of adult patients. This older patient then gains all the protection available to adult patients, including review of detention and the assistance of an independent mental health advocate.[208] The Code also warns medical teams to adopt the same approach in relation to any *Gillick* competent adolescent under the age of

---

compulsory treatment must be rigorously followed. But even if the treatment is Art. 5 compliant, it may infringe the patient's rights under Art. 3 and/or 8. See *R (on the application of Wilkinson) v. Broadmoor Hospital* [2001] EWCA Civ 1545, [2002] 1 WLR 419, esp. Hale LJ's discussion of *Herczegfalvy v. Austria* (1992) 15 EHRR 437, at [77]–[84]. See also B. Hale (2005).

[202] BMA (2001) p. 140.

[203] E.g. *Re W (a minor) (medical treatment: court's jurisdiction)* [1993] Fam 64, per Lord Donaldson MR, at 83. See also *Re K, W and H (minors) (medical treatment)* [1993] 1 FLR 854, per Thorpe J, at 857, who accepted without question that the hospital's support for 'Parental preference' explained their not using the mental health legislation to ensure treatment of one of the three girls involved in that case.

[204] I.e. *Re R (a minor) (wardship: medical treatment)* [1992] Fam 11, and *Re W (a minor) (medical treatment: court's jurisdiction)* [1993] Fam 64.

[205] Case law supports this approach. E.g. *Riverside Mental Health NHS Trust v. Fox* [1994] 1 FLR 614, per Sir Stephen Brown P, at 619: anorexia nervosa is a mental disorder under the MHA 1983, s. 63 and force-feeding an adult sufferer is a form of medical treatment for such a disorder. But see J. Tan *et al.* (2003) p. 628: anecdotal evidence suggests that child and adolescent psychiatrists in England and Wales still frequently impose treatment on minors diagnosed with anorexia nervosa on the authority of parental consent.

[206] DCA (2007) pp. 216–24: eight pages of guidance explaining the mental capacity decision-making regime for children and young people under 18; DH (2008) pp. 326–54: 28 pages of guidance, including three flowcharts explaining the mental health decision-making regime for children and young people under 18.

[207] MHA 1983, s. 131(4).   [208] MHA 1983, ss. 130A–C.

16 who refuses being informally admitted.[209] Nevertheless, as discussed below, for those *Gillick in*competent adolescents of whatever age under the age of 18, the existing 'informal' admission regime has remained largely unchanged.

Meanwhile the mental health legislation has not secured conditions of an acceptable standard for many adolescents admitted into mental health facilities for treatment.[210] A continuing shortage of specialist child and adolescent inpatient units[211] and staff[212] means that too many are admitted onto mixed sex adult mental health wards,[213] with their health and safety being seriously compromised.[214] Those admitted onto adult wards are far less likely to be treated by staff with specialist child and adolescent mental health skills,[215] are often provided with no educational arrangements even when under 16[216] and only have limited access to specialised advocacy, including explanations of their rights.[217] The amended mental health legislation may eventually ensure that the hospital environment of patients under the age of 18 'is suitable having regard to his age (subject to his needs)'.[218] The Code fleshes out the legislative duty, stressing that under 18s' needs should be met with appropriate physical facilities, appropriately trained staff, an age-appropriate hospital routine and equal access to educational opportunities as their peers. It also stresses that a young patient should only exceptionally be accommodated on an adult ward, and then only in single-sex accommodation.[219]

(C) Parental authorisation for admission and treatment

(i) Informal admission as a 'voluntary' patient

As Fennell points out,[220] the mental health legislation is based on the principle that compulsion should be only used as a last resort, with the vast majority of hospital admissions being 'informal' or voluntary.[221] But whilst an adult

---

[209] DH (2008) paras. 36.42–36.43.

[210] Inter alia: Mental Health Act Commission (2004); DH (2006); Office of the Children's Commissioner (2007). During the House of Lords debate on the Mental Health Bill 2006, concerns were repeatedly raised about deficits in the standards of treatment received by adolescents in mental health units. See HL Debs, *Hansard* 15 January 2007, esp. cols. 539–62.

[211] DH (2006) p. 34.   [212] Ibid. at p. 51.

[213] Mental Health Act Commission (2004) p. 34: only 11.5% of those adolescents admitted to adult wards were admitted on to single sex wards. See also DH (2006) p. 29: in 2005/6, whilst 141,661 bed days were spent by children and adolescents on specialist CAMHS wards, 29,306 bed days were spent by 16/17-year-olds on adult wards and 353 bed days spent by under 16s on adult wards.

[214] Office of Children's Commissioner (2007) pp. 71–3.

[215] Mental Health Act Commission (2004) pp. 24–7.

[216] Ibid. at pp. 41–2. Out of 11 under 16-year-olds visited, only two had appropriate educational arrangements. See also Office of the Children's Commissioner (2007) p. 64.

[217] Mental Health Act Commission (2004) pp. 43–7.

[218] MHA 1983, s. 131A. Implementation of this provision is expected in April 2010.

[219] DH (2008) paras. 36.67–36.74.   [220] P. Fennell (2007) p. 119.

[221] I.e. as a patient who consents to treatment, thereby obviating the need to comply with the requirements of the mental health legislation when treating patients against their wishes.

enters hospital voluntarily because he recognises that he needs treatment, matters can be very different for a child, whose parents arrange admission against his wishes. As discussed above, the government only ruled out the informal admission of competent 16 and 17-year-olds.[222] It obviously did not consider that the law governing the compulsory treatment of *Gillick in*competent patients under the age of 18 required any amendment under the mental health reforms. Doctors can still rely on parental consent to admit and treat them,[223] even against their wishes, as 'informal' or 'voluntary' patients.[224] Admittedly the Code directs doctors to take account of the child's views, and place weight on them depending on his or her maturity.[225] It also directs doctors only to rely on a parent's consent if they judge the procedure to which the parent consents, to be within the 'zone of parental control'.[226] But the 'informal patient' regime leaves these minor patients with none of the safeguards automatically available under the mental health legislation to non-consenting *Gillick* competent adolescents aged between 16 and 18. Such a situation places parents in a position of considerable power regarding unwanted treatment. It also arbitrarily assumes that it is only the onset of *Gillick* competence, combined with the adolescent's 16th birthday that produces the need for outside scrutiny.[227]

Existing case law indicates that, in the past, informal admission was, for children, often a convenient way of dealing with difficult cases, not least because of the absence of any real legal scrutiny of such decisions. Indeed, it could amount to a form of 'back door admission' organised by those with parental responsibility in situations where the criteria for detention under the mental health legislation might not be met. Although treatment units do not always use formal detention methods, such as locking their patients in,[228] it appears that many young people cooperate with their parents' arrangements and voluntarily enter and stay in mental health units,[229] as informal patients, despite their later objection to compulsory assessment and/or treatment.[230]

---

[222] MHA 1983, s. 131(4).

[223] But NB DH (2008) para. 36.35–36.36: those aged 16–17 who, by reason of mental impairment, lack capacity for decision-making, are governed by the MCA 2005 and can only be admitted on parental authority if the parents' decision to provide such authority fulfils their son or daughter's best interests, as determined by the MCA 2005, s. 4 unless such admission amounts to a deprivation of liberty, in which case the MCA 2005 is not applicable and the common law is.

[224] Under MHA 1983, s. 131.   [225] DH (2008) para. 36.47.

[226] Ibid. at para. 36.46; discussed below.   [227] B. Hale and J. Fortin (2008) p. 108.

[228] Any unit locking its doors must comply with the secure accommodation regulations; see discussed below.

[229] E.g. *Re C (detention: medical treatment)* [1997] 2 FLR 180: the director of the private eating disorders clinic indicated that most of their patients entered the clinic with the consent of their parents. See also K. Stalker *et al.* (2003) ch. 6, case histories.

[230] E.g. *Re H (a minor) (care proceedings: child's wishes)* [1993] 1 FLR 440: a 15-year-old with an obsessive compulsive disorder was unhappy over his stay in the Maudsley Hospital. Despite this, he returned there on the LA obtaining a care order, only registering his protest by intermittently refusing to eat.

Cases like *R v. Kirklees Metropolitan Borough Council, ex p C*[231] suggest that the legal framework governing the informal admission of minor patients fails to ensure that their stay in specialised units is properly scrutinised. There, a highly disturbed 12-year-old girl was admitted on to an adult ward, in a hospital nightdress, with her daytime clothes locked in a locker for over two weeks, as 'a short-term response'. Her applications for judicial review of the LA's decision to place her in the hospital and damages for false imprisonment were rejected. The court was satisfied that there is nothing in the common law to prevent the admission of a voluntary patient to hospital for assessment,[232] as long as the admission has the patient's 'consent'. In this case, consent had been supplied by the LA, on the child's behalf, it having gained parental responsibility over her through a care order. Equally, parents have similar powers.

Arguably, the situation in *Kirklees* should never have occurred – by failing to apply for a SAO, the LA had ignored the spirit of the guidance accompanying the use of the CA 1989, section 25(1), if not its actual wording.[233] The case shows how children can be 'volunteered' for admission to hospital by their parents or others, for assessment and/or treatment, with no additional check, such as a review by a mental health review tribunal.[234] Caring for handicapped or mentally disturbed children can be extremely burdensome[235] and, as has been pointed out, parents:

> are put between a rock and a hard place. As the nearest relative, when confronted by a choice between their child being sectioned and giving consent on behalf of the child, they will almost always give consent.[236]

The absence of any safeguards in these circumstances is worrying. For example, parents might consent, on their child's behalf, to his or her informal admission to an expensive private psychiatric unit and, as noted below, they might consent, on their child's behalf, to the lengthy use of sedative medication.

The informal admission of minor patients on the sole authority of parental consent will undoubtedly decrease. Whilst the admission of competent but resisting 16 and 17-year-olds is banned entirely, the Code directs doctors not to rely on parental authority for the informal admission of resisting *Gillick* competent under-16-year-olds. For the *Gillick incompetent* under 18s, like the

---

[231] [1993] 2 FLR 187.

[232] Because she was admitted for assessment and not *treatment* for a mental disorder, she was not deemed to be a voluntary patient under the MHA 1983, s. 131.

[233] Discussed below.

[234] If the unit is a nursing home or mental nursing home, those running the home must notify the LA of any child who is accommodated by them for more than three months. The LA must then determine whether his welfare is being adequately safeguarded and promoted: CA 1989, s. 86. But per P. Bartlett and R. Sandland (2000) p. 89: 'such post facto investigation is not a substitute for admission standards'.

[235] Parents may encounter considerable difficulties trying to contain aggressive and sometimes violent behaviour at home before finally agreeing to an admission to a long-term mental health establishment. See K. Stalker *et al.* (2003) pp. 54–5, describing the reasons for three male young people being admitted to a long-stay learning disability hospital.

[236] Earl Howe, HL Deb on the Mental Health Bill, *Hansard* 15 January 2007, col. 546.

girl in the *Kirklees* case, the government apparently sees no need to amend the law. It is obviously relying on the ECtHR's decision in *Nielsen v. Denmark*[237] for its assumption that parents can supply the necessary legal authority for admission and treatment, even when opposed by the patient herself. The Code's interpretation of that decision underlies its warning to a doctor only to rely on a parent's consent if he judges the procedure to which the parent is consenting, to be within the 'zone of parental control'.[238] This obscure phrase is presumably an approximation of the ECtHR's concept of 'proper purpose' which restricts a parent's decision-making rights under Article 8. In *Nielsen*, the mother's decision to have her son placed in the closed psychiatric ward of a state hospital for five and a half months, against his wishes, despite the fact that he was not even mentally ill, albeit he had a 'nervous condition', was deemed to have been for a 'proper purpose'.[239] Had it not been, the boy's challenge under Article 5 would have succeeded.

The scope of the 'proper purpose' concept is obscure; the 'zone of parental control' concept is even less helpful. A doctor is told to ask first whether the decision is 'one that a parent would be expected to make, having regard both to what is considered to be normal practice in our society and to any relevant human rights decisions by the courts'. Second he must ask whether there are 'no indications that the parent might not act in the best interests of the child or young person'.[240] When deciding whether the parent's decision is within the zone, a doctor should consider a range of factors,[241] including the invasiveness of the procedure.[242] The 'less confident a professional is that they can answer both questions in the affirmative' the more likely it is that the parent's decision falls outside the zone.[243] In the context of informal admissions, it might be safer for doctors to take note of the minority view of the ECtHR that the boy's incarceration had clearly infringed his rights under Article 5 and that the medical team, as an agent of the state, should not be allowed to shelter behind the mother's authority. Judge Pettitt in his dissenting judgment stated that:

> In a field as sensitive as that of psychiatric committal, within the framework of the European Convention, in particular under Article 5 thereof, unremitting vigilance is required to avoid the abuse of legislative systems and hospital structures.[244]

The domestic courts might well agree with these sentiments.

(ii) Treatment

A treatment unit cannot avoid using the mental health legislation where a competent patient aged between 16 and 18 refuses to enter a treatment unit

---

[237] (1988) 11 EHRR 175; discussed further in Chapter 3.
[238] DH (2008) paras. 36.9–36.15.   [239] (1988) 11 EHRR 175 at para. 69.
[240] DH (2008) para. 36.10.   [241] Ibid. at para. 36.12.
[242] Ibid. at para. 36.83, Examples A and B: parental consent to medical treatment for a mental disorder suffered by a 13-year-old *Gillick* incompetent girl is within the zone of parental control, but not to the force-feeding of a severely anorexic *Gillick* incompetent girl of 14.
[243] Ibid. at para. 36.11.   [244] (1988) 11 EHRR 175 at 199, para. 3.

voluntarily. It is not uncommon, however, for young patients to acknowledge that they need assistance and voluntarily enter a specialised treatment unit, but then to object vehemently to the form of treatment advised. The decision in *Re K, W and H (minors) (medical treatment)*[245] demonstrates the dangerously vulnerable position adolescent mental health patients may find themselves in, given that a clinical team can obtain consent from any adult with parental responsibility.[246] They have none of the legal safeguards available to adult mental health patients undergoing compulsory treatment. As noted above, the Code advises doctors not to rely on parental authority for treating *Gillick* competent 16 and 17-year-old patients against their will, unless it is an emergency in order to avoid death or severe permanent injury.[247] Similar advice is given in relation to *Gillick* competent but uncooperative under-16-year-olds.[248] In each case doctors are advised to use the mental health legislation or seek court authority, except in an emergency, when the refusal 'would in all likelihood lead to their death or severe permanent injury'.[249]

The government's assumption is that only competent minors who resist treatment should be protected by the mental health legislation, with its special safeguards. But this overlooks the fact that none of those under 18 who are *Gillick* incompetent will have independent representation, despite their feeling unable to voice their opposition to treatment. The treatment of 16 and 17-year-olds suffering from 'an impairment or disturbance in the functioning of the mind or brain' is controlled by the MCA 2005.[250] But if their incapacity for consent does not stem from such an impairment, but is perhaps attributable to their being overwhelmed by the implications of the decision, their treatment remains governed by the common law, including the principle that their parents can authorise it.[251] A similar situation applies to *Gillick* incompetent under-16-year-olds.[252] We know, however, that parents may not pay proper attention to the rights of their mentally disturbed offspring; indeed, the interests of members of the family may often be at complete variance with those of the patient.[253] Admittedly the Code warns doctors of the possible limitations on parents' power of consent.[254] They are advised only to rely on parental authority for treatment if they are convinced that by authorising it parents would be acting within their zone

---

[245] [1993] 1 FLR 854.

[246] Ibid., per Thorpe LJ, at 859: the law was perfectly clear; it was unnecessary for a specialised treatment unit to gain specific issue orders to authorise 'emergency medication' against the wishes of three 15-year-olds, because their mothers had consented in writing to the treatment. They were too highly disturbed to be *Gillick* competent, but even if they had been competent, parental consent was sufficient to exempt the head of the unit from civil or criminal liability.

[247] DH (2008) paras. 36.33–36.34.   [248] Ibid. at paras. 36.43–36.44.   [249] Ibid. at para. 36.34.

[250] But NB ibid. at para. 36.36: if the treatment amounts to a deprivation of the patient's liberty, the MCA 2005 does not apply.

[251] Ibid. at para. 36.37.   [252] Ibid. at paras. 36.45–36.50.   [253] Council of Europe (2000) para. 4.5.

[254] DH (2008) paras. 36.37 and 36.50: parents can only authorise treatment which is within the 'zone of parental control'; discussed above.

of parental control.[255] But this assumes that doctors will rigorously interpret such a concept and seek judicial authority for any treatment they feel unsure about. Leaving the law largely unchanged for these mentally disturbed patients fails to address concerns regarding the absence of controls over specialised units who provide treatment for disturbed adolescents, particularly when compulsory sedating medication is used. The three girls involved in *Re K, W and H (minors) (medical treatment)*[256] were all under the age of 16 and their parents had consented to the use of 'emergency medication'.

Well-run treatment units adopt their own regulations regarding its use, for example, restricting it to situations 'where the young person is at serious risk of self-harm and/or harming others, and other alternative approaches have been attempted and have failed to manage the difficulty'.[257] But there is no legal compulsion on all units to adopt similar controls. In particular, there is the danger that 'emergency medication' becomes a means of control rather than treatment – on parental authority. Only the use of electro-convulsive therapy (ECT) has, at last, been restricted for patients under the age of 18.[258]

(D) The courts – gaining authority for admission and/or treatment

(i) The inherent jurisdiction – compulsory admission and treatment

Parents may find it impossible to persuade a mentally disturbed adolescent to enter a specialised treatment unit – indeed, they may have little or no control over their offspring. Instead, it is not uncommon for a LA to take over responsibility for ensuring that emotionally disturbed adolescents obtain the treatment they need. As discussed below, some LAs apply for a SAO as a means of ensuring that a young person enters the unit and then does not abscond. Others apply for a care order, hoping that the adolescent will cooperate with their plans for his or her admission to a mental health facility. But even if they can persuade the potential patient to enter a unit, he or she may refuse to stay long enough to be treated, choosing to abscond home. So some LAs and clinics have, in the past, invoked the High Court's traditional powers available for the protection of children ('the inherent jurisdiction') to force an adolescent to

---

[255] Discussed above.   [256] [1993] 1 FLR 854.

[257] Excerpt from the written guidance governing the use of emergency medication in the John Clare unit, part of St Andrews Hospital, Northampton, whose treatment programme was considered in *Re K, W and H (minors) (medical treatment)* [1993] 1 FLR 854.

[258] DH (2008) paras. 36.55–36.62. ECT cannot be used on any patient under the age of 18, whether detained under the mental health legislation or not, unless either: (i) he or she consents to the treatment and a second opinion appointed doctor (SOAD) certifies both that the patient is capable of understanding the nature, purpose and likely effect of the treatment and has consented to it and that it is an appropriate form of treatment (MHA 1983, s. 58A(4)); or (ii) legal authority is gained in some other way, e.g. in relation to 16 and 17-year-olds, under the MCA 1983, or from parents (MHA 1983, ss. 56(5) and 58A(5) and (7)) and it is approved by a SOAD as an appropriate form of treatment. Patients under the age of 18 are entitled to independent advocacy to support them in any discussions involving the possible use of ECT (MHA 1983, ss. 130A–C).

enter the unit and then to prevent him or her leaving.[259] In doing so, they sidestep
the statutory ban on *Gillick* competent children being forced to undergo exami-
nations or assessments against their will in the course of protective litigation.[260]

Even before implementation of the HRA 1998, case law indicated that the
judiciary were becoming more aware of the need to respect the rights of young
patients whose admission and treatment they were being asked to authorise
under the inherent jurisdiction.[261] Today, a court knows full well that, as a public
authority[262] it must not itself infringe an adolescent's rights under the ECHR.
Arguably, the judiciary should now be far more critical of claims that the mental
health legislation is inappropriate and refuse to allow the inherent jurisdiction to
be used as a panacea to solve the problems of treatment units and LAs. Hopefully,
the High Court would today be reluctant to allow a LA to 'take all necessary steps'
to remove a *Gillick* competent girl from her home,[263] conscious that a direction of
this kind would risk infringing her rights under Article 5 of the ECHR.

When authorising treatment under the inherent jurisdiction, the courts have
not often included any restrictions over the methods of treatment adopted
by the unit. As in *Re R* and *Re W*, they leave the medical practitioners to use
whatever forms they consider appropriate.[264] But in *Re C (detention: medical
treatment)*,[265] whilst specifically authorising those administering treatment to
use force,[266] Wall J acknowledged that the patient's civil liberties would
undoubtedly be protected by the imposition of stringent safeguards.[267] Such a
view adds credence to the argument that the safeguards available under the
mental health legislation justifies regarding *all* children in psychiatric hospitals
or secure facilities as detained patients for the purposes of compulsorily treating
them.[268] Again, adolescents might claim that the use of the inherent jurisdiction
to authorise compulsory treatment infringes their rights under the HRA 1998.

(ii) Admission and restraint by secure accommodation orders

The CA 1989, section 25(1) limits LAs' power to restrict children's liberty for
more than 72 hours in any 28 days without obtaining a court order to that

---

[259] E.g. *South Glamorgan County Council v. W and B* [1993] 1 FLR 574.

[260] CA 1989, s. 38(6): although, when making an interim supervision order or an interim care order,
a court may include a direction for the child to undergo a medical or psychiatric examination or
other assessment, a child who is 'of sufficient understanding to make an informed decision' may
refuse to submit to it.

[261] E.g. *Re C (detention: medical treatment)* [1997] 2 FLR 180 , per Wall J, at 200: authorised the
enforced detention and treatment of a severely anorexic girl of 16; but to safeguard her liberty, her
stay in the unit was to be limited to four months and treatment provided in accordance with the
views of her doctors 'to ensure that (she) suffers the least distress and retains the greatest dignity'.

[262] HRA 1998, s. 6(1).

[263] I.e. the terms of the direction in *South Glamorgan County Council v. W and B* [1993] 1 FLR 574,
per Douglas Brown J, at 584.

[264] See also *A Metropolitan Borough Council v. DB* [1997] 1 FLR 767, per Cazalet J, at 777:
authorised the use 'reasonable force for the purpose of imposing intrusive necessary medical
treatment' on a 17-year-old crack cocaine addict.

[265] [1997] 2 FLR 180.   [266] Ibid. at 200.   [267] Ibid. at 190.   [268] B. Hoggett (1996) p. 66.

effect.[269] Government guidance stresses that the restriction of a child's liberty 'is a serious step which should only be taken where the needs of the child cannot be met by a more suitable placement elsewhere', but that it should *not* be considered as a 'last resort', but one of a range of positive options.[270] SAOs are often sought by LAs wishing to restrict the liberty of children they are looking after,[271] not for medical reasons but to control their aggressive and violent behaviour, both for their own sake, and for the sake of the public. Such orders are usually made without any intention of ensuring that they receive specialised treatment, though they may need it.[272] The dearth of case law suggests that less well known is the use of SAOs to ensure the admission to and detention of children in specialised secure psychiatric units. Many of these units routinely make the use of security and enforced detention a part of the treatment regime to control and modify aggressive and violent behaviour[273] and such restrictions will normally trigger the need to fulfil the secure accommodation procedure and regulations.[274]

An application for a SAO under section 25 to authorise detention for treatment purposes normally involves arguing that the adolescent is likely to injure him or herself or other persons,[275] unless their liberty is restricted.[276] The relevant regulations clearly attempt to safeguard the liberty of all those requiring compulsory treatment. They prevent the admission of an adolescent to a unit intended to restrict his or her liberty unless *either* the mental health legislation is employed, or a SAO is obtained under the CA 1989, section 25. The two sets of legislation are intended to be exclusive, so that section 25 does

---

[269] CA 1989, s. 25(1): a SAO may not be made regarding a child who is being looked after by a LA unless it appears that: (a) he has a history of absconding and he is likely to abscond from any other description of accommodation, and if he absconds, he is likely to suffer significant harm; or (b) that if he is kept in any other type of accommodation, he is likely to injure himself or other persons. See M. Parry (2000) and J. Fortin (2001) pp. 257–60; further discussed in Chapter 16.

[270] DCSF (2008) para. 5.2.

[271] A LA may only apply for a SAO in relation to a child already being 'looked after' under the CA 1989, s. 22.

[272] Discussed in more detail in Chapter 16.

[273] E.g. K. Stalker *et al.* (2003) pp. 54–5: the methods used for managing 15-year-old 'Alan', as an inpatient in a low security (locked) unit. See also Office of the Children's Commissioner (2007) pp. 26–30: 'patient profiles'.

[274] Children (Secure Accommodation) Regulations 1991, SI 1991/1505, reg. 7(2) and (3) extended CA 1989, s. 25 to govern any child being provided with accommodation by health authorities and in residential care homes, nursing homes and mental nursing homes, i.e. s. 25 governs any such accommodation involving the restriction of liberty for more than 72 hours in any 28 days.

[275] I.e. under CA 1989, s. 25(1)(b). *Re D (secure accommodation order)* [1997] 1 FLR 197, per Singer J: the grounds contained in s. 25(1)(a) and (b) are disjunctive and not conjunctive. So a SAO can be made under s. 25(1)(b) where, despite no history of absconding, there is clear evidence that if the child is kept in any other description of accommodation, he/she is likely to injure him/herself or other persons.

[276] E.g. *A Metropolitan Borough Council v. DB* [1997] 1 FLR 767: the court accepted that a 17-year-old crack-cocaine addict who had just given birth to a baby would injure herself if allowed to discharge herself from the maternity unit.

not apply to any minor detained under the mental health legislation.[277] For those not admitted under the mental health legislation, the restrictions imposed by section 25 and the secure accommodation regulations are intended to protect them from being deprived of their liberty unjustifiably. A minor should not therefore be kept in accommodation 'provided for the purpose of restricting liberty', for more than the authorised 72 hours without this being authorised by a SAO. The statutory guidance suggests that this formula could include taking any measure to prevent a child leaving a room or building of his or her own free will.[278] It also emphasises that any of the more obvious methods, such as locking the child in a room or in part of a building, amounts to 'restriction of liberty' and requires a SAO by way of justification. Consequently, keeping a minor in a locked ward without an order would obviously be a clear breach of the provisions. The guidance acknowledges that there are other practices which are 'not so clear cut'.[279] It is arguable that amongst these might be keeping a patient in a ward in her night clothes, as in the *Kirklees* case.[280] Judicial uncertainty has been expressed over whether a unit not normally designed or intended to provide secure accommodation, is governed by these regulations, if it prevents individual patients leaving the unit against their will.[281] Since their intention is to prevent children being locked up without supervision or restriction, it is arguable that the regulations should be interpreted as generously as possible.

The need for a LA to obtain a court order to restrict the liberty of young people reflects awareness that such a practice must be regulated properly and strictly limited, even when it is to ensure that they obtain essential treatment. The subject of the application must be given the opportunity of having legal representation and a children's guardian will normally be appointed for him or her.[282] Even with these safeguards, the forcible detention of an adolescent patient in a psychiatric unit against his or her will is a Draconian measure. Although the impact of being locked up may be severe, the court need not consider the child's welfare to be its paramount consideration when deciding whether to make such an order.[283] Furthermore, although case law indicates that the court may properly expect psychiatric evidence substantiating the need to admit a child for treatment in a psychiatric unit,[284] it is unclear how often this is insisted upon in practice.

---

[277] The Children (Secure Accommodation) Regulations 1991, SI 1991/1505, reg. 5(1).
[278] DH (1991) para. 8.10.   [279] Ibid.
[280] *R v. Kirklees Metropolitan Borough Council, ex p C* [1993] 2 FLR 187, discussed above.
[281] E.g. in *A Metropolitan Borough Council v. DB* [1997] 1 FLR 767 the maternity ward had security locks on the doors designed to prevent outsiders entering the unit. Per Cazalet J, because DB had not been given a key or pass, the unit intended to restrict her liberty and therefore was governed by the secure accommodation regulations. But see *Re C (detention: medical treatment)* [1997] 2 FLR 180, per Wall J, at 193: secure accommodation should be 'designed for, or have as its primary purpose' the restriction of liberty.
[282] Discussed in Chapter 7.   [283] *Re M (secure accommodation order)* [1995] 1 FLR 418.
[284] *Oxfordshire County Council v. R* [1992] 1 FLR 648, per Douglas Brown J, at 655–6.

Case law makes it clear that a SAO authorising detention in a treatment unit providing wholly inadequate educational supervision can be challenged as being incompatible with Article 5 of the ECHR.[285] Unfortunately, the possibility of challenges brought by minors detained under SAOs does not appear to have provoked consistent provision of educational facilities in secure treatment units.[286] Indeed, in this respect, international guidance is being ignored. The report of the Council of Europe Working Party stressed that every minor placed as an involuntary patient in a psychiatric establishment should be individually assessed and receive, if possible, an individualised educational or training programme, to be organised by the relevant education departments in consultation with the psychiatric establishment.[287]

The legal restrictions imposed by section 25 and its attendant regulations protect a mentally disturbed adolescent's liberty to a degree, in so far as it imposes legislative controls on the circumstances and duration of his or her confinement in the unit. It cannot, however, restrict the form of treatment or provide authority for compulsory treatment. Consent to treatment will often be obtained from the parents, whose parental responsibility is unaffected by the SAO.[288] But since, as discussed above, parents may not assess the child's real needs particularly objectively, the mental health legislation offers far better protection for the rights of the patient once restrained within the unit itself.

Conclusion

The law relating to adolescents' decision-making powers over their health is confusing and arbitrary. On the one hand, the principle of *Gillick* competence recognises their capacity for choice and encourages them to take a responsible attitude to such matters as contraception and other medical procedures that they wish to undergo. But, on the other hand, the law attempts to maintain the right to override their choice to refuse all treatment. Whilst it might be comprehensible for the law to refuse them the right to make life-threatening mistakes, it goes much further and enables parents and doctors to correct any decision they consider to be irrational or unreasonable, and not in the patient's best interests. Such provisions may come under fierce attack from adolescents objecting to their rights under the ECHR being infringed.

Further uncertainty has undermined the legal principles governing contraception and abortion. Case law has confirmed that adolescents are entitled to seek medical advice and treatment free of parental interference with their sexual privacy – but this depends on their legal competence. Meanwhile, for

---

[285] *Re K (a child) (secure accommodation order: right to liberty)* [2001] 2 All ER 719; discussed further in Chapter 16.

[286] As discussed above, educational provision for young patients in many mental health units is minimal or non-existent.

[287] Council of Europe (2000) para. 8.4.

[288] E.g. as in *Re K, W and H (minors) (medical treatment)* [1993] 1 FLR 854.

those with behavioural problems, the common law offers few obvious safe-guards to ensure that their rights to bodily integrity and liberty are fully respected. It appears that only a more consistent use of the mental health legislation will ensure that compulsory restriction of liberty and compulsory forms of treatment are well regulated and subject to appropriate external scrutiny. It is ironic that a minority status deprives younger adolescents of a respect for the civil liberties currently available to all other mental patients. Overall the law certainly no longer matches up to the promise implicit in Lord Scarman's judgment in *Gillick v West Norfolk and Wisbech Area Health Authority*[289] that adolescents had gained a degree of autonomy over their own bodies.

BIBLIOGRAPHY

NB many of these publications can be obtained on the relevant organisation's website.

Bartlett, P. and Sandland, R. (2000) *Mental Health Law, Policy and Practice*, Blackstone Press Ltd.

BMRB International (2004) *Tracking Survey Wave 12 Evaluation of the Teenage Pregnancy Strategy, Report of results of twelve waves of research*, BMRB International.

Bradshaw, J., Kemp, P., Baldwin, S. and Rowe, A. (2004) *The Drivers of Social Exclusion: A Review of the Literature for the Social Exclusion Unit in the Breaking the Cycle Series*, Social Exclusion Unit.

Brazier, M. and Bridge, C. (1996) 'Coercion or Caring: Analysing Adolescent Autonomy' 16 *Legal Studies* 84.

Bridge, C. (1999) 'Religious Beliefs and Teenage Refusal of Medical Treatment' 62 *Modern Law Review* 585.

British Medical Association (BMA) (2001) *Consent, Rights and Choices in Health Care for Children and Young People*, BMJ Books.

British Medical Association (BMA) and the Law Society (2004) *Assessment of Mental Capacity: Guidance for Doctors and Lawyers*, BMJ Books.

Bynner, J. and Londra, M. (2004) *The Impact of Government Policy on Social Exclusion Among Young People: A Review of the Literature for the Social Exclusion Unit in the Breaking the Cycle Series*, Social Exclusion Unit.

Cater, S. and Coleman, L. (2006) *'Planned' Teenage Pregnancy: Perspectives of Young Parents from Disadvantaged Backgrounds*, Joseph Rowntree Foundation.

Collishaw, S, Maughan, B., Goodman, R. and Pickles, A. (2004) 'Time Trends in Adolescent Mental Health' 45 *Journal of Child Psychology and Psychiatry* 1350.

Committee on the Rights of the Child (2002) *Concluding Observations of the Committee on the Rights of the Child: United Kingdom of Great Britain and Northern Ireland* CRC/C/15/Add 188 2002, Centre for Human Rights, Geneva.

Committee on the Rights of the Child (2008) *Concluding Observations of the Committee on the Rights of the Child: United Kingdom of Great Britain and Northern Ireland* CRC/C/GBR/CO/4, Centre for Human Rights, Geneva.

---

[289] [1986] AC 112.

Council of Europe (2000) 'White Paper' on the Protection of the Human Rights and Dignity of People Suffering From Mental Disorder, Especially Those Placed as Involuntary Patients in a Psychiatric Establishment, CM (2000) 23 Addendum.

Cyranowski, J., Frank, E., Young, E. and Shear, K. (2000) 'Adolescent Onset of the Gender Difference in Lifetime Rates of Major Depression' 57 Archives of General Psychiatry 21.

Department for Children, Schools and Families (DCSF) (2008) The Children Act 1989 Guidance and Regulations, Volume I, Court Orders, The Stationery Office.

Department for Children, Schools and Families (DCSF) and Department of Health (DH) (2008) Teenage Parents: Who Cares?, DCSF.

Department for Constitutional Affairs (DCA) (2007) Mental Capacity Act 2005: Code of Practice, The Stationery Office.

Department for Education and Skills (DfES) (2006a) Teenage Pregnancy Next Steps: Guidance for Local Authorities and Primary Care Trusts on Effective Delivery of Local Strategies, DfES.

Department for Education and Skills (DfES) (2006b) Teenage Pregnancy: Accelerating the Strategy to 2010, DfES.

Department of Health (DH) (1986) Circular HC (86) 1, DH.

Department of Health (DH) (1991) Residential Care, Volume 4 of The Children Act 1989 Guidance and Regulations, HMSO.

Department of Health (DH) (2004a) Best Practice Guidance for Doctors and Other Health Professionals on the Provision of Advice and Treatment to Young People Under 16 on Contraception, Sexual and Reproductive Health, Reference Number 3382, DH.

Department of Health (DH) (2004b) National Service Framework for Children, Young People and Maternity Services, Executive Summary, DH.

Department of Health (DH) (2006) Report on the Implementation of Standard 9 of the National Service Framework for Children, Young People and Maternity Services, DH.

Department of Health (DH) (2008) Code of Practice: Mental Health Act 1983, The Stationery Office.

Department of Constitutional Affairs (DCA) (2007) MCA 2005: Code of Practice, The Stationery Office.

Douglas, G. (1992) 'The Retreat from Gillick' 55 Modern Law Review 569.

Downie, A. (1999) 'Consent to Medical Treatment – Whose View of Welfare?' 29 Family Law 818.

Eekelaar, J. (1993) 'White Coats or Flak Jackets? Doctors, Children and the Courts – Again', 109 Law Quarterly Review 182.

Feldman, D. (2002) Civil Liberties and Human Rights in England and Wales, Oxford University Press.

Fennell, P. (2007) Mental Health: The New Law, Jordans.

Ferguson, L. (2004) The End of an Age: Beyond Age Restrictions for Minors' Medical Treatment Decisions, Law Commission of Canada.

Fortin, J. (2001) 'Children's Rights and the Use of Physical Force' 13 Child and Family Law Quarterly 243.

    (2006a) 'Accommodating Children's Rights in a Post Human Rights Act Era' 69 Modern Law Review 299.

    (2006b) 'Children's Rights – Substance or Spin?' Family Law 759.

Freeman, M. (2005) 'Rethinking *Gillick*' 13 *International Journal of Children's Rights* 201.

General Medical Council (GMC) (2007) *0–18 Years: Guidance for All Doctors*, GMC.

Gostin, L. (1992) 'Consent to Treatment: The Incapable Person' in Dyer, C. (ed.) *Doctors, Patients and the Law*, Blackwell Scientific Publications.

Green, H., McGinnity, A., Meltzer, H., Ford, T. and Goodman, R. (2004) *Mental Health of Children and Young People in Great Britain, 2004*, Palgrave Macmillan.

HM Government (2008) *Information Sharing: Guidance for Practitioners and Managers*, Department for Children, Schools and Families.

Hale, B. (2005) 'What Can the Human Rights Act 1998 do for My Mental Health?' 17 *Child and Family Law Quarterly* 295.

Hale, B. and Fortin, J. (2008) 'The Legal Principles Governing the Care and Treatment of Children with Mental Health' in Rutter, M., Bishop, D., Pine, D., Scott, S., Stevenson, J., Taylor, E. and Thapar, A. (eds.) *Rutter's Child and Adolescent Psychiatry*, Blackwell Publishing.

Healthcare Commission (2007) HC 97, *State of Healthcare 2007*, The Stationery Office.

Health Development Agency (2004) *Teenage Pregnancy: an Overview of the Research Evidence*, Health Development Agency.

Health Protection Agency (2006) *Diagnoses of Selected STIs by Region, Sex and Age Group. United Kingdom: 1996–2005*, Health Protection Agency.

Hobcraft, J. and Kiernan, K. (2001) 'Childhood Poverty, Early Motherhood and Adult Social Exclusion' 52 *British Journal of Sociology* 495.

Hoggett, B. (1996) *Mental Health Law*, Sweet and Maxwell.

Huxtable, R. (2000) '*Re M (Medical Treatment: Consent)* Time to remove the "flak jacket"?' 12 *Child and Family Law Quarterly* 83.

Jones, R. (2006) *Mental Health Act Manual*, Sweet and Blackwell.

Kennedy, I. (1992) *Treat Me Right: Essays in Medical Law and Ethics*, Clarendon Press.

Lansdown, R. (1998) 'Listening to Children: Have We Gone Too Far (or Not Far Enough)?' 91 *Journal of the Royal Society of Medicine* 457.

Lee, E., Clements, S., Ingham, R. and Stone, N. (2004) *A Matter of Choice? Explaining National Variations in Teenage Abortion and Motherhood*, Joseph Rowntree Foundation.

Lewis, P. (2001) 'The Medical Treatment of Children' in Fionda, J. (ed.) *Legal Concepts of Childhood*, Hart Publishing.

Loughrey, J. (2008) 'Can You Keep a Secret? Children, Human Rights, and the Law of Medical Confidentiality' 20 *Child and Family Law Quarterly* 312.

Lowe, N. and Juss, S. (1993) 'Medical Treatment – Pragmatism and the Search for Principle' 56 *Modern Law Review* 865.

McCafferty, C. (1999) 'Won't Consent? Can't Consent! Refusal of Medical Treatment' 29 *Family Law* 335.

Mason, J. and Laurie, G. (2006) *Mason and McCall Smith's Law and Medical Ethics*, Oxford University Press.

Masson, J. (1993) 'Re W: Appealing from the Golden Cage' 5 *Journal of Child Law* 37.

Mental Health Act Commission (2004) *Safeguarding Children and Adolescents Detained Under the MHA 1983 on Adult Psychiatric Wards*, The Stationery Office.

Moffitt, T. and the E-Risk Study Team (2002) 'Teen-aged Mothers in Contemporary Britain' 43 *Journal of Child Psychology and Psychiatry* 727.

Montgomery, J. (2003) *Health Care Law*, Oxford University Press.

National Statistics (2007) *Social Trends No 37*, The Stationery Office.

Office for National Statistics (ONS) (2008) *Social Trends No 38*, Palgrave Macmillan.

Office of the Children's Commissioner (2007) *Pushed into the Shadows: Young Peoples' Experience of Adult Mental Health Facilities*, Office of the Children's Commissioner.

Parliamentary Office of Science and Technology (2004) *Teenage Sexual Health. Postnote*, 217, 1–4.

Parry, M. (2000) 'Secure Accommodation – the Cinderella of Family Law' 12 *Child and Family Law Quarterly* 101.

Social Exclusion Unit (SEU) (1999) *Teenage Pregnancy* Cm 4342, Cabinet Office.

Social Exclusion Unit (SEU) (2000) *Young People*, Report of the Policy Action Team 12, Cabinet Office.

Stalker, K, Carpenter, J., Phillips, R., Connors, C., MacDonald, C. and Eyre, J. (2003) *Care and Treatment? Supporting Children With Complex Needs in Healthcare Settings*, Joseph Rowntree Foundation.

Tabberer, S., Hall, C., Prendergast, S. and Webster, A., (2000) *Teenage Pregnancy and Choice, Abortion or Motherhood: Influences on the Decision*, Joseph Rowntree Foundation.

Tan, J., Hope, T., Steward, A. and Fitzpatrick, R. (2003) 'Control and Compulsory Treatment in Anorexia Nervosa: the Views of Patients and Parents' 26 *International Journal of Law and Psychiatry* 627.

Taylor, R. (2007) 'Reversing the Retreat From *Gillick*? *R (Axon) v Secretary of State for Health*' 18 *Child and Family Law Quarterly* 81.

UNICEF, Innocenti Research Centre (2001) *A League Table of Teenage Births in Rich Nations*, Innocenti Report Card Issue No. 3 July 2001, UNICEF.

UNICEF, Innocenti Research Centre (2000) *A League Table of Child Poverty in Rich Nations*, Innocenti Report Card Issue No. 1 June 2000, UNICEF.

UNICEF, Innocenti Research Centre (2007) *Child Poverty in Perspective : An Overview of Child Well-being in Rich Countries*, Innocenti Report Card Issue No. 7, UNICEF.

Wiggins, M., Oakley, A., Sawtell, M., Austerberry, H., Clemens, F. and Elbourne, D. (2005) *Teenage Parenthood and Social Exclusion: a Multi-method Study*, Summary Report of Findings, Social Science Research Unit Report, Institute of Education.

Chapter 6

Promoting consultation and decision-making in schools

(1) Introduction

Views about the proper aims of education often depend on the perspectives of those considering the question. Policy-makers may stress the needs of a commercially sophisticated society,[1] whilst others assert the potential value to the individual pupil of a good education.[2] The Warnock Committee perceived the tensions in these two approaches. In their view, education is not an end in itself, but also a means to an end. It has dual aims: to enlarge the 'child's knowledge, experience and imaginative understanding, and thus his awareness of moral values and capacity for enjoyment' and also to enable the child 'to enter the world after formal education is over as an active participant in society and a responsible contributor to it, capable of achieving as much independence in it as possible'.[3]

School life may enable some children to escape from narrow and stultifying home environments and help them assess critically the ideologies with which they have been brought up. But the principles of education law are only slowly adjusting to the maturing pupil's capacity for undertaking responsibilities in school and reaching important decisions over his or her education, without parental interference. Indeed, the efforts of policy-makers to cast parents in the role of the consumers of education has produced a system of education law which, more often than not, treats children as adjuncts of their parents, rather than as responsible agents in their own right.

This narrow approach is surprising given the events of the late 1960s and early 1970s, when a pupils' rights movement made a brief appearance in British schools.[4] Student militancy had spread from universities into the schools. Various student bodies[5] started discussing and asserting a range of pupils' rights in schools, including the right to educational democracy through the

---

[1] E.g. DfES (2007a), Executive Summary, paras. 1 and 1.1.

[2] E.g. inter alia: Universal Declaration of Human Rights, Art. 26(2); United Nations Convention on the Rights of the Child (CRC), Art. 29; National Advisory Committee on Creative and Cultural Education (1999) para. 21; M. Dowling *et al.* (2006) pp. 153–6.

[3] H.M. Warnock (1978) para. 1.4. See also Committee on the Rights of the Child (2001) para. 2.

[4] S. Cunningham and M. Lavalette (2002) pp. 178–82.

[5] The Schools' Action Union (SAU) and the National Union of School Students (NUSS).

establishment of school councils, the abolition of school uniform and physical punishment and the right to freedom of expression. On 10 May 1972, up to 1,500 striking children marched to County Hall London,[6] and handed in a letter demanding, amongst other things, the right to publish school magazines without censorship, to organise student meetings during lunch breaks and after school on school premises, to join student unions and engage in political activity, including strikes. Further demonstrations followed.[7]

It is unclear why the children's rights movement in English schools ran out of steam so rapidly.[8] Possibly it was because, unlike in the US, the boundaries to children's rights could not be tested out in a school setting against the provisions of a written constitution. There, Supreme Court decisions like *Tinker v. Des Moines Independent Community School District*[9] and *Goss v. Lopez*[10] emphasised the right of school children to be treated with respect.[11] In *Tinker*, the Supreme Court found that the First Amendment rights of three students had been violated when school authorities suspended them from school for wearing black armbands to protest over the government's policy in Vietnam. The court explained that: 'Students in school as well as out of school are "persons" under our Constitution. They are possessed of fundamental rights which the State must respect.'[12] In *Goss*, the Supreme Court held that students facing disciplinary action by school officials were entitled to due process protection, such as prior notice of the action and a chance to be heard before punishment. Meanwhile, in the UK, the House of Lords' decision in *Gillick v. West Norfolk and Wisbech Area Health Authority*[13] had relatively little impact on education law. Schools were left virtually unaffected by the concept of according legal competence to young people in a variety of contexts.

Education legislation could do far more to promote children's need to be treated as individuals and to reach responsible decisions over their own education, particularly as they reach adolescence. After briefly considering the concept of a right to education per se, this chapter devotes more detailed discussion to four further topics particularly relevant to young people. It first considers the law's response to the problem of truancy; the second discusses the methods for dealing with disruptive children in school; the third assesses the extent to which children are involved in school policy and administration; and the fourth relates to the provision of sex education in schools. A possible fifth topic, concentrating on the legal principles governing the provision of religious education and collective worship in schools, is discussed elsewhere, in the

---

[6] The headquarters of the then, Greater London Council.

[7] E.g. on 17 May 1972, approximately 2,500 pupils absented themselves from school to attend a 'Schools Demo' in Trafalgar Square mounted by the SAU.

[8] Militant action occurred again briefly in 1985. S. Cunningham and M. Lavalette (2002) pp. 182–6.

[9] 393 US 503 (1969).   [10] 419 US 565 (1975).

[11] But per B. Hafen (1976) p. 646, the decision in *Tinker* protected *parents'* rights to teach and influence their children against state claims that would limit them. The parents of the students involved had encouraged their children to wear the armbands and were obviously instrumental in bringing the litigation that ensued.

[12] 393 US 503 (1969) at 511.   [13] [1986] AC 112.

context of the educational rights of minority children.[14] Regarding the terminology used, the introduction of children's trusts up and down the country has led to the duties of many local education authorities (LEAs) being assumed by children's services authorities; consequently the term used throughout this chapter is local authority (LA), not LEA.[15]

(2) A right to education

The right to be educated is probably one of the most important of children's moral and legal rights; without it they may be unable to develop their 'personality, talents and mental and physical abilities to their fullest potential'.[16] The notion that the right to education is a fundamental human right is embedded in many international documents, notably the International Covenant on Economic, Social and Cultural Rights (ICESCR), which requires all states parties to 'recognize the right of everyone to education',[17] and then expands on the ways in which this should be fulfilled.[18]

Meanwhile the huge body of English education legislation is oddly perverse in the way it largely ignores those who are the reason for its existence. Indeed, little has changed since, nearly a decade ago, Tomaševski, UN special reporter, criticised the failure of the educational system here to promote children's human rights in education. She caustically observed of the domestic legislation:

> Statutory enactments relating to education do not use human rights language nor do they mention international human rights law. Where individual rights are mentioned, these relate to parents who have been allowed to challenge school admissions as of 1980.[19]

She considered that whilst a great deal of jurisprudence had developed on interpreting parental challenges on admissions, conditions in schools, methods of teaching and discipline, this was in the narrow context of education law, rather than as a means of exploring the human right of education itself. She saw the provision of schooling in the UK being treated as a relationship between school and parents, without children having a legal standing – 'children are thus absent as actors in this process although it is aimed at their learning'.[20] Since then, the government is showing a burgeoning awareness of children 'as actors in this process'. There is, for example, the new need for schools to consider their wider role within the community and to promote pupils' well-being.[21] Of even

---

[14] See Chapter 11.
[15] The same term is also used in Chapters 11 and 12, both of which deal with aspects of education law.
[16] Phrasing used in Art. 29(1)(a) of the CRC.   [17] ICESCR, Art. 13(1).
[18] ICESCR, Art. 13(2)(a)–(d). These provisions are largely mirrored by Art. 28 of the CRC.
[19] K. Tomaševski (1999) para. 29.   [20] Ibid. at para. 31.
[21] Education Act (EA) 2002, s. 21(5)–(9) (as inserted by Education and Inspections Act (EIA) 2006): the duty to promote the 'well-being' of pupils at the school must be interpreted by school governing bodies as meaning their well-being, as interpreted by the Children Act (CA) 2004, s. 10(2)(a)–(e), i.e. the five Every Child Matters outcomes. See T. Chamberlain *et al.* (2006).

greater importance is schools' new duty to invite and consider pupils' views over 'the conduct of the school'.[22] Such reforms may gradually produce a sea change in educationalists' approach to their pupils.

Tomaševski is not the only commentator to have criticised the way in which English education law treats parents as the consumers of education, whilst ignoring children's own educational rights.[23] In an increasingly rights orientated society, education legislation astonishingly fails to acknowledge openly that children have any 'rights' to education. For example, it refers instead to the duties imposed on every LA. LAs must secure that there are 'sufficient schools' in their area for providing full-time[24] primary and secondary education,[25] so that all pupils have the opportunity to gain an 'appropriate education'.[26] Despite failing to use 'rights language', one can surmise from these legislative duties that all children do have a *right* to free full-time and appropriate education. Furthermore, it should be noted that LAs are now specifically required to promote high standards, a fair access to educational opportunity,[27] and also 'the fulfilment by every child concerned of his educational potential'.[28] Since, in the past, such 'target duties' have not proved easy for individuals to enforce,[29] it seems unlikely that such vague aspirational phrases have added significantly to an individual child's ability to obtain a high standard of education.

It seems that the Human Rights Act (HRA) 1998 gives these domestic duties extra teeth – but only up to a point. The inclusion of the right to education within the European Convention for the Protection of Human Rights and Fundamental Freedoms (1950) (ECHR) was derived largely from a concern to protect parents' right to educate their children according to their own beliefs, free from interference by totalitarian regimes.[30] Despite the negative phraseology adopted by Article 2 of the First Protocol (hereafter A2P1) of the ECHR,[31]

---

[22] EA 2002, s. 29B, as inserted by Education and Skills Act (ESA) 2008, s. 157. See also EA 2002, s. 176(1)(a); both provisions are discussed in more detail below.

[23] Inter alia: P. Meredith (2001) esp. pp. 203–8; D. Monk (2002) esp. pp. 50–6; N. Harris (2007) esp. pp. 48–63.

[24] Education Act (EA) 1996, s. 2(1), (2).

[25] The schools must be sufficient in number, character and equipment: EA 1996, s. 14(2).

[26] EA 1996, s. 14(2). S. 14(3)(a) and (b): education is 'appropriate' if it offers such variety of instruction and training (including practical instruction and training appropriate to their different needs) as may be desirable in view of (a) the pupils' different ages, abilities and aptitudes and (b) the different periods for which pupils may be expected to remain in school.

[27] EA 1996, s. 13A(1)(a)–(b).   [28] EA 1996, s. 13A(1)(c).

[29] E.g. *R v. Inner London Education Authority, ex p Ali and Murshid* [1990] 2 Admin LR 822: unsuccessful application for judicial review by a parent whose child, along with others, had no school place due to staff shortages. Held: the LA's duty under EA 1944, s. 8 (now EA 1996, s. 14) to provide 'sufficient' places is only a 'target' duty, not an absolute duty. N. Harris (2007) pp. 40–6 discusses the difficulties faced by individuals attempting to enforce the educational duties of public agencies.

[30] N. Harris (2005a) pp. 83–8. Thus Art. 2 of the First Protocol (A2P1) of the ECHR refers to states' obligation to respect the 'right of parents to ensure such education and teaching in conformity with their own religious and philosophical convictions'. Discussed further in Chapter 11.

[31] 'No one shall be denied the right to education.'

it guarantees a right of access to an 'effective' form of education.[32] In effect this comprises three separate rights: the right of access to such educational establishments as exist; a right to effective (but not the most effective possible) education; and the right to official recognition of academic qualifications. Nevertheless, states are left with complete discretion to determine for themselves issues about resourcing and delivering the educational system.[33] According to recent domestic case law, unless the education provided is so grossly inadequate that it fails to reach a minimum standard, it offers little succour to those wishing to complain, for example, about the standard of teaching in any particular school.[34] Nor does the Convention entitle a pupil access to, or to remain in, any particular educational institution.[35]

Despite these limitations, the HRA 1998 has given an individual child wrongfully denied an existing school place a right of action based on A2P1 of the ECHR, with damages or a declaration available against the relevant public authority.[36] Consequently, it seems that the pupil who has not been provided with any school place at all might also claim that the LA's failure amounts to an infringement of his or her rights under A2P1 of the ECHR. Indeed, the domestic courts might now show less sympathy with an LA's argument that it has not deliberately withheld educational places and that the lack of resources will only be temporary.[37]

(3) School attendance

(A) The merits of compulsory school

If children attend school regularly, it will probably have a profound influence on their lives. Under the current regime, they will spend approximately 2,000 days there between the ages of 5 and 16.[38] This total will expand dramatically when the government's current plans come to fruition: to establish a nation-wide system of extended schools[39] and to keep teenagers in school or training

---

[32] *Belgian Linguistics Case (No. 2)* (1968) 1 EHRR 252 at 280–3, esp. para. 4.   [33] Ibid. at para. 3.

[34] *Ali v. Head Teacher and Governors of Lord Grey School* [2006] UKHL 14, [2006] 2 All ER 457, per Lord Bingham, at [24]: the guarantee contained in A2P1 of the ECHR is 'a weak one, and deliberately so', providing no Convention guarantee of education of a particular kind or quality. See also *A v. Essex County Council* [2008] EWCA Civ 364, [2008] 321, per Sedley LJ, at [10]; *R (O) v. London Borough of Hackney* [2006] EWHC 3405, [2007] ELR 405, per Kenneth Parker QC, at [35]. Discussed further in Chapter 12.

[35] *Simpson v. United Kingdom* (1989) 64 DR 188.

[36] *Ali v. Head Teacher and Governors of Lord Grey School* [2006] UKHL 14, [2006] 2 All ER 457: a right of action lies if a pupil has been wrongfully excluded from school and provided with no other form of education; discussed below.

[37] As in *R v. Inner London Education Authority, ex p Ali and Murshid* (1990) 2 Admin LR 822. See fn 29 above.

[38] EA 1996, s. 8: 16-year-olds must wait for the next 'school-leaving date' before they can leave school.

[39] DfES (2005a) ch. 8: extended schools must provide – 'wraparound' childcare from 8a.m. to 6p.m. all year round; various activities, e.g. after school clubs; parenting support; referral to specialist support services; community access to local facilities, e.g. sports and IT. The government wants all schools to offer access to extended services by 2010.

until their 18th birthday.[40] Indeed, the notion of remaining on school premises for 10 hours per day until they attain such an age reproduces many child's worst nightmare.

Even under the current regime, it is difficult to convince all children that attending school will benefit them when they can think of far better ways to spend their time. Since the right to free state education is wasted on a child who refuses to attend school, the law imposes an absolute duty on parents to see that their children of compulsory school age receive a full-time education. Not all are successful. Truancy in schools has, over the last 15 years, become an intractable problem.[41] It seems clear that the total number of children who were missing school is probably much higher than official figures suggest,[42] and that official targets aiming for reductions have been over-optimistic.[43] Ironically, those children who stay away from school because they consider that it has nothing to offer them may eventually be barred from attending altogether. This is because when disaffected pupils do attend they often behave so disruptively that they are permanently excluded.

In the face of such problems, should the law attempt to make pupils stay at school if they decide that education is not for them? Children's liberationists such as Holt and Farson urged that children of all ages should have adult freedoms, including the right to decide whether they go to school and what lessons to attend.[44] Today such attitudes seem extreme. Contemporary children's liberationists acknowledge that allowing young children to choose whether they wish to attend school might actually reduce their chances of developing a capacity for autonomy later.[45] Indeed, the international treaties make no attempt to accommodate children's wishes in the matter of school attendance. Thus the CRC requires states to make primary education 'compulsory and available free to all'[46] and to 'take measures to encourage regular attendance at schools and the reduction of drop-out rates'.[47]

What, however, of those who are often too large to frog-march to school? Some argue that compulsion for this older group is not only counterproductive but brings education and teaching into disrepute.[48] Since they can take legal

---

[40] Discussed below.

[41] Despite efforts to reduce levels of truancy, the rates of unauthorised absences remain stubbornly high. The percentage of half days missed in maintained secondary schools in 2005/6 due to unauthorised absence was 1.42% (0.33% increase over figures published in 2006). DfES (2007b). In 2005, 7.8% of secondary school pupils missed 20% or more of their schooling.

[42] Official measures of truanting in primary schools may significantly underestimate the true rates. H. Malcolm *et al.* (2003) found (at p. 61) that 27% of primary pupils admitted missing school at some point.

[43] A series of official truancy reduction targets have not been met. E.g. SEU (1998) para. 4.2, truancy rates should be reduced by one-third by 2002 – not achieved; DfES Public Service Agreement target to reduce 2003 levels absence in school by 8% by 2008 – not achieved.

[44] J. Holt (1974) and R. Farson (1978). The ideas of Holt and Farson are discussed in Chapter 1.

[45] E.g. R. Lindley (1989) p. 85.   [46] Art. 28(1)(a).   [47] Art. 28(1)(e).

[48] T. Jeffs (2002) esp. p. 56. See also R. Lindley (1989) pp. 88–92: suggests that those between 13 and 16 should be allowed to take full-time employment.

responsibility for seeking contraceptive help, should they not also be allowed to decide whether to attend school, without involving their parents?[49] Despite the plausibility of these arguments, the House of Lords in the *Gillick* decision[50] had not intended to introduce a blanket liberality regarding a fundamental aspect of the lives of all those over a specified age. It introduced the sophisticated and difficult notion of individual children acquiring legal maturity on an incremental and case-by-case basis – a concept which would cause chaos if applied to school attendance. Allowing 13-year-olds to decide for themselves whether to attend school would probably merely swell the numbers of truanting pupils who generally go home or go to friends' houses 'to do nothing in particular'.[51] For many of those who truant, 'doing nothing' involves becoming involved in crime.[52] Since an adolescent's ability to reach wise decisions over whether to attend school may be undermined by a variety of factors, ranging from parental illness to peer pressure or bullying, it seems entirely justifiable for the state to insist on their school attendance, at least until they attain the age of 16. It is questionable, however, whether the government is wise to extend the age of compulsory participation in school or workplace training to the age of 18.[53]

(B) Tackling truancy

(i) Criminal sanctions

The government is strongly committed to tackling truancy. Claiming that small numbers of 'persistent absentees' are largely responsible for the continuing high rates,[54] it has ambitious new targets for reducing their numbers.[55] Despite its producing ever more authoritarian sanctions, the law cannot play a particularly constructive part in coercing physically mature young people into school, if they are determined not to attend. Even so, an official determination to provide legal sanctions which bite has led to truancy becoming excessively criminalised, both for children and parents. As a last resort, LAs can prosecute a truant's parents for failure to comply with their duty[56] to ensure that their children

---

[49] M. Grenville (1988) p. 18.

[50] *Gillick v. West Norfolk and Wisbech Area Health Authority* [1986] AC 112.

[51] Audit Commission (1996) p. 68.

[52] J. Fionda (2005) pp. 220–1: summary of the research linking school non-attendance and crime. See also S. Bhabra *et al.* (2006) p. 101. Youthful truants typically commit their first offence at the age of 11 or under.

[53] The 'participation age' is to be raised in stages: from 2013 – until the end of the academic year young people attain 17; from 2015 – until the attainment of 18. See inter alia: DfES (2007a), DCSF (2008a), DCSF (2008f), ESA 2008, ss. 1–2. Discussed below and in Chapter 4.

[54] DCSF (2007g) para. 4.105.

[55] Ibid. at para. 4.107: all LAs should reduce the number of persistent absentees to 5% of their secondary school population by 2011.

[56] EA 1996, s. 7. But note that since a child can receive suitable full-time education by regular attendance at school 'or otherwise', parents may choose to educate their children at home. Nevertheless, they must provide education suitable to the child's age, ability and aptitude – a condition not satisfied if the child is allowed to choose what he or she learns. E.g. *Baker v. Earl* [1960] Crim LR 363.

attend school,[57] preceded by due warning.[58] Parents may be convicted, whether or not they knew of their child's absences and irrespective of his or her attitude to attendance.[59] The law makes no concessions and simply expects them to overcome any reluctance on the child's part.

It remains unclear whether the procedural 'alternatives to prosecution', such as the issuing of fixed penalty notices[60] and fast-track prosecution schemes,[61] achieve an improvement in pupils' attendance.[62] Although they thereby allow parents of truants to avoid prosecution, data show that schools and LAs vary enormously in their use.[63] The incipient criminalisation of truancy was also reinforced when the police became involved, with power to issue penalty notices[64] and carry out 'truancy sweeps'. They can collect up children of compulsory school age whom they find in public places during school hours and take them to 'designated premises' or back to their schools.[65] Some police officers also work in schools on a regular basis, offering advice and support over a variety of issues, including deterring truancy. Researchers found very mixed feelings amongst LAs and the police over the efficacy of a police presence in schools,[66] and more particularly of truancy sweeps and other similar measures.[67] As discussed below, the governing bodies of schools and LAs may prefer to avoid resorting to criminal remedies by asking parents of truants to enter into a parenting contract. But these too have an authoritarian flavour.

The fact that criminal sanctions against parents have become more Draconian arises largely from the policy-makers' abiding conviction that some parents not

---

[57] EA 1996: s. 443(1) – failure to comply with a school attendance order; s. 444(1) – failure to ensure the child's regular attendance at school. Both are absolute offences, with no defence available to the parent even if they were unaware of the child's absence and even if they could not make the child attend had they been aware of it. E.g. *Barnfather v. Islington LBC* [2003] ELR 263 and *Hampshire County Council v. E* [2007] EWHC 2584 (Admin), [2008] ELR 260. Cf. s. 444(1A) – failure to ensure that the child attends school regularly, knowing that he is failing to do so, unless (under s. 444(1B)) the parent can show that he had reasonable justification for such failure. E.g. *R (P) v. Liverpool City Magistrates* [2006] EWHC 887 (Admin), [2006] ELR 386. But NB a parent can be convicted under s. 444(1), even if he establishes a defence to an offence under s. 444(1A). Penalties include: fine up to £2,500; imprisonment for up to 3 months; community penalties, e.g. electronic tagging.

[58] EA 1996, s. 437: prosecution under s. 443 must be preceded by a school attendance order served on the parent requiring him to satisfy the LA within a specified time (not less than 15 days) that the child is regularly attending school.

[59] *Crump v. Gilmore* (1969) 113 Sol Jo 998.

[60] I.e. parents can avoid prosecution altogether if they pay fixed penalties (£50 if paid within 28 days, rising to £100 if paid after 28 but within 42 days) before/instead of criminal proceedings under EA 1996, s. 444 being brought against them. Such notices can be issued by LAs, head teachers and police officers. Education (Penalty Notices) (England) Regulations 2007 (SI 2007/1867) and DCSF (2007a) ch. 5. See also DfES (2007c).

[61] Under 'Fast-track management schemes' for truancy, a court date is set at the beginning of a fixed period, during which the LA works with parents to improve their children's attendance, the prosecution being dropped if matters improve.

[62] K. Halsey *et al.* (2004).   [63] DfES (2007c).   [64] See fn 60 above.

[65] Crime and Disorder Act (CDA) 1998, s. 16.   [66] S. Hallam *et al.* (2005) pp. 110–12.

[67] National Audit Office (2005) paras. 3.16–3.19 and Action on Rights for Children (2005).

only condone their children's truanting but actively encourage it.[68] In reality, research indicates that very few parents condone truancy, that most take regular attendance at school very seriously and that they are often unaware of their child's truancy.[69] Few pupils themselves, when asked, admit skipping school with parental consent; pupils of all ages most often identify school-based causes, such as extreme boredom, bullying and problems with teachers.[70] In any event, well-publicised criminal sanctions do not appear to deter the small proportion of irresponsible parents from repeatedly condoning their children's long-term truancy.[71] Furthermore, utilising the criminal justice system to combat truancy will not necessarily accomplish any change in the attitudes or habits of truants themselves.[72] Nor, indeed, is it likely to enhance their relationship with their parents, which may be extremely poor already – a factor which may itself underlie their disenchantment with school.[73]

A real concern about the new legislation requiring full participation in education or training up to the age of 18[74] is that high numbers of young people and their parents may be criminalised as a result.[75] Alongside a new legal duty to participate are criminal penalties for disobedience.[76] Admittedly, the planned expansion of work-based training schemes and apprenticeships will provide young people with an alternative to remaining in school itself for an extra two years.[77] Nevertheless, in areas of high unemployment and deprivation, LAs may struggle to provide enough good quality accredited schemes for all their young people, many of whom become disaffected with school long before they reach the age of 16. Even so, LAs must ensure that 16 and 17-year-olds regularly attend their education or training, identify those failing to comply and take steps to force them to do so.[78] Consequently, a young person in breach of this duty will, following a written warning notice,[79] be issued with an attendance notice[80] specifying the time and place at which he or she is required to attend. Failure to comply with the notice, without reasonable excuse, is a criminal offence[81] leading to a penalty such as a fixed penalty notice,[82] with defaults being dealt with through fines in the youth court.

It is not entirely clear how young people are to pay the fixed penalties, given their inability to take full-time employment instead of participating in some

---

[68] DfES (2005c) paras. 7.32–7.33.

[69] H. Malcolm *et al.* (2003) ch. 4 and p. 63 and D. Dalziel and K. Henthorne (2005) ch. 4.   [70] Ibid.

[71] E.g. *Guardian*, 7 June 2008: mother jailed for 28 days; her 15-year-old daughter had attended seven times in the last 195 school days; it was the mother's fourth time in court.

[72] The National Audit Office (2005) para. 3.25: views are extremely mixed over whether prosecution improves attendance rates.

[73] Complaints about behaviour at school can increase existing tension between young people and their parents. School-based problems often underlie young runaways' decision to leave home; discussed in Chapter 4.

[74] Inter alia: DfES (2007a), DCSF (2007h), DCSF (2008a) and Education and Skills Act (ESA) 2008, ss 1–2. These reforms are to be fully implemented by 2015; discussed further in Chapter 4.

[75] E. Welton (2008) p. 11.   [76] ESA 2008, ss. 40–58.

[77] DfES (2007a) chs. 3–6.   [78] ESA 2008, ss. 10–13.   [79] ESA 2008, s. 45.

[80] ESA 2008, s. 46–7.   [81] ESA 2008, s. 51.   [82] ESA 2008, s. 53.

accredited training scheme or apprenticeship. Regarding an unpaid fine, the government suggests, without a hint of irony, that 'the Youth Court cannot use custody as a means of enforcing it'.[83] Instead, 'taking money from wages or imposing an unpaid work requirement' are to be alternatives.[84] It would certainly be unwise to assume that parents will willingly pay the fines of their older offspring who simply refuse to participate in any form of education or training. In any event, they themselves have probably already been involved in civil sanctions relating to their son or daughter's non-participation;[85] a factor which may undermine any willingness to cooperate with the authorities in this way. It is worrying that a scheme intended to produce a more knowledgeable and skilled workforce[86] may end up criminalising large numbers of disaffected young people who grow up in deprived areas where they quite reasonably consider qualifications to be unimportant.

(ii) Civil remedies

The civil law provides less punitive sanctions against parents for their children's failure to attend school. Before prosecuting the parent, the LA must consider the appropriateness of applying to the family courts for an education supervision order (ESO).[87] This order was created by the Children Act (CA) 1989 to replace the old method of applying for a care order regarding persistent truants, the sole ground being that 'the child is of compulsory school age and is not being properly educated'.[88] Since truancy is often attributable to family difficulties, prior consultation with children's services should enable social workers to establish what can be done to support the family and avoid criminal proceedings against the parents for their child's school absences, which may make matters worse. The ESO was intended to help parents who find it difficult to exercise a proper influence over their child, by giving court backing to the efforts of the supervising officer whilst working with the family and child.[89] The order involves the child being placed under the supervision of the 'designated authority'[90] for its duration[91] and a social worker or education welfare officer being appointed to 'advise, assist and befriend' the child and his or her parents and give them directions intending to achieve the child's proper education.[92] But although its creation indicated a well-intentioned effort to ensure that the individual needs of the non-attending child were considered and addressed, the ESO has proved

---

[83] DCSF (2007h) para. 4.34.   [84] Ibid.

[85] E.g. a parenting contract or parenting order, discussed below.

[86] Discussed in Chapter 4.   [87] EA 1996, s. 447(1).

[88] CA 1989, s. 36(3). Such a step should only be contemplated after having consulted children's services.

[89] DH (1991) para. 3.9.   [90] CA 1989, s. 36(7).

[91] CA 1989, Sch. 3, para. 15(1) – in the first place not more than one year, although it can be extended for a further three years.

[92] CA 1989, Sch. 3, para. 12(1).

unpopular with LAs.[93] This is probably because LAs will usually try most strategies authorised by such an order, without going to the trouble and expense of making a court application.[94] The LA will sometimes obtain an ESO in the first instance, but follow it up with criminal sanctions against the parent if the child refuses to cooperate with his or her supervisor.[95]

Parenting contracts and parenting orders are more recent legislative creations, again of a civil nature.[96] Parenting contracts[97] are designed to ensure that parents of truanting children[98] obtain professional help with attendance problems[99] and to promote a better working relationship between them and the school. A school may 'suggest' to parents of a truanting child that they enter into a parenting contract and although theoretically voluntary, a parent's refusal to sign such a document must be considered by the court in any future criminal proceedings linked to the child's continuing truancy.[100] In those circumstances, parents may feel that the description of a parenting contract as 'a voluntary agreement' is misleading.[101] Although it is difficult to assess the effectiveness of parenting contracts, given the various factors which may play a part in any improvement, schools and parents who use them appear to consider them beneficial both in improving children's attendance and parents' relationships with the school.[102]

Parents who are successfully prosecuted for their children's truancy[103] may find that they additionally become the subject of a parenting order[104] requiring compliance with various strategies designed to moderate their own behaviour and that of their children. Although civil in nature, these may have an extensive impact on families. They have two elements: the parents may be required to attend counselling or guidance sessions for up to three months and to fulfil various provisions designed to address the

---

[93] Very few orders are ever made. Only 282 were made in 2005, 244 in 2004 and 187 in 2003. Figures supplied by the former Department of Constitutional Affairs.

[94] E.g. *Re O (a minor) (care order: education: procedure)* [1992] 2 FLR 7.

[95] E.g. *Graves v. London Borough of Islington* [2003] EWHC 2817 (Admin), [2004] ELR 1.

[96] Governed by Education (Parenting Contract and Parenting Orders)(England) Regulations 2007 (SI 2007/1869). See also DCSF (2007a).

[97] Anti-Social Behaviour Act (ASBA) 2003, s. 19(4): a parenting contract is a two-sided formal agreement setting out the parents' undertakings regarding their child's future attendance and the undertakings of the LA or school regarding future support for the parent and child.

[98] ASBA 2003, s. 19(2). NB parenting contracts and orders may also be used by schools in situations where a pupil is in danger of being excluded due to his bad behaviour; discussed below.

[99] ASBA 2003, s. 19(5) and (6). E.g. parents may be offered parenting skills courses and children provided with mentors.

[100] ASBA 2003, s. 21(1)(a) and (b): when deciding whether to make a parenting order the court must consider (a) the parent's refusal to enter into a parenting contract and (b) the parent's breach of any terms of a parenting contract.

[101] DCSF (2007a) para. 38.

[102] L. Evans *et al.* (2008) chs. 6–7. The parents largely found the parenting skills courses helpful.

[103] I.e. under EA 1996, s. 443–4, discussed above.

[104] CDA 1998, s. 8(1)(d): a parenting order (lasting up to 12 months) can be made against any parent convicted of an offence under EA 1996, ss. 443–4.

non-attendance.[105] The order may even, in limited circumstances, require parents to attend a residential counselling or guidance course.[106] Breach of a parenting order is a criminal offence,[107] with sanctions being a caution or a criminal prosecution, leading to a fine or community sentence.[108] There is a risk that parents will be alienated by schools intervening in ways which result in their being taken to court, particularly if they have been doing their best to make their children attend school regularly. Fionda describes this as 'an anti-partnership approach, which seeks to coerce parents into compliance with their statutory responsibilities' and involves school in policing their behaviour.[109]

With education or training becoming compulsory up to the age of 18, LAs may turn to parenting contracts and parenting orders as a first step towards forcing this older age group to participate.[110] One wonders whether it is wise to place such store on parents' ability to force disaffected young people of such an advanced age to attend regularly. Parents may have been at a loss to know how to handle their children's attendance problems long before they attained 16. The anxiety of a prosecution hanging over them for even longer might simply exacerbate an existing stressful relationship.[111]

(iii) Non-legal strategies

Researchers all agree that persistent truants start missing school at an early age and that this behaviour gets more entrenched as they get older.[112] There is now a wide range of non-legal strategies being used by schools themselves to address this problem, supported by extensive official guidance.[113] They are required to set their own attendance targets for authorised and unauthorised absences,[114] and most LAs assist them by working with a range of agencies to combat poor attendance.[115] A majority of schools has introduced effective procedures for registering pupils,[116] with well-developed follow-up services. They often adopt various ways of supporting and reintegrating poor

---

[105] E.g. to escort their children to school every day; to impose boundaries at home; sign regular behaviour reports; attend meetings with the child's education provider etc. See DCSF (2007a) pp. 25–8.

[106] CDA 1998, s. 8(7A): a residential requirement may be imposed only if the court considers: (a) that such a course would be more effective than their attendance at a non-residential course in preventing their child from engaging in a repetition of the behaviour which led to the order; and (b) any likely interference with family life is proportionate in all the circumstances. E.g. if the 'parent's home life is so chaotic that they need a structured setting where sustained counselling and guidance can be undertaken': DCSF (2007a) para. 127.

[107] CDA 1998, s. 9(7).   [108] DCSF (2007a) pp. 28–32.   [109] J. Fionda (2005) p. 229.

[110] ESA 2008, ss. 40–1.   [111] Discussed further in Chapter 4.

[112] Mori (2004) p. 62 and H. Malcolm et al. (2003) para. 7.3.   [113] E.g. DCSF (2008b).

[114] Governed by the Education (School Attendance Targets) (England) Regulations 2007 (SI 2007/2261). See also DCSF (2007b).

[115] Inter alia: police and young offender team (YOT) workers; children's services; health boards; housing associations; local religious leaders etc. H. Malcolm et al. (2003) p. 50.

[116] I.e. by high-tech electronic registration systems which generate automatic phone calls to parents when pupils are missing. National Audit Office (2005) paras. 4.10–4.12.

attenders.[117] Overall, LAs and schools devote considerable resources to 'managing absence'.[118] Indeed many teachers think that they spend too much time implementing procedures dealing with truancy, with little real return.[119] Perhaps the reality is that however efficient such systems are, the most determined pupils will continue to skip classes.

The government has also launched a variety of broader initiatives designed to address truancy and other aspects of poor discipline in schools, which appear to be having an impact.[120] Such problems may also improve with the establishment of a new personal tutor scheme for all secondary school pupils.[121] Nevertheless, it is arguable that little progress will be made whilst policy-makers routinely attribute truancy largely to irresponsible parenting. As noted above, truants themselves most frequently refer their behaviour to school-based problems. Research indicates that ineffective schooling may contribute greatly to pupils' reluctance to attend regularly.[122] The National Audit Office observes that poorly performing schools produce a combination of the same indicators, including weak leadership, high rates of pupil absence and disruption in the classroom, bullying and/or even violence, possibly accompanied by high exclusion numbers.[123] Indeed, in 2006, it estimated that around 980,000 pupils[124] were receiving 'an unsatisfactory education'.[125] These problems are often worse in areas of severe deprivation. MacDonald and Marsh report that school was seen by the young people in their study, who lived in a deprived area with high unemployment, as being 'pointless', 'meaningless' and 'menial'. They considered that being in a low-achieving school, especially being in a low-achieving class in a low-achieving school, resulted in their receiving education of a low quality.[126] They particularly resented being seen as being

---

[117] E.g. work by education welfare officers (EWOs), home-school liaison workers, learning mentors, social inclusion units, pastoral systems, counselling, befriending and collections schemes etc. H. Malcolm *et al.* (2003) p. 60.

[118] National Audit Office (2005) para. 1.16. LAs' education welfare services alone cost £108 million per annum, ibid.

[119] H. Malcolm *et al.* (2003) p. 65.

[120] E.g. inter alia: Behaviour Improvement Programmes (BIPs); Behaviour and Education Support Teams (BESTs). S. Hallam *et al.* (2005) p. 109, these initiatives had an overall impact on attendance in individual schools. See also the National Behaviour and Attendance Strategy which produced the Social and Emotional Aspects of Learning (SEAL) and the Social, Emotional and Behavioural Skills (SEBs) programmes. Given SEAL's success in primary schools (Ofsted (2007a)), government money was provided to extend it to secondary schools.

[121] DCSF (2007g) paras. 3.74–3.77: each pupil will have a single member of staff as a personal tutor, who becomes familiar with their needs, identifies their barriers to learning and supports them through transitions.

[122] National Audit Office (2005) paras. 2.6–2.23, analyses the reasons for huge variations in schools' absence rates and notes that good Ofsted assessments are broadly linked to lower absence.

[123] Ibid. at p. 4.   [124] Around 13% of the 7.4 million pupils in maintained schools in England.

[125] National Audit Office (2006) pp. 3–4 and para. 1.5. See also Ofsted (2007c) para. 65: only 52% of maintained secondary schools provided good or outstanding teaching and learning, with 35% rated satisfactory. Cf. Ofsted (2008) para. 65: 58% of maintained secondary schools provided good or outstanding teaching and learning, with 37% rated satisfactory.

[126] R. MacDonald and J. Marsh (2005) p. 50.

too unintelligent to warrant being given stimulating material. Since many of them also reported being bullied,[127] it is hardly surprising that they frequently truanted. Indeed, one of their interviewees described leaving school as 'the happiest time of my life'.[128]

On a more positive note, the government is well aware that a conventional academic curriculum does not suit large numbers of those who are over 14 and that boredom features strongly in their explanations for truanting. Many who currently see little point in attending school may be tempted to stay on with the introduction of work-related courses and diploma qualifications.[129] The intention is to ensure that as many as possible will develop craft and technical skills, thereby preparing them for progression to apprenticeships and other accredited training at the age of 16. Whether the government achieves its ambition to have its '14–19 reform programme' fully operational by 2013, depends, amongst other things, on those responsible for its delivery[130] being able to overcome the many logistical problems hampering their providing a wide range of new diploma courses.[131] Meanwhile, young people's lives in the very disadvantaged areas of the country may soon be improved by LAs' new duty to secure 'so far as reasonably practicable' sufficient educational and recreational leisure activities (and sufficient facilities for these activities) for improving the well-being of those aged 13–19.[132] Whilst the educational activities may include homework clubs, out-of-school coaching and outdoor activities, the recreational activities could include a wide variety of sports, music and performing arts.[133] LAs must take account of the views of young people themselves before establishing these services,[134] and may assist them over transport arrangements.[135]

(4) Pupils and school discipline

(A) Schools' powers and duties

(i) The background

Bored children, who cannot see the point of classes, may either stay away or behave disruptively. 'The antipathy between school and the disruptive child is usually mutual, and disaffected young people who are not excluded often truant from school.'[136] Whatever the causes, schools are experiencing increasing

---

[127] Discussed below.   [128] R. MacDonald and J. Marsh (2005) p. 53.

[129] Adopting the reforms promised by DfES (2005b), the Qualifications and Curriculum Authority (now the Qualifications and Curriculum Development Agency) redesigned the secondary curriculum to include more practical subject content and a series of work-related diplomas made available as from September 2008.

[130] The government expects 'collaborative delivery' of the 14–19 programme to be fulfilled by LAs, consortia and 14–19 partnerships. See generally DCSF (2008f), ch. 4. See also Apprenticeships, Skills, Children and Learning (ASCL) Bill 2009, Part 2.

[131] National Audit Office (2007) para. 52: e.g. the need to overcome transport problems in rural areas, thereby enabling young people to travel rapidly from institution to institution.

[132] EA 1996, s. 507B; discussed in Chapter 19.   [133] HM Treasury and DCSF (2007).

[134] EA 1996, s. 507B(9).   [135] EA 1996, s. 507B(6).   [136] Audit Commission (1996) p. 67.

difficulties over disciplining a small but growing minority of violent and aggressive pupils.[137] Those exhibiting aggressive and anti-social behaviour may intimidate class-mates and teachers alike.[138] Indeed, a couple of violent ill-disciplined pupils in a class can create a highly charged and frightening atmosphere for their peers. Nevertheless, schools must find a balance between over-harsh discipline, which can be counter-productive, and a lax and incon-sistent approach. The CRC recognises this and requires states to 'take all appropriate measures to ensure that school discipline is administered in a manner consistent with the child's human dignity'.[139] Similarly the right to education guaranteed by A2P1 of the ECHR does not exclude recourse to disciplinary measures.[140] Domestic law clearly requires schools to maintain discipline, in so far as it imposes a duty of care on schools and their staff, just as it does on parents. A teacher is required to show the same standard of care as that of 'a reasonably careful parent', taking into account the school context and number of pupils.[141] A failure to do so may be actionable in tort by a pupil if it has led to his or her physical or psychological injury.[142]

(ii) Bullying in schools

As noted above, the National Audit Office maintains that problems like truancy and bullying are far more prevalent in poorly performing schools.[143] Some badly behaved pupils delight in persecuting their peers. As the Committee on the Rights of the Child has noted with concern,[144] bullying of all kinds[145] has become increasingly common in UK schools.[146] Nevertheless, its actual prev-alence is difficult to estimate. This is partly because of victims' reluctance to tell anyone of its occurrence, and partly because teachers themselves underestimate

---

[137] Self reports indicate that 15% of boys carry a knife to school. But 39% of those children reported that they had been the victims of physical attack themselves. D. Armstrong *et al.* (2005) pp. 12 and 28.

[138] E.g. *Leeds City Council and ors v. Channel 4 Television Corporation* [2007] 1 FLR 678, Munby J, at [5] describes the secretly filmed scenes of poor discipline in three schools, with pupils fighting each other in class, running round the classroom jumping from desk to desk and adopting a 'grossly insubordinate and offensive attitude to their teacher'.

[139] Art. 28(2).

[140] *Sahin v. Turkey* [2006] ELR 73, per Grand Chamber of the European Court of Human Rights (ECtHR), at para. 156.

[141] *Van Oppen v. Clerk to the Bedford Charity Trustees* [1989] 3 All ER 389, per Balcombe LJ, at 401 and *Gower v. London Borough of Bromley* [1999] ELR 356, per Auld LJ, at 359.

[142] Discussed below.   [143] See also C. Oliver and M. Candappa (2003) p. 19.

[144] Committee on the Rights of the Child (2002) para. 47; ibid (2008) para. 66.

[145] Including homophobic and racist abuse. See generally N. Harris (2005b) pp. 31–41. See also: Office of the Children's Commissioner (2006a) paras. 4.6–4.12; C. Oliver and M. Candappa (2003) pp. 50–7; Mencap (2007): high rates of bullying of children with learning difficulties – discussed further in Chapter 12.

[146] UNICEF (2007) Figure 5.3b: a relatively high percentage of 11, 13 and 15-year-olds reported being bullied in the previous 2 months in the UK. Only five other OECD countries had higher scores. Ibid. Figure 4.3: the UK had the lowest percentage of 11, 13 and 15-year-olds reporting having 'kind and helpful' peers.

its frequency.[147] It is clearly more common in some schools than in others. Bullying can certainly blight a child's school days[148] with victims often suffering serious psychological problems, becoming school phobic and even suicidal.[149] It is being taken increasingly seriously[150] with schools being provided with extensive guidance over how to tackle the problem.[151] Schools must establish written policies designed to 'promote good behaviour and discipline on the part of its pupils'.[152] Head teachers must also determine measures promoting amongst pupils 'self-discipline and proper regard for authority', encouraging good behaviour and, in particular, 'preventing all forms of bullying among pupils'.[153] The guidance stresses that all forms of bullying, including non-physical bullying, such as homophobic and cyberbullying should be addressed.[154] The legislation and guidance also reflects case law establishing that a school's duty of care towards a pupil does not necessarily end at the school gate and that in rare circumstances, a school may be liable in tort for failing to take effective steps to prevent bullying outside school, for example on the bus home.[155] Thus, behaviour policies should also aim to control behaviour off the school premises 'to such extent as is reasonable', even when pupils are not under the control of any member of staff.[156]

Legislation and official guidance does not necessarily produce results. Victims of bullying sometimes find it difficult to force schools to take effective action – schools may even simply ignore their complaints.[157] Both criminal[158] and civil sanctions[159] are theoretically available. Nevertheless, bringing a claim in

---

[147] See inter alia: C. Oliver and M. Candappa (2003) pp. 18–19: the difficulties of estimating accurately the prevalence of bullying in schools and the general underlying trends; Office of the Children's Commissioner (2006a) para. 4.2: very high local statistics on the prevalence of bullying; House of Commons Education and Skills Committee (2007) paras. 54–6: no robust system for collecting data on bullying.

[148] ChildLine (2005) records (at p. 15) that, for the ninth year running, bullying was the single most common reason for children and young people calling ChildLine.

[149] N. Harris (2005b) pp. 39–41.

[150] House of Commons Education and Skills Committee (2007) esp. paras. 7–10.

[151] Schools must adopt 'a Whole School Approach' with assistance from the *Safe to Learn: Embedded Anti-bullying Work in Schools* web-based package. See also Ofsted (2003) and DfES (2007e).

[152] EIA 2006, s. 88: the governing body of every mainstream school must draw up a written statement on discipline and good behaviour, having consulted the head teacher, relevant school employees, parents and pupils.

[153] EIA 2006, s. 89(1)(a) and (b). EIA 2006, s. 89(6): these measures, must, in the form of a written document, be widely publicised within the school.

[154] DfES (2007e) para. 3.1.2.

[155] *Bradford-Smart v. West Sussex County Council* [2002] EWCA Civ 07, [2002] ELR 139, per Judge LJ, at [34]–[36].

[156] EIA 2006, s. 89(5). See also DfES (2007e) para. 3.4.4.

[157] Office of the Children's Commissioner (2006b) pp. 13–14.

[158] E.g. 10 pupils in a Doncaster school were charged with a total of 35 offences, including blackmail, robbery, affray, assault and theft after a police investigation into school bullying: *The Guardian*, 16 May 1997. Anti-social behaviour orders (ASBOs) might also be obtained against children over the age of 10; discussed in Chapter 18.

[159] I.e. an action in negligence against the school for breach of its duty of care. E.g. *Bradford-Smart v. West Sussex County Council* [2002] EWCA Civ 07, [2002] ELR 139.

negligence is no easy matter[160] and some schools are unwilling to involve the police for bullying incidents in school. Even when they do, the CPS may be reluctant to prosecute.[161] Responding to calls for reform, a new scheme for dealing with parents' complaints by the Local Government Ombudsman will assist those who do not consider that the headteacher has responded satisfactorily to their concerns about bullying.[162] Sometimes, a child may have been bullied by a teacher, in which case, it may be particularly difficult for his or her parents to force the school to take action.[163] Even more dangerous is the abusive teacher, particularly because head teachers normally trust their staff implicitly. Nevertheless, LAs and schools are obliged to make arrangements 'with a view to safeguarding and promoting the welfare of the children'.[164] They are expected to follow detailed official guidance designed to ensure that no one is employed in a school as a teacher or other ancillary worker who is a danger to children and that all suspicions and allegations of abuse are properly investigated and followed up.[165]

(iii) Partnership with parents

Successive governments have placed considerable store on gaining parents' support in their efforts to promote good behaviour and discipline in schools. Nevertheless, in Ofsted's view, some schools do not place enough emphasis on sharing with parents the successes of pupils with challenging behaviour, so that most contact with them is about unacceptable behaviour.[166] There is a risk that the more authoritarian approaches now available to schools may exacerbate this situation. Largely on the recommendations of the Steer Committee,[167] the Education and Inspections Act (EIA) 2006, accompanied by a plethora of new guidance documents, subtly distorted the balance between schools and parents. For example, although extending the availability of parenting contracts was initially seen simply as a means of averting the risk of a badly behaved pupil's education being disrupted by permanent exclusion,[168] schools[169] thereby acquired considerable power over parents. Parents can now be asked to enter into a parenting contract merely because a pupil is believed to have engaged in behaviour '*likely* to cause significant disruption to the education of

---

[160] N. Harris (2005b) pp. 49–51: to succeed in an action for educational negligence a pupil must establish that bullying occurred, that the school owed a duty of care, that the pupil suffered loss and that there was a causal connection between the bullying and the loss.

[161] Office of the Children's Commissioner (2006b) p. 14. But cf. Rod Morgan, the then Chairman of the Youth Justice Board for England and Wales, *The Times*, 21 August 2006: criticised teachers and children's homes for too often resorting to the police to curb bad behaviour, rather than dealing with it themselves.

[162] Office of the Children's Commissioner (2006b) p. 23. ASCL Bill 2009, Part 10, Ch. 2.

[163] Ibid. at p. 8.   [164] EA 2002, s. 175.   [165] DfES (2007f).   [166] Ofsted (2005a) para. 82.

[167] A. Steer (2005).   [168] A. Steer (2005) para. 178 and DfES (2005c) para. 7.11.

[169] I.e. the school's governing body. See Education (Parenting Contracts and Parenting Order) (England) Regulations 2007 (SI 2007/1869).

other pupils … or to the health or safety of any staff, or forms part of a pattern of behaviour *which (if continued) will give rise to a risk of future exclusion* from the school'.[170] Admittedly the majority of schools will not over-exploit this power. Nevertheless, as some LAs and schools appreciate,[171] imposing a parenting contract on an already over-stressed and inadequate parent may result in relations between parent and school deteriorating rapidly. Meanwhile the children themselves may thereby become labelled as troublemakers, with little chance of clearing their name at such an early stage.

Less threatening are the 'home-school agreements' that parents are required to sign,[172] setting out the school's responsibilities and indicating parents' own commitment to ensuring that their children keep the rules on such matters as attendance, discipline and homework.[173] Some schools sensibly adopt a system whereby such agreements are drawn up between teachers and pupils after consultation together, with each child signing his or her part of the agreement. This is an obvious way of encouraging pupils to take responsibility for their behaviour, rather than appearing to confine issues of discipline to an adult regime of coercion. Regrettably, however, government guidance merely strongly encourages this practice,[174] without the legislation making it obligatory.[175]

(iv) Sanctions

In the event of these preventative measures failing, a teacher may wish to punish a pupil for his or her bad behaviour. The law relating to discipline in schools has become increasingly complex, having been the subject of various reports,[176] with the use of sanctions by teachers now being extensively regulated. It has been statutorily confirmed that teachers[177] have a legal power to discipline their pupils.[178] Disciplinary penalties can be imposed on bad behaviour[179] in school,[180]

---

[170] Emphasis added. ASBA 2003, s. 19(1A). See also s. 19(2A): more serious misbehaviour (justifying immediate exclusion) entitles the school to apply to a magistrates' court for a parenting order against the parent; discussed below.

[171] L. Evans *et al.* (2008) p. 37.

[172] School Standards and Framework Act (SSFA) 1998, s. 110(3): the governing body must 'take reasonable steps to secure that the parental declaration is signed by every qualifying parent'.

[173] SSFA 1998, ss. 110–11 and DfEE (1998).

[174] DfEE (1998) para. 42. See also discussed by N. Harris (2007) p. 51.

[175] SSFA 1998, s. 110(5). Schools 'may' but not 'must' invite pupils they consider to have 'a sufficient understanding' of the agreement to sign the parental declaration as well, to indicate that they acknowledge and accept the school's expectations of its pupils.

[176] Inter alia: R. Elton (1989) and A. Steer (2005).

[177] EIA 2006, s. 91(4): any paid member of staff (unless specifically prohibited by the head teacher) and any other member of staff so authorised by the headteacher.

[178] EIA 2006, ss. 90–1, supported by official guidance, DfES (2007e).   [179] EIA 2006, s. 90(1).

[180] EIA 2006, s. 91(5)(b): the penalty may also be imposed for bad behaviour out of school if the pupil was under the lawful control or charge of a member of staff. EIA 2006, s. 90(2)(a): a penalty may be imposed even if the pupil was neither on the school premises nor under the lawful control or charge of a member of staff, but only to the extent that this is reasonable.

providing the penalty in question[181] is lawful[182] and reasonable in all the circumstances.[183] However bad a pupil's behaviour, teachers in all schools, maintained and private alike, are prohibited from using physical punishment.[184] Some wrongly assume from this that teachers can never use force, whatever the circumstances. But as legislation emphasises, forceful measures can be taken by teachers confronted by disruptive and aggressive pupils.[185] Teachers have the power to use 'such force as is reasonable in the circumstances' to prevent behaviour so bad that it would have a serious effect on the school and/or other pupils.[186]

The official guidance attempts to address the fact that this ostensibly very broad formula might lead to a disproportionate use of force.[187] It stresses that it must not be used to prevent a pupil committing a trivial misdemeanour, it must only be used as a last resort, and must always be very carefully justified. Above all, force should never be used as a punishment.[188] Schools' ability to prevent dangerous violence has been reinforced by legislation giving head teachers[189] the power to search pupils without their consent if they have reasonable grounds for suspecting that they have knives, blades or other offensive weapons in their possession.[190] One wonders, however, whether teaching staff will wish to become involved in such policing tactics.

(B) Exclusions

(i) The background

Teachers clearly cannot pick and choose which children they are prepared to teach and which they are not. Nevertheless, a disruptive child's right to be educated in a mainstream school may seriously undermine a studious child's right to receive instruction in an atmosphere conducive to learning. In cases of serious infringements of discipline, schools may feel that they have little option but to resort to excluding pupils they are unable to control. Most exclusions are

---

[181] E.g. a detention.

[182] EIA 2006, s. 91(3)(a). I.e. does not infringe any statutory requirement, such as the racial discrimination legislation.

[183] EIA 2006, s. 91(3)(b) and (6): the reasonableness must be determined, taking account of whether the penalty is proportionate in the circumstances, and of the pupil's own particular circumstances, e.g. age, special educational needs, disability and religious requirements. See also DfES (2007e) paras. 3.9.1–3.9.51.

[184] EA 1996, ss. 548–9. Discussed in Chapter 9.

[185] EIA 2006, s. 93, supported by guidance DCSF (2007e).

[186] EIA 2006, s. 93(1): such force as is reasonable in the circumstances to prevent a pupil from: (a) committing any offence; (b) injuring anyone or damaging anyone's property; (c) prejudicing good order and discipline at the school or among any pupils receiving education at the school, whether during classes or otherwise.

[187] Joint Committee on Human Rights (2006) para. 52.

[188] DCSF (2007e) para. 17. The guidance provides a list of clearly described factual examples of situations where force may be justified: see para. 28.

[189] Or other authorised member of staff.

[190] EA 1996, s. 550AA. See DfES (2007g). See also ASCL Bill 2009, Part 11.

for short periods of a few days,[191] but the dramatic increase in the use of permanent exclusions during the 1990s[192] provoked government alarm.[193] Research suggested that some pupils were being excluded to avoid their poor academic skills lowering their school's performance tables and local image.[194] Nevertheless, the Labour government was also concerned by the wider debate about social exclusion and 'the view that educational disaffection, as manifested by exclusion and truancy, underpins many other social problems', including long-term socioeconomic disadvantage.[195] In particular, research shows a marked correlation between truancy, exclusion and youth offending.[196] Whilst it is unclear whether permanent exclusion is a cause of criminal behaviour, rather than a consequence of it, excluded children clearly have more time on their hands to associate with other excluded and delinquent peers in the community.[197]

The Labour government's efforts to reduce the rate of exclusions initially bore fruit.[198] Nevertheless, rates remain relatively high, as noted with concern by the Committee on the Rights of the Child.[199] Indeed, it appears that the reduction in permanent exclusions is being masked by other factors.[200] There has been a dramatic increase in suspensions or fixed period exclusions,[201] and despite its official prohibition, there appears to be a continued and widespread use of 'unofficial or informal exclusion',[202] either through pupils being sent home without the procedures for formal exclusion being followed or through parents being invited to remove their children rather than facing formal exclusion.[203] Furthermore, although the majority of schools are

---

[191] Fixed period exclusions can last up to a maximum of 45 days in any one school year. See Education (Pupil Exclusion and Appeals) (Maintained Schools) (England) Regulations 2002 (SI 2002/3178).

[192] From 1990/91, when the level of permanent exclusions was 2,910, the rate rose to a peak of 12,700 in 1997.

[193] The Social Exclusion Unit's first brief was to consider the linked problem of truancy and permanent exclusion. SEU (1998). Measures introduced included official targets for schools to reduce their use of permanent exclusion.

[194] SEU (1998) paras. 2.15, 5.11 and 5.12.

[195] D. Berridge et al. (2001) pp. 1–10: excellent analysis of the background to school exclusion and the research on the topic and government responses to the problem. See also J. Bradshaw et al. (2004) ch. 4.

[196] Inter alia: D. Berridge et al. (2001) pp. 7–10: summary of the research on this correlation; K. Hansen (2003); Mori (2004) p. 63: 46% of young (self-reporting) offenders had been given both temporary and permanent exclusions, cf. 28% of non-offenders.

[197] D. Berridge et al. (2001) ch. 5 and pp. 48–9.

[198] In 2001 schools were no longer required to comply with further targets to cut exclusions.

[199] Committee on the Rights of the Child (2002) para. 48(b); ibid. (2008) para. 66(d).

[200] DCSF (2008e): the number of permanent exclusions from maintained primary, secondary and special schools in 2006/7 (8,680) had reduced by nearly 7% on the previous year. NB there were slight changes in the coverage of the tables, cf. DfES (2007h).

[201] Ibid: in 2006/7 there were 363,270 fixed period exclusions, an increase of 4% over the previous year. In 2005/6, there had been a similar 4% increase; see DfES (2007h).

[202] Discussed below.

[203] A. Steer (2005) paras. 144–145. See also C. Parsons et al. (2004) p. 96, indicating that nearly half the pupils interviewed reported being asked to stay at home without an official exclusion.

apparently using permanent exclusion more appropriately, schools appear to lack consistency over its use[204] In particular, the apparently large numbers of disruptive pupils being expelled by academies[205] is becoming increasingly controversial.[206]

A growing body of research suggests that a variety of factors is often associated with bad behaviour leading to exclusion.[207] These include poor basic skills, limited aspirations, strained or traumatic home circumstances and poor relationships with teachers and other pupils.[208] This complex picture partly explains why exclusion rates vary from school to school, both at secondary and primary level and from LA to LA.[209] Particular groups of pupils remain at much greater risk of permanent exclusion than others. These include black-Caribbean pupils,[210] children looked after by LAs[211] and those with special educational needs (SEN).[212] The anti-discrimination legislation should ensure that pupils are not excluded for reasons relating to race or disability,[213] but compliance has been patchy. In relation to SEN pupils, teachers may not recognise or understand that their poor behaviour may be attributable to learning difficulties.[214] Concern has also been expressed from a variety of sources over the high rates of permanently excluded black-Caribbean boys. Some professionals consider that young black and ethnic minority pupils are more frequently labelled as troublemakers[215] and many black young people consider racism or racial stereotyping to play a role in their exclusion from

---

[204] F. Taylor (2005) p. 17.

[205] A. Asthana, *The Observer*, 12 August 2007: quotes statistics released under the Freedom of Information legislation showing that 8.7 pupils per 1,000 were excluded from a sample of 14 academies during the previous school year, cf. 3.2 pupils per 1,000 excluded from secondary schools in neighboring areas.

[206] A. Curtis *et al.* (2008) p. 36.

[207] In 2006/7, some 31% of permanent exclusions and 23% of fixed period exclusions were due to persistent disruptive behaviour; DCSF (2008e). See also Ofsted (2005a) p. 8, indicating that an increasing number of pupils display poor behaviour linked to medical needs such as autistic spectrum disorders.

[208] D. Berridge *et al.* (2001) pp. 4–6 for a summary of the research, and ch. 3 for the background of the excluded young people interviewed.

[209] See C. Parsons *et al.* (2004) ch. 4 for a detailed analysis of school variations in the use of exclusions. NB there is a clear link between schools with high rates of free school meals and high permanent exclusion rates.

[210] Official statistics indicate that although the rate of exclusions for black-Caribbean pupils has dropped since 1995/6, 41 black-Caribbean in every 10,000 pupils are permanently excluded, cf. 14 in every 10,000 pupils overall (DfES (2006a)) and cf. 2 Chinese in every 10,000 pupils DfES (2006b) Chart D.

[211] Current exclusion statistics do not give figures for exclusions of children in care but in 2003, the SEU noted that children in care were 10 times more likely to be excluded than other children.

[212] DCSF (2008e): in 2006/7, 36 in every 10,000 pupils with statements of SEN and 42 in every 10,000 SEN pupils without statements were permanently excluded from school, cf. 4 in every 10,000 pupils with no SEN.

[213] I.e. under the Race Relations Act 1976, as amended by the Race Relations (Amendment) Act 2000 and the Disability Discrimination Act (DDA) 1995, as amended by the Special Educational Needs and Disability Act 2001 and the Disability Discrimination Act 2005.

[214] F. Taylor (2005) pp. 18–19.   [215] Ibid. at p. 20.

school.[216] Indeed it is maintained that black pupils are 'routinely punished more harshly, praised less and told off more often'.[217] Despite many schools addressing this problem, researchers concluded that 'in a significant minority' of schools, general and specific legislative duties were not being complied with under the race relations legislation and that 'institutional racism' was evident in processes being administered differentially.[218]

(ii) Prevention

Schools are warned, when deciding how to enforce their behaviour policies, to take account of individual pupils' needs, especially their race, religion and culture, and any physical or mental impairment which might affect their ability to behave appropriately.[219] The official guidance also emphasises that permanent exclusion should be exceptional for children whose difficult behaviour may stem from a variety of factors over which they themselves have little control.[220] Considerable attention is paid to reducing the exclusion rates of children being looked after by LAs.[221] Schools are also reminded that exclusion rates amongst black-Caribbean pupils, especially boys, though reduced, remain significantly higher than those for other pupils and are warned against discriminating against pupils on racial grounds when deciding whether to exclude.[222] Similarly, attention is drawn to the need to address the behavioural problems of SEN children rather than excluding them[223] and schools' legal obligations not to discriminate against disabled pupils by punishing them for behaviour related to their disability.[224]

Considerable effort has been made, over the years through official regulation[225] and a series of guidance documents,[226] to persuade schools to take adequate preventative measures to ensure that permanent exclusion is utilised only as a remedy of last resort. They are directed to put alternatives in place well in advance of turning to exclusion.[227] They should identify pupils who are so badly behaved that they are at serious risk of permanent exclusion and arrange support programmes for them, perhaps through mentoring, or alternative provision in a school-based learning support unit or pupil referral unit (PRU).[228] A wholly inadequate alternative is, unfortunately, condoned by the judiciary.[229] This is a form of 'internal exclusion' whereby the pupil is removed to an informally designated area within the school, with appropriate support and supervision.[230] It is a half-way house which effectively allows schools to

---

[216] Ibid. at pp. 10–11 and C. Wright *et al.* (2005) pp. 10–14.   [217] P. Wanless (2006) p. 22.

[218] C. Parsons *et al.* (2004) p. 107. See also P. Wanless (2006) p. 26.   [219] DfES (2007e) section 3.9.

[220] DCSF (2008g); discussed below.   [221] DCSF (2008g) paras. 77–83.

[222] Ibid. at paras. 73–6.   [223] Ibid. at paras. 63–7.   [224] Ibid. at paras. 68–72.

[225] Education (Pupil Exclusions and Appeals) (Maintained Schools) (England) Regulations 2002 (SI 2002/3178).

[226] DfES (2007e), DCSF (2007c) and DCSF (2008g)

[227] DCSF (2008g) Part 1.   [228] Ibid. at para. 5.

[229] *R (L (a minor)) v. Governors of J School* [2003] UKHL 9, [2003] 2 AC 633, discussed below.

[230] DCSF (2008g) para. 11.

avoid complying with the formal exclusion procedures, thereby denying pupils and parents the right of appeal.

Whether or not they eventually adopt some alternative strategy, the school should immediately establish a formal 'Pastoral Support Programme' (PSP), which identifies 'precise and realistic outcomes for the child or young person to work towards'.[231] The school, in conjunction with the LA, is expected to involve parents and outside agencies in such a programme, such as children's services, health, housing, and ethnic minority community groups to help resolve family difficulties and provide additional support.[232] Sensible though this advice is, schools are unlikely to heed the encouragement to involve outside agencies in managing difficult behaviour when the response is often very poor.[233] Hopefully, the integration of children's services under children's trusts will gradually improve this situation.

The exclusions guidance emphasises the importance of schools 'engaging with parents' to minimise the number of pupils at risk of exclusion.[234] It is questionable whether schools' power to 'offer' a parenting contract as a form of early intervention is a good forum for engagement.[235] As noted above, whilst apparently voluntary, the parents' refusal to sign one must be considered by the court if an application for a parenting order is later made. Admittedly, the support provided by the school or LA may prove helpful.[236] It is also possible that the counselling and guidance sessions offered to parents receiving parenting orders[237] are equally valuable, despite the absence of robust research supporting such a view.[238] Nevertheless, it is worrying that schools have acquired such extensive powers over parents on the basis of little more than government guesswork.

The government's authoritarian approach to prevention is particularly surprising given some schools' own unimpressive past record. It seems that not all schools are particularly good at preventative work. Many fail to identify and then track a pupil's difficult behaviour,[239] and 'in many settings' pupils receive 'limited or unhelpful oral and written comments' on their work. In a few schools, some staff 'show a lack of respect by shouting at pupils, making fun of them, making personal remarks or using sarcasm. Some pupils react badly to such comments … Those with the most difficult behaviour often respond with verbal abuse.'[240] Furthermore, in a 'significant number of the schools behaviour

---

[231] Ibid. at para. 7 and DfES (2007i).   [232] DfES (2007i).

[233] Ofsted (2005a): in 2002/3 only 1 in 5 LEAs provided schools with good or very good support (para. 93); at least half of the schools reported difficulties in accessing support from educational psychologists (para. 96); support from social services departments was 'inadequate in most' early years settings and schools (para. 97); partnership with the health services was weak in at least a third of all the schools and units observed (para. 101).

[234] DCSF (2008g) para. 5.   [235] ASBA 2003, s. 19(1A). Discussed above.

[236] L. Evans et al. (2008) ch. 6.   [237] DCSF (2007a) paras. 119–20.

[238] S. Hallam et al. (2006) p. 113, stress the need for robust research examining the effectiveness of parenting programmes in an educational context.

[239] Ofsted (2005a) para. 107: about two-thirds of the secondary schools inspected.

[240] Ibid. at paras. 70–1.

targets are often vague and unhelpful to both pupils and staff. Insufficient attention is given to variation in children's responses to different lessons, members of staff and times of the day and little consideration is given to the events leading up to episodes of particularly challenging behaviour.[241] In Ofsted's view, neglect of these factors means that simple adaptations are not made which could help pupils manage and improve their difficult behaviour.[242] Parents of pupils treated in this way might quite reasonably feel aggrieved at being expected to sign a parenting contract agreeing to persuade their child to behave better.

(iii) Grounds for permanent exclusion

Children who constantly behave in an anti-social and disruptive way in school must expect their behaviour to be treated seriously. Indeed, they may find that they are deprived permanently of their right to education in a mainstream school to enable their more studious peers to be educated without fear of bullying and classroom violence. Teachers obviously have a difficult task in maintaining discipline in schools; but they may not always be fair when reacting to disruptive behaviour or in identifying the right pupils to be disciplined.[243]

The official guidance, which governs pupil referral units (PRUs), as well as schools, stresses that permanent exclusion should be resorted to only after all other strategies have been tried and failed.[244] A decision to exclude a child permanently is a serious one which should only be taken 'where the basic facts have been clearly established on the balance of probabilities'[245] and then only '(a) in response to serious breaches of a school's discipline policy; and (b) if allowing the pupil to remain in school would seriously harm the education or welfare of the pupil or others in the school'.[246] Such a punishment should be reserved for serious misbehaviour, as opposed to minor incidents.[247] The guidance that permanent exclusion should only be used in exceptional circumstances to punish a 'first or "one off" offence',[248] presents problems if schools wish to operate a policy of 'zero tolerance' regarding the possession of drugs.[249] Cases involving a one-off assault also illustrate the serious dilemmas produced

---

[241] Ibid. at para. 107.   [242] Ibid.

[243] Many excluded pupils consider that they have been blamed unfairly for incidents in school. Inter alia: Mori (2004) p. 65: 40% of the young excluded pupils believed their exclusion to have been unfair; F. Taylor (2005) pp. 18–20; C. Wright *et al.* (2005) pp. 11–14.

[244] DCSF (2008g) para. 16.   [245] Ibid.   [246] Ibid. at para. 13.

[247] Ibid. at para. 26 : minor breaches not warranting exclusion include: breaches of school uniform; failure to do homework or bring dinner money; poor academic performance; lateness or truancy; pregnancy; punishing pupils for the behaviour of their parents.

[248] Ibid. at para. 17 : serious actual or threatened violence against another pupil/member of staff; sexual abuse or assault; supplying an illegal drug; carrying an offensive weapon.

[249] E.g. *R (S and B) v. Independent Appeal Panel of Birmingham City Council* [2006] EWHC 2369 (Admin), [2007] ELR 57: two boys permanently excluded by their school for their part in a one-off incident involving experimentation with cannabis. Beatson J, at [69], set aside the Independent Appeal Panel's (IAP) decision confirming the permanent exclusion; an IAP should explain fully why it decides to depart from the official guidance on exclusions (re one-off offences) in order to support a school's 'Draconian' local policy of zero tolerance.

by the availability of permanent exclusion. The head teacher must find a balance between a victim's right to be educated without fear, and the culprit's need to return to mainstream education as soon as possible.[250]

The anti-discrimination legislation is intended to protect pupils from being excluded unfairly for reasons relating to their sex, race, religion or disability.[251] As the official guidance explains,[252] a disabled pupil has a right to protection from unjustifiable exclusion for poor behaviour over which he or she has no control, it stemming from some form of learning disability or mental disorder.[253] Nevertheless, as it makes clear,[254] recent case law has dramatically changed the way in which courts consider discrimination complaints,[255] thereby reducing the protection available for disabled pupils when, and if, permanently excluded. Under previous case law, if a mentally disabled pupil argued that, by permanently excluding him for bad behaviour stemming from his mental impairment, the school had discriminated against him unlawfully, courts would use, as a 'comparator', a pupil who was neither disabled nor behaving badly.[256] If, as was likely, the court found that the school would not have excluded an unimpaired pupil who had not behaved badly, it would conclude that the exclusion was 'less favourable treatment' and therefore prima facie discriminatory. At that point, however, the school might be able to justify such a punishment.[257]

---

[250] E.g. *R v. London Borough of Camden and the Governors of the Hampstead School ex p H* [1996] ELR 360: the Court of Appeal (disagreeing with the High Court) set aside the decision of the Committee of Governors that two 13-year-old boys should not be permanently excluded for their part in an incident in which an 11-year-old boy with a statement of SEN had been injured by an air gun pellet. The governors had been over influenced by the culprits' hitherto unblemished school record and had not adequately considered the impact on the now traumatised victim of the perpetrators being allowed to return to school.

[251] See Chapter 11 for further discussion of protection for disabled pupils. See also N. Harris (2007) pp. 147–86.

[252] DCSF (2008g) para. 68.

[253] E.g. *R (T) v. Independent Appeal Panel for Devon County Council, The Governing Body of X College* [2007] EWHC 763 (Admin), [2007] ELR 499: Walker J quashed on judicial review the IAP's decision to approve the permanent exclusion of a 15-year-old boy with severe Asperger's Syndrome for assaulting a teacher, given its failure to adequately consider the evidence of discrimination, provocation and bullying and its failure to grapple with the requirements of the DDA 1995.

[254] DCSF (2008g) esp. para. 70(c).

[255] *Lewisham London Borough Council v. Malcolm* [2008] UKHL 43, [2008] 4 All ER 525, per the House of Lords (Baroness Hale of Richmond dissenting on the 'comparator' point): a housing authority had not discriminated unlawfully against a schizophrenic secure tenant by commencing possession proceedings against him (he having breached his tenancy agreement by sub-letting his flat whilst mentally ill); the correct comparator was a mentally *un*impaired tenant who had sub-let unlawfully.

[256] Per Silber J in *McAuley Catholic High School v. C and ors* [2003] EWHC 3045 (Admin), [2004] 2 All ER 436 at [45]–[46].

[257] DDA 1995, s. 28B(1)(b). But see also s. 28B(7) – less favourable treatment such as a permanent exclusion can only be justified if it is 'for a reason material to the circumstances of the case and substantial' and s. 28B(8) – the less favourable treatment cannot be justified if the school has not made reasonable adjustments for the pupil's disabilities (i.e. under s. 28C) unless the exclusion could be justified despite reasonable adjustments being made. See *R (T) v. Independent Appeal Panel for Devon County Council, The Governing Body of X College* [2007] EWHC 763 (Admin), [2007] ELR 499, per Walker J, at [43].

Arguably against the original intention of Parliament,[258] the courts must now compare the way in which the school dealt with the disabled pupil with the way in which the school would have dealt with a pupil who had behaved equally badly but who was not disabled. Under the new approach, disabled pupils will find it hard to prove less favourable treatment when complaining against exclusions. For example, pupils with behavioural difficulties stemming from severe autism are less likely to succeed when they argue that by excluding them for behaving in a manner prompted by their disability, they have been dealt with less favourably than pupils without autism.[259] Admittedly, the pupil may be able to show that the school had failed to make reasonable adjustments for his or her disability as required by the legislation;[260] for example, it has not arranged lunch for the pupil at a time when the crowd has died down in the canteen.[261] But the school may still succeed by showing that, having made reasonable adjustments, the permanent exclusion remained necessary, for example, to protect other pupils in the school.[262]

A school may resort to permanent exclusion in response to persistent breaches of its school uniform policy. If it does, as explained below, it runs the risk of discriminating against the pupil on racial and/or religious grounds. Nevertheless, the exclusion guidance fails to explain this adequately, leaving it to the uniform guidance to tackle the fact that some young pupils take the requirements of their religion extremely seriously.[263] The official guidance on school uniforms[264] warns schools that a pupil may succeed in a claim of *racial* discrimination if a ban on certain dress is found to be unjustifiable.[265] Furthermore, there is a reminder of the human rights of religious adherents wishing to conform with a particular dress code,[266] combined with a reference to the recent case law on this issue.[267] Whilst suggesting that exclusion is not an appropriate response, it suggests that it might be where breaches are 'persistent

---

[258] *Lewisham London Borough Council v. Malcolm* [2008] UKHL 43, [2008] 4 All ER 525, per Baroness Hale, at [77]–[81]. See also ACE (2008a) p. 27.

[259] ACE (2008a) p. 26.   [260] I.e. under the DDA 1995, s. 28C.   [261] ACE (2008a) p. 26.

[262] E.g. *R (T) v. Governing Body of OL Primary School* [2005] EWHC 753 (Admin), [2005] ELR 522: exclusion of an 8-year-old girl with global developmental delay and associated behavioural difficulties was justified, the school having taken outside advice and involved outside agencies. The school was obliged to protect other pupils from the girl's violent and disruptive behaviour.

[263] Discussed in Chapter 11.   [264] DCSF (2007d) para. 25.

[265] E.g. *Mandla v. Lee and ors* [1983] 2 AC 548: per House of Lords a headmaster's unjustifiable refusal to allow a Sikh boy to wear a turban to school amounted to unlawful discrimination under the Race Relations Act (RRA) 1976; *R (Watkins-Singh, a child acting by Sanita Kumari Singh, her mother and litigation friend) v. The Governing Body of Aberdare Girls' High School and Rhondda Cynon Taf Unitary Authority* [2008] EWHC 1865 (Admin), [2008] ELR 561, per Silber J: the school's refusal to allow a Sikh girl to wear a Kara (a small steel bangle) as a visible sign of her Sikh identity and faith amounted to unlawful discrimination under the RRA 1976 and the Equality Act 2006. See also the issue of constructive exclusion discussed below.

[266] DCSF (2007d) paras. 17–22.

[267] E.g. *R (on the application of Begum) v. Head Teacher and Governors of Denbigh High School* (hereafter *Begum*) [2006] UKHL 15, [2007] AC 100; discussed further in Chapter 11.

and defiant'.[268] In such circumstances, the guidance warns of the need to justify such a step,[269] for example by showing that the response was necessary to promote health and safety or the rights and freedoms of others.[270] The guidance fails to warn schools that by establishing a rigid uniform policy barring certain forms of religious dress, they not only risk infringing the anti-discrimination legislation, but, as discussed further below, the discipline in question might be interpreted as a form of constructive and illegal exclusion.[271]

(iv) Procedural fairness in permanent exclusion

The plethora of statutory provisions, regulations and official guidance acknowledges the serious implications of permanent exclusion and provides a carefully regulated procedure which must be complied with, to the letter.[272] Nevertheless, as noted above, schools apparently still persist in adopting an 'unofficial or informal exclusion' process,[273] despite the official guidance emphasising its illegality.[274] The Strasbourg authorities' narrow interpretation of the right to a fair trial under Article 6 of the ECHR undermines its usefulness to a pupil excluded without his or her school following the required formalities.[275] A pupil might, however, instead claim damages or a declaration against a school or LA (under the HRA 1998) arguing that, by being excluded unlawfully, his or her right to education under A2P1 of the ECHR has been infringed. It appears that such an application would fail only if the pupil rejected out of hand the offer of alternative education.[276] Even then, a *wrongfully* excluded pupil might

---

[268] DCSF (2007d) para. 13.   [269] I.e. under Art. 9(2) ECHR.   [270] DCSF (2007d) para. 22.

[271] *R (Watkins-Singh, a child acting by Sanita Kumari Singh, her mother and litigation friend) v. The Governing Body of Aberdare Girls' High School and Rhondda Cynon Taf Unitary Authority,* [2008] EWHC 1865 (Admin), [2008] ELR 561. NB see Equality Act 2006, s. 49(1)(c): it is unlawful for a school to discriminate against a pupil on grounds of his religion or belief by excluding him or her. But NB s. 50 exempts maintained faith schools from s. 49's operation.

[272] SSFA 1998, s. 64; EA 2002, s. 52; Education (Pupil Exclusions and Appeals) (Maintained School) (England) Regulations 2002 (SI 2002/3178); Education (Pupil Exclusions) (Miscellaneous Amendments) (England) Regulations 2004 (SI 2004/402); Education (Pupil Exclusions and Appeals)(Miscellaneous Amendments) (England) Regulations 2006 (SI 2006/2189) and DCSF (2008g) Part 3.

[273] I.e. through pupils being sent home informally 'to cool off' or through parents being invited to remove their children.

[274] DCSF (2008g) para. 27.

[275] *Simpson v. United Kingdom* (Application No. 14688/89) (1989) 64 DR 188: the European Commission on Human Rights (EComHR) rejected a mother's claim that the procedures used to determine her son's special educational needs were in breach of Art 6 – his right to education was not of a 'civil' nature (as required by Art. 6), falling as it did within the domain of public law. Newman J in *R (on the application of B) v. Head Teacher of Alperton Community School* [2001] EWHC Admin 229, [2001] ELR 359, at paras. 46–9, applied *Simpson* on this point. Cf. *S, T and P v. London Borough of Brent* [2002] EWCA Civ 693, [2002] ELR 556, per Schiemann LJ, at [30], that it was a 'perfectly tenable assumption' that domestic human rights law and, arguably, the jurisprudence of the ECtHR, would today regard the right not to be permanently excluded from school without good reason a civil right for Art. 6 purposes.

[276] *Ali v. Head Teacher and Governors of Lord Grey School* [2006] UKHL 14, [2006] 2 All ER 457: per majority of the House of Lords (Baroness Hale of Richmond dissenting), although a

take his appeal to the ECtHR in Strasbourg, adopting the view of Baroness Hale of Richmond that alternative education, for example in a PRU, is 'no substitute for ordinary access to the full national curriculum as a pupil at an ordinary school'.[277]

A school may be challenged for failing to comply with formal exclusion procedures in a dispute over school uniform. In such a case, the school argues that the pupil has not been excluded as such; she has merely been told not to attend school wearing the item in question – which may be a justifiable stance if the uniform rule is interpreted as being lawful.[278] Meanwhile, the pupil argues that this is a form of exclusion, without the school having complied with the appropriate exclusion procedures. The pupil might further argue that not only has she suffered religious and/or racial discrimination, but has also been unlawfully deprived of her right to education under A2P1 of the ECHR. As Silber J points out, questions of procedural unfairness appertaining to exclusion can only arise if the uniform policy is *un*lawful.[279] Until his decision in *R (Watkins-Singh, a child acting by Sanita Kumari Singh, her mother and litigation friend) v. The Governing Body of Aberdare Girls' High School and Rhondda Cynon Taf Unitary Authority*,[280] there was no direct authority on this point. In *R (on the application of Begum) v. Head Teacher and Governors of Denbigh High School*,[281] the school's uniform policy was held by the House of Lords to be justified under Article 9(2) of the ECHR, in order to accommodate the needs of the other pupils,[282] so the question did not directly arise.[283] According to Lord Bingham, however, he might have upheld Shabina Begum's claim of constructive exclusion and breach of her right to education under A2P1 of the ECHR had he found the uniform rule to be unjustified.[284] Silber J dealt with this question directly in *Watkins-Singh*.[285] He ruled that if the school's uniform policy cannot be justified, and so amounts to illegal racial and/or religious discrimination,[286] a school's direction to a pupil not to attend school wearing the item of clothing in question constitutes an exclusion which not only fails to comply with the exclusion regulations,[287] but also unlawfully discriminates against the pupil.[288]

13-year-old boy had been excluded unlawfully (without the formalities being fully complied with), his right to education under A2P1 of the ECHR had not been violated because his parents had not considered the offer of alternative educational facilities at a PRU (discussed below) on his behalf.

[277] Per Baroness Hale ibid. at [81].   [278] *Spiers v. Warrington Corporation* [1954] 1 QB 61.
[279] [2008] EWHC 1865 (Admin) [2008] ELR 561(hereafter *Watkins-Singh*), per Silber J, at [150].
[280] Ibid.   [281] [2006] UKHL 15, [2007] AC 100.   [282] Discussed more fully in Chapter 11.
[283] But the Court of Appeal's unanimous view in *R (on the application of SB) v. Governors of Denbigh High School* [2005] EWCA Civ 199, [2005] 2 All ER 396 was that the respondent had been wrongfully excluded; see R. McManus (2006) pp. 99–100.
[284] Ibid. at [39]. See also Lord Hoffmann at [70]: the exclusion question was inappropriate in the light of the Art. 9 arguments; per Lord Scott [82]: the school had not excluded her because the head teacher wished her to attend school, but not wearing the jilbab. Neither Baroness Hale nor Lord Nicholls considered the point.
[285] [2008] EWHC 1865 (Admin) [2008] ELR 561.   [286] Discussed further in Chapter 11.
[287] [2008] EWHC 1865 (Admin) [2008] ELR 561, at [153].   [288] Ibid. at [158].

Even without the assistance of human rights law, a significant body of domestic case law emphasises that the exclusion procedures must comply with basic notions of fairness.[289] An elaborate appeals process[290] provides for the headteacher's decision to be subjected to objective review. The hearing before an Independent Appeal Panel (IAP) creates 'an arms length relationship between the LEA, the school and the panel'.[291] One of the most difficult aspects of the exclusion process lies in establishing whether the offence underlying the exclusion occurred at all. It is notable that the official guidance on the correct standard of proof to use has not been adjusted to reflect the standard of proof now governing care proceedings. The House of Lords stressed that neither the seriousness of the allegations grounding care proceedings nor the seriousness of the consequences should affect the standard of proof, which remains the simple balance of probabilities.[292] Meanwhile, the exclusion guidance retains the advice now rejected in the context of care proceedings.[293] Thus it directs that a pupil should only be permanently excluded if the allegations against him or her are established on the balance of probabilities. But, as before,[294] it warns that the more serious the allegation and thus the possible sanction, the more convincing the evidence substantiating the allegation must be.[295] Arguably, given that the standard of proof used in other civil proceedings (including exclusions) need not accord with that used in care proceedings,[296] the penal consequences of permanent exclusion justifies the retention of a higher standard of proof.

---

[289] E.g. *R v. Headteacher and Independent Appeal Committee of Dunraven School, ex p B* [2000] ELR 156: pupils facing possible expulsion have the right to know the nature of the accusation against them, disclosure of all evidence relied on by the discipline authorities, the opportunity to answer it through their parents, and the right for their parents to appear before the tribunal dealing with the matter. See also DCSF (2008g), para 20: pupils should be invited and encouraged to state their case at all stages of the exclusion process, where appropriate, taking account of their age and understanding. See also para 23(c): before deciding on exclusion, the head teacher should allow and encourage pupils to give their version of events.

[290] See DCSF (2008g), Parts 3–5. Pupils' parents can appeal (on the pupil's behalf) to the school discipline committee, established by the school governors to review all exclusions; appeals from that body go to the IAP established by the LA. In some circumstances, judicial review can be sought of either appeal committee's decision to uphold an exclusion.

[291] *S, T and P v. London Borough of Brent* [2002] EWCA Civ 693, [2002] ELR 556, per Schiemann LJ, at para 17. See also *R v. Headteacher and Independent Appeal Committee of Dunraven School, ex p B* [2000] ELR 156, per Sedley LJ, at 182: the governing body is there to provide an essential independent check on the headteacher's judgment.

[292] *Re B (children)(sexual abuse: standard of proof)* [2008] UKHL 35, [2008] 4 All ER 1, per Baroness Hale of Richmond, at [69]–[70]. See also Lord Hoffmann at [13]–[15]; discussed further in Chapter 15.

[293] *Re H (minors) (sexual abuse: standard of proof)* [1996] 1 All ER 1, per Lord Nicholls.

[294] DCSF (2007c) paras. 22, 96 and 144.

[295] DCSF (2008g) paras. 24, 106 and 155. ACE (2008b) p. 14: points out the very slight and confusing differences in wording between the guidance given to headteachers (para. 24), the governing body (para. 106) and the IAP (para. 155).

[296] *Re B (children)(sexual abuse: standard of proof)*, per Baroness Hale of Richmond, at [69].

Maintaining procedural fairness can be a particularly complicated matter for schools if a criminal investigation has commenced, with a possible prosecution pending, since further and more detailed evidence may emerge in the criminal proceedings.[297] Fairness is also especially important when more than one pupil is permanently excluded, all having been involved in a single incident involving a serious breach of discipline. Case law suggests that injustice can arise when differently constituted IAPs respond to their separate appeals against exclusion in different ways.[298] The official guidance suggests that the IAP should either combine all the appeals arising out of the one incident or ensure that the same members hear all the appeals.[299]

Astonishingly, in spite of the government's concern to ensure that the exclusion process is a fair one, it has doggedly resisted amending the law to give excluded pupils formal party status in any of the exclusion procedures, except in the unlikely situation of their being aged 18 or over. Despite being the focus of the proceedings, a child under 18 is not defined as the 'relevant person' for these purposes, his or her parents being named instead.[300] It is they, not the excluded child, who have a right to appeal against a permanent exclusion, attend the proceedings, be represented and offer written or oral submissions. The government has remained unmoved by the repeated criticisms of the Committee on the Rights of the Child regarding this aspect of English law.[301] It is particularly unjust where, for example, a teenager lives independently away from home, with no contact with his or her parents or where parents are too nervous to pursue an appeal on their son or daughter's behalf. In any event, the excluded pupil is well aware that a parent does not always act as his or her advocate particularly effectively during the appeals process.[302]

Unless pupils can persuade the domestic courts to expand the ambit of Article 6 of the ECHR, this gap in the legislation will remain unchallenged.[303] Meanwhile, the official guidance states that the governors' discipline committee and the IAP should encourage an excluded pupil under the age of 18 'to attend the hearing and to speak on his or her own behalf, if he or she wishes to do so'.[304] Fortunately, the guidance has now dropped its insistence on parents agreeing to the pupil's involvement.[305] Such a requirement had reinforced the perceptions of many excluded young people that 'the exclusion process was

---

[297] See further DCSF (2008g) Part 6.

[298] E.g. *R (S and B) v. Independent Appeal Panel of Birmingham City Council* [2006] EWHC 2369 (Admin), [2007] ELR 57: the IAP turned down the appeals of two boys against permanent exclusion for their part in a one-off incident involving experimentation with cannabis. A differently constituted IAP upheld the appeal of a third boy involved in the same incident.

[299] DCSF (2008g) paras. 121–2.

[300] Education (Pupil Exclusion and Appeals) (Maintained School) (England) Regulations 2002 (SI 2002/3178), reg. 2(1)(b).

[301] Committee on the Rights of the Child (1995) paras. 14 and 32; ibid. (2002) para. 48(b); ibid. (2008) para. 66(a).

[302] F. Taylor (2005) p. 39.   [303] Discussed above.

[304] DCSF (2008g) paras. 102 and 139.   [305] DCSF (2007c) paras. 92 and 129.

something that happened around them and about them, but did not directly involve them other than incidentally'.[306] The government's position over the child's lack of legal status in the exclusion procedures is unsustainable, given the fact that all Welsh children over the age of 11, have, since 2004, had full rights of appeal with or without permission from their parents.[307]

(v) The appeal decision

During the late 1990s, the ability of the appeal bodies to overrule headteachers wishing to exclude pupils from their schools increasingly fomented friction between teachers, school governors and parents.[308] The decisions of IAPs to reinstate children expelled for offences as serious as assaults on pupils and staff or drug-taking often appeared perverse.[309] Such decisions had serious repercussions for headteachers struggling to enforce discipline codes, with teaching unions threatening industrial action if their members were forced to teach reinstated pupils considered to be a threat to their safety. The government curbed the IAPs' enthusiasm for reinstating pupils on appeal through changing their composition to include more members with 'current or recent direct experience of schools'.[310] The government's evident satisfaction that this change had reduced the numbers of reinstatements on appeal arguably reflects an assumption that the large majority of exclusions are fully justified and that appellants are timewasters.[311]

Whilst ostensibly retaining their independence, IAPs are now given considerable government 'assistance' when deciding whether to reinstate the excluded pupil. Having decided, on the balance of probabilities, that the pupil is guilty of the misconduct alleged, the panel must balance his or her interests against those of the rest of the school.[312] IAPs must not reinstate a pupil '*merely* because of a failure to comply with any procedural requirement[s]',[313] unless the process was 'so flawed that important factors were not considered or justice clearly was not done'.[314] They are also directed to guard against 'the risk of undermining the headteacher's authority and the general climate of discipline

---

[306] F. Taylor (2005) p. 32.   [307] A. Sherlock (2007) pp. 177–9.   [308] I. Sutherland (2002).

[309] E.g. *R v. Independent Appeal Panel of Sheffield City Council, ex p N* [2000] ELR 700: Moses J criticised an IAP for directing a boy's reinstatement, without considering the claims of a girl pupil that he had sexually assaulted her.

[310] Schedule to Education (Pupil Exclusion and Appeals) (Maintained Schools) (England) Regulations 2002 (SI 2002/3178), reg. 2.

[311] DfES (2005c) para. 7.16: of nearly 10,000 permanent exclusions in 2003/4, there had been only 130 students reinstated on appeal. NB DfES (2007h): in 2005/6, there was a 3% increase in successful exclusion appeals and reinstatement occurred in 6% more cases than in the previous year, cf. DCSF (2008e): in 2006/7, the number of exclusion appeals had reduced by almost 1%, with the number of reinstatements reducing by 16% on the previous year.

[312] Education (Pupil Exclusion and Appeals) (Maintained Schools) (England) Regulations 2002 (SI 2002/3178), reg. 6(3).

[313] Ibid. reg. 6(4). Emphasis added.   [314] DCSF (2008g) para. 156(a).

within the school'.[315] Such heavy-handed guidance has the potential for turning the appeals system into a rubber stamp for head teachers' decisions.[316]

Most excluded pupils expect that the IAP will either confirm their exclusion or direct their reinstatement. They may be unaware that a direction to reinstate a pupil need not be interpreted literally by the school. As the case law shows, headteachers sometimes exclude children in response to the vociferous complaints of the teachers' unions who resent their members being forced to teach unruly pupils.[317] But now there is an alternative tactic. 'Reinstatement' need not involve the excluded pupil being provided with the same facilities as any other pupil.[318] Indeed, the school may put in place a regime which, far from true reinstatement, merely restores a purely formal relationship between school and child.[319] Even more worryingly, IAPs may, in exceptional cases, produce a decision which, whilst allowing the appeal against permanent exclusion, also states that reinstatement in the excluding school 'is not a practical way forward in the best interests of all concerned'.[320] This 'half-way house' allows IAPs to bow to precisely the same pressure from teaching unions that produced the exclusion in the first place. Case law suggests that excluded pupils and their parents find it difficult to understand how an appeal panel can, at one and the same time, consider that the exclusion decision was ill-founded but that reinstatement is impossible. These two findings must be dealt with discretely and each must be very carefully justified and explained.[321] The guidance now warns that schools cannot simply repeat their reasons for wishing to exclude the pupil when explaining why the pupil should not be reinstated. It also warns that it is contrary to the rules of natural justice for the parents not to be informed of the specific arguments directed at reinstatement.[322] An overall assessment of the current exclusion process produces the unfortunate impression that from start to finish excluded pupils are assumed to be troublemakers and that too much valuable time is being wasted over baseless appeals.[323]

---

[315] Ibid. at para. 159.   [316] D. Monk (2005) esp. pp. 402–5.

[317] E.g. *R (L (a minor) v. Governors of J School* [2003] UKHL 9, [2003] 2 AC 633 and *R (O) v. Governing Body of Park View Academy and ors* [2007] EWCA Civ 592, [2007] ELR 454.

[318] *R (L (a minor)) v. Governors of J School* [2003] UKHL 9, [2003] 2 AC 633: House of Lords (Lord Bingham and Lord Hoffmann dissenting) held that 'reinstatement' does not necessarily involve full reintegration within the class. The IAP's decision that an excluded pupil should be 'reinstated' was therefore fulfilled by the school arranging for L to be taught in a separate room approximately 10 foot square, isolated from the rest of the staff and pupils throughout the school day. See also *R (O) v. Governing Body of Park View Academy and ors* [2007] EWCA Civ 592, [2007] ELR 454.

[319] *R (L (a minor)) v. Governors of J School* [2003] UKHL 9, [2003] 2 AC 633, per Lord Bingham dissenting, at [20] and [23]. See also critique by D. Monk (2005) pp. 410–12.

[320] DCSF (2008g) para. 165.

[321] *D v. Independent Education Appeal Panel of Bromley London Borough and anor* [2007] EWCA Civ 1010, [2008] ELR 12.

[322] DCSF (2008g) para. 166.

[323] Per A. Steer (2005) para. 140: 'Whilst there is a need to maintain an appropriate balance of interests, some of the intended safeguards for the parent or carer and pupil have become unhelpful obstacles.'

(vi) The impact of exclusion

The impact on pupils and their families of permanent exclusion is often considerable. Researchers note that most excluded children regret being excluded and worry about its effect on their ability to pass exams and later to obtain jobs.[324] They feel isolated[325] and greatly miss their school friends.[326] The exclusion itself is a traumatic experience and a blow to their self-esteem.[327] The families of excluded pupils also suffer, both in terms of their relationships with each other and with the community at large.[328] In the past, delays in finding excluded pupils alternative education outside school left many of them free to roam the streets. Efforts to prevent exclusion being seen as a reward for bad behaviour[329] led to legislation and regulations obliging LAs to provide all permanently excluded pupils with full-time education[330] from the sixth day of their exclusion.[331] To reinforce this message, parents may be fined[332] if they fail, without reasonable cause, to ensure that their excluded child is kept away from any public place 'at any time during school hours'[333] during the first five days of his or her exclusion.[334] It is questionable whether such a coercive approach will be beneficial in the long term, given that parents may be obliged to take time off work to ensure that their child remains under what amounts to house arrest.[335] Admittedly schools' obligation to provide the excluded pupil with homework during those five days[336] provides him or her with some diversion.

Past failures to provide excluded pupils with alternative education was often attributable to a lack of resources, both in terms of financial resources and facilities available.[337] Case law indicates that LAs cannot appeal to a lack of resources to justify not providing 'suitable' and 'efficient' education outside mainstream school.[338] Nevertheless, in practice, the expense of 'education otherwise' and the shortage of places in PRUs and other facilities resulted in some excluded pupils being provided with educational provision for only a very few hours each week.[339] These resource issues are gradually being tackled, in the first place by the government funding more learning support units (LSUs) to

---

[324] F. Taylor (2005) pp. 22–3.   [325] C. Wright *et al.* (2005) pp. 47–9.

[326] F. Taylor (2005) pp. 23–4.   [327] C. Wright *et al.* (2005) pp. 16–17.

[328] Ibid. at pp. 34–5.   [329] A. Steer (2005) para. 147.

[330] DCSF (2007f) para. 3: at least 21 hours per week for key stage 1 pupils; 23.5 hours per week for key stage 2 pupils; 24 hours per week for key stage 3 pupils; 25 hours per week for key stage 4 pupils.

[331] EA 1996, s. 19(3A) and Education (Provision of Full-Time Education for Excluded Pupils) (England) Regulations 2007 (SI 2007/1870).

[332] EIA 2006, s. 105: parents may avoid a court appearance by receiving a penalty notice – see Education (Penalty Notices) (England) Regulations 2007 (SI 2007/1867).

[333] EIA 2006, s. 103(2).   [334] EIA 2006, s. 103(3) and (5).

[335] Joint Committee on Human Rights (2006) para. 57: this provision infringed the parent's rights under Art. 8 ECHR in a disproportionate manner and furthermore would discriminate against single parents or parents in low paid employment.

[336] DCSF (2008g) para. 51.   [337] Ofsted (2004) p. 34.

[338] *R v. East Sussex County Council, ex p Tandy* [1998] 2 All ER 769.   [339] Ofsted (2004) p. 26.

be attached to mainstream schools themselves, where problem pupils can be assisted. But they are not appropriate for the most disturbed children since they may involve schools coping with the continued presence on the school premises of a violent or drug abusing or dealing pupil.

The number of educational facilities outside schools has also slowly increased and some certainly provide excluded pupils with an environment far more conducive to learning than do mainstream schools.[340] Nevertheless, many such facilities have experienced considerable problems both in retaining staff[341] and in providing a good standard of education.[342] Ofsted found that many PRUs had to cope with very inadequate accommodation,[343] and with pupils of diverse age and need arriving in an unplanned way with insufficient information provided by their previous schools about their educational background.[344] The government followed up its promise to improve on alternative provision generally, more particularly the standard of education provided by PRUs,[345] with a White Paper setting out extensive plans for redesigning the whole system.[346] Whether or not these ambitions are fulfilled, at the very least, systems should be put in place, as promised, to ensure greater LA accountability for pupils' needs to be properly assessed and provision arranged to fulfil them.[347] The repackaging of PRUs under another name is certainly not enough[348] – to many they are still seen as 'sin bins'.[349]

Although most excluded pupils want to return to mainstream education as soon as possible,[350] at present, some pupils never do so, particularly the older ones.[351] Indeed, Ofsted found that the absence of proper reintegration procedures meant that if pupils in PRUs had not been reintegrated by the end of Key Stage 3, they remained there and never returned to a mainstream school.[352] In the past, the difficulty has been to persuade other schools in the area to admit a permanently excluded pupil. But even the worst behaved pupil has a right to education of some form.[353] Indeed, the government is well aware that an excluded pupil left with no educational provision at all can mount a challenge under the HRA 1998 arguing a violation of his or her right to education under A2P1 of the ECHR.[354] Admission cannot now be refused on the basis of a

---

[340] F. Taylor (2005) pp. 24–6.   [341] Ofsted (2005a) para. 43.

[342] R. MacDonald and J. Marsh (2005) pp. 50–1. See also Ofsted (2007c) para. 45: the proportion of 'inadequate' PRUs (14%) is 'too high'. DCSF (2008c) para. 4.9: in 2008, 11 PRUs were in special measures.

[343] Ofsted (2007d) paras. 8–9.   [344] Ibid. at paras. 17 and 29–30.

[345] DCSF (2007g) paras. 4.94–4.103.   [346] DCSF (2008c).   [347] Ibid. at chs. 2 and 4.

[348] Ibid. at para. 1.14. Re-named 'Short-stay schools' – ASCL Bill 2009, Part 11.

[349] *The Guardian*, 21 May 2008.   [350] F. Taylor (2005) pp. 22–3.

[351] Ibid. at p. 27 and D. Berridge *et al.* (2001) p. 30.   [352] Ofsted (2007d) para. 39.

[353] LAs have the power under SSFA 1998, ss. 96–7 to direct a much-excluded pupil's admission by a school (for which the LA is not the admission authority) within a reasonable distance of his or her home. This power's availability is, however, so strictly limited that its usefulness is questionable. See N. Harris (2007) p. 284.

[354] *Ali v. Head Teacher and Governors of Lord Grey School* [2006] UKHL 14, [2006] 2 All ER 457, discussed above.

child's poor record elsewhere or because the child is thought to be potentially disruptive.[355] Nevertheless, admission authorities are entitled to ignore parents' expressed preference for a particular school if their child has, within the last two years, been already excluded from two or more other schools.[356] The government therefore encourages groups of local schools to cooperate over taking their fair share of excluded pupils, thereby avoiding disproportionate numbers being placed in any one school.[357]

Guidance stresses the need for permanently excluded children to be reintegrated into some form of schooling quickly and directs schools to draw up individual reintegration plans for each excluded pupil in consultation with the LA, the pupil and parent within one month of a permanent exclusion.[358] In an effort to prevent pupils vanishing from the educational system once they are permanently excluded,[359] LAs are now legally obliged to identify all children of compulsory school age not registered at any school and not receiving suitable 'education otherwise'.[360] Hopefully, permanently excluded pupils will remain in view at least until they attain the age of 16. But as the government is itself aware, with the raising of the school leaving age to 18, there is a much more urgent need for well thought out 'alternative provision' for the 16 to 18-year-olds who refuse to participate in either mainstream schools or accredited training.[361]

(5) School administration

As discussed above, high rates of pupil absence and disruption in the classroom, bullying and high exclusion numbers often combine in failing schools. Were all schools to appeal to the strengths of the pupil population, they might find pupils working with them instead of against them. There is accumulating evidence that punitive regimes are associated with worse rather than better standards of behaviour;[362] furthermore that successfully performing schools adopt systems which reward good work and behaviour rather than focus on negative behaviour and punishments.[363]

The educational authorities accept that the schools which encourage pupils to take responsibility for various aspects of their school life produce better relationships between staff and pupils and between pupil and pupil.[364] Head teachers must not only consult parents before drawing up each school's

---

[355] DCSF (2009) para. 3.31. NB the statutory Admissions Code of Practice has binding authority. See SSFA 1998, s. 84(3) as amended by EIA 2006, s. 40(4).

[356] SSFA 1998, s. 87. The duty to admit such a pupil is suspended for a period of two years from the date of the last exclusion; discussed by N. Harris (2007) pp. 282–5.

[357] DCSF (2009) paras. 3.43–3.47 and DCSF (2007f) para. 37: i.e. through local 'Fair Access Protocols'.

[358] DCSF (2007f) paras. 23–4.   [359] Ofsted (2004) p. 27.   [360] EA 1996, s. 463A.

[361] DCSF (2008c) para. 1.22.   [362] Inter alia R. Elton (1989); M. Rutter *et al.* (1979).

[363] Ofsted (2005a) para. 77 and Ofsted (2006a) para. 12.

[364] Ofsted (2006a) para. 12. See also para. 13: some schools provide pupils with training to help others with advice or unofficial support, leading to younger pupils feeling safer.

behaviour policy but also all registered pupils at the school.[365] Whilst this progress has been made in the context of discipline, the government has been far more ambivalent over consulting pupils more widely over schools' administration. As the Crick committee recognised, engaging children in the more practical aspects of running their school encourages a sense of responsibility for and pride in the institution. The committee hoped that schools' new obligation to provide citizenship education[366] would encourage more schools to explore ways of involving their pupils in operational matters. It recommended that schools should consult with pupils over aspects of school life and 'wherever possible to give pupils responsibility and experience in helping to run parts of the school'.[367]

The most obvious way in which such advice can be followed is for schools to establish school councils. Many schools do so,[368] with their councils proving to be extremely effective, becoming involved in a wide range of school governance, including the appointment of teachers.[369] The way in which school councils are even able to influence particular areas of spending, controlling their own budgets[370] undoubtedly enhances pupils' own perception of the value of such entities. Some schools link membership of school councils with membership of local youth forums and parliaments[371] and even, through associate membership,[372] with the school's governing body.[373]

But until recently, schools were under no legal obligation in this respect. Indeed, the legislation merely rather vaguely required them to 'have regard to any [statutory] guidance … about consultation with pupils in connection with the taking of decisions affecting them'.[374] There was no binding legal obligation on English schools to consult pupils over any matter regarding school administration.[375] The UN Committee on the Rights of the Child criticised the fact that schoolchildren were 'not *systematically* consulted in matters that affect them'.[376] Indeed, research suggests that some teachers had reservations

---

[365] EIA 2006, s. 88(3)(c) and (d).

[366] Citizenship education was made, in September 2000, part of the Personal, Social and Health Education framework for primary schools (which became the PSHE and Citizenship programme). It became part of the national curriculum for secondary schools from September 2002.

[367] B. Crick (1998) p. 36.   [368] G. Whitty and E. Wisby (2007) p. 37 summarise the statistics.

[369] Ibid. esp. at chs. 7 and 8.   [370] Ibid. at pp. 74–5.

[371] Ibid. at p. 49.

[372] Education (No. 2) Act 1986, by setting the minimum qualifying age for becoming a school governor at 18, thereby abolished schools' ability to have pupil governors. Pupils under 18 can now be made associate members of the committee of governors, but have no voting rights.

[373] G. Whitty and E. Wisby (2007) pp. 40–1 and 76–8.

[374] EA 2002, s. 176(1) (partly repealed by ESA 2008, Sch. 2). DCSF (2008d) provided statutory guidance on this duty.

[375] Cf. the regulations governing Welsh schools; discussed below.

[376] Committee on the Rights of the Child (2002) para. 29, emphasis added; para. 30: further steps should be taken to promote participation more effectively, 'for example though school councils'. See also ibid. (2008) paras. 32, 66(a) and 67(g).

about the extent to which pupils could or should become involved in school matters beyond facilities/environment issues.[377] Meanwhile, pupils were bound to assume their school council to be purely tokenistic[378] if it was confined to dealing only with school facilities, school uniform, food and related matters.[379]

The law has at last been changed, with the introduction of a clear legislative duty on all schools to 'invite and consider pupils' views about prescribed matters' having regard to their age and understanding.[380] Indeed, although such matters as staff appointments and school budgets are unlikely to be within their purview,[381] the government intends to produce regulations requiring governing bodies to 'seek and take account of pupils, views on policies on the delivery of the curriculum, behaviour, the uniform, school food, health and safety, equalities and sustainability, not simply on what colour to paint the walls'.[382] When drafting such regulations it should take note of the Welsh Assembly's clear template for the establishment and running of school councils in all maintained schools in Wales.[383]

(6) Sex education in schools

The provision of high quality sex education is essential, in view of the high level of sexual activity amongst teenage children here in the UK,[384] compared with other European countries.[385] The role of schools is particularly important. Most research suggests that British teenagers and their parents today find it easier to talk to each other about sex, relationships and contraception than did their forbears.[386] Nevertheless, both parents and young people still rely on schools as the main source of reliable information about sexual matters.[387] Rather than encouraging young people to start sex young, as some maintain, both they and their parents consider that a sound sex education helps them adopt a more responsible attitude to sexual relationships.[388] This may explain why the countries in Western Europe with extremely well-developed sex

---

[377] G. Whitty and E. Wisby (2007) at pp. 78–9.   [378] Ofsted (2006b) para. 42.

[379] G. Whitty and E. Wisby (2007) pp. 46–8.

[380] Education Act 2002, s. 29B, as inserted by ESA 2008, s. 157.

[381] Per Baroness Morgan of Drefelin, Parliamentary Under-Secretary of State for the DCSF, HL Debs, *Hansard* 11 November 2008, col 573.

[382] Ibid.

[383] Under the School Councils (Wales) Regulations 2005 (SI 2005/3200), reg. 3(2), a head teacher must ensure that school council meetings are held six times per annum, the first of such meetings to be held by 1 November 2006. A. Sherlock (2007) pp. 170–2.

[384] Discussed further in Chapter 5.   [385] UNICEF (2007) Figure 5.2e.

[386] Ofsted (2007b) Figure 8. But see para. 21, indicating that many parents are still unable to address these issues directly or sensitively and R. French *et al.* (2005), discussed below in relation to Asian pupils.

[387] Inter alia: BMRB (2004) para. 2.7; Health Development Agency (2004) p. 4; J. Bynner and M. Londra (2004) pp. 50–1; Ofsted (2007b) Figure 9.

[388] Health Development Agency (2004) p. 4.

education programmes, in both secondary and primary schools, have the lowest rates of teenage pregnancy.[389]

The government's policy on the provision of sex education in schools has, until recently, been curiously ambivalent.[390] On the one hand, it has been determined to reduce the level of teenage pregnancy,[391] through a raft of measures, including improving the provision of sex education in schools. But, on the other hand, sex and relationships education (SRE) has remained outside the national curriculum. The government's concern to reduce the level of teenage pregnancies is understandable, given that the UK currently has the highest level of teenage birth-rate in Europe; indeed, the third highest in all OECD countries.[392] The SEU's extremely comprehensive report on teenage pregnancy painted a depressing picture of the way in which quite young teenagers 'drift into pregnancy'.[393] It found that ignorance about sex was a key risk factor in teenage pregnancy and that young people in this country were frequently ignorant or misinformed about sex and their own physical development, despite having received some sex education in school.[394] In relation to the quality of school sex education, however, the vast majority of the young people consulted considered that they had been told 'too little, too late'.[395]

Controversially, only the biological aspects of reproduction, contraception and sexually transmitted infections have been included in the national curriculum.[396] This means that education about sexual relationships has only been part of the non-statutory Personal, Social and Health Education (PSHE) programme, with schools being entitled to decide for themselves the content of the classes. As Ofsted observed in 2005:

> Some schools do not provide PSHE in any form … In some of these schools, headteachers offer the view that parents should play the key role in ensuring the personal and social development of their children. To say that schools should not play their part is to take an untenable position.[397]

It now appears that the government has at last heeded the repeated calls for PSHE to become part of the national curriculum.[398] Under proposals expected to come into force in 2010, SRE will be compulsory for all 5 to 16-year-old pupils.[399] Whilst such a move will at last ensure that all pupils receive up-to-date sex education, it will not necessarily improve the quality of SRE teaching, unless considerable efforts are made to overhaul its delivery. Although

---

[389] UNICEF (2001) pp. 20–2: e.g. Denmark and The Netherlands.

[390] N. Harris (2007) pp. 401–18.

[391] The problem of teenage pregnancy (including statistics on rates of teenage conception and abortion) is discussed in more detail in Chapter 5.

[392] Ibid.   [393] SEU (1999) para. 5.21.   [394] Ibid. at ch. 5.   [395] Ibid. at para. 5.16.

[396] I.e. as part of the science curriculum.   [397] Ofsted (2005b) para. 52.

[398] E.g. Independent Advisory Group on Teenage Pregnancy and Independent Advisory Group on Sexual Health and HIV (2006) para. 4.1.1.

[399] Announcement by Jim Knight, Minister of State for Schools and Learning, on 23 October 2008.

the quality of PSHE has apparently improved significantly in recent years,[400] this is from a very low base level, particularly in relation to SRE.

It appears that the problems underlying the teaching of SRE cannot be attributed to the official guidance. Backed up by legislation,[401] the guidance encourages open discussion about relationships,[402] and emphasises that each school's sex education should include full information about contraception and how it is to be accessed, including information about local services. It sensibly acknowledges that pupils under 16 may at times confide in their teachers and makes suggestions for handling this when it happens.[403] Admittedly, the guidance has its weaker aspects. It fails to acknowledge that young people find sexual activity pleasurable and constantly advises that they should learn the benefits of delaying sexual involvement.[404] Controversially, children must learn about the nature of marriage and its importance for family life and for bringing up children.[405] This may contribute to the fact that teachers feel discouraged from including in SRE programmes any discussion of gay or lesbian relationships.[406] Nevertheless, the criticisms of SRE largely relate to the way schools teach it. The coverage is often superficial,[407] its delivery by non-specialist teachers is often poor[408] and its assessment even worse.[409] Regarding the persistent use of non-specialist class tutors to teach SRE, Ofsted observes that 'Pupils quickly notice a teacher's lack of knowledge or enthusiasm for the subject; they react negatively or are simply embarrassed'.[410]

Although the government is now determined to make sex education a compulsory part of the school curriculum, it is unclear whether the 'parental opt-out' will be retained.[411] Currently, the assumption made by education legislation that the interests of parents and children are identical is nowhere more apparent than in this area of the law. Since 1993, parents have had an absolute right to withdraw their children from sex education classes,[412] apparently as a means of addressing the needs of those objecting on religious grounds.[413] But research published over a decade later suggests that although

---

[400] Ofsted (2007b) paras. 26 and 62.

[401] Learning and Skills Act 2000, s. 148 amending EA 1996, s. 403.

[402] DfEE (2000).   [403] Ibid. at paras. 2.11 and 7.11.

[404] D. Monk (2001) pp. 278–9. See also P. Meredith (2001) pp. 210–20.

[405] DfEE (2000) para. 1.21 and EA 1996, s. 403(1A)(a).

[406] Ofsted (2002) para. 44: according to pupils, this was one of the 'no-go areas' in their SRE classes.

[407] Ofsted (2007b) para. 26: in a majority of the SRE lessons in primary schools, pupils' knowledge and understanding of factual aspects were no better than adequate; in secondary schools, their knowledge and understanding was good in only two lessons in three at Key Stage 3.

[408] Ofsted (2005b) para. 7: at Key Stage 3, the quality of teaching was unsatisfactory in twice as many lessons taught by non-specialist class tutors as by specialist teachers. See also Ofsted (2007b) paras. 32–4.

[409] Ofsted (2005b) para. 21: 'Assessment is the weakest aspect of PSHE teaching and is often either poor or entirely absent'; Ofsted (2007b) para. 40: 'Assessment continues to be the weakest aspect of PSHE teaching. It is sufficiently rigorous in only a minority of schools and unsatisfactory in half.'

[410] Ofsted (2007b) para. 34.   [411] The government intends to consult on this question.

[412] EA 1996, s. 405.   [413] Baroness Blatch, HL Debs, 1993, Vol. 547, col. 140.

Bangladeshi and Indian children born in this country often feel unable to discuss sexual matters with their parents, they do obtain information about the act of sex from a range of sources, including SRE classes, friends, older siblings, media and magazines.[414] Many of the young people interviewed considered that not enough time was devoted by schools to SRE.[415] They also considered that when teaching SRE, schools should take account of traditional beliefs, and consider keeping the genders separate in such classes.[416] There was little indication in the research that the young people or their parents considered that the inclusion of SRE instruction in school was offensive.

The religious objections of parents aside, the government also argued that the right of parental withdrawal was necessary in order to comply with A2P1 of the ECHR.[417] In fact, government nervousness about infringing this international provision appears to have been misplaced. In *Kjeldsen, Busk Madsen and Pedersen v. Denmark*,[418] the ECtHR decided that the Danish government had not violated that provision by providing compulsory sex education in schools, since it had been conveyed in a balanced and objective manner, with no element of indoctrination. The fact that the parents had no right to exempt their children from such education did not amount to a breach of A2P1 of the ECHR. So it seems, the government here could introduce compulsory sex education with no parental right of withdrawal, as long as it imparts information 'in an objective, critical and pluralistic manner'.

Today, the high level of teenage pregnancies justifies withdrawing the parental opt-out and making sex education compulsory for all, particularly if it includes advice on contraception and protection against HIV infection. The existence of a parental right to withdraw children from SRE attracted criticism from the Committee on the Rights of the Child[419] and creates serious anomalies in the law. Indeed, the law's extreme incoherence is increased by sixth form pupils being allowed to override their parents' views on whether they attend religious education or worship in school.[420] Similarly, the common law allows even teenagers under the age of 16, who understand the dangers of unprotected sex, to seek contraceptive advice without their parents' knowledge or consent.[421] Meanwhile, education law allows parents to leave their children in a state of ignorance over the implications of sexual activity right up to the age of 18. A teenager might now argue that the parental right to withdraw a pupil from sex education classes infringes his or her rights under a variety of international human rights treaties. It not only

---

[414] R. French *et al.* (2005) pp. 33–4.   [415] Ibid. at p. 34.   [416] Ibid. at p. 35.

[417] Baroness Blatch, HL Debs, 1993, Vol. 547, col. 1292.   [418] (1976) 1 EHRR 711.

[419] Committee on the Rights of the Child (1995) para. 14.

[420] EIA 2006, s. 55 and EA 1996, s. 342(5A) (inserted by ESA 2008, s. 143); discussed further in Chapter 11.

[421] *Gillick v. West Norfolk and Wisbech Area Health Authority* [1986] AC 112; discussed further in Chapters 3 and 5.

ignores the right to be consulted,[422] but also the right to freedom of expression,[423] more particularly under Article 10 of the ECHR. It is astonishing that an area of law involving children whose sexual activity may have long-term implications for themselves and others, through teenage pregnancy and HIV infection, is still locked in the past. Although little used,[424] the existence of a parental right to withdraw their children from sex education classes ignores an important point of principle – it is short-sighted and wrong to treat them as appendages of their parents.

(7) Conclusion

Throughout the reforming activity of the 1980s, the education legislation consistently treated parents as the 'consumers' of education, and as their children's proxies or representatives when making educational choices. It progressively increased parental powers over making choices, but without suggesting that children should be involved in the process. More recently, the law has become increasingly authoritarian in its approach to parents, attributing to them most problems experienced by schools, such as truancy and serious misbehaviour. Indeed, the sanctions made available to schools may have started subtly distorting the balance of power between schools and parents. Furthermore, through their use, schools may unwittingly exacerbate the pressures experienced by many families already suffering various forms of social exclusion. The volumes of guidance on matters relating to discipline and exclusion reinforce this new authoritarian ethos pervading education law and practice.

Alongside this changing climate of opinion, we have a new body of older pupils aged 16–18 being siphoned into education or training, bringing with them their own discrete issues and problems, some inevitably relating to attendance and discipline. One wonders how well prepared educationalists will be for the large numbers attending only on sufferance. Indeed, the assumption that all children are and should remain under their parents' complete control, which so clearly permeates the huge body of education legislation, ill accords with the needs of this much older group of pupils.

BIBLIOGRAPHY

NB many of these publications can be obtained on the relevant organisation's website.

Advisory Centre for Education (ACE) (2008a) 'Disability Discrimination: Housing Case Has Wide Potential Impact' 2 (2) *ASKACE* 26.

---

[422] Art. 12 of the CRC.

[423] Art. 13 of the CRC. See also Art. 17 of the CRC which recognises that children need access to information and material from a variety of sources.

[424] Ofsted (2002) recorded (p. 6) that only about 4 in every 10,000 pupils were currently withdrawn from the non-statutory aspects of SRE.

Advisory Centre for Education (ACE) (2008b) 'Exclusions – 2008 revised guidance' 2 (2) *ASKACE* 14. Action on Rights for Children(2005) *How Effective Are Truancy Sweeps?*, ARCH.

Armstrong, D, Hine, J., Hacking, S., Armaos, R., Jones, R., Klessinger, N. and France, A. (2005) *Children, Risk and Crime: the On Track Youth Lifestyles Surveys*, Home Office Research Study 278, Home Office Research, Development and Statistics Directorate.

Audit Commission (1996) *Misspent Youth: Young People and Crime*, Audit Commission Publications.

BMRB International (2004) *Tracking Survey Wave 12 Evaluation of the Teenage Pregnancy Strategy, Report of Results of Twelve Waves of Research*, BMRB International.

Berridge, D., Brodie, I., Pitts, J., Porteous, D. and Tarling, R. (2001) *The Independent Effects of Permanent Exclusion From School on the Offending Careers of Young People* RDS Occasional Paper no 71, Home Office.

Bhabra, S., Dinos, S. and Ghate, D. (2006) *Young People, Risk and Protection: A Major Survey of Secondary Schools in On Track Areas*, DfES Research Report RR 728, Policy Research Bureau.

Bradshaw, J., Kemp, P., Baldwin, S. and Rowe, A. (2004) *The Drivers of Social Exclusion: a Review of the Literature for the Social Exclusion Unit in the Breaking the Cycle Series*, Social Exclusion Unit.

Bynner, J. and Londra, M. (2004) *The Impact of Government Policy on Social Exclusion Among Young People: a Review of the Literature for the Social Exclusion Unit in the Breaking the Cycle Series*, Social Exclusion Unit.

Chamberlain, T., Lewis, K., Teeman, D. and Kendall, L. (2006) *How is the Every Child Matters Agenda Affecting Schools?* NFER.

ChildLine (2005) *Annual Review 2005*, ChildLine.

Committee on the Rights of the Child (1995) *Concluding Observations of the Committee on the Rights of the Child: United Kingdom of Great Britain and Northern Ireland* CRC/C/15/Add 34, Centre for Human Rights, Geneva.

Committee on the Rights of the Child (2001) *General Comment No.1, The Aims of Education*, UN Doc CRC/GC/2001/1, Centre for Human Rights, Geneva.

Committee on the Rights of the Child (2002) *Concluding Observations of the Committee on the Rights of the Child: United Kingdom of Great Britain and Northern Ireland* CRC/C/15/Add 188, Centre for Human Rights, Geneva.

Committee on the Rights of the Child (2008) *Concluding Observations of the Committee on the Rights of the Child: United Kingdom of Great Britain and Northern Ireland* CRC/C/GBR/CO/4, Centre for Human Rights, Geneva.

Crick, B. (Chairman)(1998) *Education for Citizenship and the Teaching of Democracy in Schools*, Final report of the Advisory Group on Citizenship, Qualifications and Curriculum Authority.

Cunningham, S. and Lavalette, M. (2002) 'Children, Politics and Collective Action: School Strikes in Britain' in Goldson, B., Lavalette, M. and McKechnie, J. *Children, Welfare and the State*, Sage Publications.

Curtis, A., Exley, S., Sasia, A., Tough, S. and Whitty, G. (2008) *The Academies Programme: Progress, Problems and Possibilities*, The Sutton Trust.

Dalziel, D. and Henthorne, K. (2005) *Parents'/Carers' Attitudes Towards School Attendance*, TNS Social Research, DfES Research Report RR 618, DfES.

Department for Children, Schools and Families (DCSF) (2007a) *Guidance on Education-Related Parenting Contracts, Parenting Orders and Penalty Notices*, Revised September 2007, DCSF.

Department for Children, Schools and Families (DCSF) (2007b) *Guidance on the Education (School Attendance Targets) (England) Regulations 2007*, DCSF.

Department for Children, Schools and Families (DCSF) (2007c) *Improving Behaviour and Attendance: Guidance on Exclusion from Schools and Pupil Referral Units*, DCSF.

Department for Children, Schools and Families (DCSF) (2007d) *DCSF Guidance to Schools on Uniform and Related Policies*, at http://www.teachernet.gov.uk/management/atoz/u/uniform/

Department for Children, Schools and Families (DCSF) (2007e) *The Use of Force to Control or Restrain Pupils*, DCSF.

Department for Children, Schools and Families (DCSF) (2007f) *Local Authority Responsibility to Provide Full Time Education and Reintegrate Permanently Excluded Pupils*, DCSF.

Department for Children, Schools and Families (DCSF) (2007g) Cm 7280, *The Children's Plan: Building Brighter Futures*, TSO.

Department for Children, Schools and Families (DCSF) (2007h) *Raising Expectations: Staying in Education and Training Post-16. From Policy to Legislation*, DCSF.

Department for Children, Schools and Families (DCSF) (2008a) Cm 7348, *Raising Expectations: enabling the system to deliver*, TSO.

Department for Children, Schools and Families (DCSF) (2008b) *Absence and Attendance Code: Guidance for Schools and Local Authorities*, DCSF.

Department for Children, Schools and Families (DCSF) (2008c) Cm 7410, *Back on Track: A Strategy For Modernising Alternative Provision For Young People*, TSO.

Department for Children, Schools and Families (DCSF) (2008d), *Working Together: Listening to the Voices of Children and Young People*, DCSF.

Department for Children, Schools and Families (DCSF) (2008e) SFR 14/2008, *Permanent and Fixed Term Exclusions from Schools and Exclusion Appeals in England, 2006/7*, DCSF.

Department for Children, Schools and Families (DCSF) (2008f) *Delivering 14–19 Reform: Next Steps*, DCSF.

Department for Children, Schools and Families (DCSF) (2008g) *Improving Behaviour and Attendance: Guidance on Exclusion from Schools and Pupil Referral Units*, DCSF.

Department for Children, Schools and Families (DCSF) (2009) *School Admissions Code*, TSO.

Department for Education and Employment (DfEE) (1998) *Home-School Agreements: Guidance for Schools*, DfEE.

Department for Education and Employment (DfEE) (2000) *Sex and Relationship Education Guidance 0116/2000*, DfEE.

Department for Education and Skills (DfES) (2005a) *Extended Schools: Access to Opportunities and Services for All. A Prospectus*, DfES.

Department for Education and Skills (DfES) (2005b) Cm 6476, *14–19 Education and Skills*, HMSO.

Department for Education and Skills (DfES) (2005c) Cm 6677, *Higher Standards, Better Schools for All*, DfES.

Department for Education and Skills (DfES) (2006a) SFR 24/2006 *Permanent and Fixed Term Exclusions from Schools and Exclusion Appeals in England, 2004/05*, DfES.

Department for Education and Skills (DfES) (2006b) *Trends in Education and Skills*, DfES.

Department for Education and Skills (DfES) (2007a) Cm 7065, *Raising Expectations: Staying in Education and Training Post-16*, TSO.

Department for Education and Skills (DfES) (2007b) SFR 11/2007, *Pupil Absence in Secondary Schools in England, 2005/06*, DfES.

Department for Education and Skills (DfES) (2007c) *Parental Responsibility Data, Data on Penalty Notices, Fast-track to Attendance, Parenting Orders and Parenting Contracts*, DfES.

Department for Education and Skills (DfES) (2007d) *Statutory Guidance on EIA Section 6 (Positive Activities for Young People)*, DfES.

Department for Education and Skills (DfES) (2007e) *School Discipline and Pupil Behaviour Policies: Guidance for Schools*, DfES.

Department for Education and Skills (DfES) (2007f) *Safeguarding Children and Safer Recruitment in Education*, DfES.

Department for Education and Skills (DfES) (2007g) *Screening and Searching of Pupils for Weapons: Guidance for School Staff*, DfES.

Department for Education and Skills (DfES) (2007h) SFR 21/2007, *Permanent and Fixed Term Exclusions from Schools and Exclusion Appeals in England, 2005/6*, DfES.

Department for Education and Skills (DfES) (2007i) *Pastoral Support Programme*, DfES.

Department of Health (DH) (1991) *Guardians Ad Litem and other Court Related Issues Vol 7 Children Act 1989 Guidance and Regulations*, HMS0.

Dowling, M., Gupta, A. and Aldgate, J. (2006) 'The Impact of Community and Environmental Factors' in Aldgate, J., Jones, D., Rose, W. and Jeffrey, C. (eds.) *The Developing World of the Child*, Jessica Kingsley Publishers.

Elton, R. (Chairman)\(1989) *Discipline in Schools, Report of the Committee of Enquiry into Discipline in Schools*, HMSO.

Evans, L., Hall, L. and Wreford, S. (2008) Research Report DCSF-RR030, *Education-Related Parenting Contracts Evaluation*, DCSF.

Farson, R. (1978) *Birthrights*, Penguin.

Fionda, J. (2005) *Devils and Angels: Youth Policy and Crime*, Hart Publishing.

French,. S. Joyce, L., Fenton, K., Kingori, P., Griffiths, C., Stone, V., Patel-Kanwal, H., Power, R. and Stephenson, J. (2005) *Exploring the Attitudes and Behaviour of Bangladeshi, Indian and Jamaican Young People in Relation to Reproductive and Sexual Health, A Report for the Teenage Pregnancy Unit*, UCL/BMRB.

Grenville, M. (1988) 'Compulsory School Attendance and the Child's Wishes' *Journal of Social Welfare Law* 4.

HM Treasury and Department for Children, Schools and Families (DCSF) (2007) *Aiming High for Young People: a Ten Year Strategy for Positive Activities*, HM Treasury.

Hafen, B. (1976) 'Children's Liberation and the New Egalitarianism: Some Reservations About Abandoning Youth to Their "Rights"' *Brigham Young University Law Review* 605.

Hallam, S., Castle, F. and Rogers, L., with Creech, A., Rhanie, J. and Kokotsaki, D. (2005) *Research and Evaluation of the Behaviour Improvement Programme* DfES Research Report No 702, DfES.

Hallam, S., Rogers, L. and Shaw, J. (2006) 'Improving Children's Behaviour and Attendance Through the Use of Parenting Programmes: an Examination of Practice in Five Case Study Local Authorities' 33 *British Journal of Special Education* 107.

Halsey, K., Bedford, N., Atkinson, M., White, R. and Kinder, K. (2004) *Evaluation of Fast-Track to Prosecution for School Non-Attendance*, Research Brief No RR 567, DfES.

Hansen, K. (2003) 'Education and the Crime-Age Profile' 43 *British Journal of Criminology* 141.

Harris, N. (2005a) 'Education: Hard or Soft Lessons in Human Rights?' in Harvey, C. (ed.) *Human Rights in the Community*, Hart Publishing.

(2005b) 'Pupil Bullying, Mental Health and the Law in England' in Harris, N. and Meredith, P. (eds.) *Children, Education and Health: International Perspectives on Law and Policy*, Ashgate.

(2007) *Education, Law and Diversity*, Hart Publishing.

Health Development Agency (2004) *Teenage Pregnancy: an Overview of the Research Evidence*, Health Development Agency.

Holt, J. (1974) *Escape from Childhood: The Needs and Rights of Childhood*, E P Dutton and Co.

House of Commons Education and Skills Committee (2007) HC 85, *Bullying, Third Report of Session 2006–07*, The Stationery Office.

Independent Advisory Group on Teenage Pregnancy and Independent Advisory Group on Sexual Health and HIV (2006) *Personal, Social and Health Education (PSHE) in Schools: Time for Action*, IAG TP and IAG SH.

Jeffs, T. (2002) 'Schooling, Education and Children's Rights' in Franklin, B. (ed.) *The New Handbook of Children's Rights: Comparative Policy and Practice*, Routledge.

Joint Committee on Human Rights (2006) HL Paper 177/HC 1098, *Legislative Scrutiny: Ninth Progress Report*, The Stationery Office.

Lindley, R. (1989) 'Teenagers and Other Children' in Scarre, G. (ed.) *Children, Parents and Politics*, Cambridge University Press.

MacDonald, R. and Marsh, J. (2005) *Disconnected Youth? Growing Up in Britain's Poor Neighbourhoods*, Palgrave Macmillan.

Malcolm, H. Wilson, V., Davidson, J. and Kirk, S. (2003) *Absence from School: A Study of its Causes and Effects in Seven LEAs*, DfES Research Report No 424, DfES.

McManus, R. (2006) 'School Uniform and the European Convention on Human Rights' 7 *Education Law Journal* 87.

Mencap (2007) *Don't Stick it: Stop it!*, Mencap.

Meredith, P. (2001) 'Children's Rights and Education' in Fionda, J. (ed.) *Legal Concepts of Childhood*, Hart Publishing.

Monk, D. (2001) 'New Guidance/Old Problems: Recent Developments in Sex Education' 23 *Journal of Social Welfare and Family Law* 271.

(2002) 'Children's Rights in Education – Making Sense of Contradictions' (2002) 14 *Child and Family Law Quarterly* 45.

(2005) '(Re)constructing the Head Teacher: Legal Narratives and the Politics of School Exclusions' 32 *Journal of Law and Society* 399.

Mori (2004) *Youth Survey 2004*, Youth Justice Board.

National Advisory Committee on Creative and Cultural Education (1999) *All Our Futures: Creativity, Culture and Education*, DfEE.

National Audit Office (2005) *Improving School Attendance in England*, Report by the Comptroller and Auditor General, HC 212 Session 2004–5, TSO.

National Audit Office (2006) *Improving Poorly Performing Schools in England*, TSO.

National Audit Office (2007) *Partnering for Success: Preparing to Deliver the 14–19 Education Reforms in England*, TSO.

Office for Standards in Education (Ofsted) (2002) HMI 433, *Sex and Relationships: A Report from the Office of Her Majesty's Chief Inspector of Schools*, Ofsted.

Office for Standards in Education (Ofsted) (2003) HMI 465, *Bullying: Effective Action in Secondary Schools*, Ofsted.

Office for Standards in Education (Ofsted) (2004) HMI 2294, *Out of School: A Survey of the Educational Support and Provision for Pupils Not in School*, Ofsted.

Office for Standards in Education (Ofsted) (2005a) HMI 2363, *Managing Challenging Behaviour* Ofsted.

Office for Standards in Education (Ofsted) (2005b) HMI 2311, *Personal, Social and Health Education in Secondary Schools*, Ofsted.

Office for Standards in Education (Ofsted) (2006a) HMI 2377, *Improving Behaviour*, Ofsted.

Office for Standards in Education (Ofsted) (2006b) HMI 2666, *Towards Consensus? Citizenship in Secondary Schools*, Ofsted.

Office for Standards in Education (Ofsted) (2007a) Ref no. 070048, *Developing Social, Emotional and Behavioural Skills in Secondary Schools*, Ofsted.

Office for Standards in Education (Ofsted) (2007b) Ref no. 070049, *Time for Change? Personal, Social and Health Education*, Ofsted.

Office for Standards in Education (Ofsted) (2007c) HC 1002, *The Annual Report of Her Majesty's Chief Inspector of Education, Children's Services and Skills 2006/07*, TSO.

Office for Standards in Education (Ofsted) (2007d) Ref no. 070019, *Pupil Referral Units*, Ofsted.

Office for Standards in Education (Ofsted) (2008) HC 1114, *The Annual Report of Her Majesty's Chief Inspector of Education, Children's Services and Skills 2007/08*, TSO.

Office of the Children's Commissioner (2006a) *Bullying Today*, Office of the Children's Commissioner.

Office of the Children's Commissioner (2006b) *Bullying in Schools in England: A Review of the Current Complaints System and a Discussion of Options for Change*, Office of the Children's Commissioner.

Oliver, C. and Candappa, M. (2003) *Tackling Bullying: Listening to the Views of Children and Young People*, DfES Research Report No. 400, HMSO.

Parsons, C., Godfrey, R., Annan, G., Cornwall, J., Dussart, M., Hepburn, S., Howlett, K. and Wennerstrom, V. (2004) *Minority Ethnic Exclusions and the Race Relations (Amendment) Act 2000*, DfES Research Report RR 616, HMSO.

Pleace, N., Fitzpatrick, S., Johnsen, S., Quilgers, D., Sanderson, D. (2008) *Statutory Homelessness in England: The Experience of Families and 16–17 Year Olds*, Department for Communities and Local Government.

Rutter, M., Maughan, B., Mortimore, P. and Ouston, J., with Smith, A. (1979) *Fifteen Thousand Hours: Secondary Schools and Their Effects on Pupils*, Open Book.

Sherlock, A. (2007) 'Listening to Children in the Field of Education: Experience in Wales' 19 *Child Family Law Quarterly* 161.

Social Exclusion Unit (SEU) (1998) Cm 3957, *Truancy and School Exclusion: Report by the Social Exclusion Unit.*

Social Exclusion Unit (SEU) (1999) Cm 4342, *Teenage Pregnancy.*

Steer, A. (Chairman) (2005) *Learning Behaviour: The Report of the Practitioners' Group on School Behaviour and Discipline*, DfES.

Sutherland, I. (2002) 'Advances in Exclusions Law?' 3 *Education Law Journal* 216.

Taylor, F. (2005) *A Fair Hearing? Researching Young People's Involvement in the School Exclusion Process*, Save the Children.

Tomaševski, K. (1999) *'Special Rapporteur on the Right to Education' Addendum*, Mission to the of Great Britain and Northern Ireland (England) 18–22 October 1999 Report to UN Commission on Human Rights E/CN.4/2000/6/Add 2, Centre for Human Rights, Geneva.

UNICEF (2001) Innocenti Research Centre, *A League Table of Teenage Births in Rich Nations*, Innocenti Report Card Issue No 3 July 2001, UNICEF.

UNICEF (2007) Innocenti Research Centre, *Child Poverty in Perspective: An Overview of Child Well-being in Rich Countries*, Report Card 7, UNICEF.

Wanless, P. (2006) *Priority Review: Exclusion of Black Pupils 'Getting it. Getting it right'*, DfES.

Warnock, H.M. (Chairman) (1978) Cmnd 7212, *Special Educational Needs Report of the Committee of Enquiry into the Education of Handicapped Children and Young People*, HMSO.

Welton, E. (2008) 'Laying Down the Law: an Analysis of the Education and Skills Bill' 245 *Childright* 11.

Whitty, G. and Wisby, E. (2007) Research Report DCSF-RR001, *Real Decision Making?* School Councils in Action, DCSF.

Wright, C., Standen, P., John, G., German, G. and Patel, T. (2005) *School Exclusion and Transition into Adulthood in African-Caribbean Communities*, Joseph Rowntree Foundation.

Chapter 7

Children's involvement in family proceedings – rights to representation

(1) Introduction

English law allows mature children a remarkable degree of procedural autonomy by allowing them to initiate proceedings themselves, in order to enforce their own substantive rights.[1] They may, for example, apply for an order under the Children Act (CA) 1989 relating to their own health care, or gain the right to live with some adult other than their parents.[2] It is, however, relatively unusual for children to initiate their own litigation. Far more are drawn into legal proceedings by parents disagreeing over their upbringing in the context of divorce and separation. Indeed, increasing numbers of children find that 'the taken-for-grantedness of family life'[3] is shattered by their parents breaking up. These children may find that the legal system makes it only too easy for their parents not to involve them in any arrangements made for their future upbringing. Indeed, a growing body of authors criticise what they see as the law's outdated view of children as the passive victims of parental and adult quarrels.[4] Instead, those concerned with the 'new sociology of childhood' argue that children should be acknowledged as having agency – as autonomous individuals with a right to participation[5] in all aspects of family life, including post-divorce arrangements for their care. Such views are debatable.[6] Whatever conceptualisation of childhood is adopted, however, children should be allowed to challenge any infringements of their substantive rights through the court process. Otherwise, the fact that they are rights-holders may be of little comfort to them.

As the following assessment demonstrates, despite reforms, the system providing children with procedural rights not only remains confused but is unfair. This is largely due to government reluctance to devote sufficient resources to establishing better support. Financial restraints have ensured that provision remains variable and arbitrary; whilst some children are enabled to convey

---

[1] Discussed in Chapter 4.
[2] By applying for an Art. s 8 order under the CA 1989; discussed in Chapter 4.
[3] C. Smart (2006) p. 167.
[4] These ideas are summarised by A. Diduck (2003) pp. 80–3 and F. Kaganas and A. Diduck (2004) pp. 961–4.
[5] A. James (2003) p. 145 and J. Roche (1999) pp. 70–1.   [6] Discussed below.

their wishes to the courts, others are not, even for those caught up in similar circumstances. Depending on the way the litigation started, the courts receive information about some but not all children, with some children being separately represented and others not. The establishment of the Children and Family Court Advisory and Support Services, (formerly officially abbreviated to CAFCASS, more recently abbreviated to 'Cafcass')[7] appears to have been prompted, at least in part, by the government's hope to produce efficiency savings. Indeed, a failure to give budgetary priority to children's representation may explain the continuation of a system which still requires considerable improvement.

This chapter, whose overall theme is children's involvement in civil proceedings,[8] is divided into three parts. The first considers the provisions of international law recognising children's rights to participate in legal proceedings over their future. The second assesses the extent to which children whose parents separate or divorce can obtain external support services. The third considers children's involvement in family proceedings. This third section is itself divided into two parts. The first considers the methods used for ascertaining the views of children involved in private law disputes over their upbringing, including the procedures governing children wishing to instruct their own solicitors and litigate on their own behalf. The second section assesses the system of representation for children involved in public law proceedings.[9]

(2) The requirements of international instruments

The provision made by English law for the involvement of children in family proceedings does not match up to international requirements, despite improvements since the establishment of Cafcass in 2001. Fortunately, those urging further reform can use the provisions of international human rights law to clarify the defects in English procedures. Article 12 of the United Nations Convention on the Rights of the Child (CRC) is of overriding importance because of the way it affirms that children should not be seen as passive individuals but as fully fledged people with rights to express their own views on all matters affecting them.

Article 12(1) requires governments to:

assure to the child who is capable of forming his or her own views the right to express those views freely in all matters affecting the child, the views of the child being given due weight in accordance with the age and maturity of the child.

Article 12(2) further provides that for this purpose:

the child shall in particular be provided with the opportunity to be heard in any judicial and administrative proceedings affecting the child, either directly, or

---

[7] Established on 1 April 2001 by the Criminal Justice and Courts Services Act 2000, Ch. II and Sch. 2.
[8] The involvement of children in criminal proceedings is considered in Chapter 17.
[9] These issues are all considered in the context of applications brought under the CA 1989, since this is the litigation which most commonly affects children. The extent to which the courts take account of children's wishes and feelings is considered in Chapter 8.

through a representative or an appropriate body, in a manner consistent with the procedural rules of national law.

It should be noted that Article 12 does not promise autonomy to children – indeed, neither paragraph promises that children's wishes are to be acceded to. The article is about consultation and participation, not about self-determination. The fact that English law reserves the final decision to the courts fully accords with this provision, but it should also provide children with an opportunity to be heard in *any* judicial and administrative proceedings affecting the child.

How children are to be heard is not clearly specified. Article 12(2) makes no promise that the child will be heard in person, or even by a representative designated to act for that child. It merely refers to the child's views being transmitted either directly or through 'a representative or an appropriate body'. This formula does not specifically rule out the child's own parent claiming to represent the child, despite the obvious conflict of interest in most family proceedings involving both child and parent. Furthermore, Article 12 should be interpreted in the light of the child's best interests;[10] this might dictate the exclusion of a child from court whilst damaging evidence against his or her parents is produced. It does not, however, justify diluting the aims of Article 12 by interpreting it in a way which suits parents or the state, for example, by imposing an age restriction on its application. Indeed, Article 12(1) assures the rights set out to *any* child 'capable of forming his or her own views', however young. Its phrasing thereby makes it clear that specific age barriers are not acceptable.[11]

Despite its rather vague phrasing, the UN Committee on the Rights of the Child is in no doubt that the terms of Article 12(2) should be interpreted purposefully. In 2002, it criticised the UK for not ensuring that its obligations were more consistently incorporated in legislation in private law proceedings involving divorce.[12] It called on the government to take 'further steps' to reflect more consistently the obligations of both paragraphs of Article 12.[13] So far, as discussed below, there is little indication that the government takes this recommendation particularly seriously. Some might argue that if ratified, the European Convention on the Exercise of Children's Rights (ECECR) would be a much more effective tool than Article 12 of the CRC.[14] Indeed, it was specifically drafted to remedy a perceived weakness of the CRC, that children may not be able to exercise their substantive rights without appropriate procedural measures to back them up.[15] Article 1(2) explains that:

> The object of the present Convention is, in the best interests of children, to promote their rights, to grant them procedural rights and to facilitate the exercise

---

[10] I.e. Art. 12 is governed by Art. 3 CRC.   [11] R. Hodgkin and P. Newell (2007) pp. 153–4 and 157.
[12] Committee on the Rights of the Child (2002) para. 29.   [13] Ibid. at para. 30.
[14] Adopted by the Council of Europe in 1995 and open to signature January 1996. Neither the UK nor many other European counties have yet signed or ratified this instrument.
[15] M. Killerby (1995) p. 127. See also Council of Europe (1997) pp. 18–19.

of these rights by ensuring that children are, themselves or through other persons or bodies, informed and allowed to participate in proceedings affecting them before a judicial authority.

The ECECR goes into some detail regarding the kind of provision children should have.[16] It confines its application to 'family proceedings, in particular those involving the exercise of parental responsibilities such as residence and access to children'.[17] Within this context, it secures for children involved in such proceedings[18] the right to be granted and indeed, entitles them to request certain specific rights: to receive all relevant information;[19] to be consulted and express their views;[20] to be informed of the possible consequences of compliance with these views and the possible consequences of any decision;[21] and the right to apply for the appointment of a special representative,[22] if those with parental responsibilities cannot represent the child due to a conflict of interest.[23]

Although more detailed, in many respects, as Sawyer points out, the ECECR back-pedals on the aims of Article 12 of the CRC. Thus many of the rights secured only extend to those children who are 'considered by internal law as having sufficient understanding'.[24] This phrase deliberately invites states to specify a qualifying age for children benefiting from the Convention.[25] A state is thereby entitled to adopt an arbitrary and extremely high qualifying age before children can be deemed of 'sufficient understanding', irrespective of their actual competence.[26] Furthermore, since most of the protective provisions apply only to those with 'sufficient understanding', the interests of those excluded are extremely weak, with no rights, inter alia, to information, to be consulted, or express their views.[27] Indeed, the phrase is substantially more restrictive than that used in Article 12(1) of the CRC. Of equal concern is that the child's right to the appointment of a special representative only exists 'where internal law precludes the holders of parental responsibilities from representing the child as a result of a conflict of interest with the latter'.[28] Consequently, children involved in proceedings where a conflict of interest is not formally recognised by internal law cannot demand separate representation. There might, for example, be a conflict of interest if either parent involved in a parental contact dispute attempted to convey their child's views to the court. But unless the ratifying country's internal law formally recognises this, the child is not entitled to demand separate representation under Article 4. Where the internal law does admit a conflict of interest, the ECECR usefully fleshes out the

---

[16] For a detailed discussion of the Convention's provisions, see C. Sawyer (1999).   [17] Art. 1(3).
[18] But see the qualifying condition applying to certain rights, fn. 24 below.
[19] Art. 3(a).   [20] Art. 3(b).   [21] Art. 3(c).   [22] Art. 4(1).   [23] Ibid.
[24] I.e. the rights listed in Arts. 3, 6(b), 10(1)(a) and (b) contain this qualification. States are also invited to limit the right to a special representative to those children considered by internal law to have sufficient understanding. See Art 4(1) and (2).
[25] M. Killerby (1995) p. 130.   [26] C. Sawyer (1999) p. 156.
[27] Ibid. at pp. 163–4.   [28] Arts. 4(1) and 9(1).

way in which such representation should be provided.[29] Nevertheless, special representatives are given worrying leeway in interpreting their duties. For example, they need not convey to the court the child's views if they consider this to be 'manifestly contrary to the best interests of the child'.[30] As Sawyer points out, there is no indication of what a young child can do if 'represented' by an adult with whom he or she disagrees over the desired outcome of the proceedings.[31]

The ECECR appears to be gathering dust, not without reason. The European Convention for the Protection of Human Rights and Fundamental Freedoms (1950) (ECHR) is potentially of greater potential value to children. Nevertheless, the Strasbourg case law is strangely defective on this score. At first sight, Article 6, the right to a fair trial, might promote an improved system of representation for children. But although it encompasses a variety of rights revolving round a minor litigant's right to participate effectively in litigation, the case law is largely confined to a consideration of the rights of those involved in criminal proceedings.[32] The right to participate effectively in legal proceedings clearly also applies to civil proceedings; indeed where family relationships are at stake, adult litigants might certainly argue that in the absence of free legal aid they have no effective right of access to the courts.[33] But whilst children who are the subject of parents' disputes might claim that Article 6 entitles them to be represented in court or to be present themselves at a hearing, there is no relevant case law supporting such an argument. Indeed, the procedural rights of Article 8 hold greater potential and have proved useful in the context of public law proceedings.[34] As discussed by Munby J,[35] the ECtHR has indicated that the absence of representation for a parent and her child in freeing for adoption proceedings amounts to an infringement of their respective rights under Article 8.[36] Furthermore, any child involved in administrative proceedings, the outcome of which might affect his or her future upbringing, should be adequately represented.[37]

For children involved in parental disputes, the procedural benefits of Article 8 are less well established. Since the outcome of parental disputes will affect their family lives, children might argue that their own procedural rights under Article 8 would be infringed were they not provided with any chance to

---

[29] The duties of the child's representative are listed in Art. 10.

[30] Art. 10(1).   [31] C. Sawyer (1999) p. 155.

[32] *V and T v. United Kingdom* (1999) 30 EHRR 121 (paras. 85–91); discussed further in Chapter 18.

[33] *Airey v. Ireland* (1979) 2 EHRR 305.

[34] *McMichael v. United Kingdom* (1995) 20 EHRR 205: the European Court of Human Rights (ECtHR) upheld the right of all parties to disclosure of all documents in children's hearings in Scotland.

[35] Munby J (2004) p. 428.   [36] *P, C and S v. United Kingdom* [2002] 2 FLR 631 at para. 137.

[37] *CF v. Secretary of State for the Home Department* [2004] EWHC 111(Fam), [2004] 2 FLR 517 at paras. 167–8: the prison authorities should not decide to separate an imprisoned mother from her baby without considering the baby's interests, as expressed by his or her separate representative.

influence the outcome directly. But although the ECtHR has upheld adults' claims that their own applications involving their children have been dealt with unfairly, thereby infringing their procedural rights under Article 8,[38] similar arguments have not been developed on behalf of children.[39] The absence of Strasbourg case law makes it impossible to assert that all children involved in parental disputes must be separately represented. Nevertheless, as discussed below, the implementation of the Human Rights Act (HRA) 1998 undoubtedly encouraged a growing judicial appreciation that respect for children's rights demands an increasing use of separate representation in parental proceedings.[40] Similarly Thorpe LJ in *Mabon v. Mabon*[41] suggested that an older child's right to family life under Article 8 of the ECHR and to be consulted under Article 12 of the CRC, compels a right to participate directly in the court's decision-making process. Nevertheless, the domestic courts' appreciation of these international rights is inconsistent.[42] Furthermore, as discussed below, the government has indicated little sympathy with judicial efforts to provide separate representation for more children involved in private disputes between their parents. The much needed legislative reforms lie idle, awaiting activation by rules of court.[43]

(3) Children whose parents split up

(A) The right to consultation

Disputes between parents over aspects of their children's upbringing may arise at any time during their children's lives, but are most likely to occur when their own relationship is breaking up. Some disputes arise in the course of divorce proceedings, which tend to polarise existing adult hostilities to such an extent that parents fight over their children as if they were items of property. Others arise when married or cohabiting parents first separate. Certainly, it is at this stage of family life that the conflict between children's rights and parents' rights is very obvious. Parents may claim the right to put an unhappy relationship behind them by severing all connections between each other. But children may require their attachments with each parent to be maintained. Admittedly, the concept of children's rights will probably have little influence over parents'

---

[38] E.g. *Elsholz v. Germany* [2000] 2 FLR 486.

[39] *Sahin v. Germany* [2003] 2 FLR 671, per the Grand Chamber of the ECtHR, at [73]: a domestic court need not always hear a child in court in every case.

[40] *Re A (Contact: Separate Representation)* [2001] 1 FLR 715, per Dame Elizabeth Butler-Sloss P, at paras. 21–2 and Hale J, paras. 31–2. See also *Re L (family proceedings court) (appeal: jurisdiction)* [2003] EWHC 1682 (Fam), [2005] 1 FLR 210 at [28]; discussed below.

[41] *Re L (family proceedings court) (appeal: jurisdiction)* [2005] EWCA Civ 634, [2005] 2 FLR 1011.

[42] E.g. *S v. B (abduction: human rights)* [2005] EWHC 733 (Fam), [2005] 2 FLR 878: 13-year-old half-sibling of the child subject of a Hague Convention application was denied separate representation in the proceedings, with no mention of participation rights under the ECHR and the CRC.

[43] The vehicle for these changes was the Adoption and Children Act 2002, s. 122; discussed below.

plans for their own future lives. For example, the law could not prevent parents from separating because their children would prefer them to stay together. Nevertheless, a commitment to children's rights can play an important part in the various stages leading up to resolution, if cast in terms of children's rights to be involved, consulted, and later to be represented in any court proceedings, as emphasised by Article 12 of the CRC.

Parents and professionals alike should remember that children could probably give them an extremely clear and insightful account of their own needs, if adults took the trouble to ask. Indeed, a greater appreciation of the aims of Article 12 of the CRC might persuade them to do so. Children's wishes are often disregarded by adults who consider that they know what these wishes will be, without any consultation. Plainly, a growing body of research consistently supports the view that a damaging aspect of parental separation for children is the considerable shock that they suffer on the break-up, often exacerbated by their parents' failure to prepare them adequately for it, or give them any proper explanation. As has been observed: 'Children are amazingly perceptive about what is going on, and not talking to them about the changes in their lives only raises their anxieties.'[44] Few parents, whether they are married or unmarried, are particularly adept at breaking such news sensitively.[45] Furthermore, they often delude themselves over the extent to which their children understand what they are being told regarding an impending separation and how they react to such news.[46]

These research findings reinforce the need to consider adult disputes from a child's point of view. Regrettably, under English law, no child, whatever his or her age, has a legal *right* to be consulted over the arrangements to be made for their future. By way of contrast, as discussed earlier,[47] Scottish law obliges parents, depending on their children's age and maturity, to consult them over any 'major decision' within their parental responsibility.[48] A statutory obligation on English parents to consult their children over all important matters might promote a family culture of participation which would continue to operate when the adults' own relationships run into difficulties. As discussed below, the children whose parents were married and who now intend to divorce, have a narrow advantage over the children of cohabiting couples who separate. The former group has a limited form of protection designed to ensure that they make appropriate plans for their children's future upbringing.[49] Without marriage and divorce, however, unmarried parents are free to decide for themselves the future arrangements for their children's care, without

---

[44] I. Gee (1999) p. 50. See also L. Parkinson (2006) p. 484.
[45] I. Butler *et al.* (2003) p. 42: some children were told about the separation over the phone.
[46] Ibid. at p. 35: although every parent, bar one, stated that they had told their children about their separation, 29% of the children indicated that they had not been told. See also research summarised by L. Parkinson (2006) p. 483.
[47] See Chapter 3.   [48] Children (Scotland) Act 1995, s. 6(1).
[49] I.e. the procedure under Matrimonial Causes Act 1973, s. 41; discussed below.

any encouragement to consult their children or warn them what to expect. A limited, though unenforceable, means of improving this situation would be to amend the law along the lines of the Scottish legislation. Not only is it imperative for parents and professionals to consult all children early on and listen carefully to their views, but also, if a parental dispute is later translated into litigation, to give them a genuine voice through competent representation.

(B) Support for children on separation and divorce

(i) Parental support?

Children are frequently not consulted over arrangements made by their parents for their future care or contact with the non-residential parent.[50] Most children consider that, at the very least, they should have been consulted by their parents, though not necessarily involved in the actual decision-making.[51] Butler *et al.* conclude from their research that 'there is abundant evidence to show that it is both desirable and possible to consult children, even as young as 5 years old, when decisions are being made about their future'.[52]

This research evidence supports those who criticise the way that the law seemingly treats children of divorcing and separating parents as passive victims, protecting them from involvement in adult conflict rather than ensuring their participation in arrangements for their future care.[53] As Diduck explains, the proponents of the 'new sociology of childhood'[54] seek to understand childhood from children's perspectives.[55] They argue that the legal system itself encourages parents to see divorce and separation as private adult matters[56] and, by defining children as 'non-adults', creates barriers against practitioners treating them as individuals.[57] Some refer to international human rights, notably Article 12 of the CRC, as reinforcing their view that children should be consulted over parental disputes. Thus James argues that constructions of childhood based on seeing children as the product of parenting, rather than as individuals in their own right, 'effectively deny children a voice' to which they not only have a right, but are quite capable of providing.[58] These writers support their ideas by referring to the research establishing that children are surprisingly self-sufficient

---

[50] I. Butler *et al.* (2003) p. 120: 56% of children reported not having been consulted over residence; 52% reported not having been consulted over 'seeing contact'; 58% reported not having been consulted over 'staying contact'. See also A. Smith *et al.* (2003) p. 206: 19% reported being consulted over their initial residence arrangements and 37% reported being consulted over their initial contact arrangements.

[51] I. Butler *et al.* (2003) pp. 124–5 and A. Smith *et al.* (2003) p. 207.

[52] I. Butler *et al.* (2003) p. 203.

[53] E.g. S. Day Sclater and C. Piper (2001) pp. 413–22 and A. James (2003) pp. 145–6.

[54] E.g. A. James, C. Jenks and A. Prout (1998).

[55] A. Diduck (2003) pp. 80–3. See also F. Kaganas and A. Diduck (2004) pp. 961–4 and J. Pryor and B. Rodgers (2001), ch. 3.

[56] S. Day Sclater and C. Piper (2001) pp. 420–1.

[57] A. James, A. James and S. McNamee (2004) p. 200.   [58] A. James (2003) p. 145.

and competent,[59] with a 'self-awareness and resourcefulness,' in the face of family disruption.[60]

Such ideas do not tell the whole story. It would after all be folly to deny the increasing body of international research indicating that many children do suffer adverse outcomes from their parents' separation and divorce and emerge in a very vulnerable state.[61] Indeed, although the divorce rate has dropped since the early 1990s,[62] many thousands of children under the age of 16 are still affected by parental divorce every year, with significant numbers of these being under 5 years old.[63] But as Diduck and others point out, neither approach need be mutually exclusive; children may neither want complete autonomy nor to be treated as objects.[64] Smart too urges caution, on the basis that although all children need information, not all want participation and some actively oppose professional intervention.[65] Pryor and Rodgers observe:

> It is clear when children are asked, that they want adults to listen to their views and feelings about what is happening in their lives. This does not, though, necessarily mean listening to them in the same way as to adults; there are developmental differences in the ways children make sense of families and family change, and *not* to acknowledge these differences may be to fail to empower them by not communicating and listening in appropriate ways. It does, though, mean according them the respect given to adults by listening to them seriously.[66]

Ideally, of course, divorcing parents should always talk to their children about their breakup *before* they apply for a divorce; once arrangements have been made children are often presented with a fait accompli.[67] The law does little, however, to ensure that children are consulted by their parents, or by anyone else, about their parents' future plans for their upbringing. One might have imagined that compliance with the 'section 41 procedure' would prompt parents into doing so. The fact that all divorcing couples with children under the age of 16 are obliged to complete and file a 'statement of arrangements'[68] suggests that the state has an interest in the future welfare of their children. But Cardiff researchers have found that the system is severely flawed.[69] District judges very seldom withhold divorce decrees even in cases where the statements

---

[59] C. Smart *et al.* (2001) pp. 73–4.   [60] A. Wade and C. Smart (2002) p. 22.

[61] J. Pryor and B. Rodgers (2001) chs. 3 and 4. See also G. Harold and M. Murch (2005) pp. 188–95.

[62] Office for National Statistics (2008) p. 21: 155,000 divorces were granted in 2005, compared with an overall peak of 180,000 in 1993.

[63] The number of children under 16 affected by parental divorce in 2005 was 136,000, one-fifth of whom were under 5, and two-thirds were aged 10 or under. Ibid.

[64] A. Diduck (2003) p. 101. See also J. Pryor and B. Rodgers (2001) pp. 135–8.

[65] C. Smart *et al.* (2001) p. 121.   [66] J. Pryor and B. Rodgers (2001) p. 135.

[67] I. Butler *et al.* (2003) p. 123.

[68] Matrimonial Causes Act 1973, s. 41. The statement of arrangements details a divorcing couple's arrangements for their children's future upbringing and welfare. For a summary of the history and purpose of the procedure, see G. Douglas *et al.* (2000) pp. 180–4.

[69] M. Murch *et al.* (1999): research into the working of the s. 41 procedure was carried out in 1997.

disclose worrying information about the parents' plans for their children, quite simply because they think that doing so will make little difference in the long-run.[70] More to the point, the procedure's requirements appear to have little real impact on many divorcing parents, relatively few of whom discuss with their children the arrangements placed before the court.[71] Regrettably despite this research establishing clearly that the section 41 procedure in its present form fails to exploit its potential usefulness, so far as children are concerned, it remains unchanged. Nothing came of governmental promises that the state-ment of arrangements forms would be redesigned to ensure that the courts receive far more information relevant to the children themselves and the extent to which they are coping with the parental breakup.[72]

(ii) Mediation[73]

Many children feel quite unable to confide in anyone over their distress at their parents' breakup and over the future arrangements being made for their upbringing. Researchers increasingly raise concerns over the sense of deep isolation often experienced by the children of divorcing couples and the lack of any obvious source of support for them.[74] Whilst parents may come into contact with various practitioners as they proceed through the divorce process, few of these practitioners consider it their job to support the children. Some parents decide to go to court over their disputes over their children but only a small number will end up in the courtroom. Today, many of these disputes are settled with the help of various forms of mediation. There is, however, a risk that these settlements are arrived at without proper reference to the children's wishes or interests. Indeed, it is arguable that the children whose parents refuse to settle and obtain a court order regarding their upbringing are better served by the law than those whose parents ultimately resolve their differences with the assistance of solicitors and mediators. The CA 1989 directs the courts, when determining any dispute over children's upbringing, to have regard to their ascertainable wishes and feelings.[75] But there is no law obliging other practi-tioners to do so at any stage of the dispute.

The government has long seen family mediation as a way of reducing the conflict underpinning most divorces. Indeed, many divorcing parents will be

---

[70] G. Douglas *et al.* (2000) p. 189.

[71] M. Murch *et al.* (1999) p. 186: only 34% of parent petitioners in this research study had discussed the arrangements with their children.

[72] Lord Chancellor's Department (2002) *Facilitation/Enforcement Response* (p. 7 website document), responding to recommendations for reform of the s. 41 procedure made by the Children Act Sub-Committee of the Advisory Board on Family Law (2002) paras. 3.38–3.43.

[73] The term 'mediation' is still preferred by the out-of-court family mediation services (which assist only 5% of separating couples DCA/DfES/DTI (2004) para. 64) whilst the term 'conciliation' or 'dispute resolution' is favoured by the in-court services (discussed below).

[74] I. Butler *et al.* (2003) p. 63: 30% of children had told no one about their parents' separation.

[75] CA 1989, s. 1(3)(a).

sucked into state-funded mediation[76] at some stage of the divorce process. This is the case if they desire public funding for the legal costs of their involvement in disputes over family matters, whether these disputes involve money or children or both.[77] Given the overriding principles governing divorce law,[78] privately funded clients may also be encouraged by their solicitors to consider mediation. Whether or not they are divorcing, most parents intending to litigate over their children also find themselves channelled into some form of mediation. Doubtless alarmed by the rising number of contact disputes going to court,[79] the government is convinced that 'Collaborative agreements made between parents should be favoured, as they are likely to work better than those achieved by court-based resolutions.'[80] It is determined to ensure that the majority of would-be litigants are diverted into some form of mediation. The government 'does not plan to make mediation compulsory, but will strongly promote its use' both through out of court mediation and in-court conciliation.[81]

Underlying these developments is the government's assumption that enduring agreements between parents 'are responsive to children's interests and wishes'.[82] There is, however, no research substantiating such a view. The fact that separating parents agree does not ensure that the arrangements agreed upon will always be in their children's best interests, given that they are reached at a time of stress and conflict. Nor will mediators necessarily produce an outcome which takes account of the children's views. In the past, not-for-profit mediation services had, in any event, been ambivalent over whether mediators should consult children directly over parental disputes involving them. Some, like Richards, strongly opposed such a proposition. In his view, 'mediation is adult business'.[83] Indeed, research carried out in the late 1990s indicated that the majority of family mediators did not consider it appropriate to address the child's needs by talking to them directly, but instead encouraged

---

[76] This may be provided by a 'not-for-profit' organisation affiliated to the National Family Mediation, or a 'private sector' provider, usually local solicitors with mediation training, e.g. through the Legal Services Commission's Family Advice and Information Service (FAInS). See J. Walker (2004).

[77] Under the Family Law Act 1996, s. 29, now replaced by the Access to Justice Act 1999, s. 8, those requiring public funding to assist with legal costs relating to private family disputes, will normally be required to undergo assessment for suitability for mediation before public funding is granted. See generally A. Diduck and F. Kaganas (2006) pp. 427–8 and ch. 11.

[78] Family Law Act 1996, s. 1(b) requires courts and practitioners to note 'that the parties to a marriage which may have broken down are to be encouraged to take all practicable steps, whether by marriage counselling or otherwise, to save the marriage'; and '(c) that a marriage which has irretrievably broken down and is being brought to an end should be brought to an end – (i) with minimum distress to the parties and to the children affected; (ii) with questions dealt with in a manner designed to promote as good a continuing relationship between the parties and any children affected as is possible in the circumstances'.

[79] In 2005, 60,294 contact orders were made and 26,523 residence orders – Department for Constitutional Affairs statistics.

[80] DCA/DfES/DTI (2005) para. 2, emphasis as in original. See also DCA/DfES/DTI (2004) para. 23.

[81] Ibid. at para. 49.   [82] Ibid. at para. 51.   [83] M. Richards (1995) p. 225.

the parents to do so themselves.[84] Today, things have changed somewhat. Mediators fully recognise that sometimes children will wish to voice their independent perspectives on their parents' disputes but may need support before doing so.[85] A significant number of not-for-profit mediation services around the country do currently offer services for children[86] and consider them to be immensely valuable to their young recipients.[87] Nevertheless, some offer none,[88] partly due to its costly training implications[89] and undoubtedly because the Legal Services Commission do not provide separate funding for direct work with children.[90]

(iii) Support from Cafcass?

Rather than seeing an out-of-court family mediator, increasing numbers of litigating parents are being channelled into the greatly extended in-court dispute resolution procedures.[91] These are intended to facilitate agreement in the very early stages of litigation, with the assistance of a Cafcass practitioner.[92] As discussed below, it is increasingly doubtful whether these procedural developments necessarily benefit children. Matters are not improved by the reluctance of practitioners involved in the family justice system to accept any responsibility for supporting the children of divorced and separating parents. Indeed, researchers have observed mediators, solicitors, and district judges all considering that someone else, but not themselves, should take on the task of talking to children directly.[93] The government had hinted that the establishment of Cafcass might solve the problem – that Cafcass's remit 'could be extended to take on additional functions on behalf of children involved in family court proceedings and their families'.[94] So, in addition to providing a strictly court-based service, it was envisaged that Cafcass might eventually take on wider family support functions, thereby justifying its name. It would 'be a service which, through its other responsibilities, makes a wider contribution to the welfare of families likely to be involved in family proceedings'.[95] Regrettably, its organisational difficulties and increasing volume of work have undermined Cafcass' ability to provide a more generalised support service.

Designing a better support system for children is not, in any event, an easy matter. Some children may become more truly involved in parental negotiations now that family mediators seem more willing to do 'direct work' with

---

[84] M. Murch et al. (1999) paras. 7.4.1–7.5.5.   [85] National Family Mediation (2005).
[86] L. Parkinson (2006) pp. 484–6.   [87] Ibid. at p. 488.   [88] E. Greenall (2005) ch. 2.
[89] L. Parkinson (2006) pp. 486–7.   [90] Legal Services Commission (2007) para. 5.9.
[91] DCA/DfES/DTI (2005) para. 70: Cafcass conducts more than 38,000 dispute resolution appointments per annum, cf. 12,000–14,000 mediations undertaken by the independent and voluntary sector.
[92] Under *The Private Law Programme: Guidance issued by the President of the Family Division* (2005) setting out the process underpinning the First Hearing Dispute Resolution Appointment (FHDRA).
[93] M. Murch et al. (1999) para. 8.3.5.   [94] LCD Press Release No. 199–99, 27 July 1999.
[95] Department of Health (DH) et al. (1998) para. 3.3

children.[96] An overriding problem, however, is that children's needs vary considerably according to their individual circumstances.[97] As Day Sclater and Piper observe, they cannot be 'treated as a homogenous group in relation to whether and how they wish to participate in decision-making'.[98] A variety of research projects suggest that children who are the focus of parental disputes would like some kind of neutral supporter, perhaps someone trained and/or experienced in working with children/young people and divorce, with a background in counselling or medicine where the emphasis is on listening.[99] But whilst some would like an outside 'advocate', to listen to their concerns and even to be present in discussions over their future,[100] others would prefer not to participate at all if it means involving outside agencies.[101] Indeed, there are children who greatly resent being 'made to' talk to outsiders or become involved in therapeutic intervention and feel unable to confide in anyone involved in the legal process, because of the lack of confidentiality.[102] Similarly, not all children are comfortable with their teachers trying to provide support and understanding.[103] Consequently the government's suggestion that those teaching Personal, Social and Health Education in schools should provide children with 'the opportunity to learn about and examine the issue of parental separation',[104] might not be universally welcome.

An obvious problem is that adults are normally the gatekeepers to whatever support is made available to children whose parents are in conflict. The age-appropriate leaflets about divorce and separation developed by Cafcass will not reach the children for whom they were designed unless solicitors encourage their clients to pass them on. Even the specially designed internet websites may not necessarily be found by the children who might appreciate them.[105] Equally, the redeveloped Parenting Plan leaflets[106] depend on parents accepting their strong underlying message that parents should not enter into detailed arrangements regarding their children's future without discussing them with their children first.[107] Whatever route is followed, it should ensure that children are provided with support early in the process of their parents' separation.

It is ironic that Cafcass, the service established to improve the lot of children, is now devoting much of its time to adult-centred in-court conciliation work,[108] quite possibly at the expense of resources which should be devoted to children.

---

[96] See above.   [97] A. O'Quigley (2000) ch. 3.   [98] S. Day Sclater and C. Piper (2001) p. 427.

[99] J. Fortin et al. (2006) p. 221; A. Buchanan et al. (2001) p. 67, G. Douglas et al. (2006) para. 7.49.

[100] A. Buchanan et al. (2001) p. 67.   [101] C. Smart et al. (2001) pp. 162–73.

[102] Ibid. at pp. 160–4. See also G. Douglas et al. (2006) paras. 3.27 and 3.84; a number of the children interviewed resented the lack of confidentiality.

[103] I. Butler et al. (2003) pp. 77–9. See also J. Hawthorne et al. (2003) pp. 34–5.

[104] DCA/DfES/DTI (2005) para. 35.   [105] J. Hawthorne et al. (2003) p. 49.

[106] Developed by the National Council of Voluntary Childcare Organisations and launched in 2002. These were redeveloped and relaunched by the Department for Education and Skills (DfES) (2006).

[107] DfES (2006) esp. p. 18.   [108] Discussed further below.

It is clear that family assistance orders (FAOs),[109] can at times provide families with much needed support,[110] but they are normally used to provide families with short-term support in the context of contact orders.[111] They are not intended to provide children with the dedicated one-to-one support that many of them need outside the context of court proceedings. As noted above, many researchers have found that children would like someone in the family justice system in whom they can trust and whose job it is to support them.[112] Douglas et al. argue that there is a real need, at the very least, for these children to have the legal processes explained to them sympathetically. In their view, child friendly leaflets are not enough.[113] They require a sophisticated and personal source of support and information from the point at which a case first enters the dispute resolution system.[114] Furthermore:

> CAFCASS should have responsibility to ensure that they [children] are given the opportunity to meet a member of CAFCASS staff who can explain the nature not only of conciliation, if that is to be attempted, but also the family litigation process.[115]

Instead, it appears that in-court conciliation work is being developed by Cafcass with great speed, on the assumption that children will automatically benefit from parental agreements.

(4) Children's involvement in family proceedings

(A) The background

The system provided for representing children in family proceedings is extraordinarily complicated and is considered in some detail in the next three sections of this chapter. The emergence of Cafcass from three merged services[116] immediately simplified the way that children's representation was managed. It is now provided by a unified body, governed by a single set of standards and objectives.[117] There were hopes that the new service would, in future,

---

[109] CA 1989, s. 16(1): in the course of family proceedings the court may make a FAO requiring the officer (often a Cafcass officer) concerned to 'advise, assist and (where appropriate) befriend any person named in the order'.

[110] HMICA (2007a) Section 2.

[111] Ibid. at para. 3.2: FAOs are normally made to help re-establish contact, arrange or facilitate contact, support contact or supervise it.

[112] J. Fortin et al. (2006) p. 221; A. Buchanan et al. (2001) p. 67; Douglas et al. (2006) para. 7.49.

[113] G. Douglas et al. (2006) para. 7.9.

[114] I.e. when it is first set down for a FHDRA under the Private Law programme. See fn 93.

[115] G. Douglas et al. (2006) para. 7.11.

[116] I.e. the Official Solicitor (OS)'s department, which had formerly acted for children requiring separation representation; the guardian ad litem and reporting officer services who represented children in public law proceedings; the court welfare service which provided in-court conciliation work for parents involved in private disputes over children and carried out the reporting function by preparing 'welfare reports' for the courts if requested to do so under CA 1989, s. 7.

[117] Since Cafcass practitioners often act in various capacities, they are increasingly being referred to as family court advisers (FCAs).

always ensure that the courts could consider the child's wishes and feelings in all family proceedings, bearing in mind his or her age and understanding.[118] This direction was included in the CA 1989 due to the Law Commission's view that although children should not be forced to 'choose' between their parents, it is 'pointless to ignore the clearly expressed wishes of older children'.[119] Nevertheless, nearly a decade into the new Cafcass regime,[120] the methods provided whereby children's wishes are conveyed to the court are still extremely fragmented and arbitrary. The courts still receive information from some but not all children, under an archaic set of rules and procedures whose complexity defy simple explanation.

Perhaps most disappointing is the continuation of the unsatisfactory contrast between the very good system of representation for children involved in public law proceedings and their relative lack of representation in private law proceedings. One of the reasons for establishing Cafcass was a general acknowledgement that there was 'scope for improvement of the present arrangements in private law proceedings'.[121] Nevertheless, despite the reorganisation, it still varies enormously how, if at all, the court discovers information about the children involved in private law disputes.

(B) Private law proceedings

(i) An arbitrary system

Parents who go to court because of an inability to agree over their children's future upbringing will normally have legal representation – not so the children who are the focus of their disputes. The 'ladder' of these children's involvement appears to have five rungs. On the ladder's bottom rung, there is no court hearing because the parents' dispute is resolved in its early stages, under the in-court conciliation procedures established under the Private Law Programme.[122] On the next rung up, the case has proceeded to litigation but the court relies on the parents' own assessments of what is in the child's best interests. On the third rung of the ladder is the child regarding whom a welfare report is prepared by the children and family reporter (CFR). This will include an account of the child's own wishes and feelings. On the fourth rung of the ladder are children provided with party status and separate representation. On the top rung, children litigate on their own behalf, possibly even having initiated the proceedings themselves. Disappointingly, despite the reorganisation of the system for representing children in family proceedings, the rules governing these situations remain arcane.[123]

---

[118] CA 1989, s. 1(3)(a) directs the court to have regard to 'the ascertainable wishes and feelings of the child concerned (considered in the light of his age and understanding)'.

[119] Law Commission (1988) para. 3.23.   [120] See fn. 7.

[121] DH *et al.* (1998) para. 1.8.   [122] See fn 92.

[123] E.g. Solicitors Family Law Association (2002) pp. 4–5: explains the various meanings of the term 'guardian' for the purposes of litigation involving children.

The fact that the CA 1989 discriminates against children involved in private law proceedings has been a constant source of criticism. Unlike those who are the subject of public law proceedings, the legislation contains no presumption that these children will be separately represented. This feature of the system remains unchanged. The court can (but need not) ask for a welfare report to be prepared,[124] which will give it a great deal of background information about the child. The court may decide not to call for such a report, either because the case has been settled in its early stages, or because it is concerned about the potential delays involved, or because it considers that there is no need for one. Without a report, the court has no means of obtaining a true picture of the child's views regarding the outcome of his or her parents' dispute. Since the parents are unlikely to provide the court with a totally impartial account of the child's wishes, these children are nearly at the bottom of the ladder. But those on the bottom rung are those whose parents are persuaded to settle their dispute – the children may have been involved in their discussions, but may not. If they were not, their wishes regarding the outcome of their parents' dispute will remain unknown. Depending on their age, Article 12(2) of the CRC has certainly been infringed in relation to the children on the bottom two rungs of the ladder. A crucial decision has been reached regarding their future, without their participation. Despite the absence of Strasbourg case law substantiating such a claim, as discussed above, it could be argued that it would also infringe their rights to a fair trial under Article 6 of the ECHR and, because the outcome will affect their family lives, their procedural rights under Article 8.

(ii) 'In court-conciliated children'

As noted above, today increasing numbers of litigating parents are being channelled into the greatly extended in-court dispute resolution procedures.[125] These are intended to facilitate agreement in the very early stages of litigation, with the assistance of a Cafcass practitioner, now often called a Family Court Adviser (FCA).[126] Indeed, with their help, many contested private disputes are now resolved before getting to court at all. The government's hopes that these services would be used routinely before a court hearing appear to have borne fruit.[127] There are various concerns underlying these procedural developments. In the first place, there is a grave risk that

---

[124] CA 1989, s. 7: prepared by a CFR, formerly a child welfare officer (CWO). NB these reports, formerly named 'welfare reports' appear to have been renamed 'Cafcass reports' or 'court reports'. See J. Doughty (2008) for a historical assessment of the family court welfare service.

[125] Cafcass (2007d) p. 6: in 2006/7, Cafcass practitioners increased the time spent on 'early intervention' (dispute resolution schemes) by 33.6% over the previous year.

[126] I.e. under the Private Law Programme – see fn 92.

[127] Cafcass (2007d) p. 6: around 60% of Cafcass 'interventions' achieve full or partial agreement. See also L. Trinder *et al.* (2006) p. 40: 72% of parents reported reaching some agreement in conciliation; J. Hunt and A. Macleod (2008) pp. 168–88.

parents and FCAs may overlook the children's own perspectives on any arrangements reached. As HM Inspectorate of Court Administration (HMICA) observe, the in-court conciliation process involves the FCA establishing what each party wants and then trying to find a compromise between the two positions.[128] The inspectors urge:

> In law, children's needs are paramount. But where the emphasis is on agreement-seeking, there is a risk that their views become marginalised as their parents' dispute takes centre stage.[129]

The extent to which children are directly involved in the in-court conciliation services appears to be rather patchy.[130] In 2003 HM Inspectors criticised those schemes that excluded children on the basis that they were making assessments from the parents' perspectives only. It suggested that Cafcass should 'take forward the debate about inclusion (or exclusion) of children in [conciliation] schemes beyond claim and counter-claim' and embrace the demands of Article 12 of the CRC.[131] This recommendation was not followed. The fact that children have continued to be involved in 'facilitated discussions in dispute resolution work in some but not in others'[132] apparently reflects 'a long-standing and unresolved debate' within Cafcass itself over the extent to which children *should* be involved in what many see as an essentially adult process.[133] Research indicates that in many areas of the country children are still not invited to court and are not interviewed if parents do bring them along.[134] This unresolved debate is not surprising, given the practical difficulties inherent in involving children. After all, the in-court schemes are intended to provide adult-focused rapid intervention work; in such a context there is surely insufficient time for the gentle and skilled sessions necessary for young and very vulnerable children.

Some researchers have criticised the in-court schemes that do involve children for not doing so more sensitively.[135] Trinder *et al.* criticise the way that children are interviewed on court premises, considering such an environment to be too stressful and unfamiliar for them.[136] The very short interview

---

[128] HMICA (2006) para. 2.29.   [129] HMICA (2005a) para. 3.75.

[130] HM Magistrates' Courts Service Inspectorate (2003) p. 49: out of seven conciliation schemes operated by Cafcass, only one systematically involved children, although some other schemes interviewed children at the request of parents or courts. Cafcass practitioners working in the other schemes indicated deep ambivalence over the appropriateness of involving children.

[131] Ibid. at paras. 4.46–4.47.

[132] Cafcass (2005a) para. 26. Anecdotal information suggests that practice now (2008) varies enormously on a regional basis, with a few Cafcass teams routinely involving children in at least one of the dispute resolution sessions.

[133] HMICA (2005b) para. 2.28.

[134] L. Trinder *et al.* (2006) pp. 18–19 and 25: two of the three areas examined made no provision for children's involvement in the in-court conciliation process.

[135] HMICA (2006) paras. 2.47–2.63: Inspectors observed very variable standards of interviewing techniques.

[136] L. Trinder *et al.* (2006) p. 97.

sessions[137] also preclude interviewers from finding an appropriate balance between consulting children and involving them in decision-making themselves. Trinder *et al.* comment:

> The very task-focused approach of conciliation risks placing responsibility for decision making, or resolving the dispute, on children's shoulders. Children are typically seen for a very short interview which inevitably seeks views on the (adult-defined) matters in dispute. Our observations and interviews with professionals confirmed that what children say is often highly influential in determining the outcome, even down to specific details of the contact timetable. It is worth noting that children are not interviewed if the parents are able to reach agreement, suggesting that children's involvement relates to an inability to break an adult impasse rather than a general principle that all children should have their say.[138]

These researchers are not alone in suggesting that placing such obvious weight on children's views may be mistaken, that the onus on them is too great and that they may lack the foresight or maturity of age to understand the consequences of their decisions.[139] Children should not be rushed into decision-making, especially by FCAs who have insufficient time to put them at ease or to rehearse with them their genuine concerns. Such a view is supported by a number of research projects which have all found that children often have reservations about talking to someone whom they do not know at all, especially in a formal setting.[140] Children may feel very inhibited from telling a FCA what their true views are, even when alone with him or her, because of their fear of repercussions from one or other parent afterwards.[141] When there is a member of the family in the room, this problem is greatly exacerbated.[142]

In the schemes which do not involve children being interviewed, the emphasis is on facilitating discussions between parents and children, to ensure that the parents 'are better enabled to heed what their children are saying'.[143] Whilst such an objective is admirable, one wonders how the FCAs monitor its practical effectiveness. Recent official guidance to FCAs does not suggest that they are routinely expected to involve children in the short court-based conciliation work undertaken with parents in private law disputes.[144] Perhaps the view is that without any clear consensus on how best to do so, there is little point in

---

[137] Ibid. at p. 65: the Principal Registry of the Family Division routinely requires all children over the age of 9 to attend court. They are seen alone (though on occasion with a parent present) by a Cafcass officer, the length of session being, on average 12.5 minutes; HMICA (2006) paras. 2.50 and 2.52: Cafcass practitioners rarely considered interviewing a child more than once, and the length of interviews seemed arbitrary – one lasting 16 minutes, another over an hour.

[138] L. Trinder *et al.* (2006) pp. 97–8.   [139] R. Emery *et al.* (2005).

[140] J. Fortin *et al.* (2006) p. 221;   [141] A. Buchanan *et al.* (2001) p. 66.

[142] Ibid.   [143] Cafcass (2005a) para. 35.2.4.

[144] Cafcass (2007a) p. 9. See also Cafcass (2007b) Standard 5 (Children's active involvement): '5.1: Children will always be seen, including in extended dispute resolution programmes (private law) ... *The only exceptions to this area* [are] ... in short court-based resolution appointments where no further assessment or continuing work is required ... The reason for not seeing a child will be recorded on the case file.' Emphasis added. See also Cafcass (2007c).

attempting to introduce standardised methods of involving children through-out the country.

(iii) Identifying domestic violence?

The rushed and highly charged atmosphere of in-court conciliation work may be particularly dangerous for children in cases involving domestic violence.[145] In two hard-hitting reports,[146] HM Inspectors criticised the way that FCAs working with parents[147] were often downplaying the importance of risk assessment, in favour of agreement seeking. As earlier research had shown,[148] practitioners who see their primary role as persuading parents to reach agreement, seem particularly poor at addressing allegations of domestic violence.[149] As the inspectors observed, such practice produced unsafe agreements.[150] Following these reports, detailed guidance was produced directing FCAs to make risk assessments whenever issues of domestic violence emerged.[151] It stresses the need for FCAs to talk to children about their own experience of domestic violence and to understand it from the child's own perspectives.[152] Nevertheless, it does not appear that this guidance is being systematically followed,[153] with cases involving domestic violence still being handled inadequately in some areas. Issues surrounding domestic violence are, in some cases, simply being left unaddressed,[154] or its impact on children is not being adequately explored.[155] In other cases, child protection concerns are not adequately dealt with.[156]

The new need for all FCAs to make risk assessments (and pass them on to the court) where, in the course of their involvement in any family proceedings, they suspect that the child concerned is at risk of harm, will hopefully produce a more consistent approach.[157] Nevertheless, an underlying difficulty is that children brought up in a violent household are not always willing to tell adults the truth about conditions at home. Research with young adults asked to recall how their parents' disputes had been handled during their childhood showed

---

[145] Contact disputes involving domestic violence are discussed in more detail in Chapter 13.

[146] HMICA (2005a) esp. paras. 3.29–3.34 and HMICA (2006) esp. paras. 2.40–2.45.

[147] Mainly in the context of report writing work.

[148] D. Greatbatch and R. Dingwall (1999), described mediators 'sidelining' allegations of domestic violence in mediation sessions and concluded (at p. 187) that such an approach would endanger victims of domestic violence, especially if mediation was expanded. See also G. Davis *et al.* (2000) p. 58: mediators running mediation intake assessments assessed 57% of parents who indicated a fear of domestic violence as being suitable for mediation.

[149] HMICA (2005a) esp. paras. 2.15–2.30, 3.33 and 3.41 and HMICA (2006) paras. 2.62–2.63 and para. 3.14.

[150] HMICA (2005a) para. 3.77. For similar criticisms of Cafcass' failure to establish robust risk assessment and risk management procedures, see L. Trinder *et al.* (2006) pp. 94–7.

[151] Cafcass (2005b) chs. 5 and 6.

[152] Cafcass (2005b) paras. 3.2.1–3.6.4 and 5.10.2–5.10.8. The guidance suggests that in 'most circumstances' one interview with such a child will not be enough. Ibid. at para. 5.10.8.

[153] Ofsted (2008a) para. 58.   [154] Ofsted (2008b) paras. 32 and 40.   [155] Ofsted (2008a) para. 58.

[156] Ofsted (2008b) paras. 26, 40 and 45 and Ofsted (2008a) paras. 59–61 and p. 25.

[157] CA 1989, s. 16A.

that some, as children, had deliberately disguised the existence of domestic violence from the CWOs whose job it was, under the pre-Cafcass regime, to interview them. Some children did so because they valued their contact with their father. One hid the truth because of his fear of his father's anger.[158] Only well-trained FCAs with plenty of time to reflect on the issues will be able to extract from children involved in such situations the information that they need.[159]

The pressure to persuade parents to agree contact arrangements does not fall on Cafcass practitioners alone. There was a ring of truth to the accusations that the judiciary tended to welcome any agreed parental settlement, whether or not there might be underlying domestic violence, and so rubber-stamped agreed contact in the form of consent orders without adequately checking on the safety of their terms.[160] Guidance from the Family Justice Council[161] and a new and detailed Practice Direction[162] on contact disputes involving domestic violence allegations were soon to follow. The judiciary must not make any consent orders unless they are satisfied that there is risk of harm to the child and should ask for a welfare report[163] if they need more information.[164] The Family Justice Council pointed out that courts may be presented with an agreement for approval without anyone knowing the child's own wishes and feelings. Its recommendation that 'steps should be taken to ascertain the wishes and feelings of the child or children concerned before a contact order is made',[165] though sensible, did not spell out precisely who should take on this role. Solicitors seem well placed to do so but many seem relatively uninterested in this part of the process. Piper's research in the late 1990s showed that solicitors did not consider it their job to discover children's wishes before they finalised negotiated settlements with their clients.[166] More recently, research for the Family Justice Council on solicitors' practice in cases which might involve domestic violence indicated that few solicitors apparently considered it appropriate to dissuade their clients from agreeing to contact arrangements (leading to consent orders), despite their view that such orders put children at risk of harm.[167] There are obvious unaddressed training issues here.

[158] J. Fortin *et al.* (2006) p. 222.

[159] HMICA (2006) paras. 2.47–2.63, criticise the interviewing techniques of many FCAs, often with limited time being spent with children. See also Ofsted (2008a) paras. 71–74.

[160] H. Saunders (2004); discussed further in Chapter 13.

[161] J. Craig (2007a) pp. 5–6. See also J. Craig (2007b) and N. Wall (2006) paras. 8.21 and 8.27.

[162] *Practice Direction: Residence and Contact Orders: Domestic Violence and Harm* [2009] All ER (D) 122 (Jan).

[163] I.e. under CA 1989, s. 7; see discussed below.

[164] *Practice Direction: Residence and Contact Orders: Domestic Violence and Harm* [2009] All ER (D) 122 (Jan) at [4]–[5].

[165] J. Craig (2007a) p. 8.   [166] C. Piper (1997) and C. Piper (1999).

[167] J. Masson (2006) p. 1044: 40% of solicitors had experience during their career of consent orders which they thought put children at risk of harm; 8% considered that the court never had sufficient information about the children's wishes and feelings when making such consent orders.

(iv) The welfare reporting process

There are relatively few parents who slip through the in-court conciliation net and obtain a court hearing for their dispute.[168] When they do, the most serious procedural weakness undermining the courts' duty to consider the child's wishes and feelings[169] is that there is no guarantee that a court will receive any evidence indicating what those wishes are. The most obvious way for information about this to be conveyed to the court is through a 'welfare report'[170] – but there is no obligation on the court to request one, even in long-running, bitterly contested disputes involving older children. Furthermore, the enthusiasm for diverting disputing couples from court has had a direct impact on Cafcass' report writing function. The government's hope that the judiciary would appreciate the need for Cafcass to devote greater resources to the new in-court conciliation schemes, by substantially reducing the frequency with which they ask FCAs to prepare reports, seems to have borne fruit.[171] This down-grading of Cafcass' report writing function ignores the fact that the cases that do end up in court are the most intractable, with the child's own position often being well-nigh forgotten by highly conflicted parents. As noted elsewhere,[172] if a FCA is not obliged to produce a court report, it is unlikely that any Cafcass practitioner will carry out an in-depth assessment of the child's background and needs, addressing the factors in the welfare checklist.[173] Since the courts' primary source of information about the children's real wishes and feelings will be the parents, there may be little reliable evidence regarding the children's own perspectives in the dispute. It is notable that new judicial guidance directs the courts to consider calling for a welfare report in any case involving allegations of domestic violence.[174]

When a welfare report is called for, the FCA, acting in the role of children and family reporter (CFR), prepares a detailed assessment of the child's background and presents it to the court. The CFR's duties do not involve him or her representing the child. In pre-Cafcass days, parents and children were not always happy with the approach adopted by the court welfare officers (CWOs) whose duty it was then to prepare welfare reports. They complained that the CWOs did not spend long enough with children to assess their views accurately,[175] and that children's views were being reinterpreted by the CWOs when preparing the welfare report.[176] Recent research suggests that much work needs to be done to

---

[168] DCA/DfES/DTI (2004) para. 14: only 10% of contact arrangements are underpinned by court orders.

[169] I.e. CA 1989, s. 1(3)(a).

[170] I.e. under CA 1989, s. 7; alternatively referred to as a 'section 7 report' or a 'Cafcass report'.

[171] DCA/DfES/DTI (2004) para. 73; DCA/DfES/DTI (2005) paras. 67 and 72. See Cafcass (2008) p. 16: there was a 15.3% reduction in the number of requests for section 7 reports in 2007–8, on figures for the previous year (with a 8.4% reduction in 2006–7 and a 7.2% reduction in 2004–5). See also J. Hunt and A. Macleod (2008) pp. 112 and 187.

[172] J. Fortin *et al.* (2006) pp. 226–7.   [173] CA 1989, s. 1(3).

[174] *Practice Direction: Residence and Contact Orders: Domestic Violence and Harm* [2009] All ER (D) 122 (Jan) at [16].

[175] A. Buchanan *et al.* (2001) pp. 85–6 and 94.

[176] Ibid. at p. 65. See also J. Fortin *et al.* (2006) p. 220–1.

avoid CFRs replicating these very same problems with fresh groups of children, by filtering out the children's messages that are inconsistent with their own adult perspectives of the case[177] or by concluding that they are simply too young to be involved.[178] Some critics argue that the family justice system itself encourages Cafcass practitioners to place an adult construction on children's wishes and feelings in an effort to produce an 'objective' judgement of the child's capacities, often based on their own perceptions of chronological age.[179]

The case of *Re W (leave to remove)*,[180] provides a recent example of such an approach. There three children, aged 15, 13, and 11 were caught up in their divorcing parents' battle over whether the mother should be allowed to relocate to Sweden, taking the children with her. The Cafcass officer assigned to the case had considered the possibility of separate representation for the children but cast this option aside because it would lead to an adjournment of the trial.[181] Instead she soldiered on with her report summarising for the court, what she considered to be the children's wishes and feelings about the proposed move. She then proceeded to apply her own analysis of the situation, warning the court, to 'exercise a degree of caution in evaluating the children's stated wishes and feelings'.[182] This, as Thorpe LJ pointed out, was unsatisfactory; the children had understood that the Cafcass officer would advance the formulation that they had agreed on with her. She had not returned to explain to them her intention to 'finesse away their stated position by her own analysis'.[183] In particular, the youngest child would have felt that her wishes and feelings were insufficiently considered by the judge due to their having been 'diminished by the very professional whom she trusted to advance them'.[184] Children involved in such disputes are not permitted to give affidavit evidence setting out their own views.[185] But in decisions of this kind, they are effectively denied any voice over their own future, other than through the voice of a Cafcass officer, with whom they may fundamentally disagree.

CFRs should explain to each child, depending on his or her age and understanding, what they are including in their report and the outcome that they are recommending, 'in a manner appropriate to his age and understanding'.[186] Research suggests that most CFRs do explain to children very carefully what will go into their report and the recommendations being made.[187] But, as acknowledged by Scottish law,[188] it is arguable that children should receive

---

[177] Inter alia: HMICA (2005b) para. 2.29; G. Douglas *et al.* (2006) ch. 3; Ofsted (2008a) para. 74; Ofsted (2008b) para. 31 and paras. 49–50.

[178] Ofsted (2008a) para. 46 and Ofsted (2008b) para. 32.

[179] A. James *et al.* (2004) esp. pp. 199–200.   [180] [2008] EWCA Civ 538, [2008] 2 FLR 1170.

[181] Per Thorpe LJ, at [25].   [182] Ibid. at [27].   [183] Ibid. at [28].   [184] Ibid. at [33].

[185] *Re M (family proceedings: affidavits)* [1995] 2 FLR 100, per Butler-Sloss LJ, at 103.

[186] FPC (CA 1989) r. 11B(1)(a) and (b) (hereafter FPC (CA 1989) R 1991) and FPR 1991, r. 4.11B (1)(a) and (b) (hereafter FPR 1991).

[187] G. Mantle *et al.* (2006) pp. 14–15.

[188] Responding to *McMichael v. United Kingdom* (1995) 20 EHRR 205, copies of all reports and papers relating to children's hearings are given both to the child and to his parents. See *S v. Principal Reporter and Lord Advocate* [2001] UKHRR 514 at [28]–[29].

complete copies of these reports. Indeed, in *Re W (leave to remove)*[189] it was suggested not only that they should be sent a copy of the entire report but also asked to provide written comments on it before its submission. That case suggests that children should, at the very least, be told in advance *why* the CFR is adopting a particular approach, especially when it is inconsistent with their wishes.

It is, of course, essential that all CFRs are trained to carry out high quality report writing work – to interview children skilfully and to obtain detailed assessments of their needs, with plenty of time in which to do so.[190] This does not always happen. It appears that the judiciary sometimes order separate representation of children to remedy perceived defects in report writing.[191] Regrettably, the power to commission expert opinion on children who are the subject of their reports, in order to inform their own assessments,[192] appears to have been ignored by Cafcass.[193] It had been hoped that the ability, for example, to obtain a psychiatric report, would enable CFRs to focus far more on the children, rather than on their parents and to adopt a more therapeutic, rather than purely investigative, approach.[194] Allowing the CFR to adopt a more active role might also obviate the need to order separate representation in some cases.

(v) Separate representation

(a) The procedural context

Before proceeding to discuss this arcane area of law in more detail, it should be explained briefly that children can become more actively involved in litigation in a number of ways. First, as discussed below, the court may direct separate representation for the child under rule 9(5).[195] If this occurs, the child is made 'a party' to his/her parents' litigation over the child's upbringing and the child is given his/her own guardian and solicitor[196] (just as in public law proceedings)

---

[189] [2008] EWCA Civ 538, [2008] 2 FLR 1170, per Wilson LJ, at [56].

[190] HMICA (2005a) para. 3.41: over a third of the court reports considered did not reach the minimum standard; a quarter did not provide the court with full information about the case; over a third did not assess the impact of violence or the risk of future harm to children or adults (with consequent risk to their safety); in nearly a third, significant facts were not verified, and 1 in 10 were produced without the children being seen by Cafcass. See also the criticisms reported in Ofsted (2008a) para. 46 and Ofsted (2008b) para. 32.

[191] G. Douglas *et al.* (2006) para. 5.17.

[192] The Family Proceedings Courts (Children Act 1989) Rules 1991 (SI 1991/1395) (as amended), r. 11(2)(b) and Family Proceedings Rules 1991 (SI 1991/1247) (as amended), r. 4.11(2)(b).

[193] Anecdotal evidence suggests that few Cafcass practitioners know of the rule's existence.

[194] DH *et al.* (1998) para. 4.9: such a power would give 'caseworkers a more proactive role'; Children Act Sub-Committee of the Advisory Board on Family Law (1999) Annex D, p. 25: it was important for the unified service to have an 'in house budget' to purchase specialised services. See also A. Buchanan *et al.* (2001) p. 94.

[195] FPR 1991, r. 9.5.

[196] *L v. L (minors)(separate representation)* [1994] 1 FLR 156, per Butler-Sloss LJ, at 159: ordering separate representation involves a child being made party to their parents' proceedings.

and the guardian instructs the solicitor, not the child. More rarely, children may instruct their own solicitors, just as an adult would. This can occur in three situations. First, the court gives the child party status in the parents' litigation over his or her future upbringing and considers the child mature enough to have his or her own solicitor without the added assistance of a guardian. Second, the child initiates the litigation by instructing a solicitor and then applies for a section 8 order, for example, a residence order to 'divorce' his or her parents.[197] Third, in public law proceedings, where the child disagrees with the advice of the children's guardian and is deemed sufficiently mature to instruct his or her own solicitor.

(b) No automatic separate representation

A strong sense of unease is generated by cases like *Re W (leave to remove)*;[198] children may have no chance of refuting the Cafcass officer's view in a welfare report that they do not know what is good for them. One of the reasons for establishing Cafcass was the view that large numbers of children were the subject of private law applications every year, whose wishes and views were not being conveyed to the courts in any way. Nevertheless, when the new organisation was set up, the amended court rules still failed to give automatic party status to children whose parents were fighting over them in private proceedings, despite the outcome materially affecting their future. Some little improvement was apparently achieved for this group, in that the rules now oblige CFRs to advise the court in every case whether it 'is in the best interests of the child to be made a party to the proceedings'.[199] But, the value of such a best interests test is dubious if, as in *Re W*, they avoid doing so, for fear of producing delays in the litigation.[200] Since in many cases, the judiciary rely on the CFR to alert them to the need for direct separate representation, rather than acting on its own initiative, it is essential that CFRs interpret this duty from the perspectives of the children involved, rather than in an adult-focused manner. Nevertheless, as discussed above, the judiciary are now being expected to exercise restraint over calling for welfare reports. If none is required, a CFR may not discover enough about the case to know that the child requires separate representation.

Before discussing when separate representation might be ordered for children, it is worth considering the reasons for children in private law proceedings being deprived of *automatic* separate representation. Before the CA reforms, although sympathetic to the concept of children receiving separate representation in private proceedings, the Law Commission had provisionally concluded that there was no need for automatic separate representation, as in public

---

[197] Discussed in Chapter 4.   [198] [2008] EWCA Civ 538, [2008] 2 FLR 1170, discussed above.

[199] FPC (CA 1989) R 1991, r. 11B(5) and (6) and FPR 1991, r. 4.11B(5) and (6), which place the CFR under a specific duty to consider whether the child should be given party status and advise the court accordingly. Discussed above.

[200] The CFR failed to promote the children's separate representation for fear of its causing an adjournment.

proceedings.[201] Whilst children involved in public law proceedings might feel a strong sense of injustice if they were not given some voice,[202] in private law proceedings the welfare officer's report would normally suffice.[203] Consequently, rule 9.5 of the court rules accompanying the CA 1989 duly enabled the superior courts to exercise such a power, but only on an ad hoc basis. A court can make a rule 9.5 direction for separate representation (and automatic party status) when-ever it is satisfied that 'it is in the best interests of any child', and these rules remain unchanged today.[204]

The fact that the courts have the power to ensure that a child involved in private law proceedings is separately represented does not alter the fact that these children are less generously dealt with than those caught up in public law proceedings. Indeed, preceding the establishment of Cafcass there had been growing criticism of the failure of the CA 1989 to ensure that the views of *all* children caught up in parental disputes were conveyed to the courts. The critics used the Adoption and Children Act 2002 as a vehicle for reform. Section 122 apparently treats all applications for section 8 orders as 'specified proceedings' for the purposes of section 41 of the CA 1989 – thereby providing all the children involved with automatic separate representation, like children involved in public law applications. But the provision requires implementation by the introduction of rules of court detailing the circumstances in which such separate representation would apply. Contrary to expectations, these rules did not appear soon after the 2002 Act's introduction. Indeed, as discussed below, consultation over their possible format was delayed until 2006.[205]

Without court rules implementing the new provision, the family judiciary were left to work out for themselves when to exercise their existing power under rule 9.5 to direct separate representation for children on an ad hoc basis. Spurred on by official guidance,[206] they started using the power more often,[207] obviously appreciating that the impact on children of private law decisions might be just as great as in public law cases. This increased use of rule 9.5 had resource implications, given the fact that by 2004, Cafcass had improved the system of representation for children gaining such a service. Before, children provided with separate representation under rule 9.5 would be represented by a solicitor, often assisted by an independent social worker. Now Cafcass were

---

[201] Law Commission (1988) para. 6.26.   [202] Ibid. at para. 6.28.
[203] Ibid. at para. 6.26.   [204] FPR 1991, r. 9.5.   [205] DCA (2006), discussed below.
[206] *Practice Direction (Family Proceedings: Representation of Children)* [2004] 2 All ER 459, para 3 lists situations which might justify separate representation, including: '(1) where a Cafcass Officer has notified the court that in his opinion the child should be separately represented (2) where the child has a standpoint or interests which are inconsistent with or incapable of being represented by any of the adult parties (3) where there is an intractable residence or contact dispute, including where all contact has ceased, where there is irrational but implacable hostility to contact or where the child may be suffering harm associated with the contact dispute (4) where the views and wishes of the child cannot be adequately met by a report to the court (5) where an older child is opposing a proposed course of action.' See J. Whybrow (2004) pp. 507–9.
[207] G. Douglas *et al.* (2006) paras. 5.7–5.15.

replicating the public law system of tandem representation as closely as possible for children in private law cases. So today such a child is normally assisted by a Cafcass officer acting as his guardian ad litem, together with a private solicitor (or a solicitor from Cafcass Legal) acting as his legal advocate.[208] Continued resource problems led to long delays in the appointment of Cafcass guardians for children provided with party status.[209] These difficulties were the focus of the government's consultation on the possible format of new court rules activating section 122 of the Adoption and Children Act 2002.[210] The government controversially indicated that far from extending the availability of separate representation for children involved in private law cases, it now wished to introduce new court rules restricting its use.[211] It is unclear how the government intends to respond finally to the strong opposition to such a step.[212] Meanwhile the availability of rule 9.5 is unrestricted and the number of appointments thereunder continues to rise.[213]

(c) Separate representation for some?

Research reinforces the view that children who do obtain separate representation find the support they receive thereby extremely helpful.[214] In particular, a separate representative may be able to gain children's confidence and support them in long-running intractable contact disputes.[215] Nevertheless, it appears that, just as they do when writing court reports,[216] CFRs sometimes reinterpret the child's views by reference to their own ideas about what is in their best interests. Again, children themselves indicate their frustration if the CFR appears to misunderstand them or does not convey their strong views to the court in their original form.[217]

It remains unclear exactly what criteria the courts use for making a rule 9.5 appointment. The guidance, though lengthy, is not particularly specific;[218] except that the courts are also directed to consider providing children with separate representation in cases involving serious allegations of domestic violence.[219] A heightened appreciation of human rights law seems to have provoked

---

[208] *Practice Direction (Family Proceedings: Representation of Children)* [2004] 2 All ER 459 at 460, entitled *Practice Note (CAFCASS)*.

[209] C, Bellamy (2006) pp, 300–1.   [210] DCA (2006).   [211] N. Wall (2007) and J. Fortin (2007).

[212] Ministry of Justice (2007) pp. 16–17: 68% of respondents to the consultation opposed restrictions on the broad judicial discretion to utilise r. 9.5.

[213] Cafcass (2008) p. 16: there has been an increase of 22.6% of r. 9.5 appointments over the three years between 2005 and 2008, to which Cafcass has responded. NB *Practice Direction: Residence and Contact Orders: Domestic Violence and Harm* [2009] All ER (D) 122 (Jan) at [17]: in cases involving allegations of domestic violence, depending on the seriousness of the allegations and the difficulty of the case, courts should always consider making a child party to the proceedings

[214] G. Douglas *et al.* (2006) para. 7.18.

[215] E.g. *Re H (National Youth Advocacy Service)* [2006] EWCA Civ 896, [2007] 1 FLR 1028. See also R. Davies and S. Mason (2007) pp. 1096–8.

[216] Discussed above.   [217] G. Douglas *et al.* (2006) paras. 3.30, 3.27–3.28, 3.53–3.54, 3.57, 3.76.

[218] *Practice Direction (Family Proceedings: Representation of Children)* [2004] 2 All ER 459, para 3.

[219] *Practice Direction: Residence and Contact Orders: Domestic Violence and Harm* [2009] All ER (D) 122 (Jan) at [17].

a judicial acknowledgement that children may have a 'right' to participate in judicial proceedings involving them. Thus in 2001, the Court of Appeal took the unusual step of directing separate representation for a girl aged only 4½.[220] Dame Elizabeth Butler-Sloss P observed that it was unusual for a court to direct separate representation for a child, but she went on:

> There are cases where they do need to be separately represented and I suspect as a result of the European Convention ... becoming part of domestic law ... there will be an increased use of guardians in private law cases. Indeed, in the right case I would welcome it.[221]

In the slightly different context of children being allowed to instruct their own solicitors,[222] Thorpe LJ in *Mabon v. Mabon*[223] obviously favoured a similar approach in the case of older children. In his view:

> Unless we in this jurisdiction are to fall out of step with similar societies as they safeguard Art 12 rights [UNCRC], we must, in the case of articulate teenagers, accept that the right to freedom of expression and participation outweighs the paternalistic judgment of welfare.[224]

More recently, and again, in the context of older children, Munby J stressed in *Re L (family proceedings court) (appeal: jurisdiction)*[225] that by making a formal declaration regarding a 15-year-old child's parentage, without giving her notice of the hearing or party status, the court had infringed her procedural rights under Articles 6 and 8 of the ECHR.[226] Similarly, having considered the decision in *Mabon*, Ryder J emphasised that it would be 'extraordinarily paternalistic' not to allow C, an articulate, mature and intelligent 16-year-old, to respond, through a separate representative, to his father's application to remove him to France.[227]

Nevertheless, it is not always clear why one case justifies separate representation and another does not.[228] According to Douglas *et al.*, the case law illustrates the judiciary adopting one of two approaches when deciding whether to direct separate representation for a child. With the former, the 'welfare approach', by making a rule 9.5 appointment, the court hopes to achieve a better and more informed outcome for the child, with the guardian often instructing experts to assist the process. With the second, the 'voice' approach, the court decides that more needs to be known about what the child wants and

---

[220] *Re A (Contact: Separate Representation)* [2001] 1 FLR 715.   [221] Ibid. at para. 22.

[222] Discussed below.   [223] [2005] EWCA Civ 634, [2005] 2 FLR 1011   [224] Ibid. at para. 28.

[225] [2003] EWHC 1682 (Fam), [2005] 1 FLR 210: girl given permission to appeal out of time against the declaration of non-parentage made by the family proceedings court under Family Law Act 1986, s. 55A(1) regarding the man hitherto always considered to be her father.

[226] Ibid. at [24]–[25] and [28].

[227] *Re C (abduction: separate representation of children)* [2008] EWHC 517 (Fam), [2008] 2 FLR 6 at [38]. NB C was the oldest of five children, and, due to his age, was not the subject of the Hague Convention, unlike his younger siblings, whose position is discussed below, in the context of international abduction cases.

[228] J. Whybrow (2004) pp. 507–9 and J. Fortin (2007) pp. 505–7.

thinks.[229] The former type of appointment, which often involves relatively young children, reflects the courts' concern to ensure that the parents' own needs and obvious conflict of interest do not obscure the real needs of the child.[230] Despite more use when children implacably oppose contact,[231] there have, in the past, been surprisingly few reported examples of the 'voice' approach to separate representation under rule 9.5.[232]

The absence of more case law concerning older children may be explained by the availability of the rule 9.2A form of representation, where, as in *Mabon* itself, the mature older child obtains leave to instruct his own solicitor himself.[233] So those cases where the older child disagrees strongly with what the CFR recommends in his or her welfare report are dealt with procedurally, through a different form of representation being made available. In this way, as discussed below, the cases involving these older children often focus on whether they have the maturity to instruct their own solicitor, rather than on whether they should receive separate representation at all.

(d) Separate representation in international abduction cases?

There is one group of older children who, in the past, seldom obtained separate representation, despite their strong opposition to their parent's plans. These are the children caught up in international child abduction cases.[234] The domestic courts have always stressed the summary nature of Hague Convention proceedings and the need to ensure a prompt return of all abducted children to the country of their habitual residence.[235] Concerned therefore with the practical implications of giving children separate representation, with all the delays that this might entail, the judiciary have considered it a highly unusual step to take[236] and have confined its use to 'exceptional cases'.[237] Even the fact that

---

[229] G. Douglas *et al.* (2006) para. 2.3.

[230] E.g. *Re A (Contact: Separate Representation)* [2001] 1 FLR 715: 4½-year-old girl had made allegations of sexual abuse against her father; *Re K (replacement of guardian ad litem)* [2001] 1 FLR 663: 11-year-old child had been the subject of litigation between his parents since his first birthday; *Re F (contact: restraint order)* [1995] 1 FLR 956: two children aged 7 and 6 had been involved in parental contact litigation for many years; the children should be separately represented, largely to allow them to examined by a child psychiatrist.

[231] J. Hunt and A. Macleod (2008) pp. 199 and 218.

[232] E.g. *L v. L (minors)(separate representation)* [1994] 1 FLR 156: separate representation directed for three children aged just under 14, 12 and 9 to discover their true views, given that their father, who had a dominant personality and who wished to relocate with them in Australia, might be pressurising them to fall in with his wishes.

[233] Discussed below.

[234] As governed by the Hague Convention on the Civil Aspects of International Child Abduction 1980. See also discussed in Chapter 8.

[235] *Re P (abduction: minor's views)* [1998] 2 FLR 825, per Butler-Sloss LJ, at 827.

[236] Per Wall J in *Re S (abduction: children: separate representation)* [1997] 1 FLR 486 at 493; Wall LJ in *Re J (abduction: child's objections to return)* [2004] EWCA Civ 428, [2004] 2 FLR 64 at para. 63.

[237] *Re H (abduction)* [2006] EWCA Civ 1247, [2007] 1 FLR 242: per Thorpe LJ, at [16].

a much older child objected to returning did not, in the past, render the case sufficiently exceptional to justify him or her gaining party status.[238]

It is surprising that the courts have been so reluctant to order separate representation for children even in cases involving the Article 13 defence, given its special focus on the child's wishes. The defence authorises the court to refuse to order the child's return if 'it finds that the child objects to being returned and has attained an age and degree of maturity at which it is appropriate to take account of its views'.[239] The courts acknowledged that they should not reject a parent's claim under Article 13 without carefully considering and commenting on the child's wishes and maturity. But although the court should ensure that 'all appropriate steps have been taken to ensure that the information required … is before the court',[240] the judiciary commonly relied on FCAs[241] to advise them on children's maturity (and thence the relevance of their views), rather than directing separate representation.[242] As Schuz asserts, relying on interviews with the children is less than ideal, given that Cafcass officers are not there to represent the child, but to provide an opinion which may be far from objective.[243] Such officers often provided the court with firm opinions without always spending very long with the child.

A changed approach to separate representation in abduction cases may have been provoked by two recent decisions reached by Baroness Hale of Richmond – in *Re D (a child) (abduction: rights of custody)*[244] and *Re M and anor (children) (abduction)*.[245] They have undoubtedly produced a greater judicial willingness to ensure that children's views are elicited more often and more carefully than hitherto. In the former she emphasised that children should be far more frequently heard in *all* Hague Convention cases, not merely those involving an Article 13 defence.[246] In adopting this approach, she was influenced by the terms of Article 11(2) of the Brussels II Revised Regulations,[247] which governs the way that all EU countries handle international abduction

---

[238] Ibid. per Wall LJ, at [33]. The Court of Appeal confirmed that the trial judge's refusal to provide a 15-year-old abducted girl with separate representation.

[239] Sometimes described as Art. 13(c), despite its not being specifically given a sub-paragraph. This exception is sometimes combined with the abducting parent's claim under Art. 13(b) that there is a grave risk that the child's return would 'expose the child to physical or psychological harm or otherwise place the child in an intolerable situation'.

[240] *Re J (abduction: child's objections to return)* [2004] EWCA Civ 428, [2004] 2 FLR 64, per Wall LJ, at [94].

[241] Under the pre-Cafcass system, CWOs.

[242] *Re M (a minor) (child abduction)* [1994] 1 FLR 390, per Butler Sloss LJ, at 394: separate representation would be exceptional because a CWO could advise the court on the child's maturity and also convey to the court the child's views. See also Sir Thomas Bingham MR, at 397: it is very rarely right to join a child as a party.

[243] R. Schuz (2004) p. 727.   [244] [2006] UKHL 51, [2007] 1 All ER 783.

[245] [2007] UKHL 55, [2008] 1 All ER 1157.   [246] Ibid at [58].

[247] Council Regulation (EC) No. 2201/2003 Concerning Jurisdiction and the Recognition and Enforcement of Judgments in Matrimonial Matters and the Matters of Parental Responsibility (2003) OJ L 338/1. Shortly discussed by P. Beaton (2004).

cases. This specifically requires that when deciding whether a child shall be returned under Articles 12 or 13 of the Hague Convention:

> it shall be ensured that the child is given the opportunity to be heard during the proceedings unless this appears inappropriate having regard to his or her age or degree of maturity.

Acknowledging that this provision only applies to EU cases, Baroness Hale maintained that the principle itself has a universal application, consistent as it is with the terms of Article 12 of the CRC.[248] She pointed out that there is now:

> a growing understanding of the importance of listening to the children involved in children's cases. It is the child, more than anyone else, who will have to live with what the court decides. Those who do listen to children understand that they often have a point of view which is quite distinct from that of the persons looking after them.[249]

She stressed that a child should gain 'full scale legal representation' whenever it is likely that a child's views and interests are not being properly presented or legal arguments are being overlooked by the adult parties.[250] She also suggested that delays would be avoided if the question of party status was considered at the beginning of the case, not at the end.[251]

Whilst these views are welcome, Baroness Hale stressed that separate representation would only be necessary 'in a few cases'. In most cases it should be enough for the child to be interviewed by a Cafcass officer or, alternatively, the child might want to see the judge, who should then hear him or her.[252] By the time she revisited this issue in *Re M and anor (children) (abduction)*,[253] it was clear that the judiciary were showing a heightened appreciation that a child's views should be explored adequately and given sufficient weight in both EU and Hague Convention abduction cases.[254] In *Re M*, Baroness Hale emphasised that separate representation should be ordered as a matter of 'routine' in those rare cases governed by Article 12 of the Hague Convention – where the abductor claims that the child has become 'settled' in his or her new environment.[255] For all *other* cases, it would send children 'the wrong message' to always order separate representation, even where they are objecting to return.[256] Nevertheless, rather than asking whether the case is sufficiently 'exceptional' to justify separate representation, the court should ask:

> whether separate representation of the child will add enough to the court's understanding of the issues that arise under the convention to justify the

---

[248] [2006] UKHL 51, [2007] 1 All ER 783 at [58].   [249] Ibid. at [57].

[250] Ibid. at [60].   [251] Ibid. at [61].   [252] Ibid. at [60] .

[253] [2007] UKHL 55, [2008] 1 All ER 1157.

[254] Inter alia: *Re F (abduction: child's wishes)* [2007] EWCA Civ 468, [2007] 2 FLR 697, per Thorpe LJ, at [16]–[17] and [22]; *Re M (abduction: child's objections)* [2007] EWCA Civ 260, [2007] 2 FLR 72, per Sir Mark Potter P, at [61].

[255] [2007] UKHL 55, [2008] 1 All ER 1157, at [20]. See inter alia: *Re C (abduction: settlement)* [2004] EWHC 1245 (Fam), [2005] 1 FLR 127; *Cannon v. Cannon* [2004] EWCA Civ 1330, [2005] 1 FLR 169; *Re C (abduction: settlement) (No. 2)* [2005] 1 FLR 938 and R. Schuz (2008).

[256] I.e. the Art. 13 (c) cases.

intrusion, the expense and the delay which may result. I have no difficulty in predicting that in the general run of cases it will not.[257]

Subsequent case law suggests a lack of judicial consistency on this matter. Whilst some members of the judiciary continue to assert the existence of a 'general rule' in Convention cases that 'only in exceptional circumstances will children be joined as parties to the case',[258] others follow Baroness Hale's guidance on the matter.[259] Nevertheless, it appears that although children's views are now being 'routinely' elicited by specialist Cafcass officers at the Royal Courts of Justice,[260] there is some judicial acknowledgement that such a process is, from the child's perspective, greatly inferior to obtaining separate representation. As Ryder J accepted, echoing Schuz's views,[261] a Cafcass officer cannot advocate the child's views, or respond to the evidence and submissions as they unfold, giving the child's position where appropriate. Such a process 'does not allow a child to engage in the proceedings'.[262] But it also seems that some members of the judiciary are more likely to adopt Baroness Hale's suggestion that they should talk to an abducted child themselves in private, than order separate representation. This is a worrying development. As discussed below, it is questionable whether judges, who are untrained to speak sensitively to children, will be able to extract from them in the space of a very brief period,[263] their real views and the reasons for them on such an important issue. Certainly, it would be regrettable if they were to start doing so routinely, instead of the child being interviewed by a Cafcass officer.[264]

(vi) Children instructing their own solicitors under rule 9.2A of the Family Proceedings Rules 1991

(a) The background

Rule 9.2A of the Family Proceedings Rules 1991[265] was apparently introduced without anyone realising its radical nature and significance.[266] It covers two situations. First, as discussed above, a child may be granted party status in a

---

[257] *Re M and anor (children) (abduction)* [2007] UKHL 55, [2008] 1 All ER 1157, per Baroness Hale of Richmond, at [57].

[258] *Re F (abduction: removal outside jurisdiction)* [2008] EWCA Civ 842, [2008] 2 FLR 1649, per Thorpe LJ, at [12].

[259] *Re C (abduction: separate representation of children)* [2008] EWHC 517 (Fam), [2008] 2 FLR 6, per Ryder J, at [31].

[260] *Re M and anor (children) (abduction)* [2007] UKHL 55, [2008] 1 All ER 1157, per Baroness Hale of Richmond, at [57].

[261] See above.

[262] *Re C (abduction: separate representation of children)* [2008] EWHC 517 (Fam), [2008] 2 FLR 6 at [44].

[263] E.g. in *JPC v. SLW and SMW (abduction)* [2007] EWHC 1349 (Fam), [2007] 2 FLR 900 at [47]: Sir Mark Potter P reported talking privately to a 13-year-old abducted girl (whose views had been conveyed to the court in two written statements) in his room for 15–20 minutes in the presence of solicitors representing her and her mother.

[264] See Family Justice Council (2008) p. 433, in the context of family proceedings.

[265] Introduced through amendments made to the FPR 1991 in 1992.

[266] Thorpe J (1994) pp. 20–1.

parental dispute under rule 9.5. But the child may object to the CFR's approach to the case, perhaps because he is recommending a course of action with which the child disagrees. The child may then seek court leave to remove the next friend or guardian ad litem, thereby allowing him or her to proceed without such assistance.[267] Permission will only be granted if the court considers the child sufficiently mature to instruct a solicitor. Second, a child may wish to initiate proceedings to gain a judicial perspective on a family dispute by obtaining a section 8 order under the CA 1989.[268] In such circumstances, rule 9.2.A(1) allows the child to instruct a solicitor if the latter considers the child sufficiently mature to do so. Arguably, these two procedural methods reflect a remarkable legal acknowledgement of children's capacity to take responsibility for certain aspects of their own upbringing. They certainly promote the aims of Article 12 of the CRC in a radical fashion.

Children deemed to have sufficient understanding to instruct their own solicitor will be assisted by a lawyer whose duties do not encompass those of a children's guardian in public law proceedings. Indeed, a solicitor acting for a child in these circumstances is under no legal duty to provide his client with any emotional support, or to mediate between the child and his or her family. Moreover, since the child is treated as an adult client, the solicitor need not provide the court with any information about his perceptions of the child's best interests. Obvious judicial misgivings about these changes led to the senior judiciary ensuring that they maintained supervisory powers over children instituting legal proceedings. All applications made by children for leave under the CA 1989, section 10(8) were swiftly confined, by practice direction, to determination in the High Court.[269] Case law also established that the courts have the final word over whether children are indeed sufficiently competent to instruct a solicitor without the services of a guardian ad litem.[270] The judiciary then set about establishing what level of understanding a child requires to undertake such a task.

(b) Competence of children to instruct their own solicitors

A court can only allow a child, who is already party to his or her parents' dispute, to dispense with the services of his guardian ad litem under rule 9.2A (6), if it considers that the child 'has sufficient understanding to participate as a party in the proceedings concerned without a next friend or guardian ad litem'. Similarly, a solicitor can only accept instructions from a child who wishes to initiate his own litigation under rule 9.2A (1)(b) if he considers that the child

---

[267] FPR 1991, r. 9.2A(4) and (6). In which case the child will instruct his or her own solicitor, who will act for the child, thereby supplanting the guardian ad litem, who in pre-Cafcass days would normally have been the OS.

[268] But they must first obtain court leave to do so under CA 1989, s. 10(8); discussed further in Chapter 4.

[269] *Practice Direction* [1993] 1 All ER 820.

[270] *Re T (a minor) (child: representation)* [1993] 4 All ER 518, per Waite LJ, at 530.

'is able, having regard to his understanding, to give instructions in relation to the proceedings'.

Although these formulae are sufficiently similar to be treated together when considering the qualifying competence required from a child, most of the case law has arisen in the context of interpreting rule 9.2A (6). These children have already been provided with separate representation under rule 9.5,[271] but they want to dispense with the services of their guardian ad litem and instruct a solicitor on their own behalf. One might assume that when assessing the level of competence required of such a child, the courts would interpret the word 'understanding' taking account of the tasks required of someone in that situation. Thus, albeit in the context of public law proceedings,[272] Thorpe J indicated that a child should have sufficient rationality to instruct a solicitor, sufficient for 'coherent and consistent instruction'.[273] Similarly Booth J in *Re H (a minor) (guardian ad litem: requirement)*[274] considered that a child should not only be able to instruct a solicitor regarding his or her own views on the desired outcome, but also have an ability to enter the court arena alongside the adult parties, to give evidence and be cross-examined.[275]

Much of the case law establishing the level of competence required of these children, however, does something rather different. It shows the judiciary interpreting the word 'understanding' in a way designed to prevent children being damaged by becoming involved more actively in litigation between their parents. It reflects a judicial anxiety over the likely outcome of allowing them to dispense with the services of a guardian ad litem. A court may be particularly reluctant to allow the child to proceed in this way, if it suspects that he or she is being manipulated by a forceful parent into making such an application. Parents sometimes try to exploit their children's capacity to litigate themselves, in order to improve their own position in their battle with the other parent. When children 'sack' their guardian, they become involved in litigation on their own behalf. The court is aware that thereafter they are instructing a solicitor, without a guardian to shield them from the influence of a domineering parent or provide them with emotional support and advice. The court is also deprived of the services of an officer who provides it with independent advice over the child's best interests, often assisted by a consultant child psychiatrist and other practitioners. The wording of the rules, set out above, do not appear, however, to take account of these anxieties. Nor is it clear whether questions regarding the child's intellectual capacity to instruct a solicitor should be detached from broader questions regarding the child's overall maturity and welfare.

Today, courts must interpret the rule 9.2A formula taking careful account of the Court of Appeal's approach in *Mabon v. Mabon*.[276] Indeed, the decision of

---

[271] Discussed above.   [272] Discussed below.
[273] *Re H (a minor) (care proceedings: child's wishes)* [1993] 1 FLR 440 at 449.
[274] [1994] 4 All ER 762.   [275] Ibid. at 765.
[276] [2005] EWCA Civ 634, [2005] 2 FLR 1011.

the trial judge and that of the Court of Appeal in that case demonstrates well how the formula can produce very different interpretations. The Court of Appeal rejected the trial judge's interpretation which had been dictated by his anxieties about the damaging effect of a child becoming actively involved in parental litigation. Thorpe LJ was in little doubt that the formula in rule 9.2A(6) should be interpreted liberally, taking account of the right of children to participate in litigation affecting them.

> Unless we in this jurisdiction are to fall out of step with similar societies as they safeguard Art 12 rights [UNCRC], we must, in the case of articulate teenagers, accept that the right to freedom of expression and participation outweighs the paternalistic judgment of welfare.[277]

In contrast, the trial judge had been worried about the likely impact on the three elder siblings in a six-sibling family, of their becoming actively embroiled in their parents' residence dispute through dispensing with their guardian ad litem and instructing their own solicitor under rule 9.2A. Despite their ages, 17, 15 and 13, and their being intellectually able, articulate and perceptive, His Honour Judge Dixon refused to allow them to rid themselves of their guardian in order to instruct a solicitor themselves. He thought that little benefit would be derived from allowing them to become more directly involved in their parents' dispute and numerous disadvantages, including 'Delay from the pro-longation of the proceedings, unquantifiable emotional damage from contact with the material in this case, and exposure to the harshness of the litigation process'.[278] Nor did His Honour Judge Dixon believe that these young men were voicing their own views, independently from those of their father.

Much of the earlier case law reflects similar judicial anxieties about the danger of allowing children to become too involved in their parents' disputes, particularly if they appear to be influenced by a domineering parent. Sir Thomas Bingham MR's seminal judgment in *Re S (a minor) (independent representation)*[279] is a classic example of interpreting a child's 'understanding' restrictively, in the light of the outcome feared for him.[280] In his view, to have sufficient understanding, a child must show 'sound judgment on these issues'; this calls for insight and imagination which only maturity and experience can bring.[281] He could not allow this 11-year-old, who was strongly influenced by his father, to participate, without the services of a guardian ad litem, in such emotionally complex and highly fraught proceedings. Ten years later, in *Re N (contact: minor seeking leave to defend and removal of guardian,*[282] Coleridge J, for not dissimilar reasons, refused to allow an 11-year-old to dispense with the services of his solicitor guardian. Like S, he had been involved for many years in his parents' highly charged and long-running contact dispute. Influenced by the child and adolescent psychiatrist's strongly worded view that the boy was not

---

[277] Ibid. at [28]   [278] Ibid. at [18].   [279] [1993] 3 All ER 36.   [280] Discussed in Chapter 1.
[281] [1993] 3 All ER 36 at 43–4.   [282] [2003] 1 FLR 652.

sufficiently mature to participate in his parents' proceedings,[283] Coleridge J refused to allow him to divest himself of his guardian ad litem. In his view, a child would only have sufficient understanding to participate as a party to the proceedings if he has an ability to give fully considered instructions and a comprehension of their implications.[284] Although his reasons for refusing the boy's application are comprehensible, given the circumstances, such an interpretation of rule 9.2A(6) seems over restrictive. If adults were obliged to overcome a similarly worded hurdle before commencing litigation, the legal aid bill would be very small indeed.

Thorpe LJ in *Mabon*[285] considered that the approach adopted in *Re S*[286] was now outdated, pointing out that it had been decided before the true impact of the CRC, in particular Article 12, was realised. He also implied that things might be different today if a court were confronted, as the court had been in *Re N*[287] with an 11-year-old.[288] For older children, in his view, rule 9.2A(6) is sufficiently widely framed to enable the courts to meet their obligations to comply both with Article 12 and with Article 8 of the ECHR. When considering the sufficiency of the child's understanding, the courts should:

> reflect the extent to which, in the twenty-first century, there is a keener appreciation of the autonomy of the child and the child's consequential right to participate in decision-making processes that fundamentally affect his family life.[289]

The Court of Appeal's decision in *Mabon* was probably predictable, given the ages of the boys in question. Nevertheless, Thorpe LJ stressed that in testing a child's understanding:

> I would not say that welfare has no place. If direct participation would pose an obvious risk of harm to the child, arising out of the nature of the continuing proceedings and, if the child is incapable of comprehending that risk, then the judge is entitled to find that sufficient understanding has not been demonstrated.[290]

As discussed elsewhere, there are difficulties with Thorpe LJ's interpretation of rule 9.2A(6), both at a theoretical level and at a more technical interpretational level.[291] At a theoretical level, his words suggest that a child's 'rights' and his or her welfare are entirely discrete concepts – a proposition that is hard to accept.[292] In any event, since Article 12 of the CRC is itself subject to Article 3 of the Convention, it must be interpreted consistently with a child's welfare. Thus a court would not be infringing a child's rights under Article 12 if it decided not to provide a child with party status because, for example, it would entitle him to see particularly distressing and intimate evidence about one of his parents. But the real question is whether at an interpretational level, rule 9.2A

---

[283] Discussed below.   [284] Ibid. at p. 659.   [285] [2005] EWCA Civ 634, [2005] 2 FLR 1011.
[286] [1993] 3 All ER 36.   [287] [2003] 1 FLR 652.
[288] [2005] EWCA Civ 634, [2005] 2 FLR 1011 at [28].   [289] Ibid. at [26].   [290] Ibid. at [29].
[291] J. Fortin (2007) pp. 507–9.   [292] J. Fortin (2006) esp. pp. 310–12. See also Chapter 1.

can be interpreted credibly, allowing the courts such flexibility. As drafted, despite Thorpe LJ's words above, the word 'understanding' does not appear to allow them to do so without distorting its meaning. That point apart, it appears that His Honour Judge Dixon, the judge below, had carried out precisely the test that Thorpe LJ indicated, in his words quoted above, that he was entitled to do. He had decided that direct participation would harm the young men in question. Presumably, they were incapable of comprehending that risk otherwise they would not have proceeded with their application. Consequently, using Thorpe LJ's test, the judge was entitled to conclude that they had not demonstrated sufficient 'understanding'. It is therefore difficult to understand quite why the Court of Appeal considered that His Honour Judge Dixon's decision had been 'plainly wrong'.[293]

Despite these difficulties, the strength of the Court of Appeal's decision in *Mabon* suggests that in future, few courts will prevent 'elderly' children from dispensing with the services of a guardian ad litem in cases where they are already involved in parental litigation. This liberal approach is, on the whole, to be welcomed, since in many cases it is too late to impose protective restrictions. Indeed, for many children, they achieve little more than shutting the stable door after the horse has bolted. Nevertheless, as discussed elsewhere, it would be a worrying development if younger children were also allowed more freely to dispense with the services of much needed guardians ad litem, despite it being clear that they have been manipulated into litigating on their own behalf by a dominating parent.[294]

So far the discussion has concentrated on the problems thrown up by children who are already parties to their parents' disputes but who wish to instruct a solicitor free of the services of a guardian ad litem. For children seeking section 8 orders, matters are slightly different. They must first persuade a solicitor that they have sufficient understanding to instruct him under rule 9.2A(1)(b). Although the courts have the right to override a solicitor's view that a child has sufficient understanding to instruct him,[295] there is little case law indicating that solicitors blatantly misjudge children's competence. Indeed, Sawyer's research carried out in the mid-1990s, suggested that solicitors experienced in children's cases are relatively conservative in their views regarding the competence of a child to instruct them. Their assessment of competence appears to be based on a number of factors, including the child's ability to cope with the tasks and emotional difficulties involved in litigation.[296] Having persuaded a solicitor to represent him or her, a child must apply for leave under section 10(8) of the CA 1989. What little case law there is appears to show the

---

[293] [2005] EWCA Civ 634, [2005] 2 FLR 1011 at [24].   [294] J. Fortin (2007) p. 509.

[295] *Re T (a minor) (child: representation)* [1993] 4 All ER 518, per Waite LJ, at 530.

[296] C. Sawyer (1995) pp. 114–22: the solicitors interviewed were reluctant to accept instructions from children under 10; in their experience, the senior judiciary required children to be aged between 13 and 15, with the magistrates being prepared to accept competence in children from 10.

courts taking a relatively relaxed approach in relation to the type of under-standing required of children seeking leave to apply for section 8 orders.[297]

(vii) Is private law litigation bad for children?

It seems reasonably self-apparent that litigation in itself is not the root of family dissension and that happy well-functioning families do not produce children willing to take part in legal proceedings. In any event, children in this country are educated in a way which should qualify them for citizenship in a sophisti-cated and technologically advanced society. It is impossible to reverse this trend; these same children naturally want active involvement in disputes that threaten to disrupt their lives fundamentally. Allowing children to gain a much wider access to the courts to resolve family disputes is undoubtedly an important way of fulfilling the notions underlying *Gillick*.[298] A legal system which recognises the right of mature children to reach decisions for themselves, free from parental veto should also enable them to obtain court affirmation for their decision-making. Indeed, today, as Thorpe LJ emphasised in *Mabon v. Mabon*,[299] there is a far greater appreciation of their participation rights under article 12 of the CRC. None of the provisions enabling children to conduct their own litigation gives them the ability to determine the outcome of legal disputes for themselves; this rests with the courts. Plainly there is an important dis-tinction between providing children with access to the courts and considering their wishes once there.

Despite the undoubted benefits of these procedural rights, there remain considerable and well-reasoned doubts about allowing children to become heavily involved in private law proceedings. In future, children may feel extremely intimidated by the knowledge that the press will be able attend and report on the hearing of their parents' litigation in the family courts. The fact that there will be reporting restrictions may not convince them that their anonymity will be preserved.[300] Sawyer's research showed that the solicitors experienced in acting for children considered the whole process of litigation to be a damaging one. In their view, it inevitably reinforces existing tensions and polarises dissension, makes agreement impossible and undermines the ability of the family to function adequately in the future. Although many cases never get to court, the preparation for litigation may, in itself, be stressful. Solicitors must obtain instructions from their child clients on the evidence being given by the adults in the case and the ways in which they might be cross-examined on this evidence. Children may have to challenge their parents' veracity, or at least

---

[297] Discussed in Chapter 4.

[298] *Gillick v. West Norfolk and Wisbech Area Health Authority* [1986] AC 112.

[299] [2005] EWCA Civ 634, [2005] 2 FLR 1011 at [28].

[300] Statement made to the House of Commons 16 December 2008 by Jack Straw, Lord Chancellor and Secretary of State for Justice: rules of court are to be introduced which will allow 'accredited' media to attend family court hearings but parties will be allowed to make representations to the court for the media to be excluded. See MOJ (2008a).

criticise them to an outsider and have their own views written down and presented to each parent.[301] By the time of the hearing, it is probably too late to protect the child from experiencing unpleasant evidence – the damage has already been done.[302] Even the most 'children's rightist' solicitors who have considerable experience in representing children in court are ambivalent over the wisdom of allowing children to pursue private proceedings, in so far as they may have a corrosive effect on the whole structure of the family.[303]

The judiciary also express concerns that children litigating on their own behalf in private law proceedings may end up traumatised by the experience. Such cases tend to arise in the context of bitter and long drawn out parental litigation. As discussed above, parents may persuade their children to litigate on their own behalf in order to improve their own position in their battle with the other parent. The child's application may be used to reopen issues already dealt with by an earlier order.[304] As in *Re HB (abduction: children's objections)*,[305] by dint of instructing a solicitor independently and then appealing against an earlier order obtained by one parent against the other, a child effectively takes over one side of a parental dispute. The impact of becoming involved in such acrimonious litigation can be immense. In that case, the court welfare officer considered that 11-year-old C was now 'much more burdened and sad about the legal contest, in which her parents, and now she herself, are engaged'.[306] Thorpe LJ observed that the 'case illustrates only too vividly the enormous price that is paid when children are permitted to litigate'.[307] Hale J later reconsidered whether C should return to Denmark, against her wishes and in the light of changed circumstances. She too expressed concern over C's active involvement in her parents' litigation and although she did not criticise C's solicitor for accepting instructions from C, she referred to the CWO's view that C was:

> not mature enough to be other than anecdotal in her taking up of a position. She is not capable of comparative analysis of her own life history or current circumstances. She is strongly influenced in her perception of right and wrong by very strong judgmental and monolithic feelings typical of a child of her age.[308]

Similarly in *Re N (contact: minor seeking leave to defend and removal of guardian)*,[309] a well-known child psychiatrist stated:

> Children commonly have very impassioned views, indeed the younger the child the more this is so as exemplified by infantile temper tantrums. This does not

---

[301] C. Sawyer (1995) p. 155.   [302] Ibid. at pp. 155 and 175.   [303] Ibid. at p. 162.

[304] E.g. *Re S (a minor) (independent representation* [1993] 3 All ER 36 and *Re K (replacement of guardian ad litem)* [2001] 1 FLR 663.

[305] [1998] 1 FLR 422: Butler-Sloss LJ (at 429) criticised the father for allowing his 11-year-old daughter to fight his battles with her mother for him.

[306] Ibid. at 427.   [307] Ibid.

[308] *Re HB (abduction: children's objections) (No 2)* [1998] 1 FLR 564 at 567.

[309] [2003] 1 FLR 652.

bespeak mature thought. On the contrary, children have little perspective or balance. Hence their need for parental guidance and in the legal field their need for guardians. It would empower L beyond his years to act up legally. Children may commonly seek such autonomy, but seldom do they benefit from it.[310]

Coleridge J concluded that the boy in *Re N* would be damaged by being allowed to litigate without a guardian ad litem – he would become totally embroiled in the detail of his parents' dispute.[311]

These concerns about children's psychological vulnerability should be taken seriously. Few would deny that a right to be fully involved in legal proceedings may, in certain circumstances, be of sufficient importance to the child to outweigh the risks of being involved in the litigation process. But it is dangerous to assume that by promoting children's 'right' to have their say in court, with a view to promoting their autonomy, their position will be improved. There is little comfort to be drawn from the knowledge that, once children get to court, their capacity for independence will depend on the court's own paternalistic perceptions of their best interests. Indeed, as King and Piper warned, using the language of rights when dealing with disputes relating to children, may result in them being treated like little adults without childlike characteristics.[312]

These concerns do not necessarily indicate that children's rights to litigate should be withdrawn or, indeed, that the judiciary should restrict children's rights to instruct their own solicitors in a way that undermines the whole point of allowing children to litigate at all. For competent children, the procedural right to initiate their own application for a section 8 order is a particularly important one; it provides them with a route into having their views advocated in court. At the very least this process ensures that the child's views are taken seriously by his or her parents, leading to the possibility of a better mode of operating within the family. But the fact that children need to be heard in disputes, or even to initiate them, should not disguise the fact that the process of litigation may itself exacerbate relations at home and prevent existing rifts from healing over. It is essential therefore to consider carefully whether sufficient effort is being made in the early stages of such applications to avoid children becoming involved in a damaging process before it is too late.

An early referral to well-constructed child-centred mediation could provide a good means of protecting children, before the damaging process of preparation for litigation is started.[313] Despite the inherent dangers of looking on mediation as a universal panacea for all ills connected with litigation, it may avoid children becoming involved in a process which has a dangerous ability to polarise attitudes and reinforce hostility. But, as Sawyer points out, such a change should only be introduced with great care, to avoid children being thereby excluded from access to the courts. They might, for example, be threatened with the prospect of facilities for litigation being withdrawn, in the event of

---

[310] Ibid. at 658.   [311] Ibid. at p 659.   [312] M. King and C. Piper (1995) p. 144.
[313] C. Sawyer (1995) pp. 180–2.

proving 'unco-operative' with the mediation process. A similar result might obtain in the event of a parent refusing to cooperate. Moreover, insufficient time devoted to investigating the child's wishes and feelings might lead to his or her being silenced entirely. The kind of assistance made available under the auspices of a FAO,[314] but earlier in the litigation process, might fulfil this particular need.

(C) Public law proceedings

(i) 'The tandem system of representation'

Doubts have been expressed over the way in which Cafcass resources are gradually being diverted from providing children with representation in public law proceedings to dispute resolution work in private law proceedings.[315] There are concerns that this may weaken the system established for the representation of children involved in public law proceedings – an impressive one which fully complies with the requirements of international instruments such as the CRC and the ECECR. The child is provided with full party status, automatic public funding and, regardless of age, normally the services of a children's guardian,[316] in addition to those of a legal advocate. The children's guardian, who appoints a solicitor[317] to represent the child, provides the court with an assessment of what outcome would be in the child's best interests. Meanwhile, the solicitor acts as the child's legal representative in court and treats the child as his client. The children's guardian, who is qualified in social work, should be experienced at working with children and therefore able to provide the court with a detailed assessment of the needs of even very young children. The solicitor, whilst unable to assess the needs of the child, particularly if very young, has the legal skills necessary for representing the child in what are sometimes extremely complex legal hearings, involving a number of parties.

The rules of court envisage the children's guardian playing an important part in public law proceedings; he or she must 'safeguard the interests of the child in the manner prescribed by [court] rules'.[318] Working 'in tandem' with the child's solicitor,[319] he or she investigates the child's background in depth,[320] often recommending an expert to assess his or her needs. Prior to the procedural

---

[314] CA 1989, s.16; discussed above.   [315] J. Doughty (2006) pp. 38–9.

[316] CA 1989, s. 41(1) establishes a presumption that the child involved will, regardless of age, receive separate representation in all 'specified proceedings'. These include (see s .41(6)) most local authority (LA) interventions to protect children.

[317] Private solicitors who wish to represent children must be members of the Law Society Children Panel, having acquired the required training and accreditation to deal with children's cases.

[318] CA 1989, s. 41(2)(b). The duties listed by FPR 1991, r. 4.11A(4) and FPC (CA 1989) R, r 11A(3) include advising the court on the child's wishes and the appropriate forum for and timing of the proceedings.

[319] This dual system of representation is often called the 'tandem system' of representation.

[320] CA 1989, s. 42: the children's guardian has a right to examine and take copies of all social work records relating to the child and his or her family.

reforms introduced under the auspices of the Public Law Outline (PLO),[321] the children's guardian would normally do a great deal of detailed work prior to the final hearing, which assisted him or her to gain an exceptionally good knowledge of the background of the case, including the LA's long and short-term plans for the child.[322] The guardian then produced a lengthy report to the court for the final hearing, taking account of the child's wishes and feelings and every other item on the welfare checklist[323] and ultimately recommending an outcome deemed to be in the child's best interests. As discussed below, it is unclear to what extent the new procedural changes will change this approach and undermine guardians' ability to represent children satisfactorily.

(ii) Children's involvement in public law proceedings

As noted above, children involved in public law proceedings have full party status – quite rightly so, since the outcome of the case will often drastically disrupt their lives. Nevertheless, as Davis points out, party status for a child 'seems to have a different meaning than for everyone else'.[324] For an adult, party status entitles him to see all the evidence before the court, to put forward evidence, to be represented, to attend court, with a right to give oral evidence and with a presumption that he will be cross-examined. But this is not the case for children. Indeed, as Davis asserts, 'some parties are more equal than others'.[325]

In theory, there is nothing to prevent the court hearing evidence directly from any child, as long as the court considers that he or she understands the duty to speak the truth and has sufficient understanding to give evidence.[326] In practice, however, the courts have, in the past, been extremely reluctant to allow a child, however old, to give evidence in care proceedings,[327] preferring to hear the child's account of what occurred to be relayed to them by adults under the relaxed hearsay rules.[328] This is because they assume that for a child to appear in court and provide them with a first-hand account would be a damaging experience.[329] The fact that the child may himself wish to give evidence will not necessarily affect the court's attitude.[330]

---

[321] MOJ (2008b) and *Practice Direction: Guide to Case Management in Public Law Proceedings* [2008] 2 FLR 668.

[322] See *Re X; Barnet London Borough Council v. Y and X* [2006] 2 FLR 998, per Munby J, at [104]: it had been quite wrong of the LA not to keep the children's guardian abreast of important changes to the child's care plan despite care proceedings having already commenced.

[323] I.e. CA 1989, s. 1(3).   [324] L. Davis (2007) p. 65.   [325] Ibid.   [326] CA 1989, s. 96(1) and (2).

[327] E.g. *R v. B County Council, ex p P* [1991] 1 WLR 221 and *Re P (witness summons)* [1997] 2 FLR 447.

[328] CA 1989, s. 96(3)–(7) and Children (Admissibility of Hearsay Evidence) Order 1993 (SI 1993/621).

[329] E.g. *Nottinghamshire County Council v. P* [1993] 1 FLR 514: Ward J (at 519–520) disapproved of the two girls' attendance in court and also of the LA's plan to call the eldest, aged 16, with learning difficulties, to give evidence, rather than relying on the guardian's account of her views.

[330] E.g. *Re O (care proceedings: evidence)* [2003] EWHC 2011(Fam), [2004] 1 FLR 161: a 14-year-old boy who, with his 11-year-old sister was the subject of care proceedings, was refused the right to give evidence in his mother's favour supporting her denials of abuse. Per Johnson J, at p. 169, his evidence would have probably have carried little weight.

Such an attitude may appear over-protective when compared with the treatment of child witnesses in the criminal courts. Nevertheless, it is justifiable, given that children find it highly stressful to be cross-examined in a criminal court, even with protective procedures in place.[331] Fortunately a judicial attempt to readjust this paternalistic approach was forcefully rejected by the Court of Appeal. Influenced by the fact that a 13-year-old's false allegations of grave sexual abuse against his stepfather had had an appalling impact on his family,[332] Coleridge J had urged that serious consideration should be given to children of this age giving evidence in person.[333] In a later decision, the Court of Appeal disagreed, maintaining that Coleridge J's words should not be taken as indicating that children should now *normally* be expected to give evidence in court in public law cases. The 'correct starting point' remains that it is undesirable for children to give evidence in care proceedings and particular justification is required before such a course is taken.[334]

More problematic is practitioners' attitude to children's presence in court. Research shows that some, but not all,[335] children strongly favour being present at care or related proceedings.[336] They quite reasonably argue that, even if they cannot give evidence, they should at least be entitled to see and hear the process that determines their future.[337] Children have been automatic parties to public proceedings since 1975 and the rules appear to assume that they will attend.[338] Nevertheless, a decision whether to allow children to attend the hearing of their case is ultimately for the court, and practice, has over the years, been influenced by the senior judiciary's scepticism of the merits of allowing children to attend public law proceedings.[339]

HM Inspectors are extremely critical that this approach has remained unchanged. They found 'court staff, the judiciary and CAFCASS, both explicitly and formally' conveying the same message – that children are not encouraged

---

[331] E.g. *R (on the application of B) v. Stafford Combined Court* [2006] EWHC 1645 (Admin), [2007] 1 All ER 102; discussed in Chapter 17.

[332] *B v. Torbay Council* [2007] 1 FLR 203: by the time the boy retracted his story nearly four years later, his two step-siblings had been in foster care throughout that time on care orders to protect them from their allegedly abusive father.

[333] Ibid. at [17].

[334] *LM (by her guardian) v. Medway Council, RM and YM* [2007] EWCA Civ 9, [2007] 1 FLR 1698, per Smith LJ, at [44].

[335] J. Masson and M. Winn Oakley (1999) pp. 114–15 and J. McCausland (2000) pp. 80 and 105: some children strongly oppose the idea of attending the court hearing.

[336] E.g. applications to discharge a care order.

[337] J. Masson and M. Winn Oakley (1999) p. 115; M. Ruegger (2001) pp. 40–1; J. McCausland (2000) pp. 103–4; J. Timms and J. Thoburn (2003) p. 7.

[338] FPR 1991, r. 4.16(2) and FPC (CA 1989) R 1991, r. 16(2): the proceedings may take place in the absence of the child party, if considered to be in the child's best interests and he/she is represented by a children's guardian or solicitor. Before deciding, the court should allow the solicitor, children's guardian and the child, if of sufficient understanding, to make representations on this.

[339] Inter alia: *Re C (a minor) (care: child's wishes)* [1993] 1 FLR 832, per Waite J, at 841; *Re W (secure accommodation order: attendance at court)* [1994] 2 FLR 1092, per Ewbank J, at 1097.

to attend court.[340] With the exception of secure accommodation proceedings and (very rarely) the older child who has separated from his or her guardian and is instructing a solicitor direct, a child's attendance in court is 'very rare indeed'.[341] Some guardians and solicitors still arrange to show the children round the empty courtroom instead,[342] but it is unclear whether they find such visits particularly helpful. HM Inspectors suggest, somewhat caustically, that if children's attendance became more commonplace, the services offered by the courts and Cafcass 'might become focussed less on the convenience of these agencies and more on the needs of the children'.[343] Furthermore, they sensibly observe that through a greater involvement in family proceedings, children are likely to gain a better understanding of their situation, the roles of Cafcass and the courts in determining their future and to adjust better to the court's decision and its impact on their lives.[344] Arguably, children who are the focus of public law proceedings know better than anyone what has happened to them and it may be entirely appropriate for them to be present at the final stages of a process which will affect their lives fundamentally. It is often far too late to protect them from exposure to potentially damaging material. Admittedly, such views may change once it becomes clearer how media presence in care proceedings in all family courts affects the tenor of the hearings.[345]

It is difficult to defend barring children who are the subject of care proceedings from attending court. Indeed, Davis argues that refusing to allow competent children to play a full part in such proceedings when they wish to do so is tantamount to denying them a fair trial.[346] They might certainly claim that Article 6 of the ECHR, with its demands for a fair trial, supports their presence in court.[347] Furthermore, they might argue that since a care order removing them from their parents would materially affect their family life, their procedural rights under Article 8 would be infringed were they not provided with any chance to influence the outcome directly. Some might also point to the judicial willingness to allow children involved in secure accommodation proceedings to attend court. Though true, it is probably not a good analogy since the subject of a secure accommodation order (SAO) loses his liberty far more emphatically than a child removed from home under a care order. It is because the judiciary are well aware that a SAO is a 'Draconian measure'[348] designed to deprive children of their liberty, that they emphasise the need to comply strictly with all the procedural requirements of the CA 1989, section 25, plus the rules of natural justice.[349]

---

[340] HMICA (2005b) para. 3.4.   [341] Ibid. at para. 3.10.   [342] Ibid.
[343] Ibid. at para. 4.1.   [344] Ibid. at para. 4.3.   [345] See fn 300 above.
[346] L. Davis (2007) p. 65.   [347] Family Justice Council (2008) p. 434.
[348] Per Booth J in *Re W (a minor) (secure accommodation order)* [1993] 1 FLR 692 at 696 and per Butler-Sloss LJ in *Re M (a minor)* [1995] 1 FLR 418 at 423.
[349] E.g. *Re AS (secure accommodation order)* [1999] 1 FLR 103: interim SAO quashed; it had been made by the court below, knowing that the 12-year-old boy had not himself received notice of the application, had not instructed his solicitor or counsel and had no guardian ad litem appointed to represent him. See also *LM v. Essex County Council* [1999] 1 FLR 988.

Children are allowed to attend such proceedings[350] and are provided with legal representation.[351] Today, the subject of secure accommodation proceedings would certainly have good grounds for challenging any attempt to exclude him or her from court, on the basis this would infringe his or her rights under Article 6 of the ECHR.

(iii) Children instructing their own solicitors in public law proceedings

(a) Competence to instruct a solicitor

It is questionable whether the fact that a child has party status in public law proceedings is always taken sufficiently seriously by the practitioners working in this field. This issue can arise in the context of proceedings involving an older and more articulate child. A strong-minded teenager may disagree with his or her children's guardian over the desired outcome of the proceedings. In such a conflict, a teenager might certainly expect, under the Family Proceedings Rules, to have the right to instruct a solicitor without the intervention of a guardian. But the child's solicitor can only take instructions if satisfied that the child is 'able, having regard to his understanding, to give such instructions on his own behalf in which case he shall conduct the proceedings in accordance with instructions received from the child'.[352] A clear divergence of views between a mature child and his or her guardian should trigger a discussion between the guardian and solicitor about the child's ability to instruct the latter independently, with the guardian then seeking his own legal assistance. If they agree that the child has sufficient capacity, this matter should be brought to the attention of the court promptly.[353]

In practice, solicitors normally rely on the guardian to advise them on the child's competence to give legal instructions. When making this assessment, public proceedings throw up rather different problems to those arising in private disputes.[354] Children are often the subject of applications by the LA because of serious concerns about the level of their care at home. Abusive treatment may have produced disturbed behaviour which undermines the ability of adolescent children, however intelligent, to take part in such litigation. Thorpe J (as he then was) considered that the rules must be interpreted sensibly in such cases and that an emotionally disturbed child may not be sufficiently rational to give coherent and consistent instructions to his or her solicitor.[355]

---

[350] Inter alia: *Re C (secure accommodation order: representation)* [2001] EWCA Civ 458, [2001] 2 FLR 169: C attended the s. 25 hearing and gave evidence in person; *Re K (a child) (secure accommodation order: right to liberty)* [2001] 1 FLR 526: K allowed, on appeal, to attend the s. 25 hearing. Per Dame Elizabeth Butler-Sloss P, at para. 44: it had benefited him to play a part and understand the legal procedures depriving him of his liberty.

[351] *Re AS (secure accommodation order)* [1999] 1 FLR 103. But see *Re C (secure accommodation order: representation)* [2001] EWCA Civ 458, [2001] 2 FLR 169, discussed below.

[352] FPR 1991, r. 4.12(1) and FPC (CA 1989) R 1991, r. 12(1).

[353] Per Wall J in *Re M (minors) (care proceedings: child's wishes)* [1994] 1 FLR 749 at 753–4.

[354] Discussed above.   [355] *Re H (a minor) (care proceedings: child's wishes)* [1993] 1 FLR 440 at 449.

Nevertheless, emotional disturbance amongst clients is not confined to children, and solicitors are well able to take this factor into account when judging the capacity of a child client to give them instructions.

(b) The child's 'right' to instruct a solicitor

As discussed above, the court rules envisage that mature children who disagree with their children's guardian over the desired result of care proceedings are allowed to instruct their solicitor themselves. There is little current case law or research indicating how often this occurs. It does not appear, however, that practice has changed greatly since the late 1990s when mature children apparently seldom instructed their solicitors directly.[356] There were various reasons for this. Sawyer found that guardians might consider whether separate representation was 'good' for the child, rather than considering it from the viewpoint of the child's legal right.[357] Even in cases where a clear conflict had arisen between child and guardian, either the child's solicitor or guardian might seek to deter the child from seeking to instruct the solicitor directly, for fear of antagonising the court.[358] Some practitioners undoubtedly still leave a decision over a conflict between child and guardian until the last minute, in the hope that the child will come round to agreeing with the guardian.[359] There may also be a reluctance to change the existing arrangements for fear of losing the fixture for the hearing.[360]

In the past, the courts have not always sympathised with older children who argue that they should have been given a right to instruct their solicitor directly. Thus in *Re H (a minor) (care proceedings: child's wishes)*,[361] Thorpe J refused an appeal against a care order by an intelligent 16-year-old because although he had not been given the opportunity to be represented by his own solicitor, there was plenty of evidence justifying the care order. Consequently, although it would remove the boy's sense of grievance, a retrial would result in precisely the same result, despite having also produced delay, expense and anxiety.[362] It now appears that the courts are taking this issue much more seriously. In *Re K and H*,[363] Thorpe LJ pointed out how impossible it was for two boys aged 13 and 11 to feel that their wish to remain at home with their father was being adequately conveyed to the court whilst being represented by professionals who were urging their removal from home. He criticised a solicitor for not taking instructions from the older boy directly, despite her view that he had capacity to instruct her.[364]

---

[356] J. Masson and M. Winn Oakley (1999) p. 77.   [357] C. Sawyer (2000) p. 111.

[358] Ibid. and J. Masson and M. Winn Oakley (1999) p. 78.

[359] E.g. *Re H (a minor) (care proceedings: child's wishes)* [1993] 1 FLR 440 and *Re M (minors) (care proceedings: child's wishes)* [1994] 1 FLR 749.

[360] E.g. *Re P (representation)* [1996] 1 FLR 486: an appeal was allowed against Douglas Brown J's refusal to allow a teenage girl separate representation from that of her six siblings. He had considered that acting on the application at such a late stage would abort the hearing;

[361] [1993] 1 FLR 440   [362] Ibid. at 450.

[363] [2006] EWCA Civ 1898, [2007] 1 FLR 2043.   [364] Ibid. at [19].

The need for separate representation is easily apparent in care cases, particularly when an older child is opposing removal from home, as in the two cases discussed above. It becomes even more vital in cases involving applications for SAOs, given that the child's liberty is at stake.[365] Nevertheless, it does not appear that the child's right to an effective form of legal representation is always respected. Thus in *Re C (secure accommodation order: representation)*,[366] C, a 15-year-old girl had only two hours to instruct her solicitor, in a public area of the court building, on how to respond to a 14-page supporting statement from the LA. Despite agreeing that there had been procedural irregularities,[367] the Court of Appeal confirmed the SAO because it considered that her appeal would have resulted in such an order being made in any event. This approach was surprising bearing in mind its recognition that children's rights to a fair trial under Article 6 of the ECHR are particularly important in cases involving applications for SAOs, where a deprivation of liberty is the outcome. Despite its view that secure accommodation proceedings do not qualify as criminal proceedings for the purposes of Article 6, the court conceded that the rights accorded by Article 6(3) to those charged with criminal offences should be applied, 'as a matter of procedural fairness' to young people involved in secure accommodation proceedings.[368] But, having made such a concession, the Court of Appeal failed to refer specifically to the requirement in Article 6(3)(b) that the accused should have 'adequate time and facilities' to prepare his defence, nor to any case law supporting it.[369] Since the girl involved had very little time to oppose a well-prepared application from her 'opponent' (in this instance, the LA), her rights under Article 6(1) to 'equality of arms' were surely infringed. After all, as a party to litigation, she was at a substantial disadvantage to her opponent.[370] The Court of Appeal's response that the order should stand, since a SAO would have been the outcome of any appeal, smacks of highhandedness. As Masson observes, this approach is regrettable, given that secure accommodation applications provide little opportunity for challenge.[371] It seems unlikely that the Court of Appeal would have responded in this way to an adult making similar complaints.

(c) A good quality system of representation?

In the late 1990s the system of representation for children involved in public law proceedings was held up to European legal systems as 'far superior to all other practical solutions adopted so far'.[372] Though expensive, the virtually automatic appointment of a guardian and solicitor can still be justified with

---

[365] The grounds and usage of SAOs is discussed in more detail in Chapter 15.
[366] [2001] EWCA Civ 458, [2001] 2 FLR 169; discussed by J. Masson (2002).
[367] Ibid., particularly Brooke LJ at [38]–[41].
[368] [2001] EWCA Civ 458, [2001] 2 FLR 169, per Brooke LJ, at [34].
[369] E.g. *Goddi v. Italy* (1984) 6 EHRR 457 at para. 31.
[370] *Dombo v. Beheer B V v. Netherlands* (1993) 18 EHRR 213 at para. 33.
[371] J. Masson (2002) p. 90.   [372] L. Salgo (1998).

little difficulty. The dispute is a three-cornered one between LA, child and parents. The children involved have no choice over the initiation of the application, nor any control over the process, and the outcome will materially affect their way of life, if they are taken away from home or deprived of their liberty.

No system is perfect and problems can arise, particularly if, as noted above, children's solicitors, guardians and courts fail to respect the child's party status. It is clear that during their time working on a case, many children's guardians develop a very good rapport with the children involved. Others, however, fail to develop a comprehensive understanding of their needs through their interviewing,[373] or even spend very much time with them.[374] Nor do all guardians' reports give sufficient attention to the child's wishes and feelings.[375] These findings reflect the views of Masson and Oakley who criticised the way that many children's guardians dealt with their reports,[376] only discussing the section of the report dealing with the child's own wishes, with the remainder being withheld for fear of distressing them with its contents.[377] Although there is anecdotal evidence indicating the guardians took these criticisms very seriously and adapted their practice, there is merit in Masson and Oakley's suggestion that children's party status should be given far more of a reality.[378] As noted above, children's guardians should, at the very least, explore with the children any wish they have to attend the court proceedings.[379]

These criticisms apart, it is clear that under the pre-PLO system, most guardians' work was very highly regarded by LAs and courts alike. Indeed, the guardian's knowledge of the case not uncommonly influenced the LA's preparation of its care plan.[380] It also affected the court's own handling of the LA's application, with the guardian sometimes taking a very active role in ensuring that the child's position was adequately safeguarded.[381] The courts often relied on the guardian to remedy what they believed to be the LA's own flawed assessment of the parenting qualities of the parents.[382] It is difficult to predict how the children's guardian role will be affected by the recent procedural changes introduced under the PLO.[383] Nevertheless, as MacDonald

---

[373] HMICA (2007b) paras. 3.10–3.11.   [374] Ibid. at para. 3.16.

[375] Ibid. at para. 5.5. See also Ofsted (2008b) para. 34.

[376] The report must be filed with the court and a copy served on all the parties. FPR 1991, r. 4.11A (7) and FPC (CA 1989) R 1991, r. 11A(6).

[377] J. Masson and M. Winn Oakley (1999) pp. 103–5 and J. McCausland (2000) p. 77.

[378] J. Masson and M. Winn Oakley (1999) p. 117.

[379] Family Justice Council (2008) p. 434.   [380] T. Duncan (1998) pp. 72–3.

[381] E.g. *LM (by her guardian) v. Medway Council, RM and YM* [2007] EWCA Civ 9, [2007] 1 FLR 1698: the guardian appealed against the court's direction that the child should give oral evidence in court.

[382] E.g. *Re M-H (assessment: father of half-brother)* [2006] EWCA Civ 1864, [2007] 2 FLR 1715: care order set aside on appeal; given the trial judge's view that the LA's assessment of a potential carer for the child was inadequate and flawed, he should have permitted the preparation of an independent assessment instead of relying, as he did, on the guardian's own assessment work.

[383] MOJ (2008b) and *Practice Direction: Guide to Case Management in Public Law Proceedings* [2008] 2 FLR 668.

points out, under the new arrangements, although parents are entitled to legal assistance from a very early stage in the LA's involvement,[384] children do not receive independent representation until the later issue of the LA's application.[385] During that period, collusive agreements might have been reached between the LA and parents, which have little to do with the child's best interests.[386]

There are also fears that the extremely detailed guardian's report produced for the court at the final hearing will become a thing of the past.[387] Instead guardians are required to produce various much shorter 'analyses' of the key issues much earlier in the process, combined with recommendations, possibly before they have got to know the background to the case sufficiently well.[388] Indeed, by channelling the guardian's work into the pre-proceeding preparation stage of care proceedings, the courts may lose the guardian's broader perspective gained only by following a care case through from start to finish. Furthermore, by producing a very early position statement, the children's guardian may be seen by 'each side' as having formed an established position, thereby undermining his or her ability to broker an agreement between the LA and the child's parents.[389] The absence of the traditional detailed guardian's report at the final hearing may undermine the courts' ability to consider all the issues in the case,[390] including all aspects of the child's needs, together with an assessment of any last minute changes in care. Indeed, it is sometimes only by the end of the case that children feel they know their children's guardian sufficiently well to appreciate all the issues and to express their views candidly.[391] Only time will tell whether these changes to the guardian's role will fatally and permanently damage the way in which children are represented in public law proceedings.

(D) Children seeing the judge in private

One way of providing children with an assurance that their views over legal disputes are taken seriously is for the judiciary to see and talk to them in private. Case law[392] and research[393] indicates that some children want to see the judiciary dealing with their case in order to put their views forward, and that they feel extremely frustrated if they are refused such an opportunity.[394] It is

---

[384] I.e. at the point they receive a 'letter before proceedings'.   [385] A. MacDonald (2008) pp. 39–41.
[386] Ibid. p. 43. See also concerns listed in NAGALRO (2007).
[387] Under the PLO, the children's guardian is required to provide interim analyses and recommendations throughout the preparation process. Cafcass (2007b) Standard 2.
[388] NAGALRO (2007) esp. para. 27.   [389] NAGALRO (2007) para. 26.
[390] Ibid. at paras. 29–30.   [391] Ibid. at para. 28.
[392] E.g. Re S (a minor) (independent representation) [1993] 3 All ER 36 and Re R (a minor) (residence: religion) [1993] 2 FLR 163.
[393] M. Ruegger (2001) p. 41; G. Douglas et al. (2006) paras. 3.7 and 3.56.
[394] H. Stephens (1994) p. 908: Stephens (S's father in Re S (a minor) (independent representation) [1993] 3 All ER 36) criticised the trial judge's refusal to meet S to discuss his views and called for a practice direction requiring judges to interview all children who wish to speak to them.

well established that High Court and county court judges are entitled to see children in the privacy of their chambers despite there being no practice direction or, indeed, any specific rules on the matter.[395] Whilst the senior judiciary can see children privately if they wish, there has been some doubt over whether magistrates should do so.[396] It is difficult to understand why the senior judiciary should maintain the right to talk to children, whilst asserting that magistrates should not.

It has always been acknowledged that a judge can decide for himself whether he should see a child in private.[397] Whether this practice should become more commonplace is, however, becoming an increasingly controversial question, with members of the judiciary adopting opposing positions.[398] There is certainly a growing view that it should become more standard practice,[399] with some even arguing that a private discussion with the judge can be seen as an alternative to the child being separately represented or a welfare report being prepared by a Cafcass officer.[400] But there are good grounds for caution.[401] In the first place, whilst in many cases it might be acceptable for judges to see children in private in public law proceedings,[402] the fact that a judge cannot promise confidentiality to the children is particularly problematic in private law proceedings, since he must pass on any relevant information to each parent.[403] Indeed, it is arguable that the rules of natural justice, as reflected in the requirements of Article 6(1) of the ECHR, require the parents to be given this information and an opportunity to address

---

[395] *Re M (child)* [1993] 2 FLR 706, per Booth J, at 709.

[396] Ibid. at 710: magistrates should only see the child 'in rare and exceptional cases', particularly if the court welfare officer or guardian ad litem has already done so and reported to the court on the child's wishes.

[397] Per Ormrod LJ in *D v. D (custody of child)* (1981) 2 FLR 74.

[398] E.g. in *Re W (leave to remove)* [2008] EWCA Civ 538, [2008] 2 FLR 1170, Thorpe LJ, at [33] enthusiastically promotes this practice, considering it 'regrettable' that the trial judge had not met the children. Cf. Wilson LJ, at [57] disagrees, urging that the judiciary should not feel obliged to meet children in private more frequently than hitherto. See also Charles J, at [59], who did not consider that a private meeting between the trial judge and the children would have been appropriate.

[399] Inter alia: B. Hale (2004) pp. 6–10; M. Potter (2005); M. Potter (2006); N. Crichton (2006a) and (2006b), F. Raitt (2007); Family Justice Council (2008).

[400] *Re W (leave to remove)* [2008] EWCA Civ 538, [2008] 2 FLR 1170, per Thorpe LJ, at [33]. See also *Re D (a child) (abduction : rights of custody)*, per Baroness Hale of Richmond, at [60], albeit in the context of international abduction cases, discussed further above.

[401] L. Davis (2007), R. Hunter (2007) and N. Wilson (2007).

[402] E.g. *Re M (minors) (care proceedings: child's wishes)* [1994] 1 FLR 749, per Wall J, at 755: an intelligent and articulate 12-year-old with 'an excellent grasp of the issues' was 'entitled to see the judge who was to decide his future', but with the warning that his wishes could not be followed if they were not considered to be in his best interests.

[403] *B v. B (minors) (interviews and listing arrangements)* [1994] 2 FLR 489, per Wall J, at 495: there was an inherent contradiction in seeing the children for the purpose of ascertaining their wishes, whilst at the same time being obliged to report to the parents anything material they said.

the judge on it.[404] But even then there is an element of unfairness, unless the information provided by the child could be tested subsequently in cross-examination, an unlikely scenario.[405]

Not surprisingly, having been informed by the judge of his obligation to pass relevant information on to the parents, some children apparently then feel quite unable to provide the judge with any frank view of their wishes regarding which parent they most want to live with.[406] Nevertheless, over-coming children's concerns over their parents learning their views would not resolve matters. However tactfully children are interviewed, they are often very aware of the importance placed on their views and researchers point out the dangers of making them the final arbiters of highly conflicted parental disputes.[407] There is, of course, no obligation on the judge to take account of their wishes. In any event, unlike Thorpe LJ,[408] the Family Justice Council does not consider that the judge's conversation with the child should be seen as an alternative to the work of the Cafcass officer 'save in exceptional circumstances'[409] But if all agree that this is not the judge's task and that children's views may not influence the judge's final decision, what are the aims of their private conversation?[410] It is claimed that seeing the judge who reaches the decision empowers the child.[411] One wonders why this should be the case, given the chances that the decision will not fulfil the child's wishes?[412] Hunter suggests that there are real doubts about whether all such interviews really benefit the children or the judiciary. Children may feel bullied by the judge voicing his own views and the judge may jump to the wrong conclusions.[413] Indeed, as Hunter points out, without extensive and well-structured training, it may be extremely difficult for members of the judiciary to pick up the nuances underlying children's expressed views in a very short interview, however sympatheti-cally carried out.[414]

---

[404] Ibid., per Wall J, at 496.

[405] When discussing the draft court rules prepared under the CA 1989, the Home Office and the Department of Health voiced this concern. See also L. Davis (2007) pp. 66–7.

[406] *B v. B (minors) (interviews and listing arrangements)* [1994] 2 FLR 489, per Wall J, at 495.

[407] L. Trinder *et al.* (2006) pp. 97–8.

[408] *Re W (leave to remove)* [2008] EWCA Civ 538, [2008] 2 FLR 1170, at [33].

[409] Family Justice Council (2008) p. 433.

[410] L. Davis (2007) pp. 66–7.   [411] N. Crichton (2006a) p. 171.

[412] E.g. *Re R (a minor) (residence: religion)* [1993] 2 FLR 163: per Purchas LJ (at 174), who indicated that since the judge at first instance had been perfectly aware of the 9-year-old child's views, transmitted to the court by the court welfare officer, to interview him would have been 'totally counter-productive'; *H v. F (refusal of leave to remove a child from the jurisdiction)* [2005] EWHC 2705 (Fam), [2006] 1 FLR 776: mother's relocation application refused. Per J Richardson QC, his conversation in private with her 9-year-old son ranged over 29 points – the boy's views, including his wish to relocate with his mother to Jamaica, were 'welcome, interesting and valuable but not decisive' (at [53]).

[413] R. Hunter (2007) pp. 290–8.   [414] Ibid. at pp 294–5.

Hopefully the questions raised by Charles J in *Re W (leave to remove)*[415] will be fully debated before any formal guidance is issued urging the judiciary to consider meeting children privately more often before they reach their decisions. As he points out, clarification is required on the following: the meeting's format, structure, content and purpose; the judge's role; the involvement of others in the meeting; what information is to be passed on to others not present or represented at the meeting; how matters asserted by child to the judge are to be tested; whether anything not passed to the parties can be taken into account by the judge; what explanation is to be given to the child before and after the meeting.

(5) Conclusion

This chapter assesses the extent to which the legal system helps children cope with family disputes which may end up in court. The demands of Article 12 of the CRC are relatively simple. Children should be consulted over decisions reached regarding their future upbringing. But the extent to which domestic law fulfils this ideal is extremely variable. Although we know that many children whose parents separate and divorce suffer considerable psychological distress, large numbers are left entirely to their own devices. Indeed, the pressure imposed on separating parents to settle their disputes out of court often reinforces their children's isolation, ensuring that outsiders are kept totally unaware of their unhappiness and helplessness, with plans for their upbringing being made over their heads. Meanwhile, the various groups of practitioners called in to assist parents sort out their affairs on separation and divorce all dodge responsibility for supporting and counselling the children whose futures are being decided. Whilst Cafcass might have plugged this particular gap, the government has been reluctant to give it sufficient resources to become well founded, far less to initiate a support service for the adults and children caught up in acrimonious battles.

For the children who become the focus of litigation of varying kinds, the contrast between provision for children involved in public law proceedings and those who are the subject of private parental litigation has started diminishing. Nevertheless, whilst the first group is served by a system of representation widely considered to be ideal, the second group remain lucky to be represented at all. Finally, at the other end of the spectrum, mature children are empowered to litigate on their own behalf, as if they were adults, irrespective of the damage that doing so may have on their relationships with members of their families. Overall, the incoherence in the law and procedures gives the impression that children's well-being is not particularly high on the policy-makers' agenda.

---

[415] [2008] EWCA Civ 538, [2008] 2 FLR 1170, at [61].

BIBLIOGRAPHY

NB many of these publications can be obtained on the relevant organisation's website.

Bellamy, C. (2006) 'Rule 9.5: Further Reflections' 36 *Family Law* 298.

Beaton, P. (2004) 'Brussels II – The Sequel' 34 *Family Law* 170.

Buchanan, A., Hunt, J., Bretherton, H. and Bream, V. (2001) *Families in Conflict: Perspectives of Children and Parents on the Family Court Welfare Service*, The Policy Press.

Butler, I., Scanlan, L., Robinson, M., Douglas, G. and Murch, M. (2003) *Divorcing Children: Children's Experience of Their Parents' Divorce*, Jessica Kingsley Publishers.

Children Act Sub-Committee of the Advisory Board on Family Law (1999) *Second Annual Report 1998/99*, Lord Chancellor's Department.

Children Act Sub-Committee of the Advisory Board on Family Law (2002) *Making Contact Work* Report of the Children Act Sub-Committee, Lord Chancellor's Department.

Children and Family Court Advisory Support Service (Cafcass) (2005a) *Every Day Matters: New Directions for CAFCASS: A Consultation Paper on a New Professional and Organizational Strategy*, Cafcass.

Children and Family Court Advisory Support Service (Cafcass) (2005b) *Domestic Violence Policy and Standards*, Cafcass.

Children and Family Court Advisory Support Service (Cafcass) (2007a) *Responding to the Challenges in Private Law: The Key Steps of Cafcass Intervention*, Cafcass.

Children and Family Court Advisory Support Service (Cafcass) (2007b) *Cafcass National Standards* June 2007, Cafcass.

Children and Family Court Advisory Support Service (Cafcass) (2007c) *Cafcass Summary of Early Intervention and Identification of Key Issues*, Cafcass.

Children and Family Court Advisory Support Service (Cafcass) (2007d) *Annual Report and Accounts 2006–2007*, Cafcass.

Children and Family Court Advisory Support Service (Cafcass) (2008) *Annual Report and Accounts 2007–2008*, Cafcass.

Committee on the Rights of the Child (2002) *Concluding Observations of the Committee on the Rights of the Child: United Kingdom of Great Britain and Northern Ireland* CRC/C/15/Add 188, Centre for Human Rights, Geneva.

Council of Europe (1997) *Explanatory Report to the European Convention on the Exercise of Children's Rights*, Council of Europe Publishing.

Craig, J. (Chair) (2007a), The Family Justice Council's Report and Recommendations to the President of the Family Division, *'Everybody's Business' – How Applications for Contact Orders by Consent Should be Approached by the Court in Cases Involving Domestic Violence*.

Craig, J. (2007b) 'Everybody's Business: Applications for Contact Orders by Consent' 37 *Family Law* 26.

Crichton, N. (2006a) 'Children's Involvement in Court' 36 *Family Law* 170.
    (2006b) 'Listening to Children' 36 *Family Law* 849.

Davies, R. and Mason, S. (2007) 'NYAS: The Voice and Ears of the Child' 37 *Family Law* 1095.

Davis, G. Bevan, G., Dingwall, R., Finch, S., Fitzgerald, R. and James, A. (2000) *Monitoring Publicly Funded Family Mediation: Report to the Legal Services Commission* Legal Services Commission.

Davis, L. (2007) 'Children in Court' 37 *Family Law* 65.

Day Sclater, S. and Piper, C. (2001) 'Social Exclusion and the Welfare of the Child' 28 *Journal of Law and Society* 409.

Department for Constitutional Affairs (DCA) (2006) *Separate Representation of Children: Consultation Paper*, CP/2O/06, DCA.

Department for Constitutional Affairs/Department for Education and Skills/ Department for Trade and Industry (DCA/DfES/DTI) (2004) Cm 6273, *Parental Separation: Children's Needs and Parents' Responsibilities*, TSO.

Department for Constitutional Affairs/Department for Education and Skills/ Department for Trade and Industry (DCA/DfES/DTI) (2005) Cm 6452, *Parental Separation: Children's Needs and Parents' Responsibilities: Next Steps*, TSO.

Department for Education and Skills (DfES) (2006) *Parenting Plans: Putting your Children First: A Guide for Separating Parents*, DfES.

Department of Health (DH), Home Office, Lord Chancellor's Department and the Welsh Office (DH et al) (1998) *Support Services in Family Proceedings – Future Organisation of Court Welfare Services* Consultation Paper, LASSL (98) 11, Department of Health Publications.

Diduck, A. (2003) *Law's Families*, LexisNexis Butterworths.

Diduck, A. and Kaganas, F. (2006) *Family Law, Gender and the State*, Hart Publishing.

Doughty, J. (2006) 'CAFCASS Moves to Private Law' 36 *Family Law* 36.

(2008) 'From Court Missionaries to Conflict Resolution : A Century of Family Court Welfare' 20 *Child and Family Law Quarterly* 131.

Douglas, G., Murch, M., Scanlan, L. and Perry, A. (2000) 'Safeguarding Children's Welfare in Non-Contentious Divorce: Towards a New Conception of the Legal Process?' 63 *Modern Law Review* 177.

Douglas, G., Murch, M., Miles, C. and Scanlan, L. (2006) *Research into the Operation of Rule 9.5 of the Family Proceedings Rules 1991*, Final Report to the Department of Constitutional Affairs, DCA.

Duncan, T. (1998) 'Guardians and Care Plans: Cutting Through the Conflict' in Thorpe LJ and Clarke, E. (eds.) *Divided Duties: Care Planning for Children Within the Family Justice System*, Family Law.

Emery, R., Otto, R. and O'Donohue, W. (2005) 'A Critical Assessment of Child Custody Evaluations: Limited Science and a Flawed System' 6 *Psychological Science in the Public Interest* 1.

Family Justice Council Voice of the Child Sub-Group (2008) 'Enhancing the Participation of Children and Young People in Family Proceedings: Starting the Debate' 38 *Family Law* 431.

Fortin, J., Ritchie, C. and Buchanan, A. (2006) 'Young adults' perceptions of court-ordered contact' 18 *Child and Family Law Quarterly* 211.

Fortin, J. (2006) 'Accommodating Children's Rights in a Post HRA Era' 69 *Modern Law Review* 299.

Fortin, J. (2007) 'Children's Representation Through the Looking Glass' 37 *Family Law* 500.

Gee, I. (1999) 'Tales of the Unexpected – A Child's Perspective on a Family Breakup' 29 *Family Law* 49.

Greatbatch, D. and Dingwall, R. (1999) 'The Marginalization of Domestic Violence in Divorce Mediation' 13 *International Journal of Law, Policy and the Family* 174.

Greenall, E. (2005) *Children in Mediation: A Review of Current UK Practice within the National Family Mediation Network*, National Family Mediation.

HM Inspectorate of Court Administration (HMICA) (2005a) *Domestic Violence, Safety and Family Proceedings: Thematic Review of the Handling of Domestic Violence Issues by the Children and Family Court Advisory and Support Service (CAFCASS) and the Administration of Family Courts in Her Majesty's Courts Service (HMCS)*, HMICA.

HM Inspectorate of Court Administration (HMICA) (2005b) *Safeguarding Children in Family Proceedings*, HMICA.

HM Inspectorate of Court Administration (HMICA) (2006) *An Inspection Undertaken Between October 2005 and March 2006 of the Children and Family Court Advisory and Support Service (CAFCASS) Concerning Private Law Front-Line Practice*, HMICA.

HM Inspectorate of Court Administration (HMICA) (2007a) *Assisting Families by Court Order*, HMICA.

HM Inspectorate of Court Administration (HMICA) (2007b) *Children's Guardians and Care Proceedings*, HMICA.

HM Magistrates' Courts Service Inspectorate (2003) *Seeking Agreement: Children and Family Court Advisory and Support Service (CAFCASS)*, DCA.

Hale, Dame Brenda (2004) 'It's My Life You're Practising With' 30 *Newsletter of the Association of Lawyers for Children*.

Harold, G. and Murch, M. (2005) 'Inter-parental conflict and Children's Adaptation to Separation and Divorce: Theory, Research and Implications for Family Law, Practice and Policy' 17 *Child and Family Law Quarterly* 185.

Hawthorne, J., Jessop, J., Pryor, J. and Richards, M. (2003) *Supporting Children Through Family Change*, Joseph Rowntree Foundation.

Hodgkin, R. and Newell, P. (eds.) (2007) *Implementation Handbook for the Convention on the Rights of the Child*, UNICEF.

Hunt, J. and Macleod, A. (2008) *Outcomes of Applications to Court for Contact Orders After Parental Separation or Divorce*, MOJ.

Hunter, R. (2007) 'Close Encounters of a Judicial Kind; Hearing Children's "Voices" in Family Law Proceedings' 19 *Child and Family Law Quarterly* 283.

James, A. (2003) 'Squaring the Circle – The Social, Legal and Welfare Organisation of Contact' in Bainham, A., Lindley, B., Richards, M. and Trinder, L. (eds.) *Children and Their Families: Contact, Rights and Welfare*, Hart Publishing.

James, A., James, A. and McNamee, S. (2004) 'Turn Down the Volume? – Not Hearing Children in Family Proceedings' 16 *Child and Family Law Quarterly* 189.

James, A., Jenks, C. and Prout, A. (1998) *Theorizing Childhood*, Polity Press.

Kaganas, F. and Diduck, A. (2004) 'Incomplete Citizens: Changing Images of Post-Separation Children' 67 *Modern Law Review* 959.

Killerby, M. (1995) Directorate of Legal Affairs, Council of Europe, 'The Draft European Convention on the Exercise of Children's Rights' 3 *International Journal on Children's Rights* 127.

King, M. and Piper, C. (1995) *How the Law Thinks About Children*, Arena.

Law Commission (1988) *Review of Child Law, Guardianship and Custody* Law Com No. 172, HC 594, HMSO.

Legal Services Commission (2007) *Legal Aid Reform: Family and Family Mediation Fee Schemes for October 2007, Consultation Response*, Community Legal Service.

Lord Chancellor's Department (LCD) (2002) *Government's Response to the Report of the Children Act Sub-Committee of the Lord Chancellor's Advisory Board on Family Law 'Making Contact Work'*, LCD.

MacDonald, A. (2008) 'The Voice of the Child – Still a Faint Cry?' 18 *Seen and Heard* 36.

Mantle, G., Moules, T. and Johnson, K. (2006) 'Whose Wishes and Feelings? Children's Autonomy and Parental Influence in Family Court Enquiries' *British Journal of Social Work* Advance Access published 17 May 2006, doi: 10.1093/bjsw/bcl035.

McCausland, J. (2000) *Guarding Children's Interests: The Contribution of Guardians ad Litem in Court Proceedings*, The Children's Society.

Masson, J. (2002) '*Re K (A Child) (Secure Accommodation Order: Right to Liberty) and Re C (Secure Accommodation Order: Representation)* Securing Human Rights for Children and Young People in Secure Accommodation' 14 *Child and Family Law Quarterly* 77.

(2006) 'Consent Orders in Contact Cases: A Survey of Resolution Members' 36 *Family Law* 1041.

Masson, J. and Winn Oakley, M. (1999) *Out of Hearing: Representing Children in Care Proceedings*, John Wiley and Sons.

Ministry of Justice (MOJ) (2007) *Separate Representation of Children: Summary of Responses to Consultation Paper*, CP (R) 20/06, MOJ.

Ministry of Justice (MOJ) (2008a) Cm 7502 *Family Justice in View*, The Stationery Office.

Ministry of Justice (MOJ) (2008b) *The Public Law Outline: Guide to Case Management in Public Law Proceedings*, MOJ.

Munby, J. (2004) 'Making Sure the Child is Heard: Part 2 – Representation' 34 *Family Law* 427.

Murch, M., Douglas, G., Scanlan, L., Perry, A., Lisles, C., Bader, K. and Borkowski, M. (1999) *Safeguarding Children's Welfare in Uncontentious Divorce: A Study of s 41 of the Matrimonial Causes Act 1973* Research Series No 7/99, Lord Chancellor's Department.

National Family Mediation (2005) *Direct Support Services to Children: Listening to Young People – Child Inclusive Mediation in NFM Services*, Information Pack, NFM.

Nagalro (2007) *NAGALRO Response to the Draft Public Law Outline*, Nagalro Council.

Office for National Statistics (2008) *Social Trends No 38*, Palgrave Macmillan.

Ofsted (2008a) *Ofsted's Inspection of Cafcass South East Region*, Ofsted.

Ofsted (2008b) *Ofsted's Inspection of Cafcass East Midlands*, Ofsted.

O'Quigley, A. (2000) *Listening to Children's Views: the Findings and Recommendations of Recent Research*, Joseph Rowntree Foundation.

Parkinson, L. (2006) 'Child-inclusive Family Mediation' *Family Law* 483.

Piper, C. (1997) 'Ascertaining the Wishes and Feelings of the Child' 27 *Family Law* 796.

Piper, C. (1999) 'Barriers to Seeing and Hearing Children in Private Law Proceedings' 29 *Family Law* 394.

Potter Sir Mark (2005) Unpublished speech to the Children Law UK Conference.
(2006) Unpublished speech to the UK Association of Women Judges.

Pryor, J. and Rodgers, B. (2001) *Children in Changing Families: Life after Parental Separation*, Blackwell Publishers.

Raitt, F. (2007) 'Hearing Children in Family Law Proceedings: Can Judges Make a Difference?' 19 *Child and Family Law Quarterly* 204.

Richards, M. (1995) 'But What About the Children? Some Reflections on the Divorce White Paper' 7 *Child and Family Law Quarterly* 223.

Roche, J. (1999) 'Children and Divorce: A Private Affair?' in Day Sclater. S, and Piper, C. (eds.) *Undercurrents of Divorce*, Ashgate.

Ruegger, M. (2001) 'Children's Experiences of the Guardian ad litem Service and Public Law Proceedings' in Ruegger, M. (ed.) *Hearing the Voice of the Child: the Representation of Children's Interests in Public Law Proceedings*, Russell House Publishing.

Salgo, L. (1998) 'Representing Children in Civil Proceedings – Lessons From a Comparative Study of the Systems Operating in the USA, Australia, France, Germany and England and Wales' *Representing Children* 225.

Saunders, H. (2004) *Twenty-nine Child Homicides: Lessons Still to be Learnt on Domestic Violence and Child Protection*, Women's Aid Federation of England.

Sawyer, C. (1995) *The Rise and Fall of the Third Party: Solicitors' Assessments of the Competence of Children to Participate in Family Proceedings*, Centre for Socio-Legal Studies.
(1999) 'One step forward, two steps back – the European Convention on the Exercise of Children's Rights' 11 *Child and Family Law Quarterly* 151.
(2000) 'An Inside Story: Professional Practices in Public Law' 30 *Family Law* 109.

Schuz, R. (2004) 'The Hague Child Abduction Convention and the United Nations Convention on the Rights of the Child' in Lødrup, P. and Modvar, E. (eds.) *Family Life and Human Rights*, Gyldendal.
(2008) 'In Search of a Settled Interpretation of Article 12(2) of the Hague Child Abduction Convention' 20 *Child and Family Law Quarterly* 64.

Smart, C., Neale, B. and Wade, A. (2001) *The Changing Experience of Childhood: Families and Divorce*, Polity Press.
(2006) 'Children's Narratives of Post-Divorce Family Life: From Individual Experience to an Ethical Disposition' *The Sociological Review* 155.

Smith, A., Taylor, N. and Tapp, P. (2003) 'Rethinking Children's Involvement in Decision-Making after Parental Separation' 10 *Childhood* 201.

Solicitors Family Law Association (2002) *Guide to Good Practice for Solicitors Acting For Children*, SFLA.

Stephens, H. (1994) 'Independent Representation' 144 *New Law Journal* 907.

Timms, J. and Thoburn, J. (2003) *Your Shout*, NSPCC.

Thorpe J (1994) 'Independent Representation for Children' 24 *Family Law* 20.

Trinder, L., Connolly, J., Kellett, J., Notley, C. and Swift, L. (2006) *Making Contact Happen or Making Contact Work? The Process and Outcomes of In-court Conciliation*, DCA Research Series 3/06, DCA.

Wade, A. and Smart, C. (2002) *Facing Family Change: Children's Circumstances, Strategies and Resources*, Joseph Rowntree Foundation.

Wall, N. (2006) *A Report to the President of the Family Division on the Publication by the Women's Aid Federation of England Entitled "Twenty-nine child homicides: Lessons still to be learnt on domestic violence and child protection" with particular reference to the five cases in which there was judicial involvement.*

(2007) 'Separate Representation of Children' 37 *Family Law* 124.

Walker, J. (2004) 'FAInS – A New Approach for Family Lawyers?' 34 *Family Law* 436.

Wilson, N. (2007) 'The Ears of the Child in Family Proceedings' 37 *Family Law* 808.

Whybrow, J. (2004) 'Children, Guardians and Rule 9.5' 34 *Family Law* 504.

Chapter 8

Children in court – their welfare, wishes and feelings

(1) Introduction

Section 1 of the Children Act (CA) 1989 requires the courts to reach decisions over children's upbringing, by giving the children's welfare their paramount consideration – a provision often described as the 'paramountcy principle'.[1] But when deciding what is in the child's welfare or best interests, the courts are directed to consider 'the ascertainable wishes and feelings of the child concerned (considered in the light of his age and understanding)'.[2] This direction accommodates the fact that children may have a better grasp of their own needs than adults. Indeed, it promotes a diluted form of the notion of autonomy by implying that a mature child's best interests may be fulfilled most effectively by the court acceding to his or her own wishes. Furthermore, its inclusion in the welfare checklist reflects a conviction that 'the increasing recognition given both in practice and in law to the child's status as a human being in his own right' should also be matched by the courts, when hearing disputes over children.[3] Whether the direction is realistic depends on children having an effective means of conveying their views to the court – not all are provided with such a facility.[4] Despite its importance, demonstrated by its foremost position in the 'welfare checklist',[5] the courts are expected to achieve a result which most accords with adult notions of children's best interests, whether or not it accords with their wishes. The overtly paternalistic welfare principle clearly justifies a court discounting information about children's views if it considers that they lack insight into their own needs. It can rely on a wealth of other factors in the welfare checklist to substantiate its decision. These principles appear to be perfectly reasonable. Children have a minor status and the final decision quite rightly remains with the court, taking account not only of a child's interest in choice but also his or her right to protection from the risk of future harm. Consulting children is very different from delegating the decision-making process to them entirely before they reach

---

[1] The terms 'paramountcy principle', 'welfare principle' and 'best interests test' are often used interchangeably.
[2] CA 1989, s. 1(3)(a).   [3] Law Commission (1988) para. 3.24.   [4] Discussed in Chapter 7.
[5] The term commonly used to describe the list of factors contained in the CA 1989, s. 1(3).

adulthood. This is implicitly acknowledged by Article 12(1) of the Convention on the Rights of the Child (CRC).

Whilst a paternalistic interpretation of the welfare principle can certainly be justified along these lines, it also absolves the courts of blame if they reach decisions which manifestly ignore children's own views on the matter. As Eekelaar observes, the section clearly requires the courts to reach such decisions in cases where they consider that a competent child's choice contravenes their own assessment of his or her welfare. As he points out, the section could be applied in such a way as to render the child's viewpoint always irrelevant.[6] Furthermore, as discussed earlier, critics increasingly castigate the courts and family justice practitioners from a sociological viewpoint, for treating children as passive victims, rather than as individuals in their own right.[7] Thus James argues that rather than acknowledging 'an individual child's experience, agency and personhood', 'what is offered is an adult construction of what is "in the best interests of the child" that is rooted in adult concepts defining the nature of childhood'.[8] Whilst such views are attractive, it would be folly to ignore children's vulnerability and need for adult assistance, especially when caught up in parental litigation.[9] Furthermore, such criticisms may not be entirely fair. As discussed below, case law suggests that the judiciary are becoming far more aware that when the final decision accords with children's own wishes, children's own self-respect is left intact – but that children may feel confused and vulnerable if the judiciary appear to ignore their strongly voiced views about the outcome.

There would, of course, be less scope for criticism if the courts showed greater clarity over the extent to which they should take account of children's wishes. An absence of clarity is hardly surprising, in view of the doubts attending the interpretation of the welfare principle itself. Before considering the weight given to children's wishes and feelings in litigation concerning them, this chapter briefly assesses the efficacy of the welfare principle, given the need to comply with the demands of the European Convention for the Protection of Human Rights and Fundamental Freedoms (1950) (ECHR). The case law is diffuse and so this chapter does not attempt to review the cases where the courts appear to take particular account of children's wishes or to ignore them. Instead, it proceeds to discuss the complex interplay between children's age, their capacity, the type of dispute and the risks involved in acceding to or ignoring their views. It then discusses briefly three problem areas involving particularly complex issues: child abduction; a child's hostility to the non-resident parent; and child abuse.

(2) The welfare principle – a reassessment

Many authors have questioned the utility of the 'best interests' or 'welfare principle'. Whilst it is arguable that the principle's innate strength lies in its

[6] J. Eekelaar (2006) p. 158.   [7] Discussed in Chapter 7.
[8] A. James (2003) p. 145. See also A. James et al. (2004) pp. 197–200.   [9] Discussed in Chapter 7.

flexibility,[10] a constant source of criticism is its extreme indeterminacy.[11] Although the welfare checklist is designed to ensure a measure of consistency, as Eekelaar says:

> the heavily subjective nature of the power granted to the judge means that, so long as he does not claim to be applying it as a conclusive rule of law, a judge can consider almost any factor which could possibly have a bearing on a child's welfare and assign to it whatever weight he or she chooses.[12]

A frequent criticism has been that the innate vagueness of the welfare principle allows the judiciary to dress up adult-related concerns under the guise of promoting children's welfare. Some critics point to the dangers of the parents' position being undermined by this slightly underhand process. Reece, for example, refers to the courts' denigration of homosexual parents' ability to care for their children, whilst asserting a concern for their children's welfare.[13]

The Human Rights Act (HRA) 1998 provoked fresh calls to reassess the welfare principle, more particularly the paramountcy principle, as set out in the CA 1989, section 1. Given the protection Article 8 ECHR provides for family life, its coexistence with section 1 has received much attention. As Herring has pointed out, contrary to Lord Oliver's view in *Re KD (a minor) (ward: termination of access)*,[14] the demands of section 1 of the CA 1989 are very different, in evidential terms, from those of Article 8.[15] There is a significant difference between starting from the premise that a parent's rights must not be infringed *unless* the court can fulfil the detailed requirements of Article 8(2) and starting from the premise that the outcome of the dispute must be determined by the child's best interests, and *then* considering the rights of the parties involved. But as observed elsewhere, it was unlikely that the latter, pre-HRA approach, considered to underpin the whole of child law, would be given up without a judicial fight.[16] The family judiciary found their way round this conundrum by developing the idea that by fulfilling the direction in section 1 of the CA 1989, the courts would automatically fulfil the requirements of Article 8 ECHR and that therefore the courts need not justify the orders they make by reference to the Convention.[17] This approach culminated with the influential judgment of Lord Nicholls of Birkenhead in *Re B*.[18] He stated firmly that the balancing exercise required by Article 8 of the Convention does not differ in substance from that undertaken by the courts when deciding whether a particular order is in the child's best interests.[19] In his view, despite the differing phraseology, the criteria to be applied when deciding whether an order is justified under Article 8

---

[10] J. Herring (2005) p. 161.

[11] Inter alia: R. Mnookin (1975); M. Fineman (1988); S. Parker (1994); H. Reece (1996).

[12] J. Eekelaar (1991) p. 125.   [13] H. Reece (1996) p. 303. See also J. Eekelaar (2002) p. 242.

[14] [1988] AC 806.   [15] J. Herring (1999) p. 231.   [16] J. Fortin (2004) p. 268.

[17] *Payne v. Payne* [2001] EWCA Civ 166, [2001] 1 FLR 1052, per Thorpe LJ, at paras. 38–9; *Re H (contact order)(No. 2)* [2002] 1 FLR 22, per Wall J, at para. 59.

[18] *Re B (a child) (adoption by one natural parent)* [2001] UKHL 70, [2002] 1 All ER 641.

[19] Ibid. at para. 31.

(2) leads to the same result as the existing tests applied under English law. Thus the courts can behave as if the HRA had made no difference at all to their existing decision-making in parental disputes involving children. The welfare principle still pre-empts every other process in children's cases – in other words, *status quo ante bellum*. Little wonder then that many reported family law cases now make no mention of adults' rights under the ECHR, let alone those of children. Furthermore, this current approach to private parental disputes encourages the family courts to concentrate on establishing issues of fact, before deciding how best to fulfil the child's best interests – as a matter for judicial discretion.[20] As John Eekelaar points out:

> the very ease of the welfare test encourages a laziness and unwillingness to pay proper attention to all the interests that are at stake in these decisions and, possibly, also a tendency to abdicate responsibility for decision making to welfare professionals.[21]

Many writers have condemned the way in which the family judiciary currently ignore the requirements of Article 8 ECHR.[22] As Harris-Short observes,[23] it effectively deters the family courts from following the detailed requirements of Article 8(2). In particular, it assumes that the principle of proportionality is automatically fulfilled.[24] The validity of her comments can be seen when one applies Lord Nicholls' approach in *Re B* to the average contact dispute. It is unlikely that the lower courts, when following his guidance, will feel obliged to consider whether an infringement of the father's contact rights is 'necessary' under Article 8(2). Nor need they carefully assess whether, if the court chooses to fulfil the father's rights, the damage suffered by the mother, and/or the child, will be greater than is strictly necessary in the circumstances. They must merely decide whether the outcome sought by the father will fulfil the child's best interests better than that desired by the mother – just as they did before the enactment of the HRA. As before, any arguments relating to the child's own position become part of a factual discussion revolving around what outcome might most suitably accommodate his or her best interests.

Persuading the family judiciary to adopt a more rigorous approach to squaring the requirements of Article 8 ECHR with those of section 1 of the CA 1989 is hampered by the example provided by the European Court of

---

[20] E.g. inter alia: *Re C (welfare of child: immunisation)* [2003] EWHC 1376 (Fam), [2003] 2 FLR 1054, per Sumner J, at paras. 27–200: a lengthy discussion of the expert medical evidence on various kinds of immunisation, with a passing reference (at para. 327) to 'the rights of both parents and children'; *Re S (specific issue order: religion: circumcision)* [2004] EWHC 1282 (Fam), [2005] 1 FLR 236, paras. 6–24 and appendix 1, per Baron J: considered with expert assistance, the detailed differences between Hindu Jainism and Islam, with no reference to the children's potential rights under the ECHR.

[21] J. Eekelaar (2002) p. 248.

[22] See inter alia: S. Harris-Short (2002) pp. 336–8; S. Choudhry (2003) pp. 128–36; D. Bonner *et al.* (2003) pp. 575–84; J. Fortin (2004) pp. 267–9; S. Choudhry and H. Fenwick (2005) pp. 462–9.

[23] S. Harris-Short (2002) pp. 336–8.   [24] Ibid. at p. 338.

Human Rights (ECtHR) itself.[25] As discussed earlier, the ECtHR has done its best to make up for the fact that there is no 'best interests' formula in the Convention, more particularly in the wording of Article 8. It has emphasised time and again the importance of the child's interests in disputes over children.[26] But despite its efforts, it fails to articulate children's own rights under the ECHR,[27] whilst remaining loyal to the need to balance one set of rights against the other, with no initial presumption favouring the child's interests. Indeed, as Eekelaar points out, a strict adherence to the wording of Article 8(2) risks placing the child's interests too low in the hierarchy of interests.[28] This view is borne out by decisions like *Elsholz v. Germany*,[29] where although the child's welfare may indicate one outcome, on a narrow reading of the 'necessity' of so doing, the ECtHR feels unable to infringe the adult's rights in order to achieve that outcome.

Considering this Strasbourg case law, the domestic judiciary might feel justifiably nervous of exposing children to the risk of losing the protection of the paramountcy principle in order to protect the rights of one or other of the adults in the case.[30] Nor would they necessarily feel particularly attracted by Fenwick's argument that in order to accord with the requirements of the ECHR, the paramountcy principle must itself be reinterpreted, or 'read down', with children's best interests being regarded as a 'primary', but not a paramount consideration.[31] There are three ways of answering this problem. The first is to point out that there is plenty of Strasbourg case law where the child's best interests have been allowed to outweigh those of his or her parents.[32] The second is to stress that the ECtHR is not particularly consistent in its approach to children's cases and need not be followed slavishly. The third is to follow the advice of various writers and start quantifying the child's position in terms of his or her own Convention rights, as opposed to his or her best interests.[33] As discussed earlier, the ECtHR has been noticeably reticent in the way it has considered the interplay between children's rights and parents' rights.[34] If it had been more willing to acknowledge that children themselves have rights of their own under Article 8, the Court might not have produced decisions like *Elsholz*.

An articulation of children's Convention rights by the family judiciary is long overdue. Indeed, the judiciary seem far less reluctant to address the demands of the ECHR in other fields of law, perhaps because these challenges often involve children as the main players, rather than as incidental to parental disputes.[35] Challenges in other fields of law rarely involve matters involving the child's

---

[25] J. Fortin (2004) p. 269.   [26] See Chapter 2.   [27] See Chapter 2.   [28] J. Eekelaar (2002) p. 241.
[29] [2000] 2 FLR 486. See also *Görgülü v. Germany* [2004] 1 FLR 894; both discussed in Chapter 2.
[30] J. Fortin (2006) p. 309.
[31] H. Fenwick (2004) p. 916. See also S. Choudhry and H. Fenwick (2005) pp. 479–81.
[32] See Chapter 2.
[33] A. Bainham (2002) pp. 288–9; J. Eekelaar (2002) pp. 241–2; J. Fortin (2004) p. 271; S. Choudhry and H. Fenwick (2005) pp. 472 and 483–6; J. Fortin (2006) pp. 305–14.
[34] See Chapter 2.   [35] J. Fortin (2006) pp. 304–5.

upbringing, so the courts are then not constrained by the paramountcy principle, as set out by CA 1989, section 1. Nevertheless, it might strengthen children's position immeasurably if in family proceedings it was argued that the rights of the adults should not be balanced against each other without considering those of the children themselves. Arguably, an articulation of children's rights, alongside those of their parents, would avoid all the evidence underpinning the relative outcomes of the dispute being vaguely categorised as 'best interests' evidence, without proper analysis. Furthermore, as explained by Lord Steyn,[36] the various rights of the adults and child would be balanced against each other, with the justifications for interfering with or restricting each right being considered[37] and the proportionality test applied – 'the ultimate balancing test'.[38]

It seems clear that this suggested new approach to children's cases holds a number of pitfalls. First, there is the danger that parents' rights simply become relabelled, as children's rights. To a degree, as Van Krieken points out, this happens already, with the child's right to contact with his or her non-resident father being aligned with the father's right to contact with his child.[39] Second, and more importantly, there is a potential degree of confusion over how the evidence relating to the child's best interests should be handled. Choudhry and Fenwick suggest that while:

> avoiding a return to the paramountcy principle as currently conceived … it should be asked whether an especially 'core' aspect of a child's private or family life is under consideration. His or her interests would be privileged within the process of reasoning described … [the balancing process].[40]

But without clearer guidance over *how* the paramountcy principle is to be avoided, this approach risks arguments about the child's rights being placed alongside arguments about his or her welfare, as if the two issues were discrete. Case law demonstrates the judiciary encountering this confusion.[41] It has been urged, however, that this course of action misconceives rights theory itself; it implies that matters pertaining to the child's welfare are outside and often opposed to matters relating to the child's rights. It also overlooks the fact that the formulations contained in the ECHR are just that – formulations of ideas about rights (sometimes awkwardly worded), which attempt to encapsulate concepts of the good life, not the bad. They should therefore be interpreted in a

---

[36] *Re S (A Child) (Identification: Restrictions on Publication)* [2004] UKHL 47, [2005] 1 AC 593, at [17].

[37] I.e. under Art. 8(2) and other similar qualifying provisions.

[38] *Re S (A Child) (Identification: Restrictions on Publication)* [2004] UKHL 47, [2005] 1 AC 593, at [17]. This balancing process is often referred to as 'the parallel analysis'. H. Fenwick (2004) p. 917 and S. Choudhry and H. Fenwick (2005) pp. 481–4.

[39] R. Van Krieken (2005) p. 36.   [40] S. Choudhry and H. Fenwick (2005) p. 485.

[41] E.g. *Leeds Teaching Hospitals NHS Trust v. A* [2003] EWHC 259 (QB), [2003] 1 FLR 1091, per Dame Elizabeth Butler-Sloss P, at [55]; discussed by J. Fortin (2006) pp. 310–12.

way which enhances children's lives, not harms them.[42] Consequently, it is urged that evidence relating to the child's welfare should be subsumed into evidence supporting his or her rights, not presented discretely.[43] A third difficulty is that an analysis of the child's rights may not be a simple process. In some cases the child has conflicting rights which must be marshalled and weighed against each other, as well as against those of the adults concerned. Whilst the feasibility of this approach is demonstrated by cases like *Re T (paternity: ordering blood tests)*,[44] the task may be a particularly difficult one in cases where adolescents are refusing life-saving medical treatment.[45] Lastly, as Bainham points out, it is impossible to predict that an articulation of children's rights, alongside those of the adults, will always produce greater certainty than the paramountcy principle[46] or that such an approach will provide children with as much protection.[47]

An articulation of children's rights, though problematic, will ensure that the courts comply with their duty under the HRA 1998 to act compatibly with the ECHR.[48] It should also produce greater transparency in judicial decision-making – a decision reached in favour of one or other adult could not be justified 'under the guise of the child's welfare'.[49] A rights perspective, involving as it does, the identification and balancing of the individual rights involved in each case, should focus judicial attention more clearly on the child's position in relation to the adults involved. In so doing, it should avoid judgments which amount to little more than a series of vague conclusions justified by reference to best interests and welfare.

(3) The interplay between welfare, wishes and feelings and age

(A) Introduction

Mnookin has pointed out that it is often unclear to a judge what questions he should be posing when trying to determine the child's best interests. Should this be considered from a short- or long-term view point? Should he be primarily concerned with the child's happiness?[50] Similar questions could be posed when weighing the impact of a child's wishes and feelings. What precise purpose is the court considering this information for in the circumstances of this case? Is it merely to reinforce the court's own decision or to provide information that may swing a finely balanced case? Was the information extracted in circumstances that indicate that the information can be relied on in the short term or the long term? What risks are involved in taking account of the child's wishes and of

---

[42] J. Fortin (2006) p. 311. I am grateful to my ex-colleague, Kenneth Campbell, for spending much time with me discussing this area of thought.
[43] Ibid. at pp. 310–13.   [44] [2001] 2 FLR 1190; discussed in Chapter 13.
[45] J. Fortin (2006) pp. 314–24.   [46] A. Bainham (2002) pp. 279 and 288.
[47] J. Fortin (2006) pp. 313–14.   [48] HRA 1998, s. 6.
[49] J. Eekelaar (2002) p. 242.   [50] R. Mnookin (1975) p. 260.

ignoring them? How should the courts treat evidence that a mother has attempted to influence her child against his or her father?

It is universally accepted that in this field of decision-making there are no 'right' answers, but judicial discretion should not be an excuse for an arbitrary approach which suggests to children that the process of seeking their views is a meaningless exercise to be completed and then forgotten. The child psychiatrists who advised the Court of Appeal on the childhood implications of contact disputes involving domestic violence had clear views about the importance of the courts respecting all children's views. They maintained that:

> it is damaging to a child to feel he or she is forced to do something against his or her will and against his or her judgment if the child cannot see the sense of it.[51]

Eekelaar has expressed some concern over the risk of the judiciary, when subjecting children to coercive paternalism, ignoring their interest in making choices in their lives and has proposed various approaches to ensure that children's views are fully considered.[52] He favours the concept of 'dynamic self-determinism' which introduces a presumption in favour of complying with children's choices as closely as possible without restricting their capacity for fulfilling their future life-goals.[53] This suggestion is useful and, if followed, might ensure that the courts paid more attention to a child's interest in choice and fulfilled the need to treat the individual child with respect. It might also ensure that the judiciary retained a measure of flexibility when confronted by a child whose strong views conflict with their own ideas about the needs of children in general.

(B) Age and its interrelationship with context and risk

Those who write critically of legal constructions of childhood strongly criticise what they see as 'a developmentally based model of childhood' rooted in 'Piaget's ideas about the "normal" stages in a child's psychological development'.[54] Nevertheless, it is surely folly to ignore the research on cognitive development indicating that children's cognitive skills differ enormously depending on their age.[55] These differences may be of crucial importance in cases involving a number of interlocking factors, some so entangled with each other that they often defy clear identification. Central to all these must be the child's age and maturity. The importance of this factor is acknowledged by the CA 1989, section 1(3)(a), which directs the courts 'to have regard to the *ascertainable* wishes and feelings of the child concerned (*considered in the light of his age and understanding*)'.[56] A court might therefore conclude, for example, that the wishes of an infant are either not reliably ascertainable or, if

---

[51] C. Sturge and D. Glaser (2000) p. 621.
[52] Eekelaar repeatedly returns to this theme in three papers: J. Eekelaar (1986), (1992) and (1994).
[53] J. Eekelaar (1994) p. 53.   [54] A. James *et al.* (2004) pp. 193–4.
[55] Discussed in Chapter 3.   [56] Emphasis supplied.

they are, they carry little weight because the child is too young to comprehend the issues. At the other end of the age spectrum, there may be little point in making court orders against the wishes of children mature enough to have strong views of their own and large enough to vote with their feet if opposed. The CA 1989 only cautiously maintains such an approach, indicating that no orders should be made regarding children over the age of 16, unless the circumstances are exceptional.[57]

Sturge and Glaser have clear views about the relevance of age, recommending that within the overall context of the child's wishes:

> the older the child the more seriously they should be viewed and the more insulting and discrediting to the child to have them ignored. As a rough rule we would see these as needing to be taken account of at any age; above 10 we see these as carrying considerable weight with 6–10 as an intermediate stage and at under 6 as often indistinguishable in many ways from the wishes of the main carer (assuming normal development).[58]

Notably, these child psychiatrists did not recommend any formal age limit similar to those adopted by some European countries such as Finland, where children over the age of 12 can veto the enforcement of court decisions concerning their custody and access.[59] Arguably, the research evidence on cognitive development supports such a cut-off point. Although there are no clear-cut rules and some children develop certain skills earlier than others, there are fundamental psychological differences between the competence of young children aged up to about 11 to 12 and that of adolescents between that age and the age of 18. Nevertheless, researchers also warn that, even at these ages, competence for decision-making will vary enormously, depending on a variety of factors, such as peer pressure and family environment.[60] There are, of course, other risks involved in giving children as young as 12 an absolute legal veto. First, it places on their shoulders the responsibility for choice for which they may not be ready. Making choices requires very different skills and maturity from those required for taking part in a consultation process. Furthermore, giving children from the age of 12 an *absolute* veto over decisions relating to their upbringing takes little account of their parents' rights, or of the balancing process required of the courts when dealing with Convention challenges. Indeed, as discussed below, in *C v. Finland*,[61] the ECtHR made clear its disapproval of children being allowed to dictate the outcome of a parental dispute.

---

[57] CA 1989, s. 9(6) and (7).   [58] C. Sturge and D. Glaser (2000) p. 624.

[59] See *K and T v. Finland* [2000] 2 FLR 79, at paras 88–9 and *C v. Finland* [2006] 2 FLR 597, at [41].

[60] See Chapter 3.   [61] [2006] 2 FLR 597, at [58]; discussed below.

Much of the judicial unease over taking account of the views of very young children centres on private law disputes and the knowledge that a young child is not only more easily subjected to the influence of others,[62] but is also vulnerable to external factors which may only have a short-term impact.[63] Many of these concerns have centred on disputed contact. In the past, well-established case law indicated that the upsets to the child caused by unwanted contact visits were usually minor and temporary and were outweighed by the long-term benefits of keeping in touch with an absent parent.[64] Indeed, the courts felt justified in making contact orders against the wishes of the children involved, unless there was 'a serious risk of major emotional harm to the child'.[65] Today, perhaps influenced by Sturge and Glaser's advice, the courts are less likely to compel even a relatively young child to have contact against his or her strongly expressed wishes.[66] In the absence of any obvious reasons underlying a relatively young child's hostility to contact, the court may consider it important to explore the child's resistance, perhaps with the help of a psychological assessment.[67] Such an approach is no longer dictated by Strasbourg case law. The Grand Chamber of the European Court soon overruled the Court's controversial decision that any child resisting contact should undergo a detailed psychological assessment or provide direct evidence in open court explaining the reasons for his resistance.[68] It is for the domestic courts to decide how to assess the facts of the case depending on the specific circumstances of each case, having regard to the child's age and maturity.[69]

Although the domestic courts are obliged to consider a child's wishes and feelings in parental disputes, child care experts consider it essential to avoid making young children feel responsible for choosing between parents, arguing that they have a right to be protected from making decisions before they are ready – indeed, they have a right to be children. Choosing can be very damaging, given that children often blame themselves for parental separation and that many feel immensely loyal to both parents.[70] Some parents even reject their children on learning, by reading the court welfare report, of their children's

---

[62] The risks of young children being indoctrinated by a residential parent are discussed below.
[63] B. Cantwell and S. Scott (1995) pp. 340–3.
[64] *Re H (minors) (access)* [1992] 1 FLR 148, per Balcombe LJ, at 153.
[65] *Re D (a minor) (contact: mother's hostility)* [1993] 2 FLR 1, per Waite LJ, at 8.
[66] J. Hunt and A. Macleod (2008) pp. 66 and 200.
[67] E.g. *Re S (contact: promoting relationship with absent parent)* [2004] EWCA Civ 18, [2004] 1 FLR 1279, per Dame Elizabeth Butler-Sloss P, at 1288–9. See also *Re M (contact: long-term best interests)* [2005] EWCA Civ 1090, [2006] 1 FLR 627. J. Hunt and A. Macleod (2008) pp. 198–9: note the importance attached by the courts to discovering the reasons for the child's opposition to contact.
[68] *Elsholz v. Germany* [2000] 2 FLR 486; *Sahin v. Germany* [2002] 1 FLR 119, *Sommerfeld v. Germany* [2002] 1 FLR 121.
[69] *Sahin v. Germany* [2003] 2 FLR 671 at [73].
[70] E.g. *B v. B (minors) (interviews and listing arrangements)* [1994] 2 FLR 489; discussed in Chapter 7.

strong criticisms of them.[71] There is also the risk of elevating the child's status within the family to a position of power. It may unnaturally skew the psycho-dynamics of the family and allow the child to play one parent off against the other.[72]

Research indicates that however carefully practitioners consult children without apparently asking them to choose, the children often consider that they *are* being asked to choose between their parents.[73] Indeed, many children are keen to have some element of choice regarding the arrangements being made for their future and, at the very least, want some involvement in the decisions reached.[74] Importantly, the research evidence about children's cognitive abilities does not indicate that an inability to weigh up complex information in order to make *choices*, also presupposes an inability to provide good explanations for any expressed inclinations. These explanations may be of vital importance, particularly in cases where there is a risk that the child has been abused by one or both parents. In such cases, the strength of the child's views may reflect the importance of what he or she is saying and the risks involved in ignoring them. The long- and short-term implications of the decision are also important, given the fact that young children's memories are very short. This may be particularly relevant to decision-making that the courts themselves consider has only a short-term impact. For example, when dealing with applications to return children abducted from their home, the courts stress the summary nature of orders made under the Hague Convention.[75] Thus a court may justify an apparently extremely harsh decision to return a child to the country from whence he or she has been removed, arguing that it is only a short-term solution, pending a full hearing by the courts of the country to which the child is being returned. Nevertheless, to a young child, a few months can be a lifetime.

In the case of adolescents, there appear to be relatively few parental battles over those old enough to vote with their feet. The dearth of case law involving this age group probably reflects legal practitioners' view that there is little point in taking such cases to court since few courts would make decisions ignoring the wishes of much older children. The judiciary generally operate on the presumption that their wishes should be respected, since to ignore them would be counter-productive. Thus in the early 1990s, Butler-Sloss LJ made plain the importance of listening to and respecting the views of older children, whilst not necessarily doing what they want.[76] But whilst reflecting a refreshingly liberal approach to the views of a 14-year-old boy, her decision risked little. Allowing him his choice of school – a day school rather than an expensive boarding

---

[71] I. Waite and H. Stead (1998) p. 45. See also G. Douglas *et al.* (2006) p. 96.
[72] S. Bennett and S. Armstrong Walsh (1994) p. 93.   [73] A. Buchanan *et al.* (2001) pp. 64–8.
[74] I. Butler *et al.* (2003) ch. 5.   [75] Discussed below.
[76] *Re P (a minor) (education)* [1992] 1 FLR 316 at 321.

school – did not endanger his health or restrict his future choices in life. Indeed, in reality there would have been little point in the court overriding his wishes.

Contact disputes involve greater risks since, in the long term, the child may lose the chance of maintaining a relationship with his or her non-resident parent. These disputes seldom involve 'elderly' children, but when they do, the judiciary are normally reluctant to make an order against their strongly articulated wishes.[77] The courts seem far more prepared to accept the views of older adolescents without insisting on psychological assessments, particularly if they have obviously thought out their views rationally. Indeed, Judge Tyrer pointed out the futility of ordering 'ordinary teenagers' to have increased contact with their father against their wishes.

> If young people are to be brought up to respect the law, then it seems to me that the law must respect them and their wishes, even to the extent of allowing them, as occasionally they do, to make mistakes.[78]

Sometimes, as in *Mabon v. Mabon*,[79] older children may wish to take a more active part in their parents' dispute by instructing their own solicitor.[80] There, Thorpe LJ stressed that today there is a keener appreciation of the autonomy of the child and the child's consequential right to participate in decision-making processes that fundamentally affect his family life.[81] An older child's need for autonomy is inevitably tied up with his or her sense of personal identity. Thorpe LJ's judgment therefore suggests that a decision like *Re B (change of surname)*[82] is unlikely to reoccur. There the court refused to allow the mother of three children, aged 16, 14 and 12, to change their surname to that of their stepfather, as they all wished. Although this refusal did not prevent their *informally* adopting whatever surname they chose in their everyday lives,[83] the decision certainly risked exacerbating the implacable hostility they felt for their father.

The courts obviously experience far greater difficulties where physical illness or psychiatric disturbance undermines an adolescent's capacity to assess the complexities of the decision.[84] These are the cases where the courts may decide, for paternalistic reasons, to override adolescents' choices, often on the basis that

---

[77] J. Hunt and A. Macleod (2008) pp. 19 and 241: a notable feature of the research outcomes was the sharp falling off in direct contact amongst the children over 13, clearly related to the courts heeding their wishes when expressing opposition to contact.

[78] *Re S (contact: children's views)*, [2002] EWHC 540 (Fam), [2002] 1 FLR 1156, at 1171.

[79] [2005] EWCA Civ 634, [2005] 2 FLR 1011.   [80] Discussed in Chapter 7.

[81] [2005] EWCA Civ 634, [2005] 2 FLR 1011, at [26].

[82] [1996] 1 FLR 791, cf. *Re S (change of surname)* [1999] 1 FLR 672: allowing her appeal, Thorpe LJ criticised the judge at first instance for not perceiving that a 15-year-old girl was *Gillick* competent – he had refused her permission to change her surname from that of her father (against whom child sexual abuse allegations had been made by her elder sister) to that of her maternal uncle and aunt.

[83] [1996] 1 FLR 791, per Wilson J, at 795.

[84] Adolescents' decision-making in the context of health care is discussed more fully in Chapter 5.

they are not competent to reach them, or simply in order to save their lives, or at least to safeguard their future. Here, judicial decision-making reflects an awareness of the implications of overriding an adolescent's strong views, including the indignity of suffering physical compulsion. Furthermore, the temporal context of the decision is particularly important. Thus, although adolescents are, by definition, assumed to have a good ability to reach decisions about their own future, acceding to some of these may involve extremely high long-term risks, particularly if they are refusing to undergo medical treatment. But, in the short term, maturity may come from being allowed to make mistakes. The courts have a reasonably good record of paying considerable attention to an adolescent's views in cases where the outcome will seriously disrupt his or her life, whether they relate to undergoing medical treatment,[85] or going into local authority care.[86] This case law shows the judiciary implicitly adopting a 'risk analysis approach' to information regarding the wishes of older children. If acceding to such a child's wishes risks his or her death, as in some cases involving refusal of medical treatment, then the court may feel obliged to override them, whatever they think of the individual's competence to form firm and reliable views.[87]

As this discussion indicates, a child's age and competence to form views cannot be assessed *in vacuo*, since the context of the dispute and the risk involved in ignoring or acceding to his or her views will always impinge on the decision-making process. An attempt to clarify the extent to which one aspect of this information influences another may lead to a more consistent judicial approach. Whatever the context, a child may not understand why, having expressed strong views one way or the other, the court has apparently ignored them. However young, the courts should consider always including a careful explanation of their decisions in circumstances where they feel unable to comply with a child's own wishes.[88] When older, these children may wish to understand more about the legal process and discover the reasons underlying the present arrangements for their care. This is particularly important in child protection cases, where the decision may radically change a child's life. The children involved do not necessarily resent the court for not fulfilling their wishes, as long as an adult, such as their children's guardian, explains to them the terms of the order and reasons for the decision.[89]

---

[85] E.g. *Re E (a minor) (wardship: medical treatment)* [1993] 1 FLR 386.

[86] E.g. *Re H (a minor) (care proceedings: child's wishes)* [1993] 1 FLR 440.

[87] E.g. *Re W (a minor) (medical treatment)* [1993] Fam 64; discussed in Chapter 5.

[88] N. Wilson (2007) p. 819: children have a right promptly to understand not only the nature of the outcome but the main reasons for it; furthermore (p. 817) the judge presiding over private law proceedings should determine prior to their conclusion how the child is to be acquainted with his decision and the reasons for it.

[89] *Re C (a minor) (care: child's wishes)* [1993] 1 FLR 832: Waite J (at 840) hoped that the court's decision would be conveyed to the 13-year-old girl sympathetically.

(4) A child's views – some problem areas

(A) Abducted children

There is a growing body of Hague Convention[90] case law involving abducting parents who resist claims to return their children on the basis that the children themselves oppose such an action and are sufficiently mature to have their views taken seriously.[91] Unlike ordinary domestic disputes, in abduction cases the child's welfare is not paramount.[92] Indeed, a prima facie presumption underlies the Convention that a child's welfare is best served by a prompt return to the country of his or her habitual residence, leaving the decision of what should happen to the child to that country's own courts.[93] But the duty to return the child is not absolute and Article 13 authorises the court to refuse to make such an order if 'it finds that the child objects to being returned and has attained an age and degree of maturity at which it is appropriate to take account of its views'.[94]

In most family proceedings involving children, the courts have plenty of scope for offsetting the weight attributed to the child's wishes by referring to the long list of other factors contained in the statutory checklist.[95] The terms of Article 13 of the Hague Convention, however, require attention to be focused solely on the child's objections and maturity, with the court finding a mechanism for receiving information on these matters.[96] Case law has established that there are three stages to such cases.[97] The court must first establish why the child is objecting to return to the applicant's own country – his or her views will carry little weight if he or she simply objects to living apart from the abducting parent.[98] Second, the court must establish whether the child is of sufficient age and maturity for his or her views to be taken into account. On this the child must know what has happened to him or her and understand that there is a range of choice.[99] Lastly, the court must decide whether it is appropriate to exercise its discretion and depart from the usual presumption imposed by the Convention.[100] Whether a court should do so will depend, inter alia, on the strength and validity of the child's views, taking account of the child's own perspectives of his or her own interests, the reality and reasonableness of the

---

[90] The Hague Convention on the Civil Aspects of International Child Abduction 1980, given force of law by the Child Abduction and Custody Act 1985.

[91] J. Caldwell (2001).   [92] *Re R (abduction: consent)* [1999] 1 FLR 828, per Hale J, at 836.

[93] *Re P (abduction: minor's views)* [1998] 2 FLR 825, per Butler-Sloss LJ, at 827.

[94] This exception is sometimes described as Art. 13(c) despite its not being specifically given a sub-paragraph. It is sometimes combined with the abducting parent's claim under Art. 13(b) that there is a grave risk that the child's return would 'expose the child to physical or psychological harm or otherwise place the child in an intolerable situation'.

[95] CA 1989, s. 1(3)(a)–(g).

[96] Usually through an interview with a CAFCASS officer, but sometimes with the assistance of a separate representative; see Chapter 7.

[97] *Re T (abduction: child's objections to return)* [2000] 2 FLR 192, per Ward LJ, at 203–4.

[98] Ibid. at 202.   [99] Ibid. at 203.   [100] Ibid. at 204.

reasons for objection, the extent to which they have been shaped by the abducting parent and the extent to which the objections might be mediated on return.[101]

The facts of abduction cases being infinitely variable, there can be little consistency in the courts' preparedness to be influenced by children's objections to return or by the ages of the children who manage to influence them. But there are obvious tensions underlying Article 13(c) – the dilemma is to get the balance right when interpreting its terms. On the one hand, it is arguable that the provision reflects the aims of Article 12 of the CRC, to enable children, depending on their maturity, to express their views and be heard, though not to give them self-determination.[102] Furthermore, as Schuz argues, the wording of Article 13 does not dictate a stringent approach to its interpretation. Indeed, in her view, the summary nature of Convention proceedings does not negate the courts' duty to respect children's rights under Article 12 of the CRC and to uphold their views in any case where 'the children's objections represent the genuine independent views of sufficiently mature children'.[103] But on the other hand, the domestic courts are also very aware that the overall objective of the Convention, which is to ensure a summary return of abducted children, would be undermined if abducting adults exploited its terms by persuading their children to fight their battles for them.

Baroness Hale of Richmond emphasised in *Re M and anor (children) (abduction)*[104] not only that the aims of Article 12 of the CRC should be given greater credence in 'child objection cases'[105] but that the courts had formerly been getting the balance wrong. In her view, they had been interpreting the exceptions to the Convention too stringently. She disapproved of the growing body of case law[106] indicating that it was only in exceptional circumstances that a child's objections to return would be allowed to prevail.[107] This position had been reached by the Court of Appeal referring back to earlier case law stressing the need to implement faithfully the Convention's overall policy. This policy was to be treated as a very weighty factor to be brought into the scales *against* the weight attached to the child's objections – and the younger the child, the less weight his or her objections would carry.[108] This restricted interpretation of Article 13(c) had produced a situation in which the courts

---

[101] Ibid.   [102] *Re T (abduction: child's objections to return)* [2000] 2 FLR 192, per Ward LJ, at 203.
[103] R. Schuz (2004) pp. 737–8.
[104] [2007] UKHL 55, [2008] 1 All ER 1157; discussed by H. Setright *et al.* (2008).
[105] Ibid. at [46].
[106] See esp. *Zaffino v. Zaffino (abduction: children's views)* [2005] EWCA Civ 1012, [2006] 1 FLR 410: Court of Appeal upheld the father's appeal against Munby J's decision upholding (under Art. 13(c)) the objections of a 13-year-old girl and her 9-year-old brother to their return to Canada with their younger siblings.
[107] Ibid., per Thorpe LJ, at [16]-[20]. See also *Vigreux v. Michel* [2006] EWCA Civ 630, [2006] 2 FLR 1180, per Wall LJ, at [76].
[108] *Re R (child abduction: acquiescence)* [1995] 1 FLR 716, per Balcombe LJ, at 730–1 and *Re S (a minor) (abduction)* [1993] 2 All ER 683, per Balcombe LJ, at 691.

would now only exercise their discretion in the most exceptional cases, particularly if relatively young children were involved.[109] It also appeared that the traditional judicial preparedness to give very serious credence to teenagers' objections[110] had also started disappearing.[111]

Baroness Hale's decision in *Re M and anor (children) (abduction)*[112] was obviously designed to reverse this new stringency. She stressed that although the Hague Convention is there to secure the prompt return of abducted children and to deter abduction, the weight to be attached to that consideration must vary according to the circumstances of the case.[113] Above all, she strongly disapproved of the way that the courts were now requiring exceptionality to be established, as an additional test, once the other conditions for exercising discretion under Article 13(c) had been complied with.[114] The exception itself is brought into play when only two conditions are met: first the child's objections and second her maturity.[115] Baroness Hale was in no doubt at all:

> that it is wrong to import any test of exceptionality into the exercise of discretion under the convention. The circumstances in which return may be refused are themselves exceptions to the general rule. That in itself is sufficient exceptionality. It is neither necessary nor desirable to import an additional gloss into the convention.[116]

Baroness Hale also reminded the courts that it is not the policy of the Hague Convention to put children at serious risk of harm or to place them in intolerable situations.[117] In *Re M* itself, she stated that: 'These children should not be made to suffer for the sake of general deterrence of the evil of child abduction worldwide.'[118]

---

[109] E.g. *Re M (abduction: child's objections)* [2007] EWCA Civ 260, [2007] 2 FLR 72: the special circumstances of the case, including the mother's harassment by the police in Serbia, rendered this case sufficiently exceptional to warrant upholding the objections of an 8-year-old to returning to Serbia, cf. *Re J and K (abduction: objections of child)* [2004] EWHC 1985 (Fam), [2005] 1 FLR 273: no exceptional circumstances justified giving substantial weight to the objections of a 9-year-old to return to Malta.

[110] E.g. inter alia: *Re P (abduction: minor's views)* [1998] 1 FLR 825: appeal was allowed against a decision ordering the return of a 13-year-old boy to his father in the United States; *Re L (abduction: child's objections to return)* [2002] EWHC 1864 (Fam), [2002] 2 FLR 1042: court upheld a 14-year-old boy's objections to returning to France.

[111] E.g. inter alia: *Zaffino v. Zaffino* [2005] EWCA Civ 1012, [2006] 1 FLR 410: the objections of the 13-year-old girl were not to be given weight per se, especially in view of the return of her siblings to Canada; *JPC v. SLW and SMW (abduction)* [2007] EWHC 1349 (Fam), [2007] 2 FLR 900: the clearly expressed objections of a highly intelligent 14-year-old to returning to Ireland did not justify permitting her to remain in England. See also *TB v. JB (abduction: grave risk of harm)* [2001] 2 FLR 515: 14½-year-old girl's objections to returning to her abusive stepfather in New Zealand overridden.

[112] [2007] UKHL 55, [2008] 1 All ER 1157: the mother successfully opposed the return of her two daughters aged 13 and 10 to Zimbabwe, inter alia, because of their own strong objections under Art. 13(c).

[113] Ibid. at [42]–[43].   [114] Ibid. at [37].   [115] Ibid. at [46].

[116] Ibid. at [40].   [117] Ibid. at [45].   [118] Ibid. at [54].

Subsequent case law indicates the family judiciary's willingness to drop their 'exceptionality' test when dealing with Convention applications involving Article 13.[119] This changed approach is timely; the effect on individual children of a summary return to a strange country can be immense. Indeed, in the absence of any formal follow up, it is only possible to speculate what impact these judicial decisions have on the children themselves, if the courts appear to ignore their own stated wishes. For this reason, the ongoing litigation in *Re HB (abduction: children's objections)*[120] is instructive. It chronicles attempts to impose a court order on two children, originally aged 11 and 13, who were totally out of sympathy with what the court was trying to achieve. The younger child refused to return to Denmark as ordered, and, staying in England, became embroiled in her father's litigation with her mother. The older child obeyed the order and returned to Denmark, but, as he himself had predicted, again reverted to delinquent behaviour and returned to a Danish children's residential home. The litigation highlights the ease with which children can sabotage court orders that they do not consider reflect their real needs.

(B) Children's hostility to the non-resident parent

(i) Fear of domestic violence

A court's willingness to reach a decision according with the child's wishes may be undermined by its knowledge that children are extremely suggestible and can be strongly influenced by the adults around them. Dealing with children who oppose contact with non-resident parents is particularly problematic in contact disputes. The court may be convinced, when confronted with a child who is hysterically opposed to contact with the non-resident parent, that the parent with day-to-day care (normally the mother), has imposed on a young and suggestible child unwarranted fears and anxieties about the other – that she has effectively brainwashed the child.[121] Nevertheless, the reasons for children opposing contact are often extremely complex. They may simply relate to the present contact arrangements not adjusting to a growing child's changing lifestyle[122] or to a mixture of misplaced loyalties.

Children may, however, be reluctant to have contact with a non-resident parent because they fear the continuation of violent behaviour between their parents. As research shows, it is extremely damaging to grow up in a violent

---

[119] Inter alia: *Re F (abduction: rights of custody)* [2008] EWHC 272 (Fam), [2008] 2 FLR 1239, per Sir Mark Potter P, at [64]; *Re S (abduction : children's representation)* [2008] EWHC 1798 (Fam), [2008] 2 FLR 1918, per Charles J, at [23].

[120] *Re HB (abduction: children's objections)* [1997] 1 FLR 392; *Re HB (abduction: children's objections)* [1998] 1 FLR 422; *Re HB (abduction: children's objections) (No. 2)* [1999] 1 FCR 331.

[121] Discussed below.

[122] E.g. *Re O (contact: withdrawal of application)* [2003] EWHC 3031 (Fam), [2004] 1 FLR 1258, at [21]: a 12-year-old boy found frequent weekend staying contact with his father burdensome, because he could not see his friends and go to parties; he similarly disliked over-frequent telephone calls.

household; moreover there is a strong correlation between domestic violence and child abuse.[123] The strength of the 'contact presumption' has, however, led to couples being encouraged by family justice practitioners at every level to settle their disputes over contact rather than go to court. These processes risk underlying domestic violence and child protection concerns not being identified and mothers feeling coerced into agreeing contact arrangements that are unsafe.[124] As noted earlier, large numbers of couples are now funnelled into conciliation appointments with Cafcass family court advisers (FCAs) by the in-court dispute resolution procedures, with a view to reaching agreement over contact.[125] There are, however, continuing doubts over the extent to which some FCAs explore the reasons given by children for not wanting contact or the impact on the children themselves of domestic violence and/or abusive parenting.[126] Indeed, until their confidence is won over by someone they can trust, children may remain reluctant to disclose the real reasons for opposing contact.[127] Nor, apparently, do solicitors advising adults over contact disputes, consider it their job to discover children's wishes and feelings before negotiated settlements are finalised.[128] This is deeply worrying, given the research showing that two years after in-court conciliated agreements had been reached, children were just as reluctant to abide by the terms of contact arrangements as before.[129] It also showed that the well-being of many had not improved in the interim.[130] This suggests that children's concerns about unwanted contact do not simply disappear over time.

By the time a case actually gets to court, the parents' conflict will probably have become entrenched, with the tension between them seriously affecting the children. Indeed, there is no clear research evidence indicating that children benefit from court-imposed contact in circumstances poisoned by mutual parental antipathy.[131] Nevertheless, some young adults, looking back on their parents' disputes, indicated to researchers that going to court had helped and that contact orders had ensured that they had a relationship with their non-resident parents.[132] For others, particularly those with violent non-resident fathers, the court orders had made matters worse, with the fathers simply ignoring their terms.[133] Less than one-third considered that the courts had taken proper account of their views.[134]

Today, a growing willingness to direct separate representation for children in difficult contact disputes[135] coincides with an increased judicial preparedness to consider the basis for children's hostility to the non-resident parent in cases involving allegations of domestic violence. This change of heart was initially

---

[123] See research summaries in J. Hunt with C. Roberts (2004) p. 7 and S. Walby (2004) para. 7.3. See also L. Trinder *et al.* (2005) pp. 88–90.
[124] Discussed in Chapter 7 and Chapter 13.   [125] Discussed in Chapter 7.   [126] Ibid.
[127] R. Davies and S. Mason (2007) p. 1097.   [128] Discussed in Chapter 7.
[129] L. Trinder and J. Kellett (2007) pp. 28–9.   [130] Ibid. at pp. 31–2.   [131] See Chapter 13.
[132] J. Fortin *et al.* (2006) p. 218.   [133] Ibid. at pp. 218–19.
[134] Ibid. at pp. 220–1.   [135] Discussed in Chapter 7.

provoked by the 'Experts' Report' commissioned by the Court of Appeal in *Re L (a child) (contact: domestic violence)*.[136] Sturge and Glaser[137] not only stress the dangers of forcing children into continuing contact arrangements with violent fathers, but also strongly emphasise the importance of taking account of children's own views, depending on their age and the circumstances.[138] The cases dealt with in *Re L* itself reflected a far greater willingness to consider whether a child's opposition to contact stemmed from some valid reason, even when he or she was relatively young.[139] Furthermore, all courts are now required to consider very seriously all allegations of domestic violence in children's cases and to discover the children's own views underlying such cases. Whenever domestic violence allegations are made and unless they are satisfied that the children's interests do *not* need safeguarding in such a way, all courts are now obliged to consider calling for a welfare report and, depending on the seriousness of the allegations, providing them with separate representation.[140]

(ii) Indoctrinated children

Indoctrination comes in many forms and is usually not deliberate, in so far as young children often simply absorb the views of those who care for them. As Eekelaar has observed, it is arguable that children lack competence to reach decisions for themselves, if their decision is really that of the parent and not their own.[141] But on the other hand, few adults could claim that they reached their current views entirely independently of the influence of others.

> If one is to hold a person incompetent because his decision reflects socially tolerated values ingrained in his upbringing, competence could hardly ever be achieved by anyone.[142]

Religious indoctrination may be a particularly difficult factor for the courts to deal with. To what extent should a court accord freedom of choice to a child it considers has been indoctrinated into the religious tenets of his or her carers? The courts have a tradition of maintaining religious tolerance and abstain from commenting on the views of any particular religious denomination.[143] Today, a decision overriding a child's strong religious views, by, for example, removing him from his present home in a religious community,[144] might be countered by his arguing that he is entitled to religious freedom under Article 9 of the ECHR.

---

[136] [2000] 4 All ER 609.   [137] C. Sturge and D. Glaser (2000).

[138] Ibid. at p. 624. See also Appendix 2, p. 627, for a list of difficulties (contributed by J. Eekelaar) which may hamper considering a child's wishes and feelings.

[139] The children involved in the four test cases in *Re L* were all under 10.

[140] *Practice Direction: Residence and Contact Orders: Domestic Violence and Harm* [2009] All ER (D) 122 (Jan) at [17].

[141] J. Eekelaar (1994) p. 56.   [142] Ibid. at p. 57.

[143] E.g. *Re J (specific issue orders: Muslim upbringing and circumcision)* [1999] 2 FLR 678, discussed in Chapter 11.

[144] E.g. *Re R (a minor) (residence: religion)* [1993] 2 FLR 163: despite the vehement wish of a 9½-year-old boy to remain with members of the Exclusive Brethren sect, with whom he had lived for 4½ years, his care was transferred to his father.

The court might, however, respond by arguing that an infringement is necessary under Article 9(2) to preserve the child's best interests.

In contact disputes, the indoctrination may be directed at one or other parent. Indeed, a not uncommon problem arises when children simply refuse to cooperate with contact arrangements suggested by the non-resident parent. It is clear that some residential parents deliberately manipulate children emotionally against the non-resident parent. This of course makes it very difficult for FCAs, when interviewing children, to discover their 'authentic wishes and feelings'.[145] Mantle et al. point out that a common effect of brainwashing is the wholesale rejection of one parent who is effectively 'written out' of the child's life.[146] Nevertheless, as the judiciary themselves have asserted, some non-resident fathers find it easier to maintain that their children's hostility to them is attributable to the mother's behaviour than to accept their own responsibility for this attitude.[147] Possibly spurred on by some of the fathers' pressure groups, these fathers often counter their children's resistance to contact by arguing that they are suffering from a mental disorder induced by Parental Alienation Syndrome (PAS)[148] and that they need skilled psychiatric or psychological assessment and therapy.[149] A growing judicial acceptance of the syndrome in the United States has met with strong academic rejection. Echoing Bruch's detailed repudiation of the syndrome's validity,[150] Emery et al. state tersely that 'the scientific status of PAS is, to be blunt, nil'.[151] Following Sturge and Glaser's equally firm rejection of the syndrome's existence as a recognised mental disorder,[152] the judiciary here show little sign of accepting fathers' claims of PAS.[153] Nevertheless, a court may persistently attempt to overcome a child's distress if it considers it not to be well-founded.[154]

Before reaching a decision on future contact, the courts may be keen to establish, with the help of psychological experts, the real reasons underlying a

---

[145] G. Mantle et al. (2006) p. 16.   [146] Ibid. at p. 12.

[147] E.g. Re C (prohibition on further applications) [2002] EWCA Civ 292, [2002] 1 FLR 1136, per Dame Elizabeth Butler-Sloss P, at [12]–[13]; Re O (contact: withdrawal of application) [2003] EWHC 3031 (Fam), [2004] 1 FLR 1258, per Wall J, at [85]; Re Bradford; Re O'Connell [2006] EWCA Civ 1199, [2007] 1 FLR 530, per Wall J, at [94].

[148] The website of the fathers' pressure group, Families Need Fathers (www.fnf.org.uk/) contains a considerable body of information on PAS.

[149] E.g. Appeal in Re M (a child) in Re L (a child) (contact: domestic violence) and other appeals [2000] 4 All ER 609: the psychological expert in PAS had recommended, on the father's behalf, that the child undergo six sessions of therapy; Re C (prohibition on further applications) [2002] EWCA Civ 292, [2002] 1 FLR 1136: the father repeatedly applied for a mental health expert or a psychologist, expert in PAS, to be appointed to assess his daughter's state of mind, given her refusal to have contact with him; Re Bradford; Re O'Connell [2006] EWCA Civ 1199, [2007] 1 FLR 530: Mr O'Connell wanted an American expert in PAS to be appointed to assess the children.

[150] C. Bruch (2002) pp. 387–8.   [151] R. Emery et al. (2005) p. 10.

[152] C. Sturge and D. Glaser (2000) pp. 622–3.

[153] See esp. Re O (contact: withdrawal of application) [2003] EWHC 3031 (Fam), [2004] 1 FLR 1258, per Wall J, at [91]–[94];

[154] J. Hunt and A. Macleod (2008) p. 199.

child's hostility towards a non-resident parent. As noted above, such an approach is more likely with young children. In the case of contact disputes involving older children, whilst the judiciary remain vigilant for signs that their minds have been indoctrinated by the resident parent, such children seem to be given the benefit of the doubt.[155] When dealing with a relatively young child, a court may hope that, with the help of therapy, he or she can be persuaded to reopen relations with an apparently well-intentioned non-resident father. Thus, in *Re W (contact: joining child as party)*,[156] Dame Elizabeth Butler-Sloss P considered that there was no apparent reason for the increasing reluctance of a 7-year-old boy to have contact with his father. In her view he 'has a right to a relationship with his father even if he does not want it',[157] and that, with the help of a child psychiatrist or other health professional,[158] he and the parents should be given the opportunity of 'moving forward'. He would 'see it as right and proper that he should see his father and not look just at the negative side'.[159]

Critics argue that *Re W* ignored the child's right *not* to have contact with his father and demonstrated the courts' readiness to set aside children's wishes and to deny their 'agency'.[160] As commented elsewhere, this viewpoint rests on the assumption that children's rights are all about promoting their choices and fulfilling their wishes. It is arguable that the court was perfectly entitled to argue that the child had a 'right to contact' with his father, even if he himself did not want it.[161] Furthermore, the President obviously hoped that the child psychiatrist could unearth the real reason for the boy's resistance and persuade him to adopt a more cooperative frame of mind. Nevertheless, as Kaganas and Diduck point out, decisions of this kind show the courts expending effort on persuading children 'to choose the "good" post-separation family'.[162] Some practitioners are concerned over the way in which children who oppose contact may be talked to by a variety of individuals until he or she agrees to it – a process which can smack of bullying. Most agree that ultimately the court may have to give up, especially if an older child is concerned.[163]

---

[155] E.g. *Re S (contact: children's views)* [2002] EWHC 540 (Fam), [2002] 1 FLR 1156, per Judge Tyrer, at 1170: the father should take account of the views of his three children aged 16, 14 and 12; *Re Bradford; Re O'Connell* [2006] EWCA Civ 1199, [2007] 1 FLR 530, per Wall LJ, at [45]: quoting with approval Coleridge J's view (in court below) that the opposition of the children, aged 14½ and 12½ to contact with their father was rational and justifiable and (at [53]) they had no need of the psychiatric assessment requested by the father. But see *Re M (contact: long-term best interests)* [2005] EWCA Civ 1090, [2006] 1 FLR 627: a psychiatric or psychological assessment ordered on two children aged 13 and 15 whose implacable hostility towards their mother had developed under the influence of their father and stepmother.

[156] [2001] EWCA Civ 1830, [2003] 1 FLR 681. See also *Re H (a child: mother's opposition)* [2001] 1 FCR 59.

[157] *Re W*, ibid., at [16].   [158] Ibid. at [16] and [21].   [159] Ibid. at [16].

[160] A. James *et al.* (2004) p. 201.   [161] J. Fortin (2007) p. 506.

[162] F. Kaganas and A. Diduck (2004) p. 975.

[163] J. Hunt and A. Macleod (2008) pp. 199–200 and 218–20.

In some cases, as a result of parental manipulation, children simply refuse to cooperate with a contact order already in place. As discussed later in this work,[164] the courts may then resort to a variety of strategies to ensure the orders' enforcement.[165] They can justify using strong sanctions against parents who refuse to comply with contact orders by referring to the growing body of Strasbourg jurisprudence asserting the importance of facilitating a reunion between parent and child. Nevertheless, this jurisprudence is not entirely clear-cut. The ECtHR has stressed that the domestic courts' duty in this respect is not absolute.[166] It accepts that if the child has been living for some years without contact with the non-resident parent, any reunion may require preparation, perhaps with the assistance of psychologists or psychiatrists.[167] The Court has even acknowledged that reunion may be impossible, with the state's obligation to apply coercion being limited, given the need to take the best interests of the child into account and the need to strike a fair balance between the needs of the absent parent for reunion and those of the child.[168]

Nor is the ECtHR entirely consistent in its approach to young adolescents who strongly resist the enforcement of adults' claims.[169] It has stressed, on the one hand, that children's opinions should be taken into account once they attain the necessary maturity to express them.[170] But, on the other hand, it is very aware of the ability of adults to manipulate children.[171] Whilst it emphasises that measures obliging children to become reunited with a parent 'are not desirable in this sensitive area', it goes on to assert that 'such action must not be ruled out in the event of non-compliance or unlawful behaviour of the parent with whom the children live'.[172] Furthermore, as noted above, it criticised the Finnish courts for allowing children to dictate the outcome of a parental dispute. They had placed exclusive weight on the opposition of two children over 12 to reunion with their father, without taking account of the other factors

[164] See Chapter 13.

[165] E.g. inter alia: *Re M (intractable contact dispute: interim care order)* [2003] EWHC 1024 (Fam), [2003] 2 FLR 636; *Re N (sexual abuse allegations: professionals not abiding by findings of fact)* [2005] 2 FLR 340; *Re F (family proceedings: section 37 investigation)* [2005] EWHC 2935, [2006] 1 FLR 1122; *Re M (contact: long-term best interests)* [2005] EWCA Civ 1090, [2006] 1 FLR 627.

[166] The classic exposition of this principle is set out in *Hokkanen v. Finland* (1994) 19 EHRR 139, para. 58; discussed in Chapter 14.

[167] *Ignaccolo-Zenide v. Romania* (2001) 31 EHRR 7, para. 112; *Hansen v. Turkey* [2004] 1 FLR 142, para. 103.

[168] Inter alia: *Ignaccolo-Zenide v. Romania* (2001) 31 EHRR 7, para. 94; *Hansen v. Turkey* [2004] 1 FLR 142, para. 98.

[169] M. Woolf (2003) pp. 212–13.

[170] *Pini and Bertani; Manera and Atripaldi v. Romania* [2005] 2 FLR 596, at para. 164: the ECtHR sympathised with the Romanian government's refusal to force two girls, now aged 12, to live with their Italian adoptive parents. See Chapter 14.

[171] E.g. *S and G v. Italy* [2000] 2 FLR 771, para. 210.

[172] *Hansen v. Turkey* [2004] 1 FLR 142, para. 106. See also *Ignaccolo-Zenide v. Romania* (2001) 31 EHRR 7, para. 106.

in the case, in particular the father's rights.[173] This effectively gave the children 'an unconditional veto power', without the parties being given an oral hearing at which they could address the matter and other issues could be explored.[174]

As discussed above, the Grand Chamber drew back from requiring states always to clarify the reasons for a child's resistance to contact through a psychological assessment or oral evidence in court.[175] Nevertheless, there are situations where the ECtHR clearly considers that the domestic courts should have done so, as in *C v. Finland*.[176] There, it pointed out that by failing to obtain such an assessment, or any divergent interpretation of the children's resistance to contact, including the impact on them of denying them a relationship with their father, the dead mother's partner had apparently been allowed to manipulate the children and the legal system to deny the father unjustifiably of his parental role.[177] The only clear message to emerge from this body of case law is that the ECtHR expects states authorities to provide the non-resident parent with reasonable assistance in persuading the children concerned to accede to court orders, perhaps with therapeutic help.[178] Overall, the decision-making process must allow the interests of the main players involved in disputes over children to be ascertained and balanced against each other – without the children's position being allowed to dominate the outcome. Given the infinitely variable circumstances of the challenges taken to Strasbourg, the ECtHR obviously finds it as difficult to maintain any real consistency as do the domestic courts.

(C) Abused children

An abused child's right to be consulted may conflict with his or her right to be protected. Indeed, the wishes and feelings of abused children may be so extremely complex that they provide the court with some very mixed messages. As Schofield points out, abused children whose future is being determined by the courts may be so significantly harmed that they are confused about themselves and what has happened to them and therefore present a confusing picture to others:[179]

> Troubled children in crisis … very often and very understandably present entirely conflicting evidence of their wishes and feelings. They may express hopes for the future which are incompatible with what professionals and the children themselves know to be reality; for example, the wish to be at home and to be safe, the wish to be with a parent but for that parent to change.[180]

---

[173] *C v. Finland* [2006] 2 FLR 597: contrary to earlier decisions in his favour, the Finnish courts denied the father custody of and visiting rights to his children (now aged 12 and 14) once the youngest reached 12, on the basis of their wish to remain with their dead mother's partner in Finland.
[174] Ibid. at [58].   [175] *Sahin v. Germany* [2003] 2 FLR 671.   [176] [2006] 2 FLR 597.
[177] Ibid. at [58].   [178] E.g. *Hansen v. Turkey* [2004] 1 FLR 142, para. 103.
[179] G. Schofield (1998) p. 365; also discussed in Chapter 15.   [180] Ibid. at p. 364.

As she explains:

> This does not mean that we should therefore disregard those wishes and feelings but it does mean that the process of ascertaining, understanding and determining the weight to be attached to children's wishes and feelings is more problematic than it may appear from the simple words of the Act.[181]

Children, who are allegedly the victims of sexual abuse, present special problems, both in private and public law proceedings. A sexually abused child's present views may be grossly distorted by his or her damaging relationship with the abuser.[182] Whilst the court may not be sure that the child is telling the truth, research indicates that they are at least as likely to minimise or deny abuse altogether, as to lie about it.[183] Sexually abused children may not only deny or refuse to acknowledge that abuse has occurred, but also refuse to cooperate with those trying to help them.[184] Those who do disclose the abuse sometimes later deny it, due to pressure from the abuser.[185] In private law proceedings, a court may be reluctant to place a great deal of store on children's accounts of sexual abuse by a non-resident parent, especially if they are very young and if it suspects that they have been manipulated by the residential parent.[186] These difficulties may be compounded if the practitioners involved used poor interviewing techniques, including leading questions and undue pressure to obtain disclosures of the abuse.[187] Fortunately, there appears to be little sign of fathers in this country responding to allegations of child sexual abuse by asserting that the children must be victims of PAS.[188]

The courts are well aware that abused children who are the subject of child protection proceedings often strongly desire to stay at home or return home,[189] however illogical this may appear.[190] They understand that a denial of abuse may be attributable to the child's fear of breaking up the home. The courts are obviously fully justified in overriding a child's objections to removal from home if they believe him or her to have been abused; indeed, they are under a duty to consider his or her 'physical, emotional and educational needs'.[191] On the other

---

[181] Ibid.   [182] E. Jones and P. Parkinson (1995) pp. 68–75.

[183] H. Westcott (2006) pp. 179–80; discussed in Chapter 17.

[184] E.g. *Nottinghamshire County Council v. P; Re P (minors) (local authority: prohibited steps order)* [1993] 3 All ER 815: none of the teenage daughters was prepared to stay away from their sexually abusive father.

[185] E. Jones and P. Parkinson (1995) p. 64.

[186] E.g. *Re M (intractable contact dispute: interim care order)* [2003] EWHC 1024 (Fam), [2003] 2 FLR 636; *Re N (sexual abuse allegations: professionals not abiding by findings of fact)* [2005] 2 FLR 340.

[187] Discussed in Chapter 17.

[188] C. Bruch (2002) pp. 387–8: some American courts have accepted arguments of this kind in such a context.

[189] *Re F (Mental Health Act: guardianship)* [2000] 1 FLR 192, per Thorpe LJ, at 198.

[190] E.g., inter alia: *Re C (a minor) (care: child's wishes)* [1993] 1 FLR 832; *Nottinghamshire County Council v. P; Re P (minors) (local authority: prohibited steps order)* [1993] 3 All ER 815; *Re F (Mental Health Act: guardianship)* [2000] 1 FLR 192.

[191] CA 1989, s. 1(3)(b).

hand, children should not be disbelieved just because they are denying abuse, as opposed to disclosing it.[192] Sometimes, if it is too dangerous for an abused child ever to return home, he or she may be the subject of care proceedings and swiftly placed for adoption.[193] Given the impact of such a change on a child's life, it should obviously be discussed with him or her well before the adoption application is heard in court and certainly before any sudden modification in placement plans.[194] Nevertheless, since most children being placed for adoption from care are probably very emotionally vulnerable, it is arguable that they would find it difficult to consider objectively a legal right to veto any adoption application.[195] It would, in any event, be both unrealistic and unjust for the courts to ignore a child's views on the matter, particularly if he or she is reluctant to be adopted.[196]

(5) Conclusion

Children involved in litigation cannot claim complete autonomy; they must recognise their dependence on the courts for decisions determining their future. But the judiciary clearly recognise that children should not be subjected to decision-making which apparently fails to give their wishes and feelings serious weight. It would be difficult to justify such an approach to children who are being brought up in a society which constantly urges them to develop their powers of critical awareness and to act responsibly and independently. A more systematic approach to the process of considering a child's wishes in each case might emerge were the courts to show a greater willingness to articulate children's own rights under the ECHR. But this would involve the judiciary reviewing their approach to the paramountcy principle in section 1 of the CA 1989 – a task which they seem singularly reluctant to undertake.

It would be unwise to underestimate the real difficulties underlying the problem areas discussed above. Nevertheless, judicial decision-making suggests that, at times, these difficulties obscure the needs of the children who should be the focus of attention. Thus, until recently, the domestic courts seemed more

---

[192] *Leeds City Council v. YX and ZX (assessment of sexual abuse)* [2008] EWHC 802 (Fam), [2008] 2 FLR 869, per Holman J, at [127].

[193] Discussed more fully in Chapter 16.

[194] *R v. Devon County Council, ex p O (adoption)* [1997] 2 FLR 388, per Scott-Baker J, at 396–7: deplored the fact that no one had consulted a 9-year-old boy over the plans to remove him from his prospective adopters and return him to previous foster carers.

[195] The recommendation (DH (1993) para. 4.3) that the consent of children of 12 and over should be a precondition of an adoption order being made, never became the law. The Adoption and Children Act 2002, s. 1(4)(a) merely requires the court or adoption agency to have regard to 'the child's ascertainable wishes and feelings regarding the decision (considered in the light of the child's age and understanding)'. But see C. Piper and A. Miakisher (2003) who criticise this omission.

[196] E.g. *Re M (adoption or residence order)* [1998] 1 FLR 570: the mother's consent to the adoption of her emotionally disturbed and backward 11-year-old daughter was not dispensed with, given, inter alia, the girl's own lack of enthusiasm for such an outcome.

concerned to fulfil the summary nature of the Hague Convention proceedings than to protect the children themselves from distress and harm (albeit short-term). Similarly the contact presumption distracts family justice practitioners from discovering from the children embroiled in parental contact disputes what is really going on behind the closed doors of their homes. Again the procedures and processes are allowed to pre-empt the task in hand – which is to ensure that children's real wishes and feelings are conveyed to the court and given appropriate weight.

BIBLIOGRAPHY

NB many of these publications can be obtained on the relevant organisation's website.

Bainham, A. (2002) 'Can We Protect Children and Protect their Rights?' 32 *Family Law* 279.

Bennett, S. and Armstrong Walsh, S. (1994) 'The No Order Principle, Parental Responsibility and the Child's Wishes' 24 *Family Law* 91.

Bonner, D., Fenwick, H. and Harris-Short, S. (2003) 'Judicial Approaches to the Human Rights Act' 52 *International and Comparative Law Quarterly* 549.

Bruch, C. (2002) 'Parental Alienation Syndrome and Alienated Children – Getting it Wrong in Child Custody Cases' 14 *Child and Family Law Quarterly* 381.

Buchanan, A., Hunt, J., Bretherton, H. and Bream, V. (2001) *Families in Conflict: Perspectives of Children and Parents on the Family Court Welfare Service*, The Policy Press.

Butler, I., Scanlan, L., Robinson, M., Douglas, G. and Murch, M. (2003) *Divorcing Children: Children's Experience of Their Parents' Divorce*, Jessica Kingsley Publishers.

Caldwell, J. (2001) 'Child Welfare Defences in Child Abduction Cases – Some Recent Developments' 13 *Child and Family Law Quarterly* 121.

Cantwell, B. and Scott, S. (1995) 'Children's Wishes, Children's Burdens' 17 *Journal of Social Welfare and Family Law* 337.

Children and Family Court Advisory Support Service (Cafcass) (2005) *Domestic Violence Policy and Standards*, Cafcass.

Choudhry, S. (2003) 'The Adoption and Children Act 2002, the Welfare Principle and the Human Rights Act 1998 – a missed opportunity' 15 *Child and Family Law Quarterly* 119.

Choudhry, S. and Fenwick, H. (2005) 'Taking the Rights of Parents and Children Seriously: Confronting the Welfare Principle under the Human Rights Act' 25 *Oxford Journal of Legal Studies* 453.

Davies, R. and Mason, S. (2007) 'NYAS: The Voice and Ears of the Child' 37 *Family Law* 1095.

Department of Health (DH) (1993) White Paper, *Adoption: The Future* Cm 2288, HMSO.

Douglas, G., Murch, M., Miles, C. and Scanlan, L. (2006) *Research into the Operation of Rule 9.5 of the Family Proceedings Rules 1991*, Final Report to the Department of Constitutional Affairs, DCA.

Eekelaar, J. (1986) 'The Emergence of Children's Rights' 6 *Oxford Journal of Legal Studies* 161.

(1991) *Regulating Divorce*, Clarendon Press.

(1992) 'The Importance of Thinking that Children Have Rights' in Alston, P., Parker, S. and Seymour, J. (eds.) *Children, Rights and the Law*, Clarendon Press.

(1994) 'The Interests of the Child and the Child's Wishes: The Role of Dynamic Self-Determinism' 8 *International Journal of Law and the Family* 42.

(2002) 'Beyond the Welfare Principle' 14 *Child and Family Law Quarterly* 237.

(2006) *Family Law and Personal Life*, Oxford University Press.

Emery, R., Otto, R. and O'Donohue, W. (2005) 'A Critical Assessment of Child Custody Evaluations: Limited Science and a Flawed System' 6 *Psychological Science in the Public Interest* 1.

Fenwick, H. (2004) 'Clashing Rights, the Welfare of the Child and the Human Rights Act' 67 *Modern Law Review* 889.

Fineman, M. (1988) 'Dominant Discourse, Professional Language and Legal Change in Child Custody Decision-Making' 101 *Harvard Law Review* 727.

Fortin, J. (2004) 'Children's Rights: Are the Courts Now Taking Them More Seriously?' 15 *King's College Law Journal* 253.

(2006) 'Accommodating Children's Rights in a Post Human Rights Act Era' 69 *Modern Law Review* 299.

(2007) 'Children's Representation Through the Looking Glass' 37 *Family Law* 500.

Fortin, J., Ritchie, C. and Buchanan, A. (2006) 'Young Adults' Perceptions of Court-ordered Contact' 18 *Child and Family Law Quarterly* 211.

Harris-Short, S. (2002) '*Re B (Adoption: Natural Parent)* Putting the Child at the Heart of Adoption?' 14 *Child and Family Law Quarterly* 325.

Herring, J. (1999) 'The Human Rights Act and the Welfare Principle in Family Law – Conflicting or Complementary?' 11 *Child and Family Law Quarterly* 223.

(2005) 'Farewell Welfare?' 27 *Journal of Social Welfare and Family Law* 159.

HM Inspectorate of Court Administration (HMICA) (2005) *Domestic Violence, Safety and Family Proceedings: Thematic Review of the Handling of Domestic Violence Issues by the Children and Family Court Advisory and Support Service (CAFCASS) and the Administration of Family Courts in Her Majesty's Courts Service (HMCS)*, HMICA.

HM Inspectorate of Court Administration (HMICA) (2006) *An Inspection Undertaken between October 2005 and March 2006 of the Children and Family Court Advisory and Support Service (CAFCASS) Concerning Private Law Front-line Practice*, HMICA.

Hunt, J. with Roberts, C. (2004) *Child Contact with Non-resident Parents*, Family Policy Briefing 3, University of Oxford.

Hunt, J. and Macleod, A. (2008) *Outcomes of Applications to Court for Contact Orders After Parental Separation or Divorce*, Ministry of Justice.

James, A. (2003) 'Squaring the Circle – The Social, Legal and Welfare Organisation of Contact' in Bainham A., Lindley, B., Richards, M. and Trinder, L. (eds.) *Children and Their Families: Contact, Rights and Welfare*, Hart Publishing.

James, A., James, A. and McNamee, S. (2004) 'Turn Down the Volume? – Not Hearing Children in Family Proceedings' 16 *Child and Family Law Quarterly* 189.

Jones, E. and Parkinson, P. (1995) 'Child Sexual Abuse, Access and the Wishes of Children' 9 *International Journal of Law and the Family* 54.

Kaganas, K. and Diduck, A. (2004) 'Incomplete Citizens: Changing Images of Post-Separation Children' 67 *Modern Law Review* 959.

Law Commission (1988) *Review of Child Law, Guardianship and Custody* Law Com No 172, HMSO.

Mantle, G., Moules, T. and Johnson, K. (2006) 'Whose Wishes and Feelings? Children's Autonomy and Parental Influence in Family Court Enquiries' *British Journal of Social Work* Advance Access published 17 May 2006, doi: 10.1093/bjsw/bcl035.

Mnookin, R. (1975) 'Child-Custody Adjudication: Judicial Functions in the Face of Indeterminacy' 39 *Law and Contemporary Problems* 226.

Ofsted (2008) *Ofsted's Inspection of CAFCASS East Midlands*, Ofsted.

Parker, S. (1994) 'The Best Interests of the Child – Principles and Problems' 8 *International Journal of Law and the Family* 26.

Piper, C. and Miakisher, A. (2003) 'A Child's Right to a Veto in England and Russia: Another Welfare Ploy?' 15 *Child and Family Law Quarterly* 57.

Reece, H. (1996) 'The Paramountcy Principle: Consensus or Construct?' *Current Legal Problems* 267.

Schofield, G. (1998) 'Making Sense of the Ascertainable Wishes and Feelings of Insecurely Attached Children' 10 *Child and Family Law Quarterly* 363.

Schuz, R. (2004) 'The Hague Child Abduction Convention and the United Nations Convention on the Rights of the Child' in Lødrup, P. and Modvar, E. (eds.) *Family Life and Human Rights*, Gyldendal.

Setright, H., Devereux, E. and Hutchinson, A.-M. (2008) 'Discretion, Settlement and Child's Objections: *Re M (Abduction)*' 38 *Family Law* 230.

Sturge, C. and Glaser, D. (2000) 'Contact and Domestic Violence – the Experts' Court Report' 30 *Family Law* 615.

Trinder, L., Connolly, J., Kellett, J. and Notley, C. (2005) *A Profile of Applicants and Respondents in Contact Cases in Essex*, DCA Research Series 1/05, DCA.

Trinder, L., Connolly, J., Kellett, J., Notley, C. and Swift, L. (2006) *Making Contact Happen or Making Contact Work? The Process and Outcomes of In-court Conciliation*, DCA Research Series 3/06, DCA.

Trinder, L. and Kellett, J. (2007) *The Longer-term Outcomes of In-court Conciliation*, Ministry of Justice Research Series 15/07, Ministry of Justice.

Van Krieken, R. (2005) 'The "Best Interests of the Child" and Parental Separation: on the "Civilising of Parents"' 68 *Modern Law Review* 25.

Waite, I. and Stead, H. (1998) 'Reporting the Wishes and Feelings of Children' 28 *Family Law* 44.

Walby, S. (2004) *The Cost of Domestic Violence*, Women and Equality Unit, DTI.

Westcott, H. (2006) 'Child Witness Testimony: What Do We Know and Were are We Going?' 18 *Child and Family Law Quarterly* 175.

Wilson, N. (2007) 'The Ears of the Child in Family Proceedings' 37 *Family Law* 808.

Woolf, M. (2003) 'Coming of Age? – The Principle of "The Best Interests of the Child"' *European Human Rights Law Review* 205.

Part Three

Children's rights and parents' powers

Chapter 9

Children's rights versus family privacy – physical punishment and financial support

(1) Introduction

Parents are best placed to protect and promote their children's rights and the vast majority of them do so very happily. Nevertheless, the privacy of family life ensures that parents can also tyrannise and abuse their children. Indeed, the physical dependence of young children makes an imbalance in power between them and their parents inevitable. It is clear that the law could do more to ensure that parents paid greater attention to their children's rights, if it took a more interventionist role. But social policy, strongly influenced by common assumptions about family privacy and parental autonomy, reflects a distinct lack of sympathy for the view that the law should attempt to interfere with family life.

This chapter starts by assessing the extent to which the assumption that the family should be free from legal regulation underlies current legislation governing the relationship between children and their parents. It then considers two areas which, despite being very different in content, demonstrate well the law's reluctance to intervene in order to promote children's rights. It assesses first the legal principles governing parents' right to control and discipline their children as they think fit. Second, it considers the law's treatment of the child's right to financial support and to be brought up with a reasonable standard of living. Both areas of law reflect how the concept of 'private ordering' dominates policies in these fields.

(2) Family privacy and the role of the law

Article 8 of the European Convention for the Protection of Human Rights and Fundamental Freedoms (1950) (ECHR) requires the state to respect family privacy and many legal systems operate on the assumption that family life should not be interfered with unless the circumstances are exceptional. As Minow states, the basic legal framework:

> rests on a sharp distinction between public and private responsibilities for children. Using this public/private distinction, the framework assigns child-care responsi- bilities to parents, and thereby avoids public responsibility for children. Public

power becomes relevant only in exceptional circumstances, when parents default. The government is not supposed to 'intervene' in the private realm of the family, where children's needs and interests are managed by their parents.[1]

This common attitude permeated social policy culminating in the Children Act (CA) 1989. In maintaining this approach, however, the policy-makers optimistically assume that parenting styles have been sufficiently influenced by the way the law relating to the parent-child relationship has changed over the last century. Undoubtedly, the law has gradually encouraged parents to adopt a more egalitarian approach towards their children and greater regard for their welfare. Although just over a century ago fathers had absolute authority over their children, the nineteenth-century case law supporting such a principle is now 'remaindered to the history books'.[2] Twentieth-century legislation and case law firmly established the concept of the child's welfare being paramount; more important even than their parents' rights.[3] According to decisions such as *F v. Wirral Metropolitan Borough Council*,[4] parents can no longer regard their children as part of their accumulated property and thus have no independent cause of action in tort alleging an interference with their parental rights. The modern legal approach is now that since parents' rights are only derived from their duties and exist only to secure the welfare of their children, they are better described as 'responsibilities'.[5]

Despite this changed approach, parents may pay scant regard to the fact that they are only legally entitled to act towards their children in accordance with the welfare principle and can be challenged, even overridden, if they fail to do so.[6] Although the average parent inevitably brings up his or her children with the best of intentions, the essential subjectivity of the 'welfare' or 'best interests' test[7] does little to persuade repressive parents to adjust their parenting style to promote their children's rights more effectively. That parents may single-mindedly pursue their own rights, whilst arguing that they are promoting their children's best interests was demonstrated very clearly in *R (on the application of Williamson and others) v. Secretary of State for Education and Employment and others*.[8] Minow's view of the way in which the law treats families was amply borne out by the manner in which this case was litigated. By the time it reached the House of Lords, the litigation had been pursued with hardly any reference to the children who were the focus of their parents'

---

[1] M. Minow (1986) p. 7.

[2] Per Lord Scarman in *Gillick v. West Norfolk and Wisbech Area Health Authority* [1986] AC 112 at 183, when commenting on the decision in *Re Agar Ellis, Agar Ellis v. Lascelles* (1883) 24 Ch D 317. See also Lord Denning's criticisms of the same case in *Hewer v. Bryant* [1970] 1 QB 357 at 369.

[3] E.g. *J v. C* [1970] AC 668.   [4] [1991] Fam 69.   [5] Law Commission (1988) para. 2.4.

[6] Per Lord Scarman in *Gillick v. West Norfolk and Wisbech Area Health Authority* [1986] AC 112 at 184.

[7] See Chapter 8.   [8] [2005] UKHL 15, [2005] 2 All ER 1; further discussed below.

beliefs – that a strict Christian faith demanded the administration of corporal punishment for indiscipline. As Baroness Hale of Richmond noted:

> My Lords, this is, and always has been, a case about children, their rights and the rights of their parents and teachers. Yet there has been no one here or in the courts below to speak on behalf of the children ... The battle has been fought on ground selected by the adults.[9]

These parents considered that they had a right to bring their children up according to their religious tenets without state interference. The House of Lords took the opportunity to correct their view of the law. But most parents never go near the courts, thereby giving the judiciary little opportunity to urge on them a more liberal approach to their children's upbringing.

For parents who avoid the judiciary's ambit, only well-publicised legislation which directly interferes with family life can have any real effect on their parenting styles. To date, however, the government has shown a distinct lack of enthusiasm for undertaking such a task, except in the context of parents apparently quite unable to perform their role 'properly'. Thus the law certainly empowers state intervention to protect children from parental abuse,[10] and provides sanctions against parents whose children are ill-disciplined in school[11] and who become involved in anti-social and criminal activities in the wider community.[12] But in relation to the vast majority of 'good parents', whilst the government acknowledges the important role they play in their children's development, there has been little real effort to influence the type of parenting styles they adopt.[13] Alongside attempts to ensure that parents obtain practical support and advice,[14] the government colludes with and even encourages the attitude underlying the well-known saying, 'An Englishman's home is his castle', perhaps partly because it is cheaper to allow parents to operate without major interference. Arguably, in so doing, the state is showing its respect for family privacy and autonomy, as required to do by Article 8 of the ECHR, by trusting parents to bring up children with minimum state surveillance.[15] But as Baroness Hale of Richmond points out, whilst the Convention is mainly about

---

[9] Ibid. at [71].   [10] See Chapter 15.   [11] See Chapter 6.   [12] See Chapter 18.

[13] C. Henricson (2003) ch. 5, discusses these contradictions in the government's stance towards parents.

[14] E.g. recommendations on how families can be better supported have been included in a plethora of recent governmental reviews and reports, inter alia: Cabinet Office (2006) ch. 4; DfES (2007a); DCSF (2007) ch. 3; HM Treasury (2007) chs. 1 and 2; Cabinet Office (2007); Cabinet Office (2008). Government initiatives include: Sure Start, a programme aimed at improving the life chances of infants under the age of 4 in deprived areas through better family support, health services and early education – this programme led, in turn, to the Sure Start Children's Centre programme, with the government promising the establishment of 3,500 children's centres by 2010; the National Family and Parenting Institute, a charity devoted to developing and improving support for parents; Parentline Plus, a confidential 24-hour telephone advice line for parents; the National Academy for Parenting Practitioners; the appointment of a single commissioner in every local authority to 'champion' services for children. See also discussion in M. Rutter (2005) pp. 45–56.

[15] See also the Convention on the Rights of the Child (CRC), Arts. 18 and 27.

securing freedom *from* state interference, 'children often need a great deal of state interference if they are to survive, let alone thrive'.[16]

The most influential piece of legislation to emerge in recent years, which relates specifically to children, is the CA 1989. It gave official approval to the change of emphasis emerging through case law and legislation that parents were no longer to be seen as having 'rights' over their children, in the proprietorial sense, but instead were deemed to owe 'responsibilities' to them.[17] Nevertheless, in many respects this legislation maintains the essential privacy of family life. Indeed, it deliberately adopts what has been described as a 'hands-off approach', on the basis that lawyers and litigation often do more harm than good.[18] The underlying assumption seems to be that parents' interests are identical to those of their children. Regrettably, although the CA 1989 contains detailed provisions about the duties owed by local authorities (LAs) to children they look after[19] and the services they should provide for children in need,[20] it fails to set out a basic list of parental responsibilities which could be consulted by parents, children and childcare practitioners alike. Admittedly, the average parent is unlikely to refer to legislation before adopting a particular parenting regime. Nevertheless, the indirect influence that the law can have on family life should not be underestimated. The ability, for example, of Scottish childcare practitioners to refer to legislative provisions to justify advice to Scottish parents about their behaviour may gradually influence public perceptions of the parenting role.[21] By contrast, the failure of the English CA 1989 to expand on its definition of 'parental responsibilities', suggests a misplaced complacency over the existing state of family values. It is incomprehensible that this omission was not remedied by reforming provisions in subsequent legislation.[22]

The 1989 legislation not only reflects an assumption that responsible parents will automatically protect their children's interests without legislative encouragement, but seems intent on reinforcing the privatisation of family life by withdrawing the law from areas where it formerly had had some influence.[23] Indeed, by introducing what is sometimes known as 'the principle of non-intervention', the CA 1989[24] reduced the extent to which the law has any contact with parents, thereby restricting the scope of the law's persuasive influence. Significantly, it makes no attempt to change parenting styles in favour, for example, of encouraging more consultation between parents and

---

[16] B. Hale (2006) p. 351.   [17] Now enshrined in the CA 1989, s. 3.   [18] B. Hoggett (1994) p. 10.

[19] CA 1989, ss. 22–24 and the regulations made thereunder.

[20] CA 1989, Sch. 2 and the regulations made thereunder.

[21] Children (Scotland) Act 1995, s. 1(1) sets out a reasonably detailed list of parental responsibilities.

[22] Obvious vehicles for such a change would have been the Adoption and Children Act 2002 and the CA 2004.

[23] E.g. the CA 1989, Sch. 12, para. 31 scaled down the courts' role in the arrangements made by divorcing parents for their children's future upbringing under the Matrimonial Causes Act 1973, s. 41; discussed in Chapter 7.

[24] I.e. the 'no order' principle introduced by the CA 1989, s. 1(5).

children.[25] The introduction of a parenting code, as suggested by Henricson,[26] might redress the impression that society has little interest in parenting styles until things go severely wrong. It would 'reflect and provide messages about the high expectations we have about parenting, and the commensurate duty society has to help parents match these expectations'.[27]

(3) The child's right to care and control, the parents' right to discipline the child

(A) Introduction

Were a parenting code to be introduced in this country, it should explain how parents might discipline their children and how the law regulates this aspect of parenting. Attempts to draft such provisions could provoke despair. The extent to which parents should be allowed to discipline and punish their children as they think fit produces deeply polarised views over whether the use of physical punishment on children can be justified on practical and ethical grounds, and more generally, over the extent to which the state should interfere with parents' family privacy and autonomy. Children will, of course, be unable to develop the confidence to make decisions of their own if parents provide them with little opportunity to do so, by imposing on them an over-strict atmosphere of control and discipline. Nevertheless, some writers involved in the debate about children's rights are sceptical about the law's ability to persuade parents to relax their parenting methods sufficiently to promote children's decision-making capacities. Wald humorously suggests that it would be a waste of resources, for example, to introduce legislation allowing young children the right to decide 'when to go to bed, when to bathe and what to eat', due to its obvious unenforceability. He asks rhetorically whether the parents would:

> be forbidden from enforcing their request [to the child to go to bed] by cutting off allowance, setting a curfew, not buying Christmas presents, or giving the child a spanking? … [the] concept of total independence is just unrealistic unless we are prepared to place an outside monitor in every home to eliminate the authority parents have stemming from their greater strength and economic power.[28]

Implicit in this comment is the assumption that parental behaviour is beyond the reach of the law, an attitude which has contributed to the 'hands-off' approach underlying so many of the legal principles applied to children. It is this approach to family life which has consistently prevented any legislative attempt to regulate the way in which parents discipline their children.

The dilemma is that the law expects parents to impose a degree of discipline on the household. Children are naturally high-spirited and mischievous and parents may be found to be in breach of their duty to care adequately for them if

---

[25] Discussed in Chapter 3.   [26] C. Henricson (2003) ch. 6.
[27] Ibid. at p. 107.   [28] M. Wald (1979) p. 272.

they fail to control them sufficiently to prevent accidents in the home occurring. A parent or foster parent failing to maintain a standard of care which can be expected from a reasonably careful and prudent parent may be liable in tort to a child who suffers an injury as a result. In *Surtees v. Kingston-upon-Thames Borough Council; Surtees v. Hughes* the Court of Appeal warned that the courts should be cautious and avoid imposing 'an impossibly high standard', in the light of the demands of family life.[29] Indeed:

> We should be slow to characterise as negligent the care which ordinary loving and careful mothers are able to give to individual children, given the rough-and-tumble of home life.[30]

Despite this call for flexibility, parents must impose some discipline to maintain a safe level of control on the household and this may lead to their using punishment of various kinds.

(B) The current law

For many parents, the dividing line between physical abuse, which society will not condone, and reasonable physical punishment, which it will, remains unclear. The law's continued failure to clarify the extent to which physical punishment is unacceptable means that neither they nor practitioners have clear answers. For example, the mother who had punished her son by hitting him on the thigh with a wooden spoon considered that she was behaving perfectly normally.[31] When the woman police constable asked her 'Don't you think that was a little over the top?', the mother's reply was 'No, every woman corrects their child'.[32] The court refused the mother's application for judicial review of the decision to place her two children on the child protection register. Registration indicated that the LA were, at the very least, concerned about her son's future safety. Nevertheless, no criminal charges were contemplated, nor indeed, was there any suggestion that her children were to be removed from home. The mother must have been left in some confusion about society's views of her style of parenting.

The case described above occurred nearly twenty years ago. Since then, the law governing physical punishment has become far more confused. Indeed, a precocious child attempting to ascertain whether his or her parents are behaving lawfully in adopting a particular form of punishment will find that there are few clear answers. Parents will be equally puzzled. What little clarity exists relates to the protection children receive from physical punishment in schools. Since the late 1990s, school teachers using physical punishment on their pupils have been unable to defend themselves against criminal assault charges[33] by

---

[29] [1991] 2 FLR 559, per Stocker LJ, at 571.   [30] Ibid., per Browne-Wilkinson VC, at 583–4.
[31] *R v. East Sussex County Council, ex p R* [1991] 2 FLR 358.   [32] Ibid. at 360.
[33] E.g. child cruelty under Children and Young Persons Act (CYPA) 1933, s. 1(1), or (in relation to assaults), common assault or assault occasioning actual bodily harm or inflicting grievous bodily harm.

referring to the need to impose discipline.[34] The compatibility of this legal bar with the Human Rights Act (HRA) 1998 was confirmed by the House of Lords in a case referred to above – *R (on the application of Williamson and others) v. Secretary of State for Education and Employment and others*[35] (*Williamson*). There a group of fundamentalist Christian parents unsuccessfully argued that the teachers' inability to use physical punishment in the private school to which they all sent their children, infringed their own right to freedom of religion under Article 9 of the ECHR. Despite considering that the parents' rights under Article 9 had indeed been infringed by the statutory ban, the House of Lords held that its breach could be justified[36] to protect the rights and freedoms of *others* – the others here being the children involved. In their view, the legislative prohibition achieved a fair balance between the religious rights and freedoms of the parents and those of their children to be free from physical punishment. The legality of the legislation barring the use of physical punishment in schools was thereby confirmed.

When it comes to the law relating to parents, however, even the most skilled lawyer might find it difficult to explain in clear terms the current stance on smacking. The government itself, having reviewed the current state of the law, produced the following sophism:

> The current legal position is clear and appropriate, but can be difficult to under-stand. It is neither correct nor incorrect to say that 'smacking is legal'.[37]

The terms of CA 2004, section 58, which governs this area of the law, cause considerable confusion. In the first place, it fails to state clearly whether or not the law maintains parents' traditional freedom to administer reasonable punishment by way of discipline, without incurring criminal liability. Victorian case law had established that those with lawful control of a child were entitled to administer physical punishment which was 'moderate and reasonable chastisement'[38] and the survival of this defence into the twentieth century was extremely controversial. One might assume its demise, given the specific repeal of its statutory embodiment.[39] But section 58 merely prohibits such a defence being used by a parent prosecuted for having used punishment amounting to a serious assault[40] or to child cruelty.[41] Implicit, but not stated,[42] is that the defence of 'reasonable

---

[34] Education Act 1996, ss. 548–9, as amended by the School Standards and Framework Act 1998, s. 131, makes the use of physical punishment in schools unlawful not only for civil purposes but also for criminal purposes, unless there was an immediate danger of personal injury or an immediate danger to the property (s. 548(5)).

[35] [2005] UKHL 15, [2005] 2 All ER 1; discussed by B. Hale (2006).   [36] I.e. under Art 9(2) ECHR.

[37] DfES (2007b) para. 42.   [38] *R v. Hopley* (1860) 2 F & F 202.

[39] CYPA 1933, s. 1(7), which confirmed the right of any person with lawful control or charge of a child or young person to punish him, was repealed by CA 2004, s. 58(5).

[40] CA 2004, s. 58(2)(a) and (b): an assault occasioning either grievous bodily harm or actual bodily harm.

[41] CA 2005, s. 58(2)(c).

[42] CA 2004, s. 58(1): 'In relation to any offence specified in subsection (2), battery of a child cannot be justified on the ground that it constituted reasonable punishment.'

punishment',[43] still avails a parent who has punished his child with less severity, meriting only a charge of common assault, as opposed to those offences specifically listed in section 58. Little wonder that this legislation, which fails to clarify what level or type of punishment the law allows parents to adopt, is not widely understood. Even the Crown Prosecution Service (CPS) and the police required further guidance on the level at which charges should be brought,[44] it being stressed that the child's vulnerability at the hands of an adult should be treated as an aggravating factor, often justifying a more serious charge than common assault[45] – in which case, the defence of reasonable punishment is not available.

It seems unlikely that a parent will plan the force with which he or she can hit a child, in order to avoid a charge more than common assault. To do so he or she must calculate if the intended smack or blow will produce a reddening of the skin or other injury, and if so, how long it will last for. Whether charges are brought will depend on the police's discussions with the parent and, sometimes with the LA[46] – but not, it seems, with the child. If a parent is charged with common assault, the defence of reasonable punishment remains available. But both he or she and any jury may find themselves unclear over the exact point at which physical punishment is too severe to be deemed 'reasonable punishment', thereby negating the defence entirely. Many judges and juries have shown similar confusion in the past.[47] Further bewilderment is in store. When interpreting the common law, courts must consider the demands of the HRA 1998. Thus judges and juries considering whether punishment is 'reasonable' and within the common law defence, must also take into account the considerations underpinning a child's right to protection from torture or inhuman or degrading treatment or punishment under Article 3 of the ECHR. According to the Court of Appeal in *R v. H (assault of a child: reasonable chastisement)*,[48] the defence will be available only if the punishment was reasonable, taking account of the following criteria: the nature and context of the defendant's behaviour; its duration; its physical and mental consequences for the child; the child's age and personal characteristics;[49] and the reasons

---

[43] The term 'punishment' was substituted for 'chastisement' – presumably because the latter term was considered anachronistic.

[44] CPS (2004) Charging Standards, para. 1: injuries amounting only to grazes, scratches, abrasions, minor bruising, swellings, reddening of the skin, superficial cuts or a 'black eye', can all be charged as actual bodily harm (rather than the normally more appropriate charge of common assault) in cases involving a child being assaulted by an adult (due to the serious aggravating feature of the victim's vulnerability) as long as the injuries are more than transient or trifling.

[45] DfES (2007b) para. 45 and H. Keating (2006) pp. 409–10.   [46] DfES (2007b) para. 40.

[47] E.g. *B v. Harris* 1990 SLT 208: a Scottish mother was acquitted of assault for having beaten her 9-year-old daughter with a belt, leaving her thigh bruised; cf. *Peebles v. MacPhail* 1990 SLT 245: a Scottish mother was convicted of assault for having struck her 2-year-old on the side of his face hard enough to knock him over.

[48] [2001] EWCA Crim 1024, [2001] 2 FLR 431, per Rose LJ, at [31].

[49] Factors all contained in the guidance provided by the European Court of Human Rights (ECtHR) in *Costello-Roberts v. United Kingdom* [1994] 1 FCR 65 at [30] and repeated in *A v. United Kingdom* [1998] 2 FLR 959 at [20].

given by the defendant for administering the punishment.[50] This direction superimposed on the common law defence makes the law so confusing that it is extremely difficult for anyone to decide on the lawfulness of using physical punishment.

Despite finding that neither practitioners nor parents understand what the law allows and does not allow,[51] the government concluded that it would retain the law in its present form unchanged.[52] Consequently, children have been left insufficiently protected by a convoluted set of legal principles. It appears from the CPS guidance that the parents of a child who bruises easily may face prosecution without a defence, but not if there is no lasting mark, despite the same degree of force having been used. As the government itself acknowledges, practitioners working with children consider that it 'leaves the door open not just to mild smacking but to more severe punishment that would in fact not be covered by the reasonable punishment defence'.[53] The background to this unsatisfactory situation will be briefly considered below, before discussing the pressure for further reform.

(C) Physical punishment – the historical background

The current confusion in the law regarding the legality of various forms of discipline would, of course, disappear if the parental right to use physical punishment was abolished altogether. There were considerable efforts to scrap the defence of reasonable chastisement when the CA 1989 was still in Bill form, but none succeeded. A further opportunity for amending the law appeared when the government was required to respond to the landmark decision of the ECtHR in *A v. United Kingdom (human rights: punishment of child)*.[54] The Court held that the UK government had a positive obligation to provide children with practical and effective state protection against treatment or punishment contrary to Article 3. This it had manifestly failed to do, since a jury had acquitted a stepfather of assault occasioning actual bodily harm, despite his having treated his 9-year-old stepson with sufficient severity to infringe the boy's rights under Article 3 of the ECHR.[55] Reform of the law throughout the UK then appeared inevitable. The government had expressly conceded, in the course of arguing its case in *A v. United Kingdom*, that domestic law currently failed to protect children adequately from violations of their Article 3 rights and that it would require amending.

---

[50] Northern Ireland Office of Law Reform (2001) pp. 40–1, described this last requirement, added by Rose LJ in *R v. H* [2001] EWCA Crim 1024, [2001] 2 FLR 431, as an impermissible 'gloss' placed on the ECtHR's own guidance.

[51] DfES (2007b) paras. 48–9 and 56.   [52] Ibid. at para. 57.

[53] Ibid. at para. 49.   [54] [1998] 2 FLR 959.

[55] He had beaten the boy with a garden cane on several occasions thereby bruising his buttocks, thighs and calves. The jury accepted his defence that the boy's punishment amounted to 'reasonable chastisement' under CYPA 1933, s. 1(7) and *R v. Hopley* (1860) 2 F & F 202.

In 2000, the government duly established a bizarre 'consultation' exercise over how best to reform the law, but prejudged its outcome by declaring that it would be counter-productive to outlaw physical punishment. Citing views similar to those of Wald above, it saw any legislative attempt to do so as a 'heavy-handed intrusion into family life'.[56] Such laws would 'victimise parents unfairly and compromise public confidence in the legal system'.[57] The government's reluctance to change the law was influenced by the results of an opinion poll indicating that the majority of parents considered that smacking children was acceptable and that the law should allow them to do so. In the event, the government reneged on its commitment to amend English law to take account of the ECtHR's decision in *A v. United Kingdom*. It argued that reforms had been rendered unnecessary[58] because, by implementing the HRA 1998, the law already provided children with sufficient protection from infringements of their Convention rights. In reaching such a conclusion, it was influenced by the decision of the Court of Appeal in *R v. H (assault of a child: reasonable chastisement)*,[59] which, as noted above, had adapted the direction to a jury in order to comply with the HRA 1998.

Many doubted the government's confidence that the law had been brought into line with the requirements of the ECHR,[60] or the CRC.[61] Nevertheless, no further moves occurred until the passage of the CA 2004 provided yet another opportunity for law reform. At this point, section 58, introduced by Lord Lester of Herne Hill, produced a compromise between abolishing entirely parents' right to smack their children and providing children with extra legal protection against unacceptable physical violence in the home. A third opportunity for reconsidering the law then occurred in 2007, when the government fulfilled its undertaking to review the practical operation of section 58 two years after its implementation. Again, it mounted a 'consultation' exercise designed only to review the practical consequences of section 58, as opposed to mounting a principled review of the law. As made clear below, its focus was extremely narrow. Its result was predictable, to make no further changes.

> But we do not believe that the state should intervene in family life unnecessarily – unless there are clear reasons to intervene, parents should be able to bring up their children as they think fit.[62]

The government's definition of 'clear reasons' did not apparently include the need to redress the gross imbalance between parents' rights and children's rights or the law's extreme complexity.

Now, armed with the reform effected by CA 2004, section 58, the government feels more confident that the current law fulfils its promise to the ECtHR to protect children from infringements of their rights under the ECHR, as

---

[56] DH (2000) para. 2.4.   [57] Ibid. at para. 2.14.   [58] DH (2001) para. 76.
[59] [2001] EWCA Crim 1024, [2001] 2 FLR 431.
[60] Northern Ireland Office of Law Reform (2001) pp. 40–1.
[61] JCHR (2003) para. 111.   [62] DfES (2007b) para. 55.

required by *A v. United Kingdom*. But there remain doubts over whether this is the case. Admittedly, the Parliamentary Joint Committee on Human Rights (JCHR) considers that despite the retention of the defence of reasonable punishment for parents charged with common assault, the changed law, combined with the new CPS charging standard, achieves just enough. It almost certainly ensures that a parent cannot escape criminal sanction, if the discipline used was sufficiently serious to infringe Article 3 of the ECHR. Nonetheless, as discussed below, the JCHR doubts, with good reason, whether English law in its present form would survive many subsequent challenges taken to Strasbourg. Quite apart from the problems of incomprehensibility, which the JCHR also criticises,[63] it seems unlikely that the government can ignore for long the mounting pressure to reform the law more radically.

(D) Pressure for further reform

Perhaps the strongest argument in favour of finally banning the use of physical punishment entirely is that social attitudes have changed radically over the last century. Whereas in Victorian society the physical punishment of adult and child criminal offenders was routine and domestic violence in the home was condoned, society today considers both unacceptable. It is now difficult to justify the law protecting adults from assaulting each other, whilst allowing adults to assault their smaller and more vulnerable offspring. 'Children are the only people in the United Kingdom whose right to physical integrity – to protection from all forms of inter-personal violence – is not yet supported by the law and social attitudes.'[64] Furthermore, as Baroness Hale of Richmond has indicated, there is a growing body of international and professional opinion opposing its use.[65] Research shows not only that physical punishment is less effective than other forms of discipline, but also that its use is associated with long-term negative psychological effects.[66] When parents use physical punishment as a form of discipline, they indicate to their children that violent and aggressive behaviour is an acceptable method of dealing with stressful situations, thereby reinforcing violent behaviour in society.[67]

Underlying the debate over physical punishment is some uncertainty over the role that the law should be playing. Arguably, the law should 'send out a clear message about what behaviour is unacceptable in families, or what we, as a society, feel about violence'.[68] As the experience of other European countries, notably Sweden,[69] demonstrates, the law can promote attitudinal changes in society. Indeed, prohibiting physical punishment may well produce a different

---

[63] Ibid. at para. 167.   [64] Commission on Children and Violence (1995) p. 15.
[65] *Williamson* [2005] UKHL 15, [2005] 2 All ER 1, at [85].   [66] E. Gershoff (2002) pp. 544–51.
[67] Commission on Children and Violence (1995) pp. 46–55.
[68] Northern Ireland Office of Law Reform (2001) p. 42.
[69] Sweden banned all physical punishment in 1979.

approach to discipline.[70] By contrast, this government's inconsistent attitude towards promoting attitudinal change[71] has produced a confused and incoherent body of legal principles regarding punishment. On the one hand, it has clearly indicated its disapproval of the use of physical punishment by practitioners working with children. Consequently, teachers,[72] foster carers[73] and residential care workers[74] cannot physically punish children in their care. But on the other hand, the government is not prepared to interfere with parents' views on how to bring up their children. The government claims that attitudes are already changing and that younger parents are less ready to resort to smacking.[75] Nonetheless, although 'most children' consider that smacking is out of place in modern childhood,[76] it refuses to interfere more radically. It is difficult to defend this narrow interpretation of the law's proper role in society. Nor does such an approach conform with the aims of Article 8 of the ECHR, which ensures respect for family privacy. In 1982, the European Commission of Human Rights rejected an application by Swedish parents alleging that the Swedish ban on parental physical punishment infringed their rights to respect for family life. According to the Commission, Swedish law was praiseworthy since it now discouraged abuse and prevented violence against children.[77]

Until parental use of physical punishment is banned in England and Wales,[78] the law will become progressively out of step with the legal systems of many countries throughout the world.[79] As the JCHR points out, despite the 2004 reform, the UK is still failing to comply with its international human rights obligations.[80] The Committee on the Rights of the Child has made a detailed assessment of the way in which the CRC protects children against all forms of physical punishment. As it explains, Article 37 unambiguously rules out all forms of violence against children, including corporal punishment and other cruel or degrading forms of punishment.[81] Furthermore, although neither Article 19 nor 28 explicitly refer to corporal punishment, nor the *travaux préparatoires* for the Convention record any discussion of that topic during the drafting sessions, the Convention must be regarded as a living

---

[70] J. Durrant (2000) p. 9: whilst in 1965, eight years after the law reform, 50% of the Swedish population believed that corporal punishment was a necessary aspect of childrearing, by 1994, only 11% supported corporal punishment in even its mildest form.

[71] R. Smith (2004) pp. 266–71.   [72] Discussed above.

[73] Foster Services Regulations 2002 (SI 2002/57), Sch. 5, reg. 8.

[74] Discussed in Chapter 16.   [75] DfES (2007b) paras. 29–30.   [76] Ibid. at para. 35.

[77] *Seven Individuals v. Sweden* (Application No. 8811/79) (1982, unreported) 29 CDR 104.

[78] The Welsh Assembly has no power to legislate on this issue but has repeatedly stated its strong opposition to the physical punishment of children, e.g. Jane Hutt, Minister for Children, NafW Record of Proceedings/Cofnod for 23 October 2002 and NafW Record of Proceedings/Cofnod for 14 January 2004. Scottish law was reformed by the Criminal Justice (Scotland) Act 2003, s. 51 which withdraws the parental right to inflict physical punishment on children under the age of 16 in relation to blows to the head, shaking or the use of an implement.

[79] Legislation banning physical punishment by parents is in place in 16 countries of Europe.

[80] JCHR (2004) paras. 154–63.   [81] Committee on the Rights of the Child (2006) para. 18.

instrument whose interpretation develops over time.[82] The Committee further states emphatically:

> it is clear that the practice directly conflicts with the equal and inalienable rights of children to respect for their human dignity and physical integrity … The Committee emphasizes that eliminating violent and humiliating punishment of children, through law reform and other necessary measures, is an immediate and unqualified obligation of States parties.[83]

The international monitoring bodies of human rights conventions have drawn attention to the UK's failure to abide by their terms so far as the punishment of children is concerned.[84] When responding to the UK's first and second periodic reports on the implementation of the Convention, the Committee on the Rights of the Child robustly criticised the government for failing to address its international obligation to protect children's physical integrity, notably under Articles 19 and 37.[85] More recently, when responding to the UK's combined third and fourth report, the Committee indicated its dissatisfaction with the changes wrought by section 58 of the CA 2004. Noting the legislative restriction of the defence of reasonable chastisement, the Committee emphasised its concern at the government's failure to 'explicitly prohibit all corporal punishment in the home'.[86] It stressed that the existence of any defence suggests that some forms of corporal punishment are acceptable and is therefore not compliant with the CRC. Calling attention to its previous recommendations and to those of other international monitoring bodies, it urged the government to 'prohibit as a matter of priority all corporal punishment in the family'.[87]

Regrettably, because the CRC is not part of domestic law,[88] the government can continue ignoring these criticisms. By contrast, it could not ignore a future Strasbourg finding that the current legal principles governing smacking do not adequately protect children's rights under the ECHR. On this, the JCHR's view carries weight – that given the ECtHR's increasing tendency to refer to standards set out by the CRC for children, a future challenge taken to Strasbourg might produce a ruling that the UK's compromise law does not adequately comply with children's rights under the ECHR.[89] But of course, the domestic courts may themselves reach a similar conclusion. In *Williamson*,[90] Baroness Hale of Richmond rehearsed in some detail the Committee on the Rights of the Child's response to the UK's first and second reports.[91] She rejected the parents' claim that their children's own rights under Articles 3 and 8 of the ECHR would

---

[82] Ibid. at para. 20.
[83] Ibid. at paras. 21–2. See also UN General Assembly (2006) para. 98, calling on all states to prohibit the corporal punishment of children in all settings.
[84] Committee on Economic, Social and Cultural Rights (2002) para. 36; Committee on the Elimination of Discrimination against Women (2008) paras. 33–4.
[85] Committee on the Rights of the Child (1995) paras. 16 and 31 and (2002) paras. 36–7.
[86] Committee on the Rights of the Child (2008) para. 40.   [87] Ibid. at para. 42(a).
[88] Discussed in Chapter 2.   [89] JCHR (2004) para. 143.
[90] [2005] UKHL 15, [2005] 2 All ER 1.   [91] Ibid. at paras. 82–3.

not be infringed by receiving corporal punishment from their teachers, at their parents' request. Indeed, she stressed:

> A child has the same right as anyone else not to be assaulted: the defence of lawful chastisement is an exception to that right … it is clear that a universal or blanket ban may be justified to protect a vulnerable class … Above all, the state is entitled to give children the protection they are given by an international instrument to which the United Kingdom is a party, the United Nations Convention on the Rights of the Child[92]

Admittedly these comments were directed at the legality of the ban on teachers smacking their pupils. But they might also be equally relevant to a legal challenge brought by a child against the parental defence of reasonable punishment. Conscious of the significant numbers of children removed annually into public care due to parental abuse, the domestic judiciary might ignore the government's exaggerated concern not to offend parental opinion on this topic.

(4) Parental duty to support the child

(A) The state's role of non-intervention

(i) Parents' primary role

It is arguable that children are the private concern of their parents and so governments need not intervene on behalf of those requiring support. But, on the other hand, the state has an interest in the health and well-being of its next generation; their poor development will affect the whole of society. As the General Assembly of the United Nations has observed: '[C]hildren are hardest hit by poverty because it strikes at the very roots of their potential for development – their growing bodies and minds.'[93] Furthermore, since children do not choose their parents and cannot influence their household circumstances, as innocent victims, they should not be allowed to suffer serious deprivations.[94] The CRC largely reflects this opposing view. It recognises children's right to be brought up and cared for and also to be provided with a standard of living, at least adequate for their reasonable survival. But its provisions are conservative and reflect the way childcare is currently organised throughout most of the world. It accepts that children are brought up in family units and that governments should leave them in a degree of privacy, expecting the parents to provide for children out of their own resources.

The CRC's cautious approach is reflected in Article 18(1) which requires states to 'use their best efforts to ensure recognition of the principle that both parents have common responsibilities for the upbringing and development of the child'. Similarly in Article 27(1), the CRC expects parents to take primary responsibility for their children.[95] Meanwhile, Article 18(2) acknowledges that

---

[92] Ibid. at para. 80.   [93] UN General Assembly (2002) para. 18.
[94] S. Adam and M. Brewer (2004) pp. 4–5; D. Hirsch (2006) p. 15.   [95] CRC, Art. 27(2).

some parents may not be able to fulfil their duties to their children and will need extra help. States must 'render appropriate assistance to parents and legal guardians in the performance of their child-rearing responsibilities' by providing extra support for the children in the community. They must also promote children's right to enjoy an adequate standard of living.[96] The terms of these articles make it clear that state support is to be a form of safety-net assistance only. There is no suggestion in these provisions that children are to be regarded as 'children of the state'.[97]

English law and policy also adopts a conservative approach to parental responsibilities. From 1601,[98] the state expected reimbursement from a father for any public support paid over to a mother for a child who could and should have been maintained by him, and vice versa. Although parents are no longer 'liable relatives' regarding their children,[99] section 1 of the Child Support Act 1991 firmly states that parents are responsible for maintaining their own children. Those caring for children may also incur criminal liability if they ill-treat or neglect them,[100] and, more specifically, a parent is deemed to have criminally neglected a child by failing to provide him or her with adequate food, clothing, medical aid or lodging.[101] Nevertheless, as the CRC acknowledges, some parents are simply not able to fulfil their duties to their children and need extra help to do so. Research shows that families with children need considerably higher incomes to cover the additional costs of child-raising to reach a similar standard of living to that enjoyed by their childless counterparts.[102] Indeed, the costs of rearing children can fall disproportionately on families on low income, particularly if they are living in large cities, with the combination of high costs and low income pushing some families into poverty.[103] Furthermore, the amount of work that parents can do is restricted by their need to care for their children.

The generosity shown by successive governments, when recognising the state's need to assist with the financial costs of bringing up children, has varied greatly over the last 20 years. The existence of a welfare state in this country means that impoverished parents are able to rely on certain back-up services, in the form of state benefits, together with free health care, education, and subsidised housing. Indeed, the continued availability of child benefit, a weekly sum of non-means tested child benefit payable to every adult responsible for

---

[96] CRC, Art. 27(1).   [97] B. Walsh (1991) p. 173.

[98] The date when the Elizabethan Poor Law was established.

[99] Child Maintenance and Other Payments Act (CMOPA) 2008, s. 45 amends the Social Security Administration Act 1992, s. 105(3), terminating parents' public law duty to maintain their own children; N Wikeley (2008a).

[100] Under CYPA 1933, s. 1(1).

[101] CYPA 1933, s. 1(2)(a) imposes criminal liability on 'a parent or other person legally liable to maintain a child or young person'.

[102] S. Adam and M. Brewer (2004) ch. 5.

[103] L. Harker (2006a); HCWPC (2008), paras. 187–202.

any child under the age of 16,[104] retains a symbolic and financial significance.[105] In addition to a duty to provide childcare for working parents,[106] LAs must provide extra support for families with children in need,[107] and, in the last resort, may even intervene to protect children from neglect by seeking the court's authority to remove them into LA care.[108] In the event of parents having insufficient income to maintain themselves and their children, families may become entirely dependent on state support. But it is provided on the clear understanding that the primary responsibility for maintaining them is on the parents, and the state is only stepping in because the parents have failed in this respect.

It is notable that whilst the CRC expects parents to take *primary* responsibility for their children,[109] it also recognises children's right to enjoy an adequate standard of living,[110] and the state's duty to provide parents with appropriate assistance,[111] to the maximum extent of its resources.[112] By the late 1990s, despite an overall increase in the well-being of the majority of population in the UK, the UK's obvious and increasing failure on all these counts had attracted international criticism.[113] Whilst a modicum of state support was available for those in real need, the rate of families living in poverty had risen spectacularly,[114] with the child poverty rate having increased faster in the UK, between the mid 1980s and mid 1990s, than in almost any other industrialised country.[115] Whatever measures of poverty were used,[116] when the New Labour government came to power in 1997, the child poverty statistics made depressing reading, with a third of all children living in poverty, and staying in poverty for longer than in most other industrialised countries.[117]

---

[104] Including children aged between 16 and 19, in full-time non-advanced education or in approved training, or aged 19 and in full-time further education which started before their 19th birthday, or aged 16 or 17, having ceased to be in full-time education or approved training, but who is registered for work, further education or training. See Child Benefit (General) Regulations 2006 (SI 2006/223).

[105] As from 2002, claimants of child benefit have also received £250 (more for some families in receipt of child tax credit) vouchers for each child, to be paid into a child trust fund for each child, with a further £250 to be paid on the child attaining the age of 7.

[106] Discussed below.   [107] CA 1989, s. 17(1) and (10).   [108] See Chapter 15.

[109] CRC, Art. 27(2).   [110] CRC, Art. 27(1).

[111] CRC, Arts. 27(3) and 18(2).   [112] CRC, Art. 4.

[113] Inter alia: Committee on the Rights of the Child (1995) paras. 9, 15, 24 and 25, and Committee on the Rights of the Child (2002) paras. 45 and 46: both reports referring to the high proportion of children living in poverty and the need for more resources and a more effective and co-ordinated policy; Committee on Economic, Social and Cultural Rights (2002) para. 18, referring to the increasing gap between rich and poor and to the high levels of child poverty.

[114] The numbers of children living in households with below half average income tripled between 1968 and 1995/6. HCWPC (2008) para. 11: in 1998/9, there were 4.2 million children living in poverty when measured after housing costs (AFC) and 3.1 million when measured before housing costs (BHC).

[115] J. Bradshaw (2005) p. 53.

[116] Measures of child poverty differ; the conventional definition of child poverty is 60% of equivalent median income BHC. For short discussions of this topic see HCWPC (2008) paras. 11–26 and M. Magadi and S. Middleton (2007) pp. 3–8.

[117] UNICEF (2000) p. 5. See also UNICEF (2007) pp. 4–9, citing statistics dating from 2000–2003.

(ii) The battle against child poverty

The New Labour government, rightly concerned by these alarming child poverty statistics, indicated its commitment to tackle this country's dismal record. Indeed, since 1999, when the Prime Minister pledged to end child poverty within 20 years,[118] the government has worked hard to reverse these trends. A plethora of policy initiatives have emerged. The Children's Fund was launched in 2000 to assist LAs 'tackle disadvantage among children and young people'.[119] The fifth Every Child Matters 'key outcome' is children's **economic well-being**: overcoming socio-economic disadvantages to achieve their full potential in life'.[120] Assisted by the 10-year Children's Plan, the government wants 'England [by 2020] to be the best place in the world to grow up',[121] with children growing up 'free from the blight of child poverty'.[122] A new Child Poverty Unit was established in 2007 to be run by the Department for Work and Pensions and the Department for Children, Schools and Families, with a remit to co-ordinate and develop policy on the ending of child poverty.

The government is well aware that the impact of growing up in poverty is considerable. A growing body of research indicates that long periods spent dependent on state benefits is an unhappy experience for many families and more particularly, blights the upbringing of their children.[123] The current rates of state support are not high enough to prevent significant numbers of children going without items which the vast majority of parents believe to be necessary.[124] Children growing up in 'severe poverty'[125] suffer even greater deprivation.[126] Low-income families have a higher incidence of low birth weight babies, poor levels of nutrition and infant growth, poor levels of psychological health and slightly higher levels of accidental deaths. Children's lower educational attainment, higher levels of truancy, lower self-esteem and greater likelihood of being involved in criminal behaviour can be added to this list.[127] As Utting has observed:

> Living on low income in a run-down neighbourhood does not make it impossible to be the affectionate, authoritative parent of healthy, sociable children. But it does, undeniably, make it more difficult.[128]

---

[118] Tony Blair, the Prime Minister, speech at Toynbee Hall, 18 March 1999. Gordon Brown, then Chancellor, stated that 'Child poverty is a scar on Britain's soul': G. Brown (1999) p. 8. In his speech to the Labour Party Conference, 23 September 2008, Gordon Brown, the Prime Minister, undertook to enshrine in legislation the government's aim to end child poverty by 2020, thereby binding future governments to meeting this goal. The government intends to introduce a Child Poverty Bill later in 2009.

[119] K. Pinnock and R. Evans (2008).   [120] HM Treasury (2003) para. 1.3, original emphasis.

[121] DCSF (2007) p. 5.   [122] HM Treasury (2003) para. 1.8.

[123] Inter alia: T. Ridge (2006) pp. 24–32; HM Treasury, DWP and DCSF (2008) ch. 3; HCWPC (2008) ch. 2; P. Attree (2006).

[124] C.-A. Hooper et al. (2007) pp. 18–20.

[125] I.e. children in households with income below 50% of the median, in combination with 'severe' material deprivation. M. Magadi and S. Middleton (2007) p. 9.

[126] Ibid. at ch. 2.

[127] HM Treasury, DWP and DCSF (2008) paras. 3.6–3.29 and HCWPC (2008) ch. 2.

[128] D. Utting (1995) p. 40.

Of greater concern is the evidence indicating that the factors associated with growing up in poverty have a long-term impact, extending well into adult life.[129] This may be partly attributable to children from low income families 'learning to be poor'. These children are more likely to want careers with shorter training and, on the whole, they aim for lower academic qualifications than children in two-parent or non-income support families.[130] There are obvious policy implications in the evidence indicating that 'the men and women who were poor in households as teenagers are much more likely to be poor as adults in their thirties'.[131]

The New Labour government accepted responsibility for redressing child poverty[132] and rapidly increased the financial support available for families with children,[133] particularly for lone parents.[134] But whilst it proclaimed that the 'fundamental principle of the welfare state should be to support families and children', it also warned that families must be helped to help themselves, through employment.[135] As discussed below, the financial assistance available for parents was to be largely targeted at supplementing wages, not replacing them.[136]

The government's efforts to reduce child poverty made some early and impressive progress.[137] Thus in 2006, it stated, with some pride, 'Our strategy to increase the proportion of children with parents in work has been key to our success in reducing child poverty'.[138] Nevertheless, by then, it was also becoming clear that this progress was slowing.[139] Child poverty was still much higher than in other countries with similar levels of affluence.[140] Indeed, with the number of children living in poverty again on the rise, it now looks unlikely that the government can either achieve its target of halving child poverty by 2010 or eliminating it by 2020.[141] Even the 2008 budget

[129] HM Treasury, DWP and DCSF (2008) para. 3.9.

[130] J. Shropshire and S. Middleton (1999) p. 39 and P. Attree (2006) pp. 59–63.

[131] J. Blanden and S. Gibbons (2006) p. 7; see also chs. 5 and 6, for their assessment of the correlation between childhood poverty, lack of employment and low education.

[132] The Public Service Agreement target is to halve the number of children in relative low-income households between 1998/9 and 2010/11 and eradicate it by 2020.

[133] By increasing the level of child benefit, and by introducing a generous working tax credit and a child tax credit (consolidating in 2003/4 the working families' tax credit, the children's tax credit and the child-related parts of income support/income-based jobseeker's allowance).

[134] S. Adam and M. Brewer (2004) pp. 14 and 23–4.

[135] DSS (1998a) Preamble and ch. 7, para. 1.

[136] Although income support remained available as a back-stop for those genuinely unable to work and the level of child benefit (a universal benefit) was increased.

[137] DWP (2006a) p. 31: between 1998/9 and 2004/5, the number of children in absolute low income fell by 1.6 million, and the proportion of children spending a large number of years in poverty fell from 17% in 1997–2000 to 13% in 2001–04. See also L. Harker (2006b) p. 11: 'this sharp fall in child poverty has been a remarkable achievement'.

[138] DWP (2006a) p. 33.   [139] G. Palmer et al. (2007) p. 27.   [140] D. Hirsch (2006) p. 25.

[141] HCWPC (2008) paras. 37–44. See also G. Palmer et al. (2008) p. 8 and Institute of Fiscal Studies (IFS) Press Release, 10 June 2008: the number of children living in poverty rose by 100,000 to 3.9 million AHC and 2.9 million BHC in 2006/7, this being the second annual increase, with current levels being only 15% lower than in 1998/9.

assistance[142] is unlikely to ensure such an outcome without significant extra spending on child tax credit.[143] Thus, as Utting had warned, the children most easily raised above the poverty threshold were those who had been closest to the line.

> In other words, as the Government moves closer to its target, the families left below the line are likely to be those families in the deepest poverty, who are least susceptible to its welfare-to-work measures.[144]

(iii) 'Working for children'?

Many of those left in poverty are those living in large cities, such as London,[145] in 'severe poverty', in conditions of considerable deprivation.[146] Furthermore, a substantial number of those working families whose incomes are now above the poverty line were lifted out of poverty only with the help of tax credits.[147] Nevertheless, a strong component of New Labour's anti-poverty strategy has been the 'view that state responsibility should be matched by individual responsibility' – or the 'no rights without responsibilities' formula.[148] The government has stressed that it sees it as a:

> key priority to provide support to create opportunities for the most excluded ... However, the flip-side to this support is that, as far as possible, individuals need to share and take responsibility themselves.[149]

Reinforced by influential advice that work is good for physical and mental well-being and urging a move towards a 'system based on a presumption of robust self-reliance',[150] the government remains convinced that ending child poverty hinges on getting unemployed parents back into work if they can. Traditional ideas about the 'good mother' who 'stays at home caring for her children' ill accords with New Labour's emphasis on the obligation to work and be self-supporting.[151] Indeed the former has given way to the latter, because getting mothers into employment fits 'with its [the government's] conception of "active citizenship" grounded in the responsibility to work'.[152] With the development

---

[142] HM Treasury (2008) para. 4.17: increasing first child rate of child benefit; increasing the child element of the child tax credit; disregarding child benefit income in housing benefit and council tax benefit calculations.

[143] IFS Press Release, 10 June 2008: IFS estimates indicate that additional spending on child tax credit of £2.8bn a year by 2010/11 is necessary for the government to have a 50:50 chance of meeting its child poverty target. See also G. Palmer *et al.* (2008), who, at p. 13 and Tables 11A and 11B, point to the increasing numbers of children in working families needing tax credits to avoid low income.

[144] D. Utting (2003) p. 79. See also Joseph Rowntree Foundation Press Release, 18 February 2009.

[145] G. Cooke and K. Lawton (2008) pp. 19–23. See also L. Harker (2006a)

[146] M. Magadi and S. Middleton (2007) p. 24: 10.2% of children (1.3 million) are classified as being in severe poverty.

[147] L. Harker (2006b) p. 14.   [148] S. Fredman (2006) pp. 509–10.

[149] Cabinet Office (2006) p. 38.   [150] D. Freud (2007) pp. 37–8.

[151] J. Lewis (2001) p. 491.   [152] Ibid. at p. 499.

of 'wraparound' childcare throughout the country[153] for children of working parents,[154] combined with parents' ability to obtain more flexible working arrangements,[155] the government's attention is now focused on getting lone parents back to work.[156] Their traditional exemption from the need to register for work until their youngest child reached the age of 16 is being removed. Hoping to emulate the high rates of single parent employment achieved in many OECD countries,[157] the government will 'help' single parents into work by gradually restricting their automatic entitlement to income support and transferring them to a regime of 'JSA conditionality'.[158]

These changes have not only provoked concern, but some scepticism over their ability to achieve the government's targets without much more generous investment in packages of family support; in other words without a far greater redistribution of wealth to low income families.[159] For example, given the serious economic slowdown, it is unclear how inner-city LAs can fulfil their legal obligation 'to improve the well-being of young children in their area' and 'to reduce inequalities' amongst them in relation, inter alia, to their 'social and economic wellbeing'.[160] Furthermore, despite the government's assertions that 'Work is good for you',[161] work clearly does not increase the income of all poor families[162] and may not benefit their children.[163] Such assertions not only

---

[153] L. Payne (2007): through greater numbers of Sure Start Children's Centres being established throughout England, by the introduction of 'wraparound' childcare between 8a.m. and 6p.m. in extended schools and by a new legal obligation (Childcare Act 2006, s. 6) on LAs 'so far as is reasonably practicable' to provide sufficient free childcare to enable parents to work or train for work.

[154] NB every 3 and 4-year-old is entitled to 12.5 hours free nursery education for 38 weeks per annum – an entitlement being extended to 2-year-olds in deprived areas. See HM Government (2009), Part 3.

[155] Employment Rights Act 1996, s. 80F: employers of parents with children under 6 and those with disabled children must consider requests for flexible working arrangements; these requests can only be rejected on good business grounds.

[156] Through the 'welfare-to-work programme' and the New Deal for Lone Parents. DWP (2007a) p. 27: on L. Parker's recommendation ((2006b) p. 34) Jobcentre Plus is establishing a system taking account of parents' particular childcare problems, rather than persuading them to take *any* job.

[157] D. Freud (2007) p. 83 and DWP (2007b) p. 38.

[158] DWP (2007b) p. 37: as from October 2008, lone parents must transfer from income support to jobseeker's allowance (JSA) with the requirement to seek work once their youngest child is 12; as from October 2009 when the youngest is 10; and as from October 2010, when the youngest is 7. It is also intended that single parents with younger children will be placed in the 'Progression to Work' group when their youngest child attains the age of 3. For them, there will be a 'personalised conditionality regime', with their being required to undertake 'action planning' and 'work related activities', e.g. skills health checks, to improve their employment prospects. See DWP (2008) paras. 6.62–6.68 and Welfare Reform Bill (2008), Part 1.

[159] L. Harker (2006c), pp. 46–7 and D. Hirsch (2006) chs. 4–5.

[160] Childcare Act 2006, s. 1.   [161] DWP (2007b) p. 23, original emphasis.

[162] G. Cooke and K. Lawton (2008) pp. 41–6 and HCWPC (2008) paras. 316–22.

[163] L. Harker (2006b) p. 47: 48% of children in poverty are living in couple families with one parent already working.

ignore increasing levels of unemployment but the good evidence that some parents who take work find that, with the loss of the 'passported' benefits available with income support,[164] they are no better off.[165] Many lone parents take part-time work with short hours and very low pay.[166] Large numbers of poor children are Pakistani and Bangladeshi, living in couple families with unemployed mothers – whose lack of work and language skills combined with employers' discriminatory attitudes, may undermine their ability to obtain well-paid employment.[167] One in four poor children live in households with a disabled parent, who faces much higher risks of unemployment,[168] or very low pay.[169] Those parents with disabled children may also find it difficult to work because of their caring responsibilities or their inability to find appropriate and affordable childcare.[170] But even parents who are themselves disabled[171] may feel coerced into what will often be short-term insecure employment, only soon to be forced back onto benefits.

The confident claims that work produces good outcomes for children are also surprising,[172] given the lack of agreement over the potential impact on young children of long-term nursery care, rather than full-time maternal care at home.[173] It seems that good quality early childhood education and care can benefit all children through enhancing their cognitive and social development, and that it may particularly redress the disadvantages of growing up in low-income and disadvantaged households.[174] There are, however, grave concerns about the lack of a close interaction between parents and babies[175] and the effect on the cognitive and social skills of young children who spend long hours in childcare facilities.[176] Overall, it is urged that:

> the younger the child and the longer the hours spent in child care the greater the risk. In particular, long hours of child care for those under the age of one year is widely regarded as inappropriate. Inadequate care at this most critical of all stages

---

[164] E.g. housing benefit, council tax benefit, and free school means etc.

[165] HCWPC (2008) paras. 334–45 and C.-A. Hooper *et al.* (2007) pp. 20–1.

[166] D. Hirsch (2006) p. 45.

[167] Inter alia: L. Harker (2006b) pp. 28–9; HCWPC (2008) paras. 175–85; G. Cooke and K. Lawton (2008) p. 24: 50% of Bangladeshi employees were earning less than £6.50 per hour cf. 19% of White British.

[168] L. Harker (2006c) p. 45.   [169] G. Cooke and K. Lawton (2008) p. 24.

[170] IPPR (2007) p. 39 and HCWPC (2008) paras. 167–72.

[171] The Welfare Reform Act 2007 is designed to ensure that more disabled people are encouraged back into suitable employment on pain of reduction in their benefits (now 'employment and support allowance') for failing to undertake work-focused health-related assessments, work-focused interviews and work-related activities. See DWP (2007b) ch. 4.

[172] D. Freud (2007) p. 91.

[173] UNICEF (2008) pp. 6–13, assesses the international research setting out the potential benefits and the potential harm of early childhood education/care.

[174] Ibid. at p. 9.   [175] Ibid. at Box 1 and p. 12.

[176] Ibid. at p. 12: some research shows pre-school education is associated with higher levels of anti-social behaviour amongst 3–4-year-olds.

may result in weak foundations ... Overall there is a broad consensus that child care that is 'too early and for too long can be damaging'.[177]

This is worrying evidence for mothers in the UK who, because they are receiving far shorter paid maternity leave than those in many other OECD countries,[178] are returning to work much earlier and using childcare for much younger children and for longer hours than many of their European counterparts.[179]

Good outcomes for children of working parents depend on the wide availability of high quality childcare, which is appropriate for each child, especially for children with disabilities or special educational needs.[180] But establishing such a system requires considerable extra investment. Whilst government spending on pre-school education has increased dramatically, it is still low compared with many other OECD countries.[181] The current pressure on mothers to return to work results in some feeling obliged to place young children in unregulated child care facilities,[182] staffed by poorly paid and unqualified staff.[183] Many LA registered facilities offer a substandard level of care.[184] Furthermore, at a time when lone parents are being forced to take employment when their children attain 12, there 'is abundant evidence that the support system required through an expanded childcare service and extended schools and the provision of wrap around care is not in place'.[185] Sufficient places in extended schools are unlikely to become available soon enough to avoid a new generation of 'latch-key kids'.[186] Nor should it be forgotten that work may affect family life in a variety of ways, including hampering mothers' parenting abilities.[187]

As UNICEF warns, without 'specific and large-scale action' there is a danger that only the children from better off and better educated families will reap the rewards of early childhood education. It is the poorest families who come under most pressure to return as early as possible to work and, in the absence of high quality childcare, their children will suffer a 'double disadvantage' with the childcare transition becoming 'a new and potent source of inequality'.[188] It is ironic that the government's method of eradicating child poverty may be producing new generations of children who, despite not growing up poor, reach adulthood with a different set of difficulties.

---

[177] Ibid. at p. 12.   [178] Ibid. at Box 3 and pp. 14–15.
[179] Ibid. at p. 3.   [180] K Stanley et al. (2006) pp. 21–4.
[181] UNICEF (2008) pp. 26–7; see Fig. 4: the UK's spending on early childhood services is stated to be just over 0.5% of GDP, cf. 0.7% of GDP – the average for all OECD countries .
[182] Ibid. at Fig. 3: less than 30% of UK children aged 0–3 years are placed in licensed childcare facilities
[183] Ibid, p. 23. But see HM Government (2009) ch. 4: planned workforce improvements.
[184] Ofsted (2008) p. 9: only 5% of all childcare settings provided outstanding childcare in 2007/8, 56% were good, 33% were satisfactory and 6% were inadequate.
[185] CPAG (2008) p. 7.   [186] K. Buck (2007) p. 5.
[187] S. Dex (2003) ch. 3.   [188] UNICEF (2008) p. 32.

(B) The private maintenance obligation and the role of the state

(i) Privatising child support – the state's withdrawal

An increasing emphasis on children's rights might have led to the state taking a greater interest in the extent to which parents who break up fulfil their obligation to maintain their children. But the law continues to adopt the view that, in the event of separation and divorce, it is up to individual parents to decide for themselves how to redistribute their resources between them. In other words, the law trusts parents to place their children's interests in the forefront when negotiating a division of their assets. The maintenance obligation owed by parents to their children is deemed to be part of their private relationship with each other.[189] As Eekelaar and Maclean observe:

> Western countries have been tenacious in retaining the ideology that a child should look first to its parents for the retention of its living standards, even after the collapse of the family unit. The state, it is true, has been ready to move in as an ultimate guarantor against an unacceptable level of poverty, but even in this situation assistance has frequently been conditional on the instigation of legal machinery by the child's caregiver to extract support from the other parent.[190]

It is, however, when the state has to move in against 'an unacceptable level of poverty', that we see concerns about parental privacy and taxpayers' pockets coinciding to a remarkable degree.

In 2007, after a series of failed attempts,[191] New Labour reformed the disastrously complex and inefficient child support system established by the Thatcher government in the early 1990s. Its new focus is to allow (and encourage) even the poorest parents 'to make their own arrangements', with the state merely having a role 'to support and facilitate child support arrangements, and where necessary, to enforce responsibility'.[192] Indeed, Sir David Henshaw's emphasis on parents being allowed 'to sort out things for themselves'[193] implies that the chaos produced by the Child Support Agency (CS Agency) can be attributed to the state 'interfering'[194] with separating parents' innate goodwill towards each other. Instead, from now on, things will be much better because children's interests can safely be left to private ordering. Only if things go wrong, will parents receive help 'to agree, establish and maintain payments'.[195] Such an approach leaves the millions of children still living in poverty entirely at the mercy of their parents' future arrangements, with the state taking no

---

[189] See Baroness Hale of Richmond in *R (on the application of Kehoe) v. Secretary of State for Work and Pensions* [2005] UKHL 48, [2005] 4 All ER 905, at [50]–[69], for a brief history of the parental obligation to maintain children. See also N. Wikeley (2006a) chs. 3–4.

[190] J. Eekelaar and M. Maclean (1986) p. 109.   [191] Discussed below.

[192] D. Henshaw (2006) paras. 1–9 include six references to the need for parents to be able to/ allowed to/encouraged to make their own child support arrangements.

[193] Ibid. at para. 7.

[194] I.e. by forcing parents on income support to pass over their child maintenance arrangements to the CS Agency; discussed below.

[195] D. Henshaw (2006) para. 7.

obvious interest in what is agreed or whether it either reflects children's actual needs or their parents' financial circumstances. The background to this unprincipled approach is discussed below.[196]

(ii) The child support debacle – round 1

The birth of the CS Agency was not marked by any conceptual analysis of what the state's role *should* be regarding the support of children of low income parents. Nevertheless, the fact that the papers setting out the government's proposals for the child support system used titles such as '*Children Come First*'[197] and '*A New Contract for Welfare: Children's Rights …*',[198] suggested a real concern to improve children's financial support, perhaps by supplementing their provision with state subsidies, as envisaged by the Finer Committee, in the early 1970s.[199] Further reading soon dispelled such notions. The introduction of the Child Support Act (CSA) 1991 was designed 'to ensure that parents (particularly fathers[200]) honour their legal and moral responsibility to maintain their own children whenever they can afford to do so',[201] with section 1 emphasising that 'each parent of a qualifying child[202] is responsible for maintaining him'.

The CSA 1991 created a single government agency, the CS Agency, to take over from the courts the job of assessing and then collecting maintenance payments from non-resident parents. It was partly the government's impatience with the courts for producing inconsistent maintenance orders, often for unrealistically low amounts, and often lower than could be afforded by 'absent parents',[203] which led to a new administrative system being established. More important, however, the intention of the new legislation was to bring home to men their responsibility for maintaining their biological offspring. Margaret Thatcher, the Prime Minister, had been outraged to find that fathers were absconding, leaving their children to be supported by taxpayers, in the form of state benefits.[204] By the late 1980s, only 30% of lone mothers were receiving regular maintenance payments, the remainder relying on state benefits.[205] Even

---

[196] See also HCWPC (2004) chs. 1–2 and N. Wikeley (2006a) ch. 5.

[197] DSS (1990).   [198] DSS (1999). See also DSS (1998b).   [199] DHSS (1974) Pt. 5.

[200] NB for the purposes of this part of the chapter, it is assumed that the potential payer of child maintenance is the father and that the recipient is the mother. In practice, of course, the reverse may be the case.

[201] DSS (1990) vol. I, p. 5.

[202] Broadly, a 'qualifying child' is any child in relation to whom a parent can claim child benefit, as long as one parent is a non-resident parent. See N. Wikeley (2006a) pp. 217–23.

[203] DSS (1990) vol. I, para. 1.5. NB the term 'absent parent' was replaced by 'non-resident parent': Child Support, Pensions and Society Security Act (CSPASSA) 2000. This change reflected the view that 'absent' unfairly implied that maintenance payers had dropped out of their children's lives, when not all had.

[204] Margaret Thatcher's attitude is entertainingly described by Ward LJ in *R (Kehoe) v. Secretary of State for Work and Pensions* [2004] EWCA Civ 225, [2004] 1 FLR 1132, at [18].

[205] DSS (1990) vol. I, observed (at para. 1. 5) that more than 750,000 lone parents were dependent on income support, with the costs to the taxpayer having increased from £1.4bn in 1981/2 to £3.2bn in 1988/9.

those in receipt of maintenance were often paid too little to enable them to survive without further assistance. Indeed, as Lewis observes, the new law reflected the philosophy of the CA 1989; it was as much about impressing on parents that it was *they*, and not the state, who had a responsibility for their offspring, as about enforcing their responsibility for their children.[206] The underlying motive of emphasising parental responsibility was, of course, to reduce state support. Fathers were cast in their traditional role, as a source of financial support, rather than care,[207] with the legislation making no attempt to improve parent-child relationships, nor to make the child's welfare paramount.[208]

The new use of a fixed formula for calculating maintenance would, the government promised, 'produce maintenance payments which are realistically related to the costs of caring for a child'.[209] One might argue that, in so doing, the legislation was asserting the state's interest in ensuring that children received sufficient maintenance to enable them to live fulfilling lives. This, however, was not the case. In reality, the new legislation merely established a complicated and inefficient procedure aimed at moving money from one parent to another. Fathers were to be the sole source of the money – not the state. Admittedly, the fact that a state agency using this formula largely replaced the courts' jurisdiction over children's maintenance meant that official views about the standard of living required by children inevitably started permeating private ordering. Nevertheless, the arcane complication of the child support formula added considerably to the difficulties and unpopularity of the ill-fated CS Agency and resulted in relatively little child maintenance being collected. Extensive amounts of information from both parents were required by the Agency before the non-resident parent's child support liability could be calculated – a problem contributing to the delays and mounting arrears of maintenance, which quickly became chronic. The formula was extremely difficult for parents to understand, making it hard for them to predict how much they should pay. Furthermore, the calculation itself was so prone to error that many appeals against assessments sprang from mistakes made by the CS Agency. The reforms in 1995 attempting to address complaints that the child support formula was far too rigid,[210] merely tinkered with the overall scheme and did little to remedy its unpopularity. By the late 1990s, the difficulties produced by the formula resulted in CS Agency staff spending 90% of their time making assessments, keeping them up to date and making initial payment

---

[206] J. Lewis (2000) p. 95.   [207] Ibid.

[208] CSA 1991, s. 2 (unchanged by CMOPA 2008): when exercising a discretionary power the Secretary of State must 'have regard to the welfare of any child likely to be affected by his decision'. Per Thorpe J in *R v. Secretary of State ex p Biggin* [1995] 1 FLR 851 at 854: s. 2 merely requires the CS Agency to notice welfare 'in passing … Welfare is not a paramount or even a particularly significant consideration.'

[209] DSS (1990) vol. I, para. 2.1. The level set was predicated by income support rates.

[210] The CSA 1995 amended the CSA 1991; changes included the introduction of exceptions or 'departures' from the formula, in certain well-defined circumstances, e.g. exceptionally high travel to work costs.

arrangements. Indeed, only 10% of the Agency's resources were left for chasing up non-resident parents behind on their payments, with only 66% of maintenance due actually being paid.[211]

The child support system quickly attracted considerable hostility from parents up and down the country.[212] Many parents, mothers and fathers alike, would have preferred not to become involved with the CS Agency, with some considering that it exacerbated their poor relationships.[213] But the legislation insisted on any parent with care who was dependent on state support[214] cooperating with the CS Agency over tracing the father of her child.[215] This was to enable the Agency to recoup from him, in the form of child maintenance, some of the money she had been receiving from the state.[216] A mother's reluctance to involve the father was often influenced by her knowledge that unless he was earning enough to provide her with sufficient income to lift her above income support levels, forcing him to contribute to the child's maintenance would seldom benefit the child financially. This was because, under the original CS scheme, there was no income support 'disregard'. Consequently, in most cases, the mother was no better off because every pound recovered from the father merely went straight into the coffers of the Treasury, to reimburse the state for the weekly amount of income support paid to the mother. Given this feature of the scheme, the poor compliance rates were inevitable; fathers knew their children would not be lifted out of poverty because of the pound-for-pound removal of the child support payments.[217]

Theoretically, a mother was not obliged to identify the father of her child, thereby enabling the agency to pursue him; but if she refused to do so, her income support might reduce.[218] She could only escape such a penalty if she could establish that there were 'reasonable grounds for believing that ... there would be a risk of her, or any child living with her, suffering harm or undue distress as a result'.[219] Whilst this formula was allegedly relatively easy for claimants to meet,[220] a mother's motives for withholding identifying information might well be disbelieved.[221] These provisions had the 'clear legislative

---

[211] DSS (1999) p. 3.   [212] N. Wikeley (2006a) ch. 5.

[213] G. Davis, N. Wikeley and R. Young (1998) p. 192: in over 40% of cases in their study, one or both of the parents claimed that their relationship had suffered from CS Agency involvement.

[214] Income support or income-based jobseeker's allowance.

[215] Under CSA 1991, s. 6(3) (as amended by CSPASSA 2000) parents with care on benefit were assumed to have authorised the collection of child maintenance, with the result that they had specifically to object if they did not wish this to occur.

[216] CSA 1991, s. 6(1)–(3).   [217] T. Ridge (2005) p. 134.

[218] A 'reduced benefit direction' made under CSA 1991, s. 46(5) reduced the recipient's benefit by 40%, for up to three years.

[219] CSA 1991, s. 46(3). N. Wikeley (2006a) pp. 256–72.

[220] *Secretary of State for Work and Pensions v. Roach* [2006] EWCA Civ 1746, [2007] 1 FLR 2167, per Leveson LJ, at [40].

[221] Ibid., per Leveson LJ, at [45]: the tribunal had justifiably concluded that the claimant had lied and exaggerated her fears of the non-resident parent's future violent behaviour if contacted by the CS Agency; discussed by N. Wikeley (2007a).

purpose that non-resident parents should reduce the impact upon public funds of the cost of maintaining their children'.[222] There was certainly no intention to improve the relationship between father and child. Moreover, a mother might quite reasonably resent being forced to identify the father, given that she would gain nothing financially from his complying with any assessment.

(iii) The child support debacle – round 2

By the late 1990s, the CS Agency had not only still failed to get on top of its case load, but had also become a 'byword for bureaucratic incompetence'.[223] About one million families dependent on income support were headed by lone parents, with only one in five of those families receiving maintenance for their children.[224] The Agency was owed over a billion pounds in unpaid child support, with over one-half considered to be uncollectable. But the respective approaches of the Thatcher government when initiating the child support scheme and the New Labour government, when reviewing its operation in 1999, were remarkably similar. Both governments' primary concern was to reduce public expenditure on income support. The continuing poverty of one-parent families was met by a resolve to make the child support scheme more efficient, rather than to produce a more generous system of benefits for the children being brought up in such needy circumstances.

The New Labour government decided that the CS Agency could not operate more efficiently unless the child support formula was simplified. The new formula departed radically from the old.[225] The aim of the original legislation had been to produce child maintenance assessments which reflected real child-care costs, as predicated by income support rates.[226] The formula had produced relatively low sums, but symbolised a level below which child maintenance should not fall. Arguably, the state had been ensuring that children received just enough maintenance to live on – not more. But under the new system operative as from 2003, rather than attempting to link real childcare costs with the maintenance assessment, the greatly simplified formula now required the non-resident parent to pay 15% of his net income for the first child, 20% for two and 25% for three or more, irrespective of the children's age.[227] Both the income of the parent with care and of the non-resident parent's current partner was completely ignored.

The new formula seemed to have little philosophical basis. The government simply maintained that the proposed base rate of 15% of the payer's net income

---

[222] Ibid., per Leveson LJ, at [46].   [223] H. Davies and H. Joshi (2001) p. 303.

[224] DSS (1999) p. 17.

[225] CSPASSA 2000 introduced the new formula by amending CSA 1991, Sch. 1, Pt. 1.

[226] DSS (1990) vol. I, para. 2.1.

[227] The new scheme introduced four rates: the basic rate, a reduced rate, a flat rate and a nil rate. See CSA 1991, Sch. 1, Pt. I. NB Sch. 1, para. 10(3) imposed an upper statutory cap – the non-resident parent's net income of over £2,000 per week was ignored. But Sch. 1, para. 10(3), as amended by CMOPA 2008, Sch. 4 paras. 2 and 10, the non-resident's gross income of over £3,000 is ignored.

was 'roughly half the average that an intact two-parent family spends on a child', the assumption being that this is what a non-resident parent *should* also pay.[228] As Parkinson pointed out,[229] the government cited only one piece of research to substantiate such a claim.[230] The new formula not only ignored the fact that expenditure is greater for older children but also that when two-parent families spend 30% of their income on their children, fathers contribute far more to this total than mothers. In the UK, the norm is the 'one-and-a-half-earner household', with a high proportion of women working short part-time hours on low rates of pay.[231] To argue that non-resident fathers should only contribute half what two parents spend on their children was nonsensical, given that mothers' incomes, if they existed at all, were far lower than that of fathers. There was certainly no attempt to argue that the new formula would produce levels of maintenance matching actual childcare costs.

The new scheme appeared to overlook, and in some ways it exacerbated, many problems commonly experienced by mothers with care. For example, the shared care provisions became more complicated,[232] increasing the scope for disagreement.[233] Furthermore, the non-resident's new entitlement to have his responsibility for any stepchildren or children of a subsequent relationship recognised before calculating his liability to his first family[234] implied to many mothers an intention to favour the second family over the first.[235] More crucially, the new formula produced lower levels of child maintenance than before. Indeed the White Paper countered the fact that an average weekly maintenance liability would be lower under the new legislation,[236] by arguing that the new simpler rules and tougher sanctions[237] would persuade more non-resident parents to pay more child maintenance.[238] As Douglas observed:

> This reduction [in the non-resident parent's child maintenance liability] represents an acceptance that absent parents *will not* pay sums they deem unacceptable for their children, no matter how unrealistic their views on the costs of bringing up a child may be.[239]

Admittedly, the reform package included a much needed, though derisorily low, income support disregard, or 'child maintenance premium' – enabling caring parents on income support (and income-based jobseeker's allowance), to

---

[228] DSS (1999) p. 9.   [229] P. Parkinson (2007) p. 828.

[230] I.e. S. Middleton *et al.* (1997).   [231] J. Lewis (2001) p. 500.

[232] CSA 1991, Sch. 1, para. 7(4). The need for a non-resident parent to have care of his children for over 104 nights per annum was modified, with the threshold for shared care being reduced to 52 nights per annum, and fractional reductions for increased care beyond that threshold.

[233] N. Wikeley (2006a) p. 317.

[234] CSA 1991, Sch. 1, para. 2(2) allows percentage deductions for each 'relevant other child'.

[235] T. Ridge (2005) p. 129.

[236] It was predicted that the average would fall from £38 per week to £30.50 per week.

[237] E.g. much higher rates of interim and default measures and court ordered punitive sanctions, such as driving disqualifications for non-resident parents who deliberately defied maintenance calculations.

[238] DSS (1999) p. 13.   [239] G. Douglas (2000) p. 280 (footnotes omitted).

keep the first £10 per week of maintenance recovered, in addition to their benefit entitlement.[240] To the cynical, however, such a concession seemed principally motivated by a desire to encourage lone parents to cooperate with the CS Agency, rather by a new generosity of spirit.

The 'new' child support system became operational in 2003,[241] but for new cases only. Within a short time the CS Agency had established once again its peculiar ability to snatch defeat out of the jaws of victory. The government had promised that despite producing lower assessments, the new formula would produce more rapid results, more accurate assessments and increased compliance. Partly due to the failures of a new IT system, the CS Agency failed on every score; it was neither able to process new cases more rapidly,[242] reach more accurate assessments,[243] nor produce better compliance.[244] Meanwhile, the assessments were even lower than forecast.[245] Furthermore, the outstanding debt load of unpaid child maintenance was rising apace,[246] with the Agency's failure to ensure compliance by taking enforcement action producing a culture of non-compliance amongst non-resident parents.[247] Even when it did take steps to enforce payment, the calculations in the liability orders were often inaccurate.[248] The House of Commons Work and Pensions Committee described the Agency's performance as 'woefully inadequate'[249] and its failure to attain any of its targets as 'totally unacceptable ... and represents nothing less than a severe breach of trust'.[250] Furthermore, it was clear that child support was not assisting the government's fight against child poverty at a time when the government's child poverty targets were looking increasingly unrealistic.[251]

(iv) Children's rights in reverse – round 3

By 2006, although the CS Agency was becoming more cost-effective,[252] it was plain that the government had run out of patience. Now there was an opportunity to review the conceptual basis for the state's role in child support; but this

---

[240] The old scheme's regulations still governed existing cases; therefore unlike new scheme mothers with care, old scheme mothers with care dependent on income support were unable keep the first £10 per week of any maintenance recovered.

[241] Having been delayed by IT problems.

[242] National Audit Office (2006) para. 3.26: by March 2006, cases were taking 38 weeks to clear instead of the hoped for 6 weeks.

[243] HCWPC (2004) paras. 83–5.

[244] National Audit Office (2006) para. 4.6: by March 2006, compliance in new scheme cases was 67% (target 78%) cf. compliance in old scheme cases being 75%.

[245] HCWPC (2004) para. 87.

[246] National Audit Office (2006) p. 14: by 2006, there was £3.5bn of outstanding maintenance with 60% considered uncollectable. HCWPC (2004) para. 105: the average time for arrears to be paid off was 11.8 years.

[247] HCWPC (2004) para. 110.

[248] National Audit Office (2006) p. 65: 65% of cases where liability orders were sought were inaccurate.

[249] HCWPC (2004) para. 18.   [250] Ibid. at para. 31.   [251] Discussed above.

[252] N. Wikeley (2007b) p. 438: in 1995/6, £1 child support collected cost £1.55 to recover, by 2005/6, £1 collected cost 56 pence.

was clearly not on Sir David Henshaw's agenda. Regrettably, such a review had not been forced upon the government by the judiciary in *R (on application of Kehoe) v. Secretary of State for Work and Pensions*.[253] In that decision, the majority of the House avoided adopting a principled approach to a mother's claim that her inability to take her ex-husband to court to enforce the arrears of child maintenance he owed her[254] was an infringement of her rights under Article 6 of the ECHR. In their view, it had been the clear intention of the 1991 Act (which they considered had replaced the original child maintenance framework with an entirely new scheme) to preclude a person with care from playing any part in enforcing maintenance assessments against the non-resident parent. Article 6 was not available because Mrs Kehoe had no civil rights under the CS scheme.[255] Wikeley quite rightly criticises the majority opinions in *Kehoe* for being profoundly disappointing in adopting 'an unduly literalist and positivist approach to the question of statutory construction'.[256]

So far as the majority of the House of Lords was concerned in *Kehoe*, the fact that many thousands of children were suffering unnecessary child poverty, due to the CS Agency's failure to enforce vast sums of unpaid maintenance, was beside the point. Only the CS Agency could enforce the maintenance owing. It was left to Baroness Hale of Richmond, in her dissenting judgment, to reassess the concepts underlying the state's involvement in this area of law. She stressed that the matter should be considered from the child's point of view, rather than that of the parents.

> this is another case which has been presented to us largely as a case about adults' rights when in reality it is a case about children's rights. It concerns the obligation to maintain one's children and the corresponding right of those children to obtain the benefit of that obligation.[257]

But her view that children have an independent civil right under existing law to be maintained by their non-resident parents is difficult to substantiate. There is certainly no historical justification for the view that children ever had any independent and enforceable rights against non-resident parents.[258] Furthermore, unlike children in Scotland, those in England and Wales had never gained the right to seek the assistance of the CS Agency themselves.[259] Nonetheless, Baroness Hale's reminder was timely. Children have been failed

---

[253] [2005] UKHL 48, [2005] 4 All ER 905.

[254] By the time the case reached the Court of Appeal, the outstanding arrears owed by Mrs Kehoe's non-resident husband totalled well over £17,000.

[255] See also *R (Rowley) v. Secretary of State for Work and Pensions* [2007] EWCA Civ 598, [2007] 2 FLR 945, per Court of Appeal: since the claimed existence of a duty of care owed by the CS Agency to its users was inconsistent with the child support scheme which contained remedies, including judicial review, for those who had suffered loss for the Agency's deficiencies, a parent with care could not sue the Agency in negligence for its various failures in discharging its duties under the CSA 1991.

[256] N. Wikeley (2006b) p. 292.   [257] [2005] UKHL 48, at [49].

[258] N. Wikeley (2006b) p. 297–300.   [259] Discussed below.

by a system designed to provide for them – they have a moral right to maintenance which *should* have been recognised by the law. This right could serve as the basis for a more principled approach to the state's role in the child support scheme.

It was clear, however, from the pragmatic approach adopted by Sir David Henshaw[260] that a conceptual basis for child support was of little interest to him. He obviously assumed that his task was merely to address the extraordinary chaos produced by a hugely inefficient and expensive public authority. The government adopted his report, almost in its entirety,[261] with new legislation being introduced within a year of its publication.[262] The replacement of the CS Agency itself, by a new body, the Child Maintenance and Enforcement Commission (CMEC), was to symbolise a complete break with the past.[263] Nevertheless, much of the existing legislative framework was left intact,[264] with an even more simplified child support formula,[265] and even more Draconian enforcement powers.[266] Most radical of all the changes, however, was the ending of the CS Agency's role as a collection agency for the state. This was achieved by a twofold change. First, low income recipients of child support would receive an increasingly generous income support disregard.[267] Second, the rule that receipt of income support was tied to the Agency's right to collect child maintenance from the non-resident parent was abolished.[268] This, Henshaw thought, would encourage low income parents to enter into voluntary maintenance agreements.[269] So in future, whether or not they are dependent on state benefits, parents are free to make their own private arrangements for their children's future support without involving the state or the legal system. Those who wish to obtain legal ratification of any agreement reached can obtain a consent order from the courts.[270] Meanwhile, those 'unable or unwilling to agree privately or by consent' can seek help from CMEC to obtain an

---

[260] D. Henshaw (2006).   [261] DWP (2006b), DWP (2006c) and DWP (2007d).

[262] Child Maintenance and Other Payments Bill, which obtained its second reading in the House of Commons in July 2007.

[263] D. Henshaw (2006) para. 70.   [264] N. Wikeley (2007b) pp. 447–50 and 456.

[265] CSA 1991, Sch. 1, para 2(1) and (2), as inserted by CMOPA 2008, s. 16 and Sch. 4, para. 3: child support is now calculated on gross, not net income, with percentage rates for each child now being 12% for one child, 16% for two children and 19% for three or more children, with reduced percentages (9%, 12% and 15%) for non-resident parents earning more than £800 per week gross.

[266] E.g. current account deduction orders and disqualification from using travel documents, such as passports. See N. Wikeley ((2008b) pp. 1103–6 .

[267] The income support disregard was increased from £10 per week to £20 per week as from the end of 2008. As from April 2010 there will be a full child maintenance disregard in all income-related benefits. 'Old scheme' recipients were also given the right to claim the disregard, as from the end of 2008.

[268] CMOPA 2008, s. 15 repeals CSA 1991, s. 6.   [269] D. Henshaw (2006) para. 25.

[270] NB but contrary to Henshaw's recommendation (D. Henshaw (2006) paras. 57–8) the '12-month rule' was retained (DWP (2007d) para. 8) whereby a parent with a consent order can seek CMEC's assistance after 12 months of the consent order's duration, thereby preserving a parent with care's ability to escape being locked into an agreement which has broken down.

assessment of what maintenance is appropriate, and to enforce compliance, where necessary.[271]

Most, like Parkinson, consider that the most radical aspect of these changes is the 'virtual abandonment of one of the Child Support Agency's core rationales … that is for Government to recoup some of its social security expenditure on the support of the primary carers of children when parents are living apart'.[272] It had been influenced by the statistics indicating that the majority of applications to the CS Agency came from those in receipt of income support,[273] with relatively few receiving a net increase in income as a result.[274] It also accords with research indicating that the sudden involvement of the CS Agency in cases where parents have hitherto privately brokered their own financial arrangements, has, in the past, often caused immense resentment.[275] Some non-resident fathers simply had not understood why the CS Agency became involved, nor believed that the parent with care had no choice over giving their name to the Agency.[276] But although this reform receives overall approval,[277] there are deep concerns that non-resident parents may simply provide maintenance at carefully calculated low levels in order to avoid the potential involvement of CMEC.[278] Worse, they may fail to provide any maintenance at all, content to leave parents with care on benefits.[279] The government brushed these reservations aside, arguing that the new scheme would be beneficial for parents and their children.[280]

As noted above, these changes were all predicated on Henshaw's belief that parents should be allowed to organise their own arrangements for supporting their children on separation,[281] with the help of a new information and support service.[282] This assumption has provoked considerable misgivings,[283] largely because the emphasis on private ordering creates the risk that 'any existing imbalances between parents would be simply reinforced, to the detriment of children's interests'.[284] There is little research to substantiate the view that a system of private ordering can lift children out of poverty – indeed what there is[285] suggests that such a change may achieve precisely the reverse, since the parent with care often agrees to a low level of maintenance to keep good relations within the family.[286] In the context of out-of-court settlements negotiated by divorcing couples, the wish to avoid conflict has often led to long-term

---

[271] D. Henshaw (2006) para. 39.   [272] P. Parkinson (2007) p. 817.

[273] National Audit Office (2006) para. 3.4: around 70% of applications.

[274] D. Henshaw (2006) para. 10.   [275] A. Bell *et al.* (2006) p. 89.   [276] Ibid. at p. 49.

[277] HCWPC (2007) p 12–13, DWP (2007c) pp. 19–20.   [278] P. Parkinson (2007) p. 819.

[279] HCWPC (2007) para. 179.   [280] DWP (2007d) p. 15.   [281] D. Henshaw (2006) paras. 1–9.

[282] CMOPA 2008, s. 5: CMEC is obliged to provide parents with such information and guidance as it thinks appropriate to secure effective maintenance arrangements for their children.

[283] Summarised in DWP (2007c). See also HCWPC (2007) and DWP (2007d).

[284] Inter alia: HCWPC (2007) paras. 15–23; DWP (2007c) para. 2.2; DWP (2007d) para. 2; N. Wikeley (2007b) p. 446.

[285] A. Bell *et al.* (2006): research into the attitudes of parents using CSA MD (the system whereby the CS Agency calculated the level of maintenance, with the couple then choosing to organise payment themselves, to be paid direct from non-resident parent to parent with care).

[286] Ibid. at p. 31. See also HCWPC (2007) paras. 19–21.

regrets, with many feeling that they have come under pressure to negotiate and make unacceptable compromises.[287] Indeed, the judiciary are familiar with unscrupulous fathers whose reluctance to reduce their own standard of living to improve that of their children leads them to lie about the extent of their substantial resources.[288] 'Overall, non-resident parents appear to wield a disproportionate amount of power over establishing financial arrangements following separation, regardless of the type of arrangements adopted.'[289] It seems naive to assume that matters will change under the new regime merely because of the steps taken by CMEC to raise parents' awareness of the importance of taking responsibility for the maintenance of their children and of making appropriate arrangements for this to occur.[290]

On reaching greater maturity, some children may look back on their lives and decide that their mothers did not try hard enough to extract maintenance out of their fathers. Like their peers, they would have liked to have nice clothes and go on school outings, rather than managing without luxuries of any kind. In particular, they may find it difficult to understand why they themselves have no right to take their non-resident fathers to court to enforce a maintenance obligation which apparently exists, but on paper only. Incomprehensibly, the third attempt to produce a workable child support scheme contains no provision giving children in England and Wales a right to take the law into their own hands. Unlike Scottish law, which from the inception of the 1991 child support scheme, allowed children over 12 to initiate an application, no provision was made for English and Welsh children to approach CMEC themselves to obtain child maintenance from either parent. Under English law, a child support application can still only be brought by the adult providing the child with a home and day-to-day care[291] – so whether such a step is taken remains outside the child's control. Similarly unchanged are the provisions allowing a non-parent carer with a residence order to proceed in the courts against the child's parents for various financial orders outside the child support scheme,[292] an option not available to the child, except in very limited circumstances.[293]

As Ridge suggests, making children the legal beneficiaries in their own right might help reduce parental conflict, as well as establishing 'the fundamental principle that child support is first and foremost about children's rights and entitlements'.[294] Regrettably, however, three attempts were made at producing a workable scheme of child support, without the government ever reviewing the ethical issues underlying this area of law. Admittedly, towards the end of the reforming era, links were being made between an improved child support system and the battle against child poverty.[295] But there was, for example, no

---

[287] F. Wasoff (2005) p. 245.

[288] E.g. *Phillips v. Peace* [1996] 2 FLR 230; *V v. V (child maintenance)* [2001] 2 FLR 799; *Re S (unmarried parents: financial provisions)* [2006] EWCA Civ 479, [2006] 2 FLR 950.

[289] A. Bell *et al.* (2006) p. 41.   [290] CMOPA 2008, s. 5.   [291] CSA 1991, s. 3(3).

[292] See discussion below.   [293] Discussed in Chapter 4.

[294] T. Ridge (2005) p. 136.   [295] E.g. DWP (2006c) paras. 1.1–1.7.

attempt to justify, on a principled basis, the assumption that taxpayers *should* act as a financial safety net for the children of the poor. There are obvious ways of doing so; for example, one might reason that 'additional children reduce the per-capita cost of public goods and support for the growing older population'.[296] Furthermore, society has a clear need to regenerate itself with a young and healthy generation of children. Nor was there any detailed discussion of the Finer Committee's recommendation that single-parent families should receive an additional state subsidy, a Guaranteed Maintenance Allowance, designed to give single parents a genuine choice between staying at home with their children and going out to work.[297] The system of purely private ordering between parents introduced by the 2008 scheme includes no clear statutory statement that children throughout their childhood have a right to enjoy their parents' wealth and prosperity.[298] Unsuccessful efforts were made to introduce into the legislation, as a primary objective, affirmation of such a right.[299] Its inclusion would have redressed the charge that the bill was all about achieving operational efficiency and devoid of policy. Its omission reflects an official mindset incapable of considering matters from a child's viewpoint, let alone from the perspective of children's rights.

(C) The private maintenance obligation and the role of the courts

As the preceding discussion demonstrates, the law relating to children's maintenance contains few, if any, principles that promote, or even acknowledge the concept of children being rights bearers. The legal principles governing the courts' role in this area of law are even more adult-focused than those underpinning the child support legislation. Although the courts undoubtedly take a far more robust approach to ascertaining the true state of a man's income, often by making an order based on their view of what he could make available if he wished,[300] this does not reflect any judicial zeal to obtain the best for the child, *on behalf of the child*. The private nature of the maintenance obligation is reflected in the way disputes over financial provision focusing on children reach the courts – these are applications brought by adults against adults and the choice is theirs whether they bring them at all. Had the mother in *Phillips v. Peace*[301] decided that she would accept the CSA's nil assessment and depend on

---

[296] S. Altman (2003) p. 184.

[297] D. Henshaw (2006) Annex II, paras. 3–8, briefly discusses the guaranteed maintenance allowance common in some Scandinavian countries, but dismisses it as an option for England and Wales for various reasons, including expense.

[298] N. Wikeley (2007b) pp. 456–7.

[299] House of Lords Committee stage of the CMOP Bill, per Lord Kirkwood of Kirkhope, HL Debs, *Hansard*, 29 January 2008, cols GC275–80.

[300] *Phillips v. Peace* [1996] 2 FLR 230, per Johnson J, at 232. Unlike the CS Agency, Johnson J disbelieved the father's claim that he had insufficient income to pay any child support and made large lump sum orders against him to fund the purchase of a house, plus furniture and other expenses for his child.

[301] [1996] 2 FLR 230.

state assistance to bring up her daughter, no one could have forced her to apply to the courts for any of the remedies remaining outside the powers of the agency.[302] The fact that the child could have enjoyed a far higher standard of living, had the mother felt equal to proceeding against the father, would have been irrelevant.

The child support system is designed to exclude applicants' involvement with the courts in all cases involving CMEC's jurisdiction,[303] namely where a parent with care requires income from a non-resident parent for a qualifying child. In practice, however, affluent couples generally reach agreement over child maintenance liability, and will often have such agreements incorporated in the form of a consent order.[304] As discussed above, the government hopes that far more couples on low income will, in future, do the same. When advising on the terms of such agreements, legal advisers should obviously take account of the child support formula, when calculating the amount needed by the parent retaining day-to-day care of the children. This is largely because CMEC can, at the mother's request, bypass any agreement she entered into with the father, particularly if she accepted a level of income for the children less than it would have arrived at itself using the statutory formula.[305] The existence of the child support formula should, in this way, reduce the possibility of parents agreeing a figure below that approved of by the state. Nevertheless, it may not be easy to calculate the possible impact of a clean break settlement on a child maintenance assessment.[306] Similarly, it may be difficult for the judiciary to design an appropriate package of ancillary relief for a divorcing mother, given their own limited powers in relation to the children's financial support.[307]

Although the courts, as a general rule, have no power to deal with any aspect of the child's needs which could be met by income payments,[308] the child support legislation itself sets out a list of important exceptions to this principle. The courts therefore retain the power to supplement CMEC's assessments with top-up orders,[309] orders for additional educational expenses[310] and orders for

---

[302] See below.   [303] CSA 1991, s. 8(3).

[304] N. Wikeley (2006a) ch. 7: discusses the courts' residuary powers and the interrelationship between their powers and the CS Agency, in cases where maintenance agreements and consent orders exist.

[305] CSA 1991, s. 9(3). But NB s. 4(10)(aa): the mother cannot apply to CMEC for assistance within one year of the agreement being reached.

[306] E.g. *Pabari v. Secretary of State for Work and Pensions* [2004] EWCA Civ 1480, [2005] 1 All ER 287: an ex-wife unsuccessfully appealed against a reduction in the ex-husband's child maintenance assessment – his inability to comply with the terms of an order for ancillary relief on divorce without remortgaging his house led to his new mortgage payments being included as his housing costs.

[307] E.g. *V v. V (child maintenance)* [2001] 2 FLR 799, Wilson J, at [9]–[11] complained at his inability to order the father to pay child maintenance to his children at the level calculated as appropriate in the mother's package of ancillary relief.

[308] CSA 1991, s. 8(3).

[309] CSA 1991, s. 8(6). But NB the courts can only make an order to top up the amount assessed by CMEC if the non-resident parent's income exceeds the statutory limit.

[310] CSA 1991, s. 8(7).

the expenses of disabled children.[311] Parents may, of course, use the courts to obtain maintenance in situations outside CMEC's jurisdiction entirely.[312] For example, ancillary relief between divorcing parents may include lump sum orders for the children,[313] designed to meet items of capital expenditure.[314] Similarly, since the child support legislation only imposes financial responsibility in relation to children up to the age of 16,[315] the courts' powers can be invoked for older children under the matrimonial legislation[316] or the CA 1989.[317] Equally, given that parents' financial responsibilities are confined by the child support legislation to biological children, maintenance for stepchildren can be claimed through the courts.[318] Furthermore, unmarried mothers with children are increasingly turning to the courts to obtain capital and property transfers in favour of their children.[319] Indeed, this can be an extremely effective means whereby they can extract sufficient capital from wealthy fathers to obtain relatively comfortable accommodation for their children and themselves,[320] together with enough capital to equip it and an allowance for themselves, as the child's primary carer.[321]

When assessing the level of income a child requires, the judiciary acknowledge that he or she should be brought up in circumstances reflecting the father's current resources and standard of living,[322] even if those resources 'would be unrecognisable to the great majority of families'.[323] So if a teenager has been brought up in a comfortable lifestyle, she should continue to enjoy a high standard of living, if affordable.[324] A mother is treated as only applying 'in a

---

[311] CSA 1991, s. 8(8). E.g. *C v. F (disabled child: maintenance order)* [1998] 2 FLR 1.

[312] For a more detailed discussion of this area of law, see N. Lowe and G. Douglas (2007) pp. 966–76 and N. Wikeley (2006a) ch. 7.

[313] I.e. under Matrimonial Causes Act 1973, s. 23(1)(f).

[314] I.e. as opposed to awarding income, thereby avoiding the prohibition imposed by CSA 1991, s. 8(3). *Phillips v. Peace* [1996] 2 FLR 230, per Johnson J, at 235. But see Wilson J in *V v. V (child maintenance)* [2001] 2 FLR 799, at [25], who argued that a court can make lump sum orders for children to make up the short-fall where their father refuses to agree a sum of income which the court considers to be appropriate.

[315] Or 19, if in full-time secondary education.

[316] Under the Matrimonial Causes Act 1973 or the Domestic Proceedings and Magistrates' Courts Act 1978. The position of older children is discussed further in Chapter 4.

[317] CA 1989, Sch. I.

[318] I.e. on the basis that the child is a 'child of the family', under the Matrimonial Causes Act 1973 or the Domestic Proceedings and Magistrates' Courts Act 1978 or under the CA 1989, Sch. I. For the meaning of this term, see N. Lowe and G. Douglas (2007) pp. 338–40.

[319] E.g. inter alia: *Phillips v. Peace* [1996] 2 FLR 230; *J v. C (child : financial provision)* [1999] 1 FLR 152; *Re P (child: financial provision)* [2003] EWCA Civ 837, [2003] 2 FLR 865; *Re S (unmarried parents: financial provisions)* [2006] EWCA Civ 479, [2006] 2 FLR 950; *Morgan v. Hill* [2006] EWCA Civ 1602, [2007] 1 FLR 1480; *N v. D* [2008] 1 FLR 1629.

[320] The provision of a home is effected by way of a settlement of the property.

[321] *Re P (child: financial provision)* [2003] EWCA Civ 837, [2003] 2 FLR 865, per Thorpe LJ, at [48]–[49].

[322] *J v. C (child: financial provision)* [1999] 1 FLR 152, per Hale J, at 160.

[323] *Morgan v. Hill* [2006] EWCA Civ 1602, [2007] 1 FLR 1480, per Hughes LJ, at [63].

[324] *N v. D* [2008] 1 FLR 1629, per DJ Harper, at [23].

representative capacity' to obtain an order for the child's benefit and not her own,[325] the child's needs being seen as being separate from those of his or her mother.[326] The courts may even sympathise with the notion of the child being separately represented to ensure that the child's needs and interests are not lost to view.[327] Nevertheless, this body of case law contains no suggestion that children have a *right* to share their parents' wealth. Private ordering between adults remains the order of the day.

(5) Conclusion

The law could do much more to ensure that children are not treated like chattels if the policy-makers were prepared to grasp the nettle and use it to mould parental opinion more effectively. The fact that it does not do so in the context of physical punishment reflects an ambivalence over the merits of outlawing actions which large numbers of the public consider perfectly acceptable. But if the law had always been sensitive to public opinion, hanging convicted sheep stealers might still be a current form of punishment. The law's role relating to children's need for financial support appears to be similarly driven by concerns which have little to do with children's rights. Undoubtedly, children would benefit from being brought up in financially secure circumstances, but the law's respect for family privacy is exploited by a government wishing to save money. Motivated by concerns about the public purse and by policies over encouraging parents to seek employment, the state maintains only a safety-net approach to family support. Again, the need to cut costs has driven the recent reforms of the child support legislation, with parents being given complete freedom to decide how they should divide their wealth between them and their children. Such short-term policies ignore the long-term impact on society of large numbers of children being brought up in severely impoverished conditions. It also sends out unfortunate messages about the importance placed by government on the next generation's well-being.

BIBLIOGRAPHY

NB many of these publications can be obtained on the relevant organisation's website.

Adam, S. and Brewer, M. (2004) *Supporting Families: The Financial Costs and Benefits of Children Since 1975*, Policy Press.

Altman, S. (2003) 'A Theory of Child Support' 17 *International Journal of Law, Policy and the Family* 173.

---

[325] *M-T v. T* [2006] EWHC 2494 (Fam), [2007] 2 FLR 925, per Charles J, at [18]. See also *Re S (unmarried parents: financial provisions)* [2006] EWCA Civ 479, [2006] 2 FLR 950, per Thorpe LJ, at [15].

[326] *Re S (unmarried parents: financial provisions)* [2006] EWCA Civ 479, [2006] 2 FLR 950, per Thorpe LJ, at [15].

[327] Ibid., per Thorpe LJ, at [17]. See also *M-T v. T* [2006] EWHC 2494 (Fam), [2007] 2 FLR 925, per Charles J, at [22].

Attree, P. (2006) 'The Social Costs of Child Poverty: A Systematic Review of the Qualitative Evidence' 20 *Children and Society* 54.

Bell, A, Kazimirski, A. and La Valle, I. (2006) *An Investigation of CSA Maintenance Direct Payments: Qualitative Study*, DWP Research Report No. 327, DWP.

Blanden, J. and Gibbons, S. (2006) *The Persistence of Poverty Across Generations: a View From Two British Cohorts*, Joseph Rowntree Foundation.

Bradshaw, J. (2005) 'Child Poverty and Deprivation' in Bradshaw, J. (ed.) *The Well-being of Children in the UK*, Save the Children.

Brown, G. (1999) 'A Scar on the Nation's Soul' 104 *Poverty* 8.

Buck, K. (2007) *Still Home Alone: Developing 'Next Generation' Care for Older Children*, 4Children.

Cabinet Office (2006) *Reaching Out: An Action Plan on Social Exclusion*, Cabinet Office.

Cabinet Office (2007) *Reaching Out: Think Family*, Cabinet Office.

Cabinet Office (2008) *Think Family: Improving the Life Chances of Families at Risk*, Cabinet Office.

Child Poverty Action Group (CPAG) (2008) *The Social Security (Lone Parents and Miscellaneous Amendments) Regulations 2008*, Submission by the Child Poverty Action Group, CPAG.

Commission on Children and Violence (1995) *Children and Violence*, Calouste Gulbenkian Foundation.

Committee on Economic, Social and Cultural Rights (2002) *Concluding Observations of the Committee on Economic, Social and Cultural Rights: United Kingdom of Great Britain and Northern Ireland – Dependent Territories 2002* E/C 12/1/Add 79, Centre for Human Rights, Geneva.

Committee on the Elimination of Discrimination against Women (2008) *Concluding Observations of the Committee on the Elimination of Discrimination against Women: United Kingdom of Great Britain and Northern Ireland*, CEDAW/C/GBR/CO/6, Geneva.

Committee on the Rights of the Child (1995) *Concluding Observations of the Committee on the Rights of the Child: United Kingdom of Great Britain and Northern Ireland* CRC/C/15/Add 34, Centre for Human Rights, Geneva.

Committee on the Rights of the Child (2002) *Concluding Observations of the Committee on the Rights of the Child: United Kingdom of Great Britain and Northern Ireland* CRC/C/15/Add 188, Centre for Human Rights, Geneva.

Committee on the Rights of the Child (2006) *General Comment No 8 (2006) The Right of the Child to Protection From Corporal Punishment and Other Cruel or Degrading Forms of Punishment*, Centre for Human Rights, Geneva.

Committee on the Rights of the Child (2008) *Concluding Observations of the Committee on the Rights of the Child: United Kingdom of Great Britain and Northern Ireland* CRC/C/GBR/CO/4, Centre for Human Rights, Geneva.

Cooke, G. and Lawton, K. (2008) *Working Out of Poverty: a Study of the Low-Paid and the 'Working Poor'*, Institute for Public Policy Research.

Crown Prosecution Service (CPS) (2004) *Offence Against the Person, Incorporating the Charging Standard*, CPS.

Davis, G., Wikeley, N. and Young, R. (1998) *Child Support in Action*, Hart Publishing.

Davies, H. and Joshi, H. (2001) 'Who has Borne the Cost of Britain's Children in the 1990s?' in Vleminckx, K. and Smeeding, T. (eds.) *Child Well-Being, Child Poverty and Child Policy in Modern Nations: What Do We Know?*, The Policy Press.

Department for Children, Schools and Families (DCSF) (2007) Cm 7280 *The Children's Plan: Building Brighter Futures*, TSO.

Department for Education and Skills (DfES) (2007a) *Every Parent Matters*, DfES

Department for Education and Skills (DfES) (2007b) Cm 7232 *Review of Section 58 of the Children Act 2004*, TSO.

Department for Education and Skills (DfES) (2007c) *The Consolidated 3rd and 4th Periodic Report to UN Committee on the Rights of the Child*, UK Government, DfES.

Department for Health and Social Security (DHSS) (1974) Cm 5629 *Report of the Committee on One-Parent Families*, HMSO.

Department for Social Security (DSS) (1990) vols I and II, Cm 1264 *Children Come First*, HMSO.

Department for Social Security (DSS) (1998a) Cm 3805 Green Paper *New Ambitions for our Country: A New Contract for Welfare*, DSS.

Department for Social Security (DSS) (1998b) Cm 3992 White Paper *Children First: a New Approach to Child Support*, TSO.

Department for Social Security (DSS) (1999) Cm 4349 *A New Contract for Welfare: Children's Rights and Parents' Responsibilities*, TSO.

Department for Work and Pensions (DWP) (2006a) Cm 6915 *Opportunity for All, Eighth Annual Report 2006, Strategy Document*, TSO.

Department for Work and Pensions (DWP) (2006b) Cm 6895 *A Fresh Start: Child Support Redesign – the Government's Response to Sir David Henshaw*, TSO.

Department for Work and Pensions (DWP) (2006c) Cm 6979, *A New System of Child Maintenance*, TSO.

Department for Work and Pensions (DWP) (2007a) *Working for Children*, DWP.

Department for Work and Pensions (DWP) (2007b) Cm 7290 *Ready for Work: Full Employment in our Generation*, TSO.

Department for Work and Pensions (DWP) (2007c) Cm 7061 *A New System of Child Maintenance, Summary of Responses to the Consultation*, TSO.

Department for Work and Pensions (DWP) (2007d) Cm 7062 *Report on the Child Maintenance White Paper, a New System of Child Maintenance*, TSO.

Department for Work and Pensions (DWP) (2008) Cm 7506 *Raising Expectations and Increasing Support: Reforming Welfare for the Future*, TSO.

Department of Health (DH) (2000) *Protecting Children, Supporting Parents: A Consultation Document on the Physical Punishment of Children*, DH.

Department of Health (DH) (2001) *Analysis of Responses to the 'Protecting Children, Supporting Parents' Consultation Document*, DH.

Dex, S. (2003) *Families and Work in the Twenty-first Century*, Joseph Rowntree Foundation.

Douglas, G. (2000) 'The Family, Gender, and Social Security' in Harris, N. with Douglas, G., Hervey, T., Jones, S., Rahilly, S., Sainsbury, R. and Wikeley, N. *Social Security in Context*, Oxford University Press.

Durrant, J. (2000) *A Generation Without Smacking: The Impact of Sweden's Ban on Physical Punishment*, Save the Children.

Eekelaar, J. and Maclean, M. (1986) *Maintenance After Divorce*, Oxford University Press.

Fredman, S. (2006) 'Human Rights Transformed: Positive Duties and Positive Rights' *AUT Public Law* 498.

Freud, D. (2007) *Reducing Dependency, Increasing Opportunity: Options for the Future of Welfare to Work. An Independent Report to the Department of Work and Pensions*, CDS.

Gershoff, E. (2002) 'Corporal Punishment by Parents and Associated Child Behaviours and Experiences: A Meta-Analytic and Theoretical Review' 128 *Psychological Bulletin* 539.

HM Government (2009) *Next Steps for Early Learning and Childcare*, DCSF.

HM Treasury (2003) Cm 5860 *Every Child Matters*, TSO.

HM Treasury (2007) *Aiming High for Children: Supporting Families*, TSO.

HM Treasury (2008) HC 388 *Budget 2008*, TSO.

HM Treasury, Department for Work and Pensions (DWP), Department for Children, Schools and Families (DCSF) (2008) *Ending Child Poverty: Everybody's Business*, HM Treasury.

Hale, B. (2006) 'Understanding Children's Rights: Theory and Practice' 44 *Family Court Review* 350.

Harker, L. (2006a) *Closing the Gap: Combating the Causes of Child Poverty in London*, Association of London Government.

(2006b) Cm 6951 *Delivering on Child Poverty: What Would it Take?*, TSO

(2006c) 'Tackling Poverty in the UK' 13(1) *IPPR* 43.

Henricson, C. (2003) *Government and Parenting*, Joseph Rowntree Foundation.

Henshaw, D. (2006) *Recovering Child Support: Routes to Responsibility*, Cm 6894, TSO.

Hirsch, D. (2006) *What Will it Take to End Child Poverty? Firing on All Cylinders*, Joseph Rowntree Foundation.

Hoggett, B. (1994) 'Joint Parenting Systems: the English Experiment' 6 *Journal of Child Law* 8.

House of Commons Work and Pensions Committee (HCWPC) (2004) *The Performance of the Child Support Agency*, Second Report of Session 2004–05 Volume I, HC 44–1, TSO.

House of Commons Work and Pensions Committee (HCWPC) (2007) *Child Support Reform*, Fourth Report of Session 2006–07, HC 219-I, TSO.

House of Commons Work and Pensions Committee (HCWPC) (2008) *The Best Start in Life? Alleviating Deprivation, Improving Social Mobility and Eradicating Child Poverty*, Second Report of Session 2007–08, Volume I, HC 42–1, TSO.

Hooper , C.-A., Gorin, S., Cabral, C. and Dyson, C. (2007) *Living with Hardship 24/7: the Diverse Experiences of Families in Poverty in England*, The Frank Buttle Trust.

IPPR Trading Ltd (2007) *Disability 2020: Opportunities for the Full and Equal Citizenship of Disabled People in Britain in 2020*, IPPR.

Joint Committee on Human Rights (JCHR) (2003) *The UN Convention on the Rights of the Child*, Tenth Report of Session 2002–03, HL Paper 117/HC 81, TSO.

Joint Committee on Human Rights (JCHR) (2004) *Children Bill*, Nineteenth Report of Session 2003–04, HL Paper 161/ HC 537, TSO.

Keating, H. (2006) 'Protecting or Punishing Children: Physical Punishment, Human Rights and English Law Reform' 26 *Legal Studies* 394.

Law Commission (1988) *Review of Child Law, Guardianship and Custody* Law Com No 172, HC 594, HMSO.

Lewis, J. (2000) 'Family Policy in the Post-war Period' in Katz, S., Eekelaar, J. and Maclean, M. (eds.) *Cross Currents: Family Law and Policy in the US and England*, Oxford University Press.

(2001) 'Women, Men and the Family' in Seldon, A. (ed.) *The Blair Effect*, Little, Brown and Company.

Lowe, N. and Douglas, G. (2007) *Bromley's Family Law*, Oxford University Press.

Magadi, M. and Middleton, S. (2007) *Severe Child Poverty in the UK*, Save the Children.

Middleton, S., Ashworth, K. and Braithwaite, I. (1997) *Small Fortunes: Spending on Children, Childhood Poverty and Parental Sacrifice*, Joseph Rowntree Foundation.

Minow, M. (1986) 'Rights for the Next Generation: A Feminist Approach to Children's Rights' 9 *Harvard Women's Law Journal* 1.

National Audit Office (2006) *Child Support Agency – Implementation of the Child Support Reforms*, TSO.

Northern Ireland Office of Law Reform (2001) *Physical Punishment in the Home – Thinking About the Issues, Looking at the Evidence* A consultation paper for Northern Ireland, Office of Law Reform.

Ofsted (2008) *Early Years: Leading to Excellence*, Ofsted.

Palmer, G., MacInnes, T. and Kenway, P. (2007) *Monitoring Poverty and Social Exclusion 2007*, Joseph Rowntree Foundation.

(2008) *Monitoring Poverty and Social Exclusion 2008* Joseph Rowntree Foundation.

Parkinson, P. (2007) 'Reengineering the Child Support Scheme: An Australian Perspective on the British Government's Proposals' 70 *Modern Law Review* 812.

Payne, L. (2007) *Childcare Act 2006, Highlight no 234*, National Children's Bureau.

Pinnock, K. and Evans, R. (2008) 'Developing Responsive Preventative Practices : Key Messages from Children's and Families' Experiences of the Children's Fund' 22 *Children and Society* 86.

Ridge, T. (2005) 'Supporting Children? The Impact of Child Support Policies on Children's Wellbeing in the UK and Australia' 34 *Journal of Social Policy* 121.

(2006) 'Childhood Poverty: a Barrier to Social Participation and Inclusion' in Kay, E., Tisdall, M., Davis, J., Hill, M. and Prout, A. (eds.) *Children, Young People and Social Inclusion*, Policy Press.

Rutter, M. (chairman) (2005) Commission on Families and the Wellbeing of Children, *Families and the State: Two-way Support and Responsibilities*, The Policy Press.

Shropshire, J. and Middleton, S. (1999) *Small Expectations: Learning to be Poor?*, Joseph Rowntree Foundation.

Smith, R. (2004) '"Hands-off parenting?" – Towards a Reform of the Defence of Reasonable Chastisement in the UK' 16 *Child and Family Law Quarterly* 261.

Stanley, K., Bellamy, K. and Cooke, G. (2006) *Equal Access? Appropriate and Affordable Childcare for Every Child*, Institute of Public Policy Research.

UNICEF, Innocenti Research Centre (2000) *A League Table of Child Poverty in Rich Nations* Innocenti Report Card Issue No 1 June 2000, UNICEF.

UNICEF, Innocenti Research Centre (2007) *Child Poverty in Perspective: An Overview of Child Well-being in Rich Countries*, Report Card 7, UNICEF.

UNICEF, Innocenti Research Centre (2008) *The Child Care Transition: A League Table of Early Childhood Education and Care in Economically Advanced Countries*, Report Card 8, UNICEF.

United Nations General Assembly (2002) A/RES/S-27/2, *A World Fit for Children, Resolution adopted by the General Assembly*, Geneva.

United Nations General Assembly (2006) A/61/150, *Report of the Independent Expert for the United Nations study on Violence Against Children*, Geneva.

Utting, D. (1995) *Family and Parenthood: Supporting Families, Preventing Breakdown*, Joseph Rowntree Foundation.

(2003) 'Tackling Disadvantage: Families' in Darton, D. and Strelitz, J. (eds.) *Tackling UK Poverty and Disadvantage in the Twenty-first Century*, Joseph Rowntree Foundation.

Wald, M. (1979) 'Children's Rights: A Framework for Analysis' 12 *University of California Davis Law Review* 225–282.

Walsh, B. (1991) 'The United Nations Convention on the Rights of the Child' 5 *International Journal of Law and the Family* 170.

Wasoff, F. (2005) 'Mutual Consent: Separation Agreements and the Outcomes of Private Ordering in Divorce' 27 *Journal of Social Welfare and Family Law* 237.

Wikeley, N. (2006a) *Child Support: Law and Policy*, Hart Publishing.

(2006b) 'A Duty But Not a Right: Child Support After *R (Kehoe) v Secretary of State for Work and Pensions*' 18 *Child and Family Law Quarterly* 287.

(2007a) '*Secretary of State for Work and Pensions v Roach*' [2006] EWCA Civ 1746' 29 *Journal Social Welfare and Family Law* 177.

(2007b) 'Child Support Reform – Throwing the Baby out with the Bathwater?' 19 *Child and Family Law Quarterly* 434.

(2008a) 'The Strange Death of the Liable Relative Rule' 38 *Family Law* 52.

(2008b) 'Child Support: Carrots and Sticks' 38 *Family Law* 1102.

Chapter 10

Parents' decisions and children's health rights

(1) Introduction

The Convention on the Rights of the Child (CRC) recognises that without good health, children have little hope of fulfilling their potential. Article 24(1) requires states to:

> recognise the right of the child to the enjoyment of the highest attainable standard of health and to facilities for the treatment of illness and rehabilitation of health. States Parties shall strive to ensure that no child is deprived of his or her right of access to such health care services.

Article 3 requires anyone reaching a decision relating to a child to give primary consideration to his or her best interests and Article 6 requires states to recognise every child's right to life, and to promote their survival and development. These requirements should not be too onerous for the UK to fulfil, with its well-established health service and comparatively good hygiene and living conditions – better by far than those in many developing countries. Nevertheless, advances made by medical technology sometimes confront parents and doctors alike with difficult dilemmas over what is the appropriate decision to reach.

This assessment of the law is divided broadly into two sections. The first deals with the extent to which children's right to life can be endangered by decisions relating to their health. The second deals with the extent to which children's rights are jeopardised by medical procedures, which though not life-threatening, may damage their health, to a lesser or greater extent. Before these, however, there is a brief assessment of the general principles which recur in much of the case law regarding children's medical care.

(2) General principles

(A) Children's healthcare

Advances in medical technology, the availability of antibiotics and immunisation, together with a higher standard of living, have led to British children today enjoying far better general health than did their counterparts a century ago. The two main measures of health in early childhood, infant mortality and life expectancy at birth, have improved dramatically,[1] with a particularly striking reduction in the number of children's lives being lost to infectious diseases.[2] Thus the steady downward trend in infant mortality has continued into the twenty-first century, largely due to improvements in diet and sanitation, ante and post-natal medical care, infant medical care and vaccines and immunisation programmes.[3] Similarly, the rate of life expectancy has steadily increased.[4] Despite this, concerns about inequalities in the health of the population generally, highlighted by Acheson,[5] continue to focus on the way that poverty and social class affects children's early lives, more particularly on their chances of surviving to a healthy adulthood. There is, for example, a greater chance of children in deprived families suffering from low birth weight,[6] a mental health problem, obesity and diabetes.[7] Furthermore, despite rates steadily falling, the rate of infant mortality[8] and accidental child deaths[9] vary significantly according to the parents' socioeconomic classification. Indeed, it appears that rather than achieving government targets to reduce health inequalities in infant mortality and life expectancy at birth, the inequalities gap is actually widening.[10] Despite overall improvements, UK rates of infant mortality and low birth weight compare very poorly with other OECD countries.[11]

The government recognises the fact that children and young people have different health needs from adults and that it is critically important to ensure that they are healthy in their early years 'if further progress is to be made in improving the nation's quality of life'.[12] The launch, in 2004, of a programme to improve standards of health services for children,[13] coincided with the

---

[1] Healthcare Commission (2007) p. 64–5.

[2] Between 1685 and 1801, the annual incidence of smallpox peaked at 2,355 per 100,000 population and never fell below 313 per 100,000.

[3] ONS (2008) p. 96: between 1930 and 2006, the rate of infant deaths (prior to the age of one) per 1,000 live births reduced from 60 to 5.

[4] Ibid. at p. 94: between 1901 and 2006, male life expectancy increased from 45 to 77 and female life expectancy from 49 to 82.

[5] D. Acheson (1998); this report led to the establishment of the national 'Programme for Action' on health inequality, with Public Service Agreement targets to reduce health inequalities. See DH (2007).

[6] J. Maher and A. Macfarlane (2004) p. 40.   [7] Healthcare Commission (2007) pp. 68–9.

[8] ONS (2008) p. 96: the rate of infant mortality in England and Wales in 2005 among babies born inside marriage to fathers in semi-routine occupations was 6.1 per 1,000 live births, cf. 2.7 per 1,000 live births for those born inside marriage whose fathers were in large employers and higher managerial occupations. See also DH (2007) pp. 30–1: higher rates of infant mortality correlate with the mother's country of birth.

[9] Healthcare Commission (2007) p. 68: children of parents who had never worked or were long-term unemployed were 13 times more likely to die from unintentional injury than children of parents in higher managerial and professional occupations.

[10] Ibid. at p. 65. The Committee on the Rights of the Child (2002) para. 41 and ibid. (2008) para. 54: expressed concern over health inequalities, especially rates of infant mortality.

[11] UNICEF (2007) Figures 2.1a and 2.1b.   [12] Healthcare Commission (2007) p. 63.

[13] I.e. the Children's National Service Framework (DH (2004)) which set out 11 standards for the improvement of health and other services over a 10-year period.

establishment of the *Every Child Matters* reform programme.[14] Notably, the first of the five listed outcomes of the latter programme is 'being healthy'.[15] Furthermore, local authorities (LAs) are legally obliged to improve the well-being of young children in their areas and to reduce inequalities in their 'physical and mental health and emotional well-being'.[16] Nevertheless, the extent to which children's health can be improved on a national level only partly depends on better healthcare facilities and financial support for families with children.[17] It also depends on parents being educated about their children's health needs and the state's willingness to subject parents to a measure of surveillance to ensure that these needs are met. There is currently no legal compulsion on parents to allow health agencies to monitor their children's health. Indeed, the government assumes that parents are the best judges of their children's medical needs. Parents are not obliged to allow health visitors into their homes to examine their babies.[18] Similarly, although compulsory immunisation would help prevent the periodic outbreaks of serious childhood diseases,[19] public fears of vaccines producing damaging reactions in some children make future compulsion unlikely.[20] Concerns about the safety of the MMR vaccine led to a fall in the number of children vaccinated against measles, mumps and rubella.[21] Those parents who strenuously oppose immunisation[22] would undoubtedly claim not only that compulsion would infringe their own rights to respect for their family life under Article 8 of the European Convention for the Protection of Human Rights and Fundamental Freedoms (ECHR), but also their children's right to family life and bodily privacy and integrity.[23]

---

[14] HM Treasury (2003) and DfES (2004).

[15] See also Children Act (CA) 2004, s. 10(2): each children's services authority must make arrangements 'with a view to improving the well-being of children in the authority's area relating to – (a) physical and mental health and emotional well-being'.

[16] Childcare Act 2006, s. 1.   [17] Discussed in more detail in Chapter 9.

[18] R. Dingwall, J. Eekelaar and T. Murray (1995) pp. 218–21: discuss 'the liberal compromise' between state surveillance and non-intervention.

[19] ONS (2008) p. 96. E.g. the mumps epidemic of 2005.

[20] Cf. the Compulsory Vaccination Acts 1853 and 1867, which compelled parents to have their children vaccinated against smallpox within the first years of their lives and imposed fines or imprisonment for default. This was so unpopular that the Anti-Vaccination League was founded in 1867 to spearhead opposition.

[21] ONS (2008) p. 96: MMR coverage levels have fallen in the twenty-first century. J. Bridgeman (2007) pp. 108–17, discusses childhood immunisation.

[22] E.g. *Re C (welfare of child: immunisation)* [2003] EWHC 1376 (Fam), [2003] 2 FLR 1054 (decision confirmed by the Court of Appeal in *Re C (welfare of child: immunisation)* [2003] EWCA Civ 1148, [2003] 2 FLR 1095); discussed by R. Huxtable (2004).

[23] *Wain v. United Kingdom* (1987) 9 EHRR 122, per the European Commission of Human Rights: despite his son's serious reaction to the diphtheria, tetanus and whooping cough vaccination, a father's rights under Art. 8 had not been infringed by the government's failure to provide parents with detailed information about the risks of particular vaccines since the vaccination scheme was voluntary. See also the European Commission of Human Rights' decision in *Association X v. United Kingdom* (Application No. 7154/75) (1978) 14 DR 31.

There is an obvious concern on the part of the government not to interfere with parents' own views regarding the medical treatment of their children. Nevertheless, as the criminal law recognises, inactivity regarding healthcare may endanger children's lives.[24] A parent is guilty of criminal neglect if he wilfully fails to provide the child with adequate medical aid.[25] Indeed, the criminal law has shown little sympathy for a parent whose failure to ensure that his child receives medical attention has been motivated by his religious convictions[26] or for refusing to consent to what is deemed to be essential medical care.[27] Criminal sanctions may, however, be too late to protect the child's health. Furthermore, the House of Lords' strict interpretation of the wilful element of the offence of child neglect[28] has left children vulnerable to the 'stupidity or fecklessness' of their parents.[29] The child protection laws can probably achieve far more than the criminal law in terms of ensuring that a child's right to healthcare is fulfilled. LAs are legally obliged to ensure that they seek out and protect children who are suffering or are likely to suffer 'significant harm' for any reason, and this will obviously include a duty to investigate cases of ill-health due to parental inattention.[30] Young children, particularly babies, die very quickly if they become ill and are not provided with medical attention. Depending on the urgency of the situation, parental failure to seek medical attention can be dealt with by the LA seeking a child assessment order[31] or an emergency protection order.[32] Alternatively, they may seek a specific issue order regarding the child's further assessment or treatment.[33]

(B) Principles of common law

Given that the law adopts a non-interventionist approach to family life, can parents be trusted to protect adequately their young children's right to good health? English common law requires parents to reach all decisions regarding

---

[24] Children and Young Persons Act (CYPA) 1933, s. 1(1).   [25] CYPA 1933, s. 1(2)(a).

[26] E.g. *R v. Senior* [1899] 1 QB 283. See J. Bridgeman (2007) pp. 85–95 for a discussion of the criminal law's approach to parents who neglect their children's medical care.

[27] E.g. *Oakey v. Jackson* [1914] 1 KB 216.

[28] *R v. Sheppard* [1981] AC 394, per the House of Lords (majority): CPYA 1933, s. 1(1) (which imposes liability on anyone who '*wilfully* assaults, ill-treats, neglects, abandons or exposes him' – emphasis added) includes only parents able to appreciate the need to obtain medical care for their child and not parents who through stupidity, ignorance or personal inadequacy fail to do so.

[29] [1981] AC 394. See Lord Fraser's dissenting judgment, at 416–17.

[30] CA 1989, s. 47, discussed in Chapter 15.

[31] CA 1989, s. 43. A child assessment order would enable the LA to establish whether the child needs medical attention and, if so, what form it should take. But such an order is inappropriate in emergencies, since it can only be obtained on notice to the parents, and it does not confer parental responsibility on the LA.

[32] CA 1989, s. 44: an emergency protection order can be obtained rapidly ex parte and confers on the holder parental responsibility, thereby entitling the LA to consent to medical treatment. Discussed in Chapter 15.

[33] E.g. *Re C (HIV Test)* [1999] 2 FLR 1004: the LA obtained a specific issue order authorising the testing for HIV of a baby against the wishes of both her parents.

their children's upbringing, more particularly regarding medical care, in accordance with their best interests.[34] Any decisions reached which manifestly infringe such a principle, can be challenged, even overridden.[35] Indeed, case law demonstrates that the best interests test, as interpreted by parents, does not always protect children's rights, without the intervention of doctors or the courts. The real difficulty is that most parents find it relatively easy to justify their decisions by reference to their children's best interests. Since it is virtually impossible to interpret such a term objectively, it is questionable whether it provides the child with adequate protection. As Gerald Dworkin has observed, the personal views of individual parents may define the 'best interests' of their child in terms of the parent's best interests.[36]

Once a doctor is consulted, he must comply with the principles of common law, which are little different from those applying to adults.[37] Both legislation[38] and case law[39] acknowledge that it is unlawful for doctors to treat children without consent, unless it is to avoid serious harm or death, in an emergency.[40] In the case of a child too young and immature to be deemed *Gillick* competent, doctors will seek consent from the child's parents, as his or her proxies.[41] It is they who brought their child into the world and they are assumed to be the adults most likely to have his or her interests at heart.[42] In general terms, since any single adult with parental responsibility (PR)[43] can consent to a child's medical treatment,[44] consent can now be obtained from either parent, if they

---

[34] It is arguable that, for essentially trivial non-therapeutic procedures, the test is the less rigorous 'not against the child's best interests'. See *S v. S; W v. Official Solicitor (or W)* [1972] AC 24.

[35] *Gillick v. West Norfolk and Wisbech Area Health Authority* [1986] AC 112, per Lord Scarman, at 184.

[36] G. Dworkin (1982) p. 200. See also *NHS Trust v. A* [2007] EWHC 1696 (Fam), [2008] 1 FLR 70 (discussed further below), per Holman J, at [40](x): parents' wishes are 'wholly irrelevant to consideration of the objective best interests of the child save to the extent in any given case that they may illuminate the quality and value to the child of the child-parent relationship'.

[37] *Re F (mental patient: sterilisation)* [1990] 2 AC 1, per Lord Goff, at 74 and *Sidaway v. Board of Governors of the Bethlem Royal Hospital and the Maudsley Hospital* [1985] AC 871, per Lord Scarman, at 882: medical treatment of an adult without consent will normally, unless life-saving treatment is required in an emergency when it can be carried out under the doctrine of necessity, amount to a trespass to the person and to a criminal assault. See also discussed in Chapter 5.

[38] Family Law Reform Act (FLRA) 1969, s. 8(1); discussed in Chapter 5.

[39] *Gillick v. West Norfolk and Wisbech Area Health Authority* [1986] AC 112.

[40] Ibid., per Lord Scarman, at 189.

[41] Ibid., at 184: 'It is abundantly plain that the law recognises that there is a right and a duty of parents to determine whether or not to seek medical advice in respect of their child, and, having received advice, to give or withhold consent to medical treatment.'

[42] G. Dworkin (1982) p. 204.

[43] But NB, in the event of any parental dispute over immunisation (*Re C (welfare of child: immunisation)* [2003] EWCA Civ 1148, [2003] 2 FLR 1095) or circumcision (*Re J (specific issue orders: child's religious upbringing and circumcision)* [2000] 1 FLR 571), consent from a single parent is insufficient, judicial authority must be obtained.

[44] But NB CA 1989, s. 3(5): any person with care of a child, but without PR (e.g. a childminder or foster carer) can do 'what is reasonable in all the circumstances of the case for the purpose of safeguarding or promoting the child's welfare'. This might include consenting to therapeutic medical treatment.

are married,[45] and from the child's mother, if unmarried, or from anyone with whom she shares PR.[46]

Sometimes, parents and doctors disagree over how the child should be treated, in which case the dispute must be taken to court,[47] with a decision being reached over what most accords with the child's best interests. But this is an indeterminate standard which seldom produces any clear-cut answers. The court will seek the views of both the medical team and the parents and, as the case law shows,[48] these will often fundamentally differ. A doctor is influenced by medical factors, whilst the parent takes into account not only the medical advice, but also the child's psychological needs, bearing in mind the views and mores of the whole family. Indeed, the court may consider it perfectly reasonable for the parent, as a proxy for the child, to take into account non-medical issues.[49] These common law principles are now reinforced by the protection provided by human rights law, which requires practitioners to approach children's healthcare from a subtly different perspective.

(C) A rights-based approach?

Neither the medical profession nor the courts show great enthusiasm for adjusting their approach to children's healthcare by reference to a framework of rights. Admittedly, long before the implementation of the Human Rights Act (HRA) 1998, Laws J, in a decision, which was soon reversed on appeal, robustly drew attention to a child's right to life under Article 2 of the ECHR.[50] But since then, there has been little judicial acknowledgment that a rights-based approach would be helpful. Thus, in the context of refusing to override a mother's objections to her child receiving a life-saving liver transplant, Waite LJ asserted: 'It is not an occasion – even in an age preoccupied with "rights" – to talk of the rights of a child, or the rights of a parent, or the rights of a court.'[51] Nor was Butler-Sloss LJ impressed by Wilson J's references, in the court below, to the baby's own rights under the CRC, when authorising the baby to be tested for HIV against the wishes of her HIV positive mother.[52] In her view, these references were unnecessary, since it was 'all encapsulated in s1 of the Children

[45] Married parents share PR (CA 1989, s. 2(1)) and either parent can exercise it unilaterally, without the other (s. 2(7)).

[46] E.g. an unmarried father with PR through being named on the child's birth certificate or through entering a parental responsibility agreement with the mother or obtaining it by court order; CA 1989, s. 4(1)(a)–(c).

[47] By application to the High Court for a declaration under the inherent jurisdiction, or by application for a specific issue order under the CA 1989, s. 8. The child will be separately represented by Cafcass.

[48] Discussed below.

[49] *R v. Cambridge District Health Authority, ex p B* [1995] 1 FLR 1055, per Laws J, at 1062–1063; *Re T (a minor) (wardship: medical treatment)* [1997] 1 All ER 906, per Butler-Sloss LJ, at 914.

[50] *R v. Cambridge District Health Authority, ex p B* [1995] 1 FLR 1055 at 1061.

[51] *Re T (Wardship: Medical Treatment)* [1997] 1 FLR 502 at 512; discussed below.

[52] *Re C (HIV test)* [1999] 2 FLR 1004, per Wilson J (Family Division), at 1016–17.

Act'. She did acknowledge, however, that the CRC gave added strength to the child's right to be properly cared for and to discover whether the child was HIV positive herself.[53] Similarly, when considering what treatment was most appropriate for a desperately ill and disabled baby, Hedley J asserted that 'it is recognised that in this case at least the Convention now adds nothing to domestic law'.[54]

It is, however, arguable that, unlike the principles of common law which focus on issues relating to consent, and concomitant to this, on the doctor/ *parent* relationship, a rights-based framework reminds parents and medical practitioners alike that child patients have an independent status of their own. As noted above, Article 24 of the CRC entitles children to the highest attainable standard of health and all treatment decisions should be taken bearing in mind the child's best interests, as a primary consideration.[55] Furthermore Article 6 requires states to recognise every child's right to life, and to promote their survival and development. But the binding force of the ECHR makes it of greater potential relevance. At first sight, however, it does not appear that the Strasbourg jurisprudence on Article 2 of the ECHR is particularly helpful. As Bridgeman points out,[56] the ECtHR ruled inadmissible David and Carol Glass's claim that the doctors' attempt to treat their son with diamorphine amounted to a breach of Article 2.[57] Referring to a previous admissibility decision making the same point,[58] it stressed that as long as a state has made adequate provision for securing high professional standards among health professionals and the protection of patients' lives, matters such as errors of professional judgment on their part (had there been any) are not matters within the purview of a state's positive obligations under Article 2.[59] Clearly then, the domestic judiciary are correct in their view that Article 2 of the ECHR does not impose on doctors an absolute obligation to treat, where to do so would, in their view, be futile.[60]

The value of the ECHR's protection should not, however, be underestimated. Although a hospital's responsibilities under Article 2 are not engaged by ordinary medical negligence alone,[61] it is obliged thereby to adopt appropriate

---

[53] Ibid., Court of Appeal, at 1021.

[54] *Portsmouth NHS Trust v. Wyatt and Wyatt, Southampton NHS Trust intervening* [2004] EWHC 2247 (Fam), [2005] 1 FLR 21, at [25]. See also *NHS Trust v. A* [2007] EWHC 1696 (Fam), [2008] 1 FLR 70, per Holman J, at [44].

[55] CRC, Art. 3.   [56] J. Bridgeman (2005) p. 112.

[57] David Glass's mother objected to his doctors (who believed that he was dying) treating him with diamorphine to alleviate his pain and suffering and refusing to support his resuscitation.

[58] *Admissibility decision, Application no 45305/00 by William and Anita Powell v. United Kingdom* (2000) 30 EHRR CD362.

[59] *Admissibility decision, Application no 61827/00 by David and Carol Glass v. United Kingdom* (unreported), para. 1.

[60] *NHS Trust A v. M; NHS Trust B v. H* [2001] 1 All ER 801, per Dame Elizabeth Butler-Sloss P, at [37].

[61] *Savage v. South Essex Partnership NHS Foundation Trust* [2008] UKHL 74, [2009] 1 All ER 1053, per Baroness Hale of Richmond, at [97].

measures to protect the lives of its patients.[62] The ECtHR has pointed to the positive obligation placed by Article 2 on state authorities to do 'all that could be reasonably expected of them to avoid a real and immediate risk to life of which they have or ought to have knowledge'.[63] Consequently, practitioners would be unwise to stand back and take no action if they become aware of a sick child requiring attention. Furthermore, the ECtHR in *Glass v. United Kingdom*[64] acknowledged that Article 8 of the ECHR gave David Glass, a severely disabled child, the right to challenge his doctors for treating him without the consent of his mother, as his legal proxy. Indeed, the ECtHR's confirmation that *all* children have a right to physical integrity under Article 8, which will be infringed by treatment without consent, unless it can be justified under Article 8(2), has played a part in redressing the unequal balance of power between doctors and parents.

The parents' own rights under Article 8, as interpreted by *Nielsen v. Denmark*,[65] to decide whether the child should receive medical treatment and where, are also relevant. That decision provoked the Mental Health Code's advice to doctors only to rely on a parent's consent to treatment for mental disorder if they judge the parent's decision to be within the 'zone of parental control'.[66] This concept derives from the ECtHR's decision in *Nielsen* that parents only have a right to reach decisions under Article 8 which are for a 'proper purpose' under Article 8.[67] It is notable that when deciding whether the parent's decision is within the zone, doctors are advised to consider a range of factors, including the invasiveness of the procedure.[68] Furthermore Strasbourg case law clearly establishes in general terms that a parent cannot be entitled under Article 8(1) to have any measures taken that would harm the child's health and development.[69] These principles might be useful to a doctor confronted by a parent demanding invasive treatment for a child which he considers to be inappropriate.

Whilst, as explained above, Articles 2 and 8 may be of assistance, the adult orientation of the protection provided by Article 3 undermines its ability to assist child patients.[70] There seems to be no Strasbourg case law supporting the argument that Article 3 rights include the right to die with dignity.[71] Nevertheless, treatment which humiliates or debases a patient, showing a lack

---

[62] Ibid., per Lord Rodger of Earlsferry, at [45].
[63] *Osman v. United Kingdom* [1999] 1 FLR 193, at para. 116.   [64] [2004] 1 FLR 1019, at [70].
[65] (1988) 11 EHRR 175.   [66] DH (2008) paras. 36.9–36.15.
[67] Discussed in Chapter 5.   [68] DH (2008) para. 36.12.
[69] *Johansen v. Norway* (1996) 23 EHRR 33, at para. 78.
[70] *Pretty v. United Kingdom* [2002] 2 FLR 45, at [52]: Art. 3 protects an individual from the suffering flowing from a naturally occurring illness, but *only* if that suffering is exacerbated by some kind of treatment for which the authorities are responsible, e.g. poor prison conditions.
[71] Per Cazelet J in *A National Health Service Trust v. D* [2000] 2 FLR 677, at 695, referring by way of authority to *D v. United Kingdom* [1997] 24 EHRR 423. But see *Pretty v. United Kingdom* [2002] 2 FLR 45, at [52].

of respect for or diminishing his or her human dignity, may infringe Article 3 by being characterised as 'degrading'.[72]

Some, like Bridgeman, argue that invoking rights in complex medical scenarios is not helpful. When parents and professionals are seeking to do their best for the child:

> rights are not the most appropriate instrument for structuring relationships and resolving disputes. Rights make abstract claims when particular needs require investigation. They force the parties to express their positions in ways which polarise and position them in conflict when, in relation to children's healthcare, they share a goal.[73]

Nonetheless, as pointed out above, the value of a rights approach is that it reminds parents and medical practitioners of the child's independent status, with rights of his or her own. It is also a powerful way of challenging existing orthodoxies, more particularly that doctors are entitled to dictate to parents and the courts what treatment plan is best for the child.

(D) Legal competence to consent and the right to be consulted

When treating an older child, doctors will turn, in the first place, to the child for consent to treatment. Despite the legislative presumption that those over the age of 16 can legally consent to treatment,[74] according to the *Gillick*[75] principle, many adolescents under that age may also be legally capable of consenting for themselves.[76] Doctors will often assume that below adolescence they should seek consent from the child's parents, especially if the procedure has major health implications. This approach is consistent with the research on children's cognitive development which suggests that before early adolescence, younger children may be far less able to weigh up alternatives and cope rationally with important decisions affecting their upbringing.[77] Their lack of capacity for abstract thought or ability to weigh up risks and benefits of various options also indicates that the majority of young children, particularly if they are very ill, will lack the cognitive abilities and judgmental skills to make decisions that might seriously affect their healthcare.

Some refute such an approach, arguing that even very young children are capable of making far-reaching decisions about their health.[78] In Alderson's research, medical staff considered that some 3- and 4-year-old children were able to understand medical information, 'as well as the average adult' and that 'exceptional' 5- and 6-year-olds were thought able to make complex, wise decisions.[79] This led Alderson and Montgomery to suggest the introduction

[72] *Pretty v. United Kingdom* [2002] 2 FLR 45, at [52].
[73] J. Bridgeman (2007) p. 234.   [74] FLRA 1969, s. 8(1).
[75] *Gillick v. West Norfolk and Wisbech Area Health Authority* [1986] AC 112.
[76] Discussed in Chapter 5.   [77] Discussed in Chapter 3.
[78] P. Alderson and J. Montgomery (1996) ch. 2.   [79] P. Alderson (1993) p. 193.

of a new code governing healthcare for children which incorporated a legal presumption that all 5-year-olds should be deemed competent to consent to all healthcare.[80] But whilst appearing to promote the aims of Article 12 of the CRC, this would risk forcing many children into reaching important decisions about their health before they are ready to do so. Furthermore, Article 12 does not expect children to be given the right to autonomy, only the right to be involved in decisions relating to their future. Such involvement is, however, crucial, wherever possible. Although children are often too immature to *decide* such matters, they may have important views over the costs and benefits to them of the proposed treatment. It insults their dignity and self-respect for parents and doctors to make decisions which infringe their right to bodily integrity, without consulting them. By the same token, they will respond to medical treatment much better if they have been fully involved in it, understand it and have confidence in it. Current medical guidance acknowledges this and states:

> Children and young people are individuals with rights that should be respected. This means listening to them and taking into account what they have to say about things that affect them. It also means respecting their decisions and confidentiality.[81]

(3) A child's right to life: withholding or withdrawing treatment from desperately ill children

(A) The doctor/parent balance

Whilst many babies are born in hospital, most are healthy enough to go home with their mothers soon after their birth. Hopefully the majority will have no need to visit hospital again throughout their childhood. Others, however, are not so lucky and, due to severe ill health, may never leave hospital after birth. Even with improved ante-natal care, newborns are still sometimes born with very low birth weight and so massively disabled, both mentally and physically, that they have little chance of survival for more than a few days or weeks, without aggressive intervention. Some survive beyond a few months, but with such handicaps and such a low quality of life, that decisions have to be made whether to withdraw the interventions keeping them alive. The doctors treating these babies, who are far too young to speak for themselves, will seek consent to treatment, or its withdrawal, from their parents, as their proxies. Doctors traditionally wield considerable power in such situations, since ultimately it is they, as the gatekeepers to treatment resources, who decide what treatment, if any, is medically indicated. But as the trial of Dr Arthur showed, at the beginning of the 1980s doctors often deferred to parents' assessments of what

---

[80] P. Alderson and J. Montgomery (1996) ch. 5. The authors' proposed code of practice contained guidance on the factors to consider when attempting to rebut such a presumption.

[81] GMC (2007) para. 7.

was in their child's best interests, even if it meant the child dying as a result of parental decisions to withhold life-saving treatment.[82]

Today, doctors seem far more prepared to resist parents who ask for treatment they consider to be inappropriate. Most doctors will go to considerable lengths to resolve a dispute without going to court,[83] but they must act in their young patient's best interests. The law only expects them to accommodate parental wishes 'as far as professional judgment and conscience will permit'.[84] They might feel obliged to reject parental requests for treatment if they consider it to be inappropriately invasive and thereby outside the 'zone of parental control'.[85] If a court is eventually asked to decide differences between doctors and parents,[86] the former are in a powerful position.[87] Indeed, in the past the courts seemed reluctant to question their views, stressing that it would be wrong to order a doctor to act against his clinical judgement.[88] In the light of such case law, there seemed little point in parents seeking the court's judicial assessment of situations involving children – since the answer would always be that the doctors were to be guided by their own clinical judgement.[89] Such a situation had a knock-on effect. It led doctors (and their lawyers) to conclude that since a court would never direct them to act against their clinical judgement, they themselves did not need court authority to override parents' objections to any treatment they considered to be essential.[90]

The ECtHR's decision in *Glass v. United Kingdom*[91] slightly redresses this balance of power. The Court made it clear that in all but the most urgent

---

[82] *R v. Arthur* (1981) 12 BMLR 1: Dr Arthur, a well-known and respected paediatrician, placed a newly born Down's syndrome baby (whose parents did not want him to survive) on a regime described as 'nursing care only' involving suppressing his appetite with a large dose of a sedating drug and thereafter being kept comfortable. The baby died soon after birth. Dr Arthur was tried for murder, the charge being later reduced to attempted murder. Discussed by M. Gunn and J. Smith (1985) and J. Read and L. Clements (2004) pp. 484–6.

[83] M. Brazier (2006) paras. 8.48–8.51: recommends extended use being made of clinical ethics committees.

[84] *Re Wyatt* [2005] EWHC 2293 (Fam), [2005] 4 All ER 1325, per Hedley J, at [41].

[85] Discussed above.

[86] The child will be represented by Cafcass and the court will make a 'best interests declaration' indicating its view of the treatment the child should receive.

[87] E.g. *Re MM (medical treatment)* [2000] 1 FLR 224, per Black J, at 234: the Russian parents (who had originally opposed their 7-year-old son receiving treatment for his immunodeficiency) now recognised 'that in the end it will be the doctors who will determine what the appropriate treatment is'. Had the parents failed to support the suggested treatment 'I would have had no hesitation in making an order to the effect of that which has been arrived at between the parties'.

[88] *Re J (a minor)* [1990] 3 All ER 930, per Lord Donaldson MR, at 934; *Re J (a minor) (wardship: medical treatment)* [1992] 4 All ER 614, per Lord Donaldson MR, at 622 and Balcombe LJ, at 625; *Re R (a minor)(wardship: medical treatment)* [1991] 4 All ER 177, per Lord Donaldson MR, at 187; *Re C (Medical Treatment)* [1998] 1 FLR 384, per Sir Stephen Brown P, at 389–90.

[89] J. Fortin (1998) p. 416.

[90] *Glass v. United Kingdom* [2004] 1 FLR 1019, at [14]: the Official Solicitor had advised the medical team at Portsmouth hospital that no judge had ever overturned a doctor's decision to withdraw treatment/alleviate symptoms. The medical team concluded that they could give morphine to David Glass even against his mother's wishes.

[91] Ibid.

situations, an emergency court application should be made to obtain judicial authority for overriding the objections of a child's parent to a particular form of treatment.[92] Otherwise, as in *Glass* itself, a medical team will be unable to justify infringing the child's rights under Article 8, by reference to the 'necessity' of the interference.[93] Indeed, the ECtHR emphasised that a hospital team should take the initiative and go to court to 'defuse the situation in anticipation of a further emergency'.[94] *Glass* may have contributed to the perception that more disputes between parents and doctors are now going to court.[95] Case law indicates that the courts still very seldom disagree with doctors' views over what treatment is in a child's best interests. As Powell points out, when a court does disagree,[96] it leaves doctors and parents in a difficult position.[97] As noted above, well-established case law indicates that a doctor cannot be ordered by a court to carry out treatment which is contrary to his conscience and medical judgement, in which case, the parents may be obliged to find a doctor willing to provide the treatment they and the court considers appropriate – which may be difficult.[98]

(B) Treatment for newborn babies

Today, the increasingly sophisticated technology available to neonatal intensive care units has transformed the chances of survival of many desperately ill newborns. Whilst the percentage of babies born with a low birthweight has gradually increased in recent years, the rate of neonatal infant mortality amongst these babies has steadily decreased.[99] The right to life attaches to any legal person, from the moment of being born alive and separate from his mother.[100] Arguably then, however ill and disabled, a newborn baby is entitled to be kept alive by whatever means available. In the past, however, during the 1960s and 1970s, influenced by the poor quality of life of those treated, some doctors followed a deliberate policy of selective non-treatment of infants with severe medical conditions.[101] It is perhaps easier to adopt such practices in relation to newborn babies because they cannot express their wishes and have never developed relationships with other people who might speak on their behalf. As Mason and Laurie comment, such conduct came 'perilously close to

---

[92] Ibid. at [79].   [93] I.e. under Art. 8(2). Ibid. at [78]–[81].   [94] Ibid. at [79].

[95] M. Brazier (2006) para. 8.52: disputes over the care of Charlotte Wyatt (involving five legal hearings) is reported to have cost the taxpayer over £500,000. The first was *Portsmouth NHS Trust v. Wyatt and Wyatt, Southampton NHS Trust intervening* [2004] EWHC 2247 (Fam), [2005] 1 FLR 21 (hereafter *Wyatt No. 1*), discussed by M. Brazier (2005).

[96] E.g. *Re MB* [2006] EWHC 507 (Fam), [2006] 2 FLR 319, discussed below.

[97] R. Powell (2007) pp. 157–8.   [98] Ibid. at p. 158.   [99] M. Brazier (2006) pp. 30–2.

[100] *Rance v. Mid-Downs Health Authority* [1991] 1 All ER 801, per Brooks J, at 817: the criminal law protects any child 'born alive', i.e. capable of breathing and existing independently of its mother.

[101] J. Read and L. Clements (2004) pp. 489–94: discuss the practice developed by Dr Lorber, relating to the selective non-treatment of infants born with severe spina bifida and hydrocephalus. See also M. Brazier (2006) p. 135, Box 8.1: current Dutch guidelines on the practice of ending the life of severely ill newborn infants.

breaking the law'[102] since it ensured that at least some of these newborns failed to survive who could have been kept alive.[103] As the trial of Dr Arthur made plain, to end the life of a new born baby, irrespective of his disabilities, by deliberate action carries the same criminal sanctions as killing an adult.[104] This principle was later reinforced by the Court of Appeal's decision in *Re A (conjoined twins: medical treatment)*,[105] that the immensely mentally and physically disabled Mary[106] had as much right to life, as her sister, Jodie.[107] Nevertheless, it appears that the practice of 'active withdrawal of intensive care' is still very prevalent.[108]

In practice, legal disputes over the treatment of newborn babies appear to be relatively rare, with parents apparently generally content to abide by the doctors' medical advice.[109] Or they may become more prepared to adjust their own views once they fully understand what is involved in the treatment. Undoubtedly, the developing medical technology has also become increasingly difficult for parents to comprehend, undermining their ability to oppose the doctors' advice. Mason and Laurie point out that faced with medical advice that life-saving treatment should be withheld, parents of newborn babies 'are likely to agree with their medical advisers simply because they have no evidence on which to *disagree*'.[110] Nevertheless, obvious dilemmas are posed by the fact that although the lives of some extremely premature babies[111] can be saved by resuscitation and intensive care, life-saving therapies may mean lifelong severe disabilities or 'only prolong inevitable death'.[112]

As Brazier points out, the fact that legally the life of a seriously ill premature newborn baby cannot be terminated, for example, by lethal injection, does not mean that doctors are obliged to provide life-saving treatment, irrespective of the fact that he or she has no realistic prospect of survival and whose future life is considered to be full of suffering.[113] Thus, in *Re C (a minor) (wardship:*

---

[102] J. Mason and G. Laurie (2006) p. 545.

[103] It was estimated that in the mid-1980s, anything up to 30% of deaths occurred in neonatal intensive care units due to the deliberate withdrawal of life support. Ibid. at p. 546, citing A. Whitelaw (1986).

[104] *R v. Arthur* (1981) 12 BMLR 1.   [105] [2001] 1 FLR 1.

[106] She had a very poorly developed 'primitive' brain, a very poorly functioning heart and no functioning lung tissue.

[107] The Court of Appeal confirmed the authorisation by the court below of surgery separating the twins, despite the fact that it would effectively kill Mary.

[108] M. Brazier (2006) para. 6.2: cites evidence indicating that in 1995, in the UK and the Republic of Ireland, approximately 50% of the deaths of extremely premature babies were attributable to withdrawal of intensive care and 'experience would suggest that the proportion is now higher'.

[109] E.g. *Re J (a minor)* [1990] 3 All ER 930 and *Re K (medical treatment: declaration)* [2006] EWHC 1007 (Fam), [2006] 2 FLR 883.

[110] J. Mason and G. Laurie (2006) p. 543.

[111] M. Brazier (2006) para. 5.1: describes those extremely premature babies who are born alive at or before the gestational age of 25 weeks and 6 days as babies born at 'the borderline of viability'.

[112] Ibid. at paras. 3.9–3.10.   [113] Ibid. at paras. 8.21–8.22.

medical treatment)[114] the Court of Appeal confirmed that a dying baby's life does not have to be extended by artificial means, irrespective of the circumstances. The utility of the treatment is to be judged by the child's best interests, which in turn depends on the quality of life which might be achieved for the child through the proposed treatment. Many would agree with the view that if nothing is to be gained by further intervention, a dying baby has a right to die with dignity.[115] Thus in situations of this kind, the doctors may, quite lawfully,[116] adopt the doctrine of double effect.[117] Nor has the HRA 1998 provoked any adjustment to this approach.[118]

(C) Treatment for infants

As noted above, very few legal disputes appear to arise between doctors and parents over the treatment of desperately ill newborn babies. Whilst the courts have stressed that there is no legal difference between withholding or withdrawing life support,[119] these disputes are more likely to arise over the withdrawing of life-sustaining treatment from an infant who has survived for many months or even longer. Indeed, Mason and Laurie argue, it is:

> only when the bonds of adversity have been cemented between the parents and the disabled infant that the former are likely to have developed strong independent opinions as to which treatments are appropriate.[120]

Rapid advances in medical technology undoubtedly encourage parents to hope against hope that some treatment will be found to keep their ill children alive or at least delay their deaths. Furthermore, perhaps with the assistance of the internet, parents appear to be better informed[121] and more often disagree with

---

[114] [1989] 2 All ER 782, per Lord Donaldson MR, at 787: confirmed the order of court below that the medical staff were not obliged to administer antibiotics and use intravenous feeding in the event of C (a 4-month-old massively handicapped and terminally ill baby) acquiring an infection or becoming unable to take feeds by mouth; they could care for her in a way which would relieve her suffering and allow her to die peacefully and with dignity.

[115] Ibid.

[116] *Re J (a minor) (wardship: medical treatment)* [1990] 3 All ER 930, per Lord Donaldson MR, at 938.

[117] M. Brazier (2006) paras. 2.38 and 8.18: in relation to a baby, this practice might involve administering a high dose of pain relief with no intention of killing the baby, but in the knowledge that such medication might incidentally hasten his or her death.

[118] *NHS Trust A v. M; NHS Trust B v. H* [2001] 1 All ER 801, per Dame Elizabeth Butler-Sloss P, at [37] in relation to two adult permanent vegetative state (PVS) patients: the positive obligation imposed by Art. 2 of the ECHR only obliges medical teams to keep a terminally ill patient alive if, according to responsible medical opinion, this would be in the patient's best interests. It 'does not impose an absolute obligation to treat if such treatment would be futile'. See also *A National Health Service Trust v. D* [2000] 2 FLR 677, per Cazalet J, at 695: a declaration authorising the medical team not to continue with mechanical ventilation or to resuscitate a dying infant with an irreversible and worsening lung condition was not counter-indicated by Art. 2 ECHR.

[119] *Re MB* [2006] EWHC 507 (Fam) [2006] 2 FLR 319, per Holman J, [18]–[23].

[120] J. Mason and G. Laurie (2006) p. 543.   [121] M. Brazier (2006) para. 3.18.

the doctors over the proper interpretation of their view of what is in the child's best interests.[122]

On the one hand, the medical team may consider that parents who object to resuscitative treatment being withdrawn are being unrealistic. They urge that when a child is suffering a serious fatal condition, constant resuscitative intervention may not only be futile but cruel, since it will cause the child distress, not balanced by any *real* benefit, in terms of quality of life. On the other hand, the parents may argue that they are closer to their child than the doctors, and can detect improvements which others cannot see. Though tragic, an older infant whose life is undoubtedly drawing to a close presents less obvious dilemmas than one who is not yet dying but whose future, nevertheless, looks extremely bleak, even with medical intervention. The common dilemma is that these desperately ill babies and infants sometimes suffer numerous episodes of respiratory failure requiring ventilation to keep them alive – but it is unclear whether this is a steady downward process. In cases like this, the fact that the child is not dying in the short-term may encourage his or her parents to reject the medical team's pessimistic medical prognosis; they hope for a miracle and argue that their child is not ready to die.[123] If the disagreement cannot be resolved, the medical team may feel obliged to seek judicial guidance over whether such an infant's sanctity of life requires them to continue such treatment, irrespective of his or her quality of life. The dispute will often be characterised by each 'side' arguing that the other is over-influenced by their own preconceptions.

Lord Donaldson MR's decision in *Re J (a minor) (wardship: medical treatment)*,[124] remains immensely influential in this context. There the Court of Appeal held that the doctors were not obliged to resuscitate J again, having done so twice already, bearing in mind that resuscitation was an invasive process and would cause him distress. The decision in *Re J* was important in that it established that a child does not need to be actually dying before a medical team can contemplate withholding treatment. Whilst confirming the important difference between taking no steps to extend artificially the child's life, which might be lawful and taking steps to terminate the child's life, which will never be,[125] the court rejected any absolute notion of the sanctity of life. Lord Donaldson MR's words are often cited:

> But in the end there will be cases in which the answer must be that it is not in the interests of the child to subject it to treatment which will cause increased suffering

[122] Sometimes, pro-life groups support parents' applications.
[123] E.g. Charlotte Wyatt, born prematurely at 26 weeks with serious medical problems, survived to over 4 years' old and Luke Winston-Jones, diagnosed with Edward's syndrome, causing multiple defects, with a predicted life expectancy of one year, on birth was only expected to live for a few days; he survived to 10 months. Discussed by L. Jackson and R. Huxtable (2005).
[124] [1990] 3 All ER 930: apart from severe and permanent brain damage at birth, 4½-month-old J (born very prematurely) had other disabilities suggesting an extremely poor quality of life, with predicted paralysis in all his limbs, deafness, limited intellectual abilities and no speech. Although not dying, his life expectancy was uncertain but might extend to his late teens.
[125] Ibid., per Taylor LJ, at 943.

and produce no commensurate benefit, giving the fullest possible weight to the child's, and mankind's, desire to survive.[126]

The decision affirms the very strong presumption in favour of prolonging life,[127] but that continued intervention is not essential if the quality of life available to the child would be so poor that it would be against the child's best interests to strive to keep him or her alive. A balancing exercise has to be performed between what can be achieved by active intervention to keep the child alive and the burdens of such invasive procedures, and the extremely poor quality of life that survival may bring.[128] The 'ten propositions' to be applied by the courts in cases like this, summed up by Holman J in *Re MB*,[129] largely incorporate Lord Donaldson's approach in *Re J*. The judiciary currently stress that each case should be considered on its own facts, often drawing up a balance sheet of the benefits and burdens of continuing and withdrawing treatment.[130] When deciding what is in a dying child's best interests, they also stress the need for a 'good death'.[131]

(D) Best interests determination

The best interests test has been criticised in other contexts.[132] Its indeterminacy also causes difficulties in disputes of this kind. The courts constantly stress that best interests encompass medical, emotional and all other welfare issues.[133] In the past, the best interests test was often bound up with the concept of 'medical futility' and quality of life predictions – in so far as treatment was deemed to be futile and not in the child's best interests, in the face of an unacceptable or 'intolerable' quality of life. But today, the courts disapprove of attempts to place 'a gloss' on the best interests test by identifying the circumstances in which a child's quality of life might become 'intolerable'.[134] Indeed, it is questionable whether quality of life criteria are ever helpful. Jackson and Huxtable point out that arguments about such a concept are not resolved by an appeal to 'facts' and 'will remain contentious and ambiguous'.[135] Whilst disapproving of the concept of intolerability, Dame Elizabeth Butler-Sloss P finds the concept of medical

---

[126] Ibid. at 938.   [127] Ibid.   [128] Ibid. at 939.

[129] *Re MB* [2006] EWHC 507 (Fam), [2006] 2 FLR 319, at [16]. See also *NHS Trust v. A* [2007] EWHC 1696 (Fam), [2008] 1 FLR 70, at [40].

[130] *Wyatt v. Portsmouth NHS Trust* [2005] EWCA Civ 1181, [2006] 1 FLR 554, per Wall LJ, at [87]; *Re MB* [2006] EWHC 507 (Fam), [2006] 2 FLR 319, per Holman J, at [58]–[62]; *NHS Trust v. A* [2007] EWHC 1696 (Fam), [2008] 1 FLR 70, per Holman J, at [61]–[67].

[131] *Wyatt No 1* [2004] EWHC 2247 (Fam), [2005] 1 FLR 21, per Hedley J, at [28].

[132] Discussed in Chapter 8.

[133] *Re L (medical treatment: benefit)* [2004] EWHC 2713 (Fam), [2005] 1 FLR 491, per Dame Elizabeth Butler-Sloss P, at [12]; *Wyatt v. Portsmouth NHS Trust* [2005] EWCA Civ 1181, [2006] 1 FLR 554, per Wall LJ, at [87].

[134] *Re L (medical treatment: benefit)* [2004] EWHC 2713 (Fam), [2005] 1 FLR 491, per Dame Elizabeth Butler-Sloss P, at [12]; *Wyatt No 1* [2004] EWHC 2247 (Fam), [2005] 1 FLR 21, per Hedley J, at [24]; *Wyatt v. Portsmouth NHS Trust* [2005] EWCA Civ 1181, [2006] 1 FLR 554, per Wall LJ, at [76]; *Re MB* [2006] EWHC 507 (Fam), [2006] 2 FLR 319, per Holman J, at [17].

[135] L. Jackson and R. Huxtable (2005) p. 374.

futility useful. She refers to the presumption in favour of preserving life, 'but not where the treatment would be futile', emphasising that there is no obligation on medical practitioners to give treatment which is futile.[136] But there are as many doubts about the value of the concept of futility as there are about the concept of 'intolerability'.[137] Jackson and Huxtable argue that references to medical futility often tend to obscure what is the true concern. Thus, mechanical ventilation may be described as 'futile' not because it fails to help a child to breathe, but because the survival it achieves involves further suffering.[138]

As discussed above, the courts have rejected the idea that some babies have a greater right to life than others. More particularly, in *Re A (conjoined twins: medical treatment)*,[139] the fact that Mary had a very poorly developed 'primitive' brain, made no difference to her right to life. But the parents of older babies may argue that part of the best interests determination should take account of the fact that they (and sometimes other siblings) have a warm and loving relationship with the child, who recognises them and gets pleasure from their presence and that this relationship contributes to a quality of life worth sustaining for as long as possible. *Their* babies, because they have some cognitive capacity or meaningful brain activity, therefore have a quality of life which makes the treatment available to keep them alive 'worthwhile', compared with those with no cognitive capacity of any kind. Earlier case law suggested that the courts were not convinced of the need for such an approach. When doctors sought leave to withdraw life support against the wishes of parents, the courts did not distinguish between a 3-month-old dying baby with 'a very low awareness of anything, if at all',[140] and a baby of 16 months, who, despite slowly dying from spinal muscular atrophy, was conscious, able to recognise her parents and smile.[141]

More recently, however, despite his warning in *Re MB*,[142] that it is fact specific and not policy based,[143] Holman J's decision therein appears to reflect

---

[136] *Re L (medical treatment: benefit)* [2004] EWHC 2713 (Fam), [2005] 1 FLR 491, per Dame Elizabeth Butler-Sloss P, at [12].

[137] J. Mason and G. Laurie (2006) pp. 540–4.

[138] L. Jackson and R. Huxtable (2005) pp. 374–5.   [139] [2001] 1 FLR 1.

[140] *Re C (a baby)* [1996] 2 FLR 43. See also *Re C (a minor) (wardship: medical treatment)* [1990] Fam 26 and *Royal Wolverhampton Hospitals NHS Trust v. B* [2000] 1 FLR 953.

[141] *Re C (medical treatment)* [1998] 1 FLR 384: a 16-month-old baby suffering from spinal muscular atrophy whose Jewish parents vehemently, but unsuccessfully, opposed the withholding of resuscitative intervention (J. Fortin (1998)). See also *A National Health Service Trust v. D* [2000] 2 FLR 677: a 19-month-old baby, who, despite suffering from severe chronic disabilities and irreversible brain abnormality, nevertheless greeted familiar people, smiled at them and waved goodbye; parents unsuccessfully opposed the medical team's view that he should not receive intensive care.

[142] [2006] EWHC 507 (Fam), [2006] 2 FLR 319 (discussed by J. Bridgeman (2007) pp. 162–4): 18-month-old M suffered from a severe form of spinal muscular atrophy, a degenerative and progressive condition, who needed mechanical ventilation to breathe and was tube fed. Despite a limited life expectancy (probably not more than one year), he was conscious and was assumed to have normal cognitive function, including sensory awareness, but had lost the power to communicate orally, but had lost most movement.

[143] Ibid. at [106].

a markedly different approach. There the parents opposed the withdrawal of life support, arguing that 18-month-old M could see, hear and respond positively and with pleasure to family visits and familiar television programmes and music. Holman J acknowledged that parents' views on treatment are particularly valuable, bearing in mind that they spend a great deal of time with their child and know him well. Whilst their own wishes are irrelevant to an objective view of the child's best interests, they may 'illuminate the quality and value *to the child* of the child/parent relationship'.[144] Holman J proceeded on the basis that M, with age appropriate cognition, hearing, and some residuary vision, had a relationship of value to him with his family and continued to gain other pleasures from touch, sight and sound. Whilst Holman J could not value these benefits mathematically, in his view 'they are precious and real and they are the benefits, and only benefits, that M was destined to gain from his life'.[145] Since he did not consider that the routine discomfort, distress and pain caused by procedures used to keep M alive outweighed these benefits, he could not conclude that it was in M's best interests for those benefits, and life itself, immediately to end.[146]

As Brazier points out, this new approach is not without difficulties. It is arguable that the greater the cognitive function a child has, the more his suffering may be if left on life support. What weight should be placed on cognitive function and how should grave physical disabilities be weighed against mental disabilities? If the parents of a baby with normal cognitive function, but with similarly adverse physical disabilities, want him or her to be allowed to die, is the balance similarly tipped the other way?[147] Be that as it may, it is not difficult to see why a court might consider that the best interests of a child with 'an accumulation of experiences and the cognition to gain pleasure from them'[148] are very different from those of a baby with no history of this kind and no capacity to experience 'the simple pleasure of being alive'.[149]

(E) Can parents deny children the right to life?

(i) Attitudes to disability

As Bridgeman relates, Carol Glass considered that the doctors, in deciding not to resuscitate David, her 8-year-old severely mentally and physically disabled son, were influenced by their blinkered approach to him as 'a handicapped child', rather than a 'child with handicaps'.[150] David Glass confounded the

---

[144] Ibid. at [16] (x).   [145] Ibid. at [102].   [146] Ibid.
[147] M. Brazier (2006) para. 8.36.   [148] *Re MB*, ibid., at [106].
[149] *Re K (medical treatment: declaration)* [2006] EWHC 1007 (Fam), [2006] 2 FLR 883, per Sir Mark Potter P, at [57]. He compared the cognition of this premature baby (aged 5½ months) who suffered from a severe inherited neuromuscular disorder causing chronic muscle weakness and learning difficulties, with that of baby M in *Re MB*.
[150] J. Bridgeman (2007) p. 167, citing E. Day (2004); see also Bridgeman's detailed discussion of the Glass case at pp. 164–73 and in J. Bridgeman (2005).

medical prognosis that he was dying and his mother continued to care for him at home. But parents are not always so selfless. They may be dismayed at the potential sacrifices they may have to make to care for a severely disabled child[151] and deeply disappointed by not having an unimpaired child. The terms of the current abortion legislation certainly reflect an intolerance of imperfection. It authorises a termination right up to full term, as long as 'there is a substantial risk that if the child were born it would suffer from such physical or mental abnormalities as to be seriously handicapped'.[152] This provision implies that parents have a right to physical and mental 'normality' in their offspring. As noted above, when disputes go to court over whether life support treatment should be withdrawn from a desperately ill child, the courts now seem to sympathise with the view that the best interests determination should include an assessment of the child's cognitive ability. Perhaps underlying Brazier's concern about this approach is the risk of it implying that parents are entitled to refuse life-saving treatment for a mentally impaired child, not because he or she is ill or dying, but because of the child's disabilities.

Society has, in the past, seemed more tolerant of parents who rejected children born with mental impairments than of those who simply abandoned perfectly healthy babies. The response of the doctors caring for two Down's syndrome babies in the early 1980s, indicates that considerable sympathy then existed for parents who rejected otherwise healthy babies on the grounds of their mental impairment alone. A reading of decisions like *Re B (a minor) (wardship: medical treatment)*[153] and of accounts of the trial in *R v Arthur*[154] shows that such parental rejection was neither uncommon, nor considered surprising. There was the strong view that families were entitled to family privacy, with a right to raise their children as they saw fit, free from state intervention. The lives of disabled people generally were viewed as being poor in quality.[155] It was felt that parents' lives were blighted by caring for disabled children and that society needed citizens who were healthy, both in mind and body. Indeed, as Read and Clements observe:

> disabled babies and children were implicitly placed in a separate category from their non-disabled peers with the consequence that they need not be afforded the same rights or protections.[156]

Interlaced with such ideas may have been the notion that babies, particularly mentally impaired babies, lacked the characteristics and attributes commonly

---

[151] M. Brazier (2006) ch. 7, discusses the difficulties parents face when caring for severely disabled children at home.

[152] Abortion Act 1967, s. 1(1)(d).

[153] [1990] 3 All ER 927: her Down's condition apart, child B had no handicaps, bar an intestinal blockage urgently requiring uncomplicated surgery, which, if successful would give her a life expectancy of 20 to 30 years. The parents refused consent, considering it kinder to allow her to die. The LA warded her and obtained judicial authorisation for the surgery.

[154] *R v. Arthur* (1981) 12 BMLR 1.

[155] J. Read and L. Clements (2004) pp. 495–500.   [156] Ibid. at p. 506.

associated with a worthwhile existence, thereby justifying a lower order of protection.[157]

These views were underpinned by the assumption that parents had the right to determine the fate of their disabled babies – indeed that they had the power of life or death over them, once born. It was urged that the law is incapable of effectively managing the delicate and complex relationship between parent and child and that if parents refused routine, but life-saving treatment for their children, the doctors should comply with their wishes. In *Re B*, decided in 1981,[158] the surgeon who was to have performed straightforward but life-saving surgery on baby B, declined to do so when informed of her parents' objections. Even Ewbank J, at first instance, concluded that their wishes had to be respected and refused to authorise the procedure. The Court of Appeal's decision over-ruling the parents' views was itself criticised by members of the general public, who considered it unfair to foist on parents the care of mentally impaired children against their wishes.[159]

These two cases established that parents do not have the power to dictate whether their children should live or die. The law prohibits healthy, though mentally impaired, babies being allowed to die by doctors, through normal sustenance being withheld. Furthermore, parents' decisions to reject straight-forward life-saving surgery may be overridden. Public opinion has obviously changed since the early 1980s.[160] Although many parents still consider they have considerable power over their children's lives, attitudes towards mental impairment appear to have modified over the last 30 years. Down's syndrome is no longer considered to be an unacceptable handicap for parents to cope with and the concept of children having rights to protection *from* their parents has now gathered pace. Indeed, it seems unlikely that today any parents in this country would consider asking doctors to allow their mentally impaired babies to die through 'nursing care only' as in the *Arthur* case, or refuse treatment in circumstances like those arising in *Re B (a minor) (wardship: medical treatment)*.[161]

(ii) A child's right to life and parents' objections to life-saving treatment

Their horror of mental impairment led the parents of the Down's syndrome baby B[162] to refuse life-saving treatment on her behalf. No doubt they were sincere in thinking it better that she should die rather than go through life mentally impaired. In other cases, the parents may have equally strong con-victions which lead them to refuse life-saving treatment for their children, even if their survival would not be attended by mental or physical handicap. The courts most commonly encounter cases of this kind where the parents' oppo-sition to treatment stems from their religious convictions.

---

[157] C. Wells (1989) pp. 202–3. [158] But not officially reported until 1990: [1990] 3 All ER 927.
[159] J. Read and L. Clements (2004) pp. 501–4. [160] Ibid. at pp. 504–5.
[161] [1990] 3 All ER 927. [162] Ibid.

Doctors may seek the assistance of the courts in life and death situations where parents are desperately anxious to secure treatment for their sick child, but only in a way consistent with their religious beliefs. Conflicts may, for example, arise between doctors and Jehovah's Witness parents who oppose their child receiving blood transfusions, even though failure to transfuse the child may lead to his or her death. They conscientiously consider that it is in their child's best interests to die rather than receive blood. Doctors may find it difficult to sympathise with parents whose views, however sincerely held, endanger the lives of babies and infants, which could be saved by modern medical treatment. After all, these children are too young to have formed their own convictions. Although when they are older they might agree with their parents,[163] the outcome of their parents' decisions would prevent them living long enough to develop their own ideas. Justice Holmes in *Prince v. Massachusetts* put it well when he said:

> Parents may be free to become martyrs themselves. But it does not follow they are free, in identical circumstances, to make martyrs of their children before they have reached the age of full and legal discretion when they can make that choice for themselves.[164]

Legally, of course, there is no need for medical staff to obtain judicial consent before giving emergency life-saving treatment to children against the wishes of their parents. Life-saving treatment can be justified under the common law principle of necessity, backed up by the need to promote a child's right to life under Article 2 of the ECHR. Nevertheless, given the uncertain scope of the defence of necessity,[165] it would be wise always to seek judicial authority for treatment which ignores parental objections.[166] This approach would accord with the ECtHR's obvious lack of sympathy with the medical team in *Glass v. United Kingdom*[167] for not having obtained prior emergency judicial approval for treating David in a way they knew his mother opposed.

Case law indicates a general willingness on the part of the judiciary to accept medical advice that the treatment proposed is the only means of saving a sick child, even when it means overriding the religious tenets of his or her parents.[168] Thorpe J in *Re S (a minor) (medical treatment)*[169] stressed that the alternatives of transfusing the child or leaving him to die left the court with no

---

[163] E.g. *Re E (a minor) (wardship: medical treatment)* [1993] 1 FLR 386, discussed in Chapter 5.

[164] 321 US 158 at 165 (1944).

[165] *Re F (mental patient: sterilisation)* [1990] 2 AC 1, per Lord Goff, at 74.

[166] The hospital trust may seek leave from the court under the CA 1989, s. 10 to apply for a specific issue order under the CA 1989, s. 8 or seek a declaration under the inherent declaration.

[167] [2004] 1 FLR 1019, at [79].

[168] In both *Re O (a minor) (medical treatment)* [1993] 2 FLR 149 (3-month-old very low weight premature baby) and *Re R (a minor) (medical treatment)* [1993] 2 FLR 757 (10-month-old baby suffering from leukaemia) the courts authorised the use of blood transfusions.

[169] [1993] 1 FLR 376: S was a child aged 4½ suffering from leukaemia.

choice but to authorise treatment, given that its decision was governed by the welfare test. He posed the following hypothetical questions:

> are the religious convictions of the parents to deny their child a 50% chance of survival? Are those convictions to deny him that 50% chance and condemn him to inevitable and early death?[170]

Although the much criticised decision of the Court of Appeal in *Re T (a minor) (wardship: medical treatment)*[171] seemed for a time to undermine the courts' protective role, hopefully it has now been relegated to the history books. There the mother, having seen how 18-month-old C (born with a life-threatening defect) had suffered after the failure of earlier surgery, opposed his undergoing a liver transplant despite the high prospects of its success. As many critics pointed out, by suggesting that C's welfare depended on his mother[172] and that mother and child 'are one',[173] the Court of Appeal's decision carried the underlying message that the best interests test should be interpreted from the mother's perspectives. More to the point, the effect of its decision not to authorise life-saving surgery, given his mother's strong objections, was that C would die. As noted above, in his decision, Waite LJ considered it inappropriate 'even in an age preoccupied with "rights" – to talk of the rights of a child, or of a parent, or the rights of the court'.[174] Had the court been prepared to approach the case from a rights-based perspective, it would surely have acknowledged, more honestly than the Court of Appeal ever did, the outcome of their decision to abide by the mother's wishes. This was that C's right to life was to be set aside. Instead they chose death for him – on the basis that it would be better than the post-operative pain and suffering and potential complications attending the proposed surgery, bearing in mind his mother's own reluctance to cope with his post-operative care.

Admittedly the case law discussed above concerning Jehovah's Witness parents only involves blood transfusions. These are relatively simple procedures, compared with the major invasive surgery, accompanied by the pain of recovery and the possibility of long-term post-operative complications. But in both situations the choice remains equally stark – treatment or death. Fortunately, Holman J's decision in *NHS Trust v. A*,[175] which involved the possibility of very invasive treatment, suggests that the judiciary remain well aware of the need to protect children against their parents' rejection of life-saving treatment. There, strongly Christian parents opposed a bone marrow transplant (BMT) as the only form of possible cure for their seriously ill daughter A,[176] now aged 6 months. Like the mother in *Re T*, they had witnessed

---

[170] Ibid. at 380.
[171] [1997] 1 All ER 906. Discussed by S. Michalowski (1997); M. Fox and J. McHale (1997); A. Bainham (1997); J. Bridgeman (2007) pp. 137–42.
[172] [1997] 1 All ER 906, per Butler-Sloss LJ, at 915.   [173] Ibid. at 914.
[174] Ibid. at 916.   [175] [2007] EWHC 1696 (Fam), [2008] 1 FLR 70.
[176] A suffered from haemophagocytic lymphohistiocytosis (HLH), a fatal genetic defect in the immune system.

A suffering pain and distress when undergoing very strong drug treatment and wished to spare her a similar ordeal. Furthermore, they knew that the BMT might not succeed,[177] the treatment would be lengthy, painful (possibly very painful) and distressing and it would render A infertile.[178] As strong and committed Christians, they hoped that God would heal their daughter without a BMT.

Rejecting the need to approach the case from a rights-based perspective,[179] Holman J reapplied the 'ten propositions' established by existing case law.[180] These include the fact that each case depends on its own facts,[181] so in A's case, *Re T* could safely be distinguished.[182] He also stressed that although parents' views are particularly valuable, because they know their own child, their wishes are wholly irrelevant to an objective consideration of the child's best interests 'save to the extent in any given case that they may illuminate the quality and value to the child of the child-parent relationship'.[183] That being the case, in his view, Holman J could set aside the parents' religious views.[184] Having weighed up the benefits and burdens of the BMT, he concluded that a 50% prospect of A living a full, normal life, albeit infertile, outweighed the certainty of death before the age of 1 to 1½. A 'is a living human being, with a future as well as a present, to whom, despite her disease, modern medicine and science may be able to give a full life'.[185] The decision in *Re T* had dangerously undermined the clear principle that parents have no absolute right to parental autonomy, nor the final say over whether their children should live or die. *NHS Trust v. A* has restored this principle, making it clear that children's lives are too precious to be sacrificed to their parents' religious faith and fears for the future.

(4) Caring for a child's health

(A) Decisions about general healthcare

Although there is no compulsion on parents to use the healthcare services available, most are aware of the dangers of leaving sick children without medical attention. As the case law discussed above demonstrates, once they are consulted, doctors may seek judicial authority to override parental wishes and provide children with life-saving treatment. Fortunately, circumstances like these are rare. Even in non-life threatening situations, however, doctors wield considerable power and it is often they who determine the manner in which the child's right to 'the highest attainable standard of health'[186] will be

---

[177] [2007] EWHC 1696 (Fam), [2008] 1 FLR 70, per Holman J, at [1]: the BMT might achieve inter alia: approximately a 50% prospect of effecting a lasting cure with a normal life expectancy; a 10% prospect of ensuring her survival, but with some significant impairment; a 10% prospect of killing her; a 30% prospect of failing, in which case A would die of HLH.

[178] Ibid. at [45].   [179] Ibid. at [44].

[180] Ibid. at [40]. See also *Re MB* [2006] EWHC 507 (Fam), [2006] 2 FLR 319, per Holman J, at [16].

[181] [2007] EWHC 1696 (Fam), [2008] 1 FLR 70, at [40] (ix).

[182] Ibid. at [43].   [183] Ibid. at [40] (x).   [184] Ibid. at [42].

[185] Ibid. at [70].   [186] CRC, Art. 24(1).

fulfilled. They may be the effective decision-makers, despite the theoretical right enjoyed by parents, as their children's proxies, to determine their children's healthcare. Thus in *C (HIV test)*[187] it was the mother's general practitioner who, on discovering that a mother was infected with HIV, set in motion steps aimed at ensuring that her baby should be tested for HIV, against the mother's own strong wishes.

Doctors are less likely to interfere with parents' decisions when it comes to arranging for children to undergo relatively uncomplicated, non-therapeutic procedures, such as ear-piercing and minor cosmetic surgery. Although the proprietorial attitude of Victorian parents towards their children is objectionable to modern eyes, many of today's parents unconcernedly exhibit a similar approach. They quite commonly arrange for their young children to undergo procedures which infringe their children's right to bodily integrity under Article 8 of the ECHR, without always considering whether this can be justified. Brazier questions whether parents are entitled to arrange for their children to undergo cosmetic surgery, especially those with Down's syndrome.[188] Whilst she considers it would be wrong for a mother, for example, to put her son through painful surgery to advance his career as a male model, since it would not be in his best interests, she is more ambivalent over the quite common surgery on boys to redress their 'bat ears'.[189] She suggests that it is for the parents to balance the pain of the surgery against the child's misery over being taunted for his deformity. Clearly his own strong views regarding the social benefit he will gain from the procedure should be balanced against the dangers involved in surgery under a general anaesthetic.

(B) Organ and tissue donation

The prospect of having to watch a child die is one that no parent would wish to contemplate. In some cases, a seriously ill child's life might be saved by the donation of an organ, tissue or bone marrow provided by a healthy living donor. The advantages of genetic compatibility may lead parents to consider arranging for one of their healthy children to act as donor for the dying child. They may even produce a baby who can provide tissue to save an older child – the 'saviour sibling' scenario.[190] Anyone contemplating using a child as a donor must familiarise themselves with the legislation,[191] regulations[192] and codes of practice[193] now governing this area of practice. These were introduced in response to public concern about the removal and retention of organs and tissue from dead children at the Bristol Royal Infirmary and the

---

[187] [1999] 2 FLR 1004.   [188] M. Brazier (2003) pp. 357–8.   [189] Ibid. at p. 357.
[190] R. Brownsword (2005).   [191] Human Tissue Act (HT Act) 2004.
[192] Inter alia, the Human Tissue Act 2004 (Persons who Lack Capacity to Consent and Transplants) Regulations (HT Act 2004 (PLCCT) Regs) 2006 (SI 2006/1659).
[193] Issued by the Human Tissue Authority (established by the HT Act 2004, Part 2).

Royal Liverpool Children's hospital (Alder Hey),[194] without their parents' knowledge or consent.

Most practitioners have very grave reservations about children and young people being used as donors of non-regenerative organs, such as a kidney. Indeed, Mason and Laurie note that practitioners have introduced their own informal regulation and have simply stopped accepting children as donors.[195] The Human Tissue Authority (HTA) nevertheless implicitly assumes that children do exceptionally provide organs, commenting 'Children can be considered as living organ donors only in extremely rare circumstances'.[196] In its guidance[197] the HTA suggests that, in addition to complying with the common law requirements relating to consent for removal of the organ, medical practitioners and parents must overcome two hurdles. First, although the actual *removal* of the organ is not within the scope of the HT Act 2004 (it governs the *use* of the organ, with removal still being governed by the common law[198]), the HTA suggests that court approval should be obtained before the removal of a solid organ from a child.[199] Although sensible, in the absence of any reported domestic case law on this matter, it is difficult to know how this advice originated. The only reported judicial comment on children donating organs came from Lord Donaldson who considered it 'highly improbable' that an adolescent under the age of 18 wishing to become an organ donor could ever be sufficiently competent to consent on his own behalf.[200] But in any event, given the concerns over children donating tissue such as regenerative bone marrow,[201] most courts in this country would surely refuse to rule that it is in a healthy child's best interests to donate an organ or even part of an organ. In the event of a court authorising such a donation, the regulations require that before the donation can go ahead, it must be drawn to the attention of the HTA[202] and be approved by a panel of no fewer than three of its members.[203] Before the HTA panel approves the donation, it must be satisfied that no reward was provided for the donation and that the removal of the organ was otherwise lawful.[204] Given the apparent need for prior judicial authorisation,

---

[194] J. Herring (2006) ch. 7.

[195] J. Mason and G. Laurie (2006) p. 488: their inquiries indicate that only one transplant involving an identical twin aged 17 has occurred in the last 20 years.

[196] HTA (2006a) para. 30.

[197] HTA (2006a), likely to be replaced by revised guidance in a very similar format, see HTA (2008a).

[198] HTA (2006a) paras. 13 and 28.   [199] HTA (2006a) para. 28.

[200] *Re W (a minor) (medical treatment: court's jurisdiction)* [1993] Fam 64, per Lord Donaldson, at 79. Lord Donaldson's comment was apparently overlooked by the HTA, since it suggests (in HTA (2006a) para. 30) that a *Gillick* competent teenager can legally consent to donating an organ.

[201] Discussed below.

[202] HT Act 2004 (PLCCT) Regs 2006, reg. 11(2): the registered medical practitioner who has clinical responsibility for the donor must bring the proposed transplant to the attention of the HTA.

[203] HT Act 2004 (PLCCT) Regs 2006, reg. 12(1) and (2).

[204] HT Act 2004 (PLCCT) Regs 2006, reg. 11(3).

the requirement for an HTA panel decision seems otiose. Nevertheless, these complicated provisions, together with criminal sanctions,[205] will undoubtedly reinforce the general view that to use children for the donation of organs is unethical.

There is no case law in this country testing the legality of using children as donors of bone marrow or other regenerative tissue for seriously ill siblings. Despite this, according to Brazier, bone marrow donations by children, including very young children, to help treat siblings suffering from leukaemia are 'routine'.[206] This is presumably because medical practitioners are not so concerned about the ethics of children donating tissue that can be replaced quickly.[207] Furthermore, parents and medical advisers obviously assume that, by virtue of their parental autonomy, parents are entitled to use their healthy child's body to save the life of the other. It had been widely argued that regulations should be introduced in this country subjecting this practice to supervision.[208] As Mumford explained, various systems of non-judicial regulation had been introduced elsewhere.[209] As discussed below, a limited system of regulation has now been introduced in England and Wales, but it is unclear how it is working.[210]

Through a complex web of legislative provisions and regulations, donation of bone marrow[211] has been brought within the scope of the new legislation,[212] but with extra supervision by the HTA when an *incompetent* child is used as a live donor.[213] In general terms, the legislation authorises material taken from a live child to be used for transplantation only if 'appropriate consent' has been obtained first.[214] This must be obtained either from a 'competent'[215] child donor or, in relation to an incompetent child, from a person with PR for that

[205] HT Act 2004, s. 33.

[206] M. Brazier (2003) p. 423. E.g. the younger sister of the child involved in *R v. Cambridge District Health Authority, ex p B* [1995] 1 FLR 1055 provided bone marrow to help save her sister's life.

[207] Discussed generally by J. Mason and G. Laurie (2006) pp. 485–8.

[208] Inter alia: D. Feenan (1997) p. 311; S. Mumford (1998) pp. 145–6; BMA (2001) p. 164.

[209] S. Mumford (1998) pp. 138–9: e.g. in France, a committee of experts must authorise all donations.

[210] Since its establishment in September 2006, the HTA have had 137 applications for approval of bone marrow donations by incompetent children (personal communication with the HTA, April 2008). Per the Director of Bone Marrow Transplantation at Great Ormond Street Hospital (personal communication with author, April 2008): there are 300 transplants in children in the UK per annum involving approximately 100 siblings, with approximately 50 from non-*Gillick* competent children.

[211] I.e. allogeneic bone marrow and peripheral blood stem cells; see HTA (2006b).

[212] HT Act 2004, s. 1(1)(f) and Sch. 1, Part 1, 7.

[213] HT Act 2004 (PLCCT) Regs 2006, reg. 10(1)(b) and (3)(b): 'transplantable material' for the purposes of HT Act 2004, s. 33 (restrictions on transplants involving live donors), is defined as including bone marrow when it is removed from an incompetent child.

[214] HT Act 2004, s. 2.

[215] HTA (2006b) paras. 45–7: children may consent on their own behalf to the procedure if they can show *Gillick* competence for these purposes. But cf. para. 33: 'it is good practice' even with a competent child to involve the person with PR as well.

child.[216] The guidance appears to assume that even a relatively young child can be deemed *Gillick* competent for the purposes of providing bone marrow. It states:

> Young children are unlikely to have a frame of reference for understanding the procedure for donating bone marrow, PBSC [peripheral blood stem cells] and lymphocytes, or to be aware of the risks involved ... It is therefore strongly recommended that for children capable of giving consent a play therapist, psychologist or specialist nurse is involved in the communication process so that the child may better understand what is proposed and be able to give his or her fully informed consent.[217]

This guidance is worrying. Any child who needs a play therapist to help him or her 'better understand what is proposed' surely lacks the relatively sophisticated understanding necessary to weigh up the pros and cons of a bone marrow donation. Admittedly the guidance requires competent children to have explained to them 'in terms that they find easy to understand' with the help of appropriately qualified staff, a detailed list of issues relating to the procedure,[218] including the fact that donation 'is an entirely voluntary act and that they have a right to be free of any kind of coercion or pressure (for example, by family)'.[219] It also stresses that it is 'crucial to make sure that a child has consented voluntarily and has not been unduly influenced by anyone else'.[220] On this point, the revised guidance will be strengthened if it draws attention to the fact that children may have come under pressure to donate through 'feelings of guilt or a fear that love may be withdrawn if they do not proceed'.[221]

An additional risk is that medical practitioners arranging such procedures may be tempted to assume a relatively young child donor to be *Gillick* competent, knowing that a donation involving a *competent* child avoids further supervision from the HTA. Indeed, it is only when an *incompetent* child donates bone marrow that a fresh set of regulations is triggered.[222] These make it a criminal offence to remove 'transplantable material' from such a child, unless the clinician responsible for the donor makes a written referral to the HTA.[223] The procedure should not go ahead until the various parties involved have received approval from the HTA.[224] Before approving the proposed donation, the HTA must be satisfied first, that no reward has or is to be given for the procedure,[225] and second, that appropriate consents for the

---

[216] HT Act 2004, s. 2 and HTA (2006b) paras. 26–7.

[217] HTA (2006b) para. 23. It seems that the revised guidance (HTA (2008b) at para. 79) will similarly advise that even 'small children can be helped to understand some aspects of the procedure and its associated risks' with the help of play therapists etc.

[218] E.g. long- and short-term risks; potential advantages for the recipient; the right to withdraw at any time.

[219] HTA (2006b) para. 37.   [220] Ibid. at para. 29.   [221] HTA (2008b) para. 95.

[222] HT Act 2004 (PLCCT) Regs 2006.   [223] HT Act 2004 (PLCCT) Regs 2006, reg. 11(2).

[224] HT Act 2004 (PLCCT) Regs 2006, reg. 11(5). NB in this case, the HTA need not convene a panel of three to consider the application.

[225] HT Act 2004 (PLCCT) Regs 2006, reg. 11(3)(a).

procedure have been given.[226] The HTA should take account of a report prepared by an Accredited Assessor (AA),[227] whose job it is to satisfy himself (and the HTA) that the child's best interests have been properly considered and the HTA's codes of practice properly implemented.[228] Before reporting, the AA should interview the child and the person with PR over the child in order to satisfy himself, inter alia: that an adult donor is not available; that the donor's best interests have been properly considered; that the donor and recipient understand the procedure's risks and implications and that the person with PR has consented to the procedure.[229]

Although the guidance states that a child donor should only be used if it has been impossible to identify an appropriate adult donor,[230] it skates over the problems involved in assessing the best interests of a healthy child with a desperately ill sibling. The guidance points out that neither the medical practitioner nor the parent with PR should allow a child to act as a donor unless they are convinced that such a procedure is in the child's best interests. Furthermore it states that this test is not confined to the child's medical interests but should include 'emotional, psychological and social benefits'.[231] The guidance suggests, albeit in passing, that the parents should take account of the *risks* of the procedure for the child donor.[232] But, astonishingly, there is no clear warning that parents may be unable to take a dispassionate view of the donor's best interests where tissue is required to save the life of a seriously ill sibling. In contrast, earlier official guidance had specifically suggested that to counter such a risk, there should be independent scrutiny of the parents' decision by an independent assessor or by a hospital ethics committee.[233] Admittedly an AA is free to raise this question in his report. Furthermore, it appears that the revised HTA guidance will direct him or her to consider the danger of the younger incompetent donor feeling pressurised into donation. It will require the AA to discuss any feelings of pressure or duty the child holds and explore their origins.[234] Arguably, however, it should far more explicitly require AAs to balance the risks to the healthy child donor of undergoing the donation procedure against the benefits to the recipient of receiving the donated material.

By failing to draw specific attention to the parents' ambivalent position in cases like this, the HTA side-steps widely expressed doubts over whether the donation of bone marrow can ever be in the best interests of a healthy child. Parents may argue that the psychological benefits to the donor of saving his or her sibling's life will out-balance the dangers involved. Indeed, they might adopt Eekelaar's approach and claim that the potential donor, when mature, would have chosen retrospectively to save a dying sibling.[235] Furthermore, they

---

[226] HT Act 2004 (PLCCT) Regs 2006, reg. 11(3)(b). NB HT Act 2004, s. 2(3): 'appropriate consent' in relation to an incompetent child is a person with PR.
[227] HTA (2006b) para. 50. AAs are usually based in hospitals with bone marrow transplant units.
[228] Ibid. at para. 49.   [229] Ibid. at para. 50.   [230] Ibid. at paras. 22 and 50.
[231] Ibid. at paras. 25 and 27.   [232] Ibid. at para. 27.   [233] DH (2001) pp. 20–1.
[234] HTA (2008b), para. 95.   [235] J. Eekelaar (1986) p. 170.

might suggest that if they refused to allow their healthy child to be used as a donor, he or she might feel distressed on being told, when older, that the sibling had died because of the absence of a suitable donor. These arguments are all persuasive, but do they give sufficient weight to the rights of the healthy potential donor? To suggest that there are no medical or ethical problems involved because the tissue is regenerative is surely to over-simplify the issues. The procedure often involves some risk to the donor child. For example, he or she will undergo a general anaesthetic, which in itself carries risk, will be sore and bruised at the site where the tissue was removed[236] and will need hospitalising for up to two days,[237] with the attendant risks of contracting an infection. A donor child may gain little real psychological benefit from helping a dying sibling where he or she is too young to have established any emotional bond with the proposed recipient.[238] Indeed, it is unclear whether siblings truly benefit from acting as donors, particularly if the procedure does not save the ill child.[239] Furthermore, as discussed above, whilst parents may tell the medical team that the sibling donor is anxious to undergo the process, family pressure may have rendered such consent quite unreal.[240]

The HTA guidance suggests that if in real doubt about the legality of a donation from a child, a medical practitioner should consult the courts.[241] But there is little domestic authority as to how they would react to such an application. The first reported English case, *Re Y (mental incapacity: bone marrow transplant)*,[242] involved an adult donor. As Feenan points out, Connell J's decision approving the donation is a weak one.[243] He had little difficulty in deciding that it would benefit Y, a severely mentally and physically disabled woman, to provide bone marrow for her sister who was suffering from a potentially fatal degenerative bone marrow disorder. Without any detailed analysis of the dangers involved in the harvesting procedure,[244] he considered that the risks were very slight and were more than counter-balanced by the benefits to her of being able to retain close contact with her mother, given that this was a very closely knit family. There was an extremely tenuous logical connection between Y's donation to her sister, and her retaining contact with their mother – the argument being that, if the sister died, the mother's state of health would deteriorate, making it unlikely that she would be able to continue visiting Y in her residential home. To prevent Y suffering the loss of her mother's visits, she should provide her sister with bone marrow. The looseness of this judicial reasoning would be alarming if the decision was adopted as guidance for use in children's cases. It demonstrates how easily doubts over the dangers to the donor of undergoing a bone marrow harvesting procedure can be assuaged by vague assurances of it being virtually risk free.

---

[236] S. Mumford (1998) p. 135.   [237] L. Delaney (1995).   [238] Ibid. at p. 373.
[239] BMA (2001) p. 159.   [240] Ibid. at p. 162.   [241] HTA (2006b) para. 25.
[242] [1996] 2 FLR 787.   [243] D. Feenan (1997) pp. 309–10.
[244] [1996] 2 FLR 787, per Connell J, at 793: the risks of a general anaesthetic were 'extremely low', being 1 per 10,000.

It is a pity that the HTA's guidance does not deal more rigorously with the conflict of interests underlying situations of this kind. Meanwhile it is unclear how the HTA currently deals with applications involving live children as bone marrow donors for close relatives, often their own siblings. Hopefully its supervision is not purely tokenistic on the basis that the procedure 'merely' involves the removal of regenerative tissue.

(C) Parents' culture and children's bodies

Some parents obviously feel free to arrange for their children to undergo what Feldman describes as various forms of 'mutilation' carried out for religious or social reasons, such as ear piercing, circumcision and clitorectomy (female circumcision), all of which, in his view, infringe their children's right to bodily integrity.[245] He refutes the argument that religious tolerance should allow any of these practices to continue, asserting: 'This is a classic example of a case where the parent's freedom ends where the child's nose (or other anatomical protuberance) begins.'[246]

Feldman's certainty that children's rights must always prevail over parental beliefs is compelling. Nevertheless, condemnation of practices which are still widely accepted in many developing countries might be viewed as an arrogant Western refusal to acknowledge or understand long-held cultural beliefs. The practice of female circumcision, now often referred to as female genital mutilation (FGM) or, by the international community, as female genital cutting, is a case in point. The practice of FGM is not only a cultural tradition going back centuries and pre-dating Islam, but one which is still widely performed on women and children in various communities throughout Africa and the Middle East.[247] This topic proved a controversial one at the drafting stage of the CRC, with delegates from the UK and the USA wanting an outright condemnation of the practice and delegates from countries such as Senegal, wanting a more general formula.[248] The compromise which emerged is seen in the wording of Article 24(3). Whilst states are obliged to take measures 'with a view to abolishing traditional practices prejudicial to the health of children', there is no specific reference to the prohibition of FGM.

A concern not to offend community sensitivities has not weakened an international resolve to stamp out FGM.[249] Whatever form it takes, it involves girls in extreme pain and often carries long-term and serious side effects, even undermining their future child-bearing capacity.[250] There is widespread agreement

---

[245] D. Feldman (2002) pp. 270–2.   [246] Ibid. at p. 271.

[247] UNICEF (2005) p. 3: current estimates suggest that some 3 million girls and women who live in some 28 African and Middle East countries are cut each year.

[248] L. LeBlanc (1995) pp. 85–9.   [249] UNICEF (2005) ch. 4.

[250] See *K v. Secretary of State for the Home Department, Fornah v. Secretary of State for the Home Department* [2006] UKHL 46, [2007] 1 AC 412, per Baroness Hale of Richmond, at [91]–[92] for a short, but graphic, summary of the methods used in FGM and its effects.

with Feldman's condemnation of the practice on the basis that it not only infringes girls' rights to freedom from torture under Article 3 of the ECHR, but also their rights under various other international conventions.[251] Nonetheless, concerted efforts by international development agencies to persuade the relevant governments to outlaw FGM have not been particularly successful.[252] Furthermore, under the impact of post-World War II migration, it is no longer restricted to Africa but is now practised in the industrialised countries in which migrants have settled.[253] As Ford explains, families living in the communities where the practice is still prevalent are trapped. Genital cutting is considered to be an essential sign of a girl's virginity and without it she has no chance of marriage, her only route to security and prosperity. A single family cannot reject the customs of their own community if they consider that their daughters will suffer socially as a result.[254] International development agencies now widely consider that the only way to eradicate the practice is to educate communities from within and to persuade them of its dangers, rather than simply condemning it.[255] There is, however, widespread agreement in this country that girls have a right to more immediate protection from what has been described as 'an extreme and ghastly manifestation' of discrimination and subjugation.[256] Legislation making FGM a criminal offence here[257] was later re-enacted in an extended form,[258] to prevent girls resident in the UK being sent to Africa to undergo the procedure whilst on holiday there. Guidance produced by local child safeguarding boards up and down the country emphasises the criminal nature of this practice and the fact that it should be treated as a child protection issue.[259] If there are concerns that FGM is to be carried out on a child, the police and children's social care should be involved, with a section 47 investigation taking place and consideration given to obtaining an emergency protection order.[260]

Arguably, it is impossible to persuade mothers not to mutilate their daughters through FGM, whilst male circumcision is so widely tolerated, socially and legally. Male circumcision appears to have escaped both the widespread condemnation attending the 'circumcision' of females and efforts to regulate it more closely. Nevertheless, the differences between the procedures are obvious.[261] Male circumcision is far less invasive and attended by less risk

---

[251] Ibid. at [94]. See also UNICEF (2005) ch. 4.
[252] N. Ford (2005) p. 183.   [253] UNICEF (2005) p. 4.
[254] N. Ford (2005) p. 188. See also UNICEF (2005) ch. 3.
[255] Ibid. and UNICEF (2005) chs. 5–6.
[256] [2006] UKHL 46, per Lord Brown of Eaton-Under-Heywood, at [119].
[257] Prohibition of Female Circumcision Act 1985 (repealed and replaced by later legislation in 2003).
[258] Female Genital Mutilation Act 2003, s. 1: criminal offence of FGM; s. 3: criminal offence of assisting a non-UK resident to carry out FGM overseas.
[259] E.g. London Safeguarding Children Board (2007).
[260] Ibid.
[261] K v. Secretary of State for the Home Department, Fornah v. Secretary of State for the Home Department [2006] UKHL 46, [2007] 1 AC 412, per Baroness Hale of Richmond, at [93].

and pain. Whilst FGM offers no therapeutic benefit whatsoever, male circumcision does have some medical benefits for rare conditions,[262] quite apart from its being more widely practised, for religious and social reasons.[263] Medical opinion nevertheless seems divided over whether non-therapeutic male circumcision is beneficial or harmful.[264] Like any surgical procedure, it is certainly not risk free, even when carried out expertly, under medical conditions. The BMA warns that the practice should not be justified solely by reference to evidence of its health benefits – such evidence is simply insufficient.[265] At least some adults consider that they should never have been circumcised as children.[266]

The courts have shown little stomach for tackling the fraught question whether male circumcision can be justified as being in the child's best interests. Until the decision in *Re J (specific issue orders: Muslim upbringing and circumcision)*[267] there had been no legal ruling on its legality. Whilst acknowledging that much of the medical literature adopts the view that such a procedure without medical necessity is an assault on the child's bodily integrity,[268] Wall J concluded that the procedure is lawful because 'there have, historically, been a number of medical justifications put forward for male circumcision' and because 'it is insisted on by Muslim and Jews', and further that it has 'over the years, become an accepted practice amongst a significant number of parents in England'.[269] The decision, confirmed by the Court of Appeal,[270] is authority for the proposition that as long as parents agree, the law allows them to arrange for their children to be circumcised, but if they disagree over such a matter, judicial authority must be obtained from the courts.

It is questionable whether Wall J's reasoning suffices as a good legal justification. Popularity of a parental practice should not prevent the judiciary declaring it to be unlawful, if they consider it to be against children's best interests. Because in *Re J*, the divorced parents disagreed over whether their son should be circumcised, Wall J was able to weigh up the pros and cons of the procedure being carried out on their small son aged 5. He concluded that the boy was unlikely to have sufficient involvement with his Muslim father's community to justify circumcising him, given the potential medical and psychological risks, its irreversible nature and his mother's opposition.[271] But, as Fox and Thomson point out, such an approach avoids the crucial question – why should circumcision be left to parental decision?[272] It leaves the children of united parents unprotected against a practice on which they are not consulted

---

[262] A. Rickwood *et al.* (2000).   [263] M. Freeman (2001) p. 112.

[264] See inter alia: J. Hutson (2004); R. Short (2004); BMA (2004) p. 260.   [265] BMA (2004) p. 262.

[266] See letter (1996) 312 BMJ 377 (10 February) from a group of men arguing that they had been harmed by circumcision procedures carried out in their childhood.

[267] [1999] 2 FLR 678.   [268] Ibid. at 690.   [269] Ibid.

[270] *Re J (specific issue orders: child's religious upbringing and circumcision)* [2000] 1 FLR 571. See also *Re S (specific issue order: religion: circumcision)* [2004] EWHC 1282 (Fam), [2005] 1 FLR 236, per Baron J, at [76]–[78], adopting Wall J's view of the law in *Re J* [1999] 2 FLR 678.

[271] [1999] 2 FLR 678 at 699–700.

[272] M. Fox and M. Thomson (2005) pp. 165–6, citing with approval, C. Bridge (2002) p. 282.

and over which they have no control. Indeed, these authors criticise the courts for assuming that the socioreligious benefits to a child of being brought up in a Muslim or Jewish environment can outweigh the medical risks, without those medical risks ever being properly analysed.[273] They argue that the whole range of 'ethico-legal texts' on this procedure portray infant male circumcision as of low risk and therefore a matter of parental choice.

> Only limited consideration is given to the seemingly obvious fact that circumcision is the excision of healthy tissue from a child unable to give his consent for no demonstrable medical benefit.[274]

Nor does the case law show any judicial consideration of the child's own rights in such cases. Although the court in *Re J* considered and rejected the father's claimed right under Article 9 of the ECHR, to arrange for his son's circumcision according to the tenets of his religion, there was no analysis of the child's own rights. It is clear that the procedure infringes the child's right to bodily integrity under Article 8, whilst not necessarily promoting his health or morals under Article 8(2). Gilbert argues that it also infringes a child's rights under Article 3.[275] Such arguments might be countered by claiming that the procedure promotes the child's own religious rights under Article 9, combined with his rights to freedom from religious discrimination under Article 14. Indeed, Wall J implicitly accepted that a child might be at a severe social disadvantage being brought up as a member of a Muslim community without having been circumcised.

It seems unlikely that any government would contemplate prohibiting male circumcision altogether, since the result would be widespread evasion of the criminal law. A compromise would be to introduce greater protection for children by passing strict regulations requiring the procedure to be performed only by the medically qualified. In more general terms, there is a need to encourage parents to think more about their children's right to bodily integrity, rather than treating them like mere family appendages. They should avoid making any arrangements for their young children to undergo procedures, however apparently trivial, which may damage their health. Instead, they should respect their children's individuality and leave them to decide for themselves when older how to treat their own bodies.

(D) Sterilising mentally impaired adolescents

(i) The dilemmas

The sterilisation of mentally impaired girls[276] was an issue which became controversial during the late 1980s, particularly following the House of Lords'

---

[273] M. Fox and M. Thomson (2005) p. 166.   [274] Ibid. at p. 170.   [275] H. Gilbert (2007) p. 291.
[276] But see *Re A (male sterilisation)* [2000] 1 FLR 549: a parent sought to have her adult mentally impaired son sterilised. Such applications may be more common than the dearth of case law suggests but this discussion assumes that the subject for sterilisation is female.

decision in *Re B (a minor) (wardship: sterilisation)*.[277] Today, few cases involving women or adolescents appear in the law reports. This may be because more effective methods of menstrual management and contraception are being used to deal with the problems which a decade ago would have led to radical surgery. An alternative explanation may be that most of the sterilisations now being performed are allegedly for 'therapeutic' purposes, thereby escaping judicial supervision. Alternatively, as discussed below, attitudes to disability are also changing, perhaps ushering in a new willingness on the part of medical practitioners to consider far more critically parents' requests to have their daughters sterilised.

The motives underlying such requests demand serious consideration. A common concern is that severely mentally impaired girls are unable to understand or cope with menstruation.[278] Even daughters in residential care units return home from time to time and their care may be difficult once they start menstruating and becoming sexually aware. Furthermore, parents and other carers cannot supervise mentally impaired teenagers every minute of the day and, in any case, to do so would inhibit their privacy intolerably. These adolescents are as entitled as other maturing children to lead as full and as unrestricted a life as possible and to enjoy sexual relationships. Parents often consider, probably justifiably, that a mentally impaired adolescent would be incapable of coping with pregnancy, birth and motherhood. Sterilised girls, by reason of their inability to become pregnant, can be allowed more freedom in mixed units and consequently their lives may become more fulfilled. Gaining a relative degree of social freedom and well-being may involve a compromise with their other rights, such as the right to bodily integrity, but maturity always involves balancing conflicting objectives.

The arguments against such procedures are, however, more compelling. Arrangements made by parents to alter radically their daughters' bodies reflect a disturbing assumption that they have complete autonomy over their family.[279] The distasteful eugenic reasons used to justify compulsory sterilisation programmes in various countries in the world at different times in history,[280] perhaps cloud an objective approach to this topic. Nevertheless, it must be a remedy of last resort to submit a girl to a major invasion of her bodily integrity, which may be irreversible, and which may have a significant psychological impact on an already fragile personality. An inability to become pregnant will safeguard the girl neither from sexual exploitation nor sexually transmitted

---

[277] [1988] AC 199.   [278] D. Aitkenhead (2007).
[279] E.g. the American parents of severely disabled 9-year-old 'Ashley' have ensured that she remains child sized by hormone doses to limit her growth and surgery to remove her breast buds, appendix and uterus; keeping her weight down facilitates her day-to-day care.
[280] It is estimated that 70,000 mentally 'defective' people were compulsorily sterilised in the USA between the decision in *Buck v. Bell* 274 US 200, 47 S Ct 584 (1927) upholding its legality, and the late 1970s, when the practice ended.

diseases, from which she has a right to be protected.[281] The need to protect her from pregnancy might be avoided with more sensitive care, combined with a reliable form of contraception.

(ii) The human rights context

Society's attitudes to disability are gradually changing, with a growing consensus in favour of the 'social model of disability'[282] – the view that disability is a socially conditioned state[283] and that those with impairments are disabled by the barriers society puts in their way.[284] Disability rights campaigners are becoming more vigilant in detecting cases which require their involvement. For example, in late 2007, they opposed a well-publicised attempt by a mother to have a hysterectomy carried out on her 15-year-old severely disabled daughter.[285] Whilst some parents clearly hope that surgery can prevent their daughters going through the normal stages of puberty,[286] the demands of international human rights law may force medical practitioners to consider carefully the human rights of mentally impaired people.

It is notable that the UN Convention on the Rights of Persons with Disabilities[287] specifically requires states to take measures to eliminate discrimination against disabled people 'in all matters relating to marriage, family, parenthood and relationships' so as to ensure, inter alia, that: 'Persons with disabilities, including children, retain their fertility on an equal basis with others.'[288] Whilst this UN document is of considerable persuasive importance, the HRA 1998 is of greater immediate relevance to those arranging sterilisations for mentally impaired women and girls. An infringement of a girl's right to bodily integrity, as protected by Article 8 of the ECHR might be justified under Article 8(2), by reference to her other interests, including her ability to form relationships with members of the opposite sex. Thus in *Re A (male sterilisation)*[289] the Court of Appeal sympathised with the argument that a mentally impaired man's best interests might require him to be sterilised, not for any medical reasons, but to prevent his freedom of movement being restricted and his quality of life diminished.[290]

---

[281] M. Brazier (2003) pp. 275–6. See also *Re LC (medical treatment: sterilisation)* [1997] 2 FLR 258, per Thorpe LJ, at 261–2, discussed below.

[282] Discussed further in Chapter 12.   [283] M. Brazier (2006) para. 7.6.

[284] Personal communication with Scope.

[285] D. Aitkenhead (2007). In January 2008, the NHS Trust involved refused to allow the hysterectomy to go ahead.

[286] E.g. 10 October 2007, BBC news report: a Liverpool woman asked Alder Hey Children's hospital to consider the surgical options for preventing her 9-year-old daughter, with severe mental and physical disabilities, from going through puberty.

[287] Opened for signature in March 2007 and entered into force April 2008; signed by the UK in March 2007, but not yet ratified.

[288] Art. 23(1)(c).   [289] [2000] 1 FLR 549.

[290] Ibid., per Dame Elizabeth Butler-Sloss P, at 557.

An Article 3 challenge under the ECHR, would, however, be far more difficult to answer. It is hard to conceive of a form of treatment which is more inhuman and degrading than removing the reproductive organs of a mentally impaired woman or girl without her consent. Strasbourg jurisprudence clearly indicates that forcing a mental patient to undergo treatment could infringe his or her rights under Article 3, unless the measure 'is a therapeutic necessity' according to the 'psychiatric principles generally accepted at the time'.[291] It is important to note, at this point, that already under current law, the distinction between a therapeutic and non-therapeutic sterilisation is important – quite simply because the former requires no judicial authorisation and the latter does.[292] But now, as we see, there is a further reason for making this distinction. As Hale LJ emphasises, 'forcible measures inflicted upon an incapacitated patient which are *not* a medical necessity may indeed be inhuman or degrading'.[293] So a court might find it difficult to argue that a non-consensual non-therapeutic sterilisation accords with the Article 3 rights of an adolescent. Similarly, it is arguable that a parent has no right to authorise a sterilisation under Article 8 of the ECHR, even one for therapeutic purposes, because it is a decision outside the 'zone of parental control', for reasons of its disproportionate invasiveness.[294] Whilst there is no current case law supporting such arguments, disability rights campaigners might well consider appealing to these provisions, if and when they become aware of suitable test cases.[295]

(iii) Parents, sterilisations and the common law

Parents may not always fully appreciate their daughters' rights to bodily integrity and human dignity. Furthermore, their emotional involvement sometimes prevents them acknowledging their daughters' capacity for intellectual growth. In practice, there is little likelihood of a mentally impaired girl who is a candidate for sterilisation ever becoming *Gillick* competent below the age of 16. So, legally, her parents are the people to whom the doctors will turn for consent if they consider a sterilisation to be appropriate. Once a girl reaches the age of 16, she is presumed to be legally competent to consent on her own behalf to surgery,[296] but such a presumption would not be difficult to rebut in a case involving a severely mentally impaired teenager. Since her lack of capacity is probably attributable to an impairment of or a disturbance in the functioning of her mind or brain, she would almost certainly be deemed incompetent by the

---

[291] *Herczegfalvy v. Austria* (1992) 15 EHRR 437, paras. 82–6.   [292] Discussed below.

[293] *R (on the application of Wilkinson) v. Broadmoor Hospital* [2001] EWCA Civ 1545, [2002] 1 WLR 419, at [79], emphasis added.

[294] Discussed above.

[295] Furthermore, all children who are the subject of applications to obtain judicial authority for a sterilisation will be separately represented by Cafcass who might themselves present such arguments on their behalf.

[296] FLRA 1969, s. 8(1).

Mental Capacity Act (MCA) 2005.[297] According to this legislation, the medical team must still gain authority to treat 16- and 17-year-old patients from their parents,[298] but parents can only consent to the treatment if it is deemed to be in the patient's best interests, as determined by the 2005 Act[299] and its accompanying Code of Practice.[300] Thus, whether or not the sterilisation can be described as therapeutic or non-therapeutic,[301] there is now an extra level of regulation governing this older category of teenager.

The unsatisfactory absence of any legal regulation of this area of medical practice was only gradually addressed and then on an ad hoc basis. *Re D (a minor) (wardship: sterilisation)*[302] showed that, in the late 1970s, even very young children were being sterilised for non-therapeutic purposes. Other young girls were presumably undergoing similar surgery without intervention, on the assumption that parents had the right to consent on their behalf. Through an essentially informal process, matters changed when it was established that a judicial declaration of lawfulness must be obtained before sterilisations can be carried out on all patients, irrespective of age.[303] But further refinement was to come. Despite the House of Lords' view in *Re B (a minor) (wardship: sterilisation)*[304] that the distinction between therapeutic and non-therapeutic procedures was irrelevant, case law established that judicial authority is unnecessary for a *therapeutic* sterilisation, as long as it is medically indicated and the only practicable means of treating the condition.[305] So parents can still arrange for their daughters to be sterilised without court supervision, but medical advisers must be prepared to define the process as a therapeutic one, since for this narrow procedural purpose the distinction remains an important one.

Lack of court supervision over therapeutic sterilisations might matter less if there was more unanimity over how to draw the line between therapeutic and non-therapeutic procedures. A sterilisation operation which constitutes medically indicated treatment for a diseased organ is undoubtedly therapeutic and

---

[297] MCA 2005, s. 2(1); discussed in Chapter 5.

[298] Unless there is a disagreement over this, in which case a decision may be sought from the Court of Protection.

[299] MCA 2005, s. 4.   [300] DCA (2007) chs. 4 and 12.   [301] Discussed below.

[302] [1976] 1 All ER 326: a mother had arranged for her 12-year-old mentally impaired daughter to undergo a sterilisation; this was stopped by an application brought under the wardship jurisdiction.

[303] *Re F (mental patient: sterilisation)* [1990] 2 AC 1, per House of Lords: judicial authority is necessary for sterilisations; *Practice Note (Official Solicitor: declaratory proceedings: medical and welfare decisions for adults who lack capacity)* and Appendix 1: Sterilisation Cases [2001] 2 FLR 158.

[304] [1988] AC 199. Discussed below.

[305] *Re GF (medical treatment)* [1992] 1 FLR 293, per Sir Stephen Brown P, at 294: an application for leave to carry out a sterilisation is unnecessary providing two medical practitioners are satisfied that it is necessary for therapeutic purposes, it is in the patient's best interests and that there is no practicable, less intrusive means of treatment; *Re E (a minor) (medical treatment)* [1991] 2 FLR 585: no judicial authority required for the performance of a therapeutic hysterectomy on a 17-year-old mentally impaired girl who suffered from serious menorrhagia.

so requires no court authorisation. Similarly, sterilisations for contraceptive purposes are clearly non-therapeutic and do require judicial sanction. Nevertheless, some operations do not fall clearly into either category and lawyers are forced to rely on the advice of the medical profession to inform them of the correct classification. The need for 'menstrual management' can be easily invoked with a view to avoiding the judicial supervision necessary for sterilisation operations carried out for contraceptive purposes.[306] The judiciary have urged that any case 'lying near the boundary' should be referred to court.[307] Nevertheless, the introduction of a formal requirement requiring judicial authority for *all* sterilisations on minors, not merely those defined as 'non-therapeutic' would protect the rights of mentally impaired girls far more effectively.

(iv) Sterilisations, best interests and the courts

As discussed above, authorisation for non-therapeutic sterilisations became the preserve of the courts, rather than being left to parents and doctors, with decisions reached by reference to the best interests criterion. As the controversial decision of the House of Lords in *Re B (a minor) (wardship: sterilisation)*[308] demonstrates, the best interests test cannot always be relied upon to protect the rights of the adolescents involved. Their Lordships relied on the medical evidence favouring the sterilisation of Jeanette, a severely mentally impaired 17-year-old, to justify their view that it was in her best interests to authorise the procedure.[309] The only discussion of her rights was confined to 'a woman's right to reproduce', the authenticity of which is somewhat dubious. As Grubb and Pearl explain, international human rights documents protect individuals against attempts to prevent children being born for eugenic or population control reasons; they do not provide a right to reproduce.[310]

Criticisms of the decision in *Re B* abound. As critics pointed out, the indeterminate nature of the best interests test allowed the House of Lords to produce a judgment with very little attention to legal analysis.[311] Their Lordships controversially rejected La Forest J's reasoned view, in *Re Eve*,[312] that it is crucial to distinguish between 'therapeutic' and 'non-therapeutic' procedures. As discussed above, this aspect of the judgment in *Re B* has been cast aside, with medical and legal practice now hanging on this distinction. Subsequent advice issued by the Official Solicitor also stresses that a sterilisation

---

[306] Law Commission (1995) para. 6.4.

[307] *Re S (sterilisation: patient's best interests)* [2000] 2 FLR 389, per Thorpe LJ, at 405.

[308] [1988] AC 199.

[309] Jeanette, aged 17, had the intellectual ability of a child aged between 5 and 6, was epileptic and subject to mood changes and, at times, became violent and aggressive.

[310] A. Grubb and D. Pearl (1987).

[311] Inter alia: I. Kennedy (1992) ch. 20; M. Freeman (1988); J. Montgomery (1989); M. Brazier (2003) pp. 275–7 and 356–7. But see J. Mason and G. Laurie (2006) pp. 133–5, who consider that *Re B (a minor) (wardship: sterilisation)* was relatively unobjectionable on *medical* grounds.

[312] (1986) 31 DLR (4th) 1.

procedure should genuinely be a remedy of last resort.[313] Nevertheless, *Re B* fatally influenced judicial decision-making, with little attention being paid to assessing the rights actually at stake or to analysing the best interests of an adolescent in circumstances of this kind.[314] Bearing out Kennedy's criticisms, the judiciary continued to be impressed by the opinions of medical experts and ready to justify decisions to authorise sterilisations by bare assertions referring to welfare.[315] Loose reasoning is not improved upon by dire predictions of the 'disastrous' or 'catastrophic' results of a future pregnancy.[316]

Current case law suggests that judicial authority is now sought for non-therapeutic sterilisations only very occasionally and then only in relation to young adult women.[317] Perhaps adolescents are being allowed to reach formal majority before such procedures are considered. Alternatively, adolescent sterilisations are perhaps being performed under the guise of therapeutic menstrual management, thereby escaping judicial supervision. Regarding the adult cases, a rapid development of extremely reliable methods of contraception appears to be producing a more cautious response from medical experts asked to comment on parental requests for the sterilisation of their mentally impaired offspring.[318] The courts are also becoming more critical of requests to authorise the sterilisation of mentally impaired adults, both female and male.[319] The words of Thorpe J are as relevant to cases involving adolescents as they were to the young woman involved:

> It can be argued … that if there is a risk of pregnancy that cannot be eliminated by supervision, then it had better be eliminated by surgery. The contrary argument is that what would be immediately and profoundly damaging to L would be to experience again the trauma of indecent assault or worse. That is the evil against which she must be protected. Sterilisation would do nothing to protect her from that. Indeed, it might reduce the protection, either in the sense that at some level the carers would become less careful, or alternatively because the potential abuser

---

[313] *Practice Note (Official Solicitor: declaratory proceedings: medical and welfare decisions for adults who lack capacity)*, esp. *Appendix 1: Sterilisation Cases* [2001] 2 FLR 158: provides guidance on the issues practitioners should normally satisfy before seeking authorisation for such procedures.

[314] E.g. *Re M (a minor) (wardship: sterilisation)* [1988] 2 FLR 497 (general reference to the girl's need for freedom to move around in the community); *Re P (a minor) (wardship: sterilisation)* [1989] 1 FLR 182 (reference to the human right to reproduce).

[315] E.g. *Re P (a minor) (wardship: sterilisation)* [1989] 1 FLR 182.

[316] E.g. *Re HG (specific issue order: sterilisation)* [1993] 1 FLR 587, per Peter Singer QC, at 591; *Re P (a minor) (wardship: sterilisation)* [1989] 1 FLR 182, per Eastham J, at 194. See also *Re Z (medical treatment: hysterectomy)* [2000] 1 FLR 523, per Bennett J, at 534: regarding the proposed sterilisation of a 19-year-old girl.

[317] These women will undoubtedly come within the ambit of the MCA 2005, as will adolescents over the age of 16 deemed incapable of consenting to surgery on their own behalf.

[318] E.g. *Re Z (medical treatment: hysterectomy)* [2000] 1 FLR 523: the medical experts disagreed over whether contraception or sterilisation was appropriate; *Re S (sterilisation: patient's best interests)* [2000] 2 FLR 389: appeal allowed against a declaration authorising a sterilisation because the medical experts had favoured a contraceptive coil over a hysterectomy.

[319] *Re LC (medical treatment: sterilisation)* [1997] 2 FLR 258; *Re S (sterilisation: patient's best interests)* [2000] 2 FLR 389; *Re A (male sterilisation)* [2000] 1 FLR 549.

would measure the consequences of sexual invasion as reduced … I simply cannot in conscience conclude that it would be in her best interests to subject her to that as long as she is receiving the very specialist dedicated care that she is.[320]

This critical approach more obviously satisfies the courts' duty to protect the human rights of mentally impaired adolescents. La Forest J's words remain immensely persuasive:

> The grave intrusion on a person's rights and the certain physical damage that ensues from non-therapeutic sterilization without consent, when compared with the highly questionable advantages that can result from it, have persuaded me that it can never safely be determined that such a procedure is for the benefit of that person.[321]

It is also essential that those caring for mentally impaired adolescents resist sterilisation procedures being arranged under the guise of a form of therapeutic menstrual management. Indeed, as suggested above, it is arguable that judicial authorisation should be made a prerequisite of all sterilisation procedures.

(5) Conclusion

Although doctors have the expertise and training to promote children's health care, they are not necessarily in the best position to advise how children's rights should be protected, such as their right to bodily integrity and to be consulted and treated with respect. But then, nor are children's parents well equipped to protect the rights of their desperately ill children; not surprisingly, they may find it impossible to be objective over the decisions to be made. These problems are exacerbated when tiny babies are the focus of decision-making, given their inability to speak on their own behalf. Indeed, it is in the context of the medical care of young children that we find parents and doctors alike assuming that parents are entitled to reach decisions without judicial supervision, in a way that would be unthinkable in relation to older children and adults. But even when the courts are consulted, they too may lose sight of their duty to protect the child's own rights from being infringed by decisions which appear to be in a child's best interests but which may be more to do with those of his or her carers. Children's rights should not be lost somewhere in the middle, between parental, medical and judicial paternalism.

BIBLIOGRAPHY

NB many of these publications can be obtained on the relevant organisation's website.

Acheson, D. (Chair) (1998) *Report of the Independent Inquiry into Inequalities in Health*, The Stationery Office (TSO).

Aitkenhead, D. (2007) 'What Drove Alison Thorpe to Seek a Hysterectomy for her 15-year-old?' *The Guardian*, 13 October 2007.

---

[320] *Re LC (medical treatment: sterilisation)* [1997] 2 FLR 258 at 261–2.
[321] *Re Eve* (1986) 31 DLR (4th) 1 at 33.

Alderson, P. (1993) *Children's Consent to Surgery*, Oxford University Press.

Alderson, P. and Montgomery, J. (1996) *Health Care Decisions: Making Decisions with Children*, IPPR.

Bainham, A. (1997) 'Do Babies Have Rights?' *Cambridge Law Journal* 48.

Brazier, M. (2003) *Medicine, Patients and the Law*, Penguin Books.

(2005) 'An Intractable Dispute: When Parents and Professionals Disagree' 13 *Medical Law Review* 412.

Brazier, M. (Chair) (2006) *Critical Care Decisions in Fetal and Neonatal Medicine: Ethical Issues*, Nuffield Council on Bioethics.

Bridge, C. (2002), 'Religion, Culture and the Body of the Child' in Bainham, A., Day Sclater, S. and Richards, M. (eds.) *Body Lore and Laws*, Hart Publishing.

Bridgeman, J. (2005) 'Caring for Children with Severe Disabilities: Boundaries and Relational Rights' 13 *International Journal of Children's Rights* 99.

(2007) *Parental Responsibility, Young Children and Healthcare Law*, Cambridge University Press.

British Medical Association (BMA) (2001) *Consent, Rights and Choices in Health Care for Children and Young People*, BMJ Books.

British Medical Association (BMA) (2004) 'The Law and Ethics of Male Circumcision: Guidance for Doctors' 30 *Journal of Medical Ethics* 259.

Brownsword, R. (2005) 'Happy Families, Consenting Couples, and Children with Dignity: Sex Selection and Saviour Siblings' 17 *Child and Family Law Quarterly* 435.

Committee on the Rights of the Child (2002) *Concluding Observations of the Committee on the Rights of the Child: United Kingdom of Great Britain and Northern Ireland* CRC/C/15/Add 188, Centre for Human Rights, Geneva.

Committee on the Rights of the Child (2008) *Concluding Observations of the Committee on the Rights of the Child: United Kingdom of Great Britain and Northern Ireland* CRC/C/GBR/CO/4, Centre for Human Rights, Geneva.

Day, E. (2004) 'Do Not Resuscitate – and Don't Bother Consulting the Family' *Sunday Telegraph*, 14 March 2004.

Delaney, L. (1995) 'Child Bone-Marrow Donors – Victims or Volunteers?' 25 *Family Law* 372.

Department for Constitutional Affairs (DCA) (2007) *Mental Capacity Act 2005: Code of Practice*, TSO.

Department for Education and Skills (DfES) (2004) *Every Child Matters: Next Steps*, DfES.

Department of Health (DH) (2001) *Seeking Consent: Working with Children*, Department of Health Publications.

Department of Health (DH) (2004) *National Service Framework for Children, Young People and Maternity Services*, Executive Summary, DH.

Department of Health (DH) (2007) *Tackling Health Inequalities: 2007 Status Report on the Programme for Action*, DH,

Department of Health (DH) (2008) *Code of Practice: Mental Health Act 1983*, The Stationery Office. Dingwall, R., Eekelaar, J. and Murray, T. (1995) *The Protection of Children*, Avebury.

Dworkin, G. (1982) 'Consent, Representation and Proxy Consent' in Gaylin, W. and Macklin, R. (eds.) *Who Speaks for the Child*, Plenum Press.

Eekelaar, J. (1986) 'The Emergence of Children's Rights' 6 *Oxford Journal of Legal Studies* 161.

Feenan, D. (1997) 'A Good Harvest? *Re Y (mental incapacity: bone marrow transplant)*' 9 *Child and Family Law Quarterly* 305.

Feldman, D. (2002) *Civil Liberties and Human Rights in England and Wales*, Oxford University Press.

Ford, N. (2005) 'Communication for Abandonment of Female Genital Cutting: An Approach Based on Human Rights Principles' 13 *International Journal of Children's Rights* 183.

Fortin, J. (1998) '*Re C (Medical Treatment)*: A Baby's Right to Die' 10 *Child and Family Law Quarterly* 411.

Fox, M. and McHale, J. (1997) 'In Whose Best Interests?' 60 *Modern Law Review* 700.

Fox, M. and Thomson, M. (2005) 'Short Changed? The Law and Ethics of Male Circumcision' 13 *International Journal of Children's Rights* 161.

Freeman, M. (1988) 'Sterilising the Mentally Handicapped' in Freeman, M. (ed.) *Medicine, Ethics and Law*, Stevens.

(2001) 'Whose Life is it Anyway?' 9 *Medical Law Review* 259.

General Medical Council (GMC) (2007) *0-18 Years: Guidance for all Doctors*, GMC.

Gilbert, H. (2007) 'Time to Reconsider the Lawfulness of Male Circumcision' *European Human Rights Law Review* 279.

Grubb, A. and Pearl, D. (1987) 'Sterilisation and the Courts' *Cambridge Law Journal* 439.

Gunn, M. and Smith, J. (1985) '*Arthur's* Case and the Right to Life of a Down's Syndrome Child' *Criminal Law Review* 705.

HM Treasury (2003) Cm 5860 *Every Child Matters*, TSO.

Healthcare Commission (2007) HC 97 *State of Healthcare 2007*, TSO.

Herring, J. (2006) *Medical Law and Ethics*, Oxford University Press.

Human Tissue Authority (HTA) (2006a) *Code of Practice – Donation of Organs, Tissue and Cells for Transplantation*, Code 2, Department of Health.

Human Tissue Authority (HTA) (2006b) *Code of Practice – Donation of Allogeneic Bone Marrow and Peripheral Blood Stem Cells for Transplantation*, Code 6, Department of Health.

Human Tissue Authority (HTA) (2008a) *Code of Practice for Consultation – Donation of Solid Organs for Transplantation*, Code 2, Department of Health.

Human Tissue Authority (HTA) (2008b) *Code of Practice for Consultation – Donation of Allogeneic Bone Marrow and Peripheral Blood Stem Cells for Transplantation, Code 6, Department of Health*.

Hutson, J. (2004) 'Circumcision: a Surgeon's Perspective' 30 *Journal of Medical Ethics* 238.

Huxtable, R. (2004) 'Re C (A Child) (Immunisation: Parental Rights) [2003] EWCA Civ 1148' 26 *Journal of Social Welfare and Family Law* 69.

Jackson, L. and Huxtable, R. (2005) 'The Doctor-Parent Relationship: as Fragile as Glass?' 27 *Journal of Social Welfare and Family Law* 369.

Kennedy, I. (1992) *Treat Me Right: Essays in Medical Law and Ethics*, Oxford University Press.

Law Commission (1995) *Mental Incapacity* Law Com No 231, HMSO.

LeBlanc, L. (1995) *The Convention on the Rights of the Child: United Nations Lawmaking on Human Rights*, University of Nebraska Press.

London Safeguarding Children Board (2007) *Safeguarding Children at Risk of Abuse Through Female Genital Mutilation*, www.londonscb.gov.uk

Maher, J. and Macfarlane, A. (2004) 'Trends in Live Births and Birthweight by Social Class, Marital Status and Mother's Age, 1976–2000' 23 *Health Statistics Quarterly* 34.

Marshall, K. (1997) *Children's Rights in the Balance: The Participation – Protection Debate*, TSO.

Mason, J. and Laurie, G. (2006) *Mason and McCall Smith's Law and Medical Ethics*, Oxford University Press.

Meltzer, H. and Gatward, R. (2000) *Mental Health of Children and Adolescents in Great Britain* Office for National Statistics, TSO.

Michalowski, S. (1997) 'Is it in the Best Interests of a Child to Have a Life-Saving Liver Transplantation?: Re T (Wardship: Medical Treatment)' 9 *Child and Family Law Quarterly* 179.

Montgomery, J. (1989) 'Rhetoric and Welfare' 9 *Oxford Journal of Legal Studies* 395.

Mumford, S. (1998) 'Bone Marrow Donation: the Law in Context' 10 *Child and Family Law Quarterly* 135.

Office of National Statistics (ONS) (2008) *Social Trends* No 38, Palgrave Macmillan.

Powell, R. (2007) 'Medical Treatment of Children Facing Inevitable Death' *Family Law* 155.

Read, J. and Clements, L. (2004) 'Demonstrably Awful: The Right to Life and the Selective Non-Treatment of Disabled Babies and Young Children' 31 *Journal of Law and Society* 482.

Rickwood, A. *et al.* 'Towards Evidence Based Circumcision of English Boys: Survey of Trends in Practice' (2000) 321 *British Medical Journal* 792.

Short, R. (2004) 'Male Circumcision: a Scientific Perspective' 30 *Journal of Medical Ethics* 241.

UNICEF Innocenti Research Centre (2005) *Changing a Harmful Social Convention: Female Genital Mutilation/Cutting*, UNICEF.

UNICEF Innocenti Research Centre (2007) *Child Poverty in Perspective: An Overview of Child Well-Being in Rich Countries*, Innocenti Report Card 7, UNICEF.

Wells, C. (1989) '"Otherwise Kill Me": Marginal Children and Ethics at the Edges of Existence' in Lee, R. and Morgan, D. (eds.) *Birthrights: Law and Ethics at the Beginnings of Life*, Routledge.

Chapter 11

Educational rights for children in minority groups

(1) Introduction

Religious and ethnic minority groups[1] contribute to the richness of a pluralistic society. One of the most important rights for such a group is to preserve its separate identity. It cannot do so unless it maintains its continuity by educating its children to understand and respect its own customs, religion and culture. They can then mature into adult members of the group, with a commitment to its future preservation. Nevertheless, when the educational rights of the children of minority groups are considered, a number of competing considerations become apparent. Indeed, a familiar dilemma arises, although in this context it is even more acute, how to find a suitable means of ensuring that parents' rights do not override those of their children.

Overarching this discussion is a more fundamental question regarding minority groups' relationships with mainstream society. An acceptable compromise must always be found between the views of extreme pluralists who maintain the absolute right of minority groups to preserve all the elements of their cultural traditions, and those of assimilationists who expect minorities to be absorbed into the culture of the mainstream community.[2] As Poulter comments, the compromise adopted in Britain has been to promote a 'cultural pluralism within limits'.[3] This reflects the pervading view that a democratic pluralist society should support the cultures and lifestyles of its ethnic groups, whilst expecting all groups to accept a set of shared values distinctive of that society as a whole. In the field of education, this approach was embraced by the Swann Report in the 1980s, which argued that the education system should reflect the fact that a policy of pluralism must be limited by the need for a cohesive society founded on shared fundamental values.[4] Over a decade later, when setting out the aims of citizenship education, the Crick report voiced similar views. Such education should establish:

---

[1] Finding an acceptable definition of the term 'minority group' is fraught with difficulty. P. Thornberry (1991) esp. pp. 164–72. For the purposes of this work, it is assumed that a 'minority group' is numerically smaller than the majority, whose members possess ethnic, religious or linguistic characteristics different from the rest and who show a sense of solidarity directed towards preserving their culture, traditions, religion or language.

[2] S. Poulter (1998) ch. 1.   [3] Ibid. at p. 21.   [4] M. Swann (1985) p. 6.

a sense of common citizenship, including a national identity that is secure enough to find a place for the plurality of nations, cultures, ethnic identities and religions long found in the United Kingdom.[5]

Harris criticises Crick both for failing to go deeply into the nature of our 'common values' and for failing to take proper account of cultural diversity.[6] Meanwhile, as Ajegbo observes, events like 11 September 2001 and the London bombings in July 2005, have 'contributed to the debate on community cohesion and shared values, particularly because the latter were perpetrated by British-born Muslims'.[7] But the contributions that are made to the cultural wealth of society by minority groups should not be underestimated simply because some terrorists are inspired by Muslim extremism. Indeed, as Thornberry points out, most communities with any history have a complexity derived from their own divisions:

> Ethnic, religious and linguistic differences within States may be of startling complexity: religions divide into sects and denominations, languages branch into dialects, cultures flourish in diverse forms. To describe diversity in terms of a tapestry, or a hundred banners, or a coat of many colours, does inadequate justice to its richness.[8]

Nevertheless, the concept of cultural pluralism within limits provides no clear answers over how to define the fundamental values around which limits should be set.

The dilemmas are particularly acute in the field of education. One might claim that it is in the best interests of a united community for all its children to be educated in multicultural and multi-faith state schools. Such a system would undoubtedly enable children to learn about and respect the beliefs of others and equip them better to take their place in the outside world, as they grow older. Nevertheless, by refusing to allow the establishment of separate schools, the government would interfere blatantly with the freedom of minority groups, as secured by the human rights instruments referred to below. The present government is in no danger on this score; rather, it is keen to encourage the creation of more faith schools.[9] But this policy is a controversial one, opposed by some on the basis that it tends to make minority communities more exclusive, thereby leading to community fragmentation.[10] Indeed, there are concerns that society is thereby becoming more, rather than less, divided by race and religion, and that we 'are sleepwalking our way to segregation'.[11] The governing body of a school whose intake is from a single religious background

---

[5] B. Crick (1998) para. 3.14.   [6] N. Harris (2007) pp. 369–70.
[7] K. Ajegbo (2007) p. 18.   [8] P. Thornberry (1991) p. 2.
[9] DCSF (2007a) p. 4. See also the Education Act 1996, s. 14(3A): local education authorities are obliged to exercise their functions with a view to '(a) securing diversity in the provision of schools, and (b) increasing opportunities for parental choice'.
[10] Debates on the Education Bill 2002 were dominated by anxieties about the government's policy to extend maintained faith schools. E.g. HL Debs, *Hansard*, 11 March 2002, col. 592.
[11] Trevor Phillips, Chair, Commission for Racial Equality, unpublished lecture delivered in Manchester, 22 September 2005. See also N. Johnson, director of policy and public sector at

may find it extremely difficult to fulfil their legal obligation to 'promote community cohesion',[12] even with the assistance of ambitious and vaguely worded guidance.[13] Similarly problematic is the encouragement to provide 'education for diversity', meaning teaching and learning 'that addresses issues of ethnicity, culture, language and religion and the multiple identities that children inhabit'.[14] Furthermore, given the government's failure to force maintained faith schools to broaden their pupil intake,[15] these schools may become less inclusive rather than more[16] and will not represent all the communities in their local area.[17]

There is no doubt that an extension in the numbers of faith schools highlights the obvious dilemmas created by their existence; it also provokes a number of questions. For example, should society acknowledge that all minority groups have an absolute right to educate their children as they wish, even if their schools adopt educational methods that the state considers to be inward looking or even 'anti-British'?[18] How should it respond to schools which provide education considered to be inadequate and stultifyingly narrow? If children receive an education which is too restricted to enable them to leave their community and compete for a place outside its confines, then they may justifiably accuse the state of failing in its duty to ensure that they have equality of opportunity in the education they receive. Attempts by the state to interfere with the education of minority children may, however, become difficult to justify if the community's educational methods are based on their religious and racial beliefs. Members of minority groups may see any attempt to interfere with their freedom to educate their children according to their own beliefs, not only in terms of a threat to their own convictions, but amounting to religious persecution, thereby infringing their fundamental human rights, as secured by international instruments.[19]

This chapter considers the interests of minority children and their parents from three educational perspectives. First, it considers the concept of separate education from a rights perspective, looking at the international human rights

---

Commission for Racial Equality, unpublished paper, 26 April 2007, 'research suggests that schools across Britain are becoming increasingly segregated in terms of race and religion'.

[12] Education Act 2002, s. 21(5)(b). See also the Education Act 2005, s. 5, obliging school inspectors to include in their report on schools a section dedicated to the school's 'contribution to community cohesion'.

[13] DCSF (2007b).   [14] K. Ajegbo (2007) p. 15.

[15] *The Independent*, 3 November 2006: Education Secretary, Alan Johnson dropped his proposed amendment to the Education and Inspections Bill obliging all maintained faith schools to select 25% of their intake from pupils of other or non-faith backgrounds. See R. Gold (2007) pp. 11–12.

[16] N. Harris (2008).

[17] E.g. *R (E) v. Governing Body of JFS; R (E) v. Office of the Schools Adjudicator* [2008] EWHC 1535 (Admin), [2008] ELR 445, per Munby J: it is perfectly legitimate for a faith-based school to give preference in its admissions scheme to children who actively practise a particular faith or are born or raised in such a faith, even it means, as in this case, that only strictly Orthodox Jewish applicants (as so defined by the Office of the Chief Rabbi of the United Hebrew Congregation of the Commonwealth) are admitted and non-Orthodox Jewish applicants are not.

[18] K. Ajegbo (2007) pp. 90–3: the concept of 'Britishness'.   [19] Discussed below.

context and, in particular, the handling of parents' and children's rights. The way the law deals with pupils' appeals to their own religious rights is discussed in the context of current school uniform policies. Second, the chapter questions the extent to which the state should mediate between the interests of parents and children, once ethnic or religious minority groups are given the freedom to establish independent faith schools, perhaps through supervising their educational methods. Third, some minority parents may be content to keep their children within the state educational system. It is then important to consider the degree to which they should be permitted to influence the content of their children's education, particularly in those areas which may most offend their own principles, notably collective worship and religious education.

(2) Separate education – a rights perspective

(A) The international human rights context

Members of minorities obviously benefit from the well-known civil and political guarantees provided by the leading human rights instruments, such as freedom of thought, conscience and religion,[20] without discrimination.[21] Nevertheless, securing freedom from religious and racial persecution is not enough; they also need the right to bring up and inculcate their children in their own faith and traditions. The dilemma is that extreme groups might claim the right to educate their children in a manner considered by the majority to be reactionary and unenlightened. States wishing to interfere with such a regime do not derive much support from the international human rights documents, since most tend to identify children's interests with those of their parents. They were drafted at a time when religious and racial persecution before and during the Second World War was still recent history. They recognise the rights of minorities to enjoy their own culture, religion and language,[22] 'not only for the purpose of safeguarding the interests of the minorities themselves but to preserve a cultural diversity of value to the whole community'.[23] More to the point in this context, these treaties emphasise the need to avoid educational institutions being used by states to indoctrinate children in ways that undermine their allegiance to their families and their own culture and religion. Those

[20] Art. 9 ECHR employs the formula used in Art. 18 of the Universal Declaration of Human Rights (adopted in 1948 by the General Assembly of the United Nations), also used by Art. 18(1) of the International Covenant on Civil and Political Rights (ICCPR).

[21] E.g. Art. 14 ECHR ensures that all rights are enjoyed without discrimination on grounds of 'sex, race, colour, language, religion, political or other opinion, national or social origin, association with a national minority, property, birth or other status'.

[22] Notably ICCPR, Art. 27. See also the Council of Europe's Framework Convention for the Protection of National Minorities (adopted 1995 and ratified by the UK in 1998) (hereafter FCPNM esp. Arts. 4–11; discussed by E. Craig (2003) pp. 288–90 and A. Scolnicov (2007) pp. 260–3.

[23] *Chapman v. United Kingdom* (2001) 10 BHRC 48, per the European Court of Human Rights (ECtHR), at para. 93.

that contain provisions dealing specifically with children's right to education do so in a particularly adult-focused way, by protecting parents' freedom to have their children educated according to their own beliefs. For example, Article 2 of the First Protocol (hereafter A2P1) of the European Convention for the Protection of Human Rights and Fundamental Freedoms (ECHR) notably provides: 'No person shall be denied the right to education' and proceeds to require states to 'respect the right of parents to ensure such education and teaching in conformity with their own religious and philosophical convictions'.[24]

When interpreting A2P1 of the ECHR, the ECtHR obviously appreciates the need to maintain a balance between protecting pluralism and upholding the state's right to run an efficient education system reflecting society's shared values. Thus in *Kjeldsen, Busk and Pedersen v. Denmark*[25] it upheld the Danish state's right to set the curriculum and to impart information or knowledge of 'a directly or indirectly religious or philosophical kind'. This, the Court considered, was acceptable, as long as the information was conveyed in an 'objective, critical and pluralistic manner', without attempting to indoctrinate pupils in a way which does not respect their parents' religious convictions.[26] It decided that the inclusion of sex education in all primary schools' curriculum did not infringe Danish parents' rights under A2P1 of the ECHR, given the scientific and factual manner in which it was taught,[27] and given that they could dissociate their children from sex education by sending them to private schools or educating them at home.[28]

Similarly, the ECtHR indicated in the *Belgian Linguistics Case (No. 2)*[29] that A2P1 of the ECHR has clear limits when it comes to the provision of educational resources. Whilst it guarantees a right to education, including education in a national language, its scope is relatively narrow. Although in conjunction with Article 14, the protocol clearly protects minority children from being *excluded* from mainstream publicly funded state schools (by direct or indirect means[30]), it does not guarantee parents the right to obtain an education which they consider best meets their children's needs, using, for example, the language of their choice. Indeed, although international human rights law secures the

---

[24] See also Art. 5(2) of the Declaration on the Elimination of All Forms of Intolerance and of Discrimination Based on Religion or Belief (adopted by the General Assembly of the United Nations in 1981) and Art. 18(4) of the ICCPR.

[25] (1976) 1 EHRR 711. See also *Angelini v. Sweden* (1988) 10 EHRR 123 and *Folgerø and ors v. Norway* [2007] ELR 557.

[26] Ibid. at paras. 53–4.   [27] Ibid. at para. 54.   [28] Ibid. See N. Harris (2007) p. 73.

[29] (1968) 1 EHRR 252: French-speaking parents succeeded in their claim that, by excluding their children from certain schools in six communes, Belgium was discriminating against them. But they failed in their claim that by refusing to establish French-speaking schools for their children near their own homes, Belgium was infringing their rights under A2P1 of the ECHR.

[30] E.g. *DH and ors v. Czech Republic* (Application No 57325/00), [2008] ELR 17, per the Grand Chamber of the ECtHR: the system whereby disproportionately high numbers of Roma children were tested and assigned to special schools for the mentally disabled where they received a less favourable form of education amounted to a breach of their rights under Art 14 and A2P1 of the ECHR.

right of minority parents to establish their own separate schools,[31] it does not require states to finance such establishments.[32] On the other hand, when considering parents' views over what school their child should attend, the state should not ignore their religious background.[33]

(B) Parents' rights and children's rights

It is notable that the international human rights treaties discussed above promote freedom of thought and religion and the right to an education free from state indoctrination from an almost entirely adult perspective. Even the Convention on the Rights of the Child (CRC) contains compromises regarding a child's educational rights which could endanger a child's ability to break away from his or her parents' narrow beliefs through receiving a liberal education. Education could have an extremely important part to play in ensuring that children develop their own views, free of any indoctrination from their parents or indeed, from the group into which they were born. It could also help them form an ability to express their views, as promoted by Article 12. Nevertheless, children may never develop these capacities nor those required to exercise any freedom of thought, conscience or religion, as secured by Article 14(1),[34] unless the state intervenes to prevent their parents educating them in such a way that undermines their capacity for independent thought. But whilst Article 29(1)(a) stresses the need for education to develop the child's personality, talents and

---

[31] International Covenant on Economic, Social and Cultural Rights (ICESCR), Art. 13(3): parents' right to choose 'for their children schools, other than those established by the public authorities, which conform to such minimum educational standards as may be laid down or approved by the State and to ensure the religious and moral education of their children in conformity with their own convictions'. See also the UN Convention against Discrimination in Education 1962, Art. 5 (1)(b): parents' right to ensure that their children are educated in accordance with their convictions; Art. 5(1)(c): national minorities' right to have their own schools and to teach their own language.

[32] E.g. FCPNM, Art. 13(2): minorities' right to set up their own educational establishments, but its exercise 'shall not entail any financial obligation for the Parties'. NB the UK's reservation on A2P1 of the ECHR (repeating the formula in the Education Act 1944, s. 76), stating that it only accepts its terms 'so far as it is compatible with the provision of efficient instruction and training, and the avoidance of unreasonable public expenditure'. See also *R (R and ors) v. Leeds City Council Education Leeds* [2005] EWHC 2495 (Admin), [2006] ELR 25, per Wilkie J, at [45]: A2P1 of the ECHR merely obliges the state to respect parents' right to access state funded educational institutions of a religious character. So the LEA's refusal to provide Jewish children with free school transport to attend an orthodox Jewish school 45 miles away did not infringe their parents' rights under A2P1 of the ECHR; nor were Arts. 8, 9 and 14 relevant.

[33] Inter alia: *A v. Special Educational Needs and Disability Tribunal and London Borough of Barnet* [2003] EWHC 3368 (Admin), [2004] ELR 293: the tribunal's decision was flawed because it had not obviously considered how a non-Jewish school could adequately meet the needs of an orthodox Jewish child with special educational needs; *R (on the application of K) v. London Borough of Newham* [2002] EWHC 405 (Admin), [2002] ELR 390, per Collins J, at 398–9: A2P1 of the ECHR requires LEAs to identify and consider any religious convictions underlying parents' preference for a school place; here a devout Muslim father's choice of a single-sex school for his daughter was underpinned by his strong religious opposition to mixed schools.

[34] The tensions underlying children's right to religion under the CRC are discussed in Chapter 2.

abilities to their fullest potential, Article 29(1)(c) asserts that the child's education should develop a respect for the child's parents and his or her own cultural identity, language and values. Article 30 also reinforces the community rights of minority groups, as groups, rather than of their child members, as individuals. It requires states to respect the right of any child member of an ethnic, religious or linguistic minority 'in community with other members of his or her group, to enjoy his or her own culture, to profess and practise his or her own religion, or to use his or her own language'. Arguably these provisions underline parents' rights in education, rather than children's rights.

Nor have the Strasbourg institutions set the domestic courts a particularly good example when interpreting the provisions in the ECHR relevant to children's right to education. For example, in *Valsamis v. Greece*[35] the ECtHR decided that neither the parents' religious convictions under Article 9 nor their pacifist views under A2P1 of the ECHR had been infringed when their daughter was disciplined for refusing to participate in a school parade. Having rejected the arguments focusing on the parents' religious rights under Article 9, the Court thought it unnecessary to consider their daughter's own perspectives.[36] Such an approach is probably inevitable, given the wording of A2P1 of the ECHR which specifically links a child's right to education with parents' right to ensure that that education 'is in conformity with their own religious and philosophical convictions'. Thus in *Kjeldsen, Busk and Pedersen v. Denmark*, the ECtHR stressed:

> It is in the discharge of a natural duty towards their children – parents being primarily responsible for the 'education and teaching' of their children – that parents may require the State to respect their religious and philosophical convictions. Their right thus corresponds to a responsibility closely linked to the enjoyment and the exercise of the right to education.[37]

In other words, it is perfectly proper to assume that a child's interests are identical to those of his or her parents.

This approach overlooks the fact that when upholding parents' claims to have their own religious convictions respected, the state quite possibly infringes the child's own rights. This was seen only too clearly during the litigation in *R (on the application of Williamson and others) v. Secretary of State for Education and Employment and others*.[38] Admittedly, the House of Lords rejected the claim of a group of fundamentalist Christians that their rights under both Article 9 and A2P1 of the ECHR had been infringed by the law prohibiting corporal punishment in the school to which they sent their children. Nevertheless, with the exception of a passing reference by Baroness Hale of Richmond,[39] the children's own right to an education in a non-violent atmosphere was not discussed. Indeed, the case law considered above shows parents

---

[35] (1996) 24 EHRR 294.   [36] U. Kilkelly (1999) pp. 73–5 and 134–5.
[37] (1976) 1 EHRR 711 at para. 52.   [38] [2005] UKHL 15, [2005] 2 All ER 1; discussed in Chapter 9.
[39] Ibid. at [85].

exploiting their own position as rights-holders under the ECHR in an attempt to influence their children's education.

In some ways, domestic discrimination law could subtly reinforce parents' control over their children. For example, a parent may now justifiably argue, on their child's behalf, that by holding an after-school club at a time which clashes with the pupil's worship at a mosque or synagogue, a non-faith mainstream school is indirectly and unlawfully discriminating against the child on religious grounds.[40] If, due to the success of the parent's challenge, the after-school club is rescheduled, the child may thereby lose his or her much needed excuse for *not* attending the form of worship in question. As discussed below, the courts may be forced to consider a pupil's own rights under the ECHR when confronting challenges based on inflexible school uniform rules.

(C) School uniforms and pupils' rights

The government in this country considers school uniform to be an important way of 'contributing to the ethos of a school and setting an appropriate tone' and 'strongly encourages schools to have a uniform as it can instil pride ... ensure pupils of all races and backgrounds feel welcome; protect children from social pressures to dress in a particular way; and nurture cohesion and promote good relations between different groups of pupils'.[41] But despite the comparative liberality of school uniform policies adopted by most schools in this country,[42] some pupils have litigated to gain the right to wear more extreme forms of dress than those allowed. At first sight, such challenges are compelling. As noted above, schools are expected to provide an 'education for diversity' and to teach their pupils to tolerate, indeed to respect difference.[43] Schools should surely welcome pupils developing opinions of their own, more particularly their deciding for themselves how far to take their beliefs. In *R (on the application of Begum) v. Head Teacher and Governors of Denbigh High School* (hereafter *Begum*),[44] Baroness Hale of Richmond was not surprised that having attended her secondary school for two years wearing the shalwar kameez without complaint, Shabina Begum, at the age of nearly 14, decided that this form of dress was not acceptable for Muslim women. The fact that Shabina's parents had apparently accepted the school's uniform policy when they enrolled her at Denbigh High School was neither here nor there; 'it is not at all surprising to find adolescents making different moral judgments from those of their parents. It is part of growing up'.[45]

---

[40] Equality Act 2006, ss. 45 and 49. NB s. 50: maintained faith schools are excluded from these provisions.

[41] DCSF (2007c) para. 1.

[42] D. McGoldrick (2006) pp. 176–7: British schools have allowed Muslim girls to wear the Islamic headscarf for many years and, more recently, the shalwar kameez.

[43] D. McGoldrick (2006) pp. 278–82.   [44] [2006] UKHL 15, [2007] AC 100.   [45] Ibid. at [93].

Despite this, Baroness Hale, with her colleagues in the House of Lords, rejected Shabina's claim that her rights under Article 9 and those under A2P1 of the ECHR entitled her to attend school dressed in a jilbab. In the view of the majority,[46] her religious rights under Article 9 had not been interfered with because she could have attended another school which allowed pupils to wear a jilbab. In words later echoed by the official guidance on uniform codes,[47] Lord Hoffmann stressed, 'Article 9 does not require that one should be allowed to manifest one's religion at any time and place of one's own choosing'.[48] The minority[49] disagreed; in their view, the school's refusal to allow Shabina to attend school in a jilbab had interfered with her Article 9 rights. Nevertheless, all agreed that whether or not there had been an infringement of her rights, it could be justified under Article 9(2); the school's uniform policy was a proportionate response to accommodating the needs of all the pupils. Their Lordships were clearly impressed by the care the school had taken to ensure that their uniform policy satisfied the requirement of modest dress for Muslim girls.[50] Particularly influential was the headteacher's view that adherence to the school uniform policy promoted inclusion and social cohesion and that to allow new variants would encourage the formation of groups or cliques identified by their clothing.[51] Account was also taken of the girls' own concern that they might face pressure to adopt the jilbab themselves if it was allowed.[52]

Whilst it is undoubtedly important for Muslim girls to be protected from bullying fundamentalists,[53] critics of the *Begum* decision have largely focused on the issues underlying Shabina's claim – more particularly the international debates over Muslim women wearing the Islamic headscarf.[54] The approach to religious dress adopted by schools and universities here is far more liberal than the controversial ban on the headscarf by some European countries[55] – a ban not condemned by the ECtHR.[56] Nevertheless, critics argue that *Begum* not only ignores children's autonomy rights – their right to make religious choices – but also their right to education, since very orthodox believers will feel obliged to drop out of school if barred from wearing the dress they consider to be demanded by their religion.[57] Furthermore, the Committee on the Rights of the Child has itself criticised countries like France for preventing Muslim girls and teachers from wearing the Islamic headscarf.[58] But Baroness Hale of

---

[46] Lord Bingham of Cornhill, Lord Hoffmann and Lord Scott of Foscote.

[47] DCSF (2007c) para. 20.   [48] [2006] UKHL 15, [2007] AC 100, at [50].

[49] Lord Nicholls of Birkenhead and Baroness Hale of Richmond.

[50] The school governors had consulted parents, students, staff and the Imams of the three local mosques.

[51] Ibid., per Lord Bingham, at [18].   [52] Ibid., per Baroness Hale, at [98].

[53] This is the view of some Muslim women in France; D. McGoldrick (2006) pp. 272–5.

[54] Inter alia: E. Brems (2006); S. Edwards (2007); A. Pimor (2006).

[55] D. McGoldrick (2006) chs. 2–5.

[56] *Sahin v. Turkey* [2006] ELR 73 and *Dahlab v. Switzerland* [2001] ECHR 42393/98.

[57] E. Brems (2006) pp. 129–33.

[58] Ibid. See also D. McGoldrick (2006) pp. 281–2.

Richmond's judgment in *Begum* reflects her awareness of these broader issues underlying Shabina's application.[59] She appreciated that on the one hand, Muslim women may genuinely choose to wear the headscarf, but that on the other, they may be forced to do so by a male dominated code of dress.[60] Nevertheless, in her view, although all these arguments are important, 'schools are different'.

> A uniform dress code can play its role in smoothing over ethnic, religious and social divisions. But it does more than that. Like it or not, this is a society committed, in principle and in law, to equal freedom for men and women to choose how they will lead their lives within the law. Young girls from ethnic, cultural or religious minorities growing up here face particularly difficult choices: how far to adopt or to distance themselves from the dominant culture. A good school will enable and support them. This particular school is a good school.[61]

These words suggest that Baroness Hale took very seriously the headteacher's fears that Muslim pupils in her school would come under pressure from extremist groups to wear the jilbab were it to be introduced into the uniform code. And of course, the pressure may also come from pupils' own families.[62]

The *Begum* decision and subsequent case law suggests that schools may fight off challenges under Article 9 of the ECHR, by arguing that a strict uniform policy can be justified under Article 9(2).[63] Silber J's decision in *R (Watkins-Singh, a child acting by Sanita Kumari Singh, her mother and litigation friend) v. The Governing Body of Aberdare Girls' High School and Rhondda Cynon Taf Unitary Authority*,[64] suggests that a claimant may find the anti-discrimination legislation is more useful than the ECHR, particularly if he or she wishes to wear something relatively unostentatious. As Harris points out, Shabina Begum could not have brought herself within the protection of the race relations legislation[65] because Muslims are not regarded as an ethnic group per se;[66] nor was religious discrimination then banned as it is now.[67] Today, a pupil may argue that by refusing to allow him or her to attend school wearing a distinctive item of clothing as a visible sign of membership of that group or faith, the headteacher is guilty of indirect racial[68] and/or religious discrimination.[69] To

---

[59] See generally D. McGoldrick (2006).
[60] [2006] UKHL 15, [2007] AC 100, at [94]–[96].   [61] Ibid, at [97].
[62] In *Begum*, Shabina Begum's older brother appeared to be particularly influential in the stance she had adopted.
[63] *R (X) v Head Teacher and Governors of Y School* [2007] EWHC 298, [2008] 1 All ER 249: Muslim pupil unsuccessfully claimed the right to wear a niqab, not a headscarf; *R (on application of Playfoot) v. Governing Body of Millais School* [2007] EWHC 1698 (Admin), [2007] ELR 484: Christian pupil unsuccessfully claimed the right to wear a 'purity ring' despite the uniform policy prohibiting jewellery (S. Bacquet (2008)).
[64] [2008] EWHC 1865 (Admin), [2008] ELR 561
[65] E.g. *Mandla v. Lee and ors* [1983] 2 AC 548: per House of Lords, a headmaster's unjustifiable refusal to allow a Sikh boy to wear a turban to school amounted to unlawful discrimination under the Race Relations Act (RRA) 1976. The scope of the legislation was extended by RRA 1976, s. 1(1A).
[66] N. Harris (2007) p. 155.   [67] I.e. by the Equality Act (EA) 2006, Part 2.
[68] RRA 1976, s. 1(1A).   [69] EA 2006, s. 49(1).

succeed, a pupil must show that he or she is a member of a racial and/or religious group and has suffered a 'particular disadvantage'[70] or 'detriment'[71] by being prevented from wearing the item in question. According to Silber J, wearing it need not be a compulsory requirement of the group or faith,[72] but it must be shown that '(a) that person genuinely believed for reasonable grounds that wearing this item was a matter of *exceptional* importance to his or her racial identity or his or her religious belief and (b) the wearing of this item can be shown objectively to be of *exceptional* importance to his or her religion or race', even if it is not compulsory.[73]

Just as infringement of Article 9 can be justified under Article 9(2), so a school may defend its discriminatory uniform policy by showing that the ban is proportionate[74] or can be reasonably justified by the surrounding circumstances.[75] It is at this point that the visibility of the item of clothing becomes relevant. Silber J rejected the headteacher's claim that her refusal to exempt Sanika (a 14-year-old Sikh girl), from the school's jewellery ban was justified by the need to treat all the pupils in the same way. Having heard expert evidence on the importance to Sikhs of wearing the Kara (a narrow plain steel bangle) and of the importance attached to it by Sanika herself, he was not satisfied that the school had ever considered its exceptional significance.[76] Furthermore, he emphasised that the bangle is very small and unostentatious and is normally hidden from view by the claimant wearing a long-sleeved garment.[77] Consequently, the school's refusal to exempt her from the ban on jewellery was not proportionate and could not be justified.[78] If, as it seems, the item's degree of ostentation is now a relevant factor in such cases, pupils wishing to wear enveloping garments, such as the jilbab, may find it even more difficult to succeed with legal challenges.

The guidance to schools over drawing up uniform policies is far from satisfactory. The advice to consult widely before doing so, taking account of the needs of various groups and the implications of human rights law, is obviously sensible, particularly for schools with a mixed religious and racial intake.[79] The guidance quite rightly assumes from the decision in *Begum*, and later case law,[80] that a pupil with strong views about uniform is very unlikely to succeed with an Article 9 claim, if there is another school which she could attend wearing the garment of her choice.[81] But it also provides the simplistic advice that even in the absence of an alternative school, schools can enforce a

---

[70] RRA 1976, s. 1(1A)(a).   [71] EA 2006, s. 49(1)(c)(iv).
[72] [2008] EWHC 1865 (Admin), [2008] ELR 561, per Silber J, at [50]–[55].
[73] Ibid. at [56B], emphasis as in the original.
[74] RRA 1976, s. 1(1A)(c).   [75] EA 2006, s. 45(3)(d).
[76] [2008] EWHC 1865 (Admin), [2008] ELR 561, per Silber J, at [112]–[114].
[77] Ibid. at [77]–[78].   [78] Ibid. at [92].   [79] DCSF (2007c) para. 4.
[80] *R (X) v Head Teacher and Governors of Y School* [2007] EWHC 298, [2008] 1 All ER 249, per Silber J: since the pupil could have attended another school in the area which allowed the niqab, her rights under Art. 9 ECHR had not been interfered with.
[81] DCSF (2007c) para. 20.

uniform policy which infringes a pupil's religious beliefs if they can justify doing so on human rights grounds, to promote health and safety or the rights and freedoms of others.[82] Admittedly, they are warned not to discriminate unlawfully against pupils 'on the grounds of sex, race, disability, sexual orientation and religion or belief'[83] – but this is unhelpful without far more detailed explanation. As noted earlier,[84] the guidance does not warn schools that by barring certain forms of religious dress they risk infringing the anti-discrimination legislation and unlawfully excluding pupils who are members of certain racial and/or religious groups.

(3) State supervision of separate schools

As the government acknowledges, in relation to the size of their population, there are relatively few faith schools in the maintained sector that cater for the needs of Muslim, Sikh and Hindu children, compared with the provision for Christian and Jewish families.[85] In the absence of maintained schooling, some parents who are members of minority groups will feel obliged to fund their children's education themselves. Although minority groups are not obstructed from establishing independent denominational or faith schools, questions inevitably arise over the legitimacy of the state then intervening to ensure that their children obtain a well-balanced education.

A minority group may strongly resist any state interference with the content of the education offered and the methods of instruction, if the school is entirely funded by the group itself. But if, for example, the education in a minority school does not ensure that the children receive instruction in the language used by society at large, the children may be inadequately prepared for adult life if they later choose to work outside their own community or even to leave it entirely. Less dramatically, the education offered may itself preclude equality of opportunity in other ways. For example, some would argue that the Muslim practice of segregating Muslim boys and girls and providing them with a different balance of subjects, undermines the girls' equality of opportunity. Moreover, the instruction in some independent schools may be undertaken by teachers without formal educational qualifications, although they may be well qualified to teach the children about the customs and belief of the community for whom the school was established.

International human rights law recognises the right of the state to impose 'minimum standards of education' on separate schools[86] and Article 29(1) of the CRC also expects the education provided to develop the child's personality, talents and abilities to their fullest potential. It is obviously important for any liberal democracy to clarify the aims of its educational system, when laying

---

[82] Ibid. at para. 22.   [83] Ibid. at para. 23.

[84] See Chapter 6 in the context of a discussion of school exclusion.

[85] DCSF (2007a) pp. 3–4.   [86] Art. 13(3) of the ICESCR, fn 31 above.

down the 'minimum standards' it requires of the education provided. Otherwise, it could be accused of attempting to achieve an authoritarian standardisation, at the expense of the religious freedom of the group itself. Overarching these considerations is the common view that the state should not interfere with family autonomy and privacy. Matters to do with religion and education are often assumed to be within this family preserve and, as such, left to parents to determine. Such an argument is reinforced by the view that the state should not intrude into the personal lives of members of minority groups.[87]

Well-known American case law demonstrates these issues being debated by the American Supreme Court in relation to the education provided by some of their more powerful religious groups. Attempts by states to interfere with their children's schooling were seen as violations of the parents' rights to free exercise of religion, as guaranteed by the First Amendment of the American Constitution. By the time the State of Wisconsin challenged the right of the Amish community to deny education to their children beyond the eighth grade,[88] the American Supreme Court had already proclaimed its view that states had a right to interfere with parental authority over children, even in situations involving parents' religious convictions. Thus in the celebrated decision in *Prince v. Massachusetts*[89] the Supreme Court made the following observations:

> On one side is the obviously earnest claim for freedom of conscience and religious practice. With it is allied the parent's claim to authority in her own household and in the rearing of her children ... Against these sacred private interests, basic in a democracy, stand the interests of society to protect the welfare of children, and the state's assertion of authority to that end ... It is the interest of youth itself, and of the whole community, that children be both safeguarded from abuses and given opportunities for growth into free and independent well-developed men and citizens ... neither rights of religion nor rights of parenthood are beyond limitation.[90]

Despite this strong justification for state intervention to protect minority children against their parents' authority,[91] nearly 40 years later the Amish community finally gained the right to exempt their children from school after the eighth grade, contrary to Wisconsin state laws which imposed compulsory schooling up to the age of 16. In *Wisconsin v. Yoder*[92] the Supreme Court accepted that although the state had a compelling interest in the education of all its children, in this instance the state's law infringed the free exercise of Amish

---

[87] S. Poulter (1998) p. 27.   [88] *Wisconsin v. Yoder* 406 US 205 (1972).

[89] 321 US 158 (1944): US Supreme Court upheld a conviction against a Jehovah's Witness mother for allowing her two children and her 9-year-old ward to help her distribute Jehovah's Witness literature on the streets, in violation of a state child labour law.

[90] Ibid. at 165–6.

[91] Limiting previous case law such as *Meyer v. Nebraska* 262 US 390 (1923) and *Pierce v. Society of Sisters* 268 US 510 (1925), which had protected the right of parents to direct the religious upbringing of their children.

[92] 406 US 205 (1972).

parents' religion and culture. If their children attended school for two more years, instead of learning the skills and customs of the Amish community through farm and household tasks, the identity of the community would suffer. In a powerful dissenting judgment, Justice Douglas asserted that the state should be concerned with the children's religious freedoms and not those of their parents.[93] He was particularly concerned that these restrictions on an Amish child's education might damage his or her adult prospects in the outside world.

> It is the future of the student, not the future of the parents, that is imperilled by today's decision. If a parent keeps his child out of school beyond the grade school, then the child will be forever barred from entry into the new and amazing world of diversity that we have today. The child may decide that is the preferred course, or he may rebel … If he is harnessed to the Amish way of life by those in authority over him and if his education is truncated, his entire life may be stunted and deformed.[94]

Justice Douglas suggested that the answer was to consult these pupils themselves. He considered that 14- to 15-year-old teenagers were quite old enough to speak for themselves over whether they wished to attend high school, rather than their parents being allowed to speak for the entire family. Although ostensibly sensible, this suggestion overlooked the fact that children brought up in a strict and enclosed community might be too indoctrinated to have independent views, or to express them confidently. The same problem would undoubtedly have arisen had any separate representation been arranged for the children involved in *R (on the application of Williamson and others) v. Secretary of State for Education and Employment and others*.[95] It is, after all, how inward-looking minority groups renew themselves – by indoctrinating fresh generations of children.

As Harris observes, the *Yoder* decision has lost its practical significance, given the growth of the home-schooling movement in the USA, with large numbers of children now being educated at home.[96] Its wider implications are, however, obvious; it demonstrates well the tensions that arise when attempting to mediate between the needs of a minority sect and those of the state over the education of a new generation of children.[97] It certainly seems unlikely that a religious group running an independent faith school in this country would be allowed to exempt its children from the last two years of compulsory education, as the Amish were allowed to do in Wisconsin. Indeed, English law empowers the state to supervise closely and, if necessary, interfere with the operation of all independent schools in the country, irrespective of their catering for a particular religious or ethnic group.[98] Independent schools are given reasonably

---

[93] Ibid. at 242.   [94] Ibid. at 245–6; see C. Hamilton (1995) pp. 265–71.

[95] [2005] UKHL 15, [2005] 2 All ER 1, discussed above.

[96] N. Harris (2007) p. 393.   [97] Ibid. at pp. 393–4.

[98] The existing inspection scheme (Education Act 2002, Part 10) will be replaced when Education and Skills Act (ESA) 2008, Part 4 becomes operational in 2010; see fn. 100.

detailed guidance. They must provide teaching which, inter alia, fosters in pupils 'the application of intellectual, physical or creative effort, interest in their work, and the ability to think and learn for themselves'. Their education should adequately prepare pupils 'for the opportunities, responsibilities and experiences of adult life'. It should provide for their spiritual, moral, social and cultural development by enabling them 'to develop their self-knowledge, self-esteem and self-confidence' and to 'understand how they can contribute to community life'. Perhaps of greatest importance in this context, it should assist them 'to acquire an appreciation of and respect for their own and other cultures in a way that promotes tolerance and harmony between different cultural traditions'.[99]

A reading of the reports of past inspection teams[100] sent to monitor the standards of education offered by minority schools provokes fundamental questions over the state's proper role regarding its supervisory function.[101] As discussed above, despite the benefits of pursuing a policy of 'cultural pluralism within limits', doubts arise over where the limits fall.[102] More particularly, it may be difficult to determine the point at which minimum national standards are breached by a particularly traditional approach to education. If the state is to interfere with separate schooling, it is crucial for it to establish what it expects of the schools and the criteria by which it is judging them. As Cullen argues, it is important to be clear whether minority education rights are perceived as those of the individual child or the right of the community to maintain its collective identity.[103] When the education offered by faith schools is subjected to state scrutiny, its inspectors should clarify whether they are judging the education by its ability to give children equality of opportunity, preparing them to compete with others in the wider community, or by its ability to enable them take their place within their own community fully inculcated in its traditions and beliefs. Cullen suggests that a distinction should be made between an evaluation based on equality of opportunity and equality of results or outcome. In her view, if the emphasis on outcome is removed, equality of opportunity leaves more space for the operation of the value of pluralism.[104] If inspectors assume that separate education should be providing equality of outcome, rather than equality of opportunity, this would indicate a lack of sympathy with the aims of the education provided. The children emerging from these schools often cannot claim equal, or even similar skills or attainments to those who have gone through mainstream schools, quite simply because the education they receive is not intended to enable them to do so.

---

[99] Education (Independent School Standards) (England) Regulations 2003 (SI 2003/1910), Schedule.

[100] Formerly the inspection of independent denominational schools was carried out by Ofsted; this scheme is now to be replaced by 'outsourcing' their inspection to an independent inspectorate. See DSCF (2008) para. 2.11 and ESA 2008, s. 106.

[101] A. Bradney (1987).   [102] S. Poulter (1998) p. 21.

[103] H. Cullen (1993) p. 144.   [104] Ibid. at p. 152.

A lack of clarity over these fundamental questions underpinned the litigation in *R v. Secretary of State for Education and Science, ex p Talmud Torah Machzikei Haddass School Trust*.[105] A critical HMI report had led to a boys' school run by the Belz section of the orthodox Hasidic Jewish community in Hackney being threatened with closure.[106] The report had criticised the inadequacy of the buildings, the narrowness of the curriculum, the lack of encouragement of imaginative work and the staff's failure to provide a stimulating learning environment.[107] Criticism of the secular education, as opposed to the religious education, provided by such small independent faith schools is probably predictable, given their very narrow aims.[108] Nevertheless, the school challenged the competence of HMI to review its work, asserting, in judicial review proceedings, that it could only be assessed in the context of the traditions it served. Only one of the inspectors on the team understood Yiddish, the language in which many of the lessons were conducted, and even his grasp of the community's cultural traditions were insufficient for him to comprehend fully the significance of the pattern of the lessons. More fundamentally, the school argued that the standard by which it had been assessed had been wrong. On this point, counsel for the Department of Education conceded that the education provided by such a school would still be suitable if it primarily equips a child for life within the community of which he is a member, rather than for the way of life in the country as a whole. Nevertheless, this concession was qualified: the education would be suitable only as long as it does not foreclose the child's option in later years to adopt some other form of life if he wishes to do so. This echoes the concerns of Justice Douglas in the *Yoder* case,[109] that the Amish children might be barred from 'the new and amazing world of diversity' provided by society today.

Although the judicial review application failed, the decision in the *Talmud Torah Machzikei Haddass* case is an important one. The Secretary of State's concession indicated that separate schools need not be treated in precisely the same manner as maintained schools and non-denominational independent schools.[110] A similar approach was taken by HMI, nearly 20 years later, regarding the teaching provided by the Talmud Torah Yetev Lev primary school in Hackney.[111] The report clearly accepted that the school's aims were quite different to those of a mainstream school serving a mixed community. As it explained, this is:

---

[105] (1985) *Times*, 12 April.

[106] Under the inspection system then operating, as governed by the Education Act 1944, s. 71.

[107] A. Bradney (1987) provides a full discussion of the HMI report on the Talmud Torah Machzikei Haddass School. See A. Bradney (2009) for a discussion of Ofsted's inspection findings when inspecting the same school in 2007.

[108] E.g. HMI's observations (Ofsted (2001)) regarding pupils' classroom experience in the Talmud Torah Yetev Lev School.

[109] *Wisconsin v. Yoder* 406 US 205 (1972).   [110] A. Bradney (1987) p. 418.   [111] Ofsted (2001).

a school which offers a highly specialised, non-standard education. It serves a faith community which has firm ideas about the education of its children. It is primarily concerned with the transmission of particular religious ideals, values and culture, all of which have, in the recent past, been subject to the threat of extinction. For these reasons, the community that it serves is, to a large extent, inwardly focused and is committed to maintaining its traditional style of education.[112]

From an orthodox educational perspective, the school had obvious shortcomings. The pupils' knowledge of English was poor (classes being held in Yiddish), they underwent no standardised testing, the teaching of secular subjects was weak,[113] with none of the teachers of secular subjects having qualified teacher status. Nevertheless, there was no suggestion that the school should be closed down. Indeed, it was praised for the manner in which it served its community. From an adult viewpoint, such an approach is beneficial, in so far as it encourages a more tolerant assessment of the educational aspirations of minority groups. It does not, however, fulfil Hamilton's strictures. She urges that from the child's perspective, the education provided by a faith school should not be accepted as being 'suitable' if it can only equip pupils for life within the sect's community; it fails to fulfil the child's right to equality of opportunity, as protected by international human rights instruments.[114]

It does not appear that the ultra-Orthodox Jewish community which runs schools like the *Talmud Torah Machzikei Haddass* have been influenced by adverse inspection reports, such as that discussed above.[115] In any event, as Bradney points out, the regulations setting out the state's expectations for independent state schools are relatively vague in meaning.[116] As noted above, schools must prepare pupils 'for the opportunities, responsibilities and experiences of adult life',[117] but there is no clue on the type of adult life they should be prepared *for*. It is clear that neither of the Jewish schools referred to above offered an education which equipped the children to fit easily into British society. Indeed, as relatively few lessons were in English, the children might not even learn to speak English very fluently. The regulations state that where the principal language is not English, lessons in written and spoken English must be 'provided' – without specifying the extent of the provision.[118] They also expect pupils to learn how they can contribute to community life, but, as Harris

---

[112] Ibid. in section entitled 'How good are the curricular and other opportunities offered to pupils or students?'.

[113] The only non-religious subjects taught were mathematics (without geometry or algebra) and English.

[114] C. Hamilton (1995) pp. 259–63.

[115] A. Bradney (2009) discusses the aims of such schools.   [116] Ibid.

[117] Education (Independent School Standards) (England) Regulations 2003 (SI 2003/1910), Schedule, para 1(2)(j).

[118] NB Schedule, para 1(2)(d): where the principal language is not English, lessons in written and spoken English must be provided.

points out, if 'community' is interpreted narrowly, it would not safeguard pupils against an insular approach.[119] Hamilton uncompromisingly asserts:

> Allowing a child to be educated within such an ideological, social and educational enclosure cannot amount to equality of opportunity, although it undoubtedly upholds the principle of pluralism. However, the concession towards pluralism and parents' religious values and beliefs is too great.[120]

Such a view is compelling. But official involvement in the two Jewish schools discussed above demonstrates the difficulty involved in achieving a balance between the rights of a minority community to maintain its identity and the rights of children to equality of opportunity. As Cullen argues, minority educational rights should be seen in an educational context, and not as minority cultural rights. The question should then be asked whether the education fulfils the child's individual potential, rather than whether it protects the minority characteristics.[121] Nevertheless, Cullen also claims that 'the individual right to education must be understood against the background of the collective right to maintain minority identity'.[122] Herein lies the conflict. Undoubtedly, minority groups must retain their freedom to run separate schools. But the years available to fulfil children's right to a broadly based and enlightened education are very short. Unless such groups can ensure that the education they provide does not foreclose on the child's option in later years to adopt some other form of life if he or she wishes to do so, the state has a clear duty to ensure that their schools adjust their methods appropriately, or cease operating.

Whatever academic standards they achieve, separate schools may find it easier than multi-faith schools to contribute to the lives of the ethnic minority communities which they serve, through teaching the children in an informed way about their culture and religion, placing it in a historical context, and giving them a sense of pride in their cultural heritage. This may explain the present government's enthusiasm for bringing more faith schools into the maintained sector.[123] Nevertheless, it is important for the state to maintain a system of monitoring which ensures that all faith schools provide an education which develops their pupils' personality, talents and abilities to their fullest potential, as guaranteed by Article 29(1)(a) of the CRC. The current system of inspection maintains a degree of objectivity, with the result that some faith schools are found to be failing and are de-registered.[124] It is very questionable whether the planned new scheme involving an independent inspection body whose sole function is to inspect independent faith schools can uphold a wide range of

---

[119] N. Harris (2007) p. 444.   [120] C. Hamilton (1995) p. 262.
[121] H. Cullen (1993) p. 144.   [122] Ibid.   [123] Discussed above.
[124] E.g. *The Telegraph*, 11 February 2007: the Jameah Islameah School in East Sussex was one of 45 independent schools closed between 2004 and 2007 for educational failings found during Ofsted inspections. The Jameah Islammeah School was an independent secondary school for Muslim boys, with only 11 pupils, closed for 'major weaknesses'.

values and beliefs.[125] Indeed, as critics have pointed out, it may simply 'reinforce differences and divisions, damaging community cohesion'.[126]

(4) Collective worship and religious education

A fundamental aim of education should be to broaden the horizons of all pupils so that they understand the diversity of values and lifestyles now present in a multicultural society. Indeed, it is now unlawful for schools and local authorities (LAs) to discriminate against pupils on the grounds of their sex, race, disability and religion. It is difficult to deny that children's right to a broadly based and enlightened education is fulfilled better by attending multicultural and multi-faith schools, than separate schools. Although religious convictions may be an important factor in parents' choice of school for their child,[127] membership of a particular religious group does not rule out their choosing non-denominational schools for their children. Some parents who are members of religious or ethnic minority groups may even decide to send their children to non-denominational maintained schools, in the hope that they will thereby learn society's shared values and traditions and develop a respect for the beliefs of others.[128] Others who are not affiliated to any religion may choose a faith school, believing it to offer a higher standard of education than that of others in the area.[129] But some parents may be deterred from using the state system, not only by the lack of attention given by some schools to the beliefs and customs of the broad spectrum of religious and ethnic groups in the country, but also by the law's emphasis on Christian ideals.

Given the empty churches throughout the country,[130] some would be surprised to find that English law obliges all maintained schools to promote the Christian religion, through a daily act of collective worship and by providing religious instruction in class.[131] Although parents may withdraw their children from both activities,[132] the current legislation retains provisions introduced in 1988 with the specific intention of forcing all maintained schools to increase the Christian content of their religious education and collective worship.[133] Furthermore, although as a general principle, it is unlawful for a LA or school

---

[125] ESA 2008, s. 106.　[126] DCSF (2008) para. 2.11.　[127] See fn 33 above.

[128] Equality Act 2006, s. 49: prohibits maintained, non-maintained or independent schools from discriminating against a child on grounds of his religion or belief by refusing to offer him a place at the school, unless the school is a faith school and it is oversubscribed.

[129] School Standards and Framework Act (SSFA) 1998, s. 86(2) obliges all maintained school, including maintained faith schools, to offer a place to a child, whether or not he is a member of that faith, unless the school is oversubscribed. See also DCSF (2009) paras. 2.46–2.54.

[130] Office for National Statistics (2007) pp. 181–2 and Table 13.19: although in 2005, 54% of the population claimed to be Christian, and a further 6% belong to other faiths, 52% stated that they never, or practically never attended a religious service.

[131] First introduced by the Education Act 1944.　[132] SSFA 1998, s. 71(1), discussed below.

[133] Introduced by the Education Reform Act 1988. C. Hamilton (1995) pp. 271–309.

to discriminate against pupils on the grounds of their religion or belief, this prohibition does not apply to the provision of religious education or acts of collective worship.[134] Thus, in relation to the act of collective worship, every state school must arrange a daily assembly of pupils which is 'wholly or mainly of a broadly Christian character'.[135] Although schools are entitled to interpret the 'broadly Christian' requirement quite loosely, to enable pupils of a non-Christian background to take part,[136] the act of corporate worship must contain some elements which can be related specifically to the traditions of Christian belief.[137] The government seems reluctant to abolish this widely flouted legal provision,[138] despite influential calls for it to be adjusted, say by reducing the requirement from an act of daily worship to a weekly or monthly gathering.[139] If it is to be retained, the government should surely enforce it more rigorously and heed the suggestion that headteachers and teaching staff need training to run more effective religious assemblies.[140]

The same features are present in the legal principles governing religious education (RE), which must be provided for all registered pupils by all state-maintained schools.[141] As in the case of the provisions governing collective worship, the legislation shows a determination to include a clear religious ideology in the subject's content.[142] The provisions of the 1988 Act, surviving re-enactment, attempt to ensure that Christianity predominates, specifying that every agreed syllabus:

> shall reflect the fact that the religious traditions in Great Britain are in the main Christian whilst taking account of the teaching and practices of the other principal religions represented in Great Britain.[143]

---

[134] Equality Act 2006, s. 50(2)(a) and (b).

[135] SSFA 1998, s. 70 and Sch. 20, para. 3(2). See also Sch. 20, para. 3(4): not *every* act of worship need comply with this requirement, providing that, taking any term as a whole, *most* do.

[136] *R v. Secretary of State for Education, ex p R and D* [1994] ELR 495, per McCullough J, at 502: the legislation permits some non-Christian elements in the collective worship, as long as those do not deprive it of its broadly Christian character and this character would not be lost by the inclusion of elements common to Christianity and to one or more other religions.

[137] SSFA 1998, Sch. 20, para. 4(1) and Education Act 1996, s. 394: a headteacher of a school with largely non-Christian pupils may be permitted by the local Standing Council on Religious Education (SACRE) not to provide a form of collective worship at all or to provide a form more appropriate to the pupils' family backgrounds.

[138] Discussed by N. Harris (2007) pp. 437–41.

[139] As suggested by David Bell, then head of Ofsted, on 21 April 2004, in an unpublished speech in the House of Commons. He said that 76% of secondary schools were breaking the law by not complying with this legal requirement and that Ofsted inspectors struggled to enforce it.

[140] *The Guardian*, 13 June 2006: joint letter from senior representatives of the Anglican, Catholic and Baptist churches to Alan Johnson, Education Secretary, stating that although most primary schools fulfil their obligation to organise daily acts of worship, many state secondaries do not, and calling for better training for headteachers and teaching staff.

[141] Education Act 2002, s. 80 and SSFA 1998, s. 69(1). It is therefore a compulsory subject, but because it is not included in the National Curriculum, it is not subject to national assessment.

[142] C. Hamilton (1995) pp. 298–300.   [143] Education Act 1996, s. 375(3).

The objectives of that legislation may now seem anachronistic to a society which has perhaps, since the 1980s, become a little more tolerant of differences in faith and culture. Nevertheless most agree that when these objectives are interpreted broadly, through schools adopting a broadly multi-faith approach, the teaching of RE, if well taught, can achieve a great deal. It not only promotes pupils' spiritual and moral development, with a focus on 'ultimate questions and ethical issues' but also teaches them 'to appreciate their own and others' beliefs and cultures and how these impact on individuals, communities, societies and cultures'.[144] Indeed considerable efforts have been made to assist schools to teach religious education effectively, with a detailed non-statutory framework setting out what pupils should study from the ages of 3 to 19.[145] Whether the framework is adopted as a basis for the RE syllabus in maintained schools depends on local education policies. It appears, however, that syllabuses now 'overwhelmingly' take some account of the framework.[146]

These efforts are gradually bearing fruit. Ofsted research indicates that, with the help of the QCA framework,[147] and from a rather low baseline, the teaching of RE is beginning to improve, though more so in primary schools than in secondary, and with enormous variations.[148] Poor teaching is still only too common,[149] with even poorer assessment and planning.[150] There is an overall improvement in the curriculum,[151] but with a 'danger of trivialising issues of global human significance rather than developing a deeper understanding of religious perspectives on life'.[152] As Ajegbo observes, it is often simpler for teachers to fall back on 'the mechanics of religion instead of tackling the reality of being religious'.[153] Improved recruitment and training of specialist RE teachers[154] will hopefully contribute to a better quality of provision. Consideration is now also being given to the QCA Framework[155] becoming the basis for the inclusion of RE within the national curriculum.[156] This important development would largely address RE's low status. But it would also provoke a reassessment of the status of the local Standing Councils on Religious Education (SACREs) and the extent to which the content of RE course should reflect local needs.[157] This might be no bad thing, given Ofsted's trenchant criticism of their recent performance. Evidence indicated

---

[144] QCA (2004) p. 8.   [145] Ibid.   [146] Ofsted (2007) p. 34.

[147] Ibid. at pp. 27 and 33–4: many RE syllabuses have been revised, with the help of the QCA framework.

[148] Ibid. at p. 6.

[149] Ibid. at pp. 19–20: the teaching of RE in the primary schools visited was good and better in 50% of primary schools visited and outstanding in 1 in 10; the teaching of RE in secondary schools visited was good and better in just under half the schools visited and was rarely outstanding.

[150] Ibid. at p. 21: in the primary schools visited, assessment was good or better in approximately 3 out of 10 schools visited and inadequate in 1 in 10; in the secondary schools visited, assessment was good or better in only 1 in 4 schools visited and inadequate in 1 in 4.

[151] Ibid. at pp. 24–6.   [152] Ibid. at pp. 13–14.   [153] K. Ajegbo (2007) p. 68.

[154] Ofsted (2007) pp. 23–4.   [155] QCA (2004).

[156] Ofsted (2007) p. 35.   [157] Ibid. at pp. 36–8.

that across the country as a whole, the work of SACREs was having relatively little impact on schools;[158] indeed that the majority of SACREs had not offered advice to local education authorities (LEAs) in recent years 'and in this respect were neglecting one of their key responsibilities'.[159]

From a legal perspective, it is regrettable that the principles of law applying to collective worship and RE assume that parents' right to religious freedom is identical with that of their children.[160] It is clear that in adopting this stance, they have been influenced by international human rights law which guarantees the freedom of members of religious and ethnic minorities to educate their children according to their own beliefs.[161] Taking account of the need to protect children from religious indoctrination,[162] English law gives parents the right to withdraw their children from both collective worship and RE.[163] Admittedly sixth formers are now exempted from this parental power[164] and are also entitled to excuse themselves from both school assemblies and RE.[165] But these concessions do not dispel the general principle's overall message. It suggests to pupils that, until they reach the sixth form, their own views are unimportant. Withdrawing children from school activities participated in by the majority, potentially marginalises them from their contemporaries and makes them feel different. By entitling parents to withdraw them with no explanation, the law reinforces parents' perceptions that they have a right to dictate religious matters to their children.[166] There is also a greater risk of their children becoming forced further into the confines of the family and their parents' beliefs – on the basis that although the state must not indoctrinate children, parents can.

Despite this concern over a matter of legal principle, we should not discount the overall sense of optimism being displayed by educationalists over the part that RE can play in the work of schools generally. There is wisdom in the assertion that current developments in RE are taking place:

> within the context of the extraordinary increase in the political, social and cultural importance of religion in Britain in this century. Recent world events, the rise of more fundamentalist forms of religion, the growth of faith schools and the debates about the relationship between religion and British identity have given a new impetus and urgency to the subject … The notions, common until recently, that religion was quietly declining and RE had little relevance to modern life now look naïve … children and young people need to develop a more profound understanding of the importance of religious commitment and diversity. They need the opportunity to reflect on issues about personal identity, meaning and truth.[167]

---

[158] Ofsted (2004) para. 65.   [159] Ibid. in main findings.
[160] N. Harris (2007) pp. 434–7.   [161] Discussed above.
[162] *Kjeldsen, Busk Madsen and Pedersen v. Denmark* (1976) 1 EHRR 711 at para. 53. See also *Angelini v. Sweden* (1988) 10 EHRR 123 and *Folgerø and ors v. Norway* [2007] ELR 557.
[163] SSFA 1998, s. 71(1).   [164] SSFA 1998, s. 71(1A).   [165] SSFA 1998, s.71(1B).
[166] C. Hamilton (1995) pp. 303–9.   [167] Ofsted (2007) para. 132.

(5) Conclusion

The methods adopted by the state in maintaining the balance between parents' rights and children's rights should always be exercised with sensitivity. The law must respect the right of minority groups to run separate schools which instruct their children on their culture and traditions. But although aggressive interference with their educational methods can very easily be seen as religious persecution, minority children are entitled to equality of educational opportunity; further to an education which broadens their horizons, rather than narrowing their potential. Doubt over what stance is appropriate should always be resolved in favour of promoting children's rights rather than those of their parents. But on the other hand, pupils must learn that they cannot enforce their rights at any time and place at their own choosing – indeed that rights are seldom absolute and may have to accommodate those of their peers. Meanwhile, the part played by the law on religious education, with its stress on promoting the tenets of the Christian religion, appears to ignore the need to promote a cultural pluralism within limits. Religious education has its place in a multicultural society, such as our own, but it cannot ignore diversity.

BIBLIOGRAPHY

NB many of these publications can be obtained on the relevant organisation's website.

Ajegbo, K. (Chairman) (2007) *Diversity and Citizenship: Curriculum Review*, DfES.

Bacquet, S. (2008) 'School Uniforms, Religious Symbols and the Human Rights Act 1998: The "Purity Ring" Case' 8 *Education Law Journal* 11.

Bradney, A. (1987) 'Separate Schools and Ethnic Minorities and the Law' 13 *New Community* 412.

(2009) 'The Inspection of Ultra-Orthodox Jewish Schools: "The Audit Society" and "The Society of Scholars"' 21 *Child and Family Law Quarterly* 131.

Brems, E. (2006) 'Above Children's Heads: The Headscarf Controversy in European Schools from the Perspective of Children's Rights' 14 *International Journal of Children's Rights* 119.

Craig, E. (2003) 'Accommodation of Diversity in Education – a Human Rights Agenda?' 15 *Child and Family Law Quarterly* 279.

Crick, B. (Chairman) (1998) *Education for Citizenship and the Teaching of Democracy In Schools, Final Report of the Advisory Group on Citizenship*, Qualifications and Curriculum Authority.

Cullen, H. (1993) 'Education Rights or Minority Rights?' 7 *International Journal of Law and the Family* 143.

Department for Children, Schools and Families (DCSF) (2007a) *Faith in the System: The Role of Schools With a Religious Character in English Education and Society*, DCSF Publications.

Department for Children, Schools and Families (DCSF) (2007b) *Guidance on the Duty to Promote Community Cohesion, DCSF Publications*.

Department for Children, Schools and Families (DCSF) (2007c) *DCSF Guidance to Schools on Uniform and Related Policies*, www.teachernet.gov.uk/management/atoz/u/uniform/

Department for Children, Schools and Families (DCSF) (2008) *Independent Schools Inspectorates – a Consultation Document*, DCSF.

Department for Children, Schools and Families (DCSF) (2009) *School Admissions Code*, The Stationery Office.

Edwards, S. (2007) 'Imagining Islam … of Meaning and Metaphor Symbolising the Jilbab – *R (Begum) v Headteacher and Governors of Denbigh High School*' 19 *Child and Family Law Quarterly* 247.

Gold, R. (2007) 'The Education and Inspections Act 2006' 8 *Education Law Journal* 11.

Hamilton, C. (1995) *Family, Law and Religion*, Sweet and Maxwell.

Harris, N. (2007) *Education, Law and Diversity*, Hart Publishing.

  (2008) 'Editorial: Faith Schools' 9 *Education Law Journal* 167.

Kilkelly, U. (1999) *The Child and the European Convention on Human Rights*, Ashgate.

McGoldrick, D. (2006) *Human Rights and Religion: The Islamic Headscarf Debate in Europe*, Hart Publishing.

Office for National Statistics (2007) *Social Trends No 37*, Palgrave Macmillan.

Office for Standards in Education (Ofsted) (2001) *Independent School HMI Report on the Talmud Torah Yetev Lev School*.

Office for Standards in Education (Ofsted) (2004) HMI 2269, *An Evaluation of the Work of Standing Advisory Councils for Religious Education*, www.ofsted.gov.uk

Office for Standards in Education (Ofsted) (2007) Reference No 070045, *Making Sense of Religion: a Report on Religious Education in Schools and the Impact of Locally Agreed Syllabuses*, www.ofsted.gov.uk

Pimor, A. (2006) 'The Interpretation and Protection of Article 9 ECHR: Overview of the Denbigh High School (UK) Case' 28 *Journal of Social Welfare and Family Law* 323.

Poulter, S. (1998) *Ethnicity, Law and Human Rights: The English Experience*, Oxford University Press.

Qualifications and Curriculum Authority (QCA) (2004) *Religious Education: The Non-statutory Framework*, QCA Publications.

Scolnicov, A. (2007) 'The Child's Right to Religious Freedom and Formation of Identity' 15 *International Journal of Children's Rights* 251.

Swann, M. (Chairman) (1985) Cmnd 9453, *Education for All* Report of the Committee of Inquiry into the Education of Children from Ethnic Minority Groups.

Thornberry, P. (1991) *International Law and the Rights of Minorities*, Clarendon Press.

Chapter 12

Educational rights for children with disabilities

(1) Introduction

Despite many calls for improvement,[1] it is notoriously difficult to obtain accurate statistics on the prevalence and patterns of childhood disability in the UK.[2] Current estimates[3] depend on a variety of sources,[4] often depending on the extent to which families obtain services of various kinds.[5] Furthermore, any statistics on disability are undermined by varied definitions of disability. For health services, the term 'disabled children' refers to those 'children and young people who are disabled and/or those with complex health needs'.[6] Anti-discrimination law more specifically defines a 'disabled person' as someone who 'has a physical or mental impairment which has a substantial and long-term adverse effect on his ability to carry out normal day-to-day activities'.[7] The fact that many professionals working with children even lack a common language may also affect collection of data.[8] Hopefully these differences will modify as professionals work alongside each other in children's trusts, under the changes introduced by the *Every Child Matters* reform programme[9] and the Children Act (CA) 2004.[10] Similarly, data collection and information sharing about the

---

[1] Inter alia: PMSU (2005) pp. 123–4; HM Treasury and DfES (2007) pp. 28–31.

[2] The most detailed analysis of disability was carried out by the Office of Population Censuses and Surveys in the late 1980s. See OPCS (1989) esp. Report 3 and D. Gordon *et al.* (2000).

[3] HM Treasury and DfES (2007) para. 1.9: there are 570,000 disabled children in England, around 100,000 of whom have complex care needs and therefore need a wide range of services.

[4] P. Stobbs (2008) pp. 17–19.

[5] PMSU (2005) p. 123. E.g. Children Act (CA) 1989, Sch. 2, para. 2, legally obliges children's services to keep a register of disabled children in their area. But primary care trusts and education services also collect data on referrals relating to physical impairment, mental health problems and learning difficulties.

[6] DH (2004) p. 4. I.e. for the purposes of the National Service Framework standard.

[7] Disability Discrimination Act (DDA) 1995, s. 1(1) and Sch. 1. N. Harris (2007) p. 168: the extension of 'disability' to cover those infected with HIV (DDA 1995, Sch. 1, para. 6A) extends the numbers of 'disabled persons' for these purposes.

[8] Particularly regarding children in need of mental health services. See H. Green *et al.* (2004) esp. Tables 4.3 and 4.4: showing sub-categories of mental disorder, e.g. phobias and depression, which bear no relationship to the terms used by educationalists, e.g. attention deficit hyperactivity disorder (ADHD) and pupils with behavioural, emotional and social difficulties (BESD).

[9] HM Treasury (2003) and DfES (2004a).

[10] CA 2004, s. 11(2)(a), discussed in more detail in Chapter 15.

numbers and needs of disabled should also improve with the introduction of electronic health and social care records.[11] Meanwhile, official figures may always be incomplete since there is probably a high incidence of undetected childhood disabilities of various kinds. Whatever their true level, the range is considerable and there is increasing prevalence of impairment.[12] But the extent to which they hamper children from being able to benefit from educational provision varies. For all of them, of course, education is a fundamental necessity.

Long before the 1980s and 1990s which saw 'major efforts in the United Kingdom to redefine disability as a social and political issue',[13] the Warnock Committee had stressed that even the most severely disabled children had a right to be educated, because 'education as we conceive it, is a good, and a specifically human good, to which all human beings are entitled'.[14] Indeed, an enlightened education will enable them:

> to lead a life very little poorer in quality than that of the non-handicapped child, whereas without this kind of education they might face a life of dependence or even institutionalisation. Education in such cases makes the difference between a proper and enjoyable life and something less than we believe life should be.[15]

The dual aims of education, being to enlarge the child's knowledge, experience and imaginative understanding and later to enable him or her to enter the world as an active and independent participant in society, clearly apply as much to the disabled as to the unimpaired.[16] It is not only fundamentally important for education law to address these needs, but also to prevent disabled children being marginalised and discriminated against, by reason only of their difference from the unimpaired. As the Warnock Report so clearly perceived, providing education is far more than merely filling children with information, irrespective of their surroundings.

The following chapter assesses first the development of ideas about equal access to education, free from discrimination, as applied to children with learning difficulties and disabilities. It then proceeds to consider three specific areas where particular problems currently arise in promoting their rights to an appropriate and fulfilling education. The first relates to disabled children's need to access services efficiently and in due time. The second involves their right to be educated in mainstream schools alongside their unimpaired colleagues. The third relates to maintaining a balance between involving parents of children with learning difficulties in their children's educational provision and recognising the individuality and independence of their children.

It should be noted that the term 'special educational needs' or 'SEN' is used in many reports and official documents to describe those with learning difficulties.[17] This term adequately describes many intellectually impaired pupils, but

---

[11] Discussed in Chapter 15.   [12] PMSU (2005) p. 35.   [13] J. Read and L. Clements (2004) p. 504.
[14] H.M. Warnock (1978) para. 1.7.   [15] Ibid. at para. 1.8.   [16] Ibid. at para. 1.4.
[17] The law relating to children with SEN is governed by the Education Act (EA 1996) 1996, Pt. IV. See S. Oliver (2007) and N. Harris (2007), ch. 6 for a more detailed assessment.

does not necessarily correctly describe an intellectually unimpaired but physically disabled child. In this chapter, where relevant, the term pupils with 'learning difficulties and disabilities' (LDDs)[18] is used to describe both groups. It should also be noted that because the introduction of children's trusts up and down the country has led to the duties of many local education authorities (LEAs) being assumed by children's services authorities, the term used throughout this chapter is local authority (LA), not LEA.

(2) A rights perspective

As Read *et al.* observe, there is a growing consensus that:

> some of the greatest restrictions and limitations experienced by disabled children and adults are undoubtedly created by the way that society is organised to exclude them, by other people's damaging attitudes, by limited and unequal opportunities and by inadequate service provision.[19]

This is, in essence, the 'social model of disability';[20] its acceptance has been accompanied by a strengthening international movement acknowledging the human rights of all disabled people, regardless of age.[21] Alongside these developments, there has also been a gathering acceptance of the concept of 'inclusion' in education.[22] Its proponents[23] reject the practice of isolating disabled children from the rest of the community through their education and assert their right to attend, as far as possible, mainstream schools.[24] In so doing, the children can socialise with their non-disabled peers and participate in the whole range of opportunities and activities provided by schools for all their pupils. Nevertheless, international human rights law has only gradually recognised this concept. The Convention on the Rights of the Child (CRC) recognises 'the right of the child to education',[25] and also requires states to respect the rights of every child 'without discrimination of any kind, irrespective of the child's or his or her parent's or legal guardian's race, colour, sex ... disability, birth or other status'.[26] Furthermore, Article 23(1) secures the right of a mentally or physically

---

[18] As adopted by Ofsted in Ofsted (2006).   [19] J. Read *et al.* (2006) p. 32.

[20] UNICEF (2007) p. 5.   [21] Ibid. in ch. 1.

[22] There is voluminous literature about the concept of 'inclusion' which requires mainstream schools to adapt to the pupil, cf. the concept of 'integration', which expects such pupils to adapt to mainstream schools.

[23] Various international organisations are involved in the 'inclusion' movement, especially UNESCO. Its World Conference on Special Needs Education in Salamanca in 1994 produced the *Salamanca Statement and Framework for Action on Special Needs Education*. This calls for an international commitment to inclusive education and for governments to give policy and budgetary priority to improving their education systems to render them accessible to children. P. Mittler (2000) ch. 2; G. Lindsay (2007); N. Harris (2007) pp. 335–40.

[24] Despite 'inclusion' being widely adopted, the terminology has differed. The term 'mainstreaming' has been used in the USA, 'normalisation' in Scandinavia and Canada. For an assessment of the international 'inclusive schooling movement', see J. Jenkinson (1997) chs. 1–3.

[25] Art. 28(1).   [26] Art. 2(1).

disabled child 'to enjoy a full and decent life, in conditions which ensure dignity, promote self-reliance, and facilitate the child's active participation in the community'. More particularly, Article 23(3) guarantees effective access to education 'in a manner conducive to the child's achieving the fullest possible social integration and individual development'. But, as Freeman points out, these articles contain no specific reference to the disabled child's right to be educated alongside his or her peers in a mainstream school, the concept of inclusion.[27] Ignoring this omission, the Committee on the Rights of the Child consistently emphasises the need for states to recognise disabled children's rights to inclusion in regular schools and criticises states which provided segregated education.[28] When detailing its views of how the Convention should be interpreted in relation to disabled children, the Committee stresses that 'Inclusive education should be the goal of educating children with disabilities',[29] whilst also acknowledging that inclusion comes in many forms and 'should not be understood nor practised as simply integrating children with disabilities into the regular system regardless of their challenges and needs'.[30]

Despite the efforts of the Committee on the Rights of the Child to fill the gaps left by the draftsmen of the CRC, the Convention retains the weakness identified by Freeman. In contrast, the UN Convention on the Rights of Persons with Disabilities[31] specifically recognises the right of disabled persons to an 'inclusive education'[32] and requires states to ensure that they 'are not excluded from free and compulsory primary education, or from secondary education, on the basis of disability'.[33] It enlarges on these duties, stating that they should have access to such education on an equal basis to others in their communities[34] and receive the educational support they need 'to facilitate their effective education'.[35] Effective individualised support measures should also be provided 'in environments which maximise academic and social development, consistent with the goal of full inclusion'.[36]

Influential though these international documents are, they lack the practical impact of the European Convention for the Protection of Human Rights and Fundamental Freedoms (ECHR), given its incorporation into domestic law by the Human Rights Act (HRA) 1998. But Article 2 of the first protocol (A2P1) of the ECHR, even in conjunction with the right to freedom from discrimination under Article 14, merely ensures a right to an 'effective education'.[37] As the Strasbourg jurisprudence makes plain, these provisions go no further. Since they merely guarantee education to a minimum standard, they do not give a disabled child the right to attend any particular educational institution and leave the domestic authorities considerable discretion over what educational

---

[27] M. Freeman (2000) p. 283.   [28] R. Hodgkin and P. Newell (2007) pp. 335–7.
[29] Committee on the Rights of the Child (2006) para. 66.   [30] Ibid. at para. 67.
[31] Signed (but not ratified) by the UK in March 2007.   [32] Art. 24(1).
[33] Art. 24(2)(a).   [34] Art. 24(2)(b).   [35] Art. 24(2)(d).   [36] Art. 24(2)(e).
[37] *Belgian Linguistics Case (No 2)* (1968) 1 EHRR 252, discussed in Chapter 6.

services they provide.[38] Such jurisprudence has been applied by a growing body of domestic case law,[39] all of which reinforces the view that parents unhappy with their children's educational provision should use domestic education law, rather than relying on international human rights law, as the basis for any challenge.

(3) The impact of disability

On a domestic front, the notion of inclusion is not a new one,[40] and, as discussed below, the current legislation promotes it forcefully. Statistics indicate, however, that despite official encouragement, the educational and employment prospects of disabled children and young people remain relatively very poor. Children with disabilities still experience a variety of difficulties wherever they go to school. Ofsted research indicated that the majority of pupils defined as 'low attaining' at Key Stages 1 to 3 had LDDs. It concluded that although many can and do make good progress, 'Too little had been done nationally to focus schools' attention on improving the achievement of pupils in the lowest quartile'.[41]

School days may not always be a particularly happy experience. The rate of permanent and fixed-term exclusion for SEN children, whether or not they have statements of SEN,[42] continues to be far higher than that for children without such difficulties.[43] Nor does constant school attendance always produce high levels of education. Disabled people are more likely to leave school with no educational qualifications and less likely than non-disabled, to have advanced qualifications.[44] Furthermore, disabled young people are far more likely to be out of education, employment or training (NEET) than non-disabled young people of the same age.[45] Whilst one might expect the most severely impaired to encounter difficulties, these statistics show such disappointingly high levels of NEETs amongst *all* young disabled. Indeed, material

---

[38] *Simpson v. United Kingdom* (Application No 14688/89) (1989) 64 DR 188.

[39] See fn 117 below.

[40] The Education Act (EA) 1944, s. 33(2) provided for less severely handicapped children to be catered for in mainstream schools.

[41] Ofsted (2006) p. 15.   [42] Discussed below.

[43] DCSF (2008a): pupils with SEN (both with and without statements) are over nine times more likely to be permanently excluded than the rest of the school population. In 2006/7, 36 in every 10,000 pupils with statements of SEN and 42 in every 10,000 pupils with SEN without statements were permanently excluded from school, cf. 4 in every 10,000 with no SEN. See also A. Wilkin *et al.* (2005) ch. 1, Appendix 1, section 4 and Appendix 2.

[44] PMSU (2005) Tables 2.15 and 2.16. See also HCESC (2006a) para. 96 (citing Labour Force Survey 2004): 21% of disabled people aged 16–24 have no qualifications whatsoever, cf. 9% of non-disabled people of the same age.

[45] DfES (2004b) para. 3.40: in 2002, 35% of 18-year-olds with SEN and disabilities were in education, 8% in training and 35% were in employment; 23% were neither in education, training, nor employment. By the age of 19, those statistics were 33%, 13%, 30% and 24%, respectively. See also T. Burchardt (2005) pp. 30–4.

gained from research surveys shows that disabled young people have lower levels of satisfaction with their lives than non-disabled people of the same age and are less successful at making the transition to adult life. At the age of 26, disabled people are nearly four times as likely to be unemployed or involuntarily out of work than non-disabled people[46] and by the same age, many feel that the high aspirations that they had had at 16 had been frustrated and disappointed.[47]

These figures paint a gloomy picture of the educational plight of children with learning difficulties. Admittedly over the last 20 years the government has made considerable efforts, through legislation[48] and government initiatives[49] to promote the right of disabled children to participate fully in society and to access appropriate services – thereby giving them the right to 'access ordinary lives'.[50] Changes in education law reflect these efforts; notably, disabled pupils were brought under the protection of the disability discrimination legislation.[51] Nevertheless, this country remains a long way from ensuring that disabled children, young people and their families 'feel empowered and supported in the choices they make'.[52]

(4) Equal access to education free from discrimination

(A) A 'new' approach

In 2006, the House of Commons Education and Skills Committee (HCESC), having conducted a major review of the current SEN system, concluded that:

> the original Warnock framework has run its course … the SEN system is demonstrably no longer fit for purpose and there is a need for the Government to develop a new system that puts the needs of the child at the centre of provision.[53]

This swingeing criticism was not unexpected; there had been a variety of reports over the years commenting on the bureaucracy of the SEN system and the way

---

[46] T. Burchardt (2005) p. 41.   [47] Ibid. at pp. 46–7.

[48] Usefully summarised in P. Stobbs (2008) Appendix. Inter alia: CA 1989, Sch. 2, para. 6: local authorities (LAs) must provide services to minimise the effect of disabled children's disabilities and give them the opportunity to live lives 'as normal as possible'; DDA 1995: disabled people obtained the right to protection from discrimination in employment; DDA 2005: the Disability Equality Duty requires public sector organisations (including governing bodies of all maintained schools) to ensure that disabled people receive equality of opportunity, free from discrimination and are included in all aspects of policy development; the Childcare Act 2006: obliges LAs to take account of disabled children's childcare needs.

[49] Summarised in HM Treasury and DfES (2007) paras. 1.12–1.15. See particularly the mission statements contained in PMSU (2005) e.g. para. 5.3.

[50] PMSU (2005) para. 5.2.

[51] The DDA 1995 was extended to every aspect of education by Pt. 2 of the Special Educational Needs and Disability Act (SENDA) 2001. See discussion below.

[52] HM Treasury and DfES (2007) p. 9.   [53] HCESC (2006a) p. 6.

it deleteriously affected the lives of children and their families.[54] Although the government sought to head off these criticisms by introducing a new SEN 'strategy' (involving tightening up on practice),[55] and increasing investment in SEN, the basic SEN framework had remained unchanged. Matters were brought to a head in 2005, when Baroness Warnock called for a radical review of the SEN system her own committee had put in place 25 years earlier. She even showed considerable scepticism over the usefulness of the concept of inclusion and of the system of statementing, both essential cornerstones of the current SEN framework.[56] Whilst many commentators criticised her remarks,[57] the HCESC broadly agreed with her, considering that the existing system had developed 'significant cracks'.[58] The government stood firm, stating categorically that the system was in no need of fundamental review,[59] especially at a time when other major changes were being introduced.[60] In particular, it considered that the changes already put in place and the new injection of funds into the SEN system[61] were sufficient to justify such a stance.

The Education Act 1981 had implemented many of the Warnock Committee's recommendations. In establishing the current SEN system, it introduced a fundamentally new approach. It was intent on ensuring that disabled children should not be singled out by their handicaps but assessed simply as children requiring education. By using non-stigmatising terms such as 'learning difficulties' and 'special educational needs', the report emphasised that these children were no different from any others. The 1981 legislation contained certain fundamental objectives.[62] These were that all children with learning difficulties would have their educational needs fully assessed; that they would be provided with extra educational support; that the majority would be educated in mainstream schools; that parents' views would be taken into account by LEAs when assessing their children's needs; that pupils with statements would be subject to regular review.

(B) Difficulties of interpretation – 'statemented' and 'non-statemented'

Although the philosophy underpinning the Education Act 1981 has survived intact, the methods adopted for achieving its aims have needed considerable adjustment over the years. Indeed, as the HCESC declared, 'it is an old framework that is struggling to keep up with the diverse range of needs across the

---

[54] Inter alia: Audit Commission (2002a); Audit Commission (2002b); Ofsted (2004); J. MacBeath (2006).

[55] Under the auspices of DfES (2004b) esp. p. 27; see summarised in HCESC (2006b), Ev. 25–26, DfES Memorandum.

[56] M. Warnock (2005).   [57] E.g. D. Ruebain and J. Wright (2006) pp. 4–6.

[58] HCESC (2006a) para. 17.   [59] HM Government (2006) p. 3.

[60] Inter alia, through the Every Child Matters programme, see fn 9 above.

[61] HM Government (2006) p. 2 and HCESC (2006b) Ev. 16, DfES Memorandum.

[62] M. Warnock (2005) ch. 1.

1.5 million children categorised as having some sort of special educational need'.[63] As noted above, use of the system has consistently produced well-publicised difficulties for LAs, schools and parents alike. One of its most confusing and problematic aspects is the distinction, established by the Warnock Committee, between two groups of children. Central to its thinking was that the majority of children would only require special educational provision for short periods, at various stages of their school career and that there should be flexibility within mainstream education to provide for their needs quickly.[64] This first category encompasses the *majority* of children whose needs can be determined and met by ordinary schools, without specialised help from the LA.[65] The second group, the minority,[66] have exceptional needs, beyond the skills or resources of mainstream schools, at least without additional help from the LA.

Whilst LAs are under a legal duty to provide 'appropriate education' for all pupils within their area, and when doing so, to have regard to pupils' need for special educational provision,[67] Warnock's second group of children have a special status. LAs are under a clear duty to identify them and take responsibility for fulfilling their educational needs, by inter alia, identifying the school they should attend,[68] having assessed and recorded those needs in a statement.[69] But from the start, it has not been clear what level of need schools can be expected to meet, before reaching the point at which the LA is obliged to take over the responsibility for the child's education by issuing a statement. Although later legislation and guidance did not clarify the circuitous definition of the term 'special educational needs',[70] it ironed out some of the difficulties implicit in the scheme envisaged by Warnock. For example, a Code of Practice[71] now provides clear guidance explaining the fundamental principles of the legislation and its practical application.[72] The assessment and

---

[63] HCESC (2006a) para. 15.   [64] H.M. Warnock (1978) paras. 3.16–3.17.

[65] DCSF (2008b): in 2008, 17.2% of pupils across all maintained schools in England had SEN but no statements.

[66] Ibid.: in 2008, 2.8% of pupils across all maintained schools in England had statements of SEN. See also DCSF (2007a) Chart A: these numbers rose between 1994 and 2001, but have been gradually falling since.

[67] EA 1996, s. 14.   [68] Discussed below.   [69] EA 1996, ss. 321–4.

[70] EA 1996, s. 312(1) and (2): A child is deemed to have 'special educational needs' if he 'has a learning difficulty which calls for special educational provision to be made for him'. He is deemed to have a 'learning difficulty' if: '(2)(a) he has a significantly greater difficulty in learning than the majority of children of his age, (b) he has a disability which either prevents or hinders him from making use of educational facilities of a kind generally provided for children of his age in schools within the area of the local education authority, or (c) he is under the age of five and is, or would be if special educational provision were not made for him, likely to fall within paragraph (a) or (b) when of or over that age.'

[71] Issued by the Secretary of State under EA 1996, s. 313. *R (Jane W) v. Blaenau Gwent Borough Council and anor* [2003] EWHC 2880 (Admin), [2004] ELR 152, per Owen J, at [16]: although the *SEN Code of Practice* does not have to be followed, LAs and the tribunal are statutorily obliged to have regard to its provisions and explain why they decide to depart from it.

[72] DfES (2001) (hereafter *SEN Code of Practice*), recommends (chs. 5, 6 and 7) a graduated approach to SEN provision: (a) 'School Action' for the child whose needs are deemed not

statementing procedure was improved, together with the introduction of a vastly improved appeals procedure.[73] This enables parents to appeal against most aspects of the statementing process to an independent tribunal. This was formerly known as the Special Educational Needs and Disability Tribunal (SENDIST)[74] but, under a general overhaul of the tribunal system, recently became part of the Health, Education and Social Care Chamber of the First-tier Tribunal and is known as First-tier Tribunal SEND (SEND).[75]

Though welcome, none of these changes addressed the considerable doubt over the threshold of need that warrants the issuing of a statement. The duty of LAs to assess and compile a statement for a child, setting out detailed arrangements for the educational needs of a child with complex learning difficulties (which they resource and maintain) remains unchanged – despite the assistance of guidance,[76] it is a completely discretionary one.[77] Consequently, the distinction between the two categories of children with SEN, as described above, remains a fundamental feature of the whole system. The official guidance certainly provides useful pointers and suggests that, when deciding whether it is necessary to statutorily assess a child, LAs should consider the child's particular requirements and whether these can be met from existing resources in mainstream maintained schools, through school-based intervention.[78] Similarly, a LA should draw up a statement 'when it considers that the special educational provision necessary to meet the child's needs cannot reasonably be provided within the resources normally available to mainstream schools'.[79] But, as case law confirms,[80] LAs remain free to determine for themselves the extent to which schools have sufficient funding and teaching skills to provide for the educational needs of children with learning difficulties who are not statemented.

From the inception of the Warnock scheme, the statementing system has caused problems. Indeed, Warnock herself asserts that 'it turned out to be not a

---

sufficiently complex to require the school obtaining external assistance with the child; (b) 'School Action Plus' for the child whose needs, despite being more complex, can be met within the school but with external assistance and services; (c) a LA statement for the child whose needs cannot be met from within the resources available in a mainstream school.

[73] Discussed below.

[74] The jurisdiction of the Special Educational Needs Tribunal (SENT) was extended to include complaints of disability discrimination by schools and LEAs (SENDA 2001, Sch. 8, para. 2) with the tribunal adopting its present name, the Special Educational Needs and Disability Tribunal.

[75] The tribunal system was reorganised in 2008 under the changes introduced by Tribunals, Courts and Enforcement Act 2007, Part 1.

[76] SEN Code of Practice, ch. 8.

[77] EA 1996, ss. 329 and 329A: the LEA need only statutorily assess a child if it is 'necessary' so to do; EA 1996, s. 324: the LEA need only make and maintain a statement if it is 'necessary' so to do.

[78] SEN Code of Practice, para. 7.54.   [79] Ibid. at para. 8.2.

[80] E.g. R v. Secretary of State for Education and Science, ex p Lashford [1988] 1 FLR 72 and R v. Isle of Wight County Council, ex p RS; R v. Isle of Wight County Council, ex p AS [1993] 1 FLR 634 (discretion over whether to draw up a statement). See also H v. Kent County Council and the Special Educational Needs Tribunal [2000] ELR 660: discretion over whether to statutorily assess a child.

very bright idea'.[81] A recurring source of criticism[82] has been the very large variations in the extent to which LAs statement children, even taking account of population differences.[83] Parents inevitably see an inequity in the fact that in some areas pupils with lesser needs receive guaranteed specialised help, through the provision of statements, while those in their own, with greater needs do not. Indeed, since statements are often seen by parents as the only gateway to the resources needed by the child, they may not unreasonably suspect some LAs of refusing to assess or statement a child, in order to avoid the financial consequences of so doing. As the HCESC commented, there are three reasons why a LA might decide not to issue a statement: (i) that it is not necessary; (ii) that the LA is attempting to reduce its number of statements as a matter of policy; and (iii) that it is an attempt to save money. 'The first is acceptable, the second is questionable, and the third is illegal.'[84] Parents may find that they are caught in a buck-passing exercise between the LA and the local mainstream school. Mainstream schools receive funds to meet special needs and LAs may therefore refuse to statutorily assess or statement a child for this reason, considering that the local school has sufficient funds to provide for his or her needs.[85] But the funds delegated to schools for non-statemented children are not ring-fenced or earmarked to the specific child;[86] nor is there sufficient LA supervision of how they are spent.[87] Consequently, as noted by Boyle and Burton, trained experts, equipment, space and other resources are not being efficiently delivered to the unstatemented children who need them.[88] For this reason, there has been strong criticism of the government's encouragement of LAs to delegate nearly all their SEN funds to schools to spend as they will.[89]

Education legislation provides parents with a very full involvement in the various stages of determining their child's educational needs and provision. They can ask for a SEN assessment[90] and should themselves be involved in the assessment and statementing process.[91] Parents also have considerable influence over the choice of educational provision made for their child in the statement.[92] Nevertheless, many find the statementing process, more

[81] M. Warnock (2005) p. 29.

[82] Audit Commission (2002a) pp. 26–30; Ofsted (2004) paras. 32–33; J. MacBeath et al. (2006) p. 65; HCESC (2006a) para. 149.

[83] HCESC (2006a) para. 88 and Table 1: almost a fivefold difference in the proportion of pupils with statements in different authorities, ranging from 1.08% of all pupils to 4.83%.

[84] HCESC (2006a) para. 150. The illegality of such a practice is borne out by *R v. East Sussex County Council, ex p Tandy* [1998] 2 All ER 769.

[85] Audit Commission (2002b) para. 89.

[86] HCESC (2006a) para. 234: a special educational needs co-ordinator (SENCO) told the committee that SEN money transferred to her school is not ring-fenced and could therefore be spent on 'watering the garden'. See also J. Bercow (2008) paras. 3.31–3.32.

[87] J. Bercow (2008) para. 3.31.   [88] D. Boyle and E. Burton (2004) p. 19.

[89] HCESC (2006a) para. 236–7; HCESC (2006b) Ev. 157, paras. 19–26, The Advisory Centre for Education; J. Bercow (2008) para. 3.32.

[90] EA 1996, s. 329.   [91] EA 1996, Sch. 27.   [92] Discussed below.

particularly the statutory assessment process 'stressful and alienating'.[93] Despite strict time limits,[94] it often involves lengthy delays and the process runs the risk of unnecessarily 'labelling' the child.[95] Indeed, despite Warnock's wish to avoid the medicalisation of special education,[96] parents find that obtaining a specific diagnosis for their child, such as autism, establishes his or her educational need, rather than the other way round.[97] They see a conflict of interest in the fact that the LA is both obliged to assess the child's needs, with the assistance of LA funded experts, and to arrange provision for the child.[98] They may suspect that a statement which, for example, fails to name a school specialising in treating autism is attributable to the fact that the LA has no such facility. Even if the parents obtain a statement, all is not necessarily plain sailing. Research indicates that although statements dictate the type of educational provision for the child, they do not ensure quality of provision,[99] or indeed, any provision.[100] A LA may cease to maintain a statement claiming that it is no longer necessary.[101] Even so, parents' desperation to obtain a SEN statement for their child is understandable. They know that with such a document, they have formal and legally authoritative recognition of their child's needs[102] and that he or she should receive extra funding from the LA's budget.

In contrast, the governors of the school which a child attends without a statement, are merely required to 'use their best endeavours ... to secure that, if any registered pupil has special educational needs, the special educational provision which his learning difficulty calls for is made'.[103] Parents whose child is without a statement also find that no legal procedure exists whereby they can challenge a school for failing to follow LA advice[104] over how to meet their child's educational needs,[105] or for failing to design an effective

---

[93] Audit Commission (2002a) pp. 18–20.

[94] *SEN Code of Practice*, para. 8.134 and the Education (Special Educational Needs)(England) Consolidation Regulations 2001 (SI 2001/3455).

[95] Audit Commission (2002a) at p. 35. [96] Discussed above.

[97] M. King and D. King (2006) pp. 35–6. [98] HCESC (2006a) para. 99.

[99] Ofsted (2006) para. 58. [100] J. Bercow (2008) paras. 3.26–3.27.

[101] But in doing so, they must comply with a specified procedure; EA 1996, Sch. 27, paras. 10–11 and *SEN Code of Practice*, paras. 8.117–8.120. The parents have a right of appeal (EA 1996, Sch. 27, para. 11(2)(b)). E.g. *R (Jane W) v. Blaenau Gwent Borough Council and anor* [2003] EWHC 2880 (Admin), [2004] ELR 152.

[102] Audit Commission (2002a) p. 36.

[103] EA 1996, s. 317(1)(a). L. Lundy (1998) esp. pp. 47–9: LA lack of accountability.

[104] *SEN Code of Practice*, paras. 8.15–8.20: the LA may accompany its formal refusal to statement a child with a 'note in lieu' explaining its decision and detailing suitable strategies which might be taken by the school to meet the child's needs. Notes in lieu sometimes lack detail; e.g. *O v. London Borough of Harrow and Sherwin* [2001] EWCA Civ 2046, [2002] ELR 195: parents' appeal against the LEA's refusal to statement their child allowed, largely because the note in lieu was inadequate.

[105] But EA 1996, s. 496 might be utilised to complain to the Secretary of State over the LA or school's failure to perform their statutory duties.

programme of measures to address his or her problem.[106] The special educational needs co-ordinator (SENCO) in charge of such a programme may not even be a qualified teacher.[107] Although parents may argue that their child's needs are not being met by the local school, the LA may still refuse to accept responsibility by statementing the child. Challenging an LA or school for failing to address a child's learning difficulties adequately is no easy task. The complicated requirements of the law of tort make actions in negligence problematic[108] and judicial review applications are expensive and cumbersome. The SEN appeal process is infinitely preferable[109] and statistics show that parents are reasonably successful when they use it.[110] Nevertheless, it too carries difficulties. In practice, it is often costly, since if an appeal hangs on the child's condition, parents may feel obliged to commission expert reports. In many cases they will instruct their own legal representatives.[111]

The legal aspects of an appeal may be complicated, particularly if there is an overlap between SEN and disability issues.[112] Furthermore, parents must remember that LAs are under no obligation to provide a child 'with the best possible education', or 'to provide [such] a Utopian system'.[113] It is arguable that Slade LJ's robust rejection of the idea that LAs are obliged to educate such a child 'to his maximum potential' is less sustainable now that they are specifically required not only to promote 'high standards'[114] and 'a fair access to educational opportunity',[115] but also 'the fulfilment by every child concerned of his educational potential'.[116] It will be for the courts to work out the practical implications of such a duty, which in the case of a severely disabled child, could be far reaching. Meanwhile, given the relative weakness of the guarantees provided by A2P1 of the ECHR, a challenge under the HRA 1998 is unlikely to improve parents' chances. As long as a child is not being entirely denied 'effective' education, the Strasbourg jurisprudence makes it clear that detailed operational decisions over how it is delivered, within the resources available, are within the discretion of a state's own educational authorities. Indeed, recent domestic case law considering the scope of A2P1

---

[106] *SEN Code of Practice*, paras. 6.58–6.60: a school-based programme should be detailed in an individual education plan (IEP) by the school's SENCO, listing inter alia, the pupil's short-term targets, teaching strategies and provision to be made. NB Audit Commission (2007) p. 44: the targets in IEPs (and statements) are too variable and insufficiently focused on measurable outcomes to be used for measuring outcomes and progress of pupils with complex SEN.

[107] But see DCSF (2008c): the government intends to require mainstream schools to employ only qualified teachers as SENCOs.

[108] Discussed below.

[109] *O v. London Borough of Harrow and Sherwin* [2001] EWCA Civ 2046, [2002] ELR 195, per Simon Brown LJ, at [19]: parents should not be forced to use judicial review, if appealing to the SEN tribunal (now SEND) is possible instead.

[110] SENDIST (2008) p. 9: 80% of appeals decided in 2006/7 were partly/fully upheld, as in 2005/6.

[111] HCESC (2006a) paras. 211–15.   [112] Discussed below.

[113] *R v. Surrey County Council Education Committee, ex p H* (1984) 83 LGR 219 at 235.

[114] EA 1996, s. 13A(1)(a).   [115] EA 1996, s. 13A(1)(b).   [116] EA 1996, s. 13A(1)(c).

of the ECHR suggests that the term 'effective' is gradually being rendered meaningless.[117]

Meanwhile, the government disapproves of large numbers of children with learning difficulties being statemented unnecessarily,[118] especially if their needs are not complex and are well within the scope of school-based intervention. The bureaucratic statementing process is enormously expensive[119] and often involves extreme delays in producing additional resources. The government therefore considers that LAs should promote parents' confidence in the ability of mainstream schools to provide effectively for this larger group of unstatemented children.[120] Nevertheless, this is surely over-optimistic. Few schools or LAs are even particularly clear what difference their provision makes to the attainment and progress of such pupils, with inadequate monitoring mechanisms in place.[121] It is can be of no surprise that to many parents, a SEN statement remains the gold standard.

(C) The overlap between SEN and disability discrimination protection

The now extensive disability discrimination legislation may encourage parents to combine an appeal to SEND against the LA's decision about their child's learning difficulties with a complaint about the less favourable, and therefore discriminatory, provision currently made for him or her by the school.[122] Whilst the introduction of further protection for disabled children is welcome,[123] it undoubtedly confuses parents, schools and LAs alike. This must explain why the tribunal service currently deals with a tiny number of disability

---

[117] Inter alia: *Ali v. Head Teacher and Governors of Lord Grey School* [2006] UKHL 14, [2006] 2 All ER 457, per Lord Bingham, at [24]: the guarantee contained in A2P1 of the ECHR is 'a weak one, and deliberately so', providing no convention guarantee of education of a particular kind or quality; per Lord Hoffmann, at [61]: infringement of A2P1 of the ECHR requires evidence of a systemic failure of the education system leading to a denial of 'access to a minimum level of education'. See also *A v. Essex County Council* [2008] EWCA Civ 364, [2008] ELR 321, per Sedley LJ, at [7]–[15], confirming the view of Field J in the court below. A2P1 of the ECHR is not infringed if an SEN pupil is out of school for nearly 18 months (albeit being provided with two boxes of educational activities to do at home) whilst a suitable school is found for him or her; *R (O) v. London Borough of Hackney* [2006] EWHC 3405, [2007] ELR 405, per Kenneth Parker QC, at [35]: the quality of education required by A2P1 of the ECHR is set at a relatively low threshold – so offering a SEN pupil a place at a failing school does not infringe its terms.

[118] DfES (2004b) Introduction.

[119] Audit Commission (2002a) p. 14: LEAs were probably spending more than £90m pa on statutory assessments and writing statements.

[120] DfES (2004b) pp. 18–19.

[121] Ofsted (2002) para. 15; Audit Commission (2002b) paras. 104–21; Ofsted (2006) paras. 52–4.

[122] Claims can be consolidated and heard by the same tribunal if the same facts may give rise to a SEN and a disability discrimination claim. E.g. *VK v. Norfolk County Council and the Special Educational Needs and Disability Tribunal* [2004] EWHC 2921 (Admin), [2005] ELR 342.

[123] I.e. the scope of DDA 1995 was extended by SENDA 2001, Pt. 2 to every aspect of education and by the DDA 2005, amending the definition of 'disability' and imposing the 'Disability Equality Duty'.

discrimination claims, compared with the number of SEN appeals.[124] Indeed, given the complicated nature of this specialised field of law,[125] the lack of public funding for representation before SEND is a matter of some concern.[126] Schools and LAs must now identify and meet pupils' learning difficulties and also take account of the rights of disabled pupils. But not all disabled pupils have SEN and not all SEN pupils are disabled. For example, a physically handicapped child may be extremely able intellectually, but have difficulty negotiating the stairs and corridors of a local mainstream school. Meanwhile, a physically strong and fit child may have severe learning difficulties. Some children suffer a multiplicity of disabilities, with behavioural disorders and learning difficulties accompanying physical disabilities.

Many consider that the two legislative schemes do not work alongside each other effectively, with the fundamental problem being the difference in thinking behind them.[127] As Harris points out, the primary aim of the elaborate SEN framework is to identify and ensure that pupils with learning difficulties receive education appropriate for their needs. The aims of the discrimination legislation are broader. Adopting a much stronger rights-based approach, it seeks to widen access to institutions and facilities, promoting equality of opportunity, changing attitudes and generally creating a more inclusive society.[128] Every governing body of mainstream schools must now make arrangements to accommodate disabled pupils satisfactorily in their schools,[129] promote their equality,[130] publish a disability equality scheme[131] and generally take steps proactively to eliminate discrimination.[132] But time will tell whether they take their duties more seriously than those imposed by the 2001 legislation.[133]

When considering schools' more specific duties, the 'increasing confusion between SEN and disability' noted by the HCESC becomes comprehensible.[134] As Jackman observes, since both learning difficulties and clinically recognised mental illnesses are recognised in the phrase 'mental impairment', many parents assume that their child can claim the benefit of both sets of

---

[124] SENDIST (2008): in 2006/07, the Tribunal disposed of 2,013 SEN appeals, cf. only 84 disability discrimination claims.

[125] N. Harris (2007) pp. 168–76.   [126] A. Jackman (2005) p. 968.

[127] HCESC (2006a) para. 105.   [128] N. Harris (2007) p. 166.

[129] DDA 1995, ss. 28D and E (introduced by SENDA 2001): schools are required to plan to increase access to education for disabled pupils and to produce accessibility plans covering access to premises, the curriculum and written information in alternative formats (the first by April 2003). See D. Silas and D. Wolfe (2005) pp. 82–3.

[130] DDA 1995, Part 5A, s. 49A (introduced by DDA 2005): the 'general duty'.

[131] DDA 1995, s. 49D: the 'specific duty'. See DRC (2005) ch. 3: schools must assess the impact of policies and practices which directly or indirectly affect disabled pupils and set out the steps to be taken to remove any discrimination or potential discrimination.

[132] HCESC (2006b) Ev. 170, The Law Society.

[133] Ofsted (2004) para. 103: over half of the schools visited had no disability access plans and those that did exist focused only on accommodation.

[134] HCESC (2006a) para. 35.

legislation.[135] But in some cases, SEND may not consider matters to be so clear-cut, holding a preliminary hearing to decide whether the legal definition of disability is met.[136] This will depend on the individual facts and the extent to which the child's impairment affects his or her access to education.[137] Thus in the case of very severely physically and/or mentally impaired children, there will be little question of their right to receive protection from the disability discrimination legislation. It is unlawful for schools to discriminate[138] against disabled pupils or prospective pupils in relation to admissions, exclusions and the provision of education and associated services.[139] Parents may well be able to establish that the school treated their child less favourably than the other pupils,[140] but in each case, an appropriate 'comparator' must be found.[141] There are limits to the school's obligations; if less favourable treatment is made out, the discrimination may be found to have been justified[142] and it may have made reasonable adjustments to the pupil's disability.[143] In any event, it need not remove or alter a physical feature or provide auxiliary aids to avoid

---

[135] A. Jackman (2005) p. 966.

[136] DDA 1995, s. 1: a disabled person is one who 'has a physical or mental impairment which has a substantial and long-term adverse effect on his ability to carry out normal day-to-day activities'.

[137] A. Jackman (2005) p. 966. E.g. *M v. SW School and the Special Educational Needs and Disability Tribunal* [2004] EWHC 2586 (Admin), [2005] ELR 285, per Mr James Goudie QC, at [11]: 'Whether an adverse effect was "substantial" had to be assessed by considering whether the effect of the impairment on the person's ability to carry out normal day-to-day activities was more than minor or trivial.'

[138] DDA 1995, s. 28B(1)(a) and (b): a responsible body (school) 'discriminates' against a pupil if – (i) for a reason relating to his disability it treats him less favourably than it treats or would treat others to whom that reason does not or would not apply, and it cannot be shown that that treatment is justified or (ii) (s. 28C(2)): it fails, without justification, to take reasonable steps to avoid placing him or her at a substantial disadvantage – the 'reasonable adjustments' duty.

[139] DDA 1995, s. 28A.

[140] DDA 1995, s. 28A(1) and/or s. 28C(1). I.e. by producing proof that through the admissions procedure or the services provided by the school he suffered a substantial disadvantage. See generally DRC (2002) Part 5.

[141] See *Lewisham London Borough Council v. Malcolm* [2008] UKHL 43, [2008] 4 All ER 525; discussed in Chapter 6 in the context of permanent exclusions.

[142] I.e. under DDA 1995, s. 28B(1)(b). But see also s. 28B(7) – less favourable treatment can only be justified if it is 'for a reason material to the circumstances of the case and substantial'; and s. 28B (8) – the less favourable treatment cannot be justified if the school has not made reasonable adjustments for the pupil's disabilities (i.e. under s. 28C) unless the less favourable treatment could be justified despite reasonable adjustments being made. See *R (T) v. Independent Appeal Panel for Devon County Council* [2007] EWHC 763, [2007] ELR 499, per Walker J, at [43]. See also Chapter 6.

[143] I.e. under DDA 1995, s. 28C(1)(b). E.g. *K v. The School and the Special Educational Needs and Disability Tribunal* [2007] EWCA Civ 165, [2007] ELR 234, per Wall LJ, at [47]–[48]: by refusing to clean a 14-year-old paraplegic who was incontinent of faeces, the school had not discriminated against him under DDA 1995, s. 28B(2) or under s. 28C(1) because its refusal could be justified under s. 28B(1)(b) and the school had also complied with s. 28C(1)(b) by taking reasonable steps to adjust to his disability – the school had sought extra help from the LEA and had received a health and safety report indicating the risk of injury to the staff by lifting the boy.

discrimination.[144] Parents may also complain to SEND about the way in which schools discipline their children for behaviour which is solely attributable to their disability. Here they must show that the school behaved less favourably towards such a pupil compared with the way they would have disciplined a non-disabled equally badly behaved pupil.[145]

(5) Provision of timely and appropriate education

(A) A lack of inter-agency collaboration

The government constantly stresses the need for early intervention to ensure that children's learning difficulties are identified as soon as possible and provision is made to address them.[146] But it also acknowledges that this is not happening on a consistent basis.[147] Many families with disabled children spend their lives 'waiting'; they wait for equipment, which when it arrives is wrong, they wait in clinics for treatment, they wait too long for various types of assessment and therapy.[148] Disabled children often have complex needs; in addition to their need for education, they may need speech therapy, physiotherapy, occupational therapy and the whole family may need support of various kinds, such as respite care. All these services, have in the past, been delivered by separate public agencies, with early and rapid intervention being hampered by a lack of effective collaboration between them. The impact of this failure to work together can affect every aspect of a disabled child's life, and that of his or her family. 'For disabled children, young people and their families, navigating their way through the mass of services is a frustrating, time-consuming, repetitive and distressing process.'[149] Read *et al.* summarise matters well:

> The lack of commitment to joint planning and development between agencies, geographical boundaries that are not coterminous, disputes over agencies' respective responsibilities, a lack of clarity about responsibility for disabled children in some health authorities, concerns about resources, underdeveloped mechanisms for interagency cooperation and inadequate management information systems are some of the issues that have been identified as creating barriers to the delivery of coordinated services to disabled children and their families.[150]

The government recognises this and a plethora of reports and guidance documents have urged local agencies, education, social services and health, to co-ordinate the manner in which they identify and remedy the special needs of children with complex problems,[151] for example, through establishing pooled

---

[144] DDA 1995, s. 28C(2).
[145] This is the impact of *Lewisham London Borough Council v. Malcolm* [2008] UKHL 43, [2008] 4 All ER 525. See DCSF (2008d) para. 70(c); further discussed in Chapter 6.
[146] DfES (2004b) ch. 1, PMSU (2005) pp. 105–8.   [147] HM Treasury and DfES (2007) pp. 35–7.
[148] Audit Commission (2003) p. 33.   [149] Audit Commission (2003) p. 17.
[150] J. Read *et al.* (2006) p. 58.   [151] Ibid., summarised at pp. 58–9 and 81–3.

budgets.[152] Despite some progress, there remains 'inadequate provision, poor coordination of services ... resulting in anxiety, delays, multiple assessments and confusion'.[153] The government is now putting its faith in the need for all public agencies working with children to co-operate[154] and integrate their service provision under the organisational structure of children's trusts. But there remains considerable resistance to joint working across the agencies, particularly at the commissioning stage.[155] Bercow observes: 'the impression we gained from our visits around the country was that coherent strategies for children and young people using a joint commissioning framework, shared goals and integrated service delivery were rare.'[156]

Whilst education and children's social care may be forced to work together under the umbrella of a children's trust, professionals employed by primary care trusts (PCTs) receive their budgets from the Department of Health. Joint working with health has been problematic for many years. Researchers found PCT budget holders frankly admitting efforts to minimise their contributions to joint placements and there being a strong perception that 'health is not "doing its bit"'.[157] Indeed, they found that there were no pooled budgets that included health, with poor joint budget planning for services for children with complex needs between councils and local health services.[158] Bercow similarly found the tension between LAs and PCTs to be a recurrent theme, with 'limited evidence of joint working between them'.[159] Nor do the provisions of the CA 2004[160] appear to prevent health authorities relying on the strict letter of the law to justify not assisting the LA's education service with the provision of specialised health services.[161] A hard pressed PCT could still argue that such assistance is incompatible with its own statutory obligations.[162] It is not yet clear whether government plans to place children's trusts on a statutory basis will improve matters in this respect.[163]

In the context of providing effective educational services for children with learning difficulties, the official guidance emphasises that support for children

---

[152] Health Act 1999, s. 31 provides for 'partnership arrangements' between health authorities, NHS trusts, primary care trusts and LAs, involving powers to pool funds and delegate functions between agencies.

[153] HM Treasury and DfES (2007) para. 3.49.   [154] CA 2004, ss. 10–11.

[155] J. Bercow (2008) paras. 3.11–3.13; see also Audit Commission (2007) paras. 24 and 31.

[156] J. Bercow (2008) para. 4.3; see also Audit Commission (2008) paras. 94–102.

[157] Audit Commission (2007) para. 56.   [158] Ibid. at paras. 57–8.

[159] J. Bercow (2008) para. 3.28.   [160] I.e. CA 2004, ss. 10–11.   [161] EA 1996, s. 322(1).

[162] EA 1996, s. 322(3). E.g. *R v. Brent and Harrow Health Authority, ex p Harrow London Borough Council* [1997] 3 FCR 765: QBD of the High Court rejected (on judicial review brought by the education authority) that the health authority had acted unreasonably by agreeing only to assist the education authority with half the speech, language and occupational therapy sessions required by a SEN child suffering from cerebral palsy. Since the statutory forerunner of EA 1996, s. 322 only imposed an obligation on the district health authority to assist the LEA 'unless having regard to the resources available to them ... it is not reasonable for them to comply with' such a request, the health authority was entitled to ration its scarce resources by tailoring the child's needs to the resources available.

[163] Apprenticeships, Skills, Children and Learning Bill 2009, Part 9.

with SENs requires a 'concerted approach' from health, education, social services and other providers of support services. It optimistically urges the provision of an integrated service which is perceived by parents and pupils as being 'seamless'.[164] Parents of children with learning difficulties who have strong views over what school their child should attend often discover that there is no integrated 'seamless' service. Indeed, they may find themselves in the middle of a turf war between the agencies over funding the services required. A not uncommon problem for parents lies in the fact that the child's day does not end when he leaves school everyday. His behaviour at home may be impossibly stressful, especially if he needs constant supervision day and night.[165] They may therefore conclude that the only solution is for him to attend a residential school. One might imagine that if the parents nominated a maintained residential school, there would be little problem, since public resources would pay whether he stayed at home and attended a mainstream day school, assisted by further services or whether he attended a maintained residential school. Nevertheless, residential provision is normally extremely expensive[166] and endless disputes are fought out in SEND, with parents responding to the LA's education service's anxiety to avoid footing the bill.

In such a situation, the parents' lawyer will explain to them that the LA's education service is only legally obliged to arrange for (and fund) special 'educational' provision, as opposed to merely having a discretion to arrange for non-educational or 'care' provision.[167] Equally, SEND itself only has jurisdiction over educational matters[168] and so cannot direct a LA to make provision for the child's social needs or the parents' need for support.[169] This being so, the parents must satisfy the court that the services included in a 'waking-day' or 24-hour curriculum can be defined as educational, since without them their child will not acquire the skills required to reach his developmental objectives[170] – indeed, that his needs are so complex that structured residential provision is essential.[171] They can call on case law establishing that educational and care needs can, at times, overlap,[172] and that therapies and other care provided out of school hours may, depending on the circumstances, properly be

[164] SEN Code of Practice, para. 5.27.
[165] E.g. *W v. Leeds City Council and Special Educational Needs and Disability Tribunal* [2005] EWCA Civ 988, [2005] ELR 617.
[166] H. Stout (2007) p. 116.   [167] EA 1996, s. 324(5)(a)(i) and (ii).
[168] Specified in Part 3 of the statement of SEN. D. Wolfe (2003) pp. 227–8.
[169] These are set out in Parts 5 and 6 of the statement of SEN.
[170] E.g. *A v. Hertfordshire County Council* [2006] EWHC 3428 (Admin), [2007] ELR 95. See also H. Stout (2007) p. 116: the issue of whether or not such a curriculum is necessary possibly provokes more appeals to the SENDIST and the High Court than any other issue.
[171] E.g. *Oxfordshire County Council v. M and Special Educational Needs Tribunal* [2002] EWHC 2908, [2003] ELR 718.
[172] *London Borough of Bromley v. Special Educational Needs Tribunal and ors* [1999] ELR 260, per Sedley LJ, at 295–6.

described as 'educational' if the child cannot make significant educational progress without it.[173]

The LA will argue, however, that provision out of school hours is not educational and, moreover, is totally unnecessary. They will claim that their legal duties are fulfilled by their arranging for the pupil to attend a day school, with the family being provided with a non-educational 'care' or 'social' support package out of school hours, funded by the children's services arm of the LA (formerly the Social Services Department).[174] The parents may well consider that this disjointed package of support provided by education and children's services is (or is likely to be) far inferior to the consistent and structured provision available in a residential special school.[175] If, however, SEND agrees with the LA that a 24-hour curriculum cannot, in these circumstances, be described as educational, they must uphold the day school placement. But because of its narrow jurisdiction over purely educational matters, it cannot direct that the supporting care package suggested by the LA is provided. Nor can it ensure that the provision promised materialises, as it is unable to force the two public agencies to co-operate over adopting 'a holistic approach' to a child's complex set of needs.[176]

In the past, parents have been unable to argue that if their child attended a maintained residential school, the social services arm of the LA would save money – albeit through extra expense taken up by education.[177] Now, it seems, the logical impact of the integration of services under children's trusts is gradually creeping into this branch of law. Given the aims of the CA 2004, the courts may see no reason why the term 'public expenditure' should be confined to expenditure by one department alone, when the functions of the erstwhile LEA and social services department are being operated by the same corporate entity – a children's trust.[178] In other words, when considering whether the fees of a maintained residential school would amount to

---

[173] *R v. Lancashire County Council ex parte CM (a minor)* [1989] 2 FLR 279; *X and X v. Caerphilly Borough Council and Special Educational Needs and Disability Tribunal* [2004] EWHC 2140 (Admin), [2005] ELR 78. See also DfES (2001), SEN Code of Practice, para. 8.49.

[174] E.g. *London Borough of Bromley v. Special Educational Needs Tribunal and ors* [1999] ELR 260: a severely physically and mentally impaired 12-year-old pupil currently attended a special day school, fees £26,000 per annum paid from the LEA's direct budget and was accommodated in a residential respite home funded by the social services department; cf the fees of a special residential school, as requested by his parents, would be £46,000 per annum, to be paid wholly by the LEA.

[175] E.g. *W v. Leeds City Council and Special Educational Needs and Disability Tribunal* [2005] EWCA Civ 988, [2005] ELR 617: social services provision was criticised as being deficient. See also *R (LH and MH) v. London Borough of Lambeth* [2006] EWHC 1190 (Admin), [2006] 2 FLR 1275.

[176] *W v. Leeds City Council and Special Educational Needs and Disability Tribunal*, ibid., per Wall LJ, at [50]–[51].

[177] E.g. *C v. Special Educational Needs Tribunal* [1997] ELR 390 and *S v. Somerset County Council* [2002] EWHC 1808 (Admin), [2003] ELR 78.

[178] *O v. London Borough of Lewisham* [2007] EWHC 2130 (Admin), [2007] ELR 633, per Andrew Nicol QC, at [30]–[41].

'unreasonable public expenditure',[179] SEND need not distinguish between the costs saved to a council in one capacity rather than another.[180] But with the continued resistance to joint working, matters clearly will not improve overnight.[181]

(B) Legal accountability

The law of negligence reinforces the official guidance urging early identification of a child's learning difficulties. Indeed, it indicates that schools and LAs who fail to take appropriate action to diagnose and properly assess children's learning difficulties, or provide appropriate educational assistance, may be liable in damages to the children concerned. The House of Lords' decision in *Phelps v. Hillingdon London Borough Council*,[182] together with subsequent case law,[183] clearly establishes that LAs and their employees owe a duty of care to their pupils and must exercise reasonable professional skill in responding to their SENs.[184] LAs can therefore be held vicariously liable in negligence if educational practitioners, such as teachers, educational psychologists and education officers,[185] fail to exercise reasonable skill and care when diagnosing learning difficulties and when determining and delivering educational provision appropriate to address them. It remains uncertain whether LAs could also be found *directly* liable in negligence for their own actions.[186] But the issue has little practical importance, since vicarious liability could lie in all but the most exceptional circumstances.

Some deplored the decision in *Phelps*, arguing that negligence actions are an extremely expensive and inefficient way of improving educational standards.[187] Subsequent case law demonstrates, however, that concerns about it having

---

[179] Under EA 1996, s. 9; discussed below.

[180] *O v. London Borough of Lewisham* [2007] EWHC 2130 (Admin), [2007] ELR 633, per Andrew Nicol QC, at [41].

[181] E. Wright (2007) p. 91.

[182] *Phelps v. Hillingdon London Borough Council, Anderton v. Clwyd County Council, Jarvis v. Hampshire County Council, Re G (a minor)* (hereafter *Phelps*) [2000] 4 All ER 504, confirming the principles established in relation to 'the education cases' by the House of Lords in *X (minors) v. Bedfordshire County Council; M (a minor) and anor v. Newham London Borough Council and ors; E (a minor) v. Dorset County Council; Christmas v. Hampshire County Council; Keating v. Bromley London Borough Council* [1995] 2 AC 633.

[183] Discussed by T. Birtwhistle (2002) and N. Harris (2003).

[184] I.e. they must comply with the *Bolam* test, as established in *Bolam v. Friern Hospital Management Committee* [1957] 2 All ER 118.

[185] *Carty v. Croydon London Borough Council* [2005] EWCA Civ 19, [2005] 2 All ER 517: LAs may be vicariously liable for education officers' failings, despite their post carrying no formal qualifications.

[186] In *Phelps* [2000] 4 All ER 504, Lord Slynn of Hadley at 522, Lord Nicholls of Birkenhead at 531 and Lord Clyde at 538, all doubted the existence of LA direct liability. See also *Carty v. Croydon London Borough Council* [2005] EWCA Civ 19, [2005] 2 All ER 517, per Dyson LJ, at [36].

[187] Inter alia: A. Mullis (2001) p. 338; M. Harris (2001) p. 27.

opened 'floodgates' were ill founded.[188] Liability may certainly lie in a variety of situations, including the following: an educational psychologist fails to diagnose dyslexia and so fails to ensure that the pupil obtains specialised teaching; an educational psychologist diagnoses a learning difficulty that the pupil does not have and so the LA provides inappropriate provision, such as special schooling; the headteacher, knowing of a child's learning problems, does nothing about them; the LA, knowing of a child's learning problems, fails to address them in the way recommended by the educational psychologist.[189]

Whilst some litigants succeed, albeit not necessarily recovering all their costs (which may be considerable),[190] others find that there are simply too many hurdles to overcome. In the first place, since most claims are brought by 'children' once they attain adulthood, they may be statute barred.[191] Even if they are within time, the courts adopt a stringent approach to such claims, stressing that they should not be encouraged and that negligence should not be found too readily.[192] A negligence claim will fail if it rests solely on the failure of an educational practitioner to fulfil the LA's statutory duties,[193] since in those circumstances there is no common law duty of care owed to the pupil.[194] But there are further limitations. A claim in negligence cannot be brought based simply on poor quality of teaching, as opposed to the sort of cases where the diagnosis is hopelessly wrong.[195] Furthermore, it may be particularly difficult to show a direct link or 'causal connection' between the disability or suffering *presently* experienced by the child and the failure of the educational authorities in the first place.[196] Such problems are exacerbated by the need to establish facts many years after the claimed events occurred. Overall, it is clear that although the law supports the right of SEN children to have their needs diagnosed in a careful and professional manner and dealt with as early as possible, in practice, such a right may be difficult to enforce by parents during the childhood of their child, and even more difficult for the child to do so, once grown.

---

[188] D. Hay (2005) p. 535.

[189] All these scenarios are broadly similar to the cases dealt with in *Phelps* [2000] 4 All ER 504.

[190] E.g. *Clark v. Devon County Council* [2005] EWCA Civ 266, [2005] 2 FLR 747.

[191] Inter alia: *Adams v. Bracknell Forest Borough Council* [2003] EWCA Civ 706, [2003] ELR 409; *Rowe v. Kingston-upon-Hull Council and Essex County Council* [2003] EWCA Civ 1281, [2003] ELR 771; *Meherali v. Hampshire County Council* [2002] EWHC 2655, [2003] ELR 338. A claim for personal damages must normally be brought within three years of the 'child' attaining 18 years or becoming aware of having suffered significant injury and the availability of a remedy.

[192] *Phelps* [2000] 4 All ER 504, per Lord Slynn, at 519. See also *Carty v. Croydon London Borough Council* [2005] EWCA Civ 19, [2005] 2 All ER 517, per Dyson LJ, at [78].

[193] E.g. the LA's duty to reassess the claimant's educational needs after a change of circumstances, as in *Carty*, ibid.

[194] *Carty v. Croydon London Borough Council* [2005] EWCA Civ 19, [2005] 2 All ER 517, per Dyson LJ, at [51].

[195] *Phelps* [2000] 4 All ER 504, per Lord Nicholls of Birkenhead, at 531.

[196] E.g. *Meherali v. Hampshire County Council* [2002] EWHC 2655, [2003] ELR 338 and *Carty v. Croydon London Borough Council* [2005] EWCA Civ 19, [2005] 2 All ER 517.

(6) Disabled children and their right to inclusion within mainstream schools

A developing acceptance of the social model of disability was linked in this country, during the 1980s and 1990s, with the view that disabled children should be given opportunities for inclusion in mainstream services, more particularly in mainstream education.[197] Criticism was directed at the way that disabled children had been commonly segregated in special schools,[198] and provided with a narrower form of education, often of inferior quality. It was argued that this approach started such children on a course of unequal opportunities which would continue for the rest of their lives.[199] Many advocates of an inclusive education regard it as a human rights issue that *all* children should be included in mainstream schools, with the consequent closure of all special schools, a view which seems to be endorsed by the UN Convention on the Rights of Persons with Disabilities.[200] Opposing those who favour a more moderate approach to inclusion, they argue that the retention of any special schools results in considerable resources being locked within the special school system and mainstream schools 'not [being] required (or resourced) to adapt to become fully inclusive schools meeting the full range of pupil diversity'.[201] Furthermore, they claim that the retention of special schools for those with complex needs and profound impairment means that the more able children get 'creamed off', with those left behind being 'hidden away'.[202] There is also the incontrovertible view that:

> inclusion in mainstream education not only benefits many disabled children, providing the right to enjoy the same equality of opportunity as their non-disabled peers, but non-disabled children also benefit from being educated in a diverse and inclusive environment, which will lead to a reduction of oppressive attitudes towards disabled people.[203]

The current government enthusiastically embraced the concept of inclusion when it came to power,[204] declaring 'there are strong educational, as well as social and moral grounds for educating children with SEN with their peers'.[205] Subsequently, in its SEN strategy, it stressed that special schools should be regarded as a facility to be used only as a last resort for children with severe and complex needs. Furthermore, LAs should be planning on the basis that the proportion of children educated in special schools should fall, as mainstream schools developed a capacity to meet their needs.[206] This policy bore fruit, with

---

[197] J. Read *et al.* (2006) pp. 31–3.
[198] EA 1996, s. 337: a 'special school' is one 'specially organised to make special educational provision for pupils with special educational needs and is for the time being approved by the Secretary of State'.
[199] J. Read *et al.* (2006) p. 142.   [200] Discussed above.   [201] I. Lunt (2007) p. 109.
[202] HCESC (2006b) Ev. 271, Alliance for Inclusive Education.
[203] HCESC (2006b) Ev. 170, The Law Society.
[204] N. Harris (2007) pp. 332–41.   [205] DfEE (1997) p. 43.   [206] DfES (2004b) para. 2.15.

the number of statemented children attending mainstream schools increasing significantly, the number attending special schools remaining constant,[207] and the gradual closure of some maintained and non-maintained special schools.[208]

It is clear that, despite the criticisms of the SEN framework, inclusion can work well if schools are properly supported by central and local government policies, support services, funding and highly trained staff.[209] Indeed, Ofsted maintains that whilst pupils with LDDs are as likely to make good progress in their academic, personal and social development in mainstream schools as in special schools, 'pupils had the best chance of making good progress in all three areas in resourced mainstream schools'. Furthermore, 'a greater proportion of this provision was outstanding and it was seldom inadequate'.[210] Nevertheless, the experience of many parents whose children with LDDs attend mainstream schools is very different. Clearly the policy of 'total inclusion' has attracted considerable hostility, being associated with the hesitance of LAs to issue statements,[211] and the closure of the special schools that parents have fought to keep in existence.[212] Alongside Baroness Warnock,[213] its critics, including some of the charities representing disabled children,[214] now argue that attending a mainstream school is not practical or realistic for all children and, worse that it can produce deep unhappiness. A disabled child will not necessarily fit in happily into a mainstream school, especially if it is large, with noisy classrooms and playgrounds. They may find it difficult to make friends with their non-disabled peers, and need more specialised help with the social and practical skills that non-disabled children learn routinely as they grow up. Indeed, the shortage of speech and language therapists means that children with speech and communication difficulties often do not receive the help that they need to interact with their peers.[215] As they grow older, teasing may turn into bullying[216] – whereas in

---

[207] HCESC (2006a) Annex, p. 88: between 1991 and 2000, there was a 90% increase in statemented pupils attending mainstream schools, with the number of statemented pupils attending special schools remaining relatively constant. DCSF (2007a) Chart C: between 2000 and 2007, the number of SEN statemented children in mainstream schools fell by 5.7% (currently 57%); those in maintained and independent special schools and PRUs remained relatively constant (currently nearly 43%) but with the number in mainstream special schools reducing and those in independent special schools increasing by 31%.

[208] HCESC (2006a) Annex, p. 90.

[209] HCESC (2006b) Ev. 155, The Advisory Centre for Education.

[210] Ofsted (2006) paras. 12–13.

[211] DCSF (2007a) Chart D: the number of children for whom a SEN statement was made for the first time fell between 1998 and 2006 from 36,180 to 22,600.

[212] HCESC (2006a) para. 58.   [213] M. Warnock (2005) ch. 3.

[214] HCESC (2006a) para. 80: e.g. the National Autistic Society and Mencap. See also C. Low (2007): blind and partially sighted children; L. Wing (2007): severely autistic children; J. Jarvis (2007): deaf pupils – all three authors criticise the concept of 'total inclusion', arguing that many mainstream schools are unable to provide satisfactorily for these disabilities.

[215] J. Bercow (2008) paras. 1.4–1.10. One-third of the respondents reported (para. 3.41) a shortage of speech and language therapists, with a wide regional variation in provision (para. 5.8).

[216] Mencap (2007): 82% of children with learning disability have experienced bullying and are twice as likely to be bullied as other children.

special schools 'difference' is not obvious.[217] Clearly many of the appeals against permanent exclusions reflect the inability of some mainstream schools to cope with the demands of 'difficult' children[218] and the bullying that some experience, especially those with autistic spectrum disorders.[219]

Most worrying is the apparent inability of some mainstream schools to provide a stimulating education for pupils with LDDs or indeed, to include disabled pupils in an unqualified fashion. A continuing difficulty has been that many schools have no clear knowledge of what targets should be set for such pupils and therefore how well they are being helped to achieve them by the provision made.[220] Little wonder that there is 'insufficient academic challenge' and a 'fundamental weakness' in provision, if some schools still do not know what is 'satisfactory and good progress'.[221] The way in which some mainstream schools interpret the concept of inclusion has also produced concerns. As Ofsted observes, 'inclusion' is a meaningless term for children, who despite being physically on the mainstream school site, are taught by a teaching assistant outside the class group for much of the day, isolated from their peers. Such pupils have a 'lonely experience each day'.[222] Furthermore, the teaching assistants, on which mainstream schools rely so heavily for help with pupils with LDDs, are often poorly paid and may lack training, with their duties being inadequately planned or co-ordinated with class teachers.[223] Pupils 'kept engaged' by teaching assistants make little educational progress,[224] even when they are intellectually unimpaired.[225] Predictably, Ofsted research indicates that the pupils who make the greatest academic progress are those who work with specialist teachers, rather than teaching assistants.[226] But this type of provision is expensive, and apparently beyond the means of many LAs and schools. As MacBeath et al. observe: 'If inclusion means anything it is the right to be taught by a suitably qualified teacher. Currently that principle is frequently breached.'[227]

Research indicates that one reason for the failure of the inclusion movement is mainstream teachers' inability to make sufficient adjustments to their existing practice,[228] often combined with the lack of sufficient training to assist them with pupils with complex needs.[229] But even adjustments and more training[230]

---

[217] J. MacBeath et al. (2006) p. 58.   [218] Ibid. at p. 30.
[219] E.g. *McAuley Catholic High School v. C and ors* [2003] EWHC 3045 (Admin), [2004] 2 All ER 436.
[220] Audit Commission (2002b) paras. 113 and 112; Ofsted (2006) paras. 45–57; Audit Commission (2007) para. 82.
[221] Ofsted (2006) para. 52.   [222] Ofsted (2004) para. 74.
[223] Ibid. at para. 72. See also J. MacBeath et al. (2006) pp. 22–4 and 38–40.
[224] Ofsted (2004) para. 72.   [225] J. MacBeath et al. (2006) p. 39.   [226] Ofsted (2006) para. 21.
[227] J. MacBeath et al. (2006) p. 65.   [228] Ofsted (2004) paras. 29 and 81.
[229] J. MacBeath et al. (2006) pp. 37–8.
[230] DCSF (2007b) para. 3.117: the government promised £18m to fund better teacher training on the needs of children with LDDs. The government also plans to ensure that all SENCOs must have a teaching qualification.

might not overcome the problem consistently voiced by teachers in mainstream schools that some pupils are particularly disruptive or demonstrate disturbing behaviour and consequently occupy disproportionate amounts of their time.[231] Children with behavioural, emotional and social difficulties (BESD)[232] pose particular challenges, partly due to the way that their behaviour often distracts other pupils.[233] Research shows that their learning needs remain unidentified for too long, and then that inadequate provision is made for them.[234] Teaching problems are also exacerbated by the long wait experienced by many schools in obtaining appropriate support for pupils with LDDs, such as speech and language therapists, educational psychologists and physiotherapists.[235] As complaints to the Local Ombudsman show, the support may not materialise at all, even when specified in the pupil's statement of SEN.[236] Indeed, Blair comments somewhat caustically: 'Inclusion is now often characterised as a cheap alternative to special education and the funds for support in the mainstream are often fought for or simply, as in this case, not forthcoming.'[237]

Perhaps in response to this more critical outlook, the government itself now appears to be adjusting its position, asserting that it does not wish to see the closure of special schools and that they have a 'vital and continuing role' as part of an inclusive education system. It approves of the way that large numbers of special schools have links with local mainstream schools and is now funding a new series of 'SEN *specialist* schools' to 'provide outreach to mainstream schools'.[238] But although in policy terms, the government may appear confusingly ambivalent over the concept of inclusion,[239] legislation reflects its early commitment to disabled children sharing the opportunities available to their non-disabled peers. In the first place, such children should no longer find themselves effectively excluded from mainstream schools by unfavourable admissions criteria.[240] Second, there is a clear (and strengthened[241]) legal obligation on LAs to educate all children with SEN in a mainstream school,[242] unless, in the case of a statemented child, his or her parents object,[243] or it would be incompatible with the efficient education of other children.[244]

---

[231] J. MacBeath *et al.* (2006) pp. 30–7.   [232] Formerly described as 'EBSD'.

[233] A. Steer (2005) para. 132.   [234] Ofsted (2004) para. 77 and Ofsted (2006) para. 60.

[235] A. Steer (2005) para. 130; J. MacBeath *et al.* (2006) p. 26; J. Bercow (2008) para. 2.13.

[236] E.g. *Cornwall County Council* – 04/B/07871, discussed by A. Blair (2006) p. 212.

[237] A. Blair (2006) p. 213.   [238] HM Government (2006) p. 26, emphasis added.

[239] HCESC (2006a) paras. 74–87.   [240] DDA 1995, s. 28C, discussed above.

[241] Strengthened by SENDA 2001. For a discussion of the history of these amendments, see D. Silas and D. Wolfe (2005) p. 84.

[242] EA 1996, s. 316 (as amended by SENDA 2001, s. 1). NB EA 1996, s. 316(2): all SEN children *without* statements must be educated in mainstream schools.

[243] EA 1996, s. 316(3)(a). But, as explained below, the parental preference exception is secondary to the Sch. 27 process which must be exhausted first.

[244] EA 1996, s. 316(3)(b). But NB EA 1996, s. 316A(5) and (6): this exception only applies if the LA or school can show that they cannot take any reasonable steps to prevent such incompatibility. N. Harris (2007) pp. 334.

Many parents consider special schools to be a stigmatising option for their child and that he or she could cope perfectly well with the demands of mainstream education.[245] They may assume from the strengthened legislative commitment to mainstream schooling that they can choose mainstream schools for their children, just like parents of the unimpaired. Indeed, presumably in an attempt to prevent the interminable delays that often hamper the education of children with LDDs, the admissions guidance directs that such children should be placed quickly.[246] But parental frustration is caused by the legislation apparently giving them choice over the school to be named in their child's statement,[247] but then allowing the LA to discount such a choice – for the sake of other children's efficient education or the efficient use of resources.[248] Parents in this situation may benefit from the fact that once their own choice of school has been duly considered and overridden on either of these grounds, the general statutory presumption in favour of mainstream education[249] then cuts in. At that point there should be a further consideration of all the placement options, in order to decide what school should be named in the statement.[250]

Other parents may be less enthusiastic about the concept of inclusion for their child.[251] Indeed, parents of children with very complex needs may be convinced that they need the more sheltered environment of a special school, with a 'waking day' curriculum. The LA may oppose such a choice, arguing that it is too expensive and that a day school, with support at home, is preferable. As discussed above, such scenarios may be dominated by inter-agency battles over who foots the bill. But if the parents convince SEND that such provision can be defined as 'educational', the LA's duty to provide a mainstream place for their child is then suspended by the parents' rejection of such a choice.[252] Furthermore, if the parents have found a maintained special residential school, there is a presumption in favour of the LA naming their choice in their child's SEN statement, unless the LA can establish the unsuitability or incompatibility criteria.[253] But parents do not have an absolute veto over mainstream education. The LA must make 'appropriate' educational provision for a child with SEN, so if a mainstream school is appropriate, then it should be named in the statement.

---

[245] E.g. *R (MH) v. Special Educational Needs and Disability Tribunal and London Borough of Hounslow* [2004] EWCA Civ 770, [2004] ELR 424.

[246] DCSF (2009) para. 3.47.   [247] HCESC (2006a) para. 191.

[248] EA 1996, Sch. 27, para. 3(3): the parents' choice of school must be adopted in the child's statement *unless* the LA considers: (a) such a choice to be unsuitable to the child's age, ability or aptitude or to his special educational needs, or (b) the child's attendance would be incompatible with the efficient education of the other pupils with whom he or she would be educated or with the efficient use of resources. See N. Harris (2007) pp. 341–8.

[249] I.e. EA 1996, s. 316(3).

[250] *R (MH) v. Special Educational Needs and Disability Tribunal and London Borough of Hounslow* [2004] EWCA Civ 770, [2004] ELR 424, per Jonathan Parker LJ, at [68]–[80]. Discussed by D. Silas and D. Wolfe (2005) pp. 85–6.

[251] E.g. C. Moore (2007).   [252] EA 1996, s. 316(1)(a).

[253] I.e. EA 1996, Sch. 27, para. 3(3)(a) and (b); fn 248 above.

Sometimes, parents want their child to attend an expensive independent school, believing the resources offered there to be far preferable to those in any mainstream school.[254] Whilst there is nothing to prevent parents paying for such education themselves,[255] they may fail to induce the LA to fund an independent school's fees.[256] The LA must do so if the state system simply cannot provide for the child's needs,[257] even if the school is outside England and Wales.[258] But it is entitled to refuse to follow the parents' preferences if it can ensure that the child would obtain 'appropriate' education' in a maintained school,[259] thereby avoiding unreasonable public expenditure.[260] When disputes over such decisions reach SEND, the tribunal will consider whether the extra expenditure is disproportionate to the educational advantages of the parents' preference.[261]

(7) The disabled child's right to individuality and educational independence

As discussed above, the education legislation makes great efforts to ensure that the parents of children with learning difficulties are very fully involved at all stages of deciding on appropriate educational support for them. But it is doubtful whether it maintains a satisfactory balance between protecting parents' rights to be involved and children's rights to be treated as distinct individuals. Undoubtedly, in the majority of cases it will be perfectly appropriate for parents to be involved in planning for their disabled children's education, since they have a more specialised knowledge of their needs than anyone else. Nevertheless, the risks of identifying parents' interests with those of their children, as the education legislation tends to do, are greater for disabled children, than for the unimpaired. Severely disabled children are often wholly dependent on their parents and many parents shoulder overwhelming burdens in terms of the care and attention which they provide. But in such circumstances, parental attitudes are extremely important and may not always be as helpful to their children as might be desired. Indeed, their anxieties may undermine their child's self-confidence and ability to deal with demanding

---

[254] E.g. *M v. Worcestershire County Council and Evans* [2002] EWHC 1292, [2003] ELR 31.

[255] EA 1996, s. 316A(1)(a).   [256] N. Harris (2007) pp. 345–7.

[257] *Oxfordshire County Council v. GB and ors* [2001] EWCA Civ 1358, [2002] ELR 8, per Sedley LJ, at [16].

[258] EA 1996, s. 320.   [259] EA 1996, s. 324(4)(a).

[260] Whilst the parents' choice of an independent school suspends the LA's obligation under s. 316 to place the child in a mainstream school, it must specify a school in his or her statement which would be 'appropriate for the child' (s. 324(4)), bearing in mind its duty under s. 9, to take account of the parents' wishes, but only 'so far as that is compatible with the provision of efficient instruction and training and the avoidance of unreasonable public expenditure'. *Oxfordshire County Council v. GB and ors* [2001] EWCA Civ 1358, [2002] ELR 8, per Sedley LJ, at [16].

[261] Ibid.

situations. In particular, they may be unable to assess objectively their child's intellectual, physical and social abilities and these attitudes may influence a child's ability to settle happily into a mainstream school. Moreover, disabled children are particularly vulnerable to physical and sexual abuse by their carers, be they parents[262] or staff of residential homes and schools.[263] There is an obvious need to consider the disabled child as a person in his or her own right, rather than accepting the parent's view of where and how the child should be educated.

The facts of *Re V (care or supervision order)*[264] illustrate vividly that parents may sometimes be incapable of assessing impartially their disabled child's real needs. A boy, S, aged 17, suffered from cerebral palsy, spastic quadriplegia, and had speech and learning difficulties. His mother's fiercely over-protective attitude towards him as he grew up led her to control every aspect of his life, finding excuses for not allowing him to attend a special school as a weekly boarder and making it impossible for him to have any social life. She would leave him on a sofa all day, without physical or intellectual stimulation and refused to act on professional advice urging her to change her ways. The LA eventually obtained a care order over him on the evidence that she was preventing his developing his full potential, physically, socially, emotionally or educationally. Such circumstances are obviously extreme but the case provides a salutary reminder that disabled children must be regarded as individuals in their own right.

It is important to maintain a balance between utilising parents' special knowledge of their disabled child's needs and respecting the child's own individuality. The Code of Practice encourages an enlightened approach by educational practitioners, in favour of involving SEN children far more than hitherto in decisions over their education. It asserts boldly:

> All children and young people have rights … Children and young people with special educational needs have a unique knowledge of their own needs and circumstances and their own views about what sort of help they would like to help them make the most of their education[265]

The risk of parents failing to perceive their children as individuals in their own right is tackled firmly:

> Some parents may need support in seeing their children as partners in education; they may be reluctant to involve their child in education decision-making perhaps considering them ill-equipped to grasp all the relevant factors.

---

[262] E.g. *Re X (disclosure for purposes of criminal proceedings)* [2008] EWHC 242 (Fam), [2008] 2 FLR 944: care proceedings had been brought regarding an autistic girl (B) and her child, conceived when she was 13 through father-daughter incest. The father had taken the lead role in keeping B out of school and socially isolating her at home.

[263] A. Paul *et al.* (2004) pp. 14–19: summarising the research evidence on the abuse of disabled children in institutions.

[264] [1996] 1 FLR 776.   [265] SEN Code of Practice, paras. 3.1–3.2.

And it goes on to state that:

> All children should be involved in making decisions where possible right from the start of their education. The ways in which children are encouraged to participate should reflect the child's evolving maturity[266]

Cannon criticises the language used in the Code for implying 'a drift towards *Gillick*-competence like thinking', whilst merely requiring children's views to be elicited, rather than followed.[267] This seems grudging given that, by devoting a complete chapter to 'Pupil Participation',[268] the Code emphasises pupil involvement more strongly than any other form of educational guidance. Its enlightened approach has not, however, found its way into many LAs or schools. The Audit Commission found that whilst there was a genuine desire to accommodate parents' wishes over choice of school, the children's views were seldom recorded in the SEN files, even over the parents' choice of a residential school.[269] Ofsted's research also indicates that the involvement by schools of pupils with LDDs in matters to do with their educational progress was 'too variable'. In some schools, these pupils were involved in decisions about their own individual learning and behaviour and in setting their own targets. But 'too often this was done superficially: pupils did not understand the purpose of the target setting and could not read the final outcome'. This was considered to be a significant problem, since pupils' understanding of their progress was crucial to developing independence and self-esteem.[270]

Nor do the legislation and regulations underpinning the SEN framework reflect the enlightened principles in the Code of Practice, assuming instead that the interests of children with SEN are united with those of their parents. The legislative provisions and accompanying official documentation governing appeals to SEND reflect an official view that it is parents who are entitled to make all educational choices on behalf of their child and to go through the appeals process. The child is clearly not expected to play any formal part in SEND proceedings, being provided with no independent representation or party status.[271] Children with LDDs have no right to initiate appeals themselves and so cannot do so in circumstances where they are on bad terms with their parents or the latter are not interested in their education. Thus an intelligent physically impaired adolescent living in a residential school on a 52-week placement would have no right to appeal against the LA if it decided to change the named school in his or her statement. Nor would a child with significantly mentally impaired parents have a right to appeal against any statement change. Furthermore, by assuming that there is no need for the child to be made a party to appeals to SEND, the legislation seems to ignore the possibility of parents

---

[266] Ibid.   [267] L. Cannon (2005) p. 118.   [268] *SEN Code of Practice*, ch. 3.
[269] Audit Commission (2007) para. 72.   [270] Ofsted (2006) para. 34.
[271] *S v. Special Educational Needs Tribunal and the City of Westminster* [1996] ELR 228 and *London Borough of Wandsworth v. Mrs K and Special Needs and Disability Tribunal* [2003] EWHC 1424 (Admin), [2003] ELR 554.

appealing against decisions over educational provision because they want to retain control over their child.[272]

The fact that a child is not a party to the proceedings makes it all the more important that the tribunal is fully conversant with the child's own views regarding an appeal. The current regulations governing SEND contain no provisions like those contained in the CA 1989, either directing the tribunal to consider the child's welfare as being paramount or, indeed, requiring it to take account of the child's wishes and feelings, so far as they are ascertainable. Even so, SEND's current procedures do reflect an awareness of the relevance of the child's views. Thus what had been known as 'Statement of parent's case'[273] has been renamed 'Child's statement'.[274] Furthermore, the LA must discover and state to the tribunal the views of the child on the matter it appeals, or explain why it has not ascertained the child's views.[275] Even more significantly, the child is entitled to attend the hearing[276] and although the tribunal is not obliged to hear the child's views at the hearing, it can do so if it wishes.[277]

Research carried out in the mid-1990s indicated that children rarely attended SENT hearings.[278] Furthermore, extreme ambivalence was expressed by tribunal members both over children attending and giving evidence; they feared that children might hear demoralising evidence regarding their academic ability and find the proceedings lengthy and tedious. Harris suggests that if the tribunal was obliged by law to consider the child's independent views and perspectives, it might focus more on the child's own interests and become less bogged down by issues revolving around resources and technicalities.[279] One wonders, however, what real difference such a change would make to cases like *M v. Worcestershire County Council and Evans*.[280] There, the tribunal was well aware that a depressed 13-year-old boy with severe learning difficulties and a terror of attending a large mainstream school involving two hours travel each day, wished to attend a small independent residential school. Nevertheless, given the absence of any legislative direction to consider his best interests and the LA's reluctance to meet the extra cost of his choice of school (between £57,000 and £75,000 per annum), the outcome was surely inevitable.

---

[272] E.g. *Re V (care or supervision order)* [1996] 1 FLR 776, discussed above.

[273] Special Educational Needs Tribunal Regulations 2001 (SI 2001/600), reg. 9(1).

[274] *Practice Direction: Health Education and Social Care Chamber Special Educational Needs or Disability in Schools Cases*, para 2 (b); see www.tribunals.gov.uk/Tribunals/Documents/Rules/Specialeducationalneedshesc.pdf.

[275] The Tribunal Procedure (First-tier Tribunal) (Health, Education and Social Care Chamber) Rules 2008 (SI 2008/2699 (L.16)), reg. 21 (2)(e).

[276] Ibid, reg. 24(b).

[277] Ibid. Anecdotal information indicates that, in the past, the child was often only allowed to discuss his case with the SENDIST panel before the hearing, being required to leave before the full hearing starts.

[278] N. Harris (1997) pp. 146–51. Children were not then entitled to attend hearings of the SENT, but could do so at the tribunal's discretion.

[279] Ibid. at p. 149.   [280] [2002] EWHC 1292, [2003] ELR 31, cited by L. Cannon (2005) p. 114.

Unless the domestic courts can be persuaded to interpret the rights of SEN children under Article 6 of the ECHR relatively vigorously, it seems unlikely that the current failure to provide children with party status can be rectified by international human rights law. Although ostensibly such failure infringes the child's rights to a fair trial under Article 6, Strasbourg case law suggests that procedures relating to the right to education are not within the scope of that article, because the right to state education is not a 'civil right', as it requires.[281] Nevertheless, as observed by the Committee on the Rights of the Child regarding the general state of the UK's education law, to deny children the right to express their own opinions on a variety of educational matters fails to give sufficient attention to the importance of article 12 of the CRC.[282] The government will find it more difficult to justify the lack of party status for English children once children living in Wales gain the right to appeal to the SEN tribunal service in Wales on any matter, as planned.[283] Legislation fully acknowledging that English children are the focus of proceedings considering their educational future is long overdue.

(8) Conclusion

The government's 'overarching vision' that disabled children should be able to access 'ordinary lives' by 2025 is admirable.[284] Similarly its efforts, through the introduction of disability discrimination legislation, to extend their access to mainstream services, including schools, reflects its conviction that disability should not hamper the life chances of disabled people.[285] It is also difficult to deny the good intentions underlying the education legislation in this field of law. It goes to great lengths to fulfil the enlightened objectives of the Warnock Report and to ensure that children of all abilities in England and Wales receive a good education. Nevertheless, there are fundamental problems hindering such aims, with many considering the government gravely mistaken in its refusal to overhaul the enormously bureaucratic SEN framework which involves report writing and form-filling at every point in the process. Joint working arrangements provoked by the introduction of children's trusts remain in their infancy, with a grave shortage of practitioners, such as occupational and speech and language therapists, producing a postcode lottery of provision. What is worse, according to Blair, the reports of the local government ombudsman on SEN maladministration often contain 'a story not only of unfairness and indignation, but of tragic levels of neglect, disinterest and despair'.[286]

---

[281] See *Simpson v. United Kingdom* (Application No. 14688/89) (1989) 64 DR 188. Discussed further in Chapter 6.

[282] Committee on the Rights of the Child (1995) para. 14. See also Committee on the Rights of the Child (2008) paras. 32, 66(a) and 67(h).

[283] Welsh Assembly Government (2008).   [284] PMSU (2005) para. 5.2.

[285] Ibid. at p. 11.   [286] A. Blair (2008) p. 227.

The government's faith in disabled children receiving an inclusive education will also continue to lack credibility whilst children with LDDs are denied suitably qualified teaching staff to provide them with well-designed education. Meanwhile, the general weakness shared by the large body of legislation governing the education of all children results in the legal provisions governing children with LDDs consistently identifying their interests with those of their parents. They are not viewed as individuals with personalities and rights of their own. Unless disabled children, some of whom are wholly dependent on adults for many things, are treated with respect by the legislation governing their educational rights, those involved in their education will not be encouraged to do the same.

BIBLIOGRAPHY

NB many of these publications can be obtained on the relevant organisation's website.

Audit Commission (2002a) *Statutory Assessment and Statements of SEN: In Need of Review?* Audit Commission.

Audit Commission (2002b) *Special Educational Needs: A Mainstream Issue*, Audit Commission.

Audit Commission (2003) *Services for Disabled Children*, Audit Commission.

Audit Commission (2007) *Out of Authority Placements for Special Educational Needs*, Audit Commission.

Audit Commission (2008) *Are We There Yet? Improving Governance and Resource Management in Children's Trusts*, Audit Commission.

Bercow, J. (Chairman) (2008) *The Bercow Report: A Review of Services for Children and Young People (0–19) with Speech, Language and Communication Needs*, DCSF.

Birtwistle, T. (2002) 'Liability for "Educational Malpractice"' *Education Law Journal* 95.

Blair, A. (2006) 'Local Government Ombudsmen Reports' 7 *Education Law Journal* 210. (2008) 'Local Government Ombudsmen Reports' 9 *Education Law Journal* 225.

Boyle, D. and Burton, E. (2004) 'Making Sense of SEN: The Role of the Voluntary Sector' 5 *Education Law Journal* 15.

Burchardt, T. (2005) *The Education and Employment of Disabled Young People: Frustrated Ambition*, Joseph Rowntree Foundation.

Cannon, L. (2005) 'Special Educational Needs and the Case for Children's Rights' 6 *Education Law Journal* 108.

Committee on the Rights of the Child (1995) *Concluding Observations of the Committee on the Rights of the Child: United Kingdom of Great Britain and Northern Ireland* CRC/C/15/Add 34, Centre for Human Rights, Geneva.

Committee on the Rights of the Child (2006) *General Comment No 9, The Rights of Children with Disabilities*, CRC/C/GC/9, Centre for Human Rights, Geneva.

Committee on the Rights of the Child (2008) *Concluding Observations of the Committee on the Rights of the Child: United Kingdom of Great Britain and Northern Ireland* CRC/C/GBR/CO/4, Centre for Human Rights, Geneva.

Department for Children, Schools and Families (DCSF) (2007a) *Trends in Education and Skills*, DCSF.

Department for Children, Schools and Families (DCSF) (2007b) Cm 7280 *The Children's Plan: Building Brighter Futures*, TSO.

Department for Children, Schools and Families (DCSF) (2008a), SFR 14/2008 *Permanent and Fixed Term Exclusions from Schools and Exclusion Appeals in England*, 2006/7, DCSF.

Department for Children, Schools and Families (DCSF) (2008b) SFR 09/2008, *Pupil Characteristics and Class Sizes in Maintained Schools in England, January 2008 (Provisional)*, DCSF.

Department for Children, Schools and Families (DCSF) (2008c) *Consultation on Draft Education (Special Educational Needs Co-ordinators) (England) Regulations 2008*, DCSF.

Department for Children, Schools and Families (DCSF) (2008d) *Improving Behaviour and Attendance: Guidance on Exclusion from Schools and Pupil Referral Units*, DCSF.

Department for Children, Schools and Families (DCSF) (2009) *School Admissions Code*, TSO.

Department for Education and Employment (DfEE) (1997) Cm 3785 *Green Paper Excellence for all Children: Meeting Special Educational Needs*, DfEE.

Department for Education and Skills (DfES) (2001) *Special Educational Needs: Code of Practice* DfES/581/2001, DfES.

Department for Education and Skills (DfES) (2004a) *Every Child Matters: Next Steps*, DfES.

Department for Education and Skills (DfES) (2004b) *Removing Barriers to Achievement: The Government's Strategy for SEN*, DfES.

Department for Education and Skills (DfES) (2007) SFR 21/2007 *Permanent and Fixed Term Exclusions from Schools and Exclusion Appeals in England*, 2005/6, DfES.

Department of Health (DH) (2004) *Disabled Child Standard, National Service Framework for Children, Young People and Maternity Services*, DH.

Disability Rights Commission (DRC) (2002) *Disability Discrimination Act 1995 Part 4: Code of Practice for Schools*, TSO.

Disability Rights Commission (DRC) (2005) *The Duty to Promote Disability Equality: Statutory Code of Practice, England and Wales*, TSO.

Freeman, M. (2000) 'The Future of Children's Rights' 14 *Children and Society* 277.

Gordon, D. *et al.* (2000) *Disabled Children: a Re-analysis of the OPCS Disability Survey*, TSO.

Green, H. *et al.* (2004) *Mental Health of Children and Young People in Great Britain, 2004*, Palgrave Macmillan.

HM Government (2006) Cm 6940 *Government Response to the Education and Skills Committee Report on Special Educational Needs (October 2006)*, TSO.

HM Treasury (2003) Cm 5860 *Every Child Matters*, TSO.

HM Treasury and Department for Education and Skills (DfES) (2007) *Aiming High for Disabled Children: Better Support for Families*, HM Treasury.

Harris, M. (2001) 'Education and Local Authorities' 117 *Law Quarterly Review* 25.

Harris, N. (1997) *Special Educational Needs and Access to Justice*, Jordans.

(2003) 'Editorial: Negligence in Education: Where are we?' 4 *Education Law Journal* 141.

(2007) *Education, Law and Diversity*, Hart Publishing.

Hay, D. (2005) 'A Special Case of Negligence?' *New Law Journal* 534.

Hodgkin, R. and Newell, P. (2007) *Implementation Handbook for the Convention on the Rights of the Child*, UNICEF.

House of Commons Education and Skills Committee (HCESC) (2006a) HC 478-I *Special Educational Needs, Third Report of Session 2005–06*, Volume I, TSO.

House of Commons Education and Skills Committee (HCESC) (2006b) HC 478-II *Special Educational Needs, Third Report of Session 2005–06*, Volume II, TSO.

Jackman, A. (2005) 'SENDIST – a Hit and Miss Remedy?' *New Law Journal* 966.

Jarvis, J. (2007) '"Jigsawing it Together": Reflections on Deaf Pupils and Inclusion' in Cigman, R. (ed.) *Included or Excluded? The Challenge of the Mainstream for some SEN Children*, Routledge.

Jenkinson, J. (1997) *Mainstream or Special? Educating Students with Disabilities*, Routledge.

King, M. and King, D. (2006) 'How the Law Defines the Special Educational Needs of Autistic Children' 18 *Child and Family Law Quarterly* 23.

Lindsay, G. (2007) 'Rights, Efficacy and Inclusive Education' in Cigman, R. (ed.) *Included or Excluded? The Challenge of the Mainstream for some SEN Children*, Routledge.

Low, C. (2007) 'A Defence of Moderate Inclusion and the End of Ideology' in Cigman, R. *Included or Excluded? The Challenge of the Mainstream for some SEN Children*, Routledge.

Lundy, L. (1998) 'Stating a Case for the "Unstatemented" – Children with Special Educational Needs in Mainstream Schools' 10 *Child and Family Law Quarterly* 39.

Lunt, I. (2007) 'The Challenge of Meeting Additional Educational Needs With or Without Statements of Educational Need' in Cigman, R. (ed.) *Included or Excluded? The Challenge of the Mainstream for some SEN Children*, Routledge.

MacBeath, J. *et al.* (2006) *The Costs of Inclusion*, National Union of Teachers.

Mencap (2007) *Don't Stick it: Stop it!*, Mencap.

Mittler, P. (2000) *Working Towards Inclusive Education: Social Contexts*, David Fulton Publishers.

Moore, C. (2007) 'Speaking as a Parent: Thoughts about Educational Inclusion for Autistic Children' in Cigman, R. (ed.) *Included or Excluded? The Challenge of the Mainstream for some SEN Children*, Routledge.

Mullis, A. (2001) '*Phelps and Hillingdon London Borough Council*: A Rod for the Hunchbacked Teacher?' 13 *Child and Family Law Quarterly* 331.

Office of Public Censuses and Surveys (OPCS) (1989) *Surveys of Disability in Great Britain* Reports 1–6, HMSO.

Office for Standards in Education (Ofsted) (2002) HMI 737 *LEA Strategy for the Inclusion of Pupils with Special Educational Needs*, Ofsted.

Ofsted (2004) HMI 2276 *Special Educational Needs and Disability: Towards Inclusive Schools*, Ofsted.

Office for Standards in Education (Ofsted) (2006) HMI 2535, *Inclusion: Does it Matter Where Pupils are Taught?* Ofsted.

Oliver, S. (2007) *Special Educational Needs and the Law*, Jordans.

Paul, A., Cawson, P. and Paton, J. (2004), *Safeguarding Disabled Children in Residential Special Schools*, NSPCC.

Prime Minister's Strategy Unit (PMSU) (2005) *Improving the Life Chances of Disabled People*, Cabinet Office.

Read, J. and Clements, L. (2004) 'Demonstrably Awful: The Right to Life and the Selective Non-Treatment of Disabled Babies and Young Children' 31 *Journal of Law and Society* 482.

Read, J., Clements, L. and Ruebain, D. (2006) *Disabled Children and the Law: Research and Good Practice*, Jessica Kingsley Publishers.

Ruebain, D. and Wright, J. (2006) 'Warnock: A Response' 10 *Education, Public Law & the Individual* 4.

Special Educational Needs and Disability Tribunal (SENDIST) (2008) *Special Educational Needs and Disability Tribunal: President's Annual Report 2006–2007*, SENDIST.

Silas, D. and Wolfe, D. (2005) 'Four Years in the Life of the Special Educational Needs and Disability Act 2001' 6 *Education Law Journal* 82.

Steer, A. (Chairman) (2005) *Learning Behaviour: The Report of the Practitioners' Group on School Behaviour and Discipline*, DfES.

Stobbs, P. (2008), *Extending Inclusion*, Council for Disabled Children.

Stout, H. (2007) 'Comment on *A v Hertfordshire County Council* [2007]' 8 *Education Law Journal* 116.

UNICEF Innocenti Research Centre (2007) Innocenti Digest No 13 *Promoting the Rights of Children with Disabilities*, UNICEF.

Warnock, H.M., (Chairman) (1978) Cmnd 7212 *Special Educational Needs, Report of the Committee of Enquiry into the Education of Handicapped Children and Young People*, HMSO.

Warnock, M. (2005) *Special Educational Needs: a New Look*, No 11 in a series of policy discussions, Philosophy of Education Society of Great Britain.

Welsh Assembly Government (2008) *Voices and Choices: A Proposed Right for Children to Appeal to the Special Educational Needs Tribunal for Wales*, Consultation Document No: 051/; 2008, Welsh Assembly Government.

Wilkin, A. *et al.* (2005) Research Report RR 608 *Admissions and Exclusions of Pupils with Special Educational Needs*, DfES.

Wing, L. (2007) 'Children with Autistic Spectrum Disorders' in Cigman, R. *Included or Excluded? The Challenge of the Mainstream for some SEN Children*, Routledge.

Wolfe, D. (2003) 'Statements of Special Educational Needs – 20 Years on' 4 *Education Law Journal* 227.

Wright, E. (2007) 'Autism and Education Law' 8 *Education Law Journal* 83.

Chapter 13

Children's right to know their parents – the significance of the blood tie

(1) Introduction

It is increasingly common for children to be brought up in families differing greatly from the traditional unit formed by a married couple and their children. Today, society accepts that parent-child relationships can be created through adoption, fostering, reproductive technologies, unmarried birth, family breakdown and step-parenting. Indeed, the law accommodates the fact that adults caring for children may have a social relationship with them which is far more important to the children themselves than any link with their biological progenitors.[1] Nevertheless, society shows great ambivalence over what significance to attach to the biological tie between a child and birth parents. Does the tie's existence, in itself, justify the creation of a social relationship between them where none existed before, or is it enough for the child to be given accurate information about the identity of an absent parent? Furthermore, where should the law stand in relation to a growing view that all children have a right to know the identity of their birth parents?

These questions have become increasingly important, given the law's response to the technological developments which undermine old assumptions about the legal linkage between parents and children. The increasing availability of accurate DNA testing and of reproductive technologies (commonly donor conception) are probably the two developments which have provoked most debate in this context. DNA testing has an obvious significance. In the past, 'normal' childhood involved children being brought up within nuclear families by those they assumed to be their biological parents. In practice there is seldom much doubt over the identity of a child's mother – birth usually, though not always, renders it obvious.[2] Meanwhile, the absence of any foolproof method for establishing paternity led to the children of married women being protected against the shame of an illegitimate status by the common law presumption of

---

[1] Children Act (CA) 1989, s. 12(2) enables a person unrelated to the child to acquire parental responsibilities over him or her through obtaining a residence order.

[2] *The Ampthill Peerage Case* [1977] AC 547, per Lord Simon, at 577. NB Human Fertilisation and Embryology Act (HFEA) 1990, s. 27: a woman who bears a child is treated as the child's legal mother, whether or not she is the child's biological mother.

legitimacy and of marital paternity.[3] Indeed, the father-child relationship was thereby constructed through marriage.[4] Today, whilst this presumption can always be rebutted,[5] science has produced a situation where it is no longer necessary.[6] Stressing that the importance of DNA technology should not be overstated, Freeman and Richards comment:

> What is perhaps more disruptive for the traditional patriarchal order is the potential for DNA testing to challenge the ideological foundations of the marital framework itself by rendering the hidden paradoxes of paternal uncertainty visible to scrutiny ... It is evident that DNA testing has the potential both to reinforce and destabilise longstanding assumptions concerning the socio-legal status of paternity.[7]

Whilst DNA testing increasingly undermines attempts to keep secrets within families,[8] donor conception enables infertile heterosexual couples to do the opposite. Indeed, the legislation condones any attempts to pass off their children as having been conceived naturally by establishing a legal fiction. In broad terms, it treats the woman who gave birth as the legal mother[9] and her husband[10] or partner[11] as the legal father.[12] Thus any child born by donor conception looks as if he or she has been born into a 'normal' nuclear family with one mother and one father.[13] Indeed, as Freeman and Richards comment, the development of reproductive technologies has gone one step further than contraception in separating traditional links between sexuality and procreativity – 'in untying socio-legal and cultural definitions of parenthood from the reproductive process'.[14] Nevertheless, as they point out, the very existence of such technologies pays testament to people's desire 'to have their own children',[15] – to bear children into families that look conventional. Now this process is being reversed, with the child potentially gaining a second father, through a new

---

[3] *The Ampthill Peerage Case* ibid.: the presumption of legitimacy rests on the assumption that a married woman only conceives a child through intercourse with her husband.

[4] T. Freeman and M. Richards (2006) p. 72. See also C. Smart (2007) pp. 122–3.

[5] Family Law Reform Act (FLRA) 1969, s. 26: by evidence showing, that it is more probable than not that the child is illegitimate. But see *Serio v. Serio* (1983) 4 FLR 756, per Sir David Cairns, at 763, and *Re Moynihan* [2000] 1 FLR 113, per Lord Jauncey, at 120: the paternity of a child is recognised by the law as being a serious matter and the proper standard of proof is a 'standard commensurate with the seriousness of the issue involved ... more stringent than the mere tipping of the scales in favour of probability'.

[6] *Re H and A (paternity: blood tests)* [2002] EWCA Civ 383, [2002] 1 FLR 1145, per Thorpe LJ, at [30].

[7] T. Freeman and M. Richards (2006) p. 74.   [8] C. Smart (2007) pp. 126–7.

[9] HFEA 1990, s. 27 or HFEA 2008, s. 33 (re all births occurring after commencement of 2008 Act).

[10] HFEA 1990, s. 28(2) or HFEA 2008, s. 35 (re all births occurring after commencement of 2008 Act).

[11] HFEA 1990, s. 28(3) (if the mother and he received treatment services together) or HFEA 2008, ss. 36–7 (re all births occurring after commencement of 2008 Act, but only if the 'agreed fatherhood conditions' apply).

[12] See N. Lowe and G. Douglas (2007) pp. 306–20, for further details.

[13] S. Sheldon (2005) p. 541.   [14] T. Freeman and M. Richards (2006) p. 78.   [15] Ibid. at p. 82.

ability to identify the sperm donor.[16] But as Sheldon observes, the ability of children born by reproductive technology to discover the identity of their biological fathers is unlikely to dislodge the role of their social (or 'psychological') fathers.[17] We see that adoptees who trace their birth parents often simply wish to obtain information about them, for example, through obtaining copies of their original birth certificates or background medical information. Others may want to meet their birth relatives to establish their physical appearance, without wishing to develop a relationship with them.[18] Even those who have direct contact with their birth families[19] are unlikely to allow their birth parents to supplant their affection for their adoptive parents.[20] By analogy, Sheldon is probably correct in asserting that if a child born by assisted conception discovers his biological parentage, this will not necessarily disrupt his family and his relationship with his social parents.[21] After all, donors who provide licensed clinics with sperm do not intend to have a social relationship with their offspring.

Matters take on an entirely different dimension when it comes to situations involving children born through natural conception to fertile couples whose relationship breaks down or never really existed. Today, irrespective of his marital status, a man claiming to identify himself as a child's father (opposed by the mother), will undoubtedly reinforce his claim by asserting that by withholding consent to the child being DNA tested, the mother is denying the child's own right to knowledge of his or her origins,[22] and is acting against the child's best interests.[23] Add this to what Lind calls a 'long-standing obsession with the idea that there should be a genetic link between those who raise children and the children they raise'[24] – and the argument that children have a right to knowledge of their origins becomes conflated with the argument that they need a social relationship with their biological fathers.[25] Indeed, in the case of unmarried fathers, Sheldon remarks on the 'the seeming inevitability of a movement towards formal equality between all parents and a greater reliance on the genetic connection in grounding legal fatherhood and its rights and responsibilities'.[26] The fathers' rights movement has undoubtedly reinforced such ideas.[27]

---

[16] Discussed below.

[17] S. Sheldon (2005) pp. 550–1. NB the role of the 'psychological parent' is discussed further in Chapter 14.

[18] E. Neil and D. Howe (2004) chs. 4–5.

[19] PIU (2000) para. 3.142: only 20% of adopted children are likely to have direct contact with their birth parents; para. 3.145: 50% are estimated to have indirect contact (i.e. letters or telephone calls only). E. Neil (2003) p. 288: neither indirect nor face-to-face contact between birth parents and adoptees affects adoptive parents' sense of permanence in their relationships with their adoptees.

[20] D. Howe and J. Feast (2000) p. 127: noting a significant fall-off in contact between 'searching' adoptees and their birth mothers after initial contact.

[21] S. Sheldon (2005) p. 548.

[22] E.g. *Re T (paternity: ordering blood tests)* [2001] 2 FLR 1190, discussed below.

[23] J. Wallbank (2004a) p. 253.   [24] C. Lind (2006) p. 584.   [25] J. Wallbank (2004a) p. 253.

[26] S. Sheldon (2007) p. 16.   [27] Discussed below.

Not to be forgotten is the government's own interest in combating child poverty by ensuring that men identified as the fathers of impoverished children pay child maintenance.[28] In this context, the government cares not that the biological link between father and child is the only justification for seeking such payment. As Eekelaar comments, 'the man who procreates as a result of a "one-night stand" is the legal father and will be liable to support the child, whether or not he expected a child to result'.[29] DNA testing can now establish the father's identity quickly and easily; so it may, in these circumstances, fulfil two purposes. On the one hand it may prove an identified man to be the appropriate target for those administering the child support scheme, now C-MEC,[30] and on the other hand, it produces evidence fulfilling the child's need to know his or her paternity.[31]

This heady cocktail of factors propels the courts into placing even greater faith on the value of biological links between children and parents, married and unmarried alike. But the assumption that the birth tie automatically guarantees a beneficial in-built affinity between parent and child is surely naive. Certainly the cloaking of adults' claims to have a social relationship with their children on the basis of biological links alone in the language of international human rights law has a dubious merit. This chapter reflects on the extent to which the law should contribute to a situation where children and parents consider that the biological link must always be consummated by a social relationship to achieve any semblance of 'normality'.[32] In so doing, it explores areas of law where the notion of children's rights appears to be utilised to support arguments about promoting contact between children and their birth parents which perhaps have more to do with adults' rights than those of their children.

(2) A child's right to knowledge of origins

(A) Background

It seems reasonably clear that the relative ease with which it is now possible to establish the identity of a person's genetic progenitors is one of the factors driving the developing societal view that everyone has an in-built need to know the genetic 'truth' of their origins.[33] It is undoubtedly provoking a dislike of

---

[28] Discussed in Chapter 9.   [29] J. Eekelaar (2006) p. 67.   [30] Ibid.

[31] E.g. *Secretary of State for Work and Pensions v. Jones* [2003] EWHC 2163 (Fam), [2004] 1 FLR 282, per Dame Elizabeth Butler-Sloss P: the magistrates' finding that a named man was not a child's father for child support purposes was faulty because (i) it infringed the child rights under Art. 8 of the European Convention for the Protection of Human Rights and Fundamental Freedoms (ECHR) and under the Convention on the Rights of the Child (CRC) to knowledge of the identity of his father; (ii) there was no clear scientific evidence to back up their finding; (iii) they could have drawn adverse inferences from the man's refusal to undergo DNA testing under the Family Law Reform Act (FLRA) 1969, s. 23(1).

[32] See also Chapter 14, which considers the same issue from a different viewpoint.

[33] T. Freeman and M. Richards (2006) p. 75. See also C. Smart (2007) p. 36.

secrecy being allowed to mask the true situation.[34] Freeman and Richards assert that the prevalent assumptions that 'our biological origins are a significant determinant of identity and kin relationships' have been heightened by a knowledge of genetic science.[35] Whether the need to know one's origins is indeed 'a basic human right' or 'the voguish language of cod-psychology',[36] is unclear. As O'Donovan has so wisely observed in the context of adoption, the search for identity does not exist in a vacuum: 'It is produced by legal and social structures which attach value to concepts of identity linked to genitors.'[37] Be this as it may, the lessons gained from adoption research are compelling and it is tempting to apply them more generally. The research suggests that many adopted children benefit from discovering the true identity of those who brought them into the world and that this information should be provided early in life. It appears that information about children's origins gives them the ability to place themselves in a social context. They gain a continuity with the past and a complete and consistent biography.[38] Furthermore, concealment and secrecy contribute to children's sense of bewilderment if told later that they have been brought up in the incorrect belief that their present carers are their birth parents.[39] It was this research material which prompted the introduction of legislation more than 40 years ago, giving adult adoptees a procedural right to discover the identity of their birth relatives.[40]

But there are other groups with similar claims, notably those born with the assistance of donor conception. Referring to the lessons learnt from adoption, Scott Baker J, in *Rose v. Secretary of State for Health and Human Fertilisation and Embryology Authority*,[41] fully sympathised with the needs of a woman conceived through sperm donation to know the identity of her father. Indeed, by the early twenty-first century, the inability of children conceived through sperm donation and other methods of reproductive technology to obtain any information identifying their biological parents[42] was becoming increasingly controversial,[43] given our more open society and the increasing numbers of children conceived in such a way.[44] Furthermore, they might need to discover whether they have inherited a genetic disorder, before starting a family of their own.[45] Whether or not it is

---

[34] J. Eekelaar (2006) p. 74.   [35] T. Freeman and M. Richards (2006) p. 79.

[36] V. Groskop and C. Sarler (2007).   [37] K. O'Donovan (1990) p. 102.

[38] E. Haimes (1987) p. 363.

[39] J. Triseliotis (1973) p. 20: those adoptees aged between 4 and 8 years when told of their adoption experienced the greatest satisfaction; those told in adolescence and adult life experienced the greatest distress and shock.

[40] A complicated system for obtaining such information was introduced by the Adoption and Children Act (ACA) 2002, ss. 56–65. See C. Bridge and H. Swindells (2003) pp. 246–56.

[41] [2002] EWHC 1593 (Admin), [2002] 2 FLR 962, at [47].

[42] An adult could only apply to the Human Fertilisation and Embryology Authority for non-identifying information about a donor contained on its register.

[43] M. Freeman (1996).

[44] Human Fertilisation and Embryology statistics indicate that over 11,000 children are born annually though IVF treatment.

[45] E.g. *Re H (adoption: disclosure of information)* [1995] 1 FLR 236: the High Court allowed information from a sibling to be passed on to an adopted adult, alerting him to the danger of having inherited a biological disorder.

appropriate to use the analogy with adoptees,[46] Scott Baker J's acknowledgement that such claims were backed by Article 8 of the ECHR[47] made change virtually inevitable.[48] By then, the Committee on the Rights of the Child had also criticised English law for withholding information about the biological identity of donors from children born by donor conception.[49] But since few parents using donor conception tell their children the circumstances of their conception, further reforms are now urged ensuring that donor-conceived children have the method of their conception indicated on their birth certificates.[50]

(B) International human rights law

Claims that children have a right to accurate information about their biological origins are substantially reinforced by international human rights law.[51] None of the three articles of the CRC normally quoted as supporting such an argument directly substantiate such a claim. Article 7 of the CRC was inspired by a concern to redress children's statelessness. Its phrasing makes it clear that states parties must provide a method whereby the child is 'labelled' or named immediately he or she is born and thereby linked accurately and quickly to those who brought her into the world, her birth parents. Article 8 responded to the abuses committed by the military regime in Argentina during which babies were abducted from mothers at birth, before their births could be registered, and illegally given to couples associated with the armed forces and the police.[52] It therefore requires states to provide a means whereby children retain their identity, a concept which includes not only a name but also family and nationality, thereby ensuring that they are easily reunited with their parents if they become separated. Article 9 was clearly intended to bar children from being removed from their parents by the state except in situations involving abuse or neglect. Despite none of these articles specifically promoting a child's right to knowledge of origins, the UN Committee on the Rights of the Child has interpreted Article 7 in precisely such a manner. The Committee criticises legal systems which withhold such information from children born by donor conception,[53] and those which allow mothers to give birth anonymously and to keep their identity secret from their

---

[46] Discussed further below.   [47] [2002] EWHC 1593 (Admin), [2002] 2 FLR 962, at [48].

[48] Human Fertilisation and Embryology Authority (Disclosure of Donor Information) Regulations 2004 (SI 2004/1511), reg. 2(2) enables donor-conceived adults (i.e. aged 18 and over) to obtain all information (other than identifying information) held by the Authority on its register of donors about the donor; reg. 2(3) enables donor-conceived adults to obtain all information (identifying and other) held by the Authority on its register supplied to clinics from 1 April 2005. I.e. as from that date, clinics may obtain identifying information from all sperm donors. But NB the regulation changes were not retrospective, so it will not be until 2023 that the first 18-year-olds can exercise the right to discover the identity of their sperm donors. HFEA 1990, ss. 31ZA–31ZB (as amended by the HFEA 2008, s. 24) gives 16-year-olds the right to obtain non-identifying information about their genetic parents; see DH (2007) para. 68.

[49] Committee on the Rights of the Child (2002) paras. 31 and 32.   [50] Discussed below.

[51] S. Besson (2007) esp. pp. 141–3. See also R. Blauwhoff (2008) pp. 105–12.

[52] S. Detrick (1992) pp. 292–4.   [53] See fn 49 above.

offspring.[54] Although the Committee's observations are influential, the absence of any unambiguous provision in the CRC on the matter, combined with the fact that the Convention has no direct enforcement procedure, undermines its ability to provoke change in this area of law.

It is the Strasbourg jurisprudence interpreting Article 8 of the ECHR which most clearly supports the view that children have a right to establish details of their parentage. As discussed earlier,[55] the right to respect for private life has been widely interpreted. The early decision in *Gaskin v. United Kingdom*[56] reached by the European Court of Human Rights (ECtHR) secured for children the right to obtain information about themselves held by public agencies on their childhood and early development.[57] Later, in *Mikulic v. Croatia*,[58] this interpretation of Article 8 was taken further, when the Court stated that there 'appears, furthermore, to be no reason of principle why the notion of "private life" should be taken to exclude the determination of the legal relationship between a child born out of wedlock and her natural father'.[59] Clearly no rights under Article 8 are absolute, given that their infringement may be justified to promote the interests of others under Article 8(2). Here the ECtHR concluded that Croatia should have had in place a procedure striking a fair balance between the needs of a child to have eliminated without unnecessary delay any uncertainty over her personal identity (arising from ignorance of a parents' identity) and those of the alleged father not to be forced into DNA testing.[60]

In *Mikulic* the Court was fully aware of the potential tensions in such cases between the rights of the child and those of adult parties, more particularly, the alleged father's rights not to be forced into DNA testing in a disproportionate manner. Critics, agreeing with the powerful dissenting decision in *Odièvre v. France*,[61] argue that the majority of the ECtHR in that case got the balance entirely wrong between the rights of mother and child.[62] They had decided that given the flexibility introduced into the system,[63] it was within France's margin of appreciation[64] to continue allowing mothers to give birth anonymously and to retain their anonymity, even at the expense of their children being forced to remain in ignorance of their mothers' identity. But, as the dissenting judges

[54] As in France. R. Hodgkin and p. Newell (2007) p. 106.
[55] See Chapter 2.   [56] (1989) 12 EHRR 36.
[57] The Data Protection Act 1998 (as amended by the Freedom of Information legislation) imposed a general duty on local authorities (LAs) to provide full access to social work records.
[58] [2002] 1 FCR 720: a 5-year-old girl (through her mother) claimed successfully that the absence of any legal means of forcing a putative father to comply with court orders for DNA tests infringed her right to private life under Art. 8 ECHR, given that there was no independent authority to which she could turn to adjudicate her paternity claim.
[59] Ibid. at para. 53.   [60] Ibid. and at. paras. 64–6.
[61] [2003] 1 FCR 621; joint dissenting opinion by Judges Wildhaber *et al.*, esp. at paras. 5–7.
[62] Inter alia: E. Steiner (2003) and S. Besson (2007) pp. 150–2.
[63] Ibid. at para. 49: France had established an independent body to consider requests from children to have the identity of their mothers disclosed, subject only to the mothers' own consent; absent such consent, they would obtain only non-identifying information.
[64] This term is discussed in Chapter 2.

urged, this effectively made the mother's unilateral decision binding. Besson[65] argues that the significance of the dissenting judges' view in *Odièvre* was that the margin of appreciation should not prevent the ECtHR subjecting any system established for balancing competing interests to 'the fairest scrutiny' in cases where 'the very nature of the interest concerned [the right to identity]' or 'its inner core' is at stake.[66] She maintains that since the ECtHR adopted this very approach in a later case, holding that the right to know one's parentage is an *integral part* of the notion of private life,[67] *Odièvre* might not be decided along the same lines today.[68]

Clearly the ECtHR's willingness to scrutinise carefully claims involving a child's right to know her parents' identity is an important development. Nonetheless, subsequent case law continues to stress that a fair balance must be found between the child's need to have uncertainty over the identity of her father eliminated without unnecessary delay and the purported father's right not to be forced into DNA testing.[69] Furthermore, as Besson herself acknowledges, some cases involve further complexities. The child's right to information identifying his or her parents may conflict not only with the rights of other people (such as parents), but also with those of public bodies and with those of the child.[70] These complexities make it far from clear how the state, and its organs, the courts, should respond to claims that children have a *right* to knowledge of their origins under Article 8 of the ECHR. The fact remains, however, that the Strasbourg jurisprudence has considerably strengthened the view that such a right exists and should be respected by states and their judicial organs, the domestic courts.

(C) The state's response

Many would argue that English law has more than adequately fulfilled its need to promote children's right to know about their parentage, both under Article 7 of the CRC and under Article 8 of the ECHR. As discussed above, there is now in place a complicated system whereby adult adoptees can discover the identity of their birth parents. Similarly, children born by donor conception have also acquired the right to discover the identity of their gamete donors.[71] Nevertheless, as noted above, the law allows an infertile couple who have used donor conception to conceive to 'pass the child off' as their own. Indeed, given the reluctance of many such couples to tell their children their genetic history,[72] these children may grow up assuming that their legal parents are also

---

[65] S. Besson (2007) p. 151.

[66] [2003] 1 FCR 621, joint dissenting opinion by Judges Wildhaber *et al.*, at para. 11.

[67] *Jäggi v. Switzerland* (Application No 58757/00) para. 37.   [68] S. Besson (2007) p. 154.

[69] *Jevremović v. Serbia* [2007] ECHR 612 at paras. 106–11.

[70] S. Besson (2007) p. 138.   [71] See fn 48 above.

[72] S. Golombok *et al.* (2006) p. 1921: 46% of the donor insemination parents had decided against disclosing to their child the method of their conception.

their biological parents. Only when the biological truth of the deception is too obvious to go unremarked, as in *Leeds Teaching Hospitals NHS Trust v. A*,[73] do the courts interpret the legislation to ensure that biological paternity goes hand in hand with legal paternity.[74]

The introduction of new draft provisions governing donor conception[75] prompted further discussion of this issue. Bainham[76] and others strongly assert that since children have a right to know the truth about their biological parentage, the law should oblige parents to tell their children that they are donor-conceived.[77] Such a view was not received with wholehearted support,[78] although the proposal that donor conceived children should have this fact entered on their birth certificates commanded greater sympathy.[79] It was argued that the authorities should avoid 'colluding in a deception'[80] – or an erroneous birth certificate. Nevertheless, the government currently maintains that rather than the law being prescriptive, it is preferable for parents to be educated in the benefits of their children being told the truth about their birth. It has, however, undertaken to keep these issues under review.[81]

Although Bainham's arguments are persuasive, one wonders how feasible it is for the law to be entirely consistent in this context. After all, it is not only parents who conceive with the assistance of donor conception who deceive their children about their parentage. Fertile parents have been doing so since time immemorial.[82] Indeed, it is arguable that it is a question of the tail wagging the dog, with our interest in psychology and genealogy prompting the view that children who are denied information about their biological origins will inevitably suffer psychologically. Furthermore, it does not necessarily follow that research on adopted children's need for information about their birth from as early as possible translates into the need for *every* child to be given such information on birth, regardless of his or her circumstances. In relation to donor conceived children, Turkmendag *et al.* point to the absence of any robust research indicating that they should receive such information.[83] They urge that analogies with adoption are not appropriate, given that adoption involves the creation of a family around an already existing individual, whereas donor conception is a form of procreation: 'the act has its own integrity and completeness – it is the would-be parent(s)' act and the child is unquestionably their child'.[84] This is all the more the case, given that the child is normally

---

[73] [2003] EWHC 259, [2003] 1 FLR 1091: as a result of a mix up at a fertility clinic, a married white woman gave birth to mixed race twins.

[74] Ibid., per Dame Elizabeth Butler-Sloss P, at [56]–[57]; discussed by S. Sheldon (2005) pp. 544–7.

[75] I.e. the Human Tissue and Embryos Bill 2007.   [76] A. Bainham (2008a) pp. 335–6.

[77] Joint Committee on the Human Tissue and Embryos (Draft) Bill (2007) paras. 268–71: summary of evidence provided by A. Bainham and others favouring a parental duty. See A. Bainham (2008b) pp. 262–7.

[78] Joint Committee on the Human Tissue and Embryos (Draft) Bill (2007) para. 272.

[79] Ibid. at para. 276. DH (2007) paras. 69–70.   [80] Joint Committee, ibid. at para. 276.

[81] DH (2007) paras. 69–70.   [82] Discussed below.

[83] I. Turkmendag *et al.* (2008) p. 290.   [84] Ibid. at p. 289.

biologically related to at least one of his or her parents.[85] Donor conceived children were desired by their parents, whereas adopted children were relinquished.[86] In any event, as Probert points out, 'Such a right [the right to knowledge of origins] only has meaning if parents are under a duty to disclose the truth, but how is such a duty to be policed?'[87]

Less deception will be possible when new laws are implemented requiring every father's name to be entered on his child's birth certificate, irrespective of his marital status, as the government proposes.[88] Currently most birth certificates have both parents' names on them;[89] within that number, a large majority of births outside marriage are also jointly registered.[90] As discussed below, the new scheme will improve most unmarried fathers' legal status. It will also radically change the current law whereunder unmarried mothers are not obliged to register their children's birth jointly with the fathers.[91] Indeed, the government claims that joint registration will 'promote child welfare, parental responsibility and the right of every child to know who his or her parents are'.[92] Fortunately, it dropped the suggestion that it is a mark of social exclusion that mothers fail to ensure that their children's births are jointly registered.[93]

Perhaps more to the point, the government undoubtedly sees the proposal, which first emerged in the context of child maintenance reform,[94] as having a fiscal impact. Part of the child support reforms involved abolishing the rule requiring mothers on state benefits to identify the fathers of their children to the Child Support Agency, if they wished to obtain income support in full.[95] Now that this method of coercion has gone,[96] fewer mothers may turn to fathers for support, preferring to rely on state benefits, at the cost of the taxpayer. The Green Paper's reference to US research indicating that fathers who acknowledge paternity at the child's birth are more likely to pay child maintenance[97] suggests that the government's hopes are not entirely focused on children's welfare and their right to identify their fathers. Its comment that the existence of joint birth registration 'can also assist the mother in claiming child maintenance from the father to pay for the upbringing of their child' perhaps provided the clue[98] – subsequently omitted from the White Paper.

---

[85] Ibid.   [86] Ibid. at p. 290.   [87] R. Probert (2004) p. 287.
[88] Welfare Reform Bill (WRB) 2008, Sch. 6. See also DWP (2007) and DWP (2008).
[89] DWP (2007) para. 36: well over 80% in 2005.   [90] Ibid. at para. 37: 84% in 2005.
[91] Ibid. at para. 38: only 7% of all births are not jointly registered. NB existing law (Births and Deaths Registration Act 1953, ss. 2 and 10) obliges only married parents and unmarried mothers to register the child's birth within 42 days of its occurrence. The name of an unmarried father can be entered only if both parents attend to register the child's birth, or if a court order or formal declaration exists indicating his paternity. A. Bainham (2008b) pp. 450–6: discusses the current system of birth registration.
[92] DWP (2008) para. 23.   [93] DWP (2007) para. 44.
[94] DWP (2006) paras. 2.43–2.48.   [95] Discussed in Chapter 9.
[96] Child Maintenance and Other Payments Act 2008, s. 15 repeals Child Support Act 1991, s. 6.
[97] DWP (2007) para. 18.   [98] Ibid.

Under the planned new scheme, if the mother wants to register the father's name against his wishes, the registrar may contact the man she identifies, requiring him to undergo a paternity test, followed by compulsory registration – but with no sanction for his non-compliance with the test.[99] For the mother who refuses to identify her child's father, there will be broad categories of 'exemptions' from this duty,[100] but it is unclear what sanctions, if any, there will be if she does not qualify for exemption. A father can volunteer for a paternity test and, if identified, can make a declaration of paternity,[101] but he may not discover the need to do so without any sanctions against her for refusing to cooperate. The dark hints in the Green Paper of a 'range of practical measures which could be developed to complement legislation' if it went ahead,[102] were not again mentioned. Registrars are not entirely happy with their proposed role as 'interrogator' in order to challenge a woman's claim to exemption from the duty to name the child's father.[103]

Bainham argues that since the child has an independent right to know the identity of his or her parents, mothers should not be exempted from their duty to identify the child's father.[104] But even if they are forced to comply, the new legislation cannot guarantee that the 'right' men are identified and registered as fathers. So the next logical step would be to introduce compulsory DNA testing for all children and registering adults. One wonders whether, in the absence of research *outside* the field of adoption indicating that children are psychologically damaged by not knowing the identity of their biological fathers, such a bureaucratic and potentially punitive scheme could be justified. A national database listing the DNA details of every child on birth might not only fall into the wrong hands,[105] but also provide an autocratic government with a dangerous ability to invade all individuals' privacy and generally compromise their autonomy.

(D) The courts' response

Today the courts seem fully aware of the way in which a child's right to know the truth about his or her origins is protected by human rights law. In some cases, as in *Re L (family proceedings court)(appeal: jurisdiction)*,[106] doubt over a

---

[99] Births and Deaths Registration Act 1953, s. 2E(3), as inserted by the WRB 2008, Sch. 6, para. 2(4).

[100] DWP (2008) para. 27 and Births and Deaths Registration Act 1953, s. 2B(4) as inserted by the WRB 2008, Sch. 6, para. 2(4). The exemptions include: the father has died; his identity is unknown; his whereabouts are unknown; the mother fears for her safety (and/or that of the child) if the father were contacted. Discussed by A. Bainham (2008b) pp. 460–1

[101] Births and Deaths Registration Act 1953, s. 2D, as inserted by the WRB 2008, Sch. 6, para. 2(4).

[102] DWP (2007) para. 70.   [103] DWP (2008) Annex A, para. 17 and A. Bainham (2008b) p. 460.

[104] A. Bainham (2008a) p. 330 and A. Bainham (2008b) p. 460.

[105] Government departments regularly 'lose' computer discs containing the personal details of groups of individuals.

[106] [2003] EWHC 1682 (Fam), [2005] 1 FLR 210.

child's paternity is provoked by a man's desire to avoid financial responsibility for the child. There a 15-year-old girl was devastated suddenly to discover that the man she had always thought to be her father was now denying it and was refusing to pay child support for her. Munby J deplored the way that the magistrates had accepted the truth of the man's assertions and had made a declaration to that effect,[107] without the girl or her mother either being notified of the hearing, or given a chance to attend and give evidence at it. Referring to domestic and Strasbourg case law,[108] he strongly asserted that the magistrates had infringed her fundamental human rights under Article 8 of the ECHR to know the true identity of her biological father and her rights under Article 6 to a fair hearing.[109]

In *Re L*, the putative father's behaviour stemmed from his unwillingness to acknowledge his alleged daughter. More often, however, children are left in ignorance of their fathers' identity not because fathers refuse to acknowledge them, but because their mothers refuse to tell them the truth.[110] Some children never discover that their mothers lied to them over the identity of their fathers. Others, however, do so when a dispute arises between the adults involved because the putative father very much wants to acknowledge his relationship with the child but the mother objects. Then the role played by the courts, when interpreting the child's right to knowledge of origins, is crucial. Such issues arise where, despite a mother's assertions to the contrary, either of two men could have fathered her child.[111] But she refuses to acknowledge any doubt over the identity of her child's father and excludes the 'other man' – the putative father – from the child's life. Meanwhile the putative father asserts his paternity and his right to know and enjoy his child's company. But a vital first step is for him to establish his biological links with the child by asking the court to make a direction for DNA testing.[112]

It may not be too cynical to suggest that these disputes are entirely adult-centred. The men concerned do not, by seeking directions for DNA tests, want to fulfil the child's right to know the true identity of his or her father, as a right

---

[107] I.e. a declaration of non-parentage under Family Law Act 1986, s. 55A(1).

[108] *Rose v. Secretary of State for Health and Human Fertilisation and Embryology Authority* [2002] EWHC 1593 (Admin), [2002] 2 FLR 962, *Gaskin v. United Kingdom* (1989) 12 EHRR 36, *Mikulic v. Croatia* [2002] 1 FCR 720.

[109] [2003] EWHC 1682 (Fam), [2005] 1 FLR 210, at [23]–[24].

[110] C. Lind (2006) p. 584, fn 47: studies often maintain that the number of men hoodwinked into believing children to be their own offspring is much higher than society imagines. See *A v. B (damages: paternity)* [2007] 2 FLR 1051, per QBD: a man who is fraudulently persuaded that he is a child's father and to support him or her financially can sue the woman for deceit, with those sums repayable in the form of general damages.

[111] E.g., inter alia: *Re F (a minor) (paternity test)* [1993] 1 FLR 598; *Re G (a minor) (blood test)* [1994] 1 FLR 495; *Re H (paternity: blood test)* [1996] 2 FLR 65; *Re G (parentage: blood sample)* [1997] 1 FLR 360; *Re T (paternity: ordering blood tests)* [2001] 2 FLR 1190; *Re H and A (paternity: blood tests)* [2002] EWCA Civ 383, [2002] 1 FLR 1145.

[112] Under FLRA 1969, s. 20(1). In the past the courts commonly directed 'blood tests', since when DNA testing has become universal, but the current legislation refers to 'scientific tests'.

with an intrinsic value of its own. They are motivated by the assumption that biological parentage automatically carries a right to enjoy a social relationship with the child and that, once established, the court will assist in promoting such a right through court-ordered contact. In other words, the impetus for the putative father's application for paternity testing is his desire to follow this up with an application for a contact order. Equally, the mother's desire to stop him is motivated by her fear that if he establishes his paternity, the courts will force her to allow him contact. Alternatively, the mother herself seeks a direction for paternity testing, hoping that it will show that a particular man is not the father and that she can *therefore* oppose his contact application, on the basis that there is no biological tie between them and consequently no merit in granting a contact order.[113]

In purely practical terms, a mother is probably fully justified in opposing DNA tests in such situations. She recognises this from the case law surrounding women who know the true identity of their children's father, but who bring their children up to think of their stepfathers as 'Daddy'. Perhaps influenced by the research relating to adopted children,[114] the courts have referred to the dangers of a child discovering the true facts by accident. According to Holman J:

> To do and say nothing now is in truth storing up a potential bombshell for the future, which might be very damaging for J to learn and might indeed seriously undermine his sense of trust in his mother.[115]

Similarly Ward LJ has maintained that 'every child has a right to know the truth unless his welfare clearly justifies the cover-up'.[116]

Indeed, once the father is identified, the courts will almost certainly disapprove of any attempt on the mother's part either to keep this information from the child or to prevent the father from having contact with the child. A court may well direct the mother to give the child information about his true identity[117] or will expect her to produce extremely cogent reasons why she should not be required to do so.[118] In *Re R (a minor) (contact)*,[119] the mother was even told that if she could not tell her daughter the truth herself, a child psychiatrist instructed by the Official Solicitor, who was acting as guardian ad litem for the child, would do so instead.[120] Notably, this mother was not only expected to identify the child's father, but also to introduce him to the child through gradually increasing contact. Clearly these disputes over whether a child should be informed of the real identity of his or her father are almost

---

[113] See *O v. L (blood tests)* [1995] 2 FLR 930 and *Re G (parentage: blood sample)* [1997] 1 FLR 360.

[114] Discussed above.   [115] *A v. L (contact)* [1998] 1 FLR 361 at 366.

[116] *Re H (paternity: blood test)* [1996] 2 FLR 65 at 80.

[117] *Re F (paternity: jurisdiction)* [2007] EWCA Civ 873, [2008] 1 FLR 225, per Thorpe LJ, at [8] and [14], confirming that the courts have jurisdiction to make a specific issue order requiring the mother to tell her children the truth about their parentage.

[118] E.g. *Re K (specific issue order)* [1999] 2 FLR 280 and *Re J (paternity: welfare of child)* [2006] EWHC 2837 (Fam), [2007] 1 FLR 1064.

[119] [1993] 2 FLR 762.   [120] Ibid. at 768.

inevitably underpinned by assumptions that the father *should* also have contact with the child, albeit only indirect contact in some cases.[121] As Eekelaar comments it is likely that the man wants more than just knowledge that the child is his: 'He will want to have some influence over the child's life.'[122]

The fact that applications to determine paternity through DNA testing are combined with applications for contact often has a procedural basis. A man seeking to establish his paternity may find himself propelled into applying for a contact order, simply because an application for DNA testing must be brought ancillary to an application for some other order regarding the child's parentage.[123] The most obvious route for a putative father to use is to combine his application for a direction for paternity testing with one for a contact order and/or a parental responsibility order. This form of litigation immediately brings him into direct conflict with the child's mother, if she is reluctant to allow him to develop a relationship with the child. Now that the scope of the declarations of paternity procedure has been widened, he could instead apply for a direction for paternity testing, appended to an application for a declaration that he is the father of that child.[124] Theoretically, such an application might appear less threatening to a mother wishing to keep him out of the lives of herself and her child, than the alternative more obvious route, since it does not claim involvement in the child's life. But even if he chooses this more neutral strategy, it seems unlikely that a mother who is on bad terms with him will believe that he merely wants to establish the child's parentage. She will probably resolutely oppose such an application, fearing his next step.

Perhaps predictably, mothers involved in disputes over the identity of their child's father often oppose DNA testing, hoping thereby to sabotage identification attempts. Consequently, responding to suggestions that the law, as it stood, would not comply with the requirements of the Human Rights Act (HRA) 1998,[125] the government strengthened judicial powers against mothers who seek to prevent their children discovering the true identity of their fathers by simply ignoring a court's direction for paternity testing and refusing to agree to the tests.[126] Using these powers, the courts quickly overcame their early reluctance to override mothers' refusal to agree to tests.[127] As Wallbank

---

[121] E.g. *A v. L (contact)* [1998] 1 FLR 361. [122] J. Eekelaar (2006) p. 65.

[123] FLRA 1969, s. 20(1): the courts can *only* make a direction for blood tests in the course of 'any civil proceedings in which the parentage of any person falls to be determined'. See *Re E (parental responsibility: blood tests)* [1995] 1 FLR 392, per Balcombe LJ, at 400: the court had no power to deal with a free-standing application for blood tests.

[124] Family Law Act 1986, s. 55A: subject to restrictions (see s. 55A(3)–(5)), anyone can apply for a declaration of parentage regarding another person.

[125] *Re O and J* [2000] 1 FLR 418, per Wall LJ, at 434.

[126] Under FLRA 1969, s. 21(3)(b) (as amended), the court can direct paternity testing on the child, if it 'considers that it would be in [the child's] best interests for the sample to be given', irrespective of his or her carer's lack of consent.

[127] E.g. *Re F (a minor) (blood tests: parental rights)* [1993] Fam 314; discussed by J. Fortin (1994) and C. Smart (2007) pp. 124–5.

predicted, the conjunction of the child's rights to knowledge of origins with those of his or her biological father to claim paternity testing has resulted in women being seen as opposing children's best interests by refusing to cooperate with testing.[128] As discussed below, putative fathers often have little difficulty in obtaining directions for blood or DNA tests on the basis that children have a 'right' to discover their biological origins. In some cases, a rights approach is noticeably absent, replaced instead by the argument that 'the interests of justice' require the truth to be ascertained and that the court should be furnished with the best science available rather than presumptions and inferences.[129] In others, rights language is replaced by references to the child's best interests.[130]

Bodey J's decision in *Re T (paternity: ordering blood tests)*,[131] was strongly rights based. It demonstrates very clearly how, by articulating the various ECHR rights involved in these complex situations, the conflicting interests can be appropriately identified and weighed. As he indicated, the 7-year-old boy in question had a right to respect for his private life under Article 8 of the ECHR 'in the sense of having knowledge of his identity, which encompasses his true paternity'.[132] But his rights might conflict with each other – his right to know the truth might conflict with his right to security with his present de facto family (his mother and stepfather, whom he believed to be his real father). Furthermore, the child's mother and her husband had a right to respect for their private and family life, free from interference from the man claiming to be the child's real father. Such a right might be protected by refusing to direct blood tests against her wishes. Equally, the man claiming to be the boy's real father might himself have had a right to family life with his child, if he was proved to be the child's father – which in turn, he wanted further promoted by a contact order.[133] In these circumstances, Bodey J considered that greatest weight should be given to the boy's right to know 'perhaps with certainty, his true roots and identity'.[134] Consequently, any interference with the rights of the mother and her husband was justified under Article 8(2) of the ECHR, as being proportionate to the legitimate aim of furthering T's right to certainty as to his real paternity. The mother's refusal to agree to blood testing was therefore overridden by the court.[135]

By dealing with this type of dispute from a rights perspective, more particularly by considering the child's right to know his or her father's identity, the court is forced to consider the merits of an application for DNA testing independently from the possible outcome of the application for other orders, such as contact. Indeed, the judiciary seem keen to deal with the issue of biological parentage as a preliminary issue, detached from the question whether

---

[128] J. Wallbank (2004a) p. 253.

[129] *Re H and A (paternity: blood tests)* [2002] EWCA Civ 383, [2002] 1 FLR 1145, per Thorpe LJ, at [29].

[130] E.g. *Re D (paternity)* [2006] EWHC 3545 (Fam), [2007] 2 FLR 26.   [131] [2001] 2 FLR 1190.

[132] Ibid. at 1197.   [133] Bodey J quite correctly doubted the strength of this argument; see below.

[134] [2001] 2 FLR 1190 at 1198.   [135] I.e. under FLRA 1969, s. 21(3)(b).

the applicant should in future be allowed to acquire a psychological or social relationship with the child. Thus Ward LJ pointed out that if the blood test excludes the applicant from paternity, this does not necessarily prevent a future contact application succeeding; he might then convince the court that the child would benefit from continued contact with a devoted stepfather.[136] Equally, Bodey J in *Re T*,[137] emphasised that in the event of blood tests confirming the putative father's claims, it would not automatically follow that he would then succeed in obtaining a contact order or a parental responsibility order.[138]

Achieving an appropriate balance between the various sets of rights may not be easy. It is the combination of a claim for DNA testing with a claim for contact which has the potential for upsetting a child's right to security in his or her de facto family unit. It was the risk of losing this security that worried the trial judge in *Re H and A (paternity: blood tests)*.[139] He considered that it would be disastrous for the mother's husband to be excluded from paternity because twin little girls would lose their 'psychological father'. The Court of Appeal disagreed, considering that the uncertainty over their father's identity would cause greater damage. Children may be quite old enough to have strong views of their own about their parents' identity.[140] Some children, like T, the troubled 11-year-old boy in *Re D (paternity)*,[141] strongly reject adults' suggestions that they will be psychologically damaged without an accurate knowledge of their fathers' identity. T rejected the paternity claims of the putative father,[142] desiring to retain the view that he was being cared for by his paternal grandmother – and so did she. Hedley J considered that it would be against T's best interests to be forced to undergo DNA testing. But since, in his view, it was in T's long-term best interests to know the truth, he made a direction that T should undergo DNA testing, but stayed it for an unlimited time, with liberty to restore it.[143] T's guardian was asked to explain to T after the hearing that it was the view of the judge, social worker and guardian that 'this matter of paternity should be resolved and that in the end truth is easier to live with than doubt or fiction'.[144]

T's case produces a feeling of unease. Just as Munby J has asserted that it would smack 'too much of the Inquisition' to try to force a mother who has placed her child for adoption to identify the child's father,[145] so the courts should recognise that a right claimed for all children as a class, may not always

---

[136] *Re G (parentage: blood sample)* [1997] 1 FLR 360, per Ward LJ, at 366. See also *Re H (paternity: blood test)* [1996] 2 FLR 65 at 82.

[137] [2001] 2 FLR 1190 at 1198.   [138] Ibid. at 1196.

[139] [2002] EWCA Civ 383, [2002] 1 FLR 1145.

[140] E.g. *Re L (family proceedings court)(appeal: jurisdiction)* [2005] 1 FLR 210, discussed above.

[141] [2006] EWHC 3545 (Fam), [2007] 2 FLR 26.

[142] The putative father had applied for a residence order (later withdrawn), a parental responsibility order and a contact order, combined with a request for a direction for scientific testing under FLRA 1969, Part III.

[143] Ibid. at [30].   [144] Ibid. at [31].

[145] *Re L (adoption: contacting natural father)* [2007] EWHC 1771 (Fam), [2008] 1 FLR 1079, at [40].

promote an individual child's best interests. A child may have a right *not* to know the identity of his father. Furthermore, the lessons gained from adoption should not necessarily be applied in this context. After all, as discussed above, providing an adopted child with knowledge of his birth parents' identity is unlikely to be followed by a social relationship between them that will threaten the stability of his existing relationship with his adoptive parents. Cases like *Re D (paternity)* show that fulfilling the current view that *all* children have a right to know their parents' identity may sometimes achieve more harm than good, given the danger of two issues being confused, at least in the child's mind – the child's need to know about his origins and his possible need for a social relationship with his biological parent. T neither wanted any knowledge of his putative father nor contact of any kind with him, but the latter's claims had already unsettled him considerably. Just like the boy in *Re T*, his right to stability with his putative grandmother could be jeopardised by his putative father's claims. Moreover, as Hasan points out, there may also be strong cultural reasons why a child should not be told the truth of his paternity, especially if it involves his learning that he was born to unmarried parents.[146] The courts' approach to all these disputes is undoubtedly complicated by society's assumption that biological ties *should* always carry social relationships, despite the growing evidence provided by family disruption and reproductive technology that this is not always appropriate.

(3) Unmarried fathers – and 'mothers'

(A) Unmarried fathers

The law's response to the biological relationship between the unmarried father and his child informs any discussion of the extent to which the law should reinforce the link between a child and his or her biological parents. The question whether the biological tie between unmarried fathers and their children should be legally recognised in precisely the same way as that between married parents and their children continues to provoke disagreement. Meanwhile, the declining popularity of marriage and corresponding growth in unmarried cohabitation have been accompanied by increasing rates of children born outside marriage.[147] There are well-known reasons for the FLRA 1987 not matching these attitudinal changes by automatically granting all unmarried fathers an equal status to that enjoyed by their married counterparts.[148] The confused messages regarding the importance of the relationship between non-marital children and their fathers was reinforced by the legislative

---

[146] A. Hasan (2008).
[147] Office for National Statistics (2008) p. 24: in 2006, 43.7% of live births in the UK were outside marriage.
[148] N. Lowe (1997) pp. 198–201: the various attempts to reform this area of the law.

reform giving automatic parental responsibility only to those unmarried fathers whose names appear on their children's birth certificates.[149]

This reform produced a complex picture, with three groups of children enjoying subtly different legal relationships with their parents.[150] The first are the marital children, the second, the non-marital, but with 'birth certificate fathers', and the third, the non-marital children whose fathers are not identified on their birth certificates. In reality, because the change was not retrospective, a fourth group was also created. These are the children born before the reforms, who, despite their fathers' names appearing on their birth certificates, are treated in an identical manner to those in the third group. The first group, the marital children, are the most secure, with both parents having automatic parental responsibility over them as from their birth.[151] Unlike the second, their father's parental responsibility cannot be terminated by court order.[152] The third and fourth groups will have no one with parental responsibility over them in the event of their mothers dying.

Reforming the law relating to unmarried fathers and their children was obviously partly fuelled by the ease with which the paternal link can now be accurately proved by DNA testing. The secrecy which, in the past, often shrouded a non-marital child's birth and the identity of his or her father became untenable, partly due to the Child Support Agency's ability to identify him and pursue him for child support.[153] But perhaps the greatest factor provoking reform was the government's recognition that many unmarried parents were ignorant of the way in which the law discriminated against unmarried fathers.[154] Despite the growing numbers of children born outside marriage, relatively few unmarried fathers availed themselves of the legal procedures whereby they could acquire parental responsibility,[155] probably because they did not appreciate the need to apply.[156] Indeed, unmarried fathers commonly assume that, because they have lived with their partners for some years and have undertaken financial responsibility for their children, they automatically enjoy parental responsibility for them.[157]

[149] CA 1989, s. 4(1)(a), implemented as from 1 December 2003. This group of children will expand on introduction of the new birth registration scheme (WRB 2008, Sch. 6) discussed above.
[150] J. Eekelaar (2001) pp. 426–8.
[151] CA 1989, s. 2(1). See Chapter 9 for a discussion of the term 'parental responsibility'.
[152] CA 1989, s. 4(3): an unmarried father's parental responsibility can be terminated by court order on application by anyone with parental responsibility or by the child with court leave.
[153] E.g. *Secretary of State for Work and Pensions v. Jones* [2003] EWHC 2163 (Fam), [2004] 1 FLR 282; see fn 31 above.
[154] LCD (1998) paras. 51–6.
[155] I.e. under CA 1989, s. 4(1)(b) and (c): an unmarried father may enter into a parental responsibility agreement with the mother or apply for a parental responsibility order.
[156] LCD (1998) para. 53.
[157] R. Pickford (1999a) pp. 145–52. See also R. Pickford (1999b): 75% of the fathers who knew that they were financially responsible for their non-marital children were unaware that they lacked parental responsibility.

Under current law, the children whose parents jointly register their births, like marital children, have two parents with automatic parental responsibility over them. From birth, however, the third group of non-marital children lack two parents with a legal relationship with them, since only their mothers gain such legal recognition.[158] Their fathers have no legal status relating to their children. Nevertheless, their position is not as stark as this statement implies. First, by virtue of the FLRA 1987, section 1, references to 'parent' in legislation like the CA 1989[159] and the Child Support Act 1991,[160] must be interpreted as if the difference in legal status between all married and unmarried fathers is irrelevant. Second, the non-birth certificate unmarried fathers can take steps to acquire parental responsibility through obtaining a parental responsibility order (PRO).[161] Indeed, the assumption that the biological link between parent and child *normally* carries a social and legal relationship clearly underlies the ease with which many unmarried fathers obtain PROs, even when opposed by mothers. This assumption was implicit in the words of Ward LJ, who explained that the effect of such an order is to confer 'upon a committed father the status of parenthood for which nature has already ordained that he must bear responsibility';[162] furthermore, that the misuse of the PRO could be controlled by a section 8 order, if and when it occurred.

If a court adopts this approach, the unmarried father may find that it is a relatively simple task for him to satisfy the requisite 'attachment and commitment to the child' test to obtain a PRO.[163] His lack of merit as a father is irrelevant. Indeed, the woman struggling to bring up her child free from his violent attentions,[164] or without his financial help,[165] is expected to think 'calmly' about his gaining a PRO, because it merely carries the 'status of parenthood'.[166] She should understand that the PRO merely gives the father parental status and not the right to interfere with the day-to-day management of the child's life.[167] But, as various writers point out, the courts are far from consistent in their approach to applications for PROs, with some fathers

[158] CA 1989, s. 2(2).

[159] E.g. *Re B (care proceedings: notification of father without parental responsibility)* [1999] 2 FLR 408: care order was set aside because the child's unmarried father was not served with notice of the care proceedings.

[160] Child Support Act 1991, s. 1 imposes liability on the non-residential parent irrespective of legal status.

[161] CA 1989, s. 4(1)(c).

[162] *Re S (parental responsibility)* [1995] 2 FLR 648 at 657. See also *Re C and V (contact and parental responsibility)* [1998] 1 FLR 392.

[163] *Re H (illegitimate children: father: parental rights) (No 2)* [1991] 1 FLR 214, per Balcombe LJ, at 218: the court must consider the unmarried father's degree of commitment to the child, the degree of attachment existing between him and the child, and his reasons for applying for the order.

[164] E.g. *Re B J (a child) (non-molestation order: power of arrest)* [2001] 1 All ER 235.

[165] E.g. *Re H (parental responsibility: maintenance)* [1996] 1 FLR 867.

[166] *Re S (parental responsibility)* [1995] 2 FLR 648, per Ward LJ, at 657. See F. Kaganas (1996) for a critical discussion of this decision.

[167] *Re P (a minor) (parental responsibility order)* [1994] 1 FLR 578, per Wilson J, at 585.

receiving very different judicial treatment.[168] At times, the courts have implicitly accepted that such an order does not merely carry parental status[169] and that armed with PROs, fathers are all the more likely to interfere with their children's upbringing.[170] In these decisions, the courts have more critically appraised the father's application from the child's viewpoint, considering whether the PRO's potential for destabilising the family would impact deleteriously on the child.[171] As noted below, the courts seem more attracted by this position when dealing with sperm donors' applications for PROs, when opposed by lesbian parents.

Despite the reforms to date, there is a strong ground swell of opinion that the law should not discriminate against unmarried fathers in any way at all – that by forcing such a father to register his child's birth or apply to the courts for a PRO implies his lack of merit as a parent, based only on his lack of marital status.[172] Some, like Deech[173] and Wallbank[174] strongly disagree with this view, believing that such arguments concentrate on fathers' rights, without considering their children's own perspectives. In Deech's view, the biological tie between child and parent is not as important to a child as the care and love he or she receives on a day-to-day basis.[175] Wallbank strongly criticises the reform providing unmarried fathers with automatic parental responsibility merely by virtue of joint birth registration. She argues that this move was part of a response to the arguments of fathers' pressure groups that fathers are, per se, discriminated against by the legal system and that they have a right to be treated fairly.[176] In her view, since ascribing PR to unmarried fathers who jointly register their child's birth will not necessarily ensure that they act responsibly, the change will merely force victims of domestic violence into seeking revocation of a PRO whilst also seeking protective remedies.[177] Whilst this view may be an extreme one, there is the perfectly valid argument that unmarried fathers are a very diverse group, ranging from the man who, as a one-off sexual partner, subsequently has no contact with the child, to the committed and closely involved parent.[178]

---

[168] J. Wallbank (2002) and S. Gilmore (2003) discuss the case law on parental responsibility orders, together with its inconsistencies.

[169] J. Wallbank (2002) p. 287.

[170] E.g. *Re P (parental responsibility)* [1998] 2 FLR 96: PRO withheld from a man who had not only behaved in a way strongly suggesting that he might be a paedophile but whose behaviour to date indicated that he would interfere with the child's upbringing; *Re H (parental responsibility)* [1998] 1 FLR 855: PRO withheld from a father who, it appeared, had treated his 15-month-old son with deliberate cruelty and sadism.

[171] E.g. *Re J (parental responsibility)* [1999] 1 FLR 784: PRO withheld from a father largely due to the 12-year-old child's evidence that he had sought little to no contact with her since her birth and she wanted none with him now; *Re M (contact: parental responsibility)* [2001] 2 FLR 342: PRO withheld from a father largely because to date he had substantially interfered with his disabled daughter's upbringing and would misuse the PRO to interfere even more.

[172] See, inter alia: A. Bainham (1989); N. Lowe (1997); H. Conway (1996); J. Eekelaar (2001).

[173] R. Deech (1993).   [174] J. Wallbank (2002).   [175] R. Deech (1993) p. 30.

[176] J. Wallbank (2002) pp. 291–4.   [177] Ibid. at pp. 295–6.

[178] S. Sheldon (2007) p. 12. See also *B v. United Kingdom* [2000] 1 FLR 1 at 5, discussed below.

Meanwhile, further reforms in the context of citizenship law sought to eliminate one of the remaining distinctions between the status of married and unmarried men and their offspring. The old law that, unlike marital children, no non-marital child could claim British nationality from his or her father by descent arose because children of unmarried parents formerly had no legal relationship with their fathers.[179] It is difficult to maintain that reforming this extraordinary example of legal discrimination was unjustified. But as Sheldon argues, when seen as part of a general reforming movement, one may question whether the 'mere' fact of a genetic link existing between parent and child is sufficient to justify such a shift to formal equality. Until this reform, English law had not awarded rights to unmarried fathers automatically, but on the basis that the father must do more than merely provide evidence of the genetic link. They must jointly register the child's birth or obtain a PRO. In contrast, this reform, she argues, might be located 'within a broader movement towards what has been described as a "geneticisation" of paternity, with increasing weight given to genetic factors over social ones'.[180]

As is apparent, an extraordinarily inconsistent set of principles now apply to the children whose birth certificates omit their fathers' names. Of greatest concern is the fact that their mothers' death may still deprive them of the only adult with parental responsibility over them. Despite this source of discrimination, it does not appear that European human rights law will provoke further reform. Article 8 of the ECHR does indeed impose a positive obligation on states to provide legal safeguards enabling the child to be integrated within his or her marital and non-marital family from the moment of birth.[181] Nevertheless, although Article 8 protects various forms of de facto family,[182] the biological connection between father and child is not enough *per se* to justify his arguing that his rights under Article 8 have been infringed by laws which, for example, prevent his applying for contact with the child. Consequently, a sperm donor cannot pray in aid of Article 8, arguing that the law is denying him his *potential* relationship with his child.[183] On the other hand, Articles 8 and 14 combined together form a powerful weapon against discriminatory practices which inhibit the right of unmarried parents to enjoy

---

[179] See S. Sheldon (2007) pp 3–7 for a historical assessment of this rule.

[180] S. Sheldon (2007) p. 13.   [181] *Marckx v. Belgium* (1979) 2 EHRR 330, at para. 31.

[182] E.g. *Johnston v. Ireland* (1986) 9 EHRR 203: the child of a cohabiting couple was entitled to protection of her family life under Arts. 8 and 14 of the ECHR; *X, Y and Z v. United Kingdom* [1997] 2 FLR 892: the family unit existing between a transsexual, his partner and child, was a de facto family warranting the protection of Art. 8.

[183] *Lebbink v. The Netherlands* [2004] 2 FLR 463, at [36]–[38]: absent cohabitation between the parents, other factors must demonstrate that the father's relationship with the child had 'sufficient constancy and substance' to create de facto 'family ties'; mere biological kinship, without further legal or factual elements indicating the existence of a close personal relationship is insufficient to ground a claim under Art. 8.

their children's company.[184] Consequently, the ECtHR is in no doubt that the domestic courts must not treat unmarried fathers' claims to have contact with their children less favourably than those of married fathers, both substantively and procedurally.[185]

On the basis of this case law, the domestic courts are rightly anxious to protect the rights of unmarried fathers.[186] Nevertheless, the ECtHR has rejected claims that unmarried fathers' biological relationship with their children must always be reinforced by a legal status.[187] Indeed, the Court's approach to the position of unmarried fathers reflects Deech's views. The Court clearly doubts the sense of automatically providing *all* unmarried fathers with parental responsibility, irrespective of their relationship with the child or mother. The fact that the relationship between unmarried fathers and their children 'varies from ignorance and indifference to a close stable relationship indistinguishable from the conventional family-based unit' justifies any difference between their legal status and that of married fathers.[188] Thus their rights under Articles 8 and 14 of the ECHR are not infringed by English law denying them automatic parental responsibility. Nor does Article 8 provide an unmarried father with an absolute right to have his family ties with his non-marital child recognised legally, even after the mother's death.[189]

As the above discussion demonstrates, there are cogent arguments for and against reforming the law yet again, providing all unmarried fathers with an equal status to that enjoyed by their married counterparts. On the one hand, why should the man who merely had a 'one-night-stand' with a woman expect the courts to create a child-father relationship for him – does it truly promote the child's interests? This is particularly questionable if the couple never had a relationship before or after the child's birth and if the woman is now bringing the child up with her new partner acting as the child's psychological parent.[190] As Eekelaar himself asks, albeit in a slightly different context: 'So should anyone have a legally recognized interest in developing a relationship with a human being, *for no other reason than that they procreated that individual?*'[191] On the other hand, there remains a small group of children, who, through no fault of their own, have no legal relationship with their fathers either because their births were not jointly registered by both parents or because their fathers never

---

[184] *Keegan v. Ireland* (1994) 18 EHRR 342: Irish law had infringed an unmarried father's rights under Arts. 8 and 14 by denying him a right to challenge his child's adoption. See also *Kroon v. Netherlands* (1995) 19 EHRR 263.

[185] *Sahin v. Germany* [2003] 2 FLR 671, at paras 93–4, in each decision.

[186] E.g. *Re F (a child)* [2008] EWCA Civ 439, [2008] 2 FCR 93, cf. *Re L (adoption: contacting natural father)* [2007] EWHC 1771 (Fam), [2008] 1 FLR 1079; discussed further in Chapter 14.

[187] *B v. United Kingdom* [2000] 1 FLR 1.   [188] Ibid. at 5.

[189] *Yousef v. Netherlands* [2002] 3 FCR 577: the infringement of the father's rights (under Art. 8) to have his family ties between him and his daughter recognised was justified (under Art. 8(2)) by the domestic court's view that this would be against her best interests.

[190] E.g. *Re G (parental responsibility order)* [2006] EWCA Civ 745, [2006] 2 FLR 1092.

[191] J. Eekelaar (2006) p. 65 (emphasis as in the original).

obtained PROs over them. The fact that few unmarried couples realise this reinforces the problem. Furthermore, and this is the most substantial point in favour of further reform, the law fails to cater adequately for non-marital families disintegrating. The children of married parents automatically enjoy a legal relationship with their fathers, whether or not their parents separate, die, or abandon them. As discussed above, planned reforms will ensure that most unmarried fathers will be named on their child's birth certificates. But when a mother is exempted from having to identify her child's father on the birth certificate, he gains no parental responsibility for the child. If she later dies, he has no legal status and no better right to care for the child than, say, the maternal relatives.[192]

(B) Same-sex parents

Questions about the unequal legal status of unmarried fathers usually arise in the context of conventional sexual relationships between heterosexual couples. A new set of dilemmas is produced by the different parenting arrangements flowing from same-sex relationships and reproductive technologies, more particularly, sperm donation. The parenting disputes provoked by lesbian parenting illustrate exceptionally well the weight placed by society and the courts on the biological tie – or lack of it – between 'mother' and child. Thus, if a lesbian couple breaks up, the biological mother's ex-partner may find that her claim to the child's care, in her capacity as *merely* the children's 'social' or 'psychological mother', is given far less weight by the court than that given to the claim of their biological mother.[193] As Baroness Hale of Richmond emphasised in *Re G (children) (residence: same-sex partner)*,[194] as their genetic, gestational and psychological parent, the biological mother's contribution to the children's welfare is unique;[195] she is their 'natural mother … in every sense of that term'.[196] Unlike the Court of Appeal, who treated the ex-partner as a parent of equal importance to the children as their biological mother, the House of Lords, considered it self-evident that, as merely the children's social or psychological parent, the former should be denied the children's primary care.[197] Indeed, as Millbank points out, the House of Lords' decision 'established a clear "parent versus non-parent" standard for intra-lesbian disputes in English law'.[198]

Current law improves the position of such a lesbian 'psychological mother' if, prior to the child's birth, she became the biological mother's civil partner. She

---

192 E.g. *Re S (custody: habitual residence)* [1998] 1 FLR 122.   193 A. Diduck (2007).
194 [2006] UKHL 43, [2006] 4 All ER 241.   195 Ibid. at [36].   196 Ibid. at [44].
197 The non-biological mother in *Re G* retained her parental responsibility under a shared residence order, but the biological mother gained the right to provide the children's primary home.
198 J. Millbank (2008) p. 158.

can then apply for a PRO, as a step-parent;[199] presumably she must show the same degree of attachment and commitment as that expected from a male applicant.[200] But such formal action may be unnecessary.[201] Indeed, as long as lesbian mothers use the services of licensed clinics to conceive, their partners are normally treated as the children's legal parents, whether or not they have become civil partners.[202]

Meanwhile, the law is becoming increasingly incoherent in its treatment of the biological link between an unmarried father and his child. As discussed above, when a child is born to a heterosexual couple, the courts assume that they should assist the putative father establish his identity and pursue a social relationship with the child – even if the relationship between him and the mother was an essentially casual one and even if the child believes the mother's current partner to be his father.[203] But if a man becomes a father by providing sperm to lesbian parents under an informal arrangement not involving a licensed clinic he is treated very differently. Case law[204] suggests that lesbian parents do not always bargain for interference from the sperm donor,[205] and may renege on any informal assurance provided prior to the child's birth that he will have 'heaps of contact'.[206] They may argue that they are providing the child with a 'normal' two parent (albeit same-sex) household in which to grow up.[207] The courts apparently sympathise with their view that the child does not need a social father carrying out the same role as that carried out by a non-resident father in a heterosexual relationship. The sperm donor may therefore either obtain a PRO hedged around by a list of stringent limitations[208] or be refused a PRO entirely, on the basis that gaining one would be a 'threat to their [the lesbian couple's] autonomy as a family unit'.[209] He may be granted very limited contact[210] to enable the child to satisfy his natural curiosity over his father's identity, without thereby allowing the development of a parental

---

[199] CA 1989, s. 4(1)(b). Alternatively (under s. 4(1)(a)) she may enter into a parental responsibility agreement with the mother.

[200] *Re H (illegitimate children: father: parental rights) (No 2)* [1991] 1 FLR 214. See fn 163 above.

[201] HFEA 2008, s. 42: a civil partner of the mother is treated as the child's legal parent, unless she did not consent to the mother's receiving such treatment.

[202] HFEA 2008, s. 43: the female (non-civil) partner of the mother is treated as the child's legal parent, subject to the treatment being provided by a licensed clinic and subject to her and the mother formally consenting to the 'agreed parenthood conditions' at the time it is provided (i.e. under s. 44).

[203] E.g. *Re T (paternity: ordering blood tests)* [2001] 2 FLR 1190.

[204] E.g. *Re D (contact and parental responsibility: lesbian mothers and known father)* [2006] EWHC 2 (Fam), [2006] 1 FCR 556 and *Re B (role of biological father)* [2007] EWHC 1952 (Fam), [2008] 1 FLR 1015.

[205] J. Wallbank (2004b) pp. 389–91.   [206] Ibid. at p. 390.   [207] A. Diduck (2007) pp. 464–7.

[208] E.g. *Re D (contact and parental responsibility: lesbian mothers and known father)* [2006] EWHC 2 (Fam), [2006] 1 FCR 556.

[209] *Re B (role of biological father)* [2007] EWHC 1952 (Fam), [2008] 1 FLR 1015, per Hedley J, at [26].

[210] Ibid. at [30]: contact four times per annum of 2 hours' duration.

relationship.[211] Final incoherence is added to this branch of the law by the sperm donor being barred from applying for a PRO in cases where the biological mother's lesbian partner is 'treated' as a legal parent.[212] Indeed, he is written out of the family picture entirely, with the biological links between him and 'his' child being effectively erased by the new legislation.

(4) Identity and names

Children's names carry a practical as well as symbolic importance. When children are named they are identified, given membership of their family group and provided with a link to their cultural background. It is important that children's existence is recognised in this way, as soon after birth as possible, for otherwise they could be abandoned or kidnapped far more easily. As discussed above, Articles 7 and 8 of the CRC both recognise this, although it is Article 7 which specifically guarantees the child's right to a name and nationality. English law more than adequately fulfils these rights. Dame Elizabeth Butler-Sloss P emphasised the importance to children of their names, both forename and surname. In her view, by the time children reach 5, 6 or 7, they have made their names part of their identity. As she rightly observed, even a very young child is able to answer the question 'what's your name?'.[213] This led her to castigate foster parents for changing the forename of a 6-year-old foster child, because in so doing they were changing her identity.[214]

But what name should a child be given in the first place – more particularly what surname should they be given? When describing the practice in this country whereby married parents give a child the father's surname, Lord Jauncey of Tullichettle suggested that this was a way of:

> demonstrating its relationship to him. The surname is thus a biological label which tells the world at large that the blood of the name flows in its veins.[215]

Views like this regarding the importance of maintaining the blood tie between child and father through their surnames may still be common. Clearly they may be shared by many women, perhaps explaining unmarried women's predilection for ensuring that their children carry their partners' surnames whilst the relationship lasts. Eekelaar, however, robustly described Lord Jauncey's views as a 'pathetic hangover from the patriarchal era'.[216] Nor did Hale LJ consider that they accorded with the modern law.[217] She observed:

> It is also a matter of great sadness to me that it is so often assumed, and even sometimes argued, that fathers need that outward and visible link [through

---

[211] Ibid. at [29].

[212] HFEA 2008, s. 45(1): 'Where a woman is treated by virtue of section 42 or 43 as a parent of the child, no man is to be treated as the father of the child.'

[213] *Re D, L and LA (care; change of forename)* [2003] 1 FLR 339 at 346.   [214] Ibid.

[215] *Dawson v. Wearmouth* [1999] 2 All ER 353 at 361.   [216] J. Eekelaar (2006) p. 63.

[217] *Re R (surname: using both parents')* [2001] EWCA Civ 1344, [2001] 2 FLR 1358, at [13].

surnames] in order to retain their relationship with, and commitment to, their child. That should not be the case ... After all, that is a privilege which is not enjoyed by many mothers ... They have to rely on other more substantial things.[218]

In this country, parental litigation over children's surnames[219] is not a new phenomenon. Indeed, the law reports spanning more than 20 years contain accounts of such disputes.[220] Most of these arise over whether a child should now adopt a different surname, reflecting the residential parents' own change of circumstances. Notably the law gives no indication what surname the child should take on birth,[221] merely indicating who should register it and when.[222] As Eekelaar's words above suggest, the initial selection of a surname for children is strongly influenced by the now outdated customs of a patriarchal society. Women on marriage took their husbands' surnames. Furthermore, by habitually giving their children the husband's name, married couples publicly indicated that their children were legitimate, with inheritance rights and membership of their father's extended family. Historically, an unmarried woman usually retained her own surname, since she would not normally live openly with her partner. Her 'illegitimate child', as a filius nullius, was not entitled to any acknowledgment from his father and commonly took his mother's surname. Today, despite a rising divorce rate and ever-increasing rates of cohabitation outside marriage, these customs still seem to influence the initial choice of surnames. Furthermore, the custom grew up for many unmarried women to adopt their partners' surnames on entering cohabitation, rather than retaining their own surnames. Later when they have children, although they are entitled to choose what surname they please for their children,[223] some unmarried women agree to the child taking the father's surname, rather than their own.[224]

Disputes between parents over their children's surnames often occur on separation, with a mother commonly deciding to mark her changed way of

---

[218] Ibid. at [18]. See also Hale LJ's clear view (at [13]) that Lord Jauncey's views in *Dawson v. Wearmouth* [1999] 2 All ER 353, do not accord with the modern law.

[219] Parental disputes over children's names normally involve disputes over surnames. More recently disputes over forenames are becoming more common. E.g. *Re H (child's name: first name)* [2002] EWCA Civ 190, [2002] 1 FLR 973.

[220] E.g. *D v. B (otherwise D) (child: surname)* [1979] 1 All ER 92 and *Re R (surname: using both parents')* [2001] EWCA Civ 1344, [2001] 2 FLR 1358.

[221] The Registration of Births and Deaths Regulations 1987 (SI 1987/2088), reg. 9(3) merely state that the surname to be entered 'shall be the surname by which at the date of the registration of birth it is intended that the child shall be known'.

[222] The Births and Deaths Registration Act 1953, s. 2, requires the child's birth to be registered within 42 days of its birth and if the parents are married, either should do so. If the parents are unmarried, the duty is on the mother to do so. See A. Bainham (2008b) pp. 450–7.

[223] *Dawson v. Wearmouth* [1999] 2 All ER 353.

[224] E.g. *Re C (change of surname)* [1998] 2 FLR 656: dispute between an unmarried couple over whether the mother should change their daughter's surname back to that of the father, as appeared on her birth certificate. The mother had changed the child's surname to her own soon after the couple separated.

life by shedding her ex-partner's surname. She then decides that her child should carry the name she now carries – which may be that of her new partner.[225] A non-resident father may see such a change, often combined with new registration details with all official agencies, such as schools and doctors,[226] as an attempt by her to cut his links with his children. When the dispute ends up in court, the judiciary's response to the mother's application to change the child's name[227] is variable. Incidentally, it is unclear how the courts obtain any authority to be involved in such disputes at all. The legislation clearly allows a parent with parental responsibility to meet his or her responsibilities regarding the child unilaterally, without consulting the other,[228] and certainly without obtaining court permission,[229] unless a residence order is in force.[230] Nevertheless, the courts found it difficult to accept the proposition that a parent is legally entitled to go ahead with such an important change without first obtaining the other parent's consent or that of the court.[231] Through a series of self-referencing decisions, the courts laid down the proposition that if parents, married and unmarried alike, cannot agree whether to change their child's surname, they must seek judicial authority first.[232]

A court will only authorise a change in a child's surname if it considers it to be in the child's best interests.[233] But at this point, the essential subjectivity of the best interests test is demonstrated only too clearly. As Hale LJ pointed out, the court has to find a balance between the child's long-term interests in retaining an outward link with the non-resident parent, against the short-term benefits of avoiding the confusion and embarrassment of having a different surname from other members of the family.[234] The case law reflects the different judicial approaches to this balancing act. Some courts consider that a child's surname is a matter of fundamental importance because it may break the child's link with his or her non-resident father.[235] Consequently, they may give little weight to the fact that the child's surname is different from that of the

---

[225] E.g. *Re PC (change of surname)* [1997] 2 FLR 730.   [226] Ibid.

[227] Alternatively, the father may apply to force her to change the child's name back, she having made the change already, e.g. *Re C (change of surname)* [1998] 2 FLR 656.

[228] CA 1989, s. 2(7): 'Where more than one person has parental responsibility for a child, each of them may act alone and without the other (or others) in meeting that responsibility.'

[229] J. Eekelaar (1998); J. Eekelaar (2001) pp. 428–9; N. Gosden (2003) pp. 186–8.

[230] CA 1989, s. 13(1).

[231] *Re PC (change of surname)* [1997] 2 FLR 730, per Holman J, at 732–3.

[232] *Re PC (change of surname)* [1997] 2 FLR 730; *Re C (change of surname)* [1998] 2 FLR 656; *Dawson v. Wearmouth* [1999] 2 All ER 353; *Re W, Re A, Re B (change of name)* [1999] 2 FLR 930.

[233] *Dawson v. Wearmouth* [1999] 2 All ER 353, per Lord Mackay, at 359. See also *Re W, Re A; Re B (change of name)* [1999] 2 FLR 930, per Butler-Sloss LJ, at 933.

[234] *Re R (surname: using both parents')* [2001] EWCA Civ 1344, [2001] 2 FLR 1358, at [15].

[235] E.g. *W v. A (child: surname)* [1981] Fam 14 and *Re C (a child) (change of surname)* [1999] 1 FCR 318. Such a view may be strengthened by circumstances in which changing a child's surname would risk his losing his links with his racial and religious identity, e.g. *Re S (change of names: cultural factors)* [2001] 2 FLR 1005.

applicant.[236] Others consider that surnames are relatively trivial matters and that children should not be embarrassed by being forced to retain a different name to that of their mothers. That being so, the courts should therefore concentrate on fostering the father's *actual* links with the child through good contact arrangements.[237] Butler-Sloss LJ suggests that when deciding whether such a change is in the child's best interests, the courts are influenced by the parents' marital status.[238] Thus in the case of a child born to married parents, the court expects strong reasons to justify changing the surname from that registered on the birth certificate (normally that of the father). In the case of a child born to unmarried parents, given that the child's name was determined by the mother on registration of birth, the court expects evidence of the father's commitment to the child, the quality of his relationship with his child and the existence or absence of parental responsibility.[239]

It appears that in cases involving older children, the courts are more ready to take account of children's own views about what names they should carry.[240] Nevertheless, these bitter disputes will continue until parents adopt a more pragmatic approach, like that suggested by Hale and Thorpe LJJ in *Re R (surname: using both parents')*.[241] This was for the child to carry both parents' surnames on separation. Although such a solution does not prevent parents disagreeing over which surname should be listed *first*, it does overcome sexist assumptions about children bearing their fathers' names. Meanwhile, research is needed throwing light on the extent to which children's own sense of identity is bound up with the names they become familiar with in their early years.

(5) Parental contact disputes

(A) A child's 'right' to contact

(i) 'Rights talk'
Overall, official estimates state that parental separation affects '[s]ome three million of the twelve million children in this country'.[242] There is a voluminous body of research literature on the adverse outcomes suffered by children as a result.[243] One immediate outcome is that parents often disagree over their

---

[236] Per Butler-Sloss LJ in *Re W, Re A; Re B (change of name)* [1999] 2 FLR 930, at 933.

[237] E.g. *D v. B (otherwise D) (child: surname)* [1979] 1 All ER 92 and *Y v. Y (child's surname)* [1999] 2 FLR 5. See also *Yousef v. Netherlands* [2002] 3 FCR 577: the ECtHR implicitly approved of the Dutch court's view that the child might be harmed by the automatic assumption of her father's surname were he allowed formally to recognise her as his daughter. She was being brought up by her mother's family under their surname and a different surname might set her apart from them.

[238] *Re W, Re A; Re B (change of name)* [1999] 2 FLR 930 at 933.   [239] Ibid.

[240] E.g. *Re M, T, P, K and B (care: change of name)* [2000] 2 FLR 645; cf. *Re B (change of surname)* [1996] 1 FLR 791. Discussed in more detail in Chapter 8.

[241] [2001] EWCA Civ 1344, [2001] 2 FLR 1358.   [242] DCA *et al.* (2004) Ministerial Forward, p. 1.

[243] See summaries by J. Pryor and B. Rodgers (2001) ch. 3; J. Fortin *et al.* (2006) pp. 212–13; G. Harold and M. Murch (2005) pp. 186–95.

children's future upbringing. The rising number of contact disputes[244] very obviously reflects the need experienced by separated parents and children to spend time together and also an assumption that it is their right to do so, by virtue of the biological link between them. As Buchanan *et al.* observe, these disputes provoke profound debates within our society – in particular, there is the question whether a biological tie per se entitles a parent to an ongoing relationship with his child or whether the role of parent has to be earned.[245]

Few doubt that it is *normally* in children's best interests to remain in contact with the parent who leaves the home when a couple separate and international human rights law recognises this. Both the CRC[246] and the European Convention on Contact Concerning Children[247] emphasise the need for the child and parent to maintain direct and regular contact, except in circumstances where this would be against the child's best interests. Similarly, according to Strasbourg case law, the mutual enjoyment by parent and child of each other's company constitutes a fundamental element of family life under Article 8 of the ECHR, even if the parents' relationship has broken down.[248] So any infringement of such a right must be carefully justified under Article 8(2), with a fair balance being struck between the interests of the child and those of the parent, with particular importance being attached to the child's best interests, which, depending on their nature and seriousness, may override those of the parent.[249] Furthermore, the Strasbourg jurisprudence protects parents against discrimination by the courts when considering a parental dispute, both regarding the weight to be given to each parents' interests in the dispute,[250] and the handling of the evidence.[251] It should be noted that the ECtHR sees these disputes in terms of adults' rights and children's interests, with the children's position being dealt with in the context of justifying an infringement of the adults' rights, rather than in terms of their having rights of their own.[252]

The use of rights 'talk' in the context of contact disputes in this country is not unusual. Wrangham J famously described the companionship of a parent being of such immense value to a child that it should be described as 'a basic right in the child rather than a basic right in the parent'.[253] For a time, the domestic courts consistently employed the language of children's rights to justify decisions fulfilling fathers' claims to contact,[254] with such usage gradually dying out

---

[244] DCA *et al.* (2004) p. 13.   [245] A. Buchanan *et al.* (2001) p. 1.   [246] CRC, Art. 9(3).

[247] Adopted and opened for signature in 2003. See especially Art. 1.

[248] *Hoppe v. Germany* [2003] 1 FLR 384, at para. 44.

[249] Ibid. at para. 49 and *Elsholz v. Germany* [2000] 2 FLR 486, at para. 50.

[250] Inter alia: *Hoffmann v. Austria* (1993) 17 EHRR 293: the custody order to the father was primarily motivated by the mother's membership of the Jehovah's witness sect and so infringed the mother's rights under Arts. 8 and 14. See also *Palau-Martinez v. France* [2004] 2 FLR 810; cf. *Ismailova v. Russia* [2008] 1 FLR 533.

[251] *Sahin v. Germany*; *Sommerfeld v. Germany* [2002] 1 FLR 119, [2003] 2 FLR 671, at paras. 93–94.

[252] Discussed in Chapter 2.   [253] *M v. M (child: access)* [1973] 2 All ER 81 at 85.

[254] Inter alia: *Re S (minors) (access)* [1990] 2 FLR 166, per Balcombe LJ, at 170; *Re R (a minor) (contact)* [1993] 2 FLR 762, per Butler-Sloss LJ, at 767; *A v. Y (child's surname)* [1999] 2 FLR 5, per Judge Tyrer, at 8.

in the twenty-first century.[255] Today, 'rights talk' is commonly adopted by the fathers' pressure groups to justify their claims that fathers are treated unfairly by the court when dealing with contact disputes. As discussed below, their references to rights largely focus on their own rights, not on those of their children.[256]

(ii) Equal parenting presumption and joint residence orders

Much has been written about the fathers' rights movement in England and in other parts of the world.[257] Changes in attitudes towards parenting, with more mothers now working and more fathers spending increasing amounts of time with their children[258] undoubtedly underlie some of the fathers' concerns. The belligerence of the fathers' groups' campaign in this country produced a rapid response from the government in the form of a Green and White Paper reviewing the way in which contact disputes were being handled.[259] Meanwhile it is notable how the increasingly polarised and gender-based debate between the fathers' pressure groups and the women's groups has become very adult focused. Mothers often see the legal process as forcing them into apparently opposing fathers' claims to their 'legitimate' rights[260] and into asserting their own roles as 'good mothers'.[261] When opposing calls for equal parenting,[262] women's groups tend to focus on the dangers of unsafe contact, more particularly on the harm suffered by mothers and children as a result of fathers' domestic violence.[263]

Increasingly, the fathers' rights groups here and abroad[264] concentrate on issues of justice and fairness. Indeed the research literature shows non-resident fathers' pervasive sense of being controlled by their ex-partners, their feeling of powerlessness[265] and anger over the injustice of their position.[266] They commonly argue that the only acceptable solution to the rising number of contact disputes is for the law to impose on all separating parents a legal presumption of equal shared residence – an automatic 50/50 division of children's time between each parent. Only such an arrangement, they urge, will prevent mothers from restricting fathers' contact so unacceptably.[267] But as Rhoades rather caustically points out, in making such claims, fathers do not necessarily want to change their own work patterns and living arrangements to share the care of their children on a 50/50 basis with mothers. Instead, they want legal recognition for their status as parents of equal importance with mothers, 'regardless of their

---

[255] E.g. *Re W (contact: joining child as party)* [2001] EWCA Civ 1830, [2003] 1 FLR 681, per Dame Elizabeth Butler-Sloss P, at 685; discussed in more detail in Chapter 8.

[256] C. Smart (2004) p. 485.

[257] Inter alia: H. Rhoades and S. Boyd (2004); R. Collier (2005); collection edited by R. Collier and S. Sheldon (2006).

[258] DCA *et al.* (2004) paras. 35–6.   [259] Ibid. and DCA *et al.* (2005).

[260] C. Smart and B. Neale (1999) p. 163.   [261] S. Day Sclater and F. Kaganas (2003) pp. 163–6.

[262] Discussed below.   [263] H. Reece (2006).   [264] H. Rhoades and S. Boyd (2004).

[265] G. Wilson (2006) p. 302.   [266] B. Geldof (2003).   [267] Ibid. at p. 185.

past inexperience as carers or their future inability to spend significant periods of time with their children'.[268] This suggested solution, which tends to resurface from time to time,[269] has, so far, been resisted by the government here, on the basis that:

> Children are not a commodity to be apportioned equally after separation. The best arrangements for them will depend on a variety of issues particular to their circumstances: a one-size-fits-all formula will not work.[270]

The government's rejection of a presumption of equal sharing is welcome. Whilst the equal shares principle might address arguments about 'fairness', research suggests that shared parenting arrangements are not always a positive experience for the children concerned, with some finding them positively burdensome, particularly as they grow into adolescence.[271] Meanwhile, Rhoades and Boyd warn of the danger that any new legislation offering a 'one size does not fit all' approach may nevertheless give way to expectations about increased contact, with the language of shared parenting and parenting plans being widely adopted by practitioners.[272] This warning is timely, given the English courts' changing attitude to their power to grant shared residence orders.[273] They have moved from confining them to exceptional circumstances,[274] via a mid-point position of considering their availability where the children are already spending substantial amounts of time with each parent,[275] to asserting that in situations where children live nearly 50% of their time with their father, 'good reasons are required if a shared residence order is not to be made'.[276] Indeed the ability of such orders to educate parents over the need to cooperate over their parenting is now enthusiastically endorsed, even in cases where the parents are on particularly bad terms.[277] But as Gilmore points out, children in dual residence are much more likely to suffer psychologically from severe and constant friction between their parents than children in more

---

[268] H. Rhoades (2006) p. 143.

[269] Critically discussed by F. Kaganas and C. Piper (2002) and S. Day Sclater and F. Kaganas (2003) pp. 156–8.

[270] DCA et al. (2004) para. 42. See also DCA et al. (2005) para. 13.

[271] C. Smart (2004) esp. p. 495. See also B. Neale et al. (2003); H. Rhoades and S. Boyd (2004) p. 132; J. Hunt with C. Roberts (2004) pp. 6–7; S. Gilmore (2006) pp. 353–8.

[272] H. Rhoades and S. Boyd (2004) p. 138.

[273] Under CA 1989, s. 11(4). S. Gilmore (2006) assesses the changing judicial approach to joint residence orders.

[274] Re H (a minor) (shared residence) [1994] 1 FLR 717, per Purchas LJ, at 728.

[275] D v. D (shared residence order) [2001] 1 FLR 495, per Hale LJ, at [32]. See also Re F (shared residence order) [2003] EWCA Civ 592, [2003] 2 FLR 397: the fact that the parents' homes would be separated by a considerable distance (mother in Scotland and father in England) did not preclude a shared residence order.

[276] Re P (shared residence order) [2005] EWCA Civ 1639, [2006] 2 FLR 347, per Wall LJ, at [22]. See also Re K (shared residence order) [2008] EWCA Civ 526, [2008] 2 FLR 380: a shared residence order could be ordered in cases where the child's time was not shared between the parents equally, in this case 40% was to be with the father.

[277] Ibid.

conventional post-separation arrangements.[278] Furthermore, Smart's research indicates that shared parenting arrangements are sometimes imposed by a forceful parent on the other, leaving the children exposed to living half their time with an over-controlling and/or manipulative parent.[279]

(iii) The contact 'presumption'

The government was clearly at pains to soften its refusal to accede to the fathers' groups' demands to introduce an equal parenting presumption by 'firmly' asserting its belief 'that both parents should continue to have a meaningful relationship with their child after separation, as long as it is safe and in the child's best interests'.[280] It did not, however, attempt to refute the claim commonly made by the fathers' groups that the courts and the law are gender biased.[281] Hunt and Macleod found no evidence that the courts were biased against non-resident parents in contact disputes and hoped that such a 'myth' would be dispelled by their research.[282] The statistics alone establish its falsity; they show that, of the small number who apply for court orders,[283] less than one per cent of applications for contact are rejected.[284] But in any event, a growing body of case law shows that over many years the judiciary have assumed that it will 'almost always' benefit children to have as much contact with their non-resident fathers as possible.[285] More recently, Wall LJ summarised the position as follows:

> The court starts from the premise that, generally speaking, the application of the welfare test in s1 of the Children Act 1989 means: (1) that contact with a non-resident parent is in the best interests of children; and (2) that it requires compelling evidence for such contact to be refused.[286]

The courts have little patience with the 'implacably hostile mother' who has no acceptable reasons[287] for refusing to cooperate over contact.[288] In a leading case, Sir Thomas Bingham MR explained very firmly:

> Neither parent should be encouraged or permitted to think that the more intransigent, the more unreasonable, the more obdurate and the more un-cooperative they are, the more likely they are to get their own way.[289]

---

[278] S. Gilmore (2006) p. 497.   [279] C. Smart (2004) p. 491. See also B. Neale *et al.* (2003).

[280] DCA *et al.* (2005) p. 5.   [281] B. Geldof (2003) p. 181.

[282] J. Hunt and A. Macleod (2008) p. 250.

[283] DCA et al (2004), para 14: only 10% of contact arrangements are underpinned by court orders.

[284] Ibid. at para. 25. See also J. Hunt and A. Macleod (2008) p. 32: only 7% of the cases reviewed were dismissed and a further 7% ended with an order for no contact.

[285] Inter alia: *Re O (contact: imposition of conditions)* [1995] 2 FLR 124 and *Re P (contact: supervision)* [1996] 2 FLR 314.

[286] *Re Bradford; Re O'Connell* [2006] EWCA Civ 1199, [2007] 1 FLR 530, at [70].

[287] Such as domestic violence or child abuse; discussed below.

[288] *Re J (a minor) (contact)* [1994] 1 FLR 729, per Balcombe LJ, at 736.

[289] *Re O (contact: imposition of conditions)* [1995] 2 FLR 124 at 129–30.

The strength of this approach, which has led to its being described as 'the contact presumption'[290] is borne out by research. Hunt and Macleod note that all those interviewed in their research (solicitors, Cafcass officers and the judiciary) considered that 'while there is no presumption of contact in the Children Act 1989, the courts operate on a *de facto* presumption that unless there are good reasons to the contrary there should be contact'.[291] Its strength has resulted in the judiciary often stressing to mothers that contact is for the child's sake, rather than for the father, with a view to deterring them from subtly alienating their children against their absent fathers for no good reason. But by the end of the 1990s, a rising tide of criticism focusing on the courts' approach to contact disputes involving domestic violence bore fruit and led to important changes in judicial practice.[292] In all *other* cases, despite judicial efforts to change the emphasis,[293] the view remains impregnable that it is wholly exceptional not to award some kind of contact. Indeed, now that the senior judiciary feel obliged publicly to dispel fathers' claims that they unduly favour mothers in contact disputes,[294] it may have become more difficult for mothers to rebut the presumption than ever before. Cantwell doubts whether all contact orders currently being made by the courts fulfil the no order principle,[295] with its strong message that orders should only be made 'when they can be shown demonstrably to either benefit the child or protect the child from harm'.[296]

The strength of the contact presumption, combined with a 'settlement culture', can lead to couples, especially mothers, coming under considerable pressure to settle their disputes out of court. This culture has steadily strengthened over the last decade, with Hunt and Macleod finding proceedings are now 'dominated by a general preference for reaching agreed outcomes. Judges, lawyers and Cafcass officers all seemed signed up to this'.[297] Whilst refusing to introduce a legal presumption of equal contact, the government undertook to improve the manner in which contact disputes were handled.[298] For those few parents who cannot be diverted from litigation,[299] improved case management by the courts is intended to ensure that cases are heard more quickly and

---

[290] R. Bailey-Harris *et al.* (1999) pp. 114–18, historically assess the development of the contact presumption.

[291] J. Hunt and A. Macleod (2008) p. 222.   [292] Discussed below.

[293] E.g. *Re L (a child) (contact: domestic violence) and other appeals* [2000] 4 All ER 609, per Thorpe LJ, at 633–8: the language of 'rights' should be dropped and the word 'assumption', not 'presumption,' better describes the judicial preparedness to award contact.

[294] E.g. *Re O (contact: withdrawal of application)* [2003] EWHC 3031 (Fam), [2004] 1 FLR 1258, per Wall J, at [6](3)–(4); *Re S (contact: promoting relationship with absent parent)* [2004] EWCA Civ 18, [2004] 1 FLR 1279, per Dame Elizabeth Butler-Sloss P, at [18]–[22]; *Re Bradford; Re O'Connell* [2006] EWCA Civ 1199, [2007] 1 FLR 530, per Wall LJ, at [93].

[295] CA 1989, s. 1(5).   [296] B. Cantwell (2005) p. 301.

[297] J. Hunt and A. Macleod (2008) p. 187.   [298] DCA *et al.* (2005) pp. 24 *et seq.*

[299] DCA *et al.* (2004) para. 21: only 10% of parents make court applications for orders relating to their children. J. Hunt and A. Macleod (2008) p. 187: only 11% of the cases reviewed went to a contested final hearing.

efficiently.[300] But the main emphasis is to ensure that the majority of parents are diverted from litigating over contact entirely, with the assistance of mediation services or the greatly extended in-court conciliation schemes serviced by Cafcass practitioners.[301] As discussed below, mothers often feel coerced into agreeing arrangements they feel unhappy with, sometimes because they are unsafe. Worryingly, these policies have developed on the assumption that contact with the non-resident parent will virtually always benefit the child, an assumption not supported by research.

(iv) Research evidence on benefits of contact

Alongside the government, the family judiciary clearly consider that there is sufficient research evidence to justify their presuming that contact with a father is always beneficial for the children – other, that is, than in cases involving domestic violence or situations involving proved harm or risk of harm to the child.[302] There is indeed a large body of research literature indicating not only that divorce and separation has a long-term psychological impact on many children, but also that this can be mitigated by both parents remaining easily accessible to the child and involved in the parenting role.[303] If contact can occur happily, it will certainly provide the child with many benefits, including reinforcing the child's sense of identity and knowledge of origins.[304] But assuming from such research that *court ordered* contact will always be beneficial does not accord with the complexities of contact disputes.[305] Indeed, many would question whether there is sufficient research evidence to justify retaining the presumption of contact in ordinary contact disputes. Davis and Pearce robustly describe lawyers and the courts adopting 'the pro-contact presumption with a zeal hardly justified by evidence derived from the social scientific world',[306] with a self-referencing body of case law being built up, supported by little other than judicial pronouncements. Discussing the feminist critique of child contact, Reece suggests that the degree of importance placed on maintaining contact between children and their fathers is a relatively recent construction of children's welfare 'with a shaky empirical basis'. In her view, it has a social function – to reinstate the biological father into potentially fatherless families, thereby containing social anxiety about the collapse of the family.[307]

Longitudinal studies suggest that it is impossible to generalise over what is best for children after parental separation, since this will depend on the

---

[300] DCA *et al.* (2005) pp. 31–2. I.e. through rigorous attention to the various procedural requirements of the *President's Private Law Programme.*

[301] J. Hunt and A. Macleod (2008) pp. 168–88. See also discussed in Chapter 7.

[302] [2000] 4 All ER 609, per Dame Elizabeth Butler-Sloss P, at 616.

[303] B. Rogers and J. Pryor (1998) esp. pp. 42–3, summarise the research on this topic.

[304] J. Dunn (2003) and C. Sturge and D. Glaser (2000) pp. 616–17 and 627.

[305] See research summaries, inter alia: J. Hunt with C. Roberts (2004); J. Fortin *et al.* (2006) pp. 212–14; S. Gilmore (2006) pp. 347–53; G. Harold and M. Murch (2005) pp. 188–9.

[306] G. Davis and J. Pearce (1999a) p. 145.

[307] H. Reece (2006) p. 548. See also S. Gilmore (2008) pp. 1227–9.

diversity of experiences and family processes. More particularly it will depend on the extent to which children respond to inter-parental conflict,[308] which will inevitably increase if the parents go to court. The benefits of the non-resident father's involvement are clearly linked with the quality of the relationship and the degree of ongoing conflict between the parents, rather than the amount of contact.[309] The government is also unwise to assume that in-court conciliation schemes can produce agreed contact arrangements which either benefit children on a long-term basis,[310] or ensure that contact problems improve over time.[311] For parents who cannot be diverted from contact litigation, it appears that court enforced contact arrangements may actually harm some children, given that they provide further opportunities for conflict between the parents, including domestic violence.[312] There is also a growing view that many contact orders are far too inflexible to accommodate children's own developmental and practical needs.[313]

(v) Enforcement of contact

Many non-resident fathers complain that even if they obtain a favourable outcome from the courts, mothers are allowed to disobey contact orders with impunity. Indeed, part of the rhetoric of the fathers' groups is to depict mothers as vindictive and selfish, who routinely refuse to abide by contact orders.[314] This claim is not substantiated by research[315] which consistently shows that the most common reason for mothers opposing contact orders or failing to comply with them, are serious welfare concerns, including domestic violence and concerns about the fathers' parenting abilities.[316] It is clear that there are extreme examples of mothers who show implacable hostility towards the non-resident father and who behave entirely selfishly when opposing contact. Although these cases are rare,[317] they provide the fathers with useful ammunition suggesting the universal truth of such assertions. Clearly the judiciary have themselves reinforced this approach by strongly criticising the 'implacably hostile

---

[308] G. Harold and M. Murch (2005).   [309] P. Amato and J. Gilbreth (1999).

[310] L. Trinder and J. Kellett (2007) p. 31: despite parental well-being having improved during the two years after the in-court conciliation appointment, 35%–43% of the children involved in the contact arrangements continued to show borderline or abnormal 'well-being' scores, cf. 20% of children in the general population; discussed in Chapter 8.

[311] Ibid. at p. 25: at the two-year follow up, the majority of parents still reported no change or a deterioration in contact problems.

[312] J. Hunt with C. Roberts (2004) pp. 7–8; the issue of domestic violence is discussed below.

[313] C. Smart (2004) pp. 492–5.   [314] Inter alia: H. Rhoades (2002) p. 74; R. Collier (2006) pp. 63–5;

[315] H. Rhoades (2002) pp. 75–7; H. Reece (2006) p. 552.

[316] Inter alia: A. Buchanan et al. (2001) pp. 15–18; H. Rhoades (2002) pp. 75–6; L. Trinder et al. (2005) Chapter 7; L. Trinder et al. (2006) p. 94; H. Reece (2006) p. 552; A. Perry and B. Rainey (2007) pp. 36–7. See also J. Hunt and A. Macleod (2008) p. 9: 54% of the cases reviewed involved the resident parent's allegations or concerns about 'serious welfare issues' including domestic violence, child abuse or neglect, drug and alcohol abuse, mental illness, parenting capacity affected by learning ability, fear of abduction.

[317] J. Hunt and A. Macleod (2008) pp. 192–5.

mother',[318] without similarly categorising the fathers who routinely fail to fulfil contact arrangements either at all, or punctually, as 'implacably irresponsible'.[319] The violent fathers who breach the terms of contact orders[320] are less widely referred to – except by the women's groups, particularly in the context of the new enforcement measures,[321] which they strongly opposed on the basis that they might place women and children at risk.[322]

The strength of the contact presumption forces the judiciary to find sanctions for mothers who disobey contact orders, without indirectly damaging the children. Whilst rare, these cases of non-compliance cause family justice practitioners immense frustration,[323] with the common view being that the powers hitherto available to the courts were of very limited utility because of their potential impact on the children.[324] Thus the courts only exceptionally make an order uprooting the children from their home with their mother and transferring them into the father's care.[325] Fining mothers already short of money merely results in children going without. Imprisonment for contempt of court, whilst available, deprives the children of their primary carer and has traditionally been seen as a remedy of last resort.[326] The strong view is that it should never be ordered without carefully considering the effect on the children of their mother's incarceration.[327] Some maintain, however, that the Strasbourg jurisprudence in this context justifies a far more stringent approach to mothers who infringe contact orders, perhaps involving a suspended committal order with the imprisonment (if finally invoked) lasting only a very few days.[328] Although the Strasbourg case law is far from clear cut, it does establish that the state has a positive obligation to take all necessary steps as can *reasonably* be demanded in the circumstances of the case to facilitate a reunion between child and parent and as swiftly as possible.[329] Sometimes the courts adopt more indirect ways of persuading mothers to comply with contact orders, such as directing family therapy,[330] inviting a child psychiatrist or psychologist to work

---

[318] Discussed above.

[319] C. Smart and B. Neale (1997) p. 336. See also H. Rhoades (2002) pp. 78–9.

[320] J. Fortin *et al.* (2006) pp. 218–19.

[321] Introduced by CA 1989, ss. 11A–O, as inserted by Children and Adoption Act (CAA) 2006, Part 1.

[322] H. Reece (2006) pp. 549 *et seq.*   [323] J. Hunt and A. Macleod (2008) pp. 195–8 and 204–8.

[324] Prior to implementation of the CAA 2006, typical enforcement measures included: a contact order combined with a penal notice; committal to prison (or a suspended order for imprisonment); fine; transfer of residence to the non-resident parent.

[325] But see *V v. V (contact: implacable hostility)* [2004] EWHC 1215 (Fam), [2004] 2 FLR 851 and *Re C (residence order)* [2007] EWCA Civ 866, [2008] 1 FLR 211.

[326] *Re M (contact order: committal)* [1999] 1 FLR 810, per Ward LJ, at 825.

[327] *Re V (children)* [2008] EWCA Civ 635, unreported, per Wall LJ, at [36].

[328] *Re D (intractable contact dispute: publicity)* [2004] EWHC 727 (Fam), [2004] 1 FLR 1226, per Munby J, at [56]–[57]. See also *Re S (contact dispute: committal)* [2004] EWCA Civ 1790, [2005] 1 FLR 812.

[329] Inter alia: *Hokkanen v. Finland* (1994) 19 EHRR 139, para. 58; *Ignaccolo-Zenide v. Romania* (2001) 31 EHRR 7; *Sylvester v. Austria* [2003] 2 FLR 210; *Hansen v. Turkey* [2004] 1 FLR 142; discussed further in Chapter 8.

[330] *Re M (contact: committal)* [1999] 1 FLR 810, per Ward LJ, at 825.

with all members of the family,[331] or even, more dramatically, by involving the local authority,[332] with a view to the children being removed from their mother's care into foster care.[333]

When promising to 'legislate at the earliest opportunity to provide additional enforcement powers'[334] the government took account of an earlier raft of recommendations on how to improve the courts' enforcement powers in relation to contact orders.[335] Hunt and Macleod found that practitioners' views of the new legislation[336] 'ranged widely from cautious optimism to scepticism'.[337] It seems unlikely that the power to make compensation orders[338] will solve the problem presently undermining the usefulness of fines. One also wonders whether requiring a recalcitrant mother to undertake unpaid work[339] will enhance the children's view of their father. On the other hand requiring both parents to undergo 'contact activities', including receiving information, advice, counselling and/or guidance sessions[340] may well improve their ability to work together.[341] Hopefully the judiciary will bear in mind that directions can be made to address the failings of non-resident fathers, as well as those of residential mothers. They might, for example, be required to attend parenting programmes before being allowed to have very young children on overnight contact visits. Their failure to arrive on time on agreed contact visits or to spend time with the child during contact visits might be similarly dealt with.[342]

The new powers clearly carry risks. For example, there is troubling evidence from abroad that an authoritarian approach to the enforcement of contact orders produces judicial decision-making that sometimes endangers children's safety.[343] Particularly worrying is the fact that any breach of a contact order justifies the grant of an enforcement order. So non-resident fathers can now force mothers to comply with unpaid work requirements on successive occasions for technical breaches of any term.[344] Admittedly, the court must be satisfied that an enforcement order is 'necessary' to secure compliance and that the impact of the enforcement order on the recipient is 'proportionate to the seriousness of the breach'.[345] It must also consider information about the

---

[331] *Re H (a child) (contact: mother's opposition)* [2001] 1 FCR 59; *Re S (unco-operative mother)* [2004] EWCA Civ 597, [2004] 2 FLR 710. Discussed further in Chapter 8.

[332] I.e. by making a direction under CA 1989, s. 37.

[333] E.g. inter alia: *Re M (intractable contact dispute: interim care order)* [2003] EWHC 1024 (Fam), [2003] 2 FLR 636; *Re N (sexual abuse allegations: professionals not abiding by findings of fact)* [2005] 2 FLR 340; *Re F (family proceedings: section 37 investigation)* [2005] EWHC 2935, [2006] 1 FLR 1122.

[334] DCA *et al.* (2004) para. 85. See also DCA *et al.* (2005) para. 100.

[335] CASC (2002) para. 14.55.

[336] I.e. CA 1989, ss. 11A–O as inserted by Children and Adoption Act (CAA) 2006, Part 1; for details see M. Fisher and S. Whitten, with N. Arnold (2006) ch. 1.

[337] J. Hunt and A. Macleod (2008) p. 225.   [338] CA 1989, s. 11O.   [339] CA 1989, s. 11J(2).

[340] CA 1989, s. 11A(5).   [341] M. Fisher and S. Whitten, with N. Arnold (2006) p. 35.

[342] H. Reece (2006) pp. 552–3: reviews the reasons why mothers may refuse contact.

[343] Inter alia: M. Harrison (2002), H. Rhoades (2002), M. Hester (2002).

[344] CA 1989, s. 11J(2) and Sch. A1.   [345] CA 1989, s. 11L(1)(a) and (b).

person and the impact of the enforcement order on him or her.[346] Nevertheless, there is no provision making the child's welfare paramount[347] and the defendant must prove she has a reasonable excuse for failing to comply with the order.[348] How readily will the courts refuse enforcement orders in cases where the non-resident father has sufficient resources to wage a form of litigation harassment? Will they sympathise with mothers who in situations where the breaches stem from older children's own unwillingness to organise their lives around contact arrangements.[349] Furthermore, with the onus on mothers to persuade the court not to make an enforcement order, there are fears that women and children will be further subjected to various forms of domestic violence – ranging from controlling behaviour to acts of physical aggression.[350]

Overall, there remain real questions over the extent to which the new enforcement powers will improve children's well-being. They rest on the assumption that court ordered contact will benefit children in highly conflicted situations, an assumption not borne out by research.[351] As Smart and Neale commented with some prescience, 'the law is beginning to look like a lever for the powerful to use against the vulnerable, rather than a measure to safeguard the welfare of children'.[352] In truth, if the judiciary clarified more clearly their specific objectives,[353] they could probably achieve far more through an increased use of the revamped family assistance orders.[354]

(B) The exceptional cases

(i) Domestic violence

As discussed above, the majority of contact disputes are settled long before they reach court, partly because mothers are advised that given the strength of the contact presumption, there is little point in her resisting the father's application. Research shows that those few that hold out and end up in court, often do so because of concerns about domestic violence.[355] The number of contact disputes with underlying domestic violence concerns may be much higher than is

---

[346] CA 1989, s. 11L(3). Such information will be provided by Cafcass practitioners (s. 11L(5) and (6)).
[347] CA 1989, s. 11L(7): the court must 'take into account the welfare of the child who is the subject of the contact order'.
[348] CA 1989, s. 11J(4).   [349] H. Rhoades (2002) p. 79.   [350] H. Reece (2006) pp. 555 et seq.
[351] Discussed above.   [352] C. Smart and B. Neale (1997) p. 336.
[353] HMICA (2007) para. 3.13: observed that it was not clear 'in many cases' what could be achieved by Cafcass through the making of a family assistance order (FAO).
[354] CAA 2006, s. 6 amended CA 1989, s. 16: abolished the requirement of 'exceptionality'; s. 16(5) extended their duration to 12 months; s. 16(4A) enabled FAOs to be made alongside a contact order, with the view of ensuring that the family receive advice and assistance regarding establishing, improving and maintaining contact.
[355] Inter alia: A. Buchanan et al. (2001) pp. 15–17; J. Fortin et al. (2006) pp. 218 and 222; L. Trinder et al. (2005), ch. 8.

officially recognised.[356] Indeed, in many cases, it may have been the domestic violence which largely caused the separation or divorce.[357] But as Hunt points out, contrary to common perception, violence does not cease on separation and contact may be a particular dangerpoint.[358] Court orders (including consent orders) imposing contact arrangements may therefore endanger not only the women but the children in further incidents of intimidation and abuse.[359] In practice, terms designed to protect women and children may simply be ignored by violent men.[360] Sometimes post-divorce violence escalates with tragic results.[361]

Research shows that growing up in a violent household can seriously damage children psychologically[362] and there is a strong correlation between domestic violence and child abuse.[363] But until the early twenty-first century, judicial practice did not reflect an awareness of this. Courts commonly labelled mothers who opposed contact as 'implacably hostile' and incapable of appreciating their children's needs, even in cases involving domestic violence.[364] Indeed, mothers' attempts to justify opposing contact by referring to their partners' past conduct were actively discouraged – as being backward looking and irrelevant to the present dispute.[365] Eventually, prompted by a growing body of criticism,[366] an entirely new judicial approach was signalled by the Court of Appeal's decision in *Re L (a child) (contact: domestic violence)*,[367] together with the 'CASC guidelines'.[368] In *Re L*, influenced by 'the experts' report',[369] the Court of Appeal acknowledged that their response to cases involving allegations of domestic violence needed adjustment. The courts should, in future, take proper account of the impact of the father's violence on the family and the psychological dangers to children of ordering contact in such cases,[370] especially if

---

[356] DCA *et al.* (2004) para. 46: 30% of applications have safety allegations associated with them, cf. ACOP (1999) maintained that 50% of cases where a welfare report was ordered involved domestic violence. The accurate collection of these statistics is hampered by disagreement over how to define 'domestic violence'. See also H. Reece (2006) pp. 542–5 and J. Hunt and A. Macleod (2008) p. 183: 54% of the cases reviewed involved 'serious welfare issues' and 50% of these involved domestic violence allegations.

[357] L. Trinder *et al.* (2005) p. 85: over 53% of women in the study reported some form of abuse had led to the separation.

[358] J. Hunt with C. Roberts (2004) p. 7.

[359] C. McGee (2000) pp. 177–8. See also research summarised by H. Reece (2006) pp. 542–5.

[360] J. Fortin *et al.* (2006) pp. 218–19.   [361] H. Saunders (2004), discussed below.

[362] Summarised by C. Sturge and D. Glaser (2000) pp. 617–21 and S. Walby (2004) para. 7.2.

[363] See research summaries in J. Hunt with C. Roberts (2004) p. 7 and S. Walby (2004) para. 7.3.

[364] E.g. *A v. N (committal: refusal of contact)* [1997] 1 FLR 533.

[365] R. Bailey-Harris *et al.* (1999) pp. 123–4.

[366] See, inter alia: R. Bailey-Harris *et al.* (1999); CASC (2000), Section 3, summarising the responses to the consultation document.

[367] [2000] 4 All ER 609.

[368] The guidelines published by CASC (2000) Section 5, were republished in LCD (2001).

[369] C. Sturge and D. Glaser (2000).

[370] [2000] 4 All ER 609, per Dame Elizabeth Butler-Sloss P, at 616 and per Thorpe LJ, at 642–3.

children themselves oppose contact.[371] It was hoped that this strong judicial lead, reinforced by later case law,[372] and combined with the CASC guidelines,[373] would achieve much needed changes in the way that mothers opposing contact arrangements were treated.

Given that the cases that actually get to court are usually the most complex and intractable, sometimes involving dangerously violent fathers,[374] they need particularly careful handling. Controversially, however, neither the judiciary[375] nor the government were prepared to introduce a presumption against contact being granted to a violent perpetrator, as in countries like New Zealand.[376] It was considered that greater judicial attention to the official guidelines,[377] and to the broadened definition of 'harm' in the CA 1989,[378] would produce a more appropriate approach without the introduction of 'a blanket statutory presumption of no contact'.[379] Nonetheless, without a specific legislative change of this kind, it has proved hard to change the habits of family justice practitioners – whose 'contact at (almost) any cost' approach is so embedded in their every day work.[380] Large numbers of couples are now funnelled into conciliation appointments with Cafcass officers who have been strongly criticised for their failure to deal with domestic violence allegations satisfactorily.[381] Their new legal obligation to undertake an initial screening or 'risk assessment' if they suspect that the child concerned is at risk of harm[382] should provoke a better approach to child protection and safety issues, particularly in any case where allegations of domestic violence have been made or it is suspected. Nevertheless, as Trinder et al. wisely assert, the 'future-looking focus of conciliation and the pro-contact presumption' makes it more difficult for concerns to be raised and to be taken seriously.[383] Their research shows spouses feeling under pressure to agree to terms that they were unhappy with or subsequently regretted. Others left court 'still locked in conflict', despite having agreed terms and terminated their litigation[384] – with 'less than half reporting that the agreement was wholly in the child's interests'.[385]

---

[371] See Chapter 8.

[372] Inter alia: *Re G (domestic violence: direct contact)* [2000] 2 FLR 865; *M v. A (contact: domestic violence)* [2002] 2 FLR 921.

[373] LCD (2001) para. 1.2(b).

[374] E.g. *Re A (contact: witness protection scheme)* [2005] EWHC 2189 (Fam), [2006] 2 FLR 551; *Re R (secure editing of documents)* [2007] 2 FLR 759.

[375] [2000] 4 All ER 609, per Dame Elizabeth Butler-Sloss P, at 616 and per Thorpe LJ, at 643.

[376] M. Kaye (1996) pp. 289–91.   [377] LCD (2001).

[378] CA 1989, s. 31(10) (as amended by ACA 2002, s. 120) defines 'harm' as including the mental and psychological impairment of health or development caused by children seeing or hearing domestic violence. NB 'harm' in s. 1(3)(e) must also be interpreted, taking account of this type of harm.

[379] DCA *et al.* (2005) para. 22.

[380] R. Bailey-Harris *et al.* (1999) p. 122. See also J. Hunt and A. Macleod (2008) pp. 143–5.

[381] See especially Ofsted (2008a) and Ofsted (2008b); discussed in more detail in Chapter 7.

[382] CA 1989, s. 16A (as inserted by CAA 2006, s. 7).   [383] L. Trinder *et al.* (2006) p. 95.

[384] Ibid. at pp. 93–4.   [385] Ibid. at p. 94.

Cafcass officers are not the only practitioners who operate on the assumption that some contact should take place, whatever the circumstances underlying the case. Researchers report women feeling coerced into agreeing to unsafe contact arrangements by their own solicitors, in order to appear 'reasonable'.[386] Despite the efforts of the senior judiciary, some of the judiciary continue to adopt a blinkered approach to domestic violence. Research shows district judges assuming that it only occurs very exceptionally and, even then, seeing little reason to question the application of the contact presumption.[387] Indeed, the strength of the contact presumption continues to undermine some judges' willingness either to follow the official guidelines or to treat the parties' evidence impartially. Consequently, as in *Re H (contact: domestic violence)*,[388] contact orders are still being made without adequate attention to their likely impact on the mother or child. There Wall LJ robustly criticised the trial judge for adopting an increasingly polarised and hostile attitude towards the mother. Despite finding that the husband had assaulted his wife on several occasions, the trial judge downplayed their significance, concluding that she had deliberately lied about the past events and the father was the innocent victim of her unprincipled strategy to separate him from his child.[389] Furthermore, he had failed to consider the father's capacity to appreciate the impact of his violence on his wife or his capacity to change,[390] as required by the official guidance.[391] Clearly years after the changed approach signalled by *Re L (a child) (contact: domestic violence)*,[392] some courts are still making contact orders without any judicial determination of the case for violence or harassment – 'as though the Court of Appeal had never spoken on the issue'.[393]

The accusation that courts were effectively rubber stamping consent orders without investigating the underlying circumstances,[394] sometimes with tragic results – involving violent fathers killing their children during agreed contact arrangements – led to urgent review by the Family Justice Council.[395] It found that the 'no order' principle[396] was so imbued in those working in the family justice system that if two parents presented a court with an agreement about an issue or issues relating to their children, the court's normal reaction was to welcome it. It also pointed out that the pressure on judges to get through full lists, particularly in cases which are listed for in-court conciliation, did not promote detailed scrutiny of cases where contact has been agreed.[397] An emphatically worded and lengthy Practice Direction was to follow setting out yet again how courts are to deal with private law cases involving allegations of

---

[386] C. McGee (2000) pp. 175–6; J. Masson (2006) p. 1044.   [387] L. Trinder *et al.* (2006) pp. 95–6.
[388] [2005] EWCA Civ 1404, [2006] 1 FLR 943. See also *Re V (children)* [2008] EWCA Civ 635, unreported.
[389] Ibid. at [93].   [390] Ibid. at [80]–[81].
[391] DCA (2001) para. 1.6(d) and (e).   [392] [2000] 4 All ER 609.
[393] *K and S (Children)* [2005] EWCA Civ 1660, [2006] 1 FCR 316, per Thorpe LJ, at [27].
[394] H. Saunders (2004) esp. pp. 12–13.   [395] Also discussed in Chapter 7.   [396] CA 1989, s. 1(5).
[397] J. Craig (2007a) pp. 5–6. See also J. Craig (2007b) and N. Wall (2006) paras. 8.21 and 8.27.

domestic violence.[398] It stresses the need to scrutinise the terms of consent orders and re-emphasises and expands on much of the earlier guidance on the handling of cases where there is no agreement.[399] In particular, attention is again drawn to holding a fact-finding hearing[400] and to obtaining further information about the child's own views, by calling for a welfare report, or by providing him or her with separate representation.[401] If domestic violence is made out, the court should consider its effect on the child and parent in the past, the perpetrator's ability to change and his likely behaviour during future contact.[402] Above all courts are warned not to make a contact order unless satisfied that the safety of the child and parent can be secured.[403] Unfortunately, efforts to improve practice in the courts will come to naught if the women themselves feel unable to alert family justice practitioners of their plight. Even the newly designed court forms fail to ensure that the courts receive more detailed information about domestic violence and concerns about harm to children prior to a hearing.[404] Perhaps predictably, women seem reluctant to fill in complicated forms detailing incidents of domestic violence.[405]

Although the guidance stresses the need for contact orders not to endanger the mother or child, the courts continue to make considerable efforts to persuade a mother to allow direct contact.[406] Failing that, there is continued faith in indirect contact as a last resort, even in cases involving proved domestic violence,[407] with an order for supervised or supported contact at a contact

---

[398] *Practice Direction: Residence and Contact Orders: Domestic Violence and Harm* [2009] All ER (D) 122 (Jan); also discussed in Chapters 7 and 8.

[399] LCD (2001).

[400] *Practice Direction: Residence and Contact Orders: Domestic Violence and Harm* [2009] All ER (D) 122 (Jan), at [13]–[14]. J. Hunt and A. Macleod (2008) pp. 183–6: discuss the reasons for the courts' reluctance to list findings of fact hearings (out of 154 cases involving domestic violence allegations, 24 findings of fact hearings were listed and only 12 took place).

[401] Ibid. at [16]–[17]. See also Chapter 8 which discusses the extent to which the judiciary consider children's views in contact disputes involving allegations of domestic violence.

[402] Ibid. at [27].   [403] Ibid. at [26].

[404] I.e. C1A forms should accompany the application for a section 8 order in situations where applicants have indicated in the main form (C1 form), concerns about violence or abuse. See R. Aris and C. Harrison (2007).

[405] Ibid. esp. at p. 22.

[406] J. Hunt and A. Macleod (2008) pp. 190–1. See also p. 240: 79% of completed cases ended with an order or agreement for face-to-face contact, with 49% involving staying contact, 20% unsupervised contact, 4% supervised contact, 7% indirect contact; p. 32: only 7% of the cases reviewed were dismissed and a further 7% ended with an order for no contact.

[407] E.g. *Re G (domestic violence: direct contact)* [2001] 2 FCR 134: indirect contact ordered (cards and presents at Christmas and birthdays) despite the fact that the father had murdered the mother, had no understanding of his child's needs and the child's own fear of him and reluctance to see him; *Re A (contact: witness protection scheme)* [2005] EWHC 2189 (Fam), [2006] 2 FLR 551: interim provision for indirect contact (by video contact) despite the Pakistani father's violent treatment of the mother, and the risk of the child being harmed through abduction to Pakistan or by his mother being subjected to further violence by his father or his paternal extended family; *Re F (indirect contact)* [2006] EWCA Civ 1426, [2007] 1 FLR 1015: mother's appeal against an indirect contact turned down despite inter alia: the children's

centre being a preferred option.[408] The judicial assumption that children will benefit from some kind of contact with extremely violent men is puzzling, given its ability to reawaken memories of their mothers being ill-treated and the strong correlation between domestic violence and child abuse.[409] It seems that the option of refusing contact altogether is virtually always ruled out.[410] Furthermore, the judicial policy of confining indirect contact to the most extreme cases produces its own problems. It means that supervised or supported contact orders are made even in the most problematic cases, including those involving high levels of conflict, allegations of inappropriate parenting, lack of parenting ability, fear on children's part and the non-resident's severe mental illness.[411] Furniss refers to the worrying propensity of practitioners at every level to resort to supervised contact at contact centres as a remedy for patently unsuitable cases and to their ignorance of the true facilities offered.[412] Such arrangements are often far from ideal; many of the untrained volunteers maintain a pro-contact stance which prevents their paying sufficient heed to the need to protect mothers and children from violent non-resident fathers, even when alerted to the danger.[413] Few even provide safe 'handover' arrangements, such as separate entrances.[414] Arguably, the courts should pay less heed to assertions about fathers' rights and more to the experts' advice.[415] Children surely have a right *not* to have contact of any kind with extremely violent men.[416]

     guardian's recommendation against it; the father's history of serious and uncontrollable violence against the mother; his repeated failure to comply with non-molestation orders (68 breaches), leading to periods of imprisonment; findings of the risks to the mother and child if he tracked them down (the mother and child having been forced to move 10 times over 5 years to escape his attentions); the further risks to the child and mother's physical safety and emotional stability involved in indirect contact. Indirect contact to be organised by Cafcass Legal.

[408]   'Supervised contact' is provided by specialist contact centres involving contact between the non-resident parent and child in the presence of professionally trained qualified staff cf 'supported contact' is usually provided (in non-dedicated buildings) in communal contact areas, staffed by untrained volunteers.

[409]   Discussed above. See also C. Sturge and D. Glaser (2000) p. 619, who warn of the opportunities provided by indirect contact for the non-resident parent to convey 'undermining and distorting messages'.

[410]   A. Perry and B. Rainey (2007) p 29: less than 1% of their court sample.

[411]   Ibid. at p. 37. See also J. Hunt and A. Macleod (2008) pp. 190–2.

[412]   C. Furniss (2000).   [413]   C. Humphreys and C. Harrison (2003) pp. 250–2.

[414]   R. Aris *et al.* (2002) strongly criticise the lack of adequate safety arrangements at many contact centres and the paucity of well-trained staff. See esp. Sections 4, 5, 9 and 10.

[415]   C. Sturge and D. Glaser (2000) p. 624: contact would provide children with no advantage unless the non-resident parent showed inter alia: acknowledgement of the domestic violence; an awareness of the inappropriate nature of their conduct; regret; an understanding of the impact of their behaviour on their ex-partner, in the past and currently.

[416]   E.g. *Re M and B (children) (contact: domestic violence)* [2001] 1 FCR 116: an order for indirect contact was replaced, on appeal, by an order for no contact and a moratorium (under CA 1989, s. 91(14)) on the violent father reapplying for contact within two years without court leave. Per Thorpe LJ: the trial judge should have considered the impact of indirect contact on the mother's mental health, she having been subjected to six years of serious domestic violence culminating in the father's imprisonment.

(ii) Child sexual abuse

As noted above, the presumption of contact appears to have survived intact for all cases, other than those involving domestic violence or situations involving proved harm or risk of harm to the child,[417] including child sexual abuse.[418] Nevertheless, mothers will continue to encounter considerable difficulties if they refuse to agree to contact due to such fears. As Hale J (as she then was) pointed out, the mother who truly believes that her child has been sexually abused is in a difficult position. If she does nothing, she may be criticised for failing to protect the child. If she resists contact, she 'may be regarded as a wicked woman who has made it up to get rid of him [the father claiming contact]'.[419] Such a mother already faces an immensely hard task in satisfying the court that sexual abuse has occurred, since she must satisfy the court that it was more likely than not that the abuse occurred. Merely showing that there is 'a substantial risk that abuse has occurred' is not enough;[420] she must go further and establish that it occurred on the balance of probabilities. Fortunately, recent guidance from the House of Lords[421] makes it clear that the court need no longer doubt her assertions on the basis that the 'more improbable the event, the stronger must be the evidence that it did occur'.[422]

Sometimes a mother, fearing that she has insufficient evidence of sexual abuse, is persuaded to settle the contact dispute on agreed terms with her children's father. Such a decision may backfire when, many years later, the father, unencumbered by any finding of fact regarding the occurrence of child sexual abuse, reapplies for contact.[423] The moral is that, as in cases involving domestic violence allegations, a court should make findings of fact as early as possible, whenever disputed and damaging allegations are made.[424] Case law also demonstrates only too clearly the dangers of a judge failing to clarify sufficiently rigorously whether or not sexual abuse occurred. Put starkly, it means that a man, against whom there are serious allegations of sexual abuse, is allowed judicially approved contact with children who may be his victims.[425] In

---

[417] *Re L (a child) (contact: domestic violence) and other appeals* [2000] 4 All ER 609, per Dame Elizabeth Butler-Sloss P, at 616.

[418] Ibid., per Thorpe LJ, at 643.   [419] See Hale J (1999) p. 385.

[420] E.g. *Re P (sexual abuse: standard of proof)* [1996] 2 FLR 333: father allowed unsupervised contact; the mother had not shown that children had been harmed under CA 1989, s. 1(3)(e) to the required standard of proof – the balance of probabilities.

[421] *Re B (children)(sexual abuse: standard of proof)* [2008] UKHL 35, [2008] 4 All ER 1; discussed further in Chapter 15.

[422] *Re H and ors (minors) (sexual abuse: standard of proof)* [1996] AC 563, per Lord Nicholls of Birkenhead, at 586.

[423] E.g. *Re M (sexual abuse allegations: interviewing techniques)* [1999] 2 FLR 92.

[424] *Re S (contact: evidence)* [1998] 1 FLR 798, per Hale J, at 801–802.

[425] E.g. *Re F (contact: lack of reasons)* [2006] EWCA Civ 792, [2007] 1 FLR 65: rehearing ordered in a case where, despite the trial judge making a number of adverse findings against the father, a contact order had been made, the judge 'appearing to conclude' without a reasoned explanation, that allegations of the father's sexual abuse of four girls aged between 15 and 3 were untrue. See esp. Hedley J at [16].

most cases, the finding of fact investigation should be informed by information obtained through a formal investigative interview carried out conforming to ABE guidelines.[426] The mother who fails to satisfy the court that what is an essentially private form of child abuse has occurred will not find the advice to her and her family to 'try to put the allegations of sexual abuse behind them' particularly convincing or helpful.[427]

If, against all odds, the mother manages to prove her allegations of child sexual abuse to the required standard of proof, she may find the court still keen to award the father supervised or indirect contact.[428] The courts' preparedness to order some form of contact in such cases is astonishing, given the large body of research evidence indicating that victims of child sexual abuse commonly suffer serious and very long-term psychological damage and that sexual abuse is addictive behaviour.[429] Supervised contact as a means of keeping alive the link between father and child can be extremely dangerous.[430] As Furniss observes, given the lack of trained staff at most contact centres and that conversations are not generally monitored, there is little to prevent a paedophilic father 'grooming' his child.[431] The abuser may not only use contact sessions to revive the sexual relationship between him and the child,[432] but also to bring pressure to bear on the victim to retract his or her story. The old practice of resorting to indirect contact for the abusive father refused direct or supervised contact, also appears to continue.[433] Jones and Parkinson urge that before making any contact order, courts should consider the distorted and abusive relationship which exists between the sexually abusive parent and child. 'Far from ensuring continuity of the parent-child relationship, it may foster the continuance of a relationship which is aberrant and emotionally damaging to the child.'[434] It is arguable that contact orders in such circumstances merely promote a notion of fathers' rights, based on the existence of a dangerous blood tie. As urged above, the Court of Appeal should take a stronger lead and convince family practitioners and local judiciary that it may sometimes be appropriate to refuse all contact, of any kind.

(C) The blood tie – promoting or creating attachments through contact?

There is an additional reason for arguing that there is often little connection between the concept of children's rights and the presumption in favour of contact. This is that a blanket presumption fails to distinguish between two

---

[426] *D v. B and ors (flawed sexual abuse inquiry)* [2006] EWHC 2987 (Fam), [2007] 1 FLR 1295, per Stephen Wildblood QC, at [15](xiii). See discussed in more detail in Chapter 17.

[427] *Re P (sexual abuse: standard of proof)* [1996] 2 FLR 333, per Wall J, at 345.

[428] E.g. *Re S (contact: evidence)* [1998] 1 FLR 798; *Re P (Parental Responsibility)* [1998] 2 FLR 96. See also A. Perry and B. Rainey (2007) p. 30 and J. Hunt and A. Macleod (2008) p. 192.

[429] D. Jones and P. Ramchandani (1999). See also E. Jones and P. Parkinson (1995).

[430] E. Jones and P. Parkinson (1995) pp. 64–8.   [431] C. Furniss (2000) p. 258.

[432] C. Macaskill (2002) p. 60: provides a chilling description of supervised contact visits between a sexually abusive father and his 5-year-old daughter.

[433] A. Perry and B. Rainey (2007) p. 38.   [434] E. Jones and P. Parkinson (1995) p. 77.

quite separate types of situations in which contact disputes arise. If the parents lived together after the child's birth and a good relationship existed between the father and child, court ordered contact may, depending on the circumstances, be justified to keep the relationship alive and to promote existing attachments. But things are different where the child and father have never known each other, perhaps due to the parental relationship ceasing before or soon after the child's birth. Then the child is brought up by the mother alone, or with a new partner acting as a substitute father, with the child sometimes believing him to be his or her real father.[435] The judicial view has been that the long-term benefits far outweigh the 'temporary upset' caused by reintroducing children to a father with whom they have lost contact for a prolonged period;[436] further that the child should not be deprived of a fundamental 'right' to contact.[437]

This judicial confidence seems misplaced; there currently appears to be little research justifying that argument that children need a *social* relationship with a parent whose existence they have been unaware of. Notably, the experts who advised the Court of Appeal on the benefits of contact to children, emphasised that although the absence of any relationship already existing between the child and non-resident parent does not preclude trying to establish one, 'other considerations may come into play'. They suggested that in such cases the courts should consider the child's existing emotional investments, for example, with a step-parent, and what the new relationship would specifically add to the child's life and well-being.[438] Perhaps influenced by these comments, Thorpe LJ in *Re L*[439] suggested that in the past, insufficient distinction had been made between contact orders sought to maintain an existing relationship, to revive a dormant relationship and those to create a non-existent relationship. In his view, it would be wrong to assume in cases where the child has grown up unaware of his or her own father, with a psychological attachment to an 'alternative father', that a contact order would promote the child's welfare.

The assumption that the blood tie between parent and child has magical properties which, if enhanced by physical proximity, will inevitably produce a happy and long-term relationship certainly seems misguided. As Cantwell observes, there has been little discussion 'putting flesh on the bones of the presumption that contact with biological parents is invariably beneficial to the child'. Asking 'What is contact for?' might clarify matters.[440] It certainly seems foolish to argue that to fulfil a child's rights, the caring parent must undergo serious unhappiness, merely to nurture a blood tie that has no real significance for the child.

---

[435] E.g. *Re R (a minor) (contact)* [1993] 2 FLR 762; *Re W (a minor) (contact)* [1994] 2 FLR 441; *A v. L (contact)* [1998] 1 FLR 361; *Re K (specific issue order)* [1999] 2 FLR 280; *Re T (paternity: ordering blood tests)* [2001] 2 FLR 1190.

[436] Balcombe LJ in *Re H (minors) (access)* [1992] 1 FLR 148 at 153.

[437] Holman J in *A v. L (contact)* [1998] 1 FLR 361 at 365.

[438] C. Sturge and D. Glaser (2000) p. 622.   [439] [2000] 4 All ER 609.

[440] B. Cantwell (2005) p. 299.

(6) Conclusion

Considerable confusion is generated by society's assumption that children have a right to 'know' both their biological parents through a social relationship and that their childhood will be defective if no such relationship exists. This assumption is being reinforced by a growing interest in genetics and an ability to establish quickly and easily one's biological antecedents. Clearly the activities of the fathers' groups are also a factor. But whilst a loving relationship between parents and children is of inestimable value and its loss is always tragic for all concerned, its essence and value does not depend on the act of procreation or on their genetic links. Indeed, there are many parent-child relationships where no blood ties exist, which are none the worse for their absence. Children's psychological need to know about their biological origins does not imply that their relationship with their present carers is defective or needs to be replaced by a social relationship with their birth parents and it may be positively harmful to assume that this should occur.

More research is required considering the costs and benefits to children of being the subject of enforced contact arrangements. Until this is available, far greater emphasis should be placed on a child's right to protection from psychological harm. As Perry and Rainey argue, the legal system currently comes down too heavily in favour of the child's long-term interests in not losing contact with his or her non-resident parent, forgetting that short-term concerns, such as stress-related problems, are fundamentally important to his or her well-being.[441] Children's need for information about their origins could be promoted by indirect contact arrangements. In some cases, particularly those involving serious domestic violence or child abuse, no contact may be the appropriate legal response. Finally, the judiciary should suspend what appears to be a naive belief in the power of court orders to transform stressful situations into ones which will automatically benefit the child.

BIBLIOGRAPHY

NB many of these publications can be obtained on the relevant organisation's website.

Amato, P. and Gilbreth, J. (1999) 'Nonresident Fathers and Children's Well-being: A Meta-Analysis' 61 *Journal of Marriage and the Family* 557.

Aris, R. Harrison, C. and Humphreys, C. (2002) *Safety and Child Contact: An Analysis of the Role of Child Contact Centres in the Context of Domestic Violence and Child Welfare Concerns* Research Series No. 10/02, Lord Chancellor's Department.

Aris, R. and Harrison, C. (2007) *Domestic Violence and the Supplemental Information Form C1A*, Ministry of Justice Research Series 17/07, Ministry of Justice.

Association of Chief Officers of Probation (ACOP) (1999) *Response to a Consultation Paper on Contact Between Children and Violent Parents*, ACOP.

Bailey-Harris, R., Barron, J. and Pearce, J. (1999) 'From Utility to Rights? The Presumption of Contact in Practice' *International Journal of Law, Policy and the Family* 111.

---

[441] A. Perry and B. Rainey (2007) p. 39.

Bainham, A. (1989) 'When is a Parent not a Parent? Reflections on the Unmarried Father and his Child in English Law' 3 *International Journal of Law, Policy and the Family* 208.

  (2008a) 'Arguments about Parentage' 67 *Cambridge Law Journal* 322.

  (2008b) 'What is the Point of Birth Registration?' 20 *Child and Family Law Quarterly* 449.

Besson, S. (2007) 'Enforcing the Child's Right to Know Her Origins: Contrasting Approaches Under the Convention on the Rights of the Child and the European Convention on Human Rights' 21 *International Journal of Law, Policy and the Family* 137.

Blauwhoff, R. (2008) 'Tracing Down the Historical Development of the Legal Concept of the Right to Know One's Origins. Has "to know or not to know" Ever Been the Legal Question?' 4 *Utrecht Law Review* 99.

Bridge, C. and Swindells, H. (2003) *Adoption – The Modern Law*, Family Law.

Buchanan, A., Hunt, J., Bretherton, H. and Bream, V. (2001) *Families in Conflict: Perspectives of Children and Parents on the Family Court Welfare Service*, The Policy Press.

Cantwell, B. (2005) 'What is Contact For?' 35 *Family Law* 299.

Children Act Sub-Committee of the Advisory Board on Family Law (CASC) (2000) *A Report to the Lord Chancellor on the Question of Parental Contact with Children in Cases Where There is Domestic Violence*, LCD.

Children Act Sub-Committee of the Advisory Board on Family Law (CASC) (2002) *Making Contact Work Report of the Children Act Sub-Committee*, LCD.

Collier, R. (2005) 'Fathers 4 Justice, Law and the New Politics of Fatherhood' 17 *Child and Family Law Quarterly* 511.

  (2006) '"The Outlaw Fathers Fight Back"' in Collier, R. and Sheldon, S. (2006) *Fathers' Rights Activism and Law Reform in Comparative Perspective*, Hart Publishing.

Collier, R. and Sheldon, S. (2006) *Fathers' Rights Activism and Law Reform in Comparative Perspective*, Hart Publishing.

Committee on the Rights of the Child (2002) *Concluding Observations of the Committee on the Rights of the Child: United Kingdom of Great Britain and Northern Ireland* CRC/C/15/Add 188, Centre for Human Rights, Geneva.

Conway, H. (1996) 'Parental Responsibility and the Unmarried Father' 146 *New Law Journal* 782.

Craig, J. (2007a) (Chair) The Family Justice Council's Report and Recommendations to the President of the Family Division, *'Everybody's Business' – How Applications for Contact Orders by Consent Should be Approached by the Court in Cases Involving Domestic Violence*.

  (2007b) 'Everybody's Business: Applications for Contact Orders by Consent' 37 *Family Law* 26.

Davis, G. and Pearce, J. (1999) 'On the Trail of the Welfare Principle' 29 *Family Law* 144.

Day Sclater, S. and Kaganas, F. (2003) 'Mothers, Welfare and Rights' in Bainham, A., Lindley, B., Richards, A. and Trinder, L. (eds.) *Children and Their Families: Contact, Rights and Welfare*, Hart Publishing.

Deech, R. (1993) 'The Rights of Fathers: Social and Biological Concepts of Parenthood' in Eekelaar, J. and Sarcevic, P. (eds.) *Parenthood in Modern Society*, Martinus Nijhoff.

Department for Constitutional Affairs (DCA)/Department for Education and Skills/ Department for Trade and Industry (2004) Cm 6273 *Parental Separation: Children's Needs and Parents' Responsibilities*, TSO.

Department for Constitutional Affairs (DCA)/Department for Education and Skills/ Department for Trade and Industry (2005) Cm 6452 *Parental Separation: Children's Needs and Parents' Responsibilities: Next Steps* , TSO.

Department of Health (DH) (2007) Cm 7209 *Government Response to the Report from the Joint Committee on the Human Tissue and Embryology (Draft) Bill*, TSO.

Department for Work and Pensions (DWP) (2006) Cm 6979 *A New System of Child Maintenance*, TSO.

Department for Work and Pensions (DWP) (2007) Cm 7160 *Joint Birth Registration: Promoting Parental Responsibility*, DWP.

Department for Work and Pensions (DWP) (2008) Cm 7293 *Joint Birth Registration: Recording Parental Responsibility*, DWP.

Detrick, S. (ed.) (1992) *The United Nations Convention on the Rights of the Child: A Guide to the 'Travaux Préparatoires'*, Martinus Nijhoff.

Diduck, A. (2007) '"If Only We Can Find the Appropriate Terms to Use the Issue Will be Solved": Law, Identity and Parenthood' 19 *Child and Family Law Quarterly* 458.

Dunn, J. (2003) 'Contact and Children's Perspectives on Parental Relationships' in Bainham, A., Lindley, B., Richards, A. and Trinder, L. (eds.) *Children and Their Families: Contact, Rights and Welfare*, Hart Publishing.

Eekelaar, J. (1998) 'Do Parents have a Duty to Consult?' 114 *Law Quarterly Review* 337.

(2001) 'Rethinking Parental Responsibility' 31 *Family Law* 426.

(2006) *Family Law and Personal Life*, Oxford University Press.

Fisher, M. and Whitten, S., with Arnold, N. (2006) *Child Contact: Law and Practice*, The Law Society.

Fortin, J. (1994) 'The Gooseberry Bush Approach' 57 *Modern Law Review* 296.

Fortin, J., Ritchie, C. and Buchanan, A. (2006) 'Young Adults' Perceptions of Court-ordered Contact' 18 *Child and Family Law Quarterly* 211.

Freeman, M. (1996) '*The New Birth Right?: Identity and the Child of the Reproductive Revolution*' International Journal of Children's Rights 273.

Freeman, T. and Richards, M. (2006) 'DNA Testing and Kinship; Paternity, Genealogy and the Search for the "Truth" of our Genetic Origins' in Ebtehaj, F., Lindley, B. and Richards, M. (eds.) *Kinship Matters*, Hart Publishing.

Furniss, C. (2000) 'The Process of Referral to a Family Contact Centre: Policies and Practice' 12 *Child and Family Law Quarterly* 255.

Geldof, B. (2003) 'The Real Love that Dare Not Speak its Name' in Bainham, A., Lindley, B., Richards, A. and Trinder, L. (eds.) *Children and Their Families: Contact, Rights and Welfare*, Hart Publishing.

Gilmore, S. (2003) 'Parental Responsibility and the Unmarried Father – a New Dimension to the Debate' 15 *Child and Family Law Quarterly* 21.

(2006) 'Contact/Shared Residence and Child Well-Being: Research Evidence and its Implications for Legal Decision-Making' 20 *International Journal of Law, Policy and the Family* 478.

(2008) 'The Assumption that Contact is Beneficial: Challenging the "Secure Foundation"' 38 *Family Law* 1226.

Golombok, S. *et al.* (2006) 'Non-genetic and Non-gestational Parenthood: Consequences for Parent-child Relationships and the Psychological Well-being of Mothers, Fathers and Children at Age 3' 21 *Human Reproduction* 1918.

Gosden, N. (2003) 'Children's Surnames – How Satisfactory is the Current Law?' 33 *Family Law* 186.

Groskop, V. and Sarler, C. (2007) 'Do We Need to Know our Parentage?' *The Observer*, August 5.

HM Inspectorate of Court Administration (HMICA) (2005) *Domestic Violence, Safety and Family Proceedings: Thematic Review of the Handling of Domestic Violence Issues by the Children and Family Court Advisory and Support Service (CAFCASS) and the Administration of Family Courts in Her Majesty's Courts Service (HMCS)*, HMICA.

Haimes, E. (1987) '"Now I Know who I really am": Identity Change and Redefinitions of the Self in Adoption' in Honess, T. and Yardley, K. (eds.) *Self and Identity*, Routledge and Kegan Paul.

Hale, J. (1999) 'The View from Court 45' 11 *Child and Family Law Quarterly* 377.

Harold, G. and Murch, M. (2005) 'Inter-parental Conflict and Children's Adaptation to Separation and Divorce: Theory, Research and Implications for Family Law, Practice and Policy' 17 *Child and Family Law Quarterly* 185.

Harrison, M. (2002) 'Australia's Family Law Act: the First Twenty Five Years' 16 *International Journal of Law, Policy and the Family* 1.

Hasan, A. (2008) 'To Tell or Not To Tell: That is The Question' 38 *Family Law* 458.

Hester, M. (2002) 'One Step Forward and Three Steps Back? Children, Abuse and Parental Contact in Denmark' 14 *Child and Family Law Quarterly* 267.

HM Inspectorate of Court Administration (HMICA) (2007) *Assisting Families by Court Order*, HMICA.

Hodgkin, R. and Newell, P. (2007) *Implementation Handbook for the Convention on the Rights of the Child*, Unicef.

Howe, D. and Feast, J. (2000) *Adoption, Search and Reunion: The Long Term Experience of Adopted Adults*, The Children's Society.

Hunt, J. with Roberts, C. (2004) Child Contact with Non-resident Parents, *Family Policy Briefing 3*, University of Oxford.

Hunt, J. and Macleod, A. (2008) *Outcomes of Applications to Court for Contact Orders After Parental Separation or Divorce*, Ministry of Justice.

Humphreys, C. and Harrison, C. (2003) 'Focusing on Safety – Domestic Violence and the Role of Child Contact Centres' 15 *Child and Family Law Quarterly* 237.

Joint Committee on the Human Tissue and Embryos (Draft) Bill (2007) *Human Tissue and Embryos (Draft) Bill*, Volume I, HL 169-I, HC 630-I, TSO.

Jones, D. and Ramchandani, P. (1999) *Child Sexual Abuse*, Radcliffe Medical Press.

Jones, E. and Parkinson, P. (1995) 'Child Sexual Abuse, Access and the Wishes of Children' 9 *International Journal of Law, Policy and the Family* 54.

Kaganas, F. (1996) 'Responsible or Feckless Fathers? – Re S (Parental Responsibility)' 8 *Child and Family Law Quarterly* 165.

Kaganas, F. and Piper, C. (2002) 'Shared Parenting – a 70% Solution?' 14 *Child and Family Law Quarterly* 365.

Kaye, M. (1996) 'Domestic Violence, Residence and Contact' 8 *Child and Family Law Quarterly* 285.

Lind, C. (2006) '*Evans v United Kingdom* – Judgments of Solomon: Power, Gender and Procreation' 18 *Child and Family Law Quarterly* 576.

Lord Chancellor's Department (LCD) (1998) *Procedures for the Determination of Paternity and on the Law on Parental Responsibility for Unmarried Fathers: A Lord Chancellor's Department Consultation Paper*, LCD.

Lord Chancellor's Department (LCD) (2001) *Guidelines for Good Practice on Parental Contact in Cases Where There is Domestic Violence*, prepared by the Children Act Sub-Committee of the Lord Chancellor's Advisory Board on Family Law, LCD.

Lowe, N. (1997) 'The Meaning and Allocation of Parental Responsibility – A Common Lawyer's Perspective' 11 *International Journal of Law, Policy and the Family* 192.

Lowe, N. and Douglas, G. (2007) *Bromley's Family Law*, Oxford University Press.

Macaskill, C. (2002) *Safe Contact? Children in Permanent Placement and Contact With Their Birth Relatives*, Russell House Publishing.

Masson, J. (2006) 'Consent Orders in Contact Cases: A Survey of Resolution Members' 36 *Family Law* 1041.

McGee, C. (2000) *Childhood Experiences of Domestic Violence*, Jessica Kingsley Publishers.

Millbank, J. (2008) 'The Limits of Functional Family: Lesbian Mother Litigation in the Era of the Eternal Biological Family' 22 *International Journal of Law, Policy and the Family* 149.

Neale, B., Flowerdew, J. and Smart, C. (2003) 'Drifting Towards Shared Residence?' 33 *Family Law* 904.

Neil, E. (2003) 'Adoption and Contact: A Research View' in Bainham, A., Lindley, B., Richards, A. and Trinder, L. (eds.) *Children and Their Families: Contact, Rights and Welfare*, Hart Publishing.

Neil, E. and Howe, D. (2004) *Contact in Adoption and Permanent Foster Care*, BAAF.

O'Donovan, K. (1990) 'What Shall We Tell the Children?' in Lee, R. and Morgan, D. (eds.) *Birthrights*, Routledge.

Ofsted (2008a) *Ofsted's Inspection of Cafcass South East Region*, Ofsted.

Ofsted (2008b) *Ofsted's Inspection of Cafcass East Midlands*, Ofsted.

Office for National Statistics (2008) *Social Trends* No 38, Palgrave Macmillan.

Performance and Innovation Unit (PIU) (2000) *The Prime Minister's Review of Adoption*, Cabinet Office.

Perry, A. and Rainey, B. (2007) 'Supervised, Supported and Indirect Contact Orders: Research Findings' 21 *International Journal of Law, Policy and the Family* 21.

Pickford, R. (1999a) 'Unmarried Fathers and the Law' in Bainham, A., Day Sclater, S. and Richards, M. (eds.) *What is a Parent?: A Socio-Legal Analysis*, Hart Publishing.

(1999b) *Fathers, Marriage and the Law*, Family Policy Studies Centre.

Probert, R. (2004) 'Families, Assisted Reproduction and the Law' 16 *Child and Family Law Quarterly* 273.

Pryor, J. and Rodgers, B. (2001) *Children in Changing Families: Life After Parental Separation*, Blackwell Publishing.

Reece, H. (2006) 'UK Women's Groups' Child Contact Campaign: "So Long as it is Safe"' 18 *Child and Family Law Quarterly* 538.

Rhoades, H. (2002) 'The "No-Contact Mother": Reconstructions of Motherhood in the Era of the "New Father"' 16 *International Journal of Law, Policy and the Family* 71.

(2006) 'Yearning for Law: Fathers' Groups and Family Law Reform in Australia' in Collier, R. and Sheldon, S. (2006) *Fathers' Rights Activism and Law Reform in Comparative Perspective*, Hart Publishing.

Rhoades, H. and Boyd, S. (2004) 'Reforming Custody Laws: A Comparative Study' (2004) 18 *International Journal of Law, Policy and the Family* 119.

Rogers, B. and Pryor, J. (1998) *Divorce and Separation: The Outcomes for Children*, Joseph Rowntree Foundation.

Saunders, H. (2004) *Twenty-nine Child Homicides: Lessons Still to be Learnt on Domestic Violence and Child Protection*, Women's Aid Federation of England.

Sheldon, S. (2005) 'Fragmenting Fatherhood: The Regulation of Reproductive Technologies' 68 *Modern Law Review* 523.

(2007) 'Unmarried Fathers and British citizenship: the Nationality, Immigration and Asylum Act 2002 and British Nationality (Proof of Paternity) Regulations 2006' 19 *Child and Family Law Quarterly* 1.

Smart, C. (2004) 'Equal Shares: Rights for Fathers or Recognition for Children?' 24 *Critical Social Policy* 484.

(2007) *Personal Life*, Polity Press.

Smart, C. and Neale, B. (1997) 'Arguments Against Virtue: Must Contact be Enforced?' 27 *Family Law* 332.

(1999) *Family Fragments?*, Polity Press.

Steiner, E. (2003) '*Odièvre v France* – Desperately Seeking Mother – Anonymous Births in the European Court of Human Rights' 15 *Child and Family Law Quarterly* 425.

Sturge, C. and Glaser, D. (2000) 'Contact and Domestic Violence – the Experts' Court Report' 30 *Family Law* 615.

Trinder, L., Connolly, J., Kellett, J. and Notley, C. (2005) *A Profile of Applicants and Respondents in Contact Cases in Essex*, DCA Research Series 1/05, DCA.

Trinder, L., Connolly, J., Kellett, J., Notley, C. and Swift, L. (2006) *Making Contact Happen or Making Contact Work? The Process and Outcomes of In-court Conciliation*, DCA Research Series 3/06, DCA.

Trinder, L. and Kellett, J. (2007) *The Longer-term Outcomes of In-court Conciliation*, Ministry of Justice Research Series 15/07, Ministry of Justice.

Triseliotis, J. (1973) *In Search of Origins*, Routledge and Kegan Paul.

Turkmendag, I., Dingwall, R. and Murphy, T. (2008) 'The Removal of Donor Anonymity in the UK: The Silencing of Claims by Would-Be Parents' 22 *International Journal of Law, Policy and the Family* 283.

Walby, S. (2004) *The Cost of Domestic Violence*, Women and Equality Unit, DTI.

Wall, N. (2006) *A Report to the President of the Family Division on the Publication by the Women's Aid Federation of England entitled "Twenty-nine child homicides: Lessons still to be learnt on domestic violence and child protection" with particular reference to the five cases in which there was judicial involvement*.

Wallbank, J. (2002) 'Clause 106 of the Adoption and Children Bill: Legislation for the "Good" Father?' 22 *Legal Studies* 276.

(2004a) 'The Role of Rights and Utility in Instituting a Child's Right to Know Her Genetic History' 13 *Social and Legal Studies* 245.

(2004b) 'Reconstructing the HFEA 1990: Is Blood Really Thicker than Water?' 16 *Child and Family Law Quarterly* 387.

Wilson, G. (2006) 'The Non-Resident Parental Role for Separated Fathers: A Review' 20 *International Journal of Law, Policy and the Family* 286.

Chapter 14

Children's right to know and be brought up by their parents

(1) Introduction

As Wall J observed:

> The case thus raises as a central issue the classic dilemma sadly so often found in children's cases. B has become attached to people who are not her natural parents. To break that attachment will undoubtedly cause her harm. Does the harm that will be caused outweigh the benefit which B will otherwise derive from being brought up by her parents in the cultural heritage and traditions into which she was born?[1]

These words encapsulate very well the difficulties confronting the courts when dealing with disputes over children who form attachments with those who care for them and love them on a day-to-day basis, but who are not their birth parents. Schaffer warns against assuming that these affectionate ties are somehow less important to the child:

> The widespread belief in the blood bond is based on the notion that there is a natural affinity between child and biological parents which makes the latter more fit to be responsible for the child's care and upbringing than any outsider. Such fitness is assumed to be due to the common heredity found in parent-child pairs; whatever experiences a child may share with some other adult and whatever affectionate ties then develop between them are considered to be of secondary importance to the blood bond which is said to exist from the moment of conception.[2]

Having summarised the well-documented research showing only too clearly the way in which children can form positive attachments with adopters and other carers,[3] Schaffer concludes:

> It is a history of social interaction, not kinship, that breeds attachment, and to break these bonds cannot be done lightheartedly – certainly not on the basis of a myth, namely a psychological blood bond.[4]

---

[1] *Re B (adoption: child's welfare)* [1995] 1 FLR 895 at 896.   [2] H. Schaffer (1998) p. 51.
[3] See also the research summarised by I. Weyland (1997) pp. 175–8.
[4] H. Schaffer (1998) p. 62.

Very similar views led Goldstein *et al.* to coin their concept of the child's 'psychological parent'.[5] Schaffer's words make clear his disapproval of those who assume that the bonds between a child and his or her attachment figures can be broken simply because they are not linked to each other by ties of blood. Children suffer severe psychological trauma when separated from such carers,[6] whether or not they are biologically related.

Against this view has to be balanced the importance society places on the blood tie between children and birth parents and a feeling of unease generated by laws which might allow foster carers or adoptive parents to keep children in their care despite the birth parents' strong opposition. Most societies assume that 'normal' families comprise birth parents and their children and that the genetic tie between parent and child is not merely a symbolic one. The law recognises the special role that parents play in their children's lives, by giving them an initial and presumptive right to bring up their children themselves. As Eekelaar has pointed out:

> It would surely be legally wrong for a hospital to hand a child over to a stranger rather than to its mother, not simply because the child would (or might) do better with the mother, but because the mother is entitled to her child unless deprived of this right through proper legal procedures … It is surely not a matter of embarrassment to hold that parents have a prima facie right to possess their children. This must be fundamental to our social ordering.[7]

It is impossible to quarrel with this comment or with the commonly held view that, unless circumstances are exceptional, children have a corresponding right to be brought up by their birth parents. This is reflected in Articles 7, 8 and 9 of the Convention on the Rights of the Child (CRC), all of which emphasise the importance to children of retaining membership of their own families. Similarly, Article 8 of the European Convention for the Protection of Human Rights and Fundamental Freedoms (ECHR) stresses the value of family life, with the Strasbourg case law emphasising the obligation on national authorities to ensure that separated family members are reunited as soon as possible.[8]

Whilst such an approach is irrefutable so far as a newborn baby is concerned, it may not be appropriate to suggest, as some of the domestic case law does, that the child's 'right' to be brought up by his or her birth parents survives any disruption in that child's care, and even in the event of the child forming stronger emotional ties with other carers. Furthermore, some children have been removed from their birth parents, having been abused in their care. To them the blood tie may be of little value; indeed, they may need a fresh start with a new family who can provide them with security and long-term happiness.

This chapter is divided into two parts. It first traces the historical development of the legal principles now applied to disputes between birth parents and private

---

[5] J. Goldstein, A. Freud and A. Solnit (1973) p. 19.   [6] H. Schaffer (1998) pp. 90–111.
[7] J. Eekelaar (1991) p. 388.   [8] Discussed below.

foster carers. These disputes usually arise in situations developing, almost by accident, through birth parents making informal fostering arrangements for their children to be cared for temporarily. The birth parents probably had no intention of leaving their children for long, but by the time they seek their return, the children have become so attached to their foster carers, and vice versa, that the foster carers refuse to return them. This area of case law is interesting in so far as it demonstrates the varying ways in which the judiciary respond to arguments based on the value of the blood tie between child and birth parents. The chapter proceeds to consider the extent to which the courts adjust their respect for the blood tie in disputes involving applications to adopt the child.

(2) Disputes between birth parents and private foster carers

(A) Differences in approach

No one really knows how many private fostering arrangements exist up and down the country, largely because birth parents and fosterers alike fail to notify their local authority (LA) of the arrangements they are entering into.[9] Consequently LAs often find it difficult to exercise any real control over the placement or welfare of privately fostered children.[10] Many have pointed to the dangers of children being abused in such unregulated arrangements.[11] A legislative obligation on all LAs to establish registration schemes for all private foster carers awaits the introduction of enforcement regulations.[12] Large numbers of privately fostered children[13] are from ethnic minorities – some are refugees from conflict, some are fostered to allow their parents to study or work here, others come for informal visits and stay on. The early 1970s saw a considerable growth in the numbers of West African children, in particular, Nigerian children, being placed in private foster care.[14] Later, increasing

---

[9] Children (Private Arrangements for Fostering) Regulations 2005 (SI 2005/1533), regs. 3–4: foster carers are obliged to notify the LA of an intention to foster a child privately at least 6 weeks before the fostering arrangement starts. See also Children Act (CA) 1989, Sch. 8, para. 7A: every LA must promote public awareness in their area of private foster carers' obligation to notify the LA of their intention to foster. But Ofsted (2008) para. 126 notes the very slow progress made in raising awareness amongst private foster carers of the need to register with LAs.

[10] CA 1989, s. 67; Children (Private Arrangements for Fostering) Regulations 2005 (SI 2005/1533) and DfES (2005). Inter alia: the LA must visit the proposed foster carers to satisfy themselves of the suitability of the proposed arrangements; visit every 6 weeks within the first year of the arrangement and thereafter every 12 weeks.

[11] W. Utting (1997) pp. 43–6; B. Holman (2002); T. Philpot (2001); SSI (2002) paras. 1.16 and 6.4; L. Bostock (2004).

[12] CA 2004, s. 45.

[13] CA 1989, s. 66(1) and (2): a 'privately fostered child' is a child under the age of 16 who is cared for and provided with accommodation for more than 28 days by someone *other* than their parent, or someone with parental responsibility or a relative.

[14] Save the Children (1997) p. 1: by the early 1990s there were probably at least 6,000 children of West African origin privately fostered in the UK. Victoria Climbié was a recent example; she was fostered by her great aunt and brought to England from the Ivory Coast in 1999; H. Laming (2003).

numbers came from other parts of Africa[15] and from Eastern European countries, such as Bosnia.[16] Whatever their current total, it is clear that large
numbers of white British foster carers care for foster children of a different
racial and cultural origin, whose birth parents are abroad and therefore unable
to be actively involved in their children's upbringing or the type of care being
provided.

It appears that the majority of privately fostered children eventually returns
to their birth parents, but 'the consequences of their returning to a culture,
religion and language that is alien to them, and perhaps seen as inferior by them
because of experiences they have had in their placements, are plain'.[17] In a
minority of cases, the ties of affection between these children and their foster
carers strengthen over time, to such an extent that their reluctance to return the
child to their birth parents culminates in litigation.[18] When a dispute arises
between birth parents and foster carers, in the majority of cases, the court will
be faced with a single issue, whether to allow the foster carers to continue caring
for the child or to order the child's return to his or her birth parents. In
principle, there is nothing to prevent the birth parents visiting the foster carers
in person, demanding that their child be handed over to them there and then.
Unless they have already taken legal steps to protect their continued care of the
child against the birth parents' wishes,[19] foster carers confronted by birth
parents in this way have no legal authority to retain the child. In practice, the
disputes which reach the courts are probably those involving birth parents who
are too timid to take the law into their own hands in such a way.

These disputes are governed by the paramountcy principle.[20] Nevertheless,
over the last four decades there have been three different judicial approaches to
its interpretation. Though subtle, these differences would have crucially affected
any legal advice given to foster carers over the likelihood of their successfully
opposing the birth parents' claim to retrieve the fostered child. In particular,
they have materially affected the manner in which the courts have handled
evidence presented by the foster carers indicating that the child might suffer
significant psychological harm by being returned to his or her birth parents.
Some of the case law illustrates the notion of children's rights being distorted to
mask concerns over birth parents being deprived of their children's care.
Indeed, the child's right to protection from psychological harm has, at times,
been sacrificed to promoting the biological tie between children and their birth
parents.

---

[15] B. Olusanya and D. Hodes (2000) and T. Philpot (2001).   [16] Save the Children (1997) p. 12.
[17] Ibid. at p. 38.   [18] E.g. *Re B (adoption: child's welfare)* [1995] 1 FLR 895.
[19] In the past, foster carers often utilised the wardship jurisdiction to gain authority for continued
care of a foster child. Today they would apply for a residence order or special guardianship order
under the CA 1989, ss. 8 and 14A.
[20] CA 1989, s. 1 – alternatively described as the 'best interests' or 'welfare' principle.

(B) No presumption favouring the birth parents

Despite its venerable age, the House of Lords' decision in *J v. C*[21] has retained its significance. It remains one of the best factual examples of a dispute between birth parents and foster carers arising out of an informal fostering arrangement. The House of Lords considered it to be against the best interests of a 10-year-old boy to return him to his Spanish parents in Spain, after seven years in the care of English foster parents. The decision established that all the evidence relating to where the child should live should be weighed together, with no presumption favouring his birth parents. Indeed, Lord MacDermott quoted with approval the words of Wilberforce J in an earlier adoption decision:

> The tie … between the child and his natural father (or any other relative) may properly be regarded in this connexion, not on the basis that the person concerned has a claim which he has a right to have satisfied, but, only if, and to the extent that, the conclusion can be drawn that the child will benefit from the recognition of this tie.[22]

In evidential terms, the birth parents in *J v. C* were not deemed to occupy a more favourable position to retrieve their son than the foster carers. The decision established that although the claims of birth parents would often have great weight and cogency, they had to be 'assessed and weighed in their bearing on the welfare of the child in conjunction with all other factors relevant to that issue'.[23] The nearest that Lord MacDermott went to suggesting that birth parents occupied a special position in such disputes, was to comment:

> While there is now no rule of law that the rights and wishes of unimpeachable parents must prevail over other considerations, such rights and wishes, recognised as they are by nature and society, can be capable of ministering to the total welfare of the child in a special way, and must therefore preponderate in many cases.[24]

The decision in *J v. C* was controversial for a number of reasons. In particular, it suggested that the special relationship and tie between birth parents and children carried no significant weight.[25] Consequently, in disputes of this kind, there was no onus on the foster carers to overturn a legal presumption favouring continuation of the birth parents' care; rather it was the job of the court to assess which course of action would promote the child's best interests. As Eekelaar commented, 'parental claims have no independent weight but are relevant only as evidence as to what course is best for the child'.[26] *J v. C* was subsequently applied to other disputes of this kind, with birth parents being denied special treatment. The courts did not confine themselves to assessing the disruption that children would suffer when being uprooted from their homes with their foster carers after some years. They also considered it perfectly

---

[21] [1970] AC 668.   [22] *Re Adoption Application No 41/61 (No 2)* [1963] 2 All ER 1082 at 1085.
[23] [1970] AC 668, per Lord MacDermott, at 713.
[24] Ibid. at 715.   [25] J. Eekelaar (1973) p. 217.   [26] Ibid. at p. 216.

appropriate to compare the advantages of family life offered by the foster carers, with the natural care and affection that birth parents were able to offer.[27] Indeed, case law indicated the judiciary placing the blood tie between a child and his or her birth parents in the context of a variety of other factors.[28]

(C) The child's 'prima facie right' to an upbringing by birth parents

The unemotional way in which the judiciary considered the value of maintaining the blood tie between parent and child was soon to give way to a rather different approach. This utilised the concept of children's rights to promote what, in reality, appeared to be concerns about parents' rights. Indeed, the Court of Appeal now seemed to see the child-parent tie in an entirely different light, carrying a far greater significance. It produced an evidential formula which considerably favoured birth parents. In a new line of cases, starting with *Re K (a minor) (ward: care and control)*,[29] the judiciary made it clear that it was wrong for courts to weigh up the evidence relevant to the child's future life with one family rather than the other, before deciding whether to order the child's return to his or her birth parents:

> The question was not: where would R get the better home? The question was: was it demonstrated that the welfare of the child positively demanded the displacement of the parental right? The word 'right' is not really accurate in so far as it might connote something in the nature of a property right (which it is not) but it will serve for present purposes. The 'right', if there is one, is perhaps more that of the child.[30]

This mysterious change of attitude may have been influenced by the developing adoption law.[31] The judiciary's anxiety to avoid accusations of 'social engineering', when considering evidence relating to a child's future well-being with prospective adopters,[32] may have coloured their approach to similar disputes between foster carers and birth parents. It also appears that the then recent decision of the House of Lords in *Re KD (a minor) (ward: termination of access)*[33] had a powerful impact on judicial decision-making. Their Lordships

---

[27] E.g. *Re H (a minor) (custody)* [1990] 1 FLR 51: an English father brought his 8-year-old son to England from India and placed him in the care of his paternal uncle and aunt. His Indian mother failed to recover his care because he had been settled happily with his English foster carers for 2½ years and a change would be disruptive both to his home and education.

[28] E.g. *Re M (a minor) (custody appeal)* [1990] 1 FLR 291: a dispute involving an adoption application. See this type of dispute discussed below.

[29] [1990] 3 All ER 795: after his mother's suicide, a boy, now aged 4½ years had been placed by his father with his maternal aunt and uncle. After he had been in their care for one year, the foster parents refused to return him to his father.

[30] [1990] 3 All ER 795, per Fox LJ, at 798.   [31] J. Fortin (1999) pp. 436–9.

[32] E.g. Butler-Sloss LJ, in *Re K (a minor) (wardship: adoption)* [1991] 1 FLR 57 at 62 and in *Re O (a minor) (custody: adoption)* [1992] 1 FLR 77 at 79.

[33] [1988] AC 806: an application in wardship by a mother claiming that the LA was acting in breach of her parental 'right' to visit her baby whilst in LA care.

voiced some stirring views about the concept of parenthood. Indeed, it was probably Lord Templeman's eminently quotable and emotive phrases that invoked a new willingness to give the blood tie between child and parent a far greater significance:

> The best person to bring up a child is the natural parent. It matters not whether the parent is wise or foolish, rich or poor, educated or illiterate, provided the child's moral and physical health are not endangered.[34]

Lord Oliver also said:

> Parenthood, in most civilised societies, is generally conceived of as conferring on parents the exclusive privilege of ordering, within the family, the upbringing of children of tender age, with all that that entails. That is a privilege which, if interfered with without authority, would be protected by the courts.[35]

Despite this recognition of the privileges of parenthood, Lord Oliver stressed, contrary to the mother's claims in *Re KD*, that no provision in the ECHR required a reassessment of the principles established by *J v. C*[36] regarding parents' 'rights'. Indeed, he made it plain that the mother was to be given no special preference when it came to weighing the evidence regarding her claimed 'right' to access to her child. This would be determined by the child's welfare.[37] As Eekelaar comments of this outcome: 'Neither party, it seems, starts with an inherent *legal* advantage. If he or she is to "win", the erstwhile "right-holder", as much as the challenger, must establish that his or her proposals are better for the child than the competing set.'[38] Lord Oliver's confidence that this approach was consistent with Article 8 of the ECHR is difficult to accept, since it is arguable that the article creates an initial presumption in favour of upholding parents' rights, which must then be rebutted by evidence relating to the child's welfare.[39] Be that as it may, *Re KD* clearly influenced the future treatment of disputes between birth parents and foster carers.

Their Lordships' remarks in *Re KD* were later enthusiastically adopted by the Court of Appeal in *Re K (a minor) (ward: care and control)*.[40] They were taken to mean that the court should not oppose the claims of a birth parent, unless there was some evidence relating to the child's welfare which positively required that the parental rights should be suspended or superseded. The assumption was that the child had a 'prima facie right' to an upbringing by his or her birth parents and this right survived any subsequent changes in the child's care. This subtly downgraded the principle in *J v. C*, since foster carers were now required

---

[34] Ibid. at 812.

[35] Ibid. at 825. He then qualified this statement with the following words: 'but it is a privilege circumscribed by many limitations imposed both by the general law and, where the circumstances demand, by the courts or by the authorities on whom the legislature has imposed the duty of supervising the welfare of children and young persons.'

[36] [1970] AC 668.   [37] [1988] AC 806 at 827.

[38] J. Eekelaar (1988) p. 632 (emphasis in original).   [39] See discussion in Chapters 2 and 8.

[40] [1990] 3 All ER 795. See also *Re K (a minor) (wardship: adoption)* [1991] 1 FLR 57.

to produce evidence showing that the child's best interests required the *displacement* of the parents' prior claims. The court's job was not to assess the child's potential happiness in the two households, since the onus was on the foster carers to provide the court with evidence that there were 'compelling factors which required him [the learned judge] to override the prima facie right of this child to an upbringing by its surviving natural parent'.[41]

It was unfortunate that the evidential presumption favouring the birth parents was concealed behind the language of children's rights, given that its effect was to endanger children's right to protection from psychological harm. Obviously in many cases the most crucial evidence for long-term foster carers to produce relates to the psychological risks to the child of being uprooted from a home with them. The birth parents, on the other hand, would attempt to persuade the court of their love for their child and their child's love for them. They would also invite the court to bear in mind that society assumes it 'normal' and advantageous for children to be brought up by their birth parents. But the new presumption encouraged the courts to give far less serious consideration to the dangers of psychological damage being caused by removing the child from his or her present home, than to the benefits of being brought up by birth parents.[42] Indeed, as Weyland points out, in most cases, no expert evidence was produced to show that the birth parent was intrinsically better suited than the child's psychological parent to bring him or her up.[43]

Thus in *Re K (a minor) (ward: care and control)* itself[44] there was no evaluation of the relationship between father and child, although the court took account of the fact that the father had regularly visited his son. By refusing to compare the homes being offered by the birth and foster parents, the courts not only failed to apply the Children Act (CA) 1989, section 1(3) correctly,[45] but also risked endangering the child's psychological health by investing the blood tie between child and parents with undue importance.[46] Hayes and Williams suggest that to adopt the notion of children's rights in disputes of this kind actually inhibits the decision-making process. They observe:

> The child's views are likely to be coloured by the strength of his attachment to his 'natural' parents and the strength of his attachment to those who have been caring for him as substitute parents ... He certainly may not regard it as his 'right' to be brought up by his parents, who, to him may be the strangers, rather than his substitute parents whom he regards as his family.[47]

It is difficult to justify the ties of affection between the child and foster carers being automatically outweighed by concerns focusing on the blood tie and the

---

[41] [1990] 3 All ER 795, per Waite J, at 800.

[42] J. Fortin (1999) pp. 439–40 and I. Weyland (1997) pp. 180–4.

[43] I. Weyland (1997) p. 178.   [44] [1990] 3 All ER 795.   [45] I Weyland (1997) p 178.

[46] See *Re K (a minor) (wardship: adoption)* [1991] 1 FLR 57 for a similar approach in disputes involving adoption applications; discussed below.

[47] M. Hayes and C. Williams (1999) pp. 287–8.

rights of the birth parents. In such circumstances, a child surely has as much of a 'right' to continue being cared for by the foster carers, as he or she had to being cared for initially by birth parents.

(D) The 'other things being equal' formula

Judicial unease over the direction being taken by the case law regarding disputes between birth parents and foster carers marked a further change in approach. Lord Donaldson MR admitted being:

> slightly apprehensive that *Re K (a minor) (ward: care and control)*[48] may be misconstrued ... it is not a case of parental right opposed to the interests of the child, with an assumption that parental right prevails unless there are strong reasons in terms of the interests of the child ... all that *Re K* is saying, as I understand it, is that of course there is a strong supposition that, *other things being equal*, it is in the interests of the child that it shall remain with its natural parents. But that has to give way to particular needs in particular situations.[49]

Although in a number of subsequent decisions these words were adopted with approval,[50] it is unclear whether their real import was fully appreciated. What are the practical implications of Lord Donaldson's words? A strict reading suggests that a court should not assume that other things are equal, until it has made a proper comparison of the two homes available, in order to decide which would better fulfil the child's welfare. In order to make this comparison, the court might consider a number of factors, including the strength and quality of the child's relationships with his or her natural parents, comparing them with those formed with the foster parents. Indeed, Lord Donaldson's 'other things being equal' formula suggests that the value of the blood tie between parent and child should be fully assessed, in terms of the benefit to be derived by the child from the recognition of that tie. This approach would appear to be fully consistent with the intention underlying the CA 1989, section 1. The courts should consider what course would best promote the child's welfare, bearing in mind all the factors in the checklist in section 1(3), including not only any harm or risk of harm to the child through uprooting him or her from the present carers, but also the birth parents' ability for parenting.

These expectations regarding the interpretation of the 'other things being equal' formula were not borne out by the case law utilising it. Indeed, whilst avowedly taking full account of Lord Donaldson's words, the courts' attitude to foster carers' evidential burden remained very much the same as before. Rather, the formula appeared to achieve precisely the same result for them as that

---

[48] [1990] 3 All ER 795.

[49] *Re H (a minor) (custody: interim care and control)* [1991] 2 FLR 109 at 112–13 (emphasis supplied).

[50] E.g. *Re W (a minor) (residence order)* [1993] 2 FLR 625; *Re B (adoption: child's welfare)* [1995] 1 FLR 895; *Re M (child's upbringing)* [1996] 2 FLR 441.

advocated by Fox LJ in *Re K (a minor) (ward: care and control)*.[51] Furthermore, the line of cases applying this approach stretches from the early 1990s to the present day. The courts remain unshaken in their assumption that a change in the child's care makes little or no difference to the child's 'right' to be brought up by the birth parents. Consequently, there is a marked reluctance to assess and weigh all the evidence from each 'side', in order to decide what course of action would be in the child's best interests.

Re W (a minor) (residence order)[52] is a case in point. The trial judge was not persuaded that uprooting a 7-year-old boy from the home he had had with his grandparents for over three years presented 'a risk of harm that was sufficient to displace his *right* to be brought up by his father'.[53] This was despite the court welfare officer's view that there were considerable psychological risks in changing the status quo against the boy's wishes. On appeal, Balcombe and Waite LJJ wholeheartedly approved of the 'other things being equal' formula adopted by the trial judge when reaching his decision. Neither, however, indicated how, in practice, a court should decide whether other things *were* equal. There was no suggestion that the formula might allow a comparison of the relative merits of the two homes available for the child, as in much earlier case law.[54] There was no reference to the quality of relationship existing between the father and son, despite the evidence indicating the child's obvious happiness with his grandparents and his desire to stay with them.[55] Given the Court of Appeal's full approval of the decision at first instance, the boy would have been handed over to his father, were it not for the grandparents' fortuitous discovery of fresh evidence regarding the father's alleged ill-treatment of a stepson. Only in the light of that evidence was the case sent for rehearing.

It is surprising that decisions like *Re W (a minor) (residence order)*[56] and *Re M (child's upbringing)*[57] did not provoke judicial doubts about the wisdom of assuming that the blood tie between a child and his or her parent would always produce a relationship valuable to *both*. In the latter case, despite the 10-year-old Zulu boy's own strong opposition to such a step, Neill LJ stated 'he has the *right* to be reunited with his Zulu parents and with his extended family in South Africa'.[58] The Court of Appeal ignored the psychiatrist's warnings that the damage to the boy's emotional well-being, by being forced to return to his birth parents, might wholly undermine his ability to benefit from his renewed links with his Zulu heritage. Unfortunately, court orders cannot magically transform children's affections. The boy's unhappiness in South Africa forced his parents to admit defeat and to return him to his foster mother's care in England.

Despite these examples of children who reject judicial conceptions of their 'rights', the line of cases starting with *Re K (a minor) (ward: care and control)*[59]

[51] [1990] 3 All ER 795.   [52] [1993] 2 FLR 625.   [53] [1993] 2 FLR 625 at 630 (emphasis supplied).
[54] E.g. *Re H (a minor: custody)* [1990] 1 FLR 51; see above.
[55] The weight to be placed on children's own wishes is discussed more fully in Chapter 8.
[56] [1993] 2 FLR 625.   [57] [1996] 2 FLR 441.
[58] [1996] 2 FLR 441 at 454 (emphasis supplied).   [59] [1990] 3 All ER 795.

is so strong that it undermines the legal respectability of any decision which fails to follow it.[60] For example, in *Re D (care: natural parent presumption)*,[61] it led the Court of Appeal to approve of a social work placement apparently motivated solely by a belief that the blood tie between father and child would make up for the absence of any relationship between them and any flaws in the father's character. The LA explained that they had started on the basis that 'wherever possible you place the child with the natural side of the family'.[62] This approach conveniently saved the LA the task of undertaking a detailed assessment of the qualities offered by the two possible carers, the father and the grandmother.[63] The LA's stance was reinforced by the Court of Appeal's own refusal to scrutinise the respective homes on offer. Indeed, Sumner J criticised the trial judge for carrying out a 'balancing exercise' in which he weighed up the benefits the boy would be offered by the two households.[64] Instead, he should have followed the principle established by *Re K (a minor) (ward: care and control)*,[65] thereby avoiding comparing the child's prospects with the two protagonists, one being a parent, and the other only a grandmother. Although the father had no well-established relationship with his son, the trial judge should have considered whether there were any compelling factors to override the child's prima facie 'right' to live with his father.[66]

Those familiar with case law relating to children know that there will always be the odd unaccountable exception to any apparently consistent line of decisions. Despite the approach established so firmly by the Court of Appeal in *Re K (a minor) (ward: care and control)* and in subsequent cases like *Re D*,[67] the courts now and again do not refer to it at all when reaching decisions allowing children to remain with their long-term foster carers. Thus it was because an 8-year-old Down's syndrome girl considered her devoted foster carers to be her 'real' parents that the Court of Appeal refused her orthodox Jewish birth parents' application to recover her care.[68] The court accepted that she would suffer considerable psychological damage if removed from those who had cared for her almost from birth, but it provided virtually no explanation for

---

[60] E.g. *Re N (residence: appointment of solicitor: placement with extended family)* [2001] 1 FLR 1028: father's appeal allowed against an order authorising a maternal aunt and her husband to retain the care of a boy now aged 5 who had lived with them for 4 years from his mother's death. Per Hale LJ at [28]–[30]: the trial judge should have borne in mind Lord Donaldson's words in *Re H (a minor) (custody: interim care and control)* [1991] 2 FLR 109 at 112–13 (the 'other things being equal' formula) and should therefore have considered the possible medium- and long-term advantages of an upbringing in the father's family.

[61] [1999] 1 FLR 134: father with a history of abusing drugs, despite having had very little contact with his son since his birth, now wanted to care for him (with his third wife's help) together with their new baby and stepdaughter. The boy's maternal grandmother, already caring for his two half-brothers, wanted to take over the boy's care herself.

[62] Ibid. at 144.   [63] J. Fortin (1999).

[64] In favouring the grandmother over the father, the trial judge had been influenced by the fact that the boy would remain with his half-brothers if he lived with her.

[65] [1990] 3 All ER 795.   [66] [1999] 1 FLR 134 at 141.   [67] [1999] 2 FLR 1023, discussed above.

[68] *Re P (a child) (residence order: restriction order)* [2000] Fam 15.

its failure even to consider the principle in *Re K (a minor) (ward: care and control)*.[69] It is strange that in cases of this kind, the presumption is not mentioned and, more to the point, they vary very little factually from those like *Re W (a minor) (residence order)*[70] and *Re M (child's upbringing)*,[71] where there were similar risks of the children concerned undergoing very grave psychological harm by being uprooted from their foster carers on the court's direction.

(E) Convention rights

The body of case law discussed above is relatively old – does it require reassessing in the light of the Human Rights Act (HRA) 1998? Arguably, since the phrasing of Article 8 of the ECHR suggests that the interests of parents and children are united, the domestic courts may now feel under no obligation to dress up orders fulfilling parents' rights to look like orders fulfilling children's rights. Since they can now assert that the birth parents' presumption is fully justified, there is an obvious danger of the principle in *Re K (a minor) (ward: care and control)*[72] being promoted even more aggressively than before. But whilst the Strasbourg case law is not particularly coherent, it does not support the view that Article 8 will *invariably* assist parents in such disputes.

Birth parents can certainly draw support from *Görgülü v. Germany*.[73] Emphasising the biological tie between a 4-year-old boy and his father, the European Court of Human Rights (ECtHR) criticised the German domestic court for concluding that it would be against the boy's best interests for his father to take over his care.[74] In the Court's view the German court had only focused on the short-term impact on the child of separating him from his foster carers, with whom he had lived from birth, rather than on the long-term effect on him of being permanently separated from his birth father.[75] The ECtHR's conclusion that the father's Article 8 rights had been unjustifiably infringed by the German court's refusal to arrange for him to take over his son's care on an incremental basis, appeared to ignore the child's own rights under Article 8 to remain with the family he regarded as his own. It also apparently ignores the fact that by uprooting a child from the only carers he has known for many years may wholly undermine his long-term ability to benefit from the blood tie between him and his birth parent. Furthermore, such an attitude is difficult to reconcile with the ECtHR's acknowledgement in parental contact disputes that the state's obligation to facilitate meetings between a parent and child is not absolute, especially where the parent and child are still strangers to each other.[76]

---

[69] See also *Re K (adoption and wardship)* [1997] 2 FLR 230 (Fam D): no mention of the 'right' of E, an orphaned Bosnian child, now aged nearly 5, to live with her birth relatives in Switzerland, despite the loss of her cultural ties through remaining with her adoptive English parents who had become her 'primary psychological parents' (per Sir Stephen Brown P, at 248).

[70] [1993] 2 FLR 625.   [71] [1996] 2 FLR 441.   [72] [1990] 3 All ER 795.

[73] [2004] 1 FLR 894. See also discussed in Chapter 2.   [74] Ibid. at [46].   [75] Ibid.

[76] E.g. *Nuutinen v. Finland* (2002) 34 EHRR 15 at para. 128.

Meanwhile, and not surprisingly, the ECtHR seems far more swayed by objections to a change in care expressed by children old enough to have strong opinions of their own. In *Görgülü* the child was only 4 years old and so, presumably, his views could be discounted. In *Hokkanen v. Finland*,[77] the child was 12 and totally opposed to returning to her father's care, having lived with her grandparents for well over 10 years. The ECtHR held that children's attachments to their current carers may make it impossible to return them to their birth parents. So there, although the Finnish authorities were held to have infringed the father's rights under Article 8 by failing to take effective measures to overcome the grandparents' opposition and reunite him with his daughter, the ECtHR stressed that the state's obligation in this respect is not absolute.[78] The Court thereby acknowledged that there comes a time when the child has been living so long with other people that such a reunion between parent and child may not be feasible. Indeed, the state's duty to reconcile them may have to give way to the child's own interests under Article 8(2).[79] Similarly in *Pini and Bertani; Manera and Atripaldi v. Romania*,[80] the ECtHR sympathised with the Romanian government's refusal to force two 12-year-old girls to join their Italian adoptive parents[81] in Italy, given that:

> they had reached an age at which it could reasonably be considered that their personality was sufficiently formed and they had attained the necessary maturity to express their opinion as to the surroundings in which they wished to be brought up.[82]

The ECtHR agreed that since both girls, who had unknowingly been adopted at the age of 9 years old, were utterly opposed to leaving the residential home where they lived, their interests could be held to override their adoptive parents' Article 8 rights.[83] Sensible though such a decision was, it ill accords with the ECtHR's confidence in *Görgülü* that the best interests of the 4-year-old boy required his removal from his foster carers. Arguably, a very young child is likely to experience far more psychological harm from such disruption than a much older child.

Whilst the birth parent can undoubtedly turn to Article 8 of the ECHR to support a claim to retrieve his or her child, foster carers who have, as in many of these disputes, cared for a child virtually since his or her birth, might also do the same. For example, as discussed below, stepfathers have successfully claimed that their de facto family ties with their partner's child need protecting by legal

---

[77] (1994) 19 EHRR 139.   [78] Ibid. at para. 58.

[79] Ibid. at para. 64. See also *Bronda v. Italy* (2001) 33 EHRR 4 at paras. 61–2: the ECtHR acknowledged the overriding interests of a girl now aged 14, who was totally opposed to leaving her foster carers to return to her grandparents.

[80] [2005] 2 FLR 596.

[81] Ibid. at [142]: the adoption orders, having been properly made, had conferred on both sets of adoptive parents the same Article 8 rights in relation to their adopted children as those enjoyed by biological parents.

[82] Ibid. at [157].   [83] Ibid. at [155].

authority, even against the wishes of the birth father.[84] Foster carers could mount similar claims, alongside asserting a right to be treated fairly by the courts, when attempting to justify their retaining the child's care against the parents' wishes. Indeed, they might argue that a refusal to weigh their evidence in an even-handed way against that of the birth parents infringes their rights to procedural fairness under Articles 6 and 8 of the ECHR.[85] However the arguments are presented, the domestic courts should not ignore the fact that a court order is unable to put the clock back on a child's changed affections. It would be regrettable in the extreme if the ECHR were utilised to justify an outmoded myth about what Schaffer described as 'a psychological blood bond'.[86]

(F) Private foster carers and 'social engineering'

A long-term fostering arrangement arranged privately by birth parents with friends or acquaintances may work perfectly well for many years but suddenly turn sour when the parents demand the child's return against the foster carers' wishes. The foster carers' response may be to apply to adopt the child. Alternatively, the dispute may have been triggered by the foster parents' plans to adopt the child in question.[87] In either case, such a situation would not normally arise unless the child had been in the foster carers' care for at least three years.[88] Since an adoption order terminates the child's legal ties with his or her birth parents and replaces them with the adopters as the child's legal parents,[89] there is far more at stake for the birth parents than merely being unable to recover their child's care for the time being.[90] Indeed, at the mere mention by the foster carers of the possibility of adoption, the birth parents may attempt to retrieve their child before matters go any further.[91] The question then becomes a simple one – whether the foster carers can retain the child's

---

[84] E.g. *Söderbäck v. Sweden* [1999] 1 FLR 250, per ECtHR, at paras. 33–4: the need to formalise the de facto family ties between a child and her stepfather by granting him an adoption order justified the infringement of the birth father's family ties with his daughter under Art. 8. See also similar facts and similar finding in *Eski v. Austria* [2001] 1 FLR 1650, at [39].

[85] E.g. *Jucius and Juciuvienė v. Lithuania* [2009] 1 FLR 403, per ECtHR: the domestic court's failure to hear *orally* a custody dispute between an uncle and aunt and grandparents (re two orphaned girls) unfairly prevented an adequate assessment of the uncle and aunt's characters, unduly infringing their rights under Art. 8 (Art. 6 claim declared admissible). See also *Elsholz v. Germany* [2002] 2 FLR 486.

[86] H. Schaffer (1998) p. 62.

[87] E.g., inter alia: *Re K (a minor) (wardship: adoption)* [1991] 1 FLR 57; *Re O (a minor) (custody: adoption)* [1992] 1 FLR 77; *Re B (adoption: child's welfare)* [1995] 1 FLR 895; *Re M (child's upbringing)* [1996] 2 FLR 441.

[88] Adoption and Children Act (ACA) 2002, s. 42(5).

[89] ACA 2002, ss. 46 and 67.

[90] *Re B (adoption: child's welfare)* [1995] 1 FLR 895, per Wall J, at 897–9.

[91] NB ACA 2002, s. 44(3): at least 3 months before they apply for an adoption order, the foster carers must notify the LA in which they live of their intention to adopt. See also ss. 36(1) and 37: giving notice of an intention to adopt (or an application to adopt) thereafter protects the foster carers from the birth parents removing the child from their care without court leave.

care, with the backing of a court order, against the wishes of the child's birth parents. Refusal of an adoption order need not necessarily involve the foster carers handing the child back to the natural parents. The court may instead allow them to retain him or her in their care, on the authority of a residence order[92] or a special guardianship order (SGO),[93] whilst nurturing the ties with the child's birth parents by court ordered contact.[94]

Faced with an opposed adoption application, the court must be convinced that an adoption order is in the child's best interests, taking account of the welfare checklist[95] and giving paramount consideration to the child's welfare.[96] It can only dispense with the birth parents' consent if it considers that the child's welfare so requires.[97] As discussed below, the Strasbourg jurisprudence suggests that the domestic courts should treat an adoption order against a parent's wishes as an exceptional step. A domestic court may in any event be reluctant to accept that an adoption order is an appropriate order to make in favour of private foster carers, even in circumstances where the child is well settled in his or her foster home. Unlike foster carers who have been picked for the task by adoption agencies, private foster carers are chosen by parents who have no experience of gauging a person's suitability for child care. Since the initial arrangement did not envisage that the foster carers would adopt the child, the foster carers were not chosen with this purpose in mind.[98] Indeed, the law deliberately prohibits private adoption placements in order to prevent children being placed with adults who would make totally unsuitable adopters.[99]

Adoption case law shows the courts being influenced by the self-same assumptions discussed above about the value of the blood tie between child and birth parents. Again they have applied the approach established in *Re K (a minor) (ward: care and control)*[100] to justify the birth parents being permitted to retrieve their children in this type of dispute.[101] Thus in *Re K (a minor) (wardship: adoption)*[102] the Court of Appeal authorised the return of a baby to her mother after a year with prospective adopters, she having been in their care since the age of 6 weeks. According to Butler-Sloss LJ, the birth parent 'must be shown to be entirely unsuitable before another family can be considered, otherwise we are in grave danger of slipping into social engineering'.[103]

---

[92] CA 1989, s. 8.   [93] CA 1989, ss. 14A–14G.

[94] E.g. *Re O (transracial adoption: contact)* [1996] 1 FCR 540.

[95] ACA 2002, s. 1(4).   [96] ACA 2002, s. 1(2).   [97] ACA 2002, s. 52(1)(b).

[98] E.g. in *Re M (child's upbringing)* [1996] 2 FLR 441, the white South African foster carer of the Zulu boy had gained his parents' permission to bring him to England with her and her family when they left South Africa, without disclosing her intention to adopt him.

[99] ACA 2002, ss. 92–93 (replacing Adoption Act (AA) 1976, s. 11): it is a criminal offence to arrange a private adoption placement and to receive a child unlawfully placed for adoption, unless the child was initially received on a fostering basis and not for adoption (e.g. *Gatehouse v. R* [1986] 1 WLR 18) or unless the court authorises such a step (e.g. *Re P; K and K v. P and P* [2004] EWHC 1954 (Fam), [2005] 1 FLR 303).

[100] [1990] 3 All ER 795; discussed above.   [101] Discussed by I. Weyland (1997) pp. 181–2.

[102] [1991] 1 FLR 57.   [103] Ibid., per Butler-Sloss LJ, at 62.

She was plainly concerned by the way in which the mother had privately arranged the adoption placement with a couple that an official adoption agency would probably have deemed unsuitable.[104] In the circumstances, the social workers' plan to rehabilitate the baby with her mother was considered reasonable, despite posing considerable risks. After all, if this had been an officially arranged adoption, a mother's change of mind in such circumstances might well have provoked an attempt to rehabilitate the child with her.[105]

The Court of Appeal's disapproval of the informal way in which the baby's placement had been arranged, and the lack of social work support available for the mother when she first changed her mind about the adoption, clearly influenced their decision. One wonders, however, whether the court would have considered the evidence in quite the same way had they not been so convinced, on the authority of *Re K (a minor) (ward: care and control)*,[106] that this baby had a 'right' to be brought up by her birth parents.[107] The court considered it wrong to weigh up what the foster parents' family could offer the child unless it was shown that the birth parents were 'entirely unsuitable'.[108] Surprisingly, this unsuitability was not apparent to the Court of Appeal, despite the trial judge's fears, inter alia, about the mother's history of drug addiction, an unstable marriage and a husband with a criminal record, who was addicted to gambling.[109] As Eekelaar points out, Butler-Sloss LJ's use of the term 'social engineering' in a pejorative way in situations like this[110] reflected her assumption that 'natural' parenthood is far preferable to the social parenthood contrived by fostering and adoption.[111] The danger of being accused of social engineering would certainly deter any court tempted to compare a child's prospects in the two households on offer. But, as commented above, the danger is that by refusing to do so the courts risk placing an undue value on the blood tie between child and parent, at the expense of the child's psychological health.

Today, of course, foster carers seeking to adopt a privately fostered child who has been in their care for many years might point to the Strasbourg jurisprudence acknowledging that an adoption order may formalise well-established de facto family ties and that infringing a birth parent's Article 8 rights can be justified in such circumstances.[112] Nevertheless, as discussed below, the jurisprudence also stresses that depriving a birth parent of his or her family life with their child is an exceptional step which can only be justified by 'an overriding

---

[104] The adopters were childless Greek Cypriots aged 55 (husband) and 47 (wife). The birth mother, who was Irish, had met them in a Greek restaurant when eating there with her children.

[105] Ibid.   [106] [1990] 3 All ER 795.   [107] [1991] 1 FLR 57, per Butler-Sloss LJ, at 62.   [108] Ibid.

[109] The trial judge had considered that 'it would be a gamble with long odds against', to attempt rehabilitating the child with her family. She was worried by the birth mother's lack of commitment in visiting the child and her apparent lack of warmth and affection for her; [1991] 1 FLR 57, per Butler-Sloss LJ, at 61–2.

[110] The same phrase was used in *Re O (a minor) (custody: adoption)* [1992] 1 FLR 77, per Butler-Sloss LJ, at 79. See discussion below.

[111] J. Eekelaar (1994) pp. 80–2.

[112] E.g. *Söderbäck v. Sweden* [1999] 1 FLR 250 and *Eski v. Austria* [2001] 1 FLR 1650.

requirement pertaining to the child's best interests'.[113] Since an adoption order under English law has such a drastic effect on the child's relationship with his or her birth parents, it may not be a proportionate response to the situation if there are less radical methods of strengthening the foster carers' legal position.

Prior to the availability of a SGO, there was only one effective alternative to making an adoption order. This was for the court to grant the foster carers a residence order, with contact to the birth parents, buttressed by an order restraining the birth parents from constantly litigating to get their child returned. This preserved the birth parents' status as parents, whilst admitting that the foster carers were the right people to provide him or her with a home for the time being.[114] Nevertheless, from the foster carers' point of view, a residence order provides them with little security, given that it does not entitle them to make decisions relating to the child without interference from the birth parents. Now, they can instead apply for a SGO.[115] Although such an order does not confer on the foster carers the legal status of parenthood, they do thereby obtain parental responsibility,[116] and more particularly, can exclude the child's birth parents from decision-making regarding his or her upbringing.[117]

At first sight, the SGO offers a useful half-way house to a court aware of the need to abide by Strasbourg jurisprudence and produce a proportionate response which does not completely deprive the birth parents of their rights to family life with their child. Nevertheless, case law suggests that in the courts' view, adoption orders remain superior to SGOs, in so far as they alone provide the child's carers with complete security against the child's birth parents.[118] It seems very likely that practitioners will adopt the same approach, with foster carers being advised that special guardianship is an inferior legal animal. Indeed, Hall's research suggests that in the early days of their availability, SGOs were largely being applied for by kinship carers desirous of the power to exclude the parent from decision-making over the child.[119] Neither practitioners nor the courts apparently see the potential advantage of the SGO as an

[113] *Johansen v. Norway* (1996) 23 EHRR 33 at para. 78.

[114] E.g. *Re B (adoption order)* [2001] EWCA Civ 347, [2001] 2 FLR 26: father's appeal allowed against an adoption order. Per Court of Appeal, a residence order to the child's foster carer (backed by an order under CA 1989, s. 91(14) restraining the father applying himself for a residence order without court leave) would be a more proportionate response to the child's need for a permanent home than an adoption order, given the foster carer's willingness to continue caring for him on such a basis; discussed by A. Bainham (2003) p. 82. See also *Re P (a child) (residence order: restriction order)* [2000] Fam 15.

[115] CA 1989, ss. 14A–G: applicants need court leave to apply for such an order under s. 9(3), unless they can comply with the requirements of s. 14A(5) in which case they can apply as of right.

[116] CA 1989, s. 14C(1)(a). NB see *Re AJ (adoption order or special guardianship order)* [2007] EWCA Civ 55, [2007] 1 FLR 507 at 524: schedule listing the differences between adoption orders and SGOs.

[117] CA 1989, s. 14C(1)(b).   [118] Discussed in more depth in Chapter 16.

[119] A. Hall (2008) pp. 371–2.

order which easily accommodates enforceable contact arrangements between child and birth parents after the child's placement with long-term foster carers.

(3) The blood tie, birth parents and adoption placements

(A) Introduction

The discussion above concentrates on disputes arising when a child has been left with foster carers under a private arrangement, with birth parents later wanting their child returned against the wishes of the foster carers. A very different set of legal principles applies when birth parents who, having deliberately placed their child for adoption, then experience a change of heart and try to retrieve him or her. Today this seldom happens. Indeed, over the years, there has been a dramatic reduction in the proportion of children directly placed for adoption by birth parents,[120] with the vast majority of adoptees having formerly been in the care of LAs.[121] Nevertheless, such placements do still occur and a consideration of two situations allows an examination of the weight the courts place on the blood tie between child and birth parent in the course of their decision-making.

First is the traditional scenario involving the young unmarried mother who, feeling unable to care for her child herself, and wanting to ensure a better future for him or her in adoptive care, places her baby for adoption. Here, Lowe's '"gift" mindset' is apposite – the mother makes a 'gift' of her baby to the prospective adopters whom the adoption agency has carefully selected to become the baby's 'real' parents in her place.[122] But if the mother later changes her mind about the adoption, the baby may by then have formed strong attachments with the prospective adopters and vice versa. A second scenario involves an unmarried father who discovers that his child has been placed for adoption without his knowledge and who opposes the adoption proceedings on the basis that he wants to bring up the child himself.

As noted above, it is far more likely that an adopted child has been in the care of the LA. Then, if the birth parents oppose adoption, the dispute takes on an altogether different dimension, with the opposing parties not being confined to two sets of private litigants but involving the birth parents and the state – the latter acting on behalf of the child to protect him or her from the parents. Again, as discussed below, the weight attached by the courts to the blood tie between child and birth parents is of crucial importance.

(B) The adoption law context

(i) Adoption law reform

It would be unsatisfactory to examine the legal principles governing any of these situations without first placing them in the context of the changing ideas

---

[120] DH (1999) p. 4.   [121] N. Lowe and G. Douglas (2007) pp. 821–2.
[122] N. Lowe (1997) esp. pp. 371 and 382.

underlying adoption law itself.[123] According to conventional wisdom, children do best if they are brought up by their own parents. Nevertheless, adopted children often go to adoptive parents who are emotionally secure, better off and able to maintain an environment superior to that of their birth parents. This probably explains the research literature suggesting that although there are complexities underlying attempts to measure outcomes and depending on their age, many adopted children form very good attachments with their adoptive parents. It also suggests that their adoptive homes can produce considerable benefits for them.[124] But, as case law involving the upbringing of children by parents with very severe learning difficulties demonstrates,[125] this does not indicate that the state should remove children from 'inadequate' parents and place them with meritorious childless couples.[126]

The balance maintained by the law between the interests of child and parents is seen in the legal principles giving the birth parent a veto over the adoption order,[127] whilst also allowing the court to dispense with the parents' consent in certain circumstances. Under the old adoption law, if a child had already formed ties of affection with prospective adopters, the court would normally only consider dispensing with the birth parents' consent on the basis that they were withholding it unreasonably.[128] But the courts found it extremely difficult to decide how reasonable parents would behave in such circumstances and the extent to which they would take account of their child's best interests when deciding whether to agree to the adoption. The dilemmas were evident in Lord Hailsham's famous formula:

> the test is reasonableness and not anything else … It is reasonableness, and reasonableness in the context of the totality of the circumstances. But, although welfare per se is not the test, the fact that a reasonable parent does pay regard to the welfare of his child must enter into the question of reasonableness as a relevant factor.[129]

Indeed, the ability of any parent to behave reasonably when opposing an adoption order was doubtful, particularly when struggling with his or her own personal problems.[130] In truth, the concept of the reasonable parent was a fiction designed to find an appropriate balance between the child's welfare and

---

[123] J. Lewis (2004) discusses the history of adoption law reform.
[124] DH (1999) ch. 2; DH (2000) para. 1.12; D. Quinton (2006) pp. 464–6.
[125] Discussed in Chapter. 15.   [126] H. Schaffer (1998) pp. 60–2.
[127] ACA 2002, ss. 47(2) and 52(6): both parents must consent to the making of an adoption order if they are married, or if the unmarried father has parental responsibility. An unmarried father who lacks parental responsibility is nevertheless normally notified of the adoption proceedings and may be joined as a party; see discussion below.
[128] AA 1976, s. 16(2)(b). The other grounds (the parent could not be found; was incapable of signing the agreement; had abandoned or neglected the child; or had persistently or seriously ill-treated the child) were very seldom used.
[129] *Re W (an infant)* [1971] 2 All ER 49, per Lord Hailsham, at 55.
[130] See *Re S (an infant)* [1973] 3 All ER 88, per Davies LJ, at 91.

the parents' own wishes and concerns.[131] But whilst few maintained that the old formula was ideal, it reminded the courts of the need to maintain that balance as far as possible. The ACA 2002 introduced a controversially different approach by aligning all adoption decision-making with the paramountcy (or welfare) principle set out in the CA 1989, section 1. Before, the courts had been required to ask whether:

> the advantages of adoption for A appear sufficiently strong to justify overriding the views and interests of the objecting parent or parents.[132]

Now, unless the parent cannot be found or is incapable of consenting to the adoption,[133] the courts must ask a simple question when deciding whether a parent's consent should be dispensed with. Does the child's welfare require the adoption order to be made, taking account of the various factors set out in the adoption welfare checklist?[134]

The introduction of a welfare formula as a basis for dispensing with parental consent had attracted considerable opposition when adoption law reform was first mooted, long before new adoption legislation was finally introduced in 2002.[135] Critics urged that such a formula would not necessarily accommodate the complexities of adoption. Although an adoption order often ostensibly benefits a child, it deprives the child and his or her birth parents of a unique relationship in a family, which can never be retrieved.[136] The 1992 *Review of Adoption Law* had indicated its strong view that considerations of the child's welfare should not be allowed to determine whether an adoption order should be made against the parents' wishes.[137] It argued that any new legislation should achieve a balance between the interests of the child, adopters and birth parents, and suggested that a court should ask whether:

> the advantages to a child of becoming part of a new family and having a new legal status are so significantly greater than the advantages to the child of any alternative option as to justify overriding the wishes of a parent.[138]

Interestingly, had such a formula been introduced, this would have complied well with the requirements of the Strasbourg jurisprudence discussed below.

(ii) The child protection context

These concerns all perhaps carry greater cogency when considered in relation to children placed for adoption by LAs, having been removed from their parents compulsorily. In many adoption proceedings involving abused children who have been in state care, the courts will be in little doubt that their welfare

---

[131] *Re C (a minor) (adoption: parental agreement: contact)* [1993] 2 FLR 260, per Steyn and Hoffmann LJJ, at 272.
[132] *Re F (adoption: freeing order)* [2000] 2 FLR 505, per Thorpe LJ, at [22].
[133] ACA 2002, s. 52(1)(a).   [134] ACA 2002, ss. 52(1)(b) and 1(2) and (4).
[135] J. Lewis (2004) pp. 240 *et seq.*   [136] E. Cooke (1997) p. 263.
[137] Interdepartmental Working Group (1992) para. 7.1.   [138] Ibid. at para. 12.6.

requires them to be adopted. Nevertheless, some abusive parents love their children and refuse to agree to their adoption. A request from the LA to dispense with the parents' consent was, under the old adoption law, normally dealt with on the basis that the parents were withholding their consent unreasonably. As discussed above, the courts found the concept of the reasonable parent difficult to apply in practice; this was particularly the case in relation to parents whose abusive behaviour had led to the child being removed from home. The judiciary were very aware that dispensing with parental consent would not only deprive the parents of their parenthood, but also leave them bearing the stigma of unreasonableness. Sometimes, as in *Re D (grant of care order: refusal of freeing order)*,[139] a court's excessive sympathy with parents' personal difficulties undermined its ability to reach a finding of 'unreasonableness'.[140] Although humane, a refusal to dispense with parental consent to adoption might mean that a seriously abused child's chances of gaining a permanent home with prospective adopters were delayed whilst unrealistic attempts at supporting his or her parents were attempted yet again. As Thorpe LJ slightly caustically stated:

> Of course in an uncertain world almost anything can be said to be possible, but in evaluating the hypothetical reasonable parent test and in applying it, it is not open to a judge to give prominence to theoretical possibility unless the possibility has a quantifiable and realistic content. It is simply irrelevant to the judicial exercise.[141]

Despite the obvious artificiality involved in the test of unreasonableness, many organisations involved in adoption practice opposed the courts being given the power to dispense with parental consent whenever 'the welfare of the child requires the consent to be dispensed with'.[142] This, they argued, would mean that children could be removed from their families and have the legal relationship with their parents irrevocably severed 'simply because an adoption agency and court are satisfied that another family could do a better job'.[143] Critics claimed that this 'could lead to social engineering of the worst kind'.[144]

These fears should be seen in the context of the government's efforts to overhaul the whole adoption system. It had been extremely critical of the extent to which large numbers of children being looked after by LAs were 'drifting in care'.[145] The 'solution' was to ensure that far more children gained permanent

---

[139] [2001] 1 FLR 862.

[140] Ibid.: the trial judge had refused to find parents who abused heroin and alcohol unreasonable in refusing to consent to their child's adoption. If they would only take up offers of help from local substance misuse teams, one of them might be able to care for him in the future.

[141] [2001] 1 FLR 862 at [31]. See also *Re R (care: rehabilitation in context of domestic violence)* [2006] EWCA Civ 1638, [2007] 1 FLR 1830: the Court of Appeal allowed the LA's appeal against the trial judge's refusal to make a care order (but not the adoption placement order). Per Thorpe LJ, at [31]: the trial judge should not instead have pursued a rehabilitative solution which 'was both idealistic and unrealistic'.

[142] ACA 2002, s. 52(1)(b).   [143] British Association of Social Workers (2001) para. 1.

[144] National Organisation for the Counselling of Adoptees and Parents (2001) Summary.

[145] Discussed in more detail in Chapter 16.

adoptive families who would give them safety, stability and lifelong support.[146] By introducing a new, highly regulated adoption service, with adoption targets and by amending the law to introduce a more efficient and rapid legal process, the government hoped that more children could be adopted faster. In particular, the legislation ensures that applications for care orders in relation to abused children are often combined with applications for adoption placement orders.[147] Indeed, as Lewis observes, adoption has thereby become part of the care system.[148] These reforms were, however, accompanied by severe misgivings on the part of adoption practitioners who questioned whether more and quicker adoptions would necessarily benefit large numbers of children entering the care system.[149] Children with an abusive background have extremely complex needs and finding the 'right' adoptive parents for them may not be easy, appropriate or even practicable.[150] Furthermore, the adoption targets, combined with legislation making it easier to dispense with parental consent to adoption, were seen as a threat to disadvantaged and impoverished parents, who with more social work support, might eventually manage to provide a stable home for their children.[151]

Many critics argued that the adoption reforms, particularly combined with a statutory criterion based solely on the child's best interests, would infringe not only the parents' rights to respect for their family life under Article 8 of the ECHR, but also their children's rights to remain in their birth families, if at all possible.[152] These concerns have some cogency. The Strasbourg jurisprudence stresses that welfare agencies who remove children from their parents into care should treat such a measure as a temporary one; they must take all steps which could reasonably be expected of them to re-establish the parent-child relationship as soon as possible.[153] Nevertheless, the Strasbourg case law also acknowledges that a fair balance has to be struck between the child's interests in remaining in public care and those of the parent in being reunited with the child.[154] Measures depriving a birth parent of his or her family life with their child can be taken, but only in exceptional circumstances 'motivated by an overriding requirement pertaining to the child's best interests'.[155] An adoption order may eventually be an appropriate means of giving a child security, rather than leaving him or her in a state of uncertainty in temporary placements with foster carers.[156]

---

[146] PIU Report (2000) para. 4.9.   [147] See Chapter 16.   [148] J. Lewis (2004) p. 239.

[149] S. Harris-Short (2001) pp. 417–20 and 421.   [150] Family Policy Studies Centre (2000) pp. 2–3.

[151] British Agencies for Adoption and Fostering (2001) para. 11.3.

[152] Inter alia: A. Bainham (2003) pp. 82–3; S. Harris-Short (2001) pp. 423–4; S. Choudhry (2003) pp. 123–34; S. Harris-Short (2008) esp. p. 37.

[153] Inter alia: *Johansen v. Norway* (1996) 23 EHRR 33 esp. para. 78; *EP v. Italy* (2001) 31 EHRR 17 esp. para. 62. See also *Olsson v. Sweden* (1988) 11 EHRR 259; *K and T v. Finland* [2001] 2 FLR 707; *S and G v. Italy* [2000] 2 FLR 771; *Haase v. Germany* [2004] 2 FLR 39.

[154] *Johansen v. Norway* (1996) 23 EHRR 33 at para. 78.

[155] Ibid. and *Gnahore v. France* (2002) 34 EHRR 38 at para. 59; discussed by A. Bainham (2003) pp. 81–3.

[156] *Johansen v. Norway* (1996) 23 EHRR 33 at para 80 and *Scott v. United Kingdom* [2000] 1 FLR 958 at 970.

Giving the courts power to dispense with birth parents' consent if the child's welfare so demands, undoubtedly simplifies the law. But it may tempt the courts into forgetting an important legal principle – an adoption order must be a proportionate response to the child's need for permanency, given that it is the most radical form of interference with family life.[157] As discussed below, there remains legitimate anxiety about whether the new welfare test ensures that the right balance is struck between the child's position and that of the birth parents, as required by the Strasbourg jurisprudence.

(C) Vacillating mothers

The response of the courts to applications from one or other of the birth parents to stop the adoption process reflects a variety of judicial views regarding the importance of the blood tie between parent and child. The young mother who agrees to the child being placed for adoption but who later changes her mind, creates a particularly distressing situation for everyone involved. Unlike the father opposing an adoption, she is the one who instigated the adoption process and she may have done so extremely early in the baby's life, at a time when neither she nor the baby had formed any attachments with each other. By the time she agreed to the adoption she should have been sure that this was the appropriate course of action. The law not only insists on her having a period of reflection after the baby's birth before she provides any formal consent,[158] but it also attempts to ensure that she agrees to the adoption unconditionally and with a full understanding of what is involved.[159] But even with support and counselling, a mother may remain uncertain about her decision and her continuing vacillations may be very damaging if the child has meanwhile been placed for adoption and has already formed very strong attachments with the prospective adopters. In such a situation, under the old law, the court would normally consider dispensing with the mother's consent, on the basis that she was withholding it unreasonably.[160] As Ormrod LJ pointed out:

> Although it is easy to understand the difficulties of the mother as a young woman, it is equally easy to be over-indulgent in approaching her problems because, once

---

[157] *Re B (adoption by one natural parent to exclusion of other)* [2001] 1 FLR 589, per Hale LJ, at para. 37. This decision was reversed by the House of Lords, but the principle referred to by Hale LJ remains an important one. See also *Down Lisburn Health and Social Services Trust v. H* [2006] UKHL 36, [2007] 1 FLR 121, per Baroness Hale of Richmond, at [34].

[158] ACA 2002, s. 52(3): a mother cannot consent to her child's adoption within 6 weeks of the child's birth.

[159] ACA 2002, s. 52(5). See *Re A (adoption: agreement: procedure)* [2001] 2 FLR 455: the Court of Appeal stressed the need for the authorities to check prior to the court hearing that a parent fully understands the import of having consented to an adoption order. There a 15-year-old rape victim from Kosovo had signed a consent form to a freeing for adoption order over her baby without appreciating the full import of such an action.

[160] AA 1976, s. 16(2)(b). See discussion above.

she takes the step of initiating adoption proceedings, she starts a chain reaction which can only be stopped with great damage to some people.[161]

Meanwhile, as in *Re A (adoption: mother's objections)*,[162] the mother may support her opposition to the adoption by arguing that her child has 'a right' to be brought up by his or her birth mother, rather than by strangers.[163] Such a claim would find support in case law such as *Re K (a minor) (ward: care and control)*.[164] But if, as in *Re A*, the child was moved from his mother at the age of 3 days and placed with foster carers and then with prospective adopters at 2 months, the birth tie between him and his mother has little real significance – at least for the child. In *Re A* Sumner J dispensed with the mother's consent to the adoption on the basis that any reasonable mother would have recognised the risks of permanently harming her child by uprooting him from prospective adopters with whom he had lived happily from an early age. He recognised the value of the blood tie between mother and child but considered it to be outweighed by the many factors favouring his adoption.[165] It seems unlikely that the courts' new ability to dispense with a mother's consent to her child's adoption, if the child's welfare requires it, greatly affects the outcome of such decisions in future.

(D) Unmarried fathers

Perhaps the greatest swings in judicial opinion relating to the long-term value to the child of the parental blood tie can be seen in the cases involving unmarried fathers – those who endeavour to save their children from adoption by seeking permission to take over their care themselves. Today most unmarried fathers acquire parental responsibility automatically, because they are named on their child's birth certificate;[166] they are then in the same position as the child's mother and can withhold consent to the adoption.[167] Without parental responsibility, an unmarried father has no right to veto his child's adoption proceedings.[168] Nevertheless, an unmarried father who has had some involvement with the mother and his baby from the time of the child's birth has rights under Articles 6 and 8 of the ECHR[169] which normally entitles him to be identified, notified of the adoption proceedings and joined as a party if he desires.[170]

---

[161] *Re W (adoption: parental agreement)* (1981) 3 FLR 75 at 81.

[162] [2000] 1 FLR 665.   [163] Ibid. at 691.

[164] [1990] 3 All ER 795. See also *Re K (a minor) (wardship: adoption)* [1991] 1 FLR 57, discussed above.

[165] [2000] 1 FLR 665 at 694.

[166] CA 1989, s. 4(1)(a), but note only those fathers named on birth certificates after 1 December 2003; see discussed further in Chapter 13.

[167] ACA 2002, s. 47(2).   [168] ACA 2002, s. 52(6).   [169] *Keegan v. Ireland* (1994) 18 EHRR 342.

[170] *Re H; Re G (adoption: consultation of unmarried fathers)* [2001] 1 FLR 646, per Dame Elizabeth Butler-Sloss P, at [37]–[49]. See also *Re F (a child)* [2008] EWCA Civ 439, [2008] 2 FCR 93, per Wall LJ, at [37]: the LA's actions had been 'disgraceful' in deliberately placing a child for adoption knowing that his birth father had applied for a revocation of the adoption placement order and wished to take over his care himself.

Matters may be different, however, in relation to an unidentified father who has had no previous contact with the child. The courts have acknowledged that they have little sanction against a completely uncooperative mother – it would smack 'too much of the Inquisition' to try to force her to identify the father of her child.[171] Furthermore, the current adoption legislation does not place an absolute obligation on the adoption agency or the child's guardian to identify and approach the child's father and/or extended family; it should depend on the child's interests in every case.[172] Such a position is consistent with Strasbourg case law which makes it plain that an unmarried father, who has never had any contact with the child since his or her birth, has no Article 8 rights to infringe.[173] But, in any event, no right under Article 8 is absolute and infringement may be justified under Article 8(2), if deemed to be in the child's best interests.[174] So whether the father and/or the child's wider family should be sought out by the adoption agency or the child's guardian, against the mother's wishes, depends on the child's interests. This case law suggests that, depending on the circumstances, an adoption agency may justifiably respect a mother's desire for secrecy when she places her child for adoption.

In many cases, the father will be well aware of the mother's adoption plans for their child and may decide to oppose them. The remarkable differences in approach to an unmarried father's claim to bring up his child himself can be seen from a brief comparison of two cases involving very similar facts but divided by over 30 years. Thus, in the mid-1960s, Russell LJ approved of an unmarried father and his wife gaining custody of his 17-month-old son whom the father had never met. He explained:

> I myself do attach great weight to the blood tie. If a father (as distinct from a stranger in blood) can bring up his own son as his own son, so much the better for both of them, whether or not by the accident of events the legitimate relationship exists.[175]

Russell LJ clearly considered that the value of the blood tie between father and son more than counter-balanced the medical evidence spelling out the risks of uprooting this child from his home with the prospective adopters who had cared for him for 15 months, from the age of 2 months. The child psychiatrist had indicated that to move the child would 'take an unjustifiable risk with his future'.[176] Nevertheless, the majority of the Court of Appeal[177] was surprisingly

---

[171] *Re L (adoption: contacting natural father)* [2007] EWHC 1771 (Fam), [2008] 1 FLR 1079, per Munby J, at [40].

[172] *Re C (a child) v. XYZ County Council* [2007] EWCA Civ 1206, [2008] 1 FLR 1294, per Arden LJ, at [21]–[24].

[173] *Lebbink v. The Netherlands* [2004] 2 FLR 463, at [36]–[38].

[174] *Re C (a child) v. XYZ County Council* [2007] EWCA Civ 1206, [2008] 1 FLR 1294, per Arden LJ, at [33]–[39].

[175] *Re C (MA) (an infant)* [1966] 1 All ER 838, per Russell LJ, at 863.   [176] Ibid. at 855.

[177] Ibid., per Willmer LJ dissenting, at 856: the benefits to be derived by the child from being brought up by his own father were 'rather shadowy and conjectural'.

confident that the 'instinctual tie' between child and father and the qualities of
the father's wife would protect the child from the dangers of severe psychological damage.

In the years intervening between that decision and *Re O (adoption: withholding agreement)*,[178] the line of decisions commencing with *Re K (a minor)
(ward: care and control)*,[179] and establishing a child's 'right' to be brought up by
his or her birth parents, had become well known. Lord Templeman had made
his rousing assertion in *Re KD (a minor) (ward: termination of access)*[180] that
the 'best person to bring up a child is the natural parent'.[181] Judicial anxieties
had also emerged about 'social engineering',[182] in the event of a birth parent
being compared harshly with 'idealised perfect adopters'.[183] Nevertheless, in
Re O (adoption: withholding agreement)[184] the Court of Appeal adopted an
entirely different approach to that taken by Russell LJ, more than 30 years
before. It considered that, despite the presumption that it is a child's right to be
brought up by his natural family, the trial judge had been fully justified in
refusing the father a residence order. The court considered that he had quite
rightly taken full account of the psychological evidence indicating the severe
risks of uprooting this 18-month-old child, who had never met his birth father,
from his home with prospective adopters where he had been since he was
2 months old. Since the child's bonds of affection with the prospective adopters
could not be broken without adversely affecting his personality and security, his
welfare would not be promoted by his father gaining his care.[185]

It should be noted that *Re O* was complicated by the fact that, although
unmarried, the father had acquired a parental responsibility order, and so could
effectively veto the adoption proceedings, unless the court could dispense with
his consent to the adoption. This meant that the court's logical difficulties when
applying two different criteria in the same case were very obvious. The father's
application for a residence order relating to his child was governed by the
child's best interests, according to the CA 1989, section 1. But, having refused
this application, the court proceeded to consider whether to dispense with his
consent to the adoption. Although under current adoption law the best interests
test governs both applications, in this case, governed as it was by the old law, the
criterion had to shift to the reasonable parent test. Swinton Thomas LJ, having
acknowledged the unreality created by the concept of the hypothetical reasonable father, upheld the trial judge's finding that the father was unreasonable in
withholding his consent to the adoption. The court clearly rejected the notion

---

[178] [1999] 1 FLR 451.   [179] [1990] 3 All ER 795; discussed above.   [180] [1988] AC 806.
[181] Ibid. at 812.   [182] *Re O (a minor) (custody: adoption)* [1992] 1 FLR 77.
[183] Ibid., per Butler-Sloss LJ, at 79.   [184] [1999] 1 FLR 451.
[185] See also inter alia: *Re M (a minor) (custody appeal)* [1990] 1 FLR 291, per Purchas LJ, at 297:
arguments based on the blood tie between a young unmarried father and his baby daughter did
not justify the father obtaining the child's custody, thereby preventing her obtaining a stable
adoptive home. The father felt a deep sense of injustice that the LA had not informed him of the
existence of his child until the hearing of the adoption application.

that the blood tie between the child and his father could make up for the child's loss of attachments with adults who, despite being biological strangers, had become his 'real' parents. The decision is welcome because it acknowledges that it may be too late to repair a parent's sense of injustice at being deprived of the chance to have a relationship with his own 'flesh and blood', without endangering the child's own emotional stability.[186]

(E) Children adopted from care

Arguably the blood tie between them and their parents carries very little significance for seriously abused children.[187] So its existence should not necessarily deter a court from dispensing with a birth parent's consent to the child's adoption. Nevertheless, matters are not always that simple. Some parents, with more social work support, might be able to provide a good home for their children.[188] Moreover, many children, despite having been removed from home because of their parents' abusive behaviour, will retain strong ties of affection for their parents. Their relationships, albeit flawed by the child's abusive experiences, may have a value for child and parent alike. Indeed, these children may be difficult to place if adoptive parents cannot contemplate an open form of adoption involving direct contact. The law therefore has to tread a tightrope between protecting the valuable aspects of the relationships between children in care and their birth families, and ensuring that as many as possible obtain a fresh start in a new family without undue delay. This, of course, is behind the government's aggressive campaign to ensure that more children are adopted from care more rapidly.[189]

The domestic courts must, however, negotiate the tightrope designed by the Strasbourg jurisprudence discussed above. On the one hand, children cannot be expected to wait for new families indefinitely, so LAs must take adequate steps to secure for a child who has been deprived of family life with his birth family,

---

[186] See also *Re M (care order: freeing application)* [2003] EWCA Civ 1874, [2004] 1 FLR 826: father's refusal to consent to his 18-month-old son's adoption (based on his wish for his cousin and husband to care for the child) was unreasonable, given the overwhelming advantage to the child of being adopted by the foster parents who had cared for him since he was 17 days old.

[187] E.g. *Re S; Newcastle City Council v. Z* [2005] EWHC 1490 (Fam), [2007] 1 FLR 861: the 6-year-old boy subject of an adoption freeing application had been in foster care for 2 years and had since then resolutely refused to talk about his birth family, whether in connection with contact or otherwise.

[188] E.g. *Re D (grant of care order: refusal of freeing order)* [2001] 1 FLR 862: the trial judge considered that the child's parents, who abused alcohol and heroin, might, if they availed themselves of local substance abuse services, be able to take over their baby son's care. See also *Re G (a child) (interim care order: residential assessment)* [2005] UKHL 68, [2006] AC 576: care plan involving removal of a baby from her parents and adoption was foiled by the court directing a residential assessment (under CA 1989, s. 38(6)) with the mother's parenting skills improving sufficiently for the baby to be returned home; discussed by B. Hale and J. Fortin (2008) p. 102 .

[189] Discussed further in Chapter 16.

'a life with a new family who can become his new "family for life" to make up for what he has lost'.[190] On the other hand, the court should consider carefully whether an adoption order is a proportionate response to the child's need for permanency, given that an adoption order is the most radical form of interference with family life.[191] Today, few of the children adopted from care are babies;[192] indeed many of these older children have strong links with their birth parents. The factors listed in the adoption welfare checklist[193] implicitly invite the courts to consider the danger to the child of terminating all his links with his birth family through adoption.[194] In particular, they must not only consider the likely effect on the child throughout his life of ceasing to be a member of his original family,[195] but also the child's relationship with relatives and other relevant people.[196]

SB v. County Council[197] demonstrates that the courts may find it extremely difficult to uphold the value to a child of his links with his birth parents and/or siblings, alongside a consideration of whether an adoption is in the child's best interests. There the birth mother opposed adoption placement orders being made over two of her young children, largely because she wanted to retain contact with them. There was also weighty evidence that the contact enjoyed by the two siblings with each other was of great value to them both. Wall LJ, delivering the majority judgment, dealt in detail with the concerns that the new power to dispense with parental consent on the simple criterion of the child's best interests would jeopardise the balance between the rights of parents and children. He asserted that as long as the statutory guidance is followed carefully, the Strasbourg jurisprudence does not prevent a court dispensing with a parent's consent[198] if it is convinced that adoption is what the child's welfare requires.[199] He categorically rejected the mother's claim that the court has to apply an enhanced welfare test,[200] along the lines of that suggested by the 1992 *Review of Adoption Law*.[201] When deciding whether to dispense with a parent's consent, the court must consider the value of adoption in the future – an order can only be justified if the child's welfare 'throughout his life'[202] requires that he

---

[190] Per Hale LJ, in *Re W and B; Re W (care plan)* [2001] EWCA Civ 757, [2001] 2 FLR 582 at [55]. Although this decision was reversed by the House of Lords in *Re S and Re W* [2002] UKHL 10, [2002] AC 291, Hale LJ's views, in this respect, remain relevant.

[191] *Re B (adoption by one natural parent to exclusion of other)* [2001] 1 FLR 589, per Hale LJ, at para 37. This decision was reversed by the House of Lords, but the principle referred to by Hale LJ remains an important one. See also *Down Lisburn Health and Social Services Trust v. H* [2006] UKHL 36, [2007] 1 FLR 121, per Baroness Hale of Richmond, at [34].

[192] DfES (2006) p. 2: the average age at adoption is 4 years and 1 month, having remained relatively stable for the last 5 years.

[193] ACA 2002, s. 1(4).

[194] *Re C (a child) v. XYZ County Council* [2007] EWCA Civ 1206, [2008] 1 FLR 1294: per Arden LJ, at [18].

[195] ACA 2002, s. 1(4)(c).   [196] ACA 2002, s. 1(4)(f).

[197] [2008] EWCA Civ 535, [2008] 2 FCR 185.   [198] I.e. under ACA 2002, s. 52(1)(b).

[199] Per Wall LJ, at [113]–[133].   [200] Ibid. at [127].   [201] See above.

[202] ACA 2002, s. 1(2), which also governs s. 52(1)(b).

or she be adopted.[203] He acknowledged that an adoption order against the parent's wishes will be an unjustifiable infringement of her Article 8 rights under the ECHR unless such a step is proportionate to the legitimate aim of protecting the child.[204]

> In assessing what is proportionate, the court has, of course, always to bear in mind that adoption without parental consent is an extreme – indeed the most extreme – interference with family life. Cogent justification must therefore exist if parental consent is to be dispensed with.[205]

In many cases, as in *SB* itself, matters are complicated by the fact that whilst a child may need a permanent home with new carers, he or she would still greatly benefit from contact with a birth parent and/or with siblings.[206] Indeed, in that case, the children's guardian's was particularly worried by the adoption placement orders jeopardising the two children's ongoing contact with each other if placed with separate adopters. Wall LJ seemed ambivalent about the courts' role relating to post-adoption contact.[207] He acknowledged its value for some children and further that the legislation itself requires the courts to consider the value of the child maintaining links with his or her birth family.[208] He also pointed out that contact between them can be ordered alongside an adoption placement order[209] and alongside the final adoption order.[210] Nevertheless, he also re-emphasised the well-established judicial view that whilst a contact order can be attached to an adoption order,[211] 'in normal circumstances it is desirable that there should be a complete break' depending on the facts of each case.[212] Furthermore, in his view, it would be exceptional to make a contact order against the wishes of new adoptive parents.[213] Meanwhile, he stressed that the mother would almost certainly gain leave to apply for a revocation of the placement order if the adopters or foster carers with whom the child was placed failed to facilitate contact between them.[214] Notably, he did not directly acknowledge that ultimately the courts have little control over a child's adoptive parents if they renege on an agreement to fulfil post-adoption arrangements.[215]

In cases like *SB v. County Council*, it may be a daunting task for the courts to protect the blood tie between a child and his or her siblings whilst ensuring that the child gains a secure home with alternative carers. Harris-Short cogently maintains that although the question of post-adoption contact has not been dealt with explicitly by Strasbourg jurisprudence, it is arguable that both birth parents and child have a right under Article 8 of the ECHR to retain their familial links through some kind of contact, if all agree that this is beneficial to

---

203 Per Wall LJ, at [128].   204 Ibid. at [119]–[123].   205 Ibid. at [124].
206 S. Harris-Short (2008) pp. 38–43.   207 [2008] EWCA Civ 535 at [141]–[154].
208 ACA 2002, ss. 1(4)(f) and 46(6).   209 ACA 2002, ss. 26–7.
210 ACA 2002, s. 46(6).   211 *Re C (a minor) (adoption order: conditions)* [1989] AC 1.
212 [2008] EWCA Civ 535, per Wall LJ, at [143].   213 Ibid.   214 Ibid. at [150].
215 As had occurred in *SB* itself, when two younger siblings had been adopted.

them.[216] Certainly, it is arguable that 'the ability of birth parents to retain some contact with their child may also help to make compulsory adoption more Convention compliant'.[217] As Harris-Short observes, if the courts were to favour post-adoption contact orders more commonly, the support services currently offered adoptive parents would have to improve greatly.[218]

In *SB* itself, the LA sought an adoption placement order, but envisaged that if suitable adopters were unavailable, long-term fostering would be an inferior alternative. Given the fact that the courts have no sanction if adoptive parents fail to maintain post-adoption contact arrangements, it is surprising that an SGO, combined with a contact order, is not contemplated instead, in cases where such contact is considered very important to the child. Admittedly the courts are worried by the fact that an SGO does not bring the security of adoption because such an order fails to prevent birth parents taking foster carers to court challenging various decisions relating to the child's upbringing.[219] But since an SGO avoids the drastic impact of an adoption order on the child's relationship with his or her birth parents, the invocation of CA 1989, section 91(14) alongside such an order, to stop birth parents applying for section 8 orders without court leave,[220] would surely be a worthwhile solution.

(4) Conclusion

In cases outside the child protection arena, there appear to be three features common to the judicial treatment of disputes between parents and informal foster carers over a child's future. First, the courts tend to invest the blood tie between child and birth parents with considerable significance long after their relationship has been disrupted. Second, the courts appear to assume that the same set of principles should apply whether the dispute involves the child awaiting a fostering or adoption placement, who has not yet formed bonds of attachment with foster carers, or the child happily settled in a foster home. Whilst it may be more appropriate for the courts to presume that the child awaiting placement should be brought up by his or her birth parents, unless there are strong and positive reasons for this not occurring, this is not necessarily the case for the child already placed in a foster home. Third, the courts have exploited the language of children's rights to support what are often, in truth, claims to adults' rights to resume caring for their children. Ironically, when adopting this approach, the courts appear more likely to neglect making a proper assessment of the child's psychological needs or rights, than in cases where this 'rights language' is not used.

---

[216] S. Harris-Short (2008) pp. 38–41.   [217] B. Hale and J. Fortin (2008) p. 102.
[218] S. Harris-Short (2008) pp. 43–51.   [219] Discussed in Chapter 16.
[220] *Re S (adoption order or special guardianship order)* [2007] EWCA Civ 54, [2007] 1 FLR 819 at [66].

The discretionary nature of judicial decision-making in this area of child law masks a lack of clarity over the issues at stake and a failure to establish a well-defined evidential approach. A well-founded children's rights framework for decision-making might lead to a more beneficial outcome for the children who are the subject of these disputes. Paying attention to children's own rights to family life in a de facto family with foster carers would concentrate attention on their potential safety and care and a more reasoned approach to their real needs, rather than those of their birth parents. There would be no reason to discount special factors, such as a disrupted early childhood and a child's new-found happiness and security. When attempting to reach a decision, it is perfectly appropriate for the courts to place some weight on the common assumption that 'normal' family life involves children being brought up by their birth parents. Nevertheless, fulfilling the child's own rights to family life would also require careful consideration of the strength of the ties of attachment formed by children with their foster carers. The court should weigh the risks caused by breaking those ties against the benefits to be gained by being brought up by their birth parents, particularly if this maintains their links with their cultural and racial heritage.

Even greater complexities are involved in disputes over whether a child should be adopted by foster carers or prospective adopters. Here the issue is not merely whether the child should remain with the carers to whom he or she may have become firmly attached, despite their lack of kinship ties. It also involves the courts deciding whether an adoption order is the appropriate means of providing the child with security in his or her new home, given that it finally and irrevocably terminates the legal relationship between birth parents and child, irrespective of their blood ties. The law cannot provide detailed guidance on professional practice. Nevertheless, the combination of government policy and Strasbourg jurisprudence has produced, in this context, a worryingly incoherent set of aims and principles.

BIBLIOGRAPHY

NB many of these publications can be obtained on the relevant organisation's website.

Bainham, A. (2003) 'Contact as a Right and Obligation' in Bainham, A., Lindley, B., Richards, A. and Trinder, L. (eds.) *Children and Their Families: Contact, Rights and Welfare*, Hart Publishing.

Bostock, L. (2004) 'By Private Arrangement? Safeguarding the Welfare of Private Foster Children' 18 *Children and Society* 66.

British Agencies for Adoption and Fostering (2001) *Memorandum of Evidence Submitted to the House of Commons Special Select Committee on the Adoption and Children Bill*, BAAF.

British Association of Social Workers (2001) *Memorandum of Evidence Submitted to the House of Commons Special Select Committee on the Adoption and Children Bill*, BAAF.

Choudhry, S. (2003) 'The Adoption and Children Act 2002, the Welfare Principle and the Human Rights Act 1998 – a Missed Opportunity?' 15 *Child and Family Law Quarterly* 119.

Cooke, E. (1997) 'Dispensing with Parental Consent to Adoption – a Choice of Welfare Tests' 9 *Child and Family Law Quarterly* 259.

Department for Education and Skills (DfES) (2005) *Replacement Children Act 1989 Guidance on Private Fostering*, DfES.

Department for Education and Skills (DfES) (2006) SFR 44/2006 *Children Looked After in England (Including Adopters and Care Leavers), 2005–06*, DfES.

Department of Health (DH) (1999) *Adoption Now: Messages from Research*, John Wiley and Sons Ltd.

Department of Health (DH) (2000) Cm 5017, White Paper *Adoption: a New Approach*, HMSO.

Eekelaar, J. (1973) 'What are Parental Rights?' 89 *Law Quarterly Review* 210.

    (1988) 'Access Rights and Children's Welfare' 51 *Modern Law Review* 629.

    (1991) 'The Wardship Jurisdiction, Children's Welfare and Parents' Rights' 107 *Law Quarterly Review* 386.

    (1994) 'Parenthood, Social Engineering and Rights' in Morgan, D. and Douglas, G. (eds.) *Constituting Families: A Study in Governance*, Steiner.

Family Policy Studies Centre (2000) *Families and Adoption*, Family Briefing Paper 14, Family Policy Studies Centre.

Fortin, J. (1999) 'Re D (Care: Natural Parent Presumption)' 11 *Child and Family Law Quarterly* 435.

Goldstein, J., Freud, A. and Solnit, A. (1973) *Beyond the Best Interests of the Child*, Free Press.

Hale, B. and Fortin, J. (2008) 'Legal Issues in the Care and Treatment of Children with Mental Health Problems' in Rutter, M, Bishop, D., Pine, D., Scott, S., Stevenson, J., Taylor, E. and Thapar, A. (eds.) *Rutter's Child and Adolescent Psychiatry*, Blackwell Publishing.

Hall, A. (2008) 'Special Guardianship and Permanency Planning: Unforeseen Consequences and Missed Opportunities' 20 *Child and Family Law Quarterly* 359.

Harris-Short, S. (2001) 'The Adoption and Children Bill – a Fast Track to Failure?' 13 *Child and Family Law Quarterly* 405.

    (2002) '*Re B (Adoption: Natural Parent)* Putting the Child at the Heart of Adoption?' 14 *Child and Family Law Quarterly* 325.

    (2008) 'Making and Breaking Family Life: Adoption, the State and Human Rights' *Journal of Law and Society* 28.

Hayes, M. and Williams, C. (1999) *Family Law: Principles, Policy and Practice*, Butterworths.

Holman, B. (2002) *The Unknown Fostering: a Study of Private Fostering*, Russell House Publishing.

Interdepartmental Working Group (1992) *Review of Adoption Law*, A Consultative Document, HMSO.

Laming, H (2003) Cm 5730, *The Victoria Climbié Inquiry: Report of an Inquiry by Lord Laming*, The Stationery Office.

Lewis, J. (2004) 'Adoption: The Nature of Policy Shifts in England and Wales, 1972–2002' 18 *International Journal of Law, Policy and the Family* 235.

Lowe, N. (1997) 'The Changing Face of Adoption – the Gift/Donation Model Versus the Contract/Services Model' 9 *Child and Family Law Quarterly* 371.

Lowe, N. and Douglas, G. (2007) *Bromley's Family Law*, Oxford University Press.

National Organisation for the Counselling of Adoptees and Parents, (2001) *Memorandum of Evidence submitted to the House of Commons Special Select Committee on the Adoption and Children Bill*, NORCAP.

Olusanya, B. and Hodes, D. (2000) 'West African Children in Private Foster Care in City and Hackney' 26 *Child Care Health and Development* 337.

Ofsted (2008) *Safeguarding Children, the Third Joint Chief Inspectors' Report on Arrangements to Safeguard Children*, Ofsted.

Performance and Innovation Unit Report (2000) *The Prime Minister's Review of Adoption*, Cabinet Office.

Philpot, T. (2001) *A Very Private Practice: an Investigation into Private Fostering*, British Agencies for Adoption and Fostering.

Quinton, D. (2006) 'Adoption: Research, Policy and Practice' 18 *Child and Family Law Quarterly* 459.

Save the Children (1997) *Private Fostering: Development of Policy and Practice in Three English Local Authorities*, Save the Children.

Schaffer, H. (1998) *Making Decisions about Children*, Blackwell.

Social Services Inspectorate (SSI) (2002) *By Private Arrangement: Inspection of Arrangements for Supervising Children in Private Foster Care*, DH Publications.

Utting, W. (1997) *People Like Us: The Report of the Review of the Safeguards for Children Living away from Home*, DH/Welsh Office, HMSO.

Warman, A. (2006) 'An International View: Planning for Children in Long-Term Care in Other Child Welfare Systems' in Jordan, L. and Lindley, B. (eds.) *Special Guardianship: What Does it Offer Children Who Cannot Live With Their Parents?*, Family Rights Group.

Weyland, I. (1997) 'The Blood Tie: Raised to the Status of a Presumption' 19 *Journal of Social Welfare and Family Law* 173.

Chapter 15

An abused child's right to state protection

(1) Introduction

The state assumes that, because parents brought their children into the world, they will care for them and protect them from harm; indeed, it trusts them to do so. The vast majority of parents fulfil these state expectations conscientiously. They not only fulfil their children's right to protection, but bring them up in an atmosphere of love and security. Unfortunately, the children's liberationists' view of childhood as an oppressed state and parents as the chief oppressors, with the freedom to abuse their children in private, is not entirely ill-conceived. Some parents do exploit their privacy and their children's vulnerability to abuse.[1] The Committee on the Rights of the Child has indicated its deep concern over the number of child deaths each week in the UK due to violence and neglect and, more generally, over the growing levels of child neglect.[2]

The dilemma is that the degree of state surveillance and control necessary to prevent all ill-treatment would involve an unacceptable interference with the upbringing of many thousands of children, the majority of whom are perfectly well cared for by loving parents. This presents the law with the need to find a satisfactory compromise between an unwanted level of authoritarian state interference and a passive assumption that it is impossible to prevent a tiny minority of children suffering in the privacy of their homes. Indeed, it must ensure that the majority of parents continue to fulfil their parenting role on behalf of the state, without undermining their willingness or ability to do so by undue intervention.

This chapter considers first the background to this problem and proceeds to discuss the lack of clarity over what children need protection *from*. The extent to which the structural reorganisation of children's services can improve protective intervention is briefly assessed. Whether or not the law maintains

---

[1] According to NSPCC statistics (July 2007), on average between one and two children are killed by their parents or carers every week; this figure has remained reasonably constant for the last 30 years. See also H. Laming (2009) para. 1.9.

[2] Committee on the Rights of the Child (2002) para. 39; see also Committee on the Rights of the Child (2008) para. 50.

an acceptable balance between children's rights to protection from abuse and adults' right to parental autonomy is the focus of the remainder of this chapter.[3]

(2) Uncertainty over the state's role

It is a cardinal feature of western democratic legal systems that parents and families, rather than the state, have the primary right and the primary responsibility to bring up their children: to meet their claims for nurture, care and upbringing and to decide for themselves how this will be done.[4]

Nevertheless, the lengthening list of reports of inquiries into child deaths makes overwhelmingly depressing reading.[5] The Beckford Report commenting on society's resistance to acknowledging the existence of child abuse stated:

Some parents abuse, even kill their children. Throughout history, they always have, and they always will. What is new about child abuse has been the increased and still increasing public awareness of this socially unpalatable, endemic phenomenon. Realisation that the deliberate abuse of children not only occurs but is also by no means a rare occurrence is profoundly shocking both to the individual and to the body politic.[6]

Whilst the early reports into child deaths had focused on physical abuse, or 'non-accidental injuries', as they are euphemistically referred to by practitioners, towards the end of the 1980s, the Cleveland crisis suggested that child sexual abuse might be far more common than most people believe.[7] Information of this kind makes it hard for anyone to deny that children have a basic right to protection from ill-treatment and that the state must ensure that they receive it, even if it means removing them from their parents' care. Governments are unlikely to cavil at the terms of international instruments reminding them of their duties in this respect.[8]

Thus far, there is little scope for disagreement. English criminal law certainly acknowledges children's rights to protection from ill-treatment by setting a line below which parents may not descend, without risking criminal charges. The criminal process is, however, something of a blunt instrument, in so far as it can

---

[3] NB re terminology, following the structural reorganisation of local agencies working with children under the umbrella of children's trusts, the terms used to describe the former 'departments of social services' vary across the country. Early government guidance (HM Government (2006)) uses the cumbersome term 'LA children's social care' to describe the agency involved in traditional social work with children. For ease of reference, this chapter employs the term 'children's services authority' or simply local authority (LA) to describe the agency responsible for this work.

[4] B. Hale and J. Fortin (2008), p. 99.

[5] Department of Health and Social Security (1982); Department of Health (DH) (1991); H. Laming (2003); M. Bichard (2004).

[6] London Borough of Brent (1985) p. 9.   [7] Butler-Sloss LJ (1988).

[8] See esp. Arts. 19 and 37(a) of the Convention on the Rights of the Child (CRC) and Art. 3 of the European Convention for the Protection of Human Rights and Fundamental Freedoms (ECHR).

only punish adults for past abuse which should never have happened. Indeed, criminal proceedings may not improve a child victim's life and may even exacerbate the effects of the abuse if the child is called as a witness at the offender's trial.[9] The principles of civil law attempt to ensure that children are protected from abuse, if possible before it starts, or at least before it becomes very serious. But the fundamental difficulty is that the type of ill-treatment meted out to abused children occurs behind the closed doors of perfectly normal looking houses.

The law over the last century has reflected an underlying uncertainty experienced by policy-makers over finding an appropriate compromise between obliging the state to find and protect every child who is being abused and maintaining family privacy. Fox Harding's seminal analysis remains helpful.[10] According to her, it is possible to perceive four broad theoretical perspectives underlying the development of childcare policies and all four maintain distinctive positions on the state's duty to protect children from harm. There is the 'laissez-faire' and patriarchal approach, typified by case law in the late nineteenth century, which broadly took the view that power in the family should not be disturbed except in very extreme circumstances and the role of the state should be a minimal one. Writers such as Goldstein, Freud and Solnit[11] later adopted a similar position, maintaining that parents fulfil the nurturing role better than anyone else and need family privacy and autonomy in order to bring their children up without undue interference from the state.

The second and third theoretical perspectives both assume state intervention is desirable, but with a differing emphasis placed on the degree of authoritarianism accompanying it. The second perspective considers it justifiable to attribute an essentially paternalistic role to the state, by pointing to the innate vulnerability and dependence of children. The state is thereby obliged to protect them, even if it involves an authoritarian stance which undermines the biological ties between children and their parents. The third perspective defends the birth family and parents' rights. It legitimises state intervention to protect children, but also sees the dangers of targeting poorer and socially deprived parents who are thereby seen as the victims of heavy-handed state authoritarianism.[12] State intervention should therefore support families and assist them in the difficult task of bringing up children in inadequate home circumstances.

These first three perspectives appear to assume that because the state intervenes on behalf of the child there is no special need to emphasise the child's individual position. Thus, when finding a balance between over-authoritarianism and laissez-faire, the contest is between parents and state. It is assumed that once an appropriate balance is found, the state will automatically adopt the protective

---

[9] Discussed in Chapter 17.   [10] L. Fox Harding (1997) ch. 1.

[11] J. Goldstein, A. Freud and A. Solnit (1973) and (1980).

[12] For an attack couched in these terms on US state interference with parental autonomy, see M. Guggenheim (2005) ch. 6.

role for children. The fourth and last approach, is the rights approach maintained by the children's liberationists. This differs fundamentally from the others, in so far as it alone concentrates on the child's own position, seeing the contest as one between children and parents. They consider that children should be treated as independent persons in their own right with a right to adult freedoms, in order to release them from parental domination. The negative aspects of family life are used to substantiate their claim that children should be freed from adult oppression. These are exemplified by parents' ability to exploit their position of power within the family and abuse their children. This last perspective, which focuses almost exclusively on the liberationists' claims regarding children's autonomy, seems to assume that children, once emancipated, will be able to achieve their own physical protection. This emphasis during the 1980s led to the establishment of agencies which set out to 'empower' abused children to help themselves. Childline and the Children's Legal Centre were established and encouraged children to seek help on their own behalf, rather than waiting for the state to assist with their protection.

Of the four approaches, the last is perhaps the weakest. As Fox Harding points out, it is certainly unrealistic to assume that such an approach is sufficient in itself. Very young children who, by reason of their size are particularly vulnerable to abuse, are quite unable either to cope with adult freedoms or to protect themselves physically against adult abuse.[13] Older children might be expected to make choices in abusive situations and often do so, but these may be strongly influenced by their past experiences. As in so many other fields of law involving the older child, the difficulty is to find an appropriate balance between the exercise of paternalism to fulfil the child's right to protection and respecting his or her capacity for choice. Arguing that abused children's choices should be respected by the state[14] overlooks the distorted relationships that abused children often have with their abusers. In this context, the need to recognise a child's interest in choice has less obvious relevance than his or her need for protection, bearing in mind that abused children's choices may be strongly influenced by their psychological dependence on parent abusers.[15]

These very different approaches are all discernible in the violent swings in childcare policy during the last 50 years and they are all reflected, to a lesser or greater extent, by provisions of the Children Act (CA) 1989 itself. Indeed, the Act adopts an uneasy compromise between emphasising parents' rights to autonomy and privacy and fulfilling children's rights to protection. It clearly reflects the 'moral panics' arising from the child abuse inquiries of the 1970s and 1980s which led to demands for the government to 'do something about child abuse'. There is a clear commitment to ensuring that local authorities (LAs) have sufficient powers to intervene to protect children when essential. By providing

---

[13] See L. Fox Harding (1997) p. 136.   [14] E.g. F. Olsen (1992) pp. 210–13.
[15] Discussed in Chapter 8 and below.

relatively broad grounds for intervention and by strengthening the emergency powers to seek and find a child whose safety is believed to be at risk, LAs gained relatively straightforward methods for protecting children against abusive and uncooperative parents. The 'significant harm' criterion for intervention is intended to flag up the fact that children can only be removed from their parents as a measure of last resort, in order to protect children at severe risk or in potentially dangerous situations.[16] The legislation also flirts briefly with the concept of the state respecting the decision-making rights of children.[17]

Whilst the CA 1989 was intent on giving state agencies wide powers to protect children reasonably effectively, one of its other important objectives was to respond to the public fears generated by the Cleveland crisis, during which very large numbers of children were taken into state care on a suspicion of being victims of child sexual abuse.[18] This crisis had led, in the late 1980s, to a widely held perception that laws and policies then existed allowing social workers to adopt an over-authoritarian approach to families and a marked lack of respect for parents' own rights. Consequently, the 1989 Act also ensures that parents' own family rights are promoted, with clear boundaries between the family and the state. It stresses that although the state has an important part to play, it is to be residual and supportive – the primary responsibility for bringing up children remains with their parents. In the event of disagreement between parents and LAs over whether the parents are providing appropriate care for the child, state intervention against the parents' wishes is possible, but only with court authority,[19] and then only by establishing clear statutory grounds for intervention.[20] Parents retain their parental responsibilities, even in the event of their child being removed from them on the authority of a care order.[21]

The CA 1989 makes valiant efforts to maintain an appropriate balance between the child's rights and those of his or her parents, but there is now an accumulating body of government-commissioned research[22] which makes one doubt whether an appropriate equilibrium between children's interests and those of their parents can ever be found. Overall, it suggests that matters have not changed greatly since the early 1980s when Dingwall *et al.* described the child protection system as one reflecting 'a liberal compromise'. Now, as then,

---

[16] CA 1989, s. 31.

[17] E.g. CA 1989, ss. 17(4A), 22(4)–(5), 38(6), 43(8), 44(7), 46(3) and Sch. 3, paras. 4(4) and 5(5). Discussed below.

[18] Butler-Sloss LJ (1988).

[19] See *R (G) v. Nottingham City Council* [2008] EWHC 152 (Admin), [2008] FLR 1660, per Munby J, at [15]: the LA should not have directed hospital staff to separate a mother from her newly born child against her wishes and without judicial authority.

[20] LAs may not accommodate children against their parents' wishes (CA 1989, s. 20(7)) nor avoid applying for a care order (under s. 31) by using the wardship jurisdiction instead, to obtain judicial authority for removing children from their parents (s. 100).

[21] CA 1989, s. 33(3)(b).

[22] See, inter alia, the research summarised in DH (1995), DH (2001), D. Quinton (2004), J. Beecham and I. Sinclair (2007).

'The result is a system which is fully effective neither in preventing mistreatment nor in respecting family privacy but lurches unevenly between these two poles'.[23] This is probably inevitable since no system will ever achieve perfection.

(3) The rights dimension

The legal principles established by the CA 1989 for protecting children have stood the test of time. They survived the major reorganisation of children's services prompted by Lord Laming's report on the death of Victoria Climbié[24] and by the CA 2004. Nevertheless, the Human Rights Act (HRA) 1998 added a further layer of legal principles which might potentially distort the balance between children's right to protection from abuse and parents' right to family privacy. One of the aims of the CA 1989 was to reassure the public that the traditional privacy and autonomy of parents should not be undermined by over-zealous state intervention. This was very much in tune with the intentions of Article 8 of the ECHR, which reflects the post-war objectives of the Convention's draftsmen, namely to protect private individuals, including parents, from authoritarian regimes.[25] The drafting of the 1989 Act had responded to early decisions reached by the European Commission and Court in favour of parents claiming that their rights to family privacy under Article 8 of the ECHR had been infringed by state intervention to protect their children.[26] But when considering parental complaints over state intervention to protect their children, the European Court of Human Rights (ECtHR) has repeatedly emphasised the need to maintain an appropriate balance between infringing the parents' rights and protecting those of their child.[27] When considering whether state interference with parents' family life is 'necessary',[28] the fact that a child could be placed in a more beneficial environment for his or her upbringing will not on its own be deemed sufficient to justify compulsory removal from parental care.[29] The reasons for the intervention must be sufficient and the intervention itself proportionate to the aim of protecting the child in question. Nevertheless, when carrying out this balancing act, the evidence is couched in terms of the adults' rights, with a need to justify the infringement, not in terms of the children's rights, but in terms of their best interests.[30]

---

[23] R. Dingwall, J. Eekelaar and T. Murray (1983) p. 219.

[24] H. Laming (2003) para. 1.30: the legislative framework provided by the 1989 Act for protecting children is 'basically sound'. See also para. 17.79 and H. Laming (2009) para. 8.1.

[25] J. Fortin (1999) pp. 357–9.

[26] E.g. *W (and R, O, B and H) v. United Kingdom* (1987) 10 EHRR 29. The success of these parents' applications led to the abolition of the power of LAs to acquire parental responsibility over children by administrative resolution. They also provoked the CA 1989, s. 34 giving parents a right to apply for contact with their children whilst in state care.

[27] E.g., inter alia: *Johansen v. Norway* (1996) 23 EHRR 33; *K and T v. Finland* [2001] 2 FLR 707; *Z v. United Kingdom* [2001] 2 FLR 612.

[28] I.e. under Art. 8(2) of the ECHR.

[29] *Kutzner v. Germany* (2002) 35 EHRR 25, at para. 69.   [30] See Chapter 2.

Due to the wide margin of appreciation allowed states in this context, the ECtHR only rarely criticises the reasons for a child being taken into state care, taking the view that the national authorities had the advantage of seeing the parties concerned.[31] Instead it often concerns itself with scrutinising the extent to which the decision-making process provided the parent applicants with sufficient protection of their interests.[32] But this may result in the ECtHR considering the state's actions from a particularly adult-orientated viewpoint, that of the parents, again without articulating the child's own rights.[33] Once the child has been removed into state care, the ECtHR is far readier to criticise the state's approach to the child's subsequent management. Thus it has repeatedly stressed that a child's removal into state care must be seen as a temporary measure only, expecting states to make real efforts to ensure the child's rapid reintegration in his family.[34] This expectation reflects the assumption under-lying the phrasing of Article 8 itself that the family is a temporarily disrupted safe haven for the child, to which he or she should be returned as soon as possible.[35] Whilst such an approach certainly strengthens family autonomy and also prevents children being taken away from their parents unnecessarily, it does not so obviously promote an abused child's *own* rights to a happy upbringing free from parental abuse.[36]

Meanwhile the domestic courts are well aware of the danger of allowing parents to exploit their own rights to respect for their family life, at the expense of those of their children to protection from abuse. Auld LJ emphasised that:

> the advent of Article 8 to our domestic law, bringing with it a discrete right to children and parents of respect for their family life, does not undermine or weaken as a matter of public policy the primacy of the need to protect children from abuse, or the risk of abuse, from, among others, their parents.[37]

He stressed that Article 8(2) clearly precludes an Article 8(1) claim where to allow it would conflict with the need to protect children from parental abuse.[38] Furthermore, as discussed below, social workers who pay too much heed to parents' rights to respect for their family life under Article 8, risk infringing children's own rights to be protected from serious abuse under Articles 2, 3

---

[31] *Kutzner v. Germany* (2002) 35 EHRR 25, at para. 66. The examples of state intervention most commonly criticised by the ECtHR are those involving emergency intervention; see discussed below.

[32] Inter alia: *W v. United Kingdom* (1987) 10 EHRR 29, at para. 64; *Haase v. Germany* [2004] 2 FLR 39, at para. 97.

[33] Discussed further in Chapter 2.

[34] Inter alia: *Olsson v. Sweden* (1988) 11 EHRR 259; *Johansen v. Norway* (1996) 23 EHRR 33; *Scott v. United Kingdom* [2000] 1 FLR 958; *K and T v. Finland* [2001] 2 FLR 707; *S and G v. Italy* [2000] 2 FLR 771; *EP v. Italy* (2001) 31 EHRR 17; *Haase v. Germany* [2004] 2 FLR 39.

[35] But see *EP v. Italy* (2001) 31 EHRR 17, discussed in Chapter 2.   [36] J. Fortin (1999) pp. 357–9.

[37] *Lawrence v. Pembrokeshire County Council* [2007] EWCA Civ 446, [2007] 2 FLR 705, at [41].

[38] Ibid. at [42].

and 8.[39] Thus the human rights case law promotes the difficult message that whilst parents' rights to family life must be respected, children should not be left dangerously unprotected.

(4) The child protection process – what criteria should be used?

The reorganisation of children's services discussed below was accompanied by puzzling changes in terminology.[40] Through a plethora of government guidance documents we learn that the terms 'child protection' and 'child abuse' have been replaced by 'safeguarding children' and 'maltreatment'. Despite the government's explanation that the concept of 'safeguarding and promoting children's welfare' is a wider concept than child protection and includes protecting children from 'maltreatment',[41] inevitably these changes have caused confusion.[42] Terminology apart, most would agree that the real issue remains the same – 'Child abuse is an evil to which no child should be exposed'.[43] But doubts remain over how bad an abusive situation must become before the state should intervene to protect children.

The lawyer might answer the question 'which children need the attentions of a child protection service?'[44] by referring to the formula adopted by the CA 1989 – it is those children who are suffering or at risk of suffering significant harm.[45] Thus the legal framework provides the social worker with a metaphorical bottom line below which parental behaviour should not sink without child protection intervention being contemplated. But the bottom line is more apparent than real since there is no specialised definition of 'significant'.[46] Few would countenance the state intervening simply because a child's parents are not particularly adept at parenting. Indeed, Hedley J emphasised:

---

[39] *Osman v. United Kingdom* [1999] 1 FLR 193, at para. 116 : a person's rights under Art. 2 are infringed if the state agency fails to do all that could be reasonably expected of them to avoid a real and immediate risk to life of which they had or ought to have had knowledge; *Z v. United Kingdom* [2001] 2 FLR 612, at paras. 73–4: state agencies must take reasonable steps to prevent children being subjected to ill-treatment amounting to torture or inhuman or degrading treatment under Art. 3 in situations where they had or ought to have had knowledge of that ill-treatment; see also *TP and KM v. United Kingdom* [2001] 2 FLR 549; *X and Y v. The Netherlands* (1985) 8 EHRR 235: Art. 8 protects the child's moral and physical integrity and thereby entitles the child to adequate child protection measures. See also the arguments using Art. 8 presented by the Official Solicitor in *S (by the Official Solicitor) v. Rochdale MBC and Anor* [2008] EWHC 3283 (Fam), unreported, at [15]–[30].

[40] E. Munro and M. Calder (2005) p. 439.   [41] HM Government (2006) paras. 1.18–1.21.

[42] HMICA (2005) para. 2.16: 'In the absence of clarity about the meaning of the term safeguarding children' Cafcass had focused its training efforts on child protection issues rather than on safeguarding children.

[43] P. Mullen *et al.* (1996) p. 20.

[44] A similar question was posed by C. Wattam (1997) pp. 110–11.

[45] See the 'significant harm' formula used in the CA 1989, ss. 31(2) and 47.

[46] *Humberside County Council v. B* [1993] 1 FLR 257, per Booth J, at 263: the term 'significant' in s. 31 should be interpreted according to the library definition, as meaning 'considerable or noteworthy or important'.

Basically it is the tradition of the UK, recognised in law, that children are best brought up within natural families ... It follows inexorably from that, that society must be willing to tolerate very diverse standards of parenting, including the eccentric, the barely adequate and the inconsistent. It follows too that children will inevitably have both very different experiences of parenting and very unequal consequences flowing from it. It means that some children will experience disadvantage and harm, while others flourish in atmospheres of loving security and emotional stability. These are the consequences of our fallible humanity and it is not the provenance of the state to spare children all the consequences of defective parenting. In any event, it simply could not be done.[47]

In this case, as Hedley J's comment makes clear, the parenting was not ideal. Indeed, the children, who were being brought up by parents with very severe learning difficulties, were, he thought being harmed, but he did not consider the harm to be significant.[48] So in Hedley J's view, they needed state support[49] but not removal from home. Similarly, dealing with a different aspect of the same case, Ward LJ stressed that it would be impermissible social engineering to remove children from their parents into care because the parents are not sufficiently intelligent.[50]

Such an approach is laudable and has been echoed by the ECtHR itself.[51] On the other hand, children cannot be left in a flagrantly abusive situation and the fact that we have no official agreement over what constitutes child abuse in our time and our culture[52] makes the social worker's job doubly hard. Regional statistics indicate that social workers are far more likely to intervene in some areas than in others, despite the child's circumstances being similar, thereby suggesting that thresholds for bringing children into care vary considerably.[53] These regional variations may indicate uncertainty over the point at which to intervene or an anxiety over the availability of resources for large numbers of children in care. Nevertheless, when deciding whether abusive behaviour is serious enough to merit protective intervention, practitioners tend to focus on the outcomes of abuse rather than on the severity of the incident in itself. This is predictable given the need to learn from the cases involving children who die or who are very seriously injured or harmed.[54] Social workers are undoubtedly influenced by the growing body of research evidence clarifying the long-term effects well into adulthood of a variety of types of ill-treatment, such as emotional abuse and neglect and child sexual abuse.[55]

---

[47] *Re L (care: threshold criteria)* [2007] 1 FLR 2050, at [50].   [48] Ibid. at [52].

[49] They were 'children in need' under CA 1989, s. 17(1), and thus qualified for family support. See discussed below.

[50] [2006] EWCA Civ 1282, [2007] 1 FLR 1068, at [49].

[51] *Kutzner v. Germany* (2002) 35 EHRR 25, at para. 69.   [52] C. Wattam (1997) p. 110.

[53] M. Narey (2007) chs. 3–4, Ofsted (2008) para. 304 and H. Laming (2009) para. 3.11.

[54] W. Rose and J. Barnes (2008) and M. Brandon *et al.* (2008).

[55] Inter alia: M. Lynch and J. Roberts (1982); D. Cicchetti and V. Carlson (1989); D. Wolfe (1987); P. Mullen *et al.* (1996); D. Jones and P. Ramchandani (1999); D. Glaser (2000); D. Glaser (2002). See also the government commissioned research projects summarised in DH (1995), DH (2001), D. Quinton (2004), and J. Beecham and I. Sinclair (2007).

Research also shows the damaging impact on children of living in households where domestic violence is commonplace,[56] and with parents who suffer from mental illness or who abuse drugs or alcohol.[57] Overall, there is general agreement that:

> The sustained maltreatment of children – physically, emotionally, sexually or through neglect – can have major long-term effects on all aspects of a child's health, development and well-being. **The immediate and longer-term impact can include anxiety, depression, substance misuse, eating disorders and self-destructive behaviours**. Sustained maltreatment is likely to have a deep impact on the child's self-image and self-esteem, and on his or her future life.[58]

The current guidance, *Working Together*,[59] goes to some lengths to define the commonly used terms 'physical abuse', 'emotional abuse', 'sexual abuse' and 'neglect'.[60] It also endeavours to introduce greater clarity over when abusive behaviour amounts to significant harm by emphasising that although there 'are no absolute criteria to rely on', practitioners should concentrate on the outcomes for *this* child of the parents' current behaviour. It warns that all abuse must be seen in the context of this family and its wider environment.[61] Although single traumatic events can amount to significant harm, more often it is a compilation of significant events which damage the child's development. For the children whose health and development are neglected, 'it is the corrosiveness of long-term emotional, physical or sexual abuse that causes impairment to the extent of constituting significant harm'.[62] It also stresses that intervention should not be contemplated without a clear assessment of the child's developmental needs and the parent's ability to respond to them.[63]

This guidance is helpful, but, as the case law referred to above makes clear, it is the less obviously abusive behaviour that causes disagreement. Indeed, even with the assistance of legal definitions,[64] lawyers, in common with social

---

[56] M. Hester *et al.* (2007) ch. 3 summarises the body of international research. See also W. Rose and J. Barnes (2008) ch. 3, research summary; H. Cleaver *et al.* (2007).

[57] H. Cleaver *et al.* (2007).

[58] HM Government (2006) para. 9.3, emboldened as original. See also ibid., ch. 9, summarising the research on outcomes of abuse.

[59] HM Government (2006).   [60] Ibid. at paras. 1.29–1.33.

[61] Ibid. at paras. 1.25–1.26.   [62] Ibid. at para. 1.25 and para. 9.4.

[63] Ibid. at para. 5.4. Ibid. at para. 5.37: 'initial assessments' are brief assessments carried out to determine whether the child is in need, sometimes followed by a more detailed 'core assessment' using 'The Assessment Framework' (see DH, DEE and HO (2000)). Both forms of assessment are inputted electronically, using the computerised Integrated Children's System (ICS), discussed further below. NB Referrals to children's social care made by non-social work professionals, e.g. health visitors, should be carried out using the Common Assessment Framework (CAF) (see DfES (2006a)). CAF has also been electronically enabled (eCAF) thereby providing a standardised electronic assessment tool for all practitioners working with children.

[64] See CA 1989, s. 31(9), which provides the following definitions which clarify the term 'significant harm': '"harm" means ill-treatment or the impairment of health or development including, for example, impairment suffered from seeing or hearing the ill-treatment of another; "development" means physical, intellectual, emotional, social or behavioural development; "health" means physical or mental health; and "ill-treatment" includes sexual abuse and forms of ill-treatment which are not physical.'

workers, are often very ambivalent over what amounts to 'normal' and 'abnormal' parental behaviour. This was reflected in the dramatically different reactions of three sets of judiciary to information from a father that a mother and her new partner walked around nude at home in front of her two children, aged 9 and 6, and may even have bathed with the children.[65] Whilst one of the judges who had dealt with the case clearly considered this information reasonably innocuous, another not only found it alarming but considered that it raised child protection issues warranting investigation by the local children's services authority. Butler-Sloss LJ considered the latter reaction to be extreme but pointed out:

> A balance has to be struck between the behaviour within families which is seen by them as natural and with which that family is comfortable and the sincerely held views of others who are shocked by it. Nudity is an obvious example … Communal family bathing is another example. This is often entirely innocent. In other families abuse may lie behind it.[66]

Given such differing judicial responses, it is not surprising that social workers display similar uncertainty when confronted with concerns about a child's future well-being.

(5) Structural reorganisation

(A) Agency integration

Lord Laming considered that the suffering and death of Victoria Climbié was not only 'a gross failure of the system and was inexcusable' but that 'the agencies with responsibility for Victoria gave a low priority to the task of protecting children'.[67] None of the agencies involved in her case escaped censure. Lord Laming also considered that the effective support of children and families could only be provided through a number of agencies working well together on a multidisciplinary basis.[68] His report was not the first to criticise the absence of good inter-agency collaboration in child protection work but it was probably the one to prompt the greatest reorganisation of children's services in the last hundred years.

As Parton point outs, when responding to Lord Laming's report the government aimed to go far beyond simply providing a procedural response to address child protection issues.[69] Under the *Every Child Matters* reform programme[70] and the CA 2004,[71] all LAs have established children's trusts, within which the

---

[65] *Re W (residence order)* [1999] 1 FLR 869.   [66] [1999] 1 FLR 869 at 873.
[67] H. Laming (2003) para. 1.18.   [68] Ibid. at para. 1.30.
[69] N. Parton (2008) pp. 177–81. See also see C. Henricson and A. Bainham (2005) pp. 49–56.
[70] HM Treasury (2003) and DfES (2004).
[71] CA 2004, s. 10(1): each children's services authority must make arrangements to promote cooperation between themselves and their 'relevant partners' (inter alia: health, police, probation, youth offending teams, Connexions) to fulfil the five Every Child Matters outcomes

agencies providing children with specialised services are to be found, often in multi-agency teams.[72] With all children's services integrated into one agency, as in many areas, the functions of child protection and family support functions can also be combined. Joint working is assisted by the fact that professionals working with families now use a common assessment tool, with one assessment being carried out, thereby avoiding families undergoing multiple assessments for differing purposes and also ensuring that professionals work to similar goals.[73] Most children's trusts provide children and families with a full range of services, including children's centres, extended Surestart schemes, home visiting, leisure facilities and extended schools.

Even before the trial of those responsible for Baby P's death in November 2008,[74] doubts were being expressed over the effectiveness of the structural reorganisation of children's services. The Audit Commission had damningly concluded that there was:

> little evidence that children's trusts, as required by the government, have improved outcomes for children and young people or delivered better value for money, over and above locally agreed cooperation.[75]

The Commission also argued that the relatively informal standing and aims of children's trusts had produced confusion.[76] The Baby P tragedy produced further widespread questions over the extent to which Lord Laming's reforms had really improved child safeguarding arrangements. The government hopes that children's trusts will be strengthened by legislation giving them statutory status as Children's Trust Boards (CTBs).[77] Their new legal obligations will include producing the Children and Young People's Plan (CYPP) which sets out a strategy on the provision of children's services in the local area.[78] They will also monitor the work of the Local Safeguarding Children Board whose task is to organise and co-ordinate local safeguarding services established to protect children from abusive practices.[79]

At the very least, the integration of children's services should prevent 'the common picture of services protecting their boundaries and their expertise,

---

listed in s. 10(2); s. 10(5): all relevant partners must cooperate with the authority over the making of such arrangements. See also s. 11(2)(a): all relevant partners must make arrangements for ensuring that their 'functions are discharged having regard to the need to safeguard and promote the welfare of children'.

[72] DCSF (2008).   [73] I.e. the Common Assessment Framework (CAF); see fn 63 above.

[74] Baby P was a 17-month-old child who died in North London suffering over 50 injuries. Given the fact that he had been put on the child protection register and had had 60 contacts with various child professionals over 8 months, the child protection services of the London Borough of Haringey were widely criticised for safeguarding failures.

[75] Audit Commission (2008) p. 4.   [76] Ibid. at ch. 2.

[77] Apprenticeships, Skills, Children and Learning Bill 2009, Part 9. See also H. Laming (2009) para. 4.3.

[78] Children and Young People's Plan (England) Regulations 2005 (SI 2005/2149) and Children and Young People's Plan (England) (Amendment) Regulations 2007 (SI 2007/57).

[79] Established by each children's services authority under CA 2004, ss. 13–16. See HM Government (2006) ch. 3.

both because of issues around professional identity and in order to conserve resources or deal with funding problems'[80] and 'with no service having a very high opinion of each other'.[81] In the past, particularly in the context of providing services for children with special educational needs, children's needs have not infrequently been sacrificed to inter-agency turf wars.[82] Despite the clear intention of CA 1989, section 27[83] that children's services should be able to call on other public agencies, the latter have not always responded favourably to requests for extra assistance, given their own need to meet competing priorities from limited state resources. They have been assisted by the House of Lords' view of the limited force of section 27.[84] This not only undermines the ability of children's services to force another agency to assist with the provision of services, but also prevents any child or parent claiming that section 27 gives rise to a duty that they themselves can enforce against the agency in question.[85] The result has been that in some situations, the concept of inter-agency working and cooperation has completely failed to materialise.[86] It is questionable, however, whether the CA 2004 can improve matters in this respect. Under the current law, not unlike section 27 of the CA 1989, section 10(1) of the 2004 Act merely requires each children's services authority to 'make arrangements to promote co-operation' between the authority and its relevant partners. So again, like section 27, it cannot give rise to any specific obligations within agencies to cooperate with each other.[87]

Operational problems of this kind could be avoided, if as had been hoped, children's trusts would plan and commission children's services with pooled budgets and resources.[88] Previous attempts to encourage more inter-agency cooperation with pooled budgets[89] had, however, achieved little.[90] Today, whilst some children's trusts have established multi-agency teams, there are considerable regional variations,[91] and few appear to have proceeded past the

[80] D. Quinton (2004) p. 194.   [81] Ibid. at p. 200.   [82] Discussed further in Chapter 12.

[83] CA 1989, s. 27: social services departments (now termed children's services authorities) can request the help of other authorities, e.g. the local housing authority, with the exercise of any of their functions.

[84] R v. Northavon District Council, ex p Smith [1994] 2 AC 402: the House of Lords stressed that s. 27 requires public agencies, e.g. housing departments, to cooperate with social services only where 'this is compatible with their duties' and does not unduly prejudice the discharge of any of their functions. See also R (on the application of D) and ors v. London Borough of Haringey and conjoined cases [2005] EWHC 2235 (Admin), unreported, per Ouseley J, at [95]–[102].

[85] Ibid., per Ouseley J, at [97].

[86] E.g. Re T (judicial review: LA decisions concerning child in need) [2003] EWHC 2515 (Admin), [2004] 1 FLR 601, per Wall J, at paras 124–40: failure of health, education and social care to cooperate over funding a residential placement. See also R (on the application of D) and ors v. London Borough of Haringey and conjoined cases [2005] EWHC 2235 (Admin), unreported: dispute between social services and health over the funding of an extra 10 hours per week respite care for a single mother caring for a 3-year-old fitted with a tracheostomy.

[87] J. Masson (2006a) p. 241; discussed below.   [88] CA 2004, s. 10(5)–(7).

[89] Health Act 1999, s. 31 provided for partnership agreements between the various service providers.

[90] See also discussed in Chapter 12.   [91] Audit Commission (2008) ch. 3.

planning stage to implement joint commissioning of services.[92] Joint working with health still seems to be particularly problematic, with very few joint budgets involving primary care trusts (PCTs).[93] It seems naive to assume that, without new and specific legislative obligations, health trusts focusing on financial restrictions of their own[94] will be keen to fulfil requests for expensive assistance, despite the needs of children's trusts.[95] As Masson observes, when discussing Lord Laming's recommendations:

> Local agencies cannot be expected to give priority to safeguarding children when central government sets them quite different priorities and leaves them without the resources to extend their activity even though they would wish to do so.[96]

Bercow found few signs of services adopting a joint commissioning framework, shared goals or integrated service delivery.[97] But even when all practitioners are fully committed to identifying common goals, inter-professional tensions can be caused by professionals prioritising very different family needs.[98] It seems clear that the 'biggest challenge to effective joint working is that the different organisations have conflicting priorities'.[99]

(B) Information sharing

Most controversially, the government pressed ahead with Lord Laming's idea of a national database for children, ContactPoint (formerly entitled the Information Sharing Index or ISI) designed to prevent children slipping through the net or disappearing without any of the services knowing where they have gone.[100] On the face of it, such a suggestion seems sensible; indeed it is not the first time that an inquiry of this nature has pointed out the risks of crucial information held by one agency being unknown to another. This online database is intended to be a central index enabling practitioners to find out quickly if a child is obtaining support from other agencies. Thus, each children's services authority is required to establish and operate their own section,[101] providing basic identifying information on every child under 18 resident in their area,[102] together with details of all service provision relating to him or her and the professionals involved in its provision.[103]

---

[92] Ibid. at ch. 4, esp. at para. 95. See also Ofsted (2008) para. 21.   [93] See Chapter 12.

[94] A. Goveas and D. Singleton (2006) p. 12

[95] DCSF (2008a) paras. 3.12–3.16: stresses the need for PCTs to work in partnership with children's trusts. See also Local Government and Public Involvement in Health Act 2007, s. 116: requires PCTs and LAs delivering social care to cooperate over producing 'joint strategic needs assessments'.

[96] J. Masson (2006a) p. 242.   [97] J. Bercow (2008) para. 4.3; see discussed further in Chapter 12.

[98] J. Warin (2007) p. 91.

[99] Audit Commission (2008) para. 55. See also, H. Laming (2009) para. 7.6.

[100] H. Laming (2003) paras. 1.47 and 17.117.

[101] CA 2004, s. 12 and The Children Act Information Database (England) Regulations 2007 (SI 2007/2182), reg. 3(1).

[102] SI 2007/2182, Sch. 1; inter alia: name, address, gender, date of birth, etc.

[103] Ibid. inter alia: contact details for schools, GPs and other services; in the event of a CAF assessment having been carried out, the name and contact details of the person undertaking it.

The regulations governing the operation of ContactPoint reflect the government's efforts to address the wide number of concerns voiced over its establishment. Nevertheless, many of the criticisms remain unaddressed,[104] not least that the child's own right to privacy under Article 8 of the ECHR may be gravely infringed, without adequate justification in every case.[105] Whilst 'sensitive' information[106] can, in general terms, only be included on the database with the consent of the child or young person,[107] neither he nor his family has any control over what is deemed to be sensitive and therefore what must not be included. Furthermore, consent may not always be real,[108] for example if it is sought from a child at school, or it is given in the fear that services will be withdrawn if it is not forthcoming.[109] There are also concerns about unintentional breaches of privacy which could occur, for example, by the database naming a psychotherapist who specialises in supporting victims of child sexual abuse, as having had recent contact with a named child.[110] Whilst the regulations accommodate the fact that certain information should be withheld from ContactPoint's general users,[111] mistakes will inevitably be made. Widespread concerns about security have been compounded by the well-publicised 'losses' of government computer discs containing large amounts of personal information.[112]

Admittedly all users must have security identity and security clearance.[113] Nevertheless, potentially a huge range of people can access the information, with young people's right to confidentiality thereby being infringed by a range of adults and with a risk of the information falling into the wrong hands. A child's current address might become known to a violent ex-partner. Although LAs can decide for themselves who, from a long list of potential users,[114] has access to the database,[115] since virtually every type of practitioner who works with children must disclose information for inclusion in the directory, it is difficult to restrict access to only some of them.[116] Perhaps of even greater concern is the fact that a child and family could be seriously damaged by inaccurate information being recorded and information not being adequately updated.[117] Imposing a duty to correct inaccuracies or gaps in material is unlikely to repair the harm.[118]

---

[104] Inter alia: ICO (2006); R. Anderson et al. (2006); N. Parton (2008) pp. 181–5.

[105] T. Dowty (2008) pp. 397–8.

[106] SI 2007/2182, reg. 2(1): i.e. relating to sexual or mental health, or substance abuse.

[107] Ibid., reg. 11(3)(a). But see reg. 11(3)(b): such consent is unnecessary if the person providing the information has reasonable cause to believe that the child or young person is suffering or likely to suffer significant harm.

[108] R. Anderson et al. (2006) pp. 87–98.   [109] Ibid. at p. 95.

[110] Ibid. at p. 96.   [111] SI 2007/2182, reg. 6.

[112] E.g. in November 2007, two computer discs were lost with the personal details of 7.5 million families in receipt of child benefit.

[113] SI 2007/2182, reg. 10: including enhanced criminal record certification.

[114] SI 2007/2182, Sch. 3.   [115] Ibid., reg. 9(2).   [116] Ibid., Sch. 4 and CA 2004, s. 12(7).

[117] ICO (2006) p. 8. See also O. Jones (2004) p. 1296, who refers to audits disclosing worryingly inaccurate information kept on some databases, with some not even agreeing over whether people are alive or dead.

[118] SI 2007/2182, reg. 5(3).

ContactPoint will only hold basic identification data about all children. For children in need and receiving services, for those requiring protective intervention and for those already in LA care, there is a more comprehensive electronic information system, the Integrated Children's System (ICS). These electronic registers operated by every LA, allow all practitioners within each children's trust to 'access and share key information about children in need or in care, and to manage caseloads more effectively'.[119] The ICS contains a record of all children who are considered to be at continuing risk of significant harm and for whom there is a child protection plan.[120] It is intended that agencies and professionals who have concerns about a particular child, can check rapidly on the LA's system whether he or she is already the subject of practical intervention.[121] Again, there are concerns that this system allows information to fall into the wrong hands. Young people themselves have expressed a degree of ambivalence over their private information being available to other people without their consent.[122] Dowty points to the irony of placing an uncritical faith in technology 'marketed as fulfilling some kind of child protection function, when in reality it is capable of increasing the threats to children's safety and privacy'.[123]

(C) Practice issues

Parton suggests that the accumulation and exchange of information about children is only part of a move to increase surveillance over children by an increasingly interventionist state.[124] Perhaps more worryingly, as Munro and Calder observe, 'nothing in this agenda addresses directly the problems of poor practice in cases of child protection', or the professional mistakes identified by Lord Laming.[125] Anderson *et al.* note:

> The practitioners in contact with Victoria knew of each other's involvement and shared considerable amounts of information. The crucial errors arose from individuals either not paying attention to the information, or giving it a benign interpretation so that the risk to Victoria from abuse was not seen.[126]

It appears that poor practice was probably responsible for the inability of the London Borough of Haringey to prevent the death of Baby P in 2007.[127] But, as has so often been pointed out in the past, poor practice is often associated

---

[119] DfES (2006b) paras. 2.12–2.13.
[120] The ICS has thereby replaced the old documentary child protection registers maintained by every LA .
[121] HM Government (2006) paras. 5.141–5.143.
[122] Office of the Children's Commissioner (2007) p. 11.   [123] T. Dowty (2008) p. 398.
[124] N. Parton (2008) p. 185.   [125] E. Munro and M. Calder (2005) p. 445.
[126] R. Anderson *et al.* (2006) p. 17.
[127] Haringey Local Safeguarding Children Board (2008) esp. para. 3.1.10 and Section 4.

with staffing difficulties which cannot necessarily be overcome without more recruitment, combined with better pay.[128] Serious lapses in safeguarding occur when social workers carry huge case loads, not properly supervised, or cases are simply unallocated.[129] According to the Chief Inspectors, social work vacancies are falling and 'workforce strategies are starting to have a positive impact on recruitment and retention rates'. But they also note that there are still frequent changes of staff often arising from staff turnover,[130] with early intervention services being sparse in some rural areas.[131] Others see a more depressing picture, with children's social workers struggling with increased case loads and the deployment of staff insufficiently qualified to take on child protection work.[132] Nevertheless, the government considered that the *Every Child Matters* reform programme could be largely self-financing, through 'simpler and more flexible use of resources';[133] a dubious assumption.[134] Indeed, as Beecham and Sinclair observed, when considering whether the reorganisation of children's services was likely to improve child protection practice, 'the facts remain that at present a very wide range of needs are not met; that meeting them will take resources'.[135]

Poor practice comes in differing forms. Lord Laming found that nobody had followed relatively straightforward procedures on how to respond to concerns of a child being deliberately harmed.[136] This criticism was swiftly followed by the publication of clear advice to all agencies mapping out the steps that practitioners should take, depending on their profession.[137] Nevertheless, in his follow up report, Lord Laming noted that some agencies were still not ensuring that all staff know how to recognise the signs of abuse or neglect or how to act on them.[138] Another common criticism spanning the last decade or so has been the fact that social workers have allowed crisis-driven child protection work to dominate their practice, at the expense of preventative family support work. Government commissioned research has consistently argued that the balance between the provision of section 17 services and the handling of section 47 enquiries should be adjusted.[139] This issue is discussed below.

---

[128] Unison (2009).

[129] M. Brandon *et al.* (2008) pp. 93–4 and pp. 99–100. See also *S (by the Official Solicitor) v. Rochdale MBC and Anor* [2008] EWHC 3283(Fam), unreported, at [22]: the Official Solicitor's argument (unproved because the case was compromised) on behalf of S (now aged 18) that the alleged catalogue of social work failures were partly attributable to the work being carried out by an inexperienced and unqualified social worker.

[130] Ofsted (2008) para. 131.   [131] Ibid. at para. 307.

[132] Unison (2009) p. 4; H. Laming (2009) chs. 3 and 5.   [133] DfES (2004) paras. 3.20–3.24.

[134] E. Munro and M. Calder (2005) p. 444; J. Beecham and I. Sinclair (2007) p. 57.

[135] J. Beecham and I. Sinclair (2007) p. 59.   [136] H. Laming (2003) para. 1.19.

[137] DH (2003); republished (2006).   [138] H. Laming (2009) paras. 3.7–8.

[139] DH (1995) pp. 54–5 and DH (2001) pp. 42–6. See also M. Brandon *et al.* (2008) pp. 16–22.

(6) The initial referral – child protection or family support?

(A) Family support for children in need

Despite all the exhortations of the government in the guidance accompanying the CA 1989,[140] one of the main objectives of Part III of the CA 1989 has consistently remained inadequately complied with. Section 17 of the 1989 Act places a general duty on every LA 'to safeguard and promote the welfare of children within its area who are in need[141] and, so far as is consistent with that duty, to promote their upbringing by their own families'. If the initial referral indicates that the child is 'in need', the LA should then carry out careful assessment work identifying those needs,[142] analysing their extent and producing a detailed care plan setting out how the services will be delivered.[143] Some LAs apparently avoid carrying out 'children in need assessments' for fear of their resource implications.[144] A desire to avoid activating any leaving care obligations may certainly explain a LA's failure to asses the needs of an older teenager.[145] Whilst action against the LA may be brought on behalf of any child in the event of the assessment guidance not being followed adequately, such action would require legal assistance and he or she may already have suffered from a lack of adequate support in the interim.[146]

The legislation clearly intends LAs to provide parents caring for children in need with considerable state support if they desire it.[147] Support services can only be provided for the family on a voluntary basis 'in partnership'[148] with the parents. A common form of support is the provision of accommodation for a child,[149] with the parents' prior consent.[150] But a LA cannot claim that it is

---

[140] E.g. DH (1991).

[141] CA 1989, s. 17(10): 'a child shall be taken to be in need if – (a) he is unlikely to achieve or maintain, or to have the opportunity of achieving or maintaining, a reasonable standard of health or development without the provision for him of services by a local authority under this Part; (b) his health or development is likely to be significantly impaired, or further impaired without the provision for him of such services; or (c) he is disabled.'

[142] A 'core assessment'; see fn 63 above.   [143] DfES (2006a) ch. 4.

[144] Ofsted (2008) para. 303; H. Laming (2009) para. 3.11.   [145] See Chapter 4 and Chapter 16.

[146] E.g. R (LH and MH) v. London Borough of Lambeth [2006] EWHC 1190 (Admin), [2006] 2 FLR 1275 and R (S) v. Sutton London Borough Council [2007] EWHC 1196 (Admin), [2007] 2 FLR 849.

[147] I.e. under CA 1989, Part III and Sch. 2 – a wide range of family support services can be provided for families containing children in need, including, inter alia: day care (s. 18); accommodation if the child's parents are prevented from providing it (s. 20); occupational, social, cultural or recreational activities; home help; holiday provision; day centre facilities etc. See also CA 1989, Sch. 2, para. 7: work should be done to avoid the need to remove the child into care through public law proceedings.

[148] B. Hale (2000) p. 464: although the CA 1989 does not specifically express the concept of partnership between state and parents, it is an underlying principle of the Act.

[149] I.e. under CA 1989, s. 20 – a 'section 20 agreement'.

[150] CA 1989, s. 20(7): accommodation cannot be provided against the wishes of anyone with parental responsibility. E.g. R v. Tameside Metropolitan Borough Council, ex p J [2000] 1 FLR 942. See also s. 20(8): anyone with parental responsibility can remove any child under 16 (s. 20 (11)) at any time.

lawfully accommodating a child unless a parent actively consents to its doing so, rather than merely helplessly acquiescing in the LA's plans.[151]

(B) The section 47 enquiry

The focus of section 47 is very different. Although, unlike some other countries, there is no mandatory duty to report cases of suspected child abuse and neglect to children's services,[152] the law obliges LAs who 'have reasonable cause to suspect' that a child in their area 'is suffering, or is likely to suffer, significant harm' to 'make, or cause to be made, such enquiries as they consider necessary to enable them to decide whether they should take any action to safeguard or promote the child's welfare'.[153] Legally, the threshold for intervention through investigation is relatively low.[154] If a 'section 47 enquiry', which should also involve good assessment work, throws up real concerns about the child's safety, a child protection conference[155] will be convened at which it will be decided if the child is at continuing risk of significant harm.[156] If so, the child will be recorded as having been abused or neglected under one of the categories of abuse[157] and the child protection plan's format established.[158] Social workers have, in the past, often concentrated on dangerous incidents of physical abuse, failing to deal adequately with cases involving long-term chronic parental neglect and inadequate parenting.[159] The current guidance emphasises that, whatever the category of abuse, the child protection plan, which should take account of the views of the child and parents,[160] must always clarify what specific action is to be taken and by whom.[161]

Deciding what action to take based on the evidence uncovered by the investigation, confronts child protection practitioners with the dilemmas discussed above. On the one hand children must be protected from abuse by their

---

[151] *R (G) v. Nottingham City Council and Nottingham University Hospital* [2008] EWHC 400 (Admin), [2008] FLR 1668, per Munby J, at [54]–[55].

[152] B. Hale and J. Fortin (2008) p. 97.   [153] CA 1989, s. 47(1).

[154] *Re S (sexual abuse allegations: LA response)* [2001] EWHC Admin 334, [2001] 2 FLR 776, per Scott Baker J, at [36].

[155] HM Government (2006) para. 5.80: involving the child (where appropriate), family members and those professionals most involved in the family.

[156] Ibid. at paras. 5.80–5.127.

[157] Ibid. at para. 5.143. I.e. physical, emotional, sexual abuse or neglect.

[158] Ibid. at paras. 141–2. NB the child protection register (a documentary index of children deemed to be at continuing risk of significant harm and therefore in need of protective intervention) is being phased out, with the child's protection plan being entered electronically as part of his or her entry on the Integrated Children's System (ICS) (discussed above).

[159] E.g. in *Z v. United Kingdom* [2001] 2 FLR 612, despite the LA receiving numerous reports from other agencies that five children were being subjected to appalling abuse and neglect over a period of 5 years, it failed to intervene to protect them. See also D. Quinton (2004) pp. 154–6, M. Brandon *et al.* (2008) pp. 73–7, H. Laming (2009) para. 3.12.

[160] HM Government (2006) para. 5.118.

[161] Ibid. at paras. 5.116–5.127. The plan may record the intention to remove the child from his or her parents on a care order or to obtain a supervision order. Discussed in Chapter 16.

own parents, but on the other hand, parents must be protected from unnecessary interference with their family life. The legislative framework gives the LA absolute discretion over whether to act or not; it imposes no duty to take any action, despite evidence that a child is suffering from significant harm and will continue to do so unless removed from home.[162] Nevertheless, the demands of the HRA 1998 must also be addressed. The social worker who stands back and fails to prevent a child from suffering from significant harm which amounts to ill-treatment and neglect so serious that it results in the child's death or amounts to 'torture, or inhuman or degrading treatment', is not only ignoring his protective powers under the CA 1989, but also risks infringing the child's rights under Articles 2, 3 and 8 of the ECHR.[163] But the law also ensures that child protection practitioners can decide whether to intervene or not without their judgment being clouded by knowing that if their views about the abuse proved unfounded, they could be sued in negligence by distressed parents. Thus, even if protective action is taken based on a carelessly formed diagnosis of abuse, by doctors or social workers, the parents cannot sue the practitioners involved.[164]

(C) Section 17 and section 47 – getting the balance right

As noted above, following implementation of the CA 1989, research indicated that social services departments were consistently prioritising their child protection work, at the expense of providing long-term family support to families with children in need. The intention of the legislation had been for social workers to intervene early and, wherever possible, to work in partnership with the family on a voluntary basis, thereby avoiding the need for more aggressive intervention. Nevertheless, what often happened was that once cases were labelled 'child protection' cases, the need to investigate incidents of abuse overcame notions of prevention and family support. Such a situation produced a vicious circle. Because other agencies considered social services' supportive work to be inadequate, they would attempt to establish that the family posed substantial risks to the child, thereby increasing the chance of accessing services for the family.[165] But then the response was for social workers to focus almost exclusively on an assessment of risk of harm, without considering the wider needs of the child within the family.[166] Furthermore, with large

---

[162] E.g. *Nottinghamshire County Council v. P* [1994] Fam 18. But note CA 1989, s. 47(6): if, when carrying out a s. 47 enquiry, the LA is refused access to the child or is denied information about his or her whereabouts, the LA *must* apply for a protective order, unless it is satisfied that the child's welfare is satisfactorily safeguarded without such action.

[163] See fn 39 above.

[164] *D v. East Berkshire Community Health NHS Trust and ors* [2005] 2 AC 373; *Lawrence v. Pembrokeshire County Council* [2007] EWCA Civ 446, [2007] 2 FLR 705; *B v. Reading Borough Council and anor* [2007] EWCA Civ 1313, [2008] 1 FLR 797. But an action in negligence can probably be brought on behalf of a child in such circumstances – see discussed in Chapter 16.

[165] DH (2002) para. 6.15.   [166] Ibid. at para. 6.16.

numbers of section 47 referrals, staff shortages and the deployment of inexperienced and poorly supervised members of staff,[167] social services were often reluctant to undertake section 47 inquiries at all, with 'the downgrading of cases to the status of section 17, and afterwards closure, [was] becoming an attractive option to childcare teams'.[168] When considering the interrelationship of sections 17 and 47, Lord Laming stressed that it was impossible to 'separate the protection of children from wider support to families' and that the best protection for a child was often achieved through the timely intervention of the family support services. In his view referrals should not be labelled 'child protection' without good reason.[169]

The current *Working Together* does its best to emphasise that measures to safeguard children should not be seen in isolation from the wider ranger of support and services available to meet the needs of children and their families,[170] and stresses that in many cases, the two processes should march hand in hand.[171] Its detailed guidance on how to respond to a child welfare referral, stresses that supportive work may be necessary for a child in need, whether or not child protection concerns emerge.[172] Nevertheless, it seems that efforts are constantly being made to persuade child protection practitioners to concentrate less on responding to incidents of abuse and more on family support and prevention. As Parton points out, in the late 1990s, social services departments had found it very difficult to 'refocus' children's services, as was then required of them.[173] Many years later, the Green and White Papers introducing plans for improving the lives of children in care reiterated the need for social workers to do more preventative family support work with those on the edge of care thereby avoiding removing children from home.[174]

If research and guidance has been promoting this 'refocusing' message for the last decade, and it still has not occurred, one wonders why it should 'work' this time.[175] Indeed, it may be unrealistic to expect practitioners, whatever their professional training, not to focus on children in danger from abusive incidents when they are all so aware of the tragedies involving children who die from parental abuse.[176] The media outcry responding to the Baby P tragedy in November 2008 reinforced social workers' fears over not intervening soon enough. Since the risks involved in allowing children to remain with truly dangerous parents are only too obvious, it is difficult to see how a reactive child protection service can be transformed completely into a preventative family support service.[177] One wonders whether Harlow and Shardlow are

---

[167] Ibid. at para. 6.8.   [168] H. Laming (2003) para. 17.102.   [169] H. Laming (2003) para. 1.30.

[170] HM Government (2006) para. 1.12.   [171] HM Government (2006) esp. para. 5.98.

[172] Ibid. at ch. 5, esp. para. 5.46. See also DfES (2006b) ch. 2 and DfES (2007b) ch. 2.

[173] N. Parton (2008) pp. 169–70. See also J. Beecham and I. Sinclair (2007) pp. 55–7.

[174] DfES (2006b) ch. 2 and DfES (2007b) ch. 2. P. Welbourne (2008) pp. 339–44.

[175] J. Beecham and I. Sinclair (2007) pp. 55–7.

[176] See the cases reviewed by M. Brandon *et al.* (2008) and W. Rose and J. Barnes (2008).

[177] A. Gupta and J. Blewett (2007) p. 178. But see H. Laming (2009) para. 3.12.

right to argue, 'the role of social worker as social scapegoat for the abuse of children may diminish as universal services shoulder a higher level of responsibility'.[178]

From a slightly different perspective, there are concerns about the overall effectiveness of section 17. As discussed above, Masson criticises Lord Laming for concentrating too much on weaknesses in local practices, thereby over-looking the role of central government and the competing priorities of public agencies.[179] These priorities were only too apparent to the majority of the House of Lords in *R (G) v. Barnet London Borough Council and others.*[180] They held that a LA's duty under section 17 is a broad and general duty to cater for the needs of *all* children, rather than a duty to meet the specific needs of any child in particular.[181] Furthermore, in that case, although social services were obliged to accommodate a homeless child,[182] any duty to accommodate the whole family together lay within the province of the housing authority, not social services. Controversially, the House of Lords rejected the argument that a child's rights under Article 8 of the ECHR are infringed by social services accommodating a child without his parents.[183] As Cowan points out, the decision downgrades section 17, rendering it a provision with no clear purpose other than to inform the LA's broader approach in setting priorities.[184] This interpretation, combined with the substantial diminution in the force of section 27 of the CA 1989,[185] compartmentalises the functions of public agencies.[186]

Section 11(2) of the CA 2004 uses broadly similar wording to section 17 of the 1989 Act in relation to a long list of agencies involved in providing children with services. They must all arrange to discharge their functions 'having regard to the need to safeguard and promote the welfare of children'. According to Masson, however, there is no reason to think that their obligations there-under have any greater weight than those under section 17 – they are obligations to children generally and, like section 17, are unenforceable by any specific child.[187]

Meanwhile, it may be genuinely impossible to answer questions such as 'What are the circumstances in which removal [of a child from home] should be voluntary or compulsory?'.[188] This is a matter of professional judg-ment, which will only emerge with good staff management, accountability and training.

---

[178] E. Harlow and S. Shardlow (2006) p. 71.   [179] J. Masson (2006a) p. 242.
[180] [2003] UKHL 57, [2004] 2 AC 208. Lords Nicholls of Birkenhead and Steyn dissenting.
[181] Ibid., per Lord Millett, at [108].   [182] I.e. under CA 1989, s. 20.
[183] E. Palmer (2003) criticises a similar stance adopted by the Court of Appeal when dealing with the *Barnet* case.
[184] D. Cowan (2004) p. 334.   [185] See discussed above.   [186] D. Cowan (2004) p. 334.
[187] J. Masson (2006a) p 241.   [188] DH (2001) p. 42.

(7) Emergency intervention

(A) Emergency protection orders

As Munby J pointed out, it may be a terrifying experience for a child to be removed summarily from parents with whom he has lived all his life.[189] Many years before, the Cleveland report had also criticised the over-use of place of safety orders to remove children from home with little or no notice.[190] Nevertheless, it is equally terrifying to be subjected to real and immediate danger. Indeed, most children who are the subject of emergency intervention are already known to the LA, many having been on the child protection register.[191] If the initial referral indicates that a child's life is at risk of serious harm, or if a section 47 enquiry reveals such dangers, the CA 1989 provides practitioners with a range of powers to take immediate action.[192] An emergency protection order (EPO)[193] is designed to provide immediate authority to safeguard the child by removing him or her from home.[194] An application for an EPO is automatically justified when enquiries being made under section 47 are frustrated by access to the child being unreasonably refused, as long as the applicant has reasonable cause to believe that access to the child is required as a matter of urgency.[195]

The domestic courts are now very aware of the demands of the Strasbourg case law when deciding whether obtaining an EPO is really necessary.[196] The ECtHR has provided a body of trenchant advice over the use of emergency intervention,[197] emphasising that it can only be justified[198] if it is a

---

[189] *X Council v. B (emergency protection orders)* [2004] EWHC 2015 (Fam) 341, [2005] 1 FLR 341, per Munby J, at [34].

[190] Butler-Sloss (1998) ch. 1.   [191] J. Masson (2005) p. 80 and J. Masson (2008) ch. 3.

[192] Listed in HM Government (2006) Appendix 1: EPO under CA 1989, s. 44; an exclusion requirement obtained on application to the court and included in an interim care order or an EPO under ss. 38A and 44A – whereunder a perpetrator can be removed from the home instead of the child (for a discussion of the disadvantages of these exclusion requirements, see J. Fortin (2003) p. 465); police protection powers under CA 1989, s. 46. NB since child assessment orders must be applied for on notice at a full court hearing (CA 1989, s. 43(11)), they are not appropriate for use in emergencies; for details see DCSF (2008b) paras. 4.10–4.23.

[193] CA 1989, s. 44(1)(a): an order can be obtained if there is reasonable cause to believe that the child is likely to suffer significant harm if he is not removed to accommodation provided by the applicant or prevented from being removed from his present accommodation.

[194] CA 1989, s. 44(4)(c): the applicant (a LA, the police or the NSPCC) obtains parental responsibility over the child; s. 44(4)(b): the applicant can remove the child to alternative accommodation or prevent the child's removal from where he is already accommodated, e.g. a hospital; s. 45(1): the order lasts for up to 8 days, unless renewed for up to a further 7 days.

[195] CA 1989, s. 44(1)(b). See also CA 1989, s. 47(4): where enquiries are being made with respect to a child, the LA shall take reasonably practicable steps to obtain access to the child. See also DCSF (2008b) ch. 4.

[196] E.g. *Langley and ors v. Liverpool City Council and anor* [2005] EWCA Civ 1173, [2006] 2 All ER 202, per Dyson LJ, at [56]–[64]; *X Council v. B (emergency protection orders)* [2004] EWHC 2015 (Fam) 341, [2005] 1 FLR 341, per Munby J, at [34]–[35].

[197] Inter alia: *K and T v. Finland* [2001] 2 FLR 707, *P, C and S v. United Kingdom* [2002] 2 FLR 631, *Venema v. Netherlands* [2003] 1 FLR 552, *Haase v. Germany* [2004] 2 FLR 39. Discussed by J. Masson (2006b) pp. 18–20.

[198] I.e. under Art. 8(2) of the ECHR.

proportionate response to the danger that the child is considered to be in and is therefore a 'necessary' interference with the parents' family life.[199] It has criticised unnecessarily aggressive intervention methods,[200] especially in relation to older children, and if the abuse has already continued for a long period without endangering the child's life.[201] Nevertheless, it acknowledges the need in exceptional cases to obtain an order without notice (ex parte) to the parents, because of the urgency of the situation or because warning a parent who is an immediate threat to the child of such intended action may deprive the measure of its effectiveness.[202]

The senior judiciary have emphasised that LAs must pay much greater attention to the demands of the HRA 1998 and also improve their use of emergency intervention.[203] Applications for EPOs must be justified by good evidence of a 'genuine emergency'.[204] The applicant LA should also consider whether there are less drastic alternatives to emergency removal,[205] and whether they need an EPO for the full duration of 8 days.[206] In the event of an EPO being granted, the court should explain fully why it is doing so,[207] consider its duration, and whether contact with the parents during its operation need be restricted unduly.[208]

The uncritical use of ex parte applications has also been robustly criticised.[209] Despite variations in local practice, growing numbers of magistrates' courts

---

[199] *K and T v. Finland* [2001] 2 FLR 707, per Grand Chamber of the ECtHR, at [168].

[200] *Venema v. Netherlands* [2003] 1 FLR 552, at [97]–[98].

[201] E.g. in *Haase v. Germany* [2004] 2 FLR 39, at [99]–[100]: the childcare authorities' response had not been proportionate in the way six children in one family had been removed from their schools, kindergarten and home, and placed in unidentified foster homes, with contact with their parents forbidden.

[202] Ibid. at [95].

[203] E.g. in *X Council v. B (emergency protection orders)* [2004] EWHC 2015 (Fam) 341, [2005] 1 FLR 341, at [77] and [80]: Munby J criticised the LA for applying for an EPO with inadequate supporting evidence and analysis of the case; similarly in *Re X (emergency protection orders)* [2006] EWHC 510 (Fam), [2006] 2 FLR 701, at [71]: McFarlane J described the LA's decision to apply for the EPO as 'badly flawed'. See also discussed by L. Davis (2007).

[204] *Re X (emergency protection orders)* [2006] EWHC 510 (Fam), [2006] 2 FLR 701, per McFarlane J, at [72].

[205] E.g. a child assessment order (CA 1989 s. 43) or an interim care order (ibid., s. 38). *X Council v. B (emergency protection orders)* [2004] EWHC 2015 (Fam) 341, [2005] 1 FLR 341, per Munby J, at [43]–[46].

[206] Ibid., per Munby J, at [49]: many EPOs are made 'unthinkingly' and unnecessarily for the maximum period of 8 days. Per J. Masson (2006b) pp. 27–8: practice varies enormously over the length of order sought.

[207] *Re X (emergency protection orders)* [2006] EWHC 510 (Fam), [2006] 2 FLR 701, per McFarlane J, at [56].

[208] *X Council v. B (emergency protection orders)* [2004] EWHC 2015 (Fam) 341, [2005] 1 FLR 341, per Munby J, at [57] for a summary of the 14 points, described by McFarlane J in *Re X (emergency protection orders)* at [65], as 'required reading' for every magistrate and justices' clerk involved in an EPO application.

[209] Ibid., per Munby J, at [51]–[55]: EPOs should *normally* be obtained on notice to the parents; ex parte orders can only justified in real emergencies. See also *Re X (emergency protection orders)* [2006] EWHC 510 (Fam), [2006] 2 FLR 701, per McFarlane J, at [95].

have, since the implementation of the HRA 1998, been reluctant to allow applications for such orders to be heard, although they may allow an abridged notice period.[210] The ECtHR has pointed out that the absence of a court hearing not only prevents the parents producing evidence opposing the application in court, but may deny the children an opportunity to be heard.[211] The Cleveland report also stressed that it was completely inappropriate for children to be removed from their parents' care at short notice without their own views being listened to.[212] But although children should be represented on applications for EPOs, this seldom happens due to the shortage of Cafcass guardians, particularly if an application is made on abridged notice.[213]

The fact that in this country, many applications for EPOs relate to those under the age of 2,[214] suggests that practitioners are anxious about the extreme physical vulnerability of babies. Research indicates that their concerns are well founded.[215] Very young children have a right to be protected from death, fracture and brain injury – all far more common in babies than in older children and all far more likely in the first 6 months of life.[216] Much of the case law emanating from Strasbourg revolves around intervention to protect very young children. It is understandable for the ECtHR to stress that removing very young babies from their mothers soon after birth is an extremely harsh measure that can only be justified by extraordinarily compelling reasons.[217] As it has pointed out, the child's removal from his or her mother's care soon after birth will prevent the crucial formation of firm attachments between them and will also prevent the mother breastfeeding,[218] especially if there is no regular contact maintained between them after the removal. But as noted earlier in this work,[219] practitioners may have a real dilemma if they doubt a mother's ability to care for her baby.[220] Indeed, they may find the stance of the ECtHR unhelpful, given that they must address the demands of Article 3 which requires vigilance and a

---

[210] J. Masson (2006b) pp. 21 and 24–6.

[211] *Haase v. Germany* [2004] 2 FLR 39, at [97].   [212] Butler-Sloss LJ (1998) p. 245.

[213] *X Council v. B (emergency protection orders)* [2004] EWHC 2015 (Fam) 341, [2005] 1 FLR 341, per Munby J, at [37] and J. Masson *et al.* (2006b) p. 26.

[214] J. Masson *et al.* (2004) p. 3.

[215] J. Sibert *et al.* (2002) p. 270: the incidence of severe abuse in babies aged less than 1 year is six times greater than in children aged from 1–5 years, and 120 times greater than in children over 5.

[216] Ibid. at p. 274.

[217] *K and T v. Finland* [2001] 2 FLR 707, at para. 168 and *Haase v. Germany* [2004] 2 FLR 39, at para. 102.

[218] *P, C and S v. United Kingdom* [2002] 2 FLR 631, at [131]; *Haase v. Germany* [2004] 2 FLR 39, at para 101.

[219] See Chapter 2.

[220] E.g. *K and T v. Finland*, [2001] 2 FLR 707: the mother was a paranoid schizophrenic with a poor parenting record regarding her older child; *P, C and S v. United Kingdom* [2002] 2 FLR 631: the mother's first child had been removed from her by the Californian childcare authorities in the belief that he had been the victim of induced illness abuse by his mother. See also *EP v. Italy* (2001) 31 EHRR 17: an older child aged 7, had been removed from her mother in circumstances suggesting that she had been the victim of induced illness abuse (discussed in Chapter 2).

preparedness to intervene to prevent serious abuse continuing.[221] Whilst over-aggressive intervention should certainly be discouraged, social workers would be blamed by the public if they failed to avert the child's serious injury or death.[222] Although the ECtHR has acknowledged that a fair balance has to be struck between children's rights and those of their parents,[223] none of the Strasbourg case law contains a specific analysis of the child's own Convention rights which might counter-balance those of the parents.[224]

Whilst the domestic courts have taken good note of the Strasbourg case law, it is arguable that Munby J went too far in concluding that parents should have more or less daily contact with their children (supervised by the LA) during the operation of the EPO, and that a breastfeeding mother should have as much contact as she needs to continue her regime.[225] This decision certainly undermined the practicalities of many fostering arrangements.[226] Observing that foster parents might find it very difficult to organise daily contact with parents, particularly at weekends, Bodey J subsequently stated that it is not a principle of law that such generous contact has always to be arranged.[227]

As noted above, it is becoming less common for LAs to seek EPOs without notice, with practitioners apparently having become aware of the demands of the HRA 1998. Nevertheless, Masson's research suggests less high-minded reasons underlie this reduction. It appears that LAs simply bypass the need for emergency intervention.[228] They either persuade parents to agree to allow their child to be accommodated by foster carers under 'section 20 agreements'[229] or enlist the assistance of the police who may take the child into police protection.[230] Masson criticises these stratagems. Her research suggests that parents' agreement to their child being fostered may be more apparent than real, since it is often made plain to them that an EPO will be sought in the event of their refusing.[231] More to the point, she considers that a child may be protected better by the LA gaining an EPO than by relying on parental agreement. This may be the case, for example, if the child has been placed with a close

---

[221] *Z v. United Kingdom* [2001] 2 FLR 612.

[222] See the dissenting judges in *K and T v. Finland* [2001] 2 FLR 707: Judge Palm, joined by Judge Gaukur Jörundsson, (see esp. at 752) and Judge Bonello (see esp. at 755). Judge Bonello complained that those who had wanted to place the baby beyond reach of harm were now themselves 'branded violators of human rights' (at 756).

[223] *Johansen v. Norway* (1996) 23 EHRR 33, at [78].   [224] Discussed in Chapter 2.

[225] *Re M (care proceedings: judicial review)* [2003] EWHC 850 (Admin). [2003] 2 FLR 171, per Munby J, at [44].

[226] In *Kirklees Metropolitan District Council v. S (contact to newborn babies)* [2006] 1 FLR 333, per Bodey J, at [34]: this was the second appeal in 2 weeks he had heard on the issue of contact with a young baby on an EPO.

[227] Ibid. at [29]–[37].   [228] J. Masson (2005).

[229] CA 1989, s. 20; discussed further in Chapter 16

[230] I.e. under CA 1989, s. 46: if he has reasonable cause to believe that the child would otherwise be likely to suffer significant harm, a police officer may remove the child into suitable accommodation (or prevent the child's removal from suitable accommodation, e.g. a hospital) and keep him there for up to 72 hours.

[231] J. Masson (2005) p. 82.

relative who is unable to prevent intervention from an abusive parent.[232] Nor is police protection preferable to an EPO; indeed, as discussed below, there are concerns about its use.

(B) Police protection

It appears that in many areas, the reduction in the number of ex parte applications for EPOs has been masked by police protection being used instead.[233] Indeed, in some areas, the police are requested to intervene if social workers consider that they have insufficient evidence to justify applying for an EPO,[234] or if the local court is unwilling to hear cases without notice.[235] Masson *et al.'s* research on the use of police protection indicates that the interrelation-ship between social workers and the police over the use of these powers is not always an easy one,[236] with some police officers accusing social workers of opting for police protection 'as an easy way out',[237] in order to avoid going to court themselves, or in the case of teenagers, to sort out family disputes.[238] As Masson *et al.* point out, the availability of police protection as a kind of back-stop for social workers involved in child protection work may not be at all appropriate.[239] Although the legislation envisages that a child will move out of police protection into LA accommodation as soon as possible,[240] police stations have no suitable facilities for children, even for a short time.[241] Whilst the police must explain to the child what action has been taken and why[242] and discover the child's own wishes and feelings about their action,[243] the child is not entitled to any separate representation and there is no external scrutiny of the police intervention in the form of a court hearing.

Reliance on police powers appears to explain the huge reduction in out-of-hours applications for EPOs.[244] Sometimes an EPO already exists in relation to a child but the social workers may have been unable to execute it within working hours. Case law now suggests that the common practice for social workers to turn to the police for assistance in such circumstances is dubious. In *Langley and ors v. Liverpool City Council and anor*,[245] Dyson LJ emphasised the advantages of an EPO, including the fact that whilst the police officer will be a stranger to the child, the social worker may already be familiar to him or her and certainly able to remove the child from home more skilfully than even the most sensitive police officer.[246] He concluded that a police officer is legally barred from removing a child from an abusive situation if executing an EPO is practicable instead. 'In deciding whether it is practicable to execute

---

[232] Ibid. at p. 83.   [233] J. Masson (2006b) p. 23, Table 2.   [234] J. Masson (2005) p. 88.
[235] J. Masson (2006b) p. 23.   [236] J. Masson *et al.* (2001) pp. 120–35.
[237] Ibid. at p. 54.   [238] Ibid. at pp. 67–71.   [239] Ibid. at pp. 156–9.
[240] CA 1989, s. 46(3)(a) and (f).   [241] J. Masson *et al.* (2001) ch. 3.   [242] CA 1989, s. 46(3)(c).
[243] CA 1989, s. 46(3)(d).   [244] J. Masson (2005) pp. 90–2.
[245] [2005] EWCA Civ 1173, [2006] 2 All ER 202.   [246] Ibid. at [39].

the EPO, the police must always have regard to the paramount need to protect children from significant harm.'[247]

Dyson LJ went much further, holding that where an EPO already exists in relation to the child, a child should be removed from home by social workers or others who have the skills and experience to do so, unless there are compelling reasons for the police to do so.[248] In his view, a child's removal from home under police powers, which infringes both the rights of the parents and child to respect for their family life under Article 8 of the ECHR, cannot be justified under Article 8(2), despite such action being protective, since it cannot be described as being 'in accordance with the law'.[249] Consequently, before social workers obtain an EPO, they should consider carefully whether they can execute it during working hours or obtain assistance from their emergency duty team to do so. If not, they need not obtain an EPO at all, but rely instead on the police to exercise their own powers to remove the child from home after working hours.

The decision in *Langley and ors v. Liverpool City Council and anor,*[250] indicates that the argument that police protection could be challenged under Article 8 of the ECHR carries some weight.[251] Article 5 might also assist a teenager taken into police protection against his or her will, whilst the fact that there is no method of challenging this action in court might infringe the rights of parents and children alike under Article 6.

(8) Proof of significant harm – children's rights or justice for parents?

(A) The underlying issues

LAs are unlikely to initiate care proceedings precipitately, unless they consider that a crisis has arisen, in which case an application for an EPO may precede the application for an interim care order.[252] Indeed it appears that over 70 per cent of families are known to social workers prior to the application being made and most of the children involved will have been on the child protection register at some time.[253] Research indicates that social workers are wise to be vigilant over the safety of children who have already been maltreated – for them, the risks of re-abuse are relatively high.[254] Nevertheless, a great deal of professional time and energy is devoted to collecting evidence to substantiate child protection applications which may never be made and criminal charges which may never be brought.[255] The vast majority of children who are the subject of child

---

[247] Ibid. at [40].   [248] Ibid. at [52].   [249] Ibid. at [53].   [250] Ibid. at [39].
[251] J. Masson *et al.* (2001) pp. 144–6.   [252] J. Masson *et al.* (2008) ch. 2.
[253] J. Brophy (2006) pp. 11–12. See also J. Masson *et al.* (2008) pp. 24–9 and 57.
[254] M. Brandon *et al.* (2008) pp. 28–9 and 86. See also N. Hindley *et al.* (2006) p. 750: previously maltreated children are approximately six times more likely to be re-abused than children who had never been abused.
[255] Discussed in more depth in Chapter 17.

protection inquiries are never made the subject of legal proceedings of any kind, quite simply because, as discussed above, LA protection is provided in cooperation with their parents[256] under section 20 agreements.[257] Many are provided with accommodation under short-term fostering arrangements or with relatives.

Applications for care or supervision orders often never reach a final hearing or are simply not contested.[258] Indeed, the complexity of most child protection litigation means that no amount of official guidance[259] will ensure the smooth running of every case. Further efforts to reduce delays in care proceedings[260] through more effective case management assumes that with better preparation, even greater numbers of applications will be dropped.[261] It had been feared that the extremely large increases in court fees would result in LAs issuing fewer care applications or being more ready to withdraw.[262] Whilst a decrease in applications was evident for a time, the government's direction to all LAs to review their safeguarding arrangements following the death of Baby P[263] led to a significant rise both in child protection referrals and care applications.[264] It is unclear whether this increase will become a long-term trend. Meanwhile, the relatively few cases that do actually reach court involve confrontation and conflict – the battle lines are very readily drawn between the parents and the state. This may be explained by parents' knowledge that a care order will probably result in their losing contact permanently with their children.[265] Furthermore, a considerable stigma attaches 'to having a child being taken into care and being labelled an unfit parent'.[266] Indeed, when battle commences, the parents and their advisers, social workers and even the judiciary themselves, take up such formalised positions that the child at the centre is treated very much as a passive pawn.[267] But at this stage, the law's role in maintaining a balance between parents' rights to family privacy and children's rights to protection is put to a severe test. When comparing the

---

[256] J. Masson (2005) pp. 80–3.   [257] I.e. under CA 1989, s. 20.

[258] J. Brophy (2006) pp. 22, 83 and 95. See also P. Welbourne (2008) p. 345: research summary.

[259] DCSF (2008b).

[260] Official data indicated that in 2008, a s. 31 application was taking, on average, 56 weeks in care centres and 45 weeks in family proceedings courts. H. Laming (2009) para. 8.7.

[261] MOJ (2008) and *Practice Direction: Guide to Case Management in Public Law Proceedings* [2008] 2 FLR 668. The *Public Law Outline* (which replaced DCA (2003)) requires detailed LA work in the pre-proceeding stage of a care application, which, it assumes, may identify non-adversarial options, e.g. better use of extended family care, thereby obviating a final hearing.

[262] Family Proceedings Fees Order 2008 (SI 2008/1054) and Magistrates' Courts Fees Order 2008 (SI 2008/1052): an increase from £150 to a total of nearly £5,000. P Welbourne (2008) pp 353–355.

[263] Statement made by Ed Balls, Secretary of State for Children, Schools and Families on 1 December 2008.

[264] Statistics published in January 2009 showed that Cafcass had handled 693 requests for care cases, a 66% increase on December 2007. Applications had dropped to an all-time low in June 2008.

[265] DCA (2006) para. 3.5. J. Brophy (2006) pp. 95–6: research indicates that 'most' care plans for children subject to care orders involve their permanent removal from their parents.

[266] DCA (2006) para. 3.5.   [267] Discussed below.

child protection practice of English social workers with that of their colleagues in other European countries, researchers observe:

> Arrangements to secure the child's right to protection, and the due process of law protecting parents' rights against arbitrary bureaucratic interference can sometimes have the effect of cancelling each other out. English social workers in our study frequently expressed frustration about this sort of impasse ... The preeminent role of the law as protector of individual rights was ever present in the minds of the English social workers' discussion of the hypothetical case. Frequently, any action they contemplated was checked for its legality ... The possibility of using their 'professional authority' (ie that deriving from their own expertise) was less apparent in their discussions.[268]

Until recently, matters were exacerbated by the courts' own interpretation of the law. Driven by considerations of fairness to the parents, the courts had allowed a strict legalism to underlie the standard of proof for establishing the 'significant harm' formula, at the expense of the child. As discussed below, it was not until recently that the House of Lords addressed this problem.

The family judiciary's concerns about protecting adults from unfairness were undoubtedly enhanced by Angela Cannings' successful appeal against conviction for the murder of two of her four children, three of whom had died in infancy.[269] This case and others involving circumstantial evidence[270] have raised questions about the weight being placed on expert evidence[271] in criminal trials. Nevertheless, without expert medical evidence, a criminal trial may founder and it is often equally important in care proceedings.[272] Indeed, since it may throw light on whether a child has been abused or not, it should not be dismissed out of hand.[273] The courts have, however, stressed their judicial independence, with medical opinions being only part of 'the overall picture or jigsaw, albeit important parts'.[274] Cases involving allegations of child sexual abuse are often particularly difficult, given that there may be a variety of explanations for any physical evidence[275] and only the child, who may be very young, knows what really happened. A problematic aspect of care proceedings is that the child's evidence will usually be in the form of hearsay evidence.[276] Since children are not

---

[268] R. Hetherington *et al.* (1997) p. 119. See also A. Gupta and J. Blewett (2007) pp. 174–7.

[269] *R v. Cannings* [2004] EWCA Crim 1, [2004] 1 All ER 725.

[270] E.g. *R v. Holdsworth* [2008] EWCA Crim 971, (2008) 102 BMLR 112.

[271] E.g. Sally Clark's conviction for the murder of her two sons, each a few weeks after their birth, was quashed, based as it had been on the flawed evidence of Professor Sir Roy Meadow.

[272] DCA (2003) Appendix C: the duties of expert witnesses in family proceedings. See also B. Hale and J. Fortin (2008) pp. 98–9.

[273] *Re A and D (non-accidental injury: subdural haematomas)* [2002] 1 FLR 337, per Dame Elizabeth Butler-Sloss P, at [41]; *Re Y and K (split hearing: evidence)* [2003] EWCA Civ 669, [2003] 2 FLR 273, per Thorpe LJ, at [20].

[274] *Lancashire County Council v. D, E* [2008] EWHC 832 (Fam), unreported, per Charles J, at [83].

[275] E.g. *Leeds City Council v. YX and ZX (assessment of sexual abuse)* [2008] EWHC 802 (Fam), [2008] 2 FLR 869.

[276] M. Hayes (1997) pp. 5–6.

normally called to give evidence in person in care proceedings, their words and behaviour will be conveyed to the court by their adult interviewers or in the form of video-taped evidence.[277] Although hearsay evidence is admissible,[278] it does not carry as much weight as evidence provided by a witness directly, mainly because the court cannot test its weight and credibility through cross-examination. There is an obvious risk of relying only upon a child's hearsay evidence when identifying an adult as an abuser.[279]

Dame Elizabeth Butler-Sloss P emphasised that although the *Cannings* case served as a warning to the judiciary hearing care cases that they should not make orders based on insufficient evidence, the aims of the criminal jurisdiction are quite different from those of the civil.[280] This point has been made by the family judiciary many times before. Unlike the criminal law, which seeks to identify and punish the abuser, civil proceedings, with a lower standard of proof and a different aim, have a far greater chance of providing the child with a safe environment.[281] Indeed, until the introduction of a new statutory offence,[282] it was impossible to mount a prosecution when a child had been killed or injured but neither parent admitted responsibility. Defects in its drafting undermines the usefulness of this new legislation.[283] Nevertheless, the civil law is another matter. A growing body of case law shows that it is perfectly possible to obtain a care or supervision order to protect a sibling in such circumstances. A court can be satisfied that the child 'is suffering significant harm' under the CA 1989, section 31, simply because he or she is being physically or sexually abused by *somebody*.[284] A generous interpretation of the 'attributable' requirement in section 31(2)(b) allows an order to be made despite there being insufficient evidence to identify the abuser.[285] A finding that the child has suffered serious injuries at the hands of one or both of the carers, but ruling out neither, allows

---

[277] Discussed in Chapter 17.

[278] CA 1989, s. 96(3)–(7) and Children (Admissibility of Hearsay Evidence) Order 1993 (SI 1993/621). See also *R v. B County Council, ex p P* [1991] 1 WLR 221.

[279] E.g. *B v. Torbay Council* [2007] 1 FLR 203: a 13-year-old's false allegations of sexual abuse against his stepfather led to the boy's two stepsiblings being removed from home into foster care on care orders; discussed in Chapter 7.

[280] *Re U (serious injury: standard of proof); Re B* [2004] EWCA Civ 567, [2004] 2 FLR 263, at [22]–[31].

[281] E.g. *A LA v. S, W and T (by his guardian)* [2004] EWHC 1270 (Fam), [2004] 2 FLR 129, per Hedley J, at [5]–[8]: despite the father having been acquitted of murder or manslaughter of his child, family proceedings were required to decide whether the surviving child could be returned to one or both of her parents.

[282] Domestic Violence, Crime and Victims Act 2004, s. 5.   [283] Discussed in Chapter 17.

[284] Inter alia: *Lancashire County Council v. A (a child)* [2000] 2 AC 147; *In re O and anor (minors) (care: preliminary hearing)* [2003] UKHL 18, [2004] 1 AC 523; *North Yorkshire County Council v. SA* [2003] EWCA Civ 839, [2003] 2 FLR 849; *Merton London Borough Council v. K; Re K (care: representation: public funding)* [2005] EWHC 167 (Fam), [2005] 2 FLR 422.

[285] *Lancashire County Council v. A (a child)* [2000] 2 AC 147, per Lord Nicholls of Birkenhead, at 165–8: the requirement in s. 31(2) that the harm to the child must be attributable to the care given to him does not mean that the care must be attributable to the parent against whom the order is sought

the LA to mount protective measures to protect future children being cared for by any of the potential abusers, despite the possibility that one or other is wholly innocent.[286]

Whilst such an approach can be justified in child protection terms, it obviously places parents under a cloud of suspicion for unlimited periods. Furthermore, for a number of reasons, childcare practitioners' suspicions about abuse are often inextricably linked with the abuser's identity. First, the social workers carrying out the child protection investigation may be working alongside police officers who wish to identify the abuser in order to lay criminal charges. Second, LAs often use specialised treatment and assessment units to assess the parenting qualities of parents of children considered the victims of abuse. These units place considerable emphasis on the need for parents to take responsibility and blame for suspected abuse.[287] Faced with parental denial, they may not recommend that the child is safe either to return to them or to remain with them.[288] But if the parents are innocent of the abuse, they will refuse to take responsibility for it. Even if they are guilty, they may deny it,[289] fearing a criminal prosecution.[290] The LA will then consider it impossible to trust them sufficiently to contemplate their continuing to care for their child, particularly if the child is very young.[291] It is arguable that in such circumstances, and when older, an injured child also has a right to know the identity of the parent who had injured him or her.[292] A complete stalemate between parents and the LA may have to be resolved by care proceedings, with the court reaching a finding of fact one way or the other. This may be through conducting a split hearing to resolve a single disputed issue of fact, as a preliminary issue;[293] for example, the identity of the abuser.

Parents are obviously entitled to complain that their rights under Articles 6 and 8 of the ECHR have been infringed by care proceedings which treated them

---

[286] E.g. *Re K (care: threshold criteria)* [2005] EWCA Civ 1226, [2006] 2 FLR 868.

[287] E.g. *Re L (care: assessment: fair trial)* [2002] EWHC 1379 (Fam), [2002] 2 FLR 730: child psychiatrist only agreed to assess the mother for the possible rehabilitation of her baby once she had acknowledged responsibility for the death of her first child.

[288] D. Jones (1998) pp. 106–8.

[289] CA 1989, s. 98(2) provides little real protection to a parent who makes an admission in civil proceedings if the police later investigate the case. See *Re EC (disclosure of material)* [1996] 2 FLR 725 and *Re L (care: confidentiality)* [1999] 1 FLR 165.

[290] E.g. *Re U (care proceedings: criminal conviction: refusal to give evidence)* [2006] EWHC 372 (Fam), [2006] 2 FLR 690; discussed further in Chapter 17.

[291] E.g. *Re FS (child abuse: evidence)* [1996] 2 FLR 158: the mother claimed that unless she stated to the LA that she believed that her husband had abused one of their children, which she denied, she would not be trusted to continue caring for them.

[292] *Re K (non-accidental injuries: perpetrator: new evidence)* [2004] EWCA Civ 1181, [2005] 1 FLR 285, per Wall LJ, at [56].

[293] *Re S (care proceedings: split hearings)* [1996] 2 FLR 773. See also *Re B (children)(sexual abuse: standard of proof)* [2008] UKHL 35, [2008] 4 All ER 1, per Baroness Hale of Richmond, at [74]–[76]: split hearings are a useful way of separating out the factual issues which are capable of swift resolution.

unfairly.[294] Nonetheless, as the case law discussed below indicates, when it came to the need for LAs to establish the facts on which the care application hinged, there was a danger that the judicial pendulum had swung too far the other way, resulting in the child's own right to protection being compromised.

(B) The standard of proof

(i) The interrelated questions

The legislation allows a court to make a care order if it is satisfied that the child concerned 'is suffering, or is likely to suffer, significant harm'.[295] The LA will usually have plenty of evidence indicating that a child should be removed from home on the basis of what happened to him or her in the past. In rare cases, however, the child has not yet been harmed but there are fears for his or her safety in the future and the only evidence which might substantiate them relates to the past abuse (or possible abuse) of another child. This situation occurred in two cases, both dealt with by the House of Lords and separated by over 12 years: *Re H (minors) (sexual abuse: standard of proof)*[296] and *Re B (children)(sexual abuse: standard of proof)*.[297] *Re H* provoked considerable controversy over the correct standard of proof for establishing significant harm. Matters were clarified by the House of Lords in their later decision, *Re B*. In *Re H*, allegations of child sexual abuse had been made by C, a 15-year-old girl against her stepfather. She was now in foster care but the LA wished to obtain care orders over her younger sister and two younger stepsisters, all still living in the family home with the alleged abuser. Although there was no evidence at all of his yet having behaved inappropriately towards any of the three, the LA argued that, given the strength of their older sister's allegations against him, they were 'likely' to suffer significant harm in the future if left in his proximity. The likelihood of future abuse clearly hinged on the truth of C's story. In *Re B*, a not dissimilar situation had occurred, with the LA applying for care orders relating to two children aged 9 and 6, based on allegations made by their older stepsister, R, that their father,

---

[294] In *Re L (care: assessment: fair trial)* [2002] EWHC 1379 (Fam), [2002] 2 FLR 730, Munby J stressed the need for a transparently fair procedure at all stages of the care proceedings, including preparation work and meeting prior to the hearing. See also *Re G (care: challenge to LA's decision)* [2003] EWHC 551 (Fam), [2003] 2 FLR 42; *Re X; Barnet London Borough Council v. Y and X* [2006] 2 FLR 998; *Re C (breach of human rights: damages)* [2007] EWCA Civ 2, [2007] 1 FLR 1957.

[295] CA 1989, s. 31(2): a court 'may only make a care order or supervision order if it is satisfied – (a) that the child concerned is suffering, or is likely to suffer, significant harm; and (b) that the harm, or likelihood of harm, is attributable to – (i) the care given to the child, or likely to be given to him if the order were not made, not being what it would be reasonable to expect a parent to give to him; or (ii) the child's being beyond parental control.' An application for a care order under s. 31 must establish: (i) a finding of fact regarding 'significant harm'; (ii) a decision that the 'threshold criteria' under s. 31(2) are satisfied; (iii) a decision that a care order will be in the child's best interests.

[296] [1996] AC 563.   [297] [2008] UKHL 35, [2008] 4 All ER 1.

Mr B, had sexually abused her. There was insufficient evidence to justify a care order if R's allegations were untrue.

Each case provoked two interrelated questions. First, what standard of proof is required to satisfy the court that a child has suffered significant harm in the past? Second, if the court finds the evidence insufficient to indicate that significant harm has occurred in the past, can the same evidence be used to establish the likelihood of significant harm in the future?

(ii) Establishing significant harm has occurred in the past

In *Re H* the trial judge addressed the first question – what standard of proof should he use to decide whether the older sister had indeed been sexually abused? He considered 'that there was a real possibility' that the stepfather had sexually abused C, as she claimed. Indeed, in his view there was a considerable amount of evidence substantiating 'a classic unfolding revelation of progressively worse abuse'. Nevertheless, he could not be satisfied 'on the balance of probabilities' that C had suffered significant harm in the past.

The House of Lords agreed with the trial judge's conclusion in *Re H*; more was required than suspicion, however reasonably based. Lord Nicholls of Birkenhead, who delivered the majority opinion, emphasised that the correct standard of proof for proving that significant harm has occurred in the past, is the balance of probabilities. Accordingly, the court should be able to reach a finding that 'on the evidence, the occurrence of the event was more likely than not'.[298] This apparent clarity was, however, fundamentally undermined by his warning that:

> When assessing the probabilities the court will have in mind as a factor … that the more serious the allegation the less likely it is that the event occurred and, hence, the stronger should be the evidence before the court concludes that the allegation is established on the balance of probability … Deliberate physical injury is usually less likely than accidental physical injury. A stepfather is usually less likely to have repeatedly raped and had non-consensual oral sex with his under age stepdaughter than on some occasion to have lost his temper and slapped her … The more improbable the event, the stronger must be the evidence that it did occur before, on the balance of probability, its occurrence will be established.[299]

Consternation was provoked by Lord Nicholls' argument that the test remained the balance of probabilities, whilst at the same time maintaining the need for a degree of increasing scepticism the more serious the alleged behaviour. His view that intrinsically unlikely events should require stronger evidence was particularly strongly attacked, with critics pointing out that LAs only ever bring care proceedings in circumstances which, by their very nature, are unlikely to occur in normal households. The test suggested that in such a case, the courts should always require stronger evidence than they would normally require to establish that the occurrence was more likely than

---

[298] [1996] AC 563, per Lord Nicholls of Birkenhead, at 586.   [299] Ibid.

not.[300] As Ryder J pointed out, its effect was that the more serious the offence the more difficult it was to protect the child.[301] Indeed, *Re H* created an evidential strait-jacket for LAs. Admittedly, if they wished to protect children from the risk of future harm, it would only cause insurmountable problems where no clear evidence existed of any *other* worrying features in the parents' past record of care, which could justify applying for a care order. Fortunately, such cases appear to be unusual. They do, however, occur when the earlier death of a child suggests the likelihood of harm to a surviving child, but there is no evidence of the survivor having yet been ill-treated.[302] More seriously, the 'enhanced standard of proof' obliged LAs to adopt essentially diversionary tactics in cases where there were allegations of serious abuse, such as sexual abuse. Rather than basing their care application on that offence, they would exploit less serious but more certain aspects of the case to substantiate their fears of the children being at risk of abuse in the future.[303] The surer evidence of peripheral abuse would be used merely as a peg on which to hang a finding of significant harm under section 31.[304] Practitioners indicated[305] that since it had become increasingly difficult for allegations of sexual abuse or serious physical abuse to be proved, they were simply not being brought to court to be tested by fact-finding hearings.[306]

There were obvious logical difficulties underlying Lord Nicholls' assertion that although the civil standard of proof was quite unchanged and still governed care proceedings, the judiciary should be sceptical over any event deemed intrinsically unlikely. Indeed, in other branches of law, senior members of the judiciary routinely interpreted his advice as establishing a *higher* standard of proof for cases involving serious allegations. It was maintained that any differences between the standard of proof established in *Re H* and the criminal one were 'largely illusory'.[307] Matters were put on a clearer footing for child protection practitioners by the President of the Family Division who asserted resolutely that there was still an important difference in the two standards of proof which had to be maintained.[308]

---

[300] I. Hemingway and C. Williams (1997) pp. 741–2.   [301] Ryder J (2008) p. 30.

[302] E.g. *Re P (a minor) (care: evidence)* [1994] 2 FLR 751 and *A LA v. S, W and T (by his guardian)* [2004] EWHC 1270 (Fam), [2004] 2 FLR 129.

[303] E.g. *Re M and R (minors) (sexual abuse: expert evidence)* [1996] 4 All ER 239.

[304] E.g. *Re G and R (child sexual abuse: standard of proof)* [1995] 2 FLR 867. See also *JFM v. Neath Port Talbot Borough Council, TM, JM and CM (children) (by their guardian)* [2008] EWCA Civ 3, [2008] 1 FCR 97.

[305] K. Maclean and E. Hall (2008) p. 737.

[306] I.e. the first stage of a split hearing – referred to above.

[307] *B v. Chief Constable of the Avon and Somerset Constabulary* [2001] 1 WLR 340, per Lord Bingham CJ, at [31]. See also *R v. Headteacher and Independent Appeal Committee of Dunraven School, ex p B* [2000] ELR 156, per Brooke LJ, at 204–5 and *R (McCann and ors) v. Crown Court at Manchester, etc* [2003] 1 AC 787, per Lord Steyn, at [37].

[308] *Re U (serious injury: standard of proof); Re B* [2004] EWCA Civ 567, [2004] 2 FLR 263, per Dame Elizabeth Butler-Sloss P, at [13] rejecting Bodey J's view in *Re ET (serious injuries: standard of proof) Note* [2003] 2 FLR 1205, at [2] that there was little difference between the criminal and civil standard of proof in care proceedings.

Clarification by the House of Lords was long overdue, particularly when it became clear that members of the judiciary shared critics' concerns about the standard of proof established by *Re H*.[309] *Re B* provided the much-needed test case to provoke an appeal to the House of Lords. Charles J, the trial judge, had been unable to conclude either that it was more likely than not that R had been sexually abused by Mr B or that she had not. Nevertheless, since he could not conclude that there was no real possibility that Mr B had abused her, he concluded that there was a real possibility that Mr B had abused her. Such a finding failed to comply with the existing standard of proof, but if *Re H* could be overturned, it might be enough to establish the threshold for LA intervention in relation to the two younger children.

Baroness Hale of Richmond[310] rejected outright the view that evidence indicating a real possibility that abuse took place is sufficient to establish the likelihood of future harm. If Parliament had intended such a reduced standard of proof,[311] it would have said so.[312] Nor was she convinced that the civil standard of proof was out of step with the case law allowing a broad interpretation of section 31 in cases where it is impossible to identify which of the child's carers was responsible for abuse.[313] In her view, matters are completely different if it has been clearly established that the child has suffered harm in the past. Then the fact that the perpetrator's identity cannot be clarified need not prevent protective intervention.[314]

Re B put beyond doubt that the standard of proof for establishing the occurrence of past abuse remains the balance of probabilities; the LA must show that it is more likely than not that the abuse occurred. Mere suspicions or a 'real possibility' are not enough. This is the case whether or not the LA wants to use the evidence of past harm to show the likelihood of future harm.[315] Nor should there be a changed approach when, having satisfied itself that some abuse has occurred (having crossed the 'threshold stage' of the proceedings under section 31), the court progresses to the 'welfare stage' and considers, under CA 1989, section 1(3), what order to make, if any. In such a situation, the principles established by existing case law remain unchanged. If the court is not satisfied that abuse of a certain kind has occurred, it cannot at the welfare stage consider the likelihood of that abuse occurring in the future, even if it considers that there was a real possibility that it had occurred in the past.[316]

In most respects, the decision in *Re B* merely affirmed existing law. Its importance, however, lies in the way Lord Hoffmann[317] and Baroness Hale[318] rejected Lord Nicholls' suggestion in *Re H* that the more improbable the event,

---

[309] Ryder J (2008).
[310] Majority opinion with which all members of the Appellate Committee agreed.
[311] As urged by Ryder J (2008) pp. 34–6.   [312] [2008] UKHL 35, [2008] 4 All ER 1, at [54].
[313] *Lancashire County Council v. A (a child)* [2000] 2 AC 147; discussed above.
[314] [2008] UKHL 35, [2008] 4 All ER 1, at [61].   [315] Ibid. at [54].
[316] *Re M and R (minors) (sexual abuse: expert evidence)* [1996] 4 All ER 239.
[317] Ibid. at [13]–[15].   [318] Ibid. at [69]–[73].

the stronger the evidence required to establish its occurrence. This approach was consigned to the history books. Both emphasised that neither the seriousness of the allegations nor of the consequences should affect the civil standard of proof. As Baroness Hale emphasised, 'there is no logical or necessary connection between seriousness and probability'.[319] This clarification released the law from its erstwhile indefensible position that 'the worse danger a child is in, the less likely the courts are to remove her from it'.[320]

(iii) Establishing the likelihood of significant harm in the future

The first part of the decision in Re H regarding the standard of proof required to establish significant harm in the past materially affected the way in which the second question was interpreted. The LA had wished to use the evidence relating to C's allegations, despite its being too weak to show on the balance of probabilities that C had been abused by her stepfather, to show that the three younger girls were not safe with him in the future. Lord Nicholls considered that 'likely'[321] merely requires the court be satisfied that there is 'a real possibility' of the event occurring in the future, as opposed to being more likely than not.[322] This principle remains unchanged by Re B. Nor could the court conclude from the fact that there was only a real possibility of C having been abused in the past that there was also a real possibility that her sisters would be abused in the future.[323] As will be clear from the discussion above, this principle also remains the law, unchanged by Re B.

(iv) Getting the balance right

For a period of 12 years, the law appeared to favour an exaggerated fairness to parents, thereby allowing children's rights to protection to slip into second place. During this time, however, the law in other respects had adopted a more protective stance. For example, LAs had never been bound by the Re H straitjacket during the investigative stage of the intervention.[324] Furthermore, as discussed above, the House of Lords had rejected an over strict interpretation of section 31(2)(b) in cases where an abuser cannot be identified.[325] Similarly, in Re M (a minor) (care orders: threshold conditions),[326] the House of Lords rejected a restrictive interpretation of the present tense 'is suffering' as used in section 31. The use of the present tense does not mean that if a child was suffering significant harm and was rescued by the LA from such conditions, a care order cannot later be made, merely because it can no longer then be said that the child 'is suffering' significant harm. The statute should be construed 'in accordance with the spirit rather than the letter of the Act'.[327] This flexible

---

[319] Ibid. at [72].   [320] J. Spencer (1994) p. 161.   [321] I.e. CA 1989, s. 31(2)(a).
[322] [1996] AC 563 at 585.   [323] Ibid. at 589–90.
[324] The LA 's duty to investigate under s. 47 arises whenever they have reasonable cause to suspect that a child is suffering or is likely to suffer significant harm.
[325] Lancashire County Council v. A (a child) [2000] 2 AC 147.
[326] [1994] 2 AC 424.   [327] Ibid., per Lord Templeman, at 438.

interpretation of section 31 enables care applications to be brought in cases where the child was suffering significant harm at the time of the LA's initial application, despite the LA later having worked towards establishing other arrangements for his or her care prior to the court hearing.[328]

Efforts were also made to ease the rules of evidence so that the courts could be provided with all the information relevant to children's cases. In particular, expert evidence commissioned by a parent in the course of legal proceedings is not protected from disclosure by legal professional privilege and may be made available to the court even if it is unfavourable to the adult concerned.[329] Tapper suggests that the whole thrust of the evidential changes in modern legal procedure is to promote a system in which litigation is conducted 'not only with all the cards on the table, but face-up for all to see' and that it is entirely right that such changes have occurred in children's cases.[330]

The discussion above demonstrates how difficult it is for the law to maintain an appropriate balance between promoting children's rights to protection and parents' right to family privacy. Particularly problematic is our system of judicial decision-making which produces decisions like *Re H (minors) (sexual abuse: standard of proof)*[331] on an ad hoc basis, but which have an enormously wide impact throughout the family justice system.

(9) The child's own perspectives

The children's liberationists stress the importance of empowering children to free themselves of parental abuse. This is often unrealistic given the behavioural problems and depression commonly experienced by abused children. These can affect their school lives and friendships, with many worrying intensely about various aspects of their own and their parents' lives.[332] Many children who experience abuse often feel alone and confused, either having no one to confide in or feeling very reluctant to do so. This reluctance may stem from a fear of the consequences, or that they will not be believed, combined with a deep distrust of others and of anyone's ability to 'sort things out'.[333] Despite this, the liberationists' message has proved useful. The establishment of Childline and initiatives involving teaching young children in schools about acceptable and unacceptable adult familiarity do appear to have encouraged more children to tell adults about ongoing abuse.[334] Current guidance stressing that, in the

---

[328] See Lord Mackay's explanation, at 433–4.

[329] *Oxfordshire County Council v. M* [1994] 2 All ER 269; confirmed in *Re L (a minor) (police investigation: privilege)* [1997] AC 16. See also *L v. United Kingdom* [2000] 2 FLR 322, per ECtHR: a parent's obligation to disclose to the court in care proceedings an incriminating expert's report is not an infringement of his or her rights under Arts. 6 or 8 of the ECHR.

[330] C. Tapper (1997) p. 16.   [331] [1996] AC 563.

[332] S. Gorin (2004) ch. 3.   [333] Ibid. at pp. 49–51.

[334] But see R. Morgan (2007) p. 9: only 19% of children said that they would tell an adult if they had been harmed by someone else.

process of finding out what is happening to a child, practitioners must 'listen and develop an understanding of their wishes and feelings',[335] has been in place for some time. Lord Laming, however, considered that the consistent failure by a number of practitioners to communicate with Victoria Climbié was partially responsible for concealing her situation.[336] Researchers have also found that social workers, when investigating neglect and physical abuse, fail to discuss such matters with teenage family members, thereby missing information about the possible ill-treatment of younger siblings.[337] There is now a legislative duty on those undertaking section 47 enquiries, both to ascertain and to give due consideration to children's wishes and feelings, having regard to their age and understanding, over what action should be taken.[338] The qualifying phrase, 'so far as is reasonably practicable and consistent with the child's welfare' should not be taken as a reason for non-compliance.

Sadly, even when they are listened to, abused children may regret disclosing their abuse, feeling ignored and 'walked over' by those who try to protect them.[339] As the Cleveland report found, the victim of abuse is too often treated as 'an object of concern', rather than a person with a right to be involved and consulted.[340] Although child protection practitioners may listen to children in order to discover what happened to them, they may not be so enthusiastic to consult them over the outcome of protective intervention, despite the legislative obligation to do so.[341] A practical reason for the child's own position in child protection work being overlooked is the speed with which decisions to intervene are sometimes taken in the early stages, leaving practitioners feeling that they have no time to provide the child with explanations. A LA may consider it essential to take immediate steps to protect sexually abused children, particularly if a suspected abuser refuses to take responsibility for the abuse and there are fears that the child may come under pressure to withdraw his or her allegations if left at home.[342] On the other hand, children who deny that they have been sexually abused should be listened to.[343] Suspicions of serious physical abuse will also normally trigger considerable professional anxiety, particularly if a very young child is concerned, quite simply because of the fear that non-intervention may risk the child's death. But even children old enough to comprehend explanations very often experience a sense of complete bewilderment over the speed with which steps are taken to protect them, without any real effort to involve them in the arrangements being made for

---

[335] HM Government (2006) para. 5.4. See also para. 5.39.
[336] H. Laming (2003) paras. 6.652 and 8.99.   [337] W. Rose and J. Barnes (2008) p. 17.
[338] CA 1989, s. 47(5A). See also s. 17(4A) in relation to providing services for children in need and s. 22(4) in relation to services for looked after children.
[339] B. Smedley (1999) p. 115.   [340] Butler-Sloss LJ (1998) p. 245.   [341] See fn 17 above.
[342] E.g. *JFM v. Neath Port Talbot Borough Council, TM, JM and CM (children) (by their guardian)* [2008] EWCA Civ 3, [2008] 1 FCR 97.
[343] *Leeds City Council v. YX and ZX (assessment of sexual abuse)* [2008] EWHC 802 (Fam), [2008] 2 FLR 869, per Holman J, at [127].

their care.[344] Research indicates that '[T]his uncertainty and loss of control could serve to magnify the sense of powerlessness which was already a central experience for abused children'.[345]

Some feel strongly that abused children's choices over their future care after protective intervention should be respected, for otherwise they will simply retract their allegations of abuse because of their fear of the consequences.[346] But the dilemma is that an abused child's perceptions may be distorted by the abuse and adults therefore need the freedom to override their wishes and protect them. Schofield points out the temptation of assuming that because a child wants to go home or wants more parental contact, the relationship and parenting cannot be as damaging as the otherwise overwhelming evidence would suggest.[347] As she observes, however, one should not ignore the psychological factors underlying the relationship between an abused child and his or her parents:

> Troubled children in crisis, as those subject to care proceedings invariably are, very often and very understandably present entirely conflicting evidence of their wishes and feelings. They may express hopes for the future which are incompatible with what professionals and the children themselves know to be reality; for example, the wish to be at home and to be safe, the wish to be with a parent but for that parent to change.[348]

Schofield's material suggests that an abused child's right to protection by the state outweighs any right to self-determination. His or her right to make choices should be overridden if those choices will foreclose on a happy and fulfilled maturity. Consistent with this approach, the law maintains the view that the child's need for protection is more important than claims to confidentiality. Practitioners, such as social workers,[349] children's guardians,[350] and doctors[351] confided in by a child (or adult) with information indicating that a child is being abused should not promise to keep this to themselves. Indeed, they should warn the child that this information will normally be passed on to the relevant authorities and may eventually be used in court in the event of child protection proceedings commencing. Even solicitors consulted by children may feel obliged to infringe their confidentiality in the event of receiving information indicating that a child client is being abused. The child should be warned that such information may eventually have to be disclosed to the court in the event

---

[344] E. Farmer and M. Owen (1995) pp. 73–4.   [345] Ibid. at p. 72.

[346] E.g. F. Olsen (1992) pp. 210–13.   [347] G. Schofield (1998) p. 366.   [348] Ibid. at p. 364.

[349] *Re M and N (minors) (wardship: freedom of publication)* [1990] 1 All ER 205.

[350] *Re D (minors) (adoption reports: confidentiality)* [1996] AC 593.

[351] GMC (2007) para. 49: doctors must disclose information if 'it is necessary to protect the child or young person, or someone else, from risk of death or serious harm ... Such cases may arise, for example, if (a) a child or young person is at risk of neglect or sexual, physical or emotional abuse'. See also HM Government (2008) para. 3.88; discussed further in Chapter 5.

of public law proceedings being brought.[352] The controversial result is that an abused child may feel unable to confide safely in any adult.[353]

Once protective litigation is commenced, children should be given information by their social workers on what is being done on their behalf and what to expect when proceedings are issued.[354] All children who are the subject of care or supervision proceedings will be separately represented in court.[355] For some, the children's guardian is the first person available to listen to them and with whom to confide their hopes and fears regarding the outcome of the proceedings. On the whole, the tandem system of representation for children involved in public law proceedings operates extremely well, but with concerns being voiced about the procedural changes introduced under the auspices of the Public Law Outline.[356] Although the system is not perfect,[357] many children's guardians develop a very good rapport with children. Some children involved in care proceedings will tell their guardian that the court should allow them to return home. Although the care plan may involve such an arrangement,[358] as Schofield noted above, such wishes may be unreliable, indicating merely that the child's relationship with his or her abuser is a psychologically distorted one. Aware of this, the guardian may feel obliged to recommend that the child leaves home, despite his or her knowledge that the child opposes such a view. If deemed capable of instructing his or her own solicitor, the child should, at this point, be allowed to do so.[359] Critics also argue that children who are the subject of care proceedings should be allowed to take a more active role in the court proceedings, for example, by attending court and by speaking to the judge in private.[360] Consulting children over protective measures need not involve complying with their stated wishes; indeed it does not undermine the intervention for practitioners to treat children with respect and sensitivity throughout the process.

(10) Conclusion

Lord Laming considered that the legal framework for the child protection system was 'basically sound'.[361] It is still too soon to gauge whether the structural reorganisation implemented under the umbrella of the *Every Child Matters* programme can improve the state's response to concerns about children's safety. Collaboration between practitioners is not creating extra

---

[352] The solicitor may be subpoenaed and ordered to disclose documentation or divulge information.

[353] J. Loughrey (2008) discusses whether disclosure of confidential information would be a breach of a child's Art. 8 rights.

[354] DCA (2006) para. 5.7.   [355] Discussed in Chapter 7.

[356] MOJ (2008) and *Practice Direction: Guide to Case Management in Public Law Proceedings* [2008] 2 FLR 668; discussed in Chapter 7.

[357] HMICA (2007) section 3: records some criticisms of guardian practice; discussed in Chapter 7.

[358] A small minority of care plans involve the child remaining at home.

[359] Discussed in Chapter 7.   [360] Ibid.

[361] H. Laming (2003) para. 1.30. H. Laming (2009) para. 8.1.

resources.[362] Nor does it clarify ideas about how bad matters have to become in a child's home before the state must intervene. The balance between early prevention work and state intervention remains difficult to maintain. Attempts to protect children from abusive parents by removing them from home tend to polarise hostility between parents and state, with the child's own perspectives sometimes being forgotten. When practitioners' efforts are concentrated on an over-technical court process, it is understandable that protection is too often seen as a means to an end, with insufficient attention being given to dealing with children's ongoing needs, for example, for follow-up services in collaboration with other agencies.[363] Nevertheless, overall, the CA 1989 contrives reasonably well to ensure that the state's role in fulfilling children's rights to protection is promoted with some sensitivity. Finding the ideal balance between undue state interference which impinges on parents and children alike and an approach which so respects family privacy that parents are free to abuse their children in private is probably as unlikely as finding the Holy Grail.

BIBLIOGRAPHY

NB many of these publications can be obtained on the relevant organisation's website.

Anderson, R, Brown, I., Clayton, R., Dowty, T., Korff, D. and Munro, E. (2006) *Children's Databases – Safety and Privacy*, Foundation for Information Policy Research.

Audit Commission (2008) *Are We There Yet? Improving Governance and Resource Management in Children's Trusts*, Audit Commission.

Beecham, J. and Sinclair, I. (2007) *Costs and Outcomes in Children's Social Care: Messages from Research*, Jessica Kingsley Publishers.

Bercow, J. (Chairman) (2008) *The Bercow Report: A Review of Services for Children and Young People (0–19) with Speech, Language and Communication Needs*, DCSF.

Bichard, M. (chairman) (2004) *The Bichard Inquiry Report*, HC 653, The Stationery Office (TSO).

Brandon, M., Thoburn, J., Rose, S. and Belderson, P. (2005) *Living with Significant Harm: a Follow Up Study*, NSPCC.

Brandon, M., Belderson, P., Warren, C., Howe, D., Gardner, R., Dodsworth, J. and Black, J.(2008) *Analysing Child Deaths and Serious Injury Through Abuse and Neglect: What Can We Learn? A Biannual Analysis of Serious Case Reviews 2003–2005*, Research Report DCSF – RR023, DCSF.

Butler-Sloss LJ (Chairman) (1988) Cm 412 *Report of the Inquiry into Child Abuse in Cleveland 1987*, Her Majesty's Stationery Office (HMSO).

Brophy, J. (2006) *Research Review: Child Care Proceedings Under the Children Act 1989*, DCA.

Cicchetti, D. and Carlson, V. (eds.) (1989) *Child Maltreatment: Theory and Research on the Causes and Consequences of Child Abuse and Neglect*, Cambridge University Press.

---

[362] J. Beecham and I. Sinclair (2007) p. 57.   [363] Ibid. at pp. 49–51.

Cleaver, H., Nicholson, D., Tarr, S. and Cleaver, D. (2007) *Child Protection, Domestic Violence and Parental Substance Misuse: Family Experiences and Effective Practice*, Jessica Kingsley Publishers.

Commission for Social Care Inspection (CSCI) (2005) Department of Health (DH), *Safeguarding Children: The Second Joint Chief Inspectors' Report on Arrangements to Safeguard Children*, CSCI.

Committee on the Rights of the Child (2002) *Concluding Observations of the Committee on the Rights of the Child: United Kingdom of Great Britain and Northern Ireland* CRC/C/15/Add 188, Centre for Human Rights, Geneva.

Committee on the Rights of the Child, (2008) *Concluding Observations of the Committee on the Rights of the Child: United Kingdom of Great Britain and Northern Ireland* CRC/C/GBR/CO/4, Centre for Human Rights, Geneva.

Cowan, D. (2004) 'On Need and Gatekeeping – R (G) v Barnet London Borough Council etc' 16 *Child and Family Law Quarterly* 331.

Davis, L. (2007) 'Protecting Children in an Emergency – Getting the Balance Right' 37 *Family Law* 727.

Department for Constitutional Affairs (DCA) (2003) *Protocol for Judicial Case Management in Public Law Children Act Cases*, DCA.

Department for Constitutional Affairs (DCA) (2006) *Review of the Child Care Proceedings System in England and Wales*, DCA.

Department for Children, Schools and Families (DCSF) (2008a) *Children's Trusts: Statutory Guidance on Inter-agency Co-operation to Improve Wellbeing of Children, Young People and Their Families*, DCSF.

Department for Children, Schools and Families (2008b) *The Children Act 1989 Guidance and Regulations, Volume I, Court Orders*, TSO.

Department for Education and Skills (DfES) (2004) *Every Child Matters: Next Steps*, DfES.

Department for Education and Skills (DfES) (2006a) *The Common Assessment Framework for Children and Young People: Practitioners' Guide*, DfES.

Department for Education and Skills (DfES) (2006b) Cm 6932 *Care Matters: Transforming the Lives of Children and Young People in Care*, TSO.

Department for Education and Skills (DfES) (2007a) *The Consolidated 3rd and 4th Periodic Report to UN Committee on the Rights of the Child*, DfES.

Department for Education and Skills (DfES) (2007b) Cm 7137 *Care Matters: Time for Change*, TSO. Department of Health (DH) (1991) *Child Abuse: A Study of Inquiry Reports 1980–1989*, HMSO.

Department of Health (DH) (1995) *Child Protection: Messages from Research*, HMSO.

Department of Health (DH) (2001) *The Children Act Now: Messages from Research*, TSO.

Department of Health (DH) (2002) *Safeguarding Children: A Joint Chief Inspectors' Report on Arrangements to Safeguard Children*, DH Publications.

Department of Health (DH) (2003) (republished (2006)) *What to Do if You're Worried a Child is Being Abused*, DH.

Department of Health (DH) (2004) *National Service Framework for Children, Young People and Maternity Services*, Executive Summary, DH.

Department of Health (DH) Department for Education and Employment (DEE) and Home Office (HO) (2000) *Framework for the Assessment of Children in Need and their Families*, TSO.

Department of Health and Social Security (DHSS) (1982) *Child Abuse: A Study of Inquiry Reports 1973–1981*, HMSO.

Dowty, T. (2008) 'Pixie-dust and Privacy: What's Happening to Children's Rights in England?' 22 *Children and Society* 393.

Dingwall, R., Eekelaar, J. and Murray, T. (1983) *The Protection of Children: State Intervention and Family Life*, Blackwell.

Farmer, E. and Owen, M. (1995) *Child Protection Practice: Private Risks and Public Remedies*, HMSO.

Fortin, J. (1999) 'Rights Brought Home for Children' 62 *Modern Law Review* 350.

(2003) *Children's Rights and the Developing Law*, LexisNexis Butterworths.

Fox Harding, L. (1997) *Perspectives in Child Care Policy*, Longman.

General Medical Council (2007) *0–18 Years: Guidance for All Doctors*, GMC.

Glaser, D. (2000) 'Child Abuse and Neglect and the Brain – A Review' 41(1) *Journal of Child Psychology and Psychiatry* 97.

(2002) 'Emotional Abuse and Neglect (Psychological Maltreatment): a Conceptual Framework' 26 *Child Abuse and Neglect* 697.

Goldstein, J., Freud, A. and Solnit, A. (1973) *Beyond the Best Interests of the Child*, New York Free Press.

(1980) *Before the Best Interests of the Child*, Burnett Books Ltd.

Gorin, S. (2004) *Understanding What Children Say: Children's Experiences of Domestic Violence, Parental Substance Misuse and Parental Health Problems*, Joseph Rowntree Foundation.

Goveas, A. and Singleton, D. (2006) 'Every Child Matters Progress at Risk' 3–9 May, *Children Now*.

Guggenheim, M. (2005) *What's Wrong With Children's Rights*, Harvard University Press.

Gupta, A. and Blewett, J. (2007) 'Change for Children? The Challenges and Opportunities for the Children's Social Work Workforce' *Child and Family Social Work* 172.

HM Government (2006) *Working Together to Safeguard Children: A Guide to Inter-Agency Working to Safeguard and Promote the Welfare of Children*, TSO.

HM Government (2008) *Information Sharing :Guidance for Practitioners and Managers*, DCSF.

HM Inspectorate of Court Administration (HMICA) (2005) *Safeguarding Children in Family Proceedings*, HMICA.

HM Inspectorate of Court Administration (HMICA) (2007) *Children's Guardians and Care Proceedings*, HMICA.

HM Treasury (2003) Cm 5860 *Every Child Matters*, TSO.

Hale, B. (2000) 'In Defence of the Children Act' 83 *Archives of Diseases in Childhood* 463.

Hale, B. and Fortin, J. (2008) 'Legal Issues in the Care and Treatment of Children with Mental Health Problems' in Rutter, M., Bishop, D., Pine, D., Scott, S., Stevenson, J., Taylor, E. and Thapar, A. (eds.) *Rutter's Child and Adolescent Psychiatry*, Blackwell Publishing.

Harlow, E. and Shardlow, S. (2006) 'Safeguarding Children: Challenges to the Effective Operation of Core Groups' 11 *Child and Family Social Work* 65.

Haringey Local Safeguarding Children Board (2008) *Serious Case Review 'Child A'*, Executive Summary, Haringey LSCB.

Hayes, M. (1997) 'Reconciling Protection of Children With Justice for Parents in Cases of Alleged Child Abuse' 17 *Legal Studies* 1.

Hemingway, I. and Williams, C. (1997) 'Re M and R: Re H and R' 27 *Family Law* 740.

Henricson, C. and Bainham, A. (2005) *The Child and Family Policy Divide*, Joseph Rowntree Foundation.

Hester, M., Pearson, C. and Harwin, N., with Abrahams, H. (2007) *Making an Impact: Children and Domestic Violence, A Reader* Jessica Kingsley Publishers.

Hetherington, R., Cooper, A., Smith, P. and Wilford, G., (1997) *Protecting Children: Messages from Europe*, Russell House Publishing.

Hindley, N., Ramchandani, P. and Jones, D. (2006) 'Risk Factors for Recurrence of Maltreatment: a Systematic Review' 91 *Archives of Disease in Childhood* 744.

Information Commissioner's Office (ICO) (2006) *Protecting Children's Personal Information: ICO Issues Paper*, ICO.

Jones, D. (1998) 'The Effectiveness of Intervention' in Adcock, M. and White, R. (eds.) *Significant Harm: its Management and Outcome*, Significant Publications.

Jones, D. and Ramchandani, P. (1999) *Child Sexual Abuse*, Radcliffe Medical Press.

Jones, O. (2004) 'Towards a New Children Act – Part 2' *New Law Journal* 1296.

Keating, H. (1996) 'Shifting Standards in the House of Lords – Re H and Others (Minors)(Sexual Abuse: Standard of Proof)' 8 *Child and Family Law Quarterly* 157.

King, M. and Trowell, J. (1992) *Children's Welfare and the Law: The Limits of Legal Intervention*, Sage.

Laming, H. (2003) Cm 5730 *The Victoria Climbié Inquiry: Report on an Inquiry by Lord Laming*, HMSO.

(2009) HC 330 *The Protection of Children in England: A Progress Report*, The Stationery Office.

London Borough of Brent (1985) '*A Child in Trust*'. *The Report of the Panel of Inquiry into the Circumstances Surrounding the Death of Jasmine Beckford*.

Loughrey, J. (2008), 'Can You Keep a Secret? Children, Human Rights and the Law of Medical Confidentiality' 20 *Child and Family Law Quarterly* 312.

Lynch, M. and Roberts, J. (1982) *Consequences of Child Abuse*, Academic Press.

Lyons, T. (1994) 'What's Happened to the Child's "Right" to Refuse? – South Glamorgan County Council v W & B' 6 *Journal of Child Law* 84.

Maclean, K. and Hall, E. (2008) 'The Standard of Proof in Children Cases: *Re B*' 38 *Family Law* 737.

Masson, J. (2004) *Emergency Protection Orders: Court Orders for Child Protection Crises*, Executive Summary, Warwick University.

(2005) 'Emergency Intervention to Protect Children: Using and Avoiding Legal Controls' 17 *Child and Family Law Quarterly* 75.

(2006a) 'The Climbié Inquiry – Context and Critique' 33 *Journal of Law and Society* 221.

(2006b) 'Fair Trials in Child Protection' 28 *Journal of Social Welfare and Family Law* 15.

Masson, J., Winn Oakley, M. and McGovern, D. (2001) *Working in the Dark: The Use of Police Protection*, Warwick University.

Masson, J., Winn Oakley, M. and Pick, K. (2004) *Emergency Protection Orders: Court Orders for Child Protection Crises*, Executive Summary, Warwick University.

Masson, J., Pearce, J. and Bader, K. with Joyner, O., Marsden, J. and Westlake, D. (2008) Ministry of Justice Research Series 4/08, *Care Profiling Study*, Ministry of Justice.

Ministry of Justice (MOJ) (2008) *The Public Law Outline: Guide to Case Management in Public Law Proceedings*, MOJ.

Morgan, R. (2007) *Children and Safeguarding: Children's Views for the DfES Priority Review*, CSCI.

Mullen, P., Martin, J., Anderson, J., Roman, S. and Herbison, G. (1996) 'The Long-Term Impact of the Physical, Emotional, and Sexual Abuse of Children: A Community Study' 20 *Child Abuse and Neglect* 7.

Munro, E. and Calder, M. (2005) 'Where Has Child Protection Gone?' 76 *The Political Quarterly* 439.

Narey, M. (2007) *Beyond Care Matters: Future of the Care Population*, Working Group Report, DfES.

Office of Children's Commissioner (2007) *Care Matters: Transforming the Lives of Children and Young People in Care, A Response by the Children's Commissioner*, Office of Children's Commissioner.

Ofsted (2008) *Safeguarding Children, the Third Joint Chief Inspectors' Report on Arrangements to Safeguard Children*, Ofsted.

Olsen, F. (1992) 'Children's Rights: Some Feminist Approaches to the United Nations Convention on the Rights of the Child' in Alston, P., Parker, S. and Seymour, J. (eds.) *Children, Rights and the Law*, Clarendon Press.

Palmer, E. (2003) 'Courts, Resources and the HRA: Reading Section 17 of the Children Act 1989 Compatibly with Article 8 ECHR' *European Human Rights Law Review* 308.

Parton, N. (2008) 'The "Change for Children" Programme in England: Towards the "Preventive-Surveillance State"' 35 *Journal of Law and Society* 166.

Quinton, D. (2004) *Supporting Parents: Messages from Research*, Jessica Kingsley Publishers.

Rose, W. and Barnes, J. (2008) *Improving Safeguarding Practice, Study of Serious Case Reviews 2001–2003*, Research Report DCSF – RRO22, DCSF.

Ryder, Mr J. (2008) 'The Risk Fallacy: A Tale of Two Thresholds' *Family Law* 29.

Schofield, G. (1998) 'Making Sense of the Ascertainable Wishes and Feelings of Insecurely Attached Children' 10 *Child and Family Law Quarterly* 363.

Sharland, E., Seal, H., Croucher, M., Aldgate, J. and Jones, D. (1996) *Professional Intervention in Child Sexual Abuse*, HMSO.

Sibert, J., Payne, E., Kemp, A., Barber, M., Rolfe, K., Morgan, R., Lyons, R. and Butler, I. (2002) 'The Incidence of Severe Physical Child Abuse in Wales' 26 *Child Abuse and Neglect* 267.

Smedley, B. (1999) 'Child Protection: Facing up to Fear' in Milner, P. and Carolin, B. (eds.) *Time to Listen to Children: Personal and Professional Communication*, Routledge.

Spencer, J. (1994) 'Evidence in Child Abuse Cases – Too High a Price for Too High a Standard? *Re M (a minor) (appeal) (No 2)*' 6 *Journal of Child Law* 160.

Tapper, C. (1997) 'Evidential Privilege in Cases Involving Children' 9 *Child and Family Law Quarterly* 1.

Unison (2009) *Still Slipping Through the Net?*, Unison.

Warin, J. (2007) 'Joined-Up Services for Young Children and Their Families: Papering Over the Cracks or Re-Structuring the Foundations?' 21 *Children and Society* 87.

Wattam, C. (1997) 'Can Filtering Processes be Rationalised?' in Parton, N. (ed.) *Child Protection and Family Support: Tensions, Contradictions and Possibilities*, Routledge.

Welbourne, P. (2008) 'Safeguarding Children on the Edge of Care: Policy for Keeping Children Safe after the *Review of the Child Care Proceedings System, Care Matters* and the *Carter Review of Legal Aid*' 20 *Child and Family Social Work* 335.

Wolfe, D. (1987) *Child Abuse: Implications for Child Development and Psychopathology*, Sage.

Chapter 16

Right to protection in state care and to state accountability

(1) The corporate parent

Society expects parents to fulfil their children's rights to care, protection, optimum health and a good education. Parents should also promote their children's capacity for independence and take an interest in their future careers. Theoretically, when a local authority (LA) obtains a care order over a child, it is deemed to share parental responsibilities with his or her parents.[1] In practice the sharing is nominal, since parents cannot demand a right to influence events, even though they should be consulted over decisions regarding their child's future care.[2] Consequently the state effectively takes over the parenting role and should fulfil the same duties as birth parents. Indeed, the 'no order' principle[3] emphasises that by authorising an abused child's removal from home under a care order, the court is expecting the state to do a better job than the parents. The government agrees with these sentiments:

> As the corporate parent of children in care the State has a special responsibility for their wellbeing. Like any good parent, it should put its own children first. That means being a powerful advocate for them to receive the best of everything and helping children to make a success of their lives.[4]

Many children who are the subject of child protection referrals[5] are not removed from their parents' care, but are accommodated away from home with their parents' agreement[6] – on the authority of a 'section 20 agreement'.[7] Admittedly the LA's duties are less extensive in relation to this group of 'looked after children'.[8] Whilst a LA must safeguard and promote their welfare,[9] they do not assume parental responsibility for them. Nevertheless, like those removed on care orders, these children also expect their lives to improve when identified as requiring protection. But as case law and research indicates, the assumption that intervention to protect abused children will achieve a real improvement in their lives is all too often over-optimistic. Indeed, as in *Re F;*

---

[1] Children Act (CA) 1989, s. 33(3) and (5). [2] CA 1989, ss. 33(3)(b) and 22(4) and (5).
[3] CA 1989, s. 1(5). [4] DfES (2006a) p. 31. [5] Discussed in Chapter 15.
[6] M. Narey (2007) paras. 19–20: in 2006, 30% of children were in care on a voluntary basis.
[7] CA 1989, s. 20; discussed below. [8] See fn 42 below. [9] CA 1989, s. 22(3).

F v. Lambeth London Borough Council,[10] the state sometimes makes matters a great deal worse. In that case, as a result of the LA's long-term neglect of two boys whilst in care, both suffered 'significant educational, emotional, psychological, social and behavioural harm'.[11] As Munby J observed:

> it is a matter of gravity when the State's failure relates to its duties in relation to children and their families. It becomes a matter of the utmost gravity when the failure, as here, follows the intervention of the State in removing children against their parents' wishes from the parental home.[12]

The state's record as parent has been a disastrously poor one for many years. In 1998, Frank Dobson, the then Secretary of State for Health acknowledged:

> Too many children taken into care to protect and help them have received neither protection nor help. Instead they have been abused and molested. Many more have been let down, ignored, shifted from place to place, school to school and often simply turned out to fend for themselves when they turned 16.[13]

He thereby drew attention to two related problems. The first was that children were being taken into care to protect them but were not being protected adequately. The second was that the services they received once removed from home into substitute care were not adequate to meet their needs. In relation to the first, research indicates that protective intervention was not being followed up adequately, with registration on the child protection register being treated as sufficient protection, in itself. Brandon *et al.* reached the depressing conclusion that of the children initially identified as requiring protection, safety had only been achieved for three quarters of them, with 13 per cent being no safer after eight years of social work intervention,[14] and with some actually faring worse or slightly worse than prior to the intervention in terms of their overall outcomes.[15]

Some of the children in Brandon *et al.*'s research were left at home with dangerous parents, only to suffer re-abuse.[16] Others were taken into permanent care under care orders, with varying outcomes. It is the point at which children are actually removed from home that the shortcomings of the state as corporate parent become most evident. Even by 1998, as Frank Dobson acknowledged, the state's record was poor. Since then, evidence has accumulated showing that it is becoming steadily worse. In its Green Paper, *Care Matters*,[17] the government acknowledged that:

> the long term outcomes of many people who were in care as children are distressing: care leavers are over-represented in some of our most vulnerable

---

[10] [2002] 1 FLR 217: two boys aged 8 and 4, having been removed from home under care orders, were left without adequate care plans for 8 years.

[11] Ibid. at [30] (4).   [12] Ibid. at [42].

[13] Statement in the House of Commons by Frank Dobson, Secretary of State for Health, 5 November 1998.

[14] M. Brandon *et al.* (2005) p. 84.   [15] Ibid. at p. 51.

[16] Ibid. at pp. 26–31 and 86.   [17] DfES (2006a) .

groups of adults including young parents, prisoners and the homeless. They are also under-represented in further and higher education, and the proportion of young people leaving care aged 19 without any form of purposeful activity such as employment, training or education is much higher than that of their peers.[18]

The statistics cited[19] are in tune with the conclusions of a variety of reports.[20] Children experience too many foster placements,[21] often far from home[22] and are given too little say about the type of placement to which they are allocated.[23] Their overall standard of health and dental care is gradually improving,[24] but there is inadequate provision made for what are sometimes complex mental health needs.[25] Their educational attainment has been the topic of concern for many years,[26] with various targets for improving their educational qualifications being set and missed.[27]

In its 2007 White Paper,[28] the government indicated its resolve to improve matters, with a range of undertakings, most of which will take time to put in place.[29] Some of the promised changes are being piloted,[30] others are being achieved by a combination of revised performance measures[31] and new legislation,[32] to be expanded upon by regulations and guidance. Many exhortations need no official action and are only too familiar. Social workers are urged to embark on more prevention work earlier in order to support children 'on the edge of care' in their families, thereby avoiding the need to remove them from home at a later stage.[33] Particularly valuable amongst the legislative changes are LAs' new obligations regarding placements, with a new set of priorities designed to ensure that children's needs are adequately considered and met.[34]

---

[18] Ibid. at para. 22.   [19] Ibid. at ch. 1 and Annex C.

[20] Inter alia: DH (1998a); DH (1999); J. Timms and J. Thoburn (2003); H. Sergeant (2006).

[21] DfES (2006a) para. 4.5: around 1 in 10 of the children who ceased to be in care in 2005 had nine or more placements whilst in care, and only 65% of children who had been in care for over 2½ years had been in the same placement for 2 years or more.

[22] Nearly one-third of children in care are in placements outside their own LA's boundaries. Ibid. at para. 4.12.

[23] Ibid. at para. 4.22. See also R. Morgan (2006a) p. 11.

[24] DCSF (2008a): 80% had up-to-date immunisations, 86% had had dental checks and 84% had an annual health assessment.

[25] DfES (2007a) para. 5.18.   [26] E.g. SEU (2003).

[27] The Public Service Agreement (PSA) educational targets for care leavers have become less attainable rather than more. DCSF (2008a): 64% of looked after children obtained at least one GCSE or GNVQ. cf. 99% of all school children; 13% obtained at least five GCSEs (or equivalent) at grades A*–C, cf. 62% of all children. Large numbers of looked after children aged between 14 and 16 do not attend school regularly and many are excluded; discussed in Chapter 6.

[28] DfES (2007a).   [29] HM Government (2008).   [30] Ibid. at paras. 1.7 and 1.13.

[31] Ibid. at paras. 1.25–1.29.   [32] Children and Young Persons Act (CYPA) 2008.

[33] DfES (2006a) ch. 2 and DfES (2007a) ch. 2; P. Welbourne (2008), pp. 339–44. The need for more prevention work with families is discussed in Chapter 15.

[34] Inter alia: CA 1989, s. 22C (8)(a) – to find a placement close to home; s. 22C (8)(c) – to place siblings together; s. 22C (9) – to end out of area placements – in each case, so far is reasonably practicable (s. 22C(7)).

They must also provide sufficiently diverse accommodation for looked after children within their areas so that appropriate placements can be made.[35]

In the context of education, some legislative changes had already been achieved, with LAs being obliged to promote the educational achievements of looked after children.[36] Looked after children have priority over others when it comes to school admissions: LAs can direct children in care be admitted by specified schools, even when the schools in question are fully subscribed.[37] Policy-makers are only too aware that the low educational achievements of some looked after children may be attributable to the constant changes in fostering placements provoking moves from school to school. Consequently the new legislation obliges LAs not to make placements which will disrupt a child's education.[38] Furthermore, all schools must appoint a 'designated teacher' for children in care whose special role is to identify their learning needs and goals and remove barriers to their education.[39]

Although these changes should improve the lives of many looked after children, the state's poor record to date undoubtedly lends some support to the laissez-faire views of Goldstein, Freud and Solnit. They pointed out that the state cannot always offer abused children anything better or indeed compensate them for what they have missed in their own home. 'By its intrusion the state may make a bad situation worse; indeed, it may turn a tolerable or even good situation into a bad one.'[40] This chapter assesses the law's role in helping the state make a bad situation better. Far more children are placed with foster carers than in residential homes; nevertheless the latter service has been selected for special consideration due to the many reports highlighting the dangers of children suffering re-abuse whilst in residential care. The chapter considers the problems of 'control' experienced by residential establishments and the child's own perspectives whilst in state care and on leaving care. It then proceeds to consider the extent to which abused children can bring the state to account for failing to protect them at all or adequately.

(2) The courts and local authority planning for looked after children

(A) The background

There has, as discussed above, been mounting concern about the fate of 'looked after children',[41] with considerable criticism levelled at LAs' failure to plan

---

[35] CA 1989, s. 22G(4).

[36] CA 1989, s. 22(3A). See also the introduction of personal education allowances; DCSF (2008b).

[37] DCSF (2009) para. 2.8; School Standards and Framework Act (SSFA) 1998, s. 89(1a) and s. 97A and B; School Admissions (Admission Arrangements) (England) Regulations 2008 (SI 2008/3089) reg. 7.

[38] CA 1989, s. 22C(8)(b) – so far is reasonably practicable (s. 22C(7)).

[39] HM Government (2008) para. 1.35 and CYPA 2008, s. 20.

[40] J. Goldstein, A. Freud and A. Solnit (1980) p. 13.

[41] Under CA 1989, s. 22(1) and (2) a 'looked after child' is either a child who is the subject of a care order or a child being provided with accommodation under s. 20 for a continuous period of more than 24 hours. NB see *Southwark LBC v. D* [2007] EWCA Civ 182, [2007] 1 FLR 2181, per Smith

properly for their future upbringing.[42] These children fall broadly into two groups: those who are considered in sufficient danger to warrant the LA formally assuming their care with the assistance of care orders and those who are accommodated with foster carers, or in residential homes, under voluntary arrangements with their parents.[43] Concerns about their care were reinforced by the public outcry over the findings of the Waterhouse Report.[44] It suggested that far from being rescued from abuse, too many children placed in residential care were being severely re-abused, often by residential staff. Ideas about how to improve the lot of looked after children generally became linked with ideas about how to provide these children with permanent alternative homes more rapidly. Indeed, the radical reform of the adoption law was born largely out of two interlinking resolves.[45] The first was to reduce the delays and ineffective planning undermining adoption practice. The second was to ensure that far more looked after children were provided with substitute families, rather than being left to 'drift in care', at risk of abuse by unsuitable carers. These resolves were mapped out by the *Prime Minister's Review of Adoption* (PIU report),[46] and then reiterated in the White Paper on adoption.[47] The government considered that too many looked after children were waiting far too long for permanent homes and that adoption should be seen as the solution.

(B) Accommodated children

LAs often use voluntary accommodation or 'section 20 accommodation'[48] as an alternative to court proceedings.[49] In other words, despite being concerned about a child's safety, they see applying for a court order, be it a care order or a supervision order, as a last resort, with voluntary accommodation being infinitely preferable. Indeed, there is considerable pressure on LAs to avoid resorting to care proceedings unless other forms of family support have been explored and exhausted.[50] There is a presumption that, unless reasonably practicable and consistent with the child's welfare, the child will be accommodated with his or

---

LJ, at [55]: a child becomes a 'looked-after child' as soon as the LA considers that he or she requires accommodation for at least 24 hours, at which point the duty to accommodate him or her arises under s. 20(1) and the child should be provided with such accommodation under s. 23(2) or (6).

[42] CA 1989, s. 22(3)(a): a LA must 'safeguard and promote the welfare' of any looked after child.

[43] CA 1989, s. 20(1). NB s. 20(7): the LA may not accommodate the child against the wishes of anyone with parental responsibility who is able to provide the child with accommodation himself. See *R v. Tameside Metropolitan Borough Council, ex p J* [2000] 1 FLR 942.

[44] R. Waterhouse (2000).   [45] Discussed in Chapter 15.

[46] Performance and Innovation Unit (PIU) (2000).

[47] DH (2000) ch. 2.   [48] CA 1989, s. 20.

[49] J. Masson (2005) pp. 80–4; J. Brophy (2006) pp. 53–4; ibid. at p. 12: 50% of children who are the subject of care applications are already living away from their birth parents, most with foster carers under s. 20; J. Masson *et al.* (2008) p. 29: just under 40% of families whose children were later the subject of care proceedings had previously agreed to their children being accommodated under s. 20.

[50] Discussed in Chapter 15.

her own parents.[51] Failing such arrangements being appropriate, preference should be given to placements with family or friends.[52] Many parents are persuaded to agree to the child being accommodated away from home, quite often with foster carers.[53] This can cause problems, not least when parents feel coerced into agreeing such arrangements.[54] Difficulties may also arise with long-term fostering arrangements, particularly for children with uncaring parents. The only person able to exercise parental responsibility (PR) in relation to a child being accommodated voluntarily is the parent, but he or she may have completely lost interest in the child, leaving him or her in a 'legal limbo'.[55] If the LA fails to assume PR, it may feel unable to arrange a stable fostering placement for the child or arrange for appropriate psychiatric support.[56] Meanwhile, it appears that some section 20 cases may receive far less careful planning and monitoring by the LA than those involving children in care on care orders, due to the assumption that they are less serious or complex.[57] The absence of adequate monitoring may, in turn, lead to a failure to appreciate the need to assume parental responsibility by instigating care proceedings.[58] Indeed, as Ofsted found, the contribution of some LAs to ensuring children's safety is still inadequate.[59] Hopefully, the introduction of clear statutory obligations in relation to accommodated children[60] will produce more rigorous attention to their needs.

In terms of planning for accommodated children, in the past, social workers commonly rejected adoption, on the basis that there would be no parental cooperation. The PIU maintained that it was:

[51] CA 1989, s. 22C(3)(a); or failing a placement with parents (s. 22C(3)(b) and (c)) with a person with PR for the child or, if the child is already in LA care, a person with a residence order relating to the child.

[52] CA 1989, s. 22C(5), (6)(a) and (7)(a); P. Welbourne (2008) p. 342.

[53] J. Masson (2005) p. 82; discussed in Chapter 15.

[54] J. Brophy (2006) p. 54 and J. Masson (2005) pp. 80–4. See also *R (G) v. Nottingham City Council and Nottingham University Hospital* [2008] EWHC 400 (Admin), [2008] FLR 1668, per Munby J, at [54]–[55]: a parent must consent to the arrangement, rather than helplessly acquiesce to it.

[55] See *S (by the Official Solicitor) v. Rochdale MBC and Anor* [2008] EWHC 3283(Fam), unreported, Appendix A, esp. at [94]: the Official Solicitor (OS)'s allegations (unproved because the case was compromised) regarding the inadequate care of S (now aged 18) under CA 1989, s. 20, given her mother's refusal to show any interest in her.

[56] Ibid. at [21].

[57] Ibid. at Appendix A, [97] and Appendices B and C: summarising the (unproved) concerns of the OS regarding the use of inexperienced and unqualified social workers without adequate supervision for work on s. 20 cases.

[58] Ibid. at [22]. See also P. Welbourne (2008) pp. 338–9.

[59] Ofsted Press release 17 December 2008: of the 147 LAs receiving Annual Performance Assessments, 8 were assessed as providing an inadequate service in terms of children's safeguarding. E.g. Letter dated 17 December 2008 from Ofsted to the Director of Children and Young People's Services, West Sussex County Council: 'too many' children with child protection plans and those who were looked after by the council were not allocated to a qualified social worker; 78% of reviews of looked after children reviews were not completed within the year.

[60] CA 1989, Sch. 2, para. 8A.

all too easy, however, where there is no court process driving the development of the Care Plan for accommodated children to wait for long periods with no active planning for their future or consideration of whether care proceedings should be instituted.[61]

The PIU plainly considered that social work practice was hampering adoption being used more actively to improve the lives of large numbers of looked after children.[62] It also considered that the delays in the process were endangering successful placements, given the research indicating that the earlier a child is placed, the more likely the success of the placement.[63] The government hoped that the introduction of a new highly regulated adoption service, accompanied by adoption targets,[64] guidance[65] and regulations[66] would transform this situation. These changes were to be combined with the courts gaining the power to dispense with parental consent to adoption on the grounds of the child's welfare.[67] Whilst not specifically acknowledging that the new law would make it easier to force through adoption orders, the PIU stated that the changes would 'provide a very strong reinforcement throughout the legal system' of the new approach to adoption.[68] Government guidance now seeks to force social workers to consider adoption much earlier than hitherto as a means of fulfilling the child's 'need for permanence'.[69] Furthermore, the Adoption and Children Act (ACA) 2002 obliges LAs to apply for adoption placement orders in relation to children they are looking after, if they consider that such children *ought to* be adopted and if the threshold criteria for a care order can be made out.[70] Thus, as Lewis observes, adoption has become part of the care system.[71]

Clearly the choice between rehabilitation, adoption or fostering should, in practice, depend on a number of interrelating factors, such as the child's age, background, degree of contact with birth parents and extended birth family.[72] Nevertheless, the government certainly assumed that adoption was preferable to long-term fostering in terms of stability of outcome.[73] On balance, research

---

[61] PIU (2000) para. 3.30. [62] Ibid. at paras. 3.16–3.21. [63] Ibid. at paras. 2.15–2.17.

[64] DH (2000) para. 4.16. See also CSCI (2006a) para. 4.10: in 2000, a target was introduced to increase adoption of looked after children by 40% in the 5-year period to the end of March 2005. During that period, there was an increase of 38%, with 4,200 more looked after children adopted than would have been the case had adoption rates remained constant. Between 1998/ 9 and 2005/ 6, the number of looked after children adopted in England rose from 2,200 to 3,700 in 2006, with a high of 3,800 in 2004 and 2005.

[65] DfES (2005). [66] E.g. Adoption Agencies Regulations 2005 (SI 2005/ 389).

[67] Discussed in Chapter 14. [68] PIU (2000) para. 8.3.

[69] DfES (2005) ch. 2, pp. 2–3: the LA must identify 'an appropriate permanence plan' no later than by the second statutory review of the child's case (which must be held within 3 months of the first statutory review, which must take place within 4 weeks of the child being first looked after or accommodated. Review of Children's Cases Regulations 1991 (SI 1991/ 895), regs. 2–3). A permanence plan can include: 'returning the child to the parents, with support where necessary; long term placement with the child's wider family; long term placement with foster carers; residential placements until independence; placement for adoption.'

[70] ACA 2002, ss. 22(1)(c) and (d) and 21(2)(b). [71] J. Lewis (2004) p. 239.

[72] N. Lowe and M. Murch (2002) pp. 141–3. See also J. Thoburn (2006).

[73] DH (2000) para. 1.12.

appears to bear that assumption out.[74] The government did, however, acknowledge that adoption was not necessarily a universal panacea, especially for older children who do not want to be legally separated from their birth parents.[75] It accepted the widespread view that there was a clear need for a less drastic alternative.[76] The special guardianship order (SGO) was intended to provide a measure of security for children in long-term foster care, for whom adoption is considered inappropriate. Now, armed with a SGO, foster carers have parental authority over their charge,[77] with the ability to make decisions relating to a child's upbringing without parental interference.[78] Nevertheless, as discussed below, case law does not suggest that courts favour the prospect of SGOs becoming the preferred method of providing looked after children with a measure of permanence, as a half-way house between adoption and long-term fostering.

(C) Children removed into care

The comment made by the PIU report, noted above, regarding the lack of planning for accommodated children, implied that for those who were the subject of care proceedings, things were different, and better. For these children, drift and delay were avoided – because the LA would concentrate on developing comprehensive plans for the child's future upbringing. Unfortunately, research published in the late 1990s suggested that such optimism was misplaced. Indeed, care proceedings seemed often to be used primarily to ensure that assessments were done and pressure was put on parents during the preparatory period prior to litigation, with many cases not ending in a care order and less than half of the children involved going into substitute care.[79] Given the expense, financial and emotional, of court proceedings, there was some irony in researchers concluding that 'it would probably have been possible to achieve the same result, with less stress to all concerned, without making an order'.[80]

The increased numbers of children coming into care under care orders[81] faced a gloomy prospect in the 15 years or so following implementation of the Children Act (CA) 1989. Researchers, government inspection teams and case law recorded the same message. Many of these children's lives were not being improved by state intervention, despite the no order principle[82] indicating that

---

[74] D. Quinton (2006) pp. 464–6, who counters the criticisms made by J. Eekelaar (2003) pp. 258–63, of the government's assumption that adoption provides more stable outcomes than long-term fostering.

[75] DH (2000) paras. 5.8–5.11.   [76] A. Hall (2008a) pp. 365–6 and J. Thoburn (2006) esp. p. 35.

[77] CA 1989, s. 14C(1)(a); discussed further in Chapter 14.

[78] CA 1989, s. 14C(1)(b).   [79] J. Hunt (1998) p. 287.

[80] M. Brandon et al. (1999) p. 151, regarding 46% of the 28 cases in which an interim or full care order had been obtained. See also P. Welbourne (2008) p. 345: research summary.

[81] DfES (2006a) Annex C: between 1995 and 2005, the number of children coming into care on care orders increased from just under 30,000 to just under 40,000 See also M. Narey (2007) p. 13.

[82] CA 1989, s. 1(5).

care orders should not be made unless they could produce improvements. According to Hunt and Macleod, at the end of court proceedings:

> it is natural to hope that the placement plan which has been formulated will be achieved, that this will be accomplished expeditiously and without unnecessary disruption, that the placement will be stable and that the child will do well.[83]

These researchers found that only a minority of children were so fortunate. For many, the care experience had done little to ameliorate their problems and, for some, it had even exacerbated them.[84]

Since then, matters appear to have improved very little. Many LAs still fail to plan adequately for the future of children they wish to remove from home. Brandon *et al.* found that over the seven to eight years after children had first been identified as suffering or likely to suffer significant harm, some had been:

> languishing on the [child protection] register over long periods, often listed in multiple and changing categories of harm where the ongoing planning was neither promoting their well being, nor keeping them safe.[85]

Long-term planning (including the use of the courts) had taken place in only 40 per cent of the cases considered.[86] Nor is the statutory obligation on LAs to provide the court with a care plan, when applying for a care order,[87] being adequately complied with.[88] Considerable efforts are now being made to improve the quality of care proceedings through better case management, with an emphasis on appropriate assessment work and documentary evidence, including detailed care plans, all being completed before a care application is filed.[89]

Meanwhile, in response to the requirements of the ACA 2002, care planning far more often contemplates adoption. As noted above, LAs are under a statutory obligation to apply for adoption placement orders in relation to any child who is already on a care order, or the subject of a care application, if they

---

[83] J. Hunt and A. Macleod (1999) p. 189.

[84] Ibid. at p. 166. Furthermore, one-third of the children in their research sample had to cope with the insecurity and/ or disappointment of changed or unfulfilled plans. Ibid. at p. 186.

[85] M. Brandon *et al.* (2005) p. 11 and ch. 3.   [86] Ibid. at p. 43.

[87] CA 1989, s. 31A: LAs must, when applying for a care order, prepare a care plan or 's. 31A plan' to be filed with its application.

[88] DCA (2006) para. 3.10: inadequate/ delayed care plans; J. Brophy (2006) p. 42: non-completion of assessments; J. Masson (2008): in 17.4% of cases, the final care plan was only produced one week before the final hearing. See also *R (J) v. Caerphilly County Borough Council* [2005] EWHC Civ 586 (Admin), [2005] 2 FLR 860, per Munby J, at [46]. 'Any judge who sits in the Family Division will be familiar with the depressing inadequacies and deficiencies in too many of the care plans presented to the court for its approval'; *Re K and H* [2006] EWCA Civ 1898, [2007] 1 FLR 2043, per Wall LJ, at [23] and [26]: it was 'deeply dispiriting that 15 years after the implementation of the Children Act 1989 and much handing down of good practice ... that this sort of muddle appears'.

[89] *Practice Direction: Guide to Case Management in Public Law Proceedings* [2008] 2 FLR 668: the Public Law Outline requires a full assessment of the child's needs to be filed with the care application.

are also satisfied that the child 'ought to be placed for adoption'.[90] As the judiciary point out, it is deliberate statutory policy that applications for care orders are now being accompanied by applications for placement orders or by care plans involving the child being placed for adoption very soon after the care order. Arguably, it is kinder to the parent that 'the issue of adoption or no is grasped earlier rather than later, and in the course of a single set of stressful court proceedings, rather than his [the parent] having to suffer going through very similar issues in a second set'.[91]

In many ways, the statutory policy appears to provide social workers with the very powers that they need. They often favour adoption as a means of providing permanence for very young children.[92] Indeed, the dilemma is that if the authorities intervene early, before the child suffers permanent harm, the more likely that a new adoption placement can be found for him or her. The later things are left, the more harm suffered and the more difficult it is to repair the damage.[93] The courts are well aware that babies cannot wait for their mothers to change.[94] On the other hand, as discussed below, early intervention may be difficult to square with the Strasbourg jurisprudence on state intervention. Furthermore, a LA may consider that its statutory obligations require it to apply for an adoption placement order even in relation to children coming into its care who are not yet suitable for adoption.[95]

If the court is extremely unhappy about the LA's plans for fast-track adoption, considering that there is insufficient evidence showing that the parents are incapable of resuming the child's care, it might direct a parental assessment under an interim care order.[96] It may even direct the LA to undertake a residential assessment of the parents and child,[97] to obtain further evidence regarding their parenting abilities.[98] Such assessment work may not only be immensely expensive[99] but will undoubtedly take time, thereby delaying plans for a fast-track adoption. Ultimately though, it may ensure that a very young child is left with his or her birth parents rather than being adopted by strangers.[100]

---

[90] ACA 2002, s. 22(1)–(2).

[91] *Re T (placement order)* [2008] EWCA Civ 248, [2008] 1 FLR 1721, per Hughes LJ, at [16].

[92] I. Sinclair *et al.* (2007) p. 95: 54% of the children being looked after when aged less than one were adopted, with the chances of adoption reducing with every year of delay.

[93] B. Hale and J. Fortin (2008) p. 102.

[94] *A Local Authority v. J* [2008] EWHC 1484 (Fam), [2008] 2 FLR 1389, per Hogg J, at [76].

[95] As in *Re T (placement order)* [2008] EWCA Civ 248, [2008] 1 FLR 1721.

[96] CA 1989, s. 38(1).   [97] CA 1989, s. 38(6).

[98] That the courts have a power to require such an assessment in the course of interim proceedings under CA 1989, s. 38(6) was confirmed by the House of Lords in *Re C (a minor) (interim care order: residential assessment)* [1997] AC 489. But see *Re G (a minor) (interim care order; residential assessment)* [2005] UKHL 68; [2006] 1 AC 576: s. 38(6) cannot be used to produce *services* for the child or family, cf. providing the court with information from detailed assessment work.

[99] See *A Local Authority v. M (funding of residential assessments)* [2008] EWHC 162 (Fam), [2008] 1 FLR 1579, per Bodey J, at [24]–[24]: criticising the funding difficulties experienced by LAs regarding the residential assessments required by the courts.

[100] E.g. as in *Re G* [2005] UKHL 68, discussed by B. Hale and J. Fortin (2008) p. 102.

The dilemma still remains that adoption is the preferred solution precisely when the harm (or most of it) has yet to be done. This makes the professional task of accurately assessing the future risks all the more important.[101]

When considering LA applications for adoption placement orders, the judiciary are well aware that the public, including parents, may perceive LA adoption practice to be target driven. Thorpe LJ pointed out that there are 'many who assert that councils have a secret agenda to establish a high score of children that they have placed for adoption'.[102] They have therefore stressed that the proper process governing a LA's application for an adoption placement order must be rigorously followed.[103] Lowe and Murch refer to the danger that:

> authorities, keen to meet their percentage target for adoption, may too hastily rule out rehabilitation with the birth parents or wider family, particularly for young children who are likely to be thought more adoptable.[104]

Older foster children are themselves aware of the pressures on social workers to move them out of foster care into adoption.

> Some [foster children] tell us they think this is to do with targets social workers have to try to meet, rather than what each child wants. Many have told us that they are happy to stay as foster children, and not be adopted – either by their foster parents or by anyone else.[105]

(D) Care planning for permanence – is adoption the only answer?

This pressure on LAs to find adoptive homes for children received into care presents the courts with a dilemma – one which was ignored by the PIU report when it criticised some courts for hampering adoption plans by giving birth parents 'the benefit of the doubt' and insisting on repeat attempts at rehabilitation.[106] The courts must fulfil their obligation, under Article 8 of the European Convention for the Protection of Human Rights and Fundamental Freedoms (ECHR), to allow parents and children to enjoy their family life together without undue state interference. The domestic courts may not be satisfied that the initial decision to remove a child from home was a proportionate response to an abusive situation.[107] But even if all agree that the child's need for protection fully justified the LA's interference with the parents' family life, the domestic courts must consider the Strasbourg jurisprudence interpreting the states' duties regarding the children removed from home. As discussed

---

[101] B. Hale and J. Fortin (2008) p. 102.

[102] *Re F (a child)* [2008] EWCA Civ 439, [2008] 2 FCR 93, at [14]. See also *Re B (placement order)* [2008] EWCA Civ 835, [2008] 2 FLR 1404, per Wall LJ, at [14].

[103] *Re B (placement order)* [2008] EWCA Civ 835, [2008] 2 FLR 1404, per Wall LJ, at [70] *et seq.*

[104] N. Lowe and M. Murch (2002) p. 149.   [105] R. Morgan (2006a) p. 18.

[106] PIU (2000) para. 3.62. See *Re D (grant of care order: refusal of freeing order)* [2001] 1 FLR 862, for an example of such judicial optimism, at first instance.

[107] *Re C and B (care order: future harm)* [2001] 1 FLR 611, per Hale LJ, at paras. 33–5.

earlier[108] and elsewhere,[109] the European Court of Human Rights (ECtHR) has consistently stressed that when considering whether state interference with parents' family life is 'necessary',[110] the reasons for the intervention must be sufficient and the intervention itself proportionate to the aim of protecting the child in question. Furthermore, it should be seen as a temporary measure only, with efforts made to reintegrate the child at home as soon as possible.[111] More particularly, totally depriving a parent of his or her family life with a child by taking the child into care and then placing the child for adoption should only be resorted to in exceptional circumstances, in the child's best interests.[112] On the other hand, the ECtHR has acknowledged that adoption may be the only option in certain circumstances.[113]

The ECtHR is yet to comment on the scheme introduced by the ACA 2002 whereby care proceedings are often allied with adoption placement orders. As Baroness Hale of Richmond has observed, the UK is unusual amongst members of the Council of Europe in permitting the total severance of family ties by an adoption order without parental consent. She stressed that 'It is, of course, the most draconian interference with family life possible'.[114] If, and when it considers this aspect of domestic law, the ECtHR may dislike the ACA's policy, given its disapproval of the way in which, under the previous domestic provisions, a child could be freed for adoption soon after being received into state care; this decreased the possibility of exploring future rehabilitation and reunification.[115] More recently, English law has become even harsher than before, with its combination of a fast-track adoption process and laws making it easier for the birth parents' opposition to adoption to be set aside.[116] Fully aware of the Strasbourg jurisprudence, the Court of Appeal stressed in *Re B (adoption order)*[117] that turning a long-term fostering arrangement into one of adoption, even with generous contact, may not be a proportionate response to the child's

---

[108] See Chapter 14.   [109] B. Hale and J. Fortin (2008) p. 101.

[110] I.e. under Art. 8(2) of the ECHR.

[111] Inter alia: *Johansen v. Norway* (1996) 23 EHRR 33 (esp. para. 78); *EP v. Italy* (2001) 31 EHRR 17 (esp. para. 62); *Haase v. Germany* [2004] 2 FLR 39 (esp. para. 93). See also *Olsson v. Sweden* (1988) 11 EHRR 259; *K and T v. Finland* [2001] 2 FLR 707; *S and G v. Italy* [2000] 2 FLR 771. See also discussion in Chapter 14.

[112] *Johansen v. Norway* (1996) 23 EHRR 33 (para. 78) and *Gnahore v. France* (2002) 34 EHRR 38 (para. 59); discussed by A. Bainham (2003) pp. 81–3 and S. Harris-Short (2008) pp. 34–8.

[113] *Johansen v. Norway* (1996) 23 EHRR 33 (para. 80) and *Scott v. United Kingdom* [2000] 1 FLR 958 at 970.

[114] *Down Lisburn Health and Social Services Trust v. H* [2006] UKHL 36, [2007] 1 FLR 121, at [34]; B. Hale and J. Fortin (2008) p. 102. See also A. Warman (2006) for a discussion of how other countries provide for the long-term care of children unable to live with their birth parents.

[115] *P, C and S v. United Kingdom* [2002] 2 FLR 631, at paras. 98 and 104.

[116] Discussed in Chapter 14.

[117] [2001] EWCA Civ 347, [2001] 2 FLR 26: a residence order in favour of the child's foster carer was preferable to an adoption order. It would preserve the birth father's Art. 8 rights and was a more proportionate response to the child's need for a permanent home, given his strong relationship with his birth father and his foster carer's willingness to continue caring for him on such a basis.

need for permanency when he or she has a strong relationship with his or her birth parents.[118] These concerns suggest that, had it then been available, the Court of Appeal might have favoured the SGO, given that it leaves the relationship between the child and birth parents intact. This, weighed against an adoption order, might have been deemed a far more proportionate response to the child's needs under Article 8 of the ECHR.

Applying a similarly cautious approach to that adopted in *Re B*, one might imagine that, despite increased government pressure to ensure that more children are adopted from care and more quickly, care plans envisaging adoption will now be critically scrutinised by the courts, with a view to favouring a SGO in appropriate cases. Indeed, in Sir James Munby's view, bearing in mind the Strasbourg case law, adoption should be considered only if special guardianship fails to meet the child's needs – special guardianship should therefore be considered first, and adoption only if special guardianship will not suffice.[119] Nevertheless, when asked to predict the courts' response to the then forthcoming availability of SGOs, he reflected, with some prescience, that this would depend on the courts' attitude to the Strasbourg jurisprudence, with its test of necessity and proportionality. He observed:

> there is still, I fear, a continuing failure to grapple with the full implications of the Convention approach.[120]

Unfortunately, the House of Lords' decision in *Re B (a child) (adoption by one natural parent)*[121] does not suggest that there is now any real need for the courts to assess critically the LA's assertion in care applications that adoption is the better option. As critics have pointed out, the approach adopted by Lord Nicholls of Birkenhead, in that decision, is not consistent with the requirements of Article 8 of the ECHR, which requires a proportionate approach to an infringement of the birth parents' rights.[122] Indeed, Bainham suggests that the House of Lords in *Re B* (alongside the government, through its policies incorporated in the ACA 2002) took a 'cavalier attitude' to the rights of birth parents and children alike.[123] Predictably, in the light of this influential decision, the judiciary do not appear to envisage the SGO being used often as a means of softening the nature of the UK's adoption law.

The emerging case law on the relative merits of the SGO as opposed to adoption appears, with some early exceptions,[124] to play down the need to favour the less intrusive option.[125] Indeed, research suggests that it is being used to strengthen the position of kinship carers who would previously have 'made

---

[118] Ibid., per Thorpe LJ, at [20].

[119] J. Munby (2006) pp. 24–5; discussed by A. Hall (2008a) p. 368   [120] J. Munby (2006) p. 25.

[121] [2001] UKHL 70, [2002] 1 All ER 641, esp per Lord Nicholls of Birkenhead. at [31].

[122] Inter alia: S. Harris-Short (2002) pp. 419–21 and S. Choudhry (2003) pp. 132–4. See also discussed in Chapter 14.

[123] A. Bainham (2003) p. 86.   [124] E.g. *A Local Authority v. Y, Z and ors* [2006] 2 FLR 41.

[125] A. Hall (2008a) pp. 375–6 and A. Hall (2008b) pp. 245–8.

do' with residence orders over the children in their care.[126] Practitioners and the judiciary alike[127] consider the SGO to be more secure than a residence order but 'a poor second choice' to adoption.[128] Thus in *Re M-J (adoption order or special guardianship order)*[129] Wall LJ considered that the trial judge had gone too far in saying that it was 'incumbent' on the court to adopt 'the least interventionist option'; in his view, such an approach might derogate from the paramountcy of the welfare principle.[130] But, as the trial judge had perceived, an uncritical approach to the LA's assertion that an adoption order fulfils the child's welfare in the best way possible sidesteps the need to weigh up the benefits of an alternative and less draconian option. Again, in *Re S (adoption order or special guardianship order)*[131] there was little sign of the SGO being seen as an alternative to adoption. Admittedly there, the Court of Appeal approved the trial judge's decision to make a SGO, rather than the adoption order requested by the LA. Wall LJ also made it clear that a SGO is 'less intrusive' than adoption and involves less fundamental interference with the relationships protected by Article 8 of the ECHR, and is a more proportionate response to the problem. Nevertheless, his more general comments probably had a far greater impact on family law practitioners. In particular, he maintained, not unlike Lord Nicholls in *Re B*, that:

> In choosing between adoption and special guardianship, in most cases Art 8 is unlikely to add anything to the considerations contained in the respective welfare checklists [ACA 2002, s. 1(4) and CA 1989, s. 1(3)]. Under both statutes the welfare of the child is the court's paramount consideration, and the balancing exercise required by the statutes will be no different to that required by Art 8.[132]

He added:

> However, in some cases, the fact that the welfare objective can be achieved with less disruption to existing family relationships can properly be regarded as helping to tip the balance.[133]

At first sight, these additional words might suggest an acknowledgement of the force of Article 8's requirements – but that is far from the case. Article 8 requires the proportionality test to govern *all* cases, wherever alternative forms of order are available, not merely 'in some cases'. In particular Wall LJ sought to dispel the notion that a SGO would always be more appropriate than an adoption order in situations where the child is being cared for by a family member. In his view, although it may be important in some cases not to allow an adoption order to distort or 'skew' the legal status of the adopters, by renaming them 'parents', when in fact, in truth, they may be aunt and uncle, it should not

---

[126] A. Hall (2008a) pp 371–2   [127] A. Hall (2008a) p. 373..
[128] *Haringey London Borough Council v. C, E and anor* [2006] EWHC 1620 (Fam), [2007] 1 FLR 1035, per Ryder J, at [87] and [93].
[129] [2007] EWCA Civ 56, [2007] 1 FLR 691.   [130] Ibid. at [19].
[131] [2007] EWCA Civ 54, [2007] 1 FLR 819.   [132] Ibid. at [49].   [133] Ibid.

prohibit adoption being considered in any case involving such circumstances. The skewing argument should not, in his view, be overstated.[134]

An important reason for the Court of Appeal favouring adoption appears to be its concern that the SGO fails in its intentions to achieve complete permanence and security for children and their carers outside adoption.[135] The fact that the existence of a SGO cannot prevent birth parents from harassing foster carers with legal challenges to their status, by seeking section 8 orders of various kinds[136] 'in a finely balanced case, could well tip the scales in favour of adoption'.[137] Thus Wall LJ emphasised that although special guardianship might, in *some* cases, be a good way of strengthening the position of long-term foster carers, only an adoption order would enable foster carers and the children in their care to be entirely free of the threat of future litigation from uncooperative birth parents.[138] One could, however, argue that the disadvantage of having to provide a SGO holder with extra security through an order under section 91(14), does not outweigh the ECtHR's concern to limit the use of adoption expressed in the Strasbourg jurisprudence referred to above. This suggests that taking a child into state care, and then dispensing with parental consent, on the basis merely that adoption is in the child's best interests, is a draconian step to be avoided if at all possible.

The availability of the SGO could be of crucial importance in situations where a child is the subject of care proceedings and the local authority's care plan involves placing for adoption outside the family, but the child's relatives apply to take over the child's care themselves. Procedurally the order in which such claims are considered is extremely important. Thus in *Birmingham City Council v. R,*[139] the child's grandparents countered the LA's care plan for adoption by seeking a SGO. Acceding to their wishes would have interfered far less fundamentally with the child's family life and therefore with the relationships protected by Article 8 of the ECHR, than by acceding to the LA's plans for adoption by strangers. It would have been a more proportionate response to the child's need for permanence; but it might not have provided the

---

[134] *Re S (adoption order or special guardianship order)* [2007] EWCA Civ 54, [2007] 1 FLR 819, at [50]–[61]. See also *Re AJ (adoption order or special guardianship order)* [2007] EWCA Civ 55, [2007] 1 FLR 507, per Wall LJ, at [51] and *Re M-J (adoption order or special guardianship order)* [2007] EWCA Civ 56, [2007] 1 FLR 691, per Wall LJ, at [17].

[135] *Re S,* ibid., at [67]–[68].

[136] NB the holder of a SGO is protected by CA 1989, s. 14D(1), (3) and (5) – a birth parent cannot apply to vary or discharge a SGO without obtaining court leave, which can only be granted if the court is satisfied that there has been a significant change of circumstances since the SGO was made; CA 1989, s. 10(7A) – court leave must be obtained before an application can be made for a residence order relating to a child who is the subject of a SGO. But a birth parent can apply *without* court leave for any s. 8 order challenging any decisions regarding the child's upbringing not involving a change in residence.

[137] *Re S* [2007] EWCA Civ 54, [2007] 1 FLR 819, at [63]–[68].

[138] Ibid. at [65]. See also *Re AJ (adoption order or special guardianship order)* [2007] EWCA Civ 55, [2007] 1 FLR 507, per Wall LJ, at [47].

[139] [2006] EWCA Civ 1748, [2007] 1 FLR 564.

child with the security she needed. One would have expected both claims to be weighed alongside each other. Nevertheless, Wall LJ refused to consider what order the grandparents might obtain, arguing:

> The natural parents of the child concerned are ruled out as carers. The choice, accordingly, is, in real terms, between adoption outside the family, or placement with family members – in this case, the child's grandparents. In circumstances such as these, it seems to us that the first question which arises will not be the nature of the order under which the child is to live with her grandparents, but the more fundamental question: is it in M's best interests to be adopted, or is it in her best interests to live with her grandparents? If the answer to the first part of that question is that it is in M's best interests to be adopted outside the family, then its second limb does not arise. It is only if the court decides that it is in the child's interests not to be adopted outside the family, but to live with her grandparents that the question arises as to the order by which that result is to be achieved.[140]

With respect, such an approach overlooks the fact that the strength of the grandparents' position was integrally connected with their hope to gain their granddaughter's care by means of a SGO. But weighing the child's best interests in her grandparents' care, isolated from the features of a SGO, prevented the court determining whether adoption was a proportionate response to the child's needs or whether a less drastic infringement of her family connections was possible.

As Hall observes, the creation of the SGO provided a timely opportunity for practitioners and the judiciary to reassess their approach to permanency planning. Disappointingly, however, there appears to be little change in the prevailing view that adoption remains 'the "gold standard" atop the permanency hierarchy'.[141]

(E) Care proceedings – at home or away?

Social workers may decide that some abused children are very obviously not candidates for adoption because there are good chances of their being able to return home in the near future. They may sometimes even consider that abused children are in no immediate danger and can therefore be left at home with their parents. Nonetheless, they may apply for a care order, so that in the event of the home situation deteriorating, the children can be quickly removed, without going back to court. The courts may encourage LAs to seek supervision orders instead in such situations,[142] in order to comply with the principle of proportionality.[143] Nonetheless, supervision orders remain extremely unpopular with many practitioners, being seen as 'a complete waste of time' and

---

[140] Ibid. at [81].   [141] A. Hall (2008a) p. 373.

[142] To obtain a supervision order under CA 1989, s. 35, the LA must satisfy the same threshold criteria as those applying to care orders: see s. 31.

[143] *Oxfordshire County Council v. L (care or supervision order)* [1998] 1 FLR 70, per Hale J, at 76–8 and *Re O (supervision order)* [2001] EWCA Civ 16, [2001] 1 FLR 923, at [18]–[28].

'toothless'.[144] They carry less control than care orders;[145] furthermore, LAs have no real sanction when parents or relatives fail to comply with the directions they contain.[146]

In some situations, the boot may be on the other foot, so to speak.[147] Whilst the court may agree with the LA's wish to obtain a care order, considering the parents to be extremely dangerous, it may doubt the wisdom of the LA's plan to return the abused child home, once the care order has been made. The LA might argue that such a strategy would promote both the legislation's aim to encourage social workers to work in partnership with parents,[148] even with abusive parents, and with the Strasbourg case law indicating that state care should be viewed as being a short-term measure. Nevertheless, the second Inspectors' report noted:

> our inspection evidence shows that some councils have placed children on care orders at home with their parents without following regulations or sufficiently monitoring them. Returning children to parents could sometimes be seen as a way of reducing out-of-area placements, rather than ensuring the needs of the children are paramount.[149]

Even more worryingly, there is accumulating research indicating that returning an abused child home can be a high risk strategy, with some children being re-abused by their parents within a very short time.[150] In the light of this, the court may quite justifiably consider that there is insufficient evidence to indicate that the parents have changed sufficiently to make it safe for the child to be returned home.[151] Nevertheless, a court is powerless in such a situation, its role in care proceedings being only 'adjudicative', rather than 'participative'.[152] It can certainly question the format of the LA's care plan if it considers it to be based on inaccurate information.[153] It can insist on making a care order, rather than the supervision order requested by the LA, if it considers that the latter will

---

[144] J. Hunt and A. Macleod (1999) p. 237. See also, ibid., ch. 8 generally and pp. 217–18.

[145] It is *only* by obtaining a care order that the LA acquires parental responsibility over the child, which it shares with his or her parents. See CA 1989, s. 33(3). NB a supervision order leaves parental responsibility entirely with the parents.

[146] J. Hunt and A. Macleod (1999) pp. 213, 217–18 and 237.

[147] A metaphor used by Wall J to describe this situation. See Wall J (1998) p. 6.

[148] B. Hale (2000) p. 464: although the CA 1989 does not specifically express the concept of partnership between state and parents, it is an underlying principle of the Act.

[149] CSCI (2005) p. 25. See also N. Biehal (2006) pp. 44–5: research evidence indicates that return of children home is often poorly planned and supported.

[150] Inter alia: J. Hunt and A. Macleod (1999) p. 199; M. Brandon *et al.* (2005) pp. 28–29 and 86; B. Ellaway *et al.* (2004); N. Biehal (2006) ch. 8; N. Hindley *et al.* (2006) p. 750: previously maltreated children are approximately six times more likely to be re-abused than children who had never been abused; I. Sinclair *et al.* (2007) p. 107: some LAs seem more prepared to take risks by returning children home than others. See also D. Jones (2006) for a summary and discussion of the research.

[151] E.g. *Kent County Council v. C* [1993] 1 FLR 308.   [152] J. Dewar (1995) p. 16.

[153] E.g. *Re H (care plan)* [2008] EWHC 327 (Fam), [2008] 2 FLR 21.

not offer the child sufficient protection.[154] But where the LA has applied for a care order, all the court can do is decide whether the threshold criteria are made out and, if so, whether or not to make it.[155] It has no power to impose conditions on it or insist that the LA discharge their parental responsibilities in a particular way.[156]

Indeed, the judge may be faced with choosing between the lesser of two evils; if he makes a care order, the LA may implement a care plan he strongly disapproves of, but if he makes no order he may be leaving children in the care of an irresponsible or wholly inappropriate parent.[157] The latter approach is 'a potentially high-risk strategy if it means the child receives inadequate protection through the intransigence of the LA on the one hand and of the court on the other'.[158] The judiciary have expressed a degree of frustration over their inability to influence how the LA provides for the child once in care. For example, they cannot prevent the child being rehabilitated with his or her parents, if that is the LA's intention, even if they consider the parents to be inherently dangerous.[159] As discussed below, the absence of any judicial power to supervise the delivery of a care plan, or any reliable procedure whereby LAs can be called to account in cases where they wholly fail to implement such plans continues to cause frustration.

(3) Protecting children in residential care

(A) The risk of abuse

The state's intervention to protect children from abusive parents must not lead the children into more danger than before. For the child who can neither return home, nor live with anyone in the extended family, residential care is normally rejected in favour of the more natural family life provided by long-term foster carers or adoptive parents.[160] Alongside calls for recruitment of more specialised foster carers,[161] are government undertakings to improve their training and support.[162] But there are large numbers of children for whom foster care would be quite unsuitable. Some children do not want a family placement,

---

[154] E.g. Re D (a minor) (care or supervision order) [1993] 2 FLR 423.

[155] Re T (a minor) (care order: conditions) [1994] 2 FLR 423, per Nourse J, at 429.

[156] B. Hale and J. Fortin (2008) p. 101.

[157] Re S and D (children: powers of court) [1995] 2 FLR 456, per Balcombe LJ, at 464.

[158] J. Dewar (1995) p. 21.

[159] Re W and B; Re W (care plan) [2001] EWCA Civ 757, [2001] 2 FLR 582, per Thorpe LJ, at [18] (NB House of Lords' decision is reported sub nom Re S (children: care plan), Re W (children: care plan) [2002] UKHL 10, [2002] 2 All ER 192).

[160] CSCI (2008) para. 6.10: in March 2007, of the 60,000 looked after children, 60% were in foster homes, 11% with relatives/friends, 14.9% in residential care, 9% at home with parents.

[161] M. Narey (2007) para. 26. In May 2008, the Fostering Network urged LAs to reassess their recruitment targets for foster carers, asserting that over 5,000 new foster carers were needed throughout the UK.

[162] HM Government (2008) para. 1.13.

perhaps because they have had repeated bad experiences of foster care; others have complex personal and social difficulties with a need for expert treatment in a residential setting; some are a danger to themselves or others and require secure accommodation; and there are those whose abusive experiences makes it undesirable to place them in another family.[163] These are the children who need care in children's homes.

The numerous inquiries into abuse in residential care in the late 1980s and 1990s, recording the systematic abuse of children by members of staff, gave the impression that state residential care often subjects abused children to re-abuse.[164] These drew attention to the poor management, recruitment and selection procedures of care staff, which allowed small groups of paedophiles to gain access to vulnerable children. Indeed, it was the Prime Minister's response to the Waterhouse Report[165] which had prompted the review of adoption policy with a view to ensuring that far more children looked after by LAs were provided with adoptive parents.[166] As Utting chillingly pointed out:

> Persistent sexual abusers are a scourge of childhood ... sexual terrorists whose success depends, paradoxically, on their capacity to ingratiate themselves with adults and children. An outstanding characteristic is their ability to establish themselves in roles in which they are trusted to excess as friend, colleague or employee. Their subsequent activities are concealed by suborning, blackmailing and threatening their victims.[167]

Detection of abuse may be hampered because the emotional needs of many children in residential homes make them particularly vulnerable 'to the flattering attention of improperly motivated adults'.[168] Their disturbed behaviour may itself lead other staff to dismiss their complaints as fantasy or lies. Utting stressed that although over-vigilance can lead to a poisoned atmosphere, staff must be prepared to complain about their colleagues' behaviour.[169] Managers need to maintain a heightened awareness of the risks posed, not only by adults in such settings, but also by other child residents.[170]

The expense of residential child care, combined with the scandals of the 1980s and 1990s led to the closure of many children's homes. Since then,

---

[163] D. Berridge and I. Brodie (1998) pp. 90ff; I. Sinclair *et al.* (2007) pp. 148–9.

[164] Inter alia: W. Hughes (1985) (the 'Kincora' report) sexual abuse in Northern Ireland boys' hostels; G. Williams and J. Macreadie (1992) (the 'Ty Mawr' report) ill-treatment of children in the home leading to incidents of suicide and self-harm; A. Levy and B. Kahan (1991) (.the 'Pindown' report) regime adopted in some Staffordshire residential homes involving isolation, humiliation and confrontation of the children in their care; R. Waterhouse (2000) sexual abuse of children in children's homes in North Wales. See also the literature review by B. Gallagher (1999).

[165] R. Waterhouse (2000).   [166] Discussed above.   [167] W. Utting (1997) paras. 9.1–9.2.

[168] Ibid. at para. 8.36. See also R. Waterhouse (2000) para. 29.33.

[169] W. Utting (1997) paras. 15.25–15.37; see also R. Waterhouse (2000) para. 29.57.

[170] E. Farmer and S. Pollock (1998), summarised in E. Farmer and S. Pollock (1999) pp. 377ff. This research indicated that a small but significant number of sexually abused residents in children's homes (just under one in five) went on to sexually abuse other child residents.

increasingly rigorous controls on the activities and movements of sex offenders,[171] combined with efforts to regulate and improve the standard of care offered in children's homes, are gradually bearing fruit.[172] Hopefully, an even more reliable service will emerge with the promised delivery of better support and training.[173]

(B) The problems linked with 'control'

The need to maintain control in LA children's homes is a consistent theme in any commentary on residential establishments.[174] Indeed the methods used by secure training centres (STCs) to discipline young offenders have become increasingly controversial.[175] Meanwhile, in the context of LA care, disciplining residents who may be reluctant even to get up in the morning, far less attend school, clearly poses problems that some residential staff feel unable to tackle.[176] This is understandable, given the volatile mix of residents being cared for, often by young and inexperienced residential care staff. 'Some homes today have many violent, abused, abusing and self-mutilating children, rather than the orphans and truants of a bygone era and popular perception.'[177] If these highly disturbed and difficult children get 'out of control', they can be a danger to themselves, each other, the staff and those living in the vicinity of the home. Indeed, many children in children's homes suffer bullying, physical abuse and theft at the hands of other residents.[178]

The methods of control used in some Staffordshire children's homes in the 1980s[179] were, however, completely unjustifiable.[180] The official response, ruling out any degrading punishments, including corporal punishment and depriving children of food and drink, was long overdue.[181] Nonetheless, as Utting pointed out, staff in children's homes must maintain a sensitive balance. On the one hand, methods of control can very easily become abusive; but on the other, in homes accommodating volatile and disturbed children, the staff and young people may themselves feel unsafe unless reasonable control is maintained. Clearly issues of safety and control are inextricably interlinked.[182] This may be a particular problem in LA secure children's homes (SCHs) which, as

---

[171] Discussed in Chapter 17.   [172] CSCI (2008) paras. 6.26–6.31.

[173] HM Government (2008) para. 1.13.

[174] Inter alia: N. Warner (1992) p. 41; W. Utting (1997) paras. 11.11–11.28; DH (1998a) p. 28; D. Berridge and I. Brodie (1998) pp. 99ff.

[175] Discussed in Chapter 18.   [176] DfES (2006a) para. 4.48.   [177] N. Warner (1992) p. 7.

[178] W. Utting (1997) para. 7.5.   [179] A. Levy and B. Kahan (1991) esp. ch. 11.

[180] The regimes known as 'Total Pindown' or 'Sympathetic Pindown' subjected children to isolation, humiliation and confrontation, in order to discipline them and deter them from absconding repeatedly.

[181] LAs were also required to establish complaints procedures in their children's homes, a system of unannounced monthly visits to all residential homes by LA representatives, and of independent visitors for all children being looked after. See DH (1991a) chs. 5 and 6 and Children and Young Persons, Children's Homes Regulations 1991 (SI 1991/ 1506).

[182] W. Utting (1997) paras. 11.12–11.17.

discussed below, may contain a dangerous mixture of unruly young offenders and vulnerable 'welfare secures'. But those LA children's homes not designed to lock up their residents (the 'unsecure' residential homes), often confront a different problem, with rebellious and disturbed children and young people intent on absenting themselves at night.[183] Staff may be fully aware that some, too immature to resist the blandishments of pimps and paedophiles, are leaving their residential units to take part in prostitution and crime.[184]

The guidance attempts to address all these dilemmas and emphasises that sanctions and physical restraint must not be 'excessive or unreasonable' and can only be used to prevent 'likely injury to the child concerned or to others, or likely serious damage to property'.[185] The Court of Appeal, when criticising the terms of the regulations governing the methods of discipline used by staff in STCs,[186] referred favourably, and by way of contrast, to the good practice guidance developed by SCHs.[187] Buxton LJ particularly approved of the fact that, unlike STC staff, 'it is common ground' that SCH staff should not use removal from association and physical restraint merely to ensure good order and discipline.[188] Indeed, their guidance emphasises that it should only be turned to 'as a last resort where all other alternatives have been exhausted or are inappropriate'.[189] It specifically lists the circumstances where such 'last resort' interventions might be justified to prevent young people from: harming themselves; causing significant damage to property; inciting young people to cause physical harm or damage to property; absconding from within and outside the unit.[190]

A common understanding amongst SCH staff that physical restraint must be confined to last resort situations does not ensure that, when employed, the techniques adopted avoid seriously injuring the small number of recipients. The review of the use of restraint in secure homes approved of the way that SCHs appear to use restraint methods very rarely, and then with safeguards.[191] It found, however, a wide variety of different methods being employed, with some SCHs never using pain and other homes adopting the methods used in STCs. It recommended that certain techniques should be dropped immediately[192] and the safety of all others independently reviewed.[193] Given the significant

---

[183] H. Sergeant (2006) pp. 41–3.

[184] Ibid. at p. 42. E.g. *Re T (judicial review: local authority decisions concerning child in need)* [2003] EWHC 2515 (Admin), [2004] 1 FLR 601: a 14-year-old boy's second serious assault occurred because he ignored staff advice not to leave the unit with one of his earlier assailants.

[185] The Children's Homes Regulations 2001 (SI 2001/ 3967), reg. 17(1) and (6)(b) and DH (2002a) paras. 22.6–22.7. See also SAN (2005) which apply to SCHs.

[186] Discussed in Chapter 18.

[187] *R (C) v. Secretary of State for Justice* [2008] EWCA Civ 882, (2008) *Times*, October 14, per Buxton LJ, at [29].

[188] Ibid.   [189] SAN (2005) para. 1.3.   [190] Ibid. at para. 1.2.

[191] P. Smallridge and A. Williamson (2008) para. 10.38.

[192] Ibid. at para. 10.38: i.e. the nose distraction and double basket hold; discussed further in Chapter 18.

[193] Ibid. at para. 10.40

variation in the type and quality of staff training on these restraint methods, it also recommended an independent review of training and trainers.[194] These recommendations, which have found favour with the government,[195] largely reflect the views of residents themselves who, whilst appreciating the need for physical restraint in exceptional circumstances to prevent dangerous behaviour or injury, not unreasonably consider that it should only be used by well-trained staff. But they add an important caveat – they consider that restraint should not cause pain.[196] Regrettably, the review failed to recommend a complete prohibition of restraint methods which deliberately hurt children.

(C) Control through secure accommodation orders

The use of secure accommodation is normally seen as a fairly drastic remedy reserved for older children.[197] Of those who are placed in secure units, there is a significant gender imbalance in favour of girls,[198] with concerns about girls revolving mainly around sexual abuse, harm or sexual exploitation.[199] Boys' placements are normally attributable to behaviour that is considered to be a threat to others and to absconding.[200] Until recently, the official guidance on the interpretation of the CA 1989 emphasised that locking up any child or young person was such a serious step that it should only be used as a 'last resort'.[201] It appears that so many LAs took this guidance to heart, radically reducing their use of 'welfare' placements in SCHs,[202] that many have closed.[203] More specialised placements in the community are favoured by LAs for those young people with really complex difficulties.[204]

The government agreed with critics that the official guidance was unhelpful in this respect. With LAs only using SCHs when every other possible alternative had been tried, secure placements were being seen in an extremely negative light.[205] This attitude ignored the fact that secure placements could help to ameliorate risk-taking behaviour, producing more stability in the behaviour of deeply disturbed children and young people.[206] The government was also concerned that if increasing numbers of SCHs closed, LAs would be forced to

---

[194] Ibid.   [195] MOJ (2008). Discussed in more detail in Chapter 18.

[196] R. Morgan (2004)pp. 11–12.

[197] Children (Secure Accommodation) Regulations 1991 (SI 1991/ 1505), reg. 4: no child under the age of 13 can be made the subject of a SAO without the express permission of the Secretary of State.

[198] J. Held Consulting Ltd. (2006) para. 5.3.   [199] Ibid. at para. 9.32.

[200] Ibid. at para. 9.34.   [201] DH (1991b) para. 5.1.

[202] M. Graham (2006) p. 11 and J Held Consulting Ltd. (2006) para. 2.1.

[203] Whereas in 2003 there were 30 SCHs in England and Wales, now (2008) only 20 exist.

[204] J Held Consulting Ltd. (2006) para. 9.8.   [205] Ibid. at para. 7.1.

[206] Ibid. at para. 5.10: approximately half the placements discussed were deemed to have improved outcomes. See also M. Graham (2006) p. 11.

place deeply disturbed children inappropriately in the community or in secure units far from home.[207]

New official guidance stresses that although restricting a child's liberty 'is a serious step which should only be taken where the needs of the child cannot be met by a more suitable placement elsewhere', it should *not* be considered as a 'last resort'.[208] Instead it should be seen as part of a range of positive options capable of meeting the complex needs of some troubled and troublesome children and young people. Such provision may be the most suitable, both in terms of the safety and security the premises offer and the specialist programmes which a secure residential home may also provide.[209] Hopefully, the new guidance will help deter LAs from only seeking secure accommodation orders (SAOs) when they consider there is no alternative[210] – rather than doing so because there is nowhere more suitable.[211]

Revised guidance alone will not, however, cure the problems undermining the use of secure accommodation. One of the factors underlying the reduction in its use is the cost of such placements.[212] Another is the practice of mixing, within the same unit, the 'welfare secures'[213] with youth justice placements. Most LAs consider mixing to be 'unhelpful' and would be more prepared to favour secure units if more units excluded young offenders.[214] This mixing has been the subject of criticism for many years, with staff themselves stressing:

> the absurdity of seeing young people deprived of their liberty to protect them from perpetrators of abuse, sitting across the table from other young people convicted of abuse or violent offences.[215]

The use of mixed units has become more problematic over recent years, with some units containing an increased proportion of youth justice placements, compared with the welfare secures.[216] Boundaries are even more confused by young people with serious mental health disorders sometimes being referred to secure units,[217] despite it being unclear whether appropriate treatment is available for them.[218] Indeed, SAOs are sometimes used to ensure that emotionally disturbed young people receive medical treatment in secure treatment units, when the mental health legislation might be a better vehicle for ensuring that they undergo compulsory treatment.[219] It is clear that LAs would have much greater confidence in the services provided by secure units if they provided better and more specialised mental health treatment services,[220] substance abuse services, and higher quality education.[221] They would also like staff to be better qualified and trained.[222]

---

[207] DfES (2007a) paras. 3.18–3.19.　　[208] DCSF (2008c) paras. 5.2.　　[209] Ibid. at para. 5.3.
[210] J. Held Consulting Ltd. (2006) para. 9.3.　　[211] DCSF (2008c), para 5.3.
[212] Leading to an overall reduction in their use by the Youth Justice Board; discussed in Chapter 18.
[213] A. Pack (2001) p. 140.　　[214] J. Held Consulting Ltd. (2006) p. 5.　　[215] T. O'Neill (2001) p. 152.
[216] M. Graham (2006) p. 11.　　[217] J. Held Consulting Ltd. (2006) para. 5.6–5.8.
[218] Ibid. at paras. 5.9 and 9.41.　　[219] Discussed in more depth in Chapter 5.
[220] C. Simmonds (2008) pp. 1035–7.　　[221] J Held Consulting Ltd. (2006) para. 6.2.
[222] Ibid. at para. 9.65.

The law underpinning the use of SAOs is relatively straightforward. It is clear that a SAO can *only* be obtained to secure 'an absconder' if he or she is likely to abscond from non-secure accommodation and in the event of doing so is likely to suffer significant harm.[223] But LAs tend to argue that the grounds for the order are fulfilled because a young person has a history of absconding and is likely to suffer significant harm, simply by virtue of absconding again. The circularity of this argument is obvious: 'runaways are at risk because they run away'.[224] Case law indicates that the young person should only be deemed 'likely' to abscond in the future if there is 'a real possibility or a possibility that cannot sensibly be ignored' of this happening.[225] It appears that absconders are sometimes sent to secure units, without the staff in their residential homes having ever satisfactorily discovered either why they were absconding in the first place[226] or whether and how secure accommodation would address their difficulties.[227]

As the grounds of the SAO make clear, restricting the liberty of a child or young person may simply be to protect the public.[228] Indeed, case law has established that, although relevant, the welfare principle does not govern applications for SAOs.[229] Arguably this interpretation of the wording of section 25 is unduly restrictive, bearing in mind the courts' own view that these are draconian orders.[230] The application for a SAO must, however, be fully justified, not only in terms of what the order is seeking to achieve, but also in terms of the duration requested.[231] It appears that a very small number of young people are held in secure placements for more than 12 months, significant

---

[223] CA 1989, s. 25(1): a SAO may not be made regarding a child who is being looked after by a LA unless it appears that: (a) he has a history of absconding and he is likely to abscond from any other description of accommodation, and if he absconds, he is likely to suffer significant harm; or (b) that if he is kept in any other type of accommodation, he is likely to injure himself or other persons. See M. Parry (2000) and J. Fortin (2001) pp. 257–60.

[224] National Children's Bureau (1995) p. 28. Runaways are discussed in more detail in Chapter 4.

[225] *S v. Knowsley Borough Council* [2004] EWHC 491(Fam) 716, per Charles J, at [37].

[226] E.g. R. Waterhouse (2000) para. 29.59: despite the high level of absconding from several of the children's homes in North Wales, and the frequent involvement of social workers and the police, little attempt was made to ascertain the true reasons for the absconders' leaving; they were merely punished for leaving. See also discussed in Chapter 4.

[227] National Children's Bureau (1995) ch. 4.

[228] See CA 1989, s. 25(1). See also s. 25(4): if the court 'determines that any such criteria (the grounds set out by s 25(3)) are satisfied, it *shall* make an order authorising the child to be kept in secure accommodation and specify the maximum period for which he may be so kept' (emphasis supplied).

[229] *Re M (secure accommodation order)* [1995] 1 FLR 418. Discussed by P. Bates (1995).

[230] *Re W (a minor) (secure accommodation order)* [1993] 1 FLR 692, per Booth J, at 696 and *Re M (secure accommodation order)* [1995] 1 FLR 418, per Butler-Sloss LJ, at 423.

[231] Children (Secure Accommodation) Regulations 1991 (SI 1991/ 1505), regs 11–12: the maximum duration of a SAO is 3 months, extendable by a further 6 months. See *Re W (a minor) (secure accommodation order)* [1993] 1 FLR 692: Booth J criticised the magistrates for making a secure accommodation order lasting 3 months without clarifying why this was better than a 5-week order, as recommended by the guardian ad litem.

numbers for six months or more and a few with several return placements.[232] The resident's progress whilst in secure accommodation must be monitored closely by the LA, since if the grounds for the order having been made are no longer present, the order itself cannot be enforced or relied on and the young person has a right to be released.[233]

The courts have repeatedly stressed that the official guidance on the use of SAOs should be followed closely.[234] A SAO should never be used 'because the child is simply being a nuisance or runs away from his accommodation and is not likely to suffer significant harm in doing so. It should never be used as a form of punishment'.[235] Those considering that children should not be confined at all under civil orders had hoped that section 25 could itself be challenged under the Human Rights Act (HRA) 1998. These hopes were dashed by the Court of Appeal in *Re K (secure accommodation order: right to liberty)*.[236] It controversially rejected the argument that section 25 is too widely drafted to fall within any of the exemptions to Article 5 of the ECHR and is therefore incompatible with its terms.[237] The Court of Appeal ruled that as long as the secure unit to which the particular child is sent provides properly supervised educational facilities, a SAO is exempted from infringing Article 5, under the Article 5(1)(d) exemption.[238] It clearly considered it permissible for the courts to consider potential infringements of Article 5 on a purely ad hoc basis; by disallowing those SAOs not accompanied by educational facilities, they could avoid declaring section 25 incompatible with the ECHR.

In this context, the Court of Appeal's obvious anxiety to uphold a well-established legislative provision led them to ignore the central question: 'whether section 25 – as drafted – is sufficiently precise to have the quality of law which the ECHR requires.'[239] This is a surprising interpretation. As drafted, the provision plainly fails to prevent the grant of an order falling outside the boundaries of the Article 5(1)(d) exemption, since there is nothing in its wording which insists on every SAO being made for the purposes of educational supervision.[240] *Re K* establishes that as long as educational facilities are provided by the secure unit to which the child is sent, whatever the quantity and quality, a SAO is impervious to challenges under the HRA 1998. Contrarily, an order not ensuring such provision prima facie infringes the child's rights under Article 5 and can be challenged.[241] Despite the obvious weakness of this

---

[232] J. Held Consulting Ltd. (2006) para. 9.56.

[233] *LM v. Essex County Council* [1999] 1 FLR 988, per Holman J, at 994–5 and *S v. Knowsley Borough Council* [2004] EWHC 491(Fam) 716, per Charles J, at [68]–[72].

[234] *Re K (secure accommodation order: right to liberty)* [2001] 1 FLR 526, per Judge LJ, at para. 93.

[235] DCSF (2008a) para. 5.3.   [236] [2001] 1 FLR 526.   [237] J. Masson (2002).

[238] I.e. covering cases where liberty is restrained 'for the purpose of educational supervision'.

[239] AIRE Centre (2001) pp. 4–5.

[240] Ibid. at p. 5: according to Strasbourg jurisprudence, e.g. *Huvig v. France* (1990) 12 EHRR 528, this is an insufficient delineation of legal discretion.

[241] *Re K (secure accommodation order: right to liberty)* [2001] 1 FLR 526, per Dame Elizabeth Butler-Sloss P, at paras. 42–3.

argument, at the very least, the decision should focus official attention on the poor standard of educational facilities offered by some SCHs.[242]

(4) The child's own perspectives

(A) Consulting children

As Article 12 of the Convention on the Rights of the Child (CRC) makes clear, children should be consulted on all matters affecting them, and due weight should be given to their views, in accordance with their age and maturity. Most parents recognise the sense of this guidance. The LA, like any other good parent, should respect the children in their care and consult them over their future upbringing. The CA 1989 acknowledges this and encourages social workers to treat children as individuals and involve them in decision-making about their future.[243] The government has repeatedly emphasised that social workers should take this obligation seriously. The guidance on assessing children in need urges social workers, when assessing families, to communicate with the children themselves and, in so doing, talk to them:

> although this may seem an obvious part of communicating with children, it is clear from research that this is often not done at all or not done well … Children themselves are particularly sensitive to how and when professionals talk to them and consult them. Their views must be sought before key meetings.[244]

Although there have been real improvements in the extent to which social workers comply with this duty, many children indicate that they are given no choice at all over foster placements,[245] with others feeling that although they are asked for their views, they are not really being listened to.[246] The new legislation, in addition to providing LAs with detailed directions over placement decisions,[247] imposes on all LAs a duty to provide a range of accommodation sufficient to meet the needs of all looked after children within their areas.[248] Notably it does not direct LAs to give looked after children a veto over what placement is offered to them. Given the current shortage of foster carers, it is unlikely that the guidance and regulations which are to expand on the new legislation will do so either.[249] Whilst placing looked after children in placements without any choice may be attributable to shortages in foster care, sudden changes in placement with no warning or preparation is far less

---

[242] Discussed above.

[243] E.g. CA 1989, ss. 17(4A), 22(4)–(5), 38(6), 43(8), 44(7), 46(3) and Sch. 3, paras. 4(4) and 5(5).

[244] DH, DEE and HO (2000) paras. 3.41–3.42.

[245] R. Morgan (2006a) p. 11: just under half the children and young people had no choice of placement.

[246] Ibid. at pp. 6–10 and DfES (2006a) para. 4.22. See also *R v. Devon County Council ex p O (adoption)* [1997] 2 FLR 388: Scott Baker J (at 396–7) criticised the LA for failing to discover the views of a child of 9 about its plans to remove him from his foster carers with whom he had lived for 2½ years.

[247] CA 1989, s. 22C.   [248] CA 1989, s. 22G.   [249] HM Government (2008) para. 1.31.

excusable.[250] One of the ongoing problems has been LAs failure to comply adequately with their duty to review children's cases either at all, or before making changes in their placements.[251] The new legislation spells out a duty to carry out a formal review of the relevant child's case before changing a child's placement,[252] at which point the child should have a chance to make representations about the suggested change.

A common theme of commentaries on the shortcomings of state care is the fact that looked after children lack the individual attention of an adult committed to them, often due to the shortage of social workers.[253] Children who run into problems with their placements find that the social worker that they have got to know has left[254] or cancels visits or is simply unavailable to talk matters over with.[255] They also commonly complain about not being able to speak to their social worker alone without their foster carers being present.[256] Legislation,[257] to be reinforced by more detailed regulations,[258] fulfils the government's undertaking to ensure that all looked after children are visited in their placements and are then seen alone, away from their carers.[259] It has often been suggested that looked after children also need a consistent person to act as their 'champion' or mentor, to ensure that their views are heard and that agreed decisions are implemented.[260] Legislation extends the 'independent visitor' scheme[261] to a wider group of children than is presently the case,[262] giving more looked after children a chance to access advice and support from someone outside the care system.[263] Whilst this scheme does not match the objectives of appointing an individual champion, it reflects a genuine attempt to improve looked after children's feeling of powerlessness when entering the state system of care.[264] As discussed below, legislation strengthening the role of Independent Reviewing Officers (IROs) should also ensure that looked after children feel more supported if they are unhappy over decisions being made about their future care.

(B) Making complaints

Despite looked after children having very clear views about how their lives could be improved they often find it difficult to complain about any aspect of

---

[250] R. Morgan (2006a) p. 6.   [251] Discussed below.

[252] CA 1989, s. 22D(1). But see s. 22D(2) which qualifies this duty in cases of urgency.

[253] CSCI (2006b) para. 5.70: more than 5% of children in care did not have a named qualified social worker.

[254] DfES (2006a) para. 3.13: children in care experience frequent changes of social worker due to the 11% turnover rate of those involved in children's social work.

[255] J. Timms and J. Thoburn (2003) pp. 16–17; R. Morgan (2006b) pp. 9–16; CSCI (2006c) p. 33.

[256] R. Morgan (2006a) pp. 17–18.   [257] CA 1989, s. 23ZA.

[258] HM Government (2008) para. 1.30.   [259] DfES (2007a) para. 3.79–3.82.

[260] Inter alia: DH (1996) p. 31 and DH (1998b) pp. 26–7.   [261] Discussed below.

[262] CA 1989, s. 23ZA.   [263] HM Government (2008) para. 1.30.

[264] J. Timms and J. Thoburn (2003) pp. 14–15.

their care.[265] They should be informed about how to use the statutory complaints procedure,[266] but the assumption that they will feel able to do so underestimates the hurdles that they confront. This is understandable in the case of children in foster placements, because doing so would make it more difficult to continue living with their carers.[267] Many of those in residential care have emotional and/or behavioural difficulties, and a significant proportion may have been sexually abused.[268] Furthermore, countless inquiry reports find that, when re-abused in a residential setting, few children complain, fearing that complaints will go unheeded and that they may be victimised by members of staff loyal to the abuser.[269] The children in North Wales who did have the courage to complain found that either they or the member of staff involved were moved from the home, but:

> otherwise the complaint would be stifled or lost in the mists of bureaucracy. There was compelling evidence that a number of those in positions of authority did all they could to ensure that complaints did not get out of the system or at least outside the confines of the home.[270]

Research carried out many years later indicates that children still try repeatedly to get social work staff to deal with their concerns, but feel that they are not being given due weight.[271] The government is only too aware of the need to help looked after children use the complaints procedure more readily. It was overhauled in 2006, with the intention of providing children with a more accessible system.[272] But the fact that it is much more bureaucratic than before,[273] with extended time-limits for LA responses,[274] suggests concessions to LAs' concerns. Admittedly the third, review panel stage, injects greater independence into the process.[275] Nevertheless, children find the differences between the various stages of the process bewildering,[276] with the various officers involved

---

[265] R. Morgan (2005b) p. 6.

[266] CA 1989, ss. 26(3) and 24D. Residents in children's homes can also use in-house complaints procedures.

[267] R. Morgan (2005b) p. 6.   [268] DH (1998a) p. 21.

[269] Staff may be tempted to 'turn a blind eye' to what is happening or to minimise or rationalise it. See W. Utting (1997) para. 18.10; R. Waterhouse (2000) para. 29.50.

[270] E. Ryder (2000) p. 408. See also R. Waterhouse (2000) para. 29.50.

[271] A. Pithouse and C. Crowley (2007) p. 208.

[272] DfES (2006b) and the Children Act 1989 Representations Procedure (England) Regulations 2006 (SI 2006/ 1738).

[273] The procedure is a three-tiered one, with time-limits attaching to each.

[274] SI 2006/ 1738, reg. 9: an applicant must complain within one year of the grounds arising, although the LA has discretion to consider the complaint after that period has expired. SI 2006/ 1738, reg. 17: the time-limit for the LA's response time at stage 2 of the procedure is now 90 working days, including 65 days' extension (an increase on previous time-limits), cf. reg. 18: the period within which a complainant must request a review has reduced from 28 working days to 20 working days with no extension.

[275] The review panel must consist of three independent people – SI 2006/ 1738, reg. 19.

[276] R. Morgan (2005b) p. 6.

surely adding extra confusion.[277] The fact that complainants are entitled to assistance with making complaints and to independent advocacy services,[278] may prevent large numbers of children giving up in disgust at the system's complexity. As a last resort, some may find their way to the local government ombudsmen who investigate complaints of maladministration causing injustice. Thus an ombudsman may assist if the LA has defaulted in the way it carried out one of its functions or in the way it failed to do so. If the complaint is upheld, the ombudsman will recommend a remedy, normally involving returning the complainant to the position he or she should have been in, had the maladministration not occurred. If this is impossible, the ombudsman will normally recommend some financial recompense, which may be placed in trust for the child.[279]

Increasing numbers of LAs have appointed children's rights officers, whose task is to promote good practice amongst those working with children looked after by the LA. Part of their job is to ensure that children know what rights they have, how to use the statutory complaints procedure, to help them express their views over decisions they object to and provide formal advocacy if required. Not all children would, however, feel able to trust anyone who is a LA employee with disclosures about members of that LA's staff. The 'independent visitor' scheme has, until recently, been a rarely used resource. Unpaid volunteers, with no standing within the LA, are appointed to visit, advise and befriend the child in question. But LAs have not been obliged to make such an appointment in every case. The scheme was reserved for cases where communications between the child and his or her parents had become infrequent or the parents had not visited the child for more than one year and if the appointment was deemed to be in the child's best interests.[280] Legislation, reinforced by more detailed regulations and guidance, will revitalise the scheme by obliging LAs to recruit independent visitors so that more children in care can benefit from this form of outside support.[281]

(C) Leaving care

For many children, the defects in the 'parenting' provided by the state are brought home most clearly when they leave care. Some of the problems that care leavers experience are obviously attributable to their disturbed home lives, rather than what occurs whilst in care. Nevertheless, during the late 1990s, there were mounting concerns about the plight of children leaving the care of LAs

---

[277] At stage 2 of the process, the LA Complaints Manager appoints an Investigating Officer (IO) to investigate and report on the complaint, whilst his findings are considered by an Adjudicating Officer (AO).

[278] SI 2006/ 1738, reg. 11.   [279] Commission for Local Administration in England (2006).

[280] CA 1989, Sch. 2, para. 17(1) and (2).

[281] CA 1989, s. 23ZB and HM Government (2008) para. 1.30.

with far poorer life chances than those of the average teenager.[282] Particularly unforgivable, given their extreme vulnerability, was the increasing trend for LAs to discharge young people from care early, largely for financial reasons.[283] The overriding message concerned care leavers' loneliness and depression coping alone, with very little support.[284]

The Children (Leaving Care) Act 2000, which amended the CA 1989, was introduced to change matters – to ensure that young people looked after by LAs move from care into living independently, in a way that they can cope with.[285] Indeed, the aim is to provide them with the sort of support that an average child might expect from his or her own parents, including the provision of suitable accommodation and financial support.[286] The LA must therefore assess the young person's needs and prepare a 'pathway plan' covering his or her future education, training, accommodation and financial support on leaving care. Each care leaver must have a personal adviser.[287] Although this adviser is normally a social worker employed by the LA, as emphasised by case law,[288] his primary role is to enable the young person to 'identify someone as committed to their well-being and development on a long term basis',[289] and to provide him or her with advice and support. This support should last until the care leaver attains the age of 21.[290] Personal advisers should also ensure that the care leaver's pathway plan addresses his or her needs and supervise its proper implementation. They should form a 'constructive relationship' with the young person and should help him or her manage the demands of adult life.

Were LAs to meet these obligations conscientiously, the lives of many vulnerable young people would be relatively tolerable, compared with those of their peers living at home with their parents. Many young people worry most about how they will manage financially when they leave care and what accommodation they will be given.[291] Research suggests that whilst some authorities

---

[282] Inter alia: SSI (1997) esp. para. 1.2; W. Utting (1997) pp. 91–3; DH (1999) esp. para. 2.6: all referring, inter alia, to care leavers' low educational qualifications, low employment prospects, poor physical and mental health, and high levels of homelessness.

[283] DH (1999) para. 2.1: the proportion leaving care at the age of 16 increased from 33% in 1993, to 46% in 1998.

[284] J. Vernon (2000) p. 114.

[285] Discussed further in Chapter 4, in the context of care leavers' need for specialised accommodation.

[286] LAs must assess (within 3 months of attaining the age of 16) and then meet the needs of an eligible child (a looked after child now aged at least 16, who was formerly looked after by a LA for at least 13 weeks after the age of 14) through a package of support up to the age of 18, and then on to the age of 21, if in full-time further education. See CA 1989, ss. 23A–E, 24, 24A–C, and Sch. 2 para. 19A–C. See also Children (Leaving Care) (England) Regulations 2001 (SI 2001/2874). For a more detailed assessment, see A. Wheal (ed.) (2002).

[287] CA 1989, s. 23D.

[288] R (J) v. Caerphilly County Borough Council [2005] EWHC Civ 586 (Admin), [2005] 2 FLR 860, per Munby J, at [27]; discussed below.

[289] DH (2001) p. 47.

[290] The LA's duties last until the care leaver attains the age of 24, if in further education or training.

[291] Both these topics are discussed in more depth in Chapter 4.

do fulfil their duties reasonably well, providing their care leavers with relatively good support,[292] there are considerable local variations. Indeed, the Children's Rights Director found that whilst some young people appreciate their new independence, others find it overwhelming, quite simply because many LAs apparently ignore their legal obligations in almost every respect.[293] Although a pathway plan should always be drawn up by the care leaver's social worker, in liaison with the care leaver's personal adviser and care leaver himself, a significant number of young people felt that they had not had any say in their plan's content and that it was short on detail.[294] More significantly, there were numerous examples of commitments in the plan being broken. As discussed earlier in this work,[295] many experienced long delays in obtaining promised accommodation, with intervening periods in unsuitable bed and breakfast or hostel accommodation,[296] and promised funding not materialising.[297] Even worse was the fact that although the legal obligation to produce a pathway plan is intended to ensure good advance planning for the care leaver's independence, large numbers of young people reported being given very short periods of notice for leaving care, and very little preparation for it.[298] Furthermore, contrary to the intentions of the legislation, an overwhelmingly large number of young people still leave care at around 16 or 17, without feeling ready to do so and without adequate support.[299] The report concludes: 'the overall impression conveyed was distinctly that of a lottery, with some young people enjoying excellent preparation and support, whilst others received little or no help at all.'[300]

Legal challenges reinforce this rather dismal picture. Case law suggests that LAs attempt to avoid their leaving care obligations by proving that young people either do not qualify for the leaving care provisions at all,[301] or by showing that their needs are more satisfactorily met by other agencies, such as the housing authority.[302] Some LAs are reluctant to accommodate 14–18-year-olds at all, for

---

[292] J. Wade and J. Dixon (2006).   [293] R. Morgan (2006c).
[294] Ibid. at p. 11: 61% indicated that they had a pathway plan; only 55% indicated that they had had quite a bit to say about what was included in the plan.
[295] See Chapter 4.   [296] R. Morgan (2006c) p. 12.
[297] Ibid. at p. 13.   [298] Ibid. at pp. 17–19.
[299] Ibid. at p. 7 and 23. DfES (2006a) para. 7.1: whilst young people in parental care normally leave home at the age of 24, 28% of young people leave care at the age of 16.
[300] R. Morgan (2006c) p. 21.
[301] Inter alia: H, Barhanu and B v. London Borough of Wandsworth and ors [2007] EWHC 1082 (Admin), [2007] 2 FLR 822, per Holman J, esp. at [55]–[60]: the LA could not simply assert that they were providing accommodation under CA 1989, s. 17, as opposed to s. 20, thereby avoiding their leaving care obligations; R (W) v. North Lincolnshire Council [2008] EWHC 2299 (Admin), [2008] 2 FLR 2150, per HHJ Mackie QC, at [39]–[41]: the LA had taken the s. 17 route when, on the facts, they were obliged to follow s. 20; cf. R (G) v. Southwark London Borough Council [2008] EWCA Civ 877, [2008] 2 FLR 1762, per Longmore and Pill LJJ (Rix LJ strongly dissenting): depending on the circumstances, a LA is entitled to conclude that some homeless young people do not require accommodation under s. 20, but can be 'helped with accommodation' under s. 17; discussed in Chapter 4.
[302] R (M) v. Hammersmith and Fulham London Borough Council [2008] UKHL 14, [2008] 1 WLR 535.

fear of bringing them into the care system, or they de-accommodate them, in order to avoid assuming leaving care obligations.[303] Others even avoid carrying out 'children in need assessments'[304] – a strategy which can be countered by the young person applying for a declaration that the assessment guidance has not been followed adequately.[305] The judiciary have been obliged to explain to LAs their legal obligations regarding pathway plans, both in relation to time-limits,[306] and the nature of the personal adviser's true role. This is to act as the child's advocate, with a duty to negotiate with the LA on behalf of the child and to ensure that the pathway plan is implemented properly, a role which would be compromised if he were also responsible for the child's assessment and preparation of the pathway plan.[307] Case law also suggests that the contents of some pathway plans are glaringly inadequate, with no explicit and detailed information about such matters as provision for the care leaver's future accommodation, education and financial support.[308]

The government has acknowledged that the leaving care legislation has not ensured that looked after children remain in stable homes until they are 18, and that large numbers are being forced into independent living at 16 and 17 long before they feel ready. A dramatic change in the nature of state care would be achieved if all the government's many promises in its Green and White Papers were implemented.[309] Depending on the success of pilots, young people may gain the right to veto any decision that they should leave care before they attain the age of 18.[310] Even the attainment of 18 seldom brings sufficient maturity to manage complete independence without support. Legislation entitling young people over 18 who have established 'familial relationships with their foster carers' to stay in their care until they attain the age of 21, would undoubtedly provide them with far greater security.[311] The promise to ensure that young people in residential homes are not moved into 'independence' placements

---

[303] Children's Commissioner (2007) p. 9.   [304] Discussed in Chapter 15.

[305] E.g. *R (LH and MH) v. London Borough of Lambeth* [2006] EWHC 1190 (Admin), [2006] 2 FLR 1275 and *R (S) v. Sutton London Borough Council* [2007] EWHC 1196 (Admin), [2007] 2 FLR 849.

[306] E.g. *R (P) v. London Borough of Newham* [2004] EWHC 2210, [2005] 2 FCR 171: declaration granted on judicial review by Ouseley J, that the LA had not complied with its statutory duties under the leaving care legislation and regulations. Despite his grandmother's requests, the LA had not assessed or produced a pathway plan for a 17-year-old severely disabled boy despite his having been in care for many years.

[307] *R (J) v. Caerphilly County Borough Council* [2005] EWHC Civ 586 (Admin), [2005] 2 FLR 860, per Munby J, at [28]–[31] and *R (G) v. Nottingham City Council and Nottingham University Hospital* [2008] EWHC 400 (Admin), [2008] FLR 1668, esp. at [35]–[39].

[308] Ibid. [2005] EWHC Civ 586 (Admin), [2005] 2 FLR 860, per Munby J, at [39]–[40] and [47]: the first pathway plan was 'little more than worthless,' the revised pathway plan was a 'perfunctory document' and the third revision was 'still hopelessly vague'.

[309] DfES (2006a) ch. 7 and DfES (2007a) ch. 6.

[310] DfES (2006a) para. 7.10 and HM Government (2008) para. 1.7.

[311] DfES (2007a) para. 6.19; HM Government (2008) para. 1.13: such arrangements are being piloted.

before they are ready and without proper planning[312] will presumably be fulfilled through regulations and guidance.

The low number of care leavers who go into further education, employment or training must partly be explained by their lack of long-term security.[313] Those over 18 who do remain in education or training will certainly benefit from the extension of the personal adviser role from the age of 21 to 25.[314] Furthermore, as discussed earlier,[315] the standardisation of the allowances to be paid to those in higher education or training[316] should provide care leavers with much greater financial security. But an obvious reason for LAs seeking to avoid their leaving care obligations is that they are financially onerous. One wonders why new legislative obligations should be adhered to more conscientiously than before when they come unaccompanied by substantial government resources.

(5) State accountability to children?

(A) The background

Hindsight is a wonderful thing. Social workers, police officers, children's guardians and even the courts would all benefit enormously from having a crystal ball when faced with taking decisions over protecting children. Often such decisions have to be reached rapidly and in harrowing circumstances. Like those of practitioners in any field of work, some are sensible and others turn out to be unwise or plain stupid, but these decisions materially affect a child's future. Children's services authorities are alone obliged by legislation to carry out section 47 investigations and to safeguard and promote the welfare of children within their area who are in need.[317] Ultimately, it is for them to decide whether or not to initiate steps to remove children from their parents and case law makes it plain that sometimes decisions are taken far too late to avert a great deal of suffering.[318]

---

[312] DfES (2007a) paras. 6.22–6.28.

[313] DfES (2006a) para. 7.4: in 2005, only 59% of care leavers (cf. 46% in 2002) were in education, employment or training, cf. 87% of all young people aged between 18 and 19.

[314] CA 1989, s. 23D(1) supported by new regulations and guidance. See also s. 23CA: care leavers under the age of 25 who later decide to return to education or training are also entitled to such assistance.

[315] See Chapter 4.   [316] CA 1989, s. 23C(5A)–(5C).

[317] I.e. under CA 1989, s. 17(1)(a). See discussed in Chapter 14.

[318] Inter alia: *X (minors) v. Bedfordshire County Council; M (a minor) and anor v. Newham London Borough Council and ors; E (a minor) v. Dorset County Council; Christmas v. Hampshire County Council; Keating v. Bromley London Borough Council (X v. Bedfordshire County Council)* [1995] 2 AC 633: although fully aware of the appalling abuse and neglect they were suffering, Bedfordshire CC failed for five years to intervene to protect five children from further harm at the hands of their parents; *Re E (care proceedings: social work practice)* [2000] 2 FLR 254: ineffectual social work intervention spanned 20 years during which four children were emotionally, physically and sexually abused; *Re F; F v. Lambeth London Borough Council* [2002] 1 FLR 217 – see fn 10. See also *S (by the Official Solicitor) v. Rochdale MBC and Anor* [2008] EWHC 3283(Fam), unreported, at [17]–[22]: unproved allegations made by the OS that the LA had infringed S's rights under Arts. 3 and 8 of the ECHR by failing to initiate care proceedings.

(B) Children suing local authorities

By the time the ECtHR reviewed the legal principles[319] established by the House of Lords in *X v. Bedfordshire County Council*,[320] the legal landscape had changed fundamentally, principally because the HRA 1998 had been implemented. Nevertheless, for a time, the *Bedfordshire* decision indicated that children could not call LAs to account for failing to protect them when they should have done, or for intervening unnecessarily and without sufficient care.[321] Their Lordships had decided that a LA's failure to intervene to protect a child was not a justiciable matter, since it was not just and reasonable for the common law to impose a duty of care in such circumstances. Consequently, authorities could not be sued in negligence by any children they failed to protect, nor could they be sued for breach of their statutory duties. Indeed, the decision gave the unfortunate impression that the whole child protection process had become largely unaccountable.

This gap in LA accountability was eventually partly filled by the combined effect of Strasbourg case law[322] and the HRA 1998, the latter providing domestic remedies for infringements of children's human rights.[323] By then, however, the ambit of the *Bedfordshire* decision had been narrowed in only slightly different contexts, with Lord Browne-Wilkinson's reasons for rejecting common law liability receiving relatively short shrift. He had referred, amongst other things, to the multidisciplinary nature of child protection work, to its extremely sensitive nature and to the need to avert over-defensive social work practice.[324] But LAs looking after children *already* in care were later held unable to escape tortious liability, despite this area of work being only slightly less sensitive than the situation where the LA is considering whether to intervene at all.[325] Furthermore in an educational context, the multidisciplinary nature of some educational practice did not exclude public liability, since it was considered perfectly possible to 'disentangle the relevant parts played by particular individuals and identify where the alleged negligence occurred'.[326] Nor would the imposition of liability inspire a defensive attitude on the part of teachers and

---

[319] *TP and KM v. United Kingdom* [2001] 2 FLR 549 and *Z and others v. United Kingdom* [2001] 2 FLR 612. These applications were made to the ECtHR by the Official Solicitor, on behalf of the children involved in the *Bedfordshire* case, ibid..

[320] [1995] 2 AC 633.

[321] In the *Newham* case, the LA's inaccurate identification of the child's sexual abuser as her mother's boyfriend led to their removing the child unnecessarily from home for almost a year.

[322] Inter alia: *TP and KM v. United Kingdom* [2001] 2 FLR 549, *Z and others v. United Kingdom* [2001] 2 FLR 612 and *Venema v. Netherlands* [2003] 1 FLR 552.

[323] I.e. under the HRA 1998, ss. 7 and 8.

[324] [1995] 2 AC 633, per Lord Browne-Wilkinson, at 749–51.

[325] *Barrett v. Enfield London Borough Council* [1999] 3 All ER 193, per Lord Slynn, at 208.

[326] *Phelps v. Hillingdon London Borough Council, Anderton v. Clwyd County Council, Jarvis v. Hampshire County Council, Re G (a minor)* [2000] 4 All ER 504, per Lord Clyde, at 537 (discussed further in Chapter 12).

other educationalists. 'On the contrary it may have the healthy effect of securing that high standards are sought and secured.'[327]

The ECtHR in *Z v. United Kingdom*[328] dealt the *Bedfordshire* decision a final body blow. This was essential because the principle it had established had remained in being, albeit in a restricted form. The fact that children could sue LAs for allowing them to be mistreated once in LA care,[329] but not for failing to protect them in the first place was illogical and unfair. The ECtHR was in no doubt that the neglect and abuse suffered by the children in the *Bedfordshire* case amounted to an infringement of their rights under Article 3.[330] It stressed that state agencies are under a positive obligation to take measures to ensure that children do not suffer abuse of such a severity that it infringes their rights under Article 3 or, indeed, under Article 2.[331] If they fail to do so, as occurred here, the children must be provided with an effective remedy. Because the domestic law of tort excluded liability, the inability of the children to obtain redress against the LA, in the form of an award of compensation, constituted a breach of their right to an effective remedy under Article 13 of the ECHR.

By the time *Z v. United Kingdom* was decided, the introduction of the HRA 1998 had already fulfilled the government's obligation to establish an effective remedy for children involved in abusive situations occurring after its implementation in 2000.[332] It was by then plain that if the suffering was sufficiently serious, a claim could be brought on behalf of a child under the HRA 1998, claiming breach of Article 3.[333] It should, however, be noted that children are not confined to bringing claims under the HRA 1998; rather that the common law has incorporated the requirements set out in *Z v. United Kingdom*, thereby extending the principles of tort law far beyond those delineated by the *Bedfordshire* decision. Thus, whilst rejecting the argument that a duty of care is owed to parents by those involved in protecting children from abusive behaviour, the House of Lords has emphasised that they do owe a duty of care to children.[334] Having reviewed the authorities, Lord Bingham explained 'it could not now be plausibly argued that a common law duty of care may not be owed by a publicly-employed healthcare professional to a child with whom the professional is dealing'.[335] It seems clear that children are owed a duty of care by all those involved in child protection work, be they doctors, social

---

[327] Ibid. at 535.   [328] [2001] 2 FLR 612.

[329] E.g. *Barrett v. Enfield London Borough Council* [1999] 3 All ER 193 and *C v. Flintshire County Council* [2001] EWCA Civ 302, [2001] 2 FLR 33.

[330] This was conceded by the UK government.   [331] *Osman v. United Kingdom* [1999] 1 FLR 193.

[332] But children abused prior to that time could not use the HRA 1998 to gain a remedy, they were therefore forced to take their challenges to Strasbourg. E.g. *E and Others v. United Kingdom* [2003] 1 FLR 348.

[333] R. Cornwath (2001) p. 476.

[334] *D v. East Berkshire Community Health NHS Trust and Ors* [2005] 2 AC 373. See also *Lawrence v. Pembrokeshire County Council* [2007] EWCA Civ 446, [2007] 2 FLR 705, per Auld LJ, at [27].

[335] [2005] 2 AC 373, at [30] and [37]. See also Lord Nicholls of Birkenhead, at [82] and [85].

workers, the police, community health workers or those in the education service.[336] Furthermore, under the principles of vicarious liability, employers of an abusive care worker may not escape liability by simply arguing that their employee acted in an unauthorised manner when abusing the child in question. Thus an action can be brought on behalf of a child, as long as there was a sufficient connection between the abusive behaviour and the work the employee was employed to do.[337]

(C) Calling local authorities to account for failing to implement care plans

As the discussion above shows, under the combined impact of the ECtHR and the HRA 1998, the principle established by the *Bedfordshire* decision was finally rejected. It had given the impression that the child protection process was a largely unaccountable one; indeed that children who suffered in the process should not be allowed to sue their LAs because they were undertaking sensitive work as best they could. Such an approach was controversial in itself. When combined with a system which prevents the courts, or any other outside body, from monitoring the way LAs care for children it became even more questionable. The litigation in the *Bedfordshire* case started soon after the implementation of the CA 1989.[338] One wonders whether, had that decision reached the House of Lords before 1989, the draftsmen of the new legislation would have promoted such a strict separation of power between the LAs and the courts. It was their deliberate intention to ensure that LAs should not be accountable to the courts for decisions over the manner they choose to protect children. It is a controversial aspect of the statutory scheme that the courts have very little scope to prompt LA intervention, or to override or circumscribe the exercise by LAs of their statutory powers.[339] The courts are not only barred from using the inherent jurisdiction to order a child into the care of the LA,[340] but they have no supervisory powers, similar to those formerly exercised by the courts prior to the CA, over children taken into care under the wardship jurisdiction.

It must be acknowledged that the CA 1989 is not entirely consistent in its attempts to ensure that the courts, when dealing with LA applications for orders

---

[336] E.g. *Pierce v. Doncaster Metropolitan Borough Council* [2008] EWCA Civ 1416 [2008] All ER (D) 136: the Court of Appeal confirmed the decision of the court below that the claimant, now adult, had successfully proved the LA's negligence when they returned him to his mother's abusive care without proper assessment and left him with her without adequate monitoring. The LA's appeal succeeded in part, based on a limitation issue.

[337] *Lister and ors v. Hesley Hall Ltd* [2001] UKHL 22, [2002] 2 AC 215: claimants successfully sued the employers of a warden of a boarding school for children with emotional and behavioural difficulties. Per House of Lords: the warden's sexual abuse of his victims had been so closely connected with his employment as warden, that it was fair and just that his employers should be held vicariously liable for his torts.

[338] The applications were made in 1993.

[339] Applying the principle established in *A v. Liverpool City Council* [1982] AC 363.

[340] CA 1989, s. 100(1) and (2).

to protect children from harm, must always adopt what Dewar described as an 'adjudicative' role rather than a 'participative' one.[341] In particular, case law established the courts' entitlement under section 34 of the CA 1989 to force the LA to reassess the extent of contact it allows a parent to have with a child in care.[342] They also, under section 38(6), have the power to direct a LA to arrange for the child and family to undergo a residential assessment, despite the LA's strong opposition to such a course of action.[343] Furthermore, the courts can force the LA's hand, but only to a very limited extent, by making a section 37 direction,[344] together with an interim care or supervision order, pending the outcome of the LA's investigation.[345] Nonetheless, the decision in *Nottinghamshire County Council v. P*[346] demonstrated only too clearly the toothlessness of this power. At both levels, the courts made clear their intense frustration with the LA for merely complying with a section 37 direction to investigate the case, but then refusing to apply for a care order to protect two sexually abused girls from their father.[347]

These exceptions apart, the statutory regime devised by the CA 1989[348] ensures that LAs are free to decide whether to intervene and, if so, to choose the type of protection and care to offer the children they are willing to protect. In other words, the policy aspects of child protection are entirely within the LA's purview, adhering to the view that they are better placed to ascertain how and when to protect children than are the courts. Furthermore, 'Courts neither have the resources nor the expertise to act as substitute parents for children'.[349] Within a short time of the implementation of the CA 1989, the courts conscientiously emphasised the fact that with their former powers in wardship now removed, they had no ability to maintain control over children after making a care order.[350] Nevertheless, a sense of unease had been created by the courts' inability either to persuade LAs to intervene in the first place, or to control how LAs exercised their parental responsibilities over the children, once ordered into their care. A legislative scheme of this nature, with a clear division of powers, can only work well if the courts are satisfied that LAs can invariably improve a child's life. But it radically undermines the courts' ability to satisfy the no order principle[351] if they cannot be confident either that the details of the

---

[341] J. Dewar (1995) p. 16.

[342] *Re B (minors)(termination of contact: paramount consideration)* [1993] 3 All ER 524: the courts can make a contact order regarding a child in care, despite the fact that the order will interfere with the long-term plans of the LA .

[343] *Re C (a minor)(interim care order: residential assessment)* [1996] 4 All ER 871.

[344] CA 1989, s. 37(1).   [345] CA 1989, s. 38(1)(a).

[346] [1994] Fam 18.   [347] Ibid., per Sir Simon Brown P, at 43.

[348] But this approach to such a strict separation of powers pre-dated the CA 1989, being established by the House of Lords in *A v. Liverpool City Council* [1982] AC 363.

[349] B. Hale and J. Fortin (2008) p. 101.

[350] Inter alia: *Re T (a minor) (care order: conditions)* [1994] 2 FLR 423: the courts have no power to impose conditions in a care order; *Re J (minors) (care: care plan)* [1994] 1 FLR 253: interim care orders should not be used to resurrect the supervisory role enjoyed by the wardship court.

[351] I.e. CA 1989, s. 1(5).

care plan will remain substantially unchanged or that they will be fully complied with. It can also be a source of frustration to healthcare professionals if their recommendations for treatment are not adopted by the LA looking after the child.[352]

The absence of any system for calling LAs to account for failing to comply with care plans was causing judicial concern[353] well before *Re S (minors) (care order: implementation of care plan), Re W (minors) (care order: adequacy of care plan)* (hereafter *Re S and Re W*)[354] reached the House of Lords in 2001. In the years immediately preceding that decision, those involved in the family justice system were familiar with the depressing litany of LA inadequacies which continue to the present day. Then, their greatest frustration was an inability either to monitor what happened to children under care orders, or to ensure that LA care plans were complied with.[355] Not only were the care plans of low quality, with a lack of appropriate detail,[356] but, more seriously, there was an apparent inability to deliver the services set out in the plans themselves.[357] Children were understandably upset and bewildered both by the courts' inability to influence placements[358] and by planned placements not materialising and promised contact with relatives not being arranged.[359] Furthermore, compliance with the statutory review process, under which care plans should be regularly reviewed,[360] was patchy in the extreme.[361]

As the judiciary themselves fully appreciate,[362] there may be any number of reasons for LAs failing to comply with care plans, including the difficulty of complying with a child's very complex needs, and a lack of resources, particularly the availability of suitable long-term placements.[363] Nevertheless, children suffer greatly when LAs fail to make proper provision for their care. Indeed, to remove a child from his or her home in the first place constitutes a breach of the child's own rights to family life which must be very carefully justified. The Court of Appeal, when hearing *Re S and Re W*,[364] considered that

---

[352] E.g. *Re O (care: discharge of care order)* [1999] 2 FLR 119.

[353] Wall J (1998) esp. p. 8. See also *Re W and B; Re W (care plan)* [2001] EWCA Civ 757, [2001] 2 FLR 582, per Thorpe LJ, at paras. 18–21.

[354] [2002] UKHL 10, [2002] AC 291.   [355] J. Hunt and A. Macleod (1999) ch. 9.

[356] E.g. in *Re S and Re W* [2002] UKHL 10, [2002] AC 291, the trial judge described the care plan relating to the second child as being 'inchoate'.

[357] E.g. *Re S and Re W* ibid. and *Re F; F v. Lambeth London Borough Council* [2002] 1 FLR 217.

[358] M. Ruegger (2001) p. 143.

[359] J. Hunt and A. Macleod (1999), chs. 7–9 and J. Masson and M. Winn Oakley (1999) ch. 8.

[360] Under CA 1989, s. 26(1) and (2) and the Review of Children's Cases Regulations 1991 (SI 1991/895).

[361] SSI (2002) para. 6.8: 'most councils' failed to convene statutory child care reviews within statutory timescales, three councils only met timescales in 50% of cases, and in one of these there were 'weaknesses in completing the tasks laid out in the care plan'.

[362] *Re W and B; Re W (care plan)* [2001] EWCA Civ 757, [2001] 2 FLR 582 (CA), per Hale LJ, at para. 60.

[363] J. Hunt and A. Macleod (1999) pp. 229–36 and J. Harwin and M. Owen (2002) p. 71.

[364] [2001] EWCA Civ 757, [2001] 2 FLR 582, reported sub nom *Re W and B; Re W (care plan)*.

the courts should not simply overlook a LA's failure then to fulfil a child's care plan. Further such failure might constitute a breach of the LA's positive obligations under Article 8 of the ECHR to fulfil the child's rights thereunder, by providing him or her with a substitute family, or by reuniting him or her with their birth parents.[365] But the problem confronting the judiciary was the absence of any formal mechanism for bringing care cases back to court – more to the point, there was no systematic procedure available for calling LAs to account for failing to comply with the care plans upon which the courts had relied when making the original care orders.

Theoretically, when care plans are radically changed or left unfulfilled, the parents can apply for a discharge of the care order itself.[366] Although the existence of such a remedy impressed the ECtHR,[367] in practice it is more apparent than real. Few parents make discharge applications, presumably because they have little faith that the courts will consider them fit to have their children returned to them.[368] In some cases, the courts may discover the LA's failure to comply with a care plan only when, as in *Re F; F v. Lambeth Borough Council*,[369] the parents apply for increased contact,[370] thereby providing the courts with an opportunity to review what has occurred since the initial care orders were made. But parents with a history of involvement with social workers may be reluctant to take such a step. Furthermore, although older children may use the complaints system[371] or, with the help of advocacy services, take their own case back to court,[372] as Thorpe LJ pointed out in *Re S and Re W*, 'the children who are most vulnerable to breakdown and delay are the very young whose healthy future development may depend on forming a sound psychological attachment in time'.[373]

The House of Lords, perhaps predictably, rejected the Court of Appeal's radical solution to these problems. This had been simply to read into the CA 1989 a means of supervising the implementation of the fundamental elements of care plans in selected cases.[374] But, as Lord Nicholls of Birkenhead pointed out, reinterpreting the CA 1989 in a way which undermined one of its cardinal

---

[365] Ibid., see especially Hale LJ, at [52]–[59]. See also B. Hale and J. Fortin (2008) p. 102.

[366] Under CA 1989, s. 39.

[367] *Scott v. United Kingdom* [2000] 1 FLR 958: the ECtHR considered that the availability of a discharge application negated the mother's argument that when a LA abandoned the care plan to reunite the child with her, and placed the child for adoption, it had infringed the mother's rights under Art. 8, leaving her without an effective remedy.

[368] J. Hunt and A. Macleod (1999) p. 197.   [369] [2002] 1 FLR 217.

[370] Under CA 1989, s. 34(3).   [371] Discussed above.

[372] E.g. by applying for a discharge of the care order under CA 1989, s. 39 or for increased contact with their parents under s. 34(3).

[373] [2001] EWCA Civ 757, [2001] 2 FLR 582, reported sub nom *Re W and B; Re W (care plan)* at [24].

[374] These elements were to be 'starred', with an obligation imposed on the LA to report to the court or to the children's guardian on failure to implement any of them, thereby triggering an application by the children's guardian to apply for a discharge of the care order.

principles – the separation of powers between the courts and LAs – went far beyond the scope of the HRA 1998, section 3.[375] Nevertheless, their Lordships made plain their agreement with the Court of Appeal that a system which allowed LAs to fail children with impunity was quite unsatisfactory and required official review.[376]

The government's legislative response to this judicial criticism was twofold. First, LAs were now statutorily obliged to present to courts considering care applications, detailed and properly revised care plans, renamed 'section 31A plans'.[377] Second, the government recognised that the existing system involving team managers chairing their own social workers' looked after children reviews was unlikely to produce a particularly critical approach to LA plans. It instead put in place a new system whereunder the care plans of all children received into care should be rigorously reviewed by LA employees in the role of IROs.[378] Regrettably, neither of these legislative responses achieved the desired result. As noted above, the statutory obligation to produce a detailed section 31A plan alongside a care application has not greatly improved care planning over recent years. The IRO scheme also proved to be of little value. IROs are required to chair statutory reviews for children in care and detect those cases where a child's care plan is not being adequately implemented, in which case they should notify the Children and Family Court Advisory and Support Service (Cafcass). A children's guardian should then be appointed in order to apply, on the child's behalf, for some further court order, such as a discharge of the care order, or even to institute litigation against the LA.

The guidance stresses the importance of the IRO's role:

> From his/her position as the genuinely independent chair of the [review] meeting, the IRO will be well placed to identify any concerns about how a child's care is being managed … The IRO will have a key role in ensuring that the child's views are heard.[379]

As the words above make clear, the guidance suggests that IROs are independent from the LA.[380] Nevertheless, it was clear from the scheme's inception that its major weakness lay in the fact that IROs were to be drawn from the LA's own employees.[381] Sceptics doubted that they would readily identify areas of poor practice amongst their own colleagues.[382]

The IRO scheme was not established until September 2004; it was obviously unrealistic to expect these officers to produce an immediate sea change in the

---

[375] *Re S and Re W* [2002] UKHL 10, [2002] AC 291, at [34]–[44]; discussed by B. Hale and J. Fortin (2008) p. 102.

[376] Ibid., per Lord Nicholls, at [29]–[30] and [106] and Lord Mackay, at [110].

[377] CA 1989, s. 31A strengthening and clarifying the duties previously set out in DH (1999b).

[378] CA 1989, s. 26, as extensively amended by ACA 2002, s. 118. See also DfES (2004) and the Review of Children's Cases (Amendment) (England) Regulations 2004 (SI 2004/ 1419).

[379] DfES (2004) pp. 14 and 22.   [380] Ibid. at ch. 3.

[381] See Review of Children's Cases Regulations 1991 (SI 1991/ 895), reg. 2A.

[382] J. Fortin (2003) p. 513.

way that looked after children were dealt with. Nevertheless, from the start their extreme passivity proved disappointing.[383] The government itself referred to the 'widespread concern that the IRO role is not being carried out effectively across all local authorities' and more specifically to their failure to challenge LAs' decisions 'even in cases where professional practice is obviously poor and not in young people's interests'.[384] Statutory reviews were still being run without a challenging analysis of the proposals and with insufficient weight being given to the views of young people or their families – without a rigorous examination of care plans, their review 'becomes merely a sterile "box-ticking exercise"'.[385] Perhaps of greatest concern was IROs' general failure to use their power to refer cases to Cafcass, so that legal proceedings could be brought to achieve a remedy.[386] The guidance had suggested that this should be done if all other methods of resolving an identified problem had proved unsuccessful[387] and where there was danger of the child's human rights being breached.[388] By 2008, this power had never been used.[389]

The government clearly considered that there was little excuse for IROs not fulfilling their work with 'credibility and independence'.[390] An IRO must be appointed for every child prior to any statutory review,[391] with his duties being legislatively defined.[392] The new legislation strengthens the IRO's role, obliging him to monitor the LA's performance in relation to the child, rather than merely being confined to supervising reviews.[393] Referral of a child's case by the IRO to Cafcass is no longer to be seen as a last resort but a step to be taken if the IRO 'considers it appropriate to do so'.[394] The government means business. Built in to the legislation is a fail-safe mechanism, with the Secretary of State acquiring the power to establish an independent national IRO service,[395] if 'there are no significant improvements' to the existing scheme,[396] staffed as it is by LA employees.

As the discussion above makes plain, the judicial concerns which led the Court of Appeal to produce its radical solution in *Re S and Re W*, have, to date, produced little real change. Children whose experiences in care have produced grave physical and/or psychological damage, may now be able to sue LAs in negligence for their failings. But financial compensation comes after the event,

---

[383] See *S (by the Official Solicitor) v. Rochdale MBC and Anor* [2008] EWHC 3283(Fam), unreported, at [27]: the OS's allegations (unproved) regarding the IRO's failure to ensure that review meetings were properly conducted or followed up. See also Appendix A [95], describing the IRO as 'largely impotent or supine'.

[384] DfES (2007a) para. 7.29.   [385] Ibid.   [386] M. Hinchliffe (2007) p. 749.

[387] DfES (2004) p. 30. Suggested 'other methods of resolution' involve negotiation, first with the team responsible for the child and then with senior management.

[388] Ibid. at p. 32.

[389] *S (by the Official Solicitor) v. Rochdale MBC and Anor* [2008] EWHC 3283(Fam), unreported, at [96].

[390] DfES (2007a) para. 7.32.   [391] CA 1989, s. 25A.   [392] CA 1989, 25A-25C.

[393] CA 1989, s. 25B(1)(a); to be followed by regulations and guidance.

[394] DfES (2007a) para. 7.33 and CA 1989, s. 25B(3).

[395] CYPA 2008, ss. 12–13.   [396] HM Government (2008) para. 1.30.

far too late to assuage the child's suffering. Admittedly litigation may gradually provoke improvements in social work practice. Until very effective mechanisms are in place to supervise the manner in which LAs implement the care plans they agree to, the lives of at least some of the children who are 'rescued' from parental abuse will continue to be damaged even further by their experiences in state care.

(6) Conclusion

Child protection work is undoubtedly delicate and difficult, but if LAs set themselves up as being able to carry out the parenting role better than children's own parents, the children have a right to a professional service. It is clear that this is not always delivered. Many of the children coming into state care are already emotionally disturbed and extremely vulnerable. Even making allowances for this, the experience of being looked after by the state is not always a particularly beneficial one. Considerable efforts are now being made to improve the state's record regarding the children it removes from abusive birth parents. The law is largely supportive, although the courts' role is a difficult one, particularly when dealing with children who cannot return home. The assumption that adoption is always to be preferred over other options overlooks the advantages to children of their retaining their links with their birth families. Meanwhile there will always be children and young people for whom adoption or foster care is unsuitable; for them well-regulated residential care should not seen as a remedy of last resort. Finally, children have a right to hold LAs to account for their omissions and the law must provide ways in which that they are able to do so without undue delay or difficulty.

BIBLIOGRAPHY

NB many of these publications can be obtained on the relevant organisation's website.

AIRE Centre (2001) *Secure Accommodation Orders, Police Protection 'Orders', Curfews from the Convention Perspective*, AIRE Centre Family Law and European Convention on Human Rights Website Materials.

Bainham, A. (2003) 'Contact as a Right and Obligation' in Bainham, A., Lindley, B., Richards, A. and Trinder, L. (eds.) *Children and Their Families: Contact, Rights and Welfare*, Hart Publishing.

Bates, P. (1995) 'Secure Accommodation Orders – in Whose Interests?' 7(2) *Child and Family Law Quarterly* 70.

Berridge, D. and Brodie, I. (1998) *Children's Home Revisited*, Jessica Kingsley.

Biehal, N. (2006) *Reuniting Looked After Children with Their Parents: a Review of the Research*, NCB.

Bond, A. (2007) 'Special Guardianship after *Re S, Re AJ* and *Re M-J*' 37 *Family Law* 321.

Brandon, M. *et al.* (1999) *Safeguarding Children with the Children Act 1989*, The Stationery Office.

Brandon, M., Thoburn, J., Rose, S. and Belderson, P. (2005) *Living with Significant Harm: a Follow Up Study*, NSPCC.

Brophy, J. (2006) *Research Review: Child Care Proceedings under the Children Act 1989*, DCA.

Children's Commissioner (2007) *Care Matters: Transforming the Lives of Children and Young People in Care: A Response by the Children's Commissioner*, Office of the Children's Commissioner.

Choudhry, S. (2003) 'The Adoption and Children Act 2002, the Welfare Principle and the Human Rights Act 1998 – a Missed Opportunity?' 15 *Child and Family Law Quarterly* 119.

Commission for Local Administration in England (2006) *Casebook: Children and Young People*, LGO.

Commission for Social Care Inspection (CSCI), Department of Health (DH) (2005) *Safeguarding Children: The second joint Chief Inspectors' Report on Arrangements to Safeguard Children*, CSCI.

Commission for Social Care Inspection (CSCI) (2006a) *Adoption: Messages from Inspections of Adoption Agencies*, CSCI.

Commission for Social Care Inspection (CSCI) (2006b) *The State of Social Care in England 2005–6*, CSCI.

Commission for Social Care Inspection (CSCI) (2006c) *The Right People for Me: Helping Children do Well in Long-term Foster Care*, CSCI.

Commission for Social Care Inspection (CSCI) (2008) *The State of Social Care in England 2006–07*, CSCI.

Cornwath, R. (2001) 'Welfare Services – Liabilities in Tort after the HRA – Postscript' *Public Law* 475.

Department for Children, Schools and Families (DCSF) (2008a) SFR 08/ 2008 *Outcome Indicators for Children Looked After: Twelve Months to 30 September 2007, England*, DCSF.

Department for Children, Schools and Families (DCSF) (2008b) *Personal Education Allowances for Looked After Children: Statutory Guidance for Local Authorities*, DCSF.

Department for Children, Schools and Families (2008c) (DCSF) *The Children Act 1989 Guidance and Regulations, Volume I, Court Orders*, The Stationery Office.

Department for Children, Schools and Families (DCSF) (2009) *School Admissions Code*, The Stationery Office.

Department for Constitutional Affairs (DCA) (2006) *Review of the Child Care Proceedings System in England and Wales*, DCA.

Department for Education and Skills (DfES) (2004) *Independent Reviewing Officers Guidance*, DfES.

Department for Education and Skills (DfES) (2005) *Adoption Guidance: Adoption and Children Act 2002*, DfES.

Department for Education and Skills (DfES) (2006a) Cm 6932 *Care Matters: Transforming the Lives of Children and Young People in Care*, The Stationery Office.

Department for Education and Skills (DfES) (2006b) *Getting the Best from Complaints: Social Care Complaints and Representations for Children, Young People and Others*, DfES.

Department for Education and Skills (DfES) (2007a) Cm 7137 *Care Matters: Time for Change*, The Stationery Office.

Department for Education and Skills (DfES) (2007b) *The Consolidated 3rd and 4th Periodic Report to UN Committee on the Rights of the Child*, DfES.

Department of Health (DH) (1991a) *The Children Act 1989 Guidance and Regulations Vol 4 Residential Care*, HMSO.

Department of Health (DH) (1991b) *The Children Act 1989 Guidance and Regulations Vol 1 Court Orders*, HMSO.

Department of Health (DH) (1996) *Focus on Teenagers: Research into Practice*, HMSO.

Department of Health (DH) (1998a) *Caring for Children Away from Home: Messages from Research*, Wiley.

Department of Health (DH) (1998b) Cm 4175 *Children Looked After by Local Authorities: Government Response to the Second Report of the Health Committee on Children Looked After by Local Authorities: Session 1997–98*, The Stationery Office.

Department of Health (DH) (1999) *Me Survive Out There? New Arrangements for Young People Living in and Leaving Care*, DH.

Department of Health (DH) (2000) White Paper, Cm 5017 *Adoption: a New Approach*, The Stationery Office.

Department of Health (DH) (2001) *Children (Leaving Care) Act Guidance*, DH.

Department of Health (DH) (2002a) *Children's Homes, National Minimum Standards, Children's Homes Regulations*, The Stationery Office.

Department of Health (DH) (2002b) *Children Missing from Care and from Home: a Guide to Good Practice*, Department of Health.

Department of Health (DH) (2003) *Adoption: National Minimum Standards*, The Stationery Office.

Department of Health (DH), Department for Education and Employment (DEE) and Home Office (HO) (2000) *Framework for the Assessment of Children in Need and their Families*, The Stationery Office.

Dewar, J. (1995) 'The Courts and Local Authority Autonomy' 7(2) *Child and Family Law Quarterly* 15.

Eekelaar, J. (2003) 'Contact and the Adoption Reform' in Bainham, A., Lindley, B., Richards, A. and Trinder, L. (eds.) *Children and Their Families: Contact, Rights and Welfare*, Hart Publishing.

Ellaway, B. *et al.* (2004) 'Are Abused Babies Protected from Further Abuse?' 89 *Archive of Diseases of Childhood* 845.

Farmer, E. and Pollock, S. (1998) *Sexually Abused and Abusing Children in Substitute Care*, Wiley.

(1999) 'Mix and Match: Planning to Keep Looked After Children Safe' 8 *Child Abuse Review* 377.

Fortin, J. (2001) 'Children's Rights and the Use of Physical Force' 13 *Child and Family Law Quarterly* 243.

(2003) *Children's Rights and the Developing Law*, LexisNexis Butterworths.

Gallagher, B. (1999) 'The Abuse of Children in Public Care' 8 *Child Abuse Review* 357.

Gearty, L. (2001) 'Unravelling Osman' 64 *Modern Law Review* 159.

Goldstein, J., Freud, A. and Solnit, A. (1980) *Before the Best Interests of the Child*, Burnett Books Limited.

Graham, M. (2006) 'Secure Care: a Positive Option for Distressed and Damaged Young People' 222 *Childright* 11.

HM Government (2008) *Care Matters: Time to Deliver for Children in Care, an Implementation Plan*, DCSF.

Hale, B. (2000) 'In Defence of the Children Act' 83 *Archives of Diseases in Childhood* 463.

Hale, B. and Fortin, J. (2008) 'Legal Issues in the Care and Treatment of Children with Mental Health Problems' in Rutter, M., Bishop, D., Pine, D., Scott, S., Stevenson, J., Taylor, E. and Thapar, A. (eds.) *Rutter's Child and Adolescent Psychiatry*, Blackwell Publishing.

Hall, A. (2008a) 'Special Guardianship and Permanency Planning: Unforeseen Consequences and Missed Opportunities' 20 *Child and Family Law Quarterly* 359.

    (2008b) 'Special Guardianship – Themes Emerging from Case-Law' 38 *Family Law* 244.

Harris-Short, S. (2002) '*Re B (Adoption: Natural Parent)* Putting the Child at the Heart of Adoption?' 14 *Child and Family Law Quarterly* 325.

    (2008) 'Making and Breaking Family Life: Adoption, the State and Human Rights' *Journal of Law and Society* 28.

Harwin, J. and Owen, M. (2002) 'A Study of Care Plans and their Implementation and Relevance for *Re W and B and Re W (care plan)*' in Thorpe LJ and Cowton, C. (eds.) *Delight and Dole: The Children Act 10 Years On*, Family Law.

Held, J. Consulting Ltd. (2006) *Qualitative Study: The Use by Local Authorities of Secure Children's Homes*, Research Report RR 749, DfES.

Hinchliffe, M. (2007) 'CAFCASS and the Work of Independent Reviewing Officers' 37 *Family Law* 748.

Hindley, N., Rachmandani, P. and Jones, D. (2006) 'Risk Factors for Recurrence of Maltreatment: a Systematic Review' 91 *Archives of Disease in Childhood* 744.

Hoffmann, R.H.L. (1999) 'Human Rights and the House of Lords' 62 *Modern Law Review* 159.

Hughes, W. (Chairman) (1985) *Report of the Committee of Inquiry into Children's Homes and Hostels*, HMSO.

Hunt, J. (1998) 'A Moving Target – Care Proceedings as a Dynamic Process' 10 *Child and Family Law Quarterly* 281.

Hunt, J. and Macleod, A. (1999) *The Best-Laid Plans: Outcomes of Judicial Decisions in Child Protection Proceedings*, The Stationery Office.

Jones, D. (2006) 'Assessments: a Child Mental Health Perspective' 36 *Family Law* 471.

Levy, A. and Kahan, B. (Chairmen) (1991) *The Pindown Experience and the Protection of Children*, The Report of the Staffordshire Child Care Inquiry, 1990, Staffordshire County Council.

Lewis, J. (2004) 'Adoption: The Nature of Policy Shifts in England and Wales, 1972–2002' 18 *International Journal of Law, Policy and the Family* 235.

Lowe, N. and Murch, M. (2002) *The Plan for the Child: Adoption or Long-Term Fostering*, BAAF.

Masson, J. (2002) '*Re K (A Child) (Secure Accommodation Order: Right to Liberty)* and *Re C (Secure Accommodation Order: Representation)*' 14 *Child and Family Law Quarterly* 77.

    (2005) 'Emergency Intervention to Protect Children: Using and Avoiding Legal Controls' 17 *Child and Family Law Quarterly* 75.

Masson, J. and Winn Oakley, M. (1999) *Out of Hearing: Representing Children in Care Proceedings*, Wiley.

Masson, J., Pearce, J. and Bader, K. with Joyner, O., Marsden, J. and Westlake, D. (2008) Ministry of Justice Research Series 4/ 08, *Care Profiling Study*, Ministry of Justice.

Ministry of Justice (MOJ) (2008) Cm 7501, *The Government's Response to the Report by Peter Smallridge and Andrew Williamson of a Review of the Use of Restraint in Juvenile Secure Settings*, The Stationery Office.

Morgan, R. (2004) *Children's Views on Restraint: The Views of Children and Young People in Residential Homes and Residential Special Schools*, CSCI.

　(2005a) *Children's Rights Report, Part Two, How Services are Doing for Children*, CSCI.

　(2005b) *'Getting the Best from Complaints': the Children's View*, CSCI.

　(2006a) *Placements, Decisions and Reviews: A Children's Views Report*, CSCI.

　(2006b) *About Social Workers A Children's Views Report*, CSCI.

　(2006c) *Young People's Views on Leaving Care*, CSCI.

Munby, J. (2006) 'Special Guardianship: A Judicial Perspective' in Jordan, L. and Lindley, B. (eds.) *Special Guardianship: What Does it Offer Children Who Cannot Live With Their Parents?* Family Rights Group.

Narey, M. (Chairman) (2007) *Beyond Care Matters: Future of the Care Population*, Working Group Report, DfES.

National Children's Bureau (1995) *Safe to be Let Out?: The Current and Future Use of Secure Accommodation for Children and Young People*, National Children's Bureau.

O'Neill, T. (2001) *Children in Secure Accommodation: A Gendered Exploration of Locked Institutional Care for Children in Trouble*, Jessica Kingsley Publishers.

Ofsted (2008) *Safeguarding Children, the Third Joint Chief Inspectors' Report on Arrangements to Safeguard Children*, Ofsted.

Pack, A. (2001) '"Sweet and Tender Hooligans" – Secure Accommodation and Human Rights' *Family Law* 140.

Parry, M. (2000) 'Secure Accommodation – the Cinderella of Family Law' 12 *Child and Family Law Quarterly* 101.

Performance and Innovation Unit (PIU) (2000) *The Prime Minister's Review of Adoption*, Cabinet Office.

Pithouse, A. and Crowley, A. (2007) 'Adults Rule? Children, Advocacy and Complaints to Social Services' 21 *Children and Society* 201.

Quinton, D. (2006) 'Adoption: Research, Policy and Practice' 18 *Child and Family Law Quarterly* 459.

Ruegger, M. (2001) 'Seen and Heard but How Well Informed? Children's Perceptions of the Guardian Ad Litem Service' 15 *Children and Society* 133.

Ryder, E. (2000) '"Lost and Found" – Looking to the Future After North Wales' *Family Law* 406.

Secure Accommodation Network (SAN) (2005) *The Use of Restrictive Physical Interventions (RPI) in Secure Children's Homes (England and Wales)*, SAN.

Sergeant, H. (2006), *Handle with Care: an Investigation into the Care System*, Centre for Young Policy Studies.

Sinclair, I., Baker, C., Lee, J. and Gibbs, I. (2007) *The Pursuit of Permanence: A Study of the English Child Care System*, Jessica Kingsley Publishers.

Smallridge, P. and Williamson, A. (2008) *Independent Review of Restraint in Juvenile Secure Settings*, MOJ.

Simmonds, C. 'Secure Accommodation: Out of Sight, Out of Mind?' 38 *Family Law* 1033.

Social Exclusion Unit (SEU) (2003) *A Better Education for Children in Care*, SEU.

Social Services Inspectorate (SSI) (1997) '*... When leaving home is also leaving care*', DH Publications.

Social Services Inspectorate (SSI) (2002) *Fostering for the Future: Inspection of Foster Care Services*, DH Publications.

Timms, J. and Thoburn, J. (2003) *Your Shout*, NSPCC.

Thoburn, J. (2006) 'Planning for Children Who Cannot Return to Their Birth Families: Messages From Research' in Jordan, L. and Lindley, B. (eds.) *Special Guardianship: What Does it Offer Children Who Cannot Live with Their Parents?*, Family Rights Group.

Utting, W. (Chairman) (1997) *People Like Us: The Report Of The Review Of The Safeguards For Children Living Away From Home*, DH/ The Welsh Office, HMSO.

Vernon, J. (2000) *Audit and Assessment of Leaving Care Services in London*, National Children's Bureau/ Department of Health.

Wade, J. and Dixon, J. (2006) 'Making a Home, Finding a Job: Investigating Early Housing and Employment Outcomes for Young People Leaving Care' 11 *Child and Family Social Work* 199.

Wall J (1998) 'Care Plans: A Judicial Perspective' in Thorpe LJ and Clarke, E. (eds.) *Divided Duties: Care Planning for Children Within the Family Justice System*, Family Law.

Warman, A. (2006) 'An International View: Planning for Children in Long-Term Care in Other Child Welfare Systems' in Jordan, L. and Lindley, B. (eds.) *Special Guardianship: What Does it Offer Children Who Cannot Live with Their Parents?*, Family Rights Group.

Warner, N. (Chairman) (1992) *Choosing with Care: Report of the Committee of Inquiry into the Selection, Development and Management of Staff in Children's Homes*, HMSO.

Waterhouse, R. (Chairman) (2000) *Lost in Care: Report of the Tribunal of Inquiry into the Abuse of Children in Care in the former County Council Areas of Gwynedd and Clwyd since 1974*, The Stationery Office.

Welbourne, P. (2008) 'Safeguarding Children on the Edge of Care: Policy for Keeping Children Safe after the *Review of the Child Care Proceedings System, Care Matters* and the *Carter Review of Legal Aid*' 20 *Child and Family Law Quarterly* 335.

Wheal, A. (ed.) (2002) *The RHP Companion to Leaving Care*, Russell House Publishing.

Williams, G. and Macreadie, J. (Chairmen) (1992) *Ty Mawr Community Home Inquiry*, Gwent County Council.

Chapter 17

The right of abused children to protection by the criminal law

(1) Introduction

Children obviously have as much right to protection by the criminal law as adults and its use on their behalf clearly indicates that society will not condone their ill-treatment. Behaviour which leads to a child being made the subject of care proceedings under the Children Act (CA) 1989, section 31 may also result in the perpetrator facing criminal charges. Consequently, throughout a child protection investigation there should often be close collaboration between social workers and the police with a view to using both the civil and criminal law. Despite this, the criminal justice system, in many ways, casts a blight over the child protection system. There is a widespread perception amongst child-care practitioners that, as presently organised, the criminal justice system does not promote the welfare of children caught up in its processes and that its use may even victimise them over again. At every stage of the child protection process, efforts to help the child recover from the effects of abuse may be undermined by the prospect of criminal proceedings against the abuser. Sometimes the drive to obtain a conviction may prevail over the needs of the child victim.

If children, as a class, substantially benefited from criminal proceedings being brought against the perpetrators of abuse, this might justify individual children suffering in the process. The conviction rates do not, however, bear this out. It is notoriously difficult to obtain accurate statistics regarding the number of offences recorded against children.[1] Difficulties are exacerbated when attempting to establish the true extent of sexual offences against children, not least because of the varying definitions of such abuse used by researchers.[2] It seems, however, that despite all the efforts of child protection practitioners to adapt their work practices to suit the requirements of the criminal justice system, the extent of child abuse is far higher than the number of offences reported to the

---

[1] Young people are more likely to be the victims of personal crime than adults, with 10–15-year-olds being at the highest risk of being assaulted; see Chapter 18.

[2] C. Cobley (2005) pp. 33–5; D. Grubin (1998) pp. 3–12; C. May-Chahal and P. Cawson (2005) p. 980: in a research sample, 10% of children under 16 had been sexually abused (sexual contact abuse) by parents/carers or by other people.

police[3] and higher again than the number of adults convicted for such offences.[4] This problem is particularly acute in relation to child sexual abuse, with statistics showing an astonishing rate of attrition when the number of sexual offences against children first reported to the police is compared with the number of convictions obtained in the criminal courts.[5] To many of those involved in child protection work this not only seems a waste of resources, but also diverts attention from establishing whether the families involved are eligible for family support services and protection. This chapter assesses the impact on child victims of the criminal justice system's efforts to prosecute and convict the perpetrators of crimes against children. Since recent official attention has been directed at protecting children from paedophiles, the discussion will largely focus on the experiences of victims of child sexual abuse.

(2) Background

There is no offence of 'child abuse' as such, and it would be difficult to design one which was broad enough to cover all its features. Nevertheless, there is a wide range of criminal offences which protect children against what most would describe as 'abusive' behaviour. Whilst their use against those who harm children clearly acknowledges a child's right to criminal protection from such ill-treatment, the offences were not designed specifically with children in mind. Consequently, as long as an assault cannot be justified as being a form of legitimate discipline,[6] physical abuse may result in a variety of criminal charges, ranging from common assault through to actual bodily harm, to grievous bodily harm, to murder and manslaughter. Regrettably, however, as Lord Laming observed, police child protection teams did not, in the past, always devote the same resources or time and energy to investigating serious assaults against children as they would assaults against adults.[7] Furthermore, the *Cannings* case demonstrated just how difficult it may be to establish the cause of death of very young children.[8] Matters are exacerbated if a child's death could have been caused by one of a number of carers. The creation of a new

---

[3] T. Goodman-Brown *et al.* (2003) pp. 526–8: research summary; C. May-Chahal and P. Cawson (2005) p. 981: 31% of the children under 16 reporting sexual experiences against their wishes had never told anyone; ChildLine (2007) p. 20: only 2% of callers (when the perpetrator was a family member) had approached social services about their sexual abuse, only 12% had approached the police.

[4] Relatively little robust research substantiates this widely held view but see inter alia: D. Grubin (1998) pp. 5 and 12: although in 1995 there were 3,957 offenders throughout England and Wales cautioned or convicted for sexual offences against children, police crime reports suggest that as many as 72,600 cases a year of indecent assault and rape involving children may actually occur; R. Waterhouse (2000) pp. 7 and 20: the investigation of 500 complaints of physical or sexual abuse in North Wales children's homes in the 1980s led to only eight prosecutions and six convictions.

[5] HM Government (2007) para. 7.8.   [6] See Chapter 9.

[7] H. Laming (2003) paras. 13.20–13.24 and 14.14–14.15.

[8] *R v. Cannings* [2004] EWCA Crim 1, [2004] 1 All ER 725; see Chapter 15 and C. Cobley (2006) pp. 322–5.

criminal offence[9] was designed to ensure that a prosecution is possible despite the perpetrator's identity being unclear, but the legislation's efficacy is seriously weakened by drafting defects.[10]

The law recognises that there are certain types of ill-treatment which are often directed at children alone. Acknowledging that children can be as damaged by acts of omission as of commission, nineteenth-century legislation created offences regarding their neglect and cruelty; this legislation was later replaced by Part 1 of the Children and Young Persons Act 1933.[11] Although many of these provisions are technical and outdated, further reforming activity has largely focused on children's vulnerability to sexual abuse. Long before the Cleveland crisis in the late 1980s, this concern had resulted in the creation of a series of criminal offences intended to protect children from various kinds of sexual activity.[12] Some of these are couched in extremely broad language; for example, it is an offence, to take or permit to be taken any 'indecent' photograph of a child or to possess such a photograph with a view to its being distributed or 'shown' by himself or others.[13] Towards the end of the twentieth century, as more was discovered about the habits of paedophiles, the continuing inability of the law to protect children against sex abusers became increasingly evident. It was the view that children had a right to better protection, both from family members and from strangers, that led to the creation, by the Sexual Offences Act (SOA) 2003 of a new raft of specially designed offences.[14] The legislation protects children under the age of 13 from rape and sexual assaults, making the victim's consent or lack of consent irrelevant.[15] There are offences designed to prevent paedophiles befriending children,[16] with a view to eventually engaging them in sexual activities.[17] Given the 'looser structure of modern families',[18] there are also new offences replacing and extending the old offences of incest, by prohibiting sexual relations between children and people who are in positions of trust, including wider family members, such as

---

[9] Domestic Violence, Crime and Victims Act 2004, s. 5 creates the offence of causing or allowing the death of a child or vulnerable adult subject to certain conditions.

[10] M. Hayes (2005) and J. Herring (2007). See also *R v. Stephens (Jerry)* [2007] EWCA Crim 1249, [2007] 2 Cr App R 26 (CA (Crim Div)), D. Ormerod (2008).

[11] Esp. s. 1: this renders criminal all forms of wilful violent and non-violent neglect and ill-treatment which is 'likely to cause him unnecessary suffering or injury to health (including injury to or loss of sight, or hearing, or limb, or organ of the body, and any mental derangement)'.

[12] E.g. Punishment of Incest Act 1908; see now Sexual Offences Act (SOA) 2003, Part 1.

[13] Protection of Children Act 1978, s. 1. E.g. *R v. Land* [1999] QB 65. NB in s. 7(4A), the term 'photograph' as amended by Criminal Justice and Immigration Act (CJIA) 2008, s. 69(3), now includes electronic images.

[14] SOA 2003, Part I. See also CJIA 2008, s. 63 designed to outlaw various kinds of extreme internet pornography.

[15] SOA 2003, ss. 5–8. See *R v. G (Secretary of State for Home Department intervening)* [2008] UKHL 37, [2008] 1 WLR 1379: despite other criminal charges being available, a male minor under 16 can be prosecuted for raping a girl under 13, whether or not she consented to the sexual activity.

[16] E.g. through the use of internet chatrooms. HO (2002a) para. 54.

[17] SOA 2003, ss. 14–15.   [18] HO (2000) chs. 3 and 5, esp. para. 5.5.6.

step-parents and foster parents.[19] These offences are broadly drafted; even the lack of an identified victim does not prevent their biting.[20]

Hopefully, there are few types of abusive treatment of children that cannot now be slotted into a criminal offence of some kind. In some cases, however, the fact that a child's parent or parents may have been responsible for the offence means that child protection proceedings are running parallel to the criminal trial. Then the criminal process may actually hamper the proceedings designed to protect the child from further abuse.[21] At times like this, the aspects of the criminal justice system which undermine its suitability for protecting individual children from abuse become particularly obvious. In many ways its objectives are not only very different but, at times, there are direct conflicts. First, the criminal law focuses on protecting society and children as a class, not on the interests of the individual child victim. Further there is the assumption that by catching and punishing the offender, the victim's welfare will automatically be fulfilled. Second, since the focus of criminal intervention is on punishing the wrongdoer, there is considerable emphasis, not on the rights of the victim to comfort and support, but on those of the alleged perpetrator who may, after all, be innocent. Considerable effort is devoted to collecting evidence proving beyond reasonable doubt both that an offence has actually occurred and that the right person has been identified as the perpetrator. Indeed, criticising the highly tactical legal advice given to a father involved in criminal proceedings, Holman J referred to the 'huge cultural gap ... between those whose practice is predominantly in criminal courts and those who endeavour to make reliable decisions about the future of vulnerable children'.[22]

(3) Joint interviewing and the search for evidence in the investigative stages

The CA 2004 requires a long list of agencies who work with children to make arrangements to 'safeguard and promote the welfare of children'.[23] Nevertheless, the civil child protection system, as presently organised, largely

---

[19] SOA 2003, ss. 16–19. These offences protect children up to the age of 18.

[20] E.g. *R v. Jones* [2007] EWCA Crim 1118, [2007] 4 All ER 112: the offender had written graffiti messages in train toilets and stations seeking sex with girls aged 11–13, offering payment and providing a mobile telephone number. Held: SOA 2003, s. 8 applies to a person who, with the requisite intention, directly incites a child or children under the age of 13 to engage in sexual activity, despite the absence of any specific person.

[21] E.g. *Re U (care proceedings: criminal conviction: refusal to give evidence)* [2006] EWHC 372 (Fam), [2006] 2 FLR 690: given a father's pending appeal against a conviction for murdering his child and on his criminal counsel's advice, he refused to give evidence in the care proceedings concerning their two surviving children, hoping that this would weaken the mother's evidence against him.

[22] Ibid., per Holman J, at [27].

[23] CA 2004, s. 11(1)–(2). The Local Safeguarding Children Board (LSCB) is the statutory mechanism for agreeing how the relevant organisations in each area will cooperate to carry out the safeguarding duty.

depends on the work of children's social care and the police. In those cases where a criminal offence has occurred and there is a possibility of bringing the perpetrator to trial, the two agencies may work closely together from the start. The impetus for often involving the police in child protection referrals came in the late 1980s, when it was realised that far larger numbers of children were the victims of sexual abuse than had formerly been imagined. The involvement of the police in child protection work was accelerated by legislation permitting the admission in criminal trials, as their evidence-in-chief, of video-recorded interviews with child witnesses.[24]

It would be folly to suggest that relations between the police and social workers are always good. The latter often find it difficult to reconcile themselves to the features of the criminal justice system which curtail their own freedom to deal with the case as they think most appropriate. The Cleveland Report noted the deteriorating relations between social workers and the police provoked by the conflict over medical opinion and its effect on criminal proceedings.[25] In his inquiry into Victoria Climbié's murder, Lord Laming was struck by Haringey Social Services' poor working relationship with their local police force. The social workers' reluctance to involve the police in child protection investigations and their hostility towards the police had compromised the police force's own ability to carry out criminal investigations effectively in cases involving children.[26] Sir Michael Bichard similarly criticised the lack of proper co-ordination or discussion between Humberside Police and social workers over various incidents involving Ian Huntley[27] having sexual relations with under-age girls and later allegations of rape.[28] He stressed:

> One of the key failings was the inability of Humberside Police and Social Services to identify Huntley's behaviour pattern remotely soon enough. That was because both viewed each case in isolation and because Social Services failed to share information effectively with the police.[29]

Current guidance, *Working Together*, takes full account of Lord Laming's strong recommendations that the police must take complete and exclusive responsibility for any investigation into suspected injury or harm to a child.[30] It emphasises that the police should be notified as soon as possible by children's services whenever a case referred to them involves a criminal offence committed against a child or is suspected of having been so committed. It stresses that whilst this does not mean that a full investigation will be required in every case or even that there will always be further police involvement, information about these concerns should be passed on, so that the police can decide for themselves

---

[24] Criminal Justice Act (CJA) 1988, s. 32A, introduced by the CJA 1991. But see now Youth Justice and Criminal Evidence Act (YJCEA) 1999, Part II, discussed below.

[25] Butler-Sloss LJ (1988) ch. 6.   [26] H. Laming (2003) paras. 14.17–14.29.

[27] Murderer of Jessica Chapman and Holly Wells in Soham in 2003.

[28] M. Bichard (2004) paras. 1.26–1.239.   [29] Ibid. at p. 2.

[30] H. Laming (2003) recommendation 99.

whether to take further action.[31] New detailed guidance on how to deal with allegations of harm arising from underage sexual activity[32] also takes account of Sir Michael Bichard's criticism that underage sexual activity had not been taken sufficiently seriously by the Humberside police or social services.[33]

Today, in those cases where it is clear from the start that the circumstances do not warrant a criminal prosecution, a joint investigation is unnecessary.[34] But since this may not always be clear until well into the investigation process, an enquiry under section 47 of the CA 1989,[35] may, at least to start with, run concurrently with a police investigation.[36] Hopefully, current guidance, supplemented by local protocols, will redress the hitherto completely inconsistent approach to single or joint investigations.[37] With a degree of understatement, the joint Chief Inspectors referred to a 'lack of clarity' in some areas between the police and children's social care about the criteria for deciding whether an investigation should be single or joint.[38] As noted above, this 'lack of clarity' was also very evident in Humberside prior to the Soham murders. In those cases where a section 47 enquiry does run concurrently with a police investigation, the official guidance stresses the need for the police and social workers to be clear about their appropriate roles,[39] with the police taking the lead for the criminal investigation and social workers for the section 47 enquiry and the child's welfare.[40]

In the cases involving a joint investigation, the child may be jointly interviewed by a police officer and social worker, with arrangements being made for the interview to be video-recorded. As noted above, legislation introduced in the early 1990s permitted the admission of video-recorded interviews with child witnesses in criminal trials as their evidence-in-chief. The joint interviewing of victims of child sexual abuse, using video-recording equipment, quickly became standard practice. From the start, it was common for a police officer to take the lead in the investigative interview. Although the current guidance on joint interviewing stresses that this practice is not obligatory,[41] anecdotal information suggests that it is rare for a social worker to do so. Whilst joint interviewing obviates a child being interviewed separately by the two agencies, the system clearly undermines the uneasy balance between the civil child protection system

---

[31] HM Government (2006) paras. 2.102–2.103 and 5.17–5.20.   [32] Ibid. at paras. 5.23–5.30.

[33] M. Bichard (2004) para. 4.47 and paras. 4.53–4.55.

[34] Decisions about joint working are normally taken at a 'strategy discussion', followed by a core assessment carried out by children's social care. HM Government (2006) paras. 5.54–5.59.

[35] Discussed in Chapter 15.   [36] HM Government (2006) para. 5.58.

[37] HM Inspectorate of Constabulary (2005) para. 5.36: decisions as to which cases should be investigated jointly or singly varied from force to force and sometimes within the same force, with apparently arbitrary local customs, e.g. emotional abuse and minor neglect referrals *always* investigated by social services; joint investigation *always* appropriate for any allegation of a crime against a child; common assaults *always* only dealt with by social services.

[38] CSCI (2005) para. 4.33.

[39] HM Government (2006) para. 5.59: aided by protocols produced by every LSCB.

[40] Ibid.   [41] MOJ *et al.* (2007) para. 2.12.

and the criminal justice system.[42] All practitioners are only too aware of the considerable body of psychological research indicating that children can provide very accurate evidence of abuse if asked the right questions in an appropriate format.[43] Those working in the child protection field are tempted to believe a child who says that he or she has been abused. But the training of those involved in the criminal justice system, such as police officers and lawyers from the Crown Prosecution Service (CPS), requires them to probe a child's version of events and seek evidence corroborating this. Whilst social workers may wish to comfort and support a child when seeking evidence identifying the abuser, police officers and lawyers will wish to avoid suggestions that the child was encouraged, coached or bullied into identifying a defendant falsely. They may also be aware of the current research which shows that children are suggestible and may respond to leading questions and interviewer bias.[44]

When a joint interview is carried out, with the criminal investigation running alongside the child protection investigation, the child is not only a witness, but a victim as well.[45] Indeed, as Davis et al. have pointed out, the video-recorded interview must serve three very conflicting purposes, namely: (i) the initial step in a child protection investigation to ascertain whether an offence has been committed and by whom; (ii) an inquiry into whether the child needs protection; and (iii) the examination-in-chief of the child at the criminal trial, with a need to comply with strict rules of evidence. These researchers concluded that the three purposes were so difficult to reconcile that unrealistic demands were being imposed on interviewers.[46] It is clear that, even with the help of detailed guidance, interviewing a child in way which produces evidence able to fulfil these three demands is a skilled process, requiring specialised training.[47] The current official guidance on video-recorded interviewing methods, *Achieving Best Evidence in Criminal Proceedings* (ABE),[48] is the product of several revisions. It now incorporates sections on interviewing vulnerable and intimidated adults, together with detailed instructions on interviewing children.[49] It emphasises the need to plan the interview carefully[50] and to involve the child fully in the whole process – in particular to prepare him or her properly for the interview, with adequate explanations.[51] Like earlier versions, it suggests that the interviewers should follow a four-pronged phased approach to the interview,[52] with detailed guidance on how to deal with each of the four phases.[53]

In the view of Baroness Hale of Richmond, a video-recorded interview is likely to be the best evidence a child can give. It takes place close to the events in

[42] J. Brownlow and B. Waller (1997) pp. 18–21.   [43] H. Westcott (2006) pp. 177–9.
[44] Ibid. at pp. 177–8 and M. Bruck et al. (2008) pp. 84–91.
[45] MOJ et al. (2007) paras. 2.11–2.18.   [46] G. Davis et al. (1999) p. ix.
[47] H. Westcott and S. Kynan (2006) pp. 378–80.   [48] MOJ et al. (2007).
[49] Ibid. at Part 2.   [50] Ibid. at paras. 2.37–2.65.   [51] Ibid. at paras. 2.66–2.73.
[52] Ibid. at para. 2.130: i.e. establishing rapport, asking for free narrative recall, asking questions, closure.
[53] Ibid. at paras. 2.130–2.182.

question when the recollection is fresh; it is done in an informal and comfort-able setting by professionals specially trained in questioning children, first to establish that they understand the importance of telling the truth and then to elicit their story as fully as possible in language they understand without suggestion or leading questions.[54] Regrettably, this may be an idealistic version of what often happens. There is sometimes a considerable delay in making the video interview.[55] Children themselves find the interviews far more stressful than practitioners suppose, with insufficient time being devoted to explaining the process to them or involving them in the arrangements being made.[56] In some areas there is still a shortage of trained police officers to carry out inter-views with vulnerable children.[57] The technical quality of the interview may sometimes be poor, with the interview being almost inaudible.[58] Without skilled training, the detailed guidance on how to carry out a successful inves-tigative interview does not avoid interviewers making mistakes,[59] or the guid-ance sometimes being ignored almost entirely.[60] Rapport is not always established particularly well, with clumsy attempts to establish whether the child can distinguish between true and false information.[61] Despite clear guidance to the contrary,[62] interviewers appear to find it difficult to allow a child to provide information in the form of free narrative without intervening with specific questions.[63] Some interviewers distort the information provided by the child[64] and many others[65] fail to include any closure phase in the interview, without presumably even thanking the child for their efforts. It appears that the mistakes of the past[66] are still sometimes being repeated, with practitioners setting up interviews with children for therapeutic purposes to help them unburden their worries, on the assumption that abuse has occurred, without an ABE interview ever being conducted to establish the true facts.[67]

---

[54] R (on the application of D) v. Camberwell Green Youth Court; R (on the application of the Director of Public Prosecutions) v. Camberwell Green Youth Court (hereafter Camberwell Green) [2005] UKHL 4, [2005] 1 All ER 999, at [38].

[55] M. Burton et al. (2006a) p. 54: one case involved a delay of 16 months.

[56] A. Wade and H. Westcott (1997) pp. 55–8.   [57] M. Burton et al. (2006a) p. 54.   [58] Ibid.

[59] H. Westcott and S. Kynan (2006) pp. 372–8.

[60] E.g. Re B (allegations of sexual abuse: child's evidence) [2006] EWCA Civ 773, [2006] 2 FLR 1071, per Hughes LJ, at [35]–[37]: the police officer and social worker had interviewed a 5-year-old girl (about whom there were concerns of child sexual abuse by her father) almost wholly failing to follow the ABE guidelines.

[61] H. Westcott and S. Kynan (2006) pp. 376–7.

[62] HO et al. (2002) para. 2.52 and MOJ et al. (2007) para. 2.148: the interviewers should 'never' curtail the child's free narrative.

[63] H. Westcott and S. Kynan (2006) p. 376.   [64] Ibid. at p. 375: in 51% of the interviews.

[65] Ibid. at p. 377: more than half.

[66] Re D (child abuse: interviews) [1998] 2 FLR 10, per Butler-Sloss LJ, at 18: stressed the difference between interviewing a child to establish the facts and doing so to help her unburden her worries.

[67] E.g. D v. B and ors (flawed sexual abuse inquiry) [2006] EWHC 2987 (Fam), [2007] 1 FLR 1295.

Today, most social workers, police officers[68] and those working in the court system[69] consider that using video-recorded investigative interviews as children's evidence-in-chief in criminal trials is a far more efficient process than taking written statements. Children themselves consider the video-recorded interview to be less stressful and appreciate the fact that it avoids evidence-in-chief being given orally in open court.[70] Nevertheless, although guidance suggests that an older child should be given a choice over whether to being interviewed in this way, rather than by giving a written statement,[71] this seldom appears to occur.[72] The child who is the victim of a violent assault may not understand or be told that the video-recorded statement will be sent to the defence ahead of the trial, thereby identifying him or her to the defendant. In such circumstances, with the fear of reprisals from the defendant's confederates, providing a written statement and giving evidence in court behind screens might be preferred.[73] But these choices are seldom spelled out to child witnesses,[74] often because practitioners wrongly assume that there is no choice available. Providing real choice would require a good knowledge of the various options and their likely impact on the witness – but it appears that 'in general, police officers have little understanding of how special measures operate in practice'.[75] Confusion about their operation is hardly surprising, given the complexity of the legislation making them available.[76]

If given a choice, many children would prefer to provide video-recorded evidence – but they cannot do so if they are not even identified by the police as being vulnerable witnesses requiring such protection. All service providers coming into contact with vulnerable and intimidated victims[77] should identify them and pass on information about their existence to other service providers.[78] But, as the official guidance points out, the police are often the first to identify the needs and wishes of the witness and so they should activate the system for their support.[79] Although this should always happen in the case of child witnesses, research suggests that the police identify surprisingly few children who are potential witnesses at criminal trials as being vulnerable. Indeed, Burton et al. criticise the police for their inconsistent and rather arbitrary decisions not to video record interviews with a relatively high number of child witnesses. The police appear to operate a kind of sliding scale when it comes to identifying witnesses worthy of protection. Whilst child victims of

---

[68] M. Burton et al. (2006a) p. 53: three-quarters of the police officers surveyed considered video evidence to be 'very effective'.
[69] M. Hall (2009) p. 69.   [70] B. Hamlyn et al. (2004) p. 67.
[71] MOJ et al. (2007) paras. 2.9 and 5.32.
[72] J. Plotnikoff and R. Woolfson (2004) p. 16; M. Hall (2009) pp. 76.
[73] Office of Criminal Justice Reform (hereafter OCJR) (2007) Case study, paras. 4.16–4.18.
[74] M. Burton et al. (2006a) p. 42; J. Plotnikoff and R. Woolfson (2004) p. 16; M. Hall (2009) p. 76.
[75] M. Burton et al. (2006a) p. 42.   [76] Discussed below.
[77] E.g. CPS, police, youth offending teams (YOTs) etc.
[78] OCJR (2005) para. 4.11.   [79] MOJ et al. (2007) para. 5.31.

sexual abuse are virtually always assumed to be vulnerable,[80] this is not always the case where a child has witnessed a sexual offence with an adult as the victim.[81] Victims of physical abuse are even less likely to be so defined, particularly if they are adolescents.[82] Witnesses of physical assaults come fairly low on the list; these include those who have been witnesses of domestic violence, and particularly if they are witnesses for the defence.[83] The older the child, the less likely such an interview took place; but even the evidence of younger victims might not be video interviewed, if they were close in age to the defendant.[84] Accordingly, as Burton *et al.* point out, the potential benefits of the video facility now available in most courts is not realisable in the majority of cases.[85]

This rather gloomy picture of the early investigative stage is reinforced by continuing problems over ensuring that a potential child witness obtains therapy prior to the trial, if it is deemed to be necessary. The refusal to allow pre-trial therapy, often prompted by local CPS officers and prosecuting lawyers, results in severely abused and traumatised children being deprived of urgently needed therapeutic support. Refusal is to promote the aims of the criminal justice system, without any guarantee that the trial will eventually go ahead or, indeed, produce a conviction. To social workers it seems ironic that the practice of video recording children's evidence, a scheme designed to improve the treatment of child witnesses, has led to less support being given to seriously abused children in the early stages of investigations, for fear of contaminating their evidence. Such caution appears to be misplaced – current inter-agency guidance emphasises that the child's best interests must govern such decisions, which are not the preserve of the police or the CPS, but which must be taken by all the agencies responsible for the child's welfare.[86] It stresses that if the child's need for immediate therapy overrides the need for him or her to appear as a credible witness in a criminal case, then this must be arranged, even at the cost of abandoning the criminal proceedings.[87] It also points out that there are ways in which the child may receive therapy without it undermining the strength of the prosecution's case.[88] It warns, however, that the nature of the proposed therapy must be explained to the CPS beforehand, so that they can consider its likely impact on the criminal case.[89] Although such unambiguous guidance is welcome, it appears that this guidance 'is not universally known about, applied or understood. As a result, there is confusion and uncertainty over whether young witnesses can have access to pre-trial therapy'.[90]

In such a climate of uncertainty, child protection practitioners may not wish to risk jeopardising the evidential requirements by supporting the child in a way which could be exploited by the defence. Overall, one wonders whether any

[80] M. Burton *et al.* (2006a) pp. 32–3.   [81] Ibid. at p. 33.   [82] Ibid.
[83] Ibid. at p. 34.   [84] Ibid. at p. 40.   [85] Ibid. at p. 46.   [86] CPS *et al.* (2001) para. 4.5.
[87] Ibid. at paras. 4.3–4.5. See also CPS (2006) p. 13 and MOJ *et al.* (2007) paras. 5.60–5.61.
[88] CPS *et al.* (2001) chs. 5 and 6.   [89] Ibid. at para. 6.3.
[90] OCJR (2007) para. 9.10. See also MOJ (2009) p. 43.

official initiatives can overcome all the difficulties imposed by a system which, as observed by Davis et al.,[91] seeks to serve so many different functions at the same time.

(4) The decision to prosecute

In cases where a joint investigation proceeds and the team is satisfied that a child has been abused, that the abuse amounts to a criminal offence and that the abuser has been accurately identified, a decision must be taken whether criminal proceedings are appropriate. Official guidance states that this question depends on whether there is enough evidence to prosecute and whether it is in the public interest to do so.[92] Research suggests that decisions over whether jointly investigated cases should go forward for prosecution may often be reached in an unsatisfactorily idiosyncratic manner. For example, in some cases, the police may simply decide not to proceed with a criminal investigation, without obtaining CPS advice over whether the situation warranted prosecution.[93] Police normally bring allegations of more serious offences, such as sexual abuse, to the attention of the CPS. But even then, research shows that the two agencies appear to operate on a variety of assumptions about the 'seriousness' of an offence, which are, in turn, influenced by seemingly arbitrary preconceptions.[94] Thus, although it is common for sexual abuse to be regarded as very serious, a decision whether to prosecute might be influenced by such factors as the time lapse between the alleged assault and the child's complaint. Davis et al. suggest that 'it would be helpful if, across the board, the yardsticks by which the police and the CPS determine whether child abusers should be prosecuted were to be reviewed and more clearly articulated'.[95] More to the point, one would expect them to take account of the research indicating that the time taken by a child to disclose sexual abuse is significantly associated with the type of abuse and fear of the consequences. Thus children who have been abused by a family member and who fear that their disclosure will result in negative consequences take longer to disclose, as do those older children who consider themselves to be responsible for the abuse.[96] Regrettably, children and their families may receive no proper explanation from the CPS and sometimes no explanation at all, for charges being dropped or substantially altered.[97]

When deciding whether to prosecute, the CPS must first assess whether there is sufficient evidence to provide a 'realistic prospect of conviction'.[98] One might assume that this part of the Crown prosecutors' task would be greatly assisted by their ability to assess the weight of evidence, together with the child's general demeanour, by viewing his or her video-recorded interview. They might, for

---

[91] G. Davis et al. (1999) p. ix.   [92] CPS (2004) ch. 5.   [93] C. Keenan and L. Maitland (1999).
[94] G. Davis et al. (1999) pp. 41–2 and Appendix C.   [95] Ibid. at p. 83.
[96] T. Goodman-Brown et al. (2003) pp. 533–5.
[97] Ofsted (2008) para. 160.   [98] CPS (2004) para. 5.2.

example, wish to gauge the child's ability to stand up to the experience of cross-examination, still an essential part of the criminal trial. But Burton *et al.* found that the CPS often decided whether to bring a prosecution, taking account of the strength of the witness's evidence, including his or her potential strength as a witness, without first viewing the video, due to lack of time.[99] So cases were being dropped on the grounds of witness credibility, without the CPS viewing the video tapes which might enhance their view of the witness's evidence.[100] As Burton *et al.* wryly observe, if the CPS have no time to preview the limited number that do exist, they would certainly not have the time to do so if as many ABE interviews were carried out as should be.[101]

The second question, whether it is in the public interest to proceed with a prosecution, is interrelated with the first, and will obviously include a consideration of such matters as the effect of a prosecution on the victim's physical or mental health, including his or her interests and views.[102] Having considered such matters, the CPS are entitled to decide not to prosecute, despite there being sufficient evidence to obtain a conviction.[103] Many social workers and the police wish to see higher rates of prosecution than are achieved, particularly in cases involving child sexual abuse. They sometimes express considerable frustration over decisions not to prosecute reached by the CPS. This stance is understandable. In the first place, a prosecution offers the most powerful way of registering society's disapproval of the sexual abuse of children. Not only do children as a group have a right to be protected from a suspected abuser, but society as a whole also has an interest in his conviction. Indeed, the heightened public awareness of the evils of child abuse, particularly child sexual abuse, has led to a greater concern that so many child sex abusers are escaping conviction.[104] Linked to this is the fact that instigating a prosecution demonstrates to the child that he or she is believed and has support from outside the family.[105] Admittedly, although children want the abuse to stop, they often feel guilty and upset at the prospect of charges being brought against a member of their own families.[106] But a prosecution may relieve a child's sense of guilt by indicating that he or she was not responsible for what occurred and that guilt lies with the abuser.[107] In practical terms, imprisonment may provide other children and the child victim with a period of safety, during which the perpetrator is out of

---

[99] M. Burton *et al.* (2006a) pp. 44–6.

[100] M. Burton *et al.* (2006a) p. 46. See also CSCI (2005) para. 6.19 and Ofsted (2008) para. 282: the files inspected did not show that a CPS lawyer had seen and assessed the quality of video evidence given by the children.

[101] Ibid.   [102] CPS (2004) paras. 5.6–5.11.   [103] Ibid. at para. 5.7.

[104] HM Government (2007) para. 7.9.

[105] ChildLine (2007) p. 11: callers to ChildLine express considerable frustration over not being believed by the people in whom they confide over sexual abuse.

[106] Ibid. at p. 11. See also T. Goodman-Brown *et al.* (2003) pp. 527–8 and p. 537.

[107] J. Morgan and L. Zedner (1992) p. 115. The knowledge that a court has made findings of sexual abuse in care proceedings may have an equally cathartic effect on children: e.g. *Re X (disclosure of information)* [2001] 2 FLR 440, at [10]–[15]; discussed below.

circulation. Prosecution may also stop sex abusers denying their offending behaviour and the harm it has caused. By contrast, a decision not to prosecute may indicate to the abuser that, so far as the community is concerned, he did not commit the offence, in turn making it far more difficult for social workers to work with the family and secure the child's safety.[108] But the most fundamental problem is that, even with the benefit of the protection now available for many child witnesses, giving evidence against the abuser at a criminal trial can be deeply traumatic and may eventually achieve nothing, if the defendant escapes conviction.

(5) Compellability of child witnesses in criminal trials

Children become very worried and apprehensive over appearing as witnesses in criminal trials.[109] Their apprehension is often exacerbated by the long wait between the time of the initial investigation and the trial itself. The Pigot Report stated that 'one of the most substantial difficulties faced by children ... is the extraordinary and, in our view, quite unacceptable delay which they must often endure before cases come to court'.[110] Since then, successive research projects have shown that the criminal justice system seems incapable of 'fast-tracking' criminal trials involving children, with some 'fast-tracking' schemes exacerbating the 'normal' delays.[111] Delays occur at every stage of the process,[112] with children's evidence at the trial itself sometimes being weakened by their fading recollections of the offence. There is the added factor that, until the trial begins, some child witnesses are under constant fear for their safety because the defendant has been left in the community, perhaps on bail with insufficient restrictions.[113] The strain suffered by the child and family whilst awaiting the trial may be exacerbated by cases being rescheduled at the very last minute, creating further unexpected delays.[114] Even when the trial starts, and despite official guidance stressing that waiting times should be limited,[115] some

---

[108] C. Hallett (1995) p. 138.

[109] B. Hamlyn et al. (2004) p. 47; J. Plotnikoff and R. Woolfson (2004) pp. 11–14 and 33; J. Plotnikoff and R. Woolfson (2007a) p. 32: over 80% of children in the research project reported symptoms of pre-trial stress including self-harming, panic attacks, flashbacks of the offence, bed-wetting, headaches, eating and sleeping disorders, depression, mood changes, loss of concentration and of confidence.

[110] T. Pigot (1989) para. 1.20.

[111] J. Plotnikoff and R. Woolfson (1995) ch. 5: on average, cases took 10 months to complete; G. Davis et al. (1999) pp. 51–4: on average, cases took just under 58 weeks from investigation to the first day of trial, with many children bound up in the criminal process for 14 months; J. Plotnikoff and R. Woolfson (2004) p. 11: on average, witnesses in Crown Court trials waited 11.6 months before trial; witnesses in magistrates' courts waited 9.9 months and those in youth courts waited 8.6 months.

[112] E.g. A. Burton et al. (2006a) p. 54: refer to delays over making the video interview.

[113] E. Sharland et al. (1996) pp. 140–1.   [114] J. Plotnikoff and R. Woolfson (2004) p. 14.

[115] MOJ et al. (2007) paras. 5.81–5.82: arrangements should be made avoiding child witnesses waiting to give evidence, e.g. by being called as first witness on the second day of the trial; OCJR

children required to attend court for cross-examination may be kept waiting for long periods spanning more than a day.[116]

Children and their parents are well aware that giving evidence can be harrowing. Little wonder then that children are often very reluctant to appear as witnesses at a criminal trial or that their parents may strongly oppose their doing so. But like any adult, a child witness is compellable. Indeed, no matter how young, children are presumed competent to give evidence in a criminal trial, unless they cannot understand questions put to them in court or answer them in a way which can be understood.[117] Furthermore, when considering children's competence, the court will bear in mind the various special measures which can help even very young and/or disabled children comprehend the process.[118] The judiciary have, in the past, robustly emphasised children's duty to act as witnesses in criminal trials; even children who are wards of court have no special privileges in this respect.[119] The view is that the interests of the child witness cannot be allowed to prevail over the needs of society, more particularly those of other children, for protection against criminals.[120] The principle is clear, whether or not criminal proceedings will be distressing for children, it is up to the CPS and the trial judge to decide whether to call them.[121]

Although the CPS will always try to obtain agreement from a child's parents for the child to give evidence, 'there may be some very serious cases where we have to ask a child to give evidence even if a parent or carer does not agree'.[122] The official guidance implicitly counsels a sympathetic approach to reluctant child witnesses. It points out that whether or nor a witness is competent and compellable, the CPS are not obliged to insist on every witness giving evidence and need not do so if they think that a conviction can be secured without.[123] It also states that the CPS will take into account the wishes of the witness, 'although they will not necessarily defer to them'.[124] Research suggests that the CPS regard vulnerability and risk of intimidation as aggravating factors pointing to prosecution, but also recognise that the risk to the victim sometimes outweighs the benefit of going to trial.[125] The special measures available to

---

(2007) recommendation 19: listings of cases involving child witnesses should ensure that their testimony is taken at the beginning of day one when the witness is fresh with minimum waiting.

[116] J. Plotnikoff and R. Woolfson (2004) p. 32: the shortest wait was 20 minutes, the longest was over 20 hours spread over 4 days; the average wait was over 5 hours; J. Plotnikoff and R. Woolfson (2007a) p. 47: the average wait was just over 3 hours, the longest over 16 hours for a witness who attended over 3 days.

[117] YJCEA 1999, s. 53(1) and (3).   [118] Discussed below.

[119] E.g. *Re R (minors) (wardship: criminal proceedings)* [1991] 2 All ER 193 and *Re K (minors) (wardship: criminal proceedings)* [1988] 1 All ER 214.

[120] *Re S (minors) (wardship: disclosure of material)* [1988] 1 FLR 1, per Booth J, at 5.

[121] *R v. Highbury Corner Magistrates' Court, ex p D* [1997] 1 FLR 683: the High Court quashed on judicial review the magistrates' refusal to issue a witness summons requiring a 9-year-old to give evidence at the criminal trial of his father being tried for assault against his ex-partner. The final decision whether to call the child to give evidence should be left to the judge presiding over the criminal trial.

[122] CPS (2006) p. 9.   [123] MOJ *et al.* (2007) para. 2.26.   [124] Ibid.

[125] A. Burton *et al.* (2006a) p. 44.

protect child witnesses from some of the trauma of giving evidence in open court, together with the new availability of witness support schemes,[126] may have made the CPS more, rather than less, prepared to pressurise children into giving evidence. It is arguable that older children would be far more willing to give evidence in criminal trials if they were more fully involved in decisions over how they give evidence, for example, whether this should be by video-link or in person. Australian research evidence on the use of closed-circuit television for children giving evidence in criminal trials lends pragmatic support for adopting such an approach.[127] But as explained below, discussions of such choices are unlikely in many cases, due the inflexibility of the 'primary rule.' This apparently requires a video-recorded interview to be shown at the trial, as the child's evidence-in-chief, whenever charges involve a serious crime like a sexual offence, whether or not the child would prefer to give evidence in person.

The unsympathetic way child witnesses are treated in some criminal courts was demonstrated very clearly by the trial judge's actions in *R (on the application of B) v. Stafford Combined Court.*[128] He had considered that the defendant, who was being tried for sexual offences against a 14-year-old girl, must have a fair trial and that the medical records of her psychiatric treatment prior to the trial were relevant to her credibility as main prosecution witness. Consequently, he overruled the medical confidentiality objections of the local CAMHS director to the records' disclosure. Having done so, the trial judge then 'invited' the girl to miss school and attend court the following morning, to discuss these matters with him. On judicial review of these decisions, May LJ made clear his disapproval:

> I strongly deprecate what happened on 6 December 2005. It seems to me to be quite unacceptable for a vulnerable 14-year-old schoolgirl known to have attempted suicide, the victim of alleged sexual abuse and a prosecution witness in the impending trial, to be brought to court at short notice, without representation or support, to be faced personally with an apparent choice between agreeing to the disclosure of her psychiatric records or delaying a trial which was bound to cause her concern and distress.[129]

The Court of Appeal's decision makes it plain that the criminal courts should not overlook the ECHR rights of witnesses, whatever their age, but especially if they are young and vulnerable. Alongside her undoubted Article 8 rights to respect for her privacy, including her right to medical confidentiality,[130] the girl had a right to procedural fairness. Thus she should have been given notice of the defendant's application for disclosure of her medical records and also a chance to object before the order for disclosure was made.[131]

---

[126] Discussed below. [127] J. Cashmore (1992).
[128] [2006] EWHC 1645 (Admin), [2007] 1 All ER 102. [129] Ibid. at [11].
[130] Ibid., per May LJ, at [16]–[21]: disclosure of her medical records should therefore have been carefully justified under Art. 8(2) of the ECHR, by balancing her rights to medical confidentiality against the defendant's right to a fair trial.
[131] Ibid. at [25].

It is curious, when considering case law of this kind, that the law is so inconsistent in its treatment of children's potential ability to give evidence of various kinds. An extreme paternalism is shown by the courts in their reluctance to allow children to give evidence in parental disputes.[132] Similarly, they seldom allow quite mature children to give oral evidence in public law proceedings,[133] even in the event of their wishing to do so and even if they are deemed sufficiently competent to instruct their own solicitors. But this approach is not matched by a similar concern to protect a child victim from the trauma of giving evidence at the criminal trial of a possible child abuser, even when it is known that this experience may well prove distressing. So far as criminal proceedings are concerned, it is convenient for society to utilise the capacity of even very young children to recall criminal acts which have affected them.

(6) Protecting child witnesses in criminal trials

As discussed above, children experience considerable stress and anxiety waiting for cases to reach trial. It is now widely recognised that children's fears over attending court can be alleviated by their being familiarised with the courts and what will be required of them. During the 1990s, considerable efforts were made to develop age-related materials designed to provide child witnesses with information about the process.[134] Today, more is being done, with a growing official acknowledgement that young and vulnerable witnesses need support both before the trial and throughout its progress.[135] There are, however, considerable regional variations throughout the country in the type of provision made and who provides it.[136] The government funded Witness Care Units (WCUs), jointly run by the police and CPS,[137] are being established across the country, with officers providing information and exploring the type of support required for witnesses.[138] Some WCUs are still obviously struggling to fulfil their aims.[139] A number of specialist young witness support schemes have also been established on an ad hoc basis in some areas. These provide an enhanced

---

[132] Discussed in Chapter 7.

[133] *LM (by her guardian) v. Medway Council, RM and YM* [2007] EWCA Civ 9, [2007] 1 FLR 1698, per Smith LJ, at [44]: 'The "correct starting point" remains that it is undesirable for children to give evidence in care proceedings and that particular justification is required before such a course is taken'.

[134] E.g. the development of the NSPCC Young Witness Pack.

[135] MOJ *et al.* (2007) ch. 5.   [136] Ibid. at paras. 5.27–5.28.

[137] OCJR (2005) section 6: 165 WCUs operate in England and Wales providing support for victims and witnesses in a criminal context.

[138] CPS (2006) pp. 11–12: each child witness should have his or her own Witness Care Officer, whose job it is to explain every part of the criminal justice process, including inter alia: reasons for delays; organise help and support; give dates of hearings; ensure that the child knows when to attend court; explain the trial result.

[139] Ofsted (2008) para. 161.

service for child witnesses,[140] thereby ensuring that their best evidence is given, more confidently,[141] and with less attendant stress.[142] But to date, these schemes have not been developed systematically and lack national direction.[143] Critics call for the development of a national strategy for young witness care.[144]

Unfortunately, even the best of these schemes do not wholly prepare children for the experience of actually appearing in open court and confronting the defendant. This can be so distressing that, in the past, some criminal trials which hinged on a child's evidence had to be abandoned. The Pigot Committee was extremely critical of a system allowing children to suffer the trauma of giving evidence in open court and being cross-examined by defence counsel whose aim was systematically to discredit them.[145] Out of the Pigot report came the reforms of the early 1990s allowing the child's video-recorded interview to be shown in court in substitution for the child appearing in person to provide evidence-in-chief.[146] Pigot had also wanted children to be spared cross-examination in open court, by ensuring that the cross-examination would take place in advance of the trial, in a video-recorded form, with this to be shown in court at the trial (often referred to as 'full-Pigot'). Many were disappointed that this aspect of the report was not adopted. Instead, it was decided that the criminal justice system should retain the right of the defence to cross-examine all witnesses for the prosecution, irrespective of their youth. But this experience was softened in some courts, but not all, by the child being allowed to give evidence from another room by live link or protected by a screen. By the late 1990s, there was much criticism of the inconsistent approach adopted by many courts to the admission of video-recorded interviews and to the use of live-link evidence. This led to further review. It was now, however, realised that children were not the only group of witnesses who required protection from the traumas of giving evidence in open court. Recommendations for change were adopted,[147] with a range of eight 'special measures' being introduced on a phased basis,[148] for the protection of eligible vulnerable and intimidated witnesses of all ages.[149] By then, of course, the courts had already used many of these as a way of protecting child witnesses for nearly a decade.

---

[140] J. Plotnikoff and R. Woolfson (2007a) ch. 2: i.e. through the provision of personal supporters who inter alia: make pre-trial home visits; take young witness through relevant materials, including information packs and videos; take them on familiarisation visits to court; explain the style of questioning to expect in a cross-examination.

[141] Ibid. at p. 19.   [142] Ibid. at pp. 12–15.   [143] Ibid. at p. 72.   [144] Ibid. at p. 71.

[145] T. Pigot (1989) esp. paras. 2.10 and 2.12.

[146] CJA 1988, s. 32A, subject to certain age limits depending on the nature of the offence.

[147] HO (1998).

[148] The majority of the special measures introduced by YJCEA 1999, Part II, were made available to the Crown Courts in 2002, with such facilities being extended to the magistrates' courts from 2004.

[149] The special measures available for vulnerable (all children under 17 are automatically deemed to be 'vulnerable', whether they are victims of a crime themselves or witnesses to a crime involving another person) and intimidated witnesses are: screens in the courtroom (s. 23); allowing evidence by live link (where the witness gives evidence from outside the courtroom) (s. 24);

Davis *et al.* had hoped that any new legislation would stipulate 'clear statutory criteria to guide the exercise of judicial discretion' in determining whether any special pre-trial procedures for receiving the child's evidence should be used.[150] This was not to be the case. In the case of child witnesses, the legislation confusingly allows the court to treat the availability of two of the special measures differently, depending on the type of offence involved in the trial, not on the basis of the child's need for protection.[151] The courts are entirely free to ensure that child witnesses gain virtually any form of protection available.[152] There is, additionally, a legislative presumption (or 'primary rule') that a court will make a 'special measures direction' requiring a child's evidence-in-chief to be admitted in the form of a video-recording if it exists, or if not, authorising him or her to give that evidence by live link.[153] The judiciary ostensibly have no ability to set aside this primary rule if the trial involves a sexual offence[154] or an offence of kidnapping, physical violence and neglect[155] – in which case the child is automatically deemed to merit this form of 'special protection'.[156] The child then benefits from the 'primary rule' in its strengthened form – that the court *will* make such a direction. Parliament has clearly decided that it is the norm for a child needing special protection to give evidence in this way.[157] In trials *not* involving sexual offences or offences of physical violence, the primary rule becomes a more easily rebuttable presumption – a court may justify not making such a direction by arguing that 'compliance with it [the rule] would not be likely to maximise the quality of the witness's evidence so far as practicable'.[158] Furthermore, at this point, the court should consider the views of the witness.[159]

It should be noted that in 2005, doubts over the compatibility of the special measures with a defendant's right to a fair trial were put to rest by the House of Lords. They concluded, as had been urged by academic commentators,[160] that a defendant's rights under Article 6 of the European Convention for the Protection of Human Rights and Fundamental Freedoms (ECHR) are not

---

allowing evidence in private (where the courtroom is cleared of the public) (s. 25); removal of wigs and gowns by lawyers and judges (s. 26); admission of video-recorded evidence-in-chief (s. 27); admission of video-recorded cross-examination (which is recorded in advance of the trial and played on the day) (s. 28 – unimplemented); intermediaries (people who act as go-betweens to improve communication and understanding between the witness and the court, e.g. if the witness is disabled) (s. 29); aids to communication (devices used by the witness to assist in their understanding of the questions) (s. 30). Any witness may apply for a special measures direction or the court may make one on its own motion (s. 19).

[150] G. Davis *et al.* (1999) p. 85.   [151] L. Hoyano and C. Keenan (2007) pp. 625–33.

[152] YJCEA 1999, s. 19(2): the court must make a special measures direction in relation to a witness 'eligible for assistance' if it is of the opinion that such measure(s) would 'be likely to improve the quality of evidence given by the witness'. YJCEA 1999, s. 16(1)(a): all child witnesses under the age of 17 are automatically 'eligible for assistance' by reason of their age alone.

[153] YJCEA 1999, s. 21(3).   [154] YJCEA 1999, s. 35(3)(a).

[155] YJCEA 1999, s. 35(3)(b)–(d).   [156] YJCEA 1999, s. 21(5).

[157] *R (D) v. Camberwell Green Youth Court, R (DPP) v. Camberwell Green Youth Court* [2005] UKHL 4, [2005] 1 All ER 999, per Baroness Hale of Richmond, at [37] and [45].

[158] YJCEA 1999, s. 21(4)(c).   [159] YJCEA 1999, s. 19(3)(a); discussed by M. Hall (2009) p. 72.

[160] E.g. L. Hoyano (2001).

infringed by a special measures direction made under the primary rule.[161] Strasbourg jurisprudence does not insist on his having a face-to-face confrontation with the witnesses at his trial.[162]

Research shows that the special measures introduced in the early twenty-first century are gradually reducing the strain involved when children act as a witness in criminal trials.[163] Nonetheless, difficulties continue to arise. In particular, as noted above, far fewer witnesses are being identified by the police and CPS as meriting the protection available than there should be. This may be, in part, attributable to the inflexibility of the primary rule referred to above, which in turn restricts choice over the mode of giving evidence. Although children find it a relief that they can give evidence by live link (often the cross-examination), rather than in open court,[164] many would like to be given some choice over whether they should do so or not.[165] But the legislation suggests that in cases involving sexual offences or offences of physical violence, choice is simply not available – the existence of a video-recording creates the rule that the evidence-in-chief must be admitted in that format. The method of giving evidence is then not even discussed with the child. More fatally, it produces situations where interviews are being shown, even if the technical quality is so poor that obtaining a conviction on it is impossible.[166] Nevertheless, it appears that the courts may have room for manoeuvre in exceptional circumstances, if they consider this to be necessary 'in the interests of justice'.[167] In the *Camberwell Green* decision,[168] Baroness Hale of Richmond suggested that the court may allow the child to give evidence in court rather than by live link if she positively wants to and it is in the interests of justice to allow her to do so.[169] She also pointed out that the court may decide 'in the interests of justice' to exclude the whole of a video-recorded interview or any part of it;[170] for example, where the video interview is flawed for some reason.[171] Similarly, if circumstances change, the court may discharge the special direction, again if it is in the interests of justice to do so.[172] Such an approach is

---

[161] *Camberwell Green* [2005] UKHL 4, [2005] 1 All ER 999, per Lord Rodger of Earlsferry, at [11]–[15] and per Baroness Hale of Richmond, at [37] and [45].

[162] L. Hoyano and C. Keenan (2007) pp. 675–9.

[163] B. Hamlyn *et al.* (2004), J. Plotnikoff and R. Woolfson (2004), M. Burton *et al.* (2006a). See also assessment by L. Hoyano and C. Keenan (2007) pp. 679–87.

[164] J. Plotnikoff and R. Woolfson (2004) p. 39.

[165] B. Hamlyn *et al.* (2004) p. 67.   [166] A. Burton *et al.* (2006a) p. 54.

[167] YJCEA 1999, ss. 20(2), 24(3), 27(2) and (7).   [168] [2005] UKHL 4, [2005] 1 All ER 999.

[169] Ibid., per Baroness Hale of Richmond, at [34]–[35]: YJCEA 1999, s. 24(3) authorises the court to allow a child to give evidence in court rather than by live link.

[170] YJCEA 1999, s. 27(2).

[171] *Camberwell Green* [2005] UKHL 4, [2005] 1 All ER 999, per Baroness Hale of Richmond, at [25].

[172] YJCEA 1999, s. 20(2). But in *Camberwell Green*, per Lord Rodger of Earlsferry, at [7]: this discretion should only be exercised if, between making the direction and the trial, it becomes 'impossible or inappropriate to proceed' on the basis of the direction; ss. 24(3) and 27(7) should be interpreted in the same way. See also Baroness Hale of Richmond, at [32]–[37]: these departures from the primary rule are clearly intended to be 'exceptional'.

providing an escape route in some cases.[173] A further problem not cured by the special measures is the way in which young witnesses can be seen by the defendant when they give evidence by live link. Many find this very distressing and would prefer to give evidence behind a screen, if warned about it in advance and given the choice – which does not always happen.[174] Some find giving evidence by live link confusing with people speaking off-screen.[175] The layout of some courts also makes it possible for child witnesses to encounter the defendant or his supporters in public areas of the court, despite giving evidence by live link.[176]

The government has accepted that the confusion caused by the rules governing the availability of the special measures cannot continue. They plan new legislation to 'remove the present rigid special measures presumptions for young witnesses and to provide a more flexible approach, enabling young witnesses to opt out of video recorded evidence in chief and live links'.[177] A review of the special measures[178] produced overwhelming criticism of their inflexibility and the way that the eligibility criteria are rigidly categorised according to the type of case rather than the needs of the individual witness.[179] Many favoured making the special measures available to all young witnesses who need them, regardless of age or offence.[180] Further, children should be given sufficient information and support to help them make an informed independent choice over whether to give evidence in open court, rather than utilising the live link.[181] Some young witnesses may fear threats and reprisals if the defendant can watch them giving evidence by live link.[182] They might then prefer to give evidence from behind a screen in court but may not presently be given this option. The government also accepts the advantages of developing remote live links whereby witnesses give evidence from non-court locations.[183] Those that do exist seem successful[184] and ensure that the witness avoids encountering the defendant or supporters at the court itself.[185]

Full-Pigot is now on the horizon for some. Section 28 of the Youth Justice and Criminal Evidence Act (YJCEA) 1999 is to be implemented. Under this provision the witness who has provided evidence in the form of a video-recorded interview, can then undergo a video-recorded cross-examination prior to the trial, that video recording then being admitted as evidence at the trial itself.[186]

---

[173] L. Hoyano (2007) p. 857.
[174] J. Plotnikoff and R. Woolfson (2004) pp. 39–41 and A. Burton *et al.* (2006a) p. 42.
[175] M. Hall (2009) p. 79.
[176] J. Plotnikoff and R. Woolfson (2004) pp. 20–1; B. Hamlyn *et al.* (2004) p. 43; J. Plotnikoff and R. Woolfson (2007a) p. 47.
[177] MOJ (2009) p. 26; implemented by Coroners and Justice Bill (CJB) 2009, Ch. 3.
[178] OCJR (2007).   [179] MOJ (2009) para. 4.4.
[180] Ibid. CJB (2009), cl. 85: the eligibility age for special measures is extended from 17 to 18.
[181] Ibid. at para. 4.5 and CJB (2009), cl. 87(6).   [182] OCJR (2007) at pp. 22–3.
[183] MOJ (2009) pp. 14–17.   [184] NSPCC (2007) pp. 5–7.
[185] J. Plotnikoff and R. Woolfson (2007a) pp. 53–4.   [186] MOJ (2009) p. 12.

As noted above, the Pigot Committee[187] had recommended the introduction of such a scheme hoping to free child witnesses from appearance in court altogether. Nevertheless, from the start, strong and influential reservations were voiced over the scheme's theoretical and practical efficacy.[188] These doubts, which had prevented its even being piloted, let alone implemented,[189] were influential.[190] The House of Lords' ruling in *Camberwell Green*[191] suggested that there was little merit in arguing that a defendant's Article 6 rights would be infringed by admitting at the trial a video recording of the pre-trial cross-examination of a prosecution witness.[192] Most of the scheme's opponents instead concentrate on its practical and logistical difficulties. They argued that the defence could not conduct an effective cross-examination at the beginning of the investigation before the prosecution have completed their evidential work. It would cause delays, thereby undermining the objectives of full-Pigot, namely to ensure that the cross-examination is carried out as soon as possible. It might also be extremely difficult to ensure the defendant's presence at this early stage together with prosecution counsel and the trial judge.[193] Furthermore the development of more facilities for cross-examining children by live link from locations outside the court-house would obviate the need for implementing section 28 of the YJCEA 1999.[194]

Fortunately, the government heeded the scheme's supporters, who stressed the benefits for children of pre-trial cross-examination.[195] In particular, the development of more link facilities would not solve the problems created by a system apparently quite incapable of fast-tracking cases involving child-witnesses.[196] Indeed, full-Pigot will prevent the delays in the criminal justice system undermining the quality of the child's evidence. At present, young children may be cross-examined in court on aspects of their evidence-in-chief provided in an interview which perhaps took place more than a year before. The time-lag may result in their giving replies which are inconsistent with their original evidence. Even their appearance, as recorded by the video, may have changed between the initial interview and the trial itself.[197] The government was also swayed by the evidence from abroad indicating that its introduction has been highly successful in a number of countries.[198] Disappointingly, despite strong opposition to the scheme being drastically restricted,[199] it appears

---

[187] T. Pigot (1989).   [188] D. Birch and R. Powell (2004).   [189] OCJR (2007) pp. 12–13.
[190] Ibid.   [191] [2005] UKHL 4, [2005] 1 All ER 999.
[192] L. Hoyano and C. Keenan (2007) p. 678.   [193] Criminal Bar Association (2007) pp. 7–8.
[194] Ibid. at p. 8.   [195] MOJ (2009) para. 1.5 and p. 12.   [196] L. Hoyano (2007) p. 854.
[197] G. Davis *et al.* (1999) pp. 53–4.
[198] L. Hoyano and C. Keegan (2007) pp. 644–57 and MOJ (2009) pp. 10–11.
[199] L. Hoyano (2007) p. 856.

that only a small group of witnesses will be allowed to provide evidence in this way.[200]

Whilst arguments continued to rage over the merits of further protection for the child witnesses who give evidence for the prosecution, reforming legislation reversed the controversial exclusion of child defendants from protection by the special measures.[201] As critics had pointed out, it is often a matter of coincidence whether young persons are offenders or victims at any one time, particularly in cases involving gang fights.[202] Baroness Hale of Richmond had also observed that the young defendants who appear before the youth courts are often the most disadvantaged and the least able to give a good account of themselves in court.[203] Although the reforms have not yet placed child defendants on a par with child witnesses for the prosecution, in so far as their evidence-in-chief cannot take the form of a pre-recorded video interview, they may be allowed to give their evidence by live link from a venue outside the court.[204]

There are some aspects of the criminal trial that the special measures, as such, cannot address. In particular, children still often find the cross-examination harrowing, despite being able to give evidence by live link, because of the aggressive techniques adopted by defence lawyers and by questions being posed in unintelligible language.[205] The ABE guidance emphasises the fact that judges and magistrates should prevent improper or inappropriate questioning.[206] Some intervene to prevent child witnesses being bullied, but others do not.[207] Rapid change might be provoked by the introduction of a rule that no practitioner could be involved in cross-examining child witnesses without having completed an accreditation process.[208] But it is also difficult to disagree with the view that the judiciary and magistracy should be more active in controlling inappropriate cross-examination.[209]

Meanwhile, it appears that criminal justice practitioners are underestimating the extent to which many of the special measures could ensure a conviction in cases involving very young and mentally impaired children. The chief

---

[200] MOJ (2009) p. 12.   [201] YJCEA 1999, ss. 16(1) and 17(1).   [202] D. Birch (2001) p. 477.
[203] *Camberwell Green* [2005] UKHL 4, [2005] 1 All ER 999, at [56].
[204] YJCEA 1999, s. 33A (3) and (4), as inserted by Police and Justice Act 2007, s. 47: allows a live-link direction to be made in relation to an accused aged under 18 if: (a) his ability to participate effectively in the proceedings as a witness giving oral evidence in court is compromised by his level of intellectual ability or social functioning; and (b) use of a live link would enable him to participate more effectively as a witness (whether by improving the quality of his evidence or otherwise). CJB (2009) cl. 91: vulnerable defendants may give evidence through an intermediary.
[205] J. Plotnikoff and R. Woolfson (2004) pp. 51–5; J. Plotnikoff and R. Woolfson (2007a) p. 45; B. Hamlyn *et al.* (2004) pp. 53–8: two-thirds of the witnesses thought that the defence lawyer had not treated them with courtesy and over half had not been given adequate opportunity to say everything that they wanted.
[206] MOJ *et al.* (2007) para. 6.11.   [207] J. Plotnikoff and R. Woolfson (2004) pp. 53–5.
[208] OCJR (2007) Recommendation 26.   [209] Ibid. at p. 30.

inspectors note that 'In many cases, special measures were often limited to the standard special measures procedures of video links or screens'[210] – the two measures which have been available for children since the 1990s. Child witnesses would benefit from many others. For example, although enabling children to give evidence through an intermediary[211] can be very helpful, young witnesses eligible for such assistance are not being identified, the intermediary role is misunderstood and early planning is often non-existent.[212] Although intermediaries would be of particular assistance to mentally impaired victims, research indicates that many of their cases are still being dropped, often without the video tapes of their interviews even being viewed.[213] Overall, it is particularly regrettable that the current scheme is so extraordinarily complex that those preparing child witnesses for their role find it extremely difficult to establish what form of protection they are entitled to and when. It remains to be seen whether the reformed system can protect child witnesses from what the Pigot Committee described as 'a harmful, oppressive and often traumatic experience' and a form of 'secondary victimisation', through giving evidence in criminal trials.[214]

(7) Outcomes for children if the abuser is convicted

The discussion above indicates that use of the criminal justice system produces a long list of problems for the child victim. Even in the event of the abuser being tried and convicted, the outcome for the child may not always be a happy one. Despite the child's relief at the abuse being stopped, his or her sense of guilt will be exacerbated if a parent or other close relative is sent to prison, and the family may suffer further financial hardship through loss of the breadwinner. There is the added drawback that the current methods used to punish child abusers do not necessarily reduce the chance of their reoffending, particularly when sex abusers are concerned. The traditional sanction is to imprison them for long periods, depending, of course, on the severity of the abuse.[215] Indeed, the public response to well-publicised offences by highly deviant sex offenders is to demand even more incarceration and greater control on release.[216]

The advantage of sentencing child abusers to long periods in prison is that during their removal from circulation, their child victims are securely protected. Long sentences also enable prisoners to be supervised on licence in the community on their release, which, as Cobley observes, is a particularly apt way of managing sex offenders.[217] The government's determination to ensure that sex offenders deemed to be dangerous to the public are locked up for longer and supervised more closely on release is emphasised by legislation reducing the

---

[210] Ofsted (2008) para. 162.   [211] YJCEA 1999, ss. 26 and 29.
[212] J. Plotnikoff and R. Woolfson (2007b) pp. 49–50 and 62–7.
[213] A. Burton et al. (2006a) pp. 45–6.   [214] T. Pigot (1989) paras. 2.10 and 2.15.
[215] C. Cobley (2005) ch. 4: discusses sentencing policies regarding sex offenders.
[216] S. Brown et al. (2008) pp. 264–72.   [217] C. Cobley (2005) p. 228.

courts' discretion on the length of sentence.[218] So those convicted of serious sexual offences are likely to face a long period of detention.[219] Nevertheless, these 'lock them up' sentencing policies carry risks. The prison experience may cause the perpetrator to feel victimised. More crucially, in the case of sex abusers, if they receive no treatment, prison may increase the likelihood of their reoffending, by allowing them time to rehearse their sexual fantasies about children.[220] Furthermore, if perpetrators know that imprisonment will be the probable outcome of admitting abuse, they are deterred from seeking help for controlling or changing their abusive behaviour. Nevertheless, research on the effectiveness of treatment programmes for sex offenders indicates that programmes, both those operating in prisons and in the community, can reduce the risk of reoffending, in low and medium-risk offenders, although less so for high-risk offenders.[221] The last decade has seen a far greater investment in treatment programmes in the community to ensure that the probation service can provide adequately for the numbers of sex offenders allocated to them.[222] The government is also intent on exploring the use of drug treatment, combined with psychological treatment, to assist people understand their sexual thought processes and help them break the cycle of offensive behaviour.[223] But plans for the building of new residential treatment centres are often hampered by opposition from community groups concerned by fears for their personal safety.[224] The concept of sex offenders being rehabilitated in the community seems only to be acceptable if it involves *other* peoples' communities.

On the assumption that many child abusers, more particularly sex offenders, will remain in the community, improved strategies are being introduced to protect children more efficiently from their attentions. The 1990s saw a plethora of legislative initiatives. A sex offender 'register'[225] was introduced to ensure that police could keep track of sex offenders.[226] There is a legislative duty

---

[218] E.g. *R v. Terrell (Alexander James)* [2007] EWCA Crim 3079, (2008) *Times*, January 14; comment by D. Thomas (2008).

[219] Dependent on the assessment of the offender's 'dangerousness', probably on an extended sentence (the offender spends the usual term in prison with an extended licence period in the community for up to 8 years) or an indeterminate public protection sentence (offenders are not released until their level of risk is deemed to be manageable in the community). See CJA 2003, ss. 224–9 and Sch. 15. See also C. Cobley (2005) pp. 222–37.

[220] During his previous term of imprisonment, for kidnapping and indecently assaulting another child, Roy Whiting, Sarah Payne's murderer, had refused the psychiatric treatment on offer.

[221] See generally C. Cobley (2005) pp. 289–310.

[222] Ibid. at p. 295. See also F. Lösel and M. Schmucker (2005) for a summary of the international research on outcomes.

[223] HO (2007) p. 14: e.g. hormonal medication to reduce a sex offender's sexual urges or antidepressant drugs, which appear to have the same effect.

[224] C. Cobley (2005) p. 298.

[225] T. Thomas (2008). There is no separate 'register' of sex offenders; VISOR, a database recording details of all violent and sex offenders dealt with by the local MAPPA arrangements (see discussed below) includes details of sex offenders subject to the notification requirements.

[226] Now governed by SOA 2003, Part 2.

on those convicted of a very wide range of sexual (and other[227]) offences to notify the police[228] of an extensive and expanding list of identifying details,[229] with non-compliance itself being a criminal offence.[230] Although the notification requirements can have a significant impact on an offender's life,[231] thereby infringing his rights under Article 8 of the ECHR, such an infringement has been held to be proportionate to the aims pursued – those being to protect the victims of sexual offences.[232]

The considerable amount of information now held by the police about sex offenders produces regular calls from the media for such information to be made available to local communities, often triggered by highly publicised trials of child murderers.[233] But as opponents point out, evidence from the community notification schemes in the US does not substantiate claims that they have enhanced children's safety there.[234] Indeed, as Brown *et al.* observe, the government is in a difficult position.[235] It is reluctant to give the public uncontrolled access to sex offenders' notification information,[236] for fear of vigilante attacks on those identified as paedophiles.[237] It also knows that if sex offenders expect to be hounded from place to place, they will simply disappear, rather

---

[227] T. Thomas (2008) p. 234.

[228] Normally within 3 days of the conviction if the offender is not imprisoned, or date of release from prison.

[229] SOA 2003, s. 83(5): the police must be notified of the offender's: address; date of birth; national insurance number; plus (by new regulations to be made under SOA 2003, s. 83(5A)) a DNA sample (if not already given); any e-mail address; passport numbers; bank account numbers; notification if they are living in the same household as a child under the age of 18; notification of any foreign travel; report regularly to a police station if they register as homeless (see HO (2007) p. 18).

[230] SOA 2003, s. 91.

[231] E.g. *Forbes v. Secretary of State for the Home Department* [2006] EWCA Civ 962, [2006] 4 All ER 799: the claimant, who had been convicted for returning from abroad possessing video tapes containing indecent photographs of children, unsuccessfully claimed that his rights under Art. of the 8 ECHR had been infringed unjustifiably. He was permanently anxious that his status as person as 'being on the sex offender register' would become known, and was fearful of consulting a doctor because his status would then appear on his medical records. But see *R (F) and Angus Aubrey Thompson v. Secretary of State for the Justice Department* [2008] EWHC 3170, [2009] crim LR 305 per Latham LJ: the fact that the notification requirements apply for the life of an offender with no review mechanism available is incompatible with the ECHR in so far as it unjustifiably infringes an offender's rights under Art. 8.

[232] *Adamson v. UK* (1999) 28 EHRR CD 209 at 212.

[233] E.g. a campaign was started by the *News of the World* in 2000, after the murder of Sarah Payne, to introduce 'Sarah's Law', a scheme, similar to 'Megan's Law' established in the US in the aftermath of the murder of Megan Kanka, whereby the public have access to information about sex offenders.

[234] K. Fitch (2006) Part 2, esp. pp. 50–1: sex offenders 'go to ground' because of their fear of harassment.

[235] S. Brown *et al.* (2008) pp. 272–3.

[236] Home Office press release, 15 September 2000; HO (2002a) para. 19; HO (2007) p. 10.

[237] The *News of the World*'s 'naming and shaming' campaign encouraging the public to identify paedophiles, led to attacks on some men wrongly suspected of abusing children. It also disrupted ongoing work with sex offenders. See Association of Chief Officers of Probation (1998).

than registering with the police.[238] In any event, existing arrangements for managing registered sex offenders in the community[239] had already allowed the police to disclose information to a variety of people about registered sex offenders, although the extent to which they did so varied regionally.[240] But the government is also clearly reluctant to be portrayed as incompetent in relation to managing sex offenders in the community.[241] Legislation now requires the MAPPA authorities *always* to consider disclosing information about a sex offender's relevant previous convictions, including cautions, to any member of the public, whether or not they believe there is any risk to a child.[242] They are also under a presumptive legislative duty to disclose such information in cases of serious risk, whether or not requested to do so by a member of the public.[243] This change not only seems unnecessary but one wonders whether a direction to the person receiving the information not to disclose it to anyone else[244] will prevent it being leaked to the wider community.

Official policies focus on controlling the activities and movements of sex offenders, together with measures ensuring that they do not simply disappear.[245] When released from prison on licence, they are supervised by the probation service for the remainder of their sentence. They may be electronically tagged and the conditions of the licence may require them to live in approved premises, with tight controls, such as curfews and links with MAPPA.[246] Under the MAPPA scheme, the police and probation services operate local multi-agency public protection arrangements, which take responsibility for the assessment and management of sexual and violent offenders within their communities.[247] Further controls are on the horizon: polygraph testing (lie detectors) are to be piloted for offenders on licence to encourage

---

[238] HO (2007) p. 10.

[239] I.e. the Multi-Agency Public Protection Arrangements (MAPPA) (discussed below) established under Criminal Justice and Courts Services Act 2000. The MAPPA scheme requires the relevant authorities to work in partnership and share information to manage high-risk offenders in the community; discussed below.

[240] J. Cann (2007) p. 2: an offender living with or close to children 'inevitably initiated disclosure'. See also Table 2: disclosure routinely made to head teachers; employers; new/ex-partners and their family members; staff in community services (e.g. leisure facilities, parks, hospitals); family members/friends; church; children associating with offender (including victims of grooming) and parents; housing personnel, including landlords, victim and family members, local residents, GP etc.

[241] S. Brown *et al.* (2008) p. 272.   [242] CJA 2003, s. 327A (1) (as inserted by CJIA 2008, s. 140).

[243] CJA 2003, s. 327A(3): information *must* be disclosed if a particular sex offender poses a risk of causing serious harm to children generally or any child and the disclosure is necessary for protecting children generally or any child from serious harm caused by the offender.

[244] CJA 2003, s. 327A(5)(b).

[245] E.g. the Child Exploitation and Online Protection (CEOP) Centre (established in 2006), affiliated to the Serious Organised Crime Agency, with a remit to gather and co-ordinate intelligence on high-risk sex offenders; it employs specialised police officers, professionals from child protection charities and secondments from IT providers.

[246] HO (2007) p. 20.   [247] C. Cobley (2005) pp. 409–23. See also J. Wood and H. Kemshall (2007).

them to discuss more truthfully their behaviour[248] and satellite tracking to monitor the highest risk offenders' compliance with the conditions of their licence.[249] The courts may also impose a number of Draconian restrictions, for example, in the form of a sexual offences prevention order (SOPO),[250] which can last for a considerable period of time.[251]

Previous efforts to prevent sex offenders obtaining jobs involving contact with children[252] were proved faulty when Ian Huntley obtained employment as school caretaker in Soham, despite his known involvement in allegations of sexual offences with children. Not only was the Humberside police intelligence gathering, management and records system flawed, but the school had not taken sufficient care over their recruitment and vetting procedures.[253] Since then, there have been delays over establishing 'inter-operability' of police information technology systems, with a police national database now being planned for 2010.[254] Meanwhile, new legislation has simplified the process of vetting the suitability of adults for work with children by amalgamating the various (sometimes overlapping) lists of those barred from doing so,[255] whilst also introducing potentially draconian restrictions on a wide range of individuals, including volunteers.[256]

---

[248] HO (2007) p. 23.   [249] Ibid. at p. 24.

[250] SOA 2003, ss. 104–13. SOA 2003, s. 107(1)(b): a court can include in the order any prohibition considered 'necessary for the purpose of protecting the public or any particular members of the public from serious sexual harm from the defendant'. See also ss. 114–22: (prohibition of) foreign travel orders, to protect children abroad; ss. 123–9: risk of sexual harm orders (a civil order against a person who has engaged in sexual activity with a child on at least two occasions, with such an order being deemed necessary to protect children generally or any child from the defendant's behaviour). C. Cobley (2005) pp. 376–92.

[251] SOA 2003, s. 107: not less than 5 years. E.g. *R v. D* [2005] EWCA Crim 3660, [2006] 2 All ER 726, per Court of Appeal: a SOPO could be made prohibiting the defendant (who had pleaded guilty to sexually abusing his daughter when aged between 10 and 13 years) from communicating with his 10-year-old son whilst the son remained under the age of 16.

[252] Inter alia: the Protection of Children Act 1999 and the Criminal Justice and Courts Services Act 2000, both disqualifying certain categories of people from working with children and making it a criminal offence for them to apply for or fulfil such work.

[253] M. Bichard (2004) paras. 1.249–1.284. The Soham Village College hired Huntley without the recruitment agency they used following official guidance over necessary checks and before completion of the (flawed) police checks, including Criminal Records Bureau (CRB). See also Ofsted (2008) para. 34: similar vetting failures amongst public agencies working with children, though less common than before, still occur.

[254] T. Thomas (2007) pp. 8–9.

[255] Safeguarding Vulnerable Groups Act (SVGA) 2006 combined the Criminal Records Bureau's list, the Protection of Children Act (POCA) list, the 'List 99' (those barred from working in schools and other educational establishments), and the Protection of Vulnerable Adults (POVA) list. The Independent Safeguarding Authority (formerly named the Independent Barring Board) now operates a new Vetting and Barring Scheme (VBS) maintaining two lists, a children's barred list and an adults' barred list. See SVGA 2006, Sch. 3 paras. 1–9 for the offences justifying inclusion on the barred list.

[256] SVGA 2006 creates a series of offences – s. 7: when a barred individual works in a regulated activity (listed in Sch. 4, including most forms of employment with children, e.g. teaching, foster care, childcare etc); s. 11: when an employer permits an employee to work in a regulated activity without carrying out appropriate checks.

As noted above, the government has found it difficult to resist calls for the introduction of compulsory community notification for convicted sex offenders. Regrettably, however, most sex offences are not committed by strangers but by adults well known to children, perhaps because they are members of their family. These offences may remain unreported and the perpetrators unapprehended. Nevertheless strong suspicions may exist over the identity of the abuser, despite criminal charges being brought against him and dropped, or his being acquitted. An inability to bring a sex abuser to trial does not, of course, prevent child protection practitioners intervening on the basis that a child's allegations were true. As Scott Baker J pointed out, even if an alleged abuser is brought to trial and then acquitted of all criminal charges, this 'does not mean in absolute terms he has not committed the acts alleged against him', nor that the local authority is absolved from protecting the child who made the allegations against him.[257]

In situations of this kind, public agencies are forced to deal with a confused and inconsistent body of case law governing the extent to which they can share their concerns with each other. It seems reasonably clear that both children's social care and the police may disclose to third parties, such as schools and other agencies, allegations of the sexual abuse of children, subject to certain conditions.[258] Indeed, it has been stressed that the whole emphasis of section 47 of the CA 1989 is on inter-agency cooperation, enabling a local authority (LA) to pass on to other public agencies, its concerns about the existing risk posed by an individual to children in the area, and vice versa.[259] But, when reaching such a decision, the agency must demonstrate that it 'genuinely and reasonably believes that such as step is necessary to protect children in its area from the risk of sexual abuse'.[260] Furthermore, it must show that it has considered the need to maintain a balance between the public interest in protecting children and the individual's right to a private life, which should only be infringed if there is a pressing need to do so.[261] It may be difficult to justify such a requirement if the agencies' suspicions arise from uncorroborated allegations of sexual

---

[257] *Re S (sexual abuse allegations: local authority response)* [2001] EWHC Admin 334, [2001] 2 FLR 776, at [37]. See also *R (A) v. Hertfordshire County Council* [2001] EWHC Admin 211, [2001] ELR 666: a head teacher of a weekly boarding special school was acquitted of charges of indecent assault against a pupil, but was later dismissed from his post. He unsuccessfully argued (in judicial review proceedings) that the department of social services should not have written to the director of education indicating their belief that he presented a risk to children.

[258] V. Smith (2006): discusses the circumstances in which LAs should disclose to the police information obtained in the course of a child protection investigation; S. Edwards (2007): discusses the extent to which information obtained in the course of care proceedings should be disclosed to the police.

[259] *R (A) v. Hertfordshire County Council* [2001] EWHC Admin 211, [2001] ELR 666, per Keene LJ, at [28] and [31].

[260] Ibid. at [31], confirming the words of Dyson J in *R v. Local Authority and Police Authority in the Midlands, ex p LM* [2000] 1 FLR 612 at 619.

[261] [2000] 1 FLR 612 at 622–6. The 'pressing need' test was established by Lord Woolf MR, in *R v. Chief Constable of North Wales Police, ex p Thorpe and anor* [1999] QB 396.

abuse.[262] The current working environment created by children's trusts may now make it extremely difficult to prevent suspicions about named individuals being informally passed between practitioners who formerly worked in different public agencies.

If care proceedings succeed, with findings of fact made against a named abuser, practitioners may consider that the child victims should be told the details of the court's judgment, to appreciate fully that they have been believed and to make a better psychological recovery in the light of that knowledge. In *Re X (disclosure of information)*,[263] Munby J accepted this view and showed little sympathy with a sex abuser's attempt to prevent findings regarding his sexual abuse of the children in question being disclosed to his victims. Although such a disclosure would infringe the abuser's rights to privacy under Article 8 of the ECHR, Munby J held[264] that his rights were clearly outweighed by the children's own rights under Article 8 to understand fully their childhood and history.[265] The disclosure of details of care proceedings to his immediate child victims, as in *Re X*, will not prevent the abuser from seeking out other children in the future. One might have assumed that findings reached in care proceedings could also be passed over to any third-party agency involved in working with children in any capacity. Such a disclosure would appear to fulfil the 'pressing need' test since, armed with this knowledge, the agencies could protect the children in their areas from the abusers' attentions. Nevertheless, in *Re V (sexual abuse: disclosure); Re L (sexual abuse: disclosure)*,[266] the Court of Appeal allowed an appeal against directions made by two lower courts for their findings to be disclosed to local agencies. According to Butler-Sloss LJ, disclosure should not be made if there is no *immediate* need for cooperation between the agencies. Disclosure could only be justified when agencies were actually investigating matters to do with a particular child, or children who could be identified, and whose welfare would now be protected through such disclosures, rather than a more generalised future need regarding children in the community.[267]

The decision in *Re V* has been strongly criticised.[268] Cobley argues that no one will know when a pressing need arises: the LA to which a paedophile moves may be unaware that he has started grooming a particular child, and the LA in the area he left is not monitoring his movements, because he is no longer their concern.[269] There can be no 'immediate' need for cooperation *before* disclosure, because

---

[262] As in *R v. Local Authority and Police Authority in the Midlands, ex p LM* [2000] 1 FLR 612.
[263] [2001] 2 FLR 440, at [10]–[15].   [264] Ibid. at [34].
[265] As established by *Gaskin v. United Kingdom* (1989) 12 EHRR 36.
[266] [1999] 1 FLR 267: appeals against permission given by the court below for judicial findings to be passed on. In *Re V*: permission for findings of sexual impropriety by W, including an indecent assault on an 8-year-old boy (and a finding that he posed a significant risk to boys in a household in which he lived) to be disclosed to the new LA in which W was now living; *Re L*: permission for findings that L had sexually abused three children in his care and that he posed a significant threat to children in the area where he lived, to be given to the football authorities covering the junior football clubs with which he was actively involved.
[267] [1999] 1 FLR 267 at 271.
[268] V. Smith (1999); C. Cobley (2005) pp. 476–8.   [269] C. Cobley (2005) p. 476.

logically there is nothing for the agencies to cooperate about until such disclosure occurs. Smith describes the decision as 'a crushing blow to child protection'.[270] Whilst it does not prevent one LA *responding* to a request for information from another, it does prevent the information being *volunteered* by one authority to the other, with the court's permission. Its impact is particularly obvious in cases 'where abusers flit between social services' areas'.[271] It appears that *Re V* can be distinguished in cases which, in addition to complying with the 'pressing need' test, appear to be sufficiently 'exceptional' to justify disclosure to a named organisation.[272] Although welcome, this ad hoc method of side-stepping *Re V* only further confuses case law in which, as noted above, the judiciary stress that public agencies should share concerns about suspected paedophiles when investigating section 47 referrals. The government's efforts to increase the effectiveness of agency surveillance of paedophiles living in the community surely requires the courts to give far clearer guidance to agencies responsible for children's safety.

(8) Conclusion

Great efforts have been made over the last decade to ensure that the criminal law now supports, rather than seriously undermines, the work of childcare practitioners. Until recently full implementation of the Pigot scheme was still being argued over, with potential child witnesses suffering the delays of an inefficient criminal justice system. Indeed, most social workers still take some convincing that children's involvement in criminal trials can benefit them. Were it not for the risk of giving child abusers implicit permission to re-abuse with impunity, there might be some basis for arguing that a child's rights to protection would be better served by the civil law alone, without involving the criminal justice system. Time and again, commentators note the low level of convictions and the cost to the child victims of child protection workers attempting to assist in preparing cases for trials which may never occur or later collapse due to the distress of the children themselves. Many involved in the child protection process will agree with Wattam's comment:

> Protection through prosecution ... directs practices, frames intervention, and defines the kind of service that children and their families receive if they are referred as a result of an allegation of child harm or injury. Like many myths it is rarely challenged. However, it is neither achieved nor achievable, except in a tiny minority of cases. Furthermore, pursuit of it can be damaging and traumatising to children.[273]

---

[270] V. Smith (1999) p. 251.   [271] Ibid. at p. 252.

[272] *Re C (disclosure: sexual abuse findings)* [2002] EWHC 234 (Fam), [2002] 2 FLR 375, per Bodey J, at [120]: there was a pressing need for findings in care proceedings (that a sexual abuser was a considerable risk to children) to be disclosed to the housing association owning the flat in which the abuser lived, to avoid its accommodating families with young children near him. This information could not be disclosed to any other landlords to whom he might apply for accommodation in the future.

[273] C. Wattam (1997) p. 105.

BIBLIOGRAPHY

NB many of these publications can be obtained on the relevant organisation's website.

Association of Chief Officers of Probation (1998) Recent Cases of Public Disorders Around Sex Offenders which have Impeded Surveillance and Supervision.

Bichard, M. (Chairman) (2004) HC 653 The Bichard Inquiry Report, The Stationery Office.

Birch, D. (2000) 'A Better Deal for Vulnerable Witnesses' Criminal Law Review 223.
  (2001) 'Case Comment on R (on the application of DPP) v Redbridge Youth Court' Criminal Law Review 473.

Birch, D. and Powell, R. (2004) Meeting the Challenges of Pigot: Pre-Trial Cross Examination under s28 of the Youth Justice and Criminal Evidence Act 1999 – a Briefing Paper for the Home Office, Nottingham University.

Brown, S., Deakin, J. and Spencer, J. (2008) 'What People Think About the Management of Sex Offenders in the Community' 47 Howard Journal 259.

Brownlow, J. and Waller, B. (1997) 'The Memorandum: a Social Services Perspective' in Westcott, H. and Jones, J. (eds.) Perspectives on the Memorandum: Policy, Practice and Research in Investigative Interviewing, Ashgate.

Bruck, M., Ceci, S., Kulkofsky, S., Klemfuss, J. and Sweeney, C. (2008) 'Children's Testimony' in Rutter, M., Bishop, D., Pine, D., Scott, S., Stevenson, J., Taylor, E. and Thapar, A. (eds.) Rutter's Child and Adolescent Psychiatry, Blackwell Publishing.

Burton, M., Evans, R. and Sanders, A. (2006a) Are Special Measures for Vulnerable and Intimidated Witnesses Working? Evidence From the Criminal Justice Agencies. Home Office Online Report 01/06, www.homeoffice.gov.uk/rds.
  (2006b) 'Protecting Children in Criminal Proceedings: Parity for Child Witnesses and Defendants' 18 Child and Family Law Quarterly 397.

Butler-Sloss LJ (Chairman) (1988), Cm 412 Report of the Inquiry into Child Abuse in Cleveland 1987, HMSO.

Cann, J. (2007) Assessing the Extent of Discretionary Disclosure under the Multi-Agency Public Protection Arrangements, Home Office Findings 286, HO.

Cashmore, J. (1992) Children's Evidence Research Paper 1: The Use of Closed-circuit Television for Child Witnesses in the ACT, Australian Law Reform Commission.

ChildLine (2007) Casenotes: Calls to Childline about Sexual Abuse, NSPCC.

Cobley, C. (2005) Sex Offenders: Law, Policy and Practice, Jordans.
  (2006) 'The Quest for Truth: Substantiating Allegations of Physical Abuse in Criminal Prosecutions and Care Proceedings' 20 International Journal of Law, Policy and the Family 317.

Commission for Social Care Inspection (CSCI) (2005) Safeguarding Children: The Second Joint Chief Inspectors' Report on Arrangements to Safeguard Children, CSCI.

Criminal Bar Association (CBA) (2007) Improving the Criminal Trial Process for Young Witnesses, A Consultation Paper, Response by the Criminal Bar Association, CBA.

Crown Prosecution Service (CPS), Department of Health (DH), Home Office (HO) (2001) Provision of Therapy for Child Witnesses Prior to a Criminal Trial: Practice Guidance, CPS Communications Branch.

Crown Prosecution Service (CPS) (2004) The Code for Crown Prosecutors, CPS.

Crown Prosecution Service (CPS) (2006) *Children and Young People, CPS Policy on Prosecuting Criminal Cases Involving Children and Young People as Victims and Witnesses*, CPS Policy Directorate.

Davis, G, Hoyano, L., Keenan, C., Maitland, L. and Morgan, R. (1999) *An Assessment of the Admissibility and Sufficiency of Evidence in Child Abuse Proceedings*, Home Office.

Edwards, S. (2007) 'Disclosure: Sacrificing the Privilege of Self-Incrimination for the Greater Good of Child Protection' 37 *Family Law* 510.

Farmer, E. and Owen, M. (1995) *Child Protection Practice: Private Risks and Public Remedies*, HMSO.

Fitch, K. (2006) *Megan's Law: Does it Protect Children? (2)*, NSPCC.

Goodman-Brown, T, Edelstein, R., Goodman, G., Jones, D. and Gordon, D. (2003) 'Why Children Tell: a Model of Children's Disclosure of Sexual Abuse' 27 *Child Abuse and Neglect* 525.

Grubin, D. (1998) *Sex Offending Against Children: Understanding the Risk*, Police Research Series Paper 99, Home Office.

HM Government (2006) *Working Together to Safeguard Children: A Guide to Inter-agency Working to Safeguard and Promote the Welfare of Children* The Stationery Office.

HM Government (2007) *Cross Government Action Plan on Sexual Violence and Abuse*, Home Office.

HM Inspectorate of Constabulary (HMIC) (2005) *Keeping Safe, Staying Safe: Thematic Inspection of the Investigation and Prevention of Child Abuse*, HMIC.

Hall, M. (2009) 'Children Giving Evidence Through Special Measures in the Criminal Courts: Progress and Problems' 21 *Child and Family Law Quarterly* 65.

Hallett, C. (1995) *Interagency Co-ordination in Child Protection*, HMSO.

Hamlyn, B., Phelps, A., Turtle, J. and Sattar, G. (2004) *Are Special Measures Working? Evidence from Surveys of Vulnerable and Intimidated Witnesses*, Home Office Research Study 283, Home Office.

Hayes, M. (2005) 'Criminal Trials Where a Child is the Victim: Extra Protection for Children or a Lost Opportunity?' 17 *Child and Family Law Quarterly* 307.

Herring, J. (2007) 'Familial Homicide, Failure to Protect and Domestic Violence: Who's the Victim?' *Criminal Law Review* 923.

Home Office (HO) (1998) *Speaking Up for Justice: Report of the Interdepartmental Working Group on the treatment of Vulnerable or Intimidated Witnesses in the Criminal Justice System*, Home Office.

Home Office (HO) (2000) *Setting the Boundaries: Reforming the Law on Sex Offences*, Home Office.

Home Office (HO) (2002a) Cm 5668 *Protecting the Public: Strengthening Protection Against Sex Offenders and Reforming the Law on Sexual Offences*, The Stationery Office.

Home Office (HO) (2002b) Cm 5536 *Justice for All*, The Stationery Office.

Home Office (2002c) Achieving Best Evidence in Criminal Proceedings: Guidance for Vulnerable or Intimidated Witnesses, including Children, Home Office Communication Directorate.

Home Office (HO) (2003) *MAPPA Guidance*, Home Office.

Home Office (HO) (2007) *Review of the Protection of Children from Sex Offenders*, COI.

Hoyano, L. (2001) 'Striking a Balance Between the Rights of Defendants and Vulnerable Witnesses: Will Special Measures Directions Contravene Guarantees of a Fair Trial?' *Criminal Law Review* 948.

(2007) 'The Child Witness Review: Much Ado About Too Little' *Criminal Law Review* 849.

Hoyano, L. and Keenan, C. (2007) *Child Abuse: Law and Policy Across Boundaries*, Oxford University Press.

Keenan, C. and Maitland, L. (1999) '"There Ought to be a Law Against it"–Police Evaluation of the Efficacy of Prosecution in a Case of Child Abuse' 11 *Child and Family Law Quarterly* 397.

Laming, H. (2003) Cm 5730 *The Victoria Climbié Inquiry: Report of an Inquiry by Lord Laming*, The Stationery Office.

Lösel, F. and Schmucker, M. (2005) 'The Effectiveness of Treatment for Sexual Offenders: a Comprehensive Meta-analysis,' *Journal of Experimental Criminology* 117.

May-Chahal, C. and Cawson, P. (2005) 'Measuring Child Maltreatment in the United Kingdom: A Study of the Prevalence of Child Abuse and Neglect' 29 *Child Abuse and Neglect* 969.

Ministry of Justice (MOJ), Home Office, Crown Prosecution Services, Department of Health (2007) *Achieving Best Evidence in Criminal Proceedings: Guidance on Interviewing Victims and Witnesses and Using Special Measures*, Ministry of Justice.

Ministry of Justice (MOJ) (2009) *Government Response to Improving the Criminal Trial Process for Young Witness Consultation*, MOJ.

Morgan, J. and Zedner, L. (1992) *Child Victims: Crime, Impact and Criminal Justice*, Clarendon Press.

NSPCC (1998) *Young Witness Pack*, NSPCC.

NSPCC (2007) *The NSPCC's Response to Improving the Criminal Trial Process for Young Witnesses*, NSPCC.

Office for Criminal Justice Reform (OCJR) (2005) *The Code of Practice for Victims of Crime*, Office for Criminal Justice Reform

Office for Criminal Justice Reform (OCJR) (2007) *Improving the Criminal Trial Process for Young Witnesses, A Consultation Paper*, Office for Criminal Justice Reform.

Ofsted (2008) *Safeguarding Children, the Third Joint Chief Inspectors' Report on Arrangements to Safeguard Children*, Ofsted.

Ormerod, D. (2008) 'Causing or Allowing Death of a Child or Vulnerable Adult' *Criminal Law Review* 54.

Pigot, T. (1989) *Report of the Advisory Group on Video Evidence*, Home Office.

Plotnikoff, J. and Woolfson, R. (1995) *Prosecuting Child Abuse: an Evaluation of the Government's Speedy Progress Policy*, Blackstone Press.

(2004) *In Their Own Words: the Experiences of 50 Young Witnesses in Criminal Proceedings*, NSPCC.

(2007a) *Evaluation of Young Witness Support*, Lexicon Ltd.

(2007b) *The "Go-Between": Evaluation of Intermediary Pathfinder Projects*, Lexicon Ltd.

Sharland, E., Seal, H., Croucher, M., Aldgate, J. and Jones, D. (1996) *Professional Intervention in Child Sexual Abuse*, HMSO.

Smith, V. (1999) 'Passing on Child Abuse Findings – Re V and Re L', 29 *Family Law* 249.

(2006) 'In Defence of the Prosecution Disclosure Protocol' 36 *Family Law* 457.

Thomas, D. (2008) 'Sentencing: Dangerous Offenders – Imprisonment for Public Protection – Protection of Children Act 1978, s1' *Criminal Law Review* 320.

Thomas, T. (2007) 'The Bichard Inquiry: A Progress Report' 239 *Childright* 8.

(2008) 'The Sex Offender "Register": A Case Study in Function Creep' 47 *Howard Journal* 227.

Wade, A. and Westcott, H. (1997) 'No Easy Answers: Children's Perspectives on Investigative Interviews' in Westcott, H. and Jones, J. (eds.) *Perspectives on the Memorandum: Policy, Practice and Research in Investigative Interviewing*, Ashgate.

Waterhouse, R. (Chairman) (2000) *Lost in Care: Report of the Tribunal of Inquiry into the Abuse of Children in Care in the Former County Council Areas of Gwynedd and Clwyd since 1974*, The Stationery Office.

Wattam, C. (1997) 'Is the Criminalisation of Child Harm and Injury in the Interests of the Child?' 11 *Children and Society* 97.

Westcott, H. (2006) 'Child Witness Testimony: What Do We Know and Where Are We Going?' 18 *Child and Family Law Quarterly* 175.

Westcott, H. and Kynan, S. (2006) 'Interviewer Practice in Investigative Interviews for Suspected Child Sexual Abuse' 12 *Psychology, Crime and Law* 367.

Wood, J. and Kemshall, H. (2007) *The Operation and Experience of Multi-Agency Public Protection Arrangements (MAPPA)*, Home Office Findings 285, Home Office.

Chapter 18

Protecting the rights of young offenders

(1) Introduction

Children[1] who become involved in crime do not thereby lose their right to be treated as children. Indeed, as the Ingleby Committee so wisely observed, although they are 'often an appalling nuisance', young offenders are of less immediate danger to society than adult law-breakers, they are less responsible for their actions, and are more amenable to training and education.[2] The law should undoubtedly protect children from the full rigours of the criminal justice system until they are old enough to take full personal responsibility for their actions. These concepts might appear to be truisms; clearly they inspired many of the provisions of the Children Act (CA) 1908. Nevertheless, English law has increasingly become the focus of international criticism for its harsh treatment of young offenders. Since the early 1990s, successive governments have responded to a fear of juvenile lawlessness with increasingly tough measures designed to crack down on youth crime. The various legislative measures introduced by the New Labour government since it came to power in 1997 reflect this approach. Indeed, the government of England and Wales is currently infringing a variety of international instruments designed to safeguard the rights of children who offend, including their right to a form of trial adjusted to their juvenile status and to humane treatment once convicted. This area of law is far too extensive to allow an overall assessment. Instead, those aspects of the youth justice system which are currently the subject of the most stringent criticism are discussed below. First, though, there is a brief assessment of the reasons for the current and increasingly punitive response to the problem of youth crime and the apparent lack of concern for the rights of young people in an adult society.

(2) Children's rights versus society's right to protection

The Convention on the Rights of the Child (CRC) stresses the need for legal systems to respond to youth crime by respecting the legal status of juveniles and

---

[1] English criminal law uses the term 'children' to describe those under the age of 14 and 'young persons' to describe those under the age of 18.

[2] HO (1960) para. 106.

promoting their overall welfare.[3] Similarly, the United Nations Standard Minimum Rules for the Administration of Juvenile Justice 1985 (the Beijing Rules), which provide a complete and detailed framework for the operation of a national juvenile justice system, continually emphasise the importance of dealing with juvenile offenders fairly and humanely. Although not binding per se, these provide a detailed blueprint for the various processes which should be applied to children caught up in youth crime. The overall aim of these two international instruments is to ensure that young offenders are themselves protected from harm, treated justly and diverted from imprisonment and punishment into treatment and rehabilitation.[4] Further comment has been provided by the Committee on the Rights of the Child.[5] Additionally, the Human Rights Act (HRA) 1998 now reinforces the need to comply with the provisions of the European Convention for the Protection of Human Rights and Fundamental Freedoms (ECHR), a Convention which has already achieved important reforms in the law relating to young offenders.[6]

Had the policies developed in this country during the 1960s been implemented, these international instruments would have been fully complied with by English law. Instead, the UK has come under constant criticism for its treatment of young offenders.[7] It was during the 1960s that the 'welfare approach' to juvenile crime had attracted increasing support. The Ingleby Committee wanted the age of criminal responsibility raised to 12.[8] Soon afterwards, the White Paper, *The Child, the Family and the Young Offender*[9] recommended keeping young offenders out of court as far as possible, through family councils and family courts. This was quickly followed by *Children in Trouble*,[10] which emphasised that juvenile delinquency is, in most cases, no more than a phase in a child's normal development, which needs checking in a way that will not merely reinforce his or her criminal tendencies.[11] But the welfare approach lost momentum and the Children and Young Persons Act (CYPA) 1969, designed to introduce many of its ingredients, was never fully implemented. Even in the 1960s, an approach which saw children as the product of society, requiring 'treatment' to remedy their behaviour was a controversial one. Since then, it has been in almost continuous conflict with the 'justice model'.[12] The latter considers young offenders not as needing protection but as being personally responsible for their actions and therefore deserving punishment.[13]

---

[3] See particularly Art. 40, discussed in more detail below.

[4] See also the International Covenant on Civil and Political Rights, Arts. 10(2)(b) and 14(4).

[5] Committee on the Rights of the Child (2007). U. Kilkelly (2008) discusses the UN documents which protect those involved in youth crime.

[6] Discussed below.

[7] E.g. inter alia: Committee on the Rights of the Child (1995) paras. 17–18; ibid. (2002) paras. 59–60; ibid. (2008) paras. 77 and 79; T. Hammarberg (2008); discussed further below.

[8] HO (1960). See below.   [9] HO (1965).   [10] HO (1968).

[11] Ibid. at para. 6.   [12] A. Morris and H. Giller (1987) esp. ch. 8.

[13] L. Gelsthorpe and A. Morris (1994) pp. 971–3.

Many writers have described the swings between the welfare and justice models which have systematically undermined policy-makers' ability to develop any coherent youth crime strategy.[14] The 1980s and early 1990s saw concerted efforts being made to divert young people from the criminal justice system[15] and to find alternatives to custodial responses, particularly for the younger children. Nevertheless, by 1993, the year that 2-year-old James Bulger was murdered by two 10-year-old boys, a far more punitive approach was emerging. The view that the type of measures appropriate for young offenders were similar to those appropriate for abused children not only lost favour, but the justice model was being embraced far more obviously. Following the introduction of the new secure training order in 1994, the numbers of young people sentenced to prison rose spectacularly.[16] A new government then came to power in 1997. Greatly influenced by the Audit Commission's report, *Misspent Youth*,[17] it resolved to reform a youth justice system considered to be slow, inefficient, expensive and achieving little, in terms of addressing offending behaviour and preventing its reoccurrence.[18] With the assistance of the newly established Youth Justice Board (YJB)[19] to monitor the operation of the new system and provide policy guidance, an ambitious package of measures was introduced, designed to provide a clearer focus on tackling youth crime at national and local levels.[20]

The system of youth justice introduced by New Labour[21] comprises a strange blend of authoritarianism and liberalism – indeed it is permeated with contradictions and tensions. It would be simplistic to claim that it wholeheartedly adopts the justice model, given its use of 'evidence based' policies and 'what works' rationales.[22] Some of the organisational changes, particularly the multi-agency approach to youth justice, were sensible. Giving the locally based and organised multi-agency youth offending teams (YOTs)[23] the task of co-ordinating the work of various agencies, all of whom probably already deal with the same child, but in differing contexts, was a much-needed initiative. The YOTs organise and provide local community intervention programmes aimed at 'nipping crime in the bud', thereby keeping more young offenders out of the courts and preventing today's young offenders too easily becoming 'tomorrow's

---

[14] Excellently summarised by R. Morgan and T. Newburn (2007). See also J. Fionda (2005) ch. 3.
[15] I.e. through the extensive use of cautions.
[16] R. Morgan and T. Newburn (2007) p. 1031: the number of young people serving custodial sentences rose by 122% between 1993 and 1999.
[17] Audit Commission (1996).   [18] R. Morgan and T. Newburn (2007) pp. 1031–2.
[19] Later officially renamed the YJB.   [20] HO (1997c) para. 1. See also HO (1997a) Introduction.
[21] The youth justice system was largely reorganised by the Crime and Disorder Act (CDA) 1998 and the Youth Justice and Criminal Evidence Act 1999. Since then, further major changes have been introduced by the Anti-social Behaviour Act (ASBA) 2003, the Criminal Justice Act (CJA) 2003 and the Criminal Justice and Immigration Act (CJIA) 2008.
[22] B. Goldson and J. Muncie (2006) p. 207. See also R. Smith (2006) for a discussion of the use of managerial techniques to predict and divert delinquent behaviour – the new 'actuarialism'.
[23] These local teams include probation officers, social workers, police officers, education and health authority staff.

hardened criminals'.[24] The youth courts also gained a useful but bewildering armoury of non-custodial orders, some involving an element of restorative justice aimed at making the offender take responsibility for his behaviour. Nevertheless, as is discussed in more detail below, the new legislation was underpinned by the same intolerant ideas about punishment and retribution which had dominated the previous administration's approach to youth justice.

Looking back over this reforming era, Morgan and Newburn observe: 'Young offenders are today more likely to be criminalised and subject to a greater level of intervention than before the 1998 reforms.'[25] As they explain, for those dealt with pre-court, their warning is more likely to be accompanied by an intervention; but they are more likely to be prosecuted. If convicted, the sanction is more likely to be onerous and 35 per cent more children and young people are sentenced to custody today than in the years immediately preceding the 1998 legislation.[26] Furthermore, a determination to protect the public and prevent young people 'drifting into crime' has led to increasingly authoritarian attempts to control children and their families – a development strongly criticised by international observers.[27] Children are now subject to a range of civil orders and restrictions, including child safety orders, acceptable behaviour contracts (ABCs), anti-social behaviour orders (ASBOs) and local child curfews.[28]

Society is, of course, entitled to protect itself from young offenders. But it is notoriously difficult to measure the extent of youth crime,[29] with recorded crime figures often being misleading[30] and public perceptions being inaccurate.[31] It seems clear from recent self-report studies[32] that 'offending in the teenage years is relatively common'[33] and that rates remain reasonably stable.[34] Certainly public spending on youth crime is very large.[35] We now know more about the profile of young offenders. The peak ages for offending behaviour

---

[24] HO (1997a) Introduction.   [25] R. Morgan and T. Newburn (2007) p. 1046.

[26] Ibid. at pp. 1046–7. See also E. Solomon and R. Garside (2008) pp. 65–6.

[27] E.g. A. Gil-Robles (2005).   [28] Discussed below.

[29] The difficulties underlying the quest for accurate statistics on youth crime are discussed by inter alia: J. Fionda (2005) pp. 59–68; J. Muncie (2004) pp. 14–21; T. Newburn (2007) pp. 585–7; T. Bateman (2006a). More generally, see M. Maguire (2007) who considers in depth the methods used for collecting accurate crime statistics.

[30] R. Morgan (ex Chair of the YJB) (2007a): to meet crime targets, rather than pursuing serious offenders, the police are 'picking low-hanging fruit' through giving on-the-spot fines and cautions relating to relatively trivial juvenile group behaviour. See also E. Solomon and R. Garside (2008) pp. 41–2 and Nacro (2008) pp. 2–4 for a detailed explanation of the impact of government targets on police practice.

[31] Discussed below.   [32] Inter alia: D. Wilson et al. (2006); S. Roe and J. Ashe (2008).

[33] T. Newburn (2007) p. 585.

[34] S. Roe and J. Ashe (2008) p. 13: the proportion of young people who reported committing an offence (currently 20%) has shown no statistically significant change across all four waves of the Crime and Justice Survey.

[35] E. Solomon and R. Garside (2008) p. 19: between 2000/1 and 2006/7, expenditure on the youth justice system increased by 45% to £648.5m. YJB (2008) p. 17: the YJB's budget for 2008/9 was £515m. NB the YJB is not responsible for the running costs of the YOTs.

appear to be 17 for boys and 15 for girls.[36] The identification of risk factors (the factors associated with committing an offence) is a complicated science[37] and controversial.[38] Nevertheless, a growing body of research evidence supports the view that a young offender is more likely to be male, displays aggressive and hyperactive behaviour in early childhood, prone to drug and alcohol abuse, with poor relationships with family, friends and relatives, involved with the police, has a parent (and or friends) who has been in trouble with the police, and has truanted and or been excluded from school.[39] There is also a strong likelihood of a young offender having suffered from a childhood mental disorder.[40] Indeed, it was Kilbrandon's[41] perception that it is almost a matter of coincidence whether children end up in state care or being prosecuted that led to the establishment of the Scottish children's hearing system. As the research continues to show, the two groups of children suffer the same or very similar adverse life experiences.[42]

This depressing picture of marginalised young people should, however, be kept in perspective. Whipped up by media portrayals of persistent young offenders, combined with memories of the James Bulger murder, the public has exaggerated fears of increasing youth crime, not supported by the criminal statistics.[43] They presumably overlook the fact that adults are responsible for the vast majority of all detected crimes.[44] Indeed, as Fionda has pointed out: 'The "rhetoric of youth crime therefore appears at odds with the "reality".'[45] Although most of youth crime is relatively minor, mainly involving criminal damage and shoplifting,[46] it is much more visible than much adult crime. Public anxiety, which has become increasingly exaggerated, often concentrates on essentially non-criminal or relatively trivial criminal behaviour, such as hanging around on the streets, vandalism, graffiti and deliberate damage to property.[47] As Margo et al. indicate, whilst in 1992, Britons were 1.75 times

---

[36] Nacro (2008) p. 2 – figures for 2006.   [37] D. Farrington (2007) pp. 602–31.

[38] D. Armstrong (2004); K. Haines and S. Case (2008).

[39] Inter alia: D. Farrington (1996) ch. 1; J. Graham and B. Bowling (1995) esp. ch. 4; C. Flood-Page et al. (2000) esp. ch. 3; D. Armstrong et al. (2005) esp. ch. 6; D. Wilson et al. (2006) pp. 34–6; D. Farrington (2007) pp. 608–19; Nacro (2008) p. 5; J. Margo and A. Stevens (2008) pp. 36–8.

[40] H. Meltzer and R. Gatward (2000) p. 85 and Tables 7.6 and 7.7; D. Lader et al. (2000); R. Harrington and S. Bailey with P. Chitsabesan et al. (2005) pp. 37–8; discussed further in the context of imprisonment.

[41] L. Kilbrandon (1964).

[42] L. Waterhouse et al. (2004) esp pp. 167–77. See also J. McGhee and L. Waterhouse (2007) pp 112–18.

[43] T. Bateman (2006a) pp. 70–1; Nacro (2008) pp. 2–7; J. Margo and A. Stevens (2008) ch. 3.

[44] Nacro (2007a): during 2005, those under 17 committed only 12% of all detected crime. See also Nacro (2008) p. 4.

[45] J. Fionda (2005) p. 83 and discussion at pp. 82–4. See also D. Armstrong (2004) p. 101 and J. Margo et al. (2006) pp. 8–16.

[46] Nacro (2008) p. 4: but (ibid.) there has been a gradual (and slight) increase in violent crime committed by young offenders since 2003. See also A. Phillips and V. Chamberlain (2006) pp. 11–12 for self report data on violent crime.

[47] J. Mattinson and C. Mirrlees-Black (2000) p. 12.

more likely to cite young people hanging around as a problem than they were to complain about noisy neighbours, in 2006, they were more than three times more likely to do so.[48] Furthermore, by focusing its campaign to tackle anti-social behaviour on 'hoodies' and 'yobs', the government has provoked a generalised fear of young people, if not a resentment of youth generally.[49] The Committee on the Rights of the Child recently expressed concern over 'the general climate of intolerance and negative public attitudes towards children, especially adolescents' which appears to exist in this country, which may underlie further infringements of their rights.[50]

The public also fails to note that young people themselves are more likely to be victims of personal crime than adults, with 10- to 15-year-olds having the highest risk of being assaulted,[51] and many being both victims and perpetrators.[52] Adolescents are more likely to suffer harassment than adults and whilst few bring this harassment to the attention of the police, they are, themselves, more likely than adults to come into contact with the police, through being stopped and searched and being 'moved on'.[53] As the murders of Stephen Lawrence and Damilola Taylor indicate, members of ethnic minority groups may be at greater risk. Nevertheless, black people are also far more likely to be stopped by the police than white people or Asians and are more likely to be prosecuted than cautioned.[54] Ethnic minority young people certainly believe the police behave less fairly towards them than towards white people.[55]

Despite these factors which indicate that there may be almost as many young people being sinned against as are sinners, politicians continue to curry favour with the public by playing on its fears. Indeed, certain aspects of the current youth justice system reflect an implicit assumption that by becoming involved in offending behaviour, children forfeit most of their rights to a protected legal status. Much of this area of law is dominated by a legislative straight jacket with a particularly punitive aspect. Consequently, whilst legal challenges are dealt with by a judiciary very aware that young offenders have rights protected by the ECHR and CRC,[56] as some of the case law below shows, these legislative provisions are not always particularly generously interpreted.

---

[48] J. Margo et al. (2006) p. 12, citing A. Walker et al. (2006). See also J. Margo and A. Stevens (2008) ch. 2.

[49] Ibid. at pp. 13–16.　　[50] Committee on the Rights of the Child (2008) para. 24.

[51] M. Wood (2005) p. 1: 35% of children aged between 10 and 15 (surveyed in the 2003 Crime and Justice Survey) had experienced at least one personal crime in the previous year with 19% having experienced five or more incidents. See also T. Newburn (2007) pp. 593–5.

[52] S. Roe and J. Ashe (2008) pp. 28–9.　　[53] T. Newburn (2007) p. 595.

[54] C. Webster (2006) esp. pp. 33–8. See also House of Commons Home Affairs Committee (2007).

[55] Ibid. at p. 34.　　[56] K. Hollingsworth (2007).

(3) The age of criminal responsibility

(A) The international context

The youth justice system in this country has come under increasing fire from a variety of international sources, with the age of criminal responsibility attracting particular attention.[57] A crucial element in any youth justice system is the age at which offenders are obliged to take responsibility for their criminal actions. If this is too high, there is a risk that the law will be widely flouted and brought into disrepute, too low and the law risks being savagely harsh. International instruments recognise the importance of adopting an appropriate age for criminal responsibility, without being particularly helpful about what this should be. Article 40 of the CRC, which requires governments to establish special laws and procedures regarding children accused of or convicted of criminal offences, requires 'the establishment of a minimum age below which children shall be presumed not to have the capacity to infringe the penal law'. Rule 4.1 of the Beijing Rules states that:

> In those legal systems recognising the concept of the age of criminal responsibility for juveniles, the beginning of that age shall not be fixed at too low an age level, bearing in mind the facts of emotional, mental and intellectual maturity.

This rule is accompanied by the explanation that:

> The modern approach would be to consider whether a child can live up to the moral and psychological components of criminal responsibility; that is, whether a child, by virtue of her or his individual discernment and understanding, can be held responsible for essentially anti-social behaviour ... In general, there is a close relationship between the notion of responsibility for delinquent or criminal behaviour and other social rights and responsibilities (such as marital status, civil majority etc).[58]

These measures give no specific guidance as to what might be an internationally acceptable age limit below which prosecution should be impossible. Nevertheless, the UN Committee on the Rights of the Child urges states not to set it below the age of 12 and suggests between 14 and 16 as being appropriate.[59]

It is undeniably difficult to define the age at which it is appropriate to expect children to take responsibility for actions which, if committed by adults, would be punishable under the criminal law. Matters are made more complex by the lack of agreement over what the age of criminal responsibility measures, a matter returned to below. Although whatever age selected must be an essentially arbitrary one, the English government is coming under increasing international pressure to review the relatively low age of 10 presently marking the point at which children in England and Wales assume criminal responsibility.[60]

---

[57] J. Muncie (2008) pp. 108 *et seq.*   [58] Official Commentary to r. 4.
[59] Committee on the Rights of the Child (2007) para. 33.
[60] The age of criminal responsibility has been 10 since 1963. See CYPA 1933, s. 50, as amended by CYPA 1963, s. 16.

Most, but not all, European countries have adopted far higher ages.[61] Influenced by the lack of uniformity on this matter throughout Europe, the ECtHR rejected the claim made by the child killers of James Bulger that, by attributing criminal responsibility to them as 10-year-old children, the UK had infringed their rights under Article 3 of the ECHR.[62] Nevertheless, a strong minority rejected this view,[63] pointing to the vast majority of member states with far higher ages of criminal responsibility.[64] Furthermore, when visiting the UK, successive Commissioners for Human Rights have robustly criticised the low age of criminal responsibility in England and Wales[65] and have recommended that it should be raised in line with norms prevailing across Europe.[66] Gil-Robles observes that it is 'an excessive leap' to assume that a child even as old as 12 can 'measure with the full consciousness of an adult the nature and consequences of their actions'.[67] Nor is the Committee on the Rights of the Child impressed by this aspect of English law. In three sets of concluding observations it has indicated its concern at the low age of criminal responsibility and has recommended that it should be raised.[68]

(B) A source of controversy

The question whether the age of criminal responsibility should be raised has been a source of controversy in this country for many years. Although there is general agreement that society has a right to protect itself from youth crime, it is obviously inhumane and of little practical value to hold very young children responsible for breaking the law. At first sight, fixing an appropriate age for criminal responsibility might appear relevant only to the question whether a child should be found guilty of behaviour which would be criminal, if above the age selected. But the age of criminal responsibility has far greater influence than this. It governs every aspect of the youth justice system. Thus, for example, there is less obvious need for children to be protected from making incriminating admissions when being interviewed about their responsibility for certain actions if, by virtue of age, these actions cannot be defined as a criminal offence at all. An admission of guilt will not then constitute part of that child's criminal record. Equally, the type of hearing and evidential rules adopted for

---

[61] E.g. France (13); Germany, Austria, Italy, Spain and most eastern European countries (14); Scandinavian countries (15); Belgium and Luxembourg (18). See listed by J. Muncie (2008) p. 113.
[62] *T and V v. United Kingdom* (1999) 30 EHRR 121, at para. 98.
[63] A minority of five judges.   [64] Para. 1, joint partly dissenting opinion.
[65] A. Gil-Robles (2005) para. 105 and T. Hammarberg (2008) para. 8.
[66] A. Gil-Robles (2005) para. 107 and T. Hammarberg (2008), para. 50. See also T. Hammarberg (1995) p. 19 and T. Hammarberg (2006).
[67] A. Gil-Robles (2005) para. 105.
[68] Committee on the Rights of the Child (1995) paras. 17 and 36; ibid. (2002) paras. 59 and 62; ibid. (2008) paras. 77–8.

determining a child's responsibility for certain behaviour will be influenced by whether the behaviour could be described as criminal, which in turn depends on age.

The effectiveness of the criminal law might certainly be undermined by the introduction of a varying age which attempted to accommodate individual maturity, as employed by the concept of *Gillick* competence in civil law contexts.[69] There is, nevertheless, a stark contrast between the civil and criminal law regarding children's capacity for taking responsibility for the way they behave. Thus the punitive approach of the criminal law regarding a young offender's ability to be held criminally responsible at the age of 10 compares unfavourably with the civil law's overtly paternalistic approach to a child's legal competence for decision-making. Whilst the civil courts take great care to ensure that adolescents do not obtain legal capacity to reach decisions before being deemed sufficiently mature to comprehend their implications, the criminal law imposes criminal responsibility on juveniles at an extremely early age, presumably to protect society from their evident lawlessness.[70]

It is often suggested that an appropriate way of determining the age of criminal responsibility is to adopt the age at which children are commonly able to distinguish right from wrong. But as the Ingleby Committee pointed out many years ago, a capacity to do this does not necessarily indicate an ability to take personal responsibility equivalent to that in an adult.[71] Indeed, an ability to distinguish right from wrong may develop long before the child becomes sufficiently independent to take permanent personal responsibility for his or her actions, in the same way as an adult.[72] Research on the risk factors associated with youth crime[73] indicates that children are the product of their upbringing and are extremely vulnerable to influence from their environment and the climate of opinion in their immediate family and the group with which they mix. This suggests that although, for example, children of 11 may be perfectly able to distinguish right from wrong, they remain so much under the influence of their environment, that they feel obliged to join whatever criminal activity their friends are involved in.[74]

The ability to take personal responsibility for actions would suggest the need to understand their implications. Research evidence indicates that, in cognitive terms, important developmental changes occur during the teenage years.[75] It is only during the onset of early adolescence that young people become competent to think in abstract terms. With this comes the capacity to feel guilt and

---

[69] Discussed in Chapter 3.

[70] The contrast between the way in which the civil law and criminal law approach children's competence is explored by H. Keating (2007a) pp. 187–95.

[71] HO (1960) para. 81.   [72] Ibid.   [73] Discussed above.

[74] All the research on risk factors associated with youth crime indicates that having friends who have been in trouble with the police strongly correlates with adolescents' own offending behaviour; discussed above.

[75] Discussed in Chapter 3.

shame, linked with an awareness of the implications for others of the offender's wrongful actions.[76] The Royal College of Psychiatrists suggests that 'a considerable degree of intellectual development may have occurred by 14 years of age'. But it stresses that clear-cut ages are not appropriate and that there may be delays in one or more areas of development.[77] This weight of evidence reinforces the view long held by many that the current age of criminal responsibility set by English law should be increased.[78]

One of the factors hampering such an increase is the fact that the age of criminal responsibility cannot be viewed in isolation from broader considerations regarding how to deal with juvenile wrong-doing below the age chosen, and this itself has been a matter of considerable dispute. If the perception is that a child below the age specified will necessarily escape any attempt to improve his or her behaviour, despite having committed an 'offence', then the temptation will be to adopt a low age to ensure that society is able to protect itself against infant hooligans. But when the system provides a means of ensuring that children below the age of criminal responsibility can be dealt with by appropriate non-criminal methods, then there is far less need to keep it low.[79] The Ingleby Committee discussed this issue and recommended that the age of criminal responsibility be raised to 12, with the possibility of it being raised again to 14.[80] The report nevertheless stressed that such a change would not allow children below such an age to 'get off', since it was to be combined with providing the civil courts with wide powers to deal with them by other means.[81] The later White Paper, *The Child, the Family and the Young Offender*[82] more radically recommended raising the age of criminal responsibility to the age of 16 and abolishing the juvenile court. By way of a compromise, the CYPA 1969 eventually provided for the age of criminal responsibility to be raised to 14, with the retention of the juvenile court. This higher age was, however, part of the controversial package of provisions recommended by the White Paper, *Children in Trouble*[83] and was never implemented.

Subsequently, there seems to have been less sympathy for the argument that the age of criminal responsibility is too low. In a 1990 White Paper, the government indicated its satisfaction that the present legal arrangements made proper allowance for the fact that children's understanding, knowledge

---

[76] N. Tutt (1996) para. 3.10. See also Royal College of Psychiatrists (2006) pp. 30–49 and J. Margo and A. Stevens (2008) ch. 5.

[77] Royal College of Psychiatrists (2006) pp. 48–9.

[78] Inter alia: B. Goldson and E. Peters (2000) pp. 3–4; JCHR (2003) paras. 37–8; M. Rutter (2005) pp. 33–7; R. Allen (2006) p. 19; UK Children's Commissioners (2008) p. 34.

[79] As pointed out by the Scottish Law Commission (2002) para. 3.8, when recommending the age of criminal responsibility being raised from 8 to 12, a recommendation which has not been implemented by the Scottish Executive.

[80] HO (1960) para. 93.

[81] E.g. by authorising the removal of a child who needed care and protection from home into the care of a LA or an approved school.

[82] HO (1965).   [83] HO (1968); discussed above.

and ability to reason were still developing.[84] Moreover, the 1993 Home Affairs Committee took the view that 'juveniles who commit the most serious crimes must remain subject to the jurisdiction of the criminal courts in order to reassure the public that justice is done'.[85] Furthermore, ideas about reducing the age of criminal responsibility were frequently inextricably bound up with arguments about the value of the *doli incapax* presumption.

(C) Abolishing the *doli incapax* presumption

In the past, opponents to increasing the age of criminal responsibility were often influenced by the argument that the low age of 10 years was mediated by the *doli incapax* presumption, which provided an important additional safeguard for younger children. Until the presumption was abolished by section 34 of the Crime and Disorder Act (CDA) 1998, children under the age of 14 and above 10 were presumed incapable of knowing that what they had done was wrong and therefore not criminally responsible for whatever offence they might have committed. On the face of it, the presumption appeared to inject into the law a benign recognition that it was wrong to use criminal penalties to punish children under 14 who did not appreciate the wrongfulness of their actions. But it could be rebutted by the prosecution satisfying the court that the child knew, at the time of committing the offence, that it was 'seriously wrong' – as opposed to being 'merely naughty'. As the Bulger trial demonstrated, the presumption could be rebutted relatively easily, particularly in circumstances where the offence was very serious. This was illogical, since the most serious crimes are often committed by extremely emotionally disturbed children – indeed, they are the ones *least* likely to understand notions of culpability and the moral dimensions of taking responsibility for wrong-doing.[86] Despite the presumption's failure to protect these most serious wrongdoers, its existence implied that the full force of the criminal law only became fully operational at the age of 14. As Gelsthorpe and Morris point out, it had a powerful symbolic importance – 'it was a statement about the nature of childhood' and the vulnerability of children.[87]

On coming to power in 1997, prompted by judicial views that it was an anachronism,[88] the new government abolished the *doli incapax* presumption.[89] It instituted this change only three years after the Committee on the Rights of the Child had suggested that the UK should consider raising the age of criminal responsibility.[90] Adopting the views of Laws J,[91] the government asserted that whilst such a presumption might have been justified before the days of

---

[84] HO (1990) para. 8.4.   [85] House of Commons Home Affairs Committee (1993) para. 101.
[86] G. Boswell (1995) pp. 30–1.   [87] L. Gelsthorpe and A. Morris (1999) p. 213.
[88] *C v. DPP* [1994] 3 All ER 190, per Laws J, at 196–200.
[89] HO (1997b) paras. 6–13 and CDA 1998, s. 34.
[90] Committee on the Rights of the Child (1995) para. 36.
[91] *C v. DPP* [1994] 3 All ER 190, per Laws J, at 196.

compulsory education from the age of 5, today children grew up far more quickly, mentally and physically, and therefore knew right from wrong earlier.[92] The spuriousness of this argument is obvious. Developmentally, children can have changed very little, as the government's own protective stance makes clear in other contexts.[93] Children certainly remain as much a product of their home background and as prone to influence from others as they were in the nineteenth century. Indeed, the vast majority of European countries consider that this type of maturity is not present in children under the ages of 13 or 14.[94] The government also argued that children no longer needed this form of special protection from adult punishments because the reformed law would 'strengthen the capacity of the system to deal with child offenders in the most focused way, taking full account of their development' and ensuring that sentences were made age-appropriate.[95] This assertion ignores a number of issues. In particular, very young children can start being convicted for criminal offences from the age of 10, thus acquiring a criminal record – a factor which may have serious implications for them in later years. Furthermore, children over the age of 10 accused of very serious crimes may undergo a form of trial only marginally adapted to take account of their youth and, if found guilty, may receive a relatively long period in detention.[96] Finally, of course, early contact with the criminal justice system can actually prevent children growing out of crime, as many others do.[97]

The reform, which abolished a principle which had existed for over 800 years, met with a storm of critical comment.[98] The UK government's subsequent explanation (in its third, combined with its fourth, report on implementing the CRC) for this change in the law, emphasises its 'tough-on-crime' perspective. Its complaint that the doctrine of *doli incapax* had 'led to difficulties such as delaying cases *or even making it impossible for the prosecution to proceed*',[99] reflects a worrying inability to see that these outcomes demonstrated the principle's value to children. Its surprising assertion that keeping the age of criminal responsibility at the age of 10 actually *benefits* children by helping them 'develop a sense of personal responsibility for their behaviour'[100] did not impress the UN Committee on the Rights of the Child. As noted above, the Committee has again called on the government to raise the age from 10.[101]

---

[92] HO (1997b) para. 8.

[93] E.g. in October 2007, the legal age at which young people can buy tobacco was raised from 16 to 18.

[94] See the views of the five dissenting judges in *V v. United Kingdom (and T v. United Kingdom)* (2000) 30 EHRR 121; discussed further below.

[95] HO (1997b) para. 16.   [96] Discussed below.   [97] T. Bateman (2006a) pp. 74–5.

[98] Inter alia: L. Gelsthorpe and A. Morris (1999) and J. Fionda (1999) pp. 38–40.

[99] HM Government (2007) p. 160, para. 54, emphasis added.

[100] Ibid. at para. 55.   [101] Committee on the Rights of the Child (2008) para. 78(a).

(D) Reappraising the age of criminal responsibility

In the government's view, the *doli incapax* presumption had prevented child offenders undergoing the measures required to teach them to mend their ways.[102] Such a situation certainly needed reviewing – it was an obvious by-product of a low age of criminal responsibility, combined with a protective feature that ensured that children 'got off' entirely. Only a conviction could ensure that a child with criminal tendencies obtained corrective 'treatment', whereas an acquittal meant that no action at all could be taken, certainly by the criminal law. The Children Act (CA) 1989, by abolishing the old 'criminal care order'[103] and by making care or supervision orders hinge on proving that the child in question is suffering 'significant harm', or is 'beyond parental control',[104] had made early interventions by civil measures less obviously relevant to young offenders.[105] Indeed, it had contributed to a situation whereby a young offender protected by the *doli incapax* presumption might not normally receive any attention from the civil or criminal law. A more sophisticated approach would have been to adopt a similar scheme to that applying in most other European countries – establishing a far higher age of criminal responsibility, combined with well-designed civil powers to deal with child 'offenders' under that age, as proposed by the reformers in the 1960s.

Lord Lowry[106] in *C v. DPP*[107] quite clearly appreciated that the removal of the *doli incapax* presumption would have fundamental implications for the remainder of the youth justice system. Although he appreciated the principle's imperfections, including the fact that it was conceptually obscure in meaning and illogical in its effect,[108] he considered its value lay in its benevolent intentions. He rejected the view of Laws J in the court below that the presumption could be removed by the courts. Only Parliament should abolish it, but then as part of a larger review of the appropriate methods for dealing with youthful offenders. Lord Lowry stressed that any change should only be made after considering the evidence and taking account of its likely effect on the whole law relating to children's anti-social behaviour.[109] No such review ever took place; nor indeed was there any discussion of the possible impact of leaving the age of criminal responsibility at 10, detached for the first time in hundreds of years from the presumption of *doli incapax*.[110]

---

[102] HO (1997b) para. 16.   [103] CYPA 1969, s. 7(7).   [104] CA 1989, s. 31.

[105] Nevertheless, children's services have an overriding duty (under CA 1989, Sch. 2, para. 7) to reduce the need to bring criminal proceedings against children. Moreover, a child identified (e.g. by a YISP, see below) or by a YOT practitioner, as being at high risk of becoming involved in youth crime, might be found, on assessment by children's services to be 'in need' under CA 1989, s. 17, thereby justifying family support services. (Grateful thanks to T. Bateman for these points). S. Easton and C. Piper (2005) pp. 248–51 suggest that youth crime assessment work should coincide more with that carried out by children's services.

[106] Delivering an opinion with which the remainder of their Lordships agreed.

[107] [1995] 2 All ER 43.   [108] Ibid. at 57.   [109] Ibid. at 64.

[110] This point was not mentioned in the discussion of the *doli incapax* presumption in HO (1997b) paras. 6–19.

As noted above, the abolition of the presumption, which left children under the age of 14 exposed to the full rigour of the criminal law, attracted a storm of criticism. Nevertheless, since then, the judiciary have not entirely overlooked children's special vulnerability. The domestic courts have acknowledged the importance of the Strasbourg case law[111] indicating that children's right to a fair trial under Article 6 of the ECHR is infringed if their intellectual development is so impaired that they are unable to participate effectively in the proceedings.[112] Scott Baker LJ ruled that the accused must, inter alia, not only understand what he is said to have done wrong, but also have the means of knowing that what he had done was wrong.[113] Such a ruling, can in some cases, fill the gap left by the presumption of *doli incapax* – since the child who does not know that he has done wrong is also considered unable to participate effectively in a trial.[114] In the context of proving *mens rea*, unease was also expressed by the House of Lords in *R v. G*[115] over its requirements in cases involving relatively young children. More particularly, Lord Steyn warned against ignoring children's right to a special position in the criminal justice system, as protected by the CRC.[116] Consequently they should not be held guilty of 'reckless' damage, without making any allowance for their youth or lack of maturity. But this unease was expressed within the confines of an already extremely controversial test of recklessness.[117] Neither Scott Baker LJ nor the House of Lords discussed the implications of these concerns within the broader context of the principle of criminal responsibility itself.[118]

A reconsideration of this broader issue was avoided by the Court of Appeal when they rejected Smith LJ's 'tentative' and obiter suggestion in *Director of Public Prosecutions v. P (DPP v. P)*[119] that the defence of *doli incapax* had been

---

[111] *T and V v. United Kingdom* (1999) 30 EHRR 121 and *SC v. United Kingdom* (2004) 40 EHRR 10, discussed in more detail below.

[112] E.g. *R (on application of P) v. West London Youth Court* [2005] EWHC 2583 (Admin), [2006] 1 All ER 477, per Scott Baker LJ, at [9]–[11].

[113] Ibid. at [7]: the accused must *also* understand what defences are available to him, have a reasonable opportunity to make representations, and have an opportunity to consider appropriate representations once he understands the issues involved.

[114] *Director of Public Prosecutions v. P (DPP v. P)* [2007] EWHC 946 (Admin), [2007] 4 All ER 628, per Smith LJ, at [48].

[115] [2004] UKHL 50, [2004] 1 AC 1034: two boys aged 11 and 12 were charged with reckless arson. Per House of Lords, a person should not be held guilty of reckless damage without considering his particular state of mind and whether he appreciated the risk of the damage occurring; discussed by H. Keating (2007b).

[116] [2004] UKHL 50, [2004] 1 AC 1034, per Lord Steyn, at [53].

[117] Established by *R v. Caldwell* [1981] 1 All ER 961.

[118] H. Keating (2007b) pp. 547–9. See also J. Fionda (2005) p. 17.

[119] [2007] EWHC 946 (Admin), [2007] 4 All ER 628: a 13-year-old boy was prosecuted for assault and of taking and driving away a car. The CPS appealed against the district judge's stay of proceedings. The stay had been provoked by medical evidence that a combination of ADHD, a verbal IQ of 65, a mental age of 7, poor verbal reasoning and low levels of comprehension rendered the boy incapable of understanding concepts of right and wrong or of differentiating between seriously wrong and merely naughty.

left intact by section 34 of the CDA 1998.[120] In her view, although the presumption of *doli incapax* for children aged between 10 and 14 had been abolished by that provision, the defence itself remained available for those who could establish genuine incapacity.[121] Had her views been upheld, a child's incapacity would have been relevant to three different issues.[122] It could, as under existing law, negate his or her fitness to plead, thereby rendering a trial an abuse of process;[123] it could render the child entirely *doli incapax* (incapable of committing the offence); and it could, as under existing law, prevent the child participating effectively in the trial itself. The Court of Criminal Appeal did not consider that the legislative history of section 34 of the CDA 1998[124] justified Smith LJ's view that the *doli incapax* presumption remained available.[125]

The rejection of Smith LJ's views should not detract from her decision's overall importance.[126] Her detailed advice on the procedure to use in such cases remains very relevant.[127] More particularly, as Ormerod observes, her decision may also reflect a growing judicial concern over 'the heavy handedness of the criminal law in its application to children'.[128] In particular, note should be taken of her suggestion that when a child with mental health or disability problems is about to be prosecuted for an offence, the relevant agencies represented on the local YOT should consult each other over whether an application for a care or supervision order would be more appropriate.[129] It seems unlikely that this often happens given the joint Chief Inspectors' finding that a mere 54 per cent of YOTs inspected had 'sufficient or better joint working and coordination arrangements with social care services', with shortcomings being noted in numerous aspects of joint working.[130] Nevertheless, were agencies to take this suggestion seriously, they might avoid the children least able to take responsibility for their actions being sucked into the criminal justice system. Such an approach would accord with the views of critics such as Allen and Dame Elizabeth Butler-Sloss, both of whom have suggested that young offenders under the age of 14 should be dealt with, in the first instance by civil proceedings in the family courts.[131] Indeed,

---

[120] As suggested by N. Walker (1999).
[121] [2007] EWHC 946 (Admin), at [37]–[47].   [122] Ibid. at [48].
[123] Ibid. at [14]. Traditionally the accused is only found unfit to plead if he or she is suffering from a mental illness or substantial impairment of intellectual capacity; then a youth court should follow the procedure established by *R v. Barking Youth Court, ex p P* [2002] EWHC 734 (Admin), [2002] 2 Cr App R 19. I.e.: a finding of fact regarding the commission of the offence; a finding regarding the child's mental or physical condition; a hospital order (or guardianship order) under the Mental Health Act 1983, s. 37 in the event of his or her mental condition justifying such an order.
[124] Discussed in depth by M. Telford (2007).
[125] *R v. T* [2008] EWCA Crim 815, [2008] 2 Cr App R 17.
[126] D. Ormerod (2008a) pp. 170–1 and D. Ormerod (2008b) p. 723.
[127] [2007] EWHC 946 (Admin), at [51]–[58].
[128] D. Ormerod (2008a) p. 170. See also M. Telford (2007) pp. 516–17.
[129] [2007] EWHC 946 (Admin), at [32]–[36].   [130] Ofsted (2008) para. 174.
[131] R. Allen (2006) p. 19 and Dame Elizabeth Butler-Sloss (reported in C. Dyer (2005). See also Dame Elizabeth Butler-Sloss (2006).

it would achieve a system far closer to the one envisaged by the Ingleby Committee nearly 50 years ago,[132] than the present harsh approach which takes so little account of the severe mental disabilities of many very young offenders. Furthermore, the statutory focus of the youth justice system, which is to prevent offending,[133] would be achieved far more effectively and cheaply if children could be identified much earlier as requiring support, with appropriate links being made between all the relevant agencies for its provision.[134] Such an approach would also promote the YJB's aim to bring its youth crime prevention work more effectively within the *Every Child Matters* programmes established under children's trusts.[135] At the very least, Smith LJ's comments reinforce the need, highlighted by the House of Lords more than 20 years earlier in *C v. DPP*,[136] for a thorough review of the law in this area. The present government shows little interest in so doing.[137]

(E) Alternative approaches

The wide range of youth justice systems throughout the world reflect differing ideas about the age of criminal responsibility. Retaining a low age need not necessarily go hand-in-hand with a strongly punitive approach to young offenders. Indeed, although in Scotland criminal responsibility attaches to children aged 8 and over, the system of children's hearings avoids many children being dealt with by the criminal courts until they reach the age of 16. By contrast, in most European legal systems, a much higher age of criminal responsibility, combined with a welfare approach, makes it quite impossible for children under that age to be dealt with through the criminal justice system, however serious the offence with which they are charged. Thus a child under the age of criminal responsibility, who is charged with homicide, must normally be dealt with by specialised children's judges or by social welfare agencies.

There is a clear need for a thorough review of English law with an overall objective of increasing the age of criminal responsibility. Such a review should obviously encompass a consideration of what system to put in place for child 'offenders' falling below that increased age. In the countries which have adopted and retained the welfare model, whether it is presented in the form of a 'children's hearing', as in Scotland,[138] or a 'family group conference', as in Australia[139] and New Zealand,[140] the important benefit is that children are not labelled criminals by entering the system at a relatively early age. It prevents them acquiring a record of criminal offences long before they have developed a more responsible approach. Furthermore, a relatively informal procedure and non-legal style may be a far more appropriate method of dealing with children,

---

[132] Discussed above.   [133] CDA 1998, s. 38.
[134] Audit Commission (2004) pp. 92–4.   [135] YJB (2007a) pp. 24–6.   [136] [1995] 2 All ER 43.
[137] E.g. HM Government (2008) fails to mention the age of criminal responsibility.
[138] For short discussions of the Scottish children's hearing system, see inter alia: J. Fionda (2005) pp. 245–52; L. McAra (2006).
[139] C. Cunneen and R. White (2006).   [140] T. Bradley *et al.* (2006) and N. Lynch (2008).

many of whom are extremely disturbed, than a formal legal procedure. Indeed, such an approach might ensure that mentally disturbed children and those with learning difficulties obtain the services they often need so urgently, rather than attention being focused primarily on their offending behaviour.[141] Admittedly, the welfare approach has not been universally acclaimed in its practical application. Furthermore, it appears that many of the welfare based systems in Europe are changing,[142] either to a system based on principles of restorative justice, as in Belgium[143] or to a much more punitive approach, as in the Netherlands.[144] Even the Scottish children's hearing system, well known for its welfare approach, has been the subject of serious doubts. To date, however, it has survived reasonably well, despite latterly being underpinned by more punitive interventions for teenage persistent offenders, and ASBOs and parenting orders.[145]

Those countries retaining the welfare approach inevitably face challenges for infringing children's civil liberties due to their informal non-criminal procedures. With the implementation of the HRA 1998, the Scottish children's hearing system was forced to drop its opposition to providing children with free legal representation, despite considering this to be fundamentally inconsistent with the informal nature of the children's hearing.[146] But the most famous example of such a challenge occurred much earlier, when the United States Supreme Court in *Re Gault*[147] condemned a system whereby juveniles could be subjected to long periods of detention in various forms of institution, without rights to 'due process'. These are the rights to counsel, rights against self-incrimination and the other procedural protections automatically accorded to adult defendants in criminal trials.[148] The formal procedural system in England and Wales largely reflects such assumptions. Thus the present safeguards provided for children by the PACE Codes of Practice[149] are based on the view that juveniles in England and Wales should have at least as many due process rights as adults, when it comes to the police investigating a crime.[150]

There is the further problem that in welfare-based systems, decisions regarding the type of institution in which the child is accommodated and the length of stay, are usually taken on the basis of the child's future needs, not as a sanction

---

[141] As discussed above.   [142] J. Muncie and B. Goldson (2006).

[143] J. Put and L. Walgrave (2006).   [144] J. Beijerse and R. van Swaaningen (2006).

[145] L. McCara (2006) pp. 131–8, C. McDiarmid (2005), L. Piacentini and R. Walters (2006), K. Marshall (2007).

[146] *S v. Principal Reporter and the Lord Advocate* [2001] UKHRR 514: a declaration of incompatibility regarding the infringement of children's rights under Art. 6 of the ECHR.

[147] 387 US 1 (1967).   [148] B. Krisberg (2006).

[149] The Police and Criminal Evidence Act 1984 (PACE) and accompanying codes provide comprehensive regulations governing arrest and interrogation.

[150] E.g. children cannot be detained in a police station without charge for more than 24 hours; have a right to information about their rights; to contact a solicitor and receive free legal advice; to an appropriate adult to accompany them to interviews (unless they are over 17) and the right to make a telephone call.

for a past offence.[151] Consequently it may involve an equally intrusive intervention into a child's life to that allowed under the justice model, in so far as a child may be removed from his or her family for indeterminate lengths of time. Lynch points out that family group conferences in New Zealand often produce punitive outcomes.[152] Children may have little understanding of the official diagnosis that they are the product of seriously disturbed homes and that a substantial interference with their lives is required, perhaps involving removal from home for a long period. Any proposals for dealing with children below an increased age of criminal responsibility would have to take account of all these concerns. But until the calls for a full-ranging review[153] are heeded, the criminal law will continue to reflect harsh and unrealistic ideas about the capacity of very young children to take responsibility for their actions.

(4) Using the civil law to criminalise anti-social behaviour – children and parents

(A) Child Safety Orders

The reforms of the late 1990s reflected extraordinarily narrow views about how the young children who cannot conform and who behave in an anti-social way inevitably 'drift into a life of crime'.[154] Far from considering children as being vulnerable and in need of protection from adverse circumstances, as portrayed by the CA 1989, the new legislation adopted an authoritarian approach which not only kept the age of criminal responsibility at the low age of 10 but also set out to criminalise the misbehaviour of very young children.[155] The measures introduced by the CDA 1998 were grounded on ideas about young children's need for discipline and control; later they were to become even more Draconian, having gathered a further layer of civil law interventions designed to rid the nation of 'ASBO youth', 'hoodies' or 'yobs'.[156]

Initial criticism focused on the child safety order,[157] introduced to prevent children under 10 'slipping into the crime habit'.[158] The creation of these orders reflected New Labour's questionable assumption that practitioners can, with the assistance of the research on risk factors, identify even very young children as those destined for a life of crime. Indeed, as critics argued,[159] such orders risk bringing very young children within the perimeter of the criminal justice system quite unnecessarily. Whilst being ostensibly civil in nature, in so far as they are only available on the application of local authorities (LAs) to the family proceedings court, the grounds have criminal overtones.[160] The child safety

---

[151] J. Put and L. Walgrave (2006) p. 118.   [152] N. Lynch (2008) p. 222.
[153] E.g. G. Monaghan *et al.* (2003).   [154] HO (1997a) Introduction.
[155] C. Piper (1999) pp. 402–3.   [156] J. Margo *et al.* (2006) p 14.
[157] CDA 1998, s. 11.   [158] HO (1997b) para. 10.
[159] Inter alia: L. Gelsthorpe and A. Morris (1999) pp. 214–17 and C. Piper (1999) pp. 405–7.
[160] CDA 1998, s. 11(3). Such an order can be made if a child under the age of 10 commits what would be an offence if above that age, or if such an order is necessary to prevent such behaviour,

order places the child under the supervision of a responsible officer,[161] to ensure that he or she 'receives appropriate care, protection and support and is subject to proper control'.[162] Very young children are certainly unlikely to appreciate that such civil proceedings are not punitive, particularly if their parents are directed by a parenting order to enforce the conditions attached.[163] Although the court is governed by the welfare principle when deciding whether a child safety order is justified, there is no obligation to consider a welfare checklist.[164]

The conditions imposed by the order may restrict the behaviour of a young child very radically; for example, he or she may be ordered to attend a local youth programme for up to one year.[165] Furthermore, if the child breaches any of the terms of the child safety order the court can vary or discharge it,[166] make a parenting order or breach could provoke child protection proceedings.[167] Despite these features, the child is neither party to the proceedings nor entitled to separate representation in court. Arguably, a child maintaining that such failure infringes his or her rights to a fair trial under Article 6 of the ECHR has a good chance of succeeding.[168] The identification of children who should receive child safety orders has probably been assisted by the establishment of the Youth Inclusion and Support Panels (YISPs), who share information with a view to identifying those children between the age of 8 and 13 who are at 'high risk' of becoming involved in youth crime.[169] The well-intentioned remit of these multi-agency local committees is to prevent young children becoming involved in crime through assisting them and their families to access mainstream services. Nevertheless, it is arguable that their interventions, which may be based on wholly inaccurate information or an over-simplistic approach to the use of risk factors,[170] leads to more children being singled out and labelled as potential 'criminals' at an extremely young age. Such an approach is particularly questionable given recent research indicating that the vast majority of young children identified by risk factors as being at 'high risk' of future involvement in anti-social or other problem behaviour do not in fact become so involved by the time they reach the age of 8½.[171]

---

or they have breached a local child curfew, or their behaviour is harassing, alarming or distressing to local residents.

[161] A social worker, a member of a YOT, or of an LEA.   [162] CDA 1998, s. 11(5).

[163] CDA 1998, s. 8. A parenting order can be made whenever a child safety order is made; discussed below.

[164] I.e. the application is governed by CA 1989, s. 1(1) but not by s. 1(3). The court must instead obtain information about the child's family circumstances and the likely effect of the order on those circumstances. CDA 1998, s. 12(1).

[165] CDA 1998, s. 11(4), as amended by CA 2004, s. 60(3).

[166] CDA 1998, s. 12(6).   [167] I.e. by making a direction under CA 1989, s. 37.

[168] S v. Principal Reporter and the Lord Advocate [2001] UKHRR 514: per Scottish Court of Session, the failure to provide free legal representation for all children appearing before children's hearings in Scotland infringed their rights under Art. 6, despite those proceedings being civil, and not criminal, in nature.

[169] Introduced by the YJB in 2004; discussed below in Section 7C.

[170] D. Armstrong (2004) pp. 102–5.

[171] E. Bowen et al. (2008): from the sample of children identified as being at high risk, 88% had been involved in none/only one type of anti-social behaviour up to age 8½.

(B) Anti-Social Behaviour Orders

In 2004, long before the numbers of ASBOs made against children and young people had escalated out of all proportion to statistics on local crime,[172] the Commissioner for Human Rights asserted that the ASBO is the order 'which gives rise to the most human rights concerns'.[173] Although ASBOs were introduced by the CDA 1998,[174] they were little used until 2003.[175] By then, fears of escalating youth crime were being stoked by a government keen to assure the public of its determination to deal with vague concerns about social and moral decline.[176] Backed by the Prime Minister himself, the anti-social behaviour programme was reignited at various stages by further campaigns and strategies[177] reminding the public of their need to struggle against 'a tide of loutishness',[178] and by subsequent legislation extending the range of ASBOs[179] and their availability.[180] Indeed, the Commissioner for Human Rights indicated that 'excessive political encouragement' was being given by Westminster to LAs over their use.[181] Whilst acknowledging that anti-social behaviour is an urban blight which needs tackling, he doubted whether 'the excesses of the anti-social behaviour order' were fair and effective measures for combating it.[182]

The Commissioner for Human Rights hoped in 2004 that the new enthusiasm for obtaining ASBOs, what he described as 'this burst of ASBO-mania', would quieten down.[183] This, of course, was not to be the case. His very detailed concerns about these orders[184] have been followed by many other critiques,

---

[172] Between 1999/2000 and 2005 the number of ASBOs obtained accelerated from 104 to 9,853. 38% were made against young people aged 10–17. See Nacro (2007b) p. 3.

[173] A. Gil-Robles (2005) para. 83.

[174] Under CDA 1998, s. 1(1)(a) and (b), an application can be made for an ASBO if the applicant can satisfy a two-stage test showing (a) that a person (anyone over the age of 10) has acted in an anti-social way, that is in a manner that caused or was likely to cause harassment, alarm or distress to one or more persons not of the same household as himself; and (b) that such an order is necessary to protect persons from further anti-social acts by him. An application can be made by the local authority, the police, registered social landlords, county councils and housing action trusts. For a short but comprehensive summary of the current law relating to ASBOs, see Nacro (2007b)

[175] For short histories of their use in relation to children and young people, see inter alia: R. Morgan and T. Newburn (2007) pp. 1037–9 and G. Hughes and M. Follett (2006).

[176] A. Millie et al. (2005) p. ix.

[177] E.g. the Respect Action Plan, HO (2006a); the establishment of the Anti-Social Behaviour Unit and 'Trailblazers' and 'Action Areas'; the appointment of Anti-Social Behaviour Co-ordinaters etc. See National Audit Office (2006) pp. 12–16 and G. Hughes and M. Follett (2006) pp. 164–8.

[178] A. Millie et al. (2005) p. x.

[179] I.e. through the creation of the criminal ASBO (CRASBO) – any criminal conviction can be accompanied by an ASBO on evidence of the offender having caused 'harassment, alarm and distress' (not necessarily connected with the criminal offence itself) and the interim ASBO – an ASBO made prior to a full hearing, carrying the same prohibitions and the same penalty for breach as a full ASBO. See Nacro (2007b).

[180] An ASBO may now be applied for in the magistrates' court, the county court, and (in the case of a CRASBO) in the criminal court. CDA 1998, ss. 1 and 1B–1D.

[181] A Gil-Robles (2005) para. 112.   [182] Ibid. at para. 85.

[183] Ibid. at para. 113.   [184] Ibid. at paras. 108–20.

both domestic[185] and international.[186] Critics point out that despite government protestations to the contrary, the 'invention' of anti-social behaviour has seemed very much linked with youth crime.[187] They consider that this approach has encouraged fears of young people, with the media exploiting their ability to 'name and shame' the young people involved, using lurid headlines and photographs.[188] Despite much official guidance on usage,[189] there are many objectionable features of the ASBO, not least its 'flexible, ambiguous, and ultimately subjective definition' which 'necessarily invites inconsistency in application and administration'.[190] Concerns have also been expressed over the common assumption that the recipients of ASBOs have irresponsible parents who should also be taught a lesson.[191]

Perhaps the most criticised aspect of the ASBO is its hybrid nature.[192] Despite being defined as a civil order, breach is a criminal offence dealt with by the youth court, carrying a maximum penalty of a two-year detention and training order. But its civil nature means that the safeguards available for those accused of criminal offences are denied in ASBO proceedings.[193] Nevertheless, the House of Lords refused to accept that they should be classified as criminal rather than civil.[194] Their only concession was to rule that the seriousness of the matters involved justifies a heightened standard of proof rather than the normal civil standard[195] – consequently ASBO proceedings 'occupy a position mid-way between the civil and the criminal paradigms'.[196] The court is not interested in the reasons for the defendant's behaviour, nor indeed, his or her motives. This means that those with mental health problems or learning difficulties may receive ASBOs,[197]

---

[185] Inter alia: A. Ashworth *et al.* (1998); A. Ashworth (2004); J. Fionda (2005) pp. 239–45; G. Hughes and M. Follett (2006); S. Macdonald (2006); J. Margo and A. Stevens (2008) pp. 48–9; UK Children's Commissioners (2008) p. 33.

[186] Inter alia: Human Rights Committee (2008) para. 20 (regarding compliance with the UN International Covenant on Civil and Political Rights); Committee on the Rights of the Child (2008) paras. 34–5 and 79–80; T. Hammarberg (2008) paras. 29–30.

[187] Inter alia: E. Burney (2005) pp. 473–4; Nacro (2007b) p. 3; L. Koffman (2006) pp. 599–600. See also National Audit Office (2006) p. 21: 38% of their sample who had received ASBOs were under 18 and 85% were male. See generally, G. Hughes and M. Follett (2006) pp. 160–2.

[188] E. Burney (2002) p. 475. 'Naming and shaming' is discussed below.

[189] Inter alia: HO (2006b) and YJB (2005a).

[190] J. Donoghue (2007) p. 418. This inconsistency must partly explain the considerable geographical variation in the use of ASBOs by LAs and social landlords.

[191] E.g. by being given a parenting order; discussed below. See L. Koffman (2008) pp. 125–9.

[192] A. Ashworth (2004) esp. pp. 286–90.   [193] Ibid. at pp. 273–8.

[194] *R (McCann and ors) v. Crown Court at Manchester, etc* [2002] UKHL 39, [2003] 1 AC 787; critique by S. Macdonald (2006).

[195] Ibid., per Lord Steyn, at [37]: the standard of proof is 'the heightened civil standard', i.e. that set out by Lord Nicholls of Birkenhead in *Re H and ors (minors) (sexual abuse: standard of proof)* [1996] AC 563.

[196] A. Ashworth (2004) p. 277.

[197] The British Institution of Brain Injured Children (BIBIC), in its 'Ain't Misbehavin' campaign, asserted that over one-third of the children issued with ASBOs between April 2004 and April 2005 had diagnosed mental health disorders or learning difficulties. See also L. Koffman (2006) p. 603 and L. Koffman (2008) pp. 124–5.

sometimes containing restrictions that they are quite unable to understand.[198] Furthermore, as the Commissioner for Human Rights points out, since a potential recipient is not entitled to the evidential protection available to defendants in criminal trials,[199] nor to the procedural guarantees in Article 6(2) and (3) of the ECHR, he or she is 'especially vulnerable to human rights violations'.[200]

Concerns about the use of ASBOs for young people[201] include the fact that their minimum duration is two years.[202] Their impact is exacerbated if, contrary to judicial advice,[203] the order contains a number of Draconian and extremely broadly drawn restrictions.[204] Indeed, the fact that a young person must abide by such restrictions for at least two years may make breach almost inevitable, given their impact on home and social life.[205] It is surprising that the terms of ASBOs are not challenged more often, given the way in which many of the restrictions materially infringe respect for the family life of the young people involved.[206] Such extensive prohibitions might well interfere with the rights protected by Articles 8, 10 and 11 of the ECHR, and not be proportionate to the risk to the community of leaving it unprotected.[207] Further it could be argued

---

[198] A. Brown (2004) pp. 206–7.

[199] E.g. hearsay evidence may be given establishing the grounds for the ASBO. On this see *R (on application of W) v. Acton Youth Court* [2005] EWHC 954 (Admin), (2005) 170 JP 316 and *R v. W and anor* [2006] EWCA Crim 686, [2006] 3 All ER 562.

[200] T. Hammarberg (2008) para. 29.

[201] Summarised by R. Morgan and T. Newburn (2007) p. 1039.

[202] A.-R. Solanki *et al.* (2006) pp. 73–4: only 62% of the ASBOs (criminal and civil) researched were imposed for 24 months; some were for much longer, three being for up to 6 years. The new need to review annually all ASBOs made against those under 17 (introduced by CDA 1998, s. 1J and K, as inserted by CJIA 2008, s. 123) may eventually reduce the numbers of ASBOs of such long duration. See Nacro (2007d) p. 4.

[203] *R v. P* [2004] EWCA Crim 287, [2004] 2 Cr App Rep (S) 63, per Henriques J, at [34]: the terms of the order made must be precise and capable of being understood by the offender; *R v. W and anor* [2006] EWCA Crim 686, [2006] 3 All ER 562, per Aiken J, at [41](7): each separate prohibition must be *necessary* to protect others from the offender's anti-social behaviour (emphasis added).

[204] E.g. *R (W) v. Director of Public Prosecutions* [2005] EWCA Civ 1333, (2005) 169 JP 435, per Brooke LJ, at [8]: the prohibition imposed by the youth court on a young offender aged 14 committing 'any criminal offence' was unenforceable and invalid – he might not know what was a criminal offence and what was not. See also S. Macdonald (2007) for a detailed critique of the terms of five prohibitions in *Hills v. Chief Constable of Essex Police* [2006] EWHC 2633 (Admin), (2007) 171 JP 14.

[205] A.-R. Solanki *et al.* (2006) p. 75, Table 7.3, for a range of prohibitions. See also sentencers' disapproval, at pp. 65–7 and that of young offenders, pp 83–6, some of whom knew from the start that they could not comply with extensive prohibitions in their ASBOs.

[206] E.g. *R v. H, Stevens and Lovegrove* [2006] EWCA Crim 255, [2006] 2 Cr App R (S) 68, Sir Igor Judge P (QBD), at [12]: reduced in extent and duration a prohibition barring a 15-year-old youth from entering an extensive specified area (containing his family home) for 10 years – it would have undermined the chances of his rehabilitation on release from custody. See also L. Koffman (2006) p. 608: recipients of ASBOs failed to object to widely drawn prohibitions.

[207] *R v. Dean Boness and ors* [2005] EWCA Crim 2395, [2006] 1 Cr App R (S) 120, per Hooper LJ, at [37].

that the prohibitions are not strictly 'necessary',[208] since it might be possible to prevent a repeat of the behaviour by some other means.[209]

One of the most regrettable aspects of ASBO practice, deplored by successive Commissioners for Human Rights,[210] is the use of aggressive forms of publicity identifying the young recipients of such orders to the locality in which they live[211] – the 'naming and shaming' so loved by the press.[212] Hopes that the judiciary would rule such a practice an unjustifiable infringement of the Article 8 privacy rights of a young person were dashed by Kennedy LJ's decision in *R (Stanley, Marshall and Kelly) v. Metropolitan Police Commissioner*.[213] In his view, although a 'simple desire to name and shame would never be an appropriate justification for publicity',[214] a decision to identify recipients of ASBOs could be justified as being a reasonable and a proportionate breach of their Article 8 rights under the ECHR, as long as their rights had been properly considered.[215] A fact stressed by Gil-Robles, but ignored by Kennedy LJ, is that this type of publicity risks 'alienating and stigmatising children, thereby entrenching them in their errant behaviour'.[216] The Commissioner considered that stricter guidelines should be produced to prevent the indiscriminate naming and shaming which might, in certain circumstances, risk violating juveniles' Article 8 rights.[217] Instead, subsequent official guidance stresses the benefits of publicising details about the recipients of ASBOs. Whilst noting that the person's age and human rights are relevant considerations, it indicates that publicity should be the norm, not the exception.[218] But, as the international monitoring agencies point out,[219] such publicity manifestly infringes the privacy rights of young people.[220] Strongest criticism comes from Hammarberg who, having stated his deep regret over the UK government's failure to reinstate privacy safeguards for children, adds: 'It is difficult to comprehend why any civilised government would permit such a practice, let alone pro-actively pursue it.'[221]

---

[208] Therefore not justifiable under Arts. 8(2), 10(2) and 11(2) of the ECHR.

[209] E.g. by an ABC. See below.

[210] A. Gil-Robles (2005) para. 119 and T. Hammarberg (2008) paras. 30 and 51.

[211] E.g. by leaflets, newsletters, website information and local newspaper articles.

[212] E. Burney (2002) p. 475.

[213] [2004] EWHC 2229 (Admin), [2005] UKHRR 115: three teenage recipients of ASBOs sought judicial review of the local authority's (and police authority) decision to publicise their photographs, names and ages and details of their behaviour. The publicity employed inflammatory descriptions of the youths as bully boys and thugs.

[214] Ibid., per Kennedy LJ, at [39].   [215] Ibid. at [42].

[216] A. Gil-Robles (2005) para. 119.   [217] Ibid. at para. 120.

[218] HO (2005) p. 2. Serious Organised Crime and Police Act 2005, s. 141: reverses the presumption of reporting restrictions on criminal proceedings against children in hearings for breach of ASBOs. But any court has power (CYPA 1933, s. 39) to impose reporting restrictions.

[219] Inter alia: Committee on the Rights of the Child (2007) para. 64; Committee on the Rights of the Child (2008) para. 36(b); Human Rights Committee (2008) para. 20.

[220] CRC, Arts. 16 and 40(2)(b)(vii). See also the Beijing Rules, r. 8.

[221] T. Hammarberg (2008) para. 30.

ASBOs have an extremely poor track record in achieving any change of behaviour on the part of young people,[222] with punishment for breach swelling the number of young people in detention.[223] Some receive a custodial sentence for the single offence of infringing their ASBO.[224] Indeed, the Commissioner for Human Rights criticised the fact that a civil order aimed at reducing urban nuisance could bring many young people within the criminal justice system, often behind bars, without necessarily having committed a recognisable criminal offence.[225] Although ASBOs are so poorly obeyed, the courts very rarely refuse applications for them.[226] Despite clear judicial guidance to the contrary,[227] researchers suggest that the courts often leap-frog the second limb of the statutory criterion,[228] normally assuming the order to be 'necessary', merely from evidence of the defendant's past engagement in anti-social behaviour and the negative effect that this has had on the community.[229] The second requirement tends 'to play, at best, a subsidiary role in the decision-making process'.[230] Given their high rate of breach, one would have expected a very different approach, with the courts taking account of the need to consider the child's welfare[231] and insisting on applicants having explored all alternative options, with ASBOs being available only as a last resort.[232] Instead, research suggests that courts often simply assume that alternative approaches had been tried,[233] without discovering that in many cases they have not.[234] Indeed, YOT practitioners who might, if involved soon enough, offer diversionary interventions, are often left in ignorance of concerns about a young person's behaviour until after the ASBO has been made.[235]

---

[222] National Audit Office (2006) p. 21: 55% of their sample who had received ASBOs had breached their orders.

[223] D. Brogan (2005) pp. 18–20: discusses the clear link between ASBO breaches and detention with the prediction (at p. 20) that 15.5% of all ASBOs imposed on young people will result in custody. See also A.-R. Solanki et al. (2006) p. 22 for a summary of the statistics available on this link and pp. 125–6, indicating great inconsistency in the sentencing for breach of ASBOs.

[224] A.-R. Solanki et al. (2006) pp. 112–13. The Sentencing Advisory Panel (2007) para. 91: provisionally recommends that the appropriate sentence in most cases of breach of an ASBO is a community order and not a custodial sentence. See also Home Office (HO) guidance (2006d) para. 5: if the breach of an ASBO is the offender's first offence (but the breach was not flagrant), a warning may be appropriate.

[225] A. Gil-Robles (2005) para. 83; see also Human Rights Committee (2008) para. 20.

[226] T. Bateman (2007) p. 307, cites Home Office statistics indicating that less than 1% of ASBO applications had ever been refused, by year ending 2005.

[227] R v. Dean Boness and ors [2005] EWCA Crim 2395, [2006] 1 Cr App R (S) 120, per Hooper LJ, at [37]: the applicant must satisfy the court that the ASBO is 'necessary' to protect people from the defendant's anti-social behaviour, and also that the terms of the order itself are proportionate, in so far as they are commensurate with the risks to be guarded against.

[228] I.e. CDA 1998, s. 1(1)(b).   [229] I.e. the evidence provided to satisfy CDA 1998, s. 1(1)(a).

[230] T. Bateman (2007) p. 314.   [231] I.e. under CYPA 1933, s. 44.

[232] Practitioners and the courts are ambivalent over whether ASBOs should be used as a last resort or simply one, in an armoury of powers. See A.-R. Solanki et al. (2006) Section 10 and Nacro (2007b) pp. 3–4.

[233] E.g. warning letters and Anti-Social Behaviour Contracts (ABCs), discussed below.

[234] T. Bateman (2007) pp. 318–19.   [235] A.-R. Solanki et al. (2006) pp. 48–56.

Most young people consider ASBOs to be ineffective and some consider them to be counter-productive.[236] Just over half their parents also see them as achieving little, with some even considering them to be looked on as a 'badge of honour' amongst their children's friends.[237] This reflects the Human Rights Commissioner's view that the excessive use of ASBOs is more likely to exacerbate anti-social behaviour and crime amongst youths than to prevent it.[238]

(C) Acceptable Behaviour Contracts – a better alternative?

Will the government heed international calls to end the use of ASBOs as a means of controlling the anti-social behaviour of young people?[239] At present it seems ambivalent over their continued use. A new Secretary of State stated that: 'It's a failure every time a young person gets an ASBO.'[240] Nonetheless, the government does not want the public to 'suffer needlessly from anti-social behaviour'. With this in mind, a new 'Action Squad of ASB experts will troubleshoot across the country' targeting those areas which do not use the ASB measures available to them.[241] Admittedly, practitioners consider that ASBOs can be effective 'when used appropriately',[242] and the government is keen to ensure that more Individual Support Orders (ISOs)[243] are made alongside ASBOs,[244] as a way of ensuring that the recipient is given sufficient support to address the causes of his behaviour.[245] Nonetheless, it appears that a general reluctance to use ISOs[246] may be attributable to the view that 'support' should be voluntary and not underpinned by orders which, on breach, carry further penalty.[247]

The National Audit Office produced clear evidence that a range of alternative options[248] might not only be cheaper but also more effective than ASBOs.[249]

---

[236] Ibid. at pp. 135–6.   [237] Ibid. at p. 136. See also National Audit Office (2006) p. 23.

[238] A. Gil-Robles (2005) para. 118. See also T. Hammarberg (2008) para. 29: notes the absence of any research indicating that ASBOs are an effective method of dealing with nuisance behaviour.

[239] Committee on the Rights of the Child (2008) para. 80; T. Hammarberg (2008) para. 29.

[240] Interview with Ed Balls, Secretary of State for Children, Schools and Families, *The Mirror*, 27 August 2007.

[241] HM Government (2008) p. 20.   [242] A.-R. Solanki *et al.* (2006) pp. 129–35.

[243] The ISO (which lasts a maximum of 6 months) requires the recipient to become involved in a programme of intervention provided by the YOT; see YJB (2006a).

[244] CDA 1998, s. 1AA and 1C (as amended by CJIA 2008, s. 124) extend the ISO's availability by: allowing more than one to be made re the same recipient; allowing ISOs to be made subsequent to the ASBO, on application by the original applicant; allowing ISOs to be made alongside CRASBOs.

[245] DCSF (2008) p. 13.   [246] Ibid. at p. 10: fewer than 10% of ASBOs have an ISO attached.

[247] T. Lloyd (2008).

[248] E.g. warning letters and Acceptable Behaviour Contracts (ABCs) – the latter is a written voluntary agreement between a person (of any age, including those under the age of 10) who has been involved in anti-social behaviour and one or more local agencies whose role it is to prevent such behaviour.

[249] National Audit Office (2006) pp 18–25: although warning letters and ABCs had less impact on those under 18 than on older people, the younger age group were significantly less likely to re-engage in anti-social behaviour after receiving a warning letter than after receiving an ASBO.

There seems a greater governmental interest in acceptable behaviour contracts (ABCs) as the 'right intervention' for 'bringing about a positive long-term change in behaviour'.[250] In some areas they appear to be used as an earlier form of intervention to the ASBO.[251] But ABCs also raise concerns about children's human rights. Signing the written contract involves the child or young person admitting to having behaved in a specified way and agreeing to abide by a list of conditions.[252] The child has no form of legal representation and no due process safeguards regarding any admissions that he or she may feel obliged to make. Furthermore, although there are no legal penalties, evidence of breach will be used to support any future application for an ASBO. Lack of legal regulation gives local officials, such as housing officers, considerable power over families. Indeed, provoked by unsubstantiated allegations from neighbours, parents, unassisted by legal advice, may face 'informal' demands to ensure that their very young children sign contracts agreeing not to repeat behaviour that they deny responsibility for.[253]

(D) Curfews and group dispersal powers

The controlling agenda presented by the combination of child safety orders, ASBOs and ABCs is not complete without reference to the 'local child curfew schemes' introduced by the CDA 1998.[254] These were effectively replaced by the later group dispersal powers introduced in 2003.[255] The latter provisions apparently empower a police officer to remove *any* child under 16, not under the effective control of a parent or other responsible person over 18, from any public place within the prohibited locality during the hours of 9 p.m. and 6 a.m. and take him or her home.[256]

Although these dispersal powers undoubtedly infringe children's rights under Articles 5, 8, 11 and 14 of the ECHR,[257] case law suggests that the judiciary have little sympathy with arguments couched in such terms. For example, May LJ in *R (W) v. Metropolitan Police Commissioner and Another*[258] was in no doubt that the power to remove children from a designated area at night and return them

---

[250] Home Secretary Jacqui Smith, HO Press release, 23 August 2007, on the launch of new guidance, HO (2007). HO (2006c): numbers of ABCs issued increased by 70% between 2004 and 2005.

[251] L. Koffman (2006) p. 596.   [252] HO (2007) p. 12.   [253] J. Cosgrove (2003) p. 21.

[254] CDA 1998, s. 14 (as amended by the Criminal Justice and Police Act 2001): local councils are empowered to ban children under 16 from public places during specified hours between 9p.m. and 6a.m., unless under the supervision of a responsible adult.

[255] ASBA 2003, ss. 30–6; summarised in Nacro (2004a) pp. 5–6. Dispersal powers are available to the police if they reasonably believe that two or more persons have intimidated or caused harassment, alarm or distress to others by their presence or behaviour and also that anti-social behaviour is a problem in a designated locality – from which locality those persons can be ordered to disperse, and if they do not live within that locality, to leave it and not return there within 24 hours.

[256] ASBA 2003, s. 30(6).   [257] C. Walsh (2002) pp. 74–7 and K. Hollingsworth (2006) pp. 262–3.

[258] [2006] EWCA Civ 458, [2006] 3 All ER 458: a 14-year-old boy sought judicial review of the decision to authorise police to exercise the powers contained in ASBA 2003, s. 30(6) in a designated area of Richmond.

home, even against their wishes, is not punitive but designed to protect them from the anti-social behaviour of others or from taking part in it themselves.[259] There had been no removal in that particular case, so he considered it unnecessary to discuss the rights issues provoked by these legislative provisions.[260] Nevertheless, as police authorities should note, May LJ specifically ruled out a police officer exercising the power arbitrarily simply because children are in a designated area at night. The legislation does not therefore confer a power on the police to remove children *not* involved in or at risk from actual or feared anti-social behaviour. Furthermore, in order to establish reasonableness, a police officer must show he has taken account of the detailed circumstances of the case.[261]

These powers very obviously pander to the public's misconceptions about high levels of anti-social behaviour attributable to children 'hanging about on the streets'. Such measures not only have the capacity to exacerbate these fears, but also penalise children living in deprived areas, with poor home facilities, from carrying out essentially innocent activities, such as congregating in groups.[262] Research shows that although the dispersal powers can offer short-term relief to a community, they do not tackle the underlying causes of anti-social behaviour. Predictably, they not only escalate police-youth antagonism,[263] but the indiscriminate nature of dispersal orders provokes deep resentment in young people.[264] Walsh argues that the use of an ultrasonic device, the mosquito, to deter *all* teenagers from congregating in particular areas, is further evidence of society's assumption that teenagers in public places cannot act responsibly.[265] She strongly criticises the government's failure to prohibit or regulate its use.[266] Predictably, the Committee on the Rights of the Child considers that mosquito devices and other methods of dispersing children from public areas violate their right to freedom of association and peaceful assembly, as enshrined in Article 15 of the CRC.[267]

(E) Children's anti-social behaviour – parental net-widening

The New Labour government was, from the start, clearly determined to force parents to take greater responsibility for their children's behaviour.[268] This was

---

[259] Ibid. at [35].

[260] Nor did Brooke LJ, in the High Court ([2005] EWHC 1586 (Admin), [2005] 1 WLR 3706) consider the application from a rights perspective; see K. Hollingsworth (2006).

[261] [2006] EWCA Civ 458, [2006] 3 All ER 458, at [35]. E.g. the child's age, the exact time of night and the child's own explanation for his presence.

[262] Inter alia: L. Gelsthorpe and A. Morris (1999) pp. 214–17; C. Walsh (2002); K. Hollingsworth (2006); C. Walsh (2008); UK Children's Commissioners (2008) p. 33.

[263] A. Crawford and S. Lister (2007) p. 66.   [264] Ibid. at p. 69.

[265] C. Walsh (2008) pp. 123 *et seq*. The mosquito device is uncomfortable to listen to, but is normally only detected by those under 25.

[266] Ibid. at p. 131.   [267] Committee on the Rights of the Child (2008) paras. 34–5.

[268] HO (1997a) paras. 1.4–1.6 and 4.6.

not a new approach, with parents long having been regarded as a source of control.[269] What was new was the way in which the research on the risk factors associated with criminal activities was now influencing the government's approach to youth crime generally.[270] As Farrington explains 'The basic idea of risk-focused prevention is very simple', the key risk factors for offending are identified and prevention methods designed to counteract them are implemented.[271] The new legislation emphasised that the statutory aim of the youth justice system was to prevent offending.[272] The government assumed that it could prevent youth crime by identifying the risk factors which correlated with offending behaviour and then, by setting out to intervene early enough, correct those deficiencies. All risk factor research focuses on, amongst other factors, the family background of young offenders.[273] So the government controversially assumed that if parents could be corrected, so could their children.[274]

The government's later efforts to stamp out anti-social behaviour similarly reflect the view that parents are to blame for thoroughly anti-social children.[275] Indeed, the word 'support' has acquired Orwellian features in the government's commitment to helping families 'in the greatest difficulty' and who 'refuse to engage'.[276] They are to be provided with 'intensive support' with 'non-negotiable elements'[277] – meaning the issue of more ASBOs accompanied by parenting orders 'to help tackle broader family problems'.[278] Furthermore, in cases where children are 'at risk of offending', YOTs dealing with parents who do not take up much-needed support voluntarily will be expected to make this support 'non-negotiable by recommending a Parenting Order to the court' and encouraging them to make such orders against both parents, whether or not the child lives with both.[279] Whilst the value of parenting contracts is also doubtful,[280] most criticism is directed at parenting orders,[281] whose availability has gradually been extended by legislation.[282] There is a presumption that a

---

[269] Inter alia: under CYPA 1933, s. 55, courts could order parents to pay their children's fines; CJA 1991 (extended by the Criminal Justice and Public Order Act 1994), introduced a power to bind over parents to exercise proper care and control over their children. See summarised by Nacro (2004b) p. 2. See also J. Fionda (2005) pp. 211–19 and E. Burney and L. Gelsthorpe (2008) pp. 470–3.

[270] D. Armstrong (2004).   [271] D. Farrington (2007) p. 606.   [272] CDA 1998, s. 37(1).

[273] E.g. parents with criminal records themselves, lack of proper supervision etc. See D. Farrington (2007) pp. 613–26. See also research summaries in M. Rutter (2005) pp. 29–30; J. Margo *et al.* (2006) ch. 5; J. Fionda (2005) pp. 206–11.

[274] D. Armstrong (2004) pp. 102–3. See also K. Haines and S. Case (2008).

[275] L. Koffman (2008) pp. 117–20.   [276] HM Government (2008) para. 2.12.   [277] Ibid.

[278] DCSF (2008) p. 9; see also HM Government (2008) para. 2.18.

[279] HM Government (2008) p. 35.

[280] E.g. parents 'may' enter into voluntary 'parenting contracts' (ASBA 2003, ss. 19 and 25) with YOTs or with schools, with a view to ensuring that their child's behaviour improves; discussed in the context of education in Chapter 6.

[281] Inter alia: L. Gelsthorpe and A. Morris (1999) esp. pp. 218–19; M. Koffman (2008) pp. 117–21; E. Burney and L. Gelsthorpe (2008).

[282] CDA 1998, s. 8(1): a parenting order can be made against any parent whose child is the subject of: a child safety order, a parental compensation order, an ASBO, a sexual offences prevention

parenting order will be made whenever a child under 16 is convicted of any criminal offence, or receives an ASBO.[283] Furthermore, various public agencies can now obtain 'stand-alone' parenting orders; for example, as the comment above makes clear, they can be obtained by YOT practitioners to help parents prevent their children repeating anti-social or criminal behaviour.[284]

The government's faith in parenting orders and parenting 'support' is curious. Since parenting orders are often issued to single mothers,[285] they can have a considerable impact on family life, which is not necessarily beneficial. Parents may be ordered to attend counselling or guidance sessions for up to three months,[286] and even to attend a residential course.[287] Early research suggested that parenting programmes can be beneficial,[288] but as Burney and Gelsthorpe point out, there is no robust evidence indicating that obligatory programmes of this kind can have any long-term effect on children's behaviour.[289] Furthermore, although defined as a civil order, failure to comply with its terms may lead to criminal proceedings and a fine or other order.[290] Many question the threefold assumption that parents *should* shoulder responsibility for their children's offences, that they are responsible for their criminal tendencies and that they can put a stop to them. Some young people themselves strongly reject the view that their behaviour is attributable to their parents' poor parenting.[291] Furthermore, as Rutter points out, advances in genetic science indicates that children's liability to show anti-social behaviour may be at least partly attributable to their genetic makeup and not to parenting styles.[292] Making parents take responsibility for their children's acts until they attain the age of 16 is difficult to justify, alongside an insistence that children as young as 10 should take responsibility for their own criminal actions.[293] There is considerable weight in the view that:

> the abolition of *doli incapax* and the coercive nature of parenting orders have created, in effect, a questionable new reality of dual responsibility for juvenile crime.[294]

(5) Diversion from court

A number of international instruments stress the importance of diverting young offenders out of the courts, whenever possible, without resorting to

---

order, or any criminal conviction. For a discussion of school-based parenting orders to correct truancy and indiscipline, see Chapter 6.

[283] CDA 1998, s. 9(1) and (1B).   [284] ASBA 2003, s. 26.   [285] A. Holt (2008) p. 204.
[286] CDA 1998, s. 8(4).   [287] CDA 1998, s. 8(7A).
[288] D. Ghate and M. Ramella (2002) ch. 3: parents largely found the parenting programmes very helpful, even those who had been initially hostile. Nevertheless, there was little evidence indicating any measurable impact on their children's behaviour.
[289] E. Burney and L. Gelsthorpe (2008) pp. 477–9. See also P. Moran and D. Ghate (2005).
[290] J. Jamieson (2006) p. 183.   [291] A. Millie *et al.* (2005) p. 24.
[292] M. Rutter (2005) p. 30.   [293] Ibid. at pp. 33–4.   [294] Ibid. at p. 34.

formal trial.[295] Their aim is to ensure that youth justice systems not only take account of society's need for protection from juvenile lawlessness, but also promote a child's capacity for change. Children have not yet completed their growth and development. With appropriate education, training or psychological treatment, those involved in criminal acts may be helped to grow into law-abiding citizens, without the stigma of criminality attaching to them. Technical and formalistic legal procedures are ill-equipped to take account of these special factors applying to young offenders.

Such ideas are well established in this country. A growing body of research indicates that those children who enter the criminal justice system are unlikely to emerge reformed characters, particularly if they receive institutional care or custody. Indeed, since hardly any form of sentence ensures a young offender's rehabilitation, the fewer who enter the criminal justice system the better.[296] Throughout the 1980s and early 1990s, care was taken to ensure that as many young people were diverted out of the courts as possible.[297] But a new system of police reprimands and final warnings was introduced by the CDA 1998 intended to avoid '[I]nconsistent, repeated and ineffective cautioning [which] has allowed some children and young people to feel that they can offend with impunity'.[298] Under the current approach, young offenders move through a structured and an inflexible system allowing a police reprimand to be given only for a first admitted offence,[299] with subsequent offences warranting a final warning[300] or criminal charges, prosecution and conviction. A welcome feature of the scheme is the way it seeks to ensure that a warning is combined with a rehabilitation programme provided through the local YOT, which may contain elements of reparation.[301] This already complicated picture of diversion strategies is rapidly acquiring potentially confusing extra layers, with the police acquiring a youth version of the adult conditional cautioning scheme.[302]

---

[295] CRC, Art. 40(3)(b); the Beijing Rules, rr. 11.1–11.4, together with the commentary; the Riyadh Guidelines, I (5). See discussed by Baroness Hale of Richmond in *R (on the application of R) v. Durham Constabulary and anor* [2005] UKHL 21, [2005] 2 All ER 369, at [28].

[296] T. Bateman (2006a) pp. 74–5: likelihood of re-offending once young people enter the criminal justice system. See also E. Solomon and R. Garside (2008) pp. 49–52: all the government's targets on reducing re-offending have been missed.

[297] See J. Fionda (2005) ch. 5 and Baroness Hale of Richmond in *R (on the application of R) v. Durham Constabulary and anor* [2005] UKHL 21, [2005] 2 All ER 369, at [30]–[37].

[298] HO (1997a) para. 5.10.

[299] Unless the officer considers that a first offence is so serious that it warrants a warning. CDA 1998, s. 65(4). NB HO (2006d) para. 6: whenever offending behaviour occurs, the *first* response of the police should be to turn to the final warning scheme (emphasis added).

[300] CDA 1998, ss. 65–6.

[301] CDA 1998, s. 66(1)–(3). The new system adopted some of the features of the old 'caution-plus' schemes developed by some police forces, notably Northamptonshire and Thames Valley.

[302] Under CDA 1998, s. 66A (as inserted by CJIA 2008, Sch. 9) the police may give a conditional caution to a young first offender aged 16 or 17, as an alternative to prosecution, subject to his fulfilling certain conditions attached to the caution, i.e. a programme designed to address his offending behaviour; Nacro (2007d).

There are many fundamental criticisms of the current diversion system.[303] It effectively gives young offenders only two chances before appearing in the local youth court, and thereby risks undermining attempts to divert large numbers of young people from the courts.[304] Early concerns that this highly regulated early intervention scheme would prematurely launch children into criminal justice proceedings[305] were vindicated by the Audit Commission's finding that too many minor cases were being taken to the youth court.[306] As Fox *et al.* indicate, if 'discretion is curbed, the ability to use common sense is also reduced'.[307] There have been limited attempts to address this net-widening effect.[308] Nevertheless, the decision whether to administer a reprimand or final warning, combined with a referral to the YOT, is entirely in the hands of the police, who may adopt variable attitudes towards certain groups of young people, such as young women.[309] Contrary to hopes, the current system has also failed to standardise police practice, with significant variations between forces.[310]

As Baroness Hale of Richmond points out, whilst diversion policies and practice are consistent with the principles contained within instruments of human rights law, 'diversion is not to be bought at the cost of basic fairness to the child'.[311] Research indicates that the current system of pre-court interventions can operate unfairly for young first time offenders tempted to admit an offence without first obtaining legal advice, merely to stay out of court.[312] Admittedly, guidance has already attempted to address some of the concerns highlighted by *R (on the application of R) v. Durham Constabulary and Another*.[313] Police officers must now explain to young offenders and their

---

[303] Inter alia: Baroness Hale of Richmond in *R (on the application of R) v. Durham Constabulary and anor* [2005] UKHL 21, [2005] 2 All ER 369, at [37]–[43]; T. Bateman (2003); J. Fionda (2005) pp. 98–101; D. Fox *et al.* (2005).

[304] I.e. earning the 'two strikes and you're out' label.

[305] T. Bateman (2003) pp. 138–9.   [306] Audit Commission (2004) p. 20.

[307] D. Fox *et al.* (2005) p. 134. Whether to reprimand, warn or prosecute depends on the 'gravity score' of the offence, scored under the ACPO Gravity Factor System (see HO (2002) Annex D) and the type of intervention an offender receives depends on their ASSET score (i.e. the 'common assessment profile' introduced by the YJB to predict, through a risk assessment format, the risk factors associated with a young person's past and future offending behaviour and his future intervention needs). See S. Easton and C. Piper (2005) pp. 207–8.

[308] HO (2006d) para. 6: reminds the police that the penalty notice for disorder (PND) scheme offers an additional method of dealing with 'low-level, anti-social and nuisance behaviour'; para. 14: reminds the police of their 'strictly limited discretion to take informal action in exceptional circumstances'; para. 7: the warning is available even after conviction where a conditional or absolute discharge has been given. See comment by T. Bateman (2006b).

[309] R. Evans and K. Puech (2001) pp. 798–9: there was considerable inconsistency in the gravity of cases considered by police to warrant a warning. See also D. Fox *et al.* (2005) pp. 135–6: discuss the considerable increase in pre-court interventions involving young women.

[310] HO (2006d) paras. 8 and 12 and Nacro (2008) p. 7.

[311] *R (on the application of R) v. Durham Constabulary and anor* [2005] UKHL 21, [2005] 2 All ER 369, at [29].

[312] R. Evans and K. Puech (2001).

[313] [2005] UKHL 21, [2005] 2 All ER 369, per Baroness Hale of Richmond, esp. at [43] and [47]–[48]. Discussed by A. Gillespie (2005) and G. Dingwall and L. Koffman (2006).

appropriate adult the full implications of receiving a reprimand or warning, and of ensuring that the young offender's admission is voluntary and reliable.[314] But although receiving a warning may *appear* a relatively benign form of intervention, it is the cumulative effect of the consequences of the system of reprimands and warnings for the young offender that can be considered punitive.[315] Not only may such an intervention be cited in subsequent criminal proceedings involving him or her,[316] but a young offender charged with an offence within two years of receiving a warning, will probably receive a referral order, thereby progressing down the road to acquiring a criminal record. Such a response to what may be an essentially trivial offence infringes the concept of proportionality, as established by international human rights documents.[317] Anxiety has also been expressed over the absence of any right to withhold consent to the administration of a reprimand or caution, despite this having been a feature of the pre-1998 diversion scheme[318] and despite adults retaining this right.

Against the strong reservations of Baroness Hale of Richmond and Lord Steyn, and on a narrow interpretation of its phrasing, the House of Lords held that Article 6 of the ECHR cannot assist a young offender who receives a final warning.[319] Nevertheless, unhappy with the diversion scheme in its present form, Baroness Hale indicated her 'grave doubts' over the way in which it infringes children's rights under the CRC[320] and other international instruments.[321] She clearly found it difficult to sympathise with Lord Bingham's view that the system is essentially preventative and not punitive.[322]

(6) Separate courts and separate practice

One of the overriding objectives of the nineteenth-century reformatory movement was to ensure that young offenders were kept separate from adult criminals in the courts. The CA 1908 established a system of separate magistrates' courts to deal with most criminal proceedings against young offenders under the age of 16. These were to have their own informal procedures and specialised magistracy and had a duty when reaching decisions to 'have regard

---

[314] HO (2002) para. 4.12–4.14 and HO (2006d) paras. 4–4.3.

[315] [2005] UKHL 21, per Baroness Hale of Richmond, at [45]. See also A. Gillespie (2005) pp. 1008–10.

[316] CDA 1998, s. 66(5). It is also kept on the police national computer (PNC) for a minimum of 5 years until the offender reaches the age of 18, whichever is the sooner.

[317] Per Baroness Hale of Richmond, ibid., at [42].

[318] Per Latham LJ (QBD) in *R(U) v. Commissioner of Metropolitan Police; R(U) v. Chief Constable of Durham Constabulary* [2002] EWCA 2486 (Admin), [2002] All ER (D) 445 Nov, at [36]. See also A. Gillespie (2005) pp. 112–14.

[319] Article 6 is only engaged if there is a 'determination … of any criminal charge against him'. Per Lord Bingham and Baroness Hale, [2005] UKHL 21, at [12] and [45]: when the decision is made to warn, rather than to prosecute, there is no 'determination' of the charge. NB per Lord Bingham, at [11]: it is unlikely that there is *ever* any formal criminal charge made against the recipient of a warning.

[320] Especially CRC, Art. 37.   [321] [2005] UKHL 21, at [43].   [322] [2005] UKHL 21, at [14].

to the welfare of the child'.[323] Although the youth court panels are not without their critics,[324] they retain their specialised nature and are closed to the public. They are undoubtedly sufficiently separate from the adult courts at least to comply with Article 40 of the CRC.[325] Furthermore, the Criminal Justice Act 1991, by extending the jurisdiction of the youth courts to 17-year-olds, complied with the requirements of international instruments which require *all* young offenders to be dealt with by specialised authorities.

Following the ECtHR's criticism of Crown Court trials in *T and V v. United Kingdom*,[326] there is now a greater appreciation of the system of trial offered by the youth courts.[327] Acting on research findings,[328] the government directed the youth courts to adopt greater informality in the layout of their courtrooms and the procedures used.[329] Although the youth courts' proceedings are far more suitable than those in the Crown Courts, the youth court justices sometimes decline jurisdiction,[330] if they consider a custodial sentence is appropriate,[331] but the offender's youth and offending history precludes their making it themselves.[332] The senior judiciary have criticised this approach, emphasising that the youth courts should appreciate the importance, as underlined by the decision in *T and V v. United Kingdom*,[333] of trials for children fully taking account of their special needs.[334] Thus, as the Chief Justice has emphasised: 'There is no doubt that the general policy of the legislature is that young offenders should where possible be tried by a youth court.'[335]

---

[323] CYPA 1933, s. 44.   [324] See C. Ball (1995) pp. 202–5, C. Ball (2004) p. 177.

[325] See esp. Art. 40(2)(b)(iii) and (3).

[326] (2000) 30 EHRR 121. See also *SC v. United Kingdom* (2004) 40 EHRR 10, discussed below.

[327] J. Fionda (2005) pp. 116–28: the history and working of the youth court.

[328] C. Allen *et al.* (2000).

[329] HO (2001). Inter alia: reorganise the court's layout, thereby enabling them to engage young offenders more directly, by talking and listening to them and by using plain language.

[330] The youth court may decline jurisdiction (under Magistrates' Courts Act 1980, s. 24(1)) and commit a young offender charged with an indictable 'grave crime' (normally one punishable by imprisonment for at least 14 years, but see Nacro (2007e) for further explanation) to the Crown Court.

[331] I.e. by the Crown Court on indictment under Powers of Criminal Courts (Sentencing) Act (PCCSA) 2000, ss. 90 and 91.

[332] Under PCCSA 2000, s. 100, the only custodial sentence available to a youth court in relation to an offender under the age of 15 is a detention and training order, but only if he is over the age of 12 and a 'persistent offender'. Broadly, magistrates *may* commit young defendants for trial in the Crown Court, per Leveson J in *R (H, A and O) v. Southampton Youth Court* [2004] EWHC (Admin) 2912, [2005] 2 Cr App R (S) 30, at [35], if there is 'a real prospect' that a custodial sentence of or in excess of 2 years might be required or there is some unusual feature of the case justifying a sentence of less than 2 years (*and* the justices lack the power to impose a DTO).

[333] (2000) 30 EHRR 121.

[334] *R (W) v. Southampton Youth Court, R (K) v. Wirral Borough Magistrates Court* [2002] EWHC 1640 (Admin), [2003] 1 Cr App R (S) 87, per Lord Woolf CJ, at [16]. See also *R (W) v. Thetford Youth Court, R (M) v. Waltham Forest Youth Court* [2002] EWHC 1252, [2003] 1 Cr App R (S) 67, per Sedley LJ, at [43].

[335] Ibid., [2002] EWHC 1640 (Admin), per Lord Woolf CJ, at [11].

Certain crimes will always go for jury trial in the Crown Court,[336] where despite the adaptations made to address the decision of the ECtHR in *T and V v. United Kingdom*,[337] the mode of trial attracts constant criticism for infringing the rights of young offenders. In that case, the ECtHR emphasised that despite the modifications made to the trial procedure,[338] the Article 6 rights of Thompson and Venables had been infringed. The ECtHR considered that the formality and ritual of the trial by jury, which lasted three weeks, would have seemed incomprehensible and intimidating to the two 11-year-olds found guilty of murdering James Bulger. They had been unable to participate effectively in the proceedings, and had therefore been denied a fair trial.[339] The fact that the trial proceeded under a glare of publicity and that they were identified after conviction also meant that their rights under a variety of international documents were clearly infringed.[340] Furthermore, their identification made their eventual rehabilitation much more problematic and even potentially dangerous.[341]

The decision in *T and V v. United Kingdom*[342] led to Crown Court trials being adapted to take greater account of the youth of the accused.[343] Defendants must now be protected from intimidation, humiliation or distress and all possible steps should be taken to ensure that they understand and participate in the proceedings.[344] Nevertheless, it is now clear that these adaptations may not be enough to make a jury trial fair for a vulnerable young defendant. Although all these steps were followed in the later case of *SC v. United Kingdom*,[345] the ECtHR held that an intellectually impaired 11-year-old[346] should not have been tried in a Crown Court, where, despite the adaptations, he was overawed by the jury and the formalities.[347] In such circumstances, since he had been unable to participate effectively in the trial,

---

[336] E.g. homicide.   [337] (2000) 30 EHRR 121. Discussed by D. Haydon and P. Scraton (2000).

[338] Inter alia: explanations of the trial were given to the defendants and the hearing times were shortened.

[339] The majority of the ECtHR rejected the claim that the trial process had subjected Venables and Thompson to inhumane or degrading treatment under Art. 3. The minority disagreed.

[340] Inter alia: Art. 40(1) of the CRC and r. 14.2 of the Beijing Rules. See also Art. 40(2)(b)(vii) of the CRC and r. 8 of the Beijing Rules, both protecting the juvenile's privacy at all stages of the proceedings.

[341] *Venables v. News Group Newspapers Ltd* [2001] 1 All ER 908: Court of Appeal agreed that Venables and Thompson required the protection of anonymity on release to avoid the public and press mounting a witch hunt, with consequent danger to their lives.

[342] (2000) 30 EHRR 121.

[343] *Practice Note (trial of children and young persons: procedure)* [2000] 2 All ER 285.

[344] Other adaptations include: arranging the court so that the defendants are at the same level as other participants and with their family; constant explanations being given to the defendants in appropriate language; a shortened day and frequent breaks; robes and wigs dispensed with; restrictions on public and press attendance.

[345] (2004) 40 EHRR 10.

[346] With a mental age of, at best an 8-year-old, at worst a 6-year-old, who fell within the lowest 1% of his age group; ibid. at para. 26.

[347] Ibid. at para. 26.

his rights under Article 6 had been violated.[348] According to the ECtHR, when a decision is made to try a child who may not, because of his age and intellectual disabilities, be able to participate effectively in the proceedings, 'it is essential that he be tried in a specialist tribunal' able to make proper allowance for his handicaps and to adapt its procedure accordingly.[349]

It was certainly difficult for the government to justify the continuation of a system of trial involving very young children sitting in court, being stared at by a jury and cross-examined by barristers. Regrettably, they ignored Auld LJ's recommendation that no young defendant charged with murder or other grave offences should be tried by a judge and jury in the Crown Court (or be committed there for sentence). He considered that all should be tried by a specially constituted youth court.[350] SC v. United Kingdom was soon followed by a decision in which the House of Lords sympathised with the notion that some of the special measures introduced to protect vulnerable witnesses from giving evidence in criminal trials might be extended to children accused of crimes.[351] In response, the courts have acquired a new power to allow young intellectually impaired defendants to give their evidence by live link from a venue outside the court.[352] Although this form of protection can remove a great deal of the strain of the trial from young defendants, it depends on their legal representatives persuading the court of its justification.

Those conducting pre-trial hearings should surely consider far more seriously requests to stay the proceedings on the basis that a trial of this kind would be an abuse of process. Such a request had been considered in SC but was turned down. As noted above, case law has now established a reasonably rigorous test which the court should consider before ruling the accused capable of participating in a trial.[353] Nonetheless, it is questionable whether there should be a judicial assumption that proceedings should not normally be stayed before the trial starts, but only as the trial proceeds.[354] The better view must be that put forward by Smith LJ. She considers that if, before any evidence is called, it is clear that a child is so severely impaired that he or she cannot participate in the trial, then there is no useful purpose in continuing and there should be a stay in the proceedings.[355] Meanwhile, English law remains vulnerable to international criticism for retaining a system of trial so unsuitable for children. Predictably, the Committee on the Rights of the Child has expressed concern

---

[348] Ibid. at para. 33–34.   [349] Ibid. at para. 35.   [350] Auld LJ (2001) p. 216.

[351] R (on the application of D) v. Camberwell Green Youth Court; R (on the application of the Director of Public Prosecutions) v. Camberwell Green Youth Court [2005] UKHL 4, [2005] 1 All ER 999, per Lord Rodger of Earlsferry, at [16]–[17] and Baroness Hale of Richmond, at [54]–[64].

[352] Youth Justice and Criminal Evidence Act 1999, s. 33A(3) and (4), Coroners and Justice Bill (2009) cl. 91: vulnerable defendants may give evidence through an intermediary; discussed in Chapter 17.

[353] E.g. R (on application of P) v. West London Youth Court [2005] EWHC 2583 (Admin), [2006] 1 All ER 477, per Scott Baker LJ, at [7]; discussed above.

[354] Ibid. at [18].

[355] Director of Public Prosecutions v. P [2007] EWHC 946 (Admin), [2007] 4 All ER 628, at [58].

over children being tried in adult courts and has recommended that this practice should stop.[356]

Perhaps the most objectionable feature of the jury form of trial is its availability even for very young children who are accused of serious crimes. Had the age of criminal responsibility been raised, say to 12, as many recommend,[357] Thompson and Venables would have escaped trial altogether. The research information on the type of children responsible for most serious crimes throws considerable doubt on their capacity to comprehend notions of culpability or indeed the objectives of formal criminal proceedings.[358] As the experience of Thompson and Venables suggests, the presumption of *doli incapax*, when it existed, did not pose great difficulties for those intent on obtaining convictions against psychologically damaged children. But without the presumption, it is surely up to the judiciary to show a greater interest in reversing the very punitive direction in which the law has gone.

(7) Separate dispositions

(A) Underlying concepts

The CRC stresses the need for legal systems to avoid depriving young offenders of their liberty, except as a last resort,[359] and to promote their rehabilitation through reintegration in society.[360] These principles are matched by the Beijing Rules, which not only promote the idea of welfare, but also the principle of 'proportionality' in sentencing, which takes account of the offender's personal circumstances, rather than imposing punitive sanctions designed to ensure that the offender receives his 'just deserts'.[361] These international provisions also stress the need to avoid restricting a juvenile's personal liberty through the use of alternative forms of sanction, such as community rehabilitation orders and community punishment orders.[362] Their overall aim is to ensure that young offenders are treated justly and diverted from punishment combined with imprisonment, into treatment and rehabilitation.

Certain fundamental aspects of childhood underpin these sentencing principles applicable to young offenders. First, it is unjust to *blame* children for their actions when, as the research on risk factors indicates, the correlation between an inadequate home background and offending is so clear. Furthermore, children have the ability to change and grow into law-abiding adults. Consequently, the form of correction selected should ensure a successful rehabilitation of the offender into society. Nevertheless, there is disagreement over how far these ideas should be integrated into sentencing theory. Efforts to

---

[356] Committee on the Rights of the Child (2002) paras. 60 and 62; ibid. (2008) paras. 77–8.
[357] Discussed above.   [358] G. Boswell (1995). See also F. Lösel and D. Bender (2006).
[359] Art. 37(b).   [360] Art. 40(1).   [361] Rule 5.1 of the Beijing rules.
[362] CRC, Art. 40(4); Beijing Rules, rr. 5, 17 and 18 and commentary; International Covenant on Civil and Political Rights, Art. 14(4); all discussed by U. Kilkelly (2008).

achieve an enlightened approach to sentencing young offenders in this country have been undermined by the unresolved dilemma over whether sentencing should promote the child's welfare or aim to punish the child – the welfare or justice model.[363] Indeed, the commentary to the Beijing Rules expands on this dilemma by pointing out that when it comes to adjudicating on young people, there are a number of unresolved conflicts underlying a variety of objectives: rehabilitation versus just deserts; assistance versus repression and punishment; responses meeting the needs of the individual versus a reaction protecting society in general; deterrence versus individual incapacitation.[364] These questions have dogged youth justice systems across the world, with a 'repenalisation' being noted in some countries.[365]

In England and Wales, a punitive response, delivered through 'the justice model' has, since the 1960s, broadly been in the ascendant. The concept of just deserts treats the young offender, like adults, as being personally responsible for his or her actions and therefore deserving punishment, to protect society from juvenile lawlessness. Such an approach is, of course, more politically expedient since, with enthusiastic media assistance, it is more comprehensible to the public. The results are more immediately visible, as opposed to the possible achievements of a welfare approach, which must inevitably be more long term.[366] The new legislative summary of the purposes underlying the sentencing of those under 18[367] is unlikely to change existing practice, given its lack of novelty. First, it reminds sentencers that the principal aim of the youth justice system, which is to prevent offending, also applies to the sentencing stage of the process;[368] it then refers to the need to have regard to the offender's welfare.[369] Last is a list of purposes, little different to those applicable to adults.[370] This legislative guidance, by placing punishment at the top of the list of purposes, unashamedly ignores the fact that many of the children governed by these principles are very young.[371] Indeed, it makes the sentencing framework introduced for adults,[372] which ensures that the sentence or punishment[373] is

---

[363] Discussed above.

[364] Beijing Rules, commentary to r. 17 governing adjudication and disposition.

[365] J. Muncie and B. Goldson (2006) esp. pp. 204–7.

[366] Grateful thanks to J. Fionda for this point.

[367] CJA 2003, s. 142A (as inserted by CJIA 2008, s. 9).   [368] CJA 2003, s. 142A(2)(a).

[369] In accordance with CYPA 1933, s. 44; CJA 2003, s. 142A(2)(b).

[370] I.e. CJA 2003, s. 142A(3)(a)–(d): the purposes of sentencing are to achieve offenders' punishment, reform and rehabilitation, protection of the public and reparation by offenders to those affected by their offences.

[371] Grateful thanks to T. Bateman for this point.

[372] By the CJA 1991, restated by the CJA 2003, in conjunction with the PCCSA 2000.

[373] Punishment is normally measured by the degree of restriction on the offender's liberty: custodial sentence – top of the scale, community orders – middle, financial penalties – bottom. These scales or 'sentencing bands' or 'thresholds' depend on the court's assessment of the offence's 'seriousness'. J. Fionda (2005) pp. 145–7; S. Easton and C. Piper (2005) ch. 3 and Nacro (2003) pp. 3–5.

commensurate with the 'seriousness' of the offence,[374] also apply to young offenders, with a few concessions to their youth.[375]

One might assume that the principle of proportionality, which carries the full authority of international human rights law,[376] would ensure that a young offender is always dealt with humanely. But this may not occur because the court's assessment of the 'seriousness' of the child's offence is usually entirely divorced from all considerations of the child's personal circumstances. Further the new legislative guidance, by making a bare reference to the welfare factor without further comment, except for the statutory clarification that it can be overridden by the need to address prevention,[377] fails to address a fundamental and long-standing problem – the courts are unclear *how* they should incorporate the welfare direction.[378] Concerns regarding the young person's vulnerability and background are normally only considered in the context of a plea in mitigation,[379] but the courts are neither particularly consistent in their response,[380] nor always sympathetic.[381] Indeed, although research indicates that many young offenders have significant welfare needs, the courts show a deep ambivalence over the idea of departing from commensurability in sentence, in favour of a less onerous sentence, on welfare grounds.[382] Certainly the case law reflects little evidence of the courts being particularly familiar with the requirements of international human rights law.

(B) Incarcerating children

(i) International criticism

Article 37 of the CRC states that the 'arrest, detention or imprisonment of a child shall be in conformity with the law and shall be used only as a measure of last resort and for the shortest appropriate period of time'. Similarly, rule 17.1 (c) of the Beijing Rules opposes the deprivation of liberty, except as a sanction for serious acts of violence and then, only if there is no other appropriate

---

[374] CJA 2003, ss. 148 and 153. See Nacro (2007d).

[375] E.g. the statutory limits on the sentences available for those under 18. The various sentences available under English law for dealing with children who break the law justify detailed study, see J. Fionda (2005) ch. 7 and S. Easton and C. Piper (2005) chs. 7 and 9.

[376] See r. 5 of the Beijing Rules.

[377] CYPA 1933, s. 44(1A) and (1B) (as inserted by CJIA 2008, s. 9(3). Nacro (2003) pp. 1–2, discusses the inter-relationship between prevention and welfare.

[378] C. Ball *et al.* (2001) pp. 143–6.

[379] E.g. Sentencing Guidelines Council (2006) p. 8: when sentencing young offenders for robbery, courts should note that factors such as the offender's age, immaturity and group pressure, may all be of more significance than for adult offenders.

[380] C. Ball *et al.* (2001) pp. 143–6..

[381] E.g. *Attorney General's Reference (Nos 39, 40 and 41 of 2005)* [2005] EWCA Crim 1961 WL 1534605, per Holland J, at [26]: the youth (and low intelligence of one of the offenders, who had a mental age of 10½) provided no explanation and only modest mitigation for their offences which had a number of aggravating features (cited by S. Easton and C. Piper (2006) website update to ch. 9).

[382] C. Ball *et al.* (2001) p. 144.

response. Furthermore, rule 19.1 emphasises that it should 'always be a disposition of last resort and for the minimum necessary period'. But the fact that young offenders who are locked up in this country are euphemistically described as being 'detained' in young offender institutions (YOIs), as opposed to being 'imprisoned',[383] does not disguise the fact that young people constitute a significant percentage of the increase in the prison population.[384]

There is much international criticism of the UK's predilection for locking up children. Hammarberg, when Vice-Chair of the Committee on the Rights of the Child averred: 'Basically, the message of the Convention is that children should not be in prison.'[385] Successive Commissioners for Human Rights have indicated concern that the UK has amongst the highest rates of juvenile detention in Western Europe.[386] The Committee on the Rights of the Child has also robustly criticised the government for the increasingly high numbers of children in custody, at earlier ages, for lesser offences and for longer sentences. Considering that the UK is violating the terms of Article 37(b) of the CRC, in so far as custody is not being used only as a measure of last resort and only for the shortest period of time, the Committee has strongly recommended that all these matters be remedied.[387]

(ii) The courts

The government not only appears oblivious to international criticism over the use of prison for children under the age of 18, it also ignores the growing number of domestic critics who urge that imprisonment should be entirely prohibited or reserved for the most exceptional cases.[388] At present, children under the age of 15 cannot be held in YOIs, and are placed instead in LA secure children's homes (SCHs)[389] or privately run secure training centres (STCs). In the absence of sufficient places in SCHs, vulnerable 14-year-olds are decanted into YOIs on attaining 15, to make room for the younger age group. Meanwhile, there has been an ongoing controversy over the use of custodial sentences for young

---

[383] In magistrates' courts, the use of the term 'imprisonment' is only considered appropriate for those aged 21 and over. C. Piper (2001) entertainingly discusses the euphemisms employed in the field of 'youth' crime.

[384] Approximately 3% of the total prison population (statistics provided by International Centre for Prison Studies). YJB custody statistics (December 2008) show a steady rise in the use of custody for those under 18 between 2000 and 2008. See also YJB (2008) p. 18: two-thirds of the YJB's annual budget is spent on commissioning secure accommodation for 10 to 17-year-olds.

[385] T. Hammarberg (1995) p. 20.

[386] A. Gil-Robles (2005) paras. 86–7; T. Hammarberg (2008) paras. 28, 31 and 52. See also J. Muncie (2008) p. 116 and Barnardo's (2008) p. 3: international data on rates of juvenile penal custody.

[387] Committee on the Rights of the Child (2002) paras. 59 and 62; ibid. (2008) paras. 77–8.

[388] Summarised by B. Goldson (2006a) p. 451. Inter alia: HM Chief Inspector of Prisons (1997) p. 6; B. Goldson and E. Peters (2000); JCHR (2003) para. 41; Howard League (2005); Nacro (2005); Local Government Association (2006); UK Children's Commissioners (2008) p. 34.

[389] SCHs are normally used to accommodate children aged 12–14, girls up to 16 and 15-year-old boys assessed as 'vulnerable'. Such homes have steadily reduced in number, from 29 in 2003 to 20 in 2007/8; discussed in Chapter 16.

offenders; indeed, government policy has itself undergone a complete reversal on this issue since the early 1990s when youth custody was relatively unusual.[390] By the mid-1990s, a more punitive approach had emerged,[391] which was to strengthen. The youth justice system introduced by New Labour wholly endorsed the use of detention as a means of punishing young offenders. Making no fundamental change to the existing sentencing framework, the detention and training order (DTO)[392] was introduced.[393] Meanwhile much longer terms of detention could be imposed by the Crown Court on offenders aged between 10 and 18 for grave offences.[394]

Armed with these powers, the courts, particularly the youth courts,[395] are detaining larger numbers of young people than in the late 1990s,[396] particularly those in the 15- to 17-year-old age group and for longer.[397] This is despite the YJB's various targets to reduce the numbers in custody, all of which have been missed,[398] and, in some cases, despite clear evidence of severe mental health problems, including serious self-harm.[399] The reasons for this continued enthusiasm for custody are obviously complex, including the punitive attitudes of sentencers. As noted above, some youth courts decline jurisdiction to the Crown Court simply to ensure that, however young, offenders are taken out of circulation altogether. They have, however, been reminded that the limitations on their powers reflects Parliament's intention that non-custodial sentences should normally be passed.[400]

---

[390] J. Fionda (2005) pp. 164–8.

[391] I.e. with the introduction of the secure training order in 1994.

[392] CDA 1998, ss. 73–9, governed by PCCSA 2000, ss. 100–7. The DTO (which is divided into two halves, the first, the custodial element being spent in custody and the second, in the community, under supervision) directs a young offender, depending on age and circumstances, into a STC, a YOI or SCH.

[393] The DTO replaced the magistrates' power to sentence those aged 15 or over to a YOI and their power to make secure training orders for the 12- to 14-year-olds. DTOs cannot be imposed on those aged under 15 unless they are 'persistent' (see Nacro (2007c) p. 2) offenders. See PCCSA 2000, s. 100(2)(a). NB although PCCSA 2000, s. 100(2)(b) refers to the availability of DTOs for defendants under the age of 12, the power to make such orders has not been implemented.

[394] I.e. under PCCSA 2000, ss. 90–1. See J. Fionda (2005) pp. 130–9 and Nacro (2007e). NB a defendant convicted of a sexual or violent offence may receive an 'indeterminate' or 'extended' sentence under CJA 2003, ss. 226 and 228; Nacro (2006c).

[395] I.e. by making DTOs.

[396] R. Morgan and T. Newburn (2007) pp. 1046–7. See also Nacro (2006a) p. 2: the increase in the use of custody by the youth courts between 1994 and 2004 has been accompanied by a considerable increase in the length of sentences for similar offence types.

[397] Nacro (2008) p. 7. But see Barnardo's (2008) p. 3: 12- to 14-year-olds are increasingly being locked up for less serious offences.

[398] E. Solomon and R. Garside (2008) pp. 46–8.

[399] E.g. despite the court being told of his history of child sexual abuse, serious mental health problems, including suicide attempts and serious self harm, 16-year-old Joseph Scholes was given a 2-year DTO. In 2002, he hanged himself in his cell in Stoke Heath YOI, 9 days into his sentence.

[400] *R (W) v. Thetford Youth Court, R (M) v. Waltham Forest Youth Court* [2002] EWHC 1252, [2003] 1 Cr App R (S) 67, per Sedley LJ, at [42] criticising the youth court for declining jurisdiction over W, an 11-year-old, because it had considered that he merited a custodial disposal.

Many youth courts clearly have little faith in the capacity of their local YOT to deliver effective programmes of intervention in the community.[401] Nevertheless, there are other factors involved, including YOT practitioners' greater willingness to make custodial recommendations (as opposed to a community-based alternative) in pre-sentence reports[402] and the soaring figures of custodial sentences awarded for breach of community sentences.[403]

Underlying this trend is a fundamental question. Is it ever ethical to lock up young offenders, particularly those in the younger age range? The answer must be no, given the UK's human rights obligations and given every court's obligation, when dealing with children brought before them, to 'have regard to the welfare of the child or young person'.[404] If the courts were to follow rigorously the legislative guidance on the first purpose of sentencing, namely to prevent offending,[405] they would never use custody, especially in view of the consistently high reconviction rates of children discharged from prison.[406] Custodial sentences disrupt young peoples' lives, isolate them from the outside community and prevent them from growing up in a normal way, by gaining independence through employment and having families.[407] These factors may actually prevent young offenders growing out of crime, as many do, eventually. Nevertheless, it is questionable how much credence the youth courts would today give to a new statutory principle requiring custody only to be used as a remedy of last resort, as recommended by the Committee on the Rights of the Child.[408]

(iii) The impact of imprisonment

The chaotic and deprived background of many young offenders suggests that penal custody might be justified were it a worthwhile experience, but countless reports have deplored the conditions suffered by young offenders sentenced to custody.[409] The Committee on the Rights of the Child has twice censured the conditions in YOIs in this country, including the high levels of bullying, self-harm and suicides and the inadequate rehabilitative opportunities.[410] Early this century, Munby J was clearly shocked by the evidence of appalling conditions existing in some YOIs.[411] He held that although the prison service is not itself

---

[401] T. Bateman (2005) pp. 100–1.   [402] Ibid. at pp. 98–9.
[403] Ibid. at pp. 101–2.   [404] CYPA 1933, s. 44.   [405] CJA 2003, s. 142A(2), discussed above.
[406] See statistical analysis in B. Goldson (2006b) pp. 149–50 and T. Bateman (2006a) p. 74.
[407] R. Worsley (2006) pp. 25 and 61–2: while 62% of boys (52% girls) said getting a job was the thing most likely to prevent their re-offending, only 28% of boys (7% girls) had a job to go to on release and only 47% of boys (41% girls) felt that they had done something (whilst detained) which made employment more likely.
[408] Committee on the Rights of the Child (2008) para. 78(b); see also T. Hammarberg (2008) para. 48.
[409] Well summarised in B. Goldson (2006a) pp. 454–62. See also UK Children's Commissioners (2008) paras. 188–9.
[410] Committee on the Rights of the Child (2002) para. 59; ibid. (2008) paras. 28 and 77.
[411] R (Howard League for Penal Reform) v. Secretary of State for the Home Department [2002] EWHC 2497 (Admin), [2003] 1 FLR 484.

subject to the requirements of the CA 1989, children detained in YOIs are within the scope of LAs' duties under sections 17 and 47 of that legislation, 'subject to the necessary requirements of imprisonment'.[412] Given that YOIs contain large numbers of young people at serious risk of significant harm, the prison service appreciated the child protection implications of this finding. Links were rapidly established between YOIs, children's services authorities and YOTs; now that LAs have agreed to fund social workers' posts in YOIs,[413] their much needed work can develop more effectively. Perhaps more to the point, Munby J warned the prison service that although the CA 1989 does not apply to its operations as such, detained young people are nevertheless protected by Articles 3 and 8 of the ECHR:

> if it really be the case that children are still being subjected to the degrading, offensive and totally unacceptable treatment described and excoriated by HM Chief Inspector of Prisons ... then it can only be a matter of time, as it seems to me, before an action is brought under the Human Rights Act 1998 by or on behalf of a child detained in a YOI and in circumstances where, to judge from what HM Chief Inspector is saying, such an action will very likely succeed.[414]

With the encouragement of the YJB,[415] the prison service has made efforts to raise the standards of care provided,[416] albeit from a very low base line. Nevertheless, the aims listed by the YJB for secure establishments remain only aspirational,[417] except for provision in SCHs, which are much smaller units. Conditions in many YOIs remain poor, exacerbated by the current overcrowding, with HM Inspector of Prisons calling for 'increased capital investment in an estate which is over-used, under-resourced and increasingly tired'.[418] She repeatedly voices concerns over the way that many offenders undergo long journeys to these establishments and often arrive very late at night, that they are strip-searched on arrival, and over the use of segregation for disciplinary reasons.[419] Some establishments continue *all* these poor practices, despite recommendations from the prison inspectorate to desist.[420] In particular, the high number of strip

---

[412] Ibid. at [136].   [413] YJB press release 13 January 2009.

[414] [2002] EWHC 2497 (Admin), [2003] 1 FLR 484, at [173].

[415] The YJB took responsibility in 2000 for 'commissioning and purchasing' all places for 10 to 17-year-olds committed to custody. See YJB (2005b) and (2007b).

[416] Prison Service Order (PSO) No 4950, *Regimes for Juveniles*, reissued 2004. These detail the ways in which young offenders are entitled to distinctive treatment, specifying various requirements regarding their regime; e.g. ch. 6, a minimum of one hour of outside activity or recreation per day, and provision of a 'full, purposeful and active day'.

[417] YJB (2005b) p. 9: all institutions should inter alia 'have a culture centred on the child and young person...employ an approach to behaviour management that emphasises, to the greatest possible extent, positive encouragement and reward rather than physical restraint or negative sanctions'.

[418] HM Inspector of Prisons (2008a) p. 47.

[419] HM Chief Inspector of Prisons (2007a) pp. 41–4; HM Inspector of Prisons (2008a) p. 47. See also Ofsted (2008) paras. 194–5.

[420] E.g. HM Chief Inspector of Prisons, (2007b) Section 2, lists failings which had continued contrary to previous inspection recommendations, inter alia: late arrivals, one after

searches, sometimes using force, occurring in some establishments has provoked considerable criticism[421] but continues virtually unabated.[422]

Currently significant numbers of young inmates feel unsafe,[423] with increasing numbers resorting to self-harm or even suicide.[424] This must be attributable, at least in part, to the use of force by staff when keeping discipline. Indeed, the YJB has shown no enthusiasm for the view that behaviour policies excluding force might produce a less dangerously volatile atmosphere in secure establishments. Mounting criticism has been directed at the use of 'distraction techniques' designed to cause pain and distress.[425]Hammarberg states caustically that he is 'not aware of any other member state that sanctions the use of deliberate pain as a method of restraining a child'.[426] Concern over the increasing use of restraint in STCs,[427] euphemistically called Physical Control in Care (PCC), combined with evidence that at least two deaths in custody had been associated with the use of such techniques[428] led to a government commissioned review of the use of restraint in secure settings.[429] Regrettably, the review failed to recommend prohibition of behaviour policies excluding the use of 'pain compliance'. It considered that in some circumstances, without the use of pain, restraint methods may take too long and compromise the safety of young people and staff.[430] Its lengthy and detailed recommendations on the accreditation of safe restraint procedures, clarification of their legitimate use and better staff training and supervision[431] were all largely accepted by the government.[432] There were, however, fundamental gaps in the approach adopted by the review and by the government's response.

Most significantly, there was an astonishing assumption that current policies, including 'pain compliance', could comply with human rights law. This myopia

---

midnight; routine strip searching on arrival using force in uncooperative cases, with two young people having had their clothes cut off by prison officers, without these incidents having been properly documented or investigated; weak anti-bullying measures; segregation being used without proper supervision; difficulty accessing showering; no scheduled exercise sessions.

[421] Carlile (2006) ch. 8; HM Chief Inspector of Prisons (2007a) p. 41; HM Chief Inspector of Prisons (2008a) p. 48; Ofsted (2008) paras. 201–3.

[422] Lord Carlile of Berriew, *Hansard* 19 February 2007, col. 953: between January 2005 and October 2006, 6,832 strip searches were conducted at HMPYOI Huntercombe.

[423] Ofsted (2008) para. 66.

[424] Between 1990 and 2008, 30 young people committed suicide in custodial establishments.

[425] CSCI (2005) para. 5.16; Carlile (2006) p. 38; HM Inspector of Prisons (2007a) p. 41; HM Inspector of Prisons (2008a) p. 48; Ofsted (2008) paras. 200–3; JCHR (2008) pp. 3–4; Committee on the Rights of the Child (2008) paras. 38–9; T. Hammarberg (2008) paras. 33–9.

[426] T. Hammarberg (2008) para. 34.

[427] P. Smallridge and A. Williamson (2008) para. 5.6, Table 5: statistics on the use of restraints by secure establishments in April–November 2007. E.g. Oakhill STC used physical restraint 720 times between April and November 2007.

[428] On 3 May 2007, the coroner, considering the death of 14-year-old Adam Rickwood, who hanged himself in Hassockfield STC in 2004, hours after being subjected to the nose 'distraction' (subsequently banned), called for an urgent review of restraint in child prisons. Gareth Myatt, aged 15, died in 2004, 3 days after arriving at Rainsbrook STC, being restrained by three guards using the 'double seated embrace' (subsequently banned).

[429] P. Smallridge and A. Williamson (2008).

[430] Ibid. at para. 6.77.   [431] Ibid. at chs. 11–16.   [432] MOJ (2008).

had already been commented on by the Joint Committee on Human Rights[433] and by Buxton LJ.[434] More recently, when directing a fresh coroner's inquest into the death of Adam Rickwood, Blake J made similar criticisms.[435] The YJB certainly seemed unaware of the human rights of those on the receiving end of an increased use of PCC by STC staff. It had not only ignored the many calls to ban painful restraint methods, but in 2007, encouraged the government to introduce amending rules which extended their justifiable use by STC staff.[436] Before their amendment, the rules had made it clear that STC staff should only exceptionally use physical restraint methods.[437] In practice, however, PCC was increasingly used merely for the purposes of 'ensuring good order and discipline' (known as GOAD) and to ensure compliance with staff's instructions.[438] This is what had occurred in Adam Rickwood's case, but Blake J considered it to be clear from the evidence that Adam's case was not unique. It

> was a persistent practice, duly recorded, in dealing with children in detention in breach of the law, the rules, the STC contract and the training manual as well as the in-house rules. Astonishingly, none of this seems to have aroused any query or concern by the YJB[439]…this failure by the YJB can only be described as a gross failure…Some investigation and understanding of these matters may be important if the YJB are to continue to be vested with the significant public policy duties of monitoring compliance with the law. [440]

The rapid introduction of amending rules designed to legitimise the illegal use of PCC by STC staff, had provoked considerable criticism.[441] They were challenged in court and quashed by the Court of Appeal for want of due parliamentary consultation.[442] Buxton LJ emphasised that the use of PCC by staff potentially infringes a young offender's rights both under the CRC and also under the ECHR.[443] Given that the type of physical intervention used by STC staff can potentially kill or seriously endanger children 'in any normal understanding of language', such intervention is degrading and an infringement of human dignity.[444] Buxton LJ stressed that its use cannot be justified merely to enforce GOAD; unless used in cases of strict necessity, for example, to prevent injury to the trainee or to others, PCC is a breach of Article 3 of the ECHR.[445]

---

[433] JCHR (2008) paras. 30–31.

[434] *R (C) v. Secretary of State for Justice* [2008] EWCA Civ 882, *Times*, 14 October, 2008 (hereafter *R (C)*) per Buxton LJ, at [57]–[82].

[435] *R (Carol Pounder) v. HM Coroner for the North and South Districts of Durham and Darlington, the Youth Justice Board, Serco Home Affairs Limited and Lancashire County Council* [2009] EWHC 76 (Admin), unreported (hereafter *R (Carol Pounder)*) at [51]–[58].

[436] Secure Training Centre (Amendment) Rules 2007 (SI 2007/1709). The detailed history of their introduction, with YJB encouragement, is set out by JCHR (2008) ch. 3.

[437] Secure Training Centre Rules 1998 (SI 1998/472), rr. 36 (1) and 38(1): i.e. to prevent escape, damage to property or injury to the person restrained or to another person.

[438] *R (C)*, per Buxton LJ, at [13]–[14].   [439] *R (Carol Pounder)*, at [67] .

[440] Ibid. at [68].   [441] E.g. JCHR (2008) ch. 3.   [442] *R (C)*,. at [44]–[56].

[443] Ibid. at [62]–[82].   [444] Ibid. at [64].   [445] Ibid. at [79].

These judicial comments suggest that the government should reassess how it now proceeds.[446] Blake J criticised the way, when formulating their approach, the government, YJB and the authors of the review had all ignored the human rights of children as young as 14.

> The authors of the Smallridge and Williamson report to the Ministers were very much mistaken if they believed that the requirements of the UN CRC were irrelevant to the limits of restraint that could be used in the UK.[447]

It should also be noted that the government's assumption, in its response to the independent review, that the YJB would continue to monitor the use of restraint by secure establishments[448] was treated with some derision by Blake J. In his view, the YJB's past record suggested that it was 'futile' for the Secretary of State to accept the review's recommendations on this score, when it had 'so conspicuously and inexplicably failed to do so in the past'.[449]

The often inadequate provision for inmates' health, particularly their mental health, is a constant theme of many reviews of secure establishments.[450] As HM Inspector of Prisons observes 'it is in any event inappropriate to hold mentally ill children in prison'.[451] This lack of provision is particularly worrying, given the very high level of mental health problems suffered by young offenders on their arrival in such institutions.[452] Efforts are being made to improve the provision of mental health care through links with the local Child and Adolescent Mental Health Services (CAMHS) and other service providers,[453] albeit from a low base line. Mental health problems can, of course, be exacerbated if offenders are kept in isolation in a 'segregation unit'[454] or healthcare centre without any meaningful activity or recreation/or sports facilities and without support or therapeutic input.[455] Critics have condemned the way that some establishments use isolation or 'solitary' to punish sometimes very

---

[446] In November 2008, the House of Lords refused the government permission to appeal against *R (C)*.

[447] Ibid. at [51].   [448] MOJ (2008) p. 18, response to recommendation 33.

[449] *R (Carol Pounder)*, at [69].

[450] HM Inspector of Prisons (2007a) p. 44; Ofsted (2008) para. 87; T. Hammarberg (2008) para. 24.

[451] Ibid. NB Before sentencing 16-year-old Joseph Scholes to 2 years' detention, the judge at Manchester Crown Court had been alerted to his vulnerability, his history of sexual abuse and suicidal and self-harming behaviour. Despite the YJB being urged to place him in a SCH, it instead placed him in Stoke Heath YOI, where he hung himself 9 days into his sentence.

[452] D. Lader *et al.* (2000). See also R. Harrington and S. Bailey with P. Chitsabesan *et al.* (2005) pp. 37–8: almost 1 in 5 young offenders had significant depressive symptoms, 1 in 10 had anxiety or post-traumatic symptoms and almost 1 in 10 had self-harmed within the last month, with few having received any intervention for their needs, often due to inadequate initial screening. 23% had an IQ of below 70. Provision of mental health services varied geographically. Of the 15% of offenders recommended a mental health intervention, only one-third received it, with frequent long delays (at p. 41).

[453] DH (2007).

[454] HM Inspector of Prisons (2007a) pp. 41–2: notes the new euphemistic names for 'segregation units' in juvenile establishments.

[455] Prior to his suicide Joseph Scholes was kept in virtual seclusion and offered no meaningful activity or therapy.

vulnerable offenders for relatively long periods sometimes in unfurnished cells.[456] Furthermore, Moses J issued a clear warning to the prison service – 'there are clear dangers in placing young people in segregation units in relation to their rights enshrined in Article 8 [of the ECHR]'.[457] If isolation results in suicide, a challenge might also be brought under Article 2 of the ECHR on the basis that the prison authorities have failed to take sufficient steps to safeguard the young offender's life.[458]

Given the very low levels of literacy and numeracy amongst many young offenders,[459] imprisonment could become a valuable experience for young offenders if they received appropriate education. Whilst educational provision in secure establishments has improved greatly over recent years,[460] there remain logistical problems with large numbers in custody for short periods on DTOs and frequent transfers between institutions.[461] In some institutions, the hours spent in education and training is still extremely low.[462] Furthermore, the young people do not necessarily consider that the education they receive is helpful,[463] undoubtedly reflecting the very variable standards of education offered.[464] Although almost all establishments now have special educational needs co-ordinators and learning support assistants,[465] there appears to be a need for more basic remedial education,[466] on a one-to-one basis.[467] Even greater variations in educational provision may result from requiring LAs to fund and commission education for those in custody.[468]

Although conditions in the YOIs are gradually improving, overcrowding often compromises basic standards of care.[469] Overall, in Hammarberg's view,

---

[456] Carlile (2006) ch. 9; HM Inspector of Prisons (2007a) p. 42; Ofsted (2008) paras. 205 and 208; Committee on the Rights of the Child (2008) paras. 38–9.

[457] R (BP) v. Secretary of State for the Home Department [2003] EWHC 1963(Admin), [2003] All ER (D) 310 (Jul), at [34].

[458] E.g. Keenan v. United Kingdom (2001) 33 EHRR 28. NB in 2008, the government acceded to the Howard League for Penal Reform's demand for a 'right to life' inquiry under Art. 2 of the ECHR into the treatment of SP, whilst she was in custody between the ages of 17 and 19. She had severe mental health problems and despite her persistent and aggravated self-harm, resulting in hospitalisation for blood transfusions, was placed in solitary confinement for several months.

[459] R. Harrington and S. Bailey with P. Chitsabesan et al. (2005) p. 38: 23% of young offenders met the criteria for learning difficulties (IQ<70), 36% with borderline learning difficulties; mean reading age of 11.3. 75% had a history of school exclusion and 10% aged 16 or below, had failed to attend.

[460] R. Worsley (2006) pp. 19 and 57: 79% of boys (89% of girls), across the secure estate said they were in education at the time of the survey, but with considerable geographical variations.

[461] ECOTEC, chs. 5 and 7.   [462] HM Inspector of Prisons (2008a) p. 49.

[463] R. Worsley (2006) p. 20: although 98% at Brinsford YOI were in education, only 47% considered it to be helpful.

[464] HM Inspector of Prisons (2007a) p. 42.   [465] Ibid.

[466] R. Worsley (2006) pp. 20 and 58: 34% of boys (29% girls) considered they needed help with reading, writing or maths.

[467] YJB (2006b) p. 77.

[468] HM Government (2008) para. 5.7; changes to be introduced in the Apprenticeships, Skills, Children and Learning Bill 2009, Part 2.

[469] Ofsted (2008) para. 67.

given the high reoffending rates, 'serious questions' should be asked 'about the efficacy and purpose of the entire juvenile justice system in England and Wales and the use of detention in particular'.[470] Meanwhile the government shows little sign of reassessing the concept of imprisonment as a sanction for youth crime.

(C) Alternative approaches

There is a widespread view that custodial sentences are counter productive and that there must be better ways of preventing crime. Many argue that punitive attitudes towards young offenders merely divert attention from the socioeconomic background to youth offending. As researchers have pointed out, in some deprived urban areas with high unemployment, violence, drug dealing and crime are just part of everyday life.[471] The government recognises this and, under the auspices of the YJB and other government agencies, has initiated a range of community programmes in deprived high-crime areas throughout the country, designed to provide children with focused activities and support.[472]

Meanwhile, with the assistance of intervention programmes delivered through the YOTs, often as part of the final warning system,[473] the YJB's primary aim is to prevent reoffending by first time offenders. In particular, it is committed to developing community-based alternatives which inspire sufficient confidence in sentencers that they reduce their use of custody.[474] Until recently, the youth courts had a range of 'youth community orders' available to them, all with the same aim – of ensuring that young offenders remain in the community, but under some form of regulation.[475] These were all replaced by a new generic community sentence, the youth rehabilitation order (YRO) which has broadly the same purpose. But the refinement is that it allows the court to adopt a 'more targeted and tailored approach' to the offender,[476] by creating an order catering for his or her specific needs including in it a range of components chosen from a 'menu',[477]

---

[470] T. Hammarberg (2008) para. 44.

[471] J. Lyon, C. Dennison and A. Wilson (2000) pp. 76 and 10–11 and J. Pitts (2003) p. 109.

[472] Nacro (2006b) pp. 4–5: inter alia: the Youth Inclusion Programmes (YIPs) providing structured and supervised activities for young people living on particularly deprived estates; the 'holiday Splash Schemes' providing similar facilities to similar groups during the school holidays; Positive Activities for Young People (PAYP) providing a range of school holiday activities for vulnerable 8–19-year-olds; Safer Schools Partnerships (SSPs) addressing crime in and around schools in high crime areas.

[473] Discussed above.   [474] YJB (2005b) p. 8.

[475] E.g. a supervision order, attendance centre order, action plan order, curfew order, exclusion order, reparation order.

[476] I.e. using the 'scaled approach'. See YJB (2007c): to be replaced by a revised version (YJB (2009) now in draft), on implementation of the YRO in September 2009.

[477] CJIA 2008, s. 1 and Schs. 1 and 2: the 'menu' of 14 requirements includes inter alia: an activity requirement, supervision requirement, prohibited activity requirement, curfew requirement, drug treatment requirement etc, together with electronic monitoring, and, in some cases, intensive supervision and surveillance (discussed below).

all with distinct functions.[478] It remains to be seen whether the youth courts will find this new scheme more manageable than the old 'pick and mix' approach to a long list of orders, which arguably achieved much the same thing.

The high rates of youth custody suggest that youth courts believe community orders to be suitable only for trivial offences and that imprisonment is the only appropriate punishment for the more serious offender. The YJB had hoped that the introduction of the intensive supervision and surveillance programme (ISSP) would persuade the courts to allow the more serious or persistent offenders[479] to remain in the community. These programmes, first introduced in 2001, can be tacked on to a community sentence,[480] the aim being to 'bring structure to offenders' lifestyles, with a 'key element' being community surveillance, through tracking and electronic tagging.[481] The disappointingly high reconviction rates for those completing ISSPs[482] are balanced by evidence indicating that the frequency and severity of the reoffending is less.[483] Surprisingly, the extreme controls available through the ISSP have not, however, induced the youth courts to reduce their enthusiasm for custody.[484] Indeed, the ISSP may be having a net-widening effect – it is now being favoured by some youth courts over other less intensive community sentences[485] and high rates of breach are associated with the ISSP, often leading to a custodial sentence.[486]

Many of the new orders created at the end of the 1990s reflected the government's commitment to the concept of 'restorative justice'. This, in other countries, often involves techniques of mediation between offender and victim, through reparation and conferencing, as in the New Zealand 'family group conferencing' system. Dignan summarises the aims of such an approach: first, to engage with offenders to try to bring home the consequences of their actions and their impact on their victims; to encourage and facilitate the provision of

---

[478] E.g. to enable compliance, to repair harm, to help the young offender change, or to provide some form of control. YJB (2007c) pp. 12–13.

[479] In broad terms, the ISSP is available for a young offender who has been charged, warned or convicted on four or more occasions over the last 12 months and who has already received at least one community or custodial sentence. But for details see YJB (2006c).

[480] The intensive supervision involves a minimum of 25 hours contact time per week (for a minimum of 3 months) taking part in various activities, including education and training, offender behaviour programmes, recreational activities and reparation to victim and or the community.

[481] Involving at least two surveillance checks per day. YJB guidance.

[482] E. Gray et al. (2005) ch. 4: approximately 90%.

[483] Ibid.: frequency of offending reduced by 40% over 1 year, by 39% over 2 years; the seriousness of further offending reduced by 13%. See also R. Morgan and T. Newburn (2007) pp. 1051–2.

[484] E. Gray et al. (2005) p. 117: between 2000 and 2004, there was only a 2.1% reduction in the use of youth custody nationally, this being a reduction in all areas, not only those where the ISSP was available.

[485] Ibid. See also E. Solomon and R. Garside (2008) p. 49.

[486] Ibid.: 60% of young offenders on ISSP were breached, one-third of whom were recalled or sentenced to custody. See also T. Bateman (2005) pp. 101–2: custodial sentences for breach of all community penalties increased by almost four times over the last 10 years.

appropriate forms of reparation for the offence; to seek reconciliation between victim and offender.[487] Today, young offenders may be involved in a programme devised by the local YOT, involving some, or all of these elements, very early on in their criminal careers, on receiving a final warning from the police.[488] But the principles of restorative justice most obviously underlie the reparation orders,[489] and the schemes associated with the referral orders. All may involve offenders apologising to the victim in person and carrying out acts of recompense, intended to bring home to them the implications of their offence.

The referral order was part of the new youth justice framework introduced by New Labour.[490] The youth court, on making a referral order, merely decides on the programme's duration,[491] broadly reflecting its view of the seriousness of the offence.[492] The court must leave it to the local youth offender panel (YOP) to devise a programme of behaviour, based largely on principles of restorative justice, which the offender can agree to and sign – 'a youth offender contract'. By making the referral order mandatory for all 10- to 17-year-olds pleading guilty and convicted of a first offence,[493] the scheme initially ensured that *all* such offenders were automatically referred to the local YOP.[494] Initial concerns over the way the mandatory scheme was drawing in offenders whose offences were too trivial to justify a court order[495] were later addressed by an element of discretion being injected into the process.[496] These anxieties aside, referral orders were quickly accepted by all those working in the youth justice system, with the informality of the panel meetings producing encouraging levels of satisfaction for offenders and their parents.[497] The success of these orders has led to an extension of their availability.[498]

---

[487] J. Dignan (1999) p. 48.   [488] Discussed above.

[489] PCCSA 2000, ss. 73–5. Discussed by J. Fionda (2005) pp. 186–8.

[490] Introduced by the Youth Justice and Criminal Evidence Act 1999, Part 1, now governed by PCCSA 2000, Part III.

[491] At least 3 months, not more than 12 months.

[492] But see Youth Justice Board (2003) p. 14: researchers found no clear correlation between seriousness of the offence and the length of the referral orders made.

[493] But NB PCCSA 2000, s. 16(1)(b), *excluding* cases warranting a custodial sentence or a hospital order.

[494] The YOP is made up of two volunteers, drawn from the offender's local community, and one YOT practitioner.

[495] Youth Justice Board (2003) ch. 5.

[496] The Referral Order (Amendment of Referral Conditions) Regulations 2003 (SI 2003/1605), amend PCCSA 2000, s. 17: courts are only obliged to make a referral order if the offence is an imprisonable offence (but excluding offences which the court considers warrant a custodial sentence); in other cases, the court has discretion to impose a less burdensome response, e.g. a fine or conditional discharge.

[497] T. Newburn *et al.* (2002) esp. ch. 7 and p. 62.

[498] PCCSA 2000, s. 17 (as amended by CJIA 2008, s. 35): referral orders can be made despite an offender having been already convicted of one offence, for which he did not receive a referral order; a second referral order can, in exceptional circumstances, be made, on the YOT's recommendation.

Following the introduction of the referral order, concerns were voiced about the way in which the youth justice system was apparently attempting to absorb some, but not all, of the principles of restorative justice, in a peculiarly unbalanced way. The YOTs and YOPs had been given the power to produce programmes for young offenders far more intrusive and punitive than might be merited by the severity of the offence itself, thereby infringing the proportionality principle. It was also unclear how well the principles of restorative justice could work when merely spliced on to a formal court system. Elsewhere, where they had succeeded – for example, the children's hearing system in Scotland and the family group conference in New Zealand – these arrangements were substitutes for court appearances, not additional adjuncts.[499] Indeed, as critics point out, restorative justice requires cooperation and not coercion.[500] There are also doubts over the extent to which very young offenders with complex needs are capable of 'taking responsibility' for their offences, in the way expected of them.[501]

Many of these concerns proved exaggerated. Initial research suggested that young offenders did not feel coerced into agreeing programmes of behaviour designed by the YOPs.[502] Furthermore, most young people and their parents considered that the YOPs were fairer, treated them with more respect and gave them a greater opportunity to explain their side of things, than did the youth courts.[503] The government's refusal to allow young offenders legal representation before the YOPs, on the grounds that this would undermine the informality of the proceedings, was also vindicated. Indeed, the early research suggested that young people felt far more able to participate fully in the YOP meetings than in the youth court hearings,[504] presumably because of the informality of the former. Nevertheless, and despite government protestations, critics assert that the disappointingly low level of victim participation in YOP meetings,[505] prevents the referral order system being truly restorative.[506] Further it is arguable that the system merely throws a smoke screen over 'an inherently retributive and increasingly punitive youth justice system'.[507] Despite this, Rod Morgan[508] describes the referral order as the 'jewel in the crown' of the youth justice system – because it works.

(8) Conclusion

There is a wealth of research material which suggests that it is not only unjust but unrealistic to deny that child offenders are the product of their upbringing and environment. They may also mature and grow out of their offending

---

[499] C. Ball (2000) p. 217.   [500] C. Wonnacott (1999).   [501] A. Newbury (2008) pp. 140–5.
[502] T. Newburn et al. (2002) ch. 8.   [503] Ibid. at pp. 37–40.
[504] T. Newburn et al. (2002) p. 37, Table 7.1.
[505] Ibid. at ch. 8 and Youth Justice Board (2003) pp. 40–3.
[506] J. Fionda (2005) p. 185.   [507] Ibid., at p. 196. See a general critique at pp. 189–203.
[508] R. Morgan (former chair of the YJB) (2007b) p. 6.

behaviour. Certainly there seems little point in ignoring this information when attempting to deal with their wrongdoing. Nevertheless, successive governments have been reluctant to produce a youth justice system reflecting such an obvious concept. New Labour's attitude can be detected from the fact that the reorganisation of children's services[509] designed to improve the well-being of children and young people generally[510] did not include any plans to review the government's approach to young offenders.[511] Indeed, the Home Office stated its intention to 'continue to operate a distinct youth justice system broadly on present lines'.[512] Later, only a tiny part of the ten-year Children's Plan was devoted to youth crime.[513] Things may eventually change under the influence of the new Youth Justice Unit, a cross-departmental unit,[514] whose brief is not only to develop policies relating to young offenders, but also to ensure that they 'achieve all the five outcomes of Every Child Matters'.[515] Nevertheless, the government's 'comprehensive, cross-government analysis of what we need to do to tackle youth crime'[516] shows no sign of adopting a different approach.[517] Clearly no one in government openly acknowledges the lessons of the last decade – that few of the current forms of dealing with young offenders reduce the chances of their reoffending and that many achieve the reverse, and at enormous financial expense.[518]

BIBLIOGRAPHY

NB many of these publications can be obtained on the relevant organisation's website.

Allen, C., Crow, I. and Cavadino, M. (2000) *Evaluation of the Youth Court Demonstration Project* Home Office Research Study 214, Home Office.

Allen, R. (2006) *From Punishment to Problem Solving: a New Approach to Children in Trouble*, Centre for Crime and Justice Studies.

Armstrong, D. (2004) 'A Risky Business? Research, Policy, Governmentality and Youth Offending' 4 *Youth Crime* 100.

Armstrong, D., Hine, J., Hacking, S., Armaos, R., Jones, R., Klessinger, N. and France, A. (2005) *Children Risk and Crime: the On Track Youth Lifestyles Surveys*. Home Office Research Study 278, Home Office.

Ashworth, A. (2004) 'Social Control and Anti-social Behaviour: the Subversion of Human Rights?' 120 *Law Quarterly Review* 263.

Ashworth, A., Gardner, J., Morgan, R., Smith, A.T.H., Von Hirsch, A. and Wasik, M. (1998) 'Neighbouring on the Oppressive' 16 *Criminal Justice* 7.

---

[509] Under the *Every Child Matters* reform programme. DfES (2004); discussed in Chapter 15.

[510] I.e. by fulfilling the five outcomes listed in CA 2004, s. 10(2).

[511] P. Gray (2007) pp. 412–13 and R. Smith (2005) pp. 8–11.

[512] HO (2003) p. 3.   [513] DCSF (2007) paras. 6.65–6.84.

[514] Launched in November 2007, under the joint auspices of the Ministry of Justice and the Department for Children, Schools and Families, it jointly sponsors the YJB and its programmes.

[515] Ministry of Justice, press release, 13 November 2007.

[516] HM Government (2008) p. 1.   [517] Also discussed in Chapter 19.

[518] E. Solomon and R. Garside (2008) esp. chs. 2 and 4.

Audit Commission, (1996) *Misspent Youth ... Young People and Crime*, Audit Commission.

Audit Commission, (2004) *Youth Justice*, Audit Commission.

Auld, R., Lord Justice (2001) *Review of the Criminal Courts of England and Wales*, TSO.

Ball, C. (1995) 'Youth Justice and the Youth Court – the End of a Separate System?' 7 *Child and Family Law Quarterly* 196.

(2000) 'The Youth Justice and Criminal Evidence Act 1999 Part I: a Significant Move Towards Restorative Justice, or a Recipe for Unintended Consequences' *Criminal Law Review* 211.

(2004) 'Youth Justice? Half a Century of Responses to Youth Offending' *Criminal Law Review* 167.

Ball, C., McCormac, K. and Stone, N. (2001) *Young Offenders: Law Policy and Practice*, Sweet and Maxwell.

Barnardo's (2008) *Locking Up or Giving Up – Is Custody for Children Always the Right Answer?* Barnado's.

Bateman, T. (2003) 'Living with Final Warnings: Making the Best of a Bad Job?' 3 *Youth Justice* 131.

(2005) 'Reducing Child Imprisonment: A Systemic Challenge' 5 *Youth Justice* 91.

(2006a) 'Youth Crime and Justice: Statistical "Evidence", Recent Trends and Responses' in Goldson, B. and Muncie, J. (eds.) *Youth Crime and Justice*, Sage Publications.

(2006b) 'Changes to Final Warning Guidance' 6 *Youth Justice* 219.

(2007) 'Ignoring Necessity: the Court's Decision to Impose an ASBO on a Child' 19 *Child and Family Law Quarterly* 304.

Beijerse, J. and van Swaaningen, R. (2006) 'The Netherlands: Penal Welfarism and Risk Management' in Muncie, J. and Goldson, B. (eds.) *Comparative Youth Justice*, Sage Publications.

Boswell, G. (1995) *Violent Victims: The Prevalence of Abuse and Loss in the Lives of Section 53 Offenders* The Prince's Trust.

Bowen, E., El Komy, M. and Steer, C. (2008) *Characteristics Associated with Resilience in Children at High Risk of Involvement in Anti-social and Other Problem Behaviour*, Home Office Findings 283, Home Office.

Bradley, T., Tauri, J. and Walters, R. (2006) 'Demythologising Youth Justice in Aotearoa/New Zealand' in Muncie, J. and Goldson, B. (eds.) *Comparative Youth Justice*, Sage Publications.

Brogan, D. (2005) *Anti-Social Behaviour Orders: An Assessment of Current Management Information Systems and the Scale of Anti-Social Behaviour Breaches Resulting in Custody*, Youth Justice Board.

Brown, A. (2004) 'Anti-Social Behaviour, Crime Control and Social Control' 43 *The Howard Journal of Criminal Justice* 203.

Butler-Sloss, E. (2006) 'Ethical Considerations in Family Law' 2 *Web Journal of Current Legal Issues*.

Burney, E. (2002) 'Talking Tough, Acting Coy: What Happened to the Anti-Social Behaviour Order?' 41 *The Howard Journal* 469.

(2005) *Making People Behave: Anti-social Behaviour, Politics and Policy*, Willan.

Burney, E. and Gelsthorpe, L. (2008) 'Do We Need a "Naughty Step"? Rethinking the Parenting Order After Ten Years' 47 *The Howard Journal* 470.

Carlile (Chair), Lord Carlile of Berriew QC (2006) *An Independent Inquiry into the Use of Physical Restraint, Solitary Confinement and Forcible Strip Searching of Children in Prisons, Secure Training Centres and Local Authority Secure Children's Homes*, The Howard League for Penal Reform.

Commission for Social Care Inspection (CSCI) Department of Health (DH), (2005) *Safeguarding Children: The Second Joint Chief Inspectors' Report on Arrangements to Safeguard Children*, CSCI.

Committee on the Rights of the Child (1995) *Concluding Observations of the Committee on the Rights of the Child: United Kingdom of Great Britain and Northern Ireland* CRC/C/15/Add 34 Centre for Human Rights, Geneva.

Committee on the Rights of the Child (2002) *Concluding Observations of the Committee on the Rights of the Child: United Kingdom of Great Britain and Northern Ireland* CRC/C/15/Add 188 Centre for Human Rights, Geneva.

Committee on the Rights of the Child, General Comment No 10 (2007) *Children's Rights in juvenile justice*, CRC/C/GC/10 Centre for Human Rights, Geneva.

Committee on the Rights of the Child (2008) *Concluding Observations of the Committee on the Rights of the Child: United Kingdom of Great Britain and Northern Ireland* CRC/C/GBR/CO/4, Centre for Human Rights, Geneva.

Cosgrove, J. (2003) 'Easy as ABC: PlayAction Autumn 2002' 29 *Association of Lawyers for Children Newsletter* 21.

Crawford, A. and Lister, S. (2007) *The Use and Impact of Dispersal Orders*, Joseph Rowntree Foundation.

Cunneen, C. and White, R. (2006) 'Australia: Control, Containment or Empowerment?' in Muncie, J. and Goldson, B. (eds.) *Comparative Youth Justice*, Sage Publications.

Department for Children, Schools and Families (DCSF) (2007) Cm 7280 *The Children's Plan: Building brighter futures*, The Stationery Office.

Department for Children, Schools and Families (DCSF) (2008) *Youth Taskforce Action Plan*, DCSF.

Department for Education and Skills (DfES) (2004) *Every Child Matters: Next Steps*, DfES.

Department of Health (DH) (1999) *United Nations Convention on the Rights of the Child: Second Report to the UN Committee by the United Kingdom 1999*, The Stationery Office.

Department of Health (DH) (2007) *Promoting Mental Health for Children Held in Secure Settings: a Framework for Commissioning Services*, DH Publications.

Dignan, J. (1999) 'The Crime and Disorder Act and the Prospects for Restorative Justice' *Criminal Law Review* 48.

Dingwall, G. and Koffman, L. (2006) 'Diversion, Punishment and Restricting Human Rights' 57 *Northern Ireland Law Quarterly* 478.

Donaghue, J. (2007) 'The Judiciary as a Primary Definer on Anti-Social Behaviour Orders' 46 *The Howard Journal* 417.

Dyer, C. (2005) 'When Care Rather than Court is Best for Young Offenders' *The Guardian*, December 12.

ECOTEC (2001) *Report on the Audit of Educational Provision within the Juvenile Secure Estate*, Youth Justice Board.

Easton, S. and Piper, C. (2005) *Sentencing and Punishment: The Quest for Justice*, Oxford University Press.

Evans, R. and Puech, K. (2001) 'Reprimands and Warnings: Populist Punitiveness or Restorative Justice' *Criminal Law Review* 794.

Farrington, D. (1996) *Understanding and Preventing Youth Crime*, Joseph Rowntree Foundation.

(2007) 'Childhood Risk Factors and Risk-Focused Prevention' in Maguire, M., Morgan, R. and Reiner, R. (eds.) *The Oxford Handbook of Criminology* Oxford University Press.

Fionda, J. (1999) 'New Labour, Old Hat: Youth Justice and the Crime and Disorder Act 1998' *Criminal Law Review* 36.

(2005) *Devils and Angels: Youth Policy and Crime*, Hart Publishing.

Flood-Page, C., Campbell, S., Harrington, V. and Miller, J. (2000) *Youth Crime: Findings from the 1998/99 Youth Lifestyles Survey* Home Office Research Study 209, Home Office.

Fox, D., Dhami, M. and Mantle, G. (2005) 'Restorative Final Warnings: Policy and Practice' 45 *Howard Journal* 129.

Gelsthorpe, L. and Morris, A. (1994) 'Juvenile Justice 1945–1992' in Maguire, M., Morgan, R. and Reiner, R. (eds.) *The Oxford Handbook of Criminology*, Oxford University Press.

(1999) 'Much Ado About Nothing – a Critical Comment on Key Provisions Relating to Children in the Crime and Disorder Act 1998' 11 *Child and Family Law Quarterly* 209.

Ghate, D. and Ramella, M. (2002) *Positive Parenting: The National Evaluation of the Youth Justice Board's Parenting Programme*, Youth Justice Board.

Gil-Robles, A. (2005) *Report by Mr Alvaro Gil-Robles, Commissioner for Human Rights on His Visit to the United Kingdom*, CommDH 6, Council of Europe.

Gillespie, A. (2005) 'Reprimanding Juveniles and the Right to Due Process' 69 *Modern Law Review* 1006.

Goldson, B. (2006a) 'Damage, Harm and Death in Child Prisons in England and Wales: Questions of Abuse and Accountability' 45 *Howard Journal* 449.

(2006b) 'Penal Custody: Intolerance, Irrationality and Indifference' in Goldson, B. and Muncie, J. (eds.) *Youth Crime and Justice*, Sage Publications.

Goldson, B. and Muncie, J. (2006) 'Critical Anatomy: Towards a Principled Youth Justice' in Goldson, B. and Muncie, J. (eds.) *Youth Crime and Justice*, Sage Publications.

Goldson, B. and Peters, E. (2000) *Tough Justice – Responding to Children in Trouble*, The Children's Society.

Graham, J. and Bowling, B. (1995) *Young People and Crime*, Home Office Research Study No 145, Home Office.

Gray, E., Taylor, E., Roberts, C., Merrington, S., Fernandez, R. and Moore, R. (2005) *Intensive Supervision and Surveillance Programme: The Final Report*, Youth Justice Board.

Gray, P. (2007) 'Youth Justice, Social Exclusion and the Demise of Social Justice' 46 *Howard Journal of Criminal Justice* 401.

HM Government (2007) *The Consolidated 3rd and 4th Periodic Report to UN Committee on the Rights of the Child*, DCSF.

HM Government (2008) *Youth Crime Action Plan, 2008*, Home Office.

HM Chief Inspector of Prisons (1997) *Young Prisoners: A Thematic Review*, Home Office.

HM Chief Inspector of Prisons (2007a) HC 210 *Annual Report 2005/2006*, The Stationery Office.

HM Chief Inspector of Prisons (2007b) *HMYOI Werrington: Report on an Unannounced Short Follow-up Inspection 16–20 April 2007*, Her Majesty's Inspectorate of Prisons.

HM Chief Inspector of Prisons (2008a) HC 207 *Annual Report 2006/2007*, The Stationery Office.

HM Chief Inspector of Prisons (2008b) *Report on an Unannounced Inspection of the Management, Care and Control of Young People at Oakhill Secure Training Centre*, Her Majesty's Inspectorate of Prisons.

Haines, K. and Case, S. (2008) 'The Rhetoric and Reality of the "Risk Factor Prevention Paradigm" Approach to Preventing and Reducing Youth Offending' 8 *Youth Justice* 5.

Hallam, S., Rogers, L., and Shaw, J. (2006) 'Improving Children's Behaviour and Attendance Through the Use of Parenting Programmes: an Examination of Practice in Five Case Study Local Authorities' 33 *British Journal of Special Education* 107.

Hammarberg, T. (1995) 'Children, Crime and Society: Perspectives of the UN Convention on the Rights of the Child' in *Child Offenders: UK and International Practice*, The Howard League.

(2006) 'The Human Rights Dimension of Juvenile Justice', presentation by the Commissioner for Human Rights to the Conference of Prosecutors General of Europe.

(2008) *Memorandum by Thomas Hammarberg, Commissioner for Human Rights of the Council of Europe*, CommDH, Council of Europe.

Harrington, R. and Bailey, S. with Chitsabesan, P, Kroll, L., Macdonald, W., Sneider, S., Kenning, C., Taylor, G., Byford, S. and Barrett, B. (2005) *Mental Health Needs and Effectiveness of Provision for Young Offenders in Custody and in the Community*, Youth Justice Board.

Haydon, D. and Scraton, P. (2000) '"Condemn a Little More, Understand a Little Less": The Political Context and Rights Implications for the Domestic and European Rulings in the Venables-Thompson Case' 27 *Journal of Law and Society* 416.

Hollingsworth, K. (2006) '*R(W) v Commissioner of Police of the Metropolis and Another* – Interpreting Child Curfews: a Question of Rights?' 18 *Child and Family Law Quarterly* 253.

(2007) 'Judicial Approaches to Children's Rights in Youth Crime' 19 *Child and Family Law Quarterly* 253.

Holt, A. (2008) 'Room for Resistance? Parenting Orders, Disciplinary Power and the Production of the "Bad Parent"' in Squires, P. (ed.) *ASBO Nation: the Criminalisation of Nuisance*, Polity Press.

Home Office (HO) (Chairman Viscount Ingleby) (1960) Cmnd 1191 *Report of the Committee on Children and Young Persons*, HMSO.

Home Office (HO) (1965) Cmnd 2742 *The Child, the Family and the Young Offender*, HMSO.

Home Office (HO) (1968) Cmnd 3601 *Children in Trouble*, HMSO.

Home Office (HO) (1990) Cm 965 *Crime, Justice and Protecting the Public*, HMSO.

Home Office (HO) (1997a) White Paper, Cm 3809 *No More Excuses – A New Approach to Tackling Youth Crime in England and Wales*, HMSO.

Home Office (HO) (1997b) *Tackling Youth Crime* Consultation Paper, HO.

Home Office (HO) (1997c) *New National and Local Focus on Youth Crime: A Consultation Paper*, HO.

Home Office (HO) (2001) *The Youth Court 2001: The Changing Culture of the Youth Court, Good Practice Guide*, HO.

Home Office (HO) (2002) *The Final Warning Scheme: Guidance for the Police and Youth Offending Teams*, HO.

Home Office (HO) (2003) *Youth Justice – The Next Steps, Companion Document to Every Child Matters*, HO.

Home Office (HO) (2005) *Guidance on Publicising Anti-Social Behaviour Orders*, HO.

Home Office (HO) (2006a) *Respect Action Plan – Give Respect Get Respect*, Respect Task Force.

Home Office (HO) (2006b) *A Guide to Anti-Social Behaviour Orders*, HO.

Home Office (HO) (2006c) *Tackling Anti-Social Behaviour: The Story So Far and the Move to Respect*, Respect Task Force.

Home Office (HO) (2006d) *The Final Warning Scheme*, HO circular 14/2006, HO.

Home Office (HO) (2007) *Acceptable Behaviour Contracts and Agreements*, HO.

House of Commons Home Affairs Committee (1993) *Juvenile Offenders* Vol 1, Sixth Report, Session 1992–93.

House of Commons Home Affairs Committee (2007) HC 181–1, *Young Black People and the Criminal Justice System*, Second Report of Session 2006–07, The Stationery Office.

Howard League (2005) *Children in Custody: Promoting the Legal and Human Rights of Children*, Howard League for Penal Reform.

Hughes, G. and Follett, M. (2006) 'Community Safety, Youth and the "Anti-Social"' in Goldson, B. and Muncie, J. (eds.) *Youth Crime and Justice*, Sage Publications.

Human Rights Committee (2008) *Concluding Observations of the Human Rights Committee: United Kingdom of Great Britain and Northern Ireland*, CCPR/C/GBR/CO/6, Geneva.

Jamieson, J. (2006) 'New Labour, Youth Justice and the Question of "Respect"' 5 *Youth Justice* 180.

Joint Committee on Human Rights (JCHR) (2003) *The UN Convention on the Rights of the Child, Tenth Report of Session 2002–03*, HL Paper 117/HC 81, The Stationery Office.

Joint Committee on Human Rights (JCHR) (2008) *The Use of Restraint in Secure Training Centres, Eleventh Report of Session 2007–08*, HL Paper 65/HC 378, The Stationery Office.

Keating, H. (2007a) 'The "Responsibility" of Children in the Criminal Law' 19 *Child and Family Law Quarterly* 183.

(2007b) 'Reckless Children' *Criminal Law Review* 546.

Kilbrandon, L. (chairman) (1964) Cmnd 2306 *Children and Young Persons Scotland*, HMSO.

Kilkelly, U. (2008) 'Youth Justice and Children's Rights: Measuring Compliance with International Standards' 8 *Youth Justice* 187.

Krisberg, B. (2006) 'Rediscovering the Juvenile Justice Ideal in the United States' in Muncie, J. and Goldson, B. (eds.) *Comparative Youth Justice*, Sage Publications.

Koffman, L. (2006) 'The Use of Anti-social Behaviour Orders: an Empirical Study of a New Deal for Communities Area' *Criminal Law Review* 593.

(2008) 'Holding Parents to Account: Tough on Children, Tough on the Causes of Children?' 35 *Journal of Law and Society* 113.

Lader, D, Singleton, N. and Meltzer, H. (2000) *Psychiatric Morbidity among Young Offenders in England and Wales* ONS, The Stationery Office.

Law Commission (2006) Law Com No 304, HC 30, *Murder, Manslaughter and Infanticide*, TSO.

Lloyd, T. (2008) 'Super-Asbos Fail to Gain Respect', *Children and Young People Now*, 28 May–3 June 20.

Local Government Association (2006) *A Position Paper: Children in Trouble: LGA Campaign to Reduce Youth Offending*, LGA.

Lösel, F. and Bender, D. (2006) 'Risk Factors for Serious and Violent Antisocial Behaviour in Children and Youth' in Hagell, A. and Jeyarajah-Dent, R. (eds.) *Children Who Commit Acts of Serious Interpersonal Violence*, Jessica Kingsley Publishers.

Lynch, N. (2008) 'Youth Justice in New Zealand: A Children's Rights Perspective' 8 *Youth Justice* 215.

Lyon, J., Dennison, C. and Wilson, A. (2000) *"Tell Them So They Listen": Messages from Young People in Custody* Home Office Research Study 201, HO.

Maguire, M. (2007) 'Crime Data and Statistics' in Maguire, M., Morgan, R. and Reiner, R. (2007) *The Oxford Handbook of Criminology*, Oxford University Press.

Macdonald, S. (2003) 'The Nature of the Anti-Social Behaviour Order – *R (McCann & Others) v Crown Court at Manchester*', 66 *Modern Law Review* 630.

(2006) 'A Suicidal Woman, Roaming Pigs and a Noisy Trampolinist: Refining the ASBO's Definition of "Anti-Social Behaviour"' 69 *Modern Law Review* 183.

Macdonald, S. (2007) 'ASBO Prohibitions and Young People – *Hills v Chief Constable of Essex Police*' 19 *Child and Family Law Quarterly* 374.

Margo, J. and Dixon, M., with Pearce, N. and Reed, H. (2006) *Freedom's Orphans: Raising Youth in a Changing World*, IPPR.

Margo, J. and Stevens, A. (2008) *Make Me a Criminal: Preventing Youth Crime*, IPPR.

Marshall, K. (2007) 'Human Rights and Children's Rights in the Scottish Children's Hearings System' in Hill, M., Lockyer, A. and Stone, F. (eds.) *Youth Justice and Child Protection*, Jessica Kingsley Publishers.

Mattinson, J. and Mirrlees-Black, C. (2000) *Attitudes to Crime and Criminal Justice: Findings from the 1998 British Crime Survey* Home Office Research Study 200, Home Office.

McAra, L. (2006) 'Welfare in Crisis? Key Developments in Scottish Youth Justice' in Muncie, J. and Goldson, B. (eds.) *Comparative Youth Justice*, Sage Publications.

McDairmid, C. (2005) 'Welfare, Offending and the Scottish Children's Hearings System' 27 *Journal of Social Welfare and Family Law* 31.

McGhee, J. and Waterhouse, L. (2007) 'Classification in Youth Justice and Child Welfare: In Search of "the Child"' 7 *Youth Justice* 107.

Meltzer, H. and Gatward, R. (2000) *Mental Health of Children and Adolescents in Great Britain* ONS The Stationery Office.

Millie, A., Jacobson, J., McDonald, E. and Hough, M. (2005), *Anti-social Behaviour Strategies*, The Policy Press.

Ministry of Justice (MOJ) (2008) Cm 7501 *The Government's Response to the Report by Peter Smallridge and Andrew Williamson of a Review of the Use of Restraint in Juvenile Secure Settings*, The Stationery Office.

Monaghan, G., Hibbert, P. and Moore, S. (2003) *Children in Trouble: Time for Change*, Barnardos.

Moran, P. and Ghate, D. (2005) 'The Effectiveness of Parenting Support' 19 *Children and Society* 329.

Morgan, R. (2007a) 'A Temporary Respite' *The Guardian*, 19 February 2007.

(2007b) 'A New Direction' Interview, 32 *Safer Society* 5.

Morgan, R. and Newburn, T. (2007) 'Youth Justice' in Maguire, M., Morgan, R. and Reiner, R. (2007) *The Oxford Handbook of Criminology*, Oxford University Press.

Morris, A. and Giller, H. (1987) *Understanding Juvenile Justice*, Croom Helm.

Muncie, J. (2004) *Youth Crime*, Sage Publications.

(2008) 'The "Punitive Turn" in Juvenile Justice: Cultures of Control and Rights Compliance in Western Europe and the USA' 8 *Youth Justice* 107.

Muncie, J. and Goldson, B. (2006) *'States of Transition: Convergence and Diversity in International Youth Justice*' in Muncie, J. and Goldson, B. (eds.) *Comparative Youth Justice*, Sage Publications.

Nacro (2003) *The Sentencing Framework for Children and Young People*, Youth Crime Briefing, Nacro Youth Crime.

(2004a) *Anti-social Behaviour Orders and Associated Measures (Part Two)*, Youth Crime Briefing, Nacro Youth Crime.

(2004b) *Parenting Provision in a Youth Justice Context'*, Youth Crime Briefing, Nacro Youth Crime.

(2005) *A Better Alternative: Reducing Child Imprisonment*, Youth Crime Briefing, Nacro.

(2006a) *Reducing Custody: a Systemic Approach*, Youth Crime Briefing, Nacro.

(2006b) *Prevention and Youth Offending Teams*, Youth Crime Briefing, Nacro.

(2006c) *The Dangerousness Provisions of the Criminal Justice Act 2003 and Subsequent Case Law*, Youth Crime Briefing, Nacro.

(2007a) *Some Facts About Children and Young People Who Offend – 2005*, Youth Crime Briefing, Nacro Youth Crime.

(2007b) *Further Developments in Measures Related to Anti-social Behaviour*, Youth Crime Briefing, Nacro Youth Crime.

(2007c) *The Detention and Training Order: Current Position and Future Developments*, Youth Crime Briefing, Nacro Youth Crime.

(2007d) *The Criminal Justice and Immigration Bill – Some Implications for Youth Justice*, Youth Crime Briefing, Nacro Youth Crime.

(2007e) 'Grave Crimes', Mode of Trial and Long Term Detention', Youth Crime Briefing, Nacro Youth Crime.

(2008) *Some Facts About Children and Young People Who Offend – 2006*, Youth Crime Briefing, Nacro Youth Crime.

National Audit Office (2006) *Tackling Anti-social Behaviour*, The Stationery Office.

Newburn, T. (2007) 'Young People, Crime, and Youth Justice' in Maguire, M., Morgan, R. and Reiner, R. (eds.) *The Oxford Handbook of Criminology* Oxford University Press.

Newburn, T. Crawford, A., Earle, R., Goldie, S., Hale, C., Hallam, A., Masters, G., Netten, A., Saunders, R., Sharpe, K. and Uglow, S. (2002) *The Introduction of Referral Orders into the Youth Justice System: Final Report* Home Office Research Study 242, HO.

Newbury, A. (2008) 'Youth Crime: Whose Responsibility?' 35 *Journal of Law and Society* 131.

Ofsted (2008) *Safeguarding Children, the Third Joint Chief Inspectors' Report on Arrangements to Safeguard Children*, Ofsted.

Ormerod, D. (2008a) 'Young Person: Person Having Low IQ – District Judge Determining a Young Person Having Insufficient Level of Understanding to Participate Effectively in Proceedings' *Criminal Law Review* 165.

(2008b) 'Doli Incapax: Whether s34 of the Crime and Disorder Act 1998 Abolished Not Only Presumption of Doli Incapax but also Concept of Doli Incapax as a Defence' *Criminal Law Review* 721.

Phillips, A. and Chamberlain, V. (2006) *MORI Five-Year Report: an Analysis of Youth Survey Data*, Youth Justice Board.

Piacentini, L. and Walters, R. (2006) 'The Politicization of Youth Crime in Scotland and the Rise of the "Burberry Court"' 6 *Youth Crime* 43.

Piper, C. (1999) 'The Crime and Disorder Act 1998: Child and Community "Safety"' 62 *Modern Law Review* 397.

(2001) 'Who are these Youths? Language in the Service of Policy' 1 *Youth Justice* 30.

Pitts, J. (2003) *The New Politics of Youth Crime*, Russell House Publishing.

Put, J. and Walgrave, L. (2006) 'Belgium: From Protection Towards Accountability?' in Muncie, J. and Goldson, B. (eds.) *Comparative Youth Justice*, Sage Publications.

Roe, S. and Ashe, J. (2008) *Young People and Crime: Findings From the 2006 Offending, Crime and Justice Survey*, Home Office Statistical Bulletin 09/08, Home Office.

Royal College of Psychiatrists (2006) *Child Defendants* Occasional Paper OP 56, Royal College of Psychiatrists.

Rutter, M. (chairman) (2005) *Commission on Families and the Wellbeing of Children, Families and the State: Two-way Support and Responsibilities*, The Policy Press.

Scottish Law Commission (2002) *Report on the Age of Criminal Responsibility* (Scot Law Com No 185), The Stationery Office.

Sentencing Advisory Panel (2007) *Breach of an Anti-Social Behaviour Order: Consultation Paper*, Sentencing Guidelines Secretariat.

Sentencing Guidelines Council (2006) *Robbery: Definitive Guideline*, Sentencing Guidelines Secretariat.

Smith, R. (2005) 'Welfare Versus Justice – Again!' 5 *Youth Justice* 3.

(2006) 'Actuarialism and Early Intervention in Contemporary Youth Justice' in Goldson, B. and Muncie, J. (eds.) *Youth Crime and Justice*, Sage Publications.

Solanki, A.-R., Boswell, G., Hill, E. and Bateman, T. (2006) *Anti-Social Behaviour Orders*, Youth Justice Board.

Solomon, E. and Garside, R. (2008) *Ten Years of Labour's Youth Justice Reforms: an Independent Audit*, Centre for Crime and Justice Studies.

Smallridge, P. and Williamson, A. (2008) *Independent Review of Restraint in Juvenile Secure Settings*, MOJ.

Telford, M. (2007) 'Youth Justice: New Shoots on a Bleak Landscape – Crown Prosecution Service v P' 18 *Child and Family Law Quarterly* 505.

Tutt, N. (Chairman) (1996) *Children and Homicide: Appropriate Procedures for Juveniles in Murder and Manslaughter Cases*, Justice working party report, Justice.

UK Children's Commissioners (2008) *UK Children's Commissioners' Report to the UN Committee on the Rights of the Child*, 11 million.

Walker, N. (1999) 'The End of an Old Song' *New Law Journal* 64.

Walker, A., Kershaw, C. and Nicholas, S. (2006) *Crime in England and Wales 2005/06*, Home Office Statistical Bulletin 12/06, Home Office.

Walsh, C. (2002) 'Curfews: No More Hanging Around' 2 *Youth Justice* 70.

(2008) 'The *Mosquito*: A Repellent Response' 8 *Youth Justice* 122.

Waterhouse, L., McGhee, J. and Loucks, N. (2004) 'Disentangling Offenders and Non-Offenders in the Scottish Children's Hearings: A Clear Divide?' 43 *Howard Journal* 164.

Webster, C. (2006) '"Race", Youth Crime and Justice' in Goldson, B. and Muncie, J. (eds.) *Youth Crime and Justice*, Sage Publications.

Wilson, D., Sharp, C. and Patterson, A. (2006) *Young People and Crime: Findings from the 2005 Offending, Crime and Justice Survey*, Home Office Statistical Bulletin 17/06, Home Office.

Wonnacott, C. (1999) 'The Counterfeit Contract – Reform, Pretence and Muddled Principles in the New Referral Order' 11 *Child and Family Law Quarterly* 271.

Wood, M. (2005) *The Victimisation of Young People: Findings From the Crime and Justice Survey 2003*, Home Office Findings 246, Home Office.

Worsley, R. (2006) HM Inspectorate of Prisons and Youth Justice Board *Young People in Custody 2004–2006*, HM Inspectorate of Prisons.

Youth Justice Board (2003) *Referral Orders: Research into the Issues Raised in "The Introduction of the Referral Order in the Youth Justice System"*, Youth Justice Board.

Youth Justice Board (YJB) (2005a) *Anti-social Behaviour: a Guide to the Role of Youth Offending Teams in Dealing with Anti-social Behaviour*, Youth Justice Board.

Youth Justice Board (YJB) (2005b) *Strategy for the Secure Estate for Children and Young People*, Youth Justice Board.

Youth Justice Board (YJB) (2006a) *Individual Support Orders (ISO) Procedure*, Youth Justice Board.

Youth Justice Board (YJB) (2006b) *Barriers to engagement in employment, training and education*, YJB.

Youth Justice Board (YJB) (2006c) *ISSP Management Guidance*, YJB.

Youth Justice Board (YJB) (2007a) *Towards a Youth Crime Prevention Strategy*, YJB.

Youth Justice Board (YJB) (2007b) *Update on the Strategy for the Secure Estate for Children and Young People*, YJB.

Youth Justice Board (YJB) (2007c) *Youth Justice: The Scaled Approach*, YJB.

Youth Justice Board (YJB) (2008) *Corporate Plan 2008–11; Business Plan 2008/9*, YJB.

Youth Justice Board (YJB) (2009) *Youth Justice: The Scaled Approach, A Framework for Assessment and Interventions*, Post-consultation version two, draft, YJB.

Chapter 19

Conclusion – themes and the way ahead

(1) Introduction

As the preceding chapters demonstrate, in common with other minority groups, children suffer from being the focus of various specialised branches of law and policy, all with their own distinctive character. We find case law and legislation responding in an ad hoc fashion to various aspects of children's lives in a completely disparate way, which sometimes reflects a rights consciousness, but often ignores such a concept. Underlying this incoherence is a slow conversion of our legal system to one embodying a rights-based approach. The Human Rights Act (HRA) 1998, by incorporating the European Convention for the Protection of Human Rights and Fundamental Freedoms (ECHR) into domestic law, has undoubtedly enhanced public perceptions of the rights enjoyed by all individuals, both against the state and each other. Society is also becoming far more aware of the demands of the Convention on the Rights of the Child (CRC), with most public agencies attempting to comply with its broad aims. Indeed, there does appear to be a growing sympathy with a desire to promote children's rights in more realistic and practical ways. Nevertheless, the developing law does not always reflect such a desire and it would be foolish to ignore the real concerns that many retain over the wisdom of utilising the concept of rights to increase children's well-being.[1] This concluding chapter opens by considering the extent to which parents' interests hamper the law's development of children's rights. It proceeds to assess the peculiarly fragmented manner in which children are 'constructed' by law and practice to fulfil adult perceptions of their needs. The difficulties posed by society's negative attitudes towards young people, combined with the use of the concept of social exclusion, are also examined. The chapter concludes by arguing that this fragmented approach to childhood should be addressed by adopting a more vigorous rights-based perspective.

(2) The parental factor

In assessing the extent to which the developing law promotes children's rights, this work has uncovered a variety of approaches with little coherence. We must

---

[1] See Chapter 1.

accept, however, that an uncodified legal system such as our own produces legal principles in a peculiarly untidy way. The government introduces legislation and the courts case law, with scant attention to how the two bodies of law might fit together. Lawyers wishing to promote children's rights more effectively are hampered by this haphazard method of producing the legal principles governing children. Case law develops on an incremental basis, with no underlying policy or cohesion and the opportunities for remedying practical gaps and defects uncovered are very limited. The courts have to wait for further litigation on the same topic or for the government to be sufficiently motivated to deal with the matter through special legislation.

As the preceding chapters show, some branches of law reflect a good appreciation that children have their own rights that must be respected, whilst in other areas, this appears to be completely lacking. In these latter areas, it is often parents' interests which hold back a fuller legal acknowledgment of children rights. Indeed, many of the principles of child law still reflect an assumption that the state should not interfere in family life, rather that parents should be left alone to bring their children up as they see fit. This may explain the fact that overall there is relatively little case law and legislation acknowledging that children are independent rights-holders. There is, of course, some irony in the fact that decisions producing the most welcome clarification of children's rights have often been provoked by parents' attempting to enforce their own rights to control their children's lives. Thus, the group of Christian parents in the *Williamson* case[2] found to their cost that their children had a legal right to protection from the very religious views that they themselves had gone to court to promote. Victoria Gillick[3] and Sue Axon,[4] in attempting to define their own right to control their daughters' medical consultations, also unwittingly provoked a clarification of adolescents' rights to independence and medical privacy.[5]

A prime example of legal inactivity predicated by parental self-interest is the family courts' apparent inability to see the average contact dispute as anything other than a parental quarrel, thinly disguised as an argument about the child's best interests. The notion of children having their own rights in such disputes is barely ever acknowledged.[6] Similarly, in the context of social policy, the government has left virtually unscathed parents' right to use physical punishment to discipline their children in the privacy of their own homes. Its anxiety not to antagonise those upon whom it relies to bring up the next generation overcomes any notions of promoting children's right to freedom from violent

---

[2] *R (on the application of Williamson and others) v. Secretary of State for Education and Employment and others* [2005] UKHL 15, [2005] 2 All ER 1; discussed in Chapter 9.

[3] *Gillick v. West Norfolk and Wisbech Area Health Authority* [1986] AC 112.

[4] *R (Axon) v. Secretary of State for Health and the Family Planning Association* [2006] EWHC 37 (Admin), [2006] 2 FLR 206.

[5] See Chapter 5.   [6] See Chapter 13.

treatment.[7] The state's sensitivity towards parents' rights to family privacy also dictates a reluctance to intervene to protect children from parental abuse and neglect except as a last resort. Though keen to improve the way that child care and child protection agencies go about their professional work, through the introduction of integrated working, the government finds it difficult to maintain an appropriate balance between respecting parental privacy and giving child protection agencies sufficient power and resources with which to intervene.

The willingness of policy-makers to assume that children's interests are united with those of their parents is perhaps most apparent in the large body of legislation governing education. Only by avoiding the jurisdiction of the educational appeal tribunals, was Shabina Begum able to reach the House of Lords with her own claim that her school's uniform policy infringed her right to religion under the ECHR. Despite her lack of success, her action demonstrated how important it is for children to be able to test out the boundaries of their own rights.[8] But it is only very occasionally that children emerge from the cloak of parental privacy to bring challenges on their own behalf. Indeed, the fact that children still lack party status in the education appeal tribunals reflects the official view that education is a service designed for adult consumption. Admittedly some parents are tenacious enough to challenge inferior educational provision. Their success has produced judicial confirmation that children have rights to education free from discrimination and that these must be recognised by schools and local authorities (LAs).[9] There must, however, be many more parents who eschew embarking on such potentially stressful litigation, leaving their children's rights unrecognised.

The reluctance of the government and courts to see children as individuals in their own right, as opposed to adjuncts of their parents, gives way to a savage intolerance of juvenile anti-social behaviour. The youth justice system, far from respecting parental and family privacy, assumes that parents must be responsible for producing anti-social children and that through measures such as parenting orders, parenting contracts and fines, they will learn better. Alongside such an approach, the youth justice system takes a second bite at the cherry by assuming that children can take responsibility for their own wrong doing from the age of 10.[10] Overall, we see a system of law which fitfully acknowledges the concept of children having rights, with concerns about parents' interests usually far outweighing other considerations. Indeed, as discussed below, the inconsistent development of the law results in various aspects of childhood being singled out for particular attention, with little opportunity to consider children's needs holistically.

---

[7] See Chapter 9.
[8] *R (on the application of Begum) v. Head Teacher and Governors of Denbigh High School* [2006] UKHL 15, [2007] AC 100, discussed in Chapter 11.
[9] See Chapters 6, 11 and 12.   [10] See Chapter 18.

(3) The 'fragmented' child

Much has been written about the way that the law constructs children to fulfil adult preconceptions of how they fit into an adult-orientated legal framework. We have discussed, for example, the criticisms levelled at the way in which the family courts deal with private law applications, with their implicit assumption that children are the passive victims of their parents' battles.[11] There are many other ways in which law constructs children, portraying them all with group characteristics often out of tune with reality.[12] Nevertheless, in more general terms, as far as law and social policy are concerned, there appear to be two main groups of children and their treatment is at complete variance. There are the 'responsible', law-abiding children, who as they mature, are deemed perfectly able to take responsibility for their own decision-making.[13] Government policies largely leave this group well alone, trusting their parents to bring them up as they think fit. For these children, the civil law has developed the enlightened and sophisticated concept of *Gillick* competence. The House of Lords in *Gillick v. West Norfolk and Wisbech Area Health Authority*[14] saw the wisdom of harnessing the goodwill of sensible adolescents by treating them as individuals fast approaching adulthood. This legal approach promotes the idea that children, when sufficiently mature, can act responsibly if given the legal authority and freedom to do so. They may not only understand their own needs better than their parents, but society needs adolescents who know how to act sensibly without their parents' authority, for example, by taking precautions against unwanted pregnancies.

The second group of children are the troubled and the troublesome – those who create the 'headline' problems: youth crime, truancy and school exclusions, social alienation, unemployment and homelessness. Many of these have the same underlying problems,[15] but the law and policy applied to them depends entirely on the way they first attract adults' attention and whose attention they attract. For example, those who are disruptive in school, bully others and truant, may end up permanently excluded from mainstream education and in a pupil referral unit. Alternatively, their behaviour may be diagnosed as being attributable to their learning difficulties.[16] Their problems, being defined as an educational issue and dealt with under the umbrella of SEN law and policy, then gain the attention of educational psychologists, special educational needs co-ordinators and classroom assistants. They may even be sent to a special residential school. On the other hand, their disturbed behaviour may suggest mental health problems, with a referral to the CAMHS,[17] with the possibility of ending up as patients in secure children's homes, or psychiatric units, under secure accommodation orders.[18]

---

[11] See Chapter 7.   [12] C. Piper (2007) pp. 148–52.   [13] C. Piper (2008) pp. 35–50.
[14] [1986] AC 112.   [15] See Chapter 18. See also SETF (2007) pp. 9–11.   [16] See Chapter 12.
[17] Child and Adolescent Mental Health Services.   [18] See Chapter 5.

Some of the troubled children will be identified by LAs as requiring protection from abusing or neglectful parents. They may find themselves removed from home and found alternative homes, either through adoption, long-term fostering or in a children's home. A fundamental dilemma is posed by the research indicating that a proportion of the children who need protecting from abuse become involved in troublesome behaviour themselves. The type of parental behaviour which alerts social workers to the need to intervene under the civil law to protect children from their parents[19] also correlates with later criminal activity amongst children brought up in such a way.[20] Although it is recognised that abused children need state protection, the law often treats the very same children in a savagely punitive way if they become involved in offending behaviour.

The children whose offending behaviour attracts the attention of the authorities find themselves in an entirely different environment to that of child protection. Even the principles contained in the civil and criminal legal systems regarding a troublesome child's competence and ability to take responsibility for his or her actions contain utterly opposing viewpoints. The concept of *Gillick* competence not only treats children very liberally, but it also protects them from reaching decisions before they are sufficiently mature to comprehend them. The criminal law treats children in a much more punitive way, expecting them to take responsibility for their actions when they are still extremely immature. The adolescent found guilty of a serious crime may end up in a young offender institution, with little attention to his or her underlying problems. Admittedly, the criminal law has a duty to promote society's need for protection, whilst the civil law can concentrate on the needs of the individual child. This does not, however, justify the more punitive aspects of criminal law nor explain the internal incoherence of the civil law which becomes so obvious when comparing the opposing principles developed for this second group of children, through various specialised pockets of legal principles.

The extent to which a child or young person will be able to oppose any interventions with the help of separate representation depends entirely on the law relating to the process. If, for example, legal proceedings are mounted to ensure that a young person enters secure accommodation on a welfare placement,[21] he or she will be represented by a children's guardian and a solicitor. Equally, if the same young person is required to answer charges in a youth court, he or she gains legal representation. If, however, he or she is excluded from school, the parents alone are entitled to speak on behalf of their offspring, but only if they appeal. If health problems force a child under the age of 16 to seek medical attention, he or she may be treated in a psychiatric unit, on the authority only of the parents.[22] In each situation, a different set of practitioners with their own specialised training and expertise will see the child's problems

---

[19] See Chapter 15.   [20] DfES (2006) p. 14; see generally Chapter 18.
[21] See Chapter 16.   [22] See Chapter 5.

and background from an entirely different and sometimes opposing viewpoint. This fragmented approach to childhood problems encourages practitioners to categorise children according to sets of rigidly defined symptoms, rather than to view them as individuals. It promotes a simplistic approach to diagnosis, undermines an efficient co-ordination of services and prevents problems being picked up early in children's lives.

(4) The concept of 'social exclusion' and negative perceptions of 'youth'

Alongside this fragmented approach to childhood, children and young people are being portrayed in various negative ways. They are seen as irresponsible – unwilling to adopt a responsible attitude to community affairs. Concern has been voiced amongst a number of developed countries throughout Europe over the relative apathy and increasing alienation of teenagers from politics and the democratic process.[23] In this country, a small and reducing number of 18 to 24-year-olds voted in the 2001 and 2005 general elections.[24] The Crick committee received considerable evidence of negative attitudes and a general ignorance of political processes amongst young people in this country.[25] More dangerously, it is society's own attitudes towards young people which risks alienating them against an adult society which appears to view them as 'problematic' or even 'a threat'.[26] In its unconcerned use of anti-social behaviour orders (ASBOs), dispersal orders, mosquito devices and CCTV surveillance, we see symptoms of a society unwilling to tolerate young people in public spaces.[27] As the Committee on the Rights of the Child observes, young people in the UK are growing up in 'a general climate of intolerance and negative public attitudes towards children, especially adolescents'.[28] Young people are themselves keenly aware of their reputation in the community for being anti-social.[29] Raz's comment in a general context has particular resonance:

> The existence within a political society of estranged groups, who do not identify with the state, or the nation, and regard the government as an alien, potentially hostile, government, is destabilizing. Beyond that is the fact that human beings are political animals. That means more than that they can only thrive in political societies which provide the opportunities for the activities which make their lives. It also means that feeling part of a larger community, and being able to identify oneself as a member of such communities is an essential ingredient in people's well-being. Those who are second class citizens are marked by this experience which forces a flawed life on them.[30]

---

[23] R. Hodgkin and P. Newell (1996) pp. 36–8.   [24] See Chapter 4.
[25] B. Crick (1998) paras. 3.4–3.9. See also C. White *et al.* (2000) p. 44: the young people interviewed had 'depressingly low levels of political interest and knowledge'.
[26] C. Piper (2007) p. 149.   [27] See Chapter 18.
[28] Committee on the Rights of the Child (2008) para. 24.
[29] HM Treasury and DCSF (2007a) para. 1.11.   [30] J. Raz (1996) p. 125.

Raz's comment hints at some of the concerns underlying the heated debates over the existence or otherwise of an 'underclass', composed of individuals who are morally irresponsible, whose behaviour leads them into long-term unemployment, benefit dependency, single parenthood and criminal activity. One of the many weaknesses of the underclass concept is its emphasis on the make-up and behaviour of the members of the underclass, rather than on wider social factors, such as regional unemployment.[31] An off-shoot of the underclass theory is the idea of an anti-social, criminal and feckless youth underclass, distinct from and hostile to wider society.[32] Many authors, like Pearce and Hillman, not only reject the concept of an underclass as being 'simplistic and ideologically motivated' but also the notion of there being a homogenous group of disaffected young people.[33] Nevertheless, when considering the problems of young people, even the opponents of the underclass theory acknowledge the importance of addressing their growing 'disaffection and disengagement'.[34]

The government clearly recognises the weakness of the fragmented approach to childhood described above and has introduced a series of structural changes,[35] culminating in the creation in 2007 of the Department for Children, Schools and Families (DCSF).[36] But its 'cross-cutting' policy initiatives to address this problem often use the label 'social exclusion' to describe their focus.[37] This is 'a shorthand term for what can happen when people or areas suffer from a combination of linked problems such as unemployment, poor skills, low incomes, poor housing, high crime, bad health and family breakdown'.[38] Despite being less pejorative than 'underclass', this term, is, by definition exclusionary and does little to discourage the public's negative perceptions of those growing up in apparently socially excluded families. Indeed, the Social Exclusion Task Force (SETF), which replaced the Social Exclusion Unit (SEU), has largely focused on those parents who fail to conform – the 'small minority of parents who refuse offers of support'.[39] It stresses the high cost to the community as a whole of supporting this small minority of families who 'continue to experience challenging lives compared with the majority who are enjoying ever increasing prosperity and increased

---

[31] N. Pearce and J. Hillman (1998) pp. 3–4. See also SETF (2008a) chs. 1–3.

[32] See generally R. MacDonald and J. Marsh (2005) ch. 1.

[33] N. Pearce and J. Hillman (1998) p. 4. See also L. Johnston *et al.* (2000) pp. 2–3.

[34] N. Pearce and J. Hillman (1998) pp. 3–6.

[35] A number of units have been created over the last decade to tackle cross-departmental matters. Inter alia: the Social Exclusion Unit (subsequently replaced by the Social Exclusion Task Force) and the Performance and Innovation Unit, both within the Cabinet Office; the Children and Young People's Unit established in 2000 under the auspices of the DFEE, disbanded in 2004; the Home Office Family Policy Unit, subsequently transferred to DfES and then disbanded in 2004; the Child Poverty Unit created in 2007, under the auspices of DWP and DCSF; the Youth Justice Unit created in 2007, under the auspices of Ministry of Justice (MOJ) and DCSF.

[36] House of Commons (2008) paras. 9–15: reservations about the DCSF's ability to work jointly and effectively with other parts of government.

[37] HM Government (2006), SETF (2007), SETF (2008b).

[38] SEU (2001) para. 1.2.   [39] HM Government (2006) para. 5.13.

opportunities'.[40] More to the point, this small minority of socially excluded families produce vulnerable and socially excluded children, at a further cost to the taxpayer, if and when they are taken into care.[41] Families in the greatest difficulty are to be provided with 'intensive' support 'with non-negotiable elements if families refuse to engage'.[42] This condescending and punitive attitude bears out the critics who suggest that, like the term 'underclass', 'social exclusion' is merely a rather unsatisfactory shorthand reduction of a complex phenomenon. Arguably, the term has become a 'catch-all' phrase meaning all things to all people,[43] with a potential for increasing the exclusion and dis-affection of those defined as socially excluded.[44]

Greater coherence would be achieved were the government to develop policies applicable to *all* children, not just the poor and disadvantaged. As Hodgkin and Newell observe:

> The SEU has succeeded in highlighting and setting remedies for the obstacles to the social inclusion of young people ... Nonetheless its remit prevents it from celebrating the contribution of all children and thus moving our society on from negative or self-serving attitudes to children.[45]

A good education should encourage young people to feel included in, rather than excluded from society. Crick considered that citizenship education should become part of the school curriculum:

> to make secure and to increase the knowledge, skills and values relevant to the nature and practices of participative democracy; also to enhance the awareness of rights and duties, and the sense of responsibilities needed for the development of pupils into active citizens; and in so doing to establish the value to individuals, schools and society of involvement in the local and wider community.[46]

The government places great store on the ability of citizenship education to teach young people more about these matters and how to 'play a full role as active citizens' in the community.[47] At the very least, this curriculum should achieve an improvement in pupils' knowledge of the democratic process and of local and national government structures. Nevertheless, it is difficult to accept the claim that all teenagers should go through citizenship ceremonies on attaining 18 as a way of enhancing their citizenship education in schools and giving them a sense of achievement.[48] Such a coercive approach might simply reinforce feelings of disaffection and alienation.

However well designed, educational programmes alone are insufficient – they certainly cannot 'build better relationships across generations', as the government hopes to do.[49] A fundamental problem is that currently, many

---

[40] SETF (2007) para. 1.64.   [41] Ibid. at para. 1.61.

[42] HM Government (2008) para. 2.12. For parental interventions, e.g. parenting orders, see Chapters 6 and 18.

[43] L. Johnston *et al.* (2000) p. 3.   [44] R. Hodgkin and P. Newell (2001) p. 18.   [45] Ibid. at p. 19.

[46] B. Crick (1998) para. 6.6.   [47] HM Treasury and DCSF (2007a) paras. 3.29–3.30.

[48] P. Goldsmith (2007) p. 97.   [49] HM Treasury and DCSF (2007a) para. 3.54.

young people do not consider that their views are valued by decision-makers.[50] The government is fully aware that attitudes to children and young people need to change, with their competence being fully recognised.[51] A number of initiatives have been designed to help young people feel that they have a real part to play in their communities and in society generally.[52] The government hopes thereby to 'empower' young people to 'play a full role as active citizens' in their communities.[53] Whilst well meaning, the tone of the government's deliberations is prescriptive and faintly patronising, reflecting its own clear ideas about young peoples' natural inclination to fecklessness at the least, criminality at the worst. It does not intend to fund 'unstructured youth clubs' since, according to research,[54] those who attend them (and no other activities) were 'the most at risk of negative outcomes in later life',[55] whereas 'Involvement in purposeful activities as part of a group with shared goals enables young people to develop a strong sense of identity'.[56] They must also be encouraged to contribute to their communities by doing voluntary work – to help them develop a stronger sense of rights and responsibilities and improve mutual understanding between young people and the community.[57]

LAs are now obliged to provide children and young people with opportunities to participate in the design and provision of local services.[58] In particular, with some financial assistance,[59] they are expected to establish better youth facilities – more 'places to go', rather than just 'hanging around'.[60] LAs must 'so far as is reasonably practicable' secure sufficient educational and recreational leisure time activities for young people aged between 13 and 19,[61] having consulted them and taken account of their views.[62] But irrespective of the

---

[50] Unpublished research by MORI/Office for the Children's Commissioner (2006): a survey of over 2,000 11–16-year-olds revealed that 50% did not consider that they had enough say in decisions affecting them.

[51] HM Treasury and DCSF (2007a) para. 3.52.

[52] DfES (2005) ch. 4; HM Treasury and DCSF (2007a), ch. 3; HM Treasury and DCSF (2007b) pp. 48–9; DCSF (2008a) ch. 4; DCSF (2008b) ch. 5.

[53] HM Treasury and DCSF (2007a) para. 3.30.

[54] E.g. L. Feinstein et al. (2005). See also research summaries in J. Margo et al. (2006) pp. 120–7 and DCSF (2008b) pp. 4–5.

[55] HM Treasury and DCSF (2007a) para. 2.23.   [56] Ibid. at para. 2.22.

[57] DfES (2005) p. 39. See also DCSF (2008b) pp. 18–19: the National Youth Volunteering Programme run by V became operational in April 2008.

[58] E.g. Children and Young People's Plan (England) Regulations 2005 (SI 2005/2149), reg. 7(1)(a): children's services authorities must consult children and young people before preparing their Children and Young People's Plan. See CRAE (2008) esp. ch. 3 and Appendix A.

[59] DCSF (2008b) pp. 15–16. Inter alia: the Positive Activities for Young People (PAYP) programme launched in 2003, to provide 'developmental and diversionary activities' for 8–19-year-olds; the Youth Opportunity Fund (YOF) and the Youth Capital Fund (YCF) launched in 2006 providing capital and revenue budgets for young people to control and decide how funding should be spent in their areas in improving facilities; the Myplace programme launched in 2008 funding youth-led projects.

[60] HM Treasury and DCSF (2007a) pp. 45–6.

[61] Education Act 1996, s. 507B(1). NB s. 507B(2)(b): those with learning difficulties are entitled to such services up to the age of 25.

[62] Education Act 1996, s. 507B(9).

views of the young people themselves, the LA must be satisfied that the activities will improve their well-being, thereby improving their 'personal and social development' and earning the designation of 'positive leisure-time activities'.[63] These initiatives are admirable. Nevertheless, as Feinstein *et al.* emphasise, whilst the government may wish to ensure that young people attend structured activities, it may be the very lack of imposed adult structures and curricula that attracts the most challenging and at-risk young people. 'Therefore imposing structured activities risks excluding from these programmes precisely the groups targeted.'[64]

(5) A rights-based remedy

The government's ambition to turn young people into 'active citizens' might have more success if it acknowledged that involving them in local processes and consulting them over what facilities they should have is not merely a way of making them more biddable, but a means of fulfilling their rights. Indeed, greater coherence would be achieved were the government to direct their sights at *all* children, not simply the socially excluded. Approaching children's needs from a rights-based perspective is *inclusive*, without ruling out targeting the neediest within the group. Under a rights-based approach, there would be less temptation to allow the artificial distinctions between children's problems to dominate service design and delivery.[65] Practitioners would be encouraged to consider children as individuals with basic rights, rather than children whose problems fall into certain categories, including 'disadvantage' and 'deprivation'.[66] A rights-based approach might also address the feelings of disaffection and disengagement that many young people so clearly feel. The CRC would be the best vehicle for such an approach, its scope being far wider than that of the ECHR, which focuses on civil and political rights. As Newell observes:

> The particular task of the Convention is to emphasise that children too are holders of human rights. They are not possessions of their parents or of the state. They are not simply objects of concern. They are not people-in-the-making. They are individuals *now* with views, feelings and rights.[67]

But the New Labour government has fought shy of acknowledging that children have rights.[68] Neither the Green Paper, *Every Child Matters*,[69] nor *Youth Matters*,[70] contains any mention of children's rights and those who followed the progress of the Children Act (CA) 2004 know that Margaret Hodge, then the Minister for Children, Young People and Families expunged from the Bill every reference to the word 'rights', bar one. The parliamentary draftsmen found it impossible to avoid the word when referring to the duty

---

[63] Education Act 1996, s. 507B(3) and (4).   [64] L. Feinstein *et al.* (2005) p. 17.
[65] R. Hodgkin and P. Newell (2001) pp. 18–19.   [66] K. Tomaševski (1999) para. 33.
[67] P. Newell (2000) p. 18.   [68] J. Fortin (2006) p. 759.
[69] HM Treasury (2003).   [70] DfES (2005).

of the Children's Commissioner to 'have regard to the United Nations Convention on the Rights of the Child'.[71] Furthermore, despite valiant efforts by various members of the House of Commons Standing Committee to reinsert the word 'rights' into the CA 2004 when it was still in bill form,[72] the reorganisation of children's services is based on adults' ideas about children's 'well-being', not their rights.[73]

This antipathy towards the concept of children having rights is curious given the fact that the New Labour government introduced the HRA 1998, thereby signalling its intention to establish a human rights culture in this country. Attempts to persuade the government to promote children's rights more vigorously are substantially undermined by the fact that the CRC is not part of English law and so is legally unenforceable. Incorporation of the CRC into domestic law, as might now occur,[74] would address children's current special vulnerability, with 'their rights being dependent on their circumstances, rather than belonging to them, be they at home, school, looked after by the state or in custody'.[75]

Only a dramatic change of this kind will provoke a change in attitude in the various government departments which still retain traditional and hidebound assumptions about children and young people. Thus the DCSF continues to condone the permanent exclusion of many thousands of pupils from school every year[76] and the Home Office does little to discourage the public's punitive attitudes towards young offenders.[77] The way ahead must be for the government to adopt a rights-based framework, as a basis for a universal strategy for children, thereby giving all children the same entitlements. Such an approach would go some way towards achieving the goal set out by the United Nations General Assembly in 2002:

> together we will build a world in which all girls and boys can enjoy childhood – a time of play and learning, in which they are loved, respected and cherished, their rights are promoted and protected, without discrimination of any kind, in which their safety and well-being are paramount and in which they can develop in health, peace and dignity.[78]

(6) Postscript

Sadly, children are not always provided with the ideal childhood envisaged by the United Nations General Assembly above. Indeed, according to UNICEF's research, with the UK's average rank being bottom in a list of 21 OECD countries (over six dimensions of child well-being), children here have a

---

[71] CA 2004, s. 2(11).

[72] House of Commons Standing Committee B (2004), pts 2 and 3, cols 9–16.

[73] CA 2004, s. 10.   [74] Discussed in Chapter 2.

[75] JCHR (2008b) Memorandum of Evidence from the Children's Rights Alliance for England, Ev 111.

[76] See Chapter 6.   [77] See Chapter 18.   [78] UN General Assembly (2002) para 9.

particularly bad time.[79] We clearly cannot protect all children from all the pitfalls of childhood and the 'fragmented' child and the socially excluded child rightly demand our concern. Nevertheless, this should not divert attention from the far larger numbers of children who do reach adulthood very happily. The advantage of a rights-based perspective is that it avoids categorising the disadvantaged, entitling all to equal respect. It is not, however, enough for lawyers and policy-makers simply to resolve to adopt a rights-based framework for their work, without being clear what children really require to enhance their well-being. Children's rights are not promoted if adults merely deliver a rough approximation of what children need, based on their own prejudices. As this work shows, law and policy can usefully draw on a growing body of research which considers children's needs from a variety of perspectives. Practitioners who are sympathetic to the concept of fulfilling children's rights should bear in mind that to ignore this information produces principles and policies which are devoid of practical utility and which may do more harm than good.

There are, however, those who, as parents, carers or practitioners, come into contact with children every day, but who do not sympathise with the concept of children's rights. They see it as a notion which not only threatens family stability, but lacks realism and fails to produce ready solutions. They need convincing that it can improve children's lives. This work seeks to show the sceptics how a rights-based approach can be translated into workable policies and legal principles and also that a conscientious attempt to apply these is better than guesswork and intuition. Above all else, the concept of children's rights should be utilised honestly and not as a politically correct tool which only thinly disguises adult caution and narrow-mindedness.

BIBLIOGRAPHY

NB many of these publications can be obtained on the relevant organisation's website.

Children's Rights Alliance for England (CRAE) (2008) *Listen and Change: A Guide to Children and Young People's Participation Rights,* Participation Works.

Committee on the Rights of the Child (2003)*General Measures of Implementation of the Convention on the Rights of the Child* (arts 4, 42 and 44, para 6), General Comment No 5, CRC/GC/2003/5, Centre for Human Rights, Geneva.

Committee on the Rights of the Child, (2008) *Concluding Observations of the Committee on the Rights of the Child: United Kingdom of Great Britain and Northern Ireland* CRC/C/GBR/CO/4, Centre for Human Rights, Geneva.

Crick, B. (Chairman) (1998) *Final Report on Education for Citizenship and the Teaching of Democracy in Schools* Final Report of the Advisory Group on Citizenship, Qualifications and Curriculum Authority.

Department for Children, Schools and Families (DCSF) (2008a) *Youth Taskforce Action Plan*, DCSF.

---

[79] UNICEF (2007) p. 2.

Department for Children, Schools and Families (DCSF) (2008b) *Aiming High for Young People: A Ten Year Strategy for Positive Activities, Implementation Plan*, DCSF.

Department for Education and Skills (DfES) (2005) Cm 6629 *Youth Matters*, The Stationery Office.

Department for Education and Skills (DfES) (2006) Cm 6932 *Care Matters: Transforming the Lives of Children and Young People in Care*, The Stationery Office.

Feinstein, L., Bynner, J. and Duckworth, K. (2005) *Leisure Contexts in Adolescence and Their Effects on Adult Outcomes*, Centre for Research on the Wider Benefits of Learning.

Fortin, J. (2006) 'Children's Rights – Substance or Spin?' 36 *Family Law* 759.

Goldsmith, P. (2007) *Citizenship: Our Common Bond*, Ministry of Justice.

HM Government (2006) *Reaching Out: An Action Plan on Social Exclusion*, Cabinet Office.

HM Government (2008) *Youth Crime Action Plan, 2008*, Home Office.

HM Treasury (2003) Cm 5860 *Every Child Matters*, The Stationery Office.

HM Treasury and Department for Children, Schools and Families (DCSF) (2007a) *Aiming High for Young People: a Ten Year Strategy for Positive Activities*, HM Treasury.

HM Treasury and Department for Children, Schools and Families (DCSF) (2007b) *Policy Review of Children and Young People: a Discussion Paper*, HM Treasury.

Hodgkin, R. and Newell, P. (1996) *Effective Government Structures for Children* Report of a Gulbenkian Foundation Inquiry, Calouste Gulbenkian Foundation.

    (2001) *UK Review of Effective Government Structures for Children 2001* A Gulbenkian Foundation Report, Calouste Gulbenkian Foundation.

House of Commons Select Committee on Children, Schools and Families (2008) HC 213, *The Department for Children, Schools and Families and the Children's Plan, Second Report of Session 2007–08*, The Stationery Office.

Johnston, L, MacDonald, R., Mason, P., Ridley, L. and Webster, C. (2000) *Snakes and Ladders: Young People, Transitions and Social Exclusion*, The Policy Press.

Joint Committee on Human Rights (JCHR) (2008a), *A Bill of Rights for the UK? Twenty-ninth Report of Session 2007–08*, HL Paper 165-I, HC 150-I, The Stationery Office.

Joint Committee on Human Rights (JCHR) (2008b) *A Bill of Rights for the UK? Twenty-ninth Report of Session 2007–08, Volume II*, HL Paper 165-II, HC 150-II, The Stationery Office.

MacDonald, R. and Marsh, J. (2005) *Disconnected Youth? Growing up in Britain's Poor Neighbourhoods*, Palgrave Macmillan.

Margo, J. and Dixon, M., with Pearce, N. and Reed, H. (2006) *Freedom's Orphans: Raising Youth in a Changing World*, IPPR.

Newell, P. (2000) *Taking Children Seriously: A Proposal for a Children's Rights Commissioner*, Calouste Gulbenkian Foundation.

Pearce, N. and Hillman, J. (1998) *Wasted Youth: Raising Achievement and Tackling Social Exclusion*, IPPR.

Piper, C. (2007) 'Will Law Think about Children? Reflections on Youth Matters' in Invernizzi, A. and Williams,J. (eds.) *Children and Citizenship* Sage Publications.

    (2008) *Investing in Children: Policy, Law and Practice in Context*, Willan Publishing.

Raz, J. (1996) 'Liberty and Trust' in George, R. (ed.) *Natural Law, Liberalism and Morality*, Oxford University Press.

Social Exclusion Task Force (SETF) (2007) *Reaching Out: Think Family*, Cabinet Office.

Social Exclusion Task Force (SETF) (2008a) *Aspiration and Attainment Amongst Young People in Deprived Communities*, Cabinet Office.

Social Exclusion Task Force (SETF) (2008b) *Think Family: Improving the Life Chances of Families at Risk*, Cabinet Office.

Social Exclusion Unit (SEU) (2001) *Preventing Social Exclusion*, Cabinet Office.

Tomaševski, K. (1999) *Report of the Special Rapporteur on the Right to Education to the UN Economic and Social Council, Mission to the United Kingdom and Northern Ireland (England)* E/CN 4/2000/6/Add 2.

UNICEF, Innocenti Research Centre (2007) *Child Poverty in Perspective: An Overview of Child Well-being in Rich Countries*, Report Card 7, UNICEF.

United Nations General Assembly (2002) A/RES/S-27/2 *A World Fit for Children, Resolution Adopted by the General Assembly*, Geneva.

White, C., Bruce, S. and Ritchie, J. (2000) *Young People's Politics: Political Interest and Engagement Amongst 14 to 24-year-Olds*, Joseph Rowntree Foundation.

Appendix I

UN Convention on the Rights of the Child

The Convention on the Rights of the Child was adopted and opened for signature, ratification and accession by General Assembly resolution 44/25 of 20 November 1989. It entered into force 2 September 1990, in accordance with article 49.

Preamble

The States Parties to the present Convention,

Considering that, in accordance with the principles proclaimed in the Charter of the United Nations, recognition of the inherent dignity and of the equal and inalienable rights of all members of the human family is the foundation of freedom, justice and peace in the world,

Bearing in mind that the peoples of the United Nations have, in the Charter, reaffirmed their faith in fundamental human rights and in the dignity and worth of the human person and have determined to promote social progress and better standards of life in larger freedom,

Recognizing that the United Nations has, in the Universal Declaration of Human Rights and in the International Covenants on Human Rights, proclaimed and agreed that everyone is entitled to all the rights and freedoms set forth therein, without distinction of any kind, such as race, colour, sex, language, religion, political or other opinion, national or social origin, property, birth or other status,

Recalling that, in the Universal Declaration of Human Rights, the United Nations has proclaimed that childhood is entitled to special care and assistance,

Convinced that the family, as the fundamental group of society and the natural environment for the growth and well-being of all its members and particularly children, should be afforded the necessary protection and assistance so that it can fully assume its responsibilities within the community,

Recognizing that the child, for the full and harmonious development of his or her personality, should grow up in a family environment, in an atmosphere of happiness, love and understanding,

Considering that the child should be fully prepared to live an individual life in society and brought up in the spirit of the ideals proclaimed in the Charter of the United Nations and in particular in the spirit of peace, dignity, tolera. freedom, equality and solidarity,

Bearing in mind that the need to extend particular care to the child has been stated in the Geneva Declaration of the Rights of the Child of 1924 and in the Declaration of the Rights of the Child adopted by the General Assembly on 20 November 1959 and recognized in the Universal Declaration of Human Rights, in the International Covenant on Civil and Political Rights (in particular in articles 23 and 24), in the International Covenant on Economic, Social and Cultural Rights (in particular in article 10) and in the statutes and relevant instruments of specialized agencies and international organizations concerned with the welfare of children,

Bearing in mind that, as indicated in the Declaration of the Rights of the Child, "the child, by reason of his physical and mental immaturity, needs special safeguards and care, including appropriate legal protection, before as well as after birth",

Recalling the provisions of the Declaration on Social and Legal Principles relating to the Protection and Welfare of Children, with Special Reference to Foster Placement and Adoption Nationally and Internationally; the United Nations Standard Minimum Rules for the Administration of Juvenile Justice (The Beijing Rules); and the Declaration on the Protection of Women and Children in Emergency and Armed Conflict,

Recognizing that, in all countries in the world, there are children living in exceptionally difficult conditions and that such children need special consideration,

Taking due account of the importance of the traditions and cultural values of each people for the protection and harmonious development of the child,

Recognizing the importance of international co-operation for improving the living conditions of children in every country, in particular in the developing countries,

Have agreed as follows:

Part I

Article 1

For the purposes of the present Convention, a child means every human being below the age of eighteen years unless under the law applicable to the child, majority is attained earlier.

Article 2

1. States Parties shall respect and ensure the rights set forth in the present Convention to each child within their jurisdiction without discrimination of any kind, irrespective of the child's or his or her parent's or legal guardian's race, colour, sex, language, religion, political or other opinion, national, ethnic or social origin, property, disability, birth or other status.

2. States Parties shall take all appropriate measures to ensure that the child is protected against all forms of discrimination or punishment on the basis of the status, activities, expressed opinions, or beliefs of the child's parents, legal guardians, or family members.

Article 3

1. In all actions concerning children, whether undertaken by public or private social welfare institutions, courts of law, administrative authorities or legislative bodies, the best interests of the child shall be a primary consideration.
2. States Parties undertake to ensure the child such protection and care as is necessary for his or her well-being, taking into account the rights and duties of his or her parents, legal guardians, or other individuals legally responsible for him or her, and, to this end, shall take all appropriate legislative and administrative measures.
3. States Parties shall ensure that the institutions, services and facilities responsible for the care or protection of children shall conform with the standards established by competent authorities, particularly in the areas of safety, health, in the number and suitability of their staff, as well as competent supervision.

Article 4

States Parties shall undertake all appropriate legislative, administrative and other measures for the implementation of the rights recognized in the present Convention. With regard to economic, social and cultural rights, States Parties shall undertake such measures to the maximum extent of their available resources and, where needed, within the framework of international co-operation.

Article 5

States Parties shall respect the responsibilities, rights and duties of parents or, where applicable, the members of the extended family or community as provided for by local custom, legal guardians or other persons legally responsible for the child, to provide, in a manner consistent with the evolving capacities of the child, appropriate direction and guidance in the exercise by the child of the rights recognized in the present Convention.

Article 6

1. States Parties recognize that every child has the inherent right to life.
2. States Parties shall ensure to the maximum extent possible the survival and development of the child.

Article 7

1. The child shall be registered immediately after birth and shall have the right from birth to a name, the right to acquire a nationality and, as far as possible, the right to know and be cared for by his or her parents.

2. States Parties shall ensure the implementation of these rights in accordance with their national law and their obligations under the relevant international instruments in this field, in particular where the child would otherwise be stateless.

Article 8

1. States Parties undertake to respect the right of the child to preserve his or her identity, including nationality, name and family relations as recognized by law without unlawful interference.
2. Where a child is illegally deprived of some or all of the elements of his or her identity, States Parties shall provide appropriate assistance and protection, with a view to re-establishing speedily his or her identity.

Article 9

1. States Parties shall ensure that a child shall not be separated from his or her parents against their will, except when competent authorities subject to judicial review determine, in accordance with applicable law and procedures, that such separation is necessary for the best interests of the child. Such determination may be necessary in a particular case such as one involving abuse or neglect of the child by the parents, or one where the parents are living separately and a decision must be made as to the child's place of residence.
2. In any proceedings pursuant to paragraph 1 of the present article, all interested parties shall be given an opportunity to participate in the proceedings and make their views known.
3. States Parties shall respect the right of the child who is separated from one or both parents to maintain personal relations and direct contact with both parents on a regular basis, except if it is contrary to the child's best interests.
4. Where such separation results from any action initiated by a State Party, such as the detention, imprisonment, exile, deportation or death (including death arising from any cause while the person is in the custody of the State) of one or both parents or of the child, that State Party shall, upon request, provide the parents, the child or, if appropriate, another member of the family with the essential information concerning the whereabouts of the absent member(s) of the family unless the provision of the information would be detrimental to the well-being of the child. States Parties shall further ensure that the submission of such a request shall of itself entail no adverse consequences for the person(s) concerned.

Article 10

1. In accordance with the obligation of States Parties under article 9, paragraph 1, applications by a child or his or her parents to enter or leave a State Party for the purpose of family reunification shall be dealt with by States Parties in a positive, humane and expeditious manner. States Parties shall further ensure that the submission of such a request shall entail no adverse consequences for the applicants and for the members of their family.

2. A child whose parents reside in different States shall have the right to maintain on a regular basis, save in exceptional circumstances personal relations and direct contacts with both parents. Towards that end and in accordance with the obligation of States Parties under article 9, paragraph 1, States Parties shall respect the right of the child and his or her parents to leave any country, including their own and to enter their own country. The right to leave any country shall be subject only to such restrictions as are prescribed by law and which are necessary to protect the national security, public order (ordre public), public health or morals or the rights and freedoms of others and are consistent with the other rights recognized in the present Convention.

Article 11

1. States Parties shall take measures to combat the illicit transfer and non-return of children abroad.
2. To this end, States Parties shall promote the conclusion of bilateral or multilateral agreements or accession to existing agreements.

Article 12

1. States Parties shall assure to the child who is capable of forming his or her own views the right to express those views freely in all matters affecting the child, the views of the child being given due weight in accordance with the age and maturity of the child.
2. For this purpose, the child shall in particular be provided the opportunity to be heard in any judicial and administrative proceedings affecting the child, either directly, or through a representative or an appropriate body, in a manner consistent with the procedural rules of national law.

Article 13

1. The child shall have the right to freedom of expression; this right shall include freedom to seek, receive and impart information and ideas of all kinds, regardless of frontiers, either orally, in writing or in print, in the form of art, or through any other media of the child's choice.
2. The exercise of this right may be subject to certain restrictions, but these shall only be such as are provided by law and are necessary:
   (a) For respect of the rights or reputations of others; or
   (b) For the protection of national security or of public order (ordre public), or of public health or morals.

Article 14

1. States Parties shall respect the right of the child to freedom of thought, conscience and religion.
2. States Parties shall respect the rights and duties of the parents and, when applicable, legal guardians, to provide direction to the child in the exercise of his or her right in a manner consistent with the evolving capacities of the child.

3. Freedom to manifest one's religion or beliefs may be subject only to such limitations as are prescribed by law and are necessary to protect public safety, order, health or morals, or the fundamental rights and freedoms of others.

Article 15

1. States Parties recognize the rights of the child to freedom of association and to freedom of peaceful assembly.
2. No restrictions may be placed on the exercise of these rights other than those imposed in conformity with the law and which are necessary in a democratic society in the interests of national security or public safety, public order (ordre public), the protection of public health or morals or the protection of the rights and freedoms of others.

Article 16

1. No child shall be subjected to arbitrary or unlawful interference with his or her privacy, family, home or correspondence, nor to unlawful attacks on his or her honour and reputation.
2. The child has the right to the protection of the law against such interference or attacks.

Article 17

States Parties recognize the important function performed by the mass media and shall ensure that the child has access to information and material from a diversity of national and international sources, especially those aimed at the promotion of his or her social, spiritual and moral well-being and physical and mental health. To this end, States Parties shall:

(a) Encourage the mass media to disseminate information and material of social and cultural benefit to the child and in accordance with the spirit of article 29;
(b) Encourage international co-operation in the production, exchange and dissemination of such information and material from a diversity of cultural, national and international sources;
(c) Encourage the production and dissemination of children's books;
(d) Encourage the mass media to have particular regard to the linguistic needs of the child who belongs to a minority group or who is indigenous;
(e) Encourage the development of appropriate guidelines for the protection of the child from information and material injurious to his or her well-being, bearing in mind the provisions of articles 13 and 18.

Article 18

1. States Parties shall use their best efforts to ensure recognition of the principle that both parents have common responsibilities for the upbringing and development of the child. Parents or, as the case may be, legal guardians,

have the primary responsibility for the upbringing and development of the child. The best interests of the child will be their basic concern.

2. For the purpose of guaranteeing and promoting the rights set forth in the present Convention, States Parties shall render appropriate assistance to parents and legal guardians in the performance of their child-rearing responsibilities and shall ensure the development of institutions, facilities and services for the care of children.

3. States Parties shall take all appropriate measures to ensure that children of working parents have the right to benefit from child-care services and facilities for which they are eligible.

Article 19

1. States Parties shall take all appropriate legislative, administrative, social and educational measures to protect the child from all forms of physical or mental violence, injury or abuse, neglect or negligent treatment, maltreatment or exploitation, including sexual abuse, while in the care of parent(s), legal guardian(s) or any other person who has the care of the child.

2. Such protective measures should, as appropriate, include effective procedures for the establishment of social programmes to provide necessary support for the child and for those who have the care of the child, as well as for other forms of prevention and for identification, reporting, referral, investigation, treatment and follow-up of instances of child maltreatment described heretofore, and, as appropriate, for judicial involvement.

Article 20

1. A child temporarily or permanently deprived of his or her family environment, or in whose own best interests cannot be allowed to remain in that environment, shall be entitled to special protection and assistance provided by the State.

2. States Parties shall in accordance with their national laws ensure alternative care for such a child.

3. Such care could include, inter alia, foster placement, kafalah of Islamic law, adoption or if necessary placement in suitable institutions for the care of children. When considering solutions, due regard shall be paid to the desirability of continuity in a child's upbringing and to the child's ethnic, religious, cultural and linguistic background.

Article 21

States Parties that recognize and/or permit the system of adoption shall ensure that the best interests of the child shall be the paramount consideration and they shall:

(a) Ensure that the adoption of a child is authorized only by competent authorities who determine, in accordance with applicable law and procedures and on the basis of all pertinent and reliable information, that the adoption is permissible in view of the child's status concerning parents, relatives and legal guardians and that, if required, the persons concerned have given their informed consent to the adoption on the basis of such counselling as may be necessary;

(b) Recognize that inter-country adoption may be considered as an alternative means of child's care, if the child cannot be placed in a foster or an adoptive family or cannot in any suitable manner be cared for in the child's country of origin;

(c) Ensure that the child concerned by inter-country adoption enjoys safeguards and standards equivalent to those existing in the case of national adoption;

(d) Take all appropriate measures to ensure that, in inter-country adoption, the placement does not result in improper financial gain for those involved in it;

(e) Promote, where appropriate, the objectives of the present article by concluding bilateral or multilateral arrangements or agreements and endeavour, within this framework, to ensure that the placement of the child in another country is carried out by competent authorities or organs.

Article 22

1. States Parties shall take appropriate measures to ensure that a child who is seeking refugee status or who is considered a refugee in accordance with applicable international or domestic law and procedures shall, whether unaccompanied or accompanied by his or her parents or by any other person, receive appropriate protection and humanitarian assistance in the enjoyment of applicable rights set forth in the present Convention and in other international human rights or humanitarian instruments to which the said States are Parties.

2. For this purpose, States Parties shall provide, as they consider appropriate, co-operation in any efforts by the United Nations and other competent intergovernmental organizations or non-governmental organizations co-operating with the United Nations to protect and assist such a child and to trace the parents or other members of the family of any refugee child in order to obtain information necessary for reunification with his or her family. In cases where no parents or other members of the family can be found, the child shall be accorded the same protection as any other child permanently or temporarily deprived of his or her family environment for any reason, as set forth in the present Convention.

Article 23

1. States Parties recognize that a mentally or physically disabled child should enjoy a full and decent life, in conditions which ensure dignity, promote self-reliance and facilitate the child's active participation in the community.

2. States Parties recognize the right of the disabled child to special care and shall encourage and ensure the extension, subject to available resources, to

the eligible child and those responsible for his or her care, of assistance for which application is made and which is appropriate to the child's condition and to the circumstances of the parents or others caring for the child.

3. Recognizing the special needs of a disabled child, assistance extended in accordance with paragraph 2 of the present article shall be provided free of charge, whenever possible, taking into account the financial resources of the parents or others caring for the child and shall be designed to ensure that the disabled child has effective access to and receives education, training, health care services, rehabilitation services, preparation for employment and recreation opportunities in a manner conducive to the child's achieving the fullest possible social integration and individual development, including his or her cultural and spiritual development.

4. States Parties shall promote, in the spirit of international cooperation, the exchange of appropriate information in the field of preventive health care and of medical, psychological and functional treatment of disabled children, including dissemination of and access to information concerning methods of rehabilitation, education and vocational services, with the aim of enabling States Parties to improve their capabilities and skills and to widen their experience in these areas. In this regard, particular account shall be taken of the needs of developing countries.

Article 24

1. States Parties recognize the right of the child to the enjoyment of the highest attainable standard of health and to facilities for the treatment of illness and rehabilitation of health. States Parties shall strive to ensure that no child is deprived of his or her right of access to such health care services.

2. States Parties shall pursue full implementation of this right and, in particular, shall take appropriate measures:
   (a) To diminish infant and child mortality;
   (b) To ensure the provision of necessary medical assistance and health care to all children with emphasis on the development of primary health care;
   (c) To combat disease and malnutrition, including within the framework of primary health care, through, inter alia, the application of readily available technology and through the provision of adequate nutritious foods and clean drinking-water, taking into consideration the dangers and risks of environmental pollution;
   (d) To ensure appropriate pre-natal and post-natal health care for mothers;
   (e) To ensure that all segments of society, in particular parents and children, are informed, have access to education and are supported in the use of basic knowledge of child health and nutrition, the advantages of breast-feeding, hygiene and environmental sanitation and the prevention of accidents;
   (f) To develop preventive health care, guidance for parents and family planning education and services.

3. States Parties shall take all effective and appropriate measures with a view to abolishing traditional practices prejudicial to the health of children.
4. States Parties undertake to promote and encourage international co-operation with a view to achieving progressively the full realization of the right recognized in the present article. In this regard, particular account shall be taken of the needs of developing countries.

Article 25

States Parties recognize the right of a child who has been placed by the competent authorities for the purposes of care, protection or treatment of his or her physical or mental health, to a periodic review of the treatment provided to the child and all other circumstances relevant to his or her placement.

Article 26

1. States Parties shall recognize for every child the right to benefit from social security, including social insurance and shall take the necessary measures to achieve the full realization of this right in accordance with their national law.
2. The benefits should, where appropriate, be granted, taking into account the resources and the circumstances of the child and persons having responsibility for the maintenance of the child, as well as any other consideration relevant to an application for benefits made by or on behalf of the child.

Article 27

1. States Parties recognize the right of every child to a standard of living adequate for the child's physical, mental, spiritual, moral and social development.
2. The parent(s) or others responsible for the child have the primary responsibility to secure, within their abilities and financial capacities, the conditions of living necessary for the child's development.
3. States Parties, in accordance with national conditions and within their means, shall take appropriate measures to assist parents and others responsible for the child to implement this right and shall in case of need provide material assistance and support programmes, particularly with regard to nutrition, clothing and housing.
4. States Parties shall take all appropriate measures to secure the recovery of maintenance for the child from the parents or other persons having financial responsibility for the child, both within the State Party and from abroad. In particular, where the person having financial responsibility for the child lives in a State different from that of the child, States Parties shall promote the accession to international agreements or the conclusion of such agreements, as well as the making of other appropriate arrangements.

Article 28

1. States Parties recognize the right of the child to education and with a view to achieving this right progressively and on the basis of equal opportunity, they shall, in particular:
   (a) Make primary education compulsory and available free to all;
   (b) Encourage the development of different forms of secondary education, including general and vocational education, make them available and accessible to every child and take appropriate measures such as the introduction of free education and offering financial assistance in case of need;
   (c) Make higher education accessible to all on the basis of capacity by every appropriate means;
   (d) Make educational and vocational information and guidance available and accessible to all children;
   (e) Take measures to encourage regular attendance at schools and the reduction of drop-out rates.
2. States Parties shall take all appropriate measures to ensure that school discipline is administered in a manner consistent with the child's human dignity and in conformity with the present Convention.
3. States Parties shall promote and encourage international cooperation in matters relating to education, in particular with a view to contributing to the elimination of ignorance and illiteracy throughout the world and facilitating access to scientific and technical knowledge and modern teaching methods. In this regard, particular account shall be taken of the needs of developing countries.

Article 29

1. States Parties agree that the education of the child shall be directed to:
   (a) The development of the child's personality, talents and mental and physical abilities to their fullest potential;
   (b) The development of respect for human rights and fundamental freedoms, and for the principles enshrined in the Charter of the United Nations;
   (c) The development of respect for the child's parents, his or her own cultural identity, language and values, for the national values of the country in which the child is living, the country from which he or she may originate, and for civilizations different from his or her own;
   (d) The preparation of the child for responsible life in a free society, in the spirit of understanding, peace, tolerance, equality of sexes, and friendship among all peoples, ethnic, national and religious groups and persons of indigenous origin;
   (e) The development of respect for the natural environment.
2. No part of the present article or article 28 shall be construed so as to interfere with the liberty of individuals and bodies to establish and direct educational

institutions, subject always to the observance of the principle set forth in paragraph 1 of the present article and to the requirements that the education given in such institutions shall conform to such minimum standards as may be laid down by the State.

Article 30

In those States in which ethnic, religious or linguistic minorities or persons of indigenous origin exist, a child belonging to such a minority or who is indigenous shall not be denied the right, in community with other members of his or her group, to enjoy his or her own culture, to profess and practise his or her own religion, or to use his or her own language.

Article 31

1. States Parties recognize the right of the child to rest and leisure, to engage in play and recreational activities appropriate to the age of the child and to participate freely in cultural life and the arts.
2. States Parties shall respect and promote the right of the child to participate fully in cultural and artistic life and shall encourage the provision of appropriate and equal opportunities for cultural, artistic, recreational and leisure activity.

Article 32

1. States Parties recognize the right of the child to be protected from economic exploitation and from performing any work that is likely to be hazardous or to interfere with the child's education, or to be harmful to the child's health or physical, mental, spiritual, moral or social development.
2. States Parties shall take legislative, administrative, social and educational measures to ensure the implementation of the present article. To this end and having regard to the relevant provisions of other international instruments, States Parties shall in particular:
   (a) Provide for a minimum age or minimum ages for admission to employment;
   (b) Provide for appropriate regulation of the hours and conditions of employment;
   (c) Provide for appropriate penalties or other sanctions to ensure the effective enforcement of the present article.

Article 33

States Parties shall take all appropriate measures, including legislative, administrative, social and educational measures, to protect children from the illicit use of narcotic drugs and psychotropic substances as defined in the relevant international treaties and to prevent the use of children in the illicit production and trafficking of such substances.

Article 34

States Parties undertake to protect the child from all forms of sexual exploitation and sexual abuse. For these purposes, States Parties shall in particular take all appropriate national, bilateral and multilateral measures to prevent:

(a) The inducement or coercion of a child to engage in any unlawful sexual activity;

(b) The exploitative use of children in prostitution or other unlawful sexual practices;

(c) The exploitative use of children in pornographic performances and materials.

Article 35

States Parties shall take all appropriate national, bilateral and multilateral measures to prevent the abduction of, the sale of or traffic in children for any purpose or in any form.

Article 36

States Parties shall protect the child against all other forms of exploitation prejudicial to any aspects of the child's welfare.

Article 37

States Parties shall ensure that:

(a) No child shall be subjected to torture or other cruel, inhuman or degrading treatment or punishment. Neither capital punishment nor life imprisonment without possibility of release shall be imposed for offences committed by persons below eighteen years of age;

(b) No child shall be deprived of his or her liberty unlawfully or arbitrarily. The arrest, detention or imprisonment of a child shall be in conformity with the law and shall be used only as a measure of last resort and for the shortest appropriate period of time;

(c) Every child deprived of liberty shall be treated with humanity and respect for the inherent dignity of the human person and in a manner which takes into account the needs of persons of his or her age. In particular, every child deprived of liberty shall be separated from adults unless it is considered in the child's best interest not to do so and shall have the right to maintain contact with his or her family through correspondence and visits, save in exceptional circumstances;

(d) Every child deprived of his or her liberty shall have the right to prompt access to legal and other appropriate assistance, as well as the right to challenge the legality of the deprivation of his or her liberty before a court or other competent, independent and impartial authority and to a prompt decision on any such action.

Article 38

1. States Parties undertake to respect and to ensure respect for rules of international humanitarian law applicable to them in armed conflicts which are relevant to the child.
2. States Parties shall take all feasible measures to ensure that persons who have not attained the age of fifteen years do not take a direct part in hostilities.
3. States Parties shall refrain from recruiting any person who has not attained the age of fifteen years into their armed forces. In recruiting among those persons who have attained the age of fifteen years but who have not attained the age of eighteen years, States Parties shall endeavour to give priority to those who are oldest.
4. In accordance with their obligations under international humanitarian law to protect the civilian population in armed conflicts, States Parties shall take all feasible measures to ensure protection and care of children who are affected by an armed conflict.

Article 39

States Parties shall take all appropriate measures to promote physical and psychological recovery and social reintegration of a child victim of: any form of neglect, exploitation, or abuse; torture or any other form of cruel, inhuman or degrading treatment or punishment; or armed conflicts. Such recovery and reintegration shall take place in an environment which fosters the health, self-respect and dignity of the child.

Article 40

1. States Parties recognize the right of every child alleged as, accused of, or recognized as having infringed the penal law to be treated in a manner consistent with the promotion of the child's sense of dignity and worth, which reinforces the child's respect for the human rights and fundamental freedoms of others and which takes into account the child's age and the desirability of promoting the child's reintegration and the child's assuming a constructive role in society.
2. To this end and having regard to the relevant provisions of international instruments, States Parties shall, in particular, ensure that:
   (a) No child shall be alleged as, be accused of, or recognized as having infringed the penal law by reason of acts or omissions that were not prohibited by national or international law at the time they were committed;
   (b) Every child alleged as or accused of having infringed the penal law has at least the following guarantees:
      (i) To be presumed innocent until proven guilty according to law;
      (ii) To be informed promptly and directly of the charges against him or her, and, if appropriate, through his or her parents or legal guardians and to have legal or other appropriate assistance in the preparation and presentation of his or her defence;

(iii) To have the matter determined without delay by a competent, independent and impartial authority or judicial body in a fair hearing according to law, in the presence of legal or other appropriate assistance and, unless it is considered not to be in the best interest of the child, in particular, taking into account his or her age or situation, his or her parents or legal guardians;

(iv) Not to be compelled to give testimony or to confess guilt; to examine or have examined adverse witnesses and to obtain the participation and examination of witnesses on his or her behalf under conditions of equality;

(v) If considered to have infringed the penal law, to have this decision and any measures imposed in consequence thereof reviewed by a higher competent, independent and impartial authority or judicial body according to law;

(vi) To have the free assistance of an interpreter if the child cannot understand or speak the language used;

(vii) To have his or her privacy fully respected at all stages of the proceedings. 3. States Parties shall seek to promote the establishment of laws, procedures, authorities and institutions specifically applicable to children alleged as, accused of, or recognized as having infringed the penal law, and, in particular:

(a) The establishment of a minimum age below which children shall be presumed not to have the capacity to infringe the penal law;

(b) Whenever appropriate and desirable, measures for dealing with such children without resorting to judicial proceedings, providing that human rights and legal safeguards are fully respected.

4. A variety of dispositions, such as care, guidance and supervision orders; counselling; probation; foster care; education and vocational training programmes and other alternatives to institutional care shall be available to ensure that children are dealt with in a manner appropriate to their well-being and proportionate both to their circumstances and the offence.

Article 41

Nothing in the present Convention shall affect any provisions which are more conducive to the realization of the rights of the child and which may be contained in:

(a) The law of a State party; or

(b) International law in force for that State.

Part II

Article 42

States Parties undertake to make the principles and provisions of the Convention widely known, by appropriate and active means, to adults and children alike.

Article 43

1. For the purpose of examining the progress made by States Parties in achieving the realization of the obligations undertaken in the present Convention, there shall be established a Committee on the Rights of the Child, which shall carry out the functions hereinafter provided.
2. The Committee shall consist of ten experts of high moral standing and recognized competence in the field covered by this Convention. The members of the Committee shall be elected by States Parties from among their nationals and shall serve in their personal capacity, consideration being given to equitable geographical distribution, as well as to the principal legal systems.
3. The members of the Committee shall be elected by secret ballot from a list of persons nominated by States Parties. Each State Party may nominate one person from among its own nationals.
4. The initial election to the Committee shall be held no later than six months after the date of the entry into force of the present Convention and thereafter every second year. At least four months before the date of each election, the Secretary-General of the United Nations shall address a letter to States Parties inviting them to submit their nominations within two months. The Secretary-General shall subsequently prepare a list in alphabetical order of all persons thus nominated, indicating States Parties which have nominated them and shall submit it to the States Parties to the present Convention.
5. The elections shall be held at meetings of States Parties convened by the Secretary-General at United Nations Headquarters. At those meetings, for which two thirds of States Parties shall constitute a quorum, the persons elected to the Committee shall be those who obtain the largest number of votes and an absolute majority of the votes of the representatives of States Parties present and voting.
6. The members of the Committee shall be elected for a term of four years. They shall be eligible for re-election if renominated. The term of five of the members elected at the first election shall expire at the end of two years; immediately after the first election, the names of these five members shall be chosen by lot by the Chairman of the meeting.
7. If a member of the Committee dies or resigns or declares that for any other cause he or she can no longer perform the duties of the Committee, the State Party which nominated the member shall appoint another expert from

among its nationals to serve for the remainder of the term, subject to the approval of the Committee.

8. The Committee shall establish its own rules of procedure.

9. The Committee shall elect its officers for a period of two years.

10. The meetings of the Committee shall normally be held at United Nations Headquarters or at any other convenient place as determined by the Committee. The Committee shall normally meet annually. The duration of the meetings of the Committee shall be determined and reviewed, if necessary, by a meeting of the States Parties to the present Convention, subject to the approval of the General Assembly.

11. The Secretary-General of the United Nations shall provide the necessary staff and facilities for the effective performance of the functions of the Committee under the present Convention.

12. With the approval of the General Assembly, the members of the Committee established under the present Convention shall receive emoluments from United Nations resources on such terms and conditions as the Assembly may decide.

Article 44

1. States Parties undertake to submit to the Committee, through the Secretary-General of the United Nations, reports on the measures they have adopted which give effect to the rights recognized herein and on the progress made on the enjoyment of those rights:

    (a) Within two years of the entry into force of the Convention for the State Party concerned;

    (b) Thereafter every five years.

2. Reports made under the present article shall indicate factors and difficulties, if any, affecting the degree of fulfilment of the obligations under the present Convention. Reports shall also contain sufficient information to provide the Committee with a comprehensive understanding of the implementation of the Convention in the country concerned.

3. A State Party which has submitted a comprehensive initial report to the Committee need not, in its subsequent reports submitted in accordance with paragraph 1 (b) of the present article, repeat basic information previously provided.

4. The Committee may request from States Parties further information relevant to the implementation of the Convention.

5. The Committee shall submit to the General Assembly, through the Economic and Social Council, every two years, reports on its activities.

6. States Parties shall make their reports widely available to the public in their own countries.

Article 45

In order to foster the effective implementation of the Convention and to encourage international co-operation in the field covered by the Convention:

(a) The specialized agencies, the United Nations Children's Fund and other United Nations organs shall be entitled to be represented at the consideration of the implementation of such provisions of the present Convention as fall within the scope of their mandate. The Committee may invite the specialized agencies, the United Nations Children's Fund and other competent bodies as it may consider appropriate to provide expert advice on the implementation of the Convention in areas falling within the scope of their respective mandates. The Committee may invite the specialized agencies, the United Nations Children's Fund and other United Nations organs to submit reports on the implementation of the Convention in areas falling within the scope of their activities;

(b) The Committee shall transmit, as it may consider appropriate, to the specialized agencies, the United Nations Children's Fund and other competent bodies, any reports from States Parties that contain a request, or indicate a need, for technical advice or assistance, along with the Committee's observations and suggestions, if any, on these requests or indications;

(c) The Committee may recommend to the General Assembly to request the Secretary-General to undertake on its behalf studies on specific issues relating to the rights of the child;

(d) The Committee may make suggestions and general recommendations based on information received pursuant to articles 44 and 45 of the present Convention. Such suggestions and general recommendations shall be transmitted to any State Party concerned and reported to the General Assembly, together with comments, if any, from States Parties.

Appendix II

Human Rights Act 1998

1998 Chapter 42

An Act to give further effect to rights and freedoms guaranteed under the European Convention on Human Rights; to make provision with respect to holders of certain judicial offices who become judges of the European Court of Human Rights; and for connected purposes.

9th November 1998

BE IT ENACTED by the Queen's most Excellent Majesty, by and with the advice and consent of the Lords Spiritual and Temporal, and Commons, in this present Parliament assembled, and by the authority of the same, as follows: –

Introduction

1 The Convention Rights

   (1) In this Act 'the Convention rights' means the rights and fundamental freedoms set out in –

     (a) Articles 2 to 12 and 14 of the Convention,

     (b) Articles 1 to 3 of the First Protocol, and

     (c) Articles 1 and 2 of the Sixth Protocol,

     as read with Articles 16 to 18 of the Convention.

   (2) Those Articles are to have effect for the purposes of this Act subject to any designated derogation or reservation (as to which see sections 14 and 15).

   (3) The Articles are set out in Schedule 1.

   (4) The Lord Chancellor may by order make such amendments to this Act as he considers appropriate to reflect the effect, in relation to the United Kingdom, of a protocol.

   (5) In subsection (4) 'protocol' means a protocol to the Convention –

     (a) which the United Kingdom has ratified; or

     (b) which the United Kingdom has signed with a view to ratification.

   (6) No amendment may be made by an order under subsection (4) so as to come into force before the protocol concerned is in force in relation to the United Kingdom.

2 Interpretation of Convention rights

   (1) A court or tribunal determining a question which has arisen in connection with a Convention right must take into account any –

    (a) judgment, decision, declaration or advisory opinion of the European Court of Human Rights,

    (b) opinion of the Commission given in a report adopted under Article 31 of the Convention,

    (c) decision of the Commission in connection with Article 26 or 27(2) of the Convention, or

    (d) decision of the Committee of Ministers taken under Article 46 of the Convention,

whenever made or given, so far as, in the opinion of the court or tribunal, it is relevant to the proceedings in which that question has arisen.

(2) Evidence of any judgment, decision, declaration or opinion of which account may have to be taken under this section is to be given in proceedings before any court or tribunal in such manner as may be provided by rules.

(3) In this section 'rules' means rules of court or, in the case of proceedings before a tribunal, rules made for the purposes of this section –

    (a) by the Lord Chancellor or the Secretary of State, in relation to any proceedings outside Scotland;

    (b) by the Secretary of State, in relation to proceedings in Scotland; or

    (c) by a Northern Ireland department, in relation to proceedings before a tribunal in Northern Ireland –

        (i) which deals with transferred matters; and

        (ii) for which no rules made under paragraph (a) are in force.

Legislation

3 Interpretation of legislation

(1) So far as it is possible to do so, primary legislation and subordinate legislation must be read and given effect in a way which is compatible with the Convention rights.

(2) This section –

    (a) applies to primary legislation and subordinate legislation whenever enacted;

    (b) does not affect the validity, continuing operation or enforcement of any incompatible primary legislation; and

    (c) does not affect the validity, continuing operation or enforcement of any incompatible subordinate legislation if (disregarding any possibility of revocation) primary legislation prevents removal of the incompatibility.

4 Declaration of incompatibility

(1) Subsection (2) applies in any proceedings in which a court determines whether a provision of primary legislation is compatible with a Convention right.

(2) If the court is satisfied that the provision is incompatible with a Convention right, it may make a declaration of that incompatibility.

(3) Subsection (4) applies in any proceedings in which a court determines whether a provision of subordinate legislation, made in the exercise of a power conferred by primary legislation, is compatible with a Convention right.

(4) If the court is satisfied –

    (a) that the provision is incompatible with a Convention right, and

    (b) that (disregarding any possibility of revocation) the primary legislation concerned prevents removal of the incompatibility,

it may make a declaration of that incompatibility.

(5) In this section 'court' means –

    (a) the House of Lords;

    (b) the Judicial Committee of the Privy Council;

    (c) the Courts-Martial Appeal Court;

    (d) in Scotland, the High Court of Justiciary sitting otherwise than as a trial court or the Court of Session;

    (e) in England and Wales or Northern Ireland, the High Court or the Court of Appeal.

(6) A declaration under this section ('a declaration of incompatibility') –

    (a) does not affect the validity, continuing operation or enforcement of the provision in respect of which it is given; and

    (b) is not binding on the parties to the proceedings in which it is made.

5 Right of Crown to intervene

(1) Where a court is considering whether to make a declaration of incompatibility, the Crown is entitled to notice in accordance with rules of court.

(2) In any case to which subsection (1) applies –

    (a) a Minister of the Crown (or a person nominated by him),

    (b) a member of the Scottish Executive,

    (c) a Northern Ireland Minister,

    (d) a Northern Ireland department,

is entitled, on giving notice in accordance with rules of court, to be joined as a party to the proceedings.

(3) Notice under subsection (2) may be given at any time during the proceedings.

(4) A person who has been made a party to criminal proceedings (other than in Scotland) as the result of a notice under subsection (2) may, with leave, appeal to the House of Lords against any declaration of incompatibility made in the proceedings.

(5) In subsection (4) –

'criminal proceedings' includes all proceedings before the Courts-Martial Appeal Court; and

'leave' means leave granted by the court making the declaration of incompatibility or by the House of Lords.

Public authorities

6 Acts of public authorities

(1) It is unlawful for a public authority to act in a way which is incompatible with a Convention right.

(2) Subsection (1) does not apply to an act if –

    (a) as the result of one or more provisions of primary legislation, the authority could not have acted differently; or

    (b) in the case of one or more provisions of, or made under, primary legislation which cannot be read or given effect in a way which is compatible with the Convention rights, the authority was acting so as to give effect to or enforce those provisions.

(3) In this section 'public authority' includes –

    (a) a court or tribunal, and

    (b) any person certain of whose functions are functions of a public nature,

but does not include either House of Parliament or a person exercising functions in connection with proceedings in Parliament.

(4) In subsection (3) 'Parliament' does not include the House of Lords in its judicial capacity.

(5) In relation to a particular act, a person is not a public authority by virtue only of subsection (3)(b) if the nature of the act is private.

(6) 'An act' includes a failure to act but does not include a failure to –

    (a) introduce in, or lay before, Parliament a proposal for legislation; or

    (b) make any primary legislation or remedial order.

7 Proceedings

(1) A person who claims that a public authority has acted (or proposes to act) in a way which is made unlawful by section 6(1) may –

    (a) bring proceedings against the authority under this Act in the appropriate court or tribunal, or

    (b) rely on the Convention right or rights concerned in any legal proceedings,

but only if he is (or would be) a victim of the unlawful act.

(2) In subsection (1)(a) 'appropriate court or tribunal' means such court or tribunal as may be determined in accordance with rules; and proceedings against an authority include a counterclaim or similar proceeding.

(3) If the proceedings are brought on an application for judicial review, the applicant is to be taken to have a sufficient interest in relation to the unlawful act only if he is, or would be, a victim of that act.

(4) If the proceedings are made by way of a petition for judicial review in Scotland, the applicant shall be taken to have title and interest to sue in relation to the unlawful act only if he is, or would be, a victim of that act.

(5) Proceedings under subsection (1)(a) must be brought before the end of –

    (a) the period of one year beginning with the date on which the act complained of took place; or

(b) such longer period as the court or tribunal considers equitable having regard to all the circumstances,

but that is subject to any rule imposing a stricter time limit in relation to the procedure in question.

(6) In subsection (1)(b) 'legal proceedings' includes –

(a) proceedings brought by or at the instigation of a public authority; and

(b) an appeal against the decision of a court or tribunal.

(7) For the purposes of this section, a person is a victim of an unlawful act only if he would be a victim for the purposes of Article 34 of the Convention if proceedings were brought in the European Court of Human Rights in respect of that act.

(8) Nothing in this Act creates a criminal offence.

(9) In this section 'rules' means –

(a) in relation to proceedings before a court or tribunal outside Scotland, rules made by the Lord Chancellor or the Secretary of State for the purposes of this section or rules of court,

(b) in relation to proceedings before a court or tribunal in Scotland, rules made by the Secretary of State for those purposes,

(c) in relation to proceedings before a tribunal in Northern Ireland –

(i) which deals with transferred matters; and

(ii) for which no rules made under paragraph (a) are in force, rules made by a Northern Ireland department for those purposes,

and includes provision made by order under section 1 of the Courts and Legal Services Act 1990.

(10) In making rules, regard must be had to section 9.

(11) The Minister who has power to make rules in relation to a particular tribunal may, to the extent he considers it necessary to ensure that the tribunal can provide an appropriate remedy in relation to an act (or proposed act) of a public authority which is (or would be) unlawful as a result of section 6(1), by order add to –

(a) the relief or remedies which the tribunal may grant; or

(b) the grounds on which it may grant any of them.

(12) An order made under subsection (11) may contain such incidental, supplemental, consequential or transitional provision as the Minister making it considers appropriate.

(13) 'The Minister' includes the Northern Ireland department concerned.

8 Judicial remedies

(1) In relation to any act (or proposed act) of a public authority which the court finds is (or would be) unlawful, it may grant such relief or remedy, or make such order, within its powers as it considers just and appropriate.

(2) But damages may be awarded only by a court which has power to award damages, or to order the payment of compensation, in civil proceedings.

(3) No award of damages is to be made unless, taking account of all the circumstances of the case, including –

    (a) any other relief or remedy granted, or order made, in relation to the act in question (by that or any other court), and

    (b) the consequences of any decision (of that or any other court) in respect of that act,

the court is satisfied that the award is necessary to afford just satisfaction to the person in whose favour it is made.

(4) In determining –

    (a) whether to award damages, or

    (b) the amount of an award,

the court must take into account the principles applied by the European Court of Human Rights in relation to the award of compensation under Article 41 of the Convention.

(5) A public authority against which damages are awarded is to be treated –

    (a) in Scotland, for the purposes of section 3 of the Law Reform (Miscellaneous Provisions) (Scotland) Act 1940 as if the award were made in an action of damages in which the authority has been found liable in respect of loss or damage to the person to whom the award is made;

    (b) for the purposes of the Civil Liability (Contribution) Act 1978 as liable in respect of damage suffered by the person to whom the award is made.

(6) In this section –

'court' includes a tribunal;

'damages' means damages for an unlawful act of a public authority; and

'unlawful' means unlawful under section 6(1).

9 Judicial acts

(1) Proceedings under section 7(1)(a) in respect of a judicial act may be brought only –

    (a) by exercising a right of appeal;

    (b) on an application (in Scotland a petition) for judicial review; or

    (c) in such other forum as may be prescribed by rules.

(2) That does not affect any rule of law which prevents a court from being the subject of judicial review.

(3) In proceedings under this Act in respect of a judicial act done in good faith, damages may not be awarded otherwise than to compensate a person to the extent required by Article 5(5) of the Convention.

(4) An award of damages permitted by subsection (3) is to be made against the Crown; but no award may be made unless the appropriate person, if not a party to the proceedings, is joined.

(5) In this section –

'appropriate person' means the Minister responsible for the court concerned, or a person or government department nominated by him;

'court' includes a tribunal;

'judge' includes a member of a tribunal, a justice of the peace and a clerk or other officer entitled to exercise the jurisdiction of a court;

'judicial act' means a judicial act of a court and includes an act done on the instructions, or on behalf, of a judge; and

'rules' has the same meaning as in section 7(9).

Remedial action

10 Power to take remedial action

(1) This section applies if –

  (a) a provision of legislation has been declared under section 4 to be incompatible with a Convention right and, if an appeal lies –

  (i) all persons who may appeal have stated in writing that they do not intend to do so;

  (ii) the time for bringing an appeal has expired and no appeal has been brought within that time; or

  (iii) an appeal brought within that time has been determined or abandoned; or

  (b) it appears to a Minister of the Crown or Her Majesty in Council that, having regard to a finding of the European Court of Human Rights made after the coming into force of this section in proceedings against the United Kingdom, a provision of legislation is incompatible with an obligation of the United Kingdom arising from the Convention.

(2) If a Minister of the Crown considers that there are compelling reasons for proceeding under this section, he may by order make such amendments to the legislation as he considers necessary to remove the incompatibility.

(3) If, in the case of subordinate legislation, a Minister of the Crown considers –

  (a) that it is necessary to amend the primary legislation under which the subordinate legislation in question was made, in order to enable the incompatibility to be removed, and

  (b) that there are compelling reasons for proceeding under this section,

  he may by order make such amendments to the primary legislation as he considers necessary.

(4) This section also applies where the provision in question is in subordinate legislation and has been quashed, or declared invalid, by reason of incompatibility with a Convention right and the Minister proposes to proceed under paragraph 2(b) of Schedule 2.

(5) If the legislation is an Order in Council, the power conferred by subsection (2) or (3) is exercisable by Her Majesty in Council.

(6) In this section 'legislation' does not include a Measure of the Church Assembly or of the General Synod of the Church of England.

(7) Schedule 2 makes further provision about remedial orders.

Other rights and proceedings

11 Safeguard for existing human rights

A person's reliance on a Convention right does not restrict –

(a) any other right or freedom conferred on him by or under any law having effect in any part of the United Kingdom; or

(b) his right to make any claim or bring any proceedings which he could make or bring apart from sections 7 to 9.

12 Freedom of expression

(1) This section applies if a court is considering whether to grant any relief which, if granted, might affect the exercise of the Convention right to freedom of expression.

(2) If the person against whom the application for relief is made ('the respondent') is neither present nor represented, no such relief is to be granted unless the court is satisfied –

(a) that the applicant has taken all practicable steps to notify the respondent; or

(b) that there are compelling reasons why the respondent should not be notified.

(3) No such relief is to be granted so as to restrain publication before trial unless the court is satisfied that the applicant is likely to establish that publication should not be allowed.

(4) The court must have particular regard to the importance of the Convention right to freedom of expression and, where the proceedings relate to material which the respondent claims, or which appears to the court, to be journalistic, literary or artistic material (or to conduct connected with such material), to –

(a) the extent to which –

(i) the material has, or is about to, become available to the public; or

(ii) it is, or would be, in the public interest for the material to be published;

(b) any relevant privacy code.

(5) In this section –

'court' includes a tribunal; and

'relief' includes any remedy or order (other than in criminal proceedings).

13 Freedom of thought, conscience and religion

(1) If a court's determination of any question arising under this Act might affect the exercise by a religious organisation (itself or its members

collectively) of the Convention right to freedom of thought, conscience and religion, it must have particular regard to the importance of that right.

(2) In this section 'court' includes a tribunal.

Derogations and reservations

14 Derogations

(1) In this Act 'designated derogation' means –

...

any derogation by the United Kingdom from an Article of the Convention, or of any protocol to the Convention, which is designated for the purposes of this Act in an order made by the Lord Chancellor.

(2) ...

(3) If a designated derogation is amended or replaced it ceases to be a designated derogation.

(4) But subsection (3) does not prevent the Lord Chancellor from exercising his power under subsection (1) ... to make a fresh designation order in respect of the Article concerned.

(5) The Lord Chancellor must by order make such amendments to Schedule 3 as he considers appropriate to reflect –

    (a) any designation order; or

    (b) the effect of subsection (3).

(6) A designation order may be made in anticipation of the making by the United Kingdom of a proposed derogation.

15 Reservations

(1) In this Act 'designated reservation' means –

    (a) the United Kingdom's reservation to Article 2 of the First Protocol to the Convention; and

    (b) any other reservation by the United Kingdom to an Article of the Convention, or of any protocol to the Convention, which is designated for the purposes of this Act in an order made by the Lord Chancellor.

(2) The text of the reservation referred to in subsection (1)(a) is set out in Part II of Schedule 3.

(3) If a designated reservation is withdrawn wholly or in part it ceases to be a designated reservation.

(4) But subsection (3) does not prevent the Lord Chancellor from exercising his power under subsection (1)(b) to make a fresh designation order in respect of the Article concerned.

(5) The Lord Chancellor must by order make such amendments to this Act as he considers appropriate to reflect –

    (a) any designation order; or

    (b) the effect of subsection (3).

16 Period for which designated derogations have effect

(1) If it has not already been withdrawn by the United Kingdom, a designated derogation ceases to have effect for the purposes of this Act –

...

at the end of the period of five years beginning with the date on which the order designating it was made.

(2) At any time before the period –

   (a) fixed by subsection (1) ..., or

   (b) extended by an order under this subsection,

comes to an end, the Lord Chancellor may by order extend it by a further period of five years.

(3) An order under section 14(1) ... ceases to have effect at the end of the period for consideration, unless a resolution has been passed by each House approving the order.

(4) Subsection (3) does not affect –

   (a) anything done in reliance on the order; or

   (b) the power to make a fresh order under section 14(1) ...

(5) In subsection (3) 'period for consideration' means the period of forty days beginning with the day on which the order was made.

(6) In calculating the period for consideration, no account is to be taken of any time during which –

   (a) Parliament is dissolved or prorogued; or

   (b) both Houses are adjourned for more than four days.

(7) If a designated derogation is withdrawn by the United Kingdom, the Lord Chancellor must by order make such amendments to this Act as he considers are required to reflect that withdrawal.

17 Periodic review of designated reservations

(1) The appropriate Minister must review the designated reservation referred to in section 15(1)(a) –

   (a) before the end of the period of five years beginning with the date on which section 1(2) came into force; and

   (b) if that designation is still in force, before the end of the period of five years beginning with the date on which the last report relating to it was laid under subsection (3).

(2) The appropriate Minister must review each of the other designated reservations (if any) –

   (a) before the end of the period of five years beginning with the date on which the order designating the reservation first came into force; and

   (b) if the designation is still in force, before the end of the period of five years beginning with the date on which the last report relating to it was laid under subsection (3).

(3) The Minister conducting a review under this section must prepare a report on the result of the review and lay a copy of it before each House of Parliament.

Schedule 1 The Articles

Section 1(3)

Part I The Convention

Rights and Freedoms

Article 2 Right to life

1 Everyone's right to life shall be protected by law. No one shall be deprived of his life intentionally save in the execution of a sentence of a court following his conviction of a crime for which this penalty is provided by law.

2 Deprivation of life shall not be regarded as inflicted in contravention of this Article when it results from the use of force which is no more than absolutely necessary:

(a) in defence of any person from unlawful violence;

(b) in order to effect a lawful arrest or to prevent the escape of a person lawfully detained;

(c) in action lawfully taken for the purpose of quelling a riot or insurrection.

Article 3 Prohibition of torture

No one shall be subjected to torture or to inhuman or degrading treatment or punishment.

Article 4 Prohibition of slavery and forced labour

1 No one shall be held in slavery or servitude.

2 No one shall be required to perform forced or compulsory labour.

3 For the purpose of this Article the term 'forced or compulsory labour' shall not include:

(a) any work required to be done in the ordinary course of detention imposed according to the provisions of Article 5 of this Convention or during conditional release from such detention;

(b) any service of a military character or, in case of conscientious objectors in countries where they are recognised, service exacted instead of compulsory military service;

(c) any service exacted in case of an emergency or calamity threatening the life or well-being of the community;

(d) any work or service which forms part of normal civic obligations.

Article 5 Right to liberty and security

1 Everyone has the right to liberty and security of person. No one shall be deprived of his liberty save in the following cases and in accordance with a procedure prescribed by law:

(a) the lawful detention of a person after conviction by a competent court;

(b) the lawful arrest or detention of a person for non-compliance with the lawful order of a court or in order to secure the fulfilment of any obligation prescribed by law;

(c) the lawful arrest or detention of a person effected for the purpose of bringing him before the competent legal authority on reasonable suspicion of having committed an offence or when it is reasonably considered necessary to prevent his committing an offence or fleeing after having done so;

(d) the detention of a minor by lawful order for the purpose of educational supervision or his lawful detention for the purpose of bringing him before the competent legal authority;

(e) the lawful detention of persons for the prevention of the spreading of infectious diseases, of persons of unsound mind, alcoholics or drug addicts or vagrants;

(f) the lawful arrest or detention of a person to prevent his effecting an unauthorised entry into the country or of a person against whom action is being taken with a view to deportation or extradition.

2 Everyone who is arrested shall be informed promptly, in a language which he understands, of the reasons for his arrest and of any charge against him.

3 Everyone arrested or detained in accordance with the provisions of paragraph 1(c) of this Article shall be brought promptly before a judge or other officer authorised by law to exercise judicial power and shall be entitled to trial within a reasonable time or to release pending trial. Release may be conditioned by guarantees to appear for trial.

4 Everyone who is deprived of his liberty by arrest or detention shall be entitled to take proceedings by which the lawfulness of his detention shall be decided speedily by a court and his release ordered if the detention is not lawful.

5 Everyone who has been the victim of arrest or detention in contravention of the provisions of this Article shall have an enforceable right to compensation.

Article 6 Right to a fair trial

1 In the determination of his civil rights and obligations or of any criminal charge against him, everyone is entitled to a fair and public hearing within a reasonable time by an independent and impartial tribunal established by law. Judgment shall be pronounced publicly but the press and public may be excluded from all or part of the trial in the interest of morals, public order or national security in a democratic society, where the interests of juveniles or the protection of the private life of the parties so require, or to the extent strictly necessary in the opinion of the court in special circumstances where publicity would prejudice the interests of justice.

2 Everyone charged with a criminal offence shall be presumed innocent until proved guilty according to law.

3 Everyone charged with a criminal offence has the following minimum rights:

  (a) to be informed promptly, in a language which he understands and in detail, of the nature and cause of the accusation against him;

  (b) to have adequate time and facilities for the preparation of his defence;

  (c) to defend himself in person or through legal assistance of his own choosing or, if he has not sufficient means to pay for legal assistance, to be given it free when the interests of justice so require;

  (d) to examine or have examined witnesses against him and to obtain the attendance and examination of witnesses on his behalf under the same conditions as witnesses against him;

  (e) to have the free assistance of an interpreter if he cannot understand or speak the language used in court.

Article 7 No punishment without law

1 No one shall be held guilty of any criminal offence on account of any act or omission which did not constitute a criminal offence under national or international law at the time when it was committed. Nor shall a heavier penalty be imposed than the one that was applicable at the time the criminal offence was committed.

2 This Article shall not prejudice the trial and punishment of any person for any act or omission which, at the time when it was committed, was criminal according to the general principles of law recognised by civilised nations.

Article 8 Right to respect for private and family life

1 Everyone has the right to respect for his private and family life, his home and his correspondence.

2 There shall be no interference by a public authority with the exercise of this right except such as is in accordance with the law and is necessary in a democratic society in the interests of national security, public safety or the economic well-being of the country, for the prevention of disorder or crime, for the protection of health or morals, or for the protection of the rights and freedoms of others.

Article 9 Freedom of thought, conscience and religion

1 Everyone has the right to freedom of thought, conscience and religion; this right includes freedom to change his religion or belief and freedom, either alone or in community with others and in public or private, to manifest his religion or belief, in worship, teaching, practice and observance.

2 Freedom to manifest one's religion or beliefs shall be subject only to such limitations as are prescribed by law and are necessary in a democratic society in the interests of public safety, for the protection of public order, health or morals, or for the protection of the rights and freedoms of others.

Article 10 Freedom of expression

1 Everyone has the right to freedom of expression. This right shall include freedom to hold opinions and to receive and impart information and ideas without interference by public authority and regardless of frontiers. This Article shall not prevent States from requiring the licensing of broadcasting, television or cinema enterprises.

2 The exercise of these freedoms, since it carries with it duties and responsibilities, may be subject to such formalities, conditions, restrictions or penalties as are prescribed by law and are necessary in a democratic society, in the interests of national security, territorial integrity or public safety, for the prevention of disorder or crime, for the protection of health or morals, for the protection of the reputation or rights of others, for preventing the disclosure of information received in confidence, or for maintaining the authority and impartiality of the judiciary.

Article 11 Freedom of assembly and association

1 Everyone has the right to freedom of peaceful assembly and to freedom of association with others, including the right to form and to join trade unions for the protection of his interests.

2 No restrictions shall be placed on the exercise of these rights other than such as are prescribed by law and are necessary in a democratic society in the interests of national security or public safety, for the prevention of disorder or crime, for the protection of health or morals or for the protection of the rights and freedoms of others. This Article shall not prevent the imposition of lawful restrictions on the exercise of these rights by members of the armed forces, of the police or of the administration of the State.

Article 12 Right to marry

Men and women of marriageable age have the right to marry and to found a family, according to the national laws governing the exercise of this right.

Article 14 Prohibition of discrimination

The enjoyment of the rights and freedoms set forth in this Convention shall be secured without discrimination on any ground such as sex, race, colour, language, religion, political or other opinion, national or social origin, association with a national minority, property, birth or other status.

Article 16 Restrictions on political activity of aliens

Nothing in Articles 10, 11 and 14 shall be regarded as preventing the High Contracting Parties from imposing restrictions on the political activity of aliens.

Article 17 Prohibition of abuse of rights

Nothing in this Convention may be interpreted as implying for any State, group or person any right to engage in any activity or perform any act aimed at the destruction of any of the rights and freedoms set forth herein or at their limitation to a greater extent than is provided for in the Convention.

Article 18 Limitation on use of restrictions on rights

The restrictions permitted under this Convention to the said rights and freedoms shall not be applied for any purpose other than those for which they have been prescribed.

Part II The First Protocol

Article 1 Protection of property

Every natural or legal person is entitled to the peaceful enjoyment of his possessions. No one shall be deprived of his possessions except in the public interest and subject to the conditions provided for by law and by the general principles of international law.

The preceding provisions shall not, however, in any way impair the right of a State to enforce such laws as it deems necessary to control the use of property in accordance with the general interest or to secure the payment of taxes or other contributions or penalties.

Article 2 Right to education

No person shall be denied the right to education. In the exercise of any functions which it assumes in relation to education and to teaching, the State shall respect the right of parents to ensure such education and teaching in conformity with their own religious and philosophical convictions.

Article 3 Right to free elections

The High Contracting Parties undertake to hold free elections at reasonable intervals by secret ballot, under conditions which will ensure the free expression of the opinion of the people in the choice of the legislature.

Part III The Sixth Protocol

Article 1 Abolition of the death penalty

The death penalty shall be abolished. No one shall be condemned to such penalty or executed.

Article 2 Death penalty in time of war

A State may make provision in its law for the death penalty in respect of acts committed in time of war or of imminent threat of war; such penalty shall be applied only in the instances laid down in the law and in accordance with its provisions. The State shall communicate to the Secretary General of the Council of Europe the relevant provisions of that law.

Index